Exploring
Equity and Trusts

Exploring Equity and Trusts

Second edition

Sukhninder Panesar

Longman
is an imprint of

PEARSON

Harlow, England • London • New York • Boston • San Francisco • Toronto
Sydney • Tokyo • Singapore • Hong Kong • Seoul • Taipei • New Delhi
Cape Town • Madrid • Mexico City • Amsterdam • Munich • Paris • Milan

Pearson Education Limited

Edinburgh Gate
Harlow
Essex CM20 2JE
England

and Associated Companies throughout the world

Visit us on the World Wide Web at:
www.pearsoned.co.uk

First published 2010
Second edition 2012

© Pearson Education Limited 2010, 2012

ISBN: 978-1-4082-8097-3

British Library Cataloguing-in-Publication Data
A catalogue record for this book is available from the British Library

Library of Congress Cataloging-in-Publication Data
A catalog record for this book is available from the Library of Congress

10 9 8 7 6 5 4 3 2 1
15 14 13 12

Typeset in 9.5/12pt ITC Charter by 35
Printed and bound by Ashford Colour Press

Brief contents

premium
mylawchamber
unrivalled support for legal education

Your complete learning package

Visit **www.mylawchamber.co.uk/panesar** to access a wealth of resources to support your studies and teaching.

All our premium sites provide access to **an interactive Pearson eText**, an electronic version of **Exploring Equity and Trusts** which is fully **searchable**. You can **personalise** your Pearson eText with your own notes and bookmarks and extensive **links are provided to all of the resources** below. The eText page presentation mirrors that of your textbook.

Use the eText to link to **Case Navigator** for help and practise with **case reading and analysis** in **equity and trusts**.

In addition access:
- Interactive multiple choice questions to test your understanding of each topic
- Practice exam questions with guidance to hone your exam technique
- Podcasts explaining new legislation or difficult areas in more detail to keep you up to speed on how the subject is evolving
- Weblinks to help you read more widely around the subject and really impress your lecturers
- Legal newsfeed to help you read more widely, stay right up to date with the law and impress examiners

Use the access card at the back of the book to activate mylawchamber premium. Online purchase is also available at **www.mylawchamber.co.uk/register**.

Teaching support materials
- **Case Navigator** is easy to integrate into any course where case reading and analysis skills are required
- The **equity and trusts MyTest testbank** can be used to create print tests or to create tests to **download into your learning environment**. It gives you access to a wide variety of questions designed to be used in formal assessments or to check students' progress throughout the course and includes over **350** questions
- **PowerPoint** slides with visual support in explaining legal concepts

Also: The regularly maintained mylawchamber premium site provides the following features:
- Search tool to help locate specific items of content.
- Online help and support to assist with website usage and troubleshooting.

Use the access card at the back of the book to activate mylawchamber premium. Online purchase is also available at **www.mylawchamber.co.uk/register**.

Case Navigator access is included with your mylawchamber premium registration. The LexisNexis element of Case Navigator is only available to those who currently subscribe to LexisNexis Butterworths online.

Contents

Guided tour

Learning objectives at the start of each chapter outline the key concepts to be discussed, and help organise your study.

Learning objectives

After reading this chapter you should be able to:

→ understand the nature of a trust

→ understand the reasons for creating a trust

→ explain the trust as a product of fragmentation of ownership

→ understand the historical development of the trust and its modern-day significance

→ explain the respective rights of the trustee and the beneficiary

→ explain the difference of express trusts and implied trusts

→ understand how express trusts and implied trusts are classified

→ explain the role of trusts in law reform

→ understand the functions of trust law.

Setting the scene sections at the start of each chapter detail scenarios which reflect the concepts to be discussed, helping you see how the law works in real life.

SETTING THE SCENE

VISIT CASE NAVIGATOR

McPhail v Doulton [1971] AC 424: A trust for the benefit of the officers and employees or ex-officers or ex-employees of a company or to any of their relatives and dependants of any such persons as the trustees think fit

Who exactly are the beneficiaries of this trust?

The facts in McPhail v Doulton illustrate some of the concerns which are the subject matter of discussion in this chapter. The settlor, Bertram Baden, established a fund to provide benefits for the staff of Matthew Hall & Co. Ltd. Clause 9 of the trust deed authorised the trustees to apply the net income from the fund for the benefit of the officers and employees or ex-officers or ex-employees of the company or to any of their relatives and

---

Case summary boxes help you to remember the facts and legal principles arising from the leading cases in Equity and Trusts law.

CASE SUMMARY

Applying equity: two cases in the House of Lords – where lies the unconscionability?

In order to understand the importance of unconscionability and the context in which it is applied it is perhaps a good starting point to consider two decisions of the House of Lords. Although, at this stage of the book, the reader will not have been exposed to the equitable doctrines and principles in operation in the two cases, it is nevertheless a useful exercise to explore the facts of both cases and consider whether equitable relief should be given. Read the facts of these cases first and think whether the claimants in both cases should have a remedy of some sort from the court; then read what was actually decided by the House of Lords and see where the unconscionability lies, if any, in both cases. Remember, at this stage it is not crucial whether you fully understand the equitable principles applied in the cases: rather the emphasis is on identifying factual contexts which give rise to unconscionability.

Case One: Thorner v Major [2009] 1 WLR 776

The facts

In 1997 Peter Thorner made a will by which, after a number of pecuniary legacies, he left the residue of his estate, including his farm (Steart Farm, Cheddar) to his nephew,

---

Icons alerting you to more detailed examination of key cases via **Case Navigator** on the accompanying **mylawchamber** website.

VISIT CASE NAVIGATOR

In *Milroy v Lord*[5] Turner LJ identified three principal ways in which a person can make a gift to another person:

1 an outright transfer of the legal title to the property to the donee (or in the case of an equitable interest, an assignment of the equitable interest to the donee[6]);

2 a transfer of the legal title to property to trustees to hold on behalf of another;

Key statutes help you to identify and remember important aspects of legislation.

Key citations provide quotations from leading judges and judgments.

Applying the law boxes allow you to put what you have just read about into practice, helping you gain a practical understanding of the subject.

Understanding contentious or tricky elements of the law is always useful for gaining strong marks, and the **Problem area** boxes lucidly explain such difficult points

Points of departure for more detailed study are outlined in the **Further thinking** boxes.

Conclusions bring all the themes from the chapter you have just read together, helping you consolidate your learning.

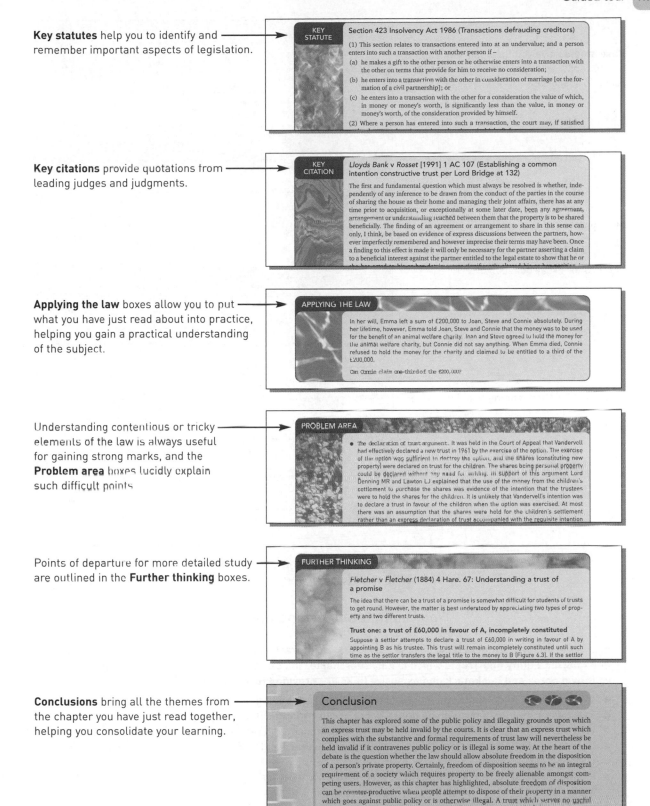

KEY STATUTE

Section 423 Insolvency Act 1986 (Transactions defrauding creditors)

(1) This section relates to transactions entered into at an undervalue; and a person enters into such a transaction with another person if –

(a) he makes a gift to the other person or he otherwise enters into a transaction with the other on terms that provide for him to receive no consideration;

(b) he enters into a transaction with the other in consideration of marriage [or the formation of a civil partnership]; or

(c) he enters into a transaction with the other for a consideration the value of which, in money or money's worth, is significantly less than the value, in money or money's worth, of the consideration provided by himself.

(2) Where a person has entered into such a transaction, the court may, if satisfied

KEY CITATION

Lloyds Bank v *Rosset* [1991] 1 AC 107 (Establishing a common intention constructive trust per Lord Bridge at 132)

The first and fundamental question which must always be resolved is whether, independently of any inference to be drawn from the conduct of the parties in the course of sharing the house as their home and managing their joint affairs, there has at any time prior to acquisition, or exceptionally at some later date, been any agreement, arrangement or understanding reached between them that the property is to be shared beneficially. The finding of an agreement or arrangement to share in this sense can only, I think, be based on evidence of express discussions between the partners, however imperfectly remembered and however imprecise their terms may have been. Once a finding to this effect is made it will only be necessary for the partner asserting a claim to a beneficial interest against the partner entitled to the legal estate to show that he or

APPLYING THE LAW

In her will, Emma left a sum of £200,000 to Joan, Steve and Connie absolutely. During her lifetime, however, Emma told Joan, Steve and Connie that the money was to be used for the benefit of an animal welfare charity. Joan and Steve agreed to hold the money for the animal welfare charity, but Connie did not say anything. When Emma died, Connie refused to hold the money for the charity and claimed to be entitled to a third of the £200,000.

Can Connie claim one-third of the £200,000?

PROBLEM AREA

● The declaration of trust argument. It was held in the Court of Appeal that Vandervell had effectively declared a new trust in 1961 by the exercise of the option. The exercise of the option was sufficient to destroy the option, and the shares (constituting new property) were declared on trust for the children. The shares being personal property could be declared without any need for writing. In support of this argument Lord Denning MR and Lawton LJ explained that the use of the money from the children's settlement to purchase the shares was evidence of the intention that the trustees were to hold the shares for the children. It is unlikely that Vandervell's intention was to declare a trust in favour of the children when the option was exercised. At most there was an assumption that the shares were held for the children's settlement rather than an express declaration of trust accompanied with the requisite intention

FURTHER THINKING

Fletcher v *Fletcher* (1884) 4 Hare. 67: Understanding a trust of a promise

The idea that there can be a trust of a promise is somewhat difficult for students of trusts to get round. However, the matter is best understood by appreciating two types of property and two different trusts.

Trust one: a trust of £60,000 in favour of A, incompletely constituted

Suppose a settlor attempts to declare a trust of £60,000 in writing in favour of A by appointing B as his trustee. This trust will remain incompletely constituted until such time as the settlor transfers the legal title to the money to B (Figure 6.3). If the settlor

Conclusion

This chapter has explored some of the public policy and illegality grounds upon which an express trust may be held invalid by the courts. It is clear that an express trust which complies with the substantive and formal requirements of trust law will nevertheless be held invalid if it contravenes public policy or is illegal in some way. At the heart of the debate is the question whether the law should allow absolute freedom in the disposition of a person's private property. Certainly, freedom of disposition seems to be an integral requirement of a society which requires property to be freely alienable amongst competing users. However, as this chapter has highlighted, absolute freedom of disposition can be counter-productive when people attempt to dispose of their property in a manner which goes against public policy or is otherwise illegal. A trust which serves no useful purpose, as for example, keeping a house locked for a long period of time and denying

Case studies give you the opportunity to further apply what you have learned to realistic scenarios.

●●● Case study

Read and analyse the following case study and answer the specific question set below.

Harriet, who died earlier this year, had made a will in which she had made the following dispositions of her property:

'My freehold property to be sold and the proceeds to be held by Derek on trust.

£60,000 to Jenny, Jill and Fiona.

The remainder of my estate to be divided equally amongst my children.'

A few weeks before Harriet's death, she visited Derek and handed him a briefcase with the instructions that the contents of the briefcase were important and that should anything happen to her he should follow the instructions in that briefcase. Harriet explained that the key to the briefcase could be obtained from her executor. When Derek opened the briefcase he found a letter instructing him that the proceeds of sale of Harriet's freehold property should be given to a named charity.

Moot points ask you to consider specific elements from the chapter you have just read in greater detail, and are excellent practice for essay questions.

●● Moot points

1 The contemporary justification for the enforcement of secret trusts is that they 'dehor the will': see the judgment of Lord Sumner in *Blackwell v Blackwell* [1929] 2 AC 318. What do you understand by the term 'dehor the will' and how far is it true to say that a secret trust is an *inter vivos* trust?

2 In a fully secret trust communication of the secret trust can be made any time up till the testator's death. It does not matter whether the communication is before or after the execution of the will. However, in the case of a half-secret trust communication must be made before or at the same time as the execution of the will. In the words of Lord Sumner, 'a testator cannot reserve to himself a power of making future unwitnessed dispositions by merely naming a trustee and leaving the purposes of the trust to be supplied afterwards . . .' [1929] 2 AC 318 at 339. What does Lord Sumner mean in this statement, and is a different rule of communication justified in the context of a half-secret trust?

Annotated **Further reading** lists feature at the end of each chapter – crucial if you wish to explore that area in more depth.

● Further reading

Hassall, N. 'Power of Advancement: How Far Can Pilkington be Stretched?' (2007) PCB 282. Looks at the meaning of benefit in *Pilkington v IRC* and considers how far the requirement of benefit in making an advancement can be extended to resettling trust property of trusts better, perhaps from a fiscal pint of view, for the beneficiaries.

Law Commission, 'Trustees' Powers and Duties' Report No. 260. Explains the inadequacies of some of the rules governing trustees' powers and duties and suggesting reform which eventually came in the form of the Trustee Act 2000.

Law Commission Supplementary Consultation Paper: Consultation Paper 191, 'Intestacy and Family Provision Claims on Death: Sections 31 and 32 of the Trustee Act 1925,' 26 May 2011.

Panesar, S. 'The Trustee Act 2000' [2001] ICCLR. Looks at some of the key sections of the Trustee Act 1925, including the power of delegation.

premium
mylawchamber
unrivalled support for legal education

Your complete learning package

Visit **www.mylawchamber.co.uk/panesar** to access an **interactive Pearson eText**, an electronic version of **Exploring Equity and Trusts** which is fully **searchable**. You can **personalise** your Pearson eText with your **own notes and bookmark** and extensive **links are provided to all of the self-study resources**:

● Interactive multiple choice questions to test your understanding of each topic
● Practice exam questions with guidance to hone your exam technique
● Weblinks to help you read more widely around the subject and really impress your lecturers
● Podcasts explaining new legislation or difficult areas in more detail to keep you up to speed on how the subject is evolving
● Legal newsfeed to help you read more widely, stay right up to date with the law and impress examiners

Preface

Ask anyone who has studied law which topic they found particularly tricky during their undergraduate degree and the chances are they'll tell you it was equity and trusts. This area of English law is seen to be notoriously difficult and often students are filled with trepidation before they've even started the module. Why should this be? I think there are two main reasons. The first is that students tend to have little by way of a general inclination or understanding of the subject matter of equity and trusts. For example, if we consider an area such as criminal law, we would expect that the student probably already understands that the subject of enquiry relates to the legal rules governing criminal wrongdoing, along with a working knowledge of what such wrongdoing might entail (murder, manslaughter, theft, etc.). With equity and trusts, however, even if the student already has some broad ideas of the nature and principle of equitable relief, they will generally not relate to the trust concept. As such, they are often approaching entirely uncharted territory, and so face the inevitable challenges that delving into any new area brings.

Secondly, the subject matter is, by its nature, broad and complex. We can see this when we consider the diverse contexts in which the trust has operated. In the social context, the trust has historically operated to deal with the rights of various groups, for example, the rights of women or the rights of illegitimate children. More recently, the trust has had an important role to play in protecting the rights of individuals in the family home (particularly in the context of increased non-marital cohabitation). The trust has also been a key factor in the world of commerce dealing with the rights, for example, of pension fund beneficiaries or the rights of beneficiaries against commercial agents who have intermeddled with trust property. It might initially appear a little daunting, but neither the student learning the law, nor the lecturer teaching it should shy away from the elaborate nature of trusts – to do so will not only short-change the student but will also hamper the effective understanding of the law. Indeed, if we embrace this fact now then I believe we can make studying equity and trusts a rich and deeply rewarding experience. This is where, I hope, this book comes in.

This book has two primary objectives. Firstly, it seeks to convey the principles of equity and trusts in a manner which the reader will find engaging and easy to understand. To achieve this, the book is divided into six parts. This fragmentation will allow the reader to understand the relevant chapters under a common theme first and then, much like a jigsaw, put all the pieces together to reveal the bigger picture. Part I of the book explores the nature of equity and the grounds for invoking equitable relief. It then examines the nature of the trust concept and the reasons for creating trusts in the contemporary world. Part II explores the substantive and formal requirements needed for the creation of express trusts. Part III looks to those trusts which are implied by law rather than created by a deliberate act on the part of an individual. Part IV looks at the law relating to the administration of trusts, in particular, the powers and duties of trustees. Part V examines the remedies available to a beneficiary for breaches of trust by a trustee. The final part of the book looks at trusts which are created in favour of the public at large, otherwise known as charitable trusts. The law relating to charitable trusts has recently undergone changes as a result of the enactment of the Charities Act 2006. Part VI explores some of the fundamental changes introduced by the Charities Act 2006 and the future direction of charitable trusts. The book also uses a number of features to help cement knowledge of the concepts and apply it at regular intervals, such as the 'Applying the law' boxes throughout each chapter, and the 'Case studies' and 'Moot points' which are at the end of each chapter. These features encourage the reader to apply the law to factual questions and think further about some of the nuances that exist within the law.

The second objective is to give the reader as much context as possible. I have tried to illustrate the significance of the trust in both its modern context and also of some of the older rules within the framework in which they were decided. This approach seeks to show the law 'in action,' and to help the reader understand not just what the law is, but also some of the reasons as to *why* it is so. To this end, each chapter opens with a 'Setting the scene' section which will introduce the reader to interesting cases that bring to light the subject matter of each chapter, and offer a frame of reference for what is to follow. Each chapter also examines the relevant cases and rulings pertinent to that area of trusts law, further reinforcing the reader's understanding of how the law has evolved.

I would like to thank Pearson Education for publishing this book. In particular, Owen Knight for his invaluable support during the writing process and his patience. I have been very fortunate to have worked with such a dedicated and professional editorial team and a lot of credit for this book belongs to them. I would like to thank all my colleagues at Coventry University for their support and encouragement.

Most importantly, I would like to thank my wife, Sandeep, and my son, Lakhdeep, for their incredible support without which book would not have been possible.

I have attempted to state the law up to and as at November 2011.

Sukhninder Panesar
Associate Head of Law
Coventry University Law School

Table of cases

Visit **www.mylawchamber.co.uk/panesar** to access unique online support to improve your case reading and analysis skills.

Case Navigator provides:

- **Direct deep links** to the core cases in **equity and trusts**.
- **Short introductions** provide guidance on what you should look out for while reading the case.
- **Questions** help you to test your understanding of the case, and provide feedback on what you should have grasped.
- **Summaries** contextualise the case and point you to further reading so that you are fully prepared for seminars and discussions.

Please note that access to Case Navigator is free with the purchase of this book, but you must register with us for access. Full registration instructions are available on the website. The LexisNexis element of Case Navigator is only available to those who currently subscribe to LexisNexis Butterworths online.

Case Navigator cases are highlighted in bold.

Table of statutes

Part I
Introduction to equity and trusts

Part I of this book explores the nature of equity and the trust concept. It is important to have a sound understanding of the nature of equity and the trust concept before moving on to a more detailed study of the law relating to trusts. Chapter 1 explores the nature of equity and its relationship with the common law. The chapter explores the historical development of equitable jurisdiction and explains the modern grounds for the application of equitable relief. The reader is encouraged to appreciate the role of unconscionability as the fundamental ground for invoking equitable relief. Chapter 2 moves on to to explore the nature of the trust concept. The chapter explores the nature of the trust, the reasons why people create trusts and the key players in the trust relationship. The purpose of this chapter is to put into context the modern social and economic significance of the trust so as to allow the reader to appreciate the concerns which form the subject matter of the remaining parts of the book. Chapter 3 looks at how the trust concept differs from other legal concepts, including powers of appointment, contracts and the rights of individuals receiving under a will or on intestacy.

1

Introduction to equity

Learning objectives

After completing this chapter you should be able to:

→ understand the origins of equity

→ understand the idea and nature of equity

→ understand the relationship between law and equity

→ understand the nature of rights in law and rights in equity

→ understand the maxims of equity

→ understand the nature of equitable relief

→ understand the contemporary role of equity.

SETTING THE SCENE

Equity and role of unconscionability

What is equity and why does the English legal system recognise a body of rules known as equity are two frequently asked questions in an undergraduate study in law. In attempting to answer these questions it is, perhaps, apt to begin with a look at two statements made some 400 years apart which provide explanation of the touchstone for application of equity and equitable doctrines to given factual situations.

The first statement is that of Lord Ellesmere who once commented in the famous *Earl of Oxford's Case* (1615) 1 Rep Ch. 1 at page 6 that 'men's actions are so diverse and infinite that it is impossible to make any general law which will aptly meet with every particular and not fail in some circumstances. The office of the Chancellor is to correct men's consciences for fraud, breaches of trust, wrongs and oppressions of what nature so ever they be, and so soften and mollify the extremity of the law.'

VISIT CASE NAVIGATOR

The idea that equity is essentially conscience driven was recently reaffirmed by the House of Lords in *Westdeutsche v Islington London Borough Council* [1996] AC 699 (HL) (at p. 705) where Lord Browne-Wilkinson commented in the context of trusts that 'equity operates on the conscience of the owner of the legal interest. In the case of a trust, the conscience of the legal owner requires him to carry out the purposes for which the property was vested in him (express or implied) or which the law imposes on him by reason of his unconscionable conduct.'

The word 'equity' is susceptible to a number of different meanings. In one sense the word means what is 'fair and just' and is, therefore, undistinguishable from the general concern of any system of laws, which is that all laws should be fair and just. However, another somewhat narrower sense of the word is that equity is that specific body of law which supplements the common law and is invoked in circumstances where the conduct of a defendant is deemed unconscionable. The unconscionability of the defendant may arise in a number of different contexts and for a number of different reasons. Additionally, the defendant's unconscionable conduct will have resulted in the defendant acquiring some advantage, whether personal or proprietary, which cannot be rightfully retained by the defendant. In most cases the defendant's unconscionability will have arisen from the strict and rigid application of a rule of common law. Where such unconscionable conduct has arisen, the role of equity is to temper the rigour of the common law by the award of an appropriate equitable remedy. Throughout this book there will be many examples where equity has intervened to prevent unconscionable conduct on the part of the defendant.

This chapter explores the nature and function of equity in the English legal system. In particular, the chapter explores the grounds for the intervention of equitable relief and the relationship between equity and the common law. It examines the role of unconscionability in equity and examines some of the important maxims of equity.

Introduction

One of the unique features of the English legal system is the duality of rights that can exist at common law and in equity. English law, like many other systems of law, allows the courts to administer two separate principles of law, which are not necessarily in conflict with each other but which seek to achieve justice on any given set of facts. The central feature of the common law is that it is based on the principle of precedent and looks to matters of form rather than substance. For example, any potential claimant wishing to pursue a remedy in the common law courts must satisfy that his complaint is a complaint which is recognised as being capable of being remedied in the common law courts, in most cases through the award of damages for loss caused to the claimant. Additionally, the common law requires that the claimant comply with all the necessary formal requirements that apply to the facts which give rise to his cause of action. This is better explained with reference to the following question.

APPLYING THE LAW

Thomas orally agreed with Victor that he would sell his house to Victor for a sum of £400,000. Victor was very pleased with the selling price and told Thomas that he would need a few months to raise the purchase price. Thomas did not hear from Victor for several months and Thomas sold his house to Betty for £500,000. Victor is not happy with the sale to Betty and wants to bring an action against Thomas for going back on his word.

Can he do this?

The above, admittedly rather simplistic set of facts, is a good staring point to illustrate whether a claimant can pursue a remedy in the common law courts. Whilst the reader may or may not be exposed to the common law rules governing contracts for the sale of land, it is a basic principle of modern land law that a contract for the sale of land is put in writing and that the written contract incorporates all the terms agreed between the parties.[1] This formal requirement is found in s. 2(1) of the Law of Property (Miscellaneous) Provisions Act 1989. Whilst it is true that Victor may feel aggrieved by the fact that Thomas did not sell his house to him, Victor would have no remedy at common law on the grounds that a contract for the sale of an interest in land is ineffective at common law if it is not in writing and incorporating all the terms and conditions of the sale.

Equity, on the other hand, is a system of law historically developed in the Court of Chancery correcting unconscionable conduct on the part of a defendant. Unlike the common law, equity is not defeated by failure to comply with form. It is often said that equity looks to matters of substance rather than form. So where there has been a failure to comply with form, equitable relief is not necessarily prevented from being given if, as a matter of substance, the court decides that equitable relief should be given. As to what matters of substance will persuade a court to grant equitable relief, the court will look to the underlying question of conscience. In particular, equity's concern is over the unconscionable conduct of a defendant. If the defendant, despite an absence of formality, has conducted himself in a manner in which he has acted unconscionably, the court will

---

[1] For more detail, see K. Gray and S. Gray, *Elements of Land Law* 5th edn (2009) at p. 1034.

grant equitable relief even where to do so would be in face of an absence of legal formality. It will be observed in this chapter that in the early days of the administration of equitable relief, the Court of Chancery was not necessarily restricted by precedent. The Lord Chancellors of the early Court of Chancery exercised equitable principles on a case-by-case analysis, the only common thread being the proof of unconscionable conduct on the part of the defendant.

A proper understanding of modern equity requires an appreciation of the common law and its shortcomings, particularly in the twelfth and thirteenth centuries. Before that, however, it is worth revisiting the question posed above regarding the sale of Thomas's house to Victor. Whilst it is established that the contract would be void at common law for failure to comply with the formal requirements of s. 2(1) of the Law of Property (Miscellaneous) Provisions Act 1989, would Victor have any relief in equity on what has been said so far about equity and the role of unconscionability? At this stage of the book the reader will not have been exposed to the very specific rules of equity governing oral contracts for the sale of land, but it is nevertheless useful to think whether the Thomas and Victor type of scenario is one which is within equity's jurisdiction to give some remedy.[2]

The common law

The origins of the common law go as far back as 1066 when the Norman Conquest introduced a new system of law for England. Towards the end of the thirteenth century two main types of courts were responsible for administering law in the country. First, there were the local courts, which were courts set up within the feudal structure and administered by the feudal lords.[3] Secondly, there were the royal courts, also known as the Courts of Common Pleas consisting of the King's Bench, Court of Common Pleas and the Exchequer. A potential litigant who felt that he had not received justice in the local courts had a right to petition the King and ask for his case to be heard in one of the royal courts. The right of an individual to petition the King arose out of the fact that the right to justice was a royal prerogative. Maitland once explained that each of the royal courts at one time had separate sphere of interest, but soon the claimant had a choice as to which court heard his case simply because each court began to administer the same law and in the same manner.[4] The Exchequer, however, was more than just a court of law; it had responsibility for fiscal matters as well as legal. Alongside the Exchequer was the Chancery Department headed by the Chancellor (who was normally a bishop).

---

[2] The detailed equitable rules relating to the enforcement of oral contracts for the sale of land are considered in Chapter 13.

[3] The feudal structure of England involved a system where the Crown acquired ownership of all land in the country, sometimes also referred as the radical title of the Crown. Under this feudal structure, the Crown's radical title served as a means by which smaller rights or ownership could vest in other persons: notably, the most powerful Lords and Knights at the top of the feudal ladder and less powerful individuals as the bottom. These smaller rights did not grant absolute ownership but limited forms of ownership. The limitation of ownership was defined by time: that is, ownership of land for defined periods of time, otherwise also known as the concepts of estates and tenures in the land. For a detailed examination of feudal tenure see F. Barlow, *The Feudal Kingdom of England 1042–1216* (4th edn, 1988) and A.W.B. Simpson, *A History of the Land Law* (2nd edn, 1986).

[4] F.W. Maitland, *Equity: A Course of Lectures* (J. Brunyate (ed.) 1936), p. 2.

The Chancery at this stage was not a court of equity that developed much later in the sixteenth and seventeenth centuries administering equitable principles and doctrines on the basis of unconscionable conduct. Rather, it was a secretarial office answerable to the King's permanent Council. The Chancellor, by way of delegation from the King, dealt with many of the petitions made to the King for justice to be given in individual cases.

The inadequacy of the writ system

The law administered by the medieval courts was partly traditional and partly statute. Traditional law was based on precedent and was termed the common law in that it was common to all areas of England and all its subjects.[5] A claimant wishing to commence an action in the Court of Common Pleas or the Kings Bench required a royal writ. A royal writ consisted of a sealed authorisation to commence proceedings in the royal courts. The office of issuing writs was given to the Chancellor who had at his disposal a number of established writs, but also had a limited power to issue new ones. It is important to note that at this point in history the Chancellor did not act in a judicial manner; his role was simply to hear the claimant's application and issue the appropriate writ. The grant of a writ did not mean that the claimant was successful, since the courts could quash the writ as being contrary to the law of the land. The power to invent new writs presented a real threat to the feudal lords and barons since new writs meant new remedies, which in turn created new rights and duties. In recognition of this problem faced by the feudal lords and barons, the Provisions of Oxford 1258 disallowed the issuing of new writs without the permission of the King's Council. In one sense this was the power of the feudal lords and barons sitting in the King's Council preventing new law, which was primarily directed at them. The net effect of the Provisions of Oxford was that a number of new cases requiring new remedies remained unresolved in the common law. The common law became rigid and incapable of dealing with the changes taking place in society requiring the recognition of new rights and remedies.

The inadequacy of an appropriate remedy

Apart from the fact that the common law was not able to redress new legal problems, there was also the fact the common law lacked an appropriate remedy in many cases. The predominant remedy at common law was, and still is today, the award of monetary damages. Thus, in the case of typical civil wrongs – for example, a breach of contract or the commission of tort such as negligence – the injured party was and still is entitled to compensation in the form of monetary damages reflecting the loss suffered by that injured party. Whilst the award of damages is appropriate in some cases it is not appropriate in all, particularly where the subject matter of the dispute involves some property: for example, land. A good example of the inappropriateness of damages is illustrated by the example of a persistent trespasser of land. In the case of a persistent trespasser a landowner can sue for damages: however, a more appropriate remedy would be an injunction preventing the commission of the trespass. The problem with the common law is that it does not recognise a remedy in the form of an injunction. It will be seen later that one of the reasons for the development of equity was primarily in response to the inadequacy of the common law remedy. Another good example is the sale of a valuable

---

[5] See, generally, S.F.C. Milsom, *A Historical Foundation of the Common Law* (2nd edn); Holdsworth, *A History of English law* (7th edn, 1956) Vol I and also J. Baker, *An Introduction to English Legal History* (2nd edn, 1979).

painting to a purchaser. It is trite law that in the event of a breach of such contract, the purchaser has a right to sue for damages for failure to deliver the painting. However, given the fact that special significance is attached to the painting in that it is something that is not readily available on the open market, a more appropriate remedy would be a decree of specific performance compelling the seller to perform the contract. Again, a primary shortcoming of the common law is that it does not recognise the remedy of specific performance. Seen in this way, one of the fundamental contributions of equity to the English legal system was the diverse range of remedies available to a claimant to enforce his rights.

 ## The origins and development of equity

Most legal systems, whether common law based or civil, have had to entertain the notion of equity.[6] The term equity is susceptible to a number of different meanings. In one sense the word equity means what is fair and just, and in this sense equity is a theme that runs through most legal systems in that all laws should strive for fairness and justice. Another sense of the word is that equity consists of a distinct body of rules that seek to introduce ethical values into the legal norms. In this respect one commentator once explained that equity consists of 'a set of legal principles entitled by the extrinsic superiority to super-sede the older law'.[7] It is this latter definition which properly explains the idea of equity in the English legal system. It will be observed in this chapter that equity in the English legal system is not a system of law based on what is necessarily fair on any given set of facts. As one judge once commented, English law does not posses a jurisdiction to administer 'palm tree justice'.[8] Modern equitable jurisdiction is exercised in well-defined circumstances which involve unconscionable conduct on the part of a defendant.

The nature of equity in the early days

In its early development, equity was developed by the Court of Chancery in the medieval ages to iron out the deficiencies of the common law and correct unconscionable conduct. The need for a separate court to administer equitable relief arose from the deficiencies of the common law in the Middle Ages, which have already been outlined above. In particular, the common law failed to address new legal problems simply because of the rigidity of the writ system: that is, the unavailability of a writ to initiate proceedings because of no recognised cause of action. Even where a recognised action existed, there was the problem of an appropriate remedy to resolve the dispute between defendant and the claimant. However, it was not simply the fact that a remedy was inappropriate; in many cases even though a remedy existed, it was simply not forthcoming for the claimant. The principal reason for this was that in many cases the rich and powerful individuals could influence both the courts and the jury, resulting in the fact that justice was simply not forthcoming for the very weak and vulnerable. Equity, as administered by the early Lord Chancellors, was not defeated by these constraints. The Lord Chancellor attempted

---

[6] For an excellent discussion of equity in the context of different legal systems, see R.A. Newman, *Equity in the World's Legal Systems: A Comparative Study* (1973).
[7] Sir Henry Sumner Maine, *Ancient Law* (1905) at p. 44.
[8] *Springette* v *Defoe* [1992] 2 FLR 388 at 393 per Dhillon LJ.

to correct abuses of fraud and unconscionable conduct by looking at each case on its merits rather than on the question of whether an appropriate course of action existed in the first place.

The Lord Chancellor

In the early development of equity the Lord Chancellor administered equitable relief. It will be recalled that when a potential litigant wished to commence proceedings against a defendant, he was required to obtain a royal writ from the Chancellor's office. Where the Lord Chancellor was unable to issue a writ because of the lack of a precedent, he could demand that the defendant appear before him and answer the charges made against him. The process by which this could happen required the complainant to issue the Lord Chancellor with a bill outlining the nature of his grievance. Having considered the bill, the Chancellor ordered the potential defendant to appear before him and answer the grievances raised by the complainant. In order to compel the defendant to appear before the Chancellor, the Chancellor issued a writ, called a *subpoena*, ordering the defendant to appear upon pain of forfeiting a sum of money, otherwise known as *subpoena centum librarum*.[9] This writ was very different from the types of writs available to commence proceedings in the common law courts, since it simply required the person against whom the complaint was made to answer to the Lord Chancellor the complaints made against him.

What started out as a mere secretarial office of government answerable to the King's Council now took on the shape of a court administering law in its own right. What law did the Chancellor administer? The Chancellor did not introduce any novelty in the law-making process and neither did he introduce laws so different in their juridical nature to the ordinary laws of the land. However, what the Chancellor did recognise was the inability of the common law to deal with the social and economic changes taking place in society. Given the fact that the Chancellor was an ecclesiastic, a man of the Church and learned in civil and canon law, he was ideally placed to deal with the legal problems put to him. The basis upon which he exercised his power was on the simple premise of what was right in any given case. If there is one word that describes how the Chancellor exercised his power to relieve aggrieved parties, that word is conscience.

The early court of equity was essentially a court of conscience. Every case was decided on its merits rather than on the question whether there existed a precedent to deal with the complaint brought by the claimant. Given the fact that the Lord Chancellor would change from time to time, each Chancellor would exercise greater or lesser power depending on his own notions of justice. In this respect most accounts of equity refer to the length of the Chancellor's foot, which was another way of saying that some Chancellors went further in the exercise of equitable relief than others. Later in the development of equity, lawyers rather than ecclesiastics were appointed to the office of Chancellor. Lord Nottingham (1673–82), Lord Hardwicke (1736–56) and Lord Eldon (1801–27) were pioneers of modern equity as we know it today. In doing so, they developed a set of principles and doctrines which were to become as fixed and rigid as the common law. In more recent times, a question that has been frequently asked is whether equity has passed child bearing and is now as established and rigid as the common law. This is a question to which this chapter will return later.

---

[9] See, F.W. Maitland, *Equity: A Course of Lectures* (J. Brunyate (ed.) 1936), p. 2.

Lord Eldon, described as one of the greatest equity lawyers[10] was primarily responsible for establishing equity as a defined body of rules and principles. He once remarked that 'nothing would inflict on me greater pain in quitting this place than the recollection that I had done anything to justify the reproach that the equity of this court varies like the Chancellor's foot'.[11] One of the many areas where Lord Eldon contributed to the development of equity was in the context of fiduciary relationships and the imposition of strict duties on persons standing in fiduciary relationships. These are analysed in more depth in Chapter 16.

Disputes in the early Court of Chancery

The types of complaints petitioned to the Chancellor at the initial stage of the development of equity were predominantly property based and centred on the most prized resource at the time, which was land. A number of examples can be give here: one of the most common complaints brought before the Lord Chancellor was the abuses of trusts. The predecessor of the modern trust, the use, was primarily employed in feudal England to overcome the taxation implications of feudal landholding.[12] Land would be put upon use by appointing trustees (called feoffees) for the benefit of beneficiaries (called *cestui que use*). Under feudal law, the heir of a deceased was required to pay feudal dues before taking possession of the land which once belonged to his father. Coupled with this problem was the fact that an individual had no freedom of testation, that is, the freedom to dispose of his land to his heirs by way of a will. These problems could, however, be avoided by the employment of a use. Typically, land would be conveyed to a number of feoffees who would be directed to hold the land for designated beneficiaries such as the oldest son of the person creating the use. The legal title would pass to the trustee; however, the Court of Chancery would recognise the rights of the beneficiary on the grounds that the conscience of the trustees would bind them to the trust. On the death of the landholder, that is the person who created the trust, the oldest son could compel the trustees to transfer the land to the oldest son on the grounds that he had equitable rights in the land. Equity would compel the trustees to transfer the land to the beneficiary. Seen in this way, a landholder could by the use of trustees convey land to his oldest son who would avoid paying feudal dues because all transfers of the land would be taking place during the lifetime of the person creating the trust and then during the lifetime of the trustees.[13]

Another notable example of the intervention of equity was in the context of a mortgage transaction. Historically, particularly in the eighteenth and nineteenth centuries, the typical mortgage transaction was very different from the type of mortgage transaction which operates today. Today, a mortgage confers upon the mortgagee (the lender) a charge on the property of the mortgagor. The charge has the effect of conferring upon the mortgagee a number of rights, not least the right to take possession of the mortgagor's land and sell it should the mortgagor default in paying the monies due under the mortgage. Historically, a typical mortgage took the form of an outright transfer of the mortgagor's land to the mortgagee. The mortgagee became the absolute owner of the land in return for the mortgage money which had been duly paid over to the mortgagor. The problem with this type of arrangement was that the common law regarded the

---

[10] J.E. Martin, *Hanbury and Martin: Modern Equity* 18th edn (2009) at p. 14.
[11] *Gee* v *Pritchard* (1818) 2 Swan. 402 at 414.
[12] The nature of the trust and its origins is discussed in more detail in Chapter 2.
[13] The concept of the use and the abuses thereof are considered in more detail in Chapter 2.

agreement to create a mortgage as an ordinary commercial one. Thus, the common law failed to redress key issues affecting the mortgagor such as his right to redeem the land once he made full payment under the terms of the mortgage. For example, if the contractual date of redemption had passed, there was nothing stopping the mortgagee from keeping the land for himself. Equity, however, intervened in a number of ways to prevent the mortgagee getting more out of the transaction other than the security for his money. Equity regarded the right of the mortgagor to get his property back on repayment of the loan money as fundamental to the mortgage agreement. The right to the return of the property, termed in equity as the mortgagor's 'equity of redemption', prevailed over and above the contractual provisions purporting to restrict it. The need for equity to intervene in mortgage transactions of the eighteenth and nineteenth centuries was influenced by the inequality of bargaining power between lender and borrower. The typical mortgage transaction at this time was in the form of money raised for some commercial venture or, as a last resort, for the poor person. Lord Chancellor Nottingham was particularly instrumental in protecting and recognising the rights of the mortgagor against abuses of power by the mortgagee.[14]

 ## Equity and the role of conscience

In the early development of equity the notion of conscience underpinned the grounds for the intervention of equitable relief. This has, perhaps, been best explained by Lord Ellesmere in the famous *Earl of Oxford's Case* where the Chancellor held that

> men's actions are so diverse and infinite that it is impossible to make any general law which will aptly meet with every particular and not fail in some circumstances. The office of the Chancellor is to correct men's consciences for fraud, breaches of trust, wrongs and oppressions of whatever nature so ever they be, and so soften and mollify the extremity of the law.[15]

The Chancellor, in administering equitable relief, did so not by interfering with the common law but rather by asking the defendant to personally appear before him. A judgment was said to be given *in personam,* which was also another way of saying that *equity acts in personam.* The Chancellor would order the defendant to do something; failure to comply with the Chancellor's order would make the defendant liable to imprisonment for contempt of court. The flexibility of the early Court of Chancery was illustrated by the fact that it was not constrained by precedent, and moreover the Chancellor could make a number of orders which were not merely monetary awards. In modern equity, the types of equitable remedies include specific performance of an obligation, injunctions, recission and rectification.

In more recent times the question has often been asked whether equity is still to be regarded as a court of conscience in the manner in which it once operated. For example, do the courts administering modern equity have the same degree of flexibility and discretion that once availed itself to the Lord Chancellors of the early Court of Chancery? In other words, are the grounds for equitable intervention dependent on a case-by-case basis looking at the merits of every case rather than by the application of some rigid process of principle and precedent? This question has received a mixed response. Lord Chancellor Eldon observed in 1818 that 'nothing would inflict on me greater pain . . .

---

[14] *Howard* v *Harris* (1681) 1 Vern. 33.
[15] (1615) 1 Rep. Ch. 1 at 6.

than the recollection that I had done anything to justify the reproach that the Equity of this Court varies like the Chancellor's foot'.[16] Some 140 years later Harman LJ remarked that equity principles had been 'rather too often bandied about in the common law courts as though the Chancellor still had only the length of his foot to measure when coming to a conclusion'.[17] In light of these remarks there have been suggestions that equity is truly beyond childbearing and that the process of creating new rights and remedies, like the way in which equity once did, should now be the responsibility of Parliament and not the courts. For example, in **Western Fish Products Ltd v Penwith District Council**[18] Megaw LJ took the same view as Harman LJ in **Campbell Discount Co Ltd v Bridge**[19] that 'the system of equity has become a very precise one. The creation of new rights and remedies is a matter for Parliament, not the judges.'[20]

Despite the above remarks, it has been equally suggested and argued that equity continues to work in the same manner that it once did, in other words, the recognition of new rights and remedies is not beyond those judges who administer equity. For example, Jessel MR explained in 1880 that

> the rules of Courts of equity are not supposed to have been established from time immemorial. It is perfectly well known that they have been established from time to time – altered, improved and refined from time to time. The doctrines are progressive, refined and improved.[21]

Despite the remarks of Jessel MR the general position in the modern equity is that equity has more become a system of principle and precedent rather than a system of ad hoc justice once administered by the Lord Chancellor. The reason for this is primarily due to the uncertainty that is created by ad hoc justice in individual cases. This is, perhaps, no better illustrated than in the context of the cohabitation and the 'deserted wife' cases of the 1970s and the attempt by Lord Denning to introduce into English law a 'new model constructive trust'.[22]

During the 1970s Lord Denning attempted to introduce broad notions of justice in resolving family property disputes. Although these matters are discussed in more detail in Chapter 13, the attempted application of broad notions of justice was primarily in response to the limited common law proprietary rights of spouses and cohabitees in the land co-occupied with their respective spouses and partners. Firstly, in a decision some 20 years earlier in **Bendall v McWhirter**[23] Denning LJ suggested that a wife who had no legal title to her husband's property and who did not make any contribution to the purchase nevertheless had a deserted wife's equity in the property capable of binding a purchaser of the land. The House of Lords in **National Provincial Bank Ltd v Ainsworth**[24] rejected this analysis of a deserted wife's equity. In the view of the House of Lords this deserted wife's equity did not have all the characteristics of a property right, namely, identifiability, stability and permanence. The House of Lords' decision illustrated the uncertainty that would have been introduced to the system of conveyancing.[25]

---

[16] *Gee v Pritchard* (1818) 2 Swans. 402 at 414.
[17] *Campbell Discount Co Ltd v Bridge* [1961] 1 QB 445 at 459.
[18] [1981] 2 All ER 204.
[19] [1961] 1 QB 445.
[20] [1981] 2 All ER 204 at 210.
[21] *Re Hallett's Estate* (1880) 13 Ch. D 696 at 710.
[22] This constructive trust is discussed in more depth in Chapter 13.
[23] [1952] 2 QB 466.
[24] [1965] AC 1175.
[25] A spouse does, however, have a statutory right of occupation now to be found in s. 30 of the Family Law Act 1996.

In 1975, when dealing with a cohabitation dispute between a husband and his wife, Lord Denning commented that 'a few years ago even equity would not have helped her. But things have altered now. Equity is not past the age of child bearing. One of her latest progeny is a constructive trust of a new model . . .'[26] What Lord Denning attempted to do was to use the new model of constructive trust as a means of doing broad justice by awarding a spouse equal ownership in the home that was in the sole name of the husband. As to the grounds upon which this could be done, Lord Denning looked to the somewhat broader and artificial notion that where a husband and wife were living jointly they both intended to share the beneficial ownership of their family home. In so far as the grounds of imposing a constructive trust, his Lordship famously commented in one case that such a trust was founded on large principles of equity and could be imposed 'whenever justice and good conscience' required it.[27] Despite Lord Denning's attempts in the 1970s to introduce wide principles of equity, the higher courts have not accepted them. The principal reason for this, as mentioned earlier, is the palm tree justice that would be served as a result of wide discretion by the courts and the resulting uncertainty that would arise.[28] For example, Bagnall J commented in **Cowcher v Cowcher**[29] '[I] am convinced that in determining rights, particularly property rights, the only justice that can be attained by mortals, who are fallible and are not omniscient, is justice according to law; the justice that flows from the application of sure and settled principles to proved or admitted facts. So in the field of equity the length of the Chancellor's foot has been measured or is capable of being measured.'[30]

More recently, however, there has been some suggestion that there may be scope for the development of a new model of constructive trust which could serve as a restitutionary remedy to reverse unjust enrichment.[31] However, English lawyers continue to demonstrate a more cautious approach to the recognition of wholly new principles of equity based on wide principles of justice and good conscience. So where does this leave modern equity? Lord Browne-Wilkinson's judgment in **Westdeutsche v Islington LBC**[32] which can perhaps be described as one of the more important equity and trusts cases of the last century, seeks to offer an explanation of modern equity. The facts of this case involved a complex interest-rate swap transaction that turned out to be *ultra vires* the council's power.[33] In an attempt to address the issue of whether a resulting trust could be imposed on payment made under a transaction which should not have taken place, his Lordship attempted to define some basic premises of the law of equity and the law of trusts. With regard to the juridical basis of equitable intervention, his Lordship explained that 'equity operates on the conscience of the owner of the legal interest. In the case of a trust, the conscience of the legal owner requires him to carry out the purposes for which the property was vested in him (express or implied trust) or which the law imposes on him by reason of his unconscionable conduct (constructive trusts).[34] In so far as the possibility of an equity introducing a broad notion of justice based on a new model constructive trust, his Lordship commented that 'although the resulting trust is an unsuitable basis for developing proprietary restitutionary remedies, the remedial constructive trust,

---

[26] *Eves* v *Eves* [1975] 1 WLR 1338 at 1341.
[27] See *Hussey* v *Palmer* [1972] 1 WLR 1286.
[28] See, for example, *Springette* v *Defoe* [1992] 2 FLR 388 at 393.
[29] [1972] 1 WLR 425.
[30] [1972] 1 WLR 425 at 430.
[31] See, for example, *Westdeutsche Landesbank Girozentrale* v *Islington LBC* [1996] AC 699.
[32] [1996] AC 699.
[33] The facts of this case are considered in more detail in Chapter 11.
[34] [1996] AC 699 at 705.

if introduced into English law, may provide a more satisfactory road forward. However, whether English law should follow the United States and Canada by adopting the remedial constructive trust will have to be decided in some future case where the point is directly in issue.'[35]

Unconscionability, fairness and the role of context

So far, it has been observed how the early Court of Chancery, which started out as a court administering equitable relief on a case-by-case basis, transformed into a court administering established principles of equity. As to the grounds for the application of the decided principles of equity, it has already been mentioned that the fundamental feature was the unconscionability of the defendant's conduct. This section explores the concept of unconscionability and how it differs from the notion of fairness. Although the term 'unconscionability' has been used widely in the sphere of equity to describe the grounds for the intervention of equitable relief, it is a term which is not always defined with exact precision.[36] When will a lawyer seeking equitable relief know whether the conduct complained of by his client has the grounds for the application of equitable principles leading to a successful remedy? In this respect, there is a lot to be said for Lord Nicholls's comment, in the context of a case concerning the liability of third parties intermeddling with trust property, that

> unconscionable is a word of immediate appeal to an equity lawyer. Equity is rooted historically in the concept of the Lord Chancellor, as the keeper of the Royal Conscience, concerning himself with conduct which was contrary to good conscience. It must be recognised, however, that unconscionable is not a word in everyday use by non-lawyers. If it is to be used in this context, and if it is to be the touchstone for liability as an accessory, it is essential to be clear on what, *in this context*, unconscionable *means*.[37]

At the present moment in time there is no universal definition of unconscionability which encapsulates all the various contexts in which equity has operated in. This statement may at first instance seem rather strange and controversial on the grounds that it questions the very fabric and foundations of equitable relief. The statement almost implies that equity lacks decided principles which allow the courts to measure whether a defendant's conduct has indeed been unconscionable. However, nothing could be further from the truth and the answer, as will be seen in the discussion in this chapter and indeed throughout this book, lies in understanding the importance of '*context*' before defining what is unconscionable and what is not unconscionable.

The absence of a universal definition of unconscionability has not proved to be a limitation in equity's ability to intervene is a diverse range of commercial and family contexts. In fact, it has been precisely because of the lack of a rigid test of unconscionability that equity has been able to resolve a number of disputes in a number of different contexts. The diversity of contexts in which equity has operated throughout the previous

---

[35] [1996] AC 699 at 716. More recently, in *Sinclair Investment Holdings SA* v *Versailles Trade Finance Ltd* [2006] 1 BCLC 60 Arden LJ did not rule out the question whether a new model constructive trust would be introduced in English law; however, that was to be decided by a further court.

[36] For an excellent discussion, see H. Delany and D. Ryan, 'Unconscionability: A Unifying Theme' (2008) Conv. 401. See more recently, N. Hopkins, 'The Relevance of Context in Property Law: A Case for Judicial Restraint' (2011) Legal Studies, Vol. 31 at 175–198.

[37] *Royal Brunei Airlines Sdn Bhd* v *Tan Kok Ming* [1995] 2 AC 378 at 392.

centuries has allowed the courts to define the notion of unconscionability with specific meanings in each context. In fact this has been one of the fundamental features of modern equity. One leading commentator on equity writes:

> The word unconscionable has lost its connection to morality and the courts try to use it as precisely as possible, in ways which vary from context to context, but it reminds us of equity's ecclesiastic origins and reminds us that equity is a broader idea than the quite narrow legal version of the concept might suggest. Language such as unconscionability sits somewhat uncomfortably in modern law, but that is a good thing for keeping the law realistically and appropriately humble about its capacity to cover every possible case by means of general rules. The language of unconscionability is highly effective at keeping the general rules open to just exceptions in particular cases and particular kind of cases.[38]

One of the fundamental reasons for the absence of a unifying definition of unconscionable conduct relates to the fact that the definition operates in so many different social and commercial contexts and, as explained by Delany and Ryan in their analysis, in each context 'the principle has been or is currently being used in a distinct manner. As such, the invocation of the principle has different implications and consequences for equitable intervention in each context.'[39] The importance of understanding the principle of unconscionability in light of the context in which it is being applied was more recently explained by Lord Neuberger *Thorner* v *Major*.[40] The facts of this case, which are considered in more detail below, concerned the question of whether a claimant, who had worked unpaid on his uncle's farm for many years, was entitled to the farm in circumstances where he had been made certain promises by his uncle that he would inherit the farm. The case involved the application of the equitable doctrine of proprietary estoppel, which prevents a person from denying a claimant a proprietary right which the claimant has been led to believe will be granted to him and one which the claimant has relied upon and suffered a detriment. The doctrine, which is explored in more detail in Chapter 13, requires the defendant to have made a clear and unambiguous assurance to the claimant that he will acquire some property right in the defendant's land. However, what amounts to a clear and unambiguous assurance depends primarily on the context in which it is made. Lord Neuberger explained that in the context of the facts of *Thorner* v *Major and Others*, the course of dealings between the uncle and nephew, although not amounting to express references that the nephew would inherit the uncle's farm, were nevertheless capable of establishing the level of unconscionability which would otherwise arise if the nephew was denied a right to inherit his uncle's farm. In the course of his judgment Lord Neuberger explained that 'in the facts of this case, it seems to me to have been an eminently sensible conclusion. Indeed, that point is a neat illustration of the fundamental importance of context to the questions of how a particular statement or action would have been understood, and whether it was "clear and unambiguous".'[41]

Whilst unconscionability is not necessarily capable of a precise definition, it is a concept which can be readily appreciated when looked at in the context in which it is being employed. At the heart of unconscionability is the element of some advantage, whether personal or proprietary, taken by the defendant, which he or she has consciously agreed belongs to the claimant. Examples of the types of context in which such unconscionable advantage has been taken by the defendant are diverse and they include the very subject

---

[38] G. Watt, *Todd and Watt's Cases and Materials on Equity and Trusts*, 7th edn (2009) Oxford at p. 3.
[39] H. Delany and D. Ryan, 'Unconscionability: A Unifying Theme' (2008) Conv. 401 at p. 402.
[40] [2009] 1 WLR 776 at 805.
[41] [2009] 1 WLR 776 at 805.

matter of this book: that is, the trust. At the heart of the enforcement of a trust is the trustee's conscience that he or she has agreed to hold trust property for the beneficiary. Where a trustee refuses to accept the rights of the beneficiary in the trust property, equity will intervene in order to prevent him from obtaining an advantage over the beneficiary's property. Another good context is that of proprietary estoppel, which prevents the owner of some property from denying the claimant some property interest in the property belonging to the owner. The doctrine of proprietary estoppel operates where the legal owner of, let's say, land encourages the claimant to believe that he will be entitled to some, if not all, of the legal owner's land and the claimant relies on that assurance and suffers some detriment as a result of the reliance.[42] Where the legal owner of land seeks to deny the existence of the proprietary right he has led the claimant to believe will be his, his conduct will be deemed as unconscionable. Equity will invoke the doctrine of proprietary estoppel in order to prevent the legal owner from taking an advantage which clearly has been given to the claimant.

Unconscionability is, however, to be distinguished from the notion of fairness. Despite what students of equity may think, unconscionability and fairness are not the same thing. Furthermore, fairness is not the basis for the intervention of equitable relief. Many factual situations may be perceived by the layman as being unfair; however, they do not necessarily provide the basis for the intervention of equitable relief. Consider the following questions.

APPLYING THE LAW

In her will Sarah left one half of her property to charity and the other half to her two youngest children equally. Sarah has, in fact, five children. The three elder children who have not been left any of Sarah's property are not happy that they have not received anything under their mother's will.

Do you think Sarah's conduct was unconscionable and that the children should seek equitable relief?

APPLYING THE LAW

Sarah, who is of very old age and suffering from a terminal illness, has two children both of which emigrated to Australia some time ago. Her nephew, Thomas, has cared for Sarah for the last seven years. Thomas qualified as an architect and was offered a high-profile job in the city. He declined the job in order to look after Sarah. Sarah assured him that she would leave her cottage to him after her death, knowing that he had cared for her and was the only important person in her life. Last year, Thomas decided to marry his girlfriend; however, Sarah persuaded him not to as it would mean that he would have to move to London and he would not be able to care for Sarah. Thomas decided not to marry and continued to live with Sarah. In her will Sarah left her cottage to her two children. When Thomas found out he was not very happy about this.

Do you think that Sarah's conduct is unconscionable? Should equity intervene here?

---

[42] Proprietary estoppel is considered in Chapter 13 in the context of constructive trusts.

In order to think more about equity and unconscionability it is convenient at this stage to investigate two cases where equitable principles have been the subject matter of discussion. The cases provide a useful insight into notions of unconscionability and the importance of understanding the context in which equity is asked to operate.

CASE SUMMARY

Applying equity: two cases in the House of Lords – where lies the unconscionability?

In order to understand the importance of unconscionability and the context in which it is applied it is perhaps a good starting point to consider two decisions of the House of Lords. Although, at this stage of the book, the reader will not have been exposed to the equitable doctrines and principles in operation in the two cases, it is nevertheless a useful exercise to explore the facts of both cases and consider whether equitable relief should be given. Read the facts of these cases first and think whether the claimants in both cases should have a remedy of some sort from the court; then read what was actually decided by the House of Lords and see where the unconscionability lies, if any, in both cases. Remember, at this stage it is not crucial whether you fully understand the equitable principles applied in the cases: rather the emphasis is on identifying factual contexts which give rise to unconscionability.

Case One: *Thorner* v *Major* [2009] 1 WLR 776

The facts

In 1997 Peter Thorner made a will by which, after a number of pecuniary legacies, he left the residue of his estate, including his farm (Steart Farm, Cheddar) to his nephew, David Thorner. The will was subsequently destroyed and Peter died intestate in November 2005. In accordance with the intestacy rules Peter's estate, including Steart Farm, was available for his blood relatives, namely, his sisters. David commenced proceedings against Peter's sisters and the personal representative to claim the farm on the grounds that he had the benefit of a proprietary estoppel against Peter and his estate. The claim was based on the grounds that Peter has made an assurance to David that the farm would be left to him after his death and that David had relied on that assurance by working for a period of some 28 years on the farm and thereby suffering a detriment.

The relevant facts in David's claim to be entitled to a proprietary estoppel begin around about 1976 when Peter's first wife died at an early age. David would help Peter in some aspects of the running of the farm; however, after Peter's second marriage failed, David worked on the farm almost on a daily basis for no remuneration at all. The work included attending to the animals, mending the fences and gates, taking cattle to and from the market, working on farm buildings and bringing in hay. Additionally, it was observed that much of the paperwork relating to the management of the farm was in a mess when David first started helping out on the farm. David took it upon himself to sort out the paperwork and continued to look after it from then on. The court was told that by 1985 David was working 18 hours a day and 7 days a week for no payment. Several witnesses remarked that David was an exceptionally hard worker and had no social life as such. Other witnesses, including a surveyor, noted that in any discussions relating to the farm, Peter would always consult with David and his father (Peter's cousin). It was further noted that, despite working punishing hours, David lived on pocket money which his own parents gave him.

▶

It was argued on behalf of David that Peter had indeed made an assurance to him that he would inherit the farm. Although it was not possible to pinpoint the exact time at which the assurance was made, it was argued that the expectation arose around about the early 1990s when Peter handed over a number of documents and discussed with David that he would take over the farm and run it. One such document was a Prudential Bonus Notice relating to two life polices worth £20,000. Peter explained to David that they would be sufficient to cover his death duties. The timing of these discussions was important because they were at a time when David was possibly thinking of pursuing his own career. The court was pointed to the fact that the timing of these discussions were duly to encourage David to stay with his parents, who lived nearby, and continue helping Peter. In 1997, Peter made a will in which he left the farm to David along with a number of pecuniary legacies to others who had helped Peter on the farm. Peter's intention was clear in that he wanted David to have the farm. In 1998, Peter fell out with some of the persons who were receiving the pecuniary legacies under his will and thus destroyed the will with the intention of making another one. In 2004 Peter suffered a stroke and David continued to look after him, but more importantly, engaging in major work on the farm. Peter died in November 2005, a couple of weeks after David's own father had died.

Having read the facts of this case do you think that David should be given his uncle's farm? If so, what factors lead you to come to that conclusion?

Case Two: *Yeoman's Row Management Ltd* v *Cobbe* [2008] 1 WLR 1752

The facts

The facts of **Yeoman's Row Management Ltd v Cobbe** involved a claimant who was unhappy about the defendant's conduct in refusing to honour an oral agreement to purchase land from the defendant. The essence of the agreement, which was conducted with one of the directors of Yeoman's, was to the effect that Mr Cobbe would seek planning permission out of his own pocket to develop land belonging to Yeoman's and that if permission was obtained, Yeoman's would sell the land to Mr Cobbe for a sum of £12 million. The agreement also made provision for Mr Cobbe to receive vacant possession of the land in order to erect six town houses. Additionally, the agreement made allowance for Yeoman's to receive further profits from the sale of the town houses should Mr Cobbe succeed in making a profit in excess of £24 million. This agreement, which was concluded 'in principle', did not cover all the matters relating to the sale of the land to Mr Cobbe – for example, matters relating to time scales regarding completion of the building of the flats and so on. The parties had deliberately not entered into a legally binding agreement because there was so much left to agree, and it was only when such matters had been agreed that the parties would enter into a legal binding written agreement. Planning permission was duly granted by the local authority; however, Yeoman's withdrew from the original oral agreement and claimed that Mr Cobbe had incurred expenditure on the land at his own risk. Mr Cobbe, however, commenced proceedings against Yeoman's on the grounds it was unconscionable for Yeoman's to withdraw from the oral agreement. In particular, he claimed that they were estopped from denying the interest in the land they had promised to give him; furthermore, he had incurred the expenditure as a result of the assurances given by Yeoman's to him. Additionally, Mr Cobbe sought to argue that a constructive trust arose in his favour on the grounds of the unconscionability of Yeoman's conduct in withdrawing from the oral agreement. Therefore, on the grounds of both proprietary estoppel and a constructive trust, Mr Cobbe argued that the terms of the oral agreement should be enforced in his favour.

Do you think that Yeoman's were acting unconscionably when they refused to honour the oral agreement? Do you think that Yeoman's had unequivocally made a promise to sell the land to Mr Cobbe?

The decision of the House of Lords in *Thorner v Major*

The House of Lords held that David was indeed entitled to his uncle's farm on the grounds of proprietary estoppel. In the context of their dealings and conduct, the requisite degree of unconscionability had arisen whereby it would be inequitable to deny David a right to the farm. Although there was no evidence of express assurances that David would inherit the farm, it was clear from the context that what David had done over the years was done in reliance that the farm would become his one day.

The decision of the House of Lords in *Yeoman's Row Management Ltd v Cobbe*

The House of Lords held that Mr Cobbe was not entitled to claim a proprietary right in the land which Yeoman's had orally agreed to sell to him. The oral agreement which had been entered into was nothing more than an agreement 'in principle'. There was still room for further negotiations and the agreement did not refer to all the terms which the parties would have wanted to include. In this respect Mr Cobbe could not be heard to be asserting that the oral agreement was enforceable but for the absence of writing. Lord Scott explained that the oral agreement did not profess to create an expectation that Mr Cobbe would be granted an interest in land. At most, the expectation Mr Cobbe had was that there would be further negotiations which would lead to a formal agreement.

Distinguishing the decision in *Thorner v Major* and *Yeoman's Row Management Ltd v Cobbe*

The facts of both cases illustrate situations where there have been promises of some sort that the claimant will acquire some interest in the defendant's land; however, only the claimant in ***Thorner v Major*** was successful. How do you distinguish the two cases?

The following extract of Lord Neuberger's judgment in ***Thorner v Major*** [2009] 1 WLR 776 at 803 may help answer the question:

> 93 In the context of a case such as Cobbe's case [2008] 1 WLR 1752, it is readily understandable why Lord Scott considered the question of certainty was so significant. The parties had intentionally not entered into any legally binding arrangement while Mr Cobbe sought to obtain planning permission: they had left matters on a speculative basis, each knowing full well that neither was legally bound – see para 27. There was not even an agreement to agree (which would have been unenforceable), but, as Lord Scott pointed out, merely an expectation that there would be negotiations. And, as he said, at para 18, an 'expectation dependent upon the conclusion of a successful negotiation is not an expectation of an interest having [sufficient] certainty'.
>
> 94 There are two fundamental differences between that case and this case. First, the nature of the uncertainty in the two cases is entirely different. It is well encapsulated by Lord Walker's distinction between 'intangible legal rights' and 'the tangible property

which he or she expects to get', in Cobbe's case [2008] 1 WLR 1752 , para 68. In that case, there was no doubt about the physical identity of the property. However, there was total uncertainty as to the nature or terms of any benefit (property interest, contractual right, or money), and, if a property interest, as to the nature of that interest (freehold, lease-hold, or charge), to be accorded to Mr Cobbe.

95 In this case, the extent of the farm might change, but, on the deputy judge's analysis, there is, as I see it, no doubt as to what was the subject of the assurance, namely the farm as it existed from time to time. Accordingly, the nature of the interest to be received by David was clear: it was the farm as it existed on Peter's death. As in the case of a very different equitable concept, namely a floating charge, the property the subject of the equity could be conceptually identified from the moment the equity came into existence, but its precise extent fell to be determined when the equity crystallised, namely on Peter's death.

96 Secondly, the analysis of the law in Cobbe's case [2008] 1 WLR 1752 was against the background of very different facts. The relationship between the parties in that case was entirely arm's length and commercial, and the person raising the estoppel was a highly experienced businessman. The circumstances were such that the parties could well have been expected to enter into a contract, however, although they discussed contractual terms, they had consciously chosen not to do so. They had intentionally left their legal relationship to be negotiated, and each of them knew that neither of them was legally bound. What Mr Cobbe then relied on was 'an unformulated estoppel . . . asserted in order to protect [his] interest under an oral agreement for the purchase of land that lacked both the requisite statutory formalities . . . and was, in a contractual sense, incomplete'.

97 In this case, by contrast, the relationship between Peter and David was familial and personal, and neither of them, least of all David, had much commercial experience. Further, at no time had either of them even started to contemplate entering into a formal contract as to the ownership of the farm after Peter's death. Nor could such a contract have been reasonably expected even to be discussed between them. On the deputy judge's findings, it was a relatively straightforward case: Peter made what were, in the circumstances, clear and unambiguous assurances that he would leave his farm to David, and David reasonably relied on, and reasonably acted to his detriment on the basis of, those assurances, over a long period.

98 In these circumstances, I see nothing in the reasoning of Lord Scott in Cobbe's case [2008] 1 WLR 1752 which assists the defendants in this case. It would represent a regret-table and substantial emasculation of the beneficial principle of proprietary estoppel if it were artificially fettered so as to require the precise extent of the property the subject of the alleged estoppel to be strictly defined in every case. Concentrating on the perceived morality of the parties' behaviour can lead to an unacceptable degree of uncertainty of outcome, and hence I welcome the decision in Cobbe's case [2008] 1 WLR 1752. However, it is equally true that focussing on technicalities can lead to a degree of strictness incon-sistent with the fundamental aims of equity.

 ## The Judicature Acts 1873 and 1875 and the relationship between law and equity

The idea of two sets of courts, that is the common law courts and the Court of Chancery, gave rise to procedural problems for potential litigants in the nineteenth century. The common law courts did not have equity jurisdiction; the Court of Chancery did not have the right to interfere or change a decision given by the common law courts. If a litigant had no redress at common law he would have to present a bill to the Lord Chancellor for his complaint to be heard in the Court of Chancery. This was even so where the common law courts acknowledged that there might be redress in equity; however, because of their limited jurisdiction, they could not award an equitable remedy such as an injunction. The same was true of the Court of Chancery, which could not award damages although it could grant an equitable remedy.[43] This meant the lodging of a new complaint in a separate court. However, it was not just the problem of procedure itself; by the nineteenth century the work of the Court of Chancery had increased considerably and this inevitably resulted in numerous delays.

To overcome the problems of two separate courts and the delays involved in litigation, the Judicature Acts 1873 and 1875 were enacted in order to restructure the court system in England. The Acts had the effect of abolishing the old courts and establishing one unified court, the Supreme Court, which was divided into a number of divisions. Initially these divisions were the Court of Chancery, King's Bench Division, Common Pleas, Exchequer, Probate and the Court of Admiralty. The Supreme Court could administer law and equity at the same time. As to whether the effect of the Judicature Acts was to fuse common law and equity is, however, a question which has been asked on many occasions and is addressed in the next section.

The modern position is re-enacted in the Supreme Court Act 1981, which divides the Supreme Court into the Court of Appeal and the High Court, the High Court consisting of the Queen's Bench Division, Chancery and Family Division.[44] These divisions are to administer law and equity together, and where there is a conflict between the rules of equity and the rules of the common law the rules of equity are to prevail. The supremacy of the rules of equity is enshrined in s. 25(11) of the Supreme Court of Judicature Act 1873 which provides: 'Generally, in all matters not hereinbefore particularly mentioned in which there is any conflict or variance between the rules of equity and the rules of the common law with reference to the same matter, the rules of equity shall prevail.' The relationship between law and equity is perhaps nowhere better explained than in the context of a lease. A lease which has a duration exceeding three years can only be created if it is in a deed.[45] Failure to comply with the requirements of a deed has the effect that no legal lease is created since no legal estate is created in the tenant. There simply is no lease capable of recognition in the common law courts. At most, where the landlord purports to act inconsistently with the terms of the lease, the purported tenant only has a right to damages for breach of contract. This is on the premise that the landlord entered into a contract with the tenant to grant a lease, albeit the contract confers no proprietary interest in the land because of the failure to comply with the requirement of a deed. At common law the tenant would not have exclusive right to possession of the land.

However, given the fact that a lease is a contract, where all the other requirements of the lease have been met, there seems to be no reason why equity should not intervene to

---

[43] There were limited reforms in the form of the Common Law Procedure Act 1854 which gave the common law courts power to grant equitable remedies. The Chancery Amendment Act 1858 gave the Court of Chancery the power to award damages.

[44] See s. 49(1) Supreme Court Act 1981. The Constitutional Reform Act 2005 has introduced a new Supreme Court of the United Kingdom to replace the House of Lords as the highest court of appeal. The Court of Appeal, the High Court and the Crown Court will be collectively called the Senior Courts of England and Wales.

[45] See s. 52 Law of Property Act 1925. A deed is a formal written document which declares it to be a deed and is signed by the parties: see s. 2(1) Law of Property (Miscellaneous Provisions) Act 1989.

compel performance of the lease. After all, as a matter of substance, as opposed to form, the landlord has done what he said he would do and the only reason why the lease is not being recognised at common law is for failure to comply with the requisite formality of a deed. Equity has long recognised that a lease, which has failed for formality at common law, could take effect in equity as a contract to grant a lease. Although it was not a legal lease, the contract to grant a lease was for all practical purposes a lease taking effect in equity. Equity could compel the purported landlord to perform his obligation to grant the lease by means of a decree of specific performance of the contract.[46] Until such time of a decree of specific performance equity recognised the lease in equity on the equitable maxim that equity regards that as done which ought to be done.[47] Thus, the substantive lease, which was purported to be created in law, would be recognised in equity as a lease for all practical purposes.

Recognition of the lease in equity did not mean that the tenant was vested with a legal estate in the land. At common law, the lease would still be merely contractual in nature, unless it could be construed as a different lease – for example, one not requiring formalities in the nature of a deed. It is a well-settled principle of property law that where a tenant pursuant to a long lease[48] moves into possession of land without compliance with the requisite formality of a deed, his tenancy will be construed at common law as a periodic tenancy. This is particularly so where the tenant is paying periodic rent, that is, month-to-month or quarter-to-quarter. A periodic tenancy requires no formality even though its duration may be longer than three years. Thus, a periodic tenancy may arise at common law even though the intentions of the parties were to create a long lease of the land.[49] It is at this point in the example that one can see the potential conflict between law and equity. The question that arises here is: what is the position where a long lease fails at common law for lack of formality but is nevertheless recognised in equity, and at common law the long lease is construed as a periodic tenancy? In other words, which one takes supremacy in the event of a dispute?

The matter is both illustrated and answered in the seminal case of **Walsh v Lonsdale**[50] where the court upheld the supremacy of equity. On the facts, a landlord had agreed in writing to grant a seven-year lease of a mill to the tenant but had failed to grant the lease by deed necessary to give it effect at common law. One of terms of the lease was that the tenant pay rent in advance. The tenant paid no rent in advance: instead he moved in and paid rent on a quarterly basis. The payment of quarterly rent was sufficient to find a periodic tenancy at common law. When the landlord demanded one year rent in advance, the tenant refused to pay. The landlord sought to exercise his right of distress which entitled him to distrain the tenant's good in order to meet the rent demanded. The tenant complained that the distress was illegal since the periodic tenancy, which arose at common law, did not contain any provision for the payment of advance rent. The landlord counter-argued that the distress was not illegal because it was the seven-year lease, which had a provision for the payment of advance rent, which determined the rights and obligations of the landlord and tenant. There was no doubt, on what has already been said above, that the seven-year lease took effect in equity as a contract to grant a lease, whilst at common law there was mere periodic tenancy. In court the tenant's action failed since the contract to grant a lease – in other words, the equitable lease – prevailed over and above

---

[46] See *Browne* v *Warner* (1808) 14 Ves. 409.
[47] This equitable maxim along with others is discussed below.
[48] Exceeding three years.
[49] See *Alder* v *Blackman* [1952] 2 All ER 41.
[50] (1882) 21 Ch. D 9.

the legal periodic tenancy. The distress by the landlord, pursuant to the terms of the seven-year lease, was therefore not illegal at all but entirely consistent with the terms of that lease.

 ## Fusion fallacy

The effect of the Judicature Acts was to allow one court to administer law and equity simultaneously. However, a question which has often been asked in many discussions on equity is whether the effect of the Acts was to fuse the principles of the common law and equity into one single coherent body of law applicable to any dispute whatsoever?[51] In other words, could a potential claimant ask the court for a common law remedy or an equitable remedy irrespective of the nature of his claim? Professor Ashburner once commented on the relationship between law and equity by describing law and equity as 'the two streams of jurisdiction though they run in the same channel run side by side and do not mingle their waters'.[52] Professor Ashburner's view very much reflected the generally understood position as to the effect of the Judicature Acts of 1873 and 1875 which was explained by the great Sir George Jessel MR in **Salt v Cooper**.[53] His Lordship commented that the main object of the Act 'has been sometimes inaccurately called the fusion of law and equity; but it is not any fusion, or anything of the kind; it was the vesting in one tribunal the administration of law and equity in every cause, action or dispute which should come before that tribunal'.[54]

However, in more recent times there have been suggestions that the rivers of law and equity are truly mingled and that there is a single coherent body of law consisting of the common law and equity. For example, in **United Scientific Holdings Ltd v Burnley Borough Council**[55] Lord Diplock, referring to Professor Ashburner's metaphor, commented:

> [M]y Lords, by 1977 this metaphor has in my view become both mischievous and deceptive. The innate conservatism of English lawyers may have made them slow to recognise that by the Judicature Act 1873 the two systems of substantive and adjectival law formerly administered by Courts of Law and Courts of Chancery were fused. As at the confluence of the Rhone and Saone, it may be possible for a short distance to discern the source from which each part of the combined stream came, but there comes a point at which this ceases to be possible. If Professor Ashburner's fluvial metaphor is to be retained at all, the waters of the confluent streams of law and equity have surely mingled now.[56]

Likewise, in other Commonwealth jurisdictions such as New Zealand the courts have been more relaxed in finding that equity and common law are truly fused into a single body of law. In one New Zealand Court of Appeal case concerning whether common law damages were available for breach of an equitable obligation, the court held that 'for all purposes now material, equity and common law are mingled or merged. The practicality of the matter is that in the circumstances of the dealings between the parties the law

---

51 See J. Martin, 'Fusion, Fallacy and Confusion: a Comparative Study' [1994] Conv. 13.
52 Ashburner, *Principles of Equity* (2nd edn, 1933) at p. 18.
53 (1880) 16 Ch. D 544.
54 (1880) 16 Ch. D 544 at 549.
55 [1978] AC 904. Much earlier, Lord Denning advocated that law and equity had truly merged; see *Errington* v *Errington and Woods* [1952] 1 KB 290 at 298.
56 [1978] AC 904 at 924.

imposes a duty of confidence. For its breach a full range of remedies should be available as appropriate, no matter whether they originate in common law, equity or statute.'[57]

Despite the approaches taken in some Commonwealth jurisdictions and what has been said by Lord Diplock in **United Scientific Holdings Ltd v Burnley Borough Council**[58] it is incorrect to suggest that the common law and equity are fused in a single coherent body of law. This is perhaps best illustrated by the subject matter of this book which is about the trust concept. In Chapter 2 the trust concept is examined in much more detail; however, suffice it is to say here that the trust concept generates two separate sets of rights. The legal title is vested in the trustee, and the equitable title to the trust property is vested in the beneficiary. The beneficiary's equitable title is only recognised in equity and enforced therein. If there is some breach of trust involving the transfer of the beneficiary's property to a third party, then that beneficiary has no right to follow that property into the hands of the third party at common law, but only in equity. If a third party negligently damages trust property, then the beneficiary has no right at common law to sue the third party for negligence.[59]

Further examples can be given to illustrate that the common law and equity remain two distinct bodies of law, but administered by one single court. It is trite law that the equitable remedy of specific performance is available to a contract which has been entered into for valuable consideration. Thus, where A enters into a contract with B to sell his painting for £3000, B can ask the court to decree specific performance instead of awarding damages. However, the equitable remedy of specific performance will not be available to a contract which is created by deed and recognised in the common law only. The common law recognises and enforces a contract entered into by deed on the grounds that the deed is the consideration.[60] Equity, however, takes the view that there is no valuable consideration and therefore refuses to recognise the contract. Thus, if A had entered into a promise by deed to transfer his painting to B, in the event of breach, B could ask the common law for an award of damages but could not ask for specific performance of the contract as the contract would not be recognised in equity.

So what then does one make of Professor Ashburner's metaphor about the two streams which run side be side and do not mingle their waters? The answer to this is neatly explained by Gary Watt, who writes: '[T]he image of two streams in single channel is not a helpful one. It would be better to see the single river of law being composed of two parts: the riverbed and the water that runs over it. The common law is the river bed, in places it is as unyielding as stone, but in those places over time it is softened by the more fluid processes of equity.'[61]

 ## Equitable maxims

It has already been seen that historically equity developed not on any formal process of precedent, but rather on the discretion of the Lord Chancellor. However, as time went on, the decisions of the Court of Chancery began to form a set of principles and doctrines, which one can say have become as rigid as the common law. What emerged in the course

---

[57] [1990] 3 NZLR 299 at 310.
[58] [1978] AC 904.
[59] *Surrey County Council* v *Bredero Homes* [1993] 1 WLR 1361. These matters are explored in more detail in Chapter 21.
[60] See *Cannon v Hartley* [1949] Ch. 213.
[61] Gary Watt, *Textbook on Trusts* 2nd edn (2006) OUP Oxford at p. 25.

of the development of equity were a set of maxims which explained the way in which equity would intervene in given situations.

Equity will not suffer a wrong without a remedy

This equitable maxim provides that, where possible, a wrong should be redressed by the courts. It does not suggest that every possible wrong complained of should be addressed, but that where there is a defect in the common law then equity should provide an answer. A good example here is the trust. In the early development of equity, the Court of Chancery readily upheld the rights of the beneficiary of the trust despite the trustee having a legal title to the trust property enforceable at common law. The trustee would be compelled to recognise the rights of the beneficiary and transfer the property to the beneficiary. Another example of the operation of this maxim is in the context of a contract. A contract may be perfectly recognised at common law in that is has satisfied all the common law requirements as to form. However, if such a contract has been entered into on grounds of fraud, mistake or undue influence, equity will allow the party affected by the fraud, mistake or undue influence to escape contractual liability. Unlike the common law, equity can put the contract to an end by the remedy of recission, which is to undo the contract and put the parties in the position had the contract not been entered into.

Equity follows the law

Equity developed as a response to the defects of the common law; however, it did not aim to override the common law. Of course, where there was a conflict between law and equity, equity would prevail. This maxim is particularly relevant in the context of land law where equitable estates and interests in land reflect legal estates and interests in the land. Thus, where a legal estate in the land fails for want of formality such as a deed, the same estate will be recognised in equity.

Equity acts *in personam*

One of the more important maxims of equity is that 'equity acts *in personam*'. This maxim has its origins in the manner in which the Lord Chancellor would seek to redress a legal wrong complained of by a claimant. The Chancellor would not interfere with the common law rule or judgment awarded by the common law courts; instead he would ask the defendant to appear before him personally. A decision would be given and an order would be made personally against the defendant to carry out what was instructed. For example, where a contract was capable of being specifically performed, an order would be made to perform that contract. Similarly, where a trustee refused to recognise the rights of a beneficiary under a trust, an order would be made compelling the trustees to so recognise the rights of the beneficiary and convey the title to the trust property in appropriate circumstances. Failure to comply with the order amounted to a contempt of court, which could lead to imprisonment; thus there was every incentive to comply such an order. What is clearly apparent from the idea of acting *in personam* is that the Chancellor and, therefore, equity did not interfere as such with the property in the hands of the defendant. For example, in the context of a trust, equity did not have the power to say that the beneficiary was the legal owner of the property, but could compel the trustee to recognise the existence of the trust, and if appropriate convey the title to the trust property to the beneficiary in the appropriate common law way.

A modern example of this maxim was illustrated in **Webb v Webb**[62] where the Court of Justice of the European Community recognised that equity acting *in personam* was sufficient to give jurisdiction over a person abroad and it made no difference that the order related to property situated abroad. On the facts, a son was ordered to hold a flat on resulting trust for his father on the grounds that his father had paid for the purchase price of the flat but did not take legal title to it.[63] Given the fact that the order related to the person and not the property, there was no conflict with the laws of the foreign country regarding ownership of the disputed property.

He who comes to equity must come with clean hands

This maxim is one that students of law become more accustomed to than any other. Unlike the common law, which is based on precedent and looks to questions of form, equitable relief is given on a discretionary basis. Indeed, all equitable remedies are given on a discretionary basis and are not available per se. Thus, even if all matters of form were complied with, the Lord Chancellor could deny the claimant a remedy if there was some impropriety in his conduct leading up to the dispute complained of. A good example is that between a landlord and tenant under a lease. Although a lease confers in the tenant an estate in the land, it is also a contractual agreement. Any attempt by the landlord to remove the tenant contrary to the terms of the lease agreement amounts to a breach of contract; the tenant can ask equity to decree specific performance of the lease. However, it is quite clear that equity will not decree specific performance where the tenant is at fault, for example, by not observing the covenants in the lease agreement.

An example of the operation of the maxim can be seen in **Lee v Haley**[64] where the claimants sought an injunction to protect their coal business. This was, however, denied by the Court of Appeal on the simple grounds that they had fraudulently sold their customers short.

It is important, however, that the wrongful conduct of the complainant must have a direct nexus with the dispute in question for the maxim to apply. For example, in **Argyll (Duchess) v Argyll**[65] the fact that the wife's adultery was the sole reason for divorce proceedings did not prevent her from obtaining an injunction stopping her former husband from publishing confidential information. Similarly, in **Tinsley v Milligan**,[66] where the House of Lords considered the maxim in detail and the extent to which it was admissible to prevent the court from awarding the claimant a remedy, the House of Lords explained that the wrongful conduct must be causally related to the particular dispute in question. On the facts of this case, a lesbian partner had joined her co-partner in the purchase of land but did not put herself on the title to the disputed property. This was done in order to make dishonest claims for social security benefits. When her co-partner denied her an interest in the disputed property, she complained that she had an equitable interest under a resulting trust by virtue of her contribution to the property. Her co-partner (the legal owner of the house) argued that her dishonest conduct in claiming social security

---

[62] [1994] QB 696. See also *Richard West and Partners (Inverness) Ltd v Dick* [1969] 2 Ch. 424 where an English court had jurisdiction to grant specific performance of a contract for the sale of land in Scotland.

[63] Resulting trusts arising on grounds of contribution to the purchase price of property are discussed in more detail in Chapter 11.

[64] (1869) 5 Ch. App. 155.

[65] [1967] Ch. 302.

[66] [1994] 1 AC 340. See Chapter 11 for a more detailed analysis of this case.

benefit was sufficient to deny her equitable relief because she was not coming to equity with clean hands. The House of Lords, however, held that the maxim only applied where the wrongful conduct of the claimant was the purpose of setting up her entitlement in the first place. On the facts, although there had been wrongful conduct by the claimant, her right to an interest in the property purchased was not influenced by the wrongful conduct put before the court.[67] In Lord Browne-Wilkinson's opinion the claimant did not need to rely on her dishonest conduct to establish an entitlement to the property: that entitlement arose by virtue of the resulting trust in her favour. In other words, if the dishonest conduct of the claimant was the only basis upon which her entitlement could be established then that would be not entertained by the court. A good example of this is illustrated in **Gascoigne v Gascoigne**[68] where a husband took a lease in the wife's name. This was sufficient to raise a presumption of advancement and infer a donative intent on his part.[69] The husband sought to rebut that presumption of advancement by arguing that the only reason he transferred the lease in his wife's name was to defraud his creditors. The Court of Appeal, however, held that he was not entitled to use evidence of an illegal nature to rebut the presumption of advancement.

Equity looks to substance as opposed to form

Equity will not be defeated by lack of compliance with form. It has already been observed in **Walsh v Lonsdale**[70] that a long lease which failed for want of formality was nevertheless recognised and upheld in equity on grounds that in substance the landlord had purported to grant a long lease. Sometimes this maxim is also explained by saying that equity looks to intent rather than form. The matter is neatly explained by Romilly MR in **Parkin v Thorold**[71] when he commented that 'courts of equity make a distinction between that which is a matter of substance and that which is a matter of form; and if it finds that by insisting on the form, the substance will be defeated, it holds it inequitable to allow a person to insist on form, and thereby defeat the substance'.[72]

Equity regards that as done which ought to be done

Equity sees that as done which ought to be done at law. Once again the decision in **Walsh v Lonsdale**[73] provides a perfect example of the operation of this maxim. The decision to uphold the long lease in that case was based on the ground that equity regarded that as done which ought to be done, and in doing so, the court regarded the long lease as having been granted even though at common law it failed for formality. The maxim also explains the grounds upon which the equitable remedy of specific performance is decreed in the case of a contract for the sale of land or some other special property. Where a contract is capable of being performed, the vendor is converted into a constructive trustee and the equitable interest in the subject matter of the contract passes to the purchaser. The basis for treating the purchaser as owner in equity is simply because

---

[67] See also *Tribe v Tribe* [1996] Ch. 107.

[68] [1918] 1 KB 223.

[69] The equitable presumption of advancement infers a donative intent when a transfer is made from father to child or husband to wife. These are considered in more detail in Chapter 13.

[70] (1882) 21 Ch. D 9.

[71] (1852) 16 Beav. 59.

[72] (1852) 16 Beav. 59 at 66.

[73] (1882) 21 Ch. D 9.

equity regards that as done which ought to be done. The decree of specific will require the vendor to transfer the legal title to the purchaser.

He who seeks equity must do equity

Where a person seeks equitable relief he must act fairly towards the other party against whom the equitable relief is being sought. For example, where an individual seeks to set aside a contract by asking the court to rescind the contract, he must be prepared to pay over any money received under the contract. Equally where a contract is set aside, for example, on grounds of undue influence, one party will be allowed to retain remuneration for work done despite having to return the profits made under the contract which is now rescinded. Thus, in **O'Sullivan v Management Agency and Music Ltd**[74] a contract between a singer and a music agency was set aside on grounds of undue influence. The Court of Appeal ordered the music company to return any profits made to the singer but also held that the company was entitled to retain some of the profits by way of remuneration for their labour and skill. A similar result was achieved in **Boardman v Phipps**[75] where a solicitor who was acting in connection with a trust advised the trustees, who were already holding shares in a private company, that they should acquire more shares in the same company with a view to exerting greater control in that company. The trustees refused to purchase further shares on the basis that the trust instrument did not authorise them to do so. After consultation with some of the trustees, the solicitor acquired a controlling interest in the company and made a substantial profit for himself as well as restructuring the company and profiting the beneficiaries. The House of Lords held by a bare majority that the solicitor was required to account for those profits made in his capacity as a fiduciary. Despite the absence of dishonesty on his part, those profits had been made in his capacity as a fiduciary and thus belonged to the beneficiaries. The decision illustrates the strict rule of equity that a fiduciary is not entitled to retain any property made in his capacity as a fiduciary. Boardman, however, was authorised to retain some of the profit by way of remuneration on the basis of *quantum meruit*. Both the Court of Appeal and the House of Lords were aware that Boardman was a man of great ability and had expended labour in reorganising the company and increasing the share therein.

**VISIT CASE
NAVIGATOR**

Equity imputes an intention to fulfil an obligation

Equity will impute an intention to fulfil an obligation. If a person intends to carry out an obligation and then does something which has the effect of fulfilling that obligation, equity will deem that obligation as being satisfied. This maxim is better explained by what has become known as the rule in **Strong v Bird**.[76] This rule holds that where a person (donor) intends to make a lifetime gift to another (donee) but fails to do so then, provided his intention to make the gift continues up until his death and he appoints the donee as his executor or administrator, the gift is said to be complete. The vesting of the donor's property in the donee as executor or administrator is deemed to impute an intention that he wanted the donee to keep what he was promised during the lifetime of the donor.

---

[74] [1985] QB 428.
[75] [1967] AC 46. The decision in *Boardman v Phipps* is considered in more detail in Chapter 17.
[76] (1874) LR 18 Eq. 315. The rule is considered in much detail in Chapter 5.

Delay defeats equity

Otherwise known as the equitable defence of laches, a person who seeks equitable relief must do so within a reasonable time.[77] If he does not assert his right to bring an action within a reasonable time then his conduct is seen as being acquiescence of the wrong complained of. The equitable defence of laches, which still applies in some cases today, must be seen in light of the Limitation Act 1980.

Where equities are equal, the first in time prevails

Where there are two competing equitable interests in the same property then the first in time will prevail. For example, if A grants an equitable mortgage to B and then subsequently grants an equitable mortgage to C, B's mortgage will take priority.[78]

Where the equities are equal, the law prevails

Unlike the last maxim, which seeks to address priority between two competing equitable rights, this maxim addresses the priority between an equitable right and a legal right in respect of the same property. The legal right takes priority over the equitable right. It does not matter whether the equitable right had pre-existed the legal right.

Where there is a conflict between law and equity, equity prevails

It has already been seen above that where there is a rule of the common law and a rule of equity, equity is said to prevail over and above the common law.

Nature of proprietary rights in law and in equity

From what has been observed so far in this chapter, it is clear that rights, particularly proprietary rights, are recognised both at common law and in equity. There is, however, a fundamental difference between those rights recognised at common law and those recognised in equity. Proprietary rights at common law are said to be rights *in rem* whereas proprietary rights recognised in equity are said to be rights *in personam*.

Legal proprietary rights: rights *in rem*

The general principle is that proprietary rights, such as legal ownership, are good against the whole world. Proprietary rights recognised at law are said to be rights *in rem*.[79] There are two meanings to the use of the word that they bind the whole world. In the first place,

---

[77] See *Smith* v *Clay* (1767) Amb. 645 and also *Lindsay Petroleum Co* v *Hurd* (1874) LR 5 PC 221.

[78] An equitable mortgage will arise, for example, where the mortgagor only has an equitable interest to mortgage. Thus, a beneficiary under a trust can only grant an equitable mortgage over the equitable interest in the trust property.

[79] Meaning that they bind the whole world.

legal rights prevail over any subsequently created legal or equitable interests.[80] A legal right, for example, affecting land will bind anyone who subsequently acquires the land irrespective of the lack of knowledge of its existence.[81] Thus if A, the owner of land, leases it to B for a term of 25 years and then subsequently sells the land to C, then C, although the freehold owner of the land, cannot take possession of the land because he will be bound by the legal lease created in B. C is, however, entitled to the receipt of rent from B.

The second aspect of the phrase that legal rights of property bind the world relates to the fact that the right in question is held against a thing rather than a person or persons. In this respect the right is good against anyone who interferes with the thing in which the right is held. Thus, the ownership of A's house is good against anyone in the world and it does not matter who has trespassed on his land. A will have an action against anyone who wrongfully interferes with his land; his right to bring an action is not limited to certain persons. In this respect Austin once commented that 'rights *in rem* may be defined in the following manner – rights residing in persons and availing against persons generally'.[82]

Equitable property rights: rights *in personam* or rights *in rem*?

Unlike common law property rights, equitable property rights are often described as rights *in personam*. This attribute arises from the historical basis that equity acts *in personam*. Conceptual problems do, however, arise when equitable property rights are described as rights *in personam*. The reason for this is that rights *in personam* have traditionally been analysed as purely personal rights. For example, parties under a contract have personal rights: for example, a personal right to see that the contract is performed. This creates the rather strange paradox that although we refer to equitable property rights as property rights, we describe them as rights *in personam*, suggesting that they are purely personal rights. However, the fact is that equitable property rights are not rights *in personam* in the sense that they are purely personal rights: they are indeed property rights.[83] For example, the right of a beneficiary under a trust is proprietary, albeit an equitable proprietary right. The fact that they are also described as rights *in personam* is attributable to the method of enforcement of the right in equity: that is, an order *in personam* in equity.

It is submitted that equitable property rights, albeit classified as rights *in personam*, are proprietary rights in the true sense of the word. The answer is arrived at if one puts aside the juridical analysis of rights and then simply asks the question of enforceability of the right. Where a right has the ability to bind a potentially large class of persons then

---

[80] The only limited exception to this rule is in the case of personal property when there may be exception to what is known as the *nemo dat quod non habet* rule. This rule holds that a person cannot give a better title to property which he does not have. Thus, a person cannot give a good title to something if he does not have it in the first place. The exceptions to the *nemo dat quod habet* rule are outside the scope of this book; however, see generally, M. Bridge, *Personal Property Law* 3rd edn (2002) at pp. 95–115.

[81] In the case of land, certain legal rights may be subject to registration where the title to land is registered. Registration of legal rights in this context is an integral and normal part of the registration process; such registration does not detract from the common law principle that legal rights bind the whole world.

[82] Austin, *Jurisprudence* (4th edn) at p. 381.

[83] Some commentators have, however, suggested that all equitable rights are personal as opposed to proprietary. See, for example, Langdell, *Brief Survey of Equity Jurisdiction* (2nd edn) who once wrote that an equitable right 'may be defined as an equitable personal obligation. It is an obligation because it is not ownership', (p. 6). See also W. Hart, 'The Place of Trust in Jurisprudence' (1912) 28 LQR at 290, where the author examines the idea of a right *in personam* in the context of the trust and the rights of the beneficiary thereunder.

it looks more like a proprietary right than a personal one. Equitable rights are not mere personal rights as, for example, those arising under a contact; they are rights which are capable of binding a potentially large class of persons. Even though equity acts *in personam*, the range of persons capable of being bound by an equitable right can be great. In this respect Megarry and Thompson write: '[E]quitable rights . . . look less and less like mere rights in personam and more and more like rights in rem. Although it is still possible to regard them as rights in personam, it is perhaps best to treat them as hybrids, being neither entirely one nor entirely the other. They have never reached the status of rights in rem, yet the class of persons against whom they will be enforced is too large for mere rights in personam.'[84]

Equitable rights and the doctrine of notice

Equitable rights, for example, the rights of a beneficiary under a trust, are governed by the doctrine of notice. This doctrine holds that equitable rights are binding on all persons except a bona fide purchaser of a legal interest without notice of the pre-existing interest.[85] Equity, acting *in personam*, clearly binds the conscience of the party against whom an equitable interest is granted. Thus, for example, a trustee is clearly bound by the trust and must recognise and respect the equitable interest of the beneficiary. However, equity goes further and binds all those persons who subsequently acquire the legal title to the property in which the equitable right is granted with notice of the equitable right. Thus, where a trustee transfers the legal title to the trust property to a third party, the equitable rights of the beneficiary will bind the third party if he has notice of the equitable interest of the beneficiary.

The doctrine of notice requires the purchaser to be a bona fide purchaser. This is no more than saying that the purchaser must be one who is innocent and acting in good faith. The absence of notice on the part of the bona fide purchaser will readily satisfy this requirement. The purchase must have given value, that is, consideration. Consideration includes the common law meaning as well as that in equity, thus money or money's worth and marriage consideration will suffice.[86] A purchaser for value need not, however, show that consideration was adequate.[87] Where a purchaser has not provided any consideration he will not be able to rely on the doctrine of notice and will be bound by the equitable right irrespective of notice. This is primarily because equity will not assist a volunteer and a volunteer is someone who has not provided consideration. The purchaser must be of a purchaser of a legal estate. In the context of real property this means that the purchaser must be a purchaser of either a freehold estate or a leasehold estate.[88] In the context of personal property the purchaser must simply be the purchaser of the legal title to such property: for example, the legal title to shares in a company or a painting. It is clear, however, that the doctrine of notice does not extend to the purchase of an equitable estate or interest in property. Here the equitable maxim 'where the equities are equal the first in time prevails' applies in order to give priority to such rights.[89]

---

[84] A.J. Oakley (ed.) *Megarry's Manual of the Law of Property*, 8th edn (2002) at p. 57.

[85] See *London and South Western Rail Co v Gomm* (1882) 20 Ch. D 562 and *Pilcher v Rawlins* (1872) 7 Ch. App. 259.

[86] Marriage consideration is considered in more detail in Chapter 6.

[87] *Midland Bank Co Ltd v Green* [1981] AC 513.

[88] Purchaser includes a legal mortgagee who, by operation of the Law of Property Act 1925, s. 87(1), is deemed as being vested with a legal estate in the land.

[89] *Re Morgan* (1881) 18 Ch. D 93; *McCarthy and Stone Ltd v Harding* [1979] 1 WLR 1547.

The central requirement of the doctrine of notice relates to the question of what constitutes notice. Three types of knowledge have been identified for the purposes of the doctrine.

1 *Actual notice*. This is the most obvious and simplest form of knowledge attributable to a purchaser. It refers to the situation where a purchaser is consciously aware of the equitable right in the property at the time of the purchase. Thus, if a trustee sells trust property in breach of trust to a third party who knows of the existence of the trust then that third party is clearly bound by the equitable right of the beneficiary.

2 *Constructive notice*. Actual notice is to be distinguished from constructive notice, which refers to knowledge which would have come to the attention of a purchaser had he carried out a reasonable inspection of the title to which he was purchasing. A good example of constructive notice was illustrated in a trust of land case ***Kingsnorth Finance Co Ltd v Tizard***.[90] On the facts, a husband held the legal title to a matrimonial home on trust for himself and his wife. After they had separated the wife discontinued to live with her husband but did visit the house on a daily basis to look after the children. The husband arranged a mortgage with the mortgagee, which was duly given after an inspection on a Sunday afternoon arranged by the husband at a time when the wife was not there. The husband told the surveyor that he had separated from his wife some time ago and that she did not have any interest in the house. When the husband later absconded with the mortgage monies, the court held that the equitable rights of the wife under the trust bound the mortgagee. The inspection by the mortgagee was simply insufficient and they were affixed with constructive notice.[91]

3 *Imputed notice*. The final type of notice is imputed notice, which arises when an agent of the purchaser has notice, actual or constructive, which is imputed to the purchaser: for example, notice which a solicitor of the purchaser may have but fails to communicate it to the purchaser. Nevertheless, the purchaser will have imputed notice by virtue of his agent.

The effect of a successful claim that a purchaser purchased the legal title without notice of the equitable right is to give him an 'absolute, unqualified, unanswerable defence'[92] against the holder of an equitable interest in the property purchased. The doctrine of notice not only gives the purchaser an unqualified defence against the holder of the equitable right but also operates in a destructive way so that the equitable interest in the property is completely destroyed. It cannot be revived against a subsequent purchaser of the legal title who may have notice of the fact that the equitable right once existed.[93]

In the context of land, the doctrine of notice has been largely superseded by a system of registration of interests. Furthermore, the doctrine of overreaching was introduced

---

[90] [1986] 1 WLR 783.

[91] The extent to which constructive notice operates in contexts other than land is debatable. It is generally understood that the level of investigation of title in personal property transactions is different from that of land transactions. Personal property has never been subject to the rigorous inspection of title that occurs in land transactions simply because there are no elaborate title deeds or a system of registration by which a purchaser can inspect title. Over a hundred years ago Lindley LJ remarked that 'the equitable doctrines of constructive notice are common enough in dealing with land and estates with which the Court is familiar; but there has always been repeated protest against the introduction into commercial transactions of anything like an extension of those doctrines and the protest is founded on perfect good sense'. See, *Manchester Trust* v *Furness* [1895] 2 QB 539 at 545.

[92] *Pilcher* v *Rawlins* (1872) 7 Ch. App. 259 at 269.

[93] *Wilkes* v *Spooner* [1911] 2 KB 473.

whereby the rights of beneficiaries under a trust were automatically transferred to the proceeds of sale, provided that the purchase money was paid over to a minimum of two trustees.[94]

Equity and social reform

In this chapter a lot has been said about the development of equity as a gloss upon the common law. It has been seen that equity played an important role in ironing out the deficiencies of the common law and thereby developing its own unique equitable principles and doctrines. However, it must also be remembered that equity played an important role in social and economic reform and recognised rights and doctrines which were not recognised at common law. Three particular examples can be given in this chapter to illustrate equity's contribution to social and economic reform.

The property rights of married women

Until the enactment of the Married Women's Property Act 1882, a married woman had no right to own property; everything she had belonged to her husband. Despite the 1882 legislation, which changed that rule, the husband usually continued in practice to be the sole owner of property.[95] It is not altogether clear why the common law denied property rights to married women. Holcombe explains that historians attribute the common law rule on grounds such as religion.[96] The medieval church regarded marriage as sacramental and the idea that two persons became one flesh justified the husband's dominion over his wife and any property she may have. Other justifications simply concentrate on the social and economic reality of the position of women in the Middle Ages. The extent of the common law rule prior to 1882 is neatly explained by Holcombe who writes: '[T]he property that a woman possessed or was entitled to at the time of the marriage and any property she acquired or became entitled to after her marriage became her husband's to control. Moreover, if a woman who accepted a proposal of marriage sought, before the marriage took place, to dispose of any property without the knowledge and consent of her intended husband, the disposition could be set aside as a legal fraud.'[97] The denial of property to married women was not something peculiar to English law; other systems of law and state followed similar patterns.[98]

Despite the denial of property rights for women at common law, equity recognised and enforced marriage settlements, protecting that property which was the subject of the settlement. Under a marriage settlement, the wife would agree to settle any property she brought into the marriage or any property acquired after her marriage upon trust. The trustees of the marriage settlement would then hold such property for her and her

---

[94] See s. 2(1) Law of Property Act 1925. For an application of the doctrine of overreaching, see *City of London Building Society* v *Flegg* [1988] AC 54. The process of registration of equitable interests in registered land is now governed by the Land Registration Act 2002.

[95] See B. Roshier and H. Teff, *Law and Society in England* (1980) at p. 173.

[96] L. Holcombe, *Wives and Property* (1983) at p. 19.

[97] *Ibid.* at p. 18. The approach of the common law to the property rights of married woman was not followed by equity jurisdiction. Equity contributed to law reform by using equitable principles, notably the trust and marriage settlements, to protect the rights of married woman in property they might acquire after marriage.

[98] See E. Sullerot, *Woman, Society and Change* (1971) at pp. 19–28.

issue.[99] The role of equity in protecting the property rights of women is best explained by Holcombe, who writes:

> In practice the Court of Chancery allowed the creation of a special category of property, the so-called separate property or separate estate of married women. At law a married woman could not own property, but in equity property could be settled upon her for her use under the management of a trustee who was responsible to the court for carrying out the terms of the trust. At first it was necessary to prove to the court's satisfaction that there was a good reason for the creation of the trust, as, for example, that the husband was a wastrel or that the woman was separated from her husband. But soon equity came to accept without inquiry any trust created for a married woman. The separate property created by the trust would be protected by the Court of Chancery against a woman's husband and all other persons according to the wishes of the donor.[100]

Freedom of testation

The system of feudal tenure discussed earlier in the chapter operated in a way in which no person, apart from the Crown, was absolute owner of land. Instead the ownership of land was fragmented vertically so that the King granted land to powerful lords who could in return grant further segments of land to tenants. The trust developed out of the use as a way in which feudal tenants could freely leave land to their heirs, without their heirs having to pay feudal dues to the overlord. By transferring the land to trustees on use of the tenant and, after death, his family, there would be no acquisition on the land of the tenant's death. Instead, the trustees would be (and would always remain) the owners of the land, but would be bound by equitable intervention to the use (this is discussed more fully in Chapter 2, under 'Historical foundations of the trust').[101]

The second advantage of the trust lay in the fact that it permitted greater freedom to the tenant in devising his property to persons other than just the heir. The common law was strict in requiring land be vested in the heir of the tenant. Where the tenant died without an heir, the overlord became entitled to the land by way of escheat.[102] Transfer to trustees, however, allowed land to be enjoyed by those designated in the terms of the use rather than on the strict principles of the common law. In recognition of the potential scope of the use in undermining the system of feudal dues and the consequential emptying of the Crown's pocket, the Statute of Uses 1535[103] was introduced which had the effect of undermining certain uses. The basic aim of the legislation was to deny the beneficiary equitable rights in the land. Rather, where the use was employed, the intended beneficiary acquired a legal title to the land and was thus subject to feudal dues in the event of the death of the tenant. In 1540 the Statute of Wills was also passed in recognition that the landowning aristocracy rejected the strict common law rule requiring land to be acquired by the heir. The statute permitted greater freedom in the disposition of property after the death of the tenant; however, such dispositions would be subject to the same feudal taxes that existed before the statute.

---

[99] See, for example, *Pullan v Koe* [1913] 1 Ch. 9. Marriage settlements are discussed at more length in Chapter 6.

[100] L. Holcombe, *Wives and Property* (1983) at p. 38.

[101] This basically involved delivery of possession in the presence of witnesses followed by ceremonial acts; see Thorne, 'Livery of Seisin' (1938) 52 LQR at 345.

[102] See Megarry and Wade, *The Law of Real Property* 7th edn (2008) at p. 17.

[103] Described as the 'most important single statute in the history of the trust's development' by G. Moffat, *Trust Law: Text and Materials*, 3rd edn (1999); see now 4th edn (2005) Cambridge, at p. 40.

● Restrictive covenants

Although in the nineteenth century it was important to keep land unfettered from burdens so as to maintain its optimal value for industry, there was also a growing recognition towards the end of the century that the pace of industrial and urban growth would seriously undermine land use in the country.[104] In the landmark decision in ***Tulk* v *Moxhay*,**[105] Lord Cottenham LC held that a successor of a negative covenant who had notice of the covenant was thereby bound in conscience to honour it. On the facts of the case, the covenantor had agreed with the covenantee that he would maintain a garden at Leicester Square uncovered with any buildings. Although the sale of the covenantor's land to his successor contained no provision in the conveyance relating to the garden, it bound the successor of the covenantor on the grounds of notice. The effect of the ruling in ***Tulk* v *Moxhay*** was to recognise a new equitable interest in land capable of binding third parties despite having its origins in contract and starting out as a personal right.

Conclusion

This chapter has explored the nature and historical development of equity. It has been observed that equity developed in response to the inadequacies of the common law in the thirteenth and fourteenth centuries. The two particular deficiencies identified in this chapter were the inadequacy of the common law remedy and the rigidity of the system of precedent. Equity developed in a manner, not so to override the common law or indeed to conflict with it: rather equity's aim was to supplement the common law system and provide a gloss on the common law. The early Court of Chancery was administered by the Lord Chancellor who sought to exercise his discretion in any given dispute by looking to the unconscionable conduct of the defendant. In this respect, equity has sometimes been described as a system of law which seeks to undo unconscionable conduct. Although the early Court of Chancery interpreted the notion of unconscionability with reference to principles of morality and applied it on a very broad discretionary basis, the modern interpretation of unconscionability is much more refined. Unconscionability in modern equity is interpreted and understood by looking at the relevant context in question. By examining the various contexts in which equity has operated and continues to operate, one can see that the courts have over time established set principles and rules which determine whether the conduct of the defendant has been unconscionable in that context.

Although the early Court of Chancery looked at cases on an individual basis, and exercised relief on the merits of every case, there has been in more recent times the debate whether equity still possesses the same degree of flexibility in developing new rights and remedies. It has been suggested that equity has gone past childbearing and now possesses the same degree of rigidity as the common law. That is to say that the rules of equity are now as determined and established as the rules of the common law. Whilst this is true to a large extent in English law, the courts have from time to time shown a willingness to use equitable jurisdiction to develop new rights and remedies. However,

---

[104] See W.R. Cornish and G. de N. Clarke, *Law and Society in England 1750–1950* (1989) at p. 150.
[105] (1884) 2 Ph. 774; 41 ER 1143.

it must be said that English law, unlike its Commonwealth partners, has remained cautious in the expansion of new equitable rights and remedies. This has primarily been in response to the perceived uncertainty in law that would arise by the creation of new rights and remedies.

This chapter has examined some of the basic maxims of equity which explain how equitable relief is administered by the courts. These maxims provide the basis upon which the discretionary nature of equitable relief is administered. As well as the maxims of equity, this chapter provides the reader with an understanding of the difference between property rights which are recognised at law and those recognised in equity. The fundamental difference lies in the fact that property rights at law are described as rights *in rem* whilst rights in equity are recognised as rights *in personam*. The distinction between the two relates primarily to the enforceability of the right against third parties. Property rights at common law bind the whole world whereas property rights in equity are governed by the equitable doctrine of notice and bind everyone except a bona fide purchaser of the legal title without notice of the equitable interest.

Finally, whilst this chapter has looked at the manner in which the common law developed as a gloss on the common law, the supremacy of equity in dealing with emerging social and economic reform cannot be underestimated. This chapter has looked at some of those areas, such as the rights of married women, the rights of a borrower under a mortgage and the restrictive covenant in planning, which demonstrate the importance of equity in meeting some of the social and economic challenges presented from time to time. Indeed, one of the notable achievements of equity has been its ability to provide legal redress in a number of quite diverse contexts ranging from social to commercial context.

●● Moot points

1 Explain the reasons for the development of the early Court of Chancery.

2 What do you understand by the term 'unconscionability' and how would you differentiate it with the notion of fairness?

3 How would you describe the relationship between the common law and equity?

4 What do you understand by the 'fusion fallacy' between common law and equity? With specific examples explain how common law and equitable remedies need to be distinguished on any given set of facts.

5 What are the fundamental differences between property rights at law and property rights recognised in equity?

6 One of the greatest achievements of equity in English law has been its ability to operate in a number of quite diverse contexts ranging from social to commercial. Explain the reasons why equity has been able to do this.

Further reading

Baker, J.H. *An Introduction to English Legal History* (3rd edn 2002). A useful resource for further investigation into the development of the common law and equity.

Delany, H. and D. Ryan 'Unconscionability: A Unifying Theme' (2008) Conv. 401. This article provides an excellent discussion surrounding the term 'unconscionability' and explores the extent to which it is possible to identify a unifying theme which explains the term.

Duggan, A.J. 'Is Equity Efficient?' (1997) 113 LQR 601.

Holmes, O. 'Early English Equity' (1885) 1 LQR 162. Provides a useful historical account of equity.

Maitland, F.W. *Equity: A Course of Lectures* (J. Brunyate (ed.) 1936). This provides an excellent read of the nature of equity and its associated principles and doctrines as delivered by Professor Maitland to his students.

Martin, J. 'Fusion, Fallacy and Confusion: A Comparative Study' [1994] Conv. 13. Examines the fusion fallacy between equity and the common law.

Worthington, S. *Equity* (Oxford: Clarendon Press, 2003). Provides a very interesting read into the nature, scope and functions of equity.

Visit **www.mylawchamber.co.uk/panesar** to access study support resources including interactive multiple choice questions, practice exam questions with guidance, podcasts, weblinks, legal newsfeed all linked to the **Pearson eText** version of Exploring Equity and Trusts which you can **search, highlight** and **personalise** with your **own notes** and **bookmarks**.

premium
mylawchamber
unrivalled support for legal education

Use Case Navigator to read in full some of the key cases referenced in this chapter with commentary and questions:

Westdeutsche Landesbank Girozentrale v Islington LBC [1996] AC 699 (HL)

Boardman v Phipps [1967] 2 AC 46

POWERED BY **LexisNexis**

2

The trust concept

Learning objectives

After reading this chapter you should be able to:

→ understand the nature of a trust

→ understand the reasons for creating a trust

→ explain the trust as a product of fragmentation of ownership

→ understand the historical development of the trust and its modern-day significance

→ explain the respective rights of the trustee and the beneficiary

→ explain the difference of express trusts and implied trusts

→ understand how express trusts and implied trusts are classified

→ explain the role of trusts in law reform

→ understand the functions of trust law.

Hambro and Others v *The Duke of Marlborough and Others* [1994] 3 WLR 341: The Blenheim Estates, the Duke of Marlborough and his irresponsible son

Many readers with an advanced understanding of the law of trust may be a little surprised and taken aback as to why the 'Setting the scene' in this chapter begins with a look at a decision of the High Court in 1994 concerning the famous Blenheim Estates. It is quite understandable why such a reader may be surprised, given the fact that litigation of the type in the case is not one which is commonplace in modern trust law. Nonetheless, the facts and the litigation concerning the Blenheim Estates and the 11th Duke of Marlborough illustrate some very important manifestations about the trust concept.

For those students who will recall their history lessons, by 1704 the French King Louis XIV had taken a powerful control over Europe in an attempt to build a massive French Empire. In order to continue with his dominance in Europe, the King formed an alliance with Bavaria. In 1704, John Churchill, the 1st Duke of Marlborough marched an English army, allied with the Dutch, some 200 miles and successfully triumphed over the French and their allies at a place called Blenheim. In recognition of this triumph, Queen Anne of England gave the Royal Manor of Woodstock, near Oxford, as a gift to the Duke of Marlborough. She instructed that a palace be built on the land. By an Act of Parliament in 1705, the land was subject to a settlement (trust) to the effect that the land be passed on to future generations of the 1st Duke of Marlborough, including female heirs. The effect of this arrangement meant that the land was held for the 1st Duke of Marlborough and his subsequent heirs.

Whilst the land continued to pass to subsequent Dukes of Marlborough, the 11th Duke of Marlborough commenced proceedings in 1994 contending that his son, the Marquis of Blandford, was financially irresponsible and that his right to the enjoyment of the Blenheim estates be subject to restrictions. These restrictions were authorised by the High Court on the grounds that the Marquis of Blandford was not in a position to take control of the Blenheim Estates.

The famous victory at Blenheim and the reward to the 1st Duke of Marlborough and the concerns of the 11th Duke provide good enough facts to illustrate some of the issues arising in trust law. First of all, the land was given by way of a gift to the 1st Duke of Marlborough, albeit subject to a settlement by an Act of Parliament in 1705. A unique feature of a trust is that it involves, in a majority of cases, a gift from one person to another. However, the gift is usually modified in some way: for example, that the enjoyment of it is only for the life of the beneficiary, as in the case of the Duke of Marlborough, or is otherwise postponed until some future time. Secondly, the land forming the subject matter of the Blenheim Estates was held by trustees for the benefit of beneficiaries in the form of the heirs of the Duke of Marlborough. Thirdly, the facts of the case illustrate that a trust often has a long duration and in the course of the duration of a trust certain things can change. When such changes take place, can the trustees or the courts change the nature of the trust which was created many years ago by the settlor? Fourthly, the case is an excellent example of what can happen when a person creating a trust, or indeed trustees administering a trust, find themselves with an irresponsible beneficiary. Is there any means by which the trust property can be protected from the irresponsible behaviour of the beneficiary? In the case of the Blenheim Estates, what do you think Queen Anne, or indeed the 1st Duke of Marlborough would have done if they knew that the estates would be under the control of an irresponsible heir? Finally, although the Blenheim Estates and the settlement of the land thereof provides an example of the use of the trust concept, the question arises as to whether the trust continues to operate in the manner it did in the case of the Blenheim Estates, or whether it has other more contemporary functions.

Moving on: thinking about trusts and trust law in the modern law

Most students doing a first degree in law will be unfamiliar with the concept of a trust. Unlike some areas of English law such as contract law or criminal law, the law of trusts is one which students will often find hard to relate to. This is not unusual since most students will not have encountered the trust concept in their lives. They will readily relate to contracts and understand criminal wrongs, but to relate to the idea that a trust allows the fragmentation of ownership of a thing is something of an alien concept. So what is it all about?

In order to understand the role and function of a trust it is best to start thinking about the following scenarios which may arise in everyday life.

Scenario One
Harry is 16 years of age and is doing very well in his studies. It is his intention to qualify as a lawyer and work with his father who has his own law firm. Harry's father has a sum of money which he would like to give to Harry so that he can use it for his studies and eventually qualify as a lawyer. Harry's father is concerned that if he simply hands over the money to Harry he may just spend it without using it for his studies. A better solution might be for someone to hold the money for Harry and make it available only for his studies. Can this be done?

Scenario Two
Victor is a wealthy businessman and has a number of shares in a number of different private and public companies. Over the past few years he has received substantial dividends on the shares. He has also had to pay tax on the profits he has made. Victor is taxed at a high rate and is wondering whether his tax liability can be lowered if he was to move some of his shares to his family members.

Scenario Three
Wayne and Hillary purchased a house in 1989 and the legal title to the house was conveyed in Wayne's name only. It was intended that the house would be their family home and Hillary contributed to the deposit of the house. Hillary also made regular contributions to the mortgage. Recently, Wayne and Hillary, who are not married, decided to split up. Hillary is concerned that she is not on the legal title to the house but feels she must have some interest in it. Hillary has no legal title to the land, but has she got some interest in the house?

As well as the famous Blenheim Estates, the above scenarios depict the type of matters which a student of equity and trusts may have to deal with. Each of these scenarios involves a solution which is provided by the trust concept. The chapter examines the concept of a trust and investigates the key features of a trust and the manner in which it operates.

Introduction

This book is primarily concerned with trusts and the law of trusts, and therefore the purpose of this chapter is to explore the concept of the trust, in particular, its nature and the means by which trusts are classified. Maitland once wrote: '[O]f all the exploits of Equity the largest and most important is the invention and development of the Trust. It is an institute of great elasticity and generality; as elastic, as general as contract. This perhaps forms the most distinctive achievement of English Lawyers. It seems to us almost essential to civilization, and yet there is nothing quite like it in foreign law.'[1] Indeed, the trust has played an important role in achieving various social and economic goals which will be explored in this chapter and throughout the course of this book. For the time being the following illustration explains the versatility of the modern trust by giving some examples of the types of socioeconomic problems that can be resolved by the use of a trust.[2] Some of the problems have already been raised above; however, the following table illustrates just how versatile the trust concept is.

The versatility of the modern trust

A problem requiring a trust solution	The trust solution
Alfred, a wealthy businessman has a number of investments which yield substantial income at the end of each tax year. Because the income exceeds the threshold for higher income tax, the question arises as to how he could possibly reduce his tax liability on the income he is earning.	The trust has, since its very beginnings, been a primary vehicle by which an individual can reduce his tax liability by settling his property for the benefit of his family members, thereby reducing the extent of tax payable on his income. For example, in the problem raised, rather than Alfred retaining beneficial ownership of the investments which yield the income, he can ask for those investments to be held by trustees on trust for his family members who will pay no tax at all or pay at a lower rate of tax.
Simone, who died recently, is survived by her three children who are all under the age of 18 years. Amongst other property, Simone has left her house to her three children. The children discover that the law does not permit a minor to hold the legal title to land.	The fact that the children cannot hold the legal title to land is not fatal to them enjoying the beneficial interest in the land. The law provides that a conveyance of a legal estate to a minor operates as a declaration of trust of that land in favour of the minor. In this way, the land is held by trustees for the benefit of the children, who on the age of majority can call for the conveyance of the land to them.
Michael, who is married to Heather, wishes to leave his property to Heather after his death. However, unknown to Heather, Michael has for a long time maintained a very close relationship with his secretary Patsy. He wishes to leave a large sum of money to Patsy after his death. He is quite happy to leave his property to Heather in his will; however, he is also aware that if he leaves a large sum of money to Patsy in the will then this will be subject of much controversy, not least, the disclosure of his relationship with Patsy.	A will is a public document and as such is available to anyone to read. It is understandable why Michael would not want to include Patsy in his will. The trust, however, is an excellent vehicle by which he can provide for Patsy without Heather or anyone else finding out about the gift to her. Michael can leave the money in his will to someone, like his solicitor, who agrees to give it to Patsy after Michael's death. This creates what is known as a secret trust. Michael's solicitor appears to receive the money absolutely; however, during his lifetime he has agreed to be a trustee for Patsy. Indeed, secret trusts, as will be seen later, were a primary vehicle for providing for mistresses and illegitimate children.

---

[1] F.W. Maitland, *Equity: A Course of Lectures* J. Brunyate (ed.) (1936) at p. 23.
[2] These are just some of the many ways in which the trust has been employed to meet different social and economic objectives.

A problem requiring a trust solution	The trust solution
Gordon is a very successful lawyer. It has long been his wish that his two sons also qualify as lawyers and continue working for the family business. He wishes to know what incentives he can create so that his sons, who are 17 and 18 respectively, enter the legal profession. Gordon also has a valuable collection of eighteenth and nineteenth century law reports which were handed down from his ancestors. He wishes to retain those reports in the family for generations to come and wishes to know how that can be achieved.	The traditional focus of trusts has been in the context of family provisions and the preservation of wealth. A trust is an excellent means by which a person can make a future gift subject to some contingency. For example, Gordon can transfer £30,000 on trust to trustees to hold for his two sons on them qualifying as lawyers. The sons would have a contingent interest in the £30,000 subject to them qualifying. At the same time he could create a settlement whereby he transfers legal title to the law reports to trustees who are to hold the law reports for Gordon for life, thereafter for his oldest son and thereafter for his grandchildren. Seen in this way, neither Gordon nor his oldest son can dispose of the law reports.
Phillip and Fiona, an unmarried couple, purchased a house sometime in the early 1990s. The intention of both Phillip and Fiona was that this would be their family home as they planned to get married. However, the house was only conveyed in Phillip's name. The house was purchased with the aid of a mortgage; however, Fiona contributed £10,000 to the deposit. Phillip and Fiona never got married and now Phillip wishes to sell the house. Fiona is not sure what rights she has in the house.	Since about the middle of the twentieth century the trust has played an important role in determining the ownership rights of cohabitees in circumstances where they have left their beneficial interests ill-defined. Particularly in cases of non-marital cohabitation, the trust has been the means by which the beneficial entitlement to land can be resolved in favour of a person who is not the legal owner of land, but has either made some contribution to the purchase price or is otherwise promised some interest in the land. In such a case the court will imply a trust so that the legal owner of the land holds the land on trust for himself and his cohabitee. The very extent of the interest of the non-legal owner depends on the type of trust the court is prepared to imply in the circumstances.
A number of law students have formed a mooting club at their law school. The club encourages the students to engage in mooting and other activities. Membership fee is £20 per year. Recently, a local firm of solicitors has donated a sum of £500 to the mooting club. The club is not a separate legal entity and the question is how the funds of the club are held and by whom.	Whereas a company, which is incorporated, acquires a separate legal entity, a club is an unincorporated association with no separate legal status. A club is nothing more than a group of individuals bound together by some common objective. A company can hold property in its own name, but a club cannot. The question arises as to who controls the property belonging to an unincorporated association. The trust is one means by which the property of the club can be transferred into the name of a few of the members who will hold the property on behalf of the other members. The ownership of property given to unincorporated associations raises a number of issues which are dealt with later in this book.
A lender wishes to lend a sum of money to a borrower. The lender is aware that, should the borrower default on payment, he will only have a personal claim to the recovery of the money loaned. In the case of the insolvency of the borrower, the lender will remain an unsecured creditor. What the lender wishes to know is whether he can loan the money to the borrower and, should the borrower fail to use the money for the purpose for which it was advanced, whether he has a right to claim back the money as his.	It has long been recognised that a trust and contract relationship can coexist. A lender can enter into a contract to loan a sum of money to a borrower who is under a personal obligation to repay the loan money. The lender can at the same time stipulate that the monies advanced under the loan are not to be used for any other purpose other than for the purpose of the loan. The effect of this arrangement will be that the borrower becomes a trustee for the lender and, should the borrower fail to use the money for the purpose of the loan, the lender can claim the money back as his property. Seen in this way, the lender will not be an unsecured creditor should the borrower be declared bankrupt.

A problem requiring a trust solution	The trust solution
Jenny has a built up a large sum of money in her current account at her bank. Her bank manager has advised her that the money would be better invested in stocks and shares where she would be able to allow her money to grow faster than in the current account. Jenny is rather concerned about the risk of investing in shares. She would rather diversify her investments and chose from a portfolio of investments, thereby reducing the risk of losing money on her investment.	In recent times the concept of the unit trust has played an important role in facilitating small-time investors, as well as larger investors, to invest in a portfolio of investments, thereby reducing the risk to their original investment. Typically, a unit trust involves a fund manager investing sums of money in particular types of companies. The investments purchased are invested by the trustee of the unit trust, who will hold any dividends for the original investors according to the amount of their initial investment or typically their units of investment. Unit trusts can have either capital growth or income growth or a combination of both. Should any holder of a unit trust investment wish to sell his investment, or typically units of investment, the value will depend on the stock market.
Mathew has recently secured a job with a large multinational company. The company has advised him that he should contribute a sum out of his salary to provide for a private pension when he retires. The company has advised him that they too will contribute a sum towards his pension and that he will be entitled to a lump sum on retirement as well as an annual pension based on his salary on retirement. Whilst Mathew is keen on this pension, he is also concerned as to how his pension contributions will be held and safeguarded.	Most private pension schemes use the trust as a means by which contributions by employees and employers are held by trustees on trust for the employees. On retirement the employee can look forward to an annual income as well as a lump sum payment. One of the advantages of using the trust is that the pension funds will be held separately from the funds of the company. Therefore, should the company encounter financial problems, the funds of the pension will belong to the beneficiaries and not form part of the assets of the company.

  ## Definition

The basic idea behind the trust lies in the fact that the management and enjoyment functions of ownership are split between different persons. The role of management is vested in a person called a trustee whilst the enjoyment of the thing subject to the trust is vested in persons called beneficiaries. The fragmentation of management and enjoyment is only possible where the legal title to the property is vested in trustees. However, because the trustees have agreed to hold and manage the legal title for the benefit of beneficiaries, their conscience binds them in equity, thereby giving the beneficiaries an equitable interest in the property subject to the trust. The net effect of fragmenting management and enjoyment is that there is a consequential fragmentation of title. The trustees hold the legal title, which is a nominal title[3], while the beneficiary holds the equitable title full of beneficial rewards from the property. The trust in this sense can be seen as a product of equity. One leading treatise on the law of trusts defines the trust as:

> an equitable obligation, binding on a person (who is called a trustee) to deal with property over which he has control (which is called the trust property), for the benefit of persons (who are called beneficiaries), of whom he may himself be one, and any one of who may

---

[3] Nominal in the sense that the trustee has no beneficial interest in the property he is holding and, therefore, is not entitled to the fruits of that property.

enforce the obligation. Any act or neglect on the part of the trustee which is not authorized or excused by the terms of the trust instrument, or by law, is called a breach of trust.[4]

   ## The key features of the trust

A trust has a number of key features, each of which requires separate discussion in this section.[5]

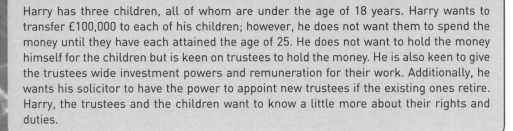

APPLYING THE LAW

Harry has three children, all of whom are under the age of 18 years. Harry wants to transfer £100,000 to each of his children; however, he does not want them to spend the money until they have each attained the age of 25. He does not want to hold the money himself for the children but is keen on trustees to hold the money. He is also keen to give the trustees wide investment powers and remuneration for their work. Additionally, he wants his solicitor to have the power to appoint new trustees if the existing ones retire. Harry, the trustees and the children want to know a little more about their rights and duties.

The settlor

Unless a trust is implied by the courts, it is usually created by a deliberate act on the part of a settlor. Where a trust is created in a will, the settlor will be referred to as the testator, or testatrix if it is woman creating the trust in the will. Where a settlor creates a trust during his lifetime, the trust is said be an *inter vivos* trust. Where the trust is created in a will, the trust is said to be a testamentary trust. There is nothing stopping a settlor also being a trustee, and indeed nothing stopping him being a beneficiary under the trust. For example, A can declare that he is a trustee of £5000 in favour of himself and his children in equal shares.

The trustee(s)

The trust property must be vested in one or more trustees who will hold the legal title to the property on trust for the beneficiaries. In principle there is nothing stopping any individual being a trustee; however, the appointment of an infant as a trustee will be void.[6] In the early days a trustee would often be a family member or a close friend who usually acted out of a sense of moral obligation. In more contemporary times, a trustee will often be a professional person, such as a solicitor or a bank, acting out of some contractual duty rather than a moral one. A trustee can be an individual or a limited company or any other body corporate. In the most typical case the trustee will be vested with the legal title to the trust property; however, it is quite possible to be a trustee of an equitable interest in favour of a beneficiary. For example, in a typical trust a settlor transfers the legal title to property to be held on trust for the benefit of a beneficiary. In such a case the trustee is

---

[4] Underhill and Hayton, *The Law Relating to Trust and Trustees* 14th edn (1987) at p. 3.

[5] For an excellent discussion of the nature of the trust, see P. Parkinson, 'Re-Conceptualising the Express Trust' (2002) 61 CLJ at 657.

[6] S. 20 Law of Property Act 1925.

vested with the legal title and the beneficiary has an equitable interest in the trust property. However, suppose that a beneficiary under a subsisting trust declares himself a trustee of his equitable interest in favour of another: in such a case, it is possible that he would become a trustee of his equitable interest in favour of another beneficiary.[7]

The trustee will be appointed by the settlor in the trust instrument, or in the case of a trust intended to take effect on the death of the testator, the will of the testator. The trustee will be required to act in accordance with the trust instrument and trust law in general as developed by cases and statute. In the course of the administration of the trust, the trustee will be conferred a number of duties and powers. With respect to his duties, the trustee has no choice but to execute them. In so far as his powers, the trustee will be given a discretion and, although he need not necessarily exercise these powers, he must from time to time show that he did consider the exercise of his powers. One particular feature of trusteeship is that a trustee stands in a fiduciary relationship to his beneficiaries. A fiduciary is someone who must act in the best interests of their beneficiary or principal. The overriding principle governing fiduciaries is that they must not allow a conflict between their duty to their beneficiary and their own personal interest. They must at all times act in the best interests of the beneficiary.[8] Once a trustee is appointed by the settler or by a testator, he may retire from the office of trusteeship, provided other trustees are left to administer the trust. If for some reason there is no trustee, for example the trustee has died, the trust will not fail as there are statutory mechanisms in place to appoint new trustees and, indeed, to remove trustees.[9] In trust law there is a maxim that a trust will not fail for want of a trustee.

The beneficiary

A trust must be created in favour of a human beneficiary who can enforce the trust obligation against the trustee. There must be some individual or individuals in whose favour the court can decree performance of the trust. Sometimes it is also said that there must be someone who has *locus standi* to enforce the trust. It is important that the trustees know exactly who their beneficiaries are and that they have been defined with a meaning which is understood by the trustee and the court, which may well have to enforce the trusts should the trustees fail to do so. Therefore, a trust for Jenny, Michael and Robert is perfectly clear. Equally a trust in favour of a class of individuals referred to by some definition will be fine provided the definition has a meaning, for example, the employees of a company. A trust which is not created for a human beneficiary is prima facie void. Thus, a trust which is not directly for the benefit of ascertainable beneficiaries but merely furthers some abstract purpose is prima facie void. The primary reason for this is that there is no one to enforce the obligation against the trustee. It is a central requirement of the law of trusts that a trust is created for the benefit of identifiable human beneficiaries. The courts will not allow a trust to exist in circumstances where it cannot control and execute that trust. The only exception to this rule is a charitable trust, which is enforced by the Attorney General through the Charity Commissioners. Charitable trusts have undergone a major change under the Charities Act 2006. The Act provides a list of purposes which qualify as being charitable, including the established categories or trusts to relieve poverty, and trusts to advance religion and education.[10]

---

[7] Such a situation will give rise to what is known as a sub-trust; see Chapter 5 for more detail.

[8] The fiduciary nature of trusteeship is explored in more detail in Chapter 17.

[9] A detailed examination of these principles is in Chapter 14.

[10] Charitable trusts are examined in more detail in Chapter 22.

Although the trustee holds the legal title to the trust property for the benefit of the beneficiary, the beneficiary's beneficial interest is substantive in terms of ownership. It is often said that the trustee's ownership is nominal and it is the beneficiary who has the full benefits of the ownership in the property. The significance of the beneficiary's equitable interest was recently highlighted in *Colour Quest Ltd* v *Total Downstream Plc*[11] where the Court of Appeal held that a beneficial owner could join in negligence proceedings against a third party who had caused damage to property held by trustees. It did not matter that the beneficial owner was not in possession of the damaged property.

The trust property

A trust must attach to some identifiable property over which the trustees have some control and over which the beneficiaries can claim an equitable interest. The identification of the trust property is important for two main reasons. Firstly, it gives the beneficiaries an equitable interest in the property. Secondly, because the equitable right is a right *in personam*, the beneficiaries can follow that property into the hands of third parties who cannot purport to show that they are bona fide purchasers of the legal title without notice of the interest. The 'bona fide purchaser principle' is explored in more detail in the next section. For the time being the basic rule is that any type of property is capable of being subject to a trust: thus, both personal and real property can be the subject matter of a trust. Students of property law will recall that personal property is divided into *choses in action* and *choses in possession* depending on whether the property is intangible and tangible respectively. It is also possible for both a legal estate and an equitable interest to be held on trust for a beneficiary. In most cases it will be a legal estate or legal interest which is vested in the trustee, for example a freehold title to land or a painting; however, a person who only has an equitable interest in property can vest that interest in a trustee to be held for the benefit of another.[12]

The trust instrument

Unless a trust is created in a will, the document purporting to create a trust is referred to as the trust instrument. However, even in the case of trust created in a will, the will may refer to the trust instrument which sets out the details of the trust created in the will. Sometimes the trust instrument is referred to as the trust deed. The nature and extent of detail in a trust instrument will vary according to the type of trust in question. There are, however, a number of general issues which will be found in all properly drafted trust instruments. As well as details of the trust, the trust instrument will refer to a number of important matters such as the power to appoint new trustees, the right of the trustees to receive remuneration and the extent to which trustees can be exonerated from liability for breach of trust. In addition, the trust instrument will refer to the powers which are conferred upon trustees: for example, the power of investment and the power to make capital or income payment to beneficiaries before the trust can be terminated by the beneficiaries.

---

[11] [2010] EWCA Civ 180.

[12] Such an assignment of an equitable interest on trust will constitute a sub-trust and will be subject to certain formalities which are discussed in Chapter 5.

The legal and equitable interest

A key feature in an effective understanding of the concept of the trust is the distinction between the legal and equitable interest. A legal interest is said to be a right *in rem* in the sense that it prevails against the whole world. A trustee who holds the legal title to trust property is capable of enforcing that legal title against the whole world. Thus, it does not matter who has interfered with the legal title to the trust property: the trustee can assert the right to recover the legal title from any third party. The same is, however, not true of equitable interests, which are said to be rights *in personam* in the sense that they are governed by the doctrine of notice. This means that such rights are binding on all persons except a bona fide purchaser of a legal interest without notice of the pre-existing equitable interest.[13] Equity, acting *in personam*, clearly binds the conscience of the party against whom an equitable right is granted. It goes further and binds all those persons who subsequently acquire the legal title to the property in which the equitable right is granted with notice of the equitable right. Thus, where a trustee transfers the legal title to the trust property to another person, the equitable right of the beneficiary may bind the transferee if she or he has notice thereof.

The doctrine of notice requires the purchaser to be a bona fide purchaser. This is no more than saying that the purchaser must be one who is innocent, and where there is an absence of notice, this requirement is easily satisfied. The purchaser must have give value, that is, consideration for the receipt of the legal title to the property. Consideration at common law means money or money's worth; in equity consideration can take the form of marriage consideration.[14] A purchaser for value need not, however, show that consideration was adequate.[15] The doctrine of notice does not extend to a person who has not furnished consideration, thus a mere donee or volunteer will be bound by equitable interests irrespective of notice.

The central requirement of the doctrine of notice relates to the question of what constitutes notice. Three types of knowledge have been identified for the purposes of the doctrine of notice. The most obvious type of notice attributable to a person is actual notice. This refers to a situation where a purchaser is consciously aware of the equitable interest in property at the time of the purchase. In such a situation the third party is more or less colluding with the trustee and will almost be acting fraudulently. Actual notice is to be distinguished from constructive notice, which refers to knowledge which would have come to the attention of the purchaser had he carried out a reasonable inspection of the title to the thing in question. It is trite law that a person buying land should carry out a reasonable inspection of the land and the title which he is he purchasing. The purpose of such an investigation is to establish whether there are equitable interests in the land which might bind him. These equitable interests may take the form of a beneficial interest in the land. A good example is ***Kingsnorth Finance Co Ltd v Tizard***[16] where a husband was holding the legal title to a matrimonial home on trust for himself and his wife. After they had separated, the wife ceased to live with her husband but did visit the house on a daily basis to look after the children. The husband arranged a mortgage with a mortgagee on a Sunday afternoon when the wife was not present. The mortgage was duly granted to the husband who later absconded with the mortgage money. The court

---

[13] See *London and South Western Rail Co* v *Gomn* (1882) 20 Ch. D 562 and *Pilcher* v *Rawlins* (1872) 7 Ch. App. 259.

[14] The concept of marriage consideration is considered in more detail in Chapter 6.

[15] *Midland Bank Co Ltd* v *Green* [1981] AC 513.

[16] [1986] 1 WLR 783.

held that the equitable right of the wife bound the mortgagee. The inspection carried out by the mortgagee was simply insufficient and it was affixed with constructive notice. The final type of notice is imputed notice, which arises when an agent of the purchaser has notice, actual or constructive, which is imputed to the purchaser.

The effect of a successful claim that a purchaser purchased the legal title without notice of the equitable interest is to give him an 'absolute, unqualified, unanswerable defence'[17] against the holder of an equitable interest in property. The doctrine of notice not only gives the purchaser an unqualified defence against the holder but also operates in a destructive way so that the equitable interest in the property is completely destroyed. It cannot be revived against a subsequent purchaser of the legal title who may have notice of the fact that the equitable interest once existed.[18]

In the case of real property the doctrine of notice has largely been superseded by a system of registration of equitable interests in the land. What is typically referred to as the 1925 legislation – culminating in the Law of Property Act 1925, Land Charges Act 1925 (now the Land Charges Act 1972) and the Land Registration Act 1925 (now the Land Registration Act 2002) – provides a framework for governing the registration of various legal and equitable interests in land.

A judicial assessment of the nature of a trust

CASE SUMMARY

VISIT CASE NAVIGATOR

Westdeutsche Landesbank Girozentrale v *Islington LBC* [1996] AC 669 (HL)

The House of Lords took the opportunity to explain the core principles of a trust, as summed up by Lord Browne-Wilkinson.

The relevant principles of trust law

(i) Equity operates on the conscience of the owner of the legal interest. In the case of a trust, the conscience of the legal owner requires him to carry out the purposes for which the property was vested in him (express or implied trust) or which the law imposes on him by reason of his unconscionable conduct (constructive trust).

(ii) Since the equitable jurisdiction to enforce trusts depends upon the conscience of the holder of the legal interest being affected, he cannot be a trustee of the property if and so long as he is ignorant of the facts alleged to affect his conscience, i.e. until he is aware that he is intended to hold the property for the benefit of others in the case of an express or implied trust, or, in the case of a constructive trust, of the factors which are alleged to affect his conscience.

(iii) In order to establish a trust there must be identifiable trust property. The only apparent exception to this rule is a constructive trust imposed on a person who dishonestly assists in a breach of trust who may come under fiduciary duties even if he does not receive identifiable trust property.

(iv) Once a trust is established, as from the date of its establishment the beneficiary has, in equity, a proprietary interest in the trust property, which proprietary interest will be enforceable in equity against any subsequent holder of the property (whether the original property or substituted property into which it can be traced) other than a purchaser for value of the legal interest without notice.

---

[17] *Pilcher* v *Rawlins* (1872) 7 Ch. App. 259 at 269.
[18] *Wilkes* v *Spooner* [1911] 2 KB 473.

 ## Trust as a product of fragmentation of ownership

An effective understanding of the trust concept requires an appreciation of some basic principles of property law. In property law, ownership is the greatest right that an individual has in relation to a thing. Furthermore ownership consists of a number of incidents. The standard incidents of ownership consist of both benefits and burdens, or rights and duties, which are vested in the person who has ownership. The common incidents of ownership include the right to possession, the right to manage, the right to capital and the right to income. Fragmentation of ownership, as the words imply, entails the splitting up of the incidents of ownership and vesting them in more than one person. The idea of splitting ownership and vesting the constituent elements of it in different persons has been a particularly notable feature in English law and other jurisdictions founded on the common law tradition.[19] There are a number of reasons for this. Unlike Roman law, English law has not treated ownership as an absolute relationship between the owner and a thing. The Roman law idea of *dominium* revolved around the fact that the owner was vested with the all the incidents of ownership, so that he alone could exercise the incidents of enjoyment and management. In English law, the development of the trust contributed to a large extent in allowing management and enjoyment functions of ownership to be distributed amongst different persons for different social and economic objectives. The trust occupies a central position in the law of fragmentation of ownership.

Another factor which has facilitated fragmentation of ownership is the nature of certain types of resources. The nature of land has allowed it to be put to different yet compatible uses at the same time by different users. Land is virtually indestructible and it can be enjoyed for a variety of purposes. An owner of land can carve smaller segments out of his full ownership and vest them in different users. Unlike land, goods and other personal property did not, from a historical point of view, feature significantly in matters of fragmentation.[20] Goods are generally less permanent than land and more movable so as to make them susceptible to simultaneous property interests. This is a factor that goes a long way in explaining the relatively fewer property interests that exist in personal property than compared to land. However, things have long changed and ownership in personal property can in many ways be fragmented in the same way as it can in land. Indeed, in the modern law of property, fragmentation of ownership of personal property is much more common and often more important than in the case of land. The relative economic significance of land has been displaced by large trust funds. The modern law of trusts generally recognises the fact that the trust operates predominantly in a commercial setting rather than land and family.[21] The idea that management and enjoyment functions can be split is very common in trusts such as pensions funds and other large investments where trustees manage assets for beneficiaries.

  ## Historical foundations of the trust

The origins of the modern trust are deeply rooted in feudal land law which existed in the Middle Ages. The trust, formerly known as a use, was employed to encounter the

---

[19] See S. Panesar, 'The Importance of Possession of Land' (2003) *Hong Kong Law Journal* Vol. 33 at 569.
[20] See F.H. Lawson and B. Rudden, *The Law of Property* 2nd edn (1982) at pp. 76–7.
[21] See G. Moffat, *Trust Law: Text and Materials* 4th edn (2005) at pp. 42–8.

problems of freedom of alienation and payment of taxes in the system of feudalism.[22] The system of tenure operated in a way in which no person, apart from the Crown, was absolute owner of land. Instead the ownership of land was fragmented vertically so that the King granted land to powerful lords who could in return grant further segments of land to tenants. A tenant, of course, could grant certain land vested in him to other tenants. If he did this, he had a dual role to play in connection with the land, for he would not only be an overlord to his tenant, but he himself would also be a tenant accountable to an overlord higher up in the feudal ladder. Within this feudal system of tenure, the death of a tenant entitled the heir of the tenant to take possession or seisin of the land, but not without first paying feudal dues to the overlord. The employment of the use allowed land to be transferred to trustees[23] during the lifetime of the tenant upon use of the tenant and after his death to members of his family, which could include the heir. The advantage of this arrangement lay in the fact that on the death of the tenant, the trustees would simply hold the land for the persons entitled after the tenant. Since there was no acquisition on the death of the tenant, the overlord had no apparent claim to dues. The land simply belonged to the trustees who at all times remained in possession. Equitable intervention, however, meant that the conscience of the trustees would bind them to the use.

In Figure 2.1, A, the owner of land, could not leave property in his will to his sons B, C and D. If A died, his land would revert back up the feudal ladder and be vested in the feudal lord.

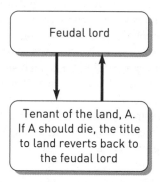

Figure 2.1 The medieval use

In Figure 2.2, having transferred the legal title to the trustees X, Y and Z, A along with B, C and D could enforce the obligation in the court of equity, compelling the trustees to recognise their interest in the land. Should A die, the land would still belong to A's sons, albeit in equity, but they could compel the trustees to transfer it to them. In this way, A could achieve what he could not achieve at common law, that is, to leave his property to his sons after his death and also avoid the payment of feudal dues by his heirs.

---

[22] See generally J.L. Barton, 'The Medieval Use' (1965) LQR 562.
[23] This basically involved delivery of possession in the presence of witnesses followed by ceremonial acts; see, Thorne, 'Livery of Seisin' (1938) 52 LQR at 345.

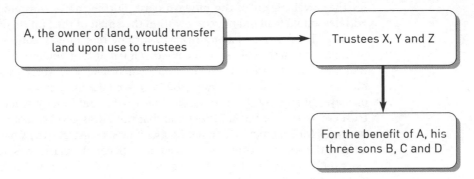

Figure 2.2

The second advantage of the trust lay in the fact that it permitted greater freedom to the tenant in devising his property to persons other than just the heir. The common law was strict in requiring land be vested in the heir of the tenant. Where the tenant died without an heir, the overlord became entitled to the land by way of escheat.[24] Transfer to trustees, however, allowed land to be enjoyed by those designated in the terms of the use rather than on the strict principles of the common law. In recognition of the potential scope of the use in undermining the system of feudal dues and the consequential emptying of the Crown pocket, the Statute of Uses 1535[25] was introduced which had the effect of undermining certain uses. The basic aim of the legislation was to deny the beneficiary equitable rights in the land. Rather, where the use was employed, the intended beneficiary acquired a legal title to the land and was thus subject to feudal dues in the event of the death of the tenant. In 1540 the Statute of Wills was also passed in recognition that the landowning aristocracy rejected the strict common law rule requiring land to be acquired by the heir. The statute permitted greater freedom in the disposition of property after the death of the tenant; however, such dispositions would be subject to the same feudal taxes that existed before the statute.

 ## Trusts and law reform

Although the Statute of Uses 1535 did not completely extinguish the use concept, it cannot be overstated that the use played a fundamental role in reforming law in medieval England. The undermining of the feudal system, which was out of touch with the needs of landowning citizens, and the recognition of the need for free alienation of land could not have been achieved without the use.[26] Uses continued to be allowed in cases where they involved the imposition of active duties on the trustees. Where, for example, a tenant put land upon use when he was absent from the land, the trustee's role was essential in collecting rents and paying debts due on the land. In this case the use was entirely genuine and not designed to avoid feudal dues. It was this type of use that paved the way

---

[24] See Megarry and Wade, *The Law of Real Property* 7th edn (2008) at p. 26.

[25] Described as the 'most important single statute in the history of the trust's development' by G. Moffat, *Trust Law: Text and Materials*, 3rd edn (1999) at p. 29; see now 4th edn (2005) at p. 40.

[26] The idea that the trust, in the course of its history, provided the means for law reform is argued by A.W. Scott, 'The Trust as an Instrument of Law Reform' (1922) 31 Yale LJ 457.

for the development of the modern trust. Furthermore, uses employed in connection with leasehold land did not come within the ambit of the Statute of Uses.

The role of trust in paving the way for law reform was not just seen in the context of feudalism. In the context of married women, it brought about legislation recognising that fact that married women could own property in their own right.[27] Before the Married Women's Property Act 1882, a wife could enjoy separate property in a number of ways. Firstly, equity recognised that a wife could enjoy a separate estate under a trust created in her favour. Providing that there was good reason for the creation of the trust – as for example, where her husband was a wastrel – the Court of Chancery would enforce the wife's separate estate in equity.[28] Secondly, marriage settlements, which were essentially a contract between husband and wife recognised and enforced in equity, allowed the wife to claim property as hers which she had acquired after marriage and which trustees of the marriage settlement held for her.

In more recent times, the trust has been a primary vehicle in determining the rights of non-marital cohabitees in circumstances where there has been no statutory framework to determine the rights of such parties. In the context of married couples there is a fairly well defined statutory framework governing the rights of such couples on separation.[29] Starting predominantly in the 1970s, implied trusts became important in determining the beneficial entitlements to property where the legal title was taken in the name of one cohabitee only but the other had contributed to the purchase or was otherwise promised an interest in the land.[30] The intervention of trusts in this context highlighted the problem facing non-married couples and prompted a Law Commission inquiry, resulting in a report published in 2006 calling for law reform by legislation.[31] More recently the Law Commission revisited this area of the law in 2007 and this time opted for a statutory regime which would address the problem of shared ownership.[32]

These examples of the role of trusts in bringing about law reform are quite unique and demonstrate the versatility of the trust in engineering the condition for reform. On a much broader note, they also illustrate the ability of equity to deal with new social and economic problems which would remain unresolved because of the rigidity of the common law. The matter is neatly explained by one commentator who argues that trusts are the primary path for statutory law reform.

> It was chiefly by means of uses and trusts that the feudal system was undermined in England, that the law of conveyancing was revolutionized, that the economic position of married women was ameliorated, that family settlements have been effected, whereby daughter and younger sons of landed proprietors have been enabled modestly to participate in the family wealth, that unincorporated associations have found a measure of protection, that business enterprises of many kinds have been enabled to accomplish their purposes, that great sums of money have been devoted to charitable enterprises; any by employing the analogy of a trust, by the intervention of the so called constructive trust, the courts have

---

[27] Married Women's Property Act 1882.

[28] See G.S. Alexander, 'The Transformation of Trusts as a Legal Category, 1800–1914' (1987) *Law and History Review* Vol. 5 at p. 320.

[29] See Part II Matrimonial Causes Act 1973.

[30] Implied trusts in the context of family property are examined in more detail in Chapters 10 and 11.

[31] Law Com. No. 307, *The Financial Consequences of Relationship Breakdown*.

[32] Law Com. No. 307, *Cohabitation: The Financial Consequences of Relationship Breakdown* (2007). For an excellent account of the Commission's proposals see D. Hughes, M. Davis and L. Jacklin, 'Come Live with Me and be my Love – Consideration of the 2007 Law Commission Proposals on Cohabitation Breakdown' (2008) Conv. 197. See also, S. Bridge. 'Cohabitation: Why Legislative Reform is Necessary' [2007] Fam. Law 911. These matters are discussed in much more detail in Chapter 14.

been enabled to give relief against all sorts of fraudulent schemes whereby scoundrels have sought to enrich themselves at the expense of other persons. Many of these reforms in the English law would doubtless have been brought about by other means; but the fact remains that it was the trust device which actually was chiefly instrumental in bringing them to pass.

A.W. Scott, 'The Trust as an Instrument of Law Reform' (1922) 31 *Yale Law Journal* 457.

Classification of trusts

Express trusts

The modern trust can be used in a wide variety of contexts to achieve different social and economic objectives. The modern trust can take a variety of forms depending on the context in which it is employed. Traditional classification of trusts has distinguished between express and imputed trusts and bare and active trusts. Express trusts are those trusts created by a deliberate act of a person called a settlor, or in the case of a trust created in a will by a testator. Express trusts can be subdivided into private and public or charitable trusts. A private trust is one that seeks to provide for private persons such as members of family, friends or other class of beneficiaries closely connected with the settlor. For example, a father of a child may transfer £2000 on trust to trustees to hold for his child until the child attains the age of 21 years. However, social behaviour dictates that a person may wish to provide for persons who are in need in terms of poverty or education. Where provision is made for purposes that are generally beneficial to the community, such provisions take effect behind a public or charitable trust. Given the importance of charitable trusts in terms of the purposes that they seek to benefit and the monies involved, these types of trust are controlled and enforced by the Attorney General and Charity Commissioners.[33]

Fixed and discretionary trusts

Express trusts can be further divided into fixed and discretionary trusts. A fixed trust is one where the beneficial interest of the beneficiaries is fixed. For example, a settlor may transfer £20,000 on trust for his three children equally. In such a case, the trust is fixed; the beneficiaries are entitled to one-third of the money and the trustees have no discretion in the manner in which the money is distributed to the children. In contrast, a discretionary trust is one where the trustees are given a discretion in the manner in which the trust property is distributed. The trust may be in favour of the children of the settlor or it may be created in favour of a class of persons: for example, a trust for the benefit of employees of a company at the discretion of the trustee. In such a trust, the trustees are under a duty to distribute; however, how they distribute and to which of the beneficiaries is left to their discretion. A discretionary trust is very similar to the concept of a power of appointment, which is discussed in the next chapter.

Bare and active trusts

The distinction between bare and active trusts relates to the duties which are imposed upon the trustee.[34] Where the trustee has only minimal duties, for example he merely

---

[33] See generally, *Tudor on Charities* 9th edn (2003).
[34] See P. Mathews, 'All About Bare Trusts' (2005) PCB at 266.

holds the trust property for the beneficiary, the trust is said to be a bare trust. The beneficiaries have paramount control over the trust property which is in the hands of the trustee. An active trust, however, is one where the trustee is under a duty to manage the trust property for the benefit of the beneficiaries. In an active trust the trustee does not merely hold the legal title: instead he is under a duty to manage the trust property in the best interests of the beneficiaries. Thus, if the trust consists of a fund, the trustee must invest the trust fund. The trustee owes fiduciary duties to the beneficiaries and is accountable for failure to manage the trust property effectively.

Protective trusts

APPLYING THE LAW

Simon wishes to create a trust of his cottage and £300,000 for his son Jacob who is 21 years of age. Simon is aware that Jacob is a spendthrift and generally irresponsible with money. He wishes to know how he can protect the trust money from being wasted by Jacob.

The beginning of this chapter explored the case of *Hambro and Others* v *Duke of Marlborough*[35] where the issue before the High Court was whether the 11th Duke of Marlborough and the trustees of the Blenheim Estates could change the nature of the Marquis of Blandford's interest in the Estates. The principal reason for this was that the Marquis had shown himself to be an irresponsible individual who was likely to harm the property subject to the settlement. The case highlights an interesting dilemma for a person creating a trust. What happens, for example, where a settlor wishes to create a trust, let's say for his son, but knows that his son is financially irresponsible? Once the trust is created, there is nothing stopping the son from using his interest in the trust property to raise money by way of mortgage of his beneficial interest. Furthermore, what happens should the son become bankrupt? In principal, the bankruptcy of the son will entitle his trustees in bankruptcy to lay hands on the trust property in order to meet the son's debts.

One way around the problems of providing for an irresponsible beneficiary is to employ a protective trust. The basic idea behind a protective trust is that a settlor, instead of conferring an absolute interest to the trust property, confers upon a beneficiary a determinable life interest only, with a gift over to others. The types of events which determine the interest of the protective beneficiary include his bankruptcy or other attempted alienation of the trust property. Where the determining event takes place, the effect is that the life interest is forfeited and the gift over takes effect. The most typical type of gift over is a direction to the trustees to hold the trust property upon a discretionary trust for members of the original beneficiary or for some other class of persons. Protective trusts can now be created by incorporating the provisions of s. 33 of the Trustee Act 1925 which provide shorthand means by which such trusts can be incorporated into a trust instrument.

Returning to the facts of the decision in *Hambro and Others* v *Duke of Marlborough*,[36] the High Court held that a protective trust could be set up for the Marquis of Blandford who would have a right to receive the income from the property; however, the land would be held for the original settlement. The facts of the case actually involved a

---

[35] [1994] 3 All ER 332.
[36] [1994] 3 All ER 332.

variation of the interest of the Marquis of Blandford and these matters are analysed in depth in Chapter 19.

Secret trusts

Secret trusts have played an important role in equity. Historically, such trusts were employed to provide for illegitimate children and a mistress. To name such beneficiaries in the will would, of course, be the subject of much unwanted publicity. In more recent times, secret trusts have been employed by a testator in circumstances where he wants to make a will but is still yet undecided as to the direction of his estate after his decease. By making a will and leaving property to a secret trustee, the testator can reserve to himself the right to make future unwitnessed dispositions of his property by merely naming a trustee and then supplying the objects of the trust closer to his death. Seen in this way, a testator can bypass the formal requirements of s. 9 of the Wills Act 1837.

In order to understand the operation of a secret trust it is best to take the following example which is explored in more detail in Chapter 7. Peter is married and has three children. He wishes to make a will leaving his property to his wife and children in equal shares. However, he also wishes to leave a sum of £60,000 to his secretary Patsy whom he has been very fond of for several years. He does not, however, want anyone to know that Patsy has received a sum of £60,000 after his death. The dilemma he faces is that if he names Patsy in the will then this will become public knowledge. One way around this is for Peter to leave the sum of money absolutely to his solicitor in his will; however, during his lifetime he secures his solicitor's agreement that he will hand the money over to Patsy after Peter's death. In this way Peter is said to have created a secret trust. Secret because, on the face of the will, Peter's solicitor is deemed to have been made an absolute gift; however, beneath the surface Peter's solicitor is really holding the money for Patsy on trust. The only person who knows of the existence of the trust is Peter's solicitor and possibly Patsy.

The principal concern over the enforcement of secret trusts is that they 'fly in the face' of the Wills Act 1837. In other words, the enforcement of a secret trust goes against the testamentary formalities in s. 9 of the Wills Act 1937, which requires that all bequests taking effect after the death of an individual must be put in a will which is in writing, signed and witnessed. The problem with a secret trust is that the secret beneficiary, who after all is receiving property from an individual after his death, is not named in the will. The secret trustee is named in the will and he or she should take the property absolutely. However, to give the property to the secret trustee, for example Peter's solicitor in the above example, would allow him to benefit from Peter's property when that was not Peter's intention. Indeed, for the solicitor to argue that the property belongs to him and not Patsy would amount to a fraud on his part. Historically, secret trusts were enforced to prevent the fraudulent conduct of the secret trustee; however, as will be explained in more detail in Chapter 7, the modern justification for secret trusts revolves around a principle which holds that they are indeed a species of *inter vivos* trusts and not in conflict with the Wills Act 1837.

Implied trusts

Trusts are not always created by a deliberate act on the part of a person; instead the law in certain circumstances may impute a trust. In other words, title to property may become fragmented by trusts which are imputed or implied by law. Implied trusts can take one of two forms: they can be either resulting trusts or constructive trusts. The fundamental distinction between resulting and constructive trusts lies in the fact that resulting trusts are implied by law whereas constructive trusts are imposed by law. Mention must also be made here to trusts which are imposed by statute; although they are often described as forms of imputed trusts, they stand as a freestanding category. They are imposed by statute in certain circumstances: for example, whenever land becomes co-owned, a statutory trust in the form of a trust of land is imposed.[37] The statutory trust of land imposed by the Trusts of Land and Appointment of Trustees Act 1996 governs the rights and duties of both trustees and beneficiaries. In addition, it provides the mechanisms by which disputes relating to co-owned land are resolved.

Resulting trusts are said to be implied by law. Unlike express trusts, they are not founded on the express intentions of the person creating the trust. The House of Lords in **Westdeutsche v Islington London Borough Council** redefined the basis upon which equity implies resulting trusts.[38] In the case, Lord Browne-Wilkinson explained that

> under existing law a resulting trust arises in two sets of circumstances: (a) where A makes a voluntary payment to B or pays (wholly or partly) for the purchase of property which is vested either in B alone or in joint names of A and B, there is a presumption that A did not intend to make a gift to B; the money or property is held on trust for A (if he is the sole provider of the money) or in the case of a joint purchase by A and B in shares proportionate to their contributions . . . (b) where A transfers property to B on express trusts, but the trusts declared do not exhaust the whole beneficial interest. Both types of trust are traditionally regarded as examples of trusts giving effect to the common intention of the parties.[39]

Prior to Lord Browne-Wilkinson's analysis, traditional trust classification had categorised circumstance (a) as a situation where the implied resulting trust was referred to as a presumed resulting trust. Circumstance (b) was a situation where the implied resulting trust was referred to as an automatic resulting trust. Lord Browne-Wilkinson, however, does not distinguish between presumed and automatic resulting trusts; instead, he argues that circumstances (a) and (b) are simply examples of trusts giving effect to the common and presumed intention of the parties.[40] Although resulting trusts are divided into two categories of presumed and automatic, the underlying theme in both trusts is the same. At the heart of the matter is the fact that a person who does not dispose of his property effectively, that is through gift or bargain, that undisposed property remains his as it does not belong to anyone else. It is a fundamental rule of property law that rights in things should not be simply abandoned but must belong to a person.

The basis of a presumed resulting trust lies in the presumed intention of a person transferring property. In other words, in certain types of property transfers, equity presumes that property transferred by a person is intended to be subject to a trust rather than, for example, to be given outright. The most common example of a situation which

---

[37] Trusts of Land and Appointment of Trustees Act 1996, s. 1.
[38] [1996] AC 699.
[39] [1996] AC 699 at 708.
[40] [1996] AC 699. This has, however, been a source of controversy since it departs from the traditional classification of Meggarry J in *White v Vandervell's Trustees Ltd (Re Vandervell's Trusts No. 2) [1974] Ch. 269* where automatic and presumed resulting trusts were clearly distinguished as being different. For further discussion, see G. Moffat, *Trust Law: Text and Materials* 4th edn (2005) at p. 184, and also R. Pearce and J. Stevens, *The Law of Trusts and Equitable Obligations* 3rd edn (2006) at p. 263. The source of the controversy relates to the fact that automatic resulting trusts are not necessarily based on the presumed or common intentions of the parties in circumstances which give rise to the trust. Thus, where a person seeks to divest himself of his beneficial interest in property, there is no real common or presumed intention that property should result back to his estate. If the beneficial interest remains unexhausted, it results back to the transferor as an automatic consequence, rather than on the implied intentions of the transferor.

VISIT CASE NAVIGATOR

may give rise to a resulting trust is where A purchases property and has it conveyed in the name of B. Where A has provided all the purchase money, the presumption is that B holds the legal title on resulting trust for A.[41] It is important to stress that this is only a presumption which, like any other presumption, can be rebutted by evidence suggesting that the transfer in the name of B was intended to take effect as a gift. The basis upon which equity makes a presumption of a resulting trust is that 'equity assumes bargains and not gifts'.[42] Furthermore, the underlying rationale seems to be that a person does not, in the absence of clear evidence to the contrary, voluntarily give away money or other property to another. An automatic resulting trust arises where property is transferred upon trust to another; however, for some reason or other, the beneficial interest in the property remains unexhausted. The most typical situation where this might happen is when A transfers property on trust, but for some reason does not identify who the beneficiary of the trust is. The only logical result here is that the property results back to the person creating the trust. The only intention, if there is an intention, is that it is the transferor's property and not anyone else's, such as the trustee.[43] The basis of an automatic resulting trust lies in the maxim that 'equity abhors a beneficial vacuum'. Just like the common law, which holds that property rights should be vested in persons rather than just abandoned, equity requires that proprietary rights be vested in persons.

The juridical basis of a resulting trust is explored in more detail in Chapter 10; however, for now it is sufficient to say that many theories have been advanced for the reasons as to why a resulting trust is imposed. Furthermore, despite the reformulation of resulting trusts by Lord Browne-Wilkinson in **Westdeutsche v Islington London Borough Council**,[44] many commentaries on the law of trusts continue to distinguish between presumed and automatic resulting trusts. One of the reasons for the continued distinction lies in the development of the case law, which prior to **Westdeutsche v Islington London Borough Council** developed a clear and neat boundary between presumed and automatic resulting trusts. It will be observed in Chapter 10 that whilst the distinction between presumed and automatic resulting trusts helps to explain the existing law, the distinction is somewhat of limited importance today on the grounds that there is a unifying theme which explains the grounds for the imposition of a resulting trust in any given type of situation. That unifying theme is the presumed intention of the donor of property in whose favour a resulting trust is implied. The presumed intention has been analysed in the form of an absence of intention on the part of a donor to part with his beneficial interest in the given circumstances which give rise to the imposition of the resulting trust. In the Privy Council in **Air Jamaica v Charlton**[45] Lord Millett explained that:

> [L]ike a constructive trust, a resulting trust arises by operation of law, though unlike a constructive trust it gives effect to intention. But it arises whether or not the transferor intended to retain a beneficial interest – he almost always does not – since it responds to any absence of intention on his part to pass a beneficial interest to the recipient. It may arise even where the transferor positively wished to part the beneficial interest, as in **Vandervell v IRC**. In that case the retention of a beneficial interest by the transferor destroyed the effectiveness of a tax avoidance scheme which the transferor was trying to implement. The

---

[41] See, for example, *Dyer* v *Dyer* (1788) 2 Cox Eq. Cas. 92 at p. 93, 30 ER 42 at 43 and *Burns v Burns* [1984] Ch. 317.

[42] *Goodfriend* v *Goodfriend* (1972) 22 DLR (3d) 699 at 703 per Spence J, quoted in K. Gray, *Elements of Land Law*, 5th edn (2009) at p. 839.

[43] See, for example, *White* v *Re Vandervell's Trustees Ltd* (*Vandervell's Trust No. 2*) [1974] Ch. 269.

[44] [1996] AC 699.

[45] [1999] 1 WLR 1399.

House of Lords affirmed the principle that a resulting trust is not defeated by evidence that the transferor intended to part with the beneficial interest if he has not in fact succeeded in doing so.[46]

Whereas resulting trusts are implied by law, constructive trusts are said to be imposed by law. Constructive trusts are not necessarily based on the presumed or common intention of parties in a property transaction.[47] Unlike in the case of a resulting trust, finding a coherent and unifying definition of a constructive trust is almost an impossible task. In the course of its history the constructive trust has operated in so many different contexts that it is impossible to find a universal definition which unifies the circumstances in which a constructive trust is imposed.[48] At the heart of the imposition of a constructive trust is the unconscionability of a defendant in respect of property which is in his hands. Whilst this goes some way towards explaining the grounds for the imposition of a constructive trust, what constitutes unconscionability, as explained in Chapter 1, can only be understood by investigating the context in which the trust is being imposed.

A further complexity in the search for a universal definition of a constructive trust lies in the fact that not all common law based jurisdictions have analysed the constructive trust in the same manner. The constructive trust has been analysed in two quite different ways. In some countries, and quite clearly in England, the constructive trust has been analysed as an 'institutional' constructive trust, whilst in some countries, most notably Canada,[49] the constructive trust has been analysed as a 'remedial' constructive trust. The distinction between an institutional and remedial constructive trust is far-reaching. The former is imposed as a result of certain facts which make it unconscionable for one person who has legal title to property to deny the beneficial ownership therein in another. It is the facts which give rise to the constructive trust. On other hand, a remedial trust is not necessarily based on unconscionable conduct of a person who acquires the legal title to property: rather the trust is imposed to reverse an unjust enrichment. The constructive trust operates as a remedy rather than recognising pre-existing property rights. The remedial constructive trust is imposed by the court in order to effect a restitution of property. The remedial constructive trust is a much more powerful property concept than an institutional constructive trust. It does not recognise pre-existing property rights; however, once imposed by the courts, it has the effect of substantially altering pre-existing property rights.[50] It is for this reason and others that the remedial constructive trust has yet to find a safe home in English law.[51]

English law takes the view that a constructive trust should only be imposed on the occurrence of certain events which make it unconscionable for the legal owner of property to deny the beneficial interest therein to another. In **Westdeutsche v Islington London Borough Council**[52] Lord Browne-Wilkinson, in an attempt to provide some generalisation about the constructive trust, commented that such a trust is imposed on a person by 'reason of his unconscionable conduct.'[53] His Lordship went on to explain that

---

[46] [1999] 1 WLR 1399 at 1412.

[47] Common intention may, however, be important in some contexts: for example, constructive trusts which are imposed in the co-ownership of land; see *Lloyds Bank v Rosset* [1991] 1 AC 107.

[48] See, generally, Oakley, *Constructive Trustees* 3rd edn (1997).

[49] See D. Waters, *The Law of Trusts in Canada* 2nd edn (1984) at pp. 379–80.

[50] As, for example, in the case of insolvency or bankruptcy of a person. Where such a constructive trust is imposed, it can grant equitable rights of property in some so as to gain priority in insolvency proceedings, whilst at the same time denying others right to the same property.

[51] See P. Birks, *The Frontiers of Liabilty* (1994) Vol. 2 pp. 163–223.

[52] [1996] AC 669.

[53] *Ibid.* at 705.

the constructive trust 'arises by operation of law as from the date of the circumstances which give rise to it: the function of the court is to merely declare that such a trust has arisen in the past'.[54] Chapter 13 of this book explores the various social and commercial contexts in which constructive trusts operate; for the time being, some examples can be given where the constructive trust is imposed by reason of the unconscionable conduct of a person. Historically, constructive trusts were imposed on persons standing in a fiduciary relationship who had made unauthorised profits as a result of the fiduciary relationship.[55] The purpose of the constructive trust was to prevent the fiduciary taking the profit which he had made as a result of an abuse of his position. For example, in the seminal case of **Keech v Sandford**[56] a trustee was holding a lease on trust for an infant beneficiary; when the lease expired, the trustee renewed the lease for his own benefit. Despite the fact that the landlord was not willing to renew the lease for the benefit of the infant, the court held that the trustee held the lease on constructive trust for the infant.[57]

In the past fifty years or so, the constructive trust has played an important role in determining the property rights of cohabitees of land. In doing so, the constructive trust has often become the only vehicle by which certain types of cohabiting individuals have been able to lay claim to ownership of cohabited land in circumstances where the common law has been unable to afford any legal rights in the land to such individuals. The primary reason for the resort to the constructive trust, and the resulting trust, has been the social and economic changes that took place after a period preceding the middle of the twentieth century in relation to home ownership. Before the Second World War, the English courts did not face the same degree of co-ownership disputes that it did after the War, particularly in the period starting in the late 1960s. With the incidence of divorce being low and title to land taken in the husband's name, there was very little by way of ownership dispute of the family home. The social and economic pattern of home ownership, however, changed significantly in the 1970s.[58] The incidence of divorce increased, thereby giving rise to ownership disputes of the house once occupied by husband and wife. As well as marital cohabitation, a significant trend which continues today, was the increased non-marital cohabitation. In the context of non-marital cohabitation, where the parties are unable to take advantage of the Matrimonial Causes Act 1973,[59] the recourse to the equitable principles and doctrine of resulting and constructive trust

---

[54] *Ibid.* at 714.

[55] *Bray v Ford* [1896] AC 44, and more recently, *Boardman v Phipps* [1967] 2 AC 46.

[56] (1726) Sel. Cas. Ch. 61.

[57] Although the constructive trust is generally imposed where a person has acted unconscionably, in the case of profits made by a fiduciary, it may not be possible to point to any unconscionable behaviour despite the imposition of the constructive trust. This stems from the strict principle of equity that no fiduciary is allowed to make a profit irrespective of honesty and good faith; see *Bray v Ford* [1896] AC 44 at 51. The policy of equity here is to take a deterrence approach rather than examine each case on its facts, since it would be a very difficult from an evidential point of view to question the fiduciary's motives and whether he acted in good faith. In *Guinness plc v Saunders* [1990] 2 AC 663 the House of Lords held that a director of company who had received an unauthorised payment of some £5.2 million was liable to account for it to the company. This liability to account was imposed irrespective of the director's honesty and good faith; the director had allowed his duty and his interest to conflict and this was sufficient to impose the constructive trust. It is precisely these varying contexts and the different policy considerations within them that have made it difficult to provide a comprehensive definition of a constructive trust. These matters are explored in more detail in Chapter 14.

[58] Some of the more recent trends on cohabitation are identified by the Law Commission in its report, *Cohabitation: The Financial Consequence of Relationship Breakdown* (Law Com. 307) 2007. See also D. Hughes. M. Davies and L. Jacklin, 'Come Live with Me and be my Love – a Consideration of the 2007 Law Commission Proposals on Cohabitation Breakdown' (2008) Conv. 197.

[59] This will be discussed in Chapter 11 under the context of purchase price resulting trusts.

became ever more pressing. A further development which saw a rise in the application of constructive trusts in land was the availability of mortgage finance. Typically, a husband may have taken out a mortgage to purchase the family home or may have remortgaged the family home in order to pick up further monies on the land. In such cases, where the husband defaulted on payment of the mortgage money, the bank sought vacant possession of the land. However, in some cases the wife asserted that a beneficial interest in the land was binding on the bank on the grounds of a constructive trust.

Whilst title to co-owned land may become fragmented by the express declarations of the co-owners of land, it often happens in practice that title to land may be vested in one person whilst the interests of other cohabitees may be silent on the legal title. There may be a number of reasons why the interests of other cohabitees of land may be undisclosed on the legal title.[60] Where it is a husband and wife, it may just so happen that the husband, who is the sole provider, takes both the legal title and mortgage on his own name. Where it is an unmarried couple, it may happen that the land may have been purchased before the relationship began, but then a partner moves in with the legal title-holder and makes some contribution towards the land, either directly through payment of the purchase price or indirectly by looking after the house. Often disputes which occur much later on after the purchase of land, or the time at which cohabitation took place, are extremely difficult for the courts to resolve. The main questions are: on what principles do such cohabitees acquire an interest in land, and, how is such an interest to be quantified? The constructive trust has been used in this context to allow cohabitees to acquire interests in land when they have acted to their detriment in reliance of a common intention that they will acquire an interest in the property.[61] Whilst in the case of marital breakdown, the Matrimonial Causes Act 1973 affords the court with a power to adjust property rights on divorce, no such power exists in relation to non-marital cohabitees.[62] In the context of non-marital cohabitation, ownership disputes can only be resolved by applying the technical and often inflexible rules of resulting and constructive trusts.

Finally, some of the other contexts in which the constructive trust has been imposed include the imposition of the trust in order to prevent a person benefiting from his crime; to find liability in the case where a stranger intermeddles with a trust either through dishonestly assisting in a breach of trust or knowingly receiving trust property;[63] to prevent a landowner from denying a claimant an interest in land where it would be inequitable to do so,[64] and where a vendor enters into a specifically enforceable contract for the sale of land.[65] All these situations are explored in more detail in Chapter 13.

Although the institutional constructive trust is firmly accepted as a trust category in English law, the English courts have generally not warmed to the remedial constructive trust. There are many reasons for this reluctance, not least the fact that it represents a very broad proposition of law. The idea that it is imposed to reverse an unjust enrichment

VISIT CASE NAVIGATOR

[60] For an excellent account of these social factors and the role of constructive trusts in family co-owned land, see A.J.H. Morris 'Equity's Reaction to Modern Domestic Relationships' in Oakley (ed.) *Trends in Contemporary Trust Law* (1996).
[61] *Lloyds Bank plc v Rosset* [1991] 1 AC 107.
[62] A similar power does, however, exist for same-sex partnerships registered under the Civil Partnership Act 2004.
[63] *Barnes v Addy* (1874) 9. Ch. App. 244; *Royal Brunei Airlines Sdn Bhd v Tan* [1995] 2 AC 378 and *Re Montagu's Settlement Trusts* [1987] Ch. 264.
[64] See *Binions v Evans* [1972] Ch. 359, see post Chapter 11.
[65] *Lsyaght v Edwards* (1876) 2 Ch. D 499, the equitable maxim, which holds that equity sees that as done which ought to be done, treats the purchaser of land as equitable owner as soon as the contract is entered into. The remedy of specific performance makes it inequitable for the vendor to deny the transfer of the land to the purchaser.

irrespective of the cause and nature of that enrichment has traditionally been regarded as being too vague a proposition. Lord Denning attempted to introduce something along the lines of a remedial constructive trust in the 1970s and it is his statement in one case which illustrates the broad nature of such a trust. In *Hussey v Palmer*[66] Lord Denning commented that a constructive trust 'is a trust imposed by law whenever justice and good conscience require it. It is a liberal process, founded on large principles of equity . . . It is an equitable remedy by which the court can enable an aggrieved party to obtain restitution.'[67] A further obstacle in the recognition of a remedial constructive trust in English law relates to the uncertainty as to the cause of action which gives rise to its imposition. An institutional constructive trust, which is imposed to reverse the unconscionable conduct of a person, requires a breach of a recognised legal duty,[68] for example, a breach of fiduciary duty. Until recently it has been unclear in the minds of English lawyers as to what is the basis of imposing a remedial constructive trust. The idea that it is a remedy without a cause of action troubles the legal mind and introduces uncertainty into law. It is submitted that these concerns and obstacles surrounding the remedial trust in English law may no longer be valid in the twenty-first century. English law has now recognised that there exists an independent law of restitution founded on the principle of unjust enrichment.[69] Where a defendant has been unjustly enriched at the expense of the plaintiff, a remedial constructive trust may be one of the remedies to effect restitution. It may well be very soon that the remedial constructive trusts finds a home in English law as a means by which restitution can be made in cases of unjust enrichment. In *Westdeutsche v Islington London Borough Council*[70] Lord Browne-Wilkinson suggested that the remedial constructive trust, if introduced into English law, would provide a suitable restitutionary remedy.[71]

 The contemporary significance of trusts

This chapter has said a lot about the historical development of the trust and its historical importance. What is equally important to stress here is that the trust has continued to play an important role throughout time and continues to do so in the contemporary world. The versatility of the trust concept has allowed both express and implied trusts to be used in a wide number of circumstances to achieve different legal, social and economic objectives. Given the flexibility of the modern trust to operate in a wide number of circumstances, mention can be made here of a few of those circumstances. It has already been seen at the outset of this chapter that, in modern practice, express trusts can be employed in family as well as commercial settings. In the context of the family, a parent may wish to provide a future gift for the child. Money can be transferred to trustees to hold for the child until he or she attains a specified age or meets any other condition specified in the instrument purporting to create the trust. Another example is where a parent wishes to provide for his children in the future in light of circumstances not yet

---

[66] [1972] 1 WLR 1286.

[67] *Ibid.* at 1289.

[68] The words 'legal duty' used here in the wider sense to include both the rules of the common law and equity.

[69] See *Lipkin Gorman* v *Karpnale Ltd* [1991] 2 AC 548 where the principle of unjust enrichment was recognised as the foundation of claims in restitution. More recently see the landmark decision of the House of Lords in *Banque Financière de la Cité* v *Parc (Battersea) Ltd* [1999] 1 AC 221.

[70] [1996] AC 669.

[71] *Ibid.* at 716.

arisen. Money can be given to trustees on trust, either at their discretion, or subject to other factors, and to be payable to children who may be in more need of money than others. Also within the family context, express trusts can be used as a means by which the incidence of tax can be reduced. Indeed, in the modern law, issues of trusts and taxation are intertwined. Liability to income tax, capital gains tax and inheritance tax can be reduced by the careful imposition of trusts to family wealth.[72] It is inevitable that a person with a high income will pay a much higher rate of income tax; however, if some of that income can be distributed to other members of the family who have only a modest income or no income at all, substantial tax savings can be made. Another example of a trust in the family context is where property is given to an infant beneficiary. An infant beneficiary is incapable of managing property on its own behalf. A trustee may be appointed to deal with the property until the beneficiary attains majority.[73]

Although express trusts historically featured dominantly in family matters where property was preserved for member of the family, in modern times the express trust plays an important role in financial and commercial matters. Rather than just providing for family members in the form of a future gift or a settlement of property, a person can make an investment of money through the use of a unit trust. A unit trust is a form of investment which allows the investor to spread the risk over a number of investments. Basically, a managing company who acts as a trustee invests money belonging to investors in a portfolio of securities such a shares. A unit trust is a particularly useful form of investment for a small investor. The reason for this is that, on his own, it is impossible to obtain the same degree of risk minimisation that is offered by pooling in funds with other investors and buying a unit of investment in the larger pool managed by the unit trust company. Along similar lines as the unit trust, there is the pension trust. Private pension schemes have become very popular in recent times as a means for providing financial provision on retirement. The basic structure of such schemes is that they operate under a trust and a contract. The trust nature of the scheme revolves around the fact that trustees invest money which is contributed by both the employer and employee during the course of an employee's occupation. The contractual nature of the scheme revolves around the fact that the employee's rights are founded upon the contract creating the entitlement to pension. It is the contract that guarantees the payment of retirement on final salary rather than the contributions made. Given the importance of pensions to those who contribute to a pension scheme and the fact that these schemes essentially lie in the control of private individuals, there is much scope for abuse of such schemes. Such abuse was apparent in the Maxwell saga in the early 1990s when pension monies, which were essentially in the control of Maxwell companies, were wrongfully appropriated and dissipated. In modern times such pensions are governed by the law of trusts alongside the Pensions Act 1995, which seeks to provide regulation of such schemes from abuse.

Imputed trusts are as important in property matters as express trusts. Imputed trusts play an important role in both commercial and family matters. In the context of the family, imputed trusts have become a very important means by which disputes relating to the ownership of land can be resolved.[74] So far mention has been made to implied trusts in the form of implied and constructive trusts; however, a form of imputed trust is one that is imposed by statute. In the context of the co-ownership of land, the Trusts of

---

[72] For an excellent account of the relationship between taxation, trusts and property see G. Moffat, *Trust Law: Text and Material* 4th edn (2005) Ch. 3.

[73] In the case of land, a conveyance to a minor has the automatic effect that the land is held upon trust by the transferor for the minor; see s. 2(6) Trusts of Land and Appointment of Trustees Act 1996 which applies to conveyances of land after 1996.

[74] See J. Dewar, 'Land, Law and the Family' Bright and Dewar (eds) *Land Law: Themes and Perspectives* (1998) at pp. 327–55.

Land and Appointment of Trustees Act 1996 imposes a trust of land in every case of the co-ownership of land. Such a trust plays an important function in spelling out the rights and duties of the co-owners of land and how disputes relating to co-ownership of land can be resolved. However, where families fail to express their intentions as to the ownership of family property such as land in a formal way, imputed trusts are the only means by which such intentions can be implied. Furthermore, where the relationship between the parties is one not founded on marriage, unlike in divorce proceedings, property law is the only way that such disputes can be resolved. Thus, as we have already seen above, where a cohabitee of land has no legal title to land, but contributes directly to the purchase of the price of the land, such cohabitee may acquire an interest under a resulting trust. The role of implied trusts in the family context and the family home are explored in more detail later in Chapters 11 and 13 of this book.

In the context of commercial matters, imputed trusts play an important role in effecting restitution of profits and money gains made by abuse of fiduciary obligations by fiduciaries. An example is the imposition of the constructive trust on a person who makes a profit by abuse of his fiduciary obligations owed to others. For example, in **A-G for Hong Kong v Reid**[75] Reid, who was the Director of Public Prosecutions in Hong Kong, had accepted bribes in the course of his employment. The bribe money was then used to purchase freehold properties in New Zealand. The Privy Council held that the freehold properties, which were purchased by Reid, were held by him on constructive trust for the Crown. The bribes had been made by the abuse of his fiduciary relationship with the Crown. More recently, however, the **Court of Appeal in Sinclair Investments (UK) Ltd v Versaille Trade Finance Ltd** [2011] 1 EWCA Civ. 347 has revisited the extent to which a constructive trust will be imposed on unauthorised gains. This is explored in Chapter 13.

 ## Some key players and concepts in the trust relationship

This chapter has explored a number of key aspects of the trust relationship and has introduced a number of key concepts which will be employed throughout this book. Therefore, it is a useful exercise at this stage to take stock of some of the key players and concepts in the trust relationship.

Key concept/player	Definition
Trust	Equitable obligation binding upon a trustee to hold property for a beneficiary.
Administrator	An individual who administers an estate of a person when there is no will.
Beneficiary	The person entitled to the equitable interest in the trust property.
Bequest	A gift which is received under a will.
Breach of trust	A failure to comply with a duty or an improper exercise of a power by trustees either conferred by the trust instrument or trust law in general.
Charitable trust	A trust which is for a charitable purpose and for the benefit of the public at large.
Constructive trust	A trust implied by law by virtue of the unconscionable conduct of the constructive trustee with respect to property in his hands.

---

[75] [1994] 1 All ER 1.

Key concept/player	Definition
Discretionary trust	A trust where the interest of the beneficiaries is at the discretion of the trustees.
Equitable interest	The interest of a beneficiary in the trust property.
Executor	Appointed under a will to administer the estate of the testator.
Fixed trust	A trust where the interests of the beneficiaries are fixed from the start, e.g. £1000 equally to A, B, and C.
Inter-vivos	An act done during the lifetime of a settlor or testator/testatrix.
Purpose trust	A trust which is for a purpose and not for ascertainable beneficiaries. Prima facie void.
Restitution	The process by which the law reverses an unjust enrichment, that is, a gain made at the expense of a claimant. Restitution is primarily effected by an account for the gain or profit or by the imposition of a constructive trust on the gain.
Resulting trust	A trust implied by law giving effect to the imputed intentions of the person in whose favour it arises.
Secret trust	A trust where the identity of the beneficiary is not disclosed and one which takes effect after the testator's death.
Settlor	A person creating a trust during his lifetime.
Testamentary	An act which takes effect on the death of an individual and complies with s. 9 Wills Act.
Testator/Testatrix	Individuals (male/female) creating a trust in a will.
Tracing	The process by which a beneficiary can follow his or her beneficial interest in property into the hands of third parties.
Trust instrument	The document creating a trust.

The functions of trust law

Having explored the nature of the trust in this chapter, it just remains to explain the functions of trust law.[76] The functions of trust law can be broken down into a number of different constituent elements. At the outset, the primary function of trust law is to govern the relationship, rights and obligations of those parties involved in the trust. For example, the rights and duties of the settlor; beneficiary and the trustees of the trust. However, trust law goes further and explores the relationship, rights and duties of other third parties who may become subject to the trust or may have some interest in the trust. These third parties include innocent third parties who may become involved in the trusts; it may also include the creditors of the trustee or the beneficiary, and it may include those third parties who intentionally intermeddle with the trust property. In addition to the primary function of trust law, the law of trusts is concerned with the substantive and formal requirements that must be fulfilled in order for the trust relationship to come about. Once the trust relationship is firmly established, the focus of the law moves to the administration of the trust. The function of the law is to govern the activities of the trustee and make sure that the trust is effectively administered in the best interests of the beneficiary. Finally, the focus of trust law shifts to an analysis of

---

[76] For an excellent account of the functions of trust law and a comparative analysis between American and European legal traditions see, Hansmann, H. and Mattei, U. 'The Functions of Trust Law' (1998) 73 NYUL Review 434. The authors also examine the differences, if any, between trust law and company law.

the remedies that are available to a beneficiary in the event of breach of trust by the trustees. These functions predominantly remain the same whether the trust is a private trust or whether it is a public trust, that is, a trust which is for the benefit of the public at large, otherwise known as a charitable trust. Indeed, the functions will equally apply to specialised trusts such as pension trusts.

Conclusion

This chapter has explored the very nature of a trust and, in doing so, has examined a number of key features relating to it. In particular, the respective positions of the trustee and beneficiaries under a trust and the nature of their interests. The chapter has examined the classification of trusts in the modern law of trust. The primary classification of trusts is between express and implied trust; however, as explained in this chapter, express and implied trusts can be further subdivided into categories. The chapter has further explored the instrumental role of trusts in achieving a number of social and economic goals and eventually contributing to law reform. It was observed that one of the main characteristics of a trust is its versatility and flexibility. It is because of this characteristic that the trust has been employed in both family and commercial settings to resolve entitlements to property. The basic feature of the trust is that it facilitates the fragmentation of ownership of property, thereby creating duality of rights in respect of the same thing. Although the legal title to the trust property is vested in the trustee, the equitable interest belongs to the beneficiary. The importance of the trust in English law cannot be underestimated and it is for this precise reason that Maitland was to comment that it is one of the greatest achievements of English lawyers.

Moot points

1 A trust is often described as a product of fragmentation of ownership. Explain exactly what aspects of ownership are fragmented when a trust is created.

2 Explain the significance of the distinction between rights *in rem* and rights *in personam*.

3 Why are equitable rights, for example, the equitable right of a beneficiary under a trust, often referred to as rights *in personam*?

4 In a system of registration of equitable interests in land, is it possible to say that equitable interests become more and more akin to rights *in rem* rather than *in personam*?

5 What were the reasons for the enactment of the Statute of Uses 1535?

6 Why has the trust concept been a primary vehicle for dealing with new social and economic problems? Can you give examples of where the trust has made a major impact in protecting the rights of certain individuals which would otherwise not be protected in the common law?

7 Identify the key differences between express and implied trust.

Further reading

Hansmann, H. and Mattei, U. 'The Functions of Trust Law' (1998) 73 NYUL Review 434. This article explores the concept of the trust, the functions of trust law and some of the differences between trust law and other areas of civil law such as contract and company law. Additionally, the authors provide a comparative analysis of trust law between American and European civil law countries.

Hayton, D. 'Developing the Obligation Characteristics of the Trust' (2001) 117 LQR. Explores the enforcement of trusts from the perspective of settlor and beneficiary.

Mathews, P. 'All About Bare Trusts' (2005) PCB at 266. Examines the nature of bare trusts and distinguishes such trusts from special trusts.

Panesar, S. 'General Principles of Property Law' (Longmans) (2001) Explores property concepts such as ownership, the nature of legal and equitable rights in addition to fragmentation of ownership.

Parkinson, P. 'Reconceptualising the Express Trust' [2002] 61 CLJ 65. For a discussion on the nature of an express trust. The author examines the express trust from a number of different angles, including the trust as a species of property as well as a species of obligation.

Scott, A.W. 'The Trust as an Instrument of Law Reform' (1922) 31 *Yale Law Journal* 457. Explores the role of trusts in law reform.

Visit **www.mylawchamber.co.uk/panesar** to access study support resources including interactive multiple choice questions, practice exam questions with guidance, podcasts, weblinks, legal newsfeed all linked to the **Pearson eText** version of Exploring Equity and Trusts which you can **search**, **highlight** and **personalise** with your **own notes** and **bookmarks**.

Use Case Navigator to read in full some of the key cases referenced in this chapter with commentary and questions:

Lloyds Bank plc v Rosset [1991] 1 AC 107
Re Vandervell's Trusts (No. 2) [1974] Ch. 269
Westdeutsche Landesbank Girozentrale v Islington LBC [1996] AC 699 (HL)

3

The trust distinguished from other legal concepts

Learning objectives

After reading this chapter you should be able to:

→ explain why it is important to distinguish the trust from other related concepts

→ understand that any purported document attempting to create a trust may also create obligations of a different kind to a trust

→ explain the difference between trusts and powers of appointment

→ explain the nature of powers of appointment

→ explain how a trust is distinguished from a power of appointment

→ understand that a trust obligation may coexist with other legal obligations, for example contractual relationships

→ understand the difference between trusts, bailment, agency and debts

→ understand some of the initial duties of trustees on appointment and the vesting of the trust property in the trustees

→ explain how the duties and discretions of trustees are controlled.

SETTING THE SCENE

Re Mills [1930] 1 Ch. 654: If you maintain the family fortune then the property is yours, but not always

The facts in *Re Mills* illustrate some of the concerns which will be the subject matter of discussion in this chapter. A testator left his residuary estate to his trustees with the express instructions that the estate be available for the benefit of all or any one of the children or remoter issue of the testator who in the opinion of one of the trustees (who also happened to be the brother of the testator) evidenced a desire and ability to maintain the family fortune. The testator provided that should the trustee fail to give the family fortune to the children or remoter issue, then the trustee could appoint the property to himself.

The testator's brother failed to give the property to any children or remoter issue and instead claimed the property for himself. The remoter issue, who happened to be the nieces and nephews of the testator claimed to be entitled to the testator's estate on the grounds that his will had created a trust in their favour.

The facts of *Re Mills* clearly illustrate that the construction of wills and trust instruments is not always an easy exercise. The real question is one of ascertaining the settlor's or testator's true intention. In *Re Mills*, the testator clearly intended his children and remoter issue to benefit from the trust, but was it a trust? Why did the testator also allow the trustee brother to appoint himself as the absolute owner of his estate? Indeed, was the brother a trustee in the first place?

Did the testator's will in *Re Mills* create a trust? It certainly looked like a trust. Did the testator create some other equitable obligation? In the course of this chapter it will be observed that a trust is to be distinguished from other legal concepts, some of which may look very similar to a trust but may have rather different outcomes.

Introduction

The previous chapter explored the nature of a trust and the trust relationship. The chapter examined some of the main reasons why trusts are created and also looked at the manner in which trusts are classified. Whilst a good understanding of the trust concept is important, it is also important to distinguish the trust from other related legal categories. There appear to be two main reasons for this. In the first place, the same act or document purporting to create a trust may also purport to create obligations which are quite different form the trust obligation. Therefore, any individual construing those acts or documents must clearly distinguish between what obligations have been created simply because the nature of those obligations will be different. For example, a person transferring property in a will or some other document may simply be making a gift to another. Alternatively, the person transferring the property may be intending that the property be held on trust for another. A gift confers absolute ownership of the recipient whereas a trust, as already observed in the preceding chapter, fragments ownership between a trustee and a beneficiary. The second reason for the need to distinguish the trust concept from other concepts relates to the fact that there may be legal categories very similar to a trust but which have rather different outcomes. For example, in this chapter, the concept of a power of appointment will be explored in detail. A power of appointment looks very similar to a trust; however, it has rather different legal consequences for the persons for whose benefit it is created. In advising the rights of any persons entitled under a trust obligation or a power of appointment it becomes imperative that the obligation is properly classified. In order to ascertain which legal obligation the settlor or testator has created requires a careful construction of the trust instrument or the will. The basic duty of the trust lawyer is to construe all the relevant facts before deciding on the outcome of a particular obligation.

 ## Contract

The element of a bargain

The basic idea behind a contract is that is creates a personal relationship between the contracting parties. The relationship arises out of some bargain where one contracting party agrees to do something in return for the other contracting party providing consideration. At the heart of a contract is the notion of an agreement between two or more persons. Contracts may take the form of simple contracts or speciality contracts. A simple contract is one where the agreement is simply made orally or is made in some form of writing. On the other hand, a speciality contract is one which is made by deed. Historically, a speciality contract was entered into by way of a deed under seal by affixing a wax seal on the document to give it its formal status as a deed. However, since the enactment of s. 1 of the Law of Property (Miscellaneous Provisions) Act 1989, the requirement of a seal has been removed and a deed obtains its status as a deed if it intended to be a deed.[1]

In contrast to a contract, a trust does not necessarily involve an element of bargain. In most cases a trust is purely gratuitous in the sense that the person settling the trust property does so voluntarily. The beneficiary of the trust does not need to furnish any consideration at all. Provided that the settlor transfers the trust property to the intended trustee, thereby constituting the trust, the beneficiary will be able to enforce the trust in equity.

It should, however, be noted that, although there are many fundamental differences between a trust and a contract, the two concepts are not mutually exclusive. The same arrangement may give rise to a contractual as well as a trust relationship. For example, a person who lends money by way of a loan has a contractual right to be repaid. However, as will be explored in more detail below, it is perfectly possible for a contractual loan to be impressed with a trust. Furthermore, in the context of employee pension funds, the arrangement will give rise to both contractual entitlements as well as those under a trust as explained by the Privy Council in **Baird v Baird** where the court held that contractual and trust entitlements were not mutually exclusive.[2]

---

[1] It should be noted, however, that a speciality contract is not truly reflective of a bargain. This is because the promise made by deed relies on form rather than consideration in the true sense. Furthermore, the legal duty arising under a speciality contract may not even be apparent to the beneficiary: see, for example, *Lady Naas v Westminster Bank Ltd* [1940] 1 All ER 485.

[2] [1990] 2 AC 548 at 560.

 A personal relationship

A contract creates a personal relationship between the parties to the contract. The general rule of contract law is that only parties to the contract can enforce it. The contractual doctrine of privity of contract prevents third parties from suing on a contract or from being sued on a contract. However, the Contract (Rights of Third Parties) Act 1999 confers upon a non-contracting party to sue upon a contract provided that the contract purports to confer a benefit on that party, or otherwise provides for that party to be able to enforce the contract.

KEY STATUTE

Contract (Rights of Third Parties) Act 1999

1 Right of third party to enforce contractual term

(1) Subject to the provisions of this Act, a person who is not a party to a contract (a 'third party') may in his own right enforce a term of the contract if –

    (a) the contract expressly provides that he may, or

    (b) subject to subsection (2), the term purports to confer a benefit on him.

(2) Subsection (1)(b) does not apply if on a proper construction of the contract it appears that the parties did not intend the term to be enforceable by the third party.

(3) The third party must be expressly identified in the contract by name, as a member of a class or as answering a particular description but need not be in existence when the contract is entered into.

(4) This section does not confer a right on a third party to enforce a term of a contract otherwise than subject to and in accordance with any other relevant terms of the contract.

(5) For the purpose of exercising his right to enforce a term of the contract, there shall be available to the third party any remedy that would have been available to him in an action for breach of contract if he had been a party to the contract (and the rules relating to damages, injunctions, specific performance and other relief shall apply accordingly).

(6) Where a term of a contract excludes or limits liability in relation to any matter references in this Act to the third party enforcing the term shall be construed as references to his availing himself of the exclusion or limitation.

(7) In this Act, in relation to a term of a contract which is enforceable by a third party –

    'the promisor' means the party to the contract against whom the term is enforceable by the third party, and

    'the promisee' means the party to the contract by whom the term is enforceable against the promisor.

The fact that a contract merely confers a personal relationship between the parties to a contract means that the right of a contracting party is essentially a right *in personam*. The right is enforceable against a specific person rather than persons at large.

In contrast to a contract, a trust does not generate a purely personal relationship between the trustee and the beneficiary. The beneficiary may enforce the trust relationship against persons other than the trustee. A third party may be bound by a trust even though he never agreed to be subject to the trust and may not even be aware of the existence of the trust. The principal reason for this is that a trust, unlike a contract, creates a proprietary relationship rather than a personal one. Once the trust is created, the beneficiary acquires a proprietary interest in the trust property. Whilst the trustee will acquire the legal title to the trust property, the beneficiary acquires an equitable interest in the property. Equitable proprietary rights are governed by the doctrine of notice. This doctrine holds that such rights bind everyone except for a bona fide purchaser of the legal title without notice of the pre-existing equitable interest.[3] Equity, acting *in personam*, clearly binds the conscience of the trustee; however, it goes further and binds all those persons who subsequently acquire the trust property with notice of the trust.[4] It is often said that the rights of a beneficiary under a trust are rights *in personam* on the basis that they, unlike rights *in rem*, do not bind the whole world. However, it is perhaps, more apt to describe the rights of a beneficiary as more akin to rights *in rem*, on the grounds that they have the potential to bind a significantly large group of persons.[5]

 A promise to create a trust or settle property for the benefit of another

A settlor who transfers the trust property to the intended trustee creates a trust which confers upon the beneficiary a right to enforce it. The trust is said to be fully constituted and that is the end of the matter. Where a settlor has not transferred the trust property to the intended trust, there is no trust and the beneficiary prima facie has no rights in the intended trust property. In such a case, however, the absence of a trust may not be the end of the matter for the intended beneficiary. The settlor may have promised to settle the trust property or covenanted that he would convey property on trust. In such a case the intended beneficiary may seek to enforce the promise or the covenant to settle. In such a case normal contractual principles will apply and the beneficiary may seek to enforce the promise if it has provided consideration. Alternatively, if the settlor has promised to settle the trust property with a potential trustee for the benefit of a beneficiary who is not party to the contract to settle, the beneficiary may be able to enforce the contract under the Contract (Rights of Third Parties) Act 1999 which was discussed above. If the contract to settle the trust property takes the form of a speciality contract, that is, a covenant by way of a deed, then the beneficiary may enforce the covenant at law.[6] These matters are discussed in more detail in Chapter 6.

Agency

An agency relationship is a contractual relationship between a principal and an agent. It has been defined as a 'relationship that exists between two persons when one, called the agent, is considered in law to represent the other, called the principal, in such a way as

---

[3] *Pilcher v Rawlins* (1872) 7 Ch. App. 259.

[4] The essential features of the doctrine of notice were explored in the preceding chapter.

[5] The labelling of equitable rights as rights *in personam* is more to do with historical factors rather than from the orthodox sense of the phrase which relates to mere personal rights. The fact that equitable rights are sometimes called right *in personam* arises from the historical basis that *equity acts in personam*: for example, the method of enforcement of a judgment of the Court of Chancery was by a personal order restraining or ordering the defendant to do something.

[6] *Cannon v Hartley* [1949] Ch. 213.

to be able to affect the principal's legal position in respect of strangers to the relationship by the making of contracts or the disposition of property'.[7] At the heart of an agency relationship is the agent's ability to bind his principal in legal relations with other third parties. The relationship of agency does have some similarities to the trust relationship. The fundamental similarity lies in the fact that both agency and trust are fiduciary relationships.[8] Thus, an agent, just like a trustee, is subject to the fiduciary obligation not to put himself in a position where his own interest conflicts with the duty he owes to the principal.[9] Where an agent makes a secret profit at the expense of his principal, he will be held to account for that profit in equity. Such an account will take the form of a restitutionary claim to reverse the unjust enrichment he will have made at his principal's expense. Similarly, a trustee who obtains an unauthorised profit from his position as a trustee will have to make proper restitution to the trust estate. In most cases this will involve either an account for profits or the imposition of a constructive trust on property acquired as a result of the breach of fiduciary duty.

Despite the fact that both agency and trust relationships are fiduciary and have been the subject of equitable jurisdiction, there are some fundamental distinctions between agency and trusts. Firstly, although an agency relationship is governed by some equitable rules, especially those relating to the fiduciary nature of the relationship, the relationship of agency is essentially a common law one. This is in contrast to a trust relationship, which is exclusively a product of equity and not the common law. Secondly, the relationship of agency is contractual and arises through some agreement. The trust relationship need not, however, arise through any agreement. Although in most cases there is an agreement between the trustee and the person creating the trust that he will hold trust property for the benefit of a beneficiary, in some cases a voluntary settlement to settle property upon trust will create a binding trust obligation in equity.[10] Thirdly, whilst an agent has the power to bind his principal in legal relations with other parties, a trustee does not represent the beneficiary and, therefore, although he may pass a valid legal title to third parties, he does not bind the beneficiary with respect to those third parties. Finally, it is not necessary in an agency relationship that the agent be vested with the legal title to the principal's property, whereas under a trust it is of utmost importance that the legal title is vested in the trustee. Indeed, without the vesting of the trust property in the intended trustee, there is no trust.[11]

 ## Bailment

Bailment involves the delivery of possession of a chattel to another person. The person bailing the property does not transfer the ownership therein, but merely the physical possession of the thing in question. The relationship of bailment arises at common law and it may be contractual, for example where property is given to another in order for it to be repaired, or it may be gratuitous, as for example a simple loan of a book to another. Once the bailor has bailed the goods, the bailee is under a duty to exercise reasonable care in respect of the bailed property. Any wrongful interference with the bailor's property will amount to a wrongful interference and the bailor may sue the bailee for

---

[7] G.H.L. Fridman, *Fridman's Law of Agency*, 7th edn, Butterworths (London) 1996 at p. 11.

[8] Fiduciary relationships are considered in detail in Chapter 14.

[9] *Parker* v *McKenna* (1874) 10 Ch. App. 96 at 118.

[10] *Fletcher* v *Fletcher* (1884) 4 Hare 67.

[11] The trust is said to be incompletely constituted: see Chapter 6.

conversion.[12] A person commits a conversion when he deals with goods belonging to another in a manner which is inconsistent with that other person's ownership of the goods.

A trust is fundamentally different from a bailment of property. Most notably, unlike a bailment, a trust requires the transfer of legal ownership of the trust property to the trustee. The trustee has the power to deal with the trust property and, indeed, can pass a valid title, albeit in breach of trust, to a third party. The same is not true of a bailment where the bailee only has possession and, therefore, cannot as a general rule deal with the bailor's legal title. A further significant difference between bailment and trust is that a bailment is confined to personal property whereas a trust can be created over any property form.

Interests under wills and administration

Perhaps one of the finer distinctions to be made is the rights of a beneficiary under a trust and the rights of those entitled under a will or the administration of a deceased's estate.[13] Such persons are frequently referred to as legatees or devisees. Furthermore, it is not just the rights of those entitled under trusts or on the death of a person that need to be distinguished, but also the rights and duties of those administering trusts and those administering the estate of a deceased. The distinction in some cases may become blurred because the same document: for example, a will, may indeed confer a dual status on a person: for example, a person may be appointed as an executor as well as a trustee. Despite the overlap between trustees and personal representatives, the distinction between trustees and personal representatives is important.

Personal representatives

Property vests in personal representatives of the deceased who are obliged to transfer that part of the estate which is left after payment of debts and expenses to the intended beneficiaries. A personal representative is a term that includes executors and administrators. In making a will the testator will appoint an executor to distribute his property after his death. In the case of a person who has died intestate, that is without having made a will, some person who is interested in the estate being administered must apply to the

---

[12] *Plasycoed Collieries Co Ltd v Partridge, Jones & Co Ltd* [1912] 2 KB 345.
[13] Administration of property of a deceased was historically regulated by the ecclesiastical courts, whereas trusts were enforced in the Court of Chancery.

court for what is known as 'letters of administration' appointing an administrator. The duties of the administrator are essentially the same as those of an executor. All the property of a deceased person vests in the personal representatives.[14] It is only after the property has vested in the personal representatives that they are able to transfer it to the intended beneficiaries. All the property of the deceased is held upon a statutory trust for sale,[15] which means that land can be sold to meet the liabilities of the deceased. Where property is left, which is not required for liabilities, the personal representatives can then transfer it to the beneficiaries. In the case of land it should be noted that there is no need for a deed to transfer the land to the beneficiaries: all that is required is a written assent.[16] Personal representatives, like trustees, stand in a fiduciary relationship to those entitled under the will or administration.[17]

There are a number of fundamental distinctions to be made between trustees and personal representatives. Firstly, the functions of a trustee are rather different from those of a personal representative. The basic duty of a trustee is to hold the trust property in accordance with the trust instrument and trust law in general. The trustee's office may well last for some considerable time, depending on the terms of the trust. For example, a settlor who directs the trustee to hold the trust property for his wife for life and thereafter for his children will inevitably impose a long-term commitment on the trustee. In contrast, a personal representative's fundamental obligation is to wind up the deceased's estate. Secondly, the power of personal representatives to dispose of personal property is rather different from that of a trustee. Trustees must act jointly in the disposition of personal property; however, in the case of personal representatives, they may dispose of personal property severally. This means that one personal representative out of many has the power to dispose of personal property. However, where a personal representative is also a trustee and his office of personal representative has come to an end, he must act jointly with the other trustees before he can deal with the trust property.[18]

The interest of a legatee or devisee

Under a trust the beneficiaries acquire a beneficial interest in the trust property as soon as the trust comes into effect. It has already been noted that this gives them a proprietary right in the trust property and is enforceable against third parties who cannot purport to show that they are bona fide purchasers of the legal title without notice of the trust. In contrast, legatees under a will or devisees under administration of an estate do not have any ownership in the property. The full ownership vests in the personal representatives until distribution is made. At most the legatees have a right to see that the estate is duly administered, which is appropriately described as a chose in action.[19] The matter is

---

[14] Administration of Estates Act 1925 ss. 1(1), 3(1).

[15] Administration of Estates Act 1925 s. 33(1).

[16] Administration of Estates Act 1925 s. 36(1).

[17] Although a personal representative who retires or renounces his executorship without having been involved in the administration of the estate will not be subject to any further fiduciary duties, see *Holder* v *Holder* [1968] Ch. 353.

[18] *Attenborough* v *Solomon* [1913] AC 76.

[19] See *Commissioner of Stamp Duties (Queensland)* v *Livingston* [1965] AC 694 where the question arose whether estate duty was payable under a Queensland statute for property situated in Queensland which became entitled to a widow under the husband's will. The widow was domiciled in New South Wales and up until his death her husband's estate had not been administered. The Privy Council held that the widow was not the owner of the property in Queensland but merely had a chose in action to see that the estate was duly administered.

neatly illustrated by the decision of the court in *Eastbourne Mutual Building Society* v *Hastings Corporation*[20] where a husband was unable to proceed with a compensation claim for the value of a house he was occupying on his wife's intestacy. The house was compulsorily purchased but, because the wife's estate had not been administered, he was not deemed to be the owner of the house.[21]

 Debts

Where one person lends money to another, a personal relationship is created between the lender and borrower. The lender has a personal right to be repaid by the borrower and his right is a right *in personam*. A loan creates a contractual debt; however, debts need not be contractual, for example, a legatee under a will has a right to be paid his legacy by the personal representatives of the deceased. In respect of a contractual debt, the rights and duties of the lender and borrower are spelt out by the contract. Despite being based on contract, a contractual debt is a rather peculiar creature because it also finds a home in the law of property. The fact that a debt is capable of assignment as a *chose in action* means it comprises a personal property interest in law. It is property for the mere fact that it is capable of assignment to third parties.[22] The proprietary essence of the debt lies in the fact that the contractual right to be paid, that is the right *in personam*, can be transferred to third parties. However, as between debtor and creditor the right is essentially personal. If A has loaned money to B, A has a personal right to be repaid by B. If B becomes insolvent, A has a personal right to be paid by the liquidator or the trustee in bankruptcy of B. The chances of being paid depend on whether the value of B's estate is capable of meeting the demands of unsecured creditors.

APPLYING THE LAW

Tim is desperately in need of some money to finance his car business. Tom is willing to advance him a loan of £50,000 but is also anxious to see that the money will be duly paid back to him. He is confident that Tim's car business will do well; however, he does not want Tim to use the loan money for any other purpose than for the car business. He wishes to transfer the £50,000 to Tim for the specific purpose of his car business and not for any other purpose. Tom knows that he is loaning the money to Tim but wishes to know whether Tim can be prevented from using the money for any other purpose.

In other words, can Tom retain some control over the loan money other than where it is used for Tim's car business?

Although a loan gives the lender a personal right to be paid by the borrower, in some circumstances the lender may have a proprietary claim to the monies loaned so as to remove those monies from the general pool of assets belonging to the borrower. This will arise when a loan is impressed with a trust relationship. For example, A may lend money to B for a specified purpose and require B to put the money in a separate account until

---

[20] [1965] 1 WLR 861.
[21] See also, *Lall* v *Lall* [1965] 1 WLR 1249.
[22] See Chapter 8.

such time as the specified purpose can be carried out. The question is whether this type of arrangement creates a loan or does B hold money upon trust for A? The question is obviously acute in the context of the insolvency or bankruptcy of B. If the money is still in the hands of B, the creditors of B will wish to see the money used to discharge the debts owed by B to the secured and other creditors. On the other hand, A will wish to argue that the money is held on trust for A because the purpose for which the money was advanced has now failed. Equally, however, there is nothing to prevent any persons who had an interest in the specified purpose to argue that they have a claim to the money; after all, they seem to be the most obvious beneficiaries of the loan.

VISIT CASE NAVIGATOR

The House of Lords in *Barclays Bank Ltd v Quistclose Investments Ltd*[23] considered the extent to which a loan and trust could coexist. On the facts of the case, Rolls Razor Ltd, who owed a large amount of money to Barclays Bank, borrowed some £209,719 from Quistclose in order to pay dividends which it had declared on its shares. The money was paid into a separate account at Barclays Bank on the understanding that it was only to be used for the specified purpose of paying the dividends. Barclays Bank had full knowledge of the arrangement between Rolls Razor Ltd and Quistclose. Before the dividends had been paid, Rolls Razor Ltd went into liquidation and the question arose whether Barclays Bank could use the money in the separate account to offset the overdraft that Rolls Razor Ltd had with it, or whether the money belonged to Quistclose on the basis that it was held on trust by Rolls Razor Ltd for them. The House of Lord unanimously held that a loan and trust relations could exist. Lord Wilberforce, delivering the unanimous decision of the court, held that the money in the separate account was impressed with a trust in favour of Quistclose as soon as the failure of the primary purpose of the trust occurred.[24] Furthermore, since Barclays Bank had notice of the trust arrangement they were clearly bound by the trust in favour of Quistclose.

The decision of the House of Lords in *Barclays Bank Ltd v Quistclose Investments Ltd* was generally accepted as appropriate by other cases and also academic writings.[25] In *Carreras Rothmans Ltd v Freeman Mathews Treasure Ltd*[26] where monies were advanced by one company to another for a specified purpose and to be kept in a separate account, the court explained that 'equity fastens on the conscience of the person who receives from another property transferred for a specific purpose only and not, therefore, for the recipient's own purpose, so that such person shall not be permitted to treat the property as his own or to use it for other than the purpose stated'.[27] Goodhart and Jones comment that '*Quistclose* is a just and commendable decision. No creditor had been misled into making a further loan by the existence of the separate dividend account; and there was no doubt that the bank knew of the agreement between the parties.'[28] Other commentators have pointed to the commercial advantages of the Quistclose trust, in particular the fact that the borrower can continue trading and avoid insolvency.[29] Continuity

---

[23] [1970] AC 567.

[24] *Ibid.* at 581–2.

[25] What is, however, unresolved is the basis upon which a Quistclose trust is enforced in favour of the original lender. Trust lawyers have generally debated whether the Quistclose trust, when enforced in favour of the original lender, is enforced on the basis of an express or implied trust. For an excellent account and review of some of the leading debates on this point see G. Moffat, *Trust Law: Text and Materials*, 4th edn (2005) at pp. 772–84. This matter fell to be decided in *Twinsectra Ltd v Yardley* [2002] 2 All ER 377, discussed in more detail below.

[26] [1985] Ch. 207, see also *Re EVTR* [1987] BCLC 646 where a Quistclose trust was accepted when money had been advanced for the specific purpose of buying machinery.

[27] [1985] Ch. 207 at 222.

[28] W. Goodhart and G. Jones, 'The Infiltration of Equitable Doctrine into English Commercial Law' (1980) 43 MLR 489 at p. 494.

[29] G. Moffat, *Trust Law: Text and Materials* 4th edn (2005) at p. 763.

of trading is obviously important from an insolvency point of view because it avoids the creation of fresh liabilities to creditors. In this respect Ulph writes:

> Quistclose trusts are frequently beneficial in the sense of providing an injection of capital which may rescue the company in financial difficulties. Moreover, these trusts are short term expediencies which cease to exist once the primary purpose is fulfilled and the provider of the funds is then in the position of an ordinary creditor, standing in line with others. The risk of a large and previously undisclosed class of claimants forcing themselves up in the insolvency queue by asserting proprietary claims under Quistclose trusts is therefore not significant as yet.[30]

Although the coexistence of a loan and trust relationship was firmly recognised by the House of Lords in *Barclays Bank Ltd* v *Quistclose Investments Ltd*[31] the main problem with the so-called Quistclose trust related to two things. First, what were the exact terms of the trust, and secondly, what was the nature of the trust in question? These matters fell to be decided by the House of Lords in *Twinsectra Ltd* v *Yardley*[32] where, until that decision, it was generally understood that the exact terms of the trust depended on the nature of the agreement between the lender and the borrower. It is only from this agreement that the terms of the trust can be construed. In some cases the terms of the trust are to the effect that the money is given to the borrower who is to hold such money on a primary trust for the purpose of the loan, and then on a secondary trust for the lender should the primary trust fail on grounds of some impossibility. This is exactly what happened in *Barclays Bank Ltd* v *Quistclose Investments Ltd* where the House of Lords held that the loan money had been received by Rolls Razor Ltd on primary trust to pay the dividends to its shareholders and that, in the event of failure of such payment, the money was to be held on a secondary trust for Quistclose Investments Ltd. In the course of judgment Lord Wilberforce commented that:

> there is surely no difficulty in recognising the coexistence in one transaction of legal and equitable rights and remedies: when the money is advanced, the lender acquires an equitable right to see that it is applied for the primary designated purpose . . . when the purpose has been carried out (i.e., the debt paid) the lender has his remedy against the borrower in debt: if the primary purpose cannot be carried out, the question arises if a secondary purpose (i.e., repayment to the lender) has been agreed, expressly or by implication: if it has, the remedies of equity may be invoked to give effect to it, if it has not (and the money is intended to fall within the general fund of the debtor's assets) then there is the appropriate remedy for recovery of a loan. I can appreciate no reason why the flexible interplay of law and equity cannot let in these practical arrangements, and other variations if desired: it would be to the discredit of both systems if they could not. In the present case the intention to create a secondary trust for the benefit of the lender, to arise if the primary trust, to pay the dividend, could not be carried out, is clear and I can find no reason why the law should not give effect to it.[33]

Whilst the principle that a loan and trust relationship could coexist was not disputed by all the judges in the case, it was the reference to the primary and secondary trust which caused much controversy, the fundamental question being: where exactly does the beneficial interest lie in a Quistclose trust? This matter received clarification in the House of Lords in 1996 in the decision in *Twinsectra Ltd* v *Yardley*.[34]

---

[30] J. Ulph, 'Equitable Proprietary Rights in Insolvency: The Ebbing Tide' (1996) JBL 482 at pp. 495–6.
[31] [1970] AC 567.
[32] [2002] 2 All ER 377.
[33] [1970] AC 567 at 581.
[34] [2002] 2 All ER 377.

KEY CITATION

Twinsectra Ltd v Yardley [2002] 2 All ER 377 (Judicial assessment of Quistclose trusts per Lord Millett)

Money advanced by way of loan normally becomes the property of the borrower. He is free to apply the money as he chooses, and save to the extent to which he may have taken security for repayment the lender takes the risk of the borrower's insolvency. But it is well established that a loan to a borrower for a specific purpose where the borrower is not free to apply the money for any other purpose gives rise to fiduciary obligations on the part of the borrower which a court of equity will enforce. In the earlier cases the purpose was to enable the borrower to pay his creditors or some of them, but the principle is not limited to such cases.

Such arrangements are commonly described as creating 'a Quistclose trust', after the well known decision of the House in **Quistclose Investments Ltd v Rolls Razor Ltd** [1970] AC 567 in which Lord Wilberforce confirmed the validity of such arrangements and explained their legal consequences. When the money is advanced, the lender acquires a right, enforceable in equity, to see that it is applied for the stated purpose, or more accurately to prevent its application for any other purpose. This prevents the borrower from obtaining any beneficial interest in the money, at least while the designated purpose is still capable of being carried out. Once the purpose has been carried out, the lender has his normal remedy in debt. If for any reason the purpose cannot be carried out, the question arises whether the money falls within the general fund of the borrower's assets, in which case it passes to his trustee in bankruptcy in the event of his insolvency and the lender is merely a loan creditor; or whether it is held on a resulting trust for the lender. This depends on the intention of the parties collected from the terms of the arrangement and the circumstances of the case.

The idea that the loan money was held under a primary and then a secondary trust was rejected by Millett LJ in **Twinsectra Ltd v Yardley**.[35] The House of Lords held that the money advanced under a loan for a specific purpose was held under a resulting trust for the lender until such time as it was used for the purposes of the loan. On the facts of the case, Twinsectra Ltd loaned money to a property dealer on the undertaking by the property dealer's solicitors that the money would only be used for property transactions and no other purposes. In breach of this undertaking, the solicitors, at the request of the property dealer, transferred the money to another solicitor who transferred the money at the request of the dealer for purposes other than property transactions. Twinsectra commenced proceedings against the property dealer as well as all of the solicitors involved in the dealings with the loan monies. The claim against the solicitors who had undertaken to make sure that the money would only be used for property transactions was one of breach of trust. As for the solicitor who transferred the loan money for purposes other than that to do with property transaction, the action was one for dishonest assistance in a breach of trust.[36] The success of both of these actions depended crucially on whether there was a trust in favour of Twinsectra. Following the decision in **Barclays Bank Ltd v Quistclose Investments Ltd**[37] the House of Lords accepted that a trust did arise in favour of Twinsectra. The House of Lords then proceeded to examine the nature of the trust

---

[35] [2002] 2 All ER 377.
[36] See generally Chapter 14. A person who dishonestly assists in a breach of trust will be liable as a constructive trustee to replace the loss.
[37] [1970] AC 567.

arising in favour of the lender by exploring the possible locations where the beneficial interest in the loan money lay during the time at which the money was in the hands of the borrower. Millett LJ identified four possible locations where the beneficial interest in the loan money could exist during the time the loan money was not being used for the purpose for which it was given. His Lordship explained that the beneficial interest could lie with the lender; the borrower; the persons for whom the loan money was taken out, or simply lie in suspense. In coming to a conclusion, Millett LJ explained that, until such time as the loan money was not being used for the purposes of the loan, the beneficial ownership in the money belonged to lender. In his Lordship's words, 'this is the only analysis which is consistent both with orthodox trust law and commercial reality'.[38]

There is much to be said for the line of reasoning taken by Millett LJ in *Twinsectra* simply because it is the only line of reasoning which puts the Quistclose trust comfortably within trust law principles. In so far as the borrower is concerned, there is no intention on the part of the lender that the money should be freely at his disposal. In so far as the intended beneficiary of the purpose of the loan is concerned, it cannot be said that there is a trust in all cases or that there was even an intention on the part of the lender that the advancement of the loan money was directly for the benefit of the beneficiaries of the loan. In some cases such as *Twinsectra* itself the loan money may not be for human beneficiaries. The absence of a human beneficiary would be fatal to the finding of a trust relationship. However, even where there are human beneficiaries who are to benefit from the loan money, for example like the shareholders in *Quistclose*, it is questionable whether it was the lender's intention to create a trust in their favour or whether the real intention was to help the borrower avoid financial problems which might in turn protect the lender who may have a vested interest in the borrower's financial position.

The Court of Appeal in *Twinsectra* was clearly of the opinion that the beneficial interest under a Quistclose trust remained in suspense until the stated purpose of the loan had been carried out or had otherwise failed. This view was rejected in the House of Lords on the grounds that it did not fit comfortably with established principles of equity. In particular, the principle that 'equity abhors a beneficial vacuum' and that the beneficial interest in property must belong to some person at all relevant times. Millett LJ explained that a resulting trust arose in favour of the lender as soon as the loan was made to the borrower. The basis for the imposition of such a trust was on grounds that the lender had an absence of intention that the loan money should belong to any other person. This absence of intention to pass the beneficial interest to any other person meant that it belonged under a resulting trust for the lender.[39]

The decision in *Barclays Bank Ltd* v *Quistclose Investments Ltd*[40] was applied in *Cooper* v *Powerhouse Ltd (in liquidation)*[41] where a company received a sum of money from an employee in order to make payment to a finance company in order to discharge the instalments due on a car purchased from a car dealer. The employee had been provided with a Mercedes car which had been purchased by way of a finance agreement with a supplier. The instalments were to be paid by the employers by way of deductions from the employee's salary. When the employee resigned, it was agreed between the employer and the employee that he could purchase the car by discharging the monies

---

[38] [2002] 2 All ER 377 at 399.
[39] The idea that a resulting trust responds to an absence of intention was explained by Millett LJ in an earlier decision of the Privy Council in *Air Jamaica Ltd* v *Charlton* [1999] 1 WLR 1399. The nature of resulting trusts are examined in much detail in Chapter 10.
[40] [1970] AC 567.
[41] [2008] BCC 588.

due to the car supplier. The employee transferred the monies due to the supplier to his employers who would then make payment on his behalf. Before the payment was made by the employers, the employers went into liquidation and the liquidator argued that the employee was an unsecured creditor in respect of the money he had given to his former employers to discharge the instalments due on his company car. The question before Evans-Lombe J was whether the employee was an unsecured creditor or whether the employer held the money under a trust for a purpose, and that, the purpose having failed, the money was held under a Quistclose-type trust for the employee. The court held that the money advanced by the employee to his former employers was indeed transferred subject to a purpose. The purpose of the loan having failed, the money was held on trust for the employee. The court held that it was not necessary that the money had not been paid into a separate account. It was important, however, that the employers knew that the money was advanced for a specific purpose and not for the general availability of the employer. In the course of his judgment, Evans-Lombe J, after a comprehensive review of the principles surrounding Quistclose trusts by Millett J in *Twinsectra Ltd v Yardley*,[42] explained that:

> it seems to me that what emerges from this passage in Lord Millett's speech is that whether or not money has been paid subject to a purpose trust is a question of fact. If a purpose trust is to be established, it is necessary for the payer to show that the arrangement pursuant to which the payment was made defined the purpose for which it was made in such a way that it was understood by the recipient that it was not at his free disposal . . . I have found that Mr Cooper's [the employee] payment was made to the company subject to a purpose trust and that accordingly the company owed him fiduciary duties in respect of it. It follows that rules of equitable tracing apply.[43]

The Quistclose trust was more recently considered by the High Court of the Isle of Man in *Habana Ltd v Kaupthing Singer & Friedlander (Isle of Man) Ltd*.[44] The question before the court was whether routine payments from one bank to another at the request of the account holder could be subjected to a Quistclose trust. The High Court held that for a Quistclose trust to arise it was necessary for new money to be received by a bank for a stated purpose. Routine acceptances and debiting of an account's money could not alone be subject to a Quistclose trust. The decision affirms the general principle that a Quistclose trust will only arise if there is an intention to create such a trust in respect of the money being loaned.[45]

A further application of the Quistclose trust was found by the High Court in *Global Marine Drillships Ltd v Landmark Solicitors LLP*[46] where Global Marine Insurance Ltd commenced proceedings against a firm of solicitors. The facts of the case are very complex; however, a solicitor had given an undertaking on 26 May 2010 personally and on behalf of her firm that money advanced by an investment company pursuant to a specific business venture by Global Marine Drillships Ltd would only be used for specific purposes outlined in the undertaking, namely the purchase of an insurance policy for the investment company. None of the monies advanced to the firm of solicitors were used for the specific purpose as identified in the undertaking. The court held that a Quistclose trust had arisen in the favour of Global Marine Drillships, which was assured that the

---

[42] [2002] 2 All ER 377.
[43] [2008] BCC 588 at paras 15 and 25.
[44] [2011] WTLR. 275.
[45] The Quistclose trust has more recently been applied in *Soutzos v Armstrong* [2010] EWHC 362 and *Aviva Insurance Ltd v Brown* [2011] EWHC 362 (Ch).
[46] [2011] EWHC 2685 (Ch).

advanced monies would only be used for specific purposes. The firm of solicitors were in breach of trust by using the money for purposes other than those specified in the undertaking. In the course of his judgment, Henderson J explained that the money 'was held by Landmark and Ms Jones upon trust for Global Marine, subject to a power to apply it for the sole purpose authorised by the Undertaking.' In other words, he submitted, the money was held on a Quistclose trust: see the well-known analysis of such trusts by Lord Millett in *Twinsectra Limited* v *Yardley* [2002] UKHL 12, [2002] 2 AC 164 at [68] and following, and the application by the House of Lords in that case of the Quistclose principle to a loan held by a solicitor in his client account subject to an undertaking given by him to the lender to use the money for a sole specified purpose. As Lord Hoffmann said at [13], the effect of the undertaking was to provide that the money in the client account should remain the lender's money until such time at it was applied for the acquisition of property in accordance with the undertaking. The money was held in trust for the lender, but subject to a power to apply it in accordance with the undertaking.[47]

VISIT CASE NAVIGATOR

Powers: general observations

One of the fundamental distinctions to be made with a trust is that of a power, in particular, a power of appointment. A power of appointment has many similar features to that of a trust; however, it creates obligations and rights of a different kind in so far as the donees and objects of the power are concerned. Distinguishing between a trust and a power of appointment is not always an easy task. The difficulty is compounded by the fact that the same document purporting to create a trust may also create a power of appointment. Further still, trustees of a trust may at the same time be conferred a power of appointment and a trust in respect of various property, and the real question is which obligation attaches to which particular property. It is fair to say that the language does not help either as some powers are also referred to as trust powers whilst others are mere powers. Before a power of appointment is examined in more detail, it is important to understand the concept of a power in general. The principal reason for this is that the concept of a power features in many legal contexts and has different meanings.

Powers in general

The concept of a power features in a number of contexts in law.[48] Often powers are said to be conferred upon public authorities or officials. Sometimes powers are said to be common law powers, as for example a power vested in another person to convey a legal estate in land not belonging to him. A good example is a power of attorney under which one person may be authorised to do certain things in respect of another person's property – for example, convey the legal title to land. Further still, powers may be conferred by statute. A good example of a power conferred by statute is that which is given to a mortgagee of land who has the power to sell land in the event of default by a mortgagor of land.[49] In the field of trusts, managerial and dispositive powers are conferred upon trustees. A managerial power entitles the trustees to do something in respect of managing the trust property, for example, delegating the duty to another person.

---

47 [2011] EWHC 2685 (Ch) at para. 23.
48 See G. Thomas, *Thomas on Powers* (1998).
49 Law of Property Act 1925 s. 101.

A dispositive power entitles the trustee to dispose of the trust property wholly or in part to the beneficiary. For example, a beneficiary may not wish to put the whole trust to an end, but may want some money for education. Trustees are usually given powers of maintenance and advancement which allow payment of money from the trust fund to the beneficiaries.[50] In all these examples, an authority is conferred upon a person to do something. A power has been described as 'an individual personal capacity of the donee of the power to do something'.[51] The exercise of a power has the effect of changing the legal relationship of persons or persons in respect of things. Thomas writes that 'a power signifies an ability to do or effect something or to act upon a person or thing'.[52] One leading treatise on the law of trusts defines a power as a 'right to exercise, in respect of property belonging to another, one or more of the rights which are the normal incidents of ownership'.[53]

Powers of appointment

Powers of appointment, like trusts, allow management and enjoyment functions of property to be fragmented. The basic idea behind a power of appointment was explained by Lord Jessel MR in one case where he commented that a power of appointment 'is a power of disposition given to a person over property not his own by someone who directs the mode in which that power shall be exercised by a particular instrument'.[54] Powers of appointment have some similar features to a trust; however, the obligation created in a power is fundamentally different from that created in a trust. A trust imposes an imperative duty on trustees to distribute the trust property in accordance with the instructions in the trust instrument. Furthermore, it grants in the beneficiaries an equitable interest as soon as the trust is up and running. A power of appointment, on the other hand, is entirely discretionary and does not impose imperative obligations on the holder of the power to distribute. In order to make sense of this distinction between powers of appointment and trusts, it is important to understand the concept of a power of appointment. The key players in a power of appointment are the donor, the donee and the objects of the power (see Figure 3.1). The donor is the person who creates a power of appointment by conferring upon the donee a right to appoint from a class of persons, called the objects of the power, who are to benefit from the donor's property. Unlike a trust, the donee is not under any obligation to make an appointment, and as shall be seen later, where the

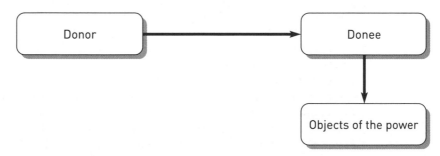

Figure 3.1 A power of appointment

---

[50] These matters are considered in more detail in Chapter 15.
[51] *Re Armstrong* (1886) 17 QBD 521 at 531, per Fry LJ.
[52] *Op. cit.* at p. 1.
[53] Parker and Mellows, *The Modern Law of Trusts* 9th edn (2008) at p. 196.
[54] *Freme v Clement* (1881) 18 Ch. D 499 at 504.

power is a mere power the donee is under no obligation to show that he acted in good faith. Unlike the beneficiaries of a trust, the objects of a power have no proprietary interest in the donor's property until such time as the donee has appointed one or more of them as the objects to benefit from the property.

Reasons for creating powers of appointment

APPLYING THE LAW

Harry is about to write his will and wishes to leave half of his property to his wife absolutely and the remainder to his children. As for the children he is not entirely sure what shares they should have in half of his property. In fact, his two older sons have had very little to do with him and it is only his daughter that has looked after him and his wife. He is confident that his two older sons will eventually change their ways and come back in the family fold. However, he is equally aware that should they not do so, he would not wish to leave any property to them and instead give the half share entirely to his daughter. So, at the time of writing the will he is not sure what will happen in the future. He does not want to create a trust in favour of his children in equal shares but wants his wife to decide on his death which of the children should get the half share in his property.

What can he do so as to have flexibility in deciding which of his children gets a share in his property?

One of the fundamental reasons for creating a power of appointment rather than a trust is the flexibility that is afforded by a power. Typically, a power will be conferred upon, for example, a wife who has been left property by her husband. The wife may have a life interest in such property whereby she is entitled to the enjoyment of her husband's property, but then is given the power to determine which of her children are to benefit from that property after her decease. The wife is not under any obligation to distribute the property to any of the children. The reason why her husband may have conferred a power of appointment upon her rather than a trust is that it allows the wife to take into account any changes that may take place in the future. For example, if the husband was to create a trust of his property for his wife for life and thereafter for his children in equal shares, it would guarantee all of the children an equal share in his property on his wife's decease. This is something that he may not want to do, particularly, if he is not sure how the children will turn out to be and whether they have any desire to maintain the family wealth. A power, on the other hand, allows the husband to leave the matter to be ultimately decided by his wife who may wish to give to all three children or to those who she feels deserve the property more than others.

Different types of power of appointment

Like trusts, powers of appointment can be classified in various ways. The principal means by which powers have been classified are, firstly, by looking at the nature of the objects under the power and, secondly, by looking at the duties imposed on the donee of the power. A further classification of a power is a trust power, which as will be seen below, operates very much like a discretionary trust.

General, special and hybrid powers

In relation to the class of objects of the power, powers have been classified as general powers, special powers and hybrid powers. A general power is usually defined as a power which entitles the donee to appoint the property to anyone in the world including itself. It is questionable whether a general power is really a case of fragmented ownership, given the fact that the donee can, if he or she decides, appoint itself as the object of the power; such a power is tantamount to absolute ownership in the donee. A special power, on the other hand, is a power which can only be exercised in favour of a defined class of objects: for example, the children of the donor. A hybrid power of appointment arises where the donor stipulates that the donee can make an appointment to anyone in the world except a specified class of persons. Usually such a power will arise where the donor does not want a specific member or members of a family to get any benefit but is otherwise not concerned who else does benefit from it.[55]

Bare powers and fiduciary powers

Powers can be further classified into bare and fiduciary powers, depending on the nature of the duties imposed on the donee. Where the donee is given a power in his capacity as a fiduciary, the power is referred to as a fiduciary power. Where the donee does not stand in a fiduciary relationship to the objects of the power, the power is a called a bare power or sometimes a personal power. The distinction between a bare and fiduciary power lies in the duties which are imposed on the donee of the power. In the case of a bare power, the donee is under no duty to exercise the power and need not even consider exercising the power. If he does decide to exercise the power, he is under a duty not to exercise it excessively or fraudulently. For example, a donee of a bare power cannot exercise the power for purposes which are inconsistent with the instrument creating the power.[56] A fiduciary power is one which is given to a donee in a fiduciary capacity. The most obvious example of a fiduciary power is one given to a trustee in the case of a trust. A modern example of a fiduciary power is one given to trustees of a pension fund to decide who is entitled to surplus funds once the entitlement of the pension beneficiaries has been met.[57] The power in such pension schemes often allows the surplus to be paid to the pensioners in the form of increased entitlements. Failure to exercise the power results in the surplus funds going into the hands of the company. Given the fiduciary nature of the power, donees of the power are under a duty to consider whether they should exercise the power, consider the range of potential objects of the power and consider appropriateness of individual appointments.[58] Although a fiduciary power like any other power is discretionary, so that the court cannot compel the donee to exercise the power, in some circumstances the court may intervene and exercise the power if there is a conflict of interest between the interests of the donee and the interests of the potential objects of the power.[59]

---

[55] *Re Byron's Settlement* [1891] 3 Ch. 474.

[56] *Vatcher* v *Paull* [1915] AC 372.

[57] *Mettoy Pension Trustees Ltd* v *Evans* [1990] 1 WLR 1587.

[58] *Re Hay's Settlement Trusts* [1982] 1 WLR 202.

[59] In *Mettoy Pension Trustees Ltd* v *Evans* [1990] 1 WLR 1587, a company had a power to appointment over surplus funds in a pension scheme in favour of the pensioners. If the company failed to exercise the power they would be entitled to the money. The company had gone into liquidation and the power was now vested in the liquidators. Warner J held that the liquidators were unable to exercise the power because of the conflict of interests that arose from the fact that they owed duties both to creditors and the pensioners under the power. Warner J explained that the court would exercise the power itself in this circumstance.

Trust powers and mere powers

A distinction is often made between trust powers and mere powers. This distinction is often confusing, particularly when considered alongside a discussion of discretionary trusts. It is suggested that the distinction between trust powers and mere powers should be substituted with a distinction between discretionary trusts and mere powers. A trust power is essentially a discretionary trust where the trustee has a discretion to select from a class of persons who should benefit from the trust property. The trustee is nevertheless required to distribute the trust property. In contrast, as already observed above, under a mere power, whether it is a bare or fiduciary power, the donee is not under any obligation to appoint amongst any of the objects. Whether, on any given set of facts, a trust power or a mere power has been created is ultimately a question of construing the intentions of the settlor or testator. In construing the intention of the settlor or testator, there are certain factors which may be taken into consideration which may aid the construction of his intention.

APPLYING THE LAW

Tim and Tom have been appointed executors as well as trustees under a will. One of the clauses in the will reads as follows:

'A sum of £20,000 at the discretion of my trustees to be distributed amongst my nieces; however, should they fail to distribute within two years after my decease, I hereby direct that the sum be given to the local dogs' home.'

Does this create a discretionary trust in favour of the testator's nieces or a mere power?

One factor which may indicate that a mere power was intended rather than a trust power is the presence of a gift over in default of appointment. A gift over in default is inconsistent with the finding of a trust power in favour of a class of objects. A gift over in default of appointment will arise where the donor of a power gives the donee a right to appoint amongst a class of objects, but then provides that if the donee fails to appoint amongst the class the property must be given to another person or persons. Take, for example, a husband who confers a power of appointment on his wife to distribute property amongst his three children, who in the opinion of the wife deserves such property, and then declares that if the wife fails to give the property to any one of the children, the property is to be given to his nephew. The fact that the husband has identified that his nephew should receive the property should the wife default in making appointments for the children is inconsistent with the finding of a trust power. The reason for this is that a trust power imposes an imperative obligation on the trustee to distribute the trust property. In the case of a gift over in default, the donee does not have to distribute because the gift over in default makes allowance for the fact that the donee may give the property elsewhere. The matter is neatly illustrated by the decision in **Re Mills**[60] where a testator conferred a power of appointment on his brother to appoint the property amongst his children and remoter issue, who in the opinion of his brother should evidence a desire to maintain the family property. There then followed a gift over in default of appointment to the testator's brother. The Court of Appeal held that the existence of a gift over in

---

[60] [1930] 1 Ch. 654.

default of appointment was inconsistent with the finding of a trust in favour of the children and remoter issue and therefore the power operated as a mere power. Lord Hanworth MR explained that 'here there is a gift over to the donee in default of appointment . . . and, therefore, it is not, to my mind, possible to construe this clause as one in which there is a gift to the possible objects of the power – namely, the children or remoter issue of the [testator]. It follows that it is not a power which is coupled with or embedded in a trust.'[61]

Whilst the presence of a gift over in default of appointment will negate the finding of a trust power in favour of objects of the power, the mere fact that there is an absence of a gift over in default of appointment does not necessarily lead to the conclusion that the power takes the form of a trust power. For example, in **Re Weekes' Settlement**[62] a wife left her residuary estate to her husband for his life with a power to appoint the property amongst the children. When the husband died without having made any appointments amongst the children, the question arose whether the children were entitled under a trust power. It was argued on behalf of the children that, in the absence of a gift over in default of appointment, the power should be construed as a trust power thereby conferring a gift upon the children. In rejecting this argument, Romer J held that:

> [T]he authorities do not show, in my opinion, that there is a hard and fast rule that a gift to A for life with a power to A to appoint among a class and nothing more must, if there is no gift over in the will, be held a gift by implication to the class in default of the power being exercised. In my opinion the cases show that you must find in the will an indication that the [wife] did intend the class or some of the class to take . . .[63]

A similar result was achieved in **Re Perowne**[64] where a wife left her estate to her husband knowing that he would make arrangements for the disposal of her estate for the benefit of her family. When the husband made an appointment, which later turned out to be defective, the question arose whether a gift should be implied in favour of the children thereby conferring upon them a trust power. The court held that the wife had only conferred a mere power on her husband and that very clear words would be required to infer a trust power in favour of the children.

Exercising a power of appointment

In order to establish whether a donee of power of appointment has exercised it properly depends primarily on whether the power in question is a mere power or a fiduciary power. It has already been observed above that a mere power is a power conferred upon a person who does not stand in a fiduciary capacity. Where, however, the power is conferred upon a trustee in his office as trustee, then the power is said to be a fiduciary power. In the case of a mere power the donee is under no obligation to exercise the power in favour of the objects. Furthermore, he owes no duties to the objects of the power and is under no duty to even consider whether to exercise the power at all. A donee of a mere power of appointment may release the power with the consequence that the property

---

[61] [1930] 1 Ch. 654 at 661.
[62] [1897] 1 Ch. 289.
[63] [1897] 1 Ch. 289 at 292.
[64] [1951] Ch. 785.

results back to the settlor or the testator's estate or to those entitled in default of appointment. The only obligation imposed on the donee of a mere power of appointment is, like any other power of appointment, not to exercise it excessively or fraudulently. The excessive and fraudulent exercise of powers of appointment is discussed below.

APPLYING THE LAW

Suppose that Tim and Tom, in their capacity as executors and trustees, have been conferred a power to appoint £30,000 amongst the testator's two sons. They are asked by the sons to exercise the power of appointment and they duly exercise it by appointing the oldest son. They inform the younger son that he was not appointed because he married without their consent.

Can the younger son challenge the exercise of the power of appointment?

Like a donee of a mere power of appointment, a donee of a fiduciary power of appointment need not exercise the power in favour of the objects. Having said that, the donee of a fiduciary power is subject to a number of duties in favour of the objects of the power. Although he need not exercise the power in favour of the objects, he is under a duty to consider from time to time whether to exercise the power. Furthermore, if he does decide to exercise the power, the court will intervene in the exercise of the power if it is made in bad faith or is otherwise unreasonable. The matter is neatly explained by Megarry VC in *Re Hay's Settlement Trusts*[65] who explained that, although the donee need not exercise the power,

[it] does not mean that he can simply fold his hands and ignore it, for normally he must from time to time consider whether or not to exercise the power, and the court may direct him to do this. Whereas a person who is not in a fiduciary position is free to exercise the power in any way that he wishes, unhampered by fiduciary duties, a trustee to whom, as such, a power is given is bound by the duties of his office in exercising that power to do so in a responsible manner according to its purpose. It is not enough for him to refrain from acting capriciously; he must do more. He must make a survey of the range of objects or possible beneficiaries as will enable him to carry out his fiduciary duty. He must find out the permissible area of selection and then consider responsibly, in individual case, whether a contemplated beneficiary was within the power and whether, in relation to the possible claimants, a particular grant was appropriate.[66]

Although a fiduciary power is a power conferred upon someone standing in a fiduciary position like a trustee, it is clear from the relatively more recent case law, primarily in the context of pension trusts, that a fiduciary power may in some circumstances be conferred on a mere donee of a power of appointment. The matter is neatly illustrated by the decision in *Mettoy Pension Trustees Ltd* v *Evans*[67] where a company, who had gone into liquidation, had a power of appointment in respect of a surplus in a pension fund. The power was held by the company and not the trustees of the fund, which would have made the power fiduciary in its nature. If the power was not exercised then the surplus would

VISIT CASE NAVIGATOR

[65] [1982] 1 WLR 202.
[66] [1982] 1 WLR at 209–10, reference having being made by Megarry VC to the decision of Lord Wilberforce in *McPhail* v *Doulton* [1971] AC 424.
[67] [1991] 2 All ER 513.

in effect belong to the company as it was entitled to the surplus under a gift over in default of appointment. If the money went back to the company it would then become available for the creditors of the company. There were two questions before the court. Firstly, whether the power could be exercised in order to increase the entitlement of the pensioners. Secondly, if the company did not exercise the power, could the court exercise the power? Both of these answers were answered in the affirmative. Warner J held that although the power was held by the company and not the trustees of the pension fund, it was nevertheless fiduciary in its nature. In coming to this conclusion, he explained that if the power conferred upon the company was not construed as being fiduciary, then its inclusion in the pension scheme would be meaningless. Warner J went on to say that if it was a mere power then the company would be making gifts of its own absolute property to those entitled under the pension fund. If such was the case, it would be meaningless to have that power in the scheme when the company could, if it wanted, make those payments without recourse to the power. Secondly, Warner J explained that the pensioners under the fund were not volunteers as they had also contributed to the surplus. In such a case, the court explained that the company held a fiduciary power and was subject to the fiduciary duties to consider whether to exercise the power. The court held that, in the absence of the exercise of the power by the company, the court could exercise the power in favour of the pensioners.[68] The decision in **Mettoy Pension Trustees Ltd v Evans**[69] further assimilates fiduciary powers of appointment with discretionary trusts. Although the court did not say that the fiduciary power held by the company should have been exercised, the fact that it borrowed similar principles relating to discretionary trusts – for example, the intervention of the court in exercising the discretion – it is questionable whether there is a distinction between discretionary trusts and fiduciary powers of appointment.

In summary, the key duties imposed on a donee of a fiduciary power are:

● to consider on a periodic basis whether to exercise the power or not;

● to survey the range of objects that fall within the power;

● to consider whether any given appointment should be made.

Excessive or fraudulent exercise of a power

It has already been observed that the donee of a mere power of appointment need not exercise the power and need not even consider whether he should exercise the power. Furthermore the donee of a mere power can release the power.[70] The donee of a fiduciary power, albeit under no duty to exercise the power, is under a duty to consider whether to exercise the power and periodically do so by considering the range of objects that may benefit from the power. However, despite this distinction between mere powers and fiduciary powers, in both cases the court can intervene if the power is exercised excessively or in a manner which is fraudulent. An excessive exercise of the power of appointment will occur when the power is exercised in favour of objects that are not intended to benefit from the power of appointment. In other words, the power is exercised by the

---

[68] See also *Schmidt v Rosewood Trust Ltd* [2003] 2 AC 709. Whether the objects have the right to challenge the decisions of the donee of a fiduciary power and inspect relevant documents, see Chapter 14.

[69] [1991] 2 All ER 513.

[70] See *Re Wills' Trust Deeds* [1964] Ch. 219.

donee in favour of objects that are clearly outside the scope of objects that can benefit from it.

A fraud on a power will occur when the donee fails to exercise the power bona fide. The matter is neatly explained by Lord Parker in **Vatcher v Paull**[71] where his Lordship explained that:

> [t]he term fraud in connection with frauds on a power does not necessarily denote any conduct on the part of the appointor amounting to a fraud in the common law meaning of the term or any conduct which could be properly termed dishonest or immoral. It merely means that the power has been exercised for a purpose, or with an intention, beyond the scope or not justified by the instrument creating the power.[72]

Similarly, in **Hillsdown Holdings plc v Pensions Ombudsman** Knox J referred to fraud on a power in circumstances where there is 'an improper use of the power for a collateral purpose'.[73] Three categories of fraud on a power have been recognised. The first situation arises when the power has been exercised for a purpose which is corrupt. For example, if the donee makes an appointment with the ultimate intention of benefiting himself, then the power will have been exercised fraudulently. It does not matter that the donee could have exercised the power in the way he did: it is the reasons for the exercise of the power which makes it fraudulent. A good example in this context is where a father makes an appointment in favour of a child who is about to die with the view that when the child does die, he will receive the property as the child's next of kin.[74]

The second category where there will be a fraud on the power is where the donee exercises the power with a view to benefiting persons who are not the objects of the power. Although this category is very similar to the circumstances that lead to excessive delegation of a power, the difference here is that the donee exercises the power in favour of objects of the power but with the consequence that the real benefactors of the exercise will be persons other than the objects. A neat illustration of this can be seen in **Re Dick**[75] where a donee exercised a power of appointment in her will in favour of her sister. At the same time as the will, the donee executed a formal document requiring her sister to pay a sum of £800 per annum to a family who were not objects of the power but nevertheless had cared for the donee. The Court of Appeal held that the sole purpose of the appointment in favour of the sister was to benefit the family who had cared for her. The sister was the means by which the money could be given to the family. The decision in *Re Dick* illustrates that the real question before the court is to weigh up the intentions of the donee in order to ascertain whether the real intention was to benefit a non-object. Of course, not every appointment in favour of an object which has the effect of benefiting a non-object will be invalidated. To suggest otherwise would produce an absurd result. For example, the exercise of a power in favour of a mother which may confer some benefit on a child will not necessarily be invalidated. However, what appears to be the main problem in the case of **Re Dick** is that a substantial amount of the money appointed by the donee to the sister was being used for the purpose of the annuity in favour of the family who had cared for the donee. In such circumstances, the court's inference is that the real intention was to benefit a non-object of the power. More recently, cases in this category have concerned the exercise of powers in pension funds, particularly where

---

[71] [1915] AC 372.
[72] [1915] AC 372 at 378.
[73] [1997] 1 All ER 862 at 883. See also *Walker v Stones* [2001] QB 902.
[74] See, for example, *Lord Hinchinbroke v Seymour* (1784) 1 Bro. CC 395.
[75] [1953] Ch 343.

there has been a surplus in the pension fund trust and the trustees of the fund have exercised the power in order to confer the surplus fund upon the employer.[76]

The final category of fraud on a power will occur when there is some prior agreement between the donee of the power and the appointee as to what will happen with the fund which is to be appointed. The most typical case is where the donee and the appointee agree that the appointee will give some of the money to the donee.[77] In the context of a pension fund trust a pension trustee may exercise a power to transfer the pension funds to another scheme in circumstances so as to allow any surplus in the fund to be returned to the employer. This is particularly so where the existing pension scheme may not have any provision as to who is entitled to the surplus. The matter is neatly illustrated in **Hillsdown plc v Pensions Ombudsman**[78] where Hillsdown plc provided a pension scheme for its employees. The pension scheme actually ended up having a surplus of some £20 million. There was nothing in the pension scheme rules which allowed for Hillsdown to become entitled to the surplus funds. With the agreement of Hillsdown plc, the trustees of the pension fund exercised their power to transfer the funds to another scheme which in fact did contain a provision entitling Hillsdown to the surplus funds. Normally the exercise of the power to allow transfer of pension funds to another scheme would be proper if it was to secure the pension rights of the members. The court held that the exercise of the power by the trustees was a fraud on the power. The main reason for the exercise of the power was to confer a benefit on Hillsdown plc as a result of the agreement it had with the trustees of the scheme. In the course of his judgment, Knox J explained that the purpose for which the power was exercised was to give 'effect to the bargain struck with Hillsdown of which a major element was that of a payment of surplus to Hillsdown. That was outside the proper ambit of r 21 which was to enable transfer of obligations and assets to other approved funds securing pension rights for members.'[79]

Consequences of not exercising a power of appointment

One final question which remains to be considered is: what are the consequences of a failure to exercise a power of appointment? It has already been observed that a donee of a power is under no imperative duty to make any appointments, although, in the case of a fiduciary power, the donee is certainly under a duty to consider whether he should exercise the power. Where the donee does not exercise the power in favour of the objects of the power, there are a number of possible outcomes that may arise.

Resulting trust for the donor or his estate

As with any surplus fund arising which does not have any designated recipient, the un-exhausted fund will be governed by the normal principles of property law, which hold that such a fund will revert back to the donor by way of a resulting trust. Where the power is created in the donor's will, the property will result back to the residuary legatees of the

---

[76] See, for example, *Re Courage Group's Pension Schemes* [1987] 1 WLR 495.
[77] *Daubeny v Cockburn* (1816) 1 Mer. 626.
[78] [1997] 1 All ER 862.
[79] [1997] 1 All ER 862 at 883.

will. In the case of a power created in an *inter vivos* instrument, the property will revert back to the donor (see Figure 3.2).

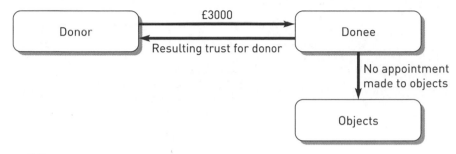

Figure 3.2

Gift over in default of appointment

The donor of a power of appointment may provide that, should the donee of the power fail to make any appointments, the property subject to the power is given to some other named beneficiary. In such a situation the donor is said to have made an express gift over in default of appointment, which is no more that saying that in the event of the donee not exercising the power some other person will be automatically entitled to the property. For example, a husband may confer a power on his wife to appoint amongst such of his children as she thinks fit. He may then provide that, should the wife fail to make any appointments to the children, the property should be given to his oldest son. The existence of a gift over in default has a number of important consequences. In the first place, it displaces any resulting trust back to the donor or his estate. Secondly, as already observed, the existence of a gift over in default is conclusive evidence that the donor only intended a power in favour of the objects and not a trust. The fact that the donor envisaged some other person to receive the property in gift over in default evidences an intention that he did not necessarily impose a mandatory obligation on the donee to make any appointments. Thus, in cases where the objects seek to argue that they should be entitled to the property by way of trust, the existence of a gift over in default will negate any such finding of a trust in their favour. The matter, as already observed, was neatly illustrated in **Re Mills**[80] where a power was conferred upon a donee to appoint property amongst children who had desired an intention to maintain the family wealth. The donor then provided that should the donee fail to make any appointments then the property was to be given to someone else. In these circumstances the Court of Appeal held that there was only a power in favour of the children and no trust. The final consequence of finding a gift over in default of appointment is that the person who is entitled in gift over is entitled by way of a trust. This is because, should the donee fail to make any appointments in favour of the objects of the power, the donee is under a mandatory obligation to give to the person entitled in gift over in default. The fact that the donee can, if he chooses to do so, exercise the power of appointment in favour of the objects does not negate the fact there is a trust in favour of the person entitled in default. If the donee does exercise the power, then the person entitled in default simply does not receive. On the other hand, should the donee fail to appoint then the person entitled in gift over will receive. This is nothing more than saying that the person entitled in gift over

---

in default is entitled under a trust, albeit that trust being in his favour is contingent on no appointments being made in favour of the objects (see Figure 3.3).[81]

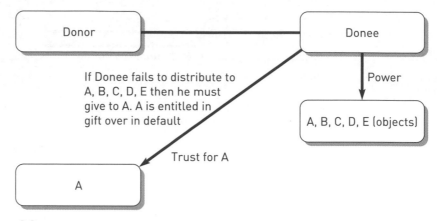

Figure 3.3

Gift in favour of all of the objects or the class

A somewhat more difficult outcome of the failure to exercise a power of appointment is that there may be an implied gift in favour of the objects of the power. In other words, the failure to exercise the power will result in a trust in default for the entire class of objects. The circumstances giving rise to such an implied gift or trust in favour of the objects was explained by Lord Cottenham in **Burrough v Philcox**.[82] The facts of the case involved a testator who provided that his surviving daughter should have the power to appoint property amongst his nephews and nieces. The daughter failed to make any appointments in favour of the nephews and nieces. Normally, in such a case of non-exercise of the power the property would result back to the donor's estate. Despite this, the court held that the nephews and nieces were entitled to the testator's property equally. It is interesting to note that the court came to the conclusion that the nephews and nieces were entitled to the property despite the absence of an express gift over in default in their favour. At first sight it is very difficult to distinguish cases such as **Re Weekes' Settlement**[83] from the decision in **Burrough v Philcox**. Both cases involve the non-exercise of a power of appointment and an absence of a gift over in default of appointment. Yet, in **Re Weekes Settlement** the court took the view that the non-exercise of the power by the donee should result in the property going back to the donor's estate whereas in **Burrough v Philcox** it was distributed equally amongst the objects of the power. The question arising here is: what is the rationale for equal distribution in favour of the class of objects of the power? The answer is provided by Lord Cottenham who explained that 'when there appears a general intention in favour of a class, and a particular intention in favour of individuals of a class to be selected by another person, and the particular intention fails, from that selection not being made, the court will carry into effect the general intention in favour of the class'.[84]

---

[81] Although it must be observed that even where appointments are made, the person entitled in gift over in default may well be entitled to some property and that will arise where there is a surplus remaining after appointments have been made.

[82] (1840) 5 My. & Cr. 72.

[83] [1897] 1 Ch. 289.

[84] (1840) 5 My. & Cr. 72 at 92.

The effect of the approach taken in **Burrough v Philcox** is to imply a trust in favour of the objects of the power. So whilst the donee of the power has a discretion to appoint amongst particular objects, failure to do so will result in an equal distribution in favour of the general class. The justification for such distribution amongst the general class of objects is the intention of the donor. In Lord Cottenham's judgment it is clear that such equal distribution is made on the basis that the donor expressed a general intention to benefit a class of objects, albeit with a power conferred on the donee to appoint particular objects within that class. The decision in **Burrough v Philcox** is very difficult to categorise because it does not fall neatly into the power category or the trust category but rather lies at the boundaries of both. Furthermore, there remain a number of questions as to its operation which are not convincingly answered. One of those questions is: why is the fund distributed equally amongst the objects? If the donor expresses an intention that the donee has a power of selection amongst a class of objects, then why is a fixed trust implied when the donor's intention is better served with the imposition of a discretionary trust? Most accounts of the rule explain that the rationale for equal distribution in the event of failure to exercise the power is based on the maxim that 'equity is equality'.[85]

Although there have been a number of analyses of the decision in **Burrough v Philcox**[86] and the nature of the trust implied in favour of the objects, it is submitted that a better analysis of the case is to regard the objects of the power as entitled to the property by way of a gift over in default of appointment. In respect of this analysis, the donee of the power has the power to appoint amongst particular objects of the class; however, should he fail to distribute then all members of the class become entitled by way of a fixed entitlement.

Conclusion

The primary purpose of this chapter has been to distinguish the trust from other concepts in law. The need to distinguish the trust from other concepts serves a very important function and is not just confined to an abstract comparative study. It has been seen in the course of this chapter that there are some concepts, notably powers of appointment, that have many similar features to a trust; yet their outcomes are rather different. In many cases it may be difficult to establish at first instance whether in fact a person intended to create a trust or a power of appointment. Ultimately the question is one of construing the intentions of the person creating the obligation. In construing the real intention of the testator or settlor the court is aided by factors such as whether there is a gift over in default of appointment, which will negate the finding of a trust in favour of objects of the power. However, the absence of a gift over in default is not conclusive that a trust was intended: everything depends on the intentions of the person creating the particular disposition. Another reason for the distinction between trusts and other legal categories is that the trust may indeed work contemporaneously alongside other legal

---

[85] See, for example, *Snell's Equity* 31st edn (Sweet & Maxwell) 2005 at p. 476 where it is commented that 'when equity executes an unexercised trust power, it usually applies the maxim that equality is equity, and divides the property amongst all members of the class equally as tenants in common, although the donee of the power may have given unequal shares'.

[86] (1840) 5 My. & Cr. 72.

categories. For example, it has been seen in this chapter that a trust relationship can coexist alongside a loan relationship between debtor and creditor. It becomes important to differentiate clearly which legal concept is being employed at any given time in order to apply the correct principles in determining the outcome of disputed facts.

Case study

Consider the following case study.

In 2007 Donald executed a deed in which he appointed Peter and Michael as his trustees. The deed contained, *inter alia*, the following clause:

> '£50,000 to be held by my trustees for my three children until the youngest attains the age of 18. Should the trustee fail to distribute the money for a period greater than 2 years, the money should be given to my youngest son James.'

Soon after the execution of the deed the £50,000 was transferred into a joint account held by Peter and Michael.

Donald's children have not yet received any of the £50,000 but would like to share it equally. All of the children are now over the age of 18 and seek your advice as to their entitlement to the £50,000.

What would your answer be if Peter and Michael gave the entire £50,000 to Donald's oldest son and refused to give the money to the other two on grounds that they had never really liked the younger two children?

Moot points

1 Suppose that S enters into an agreement with T that he will settle upon trust property for the benefit of B. At the time of the agreement B was not aware of this arrangement but learns sometime later that it was S's intention to leave the property to him. Can B enforce the agreement between S and T?

2 What are the differences between a personal representative and a trustee under a will?

3 In *Twinsectra* v *Yardley* [2002] 2 All ER 377 Millett LJ held that where there is a coexistence of a loan and trust relationship, until such time as the loan money is used for the purposes of the loan the money belongs to the lender under a resulting trust. What is the basis for imposing a resulting trust in favour of the lender? Is it the intention of the lender that the money should remain his until such time that it is used for the loan and how is that intention ascertained?

4 Explain the reason why a testator may decide to create a special power of appointment as opposed to a discretionary trust in his will.

5 What do you understand to be the main difference between a fiduciary power of appointment and a mere power of appointment? On what grounds can an object of a fiduciary power challenge its exercise?

6 What is the basis for an equal distribution of property in the *Burrough* v *Philcox* (1840) type of power where the donee fails to exercise the power of appointment?

7 Explain the circumstances in which a court will deem a power to have been exercised excessively or fraudulently.

● Further reading

Gardner, S. **'Fiduciary Powers in Toytown'** (1991) LQR 214. Examines the decision in *Mettoy Pensions Trustees Ltd* v *Evans* [1991] 2 All ER 513.

Glister, J.A. **'The Nature of Quistclose Trust: Classification and Reconciliation'** (2004) CLJ 632. Considers the way in which a Quistclose trust is classified.

Martin, J. **Editorial Casenote on** *Mettoy Pensions Trustees Ltd* v *Evans* [1991] 2 All ER 513, (1991) Conv. 364.

Millett, P. **'The Quistclose Trust: Who Can Enforce It?'** (1985) 101 LQR 269. Provides an excellent account of the situations in which a Quistclose trust can come into existence and explores the individuals who have the right to enforce the trust.

Panesar, S. **'A Loan Subject to a Trust and Dishonest Assistance by a Third Party'** (2003) JIBL 18(1) 9. Considers the nature of a Quistclose trust after the decision of the House of Lords in *Twinsectra* v *Yardley*.

Part II
Creating the trust relationship

Part I of this book examined the nature of equity and also explored the nature of the trust relationship. Having covered the nature of the trust relationship and the reasons why trusts are created, Part II of this book moves on to explore the legal requirements needed to create the trust relationship. Exactly what must a person do before a legally binding trust relationship can be said to have arisen? Chapter 4 begins with a discussion of the certainty requirements of a trust. It is a fundamental principle of trust law that a person creating a trust intends to bring about a trust relationship. The certainty requirement not only relates to the settlor's intention, but also extends to certainty of subject matter and certainty as to the beneficiaries of the trust. Once the element of certainty has been met, it is important that the person creating the trust has complied with any necessary formal requirements prescribed by statute. Chapter 5 explores the formal requirements for the creation and disposition of interests under a trust. It will be observed that, whilst much of the case law in this area has arisen in quite complex taxation contexts, the fundamental objective behind the formal requirements for trusts is to prevent fraud.

Although a trust may well comply with certainty and formality, it does not necessarily mean that the trust relationship has come into existence. The crucial point in time when a trust relationship comes into being is where the settlor has transferred the subject matter of the trust to the intended trustee or where he has unequivocally declared himself a trustee of his own property in favour of a beneficiary. The act of transferring the trust property to the intended trustee is known as constituting the trust. Until such time, the settlor can change his mind and, in the absence of unconscionability on the part of the settlor, equity will generally not assist an intended beneficiary. Chapter 6 explores the rules governing constitution of trusts.

One particular type of trust which has attracted special attention is known as a secret trust. Such a trust, as implied by its name, is secret in the sense that ▶

the identity of the beneficiaries is not disclosed to the world at large. Property is normally left to someone in a will who has agreed during the lifetime of the person creating the trust that he or she will hold it for some other third party. The function of such a trust is to hide the identity of the beneficiary, which not to do so would cause some embarrassment to the testator. It will be seen in Chapter 7 that secret trusts historically played an important role in providing for illegitimate children and mistresses of a testator.

It is a fundamental principle of trust law that a trust is created for a human beneficiary. Despite this, it is not uncommon for a person to create a trust for a mere purpose or a trust in favour of a pet, for example a cat or a dog. Chapter 8 explores the position where a trust is created for a non-human beneficiary and examines the extent to which such a trust will be allowed to exist. It will be observed that the fundamental problem with trusts created for a purpose or a non-human beneficiary is one of enforceability. Generally, equity will not permit a trust which it cannot control and enforce.

Part II of this book also looks at the question of illegality and public policy. Even where a trust complies with all of the trust law requirements, it will nevertheless be invalidated if it contains an element of illegality or public policy. For example, a trust which promotes illegal conduct will be struck down by the courts as will a trust which is created for the sole purpose of defeating the rights of the creditors of the person creating the trust. Chapter 9 explores some of the key illegality and public policy grounds for setting aside a trust.

4

The three certainties

Learning objectives

After reading this chapter you should be able to:

→ understand the rationale behind the certainty requirements of a trust

→ explain the effect of uncertainty on an intended trust

→ understand the certainties of intention, subject matter and objects

→ understand the test of certainty of intention as one of substance as opposed to form

→ distinguish between the certainty of subject matter test for ascertained property and unascertained property

→ distinguish between the constituent elements of the certainty of objects requirement and the extent to which they apply to fixed and discretionary trusts

→ understand the test of certainty of objects for a fixed trust

→ understand the test of certainty of objects for a discretionary trust.

SETTING THE SCENE

VISIT CASE NAVIGATOR

McPhail v *Doulton* [1971] AC 424: A trust for the benefit of the officers and employees or ex-officers or ex-employees of a company or to any of their relatives and dependants of any such persons as the trustees think fit

Who exactly are the beneficiaries of this trust?

The facts in *McPhail* v *Doulton* illustrate some of the concerns which are the subject matter of discussion in this chapter. The settlor, Bertram Baden, established a fund to provide benefits for the staff of Matthew Hall & Co. Ltd. Clause 9 of the trust deed authorised the trustees to apply the net income from the fund for the benefit of the officers and employees or ex-officers or ex-employees of the company or to any of their relatives and dependants of any such persons as the trustees think fit. Clause 9 continued:

(a) The trustees shall apply the net income of the fund in making at their absolute discretion grants . . . in such amounts at such times and on such conditions (if any) as they think fit . . .

(b) The trustees shall not be bound to exhaust the income of any year or other period in making such grants . . . and any income not so applied shall be . . . [placed in a bank or invested].

(c) The trustees may realise any investments representing accumulations of income and apply the proceeds as though the same were income of the fund and may also . . . at any time prior to the liquidation of the fund realise any other part of the capital of the fund . . . in order to provide benefits for which the current income of the fund is insufficient.

The executors of Bertram Baden challenged the trust created in the deed on the grounds that it was void for uncertainty. The principal claim of the executors was that the deed purported to create a discretionary trust and that it was void for non-compliance with the certainty of objects test for a discretionary trust. The argument on behalf of the executors was that the validity of a discretionary trust required the trustees to be in a position to draw up a complete list of all the beneficiaries who were intended to benefit from the trust. It was claimed that it was not possible to draw a complete list of all the beneficiaries on the grounds that terms 'officers, employees, ex-officers, ex-employees and relatives and dependants' were not certain.

The question before the House of Lords was whether the deed created by Bertram Baden created a trust, and if so, whether the trust was void for uncertainty of beneficiaries. This chapter explores the requirements of certainty which are essential to every trust: in particular, the certainty of intention to create a trust, certainty of subject matter and certainty of objects.

The decision of the House of Lords in *McPhail* v *Doulton* is considered in greater detail in this chapter; however, for the present moment it may be useful to get started by thinking about the following questions:

● Was the intention of Bertram Baden to create a trust?

● Did the terms of the trust, particularly, clause 9, require the trustees to give the income to every single member of the class?

● If the trustees had a discretion in the first place, do you think it would have been fatal to the validity of the trust if the trustees could only ascertain about 80 per cent of the class but were unsure about the other 20 per cent?

● Do you think that words such a 'dependants' and 'relatives' are definable?

Introduction

An express trust can arise in one of two ways, as illustrated in the diagrams below. Firstly, it can arise when a person, called a settlor, transfers property to trustees to hold for the benefit of a beneficiary. Where the person transferring the property to trustees does so in a will, he is referred to as a testator. This method of creating a trust is simply called a transfer to trustees and is illustrated in Figure 4.1.

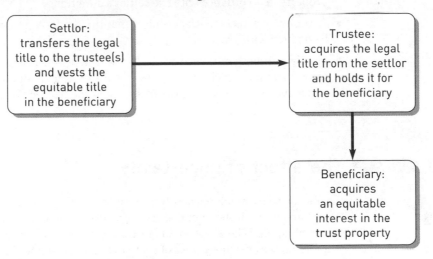

Figure 4.1

Secondly, a trust can arise when a person, that is the settlor, declares himself trustee for the benefit of a beneficiary. This method of creating a trust is often called a declaration of self as trustee and is illustrated in Figure 4.2.

Figure 4.2

Whichever method is used to create the trust, equity requires that a number of substantive and formal requirements be complied with in order for the trust to be legally binding on the trustee. The first of those requirements is that the trust complies with the three certainties. In **_Knight v Knight_**[1] Lord Langdale MR identified the three certainties as certainty of intention; certainty of subject matter; and certainty of objects.

- Certainty of intention requires the settlor to use such language, or demonstrate such conduct, that will impose an imperative obligation on the trustee to deal with the trust property in accordance with the settlor's intentions.

- Certainty of subject matter requires that the property, to which the trust is to attach, be defined with precision.

- Finally, certainty of objects requires that the beneficiaries of the trust be defined by some meaning which is understood both by the trustee and ultimately the court, which may have to enforce the trust should the trustee fail to do so.

The effect of uncertainty

If a purported trust fails to comply with any of the three certainties, there will be no trust. What happens with the intended trust property very much depends on where the property is situated. Where the intended trust property has not left the settlor, the settlor will remain the absolute owner of such property. During his lifetime the intended settlor will be able to freely deal with such property and on his death the property will devolve in accordance with his will or, where he has not made a will, according to the rule of intestate succession.[2] If the trust property has been transferred to the intended trustee, there are two possible outcomes, depending on which uncertainty has occurred. If the intended settlor transfers the trust property to the intended trustee without evincing an intention to create a trust, the intended trustee is in fact not a trustee at all but prima facie a donee of a gift. In other words, the settlor has transferred something to the donee without any further obligation. The same is true where the trust fails for uncertainty of subject matter. This is simply because the purported beneficiary cannot point to any identifiable property in the hands of the intended trustee to which equitable ownership can be attached.[3] In this respect there is also an overlap between the certainties of intention and subject matter. This is because the absence of any identifiable property in the hands of a purported trustee only goes to illustrate the lack of intention on the part of the settlor to intend a trust in the first instance. Furthermore, 'uncertainty in the subject matter of the gift has a reflex action upon the previous words, and shows doubt upon the intention of the testator, and seems to show that he could not possibly have intended his

---

[1] (1840) 3 Beav. 171.

[2] Intestate succession refers to the situation where a person dies without having made a will. In such a case, his property will pass to his personal representatives who will be required to distribute it in accordance with the statutory scheme enacted in the Administration of Estates Act 1925.

[3] The only exception here is where the trust property is identified but there is uncertainty as to the precise beneficial interest of the beneficiary in such property. For example, a settlor may transfer £3000 on trust for a beneficiary who is only to receive some of the income from the £3000. Although the £3000 is certain in itself, what is not certain is the term 'some of the income'. In such a case the trust fails and the capital sum reverts back to the settlor by way of a resulting trust.

words of confidence, hope, or whatever they may be . . . to be imperative words'.[4] Where the trust fails for uncertainty of objects, the intended trustee will hold the intended trust property on resulting trust for the settlor or his estate if he has died.

 ## The rationale for certainty

There are a number of reasons for the certainty requirements. Primarily the certainty requirements ensure that the trust is one which can be policed and enforced by the courts. In *IRC* v *Broadway Cottages Trusts*[5] Jenkins LJ explained that 'the principle can be concisely stated by saying that, in order to be valid, a trust must be one which the courts can control and execute'.[6] In other words, the requirement of certainty ensures that the trustee is under a legal as opposed to a moral obligation to execute the trust, and that there is someone in whose favour the court can decree performance. This requires that there is someone who can enforce the obligation in court, that is, someone who has *locus standi* to compel performance.

The second reason for the certainty requirements is that they allow the trust to be distinguished from other concepts, some of which may be very similar to a trust but which in fact have rather different outcomes. Given the fact that a trust usually involves the transfer of some property to a trustee for the benefit of a beneficiary, not all transfers of property, either during the lifetime of the settlor or in his will, are intended to create trusts. In the case of a will, a testator may attempt to transfer his property in a number of ways. Some of the transfers may simply amount to gifts; others may amount to powers of appointment whilst at the other end of the spectrum he may intend to create trusts. It has already been seen in previous chapters that gifts, powers of appointment and trusts confer rather different obligations on the recipients of the property.[7] A gift confers absolute ownership on the recipient while a power confers discretion on the donee of the power; a trust on the other hand creates an imperative obligation on the trustee. Distinguishing one from the other may not always be that simple, especially when the language used by the testator leaves the matter uncertain. The requirement of certainty is a yardstick to measure whether a trust has been created.

Certainty of intention

In order for a trust to come into existence it is important that the settlor intended a trust obligation, as opposed to any other type of obligation such as a power of appointment. Further still, it is important to distinguish between whether the settlor intended a simple gift to the donee, or whether he intended the donee to be subject to a trust in favour of a beneficiary. Whether the settlor intended to create a trust is essentially a matter of intention. The intention of the settlor can be ascertained from the document purporting to create the trust or from his or her conduct. Ultimately the matter is one of construing the intention of the settlor, whether that is in the form of words used by the settlor or by his conduct.

---

[4] *Mussoorie Bank Ltd* v *Raynor* (1882) 7 App. Cas. 321 at 331.
[5] [1955] Ch. 20.
[6] [1955] Ch. 20 at 30.
[7] See Chapter 3.

Equity's concern is with substance not form

Whether a trust is intended in any given circumstance is essentially a question of substance and not form. In most professionally drafted trusts there will be little doubt as to whether a trust is created. The problem is more acute in some of the older cases where a trust was created in rather informal family settings or in the context of wills. In *Re Kayford Ltd*[8] Megarry J explained that 'the question was whether in substance a sufficient intention to create a trust has been manifested'.[9] Thus, the settlor must demonstrate, either through the language used, or by his conduct that he intended a legally binding obligation, that is, an obligation enforceable by the beneficiary against the trustee.

Since equity looks at intent rather than form, there is no need to use any technical language to create a trust. The question in each case is whether on a proper construction of the relevant words the settlor intended a trust. In *Re Kayford Ltd*[10] customers of a mail-order company Kayford Ltd either paid the full price in advance for goods ordered or paid a deposit. The company's main suppliers ran into difficulty and as a consequence went into liquidation. On the advice of its chief accountants Kayford Ltd was told to open a separate account where it could put the monies advanced by customers who had not yet received their goods. The separate bank account was called the 'Customers' Trust Deposit Account'. The object of this arrangement was quite simply to protect the money belonging to the customers and to repay it back should their orders not be completed. Kayford Ltd eventually went into liquidation and the question was whether the money in the separate account formed part of the general assets of the company or whether the money was held on trust for the customers. The court held that the conduct of the company in opening a separate account evidenced an intention that they were holding the monies in the separate account on trust for the customers. The money did not form the general assets of the company.[11]

A similar approach was adopted in In *Re Farepak Foods and Gifts Ltd (in administration)*[12] where a company, Farepak, operated a Christmas savings scheme under which customers could spread the cost of Christmas over a year. The scheme was particularly designed for people on low incomes who were thus able to spread the cost of Christmas. The scheme operated through a system of agents. The agents collected money from the customers and forwarded it to Farepak. As Christmas approached, and to the mass disappointment of the customers, Farepak ceased trading and went into liquidation. Except for the last three days leading up to the administration, the money belonging to the customers had not been put into a separate account. However, in the last three days leading up to administration, the directors executed a deed that the money belonging to the customers be put into a separate account, although the identity of that account remained mistakenly unclear. The court held that despite the mistaken identity as to the account in which the customers' money was to be placed, a trust arose in favour of those customers who had paid money in the three days leading up to the administration of the company. As for the customers who had paid money during the rest of the year, there was no trust as there was no intention to hold the money advanced by such customers on trust for them.

---

[8] [1975] 1 WLR 279. See also *Richards v Delbridge* (1874) LR Eq. 11 and *Paul v Constance* [1977] 1 WLR 527.

[9] [1975] 1 WLR 279 at 282.

[10] [1975] 1 WLR 279.

[11] The same conclusion was reached in *Re Chelsea Cloisters Ltd (in liquidation)* (1980) 41 P & CR 98 and later in *Re Lewis's of Leicester Ltd* [1995] 1 BCLC 428.

[12] [2007] 2 BCLC 1.

In **Staden v Jones**[13] the Court of Appeal emphasised that in creating a trust, it was not necessary to refer expressly to the word 'trustee' but words or acts done by the settlor must have intended to have that meaning. In reaching the conclusion as to whether a trust had indeed been created on the facts, Arden LJ explained that it was important to construe the whole document purporting to create the trust. The facts of the case concerned a husband and wife who, on their separation in 1971, executed a memorandum to the effect that the wife agreed to convey her half interest in their matrimonial home to her husband in consideration that he would leave that half share to their daughter on his death. The husband remarried in 1980 and in 1991 transferred the house into the joint names of himself and his new wife. When the husband died in 1994, the title to the house vested in his new wife absolutely on the grounds that the house was held under a joint tenancy, and as a result of operation of the right of survivorship, she became entitled to the absolute ownership to the house. The question before the Court of Appeal was whether the daughter was entitled to a half share in her father's house. At first instance, the High Court held that the daughter was not entitled to any interest in the house which was now vested in her stepmother. The basis of the decision of the High Court was that the daughter was a mere volunteer and, therefore, not entitled to a half share in the house. Although, the agreement between the husband and wife was to the effect that the husband would give a half interest in the house to the daughter, the daughter was not in a position to enforce that agreement because she was not privy to it and had not provided any consideration. In this respect, the trust remained incompletely constituted.[14] It will be observed in Chapter 6 that a trust only comes into being where the trust property is vested in the trustee. If the trust property is not vested in the trustee, the intended beneficiary has no rights in the intended trust.

The Court of Appeal overturned the decision of the High Court and held that a fully constituted trust of half the share in the house had been created in favour of the daughter, who was, therefore, not a volunteer. Arden LJ explained that, in coming to the conclusion whether a trust had been created in favour of the daughter, it was important to interpret the memorandum of 1971 in substance, including any correspondence, such as letters from solicitors. In the course of her judgment Arden LJ explained that in her judgment:

> the fact that the writing refers only to the devolution of one half to Mrs Staden, and not to its being held for her in the meantime, is not necessarily an indication that the property was not being held upon trust. As I have said in my judgment, the court is entitled to look at the solicitors' letter which states that the parties' agreement was that Mrs Staden should receive a half interest in the property, without stating that she should receive it at any particular point in time . . . So in my judgment it is important to read the document as a whole; and when it is read as a whole, in my judgment, it is clear that the parties' intention was that the property should be kept for Mrs Staden, and that was so even though the only time it was to be transferred to her was in the event of Mr Jones's death. In other words she was to have a beneficial interest, albeit that it was subject to his right to continue to occupy the premises should he wish to do so, but he had no right to dispose of the property for his own benefit. His only right was to occupy it. I bear in mind that a trust is a matter which is difficult to define, but which essentially imposes an obligation to deal with property in a particular way on behalf of another person. It does not, as Jessel MR said, involve using express words of creating a trust.[15]

---

[13] [2008] 2 FLR 1931.

[14] It will be observed in Chapter 6 that an incomplete trust is one where the trust property has not been vested in the trustee. In such a case, the beneficiary has prima facie no rights.

[15] [2008] 2 FLR 1931 at paras. 24–5.

More recently in **Shah v Shah**,[16] an interesting question arose in the Court of Appeal as to whether a letter signed by a shareholder purporting to transfer shares in a private company in favour of another coupled with a signed transfer form amounted to a declaration of trust or a mere incomplete gift. Simply put in another way, could a failed transfer of shares be construed as a declaration of trust in circumstances where the transferor had manifested an intention that he would hold such shares for the transferee? The facts of **Shah v Shah** essentially involved a long-standing feud between four brothers as to the shareholding in a public limited company. Mr Dinesh Shah was one of five brothers as well as one of three shareholders in a public limited company. All three shareholders in the company were brothers and each held one-third of the shareholding. As for the other two brothers, one of them was simply not interested in acquiring any shareholding in the company; however, as for the other, a certain Mr Mahendra Shah, the three brothers who held shares in the company decided that he too should acquire some shareholding in the company so that all four of them would eventually have equal shares of 25 per cent in the company. In order to put this arrangement to effect, on 11 March 2005 Mr Dinesh Shah and another brother executed and delivered letters to Mr Mahendra Shah with the intention that they would hold shares out of their respective shareholding for the benefit of Mahendra. Additionally, they also delivered forms of transfer of 4000 shares in favour of Mahendra in August 2005, but leaving the consideration and date blank on the forms. The shares were duly registered in favour of Mahendra; however, no share certificate was actually delivered to Mahendra, thus leaving the gift of the shares imperfect. Subsequently, Dinesh had a disagreement with his brother Mr Mahendra Shah and, as well as preventing him from having anything to do with the company, he challenged the fact that Mahendra was the owner of any shares in the company. Dinesh argued that the stock transfer form was incomplete and, coupled with the fact that no actual share certificate was actually delivered to him, the disposition was ineffective on the grounds that the letter of 11 March 2005 constituted an attempt to make a gift of the shares in the company and since no share transfer form had been issued, there was an incomplete gift of the shares to Mahendra.

In the Court of Appeal it was held that a valid trust of the shares arose in favour of Mr Mahendra Shah. Arden LJ explained that the effect of the letters delivered in March 2005 to Mahendra evidenced an intention that Mr Dinesh Shah and indeed his two other brothers had created a trust of the shares in favour of their brother Mahendra. In the course of her judgment, Arden LJ explained that:

> In interpreting a document, the court should not have regard to the subjective intention of its maker but to the intentions of the maker as manifested by the words he has used in the context of all the relevant facts. Here there is no doubt that Mr Dinesh Shah manifested an intention that the letter should take effect forthwith: see the words 'as from today'. To give effect in law to those words, there has to be a disposition only of a beneficial interest, since, for the reasons given above, legal title did not pass until registration. The parties clearly intended registration to take place in due course because otherwise Mr Dinesh Shah would not have simultaneously executed and delivered a stock transfer form. Judged objectively, did the words used convey an intention to give a beneficial interest there and then or an intention to hold that interest for Mr Mahendra Shah until registration? Mr Dinesh Shah used the words 'I am . . . holding', not, for example, the words 'I am assigning' or 'I am giving' and the concept that he *holds* the shares for Mr Mahendra Shah until he loses that status on registration can only be given effect in law by the imposition of a trust. Accordingly Mr Dinesh Shah must be taken in law to have intended a trust and not a gift.[17]

---

[16] [2010] EWCA Civ 1408.
[17] [2010] EWCA Civ 1408 at para. 13.

The decision in **Shah v Shah** illustrates the need to look at all of the conduct of a settlor before deciding his actual intention. In this case the delivery of the signed letter indicated an intention to transfer the shares and coupled with the signing of a stock transfer form this amounted to an unequivocal intention to create a trust in favour of the intended donee of the shares.[18]

Precatory words

APPLYING THE LAW

In her will Veronica left her entire residuary estate to her daughter Mary on the understanding that she was fully confident that Mary would give some of the estate to Veronica's three nieces. After Veronica's death Mary refused to give any of the estate to Veronica's nieces.

Do you think that Mary was subject to a trust in favour of Veronica's nieces?

Whilst it is not necessary for a person creating a trust to use any technical language, the general rule is that the courts will not recognise a trust when the settlor uses 'precatory' words. Precatory words are expressions which are not thought to impose a legal obligation on the recipient of property. Good examples of such words are hope, desire and confidence. Thus, as a general rule a trust is not said to arise where the settlor transfers property to a person in the hope, desire or full confidence that he will give all or some part of that property to a third party. At one time the Court of Chancery took the stance that precatory words could create a trust, but this was in the context of a rather different set of succession laws to the modern ones. Prior to the Executors Act 1830, an executor who had administered an estate was entitled to keep for himself any surplus which remained undisposed of by the will. To prevent an executor from abusing this position the court was ready to find that he was a trustee of any surplus which remained at his disposal with the use of words such as hope, desire and confidence.

In the middle of the nineteenth century the Court of Chancery took a strict approach to precatory words, holding that such words would not impose a trust obligation on the person receiving property. A good example of the modern approach is illustrated in **Lambe v Eames**[19] where a testator gave his estate to his wife in a will with the use of the words that it 'be at her disposal in any way she may think best, for the benefit of herself and her family'. By her own will the wife gave part of the estate to people outside the family and when challenged by her family the court held that she was absolutely entitled to her husband's property. There was no trust in favour of the family. A similar result was achieved in **Re Adams and the Kensington Vestry**[20] when a testator left property to his wife using the words that it be for her absolute use, 'in full confidence that she will do what is right as to the disposal thereof between my children either in her lifetime or by will after her decease'. The question was whether a trust was created in favour of the

---

[18] See also, *Moore v Williamson* [2011] EWHC 672 (Ch).

[19] (1871) 6 Ch. App. 597. See also *Re Diggles* (1888) 39 Ch. D 253 where a testatrix left property to her daughter expressing her 'desire' that her daughter pay an annuity to a named relative. The daughter paid the annuity for some years but then stopped. The Court of Appeal held that there was no trust imposed on the daughter to pay the annuity to the named relative.

[20] (1884) 27 Ch. D 394.

children. The Court of Appeal held that the words used in the will were not sufficient to impose an equitable obligation on the wife and that she was absolutely entitled to her husband's estate. In so far as the use of precatory words was concerned, Cotton LJ explained that:

> some of the older authorities went a deal too far in holding that some particular words appearing in a will were sufficient to create a trust. Undoubtedly confidence, if the rest of the context shows that a trust is intended, may make a trust, but what we have to look at is the whole of the will which we have to construe, and if the confidence is that she will do what is right as regards the disposal of the property, I cannot say that this is, on the true construction of the will, a trust imposed upon her.[21]

His Lordship went on to remark that he would find it very strange for the wife's husband to put her under a trust obligation to provide for the children when he knew she would in any event.

Although the general rule is that precatory words will not create a trust, the fact that a settlor or testator uses such words does not automatically mean that there is no trust. The real question in each case is whether on a proper construction of the trust instrument or will a trust was intended. It may well be that a testator uses precatory words, but if the rest of the document makes it clear that a trust was intended then the court will find a trust. A very good illustration of this is *Comiskey* v *Bowring-Hanbury*[22] where a testator left property to his wife 'in full confidence that . . . at her death she will devise it to such one or more of my nieces as she may think fit and in default of any disposition by her thereof by her will . . . I hereby direct that all my estate and property acquired by her under my will shall at her death be equally divided among my said surviving nieces.' Despite the use of the words 'in full confidence' the House of Lords held that the testator's will created a gift to his wife subject to a trust over the remaining part in favour of the surviving nieces to be shared in accordance with the wife's will or otherwise equally. In other words, the wife was at liberty to enjoy her husband's property during her lifetime but was under an obligation to leave it to the nieces in her will, and if not, then to be divided equally amongst the nieces. The reason for this is quite simple; the testator's intention was that, come what may, should any of the property remain after his wife's death, it must go to his nieces. The case is a good example of the need to construe the document in its entirety and not to pay attention to words in isolation.

The effect of reliance on precedent

Where a testator uses a precedent to give effect to his intention then the court will recognise the existence of a trust even though the precedent in question might be viewed upon differently in the modern context. The rationale for this is that equity looks to intent rather than form, and if the reliance on a previous decision is done with a view to create a trust, then a trust will be recognised even though that previous decision would be decided differently today. A good example of this is *Re Steele's Will Trusts*[23] where a testatrix left a diamond necklace to her son, to be held by him for his eldest son, adding the words that 'I request my said son to do all in his power by his will or otherwise to give effect to this my wish.' These words along with others were reproduced in the same way from a previous disposition where the court had held that a trust had been created.[24] Therefore,

---

[21] (1884) 27 Ch. D 394 at 410.
[22] [1905] AC 84.
[23] [1948] Ch. 603.
[24] *Shelley* v *Shelley* (1886) LR 6 Eq. 540.

although the use of the words 'my wish' would not be sufficient to impose a trust obligation upon the son, Wynn-Parry J held that the words of the will had been couched in the same language *mutatis mutandis* of a previous authority upholding a trust. This was the strongest evidence that the testatrix intended the necklace to be a family heirloom.

Curing uncertainty with extrinsic evidence

In a majority of cases problems with uncertainty usually occur in the context of a will. It is up to the court to decide whether on a proper construction of the will a trust was intended by the testator. In the context of a will there are two types of evidence the court can look to in order to ascertain the true intention of the testator. The first is intrinsic evidence, that is, evidence within the will itself which sheds light on what the testator meant. For example, the testator may refer to such concepts which when looked upon objectively may be difficult to define with precision, but the testator gives his own meaning to those concepts in order to resolve the uncertainty. On the other hand, extrinsic evidence is evidence which is external to the will: for example, some statements said about the will which may be able to shed light on what his true intentions were. Where a will is uncertain as to the true intentions of the settlor, the court can admit extrinsic evidence to assist in the interpretation of the will. This is provided for by s. 21 of the Administration of Justice Act 1982 which provides that extrinsic evidence, including evidence of the testator's intention, may be admitted to assist in the interpretation of a will:

(a) in so far as any part of the will is meaningless;

(b) is so far as the language used in any part of it is ambiguous on the face of it;

(c) in so far as evidence, other than evidence of the testator's intention, shows that language used in any part of it is ambiguous in the light of the surrounding circumstances.

Sham intentions

APPLYING THE LAW

Michael is about to start a risky business and he fears that if the business does not do too well, and he finds himself bankrupt, his creditors may lay their hands on his house in order to discharge his debts owed to them. In order to avoid the possibility of losing his house, Michael has instructed that the house be conveyed upon trust to trustees to hold for the benefit of his wife and his three daughters.

Do you think the court should uphold this type of trust, which after all does meet all the requirements of certainty?

The court will not recognise a trust if the intention behind it is purely a sham. For example, a settlor may use language with such precision to make it clear that he intended to bring about a trust; however, if the purpose of that trust is to obtain some fraudulent benefit then the court will not recognise the trust. A trust can be a sham on the face of the instrument purporting to create it or it may be a sham in substance. An example of a sham taking place on the face of the instrument purporting to create it is where the settlor apparently creates a trust in favour of beneficiaries, who either have no knowledge of the existence of the trust, or have no right to control the exercise of the trustee's power or discretion. In other words, the trustee holds the property which the beneficiaries cannot control and all control is vested in the settlor. In such a case the settlor is in substance controlling the trust property which is repugnant to the very idea of a trust. It is easily seen why a settlor may resort to this type of arrangement. Vesting the property into the hands of the trustees for apparent beneficiaries who have no control is usually a fraudulent tax-planning device.[25]

A trust may be a sham in substance where, for example, the sole reason for the creation of the trust is to defraud creditors. For example, a husband may attempt to transfer his house on trust for his wife and children before entering a risky business. The effect of such a trust is simply to keep the house out of reach of the creditors should the business not succeed. A very good illustration of this is provided by **Midland Bank plc v Wyatt**[26] where a trust deed was executed by a husband in 1987 purporting to declare that the family home was to be held on trust for his wife and daughters. The document was stored in a safe place and the wife was not aware of its existence. The house was in fact jointly owned by the husband and wife who continued to obtain loans on it by way of mortgage. When the husband's business failed the bank obtained a charging order on the house. When the husband showed the trust deed to the bank with a view to denying that he had any equitable interest in it, the court held that the trust could not be upheld because it was a sham. Its main purpose was to defraud his creditors. In the course of his judgment D.E.M. Young QC explained that he did not 'believe Mr. Wyatt had any intention when he executed the trust deed of endowing his children with his interest in Honer House, which at that time was his only real asset . . . the declaration of trust was not what it purported to be but a pretence or, as it is sometimes referred to, a sham'.[27]

 Certainty of subject matter

There must be certainty as to what forms the subject matter of the trust. It is crucial to the existence of a trust that the beneficiaries can purport to show where their equitable rights lie at any given time. There must be some property to which the beneficiaries can point to, although it does not matter if that property has subsequently changed its nature or has become mixed with other property.[28]

When addressing the question of certainty of subject matter, trust law is concerned with two questions. The first is: what is the subject matter of the intended trust? The second is: what is the precise beneficial interest of the beneficiary in question? These two questions should be dealt with separately because the consequences of failure to comply with each are different. In the case where there is uncertainty of subject matter altogether, there is no trust at all. If the purported trust was attached to an absolute gift then the absolute gift remains, since there is nothing to which a resulting trust can attach itself.[29] In the case where it is clear what the property is, but there is uncertainty as to the precise beneficial interest of the beneficiary, the trust will fail and the property will revert back to the settlor or the testator's estate. An example of the latter is where a testator purports to leave four paintings out of a collection of ten for a beneficiary and the decision

---

[25] See, for example, *Re Fleet Disposal Services Ltd* [1995] 1 BCLC 345.

[26] [1995] 1 FLR 696; see also *Shalson v Russo* [2005] Ch. 281 and *Re Esteem Settlement* [2004] WTRL 1.

[27] [1995] 1 FLR 697 at 707.

[28] See Chapter 21.

[29] See below.

as to which four are to be held on trust is given to a third party. If the third party dies before a decision is made, the trust will fail for uncertainty of subject matter. In such a case the ten paintings in the hands of the purported trustee will be held on resulting trust for the testator's estate.[30]

What is the subject matter of the trust?

Any form of property can be subject to a trust. Thus, it may be an interest in land such as a freehold interest or a leasehold interest or it may be any form of personal property. Personal property can be classified either as chose in possession or chose in action. A chose in possession is a tangible form of personal property such as a painting or a car. A chose in action, on the other hand, is an intangible form of property, for example, shares in a company or a debt owed to a person. Another good example of intangible property is a covenant, that is, a promise to do something. It is quite possible for a settlor to put a covenant on trust for the benefit of another, thereby allowing that other to enforce the trust of a covenant and as a result deriving the benefits of the covenant.[31]

APPLYING THE LAW

In his will Alf left his residuary estate to his wife Vicky, subject to a trust that on her death Vicky would leave as much as possible of Alf's property to her children in equal shares. When Vicky died she left the property she had acquired from Alf to her best friend, Nancy.

Is a trust created in favour of Alf's children, and if so, what is the subject matter of that trust?

In many cases the subject matter will be relatively clear: for example, two hundred shares on trust; £3000 on trust or a house on trust. However, in some of the older cases decided in the context of wills, the subject matter of the intended trust has not always been defined with certainty. For example, in **Palmer v Simmonds**[32] a testatrix in her will left her residuary estate to a certain Thomas Harrison (the husband) 'for his own use and benefit', and expressing her 'confidence' in him that he would leave the bulk of her residuary estate to certain named persons if he should die without issue. The question was whether there was a trust of the bulk of the estate in favour of the named persons. The court held that there was no trust in favour of the named persons as it was impossible to define what was meant by the term 'bulk of my estate'. A similar result was reached in **Sprange v Barnard**[33] where a testatrix left property to her husband with the instructions that the remaining part of what was left and what he did not want for his own use to be divided equally between her brother and sister. The court held that it was impossible to say with certainty what her husband did not want for his own use and therefore the trust failed. In both **Palmer v Simmonds** and **Sprange v Barnard** the husband took the property absolutely because the property had been given absolutely in

[30] See, for example, *Boyce v Boyce* (1849) 16 Sim. 476.
[31] *Fletcher v Fletcher* (1884) 4 Hare. 67; this case is discussed at more length in Chapter 6.
[32] (1854) 2 Drew 221. See also *Anthony v Donges* [1998] 2 FLR 775 where a husband made a gift to his wife of 'such minimal part of my estate . . . as she may be entitled to under English law for maintenance purposes'. The court held that it was impossible to define what she was entitled to under English law for maintenance purposes.
[33] (1789) 2 Bro. CC 585.

the first place and there was nothing upon which to attach a resulting trust in favour of the estate of the testatrix. This is often known as the rule in **Hancock v Watson**[34] which provides that where property is left as an absolute gift subject to some trust which has failed, the legatee takes absolutely.

Cases such as **Palmer v Simmonds** and **Sprange v Barnard** need to be distinguished from a rather different set of cases which, although having very similar facts, have rather different outcomes. The first case to observe is **Re Last**[35] where a testatrix left her property to her brother with the instruction that on his death anything that was left and which came from her was to be given to her late husband's grandchildren. The brother died intestate and the question was whether the grandchildren could claim what was left. It was contended that the brother took the property absolutely; however, the court held that on a true construction of the will the brother only had a life interest in the property and that anything that remained belonged to the grandchildren. The same result was achieved in an earlier case **Re Thompson's Estate**[36] where a testator left all of his property to his wife to be disposed of as she might think proper and in the event of her death, should there be anything remaining, to certain named persons. Hall VC held that the widow took her husband's property for life only, with a power of disposition during her life but not by will and that anything remaining belonged to the named persons. It can be seen that the distinction between the two types of cases is a very fine one. The problem with the **Palmer v Simmonds**[37] type of case is that the court cannot in any way define what is to be held on trust for the intended beneficiary. In the *Re Last* type of situation the court is not faced with a problem with uncertainty of subject matter because 'what is left' is capable of definition. The only problem with the **Re Last**[38] type of case is whether the testator had the necessary intention to create a life interest followed by a remainder interest of what is left after the life tenant has died. It is submitted that the **Re Last** type of scenario is perfectly acceptable, providing it is the settlor's intention to create a life interest. It would work, for example, where a testator leaves his estate to A providing that whatever is left at his death to go to B. In such a case the testator is creating a trust for A and B and at the time of the creation of the trust it is certain what the subject matter of the trust is – that is, his estate. The fact that A can dispose of the estate is not fatal because B's interest is simply contingent on there being something left after A's death.

What is the precise beneficial interest of the beneficiary?

It some circumstances the settlor may identify with an element of certainty the property from which the beneficiary is to derive a benefit, but leave uncertain the extent of the benefit to be derived. If this happens the intended trustee will hold the property on resulting trust for the settlor or his estate. The inability to determine the extent of the beneficial interest may well be beyond the control of the settlor or testator. For example, **Boyce v Boyce**[39] a testator left two houses on trust for his daughters. The terms of the trust provided that the trustees were to convey to one of the daughters one house of her choice and the remaining house to the other daughter. The daughter with the first right of choice died without making a decision as to which house she wanted; as a consequence

---

[34] [1902] AC 14.
[35] [1958] P 137; [1958] 2 WLR 186.
[36] (1879) 13 Ch. D 144.
[37] (1854) 2 Drew. 221.
[38] [1958] P 137; [1958] 2 WLR 187.
[39] (1849) 16 Sim. 476.

the court held that there was no trust in favour of the surviving daughter. In such a case it was impossible say what the subject matter of the trust was because the right of the surviving daughter could only be determined by the decision of the other daughter. A different rule, however, will apply where the trustee has discretion as to the extent to which the beneficiary is to benefit from such property.

An element of uncertainty can be cured if the court is prepared to give some light on the matter. For example, in **Re Golay's Will Trusts**[40] a testator directed that a certain Mrs B was 'to enjoy one of my flats during her lifetime and to receive a reasonable income from my other properties'. It would appear that such a trust should fail for want of certainty of subject matter as it is impossible to define with certainty which flat the beneficiary is to enjoy and what is a reasonable income. However, Ungoed-Thomas J held that, because the court is constantly making objective assessments of what is reasonable, it could define what is meant by reasonable income. In the course of his judgment he explained that 'the yardstick indicated by the testator is not what he or some other specified person subjectively considers to be reasonable but what he identifies objectively as a reasonable income'.[41]

Unascertained property

APPLYING THE LAW

Nisha owns a wine shop in West London. Recently, she ordered a consignment of red wine of a particular make and year from a wine merchant in Scotland. Nisha was asked to pay for the wine in advance and was assured that, once the wine merchant received her money, her consignment would be held on trust for her.

Unfortunately, before delivery of the consignment, the wine merchant went into liquidation. Nisha claims that her consignment, which was 500 bottles, was held by the wine merchant on trust for her, and as such she could claim the bottles as hers.

Is there a trust of the bottles of wine in favour of Nisha?

A question that has attracted some controversy in recent times is the extent to which a trust can be created over property which is unascertained. Unascertained property is property which forms part of a bulk. For example, can a settlor create a trust over 50 bottles of wine in favour of a beneficiary when the 50 bottles form a bulk of 200 bottles? The answer to this question was given in **Re London Wine Co (Shippers) Ltd**[42] where a wine merchant held stocks of wine in its warehouses. When a customer placed an order for wine the intention was that the bottles of wine ordered should become the property of the customer and that they would be held on trust for the customer. The intention here was clearly to give some protection to the customers who had paid for their order but had not yet received delivery under the contract. The only problem with this arrangement was that there had been no segregation of the bottles of wine ordered by the customers. In other words, the customers could not point to which bottles of wine belonged to them.

---

[40] [1965] 1 WLR 969.
[41] [1965] 1 WLR 969 at 972.
[42] (1986) PCC 121.

The question in court was whether the customers who had ordered wine had a proprietary claim over bottles of wine stored in the various warehouses. The advantage of finding a trust over bottles of wine in favour of the customers was that it would give them priority over other creditors of the company. In giving judgment, Oliver J held that the intended trust in favour of the customers failed for lack of certainty of subject matter. The court held that as a general principle there can be no trust of property which is unascertained.[43]

In *Re Goldcorp Exchange Ltd*[44] the Privy Council had to consider whether a trust could be created in favour of purchasers of gold bullion which had not been segregated from the bulk. The facts of this case concerned a gold bullion exchange which went into liquidation. The exchange acted in buying gold bullion for its clients. The gold had been purchased for some clients and the specific amounts were segregated and put to one side. In the case of other buyers the gold was purchased in bulk but had yet to be segregated to the individual contracts. The Privy Council held that no trust arose in favour of the customers whose gold had not been segregated from the bulk. As a consequence those customers remained unsecured creditors when the company became insolvent.

APPLYING THE LAW

Harry owns 300 shares in a private company. Harry told his son, Charlie, that he would hold 50 shares out of his 300 shares in the private company on trust for him. Two months later, Harry sold the shares for twice their original value and transferred the proceeds to his daughter, Vicky, absolutely. Charlie claims to be entitled to some of the proceeds of the shares given to Vicky on the grounds that Harry was holding 50 shares on trust for him.

Was there a trust of 50 shares for Charlie out of the 300 held by Harry?

The general principle that there can be no trust over property which is unascertained is true only to the extent that the property in question is tangible. Where the property in question is intangible it is quite possible for a person to declare a trust over such property even though it is unascertained. The presumed rationale for this distinction is that, unlike tangible property such as bottles of wine, intangible property is by its inherent nature the same. For example, whilst in the case of bottles of wine stored in bulk, some of which may be corked and some undrinkable, intangible property such as shares of the same type in a company are identical. It does not matter that one share out of a holding of 20 is separated in order to declare a trust over that share. The leading authority is

---

[43] There is nothing stopping the customers having some co-ownership interest in the unascertained property. The Sale of Goods (Amendment) Act 1995 provides that where goods form part of a bulk and are unascertained, buyers of the goods are capable of acquiring co-ownership interests in the bulk until such time as the goods are ascertained to the particular contracts in question. The advantage of this legislation is that it will give the customers priority over other creditors of the company by declaring such customers tenants in common of whatever the property in question is.

[44] [1995] 1 AC 74.

VISIT CASE NAVIGATOR

Hunter v *Moss*[45] where Moss the absolute beneficial owner of 950 shares in company, which had an issued share capital of 1000 shares, orally declared that he would hold 5 per cent (that is, 50 shares) of the issued share capital for Hunter. When Moss refused to transfer the 50 shares to Hunter, Hunter claimed to be beneficially entitled to 50 shares out of the 950 held by Moss. The question in the Court of Appeal was whether there could be a trust of 50 shares out of 950 held by Moss. Dillon LJ held that since the shares were of the same class and in the same company and as such indistinguishable from each other, there could be a trust over part of those shares even though they had not been separated.

Whilst the tangible property rule does not apply to intangible property, the decision in *Hunter* v *Moss* is not without problems.[46] These problems relate to the consequences of finding a trust over unascertained property and subsequent dealings with such property. The matter is particularly acute in the context of intangible property such as shares. For example, what would be the position if a settlor declares himself a trust of 50 shares out of 950 he holds and then, before transferring the 50 shares to the beneficiary, transfers the 950 shares to two bona fide transferees in equal amounts? It is an essential feature of a trust that a beneficiary can identify the property in which it has a proprietary interest. Given the fact that a trust can continue to exist for a long period of time, the beneficiary must be able to locate the existence of its beneficial interest. The ability to identify the existence of the beneficial interest is fundamental to the tracing rules, which allow the beneficiary to follow the property into the hands of third parties who cannot prove that they have acquired the legal title as bona fide purchasers and without notice of the equitable interest.[47] Thus, in the question posed above, how does the beneficiary identify property to show where his or her 50 shares lie at any given time? Where the shares have been transferred in sums of 475 to A and 475 to B, against whom does the beneficiary seek to claim the 50 shares? Ockelton explains that the 'tracing rules, developed for the identification of money that has found its way into a mixed fund, are not to the point, because the shares, unlike money, have an earmark: each has a number by which it retains its identity in which it forms part'.[48]

Although the decision in *Hunter* v *Moss* has been the subject matter of criticism, it has been argued that on the facts of the case the decision is justified.[49] In the first place, Moss had agreed to hold the shares for Hunter and his subsequent refusal to do so would be regarded as well within the jurisdiction of equity to prevent unconscionable conduct. Secondly, Professor Jill Martin argues that the inability of a beneficiary such as Hunter to identify exactly where his shares are at any give time, thereby making the process of tracing difficult if not impossible, should not be decisive of whether a trust should come into existence in the first place. However, an integral part of a trust is that it creates equitable property rights in a beneficiary which, like any other form of property, belong to a person. Belonging to, or being the subject matter of ownership, presupposes that they are identifiable with a particular person. In *Hunter* v *Moss* it is difficult to see which shares belonged to Hunter out of the 950 which Moss had legal title to. A final defence in favour of *Hunter* v *Moss* is that it was, unlike some of the other cases in which the issue has arisen, a case which did not involve a claim by unsecured creditors to gain priority on

---

[45] [1994] 3 All ER 215.
[46] See M. Ockelton, 'Share and Share Alike?' (1994) 53 CLJ 448.
[47] A more detailed account of the tracing rules is provided in Chapter 21.
[48] *Ibid.* at p. 449.
[49] J. Martin, 'Certainty of Subject Matter: A Defence of *Hunter* v *Moss*' [1996] Conv. 233.

insolvency.[50] For example, in the **Re London Wine Co** case the company was insolvent and the decision to hold that the customers had beneficial interests in the stocks of wine would have interfered with the rights of the general creditors of the company.

Whatever the criticisms of the decision in **Hunter v Moss**, it remains the law in so far as a declaration of a trust over unascertained property of an intangible nature. The decision was applied in **Re Harvard Securities Ltd (in Liquidation)**[51] where it was held by the High Court that a registered securities dealer held shares on trust for various clients. On the facts of the case, Harvard, a registered securities dealer, had acquired certain US and Australian shares on behalf of his clients. The intention was that he was to hold the non-numbered shares as nominee for his clients. On the insolvency of Harvard Securities Ltd, it was held that the shares were held on trust for the clients. The decision, however, must be contrasted with a situation which is altogether different on the facts. Where the settlor simply fails to identify any assets which are to be impressed with a trust there can be no trust. For example, in **Mac-Jordan Construction Ltd v Brookmount Erostin Ltd**[52] a main contractor withheld retention money from a subcontractor until satisfactory completion of work under a contract. The intention was that the retention money would be held upon trust for the subcontractor; however, no separate retention fund was set up and on the insolvency of the company the court held that there was no identifiable assets upon which to impress a trust. The subcontractor merely had a contractual right to the return on the retention money and was therefore an unsecured creditor.

Certainty of objects: general observations

Sir William Grant MR once commented that 'there can be no trust, over the exercise of which this court will not assume a control, for an uncontrollable power of disposition would be ownership, and not trust. Every trust must have a definite object. There must be somebody in whose favour the court can decree performance.'[53] It is an essential feature of a trust that is for the benefit of human beneficiaries and that those beneficiaries are defined with a meaning which is understood by the trustee and the courts.[54] Where the settlor or testator fails to identify the objects of a trust or attempts to define them in a manner which is not understood by the trustee or the court, the intended trust property results back to the settlor or his estate under a resulting trust.

The objects of a trust can be defined by name: for example, a trust for 'Phillip and Martha' or they can be defined by reference to some class such as 'my children'; employees of a company, or 'my old friends'. Whatever method is used by the settlor, the courts require certainty so that someone has *locus standi* to enforce the trust. The question whether a given trust satisfies certainty of objects very much depends on the type of trust in question. For example, the test for certainty of objects for a fixed trust is rather different from the test for a discretionary trust. Before these tests are examined in detail it is important to appreciate that the certainty of objects requirement has a number of constituent elements to it.

---

[50] *Ibid.* at p. 227.
[51] [1998] BCC 567.
[52] [1992] BCLC 350.
[53] *Morice* v *Bishop of Durham* (1804) 9 Ves. 399 at 404.
[54] There are limited exceptions to the rule that a trust should be for human beneficiaries; these are examined in Chapter 8 under the beneficiary principle.

The constituent elements of certainty of objects

The certainty of objects requirement can be broken down into four separate requirements.[55] The extent to which they apply will depend on the type of trust in question.

Conceptual certainty

Conceptual certainty refers to the way in which the settlor has described the objects of
the trust. He may define them by name, for example Peter, Colin and Mary, or he may
refer to them by some concept such as niece and nephew or he may simply refer to some
class, for example, the employees of a company. Whatever method of description is used,
the settlor must have defined the objects with a meaning which is understood by the
trustee, the objects of the trust and ultimately the court who may be required to execute
the trust should the trustees fail to do so.[56] Conceptual certainty requires the trust
objects to be defined with a dictionary meaning. Conceptual certainty is fundamental to
the validity of any type of trust in question. Without conceptual certainty it is impossible
for the trustees to distribute the trust property as they simply have no defined beneficiaries. If there is an element of conceptual uncertainty in a trust then the trust will fail
and the property will result back to the settlor or his estate.

There will be few problems of conceptual certainty in respect of beneficiaries who
are named as individuals or who have been referred to with a term which is clearly
understood, for example 'my sons'. Problems of conceptual certainty will, however, arise
where the settlor defines the objects with reference to a class which is so hopelessly
vague. For example, in *Re Leek*[57] where a trust was created in favour of such persons as
A may consider to have a moral claim on X was said too vague and therefore conceptually uncertain. In between those categories which are defined with certainty and those
which are hopelessly vague will be categories which are almost certain but may need
clarification from the court. In *Re Gulbenkian's Settlement Trusts*[58] Lord Upjohn
explained the question of conceptual certainty in the following manner. 'Suppose the
donor directs that a fund be divided equally between my old friends, then unless there is
some admissible evidence that the donor has given some special dictionary meaning to
that phrase which enables the trustee to identify the class with sufficient certainty, it is
plainly bad as being too uncertain.'[59]

Evidential certainty

The class of objects may be defined with certainty so that the trustee understands in
whose favour the trust should be exercised. However, the trustee may find himself facing
a rather different type of problem, that is, evidential uncertainty. Suppose a settlor
directs that a fund is divided equally amongst the employees and ex-employees of a

---

[55] See C.T. Emery, 'The Most Hallowed Principle – Certainty of Beneficiaries of Trusts and Powers of
Appointment' LQR Vol. 98 551.

[56] It is not normal for the court to execute a trust should the trustees fail to do so. If the trustee fails to
execute the trust the preferred option is to appoint new trustees who will do so. This is explored later
in the chapter.

[57] [1969] 1 Ch. 563.

[58] [1970] AC 508.

[59] *Ibid.* at 528.

certain company. 'Employees and ex-employees' is a term which has a meaning and is, therefore, conceptually certain; however, because the trustee is required to distribute the fund equally amongst all the employees past and present, he would need an accurate list of all such employees. If it is impossible for the trustee to verify whether a given individual is an ex-employee because, for example, the company has failed to keep an accurate record of past employees, the trust will simply fail on grounds of evidential uncertainty.[60] The same result will arise where a trust is created in favour of relatives of a settlor. Whilst the definition of relative may be conceptually certain, there may be evidential problems as to which of, for example, ten individuals are in fact the relatives of the settlor. If the evidence is clear that only six out of the ten are relatives one can say that there is evidential certainty. On the other hand, if the evidence is insufficient then the trustees are faced with evidential problems, which may affect the validity of the trust depending on whether it is fixed or discretionary. Evidential certainty, therefore, can be said to be the extent to which it is possible to identify with certainty the full range of beneficiaries within a class.

Ascertainability

Where the objects of the trust are conceptually certain and there are no evidential problems in identifying the full range of beneficiaries, the trustee may yet face the problem of ascertainability. The trustee may well know that he has ten beneficiaries who are to benefit from the trust; however, if he is unaware of the whereabouts and continued existence of one or more of those beneficiaries, the trustee is said to have a problem of ascertainability. There is often a tendency to confuse evidential certainty with ascertainability; however, the two are rather different matters. Evidential certainty refers to the question whether somebody is, for example, a relative or an employee. Ascertainability refers to the question whether somebody who has clearly been identified as the relative of the settlor is still living and, if so, where his continued existence is.

Administrative workability

The final aspect of certainty of objects relates to the question of administrative workability. The objects of the trust may be defined with certainty so that the trustee knows exactly in whose favour the trust should be exercised; however, the problem may be that the size of the potential beneficiaries may be so hopelessly wide that the trustee could not realistically apply his mind to the size of the group. In **Re Baden's Deed Trusts (No. 1)**[61] Lord Wilberforce commented that the 'definition of beneficiaries [may be] so hopelessly wide as not to form anything like a class, so that the trust is administratively workable'.[62] The question is: when will a trust be void on grounds of administrative workability? Or, in other words, why should the size of the group make a difference? The

---

[60] This is exactly what happened in *Re Sayer* [1957] Ch. 423. Here a trust was created in favour of the employees and ex-employees of Sayer Ltd; however, since its incorporation the company had failed to keep an accurate record of its ex-employees. The trust failed on the grounds that it was evidentially impossible to identify who were the ex-employees of the company.

[61] [1971] AC 424.

[62] *Ibid.* at 457.

answer to this question is better understood in the context of the test for certainty of objects of a discretionary trust. This is considered below.

The test of certainty of objects for a fixed trust

A fixed trust arises where the settlor or testator confers upon the beneficiary or beneficiaries a fixed entitlement, for example, £10,000 to be divided equally amongst his nieces as illustrated in Figure 4.3.[63]

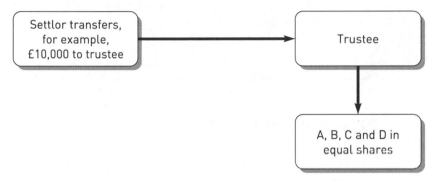

Settlor transfers, for example, £10,000 to trustee → Trustee → A, B, C and D in equal shares

Figure 4.3

In contrast to a fixed trust is a discretionary trust where the trustee has absolute discretion as to how much and when to distribute. The test of certainty of objects for a fixed trust is to be found in the case of **IRC v Broadway Cottages Trust**[64] where Wynn-Parry J held that a trustee was required to draw up a complete list of all the beneficiaries.[65] The test for certainty of objects for a fixed trust is therefore described as the 'complete list test'. Given the nature of a fixed trust, the requirement that a trustee must be able to draw up a complete list of the beneficiaries is logical. Take, for example, a trust which requires equal distribution amongst the nieces of a settlor. Unless the trustee has a complete list of all the nieces, the trust is impossible to administer. It is simply impossible to divide the fund if the trustee does not know how many nieces the settlor has. The requirement that the trustee must be able to draw up a complete list of beneficiaries does not require that the complete list be capable of being drawn up at the time of the creation of the trust, rather it is at the time of the execution of the trust. For example, it is possible for a settlor to create a trust of equal shares in favour of children not yet born, as explained by Fox LJ in **Swain v Law Society**,[66] thus making it impossible for the trustee to know exactly how many children the trust is to be exercised in favour of. This trust will not fail

---

[63] Of course there is nothing stopping the settlor from stipulating shares of some other proportion.

[64] [1954] 1 All ER 878.

[65] The facts of *IRC v Broadway Cottages* will reveal that the trust in question there was not a fixed trust at all but rather a discretionary trust. In the context of a discretionary trust pre *McPhail v Doulton* [1971] AC 424, the courts required the trustees to draw up a complete list of all of the beneficiaries in order to find the trust valid. In this sense, the law was that the test for certainty of objects of a discretionary trust is the same as that of a fixed trust: that is, the class must be capable of ascertainment or there must be a complete list of all the beneficiaries.

[66] [1981] 3 All ER 797 at 822.

simply because the trustee cannot at the time of the creation of the trust draw up a complete list. It is only when the trustee seeks to distribute the fund that he must be in a position to draw up a complete list of the children.[67]

APPLYING THE LAW

In his will Samuel David left a fund of £200,000 to be distributed equally amongst the employees and ex-employees of S.M. Ltd. The trustees of the fund have established the names of all of the present employees of S.M. Ltd; however, they are struggling to find the names of all of the ex-employees because the company has failed to keep an accurate record of its ex-employees. The present employees are keen that the money be divided equally amongst them.

Can the trustees distribute to the present employees only?

Conceptual certainty

When applying the complete list test to a fixed trust the court will require, in the first place, that the objects of the trust be conceptually certain. The settlor or testator must have described the objects with a meaning which is understood by both the trustee and the courts. A trust which requires equal distribution amongst 'my nieces' is conceptually certain. On the other hand, a trust which requires equal distribution amongst 'those who have helped me during my life' is conceptually uncertain and thus void.

Evidential certainty

It will be recalled that evidential certainty refers to the extent to which it is possible to identify every member of the class of objects to benefit from the trust. Thus, if a trust is created in favour of the settlor's seven nephews, the trustee must have a complete list of the seven nephews in order for the trust to be administered. If the trustees cannot draw up the list owing to evidential problems in establishing who the seven nephews are, then the trust fails for evidential uncertainty with the consequence that the property results back to the settlor. Another example of evidential uncertainty is where the settlor declares a fixed trust in favour of seven nephews but the trustees are confronted with nine individuals all claiming to be the nephews of the settlor or testator. If the trustees cannot establish with certainty who the real nephews are then they are said to have a problem of evidential certainty and no distribution can take place. In this respect evidential certainty is fundamental to the validity of a fixed trust. The issue of evidential uncertainty is neatly illustrated by the case of **Re Sayer**[68] where a sum of money was settled upon trust for employees, ex-employees and dependants of Sayer (Confectioners) Ltd. In applying the complete list test, Lord Upjohn held that the trust must fail because

---

[67] This is, of course, subject to the rule against perpetuities: see Chapter 8.

[68] [1957] 2 WLR 261. The facts of *Re Sayer* will show that the trust in question there was a discretionary trust rather than a fixed trust; however, as explained before, all the pre-1971 discretionary trusts had to comply with the complete list test whereby the trustees had to show that the whole class was ascertained.

since the incorporation of the company the company had failed to keep an accurate record of its ex-employees.

Ascertainability

In her will Jacky left her entire estate in equal shares on trust for her seven children on them attaining the age of 25. Jacky died last year and the trustees have established that all of her children are now over the age of 25. They have also established that one of her sons, Tom, went to live in New Zealand about 5 years ago. They have tried tracking him down in New Zealand; however, the authorities in New Zealand have no records of Tom's residence in New Zealand. They are not sure what to do with his share of his mother's estate.

Where a fixed trust is both conceptually certain and there are no evidential problems which prevent identification of all the beneficiaries in the class to be benefited, ascertainability of one or more of those beneficiaries will not invalidate the trust. The question of ascertainability refers to the extent to which it is possible to locate a particular beneficiary whose identity has been established. Take the following example: a testator creates a trust in favour of his six children in equal shares. The trustees establish the identity of the six children and know exactly who they are looking for; however, the problem is in locating one of the sons. The trustees know that the son went abroad some time ago but has since not been seen by the family. In such a case there is no reason why the trust should fail, since the trustees are in a position to divide the fund equally and allocate the respective share to the five children who have clearly been ascertained. The only question in such a case is what happens to the share of the missing son? It is submitted that in such a case the trustees have one of two options in respect of the share of the missing beneficiary. In the first place, the trustee can pay the share of that missing beneficiary into court.[69]

A second option available to the trustees is to apply for a *Benjamin* order, which allows the court to make a presumption that the missing beneficiary predeceased the testator. A presumption that the beneficiary predeceased the testator means that the gift of that beneficiary is said to lapse and the trustee is entitled to distribute the share of the missing beneficiary amongst the other beneficiaries. In the example of the six children above, the trustees under a Benjamin order are entitled to assume that the testator had only five children and not six so that distribution takes place five ways as opposed to six. The name 'Benjamin order' comes from **Re Benjamin**[70] where the testator directed his executors to distribute his residuary estate equally amongst his thirteen children. The executors were unable to ascertain the whereabouts of one of the testator's son, who had gone missing whilst on holiday one year before the testator's death. The court held that the executors were entitled to distribute the estate amongst the other children. If the missing beneficiary does subsequently appear, he is entitled to claim his share from the other beneficiaries because a Benjamin order does not destroy entitlement.[71] It is important

---

[69] See *Re Gulbenkian's Settlement* [1970] AC 508 at 524.
[70] [1902] 1 Ch. 723.
[71] *Re Green's Will Trusts* [1985] 3 All ER 455.

to appreciate that a Benjamin order is a principle of succession law and will, therefore, only apply where a fixed trust is created in a will. The rule does not apply to an *inter vivos* fixed trust.

Administrative workability

Administrative workability really does not have any operation in the field of fixed trusts. Once the trustees have identified a conceptually certain group of beneficiaries, their duty is to carry out equal distribution. Such a distribution is a mathematical exercise and, providing the fund is capable of distribution, the trust is workable.[72]

The test of certainty of objects for a discretionary trust

Unlike a fixed trust, a discretionary trust confers upon the trustee discretion in respect of distribution of the trust fund. However, unlike a power of appointment, the trustees must at some point exercise the discretion in favour of the beneficiaries (see Figure 4.4).

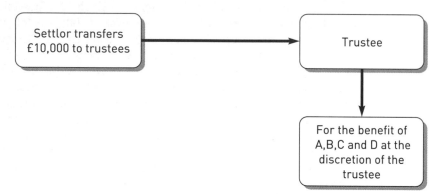

Figure 4.4

The test for certainty of objects for a discretionary trust was fundamentally changed in 1970 by the House of Lords in **McPhail v Doulton**.[73] The facts of this case concerned a deed of July 1941 which purported to establish a discretionary trust in favour of the officers and employees of a company. Clause 9 of the deed provided that 'the trustees shall apply the net income of the fund in making at their absolute discretion grants to or for the benefit of any of the officers and employees or ex-officers or ex-employees of the company or to any of the relatives or dependants of any such persons in such amounts at such times . . . as they think fit'. The question in the House of Lords was which test should be applied to determine whether the trust was valid or void for uncertainty of objects.

---

[72] For a contrary view, see I.M. Hardcastle 'Administrative Unworkability: A Reassessment of an Abiding Problem' [1990] Conv. 24.

[73] [1970] 2 All ER 228.

The position pre *McPhail v Doulton*

The test for certainty of objects for a discretionary trust prior to **McPhail v Doulton** was exactly the same as that for a fixed trust. In other words, the trustees were required to draw up a complete list of all the beneficiaries.[74] If it was not possible to identify all the beneficiaries the trust would fail for uncertainty, despite the fact that the trustees had discretion in the first place whether to give to a particular beneficiary or not.[75] The rationale behind the requirement of a complete list was twofold. In the first place, it was held that in the event of the trustee not exercising the discretion vested in him, the court would execute the trust on his behalf. The court would, on the principle that 'equity is equality', distribute the fund equally amongst the class of beneficiaries. In this respect, a complete list of all the beneficiaries was required in order for the court to both control and execute the trust. Secondly, the assumption was that for a trustee to have shown that he had properly exercised his discretion, he must have surveyed all the potential beneficiaries in the class. Both of these arguments were discarded by the House of Lords in **McPhail v Doulton**.[76] Delivering the leading judgment in the case, Lord Wilberforce explained that, in so far as the equal distribution of the fund by the court in the event of the failure of the trustee, to do so would fundamentally go against the testator's intention. In the words of his Lordship, '. . . to hold that a principle of equal division applies to trusts such as the present is certainly paradoxical. Equal distribution is surely the last thing the settlor ever intended; equal distribution among all may, probably would, produce a result beneficial to none.'[77] Secondly, in relation to the point that the trustee in exercising his discretion under a discretionary trust was required to survey the whole, this was again not founded on authority or principle. Provided the trustees made a reasonable survey of the potential range of beneficiaries, and did not act capriciously, it did not matter that they did not survey every single member of the class.[78]

The position post *McPhail v Doulton*

In **McPhail v Doulton** the House of Lords held that the complete list test for certainty of objects should be discarded and the test to be applied should be the same as that for a power of appointment.[79] It will be recalled that a power of appointment is a very similar concept to a discretionary trust.[80] The difference is that a power confers on the donee of the power a non-imperative obligation to distribute the property amongst the objects of the power, whereas under a discretionary trust the trustee must distribute the trust property, albeit at his discretion. The leading case on certainty of objects for a power of appointment is **Re Gulbenkian's Settlement Trusts**[81] where a power was created in favour of a group of objects. In the course of his judgment, Lord Upjohn explained that

---

[74] See *IRC v Broadway Cottages Trust* [1955] Ch. 20.
[75] The requirement of complete list for a discretionary trust pre-1970 had the effect that many discretionary trusts would fail where it was impossible to draw up a complete list of the beneficiaries, even though the trust was capable of being exercised in favour of a potentially large group of beneficiaries which were capable of ascertainment.
[76] [1970] 2 All ER 228.
[77] [1970] 2 All ER 228 at 241.
[78] [1970] 2 All ER 228 at 247.
[79] The test for certainty of objects of a power is to be found in *Re Gulbenkian's Settlement Trusts* [1968] 3 All ER 785.
[80] See Chapter 3.
[81] [1968] 3 All ER 785.

'a mere or bare power of appointment among a class is valid if you can with certainty say whether any individual is or is not a member of the class; you do not have to be able to ascertain every member of the class'.[82] This test has become more popularly known as the 'is or is not' or 'given postulant' test. The donee of the objects is not required to draw up a complete list of the objects, provided that he is able to say whether any given individual is or is not within the class, the test is satisfied and the power is valid.

A discretionary trust will be valid if the trustee can say with certainty whether any given individual is or is not a member of the class. The trustee is not required to draw up a complete list of all of the beneficiaries, and should the trustee fail to execute the trust the court is not required to and neither is it justified in distributing the fund equally amongst the class of objects. In the event of the trustee failing to execute the trust, the court can, in the words of Lord Wilberforce, 'execute the trust . . . in the manner best calculated to give effect to the settlor's or testator's intentions. It may do so by appointing new trustees, or by authorising or directing representative persons of the classes of beneficiaries to prepare a scheme of distribution, or even, should the proper basis for distribution appear, by itself directing the trustees so to distribute.'[83] The individual elements of certainty of objects can now be examined in respect of a discretionary trust which is subject to the given postulant test.

Conceptual certainty

In order for the trustee to be in a position to say whether any particular beneficiary is or is not within the class, the class must be defined with a dictionary meaning. Conceptual certainty is crucial to the validity of a discretionary trust. The settlor may well use meanings which are very clear to the trustee as well as meanings which are so hopelessly wide that the trust fails for want of certainty of objects. As mentioned earlier, between the very clear and the hopelessly vague cases will be cases which the courts will attempt to give some meaning to. For example in *Re Baden's Deed Trusts (No. 2)*[84] the Court of Appeal when applying the test of certainty established in the House of Lords in *McPhail v Doulton*[85] held that the words 'dependant' and 'relatives' were both conceptually certain.[86] Sachs LJ held that 'any one wholly or partly dependent on the means of another is a dependant'.[87] In so far as the word 'relative' the court explained that it meant someone who was a common ancestor and not someone who was remotely related to the settlor.

APPLYING THE LAW

In an *inter vivos* deed executed last year, Chris transferred a sum of £200,000 to his trustees to distribute at their discretion amongst his relatives, best friends, dependants and any other such persons with whom he has had a close connection.

Do you think this creates a valid discretionary trust?

---

[82] [1968] 3 All ER 785 at 790.
[83] [1970] 2 All ER 228 at 247.
[84] [1972] 3 WLR 250.
[85] [1970] 2 All ER 228.
[86] [1972] WLR 250 at 257.
[87] *Ibid.*

● Evidential uncertainty

Evidential uncertainty will never defeat a discretionary trust simply because the trustee under a discretionary trust is no longer required to ascertain the whole class. In **Re Baden's Deed Trusts (No. 2)** Sachs LJ explained that 'the court is never defeated by evidential uncertainty . . . once the class of persons to be benefited is conceptually certain it then becomes a question of fact to be determined on evidence whether any postulant has on inquiry been proved to be within it; if he is not so proved then he is not in it.'[88] Thus, a trust in favour of the employees and ex employees of a company will not fail simply because a potential beneficiary cannot prove himself to be an ex-employee of the company. Why should it fail? The failure of a particular beneficiary to show that he or she is definitely within the class has no effect on the trustee exercising his discretion in favour of the beneficiaries who have been proved to be within the class.

Although it is clear that post **McPhail v Doulton**[89] the trustees of a discretionary trust are no longer required to draw up a complete list of all of the beneficiaries of a discretionary trust, there does remain an element of uncertainty as to how the 'is or is not' test is satisfied. In **Re Baden's Deed Trusts (No. 2)**[90] the three Court of Appeal judges seem to have taken different approaches to satisfying the test. Megaw LJ was of the view that the test was satisfied if it was possible to say that a substantial number of beneficiaries fell within the class. In the course of his judgment, Megaw LJ explained that:

> to my mind, the test is satisfied if, as regards at least a substantial number of objects, it can be said with certainty that they fall within the trust; even though, as regards a substantial number of other persons, if they ever for some fanciful reason fell to be considered, the answer would have to be, not 'they are outside the trust,' but 'it is not proven whether they are in or out.' What is a 'substantial number' may well be a question of common sense and of degree in relation to the particular trust: particularly where, as here, it would be fantasy, to use a mild word, to suggest that any practical difficulty would arise in the fair, proper and sensible administration of this trust in respect of relatives and dependants.[91]

On the other hand, Stamp LJ preferred to adopt a rather strict approach. In his Lordship's opinion, although the trustees were not under a duty to draw up a complete list of beneficiaries, they nevertheless had to be in a position to carry out a comprehensive survey of the range of beneficiaries. This, therefore, required not just a substantial number of beneficiaries to fall within the class, but also a range of beneficiaries from all aspects of the class to fall within it. In the course of judgment, Stamp LJ explained that:

> the trustees ought to make such a survey of the range of objects or possible beneficiaries as will enable them to carry out their fiduciary duty, and I ought perhaps to add that he indicated that a wider and more comprehensive range of inquiry is called for in the case of what I have called discretionary trusts than in the case of fiduciary powers. But, as I understand it, having made the appropriate survey, it matters not that it is not complete or fails to yield a result enabling you to lay out a list or particulars of every single beneficiary. Having done the best they can, the trustees may proceed upon the basis similar to that adopted by the court where all the beneficiaries cannot be ascertained and distribute upon the footing that they have been . . . Validity or invalidity is to depend upon whether you can say of any individual – and the accent must be upon that word 'any,' for it is not simply the individual

---

[88] [1972] 3 WLR 250 at 255.
[89] [1970] 2 All ER 228.
[90] [1972] 3 WLR 250.
[91] [1972] 3 WLR 250 at 265.

whose claim you are considering who is spoken of – 'is or is not a member of the class', for only thus can you make a survey of the range of objects or possible beneficiaries.[92]

Ascertainability

Questions of ascertainability of a given beneficiary will not apply to a discretionary trust. You will recall that ascertainability addresses the question of the continued whereabouts of a particular beneficiary who is proved to be within the range of objects to benefit from the trust. If the trustees have a discretion in the first place, it hardly makes any sense to try to find the continued whereabouts of a beneficiary who simply cannot be found. Indeed, it would be wholly irrational for the trustee to pursue the existence of a particular beneficiary under a discretionary trust where it is usually the existence of the beneficiary and his or her particular needs that calls for the exercise of the discretion in his or her favour. In the words of one commentator, 'the whole drift of such trusts is to enable the trustee to provide for patent need; and one's need can hardly be patent to trustees if they are in irresolvable doubt as to one's continued existence or whereabouts'.[93]

Administrative workability

A discretionary trust may be held to be void on the grounds of administrative workability. Exactly what is meant by administrative workability has until recent times remained rather unclear.[94] Furthermore, there has been some debate as to the difference between the concept of administrative workability and the concept of capriciousness. Capriciousness is a term used in connection with a power of appointment. In *Re Manisty's Settlement*[95] Templeman J explained that a trust in favour of the residents of Greater London would be void on grounds on capriciousness. The rationale was that there is no sensible motive behind the gift and no sensible criteria on which the donee of the power is to consider exercising the power if he so chooses to do so. It is submitted that, just like a power of appointment, a discretionary trust can be void on grounds of capriciousness if the motive behind the trust is meaningless and there is likewise no discernable basis on which discretion is to be exercised in favour of the objects. For example, a testator who leaves a fund to be distributed at the trustee's discretion amongst the inhabitants of Greater London would prima facie be void on grounds of capriciousness.

Administrative workability, unlike capriciousness, looks to the size of the group. A settlor may well have a perfectly valid motive behind the trust; however, the size of the group may make it difficult if not impossible for the trustee to exercise a discretion which is reasonable. In *Re Baden's Deed Trusts (No. 1)*[96] Lord Wilberforce explained that there may be a case 'where the meaning of the words used is clear but the definition of the beneficiaries is so hopelessly wide as not to form anything like a class so that the trust is administratively unworkable'.[97] Although a trustee has discretion to distribute the trust

---

[92] [1972] 3 WLR 250 at 268.

[93] C.T. Emery, 'The Most Hallowed Principle – Certainty of Beneficiaries of Trusts and Powers of Appointment' LQR Vol. 98 551 at p. 578.

[94] See I.M. Hardcastle 'Administrative Unworkability: A Reassessment of an Abiding Problem' [1990] Conv. 24.

[95] [1974] Ch. 17.

[96] [1971] AC 424.

[97] [1971] AC 424 at 457.

property under a discretionary trust, he cannot simply purport to exercise that discretion in favour of those beneficiaries who claim his attention, The fact that the trustee stands in a fiduciary relationship means that he must show that his discretion was exercised both in good faith and in a reasonable manner. In *Re Hay's Settlement Trusts*[98] Megarry VC explained the extent of a trustee's duty under a discretionary trust. In the course of his judgment he explained that:

> the trustee must not simply proceed to exercise the power in favour of such of the objects as the objects as happen to be at hand or claim his attention. He must first consider what persons or classes of persons are objects of the power . . . what is needed is an appreciation of the width of the field, and thus whether a selection is to be made merely from a dozen or, instead, from thousands and millions . . . Only when the trustee has applied his mind to the size of the problem should he consider individual cases . . .[99]

The problem of administrative workability was neatly illustrated in *R v District Auditor ex p. West Yorkshire Metropolitan County Council*.[100] In this case a trust with a fund of £400,000 was created by a council in favour of the inhabitants of West Yorkshire of which there were potentially 2.5 million. The court held that the trust was void on grounds of administrative workability. The size of the class was simply too large for the trustees to properly exercise the discretion in favour of the potential beneficiaries. It is submitted that such a trust would not, however, be deemed as capricious because the intention of the council in creating the trust was a genuine one.

● Gifts subject to a condition precedent

APPLYING THE LAW

In his will Harjit left his estate, including his collection of vintage motorbikes, to his executors to be sold and the proceeds to be distributed amongst various charitable organisations. He instructed his executors to sell the motorbikes at auction, but only after his close friends had been given the opportunity to purchase the bikes at a price 25 per cent below the market price of the bikes. The executors are not too sure who are the close friends of Harjit are.

Is this condition valid?

Where a gift is subject to a condition precedent the test of certainty is not as strict as it is if the gift is in favour of a class to be selected by trustees. The gift will be valid even though it contains an element of uncertainty provided at least that an individual can show he meets the criteria set in the condition precedent. The matter is illustrated in a number of cases, although the rationale for the distinction between gifts subject to a condition precedent and gifts to a class under a discretionary trust is not one which is justified.[101] In *Re Allen*[102] a gift was made to a member of the family subject to the condition that he shall be 'a member of the Church of England and an adherent to the doctrine

---

[98] [1982] 1 WLR 202.
[99] [1982] 1 WLR 202 at 209–10.
[100] [1986] RVR 24.
[101] See, for example, L. Mckay, '*Re Barlow* and the Certainty of Objects Rule' [1980] Conv. 263.
[102] [1953] Ch. 810.

of that Church'. The question before the Court of Appeal was whether this gift was void for uncertainty. The Court held that the gift was valid on the grounds that, although there might be uncertainty surrounding the words 'adherent to the doctrine of the Church of England', it was not a term which is insoluble. Provided that one person had clearly shown himself to be within the definition, it did not matter that the definition lacked total conceptual certainty.

The decision in **Re Allen** was applied in **Re Barlow's Will Trusts**[103] where a testatrix left some valuable paintings to members of her family and instructed the trustees to sell the remainder, but subject to any member of her family or friends being allowed to purchase them at a reduced price. The question before Browne-Wilkinson J was whether the condition was void for uncertainty. In particular, what did the testatrix mean by 'friends'? The court held that the test in **Re Allen**[104] and the gift was valid. The court held that where there was a gift subject to a condition precedent, a less strict test applied, on the grounds that it was not essential to have complete conceptual certainty, provided that at least one person satisfied the description event; though as regards others the question could not be answered affirmatively. Brown-Wilkinson J explained in the course of his judgment that:

> in the case of a gift of a kind which does not require one to establish all the members of the class (e.g. 'a gift of £10 to each of my friends'), it may be possible to say of some people that on any test, they qualify. Thus in *In re Allen*, decd. at p. 817, Sir Raymond Evershed M.R. took the example of a gift to X 'if he is a tall man'; a man 6 ft. 6 ins. tall could be said on any reasonable basis to satisfy the test, although it might be impossible to say whether a man, say, 5 ft. 10 ins. high satisfied the requirement. So in this case, in my judgment, there are acquaintances of a kind so close that, on any reasonable basis, anyone would treat them as being 'friends.' Therefore, by allowing the disposition to take effect in their favour, one would certainly be giving effect to part of the testatrix's intention even though as to others it is impossible to say whether or not they satisfy the test.[105]

As for the definition of friends, the judge explained that:

> without seeking to lay down any exhaustive definition of such test, it may be helpful if I indicate certain minimum requirements: (a) the relationship must have been a long-standing one. (b) The relationship must have been a social relationship as opposed to a business or professional relationship. (c) Although there may have been long periods when circumstances prevented the testatrix and the applicant from meeting, when circumstances did permit they must have met frequently. If in any case the executors entertain any real doubt whether an applicant qualifies, they can apply to the court to decide the issue.[106]

This aspect of the decision has, however, been criticised by Professor Jill Martin who writes that 'although the "condition precedent" test is now settled, this decision illustrates the difficulty inherent in it. The trustees could be in a real difficulty in giving effect to such a disposition. The solution that trustees could apply to the court in cases of doubt is unsatisfactory. How can the court be in any better position than the trustees to pronounce on questions whether X is a "friend" or Y?'[107]

Curing conceptual uncertainty

Where a settlor or a testator uses uncertain terms to describe the beneficiaries, the trust fails outright for conceptual uncertainty and intended trust property results back to the

---

[103] [1979] 1 All ER 296.
[104] [1953] Ch. 810.
[105] [1979] 1 All ER 296 at 281.
[106] [1979] 1 All ER 296 at 282.
[107] J. Martin, *Hanbury and Martin: Modern Equity* (2009) 18th edn at p. 120.

settlor or the testator's estate. Except in cases such as **Re Allen**[108] and **Re Barlow's Will Trusts**[109] where a less strict test applies, the questions arise as to whether there are any ways in which the conceptual uncertainty can be cured. For example, is it possible for the settlor to leave the definition of an uncertain term to be decided by the opinion of a third party? Suppose that a settlor creates a trust in favour of his good friends to be determined by his trustees: can the apparently uncertain term 'good friends' be allowed on the grounds that the matter is to be determined by the opinion of the trustees? It appears that the opinion of a third party may well settle the matter, but only if the settlor has laid down sufficient criteria by which the trustees will make their decision. The matter is illustrated by the decision in **Re Coxen**[110] where a testator devised a dwelling house to his trustees with a direction to permit his wife to 'reside therein during her life, or for so long as she shall desire to reside therein', and declared that 'from and after her death or if in the opinion of the trustees shall have ceased permanently to reside therein', the house was to fall into his residuary trusts. Jenkins J held that the meaning of 'ceased to have permanently reside therein' had been left with sufficient criteria with the trustees and, therefore, the condition was not void for uncertainty. In the course of his judgment, the judge explained that:

> [i]f the testator had insufficiently defined the state of affairs on which the trustees were to form their opinion, he would not I think have saved the condition from invalidity on the ground of uncertainty merely by making their opinion the criterion, although the declaration by the trustees of this or that opinion would be an event about which in itself there could be no uncertainty. But as I have already indicated, I think the relevant double event is sufficiently defined to make it perfectly possible for the trustees (as the judges of fact for this purpose) to decide whether it has happened or not, and in my view the testator by making the trustees' opinion the criterion has removed the difficulties which might otherwise have ensued from a gift over in a double event the happening of which, though in itself sufficiently defined, may necessarily be a matter of inference involving nice questions of fact and degree.[111]

Where a settlor fails to leave any suitable criteria upon which to resolve the matter, the uncertain term remains uncertain and the trust will fail. For example, a settlor cannot simply just leave it to the unfettered opinion of a third party as to what is meant by a particular term.[112]

Conclusion

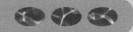

This chapter has looked at the certainty requirements needed for the creation of a trust. It is an essential requirement of trust law that a trust must be one which the courts can control, administer and eventually execute in favour of the beneficiaries. In order for the courts to be able to do this the settlor must satisfy the certainties of intention, subject matter and objects. It is paramount that the settlor intends to create a legally binding obligation on the trustee; the law requires the use of such words or conduct that imposes

---

[108] [1953] Ch. 810.
[109] [1979] 1 All ER 296.
[110] [1948] Ch. 747.
[111] [1948] Ch. 747 at 761.
[112] *Re Jones* [1953] Ch. 125.

an imperative obligation to hold the trust property for the benefit of the beneficiaries. So, whilst the settlor need not use any technical language to create a trust, he needs to evince an intention to impose an obligation on the trustee. As well as an intention to create a legally binding obligation, the settlor must identify with precision the subject matter of the trust, that is, the property on which the trust is to attach. Not only must it be clear as to what actually forms the trust property, but also the settlor must identify the extent of the beneficial interest. This chapter examined the extent to which it was possible to attach a trust to property which is not yet ascertained. A fundamental distinction was seen between unascertained property of a tangible nature and unascertained property of an intangible nature. The law allows a trust to be created over unascertained property of an intangible nature, for example shares in a company, yet it does not allow a trust over unascertained property of a tangible nature, such as bottles of wine. The basis of the distinction relates to the fact that intangible property is the same in nature, whereas tangible property can be different even though belonging to the same description. The distinction, however, makes little sense when viewed from the tracing rules of equity.

Finally, the settlor must identify the beneficiaries with precision. If he is creating a trust in favour of a large group of beneficiaries, such as a class, he must identify that class with an element of conceptual certainty. In other words, the beneficiary or class of beneficiaries must have a dictionary meaning which is understood by both the trustee and the courts. It has been seen that the rule of certainty of objects varies with the type of trust in question. Where the trust is fixed, so that the beneficial entitlement of the beneficiaries is fixed from the beginning, the trustees must be able to draw a complete list of the beneficiaries. Where the trust is discretionary the trustees will be able to execute the trust, provided that they can say with certainty that an individual is within the class of beneficiaries to benefit. Once a trust has satisfied the element of certainty, the next stage will be to see whether the trust complies with the formal requirements such as writing or deeds. Chapter 5 goes on to examine the formal requirements needed for the creation of trusts.

●●● Case study

Consider the following case study.

On her retirement as a professor of medicine at the South-Western University, Aveline executed two documents. The first document was an *inter vivos* settlement in which she settled the following property:

£60,000 to my trustees to be distributed at their unfettered discretion amongst such of my good friends and colleagues who I have known at the various universities that I have worked for.

One of my flats in London to be selected by my daughter as an absolute gift for herself and the remaining flats to be sold and the proceeds of sale to be invested for a period of 21 years in order to provide a reasonable income for my two nieces.

A sum of £200,000 to be distributed equally amongst my grandchildren, my nieces and nephews.

My cottage to be sold by my trustees and the proceeds to be distributed amongst my relatives. However, before sale, the trustees to allow any one of my good friends and associates to purchase the contents of my cottage at a price 25 per cent less than the market price.

In a second document, Aveline's will, she left her entire residuary estate to her trustees to distribute to such of her family members who in the opinion of the trustees deserved it. The will provided that, should the trustees fail to distribute to any of the family members, the estate was to be given to her best friend Valerie.

Tragically, Aveline's daughter died from a rare illness last year. She never got round to selecting one of Aveline's flats in London.

Advise on the validity of the dispositions in the two documents.

Moot points

1 What is the rationale behind the certainty requirements of a trust?

2 Does the use of precatory words by a settlor or a testator necessarily mean that a trust will not be found?

3 How do you distinguish between the decision in *Palmer* v *Simmonds* (1854) 2 Drew 221 and the decision in *Re Last* [1958] P 137; [1958] 2 WLR 186?

4 It is possible to create a trust over unascertained trust intangible property, but it is not possible to do the same in respect of tangible property. What is the justification for this distinction? You are advised to read the decision in *Hunter* v *Moss* [1994] 1 WLR 452. Additionally, read the following:

Ockleton, M. 'Share and Share Alike' (1994) CLJ 448.

Martin, J. 'Certainty of Subject Matter: A Defence of *Hunter* v *Moss*' [1996] Conv. 223.

5 Post *McPhail* v *Doulton* [1970] 2 All ER 228 it is clear that the test of certainty of objects for a discretionary trust is the 'given postulant test' or sometimes referred to as the 'is or is not' test. The validity of a discretionary trust requires the trustees to be in a position to say whether a given beneficiary is or not within the class. How was this test applied by the Court of Appeal in *Re Baden's Deed Trusts (No. 2)* [1972] 3 WLR 250? Did the three judges in the Court of Appeal take a similar view in applying the test?

6 In *Re Barlow's Will Trusts* [1975] 1 All ER 296 it was held that where a gift was created in favour of a class subject to a condition precedent, then a less strict test applied to the way in which the class was described by the person making the gift. Does the mere fact that a gift is subject to a condition precedent necessarily remove the element of conceptual uncertainty which may otherwise exist if the condition was absent?

Further reading

Emery, C.T. 'The Most Hallowed Principle – Certainty of Beneficiaries of Trusts and Powers of Appointment' (1982) LQR Vol 98 551. Provides an excellent account of the test for certainty of objects for trusts and powers and, in doing so, takes a critical look at the requisite components of the objects test such as conceptual certainty, evidential certainty, ascertainability and administrative workability.

Gbrich, Y. 'Baden: Awakening the Conceptually Moribund Trust' (1974) 37 MLR 64. Examines the decision of the Court of Appeal in *Re Baden (No. 2)*.

Harris, J.W. 'Trust, Power and Duty' (1971) LQR 31.

Hawkins, A.J. 'The Exercise by Trustees of a Discretion' [1963] Conv 117. Considers the manner in which the trustees should exercise a discretion.

Hopkins, J. 'Certain Uncertainties of Trusts and Powers' (1971) CLJ 68. Looks at the decision in *Mcphail* v *Doulton* and discusses the assimilation of the test for certainty of objects for a discretionary trust and a power of appointment.

Martin, J. 'Certainty of Subject Matter: A Defence of *Hunter* v *Moss*' [1996] Conv. 223. Identifies that the decision in *Hunter* v *Moss* was right on its facts, in particular when looked at from the point of view of unconscionability.

Mckay, L. '*Re Barlow* and the Certainty of Objects Rule' [1980] Conv. 263. Critically evaluates the decision in *Re Barlow* and explains that it is inconsistent with the ruling of the House of Lords in *Re Gulbenkian's S.T.* [1970] AC 508.

Ockleton, M. 'Share and Share Alike' (1994) CLJ 448. Provides a critique of the ruling of the Court of Appeal in *Hunter* v *Moss* and identified the impracticalities of the ruling.

5
Formalities

Learning objectives

After reading this chapter you should be able to:

→ understand and explain the importance of the formal requirements needed for the creation of trusts and dealings thereunder

→ understand the formal requirements needed for the creation of trusts intended to take effect on the death of a person

→ understand the formal requirements for *inter vivos* trusts as set out in s. 53(1) of the Law of Property Act 1925

→ explain the ambit of s. 53(1)(b) Law of Property Act 1925 and the consequences of failure to comply with the section

→ explain the ambit of s. 53(1)(c) Law of Property Act 1925 and its operation in the context of the decided cases

→ understand the interplay between trust law principles and tax considerations in the decided cases

→ understand the exemption of the formality requirements to implied trusts in s. 53(2) Law of Property Act 1925.

The Vandervell Saga 1958–1965: Formula 1 racing, the Royal College of Surgeons, the Inland Revenue and the courts

One particular litigation in trust law, which students remember more so than any other litigation, is that between the Inland Revenue Commissioners and Tony Vandervell. There are many reasons for this, not least that it reminds them of the complexities of trust law and the interplay between trust law and fiscal considerations. Before the facts of the Vandervell litigation are examined, a little more must be said about Tony Vandervell, who no doubt would have wished to have been remembered for more than just his dealings with the Inland Revenue Commissioners.

Vandervell came from a very wealthy family which was engaged in an electrical business. In the 1940s Vandervell set up his own company called Vandervell Products Ltd which produced bearings for racing cars. The success of this company made him a very wealthy individual. In the early 1950s Vandervell decided to manufacture his own racing cars and race them at Formula 1 level. He organised the Vanwall team which won six out of the nine Formula 1 races in the 1958 Formula 1 season. In addition to his love of cars and racing, Vandervell donated money to charity and it is precisely his involvement in charity that was to become the source of much litigation not only lasting several years, but also with visits to the Court of Appeal and the House of Lords until his eventual death in 1967. So, what went wrong?

The facts leading up to the litigation concerned shares in Vandervell Products Ltd, which were either held absolutely by Vandervell or on trust for him by National Provincial Bank Ltd as his nominees. In 1958 he decided to fund a chair in pharmacology at the Royal College of Surgeons. In order to do this he instructed National Provincial Bank to transfer 100,000 shares to the college who would receive the dividends in order to fund the chair. The college would then grant an option to purchase the shares once the chair was funded. In 1961 the option was exercised and Vandervell instructed his trustees to hold the shares for his children. This arrangement formed the basis of a tax avoidance scheme, which as will be observed in this chapter, proved to be more complicated than originally thought.

It is amazing how these rather simple set of facts resulted in a mass of litigation involving two trips to the House of Lords and one to the Court of Appeal. This chapter explores the formal requirements needed to create a trust and the formal requirements applicable to subsequent dealings with the interests, particularly the equitable interest under a trust. It will be observed that, like in the Vandervell litigation, the creation and subsequent dealings with equitable interests is a complicated matter. This is because the law requires in many cases strict compliance with writing in order to avoid uncertainty and fraud in relation to trusts.

The Vandervell litigation illustrates the consequences that an individual may face when failing to understand and comply with the formal requirements of trust law, in particular the taxation implications involved in the transfer of equitable interests under a trust. This chapter explores the formal requirements of trusts.

Introduction

This chapter looks at the formal requirements needed for the creation of both *inter vivos* and testamentary trusts. A trust may satisfy all elements of certainty, but its enforce-ability may well depend on formal requirements. Formality is concerned with the issue of whether the creation of the trust requires recourse to writing in some form or another. The basic rule is that a trust of pure personal property can be created without any recourse to any formality. However, a trust of land will require manifestation and proof in writing in order for it to be valid. A trust intended to take effect on the death of the testator must be put in a valid will, which as will be observed below will require the formality requirements in s. 9 of the Wills Act 1837. Formality will also be important once the trust is created and where the beneficiary attempts to deal with his or her beneficial interest without necessarily terminating the trust.

   ## Testamentary trusts

A trust which is intended to take effect on the death of a person must comply with the formal requirements of a will set out in s. 9 of the Wills Act 1837 as shown below.

> **KEY STATUTE**
>
> ### Section 9 Wills Act 1837
>
> No will shall be valid unless –
>
> 1. it is in writing, and signed by the testator, or by some other person in his presence and by his direction; and
>
> 2. it appears that the testator intended by his signature to give effect to the will; and
>
> 3. the signature is made or acknowledged by the testator in the presence of two or more witnesses present at the time; and
>
> 4. each witness either –
>   (i) attests and signs the will; or
>   (ii) acknowledges his signature,
>   in the presence of the testator (but not necessarily in the presence of any other witnesses), but no form of attestation shall be necessary.

Thus, a trust intended to take effect on the testator's death must be put in a properly executed and attested will or a codicil. A codicil is a testamentary instrument intended to add to an existing will. Codicils are common in adding to or altering an existing will. The codicil must, however, meet the same formality as that prescribed for the creation of a will.

   ## *Inter vivos* trusts

The relevant formalities governing the creation of trusts and the subsequent dealings with equitable interests are to be found in section 53 of the Law of Property Act 1925.

There are three main provisions which need investigation:

1 S. 53(1)(b) provides that 'a declaration of trust respecting any land or any interest therein must be manifested and proved by some writing by some person who is able to declare such trust or by his will'.

2 S. 53(1)(c) provides that 'a disposition of an equitable interest or trust subsisting at the time of the disposition, must be in writing signed by the person disposing of the same, or by his agent thereunto lawfully authorised in writing or by his will'.

3 S. 53(2) provides that ss. 53(1)(b) and 53(1)(c) 'do not affect the creation or operation of resulting, implied or constructive trusts'.

A contract to create a trust of land or any interest therein will be governed by s. 2(1) Law of Property (Miscellaneous Provisions) Act 1989. This section requires the contract to be made in writing and by incorporating all terms which the parties have expressly agreed in one document. The section will also apply to a contract to dispose to any equitable interest in land.

Section 53(2) exempts resulting, implied and constructive trusts from the formal requirements of s. 53(1)(b) and (c). These trusts arise by operation of law and thus do not need to comply with formality. However, it is clear that once these trust have arisen, their subsequent operation are certainly within the scope of s. 53(1).[1]

Declarations of trust

Trusts of pure personalty

A declaration of trust in respect of personal property can be made orally. Thus, a trust of a painting or shares in a private company need not require any formality. The only question in such a case is whether there is a sufficient intention to create a trust. For example, in **Paul v Constance**[2] Mr Constance, who had separated from his wife, lived with a certain Mrs Paul. In 1973 Mr Constance received a sum of £950 representing compensation for injuries he had suffered at his place of employment. Both Mr Constance and his partner Mrs Paul agreed that the money should be placed in a bank account. The account was opened in Mr Constance's name primarily because he did not want the embarrassment of opening a joint account in his and Mrs Paul's name because they were not married. For a period of some 13 months sums of money were deposited in that account representing the winnings from bingo games played by both of them. It was clearly the understanding between Mr Constance and Mrs Paul that the bingo winnings and the money in the account were as much Mrs Paul's as they were Mr Constance's. When Mr Constance died, his wife took over the administration of his estate. Mrs Paul brought an action against Mrs Constance arguing that the money in the bank account was held by Mr Constance on trust for himself and her jointly. Scarman LJ found a trust in favour of the lady beneficiary in respect of a bank account in the name of the settlor. The settlor had manifested an intention over a long period of time that the money in the account was as much hers as it was the settlor's.

It is striking that a trust of £1 million can be created orally whilst, as will be seen later, a trust of even one square foot of land needs to be evidenced in writing. Much of the

---

[1] This is discussed in much more detail later in the chapter.
[2] [1977] 1 WLR 527.

rationale behind this distinction lies in the relative importance of land both as a commodity and as the predominant subject matter of many trusts at the time of the Law of Property Act 1925. In contemporary trust law most trusts will be created in writing. Writing is particularly significant to the settlor because it is the very existence of writing that will show relevant authorities, such as the Inland Revenue, where the beneficial interest in property lies at any given time.

Trusts of land and interests therein

Section 53(1)(b) of the Law of Property Act 1925 requires that a declaration of trust respecting any land or any interest therein must be manifested and proved by some writing. The section applies to the creation of a trust of a fee simple absolute in possession as well as any other interest in land such as a lease.[3] It requires the declaration of trust to be manifested and proved by some writing. The evidence in writing of the trust need not, however, be contemporaneous with the declaration of trust. For example, it is possible for land to be conveyed to the intended trustee on the understanding that he is to hold for the beneficiary and then for the proof in writing to follow later on. Furthermore, is not necessary for the writing to be in any particular form; however, the writing must make it clear that there was an intention to create a trust.[4] The requisite signature must be that of the settlor and not that of any other person. Section 53(1)(b) specifically precludes an agent of the settlor from signing such a declaration.[5]

The effect of non-compliance with s. 53(1)(b)

APPLYING THE LAW

Thomas conveyed Ivy Cottage to his son Mathew on the understanding that Mathew would hold the cottage on trust for Sarah. This understanding was not put in writing; however, Charlotte, who happens to be Thomas's solicitor, is aware that the conveyance of Ivy Cottage to Mathew was on the understanding that he would hold it for Sarah. Charlotte has some correspondence in her possession from Mathew which suggests that Mathew is holding the cottage on trust for Sarah. Mathew is now denying that he ever agreed to hold Ivy Cottage on trust for Sarah.

What is Sarah's position?

Failure to comply with section 53(1)(b) will render the intended trust of land unenforceable but not void.[6] To hold the trust completely void would produce a rather strange result in circumstances where land is conveyed on the oral strength that the intended trustee will hold on trust, but then refuses to do so on the grounds that there is an absence of compliance with section 53(1)(b). To hold the trust void in such a situation

---

[3] S. 53(1)(b) replaces s. 7 Statute of Frauds 1677.
[4] *Smith* v *Matthews* (1861) 3 De GF & J 139 at 151.
[5] This can be contrasted with s. 53(1)(c) which allows an agent of the beneficiary to sign on his behalf in order to dispose of an equitable interest; see later.
[6] *Gardner* v *Rowe* (1828) 5 Russ. 258.

would allow the intended trustee to use the statute as an instrument to set up his own fraud. Equity will not allow a statue to be used as an instrument for fraud. In such a situation the court will enforce the trust, provided the beneficiary can produce oral evidence supporting the existence of trust. Not enforcing the trust would allow the intended trustee to walk away with an unjust enrichment.

The seminal case is that of **Rochefoucauld v Boustead**[7] which was decided under the old s. 7 of the Statute of Frauds 1677. The facts of this case involved a mortgagor who had mortgaged land (the Delmar Estates in Ceylon) to the mortgagee. The mortgagee sold the land to the defendant on the oral understanding that the defendant would hold the land on trust for the mortgagor subject to repayment to the defendant of the purchase price and any expenses. The defendant, in breach of the oral agreement, sold the land to a third party at a profit without any account to the mortgagor. The mortgagor sought an account for the profits on the grounds that the land in which the profits were made was held on trust for the mortgagor. In the Court of Appeal Lindley LJ held that:

> the Statute of Frauds does not prevent the proof of a fraud; and it is a fraud on the part of a person to whom land is conveyed as trustee, and who knows that it was so conveyed, to deny the trust and claim the land himself. Consequently, notwithstanding the statute, it is competent for a person claiming land conveyed to another to prove by parol evidence that it was so conveyed upon trust for the claimant, and that the grantee, knowing the facts, is denying the trust and relying upon the forms of the conveyance and the statute, in order to keep the land himself.[8]

Where there has been failure to comply with s. 53(1)(b) of the Law of Property Act, the intended trust is indeed unenforceable. The intended beneficiary of the settlor must purport to show by parol evidence that a trust was indeed intended and that the intended trustee did indeed take the trust property as trustee. However, the courts will not allow the enforcement of a trust which fails to comply with s. 53(1)(b) where there is simply no evidence of the trust, or where the evidence put forward to suggest that there was indeed a trust is pursuant to an unlawful act. The matter is neatly illustrated by the decision of the High Court in **Random House UK Ltd v Allason**[9] where the question before the court was whether land owned by the defendant was held on trust. The defendant owed money to the claimant and the claimant sought to set aside a number of transactions under s. 423 of the Insolvency Act 1986.[10] In respect of certain land, the defendant purported to argue that he was not the beneficial owner of the land and that he held it upon trust for others. The defendant could not provide any credible evidence to suggest that the land had indeed been held upon trust. In the course of his judgment, David Richards J held that in

> order to establish a beneficial interest in the property in favour of the trust, there must be a written declaration of trust complying with s. 53(1)(b) of the Law of Property Act 1925. In the absence of an original document complying with those requirements, the trustees had to satisfy the requirements of the secondary evidence rule before they could rely on the purported copy declaration of trust. They must satisfy the court that the original document existed or had existed, that it had been lost or destroyed and that a reasonable explanation of this had been given . . . Random House submitted that the trustees had failed to satisfy the secondary evidence rule and could not rely on the purported copy declaration of trust.

---

[7] [1897] 1 Ch. 196.
[8] [1897] 1 Ch. 196 at 206.
[9] [2008] EWHC 2854 (Ch).
[10] This section is explored in more detail in Chapter 9.

I agree. However, as stated above, the evidence goes further and satisfies me that there never has been a genuine declaration of trust.[11]

What trust is being enforced if s. 53 is not complied with?

The principle enunciated in *Rochefoucald v Boustead* allows parol evidence to enforce the trust despite the statute. It is, however, questionable why equity should totally disregard the statute and enforce the trust in favour of the beneficiary. If the fear is that a disregard of the statute will allow the trustee to be unjustly enriched, surely the unjust enrichment can be reversed by imposing a resulting trust in favour of the settlor or his estate. In this way equity can prevent both a disregard of the statute and unjust enrichment in the hands of the intended trustee. However, the courts have not taken the resulting trust avenue and have instead sought to enforce the trust in favour of the intended beneficiary.

If the court is enforcing the trust in favour of the intended beneficiary, one question which has often been asked in this context is what is the nature of the trust being enforced? Is the court enforcing the express trust despite the lack of writing, or is it enforcing an implied constructive trust to prevent the unconscionable conduct of the intended trustee? The accepted view is that the court is giving effect to the express trust, which, despite lacking evidence in writing, is being enforced in the face of parol evidence. In *Rochefoucauld v Boustead* Lindley LJ stated that 'the trust which the plaintiff has established is clearly an express trust . . . one which the plaintiff and defendant intended to create'.[12] However, despite the words of Lindley LJ it is submitted that later authorities have not necessarily sought to enforce the express trust: instead they have implied a constructive trust. The imposition of a constructive trust is justified on the grounds of the unconscionable conduct of the trustee who is seeking to use the absence of formality to set up his or her own fraud. For example, in *Re Densham*[13] Goff J commented that:

> [t]o hold such an agreement unenforceable unless in writing . . . is in my opinion contrary to equitable principles, because once the agreement is formed it would be unconscionable for a party to set up the statute and repudiate the agreement. Accordingly, in my judgment he or she becomes a constructive trustee of the property so far as necessary to give effect to the agreement. That, in my judgment, was established long ago in *Rochefoucauld v Boustead*.[14]

Declaration of sub-trust

APPLYING THE LAW

Jennifer is holding 20,000 shares in a private company on trust for her daughter Simone. Simone has orally told her niece, Amy, that she will hold her interest in the 20,000 shares on trust for Amy.

Is there a valid declaration of trust in favour of Amy?

---

[11] [2008] EWHC 2854 (Ch) at para. 46.
[12] [1897] 1 Ch. 196 at 208.
[13] [1975] 3 All ER 726; see also *Bannister v Bannister* [1948] 2 All ER 133, *Binions v Evans* [1972] Ch. 359 and *Lyus v Prowsa Developments* [1982] 1 WLR 1044.
[14] [1975] 3 All ER 726 at 732.

A rather different situation arises where a beneficiary under a subsisting trust attempts to declare himself a trustee of that interest in favour of another. For example, where T1 holds on trust for B1 and B1 declares himself a trustee of his equitable interest in favour of B2. This is illustrated in Figure 5.1.

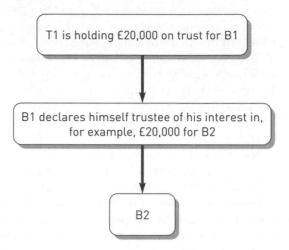

Figure 5.1

In such a case T1 is already holding the legal title for B1, and if it is the intention of B1 to divest himself of his equitable interest in the £20,000, it is B1 that should fall out of the picture as he is simply a bare trustee of his interest. T1 thenceforth holds the title for B2. However, B1 can only remove himself from the picture if he complies with s. 53(1)(c) of the Law of Property Act 1925, which requires that a disposition of an equitable interest subsisting under a trust must be in writing and signed by the person disposing of the same.[15] Thus, B1's oral declaration to the effect that he holds for B2 would be ineffective to create a trust in favour of B2.[16]

It is, however, possible for an equitable owner under a subsisting trust to effectively declare a sub-trust. In such a situation the equitable owner is not said to fall out of the picture: instead his presence is absolutely vital to the sub-trust which he has declared in favour of a new beneficiary. What distinguishes this situation from the situation discussed above is that, unlike B1 in the first diagram, who acts as a bare trustee, in the truly sub-trust situation B1 is said to have retained active duties and as such is an active trustee.[17] The illustration in Figure 5.2 can be used to explain the creation of a sub-trust where B1 does not fall out of the picture.

---

[15] S. 53(1)(c) is discussed in more detail below; see, however, *Grey* v *IRC* [1960] AC 1.

[16] This view is supported by a number of nineteenth-century cases; see *Grainge* v *Wilberforce* (1889) 5 TLR 436 where Chitty J in the course of his judgment explained that where T1 was trustee for B1, who was trustee for B2, then T1 had no option but to convey to B2. However, this would be only possible if B1 falls out of the picture by complying with s. 53(1)(c). See also *Onslow* v *Wallis* (1849) 1 Mac. and G. 506 and *Re Lashmar* [1891] 1 Ch. 258. This view is also supported by Professor Hayton in *Hayton and Marshall, Cases and Commentary on the Law of Trusts and Equitable Obligation* 12th edn (2005) at p. 84. For a rather different interpretation of these nineteenth-century cases, see B. Green 'Grey, Oughtred and Vandervell – A Contextual Appraisal' (1984) 47 MLR 385 at p. 396.

[17] *Re Lashmar* [1891] 1 Ch. 258.

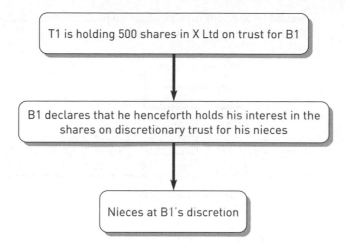

Figure 5.2

Thus, where B1 declares that he will henceforth hold his equitable interest in the 500 shares on a discretionary trust for his nieces, he remains within the picture as he retains active duties in connection with the sub-trust. B1 alone is capable of exercising the discretion in favour of his nieces. Such a declaration of sub-trust would not require any formality unless, of course, the declaration of sub-trust concerned land or an interest therein.[18]

Dispositions of equitable interests

Once a settlor has declared a trust in favour of a beneficiary, provided that the beneficiary is in a position to deal with his or her equitable interest, there is nothing stopping the beneficiary from either terminating the trust or dealing with the equitable interest. It may well be that a beneficiary does not wish to terminate the trust, but wishes to deal with the beneficial interest. The most simple thing the beneficiary can do with the beneficial interest is to transfer it, whether voluntarily or in return for consideration, to another person. This section looks at the formal requirements needed if the beneficiary attempts to deal with his or her equitable interest.

The ambit of section 53(1)(c) Law of Property Act 1925

Section 53(1)(c) deals with dispositions of equitable interests. The section requires a disposition of an equitable interest or trust[19] to be in writing and signed by the person disposing of such an interest.[20] Take, for example, Alf who is holding property on trust for Sid. Sid wishes to transfer his interest in the trust property to his son John. In such a case Sid would be regarded as disposing of his equitable interest to his son and would therefore need to comply with the formal requirements of s. 53(1)(c) (see Figure 5.3). Sid's interest in the property would only move if the disposition was put in writing and

---

[18] In which case the declaration would have to comply with s. 53(1)(b) and evidenced in writing.
[19] The use of the word 'trust' means the same thing as 'equitable interest'.
[20] This section replaced s. 9 of the Statute of Frauds 1677.

signed by Sid. Any oral direction to hold in favour of John would be ineffective in transferring his interest in the property.

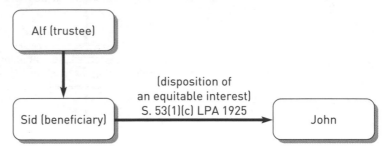

Figure 5.3

The rationale behind s. 53(1)(c), like that of its predecessor s. 9 Statute of Frauds 1677, is to prevent fraud. In **Vandervell v IRC**[21] Lord Upjohn explained that the section had a dual function. In the first place, the section was designed to prevent hidden oral transactions in equitable interests in fraud of those truly entitled. Secondly, the section was designed to help enable the trustees to establish where a beneficial interest resided at any particular time.[22] These dual functions are easily understood when it is appreciated that a beneficiary has nothing more than a mere *chose in action* to pass on to another person. A chose in action is an intangible property form and cannot be passed by delivery of possession. Thus, compliance with s. 53 (1)(c) provides the person to whom the equitable interest has been disposed with the necessary proof of ownership of that equitable interest.

The section is only satisfied if the disposition is in writing. Thus, unlike s. 53(1)(b) of the Law of Property Act 1925, which requires that a declaration of trust be manifested and proved by some writing, s. 53(1)(c) requires the actual disposition to be in writing. If the disposition is not in writing, the equitable interest simply does not move. It is quite possible, however, that the disposition may be effected by more than one document, provided there is sufficient reference to each other.[23]

The context of the s. 53(1)(c) case law

Whilst the rule contained in s. 53(1)(c) of the Law of Property Act 1925 is relatively clear, its application in the relevant cases is far from so. In the words of Lord Wilberforce in **Vandervell v IRC** the section 'is certainly not easy to apply to the various transactions in equitable interests which now occur'.[24] Much of the case law on s. 53(1)(c) has been decided in a fiscal context where owners of property have attempted to avoid paying certain forms of tax by devising schemes avoiding the need for writing. The principal form of tax in question in some of the cases is *ad valorem* stamp duty.[25] *Ad valorem* stamp duty

---

[21] [1967] 2 AC 291.

[22] [1967] 2 AC 291.

[23] *Re Danish Bacon Co Ltd Staff Pension Fund* [1971] 1 All ER 486, where it was held that a disposition in writing could be satisfied by two or more documents, provided they were sufficiently interconnected.

[24] [1967] 2 AC 291 at 329. For a detailed examination of the s. 53(1)(c) case law, see B. Green, 'Grey, Oughtred and Vandervell – A Contextual Appraisal' (1984) 47 MLR 385. See also G. Battersby, 'Formalities For the Dispositions of Equitable Interests Under a Trust' (1979) Conv. 175.

[25] Abolished by the Finance Act 1985 and now only applies to transfers of land by the Finance Act 2003.

was payable on deeds of transfer but not on the transaction itself. In other words, where a person had to use a deed to transfer an interest in property to another, the deed was chargeable with *ad valorem* stamp duty. If the transaction could be effected without the need for a written deed or other instrument, the transaction was not liable to tax. Being *ad valorem* in its nature, this meant the greater the value of the interest being transferred the greater the tax payable on the deed. In this context, it can be seen why s. 53(1)(c) provided a fertile source of litigation initiated by Inland Revenue Commissioners attempting to use written deeds used in pursuant to s. 53(1)(c) as deeds subject to *ad valorem* stamp duty.

The s. 53(1)(c) case law is generally regarded by most commentators as complex. The complexity is compounded by the fact that the cases have been decided in rather complex fiscal matters. Nevertheless, there are a number of principles which emerge from the decided cases and these are examined below.

Assignment of an equitable interest

The most simple case where s. 53(1)(c) applies is where a beneficiary assigns his or her interest to another. This is illustrated in Figure 5.4.

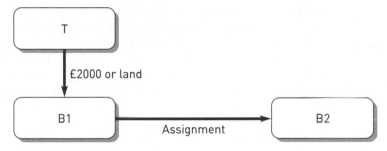

Figure 5.4

In such a case where B1 wishes to assign his or her interest to B2 then this must be in writing. It does not matter that the beneficiary's interest is in land or personal property, as the section applies to dispositions of equitable interests in both real and personal property.

Direction by equitable owner to trustee to hold for another

APPLYING THE LAW

Suresh is holding £30,000 on trust for Todd under a trust created three years ago by Todd's father. Todd is 18 years of age and fully entitled to the £30,000. Todd is about to start a business with his friend Jim who needs further capital to get started. Todd telephoned Suresh and told him to hold the £30,000 on trust for Jim until such time Jim needed the money. Tragically, Todd died last week. Jim claims to be entitled to the £30,000; however, Todd's wife claims that all of Todd's property was left to her in his will.

Who is entitled to the £30,000?

Where a beneficiary under a subsisting trust directs the trustee to hold the beneficial interest in the trust in favour of another person, he or she must do so in writing. Such a direction amounts to a disposition of the beneficiary's equitable interest and must comply with the requirements of s. 53(1)(c). This is illustrated in Figure 5.5 where B1 is entitled under a trust but directs her trustee to hold the interest for her sister B2.

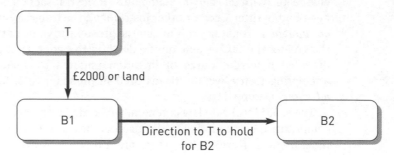

Figure 5.5

The disposition must be in writing and signed by the beneficiary disposing of the equitable interest. If the disposition complies with the formal requirements of s. 53(1)(c), the beneficiary will have divested itself of its equitable interest in the trust and thereafter have no further role in the trust. The trustee will have no choice but to hold for the new beneficiary and must convey the legal title to the property to the new beneficiary if the new beneficiary is able and willing to terminate the trust.

VISIT CASE NAVIGATOR

It is clear that an oral direction by a beneficiary to a trustee will not be sufficient to divest itself of the equitable interest in the trust. The leading authority is *Grey v IRC*[26] This case involved a somewhat strange attempt to avoid paying stamp duty on a transfer of 18,000 shares by a settlor to his grandchildren. With hindsight it can be seen that the objectives of the settlor could have been met without recourse to the events which actually took place in the case. It is not surprising, therefore, that the House of Lords described this cases as a botched-up stamp duty avoidance scheme. The facts of the case involved a transfer of 18,000 shares by Hunter to his nominees on 1 February 1955. In other words, the nominees became trustees of the 18,000 shares in favour of Hunter. Earlier, Hunter had also created six settlements of nominal sums in favour of his grandchildren. On 18 February in the presence of both his trustees and solicitor, Hunter orally directed that the trustees should thenceforth hold the shares in equal amounts for his grandchildren under the six settlements which had been created previously. The intention was that each grandchild would be entitled to 3000 shares and that Hunter would cease to have any further interest in those shares. On 25 March the trustees executed six deeds supplemental to the six settlements, declaring that since 18 February the shares were held for the children in equal amounts. The question in the House of Lords was whether the deeds of 25 March constituted voluntary dispositions of Hunter's property, thereby attracting *ad valorem* stamp duty. On the other hand, as contested by counsel for the trustees, did the direction of the 18 February in fact constitute a declaration of new trust in favour of the grandchildren?[27] If it was to be treated as a declaration of trust it would not have to comply with any formality since it involved personal property and

---

[26] [1960] AC 1.

[27] It was argued by counsel for the trustees that the transaction was not within the spirit of s. 9 of the Statute of Frauds which spoke of 'grants and assignments'. Furthermore, being a consolidating statute, the court was required to interpret s. 53(1)(c) with least change in the law. In the House of Lords, Lord Radcliffe held that, whilst the Law of Property Act was undoubtedly a consolidating statute, what was consolidated were two previous property law Acts (the Law of Property Act 1922 and the Law of Property (Amendment) Act 1924. Section 9 of the Statute of Frauds was not within the ambit of the 1922 Act and was repealed by the 1924 Act.

not land. *Ad valorem* stamp duty is only payable on deeds of transfer and not on the transfer itself.

The House of Lords held that the oral direction of 18 February constituted a disposition of Hunter's equitable interest and thus could not pass to his grandchildren unless it was put in writing. It therefore followed that the deeds of 25 March were the real and effective time of the disposition and as such they were liable to *ad valorem* stamp duty. According to Lord Radcliffe the term 'disposition' was to be given a very wide meaning, covering a situation where the beneficial owner directs his trustees to hold for another.

Grey v *IRC*[28] is a case where Hunter wanted to avoid paying stamp duty on a transfer of shares from himself to his grandchildren. Hunter and his trustees thought this could be done by creating six nominal settlements and then for Hunter to transfer his shares to his trustees only for them to then declare that they held for the grandchildren. If the intention was to transfer the shares on trust for the grandchildren then this objective could have been met without recourse to any writing by a simple declaration from the outset that he wished his trustees to hold his shares on trust for the children in the respective shares. This would not have required any formality as it would have involved a simple declaration of trust of pure personalty.

Direction by equitable owner to trustee to transfer the legal title to a third party

APPLYING THE LAW

Suppose that Steve is holding £10,000 on trust for Mark, who is absolutely entitled to the money and in a position to terminate the trust. Mark is about to enrol on a postgraduate course at his local university and needs to pay £10,000 for his fees. He has instructed Steve to transfer the £10,000, which Steve is holding on his behalf, directly to the finance department of his local university. Steve has transferred the legal title to the university.

What has happened to Mark's equitable interest in the £10,000? Is it still with Mark?

Instead of directing the trustee to hold the equitable interest for another, a beneficiary under a trust may request the trustee to transfer the legal title to a third party. For example, let us say that a beneficiary entitled under a trust is accepted on a university course and requires money to pay for her fees. She can access the trust money in one of two ways. Firstly, she can terminate the trust providing she is 18 years[29] old and ask the trustees to pay her what she is entitled to under the trust and use the money to pay her fees. Or, secondly, she can simply ask her trustees to make a direct payment to her university. In the latter case, the question arises as to whether any formality is required in order to complete the transfer. The transfer of the legal title would, of course, require the necessary formality, depending on the type of property concerned. So, a transfer of land would require a formal conveyance; a transfer of shares would require the necessary stock transfer form to be completed; whereas a transfer of money or a painting would require delivery thereof.

---

[28] [1960] AC 1.
[29] The Rule in *Saunders* v *Vautier* (1841) 4 Beav. 115.

Although the transfer of the legal title does not raise any particularly problematic issues, a question which has arisen in the case law is whether s. 53(1)(c) applies in this context, given the fact that the beneficiary had an equitable interest under the trust and can only dispose of it in favour of a third party if it is put in writing. In other words, is there a requirement for a separate assignment of the beneficiary's equitable interest? This is illustrated in Figure 5.6.

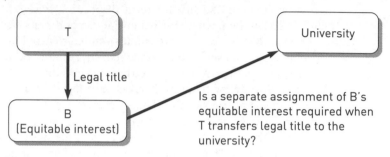

Figure 5.6

The issue arose in **Vandervell v IRC**[30] where the House of Lords held that prima facie a transfer of the legal title at the request of the beneficiary carries with it the equitable interest, thereby vesting absolute ownership in the transferee. There is no need for a separate assignment of the beneficiary's equitable interest, because in effect the trust is destroyed and the third party transferee will have acquired an absolute title to the property. On the facts of the case, Vandervell, a wealthy businessman, directed his nominee (National Provincial Bank) to transfer shares held by them for him to the Royal College of Surgeons whose intention it was to endow a chair of pharmacology. Vandervell agreed that the college could have ownership of his shares in his company and use the dividend money to finance the chair. It was also agreed that once the dividends had paid for the purpose of endowing the chair of pharmacology, the college would give an option to Vandervell to purchase the shares for a nominal sum of £5000. The bank duly transferred the legal title to the shares to the college which granted an option to purchase the shares. The option was transferred to the Vandervell Trust Company without any instructions by Vandervell as to whose benefit it was to be held for.

The Inland Revenue claimed surtax from Vandervell on the dividends declared between 1957 and 1961 (this being the period under which the shares remained with the college), on the grounds that Vandervell had not completely divested himself of his beneficial ownership in the shares even though the legal title to them had been transferred to the college. Two arguments were presented by the Inland Revenue in support of their claim. The argument which succeeded in making a case for liability for surtax related to the grant of the option to purchase the shares which had been transferred to the Vandervell Trust Company. The Revenue claimed that since Vandervell had transferred the option to the trust company without specifying who the benefactor of the option was, the option would have to be held on resulting trust for Vandervell himself. The majority of the House of Lords held that the option was indeed held on resulting trust for Vandervell who, therefore, retained some beneficial interest in the shares and therefore was liable to pay surtax on those shares.[31] The issue of liability for surtax was therefore clearly decided on this basis.

---

[30] [1967] 2 AC 291.
[31] See Income Taxes Act 1952, s. 415; the current legislation is the Income and Corporation Taxes Act 1988 ss. 684, 685.

The Revenue's primary argument was that since the bank was holding the shares as nominees for Vandervell, who, therefore, merely had an equitable interest in such shares, his equitable interest could only pass to the Royal College of Surgeons if it was put in writing pursuant to s. 53(1)(c) of the Law of Property Act 1925. The House of Lords rejected this contention, holding that s. 53(1)(c) had no application where the equitable owner, being in a position to terminate the trust, directs the trustees to transfer the legal title to a third party. Lord Upjohn explained that 'when the beneficial owner owns the whole beneficial estate and is in a position to give directions to his bare trustee with regard to the legal as well as equitable estate there can be no possible ground for invoking the section where the beneficial owner wants to deal with the legal estate as well as the equitable estate'.[32] His Lordship explained that the object of s. 53(1)(c) was to 'prevent hidden oral transactions in equitable interests . . . and making it difficult, if not impossible, for the trustees to ascertain in truth his beneficiaries'.[33] It is illogical to call upon the beneficiary to separately assign his beneficial interest to the third party, who after all would not be concerned of the absence of a s. 53(1)(c) written document purporting to show that he has been assigned the beneficiary's equitable interest. Such a third party would have the legal title to property and be able to deal with it as he or she wishes.

Section 53(1)(c) will apply in circumstances where the legal title and equitable title are moving separately. Suppose that a beneficiary under a subsisting trust directs the trustee to transfer the legal title to a third party, on the understanding that the third party will hold on trust for another. In such a situation, as illustrated in Figure 5.7, the legal and equitable titles are moving separately and as such the beneficiary must execute a separate assignment of his or her equitable interest in accordance with s. 53(1)(c). Where the beneficiary fails to do this, the result will be that the beneficiary will have merely changed one trustee for another, and the new trustee will continue to hold for that beneficiary or his estate in the event of his decease.

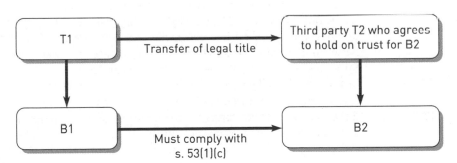

Figure 5.7

Declaration of new trusts with the consent of equitable owner

VISIT CASE NAVIGATOR

A somewhat more problematic and controversial context in which the application of s. 53(1)(c) has been questioned arose in *Re Vandervell's Trusts (No. 2)*.[34] You will recall that in the first phase of the Vandervell litigation, the Inland Revenue sought to claim surtax from Vandervell on the dividends declared on the shares that he had transferred

---

[32] [1967] 2 AC 291 and 311.

[33] [1967] 2 AC 291 and 311.

[34] [1974] Ch. 269.

to the Royal College of Surgeons.[35] This claim was on the grounds that he had not completely divested himself of his beneficial interest in the shares since the college had granted him an option to buy back the shares at a nominal price. The Inland Revenue succeeded in this claim on the grounds that the option was held on resulting trust for Vandervell. Vandervell had been granted the option in 1957 at the time of the transfer of the shares to the college and since he transferred the option to his trustees (the Vandevell Trust Company) without any express declaration as to whom it was to be held for, the orthodox trust principle meant that the option was held on an automatic resulting trust for none other than him.

In *Re Vandervell's Trusts (No. 2)*[36] it was precisely this option and its subsequent exercise thereof by the trustees which came to haunt Vandervell. On the facts of this litigation, £5000 from Vandervell's children's settlement was used to purchase back the shares from the Royal College of Surgeons with the instruction by Vandervell that the shares were to be held on trust by his trustees for the children. Between 1962 and 1964 dividends were declared on the shares in the region of £750,000. The Inland Revenue were informed of the exercise of the option and the fact that the shares were now held on trust for the children. In January 1965, just before the pending litigation in *Vandervell v IRC*, Vandervell instructed his trustees to execute a deed of release by which he transferred to his trustees (VTC Ltd) all rights in the option and declaring that the trustees were to hold such shares for the children. In other words, since 1961 the shares were held on trust for the children by virtue of an express declaration of trust by Vandervell.

Vandervell died in March 1967 having made a will which contained no express provision for his children. The lack of any provision for the children in the will was in recognition of the fact that he had already provided for them *inter vivos* by the shares, which the trustees were holding on trust for the children supposedly since 1961. At this point in time Vandervell had truly believed that he had settled his property, certainly the shares in Vandervell Products Ltd, beyond any further doubt and litigation. However, in *Re Vandervell's Trusts (No. 2)*[37] the Inland Revenue claimed surtax in respect of the period between 1961 and 1965 on the grounds that Vandevell had not completely divested himself of all interest in the shares between that period. You will recall that between 1957 and 1961 the option to purchase the shares from the Royal College of Surgeons was held by Vandervell's trustees under a resulting trust for Vandervell. Thus, in 1961 Vandervell had nothing more than an equitable right in the option. On this basis, the Revenue argued that the exercise of the option by the trustees and the subsequent direction to hold the shares for the children could only take place by compliance with s. 53(1)(c). As there was no such writing in 1961, other than an oral direction to exercise the option and hold the shares for the children, Vandervell remained the beneficial owner of the shares until such point in time when his interest had been duly disposed of in writing. No such writing came until 1965 and it was therefore the deed of 1965 which effectively transferred Vandervell's interest in the shares to his children.

The Inland Revenue's claim was against the executors of Vandervell's estate; however, when the executors realised the consequence of the Inland Revenue's claim, they sought to litigate against the trustees to recover the dividends from them on the grounds that they belonged to Vandervell between the period 1962 and 1964. At first instance, the executors' claim against the trustee succeeded on the grounds that the option was held on resulting trust for Vandervell since 1957 and that the exercise thereof and the shares

---

[35] This period being 1957 to 1961.
[36] [1974] Ch. 269.
[37] *Ibid.*

remained vested in him until the deed of 1965 which effectively released the interest in the shares to the children.[38]

The Court of Appeal reversed the judgment at first instance and held in favour of the trustees. The Court of Appeal held that the shares were held for the children since the exercise of the option in 1961. A number of grounds have been identified as the basis of the decision, all of which are not without controversy, and sometimes difficult to justify in the context of some of the established principles of trust law.

PROBLEM AREA

- **The declaration of trust argument**. It was held in the Court of Appeal that Vandervell had effectively declared a new trust in 1961 by the exercise of the option. The exercise of the option was sufficient to destroy the option, and the shares (constituting new property) were declared on trust for the children. The shares being personal property could be declared without any need for writing. In support of this argument Lord Denning MR and Lawton LJ explained that the use of the money from the children's settlement to purchase the shares was evidence of the intention that the trustees were to hold the shares for the children. It is unlikely that Vandervell's intention was to declare a trust in favour of the children when the option was exercised. At most there was an assumption that the shares were held for the children's settlement rather than an express declaration of trust accompanied with the requisite intention required by the law.[39] Furthermore, the mere use of the money from the children's settlement did not mean that the intention was to declare such a trust in their favour. At first instance, Megarry J explained the position in respect of the use of the money from the children's settlement to purchase the shares. He explained that the issue was 'whether trustees who hold an option on trust for X will hold the shares obtained by exercising that option on trust for Y merely because they used Y's money in exercising that option. Authority apart, my answer would be an unhesitating no. The option belongs to X beneficially, and the money merely exercises rights which belong to X. Let the shares be worth £50,000 so then an option to purchase the shares for £5000 is worth £45,000, and it will be seen at once what a monstrous result would be produced by allowing trustees to divert from their beneficiary X the benefits of what they hold for him merely because they used Y's money instead of X's.'[40] It is conceded that the use of the money from the children's settlement would only create a lien to the value of £5000 over the shares.[41]

- **The resulting trust argument**. In the course of his judgment Lord Denning MR explained that it was important to remember that the option was held under a resulting trust for Vandervell. As such, his Lordship explained that a resulting trust for the settlor is born and dies without any writing at all. 'It comes into existence whenever there is a gap in the beneficial ownership. It ceases to exist whenever that gap is filled by someone becoming beneficially entitled. As soon as the gap is filled by the creation or declaration of a valid trust, the resulting trust comes to an end.'[42] On this basis, his Lordship argued that the exercise of the option was to terminate the resulting trust

▶

---

[38] [1974] 1 All ER 47.
[39] See Chapter 4.
[40] [1974] 1 All ER 47 at 72.
[41] See J.W. Harris, 'The Case of the Slippery Equity' MLR Vol. 38 at 557.
[42] [1974] 3 All ER 205 at 211.

and the subsequent direction to the trustees to hold for the children was an effective declaration of a new trust. Whilst it is true to say that resulting trusts are exempt from the formal requirements of s. 53(1)(c) by virtue of s. 53(2) it is not entirely correct to say that s. 53(2) provides a blanket exemption for application of the formality requirements.[43] You will recall that s. 53(2) provides that the formal requirements in s. 53(1) do not affect the creation and operation of resulting, constructive and implied trusts. A resulting trust arises by operation of law and as such does not require any formality because it is the 'law' that puts it in place. However, once that resulting trust is put in place, it is like any other trust and as such any subsequent dealings with the beneficial ownership thereunder is clearly subject to the formality requirements in s. 53(1)(c) of the Law of Property Act 1925. Thus, the termination of a beneficial interest under a resulting trust is within the scope s. 53(1)(c) and certainly outside of the scope of the s. 53(2) exemption, which only covers creation and operation. The matter is better explained by the Further thinking box below.

- **The shares and option argument**. It was argued that the resulting trust attached to the option and not to the shares. A new express trust of the shares was created in favour of the children.[44] Although it is true to say that the resulting trust attached to the option, the fact remained that the beneficial ownership in the option and the shares remained fragmented at all times. The option belonged beneficially to Vandervell and when the trustees exercised the option the beneficial interest in the shares belonged to Vandervell because they were a direct product of the option. To argue that Vandervell merely had an equitable interest in the option and not the shares is contradictory to the assumptions made by both the Inland Revenue and the House of Lords in *Vandervell* v *IRC*[45] – where Vandervell was held to be liable for surtax on dividends declared between the period when the shares were owned by the Royal College of Surgeons. The fact that Vandervell was granted an option to purchase the shares meant that he retained a beneficial interest in the shares.[46]

FURTHER THINKING

When does s. 53(2) exempt a resulting trust from the formal requirements of s. 53(1)(b) and (c)?

Suppose Alf wishes to create a trust of Ivy Cottage in favour of Bill. In such a case, Alf will need the necessary intention to create the trust as well as complying with the formal requirements of s. 53(1)(b) of the Law of Property Act 1925. This section requires that the trust of land be manifested and proved in writing. Clearly Alf is attempting to declare an express trust of land which is caught by the formal requirements of s. 53(1)(b).

Now suppose that Alf and Bill decide to purchase Ivy Cottage together; however, the legal title to the cottage is only taken in Alf's name despite Bill providing over half of the purchase price. In such a situation, although the legal title is in Alf's name alone, Bill will have a beneficial interest in the cottage under a resulting trust in his favour. A resulting trust arises by operation of law when one person contributes to the purchase price and

---

[43] See above.
[44] See Lawton LJ [1974] 3 All ER 205 at 216.
[45] [1967] 2 AC 291.
[46] See now the ICTA 1988 ss. 684, 685.

the legal title is taken in the name of another.[47] Such a trust is implied by the law on grounds of the presumed intentions of the parties. Given that this, like the first example, is a trust of land, it should comply with s. 53(1)(b) of the Law of Property Act 1925. However, it would be nonsense to suggest that it does simply because the parties are not creating an express trust but the law imposes a resulting trust to give effect to the intentions of the parties on the basis of their conduct (i.e. the act of contributing to the purchase price).

In the two examples given above, it is clear why the formal requirements of s. 53(1)(b) do not apply to the second trust but do clearly apply to the first. If the matter is taken one stage further, it can be observed that in both cases Bill acquires a beneficial interest in Ivy Cottage. The first arises by an express declaration of trust and the latter by an implied trust in the nature of a resulting trust. Now, suppose Bill wishes to dispose of his beneficial interest to Mary. In both examples above, he would need to comply with s. 53(1)(c) of the Law of Property Act 1925 and dispose of such interest in writing. It does not matter that the second trust is a resulting trust. In both cases he has a beneficial interest, which can only be disposed of in writing. S. 53(2) of the Law of Property Act 1925 cannot be used to exempt the need for writing simply because there is a resulting trust in place. The exemption only covers the creation and operation of the resulting trusts; it certainly does not cover the termination thereof. Indeed, it would be absurd to apply s. 53(1)(c) to the first example and not to the second when there is no real difference between the two on the facts.

The decision in **Re Vandervell's Trust (No. 2)** is difficult to justify when looked at in the context of **Grey v IRC**.[48] In both of these cases, the equitable ownership in property (the shares in the case of **Grey** and the option in the case of **Vandervell**) was disposed of in favour of children of the settlor. The only noticeable difference between the two cases is that in **Grey** the trustees held the shares under an express trust for Hunter (the settlor) whereas in the case of **Vandervell**, the option (which was eventually exercised in favour of the children) was held under an implied resulting trust for Vandervell. It does not matter how the equitable ownership arose in the first place; the fact remains that Vandervell was attempting to dispose of his equitable ownership in what was initially the option and then shares in favour of his children. Such a disposition would have to comply with s. 53(1)(c). None of the arguments presented in the Court of Appeal explain how Vandervell was declaring a new trust of property when all that he had was equitable ownership to property, the legal title to which was at all times vested in trustees.

● Specifically enforceable contract for the assignment of an equitable interest

APPLYING THE LAW

Suppose that Margaret settles 10,000 shares on trust for her daughter, Lisa, for life, and thereafter for Zoe absolutely. In such a situation the trustees will hold the legal title to the shares for Lisa for her life and thereafter the whole amount for Zoe. Both Lisa and

---

[47] *Dyer* v *Dyer* (1788) 2 Cox. Eq. Cas. 92; these matters are explored in more detail in Chapter 11.
[48] [1960] AC 1.

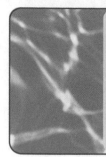

Zoe would only have an equitable interest in the shares. During her lifetime, Lisa will receive the income on the shares, whilst Zoe must await Lisa's death before she can claim the full value of the shares.

What is the position if Lisa and Zoe agree that Zoe will give her equitable interest in the shares to Lisa in return for Lisa giving her £5000?

As this is a contract to assign Zoe's equitable interest, should it comply with s. 53(1)(c) of the Law of Property Act 1925?

It is perfectly possible for a beneficiary under a subsisting trust to enter into a contract for the assignment of the equitable interest in favour of another person. Suppose Alf is already a beneficiary of 2000 shares in a private company; he then enters into a contract with Bill for the assignment of his equitable interest to Bill, who in return will give him £2000 for such shares. In such a case the assignment by Alf is not voluntary but subject to consideration provided by Bill, which is the £2000. Nevertheless, the point remains that Alf is disposing of his equitable interest to Bill, and as such the disposition must comply with s. 53(1)(c) of the Law of Property Act 1925 and be put in writing. If the disposition is not in writing then it is void.

Whilst this sounds straightforward enough, the matter is more complicated when the disposition takes the form of a contractual assignment. A basic principle of contract law is that where one person enters into a contract with another which is capable of specific performance, equity regards that as done which ought to be done. As soon as the contract is made the purchaser acquires an equitable interest in the subject matter of the contract on the grounds that the vendor becomes a constructive trustee for the purchaser. The consequence of this principle is that, if the contract to dispose of an equitable interest is capable of being made orally, the contract itself is sufficient to shift the equitable interest to the purchaser irrespective of any writing pursuant to s. 53(1)(c). The question whether an oral contact to assign an equitable interest need comply with s. 53(1)(c) fell to be decided in the House of Lords in *Oughtred v IRC*.[49] The decision of the House of Lords is not without its problems, not least because it overlooks the contractual principles of specific performance, but also because it gives way to fiscal concerns over legal doctrine. Before the decision can be analysed, it is worth going over the basic principles which govern a contract capable of specific performance.

FURTHER THINKING

Understanding *Oughtred v IRC*: contracts capable of specific performance

The decision in *Oughtred v IRC* and the subsequent criticisms of that decision are better understood if one looks at the principles of contract law which apply when a contract is capable of specific performance. It is an elementary principle of contract law that the equitable remedy of specific performance is available in circumstances where damages would be inadequate, for example, where the subject matter of the contract is unique or

---

[49] [1960] AC 206.

where it would be difficult to quantify loss. Thus, students of land law will know that a contract for the sale of land is capable of specific performance, providing it complies with s. 2(1) of the Law of Property (Miscellaneous Provisions) Act 1989. This section requires that the contract be made in writing incorporating all the terms and conditions and be signed by the parties. The basis for the grant of a decree of specific performance is that equity regards that as done which ought to be done. The vendor becomes a constructive trustee for the purchaser who is deemed to have acquired the equitable interest in the land. Of course, in the case of land, the contract is only capable of specific performance if it is in writing. However, not all contracts capable of specific performance need be in writing, for example, a contract to sell a unique painting or stocks and shares in a private company can be made orally. However, the fact remains that the oral contract is capable of specific performance on the grounds that equity regards that as done which ought to be done. Thus, the equitable interest in the subject matter of the contract passes to the purchaser as soon as the oral contract is made.

On this line of reasoning, it follows that where a beneficiary enters into a specifically enforceable contract to assign an equitable interest, that equitable interest passes to the purchaser as soon as the contract is made. There should be no requirement for any further writing in order to transfer the equitable interest. However, this line of reasoning was not followed in the House of Lords' decision in *Oughtred*.

The facts of *Oughtred* v *IRC*[50] involved a contract for the transfer of a beneficial interest in shares in a private company. Under a trust created some time ago, trustees were holding 200,000 shares in a private company on trust for Mrs Oughtred for life and thereafter for her son Peter absolutely.[51] In addition, Mrs Oughted was also the absolute owner of 72,700 shares. On 18 June, 1956, Mrs Oughted entered into an oral contract with Peter whereby she promised to give Peter her 72,700 shares in exchange for Peter assigning his reversionary interest to her. The net effect of this arrangement was to make Mrs Oughtred the absolute owner of the 200,000 shares. On 26 June, 1956, a deed of release was executed by Mrs Oughtred, the trustees and Peter which stated, *inter alia*, that since 18 June the trustees were holding the 200,000 shares absolutely for Mrs Oughtred and that they were going to transfer the legal title to Mrs Oughtred thereby ending the trust of the settlement. The 200,000 shares were duly transferred to Mrs Oughtred who, as promised in the oral agreement, transferred the 72,700 shares to nominees for Peter. The question in court was whether the deed of 26 June attracted *ad valorem* stamp duty on the grounds that it was a transfer of property on sale of Peter's interest. Certainly, the deed of 26 June made it clear that the trustees were holding the absolute interest in the 200,000 shares for Mrs Oughtred; however, was it the deed of 26 June that made Mrs Oughtred the absolute owner of the shares, or was it the oral agreement of 18 June?

At first instance, Upjohn J held that it was the oral agreement of 18 June that made Mrs Oughtred the absolute owner of the 200,000 shares.[52] Applying the principle of contracts capable of specific performance already discussed above, Upjohn J held that as soon as the oral contract had been made by Mrs Oughtred and Peter, Peter became a constructive trustee of his interest in favour of his mother. In other words, Peter's equitable

---

[50] [1960] AC 206.
[51] The effect of this was to create a settlement of the shares, making Mrs Oughtred a life tenant and her son a remainderman. Mrs Oughtred's interest in the shares would be described as a life interest and Peter's interest a reversionary interest.
[52] [1958] Ch. 383.

reversionary interest was held on constructive trust for his mother. Furthermore, given that the contract gave rise to a constructive trust, such a trust could be imposed without any recourse to writing.[53] The net effect of this was that Peter's equitable interest shifted to his mother without recourse to s. 53(1)(c) suggesting, therefore, that an equitable interest could pass to another person without recourse to writing if it was subject to a contractual transfer accompanied with the availability of specific performance.

The Court of Appeal reversed the decision at first instance[54] and the House of Lords upheld the decision of the Court of Appeal by a majority of three to two. The House of Lords held that the deed of 26 June was liable to *ad valorem* stamp duty on the grounds that the deed was implementing a transfer on sale and therefore clearly within the ambit of the Stamp Act 1891. The majority, Lords Keith, Denning and Jenkins, took the view that, even if the oral contract was sufficient to impose a constructive trust, Peter's equitable interest could not have moved without recourse to writing. The judgments of their Lordships are not entirely consistent and it is difficult to ascertain exactly what point of law is being used to justify the imposition of *ad valorem* stamp duty on the deed of 26 June. Lord Denning took the view that the oral agreement was not effective to transfer Peter's reversionary interest to his mother. According to his Lordship, 'the wording of s. 53(1)(c) of the Law of Property Act 1925 clearly made writing necessary to effect a transfer; and s. 53(2) does not do away with that necessity'.[55] With respect to his Lordship, this view merely avoids a proper construction of s. 53(2) of the Law of Property Act 1925 and fails to give any significance to the fact that the contract, which being capable of specific performance, had shifted the equitable interest as soon as the contract was made. What is more interesting is that Denning LJ suggested that s. 53(2) does not do away with the need for writing, yet some fourteen years later in **Re Vandervell's Trusts (No. 2)**[56] his Lordship was firmly of the opinion that s. 53(2) operated to exempt an implied trust from the need for writing.[57] Lord Keith in his judgment made an analogy with a contract to sell land and commented that although a purchaser of land gained some proprietary interest in the land between contract and completion,[58] 'its existence has never . . . been held to prevent a subsequent transfer, in the performance of the contract, of the property contracted to be sold from constituting for stamp duty purposes a transfer on sale of the property in question'.[59]

Lord Radcliffe gave a powerful dissenting judgment, which is regarded by most commentators as the correct position in respect of a contract to transfer an equitable interest. His Lordship paid significance to the effect of a contract capable of specific performance, already discussed above. His Lordship explained that:

> reasoning of the whole matter, as I see it, is as follows: On June 18 1956 the son owned an equitable reversionary interest in the settled shares: by his oral agreement of that date he

---

[53] See s. 53(2) LPA 1925, discussed above.
[54] [1958] Ch. 678.
[55] [1960] AC 206 at 233.
[56] [1974] Ch. 269, discussed above.
[57] It will be recalled that in *Vandervell* v *IRC (No. 2)* [1974] Ch. 269, the question was whether a declaration of a new trust by a beneficiary under a resulting trust was in essence a disposition of that beneficiary's equitable interest. Lord Denning took the view that a resulting trust is born and terminated without any recourse to writing. Surely the matter remains the same in respect of a constructive trust, no matter how it arises. Thus in the case of a contract to transfer an equitable interest to another, a constructive trust arises to shift the equitable interest to the transferee irrespective of any recourse to writing.
[58] That is, the equitable interest in the land by virtue of the vendor becoming a constructive trustee for the purchaser.
[59] [1960] AC 206 at 240.

created in his mother an equitable interest in his reversion, since the subject-matter of the agreement was property of which specific performance would normally be decreed by the court. He thus became a trustee for her of that interest sub modo: having regard to subsection (2) of section 53 Law of Property Act 1925 subsection (1) of that section did not operate to prevent that trusteeship arsing by operation of law.[60]

Despite the majority decision in **Oughtred v IRC**[61] subsequent cases have taken the approach adopted by Lord Radcliffe.[62] That is, where there is a specifically enforceable contract for the transfer of an equitable interest, that interest moves by virtue of the contract and the imposition of a constructive trust on the vendor. Where the contract can be made orally, there is no separate need to put the transfer of such equitable interest in writing. For example, in **Chinn v Collins (Inspector of Taxes)**,[63] a case involving the transfers of equitable interests in shares under a capital tax avoidance scheme, Lord Wilberforce commented that 'the legal title to the shares was at all times vested in the nominee . . . and dealings related to the equitable interest in these required no formality. As soon as there was an agreement for their sale accompanied or followed by payment of the price, the equitable title passed at once to the purchaser . . . and all that was needed to perfect his title was notice to the trustees or nominees . . .'[64] In **Neville v Wilson**[65] the Court of Appeal endorsed the view of Lord Radcliffe in **Oughtred v IRC**[66] by holding that the imposition of a constructive trust by virtue of an oral contract to transfer an equitable interest was sufficient to transfer the equitable interest without need to comply with s. 53(1)(c). The facts of the case involved the beneficial ownership of shares by one private company in a second private company. An oral agreement was made between the shareholders of the company that the shares in the second company should be distributed in proportion to their shareholding. The question before the Court of Appeal was whether the oral agreement was sufficient to transfer the equitable interest in the shares in the second company to the shareholders or whether the agreement was void for failure to comply with section 53(1)(c) of the Law of Property Act 1925. The Court of Appeal held that the imposition of the constructive trust was sufficient to transfer the equitable interest.

In light of the decisions after **Oughtred v IRC** it seems conclusive that where the transfer of an equitable interest is subject to a specifically enforceable contract for sale, the equitable interest moves without need to comply with the formal requirement of s. 53(1)(c) of the Law of Property Act 1925.

Disclaimer

Where a settlor purports to confer a beneficial interest to a beneficiary who subsequently disclaims that interest, the question arises as to whether the subsequent disclaimer is only effective if it is put in writing pursuant to s. 53(1)(c) of the Law of property Act 1925. This point of law arose in **Re Paradise Motor Co Ltd**[67] where a stepfather made a gift of

---

[60] [1960] AC 206 at 227.

[61] [1960] AC 206.

[62] See, for example, *Re Holt's Settlement* [1969] 1 Ch. 100. The facts of this case concerned an order to vary a trust under the Variation of Trusts Act 1958. The question was whether such an order approving a variation need be in writing. In the course of his judgment, Megarry J held that when there exists a specifically enforceable contract, the imposition of the constructive trust passes the equitable interest to the purchaser. See also *DHN Food Distributors v Tower Hamlets LBC* [1976] 1 WLR 852.

[63] [1981] AC 533.

[64] [1981] AC 533 at 548.

[65] [1997] Ch. 144. See also *Singh v Anand* [2007] EWHC 3346 where it was held that an equitable interest acquired a constructive trust and did not require writing under s. 52(2) of the Law of Property Act 1925.

[66] [1960] AC 206.

[67] [1968] 2 All ER 625.

shares to his stepson. The gift was technically defective at law but the technicality did not prevent the son becoming equitable owner of the shares. When the son learnt of the gift he unequivocally rejected the gift. However, when he changed his mind later he sought to claim the shares on the grounds that he did not dispose of his equitable interest in the shares as required in writing by virtue of s. 53(1)(c) Law of Property Act 1925. The Court of Appeal held that his unequivocal rejection of the gift amounted to a disclaimer and that a disclaimer operated by way of avoidance rather than a disposition within s. 53(1)(c).

Conclusion

In this chapter it has been seen that both the creation and operation of trusts are governed by formal requirements. Historically, these formal requirements have been concerned with policy issues such as the avoidance of fraud and certainty in property dealings. All testamentary trusts are governed by the formalities of a valid will. *Inter vivos* trusts of personal property can be crated orally but trusts of land must be evidenced and proved in writing. Land has been singled out because of the certainty in land dealings which finds itself central to land law legislation. Today, however, there makes very little sense in distinguishing a declaration of a trust of a fund of £1 million and a trust of one square foot of land.

Dispositions of equitable interests subsisting under a trust must be in writing. The need for writing is particularly important in this context in order to prevent fraud. A beneficiary under a trust has nothing more than a chose in action in the trust property. Thus, where a beneficiary purports to transfer his equitable interest to another, there is nothing physical that he can pass on to the third party. The third party can only rely on the writing as proof of his entitlement to the trust property. In turn the trustees will know who their true beneficiaries are. Much of the complexity surrounding this area of trust law relates to the fact that the litigation has occurred in the context of taxation. The cases have shown that sometimes the taxation issues have clouded and left unresolved the trust issues.

Case studies

Consider the following case studies:

1   Consider the formal requirements needed in each of the following.

(a) Simon is holding £2000 on trust for Paul. Paul orally declares that he will hold his interest in the £2000 upon trust for his children in equal shares.

(b) Simon is holding 5000 shares in a private company on trust for Helen. Helen agrees with Jill that she will assign her equitable interest in the 5000 shares to Jill on the understanding that Jill will act as a director of the company.

(c) Simon is holding 2000 shares on trusts for Gary. Gary, by unsigned writing, declares that he will hold any dividends received on those shares upon trust for his nephew.

(d) Simon is holding £20,000 on trust for Jenny. Jenny directs Simon to transfer the £20,000 to Peter.

2 Earlier this year Laura did the following:

(a) transferred £3000 on trust for Gavin and Vicky in equal shares

(b) transferred her shares in ICI Ltd to her trustees, informing them that she would tell them later what to do with the shares

(c) conveyed Ivy Cottage to Mike.

When Gavin found out that Laura had transferred some money on trust for him, he immediately phoned Laura and told her that he did not want anything from her. Vicky on the other hand was pleased to learn of the trust. Vicky told her daughter, Michelle, that she wanted her to have her interest in the trust fund, as this would help her with her studies.

In April Laura told her trustees to hold the shares in ICI Ltd for a local charity.

Laura died a few months ago without having made a will. Recently, Mike received a letter from Gavin informing him that he should convey Ivy Cottage to him since Mike had orally agreed with Laura that he would hold it upon trust for Gavin. Mike has refused to do so on the grounds that he never agreed to be a trustee for Gavin. Gavin, however, claims to have enough proof to show the existence of the trust. Gavin also wishes the trustees to transfer his share of the trust fund of £3000 to him even though Laura had explained in writing to her trustees that he did not want any of the money.

Advise Gavin and Michelle as to their rights to any of the property on these facts.

●● Moot points

1 Where there is a failure to comply with s. 53(1)(b) of the Law of Property Act 1925, but the beneficiary of the intended trust of land has sufficient evidence to prove the existence of the trust, what trust is being enforced by the courts? Is it the express trust, which the trustee is refusing to accept, or is it a constructive trust imposed by reason of the trustee's unconscionable conduct?

2 Do you think that the court should impose a constructive trust if there has been non-compliance with s. 53(1)(b) of the Law of Property Act 1925? Surely, to impose the trust would show some disregard to the requirement of formality in s. 53(1)(b). Is it not better to impose a resulting trust to prevent the unjust enrichment of the trustee? What do you think?

3 Does a declaration of a sub-trust need to comply with s. 53(1)(c) of the Law of Property Act 1925? There is very little case law on sub-trusts; however, the law seems to allow a sub-trust to bypass the requirements of s. 53(1)(c) when the trust involves 'active duties'. What do you understand by the term 'active duties' in this context?

4 Read the judgment of the Court of Appeal in *Vandervell (No. 2)* [1974] Ch. 269 and explain why the exercise of the option by the trustee and the subsequent holding of the shares for the Vandervell's children did not need to comply with s. 53(1)(c) of the Law of Property Act 1925.

5 Does s. 53(2) of the Law of Property Act 1925 provide a wholesale exemption for implied trusts to comply with the formality requirements in s. 53(1) of the Act?

6 It is generally argued that the decision in *Oughtred v IRC* [1960] AC 206 is wrongly decided. In particular, where there is a specifically enforceable contract for the sale of an equitable interest, the equitable interest moves as soon as the contract is made on the grounds that 'equity regards that as done which ought to be done'. Read the judgments in the case and explain why the majority of the Law Lords required that compliance with s. 53(1)(c) was necessary on the fact of *Oughtred*.

7 Do you think the decision in *Oughtred* **v** *IRC* [1960] AC 206 reflects the tensions between the application of principles of property and trusts and the general policy of paying tax?

Further reading

Battersby, G. 'Formalities for the Dispositions of Equitable Interests under a Trust' (1979) Conv. 175. Examines the nature of the formality requirements in s. 53(1) of the Law of Property Act 1925 and examines the decision in the decided cases.

Green, B. 'Grey, Oughtred and Vandervell – A Contextual Appraisal' (1984) 47 MLR 385. Provides an excellent critical analysis of the decision in Grey, Oughtred and Vandervell. The article also explores the nature of the formality requirements.

6
Constitution of trusts

Learning objectives:

After completing this chapter you should be able to:

→ understand the difference between a completely constituted trust and an incompletely constituted trust

→ understand the ways in which a trust can be constituted and the significance of constituting a trust

→ explain the maxims that equity will not perfect an imperfect gift and equity will not assist a volunteer

→ explain the position of a beneficiary under an incompletely constituted trust

→ explain the exceptions to the rule that equity will not assist a volunteer

→ explain the remedies available for breach of a covenant to settle

→ understand a trust of a promise and the circumstances in which a trust of a promise will arise.

Pennington v *Waine* [2002] 1 WLR 2075: The aunt, her nephew and a purported transfer of shares

The facts of *Pennington* v *Waine* neatly illustrate the issues which arise in the context of the constitution of trusts. The case concerned an attempted gift of shares in a private company by an aunt to her nephew. Ada Crampton executed a share transfer form in respect of 400 shares in a private company in favour of her nephew Harold Crampton. She in fact owned a total of 1500 shares out of the 2000 issued in the company. The understanding was that Harold would become a director in the company and that the 400 shares were transferred solely for this purpose. The stock transfer form was sent to the company's auditor who informed Harold that he need not do anything further about the transfer of the shares. The auditor placed the stock transfer form on the company's file and completed the necessary paperwork to appoint Harold as a director the company. A few months later Ada made a will leaving the rest of her shareholding in a will without reference to the 400 which she had intended to give to Harold. The stock transfer form remained on the company's files until Ada's death without delivery being made to Harold or registration on the company's share register.

The question before the Court of Appeal was whether there had been an assignment of the shares in favour of Harold or whether the 400 shares belonged to Ada's estate.

In the absence of a formal transfer of those shares to Harold it would be logical to assume that there had been no assignment of the shares and that the shares belonged to Ada's estate.

The same principle would apply to a settlor who attempts to create a trust by making his intentions clear, but fails to transfer the trust property to the intended trustee(s). Surely he cannot be compelled to transfer the trust property and, indeed, he may well have changed his mind.

What is the position of a beneficiary who is promised an interest under a trust, or indeed, a simple gift but then fails to receive it because the settlor or donor fails to effectively transfer the subject matter of the trust or gift to the trustee or donee? Can the beneficiary do anything about the failure of the settlor to transfer the subject matter of the trust to the trustee? This chapter explores the rules and principles which govern the situation where a settlor intends to create a trust in favour of a beneficiary, but then fails to transfer the subject matter of the trust to the intended trustee.

Introduction

It has already been observed in the preceding chapters that in order to be valid a trust requires a number of substantive and formal requirements to have been met. A settlor must have the necessary intention to create a trust and must also comply with any necessary formality. This chapter explores the next stage in the creation of a private trust, that is, the act of constituting a trust. A trust is said to be constituted when the settlor transfers the subject matter of the trust property to the intended trustee(s) or where he effectively declares himself as trustee for another. In the case of an effective transfer to trustees, the settlor divests himself of his legal interest in the property transferred. The trustee gains the legal title to the trust property and will hold so for the beneficiary who gains an equitable interest in the trust property. In the case where the settlor declares himself as trustee for the beneficiary, his ownership is said to become nominal as he will have divested himself of his enjoyment to the property in question and created in the beneficiary an equitable interest. Seen in this way, the act of constituting a trust is the most important stage in the creation of a trust. It is only at the point of constituting the trust that the trust comes into being and ownership is fragmented. It is equally clear that up until the point of constitution, the settlor can change his mind and decide not to subject his property to a trust in favour of the intended beneficiary. However, where the trust is fully constituted, the settlor falls out of the picture and retains no further say in respect of the property subject to the trust.

# Completely constituted and incompletely constituted trusts

Where a settlor has transferred the subject matter of the trust to the intended trustee or where he has effectively declared himself as trustee, the trust is said to be completely constituted. A completely constituted trust is binding on the trustee as well as his representatives. The beneficiary acquires an equitable proprietary right in the property which binds everyone except a bona fide purchaser of the legal title without notice of the trust. Whether or not a trust is completely constituted is in most cases a relatively straightforward exercise. Either the settlor will have transferred the subject matter to the trustee with the requisite intention that it be held for the beneficiary, or the settlor will have unequivocally declared himself a trustee in favour of the beneficiary. In other cases it may be a question of construction of all the relevant facts whether the settlor has indeed constituted the trust and whether the intended trustee has indeed taken the legal title to property upon trust for another person. The matter is neatly illustrated by the decision of the Court of Appeal in *Staden v Jones*,[1] where the the Court of Appeal emphasised that in creating a trust it was not necessary to refer expressly to the word 'trustee', but words or acts done by the settlor must have intended to have that meaning.[2]

Where the settlor fails to transfer the intended trust property to the trustee(s) then the trust is said to be incompletely constituted. In fact, it is rather strange to describe the trust as an incompletely constituted trust since in reality there is no trust. At most the settlor has promised to create a trust or covenanted to create a trust[3] and, like any other promise, the beneficiary cannot in the absence of consideration compel performance of it.[4] The equitable maxim operating here is: 'equity will not assist a volunteer'. An individual is described as a volunteer in the eyes of equity where he has not furnished any consideration. Furthermore, an equally important maxim operating to deny the beneficiary a right to do anything about an incompletely constituted trust is: 'equity will not perfect an imperfect gift'. This simply means that where a person intends to make

---

[1] [2008] 2 FLR 1931.
[2] [2008] 2 FLR 1931 at paras. 24–5.
[3] Sometimes also referred to as a covenant to settle.
[4] The doctrine of estoppel may be invoked where a beneficiary relies on a promise to create a trust and suffers a detriment. This is explored in more detail later on.

a gift, albeit by way of trust, that person can at any time up until the actual transfer of the subject matter of the gift change his mind. In the absence of unconscionable conduct on the part of the person making the gift, or a settlor intending to create a trust, equity will not perfect the gift or trust should the donor of the gift or settlor change his mind.

The *Milroy* v *Lord* principles of conferring a benefit on a donee

VISIT CASE NAVIGATOR

In *Milroy* v *Lord*[5] Turner LJ identified three principal ways in which a person can make a gift to another person:

1 an outright transfer of the legal title to the property to the donee (or in the case of an equitable interest, an assignment of the equitable interest to the donee[6]);

2 a transfer of the legal title to property to trustees to hold on behalf of another;

3 a declaration of self as trustee for another.

Whichever method is used, the person making the gift must do everything in his power to transfer the legal title to the property of the type in question. In *Milroy* v *Lord* Turner LJ explained the requirements of making a gift by way of a trust so as to make the trust fully constituted. His Lordship explained that:

> [i]n order to render a voluntary settlement valid and effectual, the settlor must have done everything which according to the nature of the property comprised in the settlement was necessary to be done in order to render the settlement binding upon him. He may, of course, do this by actually transferring the property to the persons for whom he intends to provide and the provision will then be effectual and it will be equally effectual if he transfers the property to a trustee for the purpose of the settlement, or declares that he himself holds it on trust for those purposes and if the property is personal, the trust may, as I apprehend, be declared either in writing or parol but, in order to render the settlement binding, one or other of these modes must, as I understand the law of this court, be restored to, for there is no equity in this court to perfect an imperfect gift.[7]

So where a person intends to make a gift of a painting to a donee, he must hand over possession of the painting. Where, in the case of a transfer of shares on trust for another, the settlor must transfer the legal title to those shares in the appropriate form. This will require the use of an appropriate stock transfer form followed by registration of the transfer in the share register of the company. Where the settlor fails to do everything in his power to transfer the legal title to the property, the gift remains imperfect and equity will not perfect the imperfect gift. Likewise the intended trust remains incompletely constituted and equity will assist the beneficiary who remains a volunteer.

It is also clear from the cases that a failed gift will not be construed as creating a trust unless there is clear manifestation that the gift was intended to take effect as a trust. The matter was elegantly explained by Maitland in his *Lectures on Equity*. Maitland wrote:

> I have a son called Thomas. I write a letter to him saying 'I give you my Blackacre estate, my leasehold house in the High Street, the sum of £1000 Consols standing in my name, the

---

[5] (1862) 4 De GF & J 264.

[6] In the case of an assignment of an equitable interest to another, it must comply with s. 53(1)(c) of the Law of Property Act 1925, which requires the disposition to be in writing and signed by the person who is capable of disposing of that interest. This was discussed in detail in the preceding chapter.

[7] (1862) 4 De GF & J 264 at 274.

wine in my cellar.' This is ineffectual – I have given nothing – a letter will not convey freehold or leasehold land, it will not transfer Government stock, it will not pass the ownership in goods. Even if, instead of writing a letter, I had executed a deed of covenant – saying not I do convey Blackacre, I do assign the leasehold house and the wine, but I covenant to convey and assign – even this would not have been a perfect gift. It would be an imperfect gift, and being an imperfect gift the Court will not regard it as a declaration of trust. I have made quite clear that I do not intend to make myself a trustee, I meant to give. The two intentions are very different – the giver means to get rid of his rights, the man who is intending to make himself a trustee intends to retain his rights but to come under an onerous obligation. The latter intention is far rarer than the former. Men often mean to give things to their kinsfolk, they do not often mean to constitute themselves trustees. An imperfect gift is no declaration of trust.[8]

For example, as will be seen in more detail below, in **Richards v Delbridge**[9] a certain Delbridge purported to make a gift of his lease and business to his grandson, Richards. No such assignment of the lease and the business was made to Richards. The court held that in the absence of a clear manifestation to create a trust in favour of Richards, there was no trust of the lease and the business in favour of Richards.[10] On the other hand, where a donor attempts to make a gift coupled with an intention that until such time as the gift is complete the subject matter of the gift should be held immediately upon trust for the donee, then the court will construe that the failed gift was accompanied with an intention to create a trust. The matter is neatly illustrated in the decision of the Court of Appeal in **Shah v Shah**.[11] The question before the Court of Appeal was whether a letter signed by a shareholder purporting to transfer shares in a private company in favour of another coupled with a signed transfer form amounted to a declaration of trust or a mere incomplete gift. Simply put in another way, could a failed transfer of shares be construed as a declaration of trust in circumstances where the transferor had manifested an intention that he would hold such shares for the transferee? The facts of **Shah v Shah** essentially involved a long-standing feud between four brothers as to the shareholding in a public limited company. Mr Dinesh Shah was one of five brothers as well as one of three shareholders in a public limited company. All three shareholders in the company were brothers and each held one-third of the shareholding. As for the other two brothers, one of them was simply not interested in acquiring any shareholding in the company; however, as for the other, a certain Mr Mahendra Shah, the three brothers who held shares in the company decided that he too should acquire some shareholding in the company so that all four of them would eventually have equal shares of 25 per cent in the company. In order to put this arrangement to effect, on 11 March 2005 Mr Dinesh Shah and another brother executed and delivered letters to Mr Mahendra Shah with the intention that they would hold shares out of their respective shareholding for the benefit of Mahendra. Additionally, they also delivered forms of transfer of 4000 shares in favour of Mahendra in August 2005, but leaving the consideration and date blank on the forms. The shares were duly registered in favour of Mahendra; however, no share certificate was actually delivered to Mahendra, thus leaving the gift of the shares imperfect. Subsequently, Dinesh had a disagreement with his brother Mr Mahendra Shah and, as well as preventing him from having anything to do with the company, he challenged the fact that Mahendra was the owner of any shares in the company. Dinesh argued that the

---

[8] F.W. Maitland, *Equity: A Course of Lectures* (J. Brunyate (ed.) 1936) at pp. 71–2.
[9] (1874) LR 18 Eq 11.
[10] See also, *Heartley* v *Nicholson* (1875) LR 19 Eq 233.
[11] [2010] EWCA Civ 1408.

stock transfer form was incomplete and, coupled with the fact that no actual share certificate was actually delivered to him, the disposition was ineffective on the grounds that the letter of 11 March 2005 constituted an attempt to make a gift of the shares in the company and since no share transfer form had been issued, there was an incomplete gift of the shares to Mahendra.

In the Court of Appeal it was held that a valid trust of the shares arose in favour of Mahendra. Arden LJ explained that the effect of the letters delivered in March 2005 to Mahendra evidenced an intention that Mr Dinesh Shah and indeed his two other brothers had created a trust of the shares in favour of their brother Mahendra. In the course of her judgment, Arden LJ explained that:

> In interpreting a document, the court should not have regard to the subjective intention of its maker but to the intentions of the maker as manifested by the words he has used in the context of all the relevant facts. Here there is no doubt that Mr Dinesh Shah manifested an intention that the letter should take effect forthwith: see the words 'as from today'. To give effect in law to those words, there has to be a disposition only of a beneficial interest, since, for the reasons given above, legal title did not pass until registration. The parties clearly intended registration to take place in due course because otherwise Mr Dinesh Shah would not have simultaneously executed and delivered a stock transfer form. Judged objectively, did the words used convey an intention to give a beneficial interest there and then or an intention to hold that interest for Mr Mahendra Shah until registration? Mr Dinesh Shah used the words 'I am . . . holding', not, for example, the words 'I am assigning' or 'I am giving' and the concept that he *holds* the shares for Mr Mahendra Shah until he loses that status on registration can only be given effect in law by the imposition of a trust. Accordingly Mr Dinesh Shah must be taken in law to have intended a trust and not a gift.[12]

The decision in **Shah v Shah** illustrates the need to look at all of the conduct of a settlor before deciding his actual intention. In this case the delivery of the signed letter indicated an intention to transfer the shares and, coupled with the signing of a stock transfer form, this amounted to an unequivocal intention to create a trust in favour of the intended donee of the shares.[13] Arden LJ referred to a passage of her own judgment earlier in the decision in **Pennington v Waine**[14] where she commented that 'accordingly the principle that, where a gift is imperfectly constituted, the court will not hold it to operate as a declaration of trust, does not prevent the court from construing it to be a trust if that interpretation is permissible as a matter of construction, which may be a benevolent construction. The same must apply to words of gift. An equity to perfect a gift would not be invoked by giving a benevolent construction to words of gift or, it follows, words which the donor used to communicate or give effect to his gift.'[15]

Declaration of trust

It has already been observed that a trust can be created in one of two ways. Firstly, by declaration of self as trustee, that is, where a settlor declares that he holds property in his hands on trust for a beneficiary. Secondly, a trust will arise where a settlor transfers property to trustees for the benefit of beneficiaries (see Figure 6.1).

---

[12] [2010] EWCA Civ 1408 at para. 13.
[13] See also, *Moore v Williamson* [2011] EWHC 672 (Ch).
[14] [2002] 1 WLR 2075.
[15] [2002] 1 WLR 2075 at 2090.

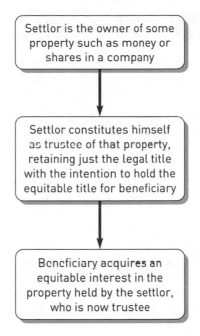

Figure 6.1

In the case of declaration of self as trustee, the settlor already has the legal title to the trust property: in other words, the property is already in his hands. The only question here is whether he has manifested a sufficient intention to create a trust. The person declaring himself trustee must use sufficient language or evidence such conduct that clearly shows that he has fragmented his ownership. In this respect, all the rules relating to certainty of intention discussed in Chapter 4 will apply. Thus in **Richards v Delbridge**[16] a certain Delbridge purported to make a gift of his lease and business to his grandson, Richards. No such lease or business was assigned over to the grandson; however, Delbridge annexed a memorandum to the lease containing the words: 'This deed and all thereto belonging I give to Edward Bennetto Richards from this time forth, with all stock in trade.' Delbridge died without making any provision for his grandson in his will. The question before the court was whether there was a gift of the lease and business to his grandson, and, failing that, whether Delbridge had declared himself a trustee of the lease and business for his grandson. Clearly, there had been no effective gift of the lease of business to the grandson as there was never any assignment thereof. As to whether Delbridge had declared himself as a trustee for his grandson, Sir George Jessel MR held that: 'It is true [Delbridge] need not use the words "I declare myself trustee" but he must do something that is equivalent to it, and use expressions that have that meaning; for, however anxious the court may be to carry out a man's intention, it is not at liberty to construe words otherwise than according to their proper meaning.'[17] On this basis no such trust of the lease and business was found in favour of the grandson.

---

[16] (1874) LR 18 Eq 11.
[17] (1874) LR 18 Eq 11 at 14.

APPLYING THE LAW

> Over a few pints of beer, Tom told Brad that he would hold his classic sports car on trust for Brad. Brad did not make too much of that statement; however, two weeks later, Brad is now asking Tom to transfer the car to him.
>
> *Is there a trust in favour of Brad?*

The courts will not recognise a declaration of self as trustee where an individual uses casual or loose language. For example, a trust will not arise if a person casually says to another 'Don't worry, this car in my possession is yours and I will give it to you.' This is precisely what happened in ***Jones v Lock***[18] where Jones, on returning from a business trip in Birmingham, was confronted by the nurse looking after his baby son for not bringing anything back for his son. In the heat of the moment, Jones produced a cheque for £900, and in the presence of his wife and the nurse said that the cheque was for his baby and that, along with the cheque, he would give a lot more to his son. The cheque was temporarily placed in the baby's hands but was never endorsed in the son's name, it being at all times payable to Jones. Whilst Jones intended to make proper provision for his baby son, he died before this could be done. The question in court was whether Jones had declared himself a trustee of the £900 for his son. Lord Chancellor Cranworth held that, although Jones intended to make a gift of £900 to his son, which remained imperfect for lack of endorsement, his conduct and loose conversation could not be interpreted to mean that he had effectively declared himself a trustee of the money. Lord Chancellor Cranworth explained that it would be a very dangerous example if mere loose conversation like the type employed by Jones would have the effect of declarations of trusts. The case also illustrates the point that, where a gift fails for lack of delivery to the recipient, the courts will not recognise that the person making the gift intends to hold the subject matter of the gift on trust for the intended recipient.

A declaration of self as trustee may, however, be found where a person's conduct over a long period of time evidences a clear intention that he intends to hold certain property on trust for another. For example, in ***Paul v Constance***[19] Mr Constance, who had separated from his wife, lived with a certain Mrs Paul. In 1973 Mr Constance received a sum of £950 representing compensation for injuries he had suffered at his place of employment. Both Mr Constance and his partner Mrs Paul agreed that the money should be placed in a bank account. The account was opened in Mr Constance's name primarily because he did not want the embarrassment of opening a joint account in his and Mrs Paul's name because they were not married. For a period of some 13 months sums of money were deposited in that account representing the winnings from bingo games played by both of them. It was clearly the understanding between Mr Constance and Mrs Paul that the bingo winnings and the money in the account were as much Mrs Paul's as they were Mr Constance's. When Mr Constance died, his wife took over the administration of his estate. Mrs Paul brought an action against Mrs Constance arguing that the money in the bank account was held by Mr Constance on trust for himself and her jointly. Scarman LJ held that this was 'a borderline case, since it was not easy to pin-point a specific moment of declaration'.[20] Nevertheless, words repeated over time evidencing

---

[18] (1865) 1 Ch. App. 25.
[19] [1977] 1 All ER 195.
[20] [1977] 1 All ER 195 at 198.

an intention that a person intends to hold for another were sufficient to create a trust. In this case Mrs Paul was entitled to half of the sum of money held in the bank account in Mr Constance's name.

A similar result was achieved in **Rowe v Prance**[21] where two cohabiting individuals purchased a boat intended to be used for their pleasure and a place to live whilst they sailed the world. The boat was purchased solely with the money of the male cohabitee who had assured his female partner that the boat was as much hers as it was his. The boat was registered in the male partner's name and, when asked why it was not also registered in the female partner's name, the male partner replied that his female partner did not have a Master's certificate. In the course of their relationship, the male partner assured the female partner that the boat belonged to them jointly. The court held that the facts were sufficient to show that the male partner had declared himself a trustee for himself and his female partner in equal shares.[22]

 ## Transfer to trustees

Where a settlor intends to create a trust by appointing a trustee in favour of the beneficiary, he must transfer the subject matter of the intended trust property to the trustee (see Figure 6.2). The manner in which the trust property is transferred to the trustee depends primarily on the type of property in question. Where the property is something like a painting or a diamond, the trustee must hand over possession in order to convey the legal title thereto. Where the subject matter of the trust is land, the settlor must transfer the land in accordance with the formal requirements of the Land Registration Act 2002, which requires a deed followed by registration.[23] If the subject matter of the trust involves shares in a company, then the appropriate way in which the transfer will be effective is if the settlor executes the appropriate stock transfer form followed by registration of the shares in the share register of the company.[24]

Figure 6.2

There must be an actual transfer of the property to the trustee

Where a settlor intends to create a trust by transferring the trust property to trustees he must do everything in his power to transfer the trust property to the intended trustees. In **Milroy v Lord**[25] a settlor executed a deed in which he made clear his intention to

---

[21] [1999] 2 FLR 787. See also *Wallbank v Price* [2007] EWHC 3001 (Ch).
[22] See S. Baughen, 'Equality is Equity: Or is It?' (2000) Conv. 58.
[23] Land Registration Act 2002, ss. 29, 30.
[24] Stock Transfer Act 1963, s. 1.
[25] (1862) 4 De GF & J 264.

transfer shares in an American bank to a certain Samuel Lord who was to hold the shares on trust for the claimant. Like any other shares, these could only be transferred to Samuel Lord by complying with the appropriate transfer forms followed by registration in the books of the bank. The settlor had created a power of attorney in Samuel Lord so as to allow the transfer of the shares to take place; however, Samuel Lord never took any steps to transfer the shares. When the claimant attempted to enforce the trust the Court of Appeal held that, although there was a sufficient intention to create a trust, there was no trust for lack of transfer of the shares to the intended trustee. The settlor had not done everything in his power to transfer the shares in the intended trustee.

It matters not that the intended trust property arrives in the hands of the trustee in some other capacity

The rule in *Milroy* v *Lord* is that the settlor must do everything in his power to vest the trust property in the hands of the intended trustee. Once the property is vested the trust is completely constituted. It matters not that the vesting of the trust property in the hands of the intended trustee happens quite incidentally. The bottom line is that when it reaches the hands of the trustee the beneficiary can enforce the trust obligation. In *Re Ralli's Will Trusts*[26] a testator left his residue on trust for his wife and then to his two daughters absolutely. One of the daughters, Helen, had entered into a marriage settlement[27] whereby she covenanted that she would settle all her existing and after-acquired property on certain trusts including for the benefit of her sister's children. Helen died before her mother and therefore was never able to transfer her remainder interest (that is, the interest she was to derive under her father's will) to the trustee of the covenant. The plaintiff, the husband of Helen's sister, was appointed as a trustee of the will of the testator. He also happened to be the trustee of Helen's marriage settlement. When Helen's mother died in 1961 the testator's residuary estate vested in him, and the question before the court was whether the plaintiff held Helen's remainder interest for her estate or whether he could, being the trustee of her marriage settlement, hold her interest subject to the terms of the marriage settlement. Buckley J held that the circumstances in which a trustee became the legal owner of the residue were irrelevant. The property subject to Helen's marriage settlement had vested in the trustee who was required to hold it on the terms of that trust, which in this case meant for the children of Helen's sister.

What is the legal position where it is an act of a third party which is required to perfect the transfer?

It is clear that the settlor must do everything in his power to transfer the property into the hands of the intended trustee. However, it may well be the position that the transfer can only be completed by some act on the part of a third party. For example, in the context of a transfer of shares in a private company, the directors may well have a right to refuse registration. The question arises: what is the position where it is a third party who is required to complete the transfer? In simple terms, if the transfer is completed by the third party then the trust is fully constituted; if not, then the trust remains incomplete.

---

[26] [1964] Ch. 288.
[27] See below for a detailed explanation of marriage settlements.

The problem is not so much whether the trust has in effect become constituted: rather the question relates to the proper time at which the transfer took place. Take, for example, a settlor who does everything in his power to transfer shares in a private company and the only thing remaining is for the company to register the shares. If the settlor dies and the shares are registered after his death, is the effective date of transfer of the shares when registration took place or when the settlor did everything in his power to transfer the shares? If the effective date of the transfer is the actual date when they are registered, then it becomes clear that the transfer may be liable to some form of tax in the nature of estate duty or inheritance tax as we know it today.

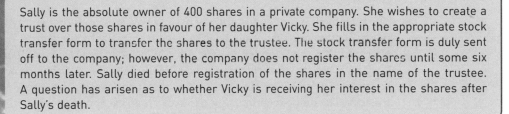

APPLYING THE LAW

Sally is the absolute owner of 400 shares in a private company. She wishes to create a trust over those shares in favour of her daughter Vicky. She fills in the appropriate stock transfer form to transfer the shares to the trustee. The stock transfer form is duly sent off to the company; however, the company does not register the shares until some six months later. Sally died before registration of the shares in the name of the trustee. A question has arisen as to whether Vicky is receiving her interest in the shares after Sally's death.

VISIT CASE NAVIGATOR

The matter fell to be decided in **Re Rose**[28] where a donor wished to make a gift of shares to his wife.[29] The appropriate share transfer form and the relevant share certificates were forwarded to the company on 30 March 1943. The company registered the transfer on 30 June 1943, some three months later. The donor died in 1947 and the question was whether the gift of the shares to his wife was subject to estate duty. If the shares had been transferred to his wife before 10 April 1943 then under the then rules of estate duty the transfer would not be subject to estate duty. The Court of Appeal held that the effective date of the transfer was 30 March 1943 and not 30 June 1943. Jenkins LJ explained that the donor had done everything in his power to transfer the shares to his wife. All that was needed was an act of a third party to perfect that transfer. It is sometimes said the rule in **Re Rose** will only apply when the donor has reached a stage in making the gift where there is no return. This is also known as the last act doctrine. In **Re Rose** the Court of Appeal gave an example of where the rule would not operate. Jenkins LJ referred to an earlier decision in **Re Fry**[30] where a settlor living in America completed share transfer forms transferring shares in a limited company in England. However, before these shares were capable of registration the settlor was required to obtain consent from the Treasury under certain Defence Regulations. Although the necessary consent forms had been filled in and sent to the relevant authorities, the settlor died before the consent was given. Romer J declined to recognise that there was any trust in favour of the intended beneficiaries. The settlor had not done everything in his power to transfer the shares on trust.

---

[28] [1952] Ch. 499.
[29] Although this case concerned a gift, the rule works equally in relation to a gift by way of a trust.
[30] [1946] Ch. 312.

The last act doctrine in **Re Rose**[31] was recently applied in **Curtis v Pulbrook**[32] where a purported transfer of shares in a company by a director to his wife and daughter failed for non-compliance with the appropriate procedures for the registration of the shares in the names of the wife and daughter. The court held that the director was not authorised to register new shareholders in the company's register and neither was he entitled to issue new share certificates. In this respect the director (the intended donor of the shares) had not done everything in his power to constitute the gift. Furthermore, the court held that no amount of benevolent construction could be given to the acts of the director so as to hold that he had declared himself a trustee of the shares for his daughter and his wife.

Equity will not strive officiously to defeat a gift

The two maxims that equity will not assist a volunteer and that equity will not perfect an imperfect gift have generally been applied rigorously by the courts. It has already been observed that the intended beneficiaries in cases such as **Milroy v Lord**[33] and **Re Fry**[34] obtain no benefit of a trust which was clearly intended for their benefit. This is simply because of a failure on the part of the settlor to transfer the intended property to the trustees. The only exception, if one is to call it an exception, is where the settlor has done everything in his power to effect the transfer and it is the act of a third party which is required to perfect the transfer. Despite this, in more recent times the courts have demonstrated a more relaxed approach to the question of transfer in the context of both gifts and gifts by way of trust. Two particular cases that have been decided relatively recently are difficult to explain within the existing principles and doctrines which have been developed in this area. Indeed these cases move away from the established doctrine that it is the last act which determines whether a gift or trust should be upheld or should fail. These cases adopt a broader notion of unconscionability in determining whether a purported gift or trust should be upheld. These can be examined in more detail.

Settlor declares a trust being one of a number of trustees

The first case is **T. Choithram International S.A. v Pagarani**[35] which involved an appeal to the Privy Council against a decision of the Court of Appeal of the British Virgin Islands. The facts of the case involved a wealthy businessman, Mr Pagarani, who having been diagnosed as suffering from cancer, decided to establish a charitable foundation which would oversee a number of charities which he had established during his lifetime. He appointed himself trustee along with nine other trustees to oversee the running of the foundation. In order to set up the foundation, Mr Pagarani, in the presence of three of the trustees, executed a deed outlining the nature and purpose of the foundation. At the same time, at his bedside, he orally made it clear that he wanted his shares and other wealth in a number of British Island's companies to be given to the foundation. Directors of the companies in which Mr Pagarani held the shares passed resolutions that the

---

[31] [1952] Ch. 499.
[32] [2011] EWHC 167 (Ch).
[33] (1862) 4 De GF & J 264.
[34] [1946] Ch. 312.
[35] [2001] 1 WLR 1.

trustees of the foundation were to be the new owners of the shares. However, Mr Pagarani, who died a month later did not make any transfer of his shares in the companies to the foundation. It was only after Mr Paragani's death that the directors of the relevant companies registered the trustees of the foundation as the new owners of the shares. Mr Paragani's family contended that the transfers were ineffectual because he had not transferred them prior to his death and so were part of his estate which devolve under the rules of intestacy. Although a trust of the shares was intended for the foundation, it remained incompletely constituted.

The leading judgment was delivered by Lord Browne-Wilkinson. His Lordship explained that the facts of the present case did not fall squarely within the two methods of making a gift by way of trust as identified in *Milroy v Lord*.[36] However, on the facts of the present case, his Lordship explained that there was no breach of the principles identified in *Milroy v Lord*.[37] In coming to his judgment, Lord Browne-Wilkinson identified a number of key facts which could only lead to one conclusion: that is, it would have been unconscionable for Mr Pagarani to recall the gift of the shares to the foundation. Firstly, the foundation, which Mr Pagarani intended to set up, was nothing more than an unincorporated association without any separate legal identity. It could not own property and hold property in its own right. Any such property belonging to the foundation could only be held for it by the trustees of the foundation. Secondly, Lord Browne-Wilkinson explained that there was no difference between the situation where a settlor declares himself as sole trustee and where he declares himself trustee being one of a number of trustees.[38] Mr Pagarani, the settlor of the shares in the various companies, had legal title to the shares and when he declared the trust deed appointing himself and nine other trustees, he had effectively constituted a trust of the shares in favour of the foundation. It did not matter that there was no formal transfer of the shares in the remaining trustees as long as they were vested in one of the trustees. In such circumstances it would be unconscionable for the settlor to recall the gift. Lord Browne-Wilkinson explained that 'although equity will not assist a volunteer, it will not strive officiously to defeat a gift'.[39] As a result of this, there was a completely constituted trust of the shares in favour of the foundation with Mr Pagarani as a trustee of the shares. The fact that the shares were formally registered in the name of the remaining trustees of the foundation after Mr Pagarani's death was not crucial.

It is true that the decision of the Privy Council in *T. Choithram International S.A.* v *Pagarani*[40] does not sit perfectly within the orthodox principles of making a gift by way of trust identified in *Milroy v Lord*.[41] The question which arises here is: what is the exact principle on which the case is decided and does that add to or vary the orthodox principles traditionally understood in *Milroy v Lord*?[42] There appear to be two central features in the decision of the Privy Council, firstly the element of unconscionability and secondly,

---

[36] (1862) 4 De GF & J 264.
[37] (1862) 4 De GF & J 264.
[38] [2001] 1 WLR 1 at 12.
[39] [2001] 1 WLR 1 at 11.
[40] [2001] 1 WLR 1.
[41] (1862) 4 De GF & J 264.
[42] (1862) 4 De GF & J 264. For a critical overview of this case and its impact on the traditional principles of making a gift by way of trust, see J. Morris, 'Questions: When is an Invalid Gift a Valid Gift? When is an Incompletely Constituted Trust a Completely Constituted Trust? Answer: After the Decisions in *Choithram* and *Pennington*', *Private Client Business* (2003) 6, 393–403. See also M. Halliwell, 'Perfecting Imperfect Gifts and Trusts: Have we Reached the end of the Chancellor's Foot?' *Conveyancer* (2003) 192–202.

the fact that the settlor was one of a number of trustees and he had declared himself as trustee. It is submitted that the principle emanating from *T. Choithram International S.A. v Pagarani*[43] is that where a settlor, who is one of a number of trustees, declares himself as trustee of some property, then it would be unconscionable for him to recall the gift despite the fact that the property is not yet vested in the other trustees. It is not unconscionability on its own which makes the trust completely constituted, but the fact that he has declared himself as trustee for another being one of a number of trustees. In this way it can be seen that the decision in *T. Choithram International S.A. v Pagarani* is an extension of the principles identified in *Milroy v Lord*.[44] The decision in this case has often been analysed as being authority for the proposition that the courts may give a benevolent construction to a failed gift if it is accompanied by an intention to create a trust.

Where it would be unconscionable to recall the gift

The decision of the Privy Council in *T. Choithram International S.A. v Pagarani*[45] was approved in a decision of the Court of Appeal in *Pennington v Waine*.[46] It is, however, submitted that the decision of the Court of Appeal in *Pennington v Waine*[47] goes much further in perfecting an imperfect gift and as such clearly does not fit within the principles of *Milroy v Lord*.[48] The case concerned an attempted gift of shares in a private company by an aunt to her nephew. Ada Crampton executed a share transfer form in respect of 400 shares in a private company in favour of her nephew Harold Crampton. She in fact owned a total of 1500 shares out of the 2000 issued in the company. The understanding was that Harold would become a director in the company and that the 400 shares were transferred solely for this purpose. The stock transfer form was sent to the company's auditor who informed Harold that he need not do anything further about the transfer of the shares. The auditor placed the stock transfer form on the company's file and necessary paperwork to appoint Harold as a director of the company. A few months later Ada made a will leaving the rest of her shareholding in a will without reference to the 400 which she had intended to give to Harold. The stock transfer form remained on the company's file until Ada's death without delivery to Harold or registration on the company's share register. The question in the Court of Appeal was whether there was a gift of the shares to Harold.

The gift of the 400 shares to Harold could only be complete if the stock transfer form had been received by the company and appropriate registration completed, followed by delivery of the share certificate to Harold. No such registration and delivery of the certificate had taken place and as such the gift remained incomplete and imperfect. In the Court of Appeal, Arden LJ explained that it was important not to detract from the principle that 'equity will not perfect an imperfect gift'; however, on the present facts there had been an equitable assignment of the 400 shares in favour of Harold. This meant that Ada Crampton held the shares on trust for Harold and as such he was entitled to them from the moment the gift was made. The difficult question which arises on the facts of this case is: on what basis could it be said that there was an equitable assignment of

---

[43] [2001] 1 WLR 1.
[44] (1862) 4 De GF & J 264.
[45] [2001] 1 WLR 1.
[46] [2002] 1 WLR 2075.
[47] *Ibid*.
[48] (1862) 4 De GF & J 264.

Ada's beneficial interest in the 400 shares to her nephew Harold? Clearly, Ada had not declared that she was to be a trustee of the shares for Harold; her only intention was to make an immediate gift of those shares to him. Clarke LJ suggested that as soon as the stock transfer form was completed with the intention of making an immediate gift of the shares then there was at this stage an equitable assignment of shares in favour of the donee. However, this line of reasoning is not without problem. The main difficulty lies in explaining how a donor can be construed as declaring himself as trustee over property which is intended to be transferred immediately to the donee. He either intends to create a trust or make an immediate gift. The rule is that equity will not construe a trust so as to save a failed gift unless there is a clear intention that the donor intended to became an immediate trustee in favour of the donee of the gift.

Arden LJ proceeded to address the issue on a rather different stance. Her Ladyship referred closely to the decision of the Privy Council in *T. Choithram International S.A. v Pagarani*[49] and paid particular emphasis to the words of Lord Browne-Wilkinson when his Lordship commented that 'although equity will not aid a volunteer, it will not strive officiously to defeat a gift'.[50] It will be recalled that in *T. Choithram International SA v Pagarani* the Privy Council held that it would be unconscionable for a settlor, who being one of a number of trustees, to declare himself a trustee in a favour of another to recall that gift. Arden LJ used this as the basis for her judgment in *Pennington v Waine*. In the opinion of her Ladyship, it would have been unconscionable for Ada Crampton to recall the gift of the shares to her nephew and as such she held the shares on trust for him. However, despite this, it is not altogether clear where the element of unconscionability lies on the facts of *Pennington v Waine*. Indeed, the judgment of Arden LJ fails to comprehensively explain why it would have been unconscionable for Ada to recall the gift of the shares to her nephew. Arden LJ commented that 'there can be no comprehensive list of factors which make it unconscionable for the donor to change his mind: it must depend on the court's evaluation of all the relevant considerations'.[51] On the facts, Ada had told her nephew that the shares were intended for his benefit and he was told that he need not take any further action. Furthermore, her nephew had agreed to act as director of the company. These factors, in the opinion of Arden LJ could only lead to one conclusion, and that was that Ada could not recall the gift of the shares to her nephew. Consequently, there had been an equitable assignment of the shares in favour of the nephew.

Undoubtedly, the decisions in *T. Choithram International S.A. v Pagarani*[52] and *Pennington v Waine*[53] illustrate a relaxation of the orthodox principles applying to imperfect gifts. The decision of the Privy Council in *T. Choithram International S.A. v Pagarani* can be explained and justified on the grounds that there the Privy Council took the view that there could be no difference between a situation where a settlor declares himself a trustee for another and where a settlor, being one of many trustees, declares himself a trustee for another; however, the decision in *Pennington v Waine* is more difficult to justify. The decision does fundamentally conflict with the principle that equity will not perfect an imperfect gift and that a donor or settlor has the right to change his mind any time up until transfer has taken place. There does not appear to be any element of unconscionability where a donor fails to do everything in his power to effect a gift.

---

[49] [2001] 1 WLR 1.
[50] [2001] 1 WLR 1 at 11.
[51] [2002] 1 WLR 2075 at 2089.
[52] [2001] 1 WLR 1.
[53] [2002] 1 WLR 2075.

Perhaps a better line of reasoning in **Pennington v Waine** would have been that, given that Harold had agreed to act as director of the company, he could perfect the imperfect gift by arguing that he was not a volunteer but had provided consideration in the form of acting as a director. As such he would be enforcing a promise to do something supported by consideration, which would have been far more in line with established principles. It is submitted that broad application of a test of unconscionability is far too dangerous a discretion to be given to the courts and one which introduces much uncertainty into an area of law which strives to achieve certainty.

Recent developments: unconscionability displaced by orthodox principles

Recent case law developments suggest that the broad test of unconscionability should be replaced by a return to the more traditional 'last act doctrine'. In other words, where the settlor has not done everything in his power to perfect the gift, then equity should not intervene to perfect an imperfect gift. For example, in **Zeital v Kaye**[54] the Court of Appeal refused to perfect an imperfect gift of shares in circumstances where the deceased transferor had nothing more than an equitable interest in the shares. The facts concerned the deceased, Raymond Zeital, who had been survived by his widow and his daughter (the appellants) and a certain Stefka Appostolova with whom he had been having a relationship for the last 20 years. Raymond died intestate in 2004 and the question arose as to the destiny of his estate. One particular aspect of his estate was a company called Dalmar, which he had formed for the purpose of property acquisitions. The two subscribed shares in the company were held by nominees on trust for Raymond. In this respect it was clear to the court that Raymond had a mere equitable interest in those shares. Before his death, it was pretty clear that Raymond's intention was to transfer the shares in the company to his partner for the last 20 years, Stefka. In order to put this into effect, Raymond filled in a stock transfer form in respect of one of the shares naming Stefka as the transferee, but in respect of the other share he merely transferred a blank transfer form to her. After Raymond's decease, Stefka claimed to be the director of Dalmar and entitled to its assets.

The Court of Appeal held that Stefka was not entitled to the purported attempt to transfer the second share on the grounds that Raymond had not done everything in his power to transfer the legal title to the shares to Stefka. At most he had a beneficial interest in the shares and he had not done all in his power to transfer that share to Stefka. If he wanted to transfer his equitable interest in the shares to Stefka, he should either have declared himself a trust of those shares for her or otherwise have directed the legal owner of the shares to hold them on trust for Stefka. Both of these options would have required a disposition of his equitable interest in writing pursuant to s. 53(1)(c) of the Law of Property Act 1925.[55] In the course of his judgment, Rimer LJ explained that:

> Raymond did *not* do all in his power to transfer the second share to Stefka. To become registered as a member, Stefka also needed the share certificate in respect of that share. The evidence was that its whereabouts were unknown. If it was lost, it was open to Mrs Kumar, as the legal owner, to procure the creation of a duplicate; and Raymond could have asked

---

[54] [2010] EWCA Civ 159.

[55] It was observed in Chapter 4 that a disposition of an equitable interest is only effective if it is in writing and signed by the person attempting to dispose of that equitable interest.

her to do so. He might perhaps first have had to procure Dalmar's restoration, but as the beneficial owner of the second share he could have asked Mrs Kumar to lend him her name for that purpose, upon giving her appropriate indemnities as to costs. But Stefka herself would not, I consider, have had any right to obtain a duplicate. Company registrars or secretaries do not ordinarily provide duplicates for lost shares to putative transferees so as to enable them to apply to be registered as members: they require such a transferee already to have a share certificate as part of his title to a claim to be registered. Raymond had not therefore equipped Stefka with the title documentation that she needed in order to be registered as a member of Dalmar, whereas he could have done. Unlike the donors in the Rose cases he had not, therefore, done all in his own power to transfer to her, or to procure the transfer to her, of the second share. For this further reason, his actions of August 2003 did not constitute her the beneficial owner of that share.[56]

The decision in **Zeital v Kaye** is a welcome development in this area of the law. Raymond's intention was to transfer the shares and give his partner of the last 20 years or so control of Dalmar and the assets or any proceeds of the assets held by that company. It was not his intention to leave those shares to his widow or his daughter. Some may argue, as was argued in the case, that just like in **Pennington v Waine**[57] it would have been unconscionable for Stefka to be denied the right to the share and that the nominees should have been ordered to hold the share on a constructive trust for her. Nevertheless, the Court of Appeal, quite rightly, held that she was not entitled to the share on the grounds that he had not done everything in his power to transfer the share to her. In the end the share vested on intestacy to his wife. The decision in this case introduces an element of certainty in the law. As for the broad notion of unconscionability, it is not clear what circumstances in this case could have given rise to unconscionability thereby requiring equity to perfect the imperfect gift.[58]

Zeital v Kaye[59] was more recently applied in **Curtis v Pullbrook**[60] where a purported transfer of shares in a company by a director to his wife and daughter failed. The correct procedure for the registration and issue of new shares in favour of the wife and daughter had not been followed by the director. The court held that in the absence of an effective transfer no amount of benevolent construction could be given to the failed transfer. **Curtis v Pullbrook** is less problematic from an unconscionability point of view because on the facts the purported transfer of the shares was a sham to defraud his creditors.

 ## Enforcing an incompletely constituted trust

A settlor must do everything in his power to transfer the trust property to the intended trustee. Where no such transfer has taken place the trust is incompletely constituted and the beneficiary has no trust in his favour. The question which arises at this stage is: what action if any can the beneficiary take to get the trust constituted? It has already been seen that equity will not assist a volunteer. Given that a settlor who intends to create a trust will normally enter into a covenant to settle, the beneficiary may well seek to enforce the

---

[56] [2010] EWCA Civ 159 at para. 43.
[57] [2002] EWCA Civ 227.
[58] See, Gerwyn Ll H. Griffiths, 'Zeital v Kaye: Doing Everything Necessary – A Recent Manifestation of an Ongoing Issue' [2010] Conv. 321.
[59] [2010] EWCA Civ 159.
[60] [2011] EWHC 167 (Ch).

covenant to settle by relying on principles outside the law of trusts, namely the law of contract.

Has the beneficiary given consideration at common law?

APPLYING THE LAW

Gary has promised to create a trust of 3000 shares in a private company in favour of Glen in return for Glen's services as an accountant. Glen has provided his accountancy services to Gary; however, Gary has not transferred the 3000 shares on trust for Glen.

Can Glen do anything about Gary's failure to transfer the shares on trust?

Where a beneficiary has provided consideration in return for a promise to create a trust or a covenant to settle property on trust, then that beneficiary may be able to enforce that covenant both at common law and in equity. Consideration at common law is defined as money or money's worth. At common law the beneficiary may sue for breach of contract and receive damages reflecting the loss he has suffered as a result of the settlor's failure to settle the trust property. In equity, the beneficiary may be able to ask the court for a decree of specific performance if the contract is capable of specific performance. Contracts are capable of specific performance where damages are inadequate, as for example, where the subject matter of the contract is rare and not readily available. Thus a contract to convey a classic painting on trust will avail itself to the remedy of specific performance. The decree of specific performance will have the effect of constituting the incompletely constituted trust.

A beneficiary who has provided consideration will be able to enforce a covenant to settle both existing and future property. It is trite law that a covenant to convey future property cannot be enforced by a beneficiary.[61] For example, in **Re Ellenborough**[62] the sister of Lord Ellenborough executed a voluntary settlement purporting to convey any property she would receive under her brother's will on trust for certain individuals. When her brother died in 1902 she refused to settle the property on trust. Buckley J held that there was no trust of future property and the trustees could not enforce the covenant in favour of the intended beneficiaries as they had not provided consideration.[63] However, where a beneficiary has given consideration in return for a promise to convey future property then that promise is capable of enforcement. For example, in **Holroyd v Marshall**[64] as part of a sale of mill machinery the purchaser agreed to assign the machinery on trust for a vendor provided he should pay £5000 to the purchaser and if not on trust for the purchaser. The terms of the assignment included both the existing machinery and any other after-acquired machinery which might be added to the existing machinery. The question in the House of Lords was whether the after-acquired machinery was capable of being used by the creditors of the vendor. The House of Lords held that any future machinery was subject to the trust.

---

[61] *Robinson* v *Macdonnell* (1816) 5 M & S 228. This is based on the simple premise that a person cannot assign something which he does not have.
[62] [1903] 1 Ch. 697.
[63] See also *Re Brooks' Settlement Trusts* [1939] Ch. 993.
[64] (1862) 10 HL Cas 191.

Marriage consideration

The common law views consideration as money or money's worth. In equity, however, consideration may take the form of marriage consideration. Marriage consideration and marriage settlements need to be understood in the context of their historical importance.

Understanding marriage settlements

Until the enactment of the Married Women's Property Act 1882, a married woman had no right to own property; everything she had belonged to her husband. Despite the 1882 legislation, which changed that rule, the husband usually continued in practice to be the sole owner of property.[65] It is not altogether clear why the common law denied property rights to married women. Holcombe explains that historians attribute the common law rule on grounds such as religion.[66] The medieval church regarded marriage as sacramental and the idea that two persons became one flesh justified the husband's dominion over his wife and any property she may have. Other justifications simply concentrate on the social and economic reality of the position of women in the Middle Ages. The extent of the common law rule prior to 1882 is neatly explained by Holcombe who writes: 'the property that a woman possessed or was entitled to at the time of the marriage and any property she acquired or became entitled to after her marriage became her husband's to control. Moreover, if a woman who accepted a proposal of marriage sought, before the marriage took place, to dispose of any property without the knowledge and consent of her intended husband, the disposition could be set aside as a legal fraud.'[67]

One way around the problem of a wife not being able to own property in her own right was to create a marriage settlement whereby the husband would covenant to convey on trust for the wife any of her existing property and any future property she may receive. Trustees of the marriage settlement would be able to enforce the covenant in equity and hold any such property subject to the covenant for the wife and any issue of the marriage, the consideration being the marriage of the husband to his wife. Normally all property of the wife, whether existing or after-acquired, would become the property of the husband; however, because of the marriage settlement the trustees could obtain specific performance and compel the husband to transfer the property to them on trust for the wife.

A classic example of marriage consideration and a marriage settlement is illustrated in *Pullan v Koe*.[68] The facts of the case involved a marriage settlement of 1859 whereby a wife agreed to settle any after-acquired property of the value of £100 or more on trust. The wife received a sum of £285 from her mother which she failed to transfer to the trustees of the marriage settlement. Some of the money was placed in her husband's bank account and some of it was used to purchase investment bonds which remained in her husband's name until his death in 1909. The question was whether the trustees of the

---

[65] See B. Roshier and H. Teff, *Law and Society in England* (1980) at p. 173.

[66] L. Holcombe, *Wives and Property* (1983) at p. 19.

[67] *Ibid.* at p. 18. The approach of the common law to the property rights of married woman was not followed by equity jurisdiction. Equity contributed to law reform by using equitable principles, notably the trust and marriage settlements, to protect the rights of married women in property they might acquire after marriage.

[68] [1913] 1 Ch. 9.

marriage settlement could takes steps to obtain the bonds from the husband's executors and hold them subject to the marriage settlement. The court held that, although the wife had failed to transfer the shares to the trustees of the marriage settlement, the trustees of the settlement could claim the bonds on behalf of the wife and her children. The court explained that as soon as the wife received the £285 it was subject to the marriage settlement and the wife and the children could claim the bonds in equity.

A marriage settlement can be enforced by the wife and her children. It cannot, however, be enforced by the next of kin of a wife who are deemed to be outside the marriage consideration. For example, in **Re Plumptre's Marriage Settlement**[69] a marriage settlement of 1878 settled the wife's after-acquired property on trust for the wife and then for the wife's next of kin. In 1884 the wife received money which was invested in various investments which remained in her husband's name until her death in 1909. The wife's next of kin sought to enforce the marriage settlement in their favour and recover the investments from the husband. Eve J held that the next of kin of the wife, being volunteers and strangers to the marriage consideration could not enforce the marriage settlement in their favour. The trustees of the marriage settlement were not bound to take any steps to obtain a transfer of the investments.[70]

Contract (Rights of Third Parties) Act 1999

The Contract (Rights of Third Parties) Act 1999, which came into force on 11 May 2000, may provide a beneficiary who has not provided consideration, and who is not privy to a settlor's covenant to create a trust, a right to enforce a covenant to settle property on trust.

APPLYING THE LAW

Charlie entered into a covenant with Peter to the effect that, in return for an annual payment of £3000, Peter would hold a sum of £200,000 on trust for Gillian until such time as she reached the age of 30 years old. Gillian was not party to the covenant, but now wishes to enforce the covenant against Charlie.

Can she do this?

KEY STATUTE

Contract (Right of Third Parties) Act 1999 section 1

(1) Subject to the provisions of this Act, a person who is not a party to a contract (a 'third party') may in his own right enforce a term of the contract if –

    (a) the contract expressly provides that he may, or

    (b) subject to subsection (2), the term purports to confer a benefit on him.

(2) Subsection (1)(b) does not apply if on the property construction of the contract it appears that the parties did not intend the term to be enforceable by the third party.

(3) The third party must be expressly identified in the contract by name, as a member of a class or as answering a particular description but need not be in existence when the contract is entered into.

---

[69] [1910] 1 Ch. 609.
[70] See also *Re D'Angibau* (1880) 15 Ch. D 228.

(4) This section does not confer a right on a third party to enforce a term of a contract otherwise than subject to and in accordance with any other relevant terms of the contract.

(5) For the purpose of exercising his right to enforce a term of the contract, there shall be available to the third party any remedy that would have been available to him in action for breach of contract if he had been a party to the contract (and the rules relating to damages, injunctions, specific performance and other relief shall apply accordingly).

Section 1(1)(b) is particularly relevant to a covenant to settle property on trust. If a settlor covenants to settle property with a trustee on trust for a beneficiary, the beneficiary can rely on s. 1 and enforce the covenant in his or her favour because, by the very nature of the covenant, the covenant is purporting to confer a benefit on the beneficiary. The beneficiary will be able to enforce a covenant to settle not only existing property but also any after-acquired property. The main requirement under the section is that the beneficiary seeking to enforce the covenant must be identified in the covenant expressly by name, as member of a class or answering a particular description. Section 1(5) makes it clear that all the normal contractual remedies will be available to the third party who is seeking to enforce the terms of the contract. However, in the case of a voluntary covenant to settle property, it is questionable whether the beneficiary will be able to obtain specific performance to enforce the provisions of the covenant. If the settlor's covenant is voluntary then equity will not recognise the contract and as such will not decree specific performance.

Consideration by use of a deed

APPLYING THE LAW

Tasmira has entered into a covenant under which she has covenanted with Jasmine and Alisha that she will transfer to both of them £4000 in twelve months' time as an appreciation of their moral support when Tasmira was going through a divorce. The covenant was between Tasmira, Jasmine and Alisha and they all signed it. Tasmira has recently received a substantial sum of money as a result of her divorce settlement; however, she refuses to transfer the money she promised to give to Jasmine and Alisha.

Can Jasmine and Alisha do anything about this?

A beneficiary who is party to the settlor's covenant to create a trust may enforce the covenant directly at common law even though it has not provided consideration in the form of money and money's worth. If the covenant is made by deed, and the beneficiary is a party to it, then the contract will be recognised at common law. The rule stems from the historical recognition of the common law that contracts entered into under seal are legally binding at common law. Historically, use of a seal gave legal significance to the deed and the deed provided the necessary consideration at common law to enforce the contract contained in the deed. Although a seal is no longer needed to give a deed its characteristic of a deed,[71] a party to a covenant in a deed can enforce the covenant

---

[71] See s. 1 Law of Property (Miscellaneous Provisions) Act 1989.

at common law. This was neatly illustrated in **Cannon v Hartley**[72] where, by a deed of separation made by a husband to whom his wife and daughter were parties, covenanted that he would convey upon trust any such property over the value of £1000 which he would receive under his parents' will for himself for life, thereafter for his wife and then absolutely for his daughter. In 1944 the husband became entitled to money under his parents' will. In 1946 the wife died and the husband refused to settle the money in accordance with the deed in favour of his daughter absolutely. Romer J held that the daughter was entitled to sue her father for breach of contract and receive damages reflecting the loss that she had suffered as a consequence of the failure to honour the promise made in the deed. Romer J explained that it was a well-established principle that a document made under seal was enforceable at law. In this case the daughter would have no right to enforce the covenant in equity by way of specific performance but was perfectly entitled to damages at common law. The reason why the daughter was not entitled to enforce the covenant in equity is simply because in the eyes of equity she would still be a volunteer. There is no consideration in substance and thus the contract will not be recognised in equity. The effect of this is that the remedy of specific performance will not be available to enforce a covenant to settle property where the beneficiary is a party to it.

Settlor covenants with the trustee to settle property on trust

A settlor may attempt to create a trust by covenanting not directly with the beneficiary but rather with the intended trustee. Thus, the parties to the covenant are the settlor and the trustee but not the beneficiary. In this situation the beneficiary is clearly a third party and not privy to the contract. The beneficiary cannot enforce the covenant at common law on the basis of **Cannon v Hartley**[73] because, although the covenant is in a deed, the beneficiary is not a party to the settlor's covenant to settle. If the covenant is created after May 2000 then the beneficiary may rely on s. 1 of the Contract (Rights of Third Parties) Act 1999, provided the contract confers a benefit on the beneficiary, which undoubtedly it will in the case of a covenant to settle. However, if the covenant is before May 2000 the question arises whether the trustee, who is clearly party to the settlor's covenant to settle, can sue on behalf of the beneficiary and recover substantial damages. There are two immediate problems which arise in this context. Firstly, the question is whether a party who is privy to a contract should be allowed to sue on behalf of another who is clearly not privy to it? Secondly, and perhaps more crucially, even if the trustee was allowed to sue the settlor in his own capacity, what loss has he suffered? The trustee's own loss would be nominal and as such would not be able to recover substantial damages for the beneficiary.

The general view that seems to come from the cases decided in this context is that trustees should not be compelled to sue on behalf of the volunteer beneficiaries. Most of the cases involve voluntary covenants to settle after-acquired property and the question has been whether the trustees can sue at common law when the settlor has failed to settle the property. In **Re Kay**[74] a spinster executed a voluntary settlement covenanting with trustees to settle any after-acquired property. She married later on and had three children. When she became entitled to property under a will she refused to settle in

---

[72] [1949] Ch. 213.
[73] [1949] Ch. 213.
[74] [1939] 1 Ch. 329. See also *Re Pryce* [1917] 1 Ch. 234 where Eve J held that trustees ought not to bring proceedings against a settlor who voluntarily covenants to settle property. To do so would allow the beneficiaries to obtain relief which they cannot do by direct procedure and have the effect of enforcing a covenant which is not recognised in equity.

accordance with the voluntary settlement. The trustees of the settlement asked the court for direction whether they could sue on behalf of the volunteer children. Simonds J held that the children, being volunteers, had no right to enforce the covenant, and therefore the trustees should not be compelled to enforce the covenant. Similarly, in **Re Cook's Settlement Trusts**[75] Buckley J held that trustees should not be allowed to sue on behalf of volunteer beneficiaries who could not enforce the covenant in their own right. Buckley J went further and explained that even if the trustees were allowed to sue the settlor, any damages received would be held on resulting trust for the settlor rather than the beneficiaries. The reason for this is that there is no trust for the intended beneficiaries and any such damages would have to be returned to the settlor. In this context it is simply wasteful and illogical for the trustee to be allowed to sue the settlor.[76] Furthermore, to leave it to the whim of the trustee to sue the settlor hardly creates a sound principle of law.

Completely constituted trust of a covenant (promise) in favour of a beneficiary

It is quite possible that a settlor can create a fully constituted trust of a promise or covenant for the benefit of a beneficiary. This somewhat difficult concept was explored by Wigram VC in **Fletcher v Fletcher**[77] where Fletcher made a voluntary deed whereby he covenanted to settle a sum of £60,000 in favour of his illegitimate sons John and Jacob on them attaining the age of 21 years. The deed contained a provision that should either of the illegitimate sons die before Fletcher then the £60,000 would be held by the trustees absolutely for the surviving son. The deed was kept with Fletcher's most valuable belongings; however, neither the trustees of the covenant nor the illegitimate sons had any knowledge of it. When Fletcher died he was survived by one of the illegitimate sons, Jacob, who had reached the age of 21. Jacob sought to enforce the covenant in his favour. The executors of Fletcher's will argued that Jacob was a mere volunteer and therefore incapable of enforcing the covenant at law or in equity. Furthermore, the trustees had not been made aware of the covenant and they were not willing to accept the office of trusteeship. Despite this, Wigram VC held that a fully constituted trust of a covenant had been created in favour of Jacob. He could vis-à-vis the trustees sue at common law and receive damages or independently recover the money in his own name in equity. The judge explained the matter as follows:

---

[75] [1965] Ch. 902.

[76] This view is echoed in D. Hayton, *Underhill and Hayton: Law of Trusts and Trustees* 17th edn (2006). One decision which appears to be inconsistent with *Re Kay's Settlement* [1939] 1 Ch. 329 and *Re Cook's Settlement Trusts* [1965] Ch. 902 is *Re Cavendish Browne's Settlement Trusts* [1916] WN 341. In this case the settlor covenanted to settle land in Canada on trust for beneficiaries who were mere volunteers. When the settlor refused to settle the land on trust, the trustees sued and received substantial damages reflecting the value of the land. This decision is often cited as authority for the view that substantial damages are recoverable by a trustee on behalf of a volunteer beneficiary who is not party to the settlor's covenant to create a trust. This is certainly the view of J. Martin, *Hanbury and Martin: Modern Equity* (18th edn 2009) Sweet & Maxwell, London at p. 141. However, it is not entirely clear why this should be the case. In *Re Cook's Settlement Trusts* [1965] Ch. 902 Buckley J distinguished *Re Cavendish Browne's Settlement Trusts* on the grounds that the settlor was attempting to settle existing property, that is, property which she was absolutely entitled to. In contrast the facts of both *Re Kay's Settlement* [1939] 1 Ch. 329 and *Re Cook's Settlement Trusts* [1965] Ch. 902 involved covenants to settle after-acquired property. However, it is submitted that there appears to be no logical reason to distinguish between voluntary covenants to settle existing property and voluntary covenants to settle after-acquired property when in both cases the beneficiaries are volunteers. Given the fact these cases have been decided at first instance, the position does remain unclear.

[77] (1844) 4 Hare. 67.

I cannot, I admit, do anything to perfect the liability of the author of the trust, if it is not already perfect. This covenant, however, is already perfect. The covenantor is liable at law, and the Court is not called upon to do any act to perfect it. One question made in argument has been whether there can be a trust of a covenant the benefit of which shall belong to a third party; but I cannot think there is any difficulty in that . . . the real question is whether the relation of trustee and *cestui que trust* is established in the present case.[78]

The decision in *Fletcher v Fletcher* is quite remarkable, given the facts that neither the settlor's son nor the trustees had any knowledge of the existence of the covenant. The covenant was voluntary in all respects and Jacob, who was seeking to enforce the trust, was a volunteer in respect of the £60,000. However, despite this, the basis of the decision in *Fletcher v Fletcher* is that Jacob was not enforcing a trust of the £60,000: rather, Jacob was enforcing a completely constituted trust of a promise to settle £60,000. In other words, the promise which his father had made in the voluntary deed had in itself become the subject matter of a trust in favour of Jacob. The following box attempts to illustrate how a trust of a promise operates.

FURTHER THINKING

Fletcher v Fletcher (1884) 4 Hare. 67: Understanding a trust of a promise

The idea that there can be a trust of a promise is somewhat difficult for students of trusts to get round. However, the matter is best understood by appreciating two types of property and two different trusts.

Trust one: a trust of £60,000 in favour of A, incompletely constituted

Suppose a settlor attempts to declare a trust of £60,000 in writing in favour of A by appointing B as his trustee. This trust will remain incompletely constituted until such time as the settlor transfers the legal title to the money to B (Figure 6.3). If the settlor does not transfer the money then A remains a volunteer and cannot really do anything to enforce the trust.

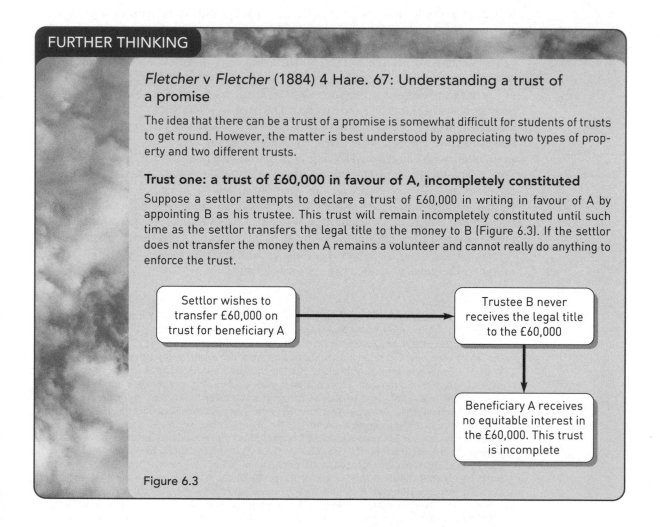

Figure 6.3

---

[78] (1844) 4 Hare. 67 and 74.

Trust two: a trust of a promise to settle £60,000 in favour of A, completely constituted

In Trust one above it has already been observed that, until such time as the £60,000 is transferred into the hands of B (the trustee) the trust is incompletely constituted. However, the fact that the settlor has made a promise (which in itself is a form of property in the nature of a *chose in action*) means that the promise attaches itself to a trust. The promise is held by the trustees on behalf of the beneficiary. The fact that the settlor has made the promise to settle the £60,000 means that the trust of the promise is fully constituted and the promise belongs to the beneficiary who can ask the trustees to compel performance by the settlor (Figure 6.4). The settlor could be said to have created a debt in favour of the beneficiary, albeit enforceable vis-à-vis the trustee at law or directly by the beneficiary in equity.

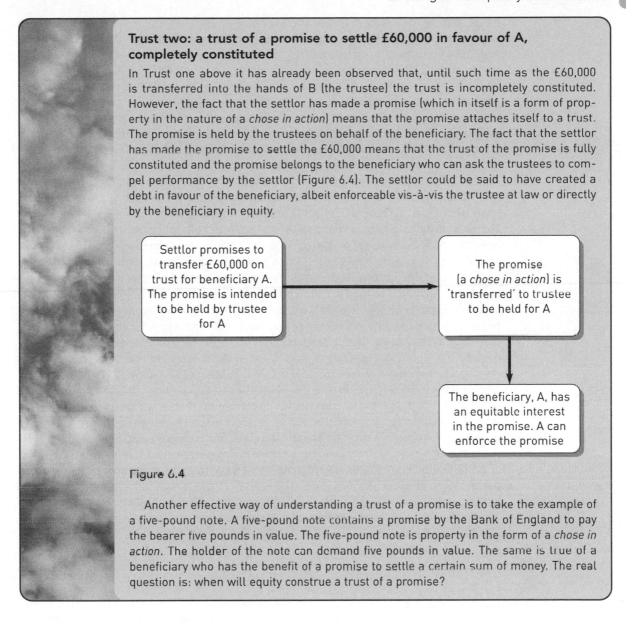

Settlor promises to transfer £60,000 on trust for beneficiary A. The promise is intended to be held by trustee for A

The promise (a *chose in action*) is 'transferred' to trustee to be held for A

The beneficiary, A, has an equitable interest in the promise. A can enforce the promise

Figure 6.4

Another effective way of understanding a trust of a promise is to take the example of a five-pound note. A five-pound note contains a promise by the Bank of England to pay the bearer five pounds in value. The five-pound note is property in the form of a *chose in action*. The holder of the note can demand five pounds in value. The same is true of a beneficiary who has the benefit of a promise to settle a certain sum of money. The real question is: when will equity construe a trust of a promise?

Although the idea of a fully constituted trust is sound in principle, it is questionable whether the facts of **Fletcher v Fletcher**[79] did give rise to a trust of a promise. You will recall that the covenant made by Ellis Fletcher was voluntary and no one including the trustees had any knowledge of the existence of the covenant. Furthermore, it is questionable whether there was any intention on the part of Ellis Fletcher to create a trust of a promise. The only intention in the voluntary deed was to pay a sum of £60,000 to trustees for the benefit of his illegitimate children. Subsequent authorities have suggested that a trust of a promise will only arise where there is a clear manifested intention

---

[79] (1844) 4 Hare. 67.

on the part of the settlor to create a trust of a covenant. Supposedly, the settlor must do something more that just attempt to declare a trust, of let's say £60,000, in favour of a beneficiary. He must go further and say that, until such time as he transfers the £60,000 on trust for the beneficiary, he wishes the covenant in which he makes the promise to be held on a trust for the beneficiary. For example, in **Re Cook's Settlement Trusts**[80] a settlement by Sir Francis Cook to settle certain property which would become his in favour of his children was said to be unenforceable. The children were mere volunteers and incapable of enforcing the voluntary covenant. Buckley J distinguished **Fletcher v Fletcher**[81] on the grounds that 'the covenant did not create a debt enforceable at law, that is to say, a property right, which, although to bear fruit only in the future and on a contingency, was capable of being made the subject of an immediate trust'.[82] This is another way of saying that there was no intention on the part of Sir Francis Cook to create an immediate trust of a covenant to settle property he would acquire later on. Indeed, most commentators have argued that a trust of a promise will only arise if there is sufficient intention on the part of the settlor to create a trust of such a promise.[83]

Although it is quite possible to have a fully constituted trust of a promise to settle property, one limitation on this is that the promise must relate to existing property and not to after-acquired property. Thus a promise to convey a sum of money or a painting is perfectly capable of being the subject matter of a trust; however, a promise to convey property which the settlor might acquire in the future is not capable of being the subject matter of a trust. In **Re Cook's Settlement Trusts**[84] Buckley J explained that one of the reasons why there was no trust of a covenant to settle property was because, unlike all the cases he had been referred to,[85] the covenant related to property which the settlor did not yet have in his possession. It is not altogether clear whether this line of reasoning is indeed correct. It does not matter whether the covenant to settle property relates to existing or after-acquired property. The fact is that a covenant is one thing and the property which it is seeking to convey is another. The covenant is clearly existing once it has been made by the settlor, and the fact that it relates to property which is not yet in possession is neither here or there. One leading authority on the matter explains that 'a covenant to pay a sum to be ascertained in the future is just as good a chose in action as a covenant to pay a specified sum, and it creates a legal property of value. The subject-matter of the trust is the benefit of the covenant, the chose in action; not the property which will be obtained in performance.'[86]

---

[80] [1965] Ch. 902.

[81] (1844) 4 Hare. 67.

[82] [1965] Ch. 902 at 913. See also, *Vandepitte* v *Preferred Accident Insurance Corpn of New York* [1933] AC 70 where the Privy Council declined to find a trust of the benefit of an insurance contract in the absence of firm evidence.

[83] The decision in *Fletcher* v *Fletcher* (1844) 4 Hare. 67 has been explained by one commentary on the grounds that it was decided at a time when the rules on certainty of intention were relaxed and that any words of hope, desire or the like were seen as creating a trust. Given the fact that Ellis Fletcher intended his sons to receive the benefit of the covenant after his death, it is not, therefore, surprising that the Court held that a trust of a promise had arisen in favour of the illegitimate sons; see T. Oakley, *Parker and Mellows, The Modern Law of Trusts* 9th edn (London: Sweet & Maxwell, 2008) at p. 187.

[84] [1965] Ch. 902.

[85] For example, *Fletcher* v *Fletcher* (1844) 4 Hare. 67, *Williamson* v *Codrington* (1750) 1 Ves. Sen. 511 and *Re Cavendish Browne's Settlement Trusts* (1916) 61 SJ 27.

[86] J. Martin, *Modern Equity* 18th edn (2009) at p. 142. See also Lee, 'The Public Policy of *Re Cook's Settlement Trusts*' (1969) 85 LQR 213; Meagher and Lehane, 'Trusts of Voluntary Covenants' (1976) 92 LQR 427 and Feltham, 'Intention to Create a Trust of a Promise to Settle Property' (1982) 98 LQR 17.

Specific performance of a covenant using the principle of *Beswick* v *Beswick*

On the facts of **Beswick v Beswick**,[87] Mr Beswick assigned to his nephew, the appellant, his business in return for the nephew paying Mr Beswick £6 per week for the remainder of his life and then to pay Mrs Beswick, the respondent, £5 per week. Mr Beswick died in 1963, and his nephew, after making one payment to Mrs Beswick, refused to pay the £5 per week as promised. Mrs Beswick sued the nephew for arrears of £175. Interestingly, on the facts Mrs Beswick was also administrator of her husband's estate. Mrs Beswick sued the nephew in both her personal capacity and in her capacity as administratrix of her late husband's estate. The House of Lords held that Mrs Beswick, in her personal capacity, was a volunteer and as such had no claim against the nephew. In other words, she had not provided any consideration in return for the nephew's promise to pay her £5 per week. However, the House of Lords held that she could in her capacity as administrator ask for a decree of specific performance to pay the £5 per week.

The decision of the House of Lords in **Beswick v Beswick**[88] suggests that a possible way around the enforcement of covenant to settle is for the trustees to obtain specific performance of the covenant. However, it is submitted that the facts of **Beswick v Beswick**[89] do not allow trustees of a voluntary covenant to obtain specific performance for the beneficiaries. On the facts, Mr Beswick had provided consideration in return for his nephew's promise to pay the agreed sum of money per week to him and then to his wife. Furthermore, what is crucial on the facts is that Mrs Beswick had been appointed administratrix of her late husband's estate and as such stood in the same 'shoes' as her husband. The decision in **Beswick v Beswick** may, however, apply in a case where a settlor covenants to create a trust in return for some consideration from the trustee: for example, if A agrees with B to settle property on trust for C in return for B giving him a sum of money or some other property. Certainly, in such a case B can obtain specific performance against A to perform the covenant. Equally, provided C is appointed as B's administrator, then C in his capacity as administrator can ask the court for specific performance, compelling A to transfer the property subject to the covenant to C.

Exceptions to the rule that equity will not assist a volunteer

Although it is well established that equity will not assist a volunteer, there are two genuine exceptions to this rule. These exceptions are wide enough to perfect an imperfect gift as well a constitute an incompletely constituted trust.

The rule in *Strong* v *Bird*

The rule in **Strong v Bird**[90] was neatly summarised by Neville J in **Re Stewart**[91] the following manner.

---

[87] [1968] AC 58.
[88] *Ibid.*
[89] *Ibid.*
[90] (1874) LR 18 Eq. 315. For a detailed discussion of the rule, see G. Kodilinye, 'A Fresh Look at the Rule in *Strong* v *Bird*' [1982] 46 Conv. 14.
[91] [1908] 2 Ch. 251.

[W]here a testator has expressed the intention of making a gift of personal estate belonging to him to one who upon his death becomes executor, the intention continuing unchanged, the executor is entitled to the property for his own benefit. The reason why this conclusion is reached is of a double character – first, that the vesting of the property in the executor at the testator's death completes the imperfect gift made in the lifetime, and, secondly, that the intention of the testator to give the beneficial interest to the executor is sufficient to countervail the equity of beneficiaries under the will, the testator having vested the legal estate in the executor.[92]

As explained by Neville J the rule in *Strong v Bird* operates to complete an incomplete gift, provided that the donee of the gift is appointed executor of the donor's will.[93] A good example is where A wishes to make a gift of his Rembrandt painting to B, but during his lifetime fails to deliver the painting to B required to make him the owner. If A's intention to make the gift continues until his death and B finds himself appointed as A's executor, the vesting of the painting in B as executor is sufficient to complete the incomplete *inter vivos* gift of the painting. The same principle will apply in the case of a trust: for example, where a settlor intends to create a trust during his lifetime in favour of another, but fails to vest the legal title in the hands of the intended trustee. In the case of the trustee being appointed executor, the vesting of the trust property in him as executor has the effect of completing the incomplete trust.

The facts of *Strong v Bird*[94] did not involve an imperfect gift but an imperfect release of a debt: however, the underlying principle is the same. On the facts of *Strong v Bird* a stepson had borrowed a sum of money from his stepmother who was living with him and paying him rent. The understanding was that the loan could be repaid through a deduction in the monthly rent that the stepmother was paying her stepson. After two reduced payments of rent the stepmother made it clear that she did not want the loan repaid. This loan could only be released at common law if it had complied with the correct formality, that is, if it was for consideration or if it was made under seal. Although the loan remained unreleased at common law despite the stepmother's intention to release, it did become released when the stepson was appointed as the executor of his stepmother's will. His appointment as executor had the effect of vesting the legal title to the debt in him. In such a situation it is absurd to suggest that the executor would sue himself to recover the debt in favour of the residuary legatees of the will. The vesting of the legal title in the executor had the effect of releasing the debt. In order for the rule in *Strong v Bird* to be invoked there are two primary requirements that must be satisfied.

APPLYING THE LAW

Colin has promised to transfer his antique paintings to Harold to be held upon trust for Kelly. He has promised to do this but never got round to transferring the paintings to Harold. Colin died last year leaving his estate to a number of charities. Harold, who has been appointed the executor of Colin's will, has been approached by Kelly who demands that Harold hand over the paintings to her.

Can Kelly demand the paintings from Harold?

---

[92] [1908] 2 Ch. 252 at 254.

[93] The juridical basis of the rule has been questioned recently by J. Jaconelli, 'Problems in the Rule in *Strong v Bird*' [2006] 70 Conv. 432.

[94] (1874) LR 18 Eq. 315.

There must be an intention to make an *inter vivos* gift up to the point of the donor's death

The donor must have an immediate intention of making an *inter vivos* gift and that intention must continue up until his death. Where the donor merely intends to make a gift in the future the rule will not apply. This principle is neatly illustrated in **Re Freeland**[95] where the donor told her friend, Hilda, who was in need of a car that she could have her Hillman car once it was made roadworthy. The car remained in the donor's garage until it was eventually repaired. The donor then lent the car to another friend, May, with Hilda's permission. The car remained in May's possession until the donor's death. Both Hilda and May were appointed as executrices of the donor's will and the question was whether Hilda was entitled to the car. The court held that Hilda was not entitled to the car as the donor had only intended to make a future gift of the car to her once it was repaired. Furthermore, the fact that the car had been loaned to May was inconsistent with the donor's intention to make an immediate gift of the car to Hilda.

The property must be vested in the executor or administrator

The rule in **Strong v Bird**[96] will only apply if the donee of the gift is appointed as the executor of the donor's will. It is immaterial whether the donee is the sole executor of the donor's will or where he is one of several executors. The question arises whether the rule in **Strong v Bird** applies to a donee who is appointed as administrator. In **Re James**[97] a donor gave furniture and the title deeds to his house, which he had inherited from his father, to his father's housekeeper. When the donor died, the housekeeper asked to be appointed as the administratrix of the donor's estate. The court held that her appointment as administratrix was sufficient to allow her to keep the property given to her by the donor. Although it has been accepted that the rule in **Strong v Bird** will apply to a donee who is granted letters of administration, it does remain rather controversial. An executor is appointed by the donor through a deliberate act on his part. An administrator is appointed by law and the initiative is on the donee to apply for letters of administration. In **Re Gonin**[98] Walton J cast doubt whether the rule should extend to administrators, because 'it is often a matter of pure chance which of many persons equally entitled to a grant of letters of administration finally takes them out'.[99]

● *Donatio mortis causa*

---

[95] [1952] Ch. 110. See also *Re Gonin* [1979] Ch. 16.
[96] (1874) LR 18 Eq. 315.
[97] [1935] Ch. 449.
[98] [1979] Ch. 16.
[99] [1979] Ch. 16 at 35.

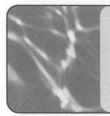

she wanted him to have the contents of the case. Beatrice died last week and Victor discovers that the briefcase contains several bank account books and a land certificate to her cottage. Victor claims that Beatrice intended him to keep the money in the accounts and the house for himself.

Can he do this? The nieces are claiming all of Beatrice's property under Beatrice's will.

A *donatio mortis causa* is a gift made in contemplation of death. The doctrine has its origins in Roman law and became incorporated into English law in the early eighteenth century.[100] The basic idea behind a *donatio mortis causa* can be best explained by reference to the following example. A is lying on his deathbed and is being cared for by B. A may well have executed a will leaving all of his property to C; however, if A gives to B some property which he wants B to keep once A has died, then B can keep that property. It does not matter that the property which A wishes to leave to B has not been properly transferred to B: the doctrine will have the effect of perfecting the gift in B because of the very circumstances in which it was made. In this sense a *donatio mortis causa* is a gift which is *inter vivos* in its nature but one which vests in the donee once the donor is dead. The matter was explained by Buckley J in **Re Beaumont**[101] where he commented that 'a *donatio mortis causa* is a singular from of gift. It may be said to be of an amphibious nature, being a gift which is neither entirely *inter vivos* nor testamentary. It is an act *inter vivos* by which the donee is to have the absolute title to the subject of the gift not at once but if the donor dies.'[102] The requirements needed to establish a *donatio mortis causa* were explained by Nourse LJ in the Court of Appeal in **Sen v Headley**.[103] His Lordship commented:

> First, the gift must be made in contemplation, although not necessarily in expectation, of impending death. Secondly, the gift must be made upon the condition that it is absolute and perfected only on the donor's death, being revocable until that event occurs and ineffective if it does not. Thirdly, there must be a delivery of the subject matter of the gift, or the essential indicia of title thereto, which amounts to a parting with dominion and not mere physical possession over the subject-matter of the gift.[104]

These requirements can now be considered in more detail.

Gift must be made in contemplation of death

The donor must have made the gift in contemplation though not necessarily in expectation of death. The donor must be expecting a near possibility of death rather than a general expectation that death will eventually come as it does to every human being. For example, in **Re Craven's Estate**[105] a donor was expecting to undergo an operation which may well prove to be fatal. She instructed her son that money and securities in her bank should be put into his name. The operation did prove to be fatal, and when the issue arose as to whether the son was entitled to the money and securities, the court held that a valid *donatio mortis causa* had been proved. Farwell J explained that there must be

---

[100] For a more detailed account see A. Borkowski, *Deathbed Gifts* (1999).
[101] [1902] 1 Ch. 889.
[102] [1902] 1 Ch. 889 at 892.
[103] [1991] 2 All ER 636; see also *Cain v Moon* [1896] 2 QB 283.
[104] [1991] 2 All ER 636 at 639.
[105] [1937] Ch. 423.

'death within the near future, what may be called death for some reason believed to be impending'.[106]

Although the donor must be expecting death from some source such as an illness or as the result of carrying out some risky expedition, it does not matter that the actual cause of the death is different from the one that was contemplated. The only requirement is that the donor made the gift in circumstances in which he was contemplating the possibility of death. For example, in **Wilkes v Allington**[107] the donor was diagnosed as suffering from cancer and as a result of this he transferred the mortgage deeds to his farm to his nieces, the intention being that should he die from cancer the farms would belong to the nieces. A month later the donor died from pneumonia. The court held that there was a valid *donatio mortis causa*.

The gift must be conditional on death

The gift must be made in circumstances that it is conditional upon death. If the donor intends to make an immediate *inter vivos* gift then there can be no room for *donatio mortis causa*. The fact that the gift is conditional upon death means that should the donor recover the gift reverts back to him. It is also for this reason that the gift is fully revocable at any time during the donor's lifetime. The donor's intention that the gift is conditional upon death is often implied from the very circumstances in which the gift is made.[108]

There must be delivery of the subject matter of the gift

The donor must transfer to the donee the subject matter of the gift or he must transfer something which enables the donee to obtain the subject matter of the gift. Sometimes it said that the donor must part with dominion over the property comprised in the gift. In the case of personal property, there must be actual delivery of possession. For example, in the case of a painting, the donor must transfer physical possession of the painting. In such a case the gift is complete as the legal title will have passed to the donee. The donor must have an intention to part with control over the subject matter of the gift. Thus, it may prove fatal to a valid *donatio mortis causa* if the donor passes physical possession of the subject matter of the gift, but still retains some degree of control over the subject matter. The matter is neatly illustrated in **Reddel v Dobree**[109] where the donor, having being diagnosed of an illness, gave to the donee a cash box with the instructions that it was hers after his death. He explained to her that the key to the box could be obtained from his son, but that the box must be brought to him every three months whilst he was still alive. In these circumstances, the court held that there could be no *donatio mortis causa* as the conduct of the donor evidenced that he did not intend to part with control over the cash box.

In the case of some forms of personal property, such as money in a bank account or some form of national savings, it will be impossible for the donor to make actual delivery of such property to the donee. In such a case, it is important for the donor to make some form of constructive delivery of the subject matter of that gift. Constructive delivery involves delivery of some indicia of title to the subject matter of the gift.[110] For example,

---

[106] [1937] Ch. 423 at 426.
[107] [1931] 2 Ch. 104.
[108] *Re Lillington* [1952] 2 All ER 184; *Gardner v Parker* (1818) 3 Madd 184; 56 ER 478.
[109] (1839) 10 Sim. 244; 59 RR 607.
[110] *Birch v Treasury Solicitor* [1951] Ch. 298.

in **Re Weston**[111] the donor transferred to the donee his Post Office Savings Book and this was held to be sufficient for a valid *donatio mortis causa*. In so far as shares in a public company are concerned, it has been held that handing over an executed share transfer form to the donee is sufficient to effect a *donatio mortis causa* of the shares.[112] However, a mere transfer of a receipt for the purchase of shares will be insufficient as this will only amount to symbolic delivery, which is not acceptable to effect a *donatio mortis causa*.[113] Other examples include handing over the keys to a safety box held at a bank[114] and handing the keys to a car.[115] However, where the donor retains a second set of keys it may be construed that he has not parted with dominium. This was certainly the view taken in **Re Craven's Estate**[116] where the court was of the opinion that the retention of a second set of keys was evidence of the lack of intention on the part of the donor to part with exclusive control over the property. It is submitted that the question is not so much whether the donor has retained a second set of keys, but whether in the circumstances the donor has indeed parted with dominium over the property. For example, in **Woodard v Woodard**[117] the donor had been in hospital for some time suffering from leukaemia. His son had been in possession of his car even though he did not have the registration document. Shortly before the donor's death, he told his son that he could keep the keys as he would not be driving the car any more. It was held that there was a valid *donation mortis causa* despite the fact that the donor had a separate set of keys for the car. The court explained that it was clear on these facts that the donor would be unlikely to drive the car again.

In **Sen v Headley**[118] the Court of Appeal held that a valid *donatio mortis causa* could be made of land. Prior to this decision there had been debate as to what the donor would need to do to effect of *donatio mortis causa* of land. **Sen v Headley** involved unregistered land, and the donor, a few days before his death, handed over to the donee a key to a steel box which contained the title deeds to his house. The Court of Appeal held that these facts were sufficient to effect a *donatio mortis causa* of land. The handing over of the title deeds to the land was a good indicia of the donor's intention to transfer the land to the donee. It follows from the decision in **Sen v Headley** that a valid *donatio mortis causa* can also be made of registered land presumably by transferring the land certificate to the donee.

The effect of a valid *donatio mortis causa* is that the donee's conditional title to the donor's property becomes unconditional. The gift is said to be completed on the donor's death. Thus, a donor who has transferred, for example, a painting to a donee in contemplation of death, the conditional gift of the painting is said be completed and the donee obtains an unconditional legal title to the painting. However, in the case of intangible property such as shares the gift of the shares does not automatically render the gift complete. In such a case the donee will need the legal title to the shares to be duly transferred to him. This can only happen if the personal representatives of the donor execute the appropriate stock transfer form and send it off for registration. In such circumstances, the donee can compel the personal representatives of the donor to complete the gift of

---

[111] [1902] 1 Ch. 680.

[112] *Staniland* v *Wilmott* (1852) 3 Mac & G 664.

[113] *Ward* v *Turner* (1752) 2 Ves. Sen. 431; 28 ER 275.

[114] *Re Wasserberg* [1915] 1 Ch. 195.

[115] *Woodard* v *Woodard* [1995] 3 All ER 980.

[116] [1937] Ch. 423.

[117] [1995] 3 All ER 980.

[118] [1991] Ch. 425. See, N. Lesley and P. Welsh, 'Is the *Donatio Mortis Causa* of Land Dead or Alive' Tru. & E.L.J. (2001) at 1–3.

the shares by duly executing the stock transfer form. Until such time as this is done, the personal representatives of the donor will hold the legal title to the property on trust for the donee.[119]

   ## Proprietary estoppel

A discussion of constitution of trusts would not be complete without reference to the equitable doctrine of proprietary estoppel. It is quite possible for a claimant to enforce a covenant or a promise to create a trust where the claimant establishes an estoppel claim against a settlor. The estoppel claim will arise where the claimant is made a promise that a trust will be created in his or her favour, and in reliance on that promise, suffers some detriment. The essence behind proprietary estoppel is to prevent a legal owner of land from denying a proprietary right in land or other property which he has led the claimant to believe will become his. The doctrine is neatly explained by one leading commentary on land law which explains that 'the doctrine of proprietary estoppel gives expression to a general judicial distaste for any attempt by a legal owner unconscientiously to resile from assumptions which were previously understood, and acted upon, as the basis or relevant dealings in respect of his land. In curtailing the unconscionable disclaimer of such underlying assumption, the estoppel principle is ultimately directed against the abuse of power.'[120] Judicially, Oliver J explained the doctrine as one which:

> requires a very much broader approach which is directed rather at ascertaining whether, in particular individual circumstances, it would be unconscionable for a party to be permitted to deny that which, knowingly, or unknowingly, he has allowed or encouraged another to assume to his detriment than to inquiring whether the circumstances can be fitted within the confines of some preconceived formula serving as a universal yardstick for every form of unconscionable behaviour.[121]

A successful claim to an interest under proprietary estoppel requires that the defendant make some assurance or representation that the claimant will acquire an interest in the defendant's property. Secondly, the claimant must have relied on the assurance or representation by changing his position. Finally, as a result of the representation and subsequent change of position, the claimant must have suffered a detriment which makes it unconscionable for the defendant to deny the very rights in the property which he led the claimant to believe would be his.

Conclusion

This chapter has examined one of the most important requirements needed to create a trust. A settlor may have a very clear intention to create a trust and that intention may well be defined in a well-written trust document; however, what brings the intended trust into being is the act of constituting the trust. The settlor must either declare himself as a trustee, or he must transfer the subject of the trust to another trustee. If he fails to

---

[119] *Re Wasserberg* [1915] 1 Ch. 195.
[120] K. Gray and S. Gray, *Elements of Land Law* 6th edn (2009) at p. 1197.
[121] *Taylor Fashions* v *Liverpool Victoria Trustees Co Ltd* [1982] QB 133 at 151.

transfer the trust property to the trustee, the trust is said to be incompletely constituted and prima facie the beneficiaries have no immediate right to demand that the trust be constituted. The beneficiaries are, after all, volunteers in the sense that they have not given consideration in return for the trust. Furthermore, in the absence of unconscionable conduct on the part of the settlor, the settlor is free to change his mind. Where a trust is incompletely constituted, the beneficiaries will have to examine other options available to them in order to get the trust constituted. They may rely on the law of contract and try to enforce the settlor's promise to create a trust. However, the success of this very much depends on whether they have the appropriate contractual requirements to enforce the trust. In the absence of contract law, there are two exceptions to the general rule that equity will not perfect an imperfect gift. These exceptions lie at the boundaries between *inter vivos* and testamentary gifts.

Finally, it must be noted that in some cases, the courts have adopted a somewhat more liberal and relaxed approach to failed gifts and incomplete trusts. This liberal approach seems to be based on a broad notion of unconscionability. Where it would be unconscionable for the donor to recall a gift or where he has failed to complete a trust, both the Privy Council and the Court of Appeal have upheld gifts which have remained incomplete. Whether this broad policy of unconscionability warrants the justification of enforcing failed gifts is a matter which remains very much unsettled. Recent authorities such as *Zeital v Kaye*[122] suggest a return to more orthodox principles.

●●● Case studies

Read and analyse the following case studies.

1   Under a voluntary settlement made last year Mathew covenanted that he would convey any property he would acquire under his mother's will to his son Kirk. The covenant was made between himself and his trustee. The covenant, *inter alia*, contained the following clause:

> 'Until such time as I transfer the property which I expect to receive under my mother's will, I hereby declare that my trustees are to hold the benefit of this covenant upon trust for my son Kirk.'

A few months later, Mathew visited his brother Linden. He told Linden that he wanted Linden to keep his classic paintings as a gift. Mathew told him that he would always hold the paintings for him although he never transferred them to Linden. On a number of occasions Linden would visit Mathew and Mathew would insist that Linden take the paintings, but he never did.

Recently, after having received a valuable painting under his mother's will, Mathew was diagnosed as suffering from a serious illness. On one occasion, when he was very sick, Mathew handed over a briefcase to his nurse, Patty. He told her that he wanted her to keep the contents of the briefcase. Three days later Mathew died. When Patty opened the briefcase she found a bankbook and the title deeds to Mathew's House.

Advise Kirk, Linden and Patty, Mathew having made a will in which he left all of his property to Linden as his executor.

---

[122] [2010] EWCA Civ 159.

2 In June 2007 Magda executed a voluntary covenant in which she promised to transfer on trust valuable paintings to her cousin Sonya. Sonya was not aware of this covenant, which Magda had safely kept alongside her will at her solicitor's office. The trustee of this covenant was her solicitor who had drafted the covenant. At the same time Magda got her solicitor to execute a deed to the effect that until such time as she transferred her valuable paintings to her trustee, the trustee was to hold the benefit of the covenant on trust for Sonya.

In the same month Magda opened a bank account depositing £2000. She told Sonya that the money was for both of them to spend on a forthcoming holiday and that because Sonya was under age the account could not be opened in her own name. Magda did, on many occasions, make it clear to Sonya that the money in the account was as much hers as it was Magda's.

On her 75th birthday Magda asked her three children Victor, Aran, and Jessy to visit her. To Victor she said, 'Here is an envelope for you but don't open it until you have left me.' The envelope contained a cheque for £2000. She told Aran, 'Here is my share certificate to 3000 shares in ICI Ltd, together with a stock transfer form in your favour which I have duly signed.' To Jessy she said, 'I want you to have everything else including this house and all my furniture. All the necessary papers are in this deed box underneath my bed. Here is the only key.' The box contained the title deeds to the house and a savings book.

Magda died in her sleep that very night. In her will she appointed Sonya as her executor and left all her property to the local dogs' home.

Aran has sent the share transfer form to the company but the directors, who have a right to refuse registration, have refused registration.

Advise Sonya and Magda's children as to what entitlement they have to Magda's property.

●● Moot points

1 In *Paul v Constance* [1977] 1 All ER 195 Scarman LJ held that the settlor had declared himself a trustee of a bank account in favour of himself the beneficiary. At what point in time did the settlor declare himself a trustee in favour of the beneficiary? Do you think, given the fact that a trust generates an equitable proprietary interest in a beneficiary which binds everyone except a bona fide purchaser of the legal title without notice, that it is important to know exactly at what point in time a trust is in operation?

2 The decisions in *T. Choithram International S.A. v Pagarani* [2001] 1 WLR 1 and *Pennington v Waine* [2002] 1 WLR 2075 illustrate a relaxation of the orthodox principles applying to imperfect gifts. The view is that the courts should uphold failed gifts where it would be unconscionable for the donor of the gift to complete the failed gift. Is a broad-based test of unconscionability a satisfactory principle in upholding failed gifts?

3 In *Fletcher v Fletcher* (1844) 4 Hare. 67 the court held that a settlor could create a trust of a covenant in favour of a beneficiary. Do you think that in that case there was ever any real intention on the part of the settlor to create a trust of a covenant? Can you think of any other reasons why the case may have decided in the way it did?

4 Should the rule in *Strong v Bird* (1874) LR 18 Eq 315 apply to a person who has appointed as the administrator of the donor's estate?

5 Read the decision of the Court of Appeal in *Zeital v Kaye* [2010] EWCA Civ 159 and explain why the court refused to perfect an imperfect gift of a share in favour of the deceased's

partner for the last 20 years. Do you think that the facts in *Zeital* v *Kaye* were fundamentally different from the facts in *Pennington* v *Waine* [2002] 1 WLR 2075 where the Court of Appeal upheld a gift of shares in favour of a nephew on grounds of unconscionability? What does the decision in *Zeital* v *Kaye* tell you about equity's response to imperfect gifts?

Further reading

Barton, J.L. 'Trusts and Covenants' (1975) 91 LQR 236. Explores the relationship between trusts and covenants to settle property.

Elliot, D.W. 'The Power of Trustees to Enforce Covenants in Favour of Volunteers' (1960) 76 LQR 100. Examines the right of trustees to enforce covenants on behalf of volunteers who are not privy to the covenant to create a trust between the original settlor and the trustee.

Halliwell, M. 'Perfecting Imperfect Gifts and Trusts: Have We Reached the End of the Chancellor's Foot?' [2003] Conv. 192. Examines whether the decisions in *Choithram International S.A.* v *Pagarani* [2001] WLR 1 and *Pennington* v *Waine* [2002] 4 All ER 214 have gone too far in giving the courts an unfettered discretion to perfect imperfect gifts.

Jaconelli, J. 'Problems in the Rule in *Strong* v *Bird*' [2006] Conv. 432. This article offers a critical re-examination of the theoretical grounds for invoking the rule in *Strong* v *Bird* and argues that the rule is at odds with the general law of making gifts.

Kodilinye, G. 'A Fresh Look at the Rule in *Strong* v *Bird*' [1982] Conv. 14. Examines the nature and the grounds for invoking the rule in *Strong* v *Bird*.

Visit **www.mylawchamber.co.uk/panesar** to access study support resources including interactive multiple choice questions, practice exam questions with guidance, podcasts, weblinks, legal newsfeed all linked to the **Pearson eText** version of Exploring Equity and Trusts which you can **search**, **highlight** and **personalise** with your **own notes** and **bookmarks**.

premium
mylawchamber
unrivalled support for legal education

Use Case Navigator to read in full some of the key cases referenced in this chapter with commentary and questions:

Milroy v *Lord* (1862) 4 De GF & J 264
Re Rose [1952] Ch 499

CASE NAVIGATOR

POWERED BY LexisNexis®

7

Secret trusts and mutual wills

Learning objectives

After reading this chapter you should be able to:

→ understand the nature of a secret trust

→ distinguish between a fully secret trust and a half-secret trust

→ explain the status of secret trusts in relation to *inter vivos* and testamentary trusts

→ explain the justifications for the enforcement of secret trusts

→ understand the requirements needed for the creation of secret trusts

→ explain the consequences of failure of a secret trust

→ explain residual matters, for example the effect of decease of the secret trustee or beneficiary as well as whether a secret trustee can benefit under a secret trust

→ explain the nature of secret trusts as express or constructive trusts

→ explain mutual wills and the effect of mutual wills.

SETTING THE SCENE

Re Boyes (1884) 26 Ch. D 531: The mistress and the illegitimate child

The facts of *Re Boyes* decided towards the end of the nineteenth century neatly explain one important role served by secret trusts. George Boyes made a will in which he left his entire residuary estate to his solicitor Mr Carritt. George Boyes had previously told Mr Carrit that he wished him to hold the property in accordance with instructions which he would communicate to him later. In fact no communication of any instructions was made to Mr Carrit and it was only after the death of George Boyes that two unattested documents were found explaining how the property, which had been duly left to Mr Carrit, should be dealt with. The two unattested documents revealed that the property should be held upon trust for George Boyes's mistress and illegitimate child. On the other hand, George Boyes's next of kin argued that Mr Carritt should return the property to them on the grounds that Mr Carritt had not been made a gift of the property.

The facts of *Re Boyes* illustrate a number of issues and problems arising in the context of secret trusts.

- Why did George Boyes not simply provide for his mistress and illegitimate child in his will?

- Why was Mr Carrit not entitled to keep George Boyes's property left to him in a duly executed will? In other words, the will had clearly left him the property and the will was witnessed and attested by two witnesses.

- When the two documents were found after the death of George Boyes, it became clear that the mistress and the illegitimate child were to receive the property, why could Mr Carrit not hand the property over to them?

These issues are addressed in this chapter which explores the rules and principles governing secret trusts. In addition this chapter also looks at the doctrine of mutual wills.

Introduction

It has already been observed that a trust can be created either during the lifetime of a testator or on his death. A trust intended to take effect in the lifetime of testator must comply with certainty and satisfy the formal requirements founded in s. 53(1) of the Law of Property Act 1925.[1] Furthermore, the settlor must do everything in his power to transfer the subject matter of the trust to the trustees. Once this has been done, the trust is said to be fully constituted and the beneficiary acquires an equitable interest in the subject matter of the trust. A trust, which is intended to take effect after the death of the testator, must comply with the formal requirements of s. 9 of the Wills Act 1837. This section requires that a will be made in writing, signed by the testator and witnessed. Failure to put a testamentary trust in writing is fatal to the trust since the intended trust

---

[1] Discussed in detail in Chapter 5.

property will form part of the testator's estate and pass to residuary legatees of his will if he has made a will, or in the absence of a will, to his next of kin in accordance with the rules of intestate succession.

A particular type of trust which does not fit neatly into the categories of *inter vivos* and testamentary trusts is a secret trust. Instead, such a trust sits between the boundaries of *inter vivos* trusts and testamentary trusts. A secret trust is a trust which is created during the lifetime of a settlor; however, unlike a normal *inter vivos* trust, which comes into operation during the lifetime of the settlor, a secret trust does not come into operation until after the death of the settlor. This does create a rather strange paradox in that a trust which is intended to confer a benefit on an individual after the death of a settlor must comply with s. 9 of the Wills Act 1837. This section makes it absolutely clear that the settlor, indeed now the testator, must identify in writing the existence of the trust, the identity of the beneficiary of the trust and finally the property to which the trust is to attach. However, a secret trust need not comply with any formal requirements of s. 9 of the Wills Act 1837. So why is a secret trust enforced when it clearly flies in the face of the Wills Act 1837? This fundamental question is answered below; firstly though, it is important to have some basic understanding of the rules of succession in order to understand the operation of secret trusts.

Succession

Testamentary transfers of property can arise in one of two ways. Firstly, where a person dies without having made a will, his property devolves to others by way of statute in the form of the intestacy rules. Secondly, where a person dies having made a will during his lifetime then the devolution of his property is governed by the will which he has executed.

Intestate succession

A person who dies without having made a will is said to have died intestate (Figure 7.1). Intestacy can take one of two forms: total or partial intestacy. Total intestacy occurs where a person dies without having made a will or where he has made a will but the will is invalid because of improper execution of the will.[2] A partial intestacy occurs where a person dies having made a will but, for some reason or another, fails to effectively deal with all of his property in the will. For example, a person may well think he has dealt appropriately with all of his property but in fact may have forgotten about some property and how it is to be distributed on his death. The rules governing the devolution of his property are to be found in the Administration of Estates Act 1925.[3] Once the debts and expenses of administering the estate are met, the remaining estate[4] is available for

---

[2] Section 9 of the Wills Act 1937 requires a will to be in writing, signed by the person making the will and attested by two witnesses; see below.

[3] This Act has been amended by the Intestates' Estates Act 1952, the Family Provision Act 1966, the Family Law Reform Act 1969, Administration of Justice Act 1977 and the Family Provision (Intestate Succession) Order 2009 sets out the current levels of statutory legacies.

[4] The use of the word 'estate' here is used to describe the total sum of assets and liabilities of the deceased. It is not used in the technical sense of denoting an estate in land.

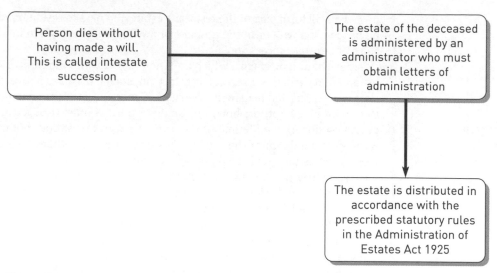

Figure 7.1

distribution in accordance with the statutory scheme found in the Act. The spouse has a primary right of succession, but where the deceased is survived by a spouse and children then right of succession is divided amongst them.[5] The rules relating to beneficial entitlement on intestacy are designed to reflect the wishes of the average testator.[6] The word 'testator' is used to describe a person who makes a will. The intestacy rules attempt to deal with three common situations which may arise after the death of a person. Firstly, where the deceased leaves behind a spouse without children, in which case the spouse takes all. Secondly, where the deceased leaves behind a spouse with children, in which case, where the estate is worth more than £75,000, the property is divided amongst the spouse and the children. Finally, where the deceased leaves behind no spouse or children, in which case the estate is given to near relatives.[7]

Testate succession

If an individual wishes to leave property to designated people after his death he or she needs to make a valid will. A person making a will is described as a testator, or testatrix in the case of a female. The effect of a will is to designate the persons to whom the property of the testator should vest after his death. The will itself does not provide the mechanism of transfer; it merely provides evidence of the testator's intentions (Figure 7.2). The transfer of the property occurs through the vesting of the property in the personal representatives of the deceased. A will is to be distinguished from an *inter vivos* gift as regards both the time when it takes effect and the formalities required. With respect to time, an *inter vivos* gift usually takes effect forthwith whereas a gift in a will only takes place on death of the donor. With regard to formalities, *inter vivos* gifts

---

[5] For a detailed account of how property devolves on intestacy, see Kerridge, Parry and Kerridge, *The Law of Succession* (2009) 12th edn.

[6] See Mellows, *The Law of Succession* (1993) 5th edn at p. 173.

[7] It is not in the ambit of this book to examine the rules of intestacy in depth; however, an excellent account of these rules can be found in Kerridge, Parry and Kerridge, *The Law of Succession* (2009) 12th edn.

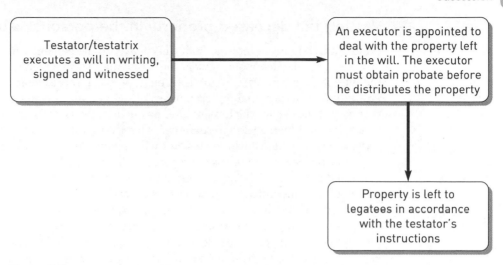

Testator/testatrix executes a will in writing, signed and witnessed

An executor is appointed to deal with the property left in the will. The executor must obtain probate before he distributes the property

Property is left to legatees in accordance with the testator's instructions

Figure 7.2

usually require the use of deeds, for example a gift of land, and then followed by registration. A will, on the other hand, need only meet the requirement of formality laid down in s. 9 of the Wills Act 1837.[8] Although a will need not be in any particular legal language or form, s. 9 requires a will to be in writing, signed by the testator and witnessed. The essence of a will is that it is only a declaration of the intentions of the testator; it is sometimes said that a will is ambulatory in nature. The consequence of this is that a person making a will is perfectly free to deal with his property after making the will, and if he or she should so desire, can transfer the property during his or her lifetime to other persons other than those identified in the will. From the viewpoint of the persons entitled in the will, called legatees under the will, they acquire no interest in the property.[9] It is only when the personal representatives of the deceased distribute the property to the intended beneficiaries that they acquire any proprietary rights in the deceased estate. It may, however, be the case that the liabilities of the deceased estate are so large that the assets are used to meet those liabilities, in which case many dispositive parts of the will become fruitless.

There are two important sections of the Wills Act 1837 which need to be understood when attempting to deal with secret trusts. The first is s. 15, which provides that a person witnessing a will cannot derive any benefit thereunder. Thus, where a person witnesses a will, any gift left to him in the will becomes utterly null and void. The rationale behind this rule is that the person witnessing the will should be impartial and neutral and be in a position to give impartial evidence when issues arise about the due execution of the will. Certainly, if the witness has an interest in upholding the will in which he is deriving an interest, he cannot be said to be acting impartially. The second section is s. 25 which provides that, subject to certain exceptions, a gift will lapse if the legatee should predecease the testator. Thus, if A leaves property to B and B dies before A, B's gift is said to lapse and there is nothing which B's personal representatives can claim from A's personal representatives when A should die.

---

[8] As amended by the Administration of Justice Act 1982, s. 17.
[9] *Commissioner of Stamp Duties (Queensland)* v *Livingstone* [1965] AC 694.

Vesting the deceased property in the personal representatives

Whilst rules relating to intestacy and wills deal with the persons who become entitled to property after the death of a person, the actual manner in which transfer of property to the intended beneficiaries occurs is through personal representatives of the deceased. Property vests in personal representatives of the deceased, who are obliged to transfer that part of the estate which is left after payment of debts and expenses to the intended beneficiaries. A 'personal representative' is a term that includes executors and administrators. When making a will the testator will appoint an executor to distribute his property after his death. In the case of a person who has died intestate, the person who is interested in the estate being administered must apply to the court for what is known as 'letters of administration' appointing an administrator. The duties of the administrator are essentially the same as those of executors. All the property of the deceased will vest in the personal representatives.[10] It is only after the property has vested in the personal representatives that they are able to transfer it to the intended beneficiaries. All the property of the deceased is held upon a statutory trust for sale,[11] which means that land can be sold to meet the liabilities of the deceased. Where property is left which is not required for liabilities, the personal representatives can then transfer to the beneficiaries. In the case of land it should be noted that there is no need for a deed to transfer the land to the beneficiaries; all that is required is a written assent.[12]

 ## Definition of a secret trust

Snell's *Equity* defines a secret trust as:

> one which gives effect to the express intentions of a testator which are not contained in a written document duly executed as a will. A will is a public document. The advantage of a secret trust is that the testator may use a will to implement his wish to establish a trust on his death without disclosing the intended beneficiary or the terms under which he holds.[13]

A secret trust normally operates in conjunction with a will.[14] The following example can be used to explain the operation of a secret trust. Peter is married and has three children. He wishes to make a will leaving his property to his wife and children in equal shares. However, he also wishes to leave a sum of £60,000 to his secretary Patsy whom he has been very fond of for several years. He does not, however, want anyone to know that Patsy has received a sum of £60,000 after his death. The dilemma he faces is that if he names Patsy in the will then this will become public knowledge. One way around this is for Peter to leave the sum of money absolutely to his solicitor in his will; however, during his lifetime he secures his solicitor's agreement that he will hand the money over to Patsy after Peter's death. In this way Peter is said to have created a secret trust. Secret because, on the face of the will, Peter's solicitor is deemed to have been made an absolute

---

[10] Administration of Estates Act 1925 ss. 1(1), 3(1).
[11] Administration of Estates Act 1925 s. 33(1).
[12] Administration of Estates Act 1925 s. 36(1).
[13] J. McGhee, *Snell's Equity*, 31st edn, (London, Sweet & Maxwell, 2005) at p. 555.
[14] A secret trust can also arise on intestacy. For example, if a dying person is encouraged not to make a will by the person who is to receive his property under the intestacy rules in circumstances that that person will give the deceased's property to another, then equity will compel the enforcement of the secret trust. See, for example, *Sellack* v *Harris* (1708) 2 Eq. Cas. Abr. 46.

gift; however, beneath the surface Peter is really holding the money for Patsy on trust. The only person who knows of the existence of the trust is Peter's solicitor and possibly Patsy.

A secret trust can take one of two forms. A fully secret trust arises where a testator makes a will and leaves property in a will absolutely to a legatee, for example '£60,000 to my solicitor absolutely'. Thus, on the face of the will, the legatee is made an absolute gift. However, during the lifetime of the testator, the legatee has agreed to hold the property on trust for a designated beneficiary. The trust is said to be fully secret since there is nothing to conceal the existence of a trust. A fully secret trust is explained in Figure 7.3.

In his will:

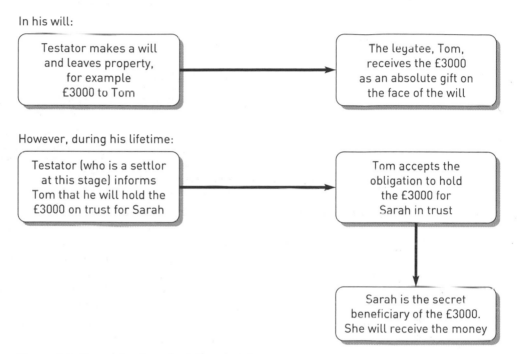

Figure 7.3 The operation of a fully secret trust

On the other hand, a half-secret trust is said to arise when a testator makes a will and leaves property in his will on trust to a named trustee, for example '£60,000 to my solicitor on trust'. What is clearly not evident on the face of the will is the identity of the beneficiary (Figure 7.4). The reason why a testator may wish to make a half-secret trust instead of a fully secret trust is to reduce the risk of fraud. In the case of a fully secret trust, there is every possibility that the secret trustee may keep the property for himself in fraud of the true beneficiary. On the face of the will the secret trustee has been given the property absolutely and he may, in the absence of anyone contesting the existence of the trust, keep the trust property absolutely for himself. In the case of a half-secret trust there is no possibility for the secret trustee to keep the trust property absolutely. Thus, if the secret trust is not enforced the secret trustee has no option but to return the property to the estate of the testator. The secret trustee has received the trust property on trust and cannot, on the face of the will or otherwise, argue that it was his absolutely.

Secret trusts have played an important role in equity. Historically, such trusts were employed to provide for illegitimate children and a mistress. To name such beneficiaries

In his will:

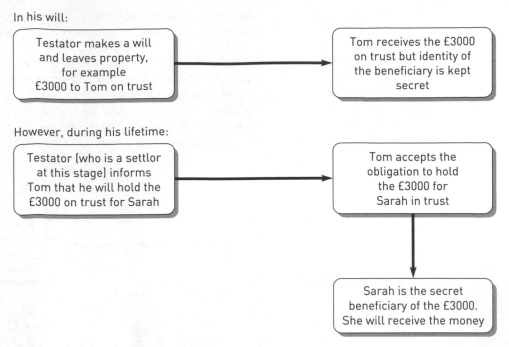

Figure 7.4 The operation of a half-secret trust

in the will would be the subject of much unwanted publicity. In more recent times, secret trusts have been employed by a testator in circumstances where he wants to make a will but is still yet undecided as to the direction of his estate after his decease. By making a will and leaving property to a secret trustee, the testator can reserve to himself the right to make future unwitnessed dispositions of his property by merely naming a trustee and then supplying the objects of the trust closer to his death. Seen in this way, a testator can bypass the formal requirements of s. 9 of the Wills Act 1837.

Although secret trusts have been very popular in the eighteenth and nineteenth centuries, in more recent times it has been questioned whether they retain the same degree of importance they once did and whether they are frequently employed by modern testators. One of the reasons for this is the relatively few cases which have been decided in the twentieth century, suggesting the possibility that they are not used and are unreliable. One commentator described the subject of secret trusts as one which was 'esoteric' and commented that they were rare in practice.[15] However, more recently, a survey has indicated that, despite the relatively few cases emerging in the caselaw, secret trusts remain popular with testators.[16]

The theoretical justification of secret trusts

From what has been seen so far, secret trusts fly in the face of the Wills Act 1837. In the case of a fully secret trust the secret trustee is left the trust property absolutely in the will. The secret trustee is in essence a legatee under the testator's will. Strictly speaking,

---

[15] B. Perrins, 'Secret Trusts: The Key to the Dehors?' [1985] Conv. 248 at 248.
[16] See, for example, R. Meager, 'Secret Trusts – Do They have a Future?' [2003] Conv. 203.

and as a matter of form, the secret trustee should take the property absolutely under the will. In the case of a half-secret trust, property is left in a will to a person who is clearly identified as a trustee. All that is missing is the identity of the beneficiary of the intended trust. Seen in this way, what the testator has done in his will is to declare a trust without declaring the objects of the trust. The orthodox trust rule is that the intended trust property should result back to the testator's estate for lack of certainty of objects.

Despite the Wills Act 1837, secret trusts are nevertheless enforced in order to give the intended trust property to the secret beneficiaries even though to do so would conflict with the terms of the will. Two justifications have been given for the enforcement of secret trusts: namely, the fraud justification and, secondly, something called the 'dehor' theory. These can be examined in more detail.

Fraud justification for the enforcement of secret trusts

APPLYING THE LAW

Suppose that William creates a will leaving his entire estate to his best friend Luke absolutely in the will on the understanding that Luke will give the property to Samantha when William dies.

What would the position be if Luke refused to give the property to Samantha? Is Luke under any obligation to give the property to Samantha when it has been left to him absolutely in the will?

The earliest justification for the enforcement of secret trusts turned on the question of fraud. Where a legatee had received property in a will on the understanding that he would hold it for the benefit of another person, allowing him to retain the property absolutely on the face of the will would allow him to benefit from his own fraud. It would surely be a fraud for the legatee to use the provisions of the Wills Act 1837 to argue that he has received the property absolutely when in substance he agreed to hold it on trust. Equity will not allow a statute to be used as an instrument for fraud. The fraud justification for enforcement of secret trusts was explained by Lord Chancellor Hatherley in *McCormick v Grogan*.[17] His Lordship explained the enforcement of secret trust required a departure from the Wills Act 1837 in order to avoid fraud. His Lordship commented that, 'only in clear cases of fraud has this doctrine been applied – cases in which the court has been persuaded that there has been a fraudulent inducement held out on the part of the apparent beneficiary in order to lead the testator to confide to him the duty which he so understood to perform'.[18] On the facts of the case McCormick had left his estate in a will to Grogan. On his deathbed McCormick informed Grogan of the existence of his will and that, along with the will, he would find a letter which would tell him what to do with the estate which he was leaving to Grogan. The letter contained instructions relating to numerous gifts to named individuals and ended with the words: 'I do not wish you to act strictly on the foregoing instructions, but leave it entirely to your

---

[17] (1869) LR 4 HL 82.
[18] (1869) LR 4 HL 82 at 89.

own good judgement to do as you think I would, if living, and as the parties are deserving.' The terms of the letter were accepted by Grogan. When challenged by a potential beneficiary, the House of Lords held that no trust was established. Fraud had not been established on the facts and Grogan had not taken the property on any trust. Similarly, in **Blackwell v Blackwell**[19] Lord Sumner commented that, 'for the prevention of fraud, Equity fastens on the conscience of the legatee a trust, a trust, that is, which would otherwise be inoperative; in other words it makes him do what the will in itself has nothing to do with, it lets him take what the will gives him and then makes him apply it, as the Court of Conscience directs, and it does so in order to give effect to the wishes of the testator, which would not otherwise be effectual.'[20] However, as will be seen below, Lord Sumner also offered an alternative reason for the enforcement of secret trusts, commenting that they 'dehored' the will.

Whilst the fraud justification occupied a central role in the enforcement of secret trusts in the nineteenth century, in the twentieth century it became clear for a number of reasons that fraud alone could not provide the justification for the enforcement of a secret trust. Firstly, in the case of a half-secret trust, where the will makes it absolutely clear that property is given to a trustee, there can be no question of the trustee taking the trust property absolutely in fraud of the secret beneficiary. In such a case, as explained above, the will attempts to declare a trust which fails for want of a beneficiary and thus the property should in principle result back to the testator's estate. Despite this, a half-secret trust is enforced in equity but not on any fear of fraud by the secret trustee. Secondly, as Pearce and Stevens argue, if fraud is the basis upon which a secret trust is enforced, then why does the court not impose a resulting trust in favour of the testator's estate should the secret trustee act fraudulently.[21] Surely, all that is needed is a resulting trust in favour of the testator's estate to prevent the trustee from taking absolutely. This argument is certainly a powerful one and one which avoids a conflict with the Wills Act 1837. Pearce and Stevens write: 'fraud could equally be prevented if the trustee was required to hold the property on resulting trust for the residuary legatees under the will or the testator's next of kin. This would prevent the trustee benefiting by his fraud, but would not contradict the provisions of the Wills Act.'[22]

● Secret trusts dehor the will

The contemporary justification for the enforcement of secret trusts centres on what has been described as the 'dehor theory'. 'Dehor' means to operate outside of something: thus, a secret trust is said dehor the will, that is, it is said to operate outside the will and thus not in conflict with the Wills Act 1837. This theory was first articulated by Lord Sumner in **Blackwell v Blackwell**[23] where the House of Lords had to consider the validity of a half-secret trust. On the facts of this case, a testator left a sum of £12,000 in a codicil to five persons to invest and 'to apply the income . . . for the purposes indicated by me to them'. Before the execution of the codicil, the testator had communicated the terms of the trust to all five individuals who had duly accepted the terms of the trust. The residuary legatees of the testator argued that there was no trust in favour of the objects on the grounds that parol evidence was inadmissible to establish the trust intended by

---

[19] [1929] AC 318.
[20] [1929] AC 318 at 334.
[21] R. Pearce and J. Stevens, *The Law of Trusts and Equitable Obligations*, 5th edn (2010) at p. 259.
[22] R. Pearce and J. Stevens, *The Law of Trusts and Equitable Obligations*, 5th edn (2010) at p. 259.
[23] [1929] AC 318.

the testator. The House of Lords held that such evidence was admissible to establish a trust in favour of the objects and a valid half-secret trust had been created in favour of the objects. In the course of his judgment Viscount Sumner held that 'it is communication of the purpose to the legatee, coupled with acquiescence or promise on his part, that removes the matter from the provisions of the Wills Act and brings it within the law of trusts, as applied in this instance to trustees, who happen to be legatees'.[24] Similarly, in *Re Snowden*[25] Megarry VC explained that 'the whole basis of secret trusts, as I understand it, is that they operate outside the will, changing nothing that is written in it, and allowing it to operate according to its tenor, but then fastening a trust on to the property in the hands of the recipient'.[26]

So, how does the 'dehor justification' work? In order to understand the dehor justification of secret trusts it is important to distinguish between two stages in the creation of a secret trust. The first stage is the *inter vivos* declaration of trust. This happens when the testator approaches the secret trustee during his lifetime and tells him that he is either receiving property in his will absolutely or on trust. He then communicates not only his intention that he is creating a trust but also the purpose of the trust to the secret trustee. In this respect this declaration of trust is like any other *inter vivos* declaration of trust and it can be said that the testator is in fact creating an *inter vivos* trust. However, at this moment in time, and indeed during the remainder of his lifetime, that intended trust is said to be incompletely constituted. As was seen in Chapter 6, an incompletely constituted trust is one where the settlor has yet to transfer the trust property to the trustee. The second stage in the creation of a secret trust is the devise of the trust property to the secret trustee in the will. Thus, in the case of a fully secret trust the testator will leave the trust property to the secret trustee absolutely as a legatee. In the case of a half-secret trust the property will be left to the secret trustee on trust. However, all that the will is attempting to do is to constitute an *inter vivos* trust by vesting the trust property in the trustee. Seen in this way, it has been argued that a secret trust dehors the will and has nothing to do with the will. It is simply a trust which has been declared during the lifetime of the settlor (Figure 7.5).

One case which is often cited as an example of a secret trust dehoring the will is *Re Young*.[27] In this case a testator left property to his wife in a will with a direction that she would leave the property on her death for purposes which he had communicated to her. During his lifetime and before the execution of the will the testator had informed his wife that his chauffeur was to receive a sum of £2000. The chauffeur had witnessed the will and the question was whether he had forfeited his right to the £2000. You will recall that a person who witnesses a will forfeits any benefits in the will by virtue of s. 15 of the Wills Act 1837. The court in this case held that the chauffeur had not forfeited his right to the £2000 because his entitlement to that sum arose not under a will but under an *inter vivos* trust created during the lifetime of the settlor. Danckwerts J explained: 'The whole theory of the formulation of a secret trust is that the Wills Act has nothing to do with the matter because the forms required by the Wills Act are entirely disregarded, since the persons do not take by virtue of the gift in the will, but by virtue of the secret trusts imposed upon the beneficiary, who does in fact take under the will.'[28]

---

[24] [1929] AC 318 at 339.
[25] [1979] 2 All ER 172.
[26] [1979] 2 All ER 172.
[27] [1951] Ch. 344.
[28] [1951] Ch. 344 at 350.

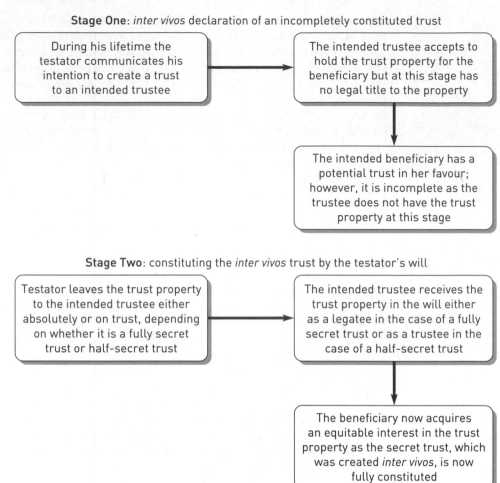

Stage One: *inter vivos* declaration of an incompletely constituted trust

During his lifetime the testator communicates his intention to create a trust to an intended trustee

The intended trustee accepts to hold the trust property for the beneficiary but at this stage has no legal title to the property

The intended beneficiary has a potential trust in her favour; however, it is incomplete as the trustee does not have the trust property at this stage

Stage Two: constituting the *inter vivos* trust by the testator's will

Testator leaves the trust property to the intended trustee either absolutely or on trust, depending on whether it is a fully secret trust or half-secret trust

The intended trustee receives the trust property in the will either as a legatee in the case of a fully secret trust or as a trustee in the case of a half-secret trust

The beneficiary now acquires an equitable interest in the trust property as the secret trust, which was created *inter vivos*, is now fully constituted

Figure 7.5 Understanding the dehor theory of secret trusts

Requirements for a fully secret trust

The requirements for a fully secret trust were explained by Brightman J in **Ottaway v Norman**.[29] On the facts of the case Harry Ottoway, who was cohabiting with his housekeeper Miss Hodges, left his bungalow in his will to Miss Hodges. Before his death, Harry had explained to Miss Hodges that he was leaving the bungalow to her in his will on the understanding that she would, in her will, leave it to his son William Ottoway. Despite this oral understanding, Miss Hodges left the bungalow in her will to Mr and Mrs Norman. William Ottoway commenced proceedings against the Normans on the grounds that a fully secret trust of his father's bungalow had been created in his favour and that Miss Hodges had left the bungalow in breach of trust to the Normans. Given the fact that the Normans were mere volunteers of the bungalow, and not bona fide purchasers of the legal title to the house, William could claim it from them. In other words, the bungalow did not form any part of Miss Hodges's estate. Brightman J held that a valid secret trust

---

[29] [1972] 2 WLR 50.

had been created in favour of William Ottoway who was entitled to the bungalow after Miss Hodges's death. In the course of his judgment, Brightman J described Miss Hodges as the primary donee and William the secondary donee. Miss Hodges could have used the bungalow during her lifetime but was under a duty to give it to William on her death. Despite the rather confusing terminology of a primary donee and a secondary donee, Brightman explained the vital requirements needed to create a fully secret trust.

> The essential elements which must be proved to exist are: (i) the intention of the testator to subject the primary donee to an obligation in favour of the secondary donee; (ii) communication of that intention to the primary donee; and (iii) the acceptance of that obligation by the primary donee either expressly or by acquiescence. It is immaterial whether these elements precede or succeed the Will of the donor.[30]

It is perhaps better to avoid the use of the words primary donee and secondary donee and substitute them for trustee and beneficiary. In this respect the requirements for a fully secret are essentially threefold:

1 an intention to create a trust in favour of a beneficiary
2 communication of that intention to the trustee
3 and acceptance by the trustee thereof.

Intention to create a trust

Suppose that William creates a will leaving his entire estate to his best friend Luke absolutely. During William's lifetime he visits Luke and tells him that he has left all his property to Luke in his will. William also tells Luke that he is fairly confident that Luke will give some of the property to his younger sister, Samantha.

Is there a secret trust in favour of Samantha?

The testator must, during his lifetime, intend to create a trust in favour of the secret beneficiary. In this respect all of the rules of intention, which were explored in Chapter 4, apply equally here. The testator need not use any technical language to create the trust but must show in substance that he intended to confer a benefit on the secret beneficiary and an imperative obligation on the secret trustee. Thus, where a testator uses precatory words, such as 'fully confident that the intended trustee will do as he wishes', he will not create a trust. For example, in **Re Snowden**[31] a sister left her entire estate to her brother in her will using the words that 'he will know what to do'. The brother died shortly after his sister and the niece and nephew of the sister contended that a secret trust of her property had been created in their favour. In the High Court Megarry VC explained that no legal obligation had been imposed on her brother, at most only a moral obligation, and therefore the property had been given to her brother absolutely and passed under the terms of his will. A similar result was achieved in **McCormick v**

---

[30] [1972] 2 WLR 50 at 62.
[31] [1979] 2 All ER 172.

Grogan[32] where a testator made a will leaving his property to Grogan. Having being diagnosed of a serious illness, the testator called for Grogan and explained to him that he had left his property to him and that he should follow the instruction contained in a letter which was kept alongside the will. The letter referred to certain bequests and one section of the letter read: 'I do not wish you to act strictly to the forgoing instructions, but leave it entirely to your own good judgment to do as you think I would if living, and as the parties are deserving.' McCormick commenced proceedings against Grogan arguing that the testator would have regarded him as deserving and that Grogan had failed to consider him as a potential beneficiary under the secret trust. The House of Lords held that no secret trust had been created, because the words used in the letter were not sufficient to put Grogan under an imperative obligation to distribute. At most there might have been a moral obligation on Grogan.

In *Kasperbauer v Griffith*[33] a testator, in the presence of his family members, told his wife that he would leave his house and a pension benefit to his wife. He told the wife that she was to use the pension money to discharge the mortgage on the house and then to sell the house and divide the proceeds of sale equally amongst children of his previous marriage. The wife did not say anything further regarding this matter, although the testator explained that the wife knew what she had to do with his property. Later on the testator executed a will quite different from the one envisaged by the wife. Furthermore, the testator made no attempt to direct the trustees of his pension fund to pay the pension to his wife so as to allow her to discharge the mortgage as originally intended. In the will he left all his property to her without any reference to the children. The children argued that a fully secret trust of the proceeds of the house had been created in their favour. The Court of Appeal, however, held that no trust had been created in their favour. The testator's will was simply inconsistent with his intentions to create a trust in favour of the children. The will suggested that he had changed his mind and now intended his wife to receive his entire estate absolutely. Furthermore the use of the words 'knowing what she had to do' were insufficient to impose a legal obligation. The case neatly illustrates the point that the testator must seek to impose on the intended trustee an imperative obligation to deal with his property subject to a secret trust.

Communication of the secret trust

The testator must communicate the existence of the trust to the intended trustee who on the face of the will is receiving as a legatee. There are various aspects to the communication rules and these can be explained as follows.

Communication must be before the testator's death

APPLYING THE LAW

In his will Barry left his entire estate to his brother, Charles. When Barry died, Charles was approached by a local charity who claimed that they had written evidence from Barry that Charles would hold Barry's estate on trust for them. Charles is not too happy about the prospect of having to hand over the estate to charity.

Is Charles a trustee of Barry's estate?

---

[32] (1869) LR 4 HL 82.
[33] [2000] WTLR 333. See also *Margulies v Margulies* [2008] WTLR 1853.

The testator must communicate the secret trust before his death. If the intended trustee, who after all will be receiving the testator's property as legatee under his will, finds out the existence of the trust after the testator's death then there can be no trust. The legatee's conscience has simply not been affected and he has received the testator's property absolutely in the will without any further obligation. The matter was neatly illustrated in *Wallgrave v Tebbs*[34] where a testator left a sum of £12,000 to a certain Tebbs and Martin as joint tenants. After the testator's death it appeared through oral and written evidence presented to the court that the testator wished the money to be used by Tebbs and Martin for certain charitable objects. Tebbs and Martin argued that they were never made aware of the existence of the testator's intentions and sought an order that they were absolutely entitled to the £12,000. Wood VC held that no secret trust had been imposed on Tebbs and Martin, as the testator had failed to communicate his intention to them.

Communication can be before or after the execution of the will

Although the testator must communicate his intention before his death, it does not matter that the communication is before or after the execution of the will.[35] For example, it is perfectly possible for a testator to execute a will and then inform the legatee that he is to be trustee of property left to him in the will in favour of a secret beneficiary. If the legatee declines the trust then the onus is on the testator to change his will and appoint a new legatee who will be willing to be bound by the secret trust.

Testator must communicate both the existence of the trust and the fact of the trust

APPLYING THE LAW

Vicky creates a will leaving a sum of £40,000 to Jessica absolutely. During her life, Vicky told Jessica that she had left £40,000 to Jessica in her will and would tell her later what to do with the money. In fact, Vicky never got round to telling Jessica as to what was to happen with the money. When Vicky died, a letter addressed to Jessica was found alongside her will which instructed Jessica to give the money to charity.

What should be done with the £40,000?

A secret trust will arise in favour of the intended secret beneficiary if the testator communicates both the existence of the trust and the terms of that trust. This means that the intended secret trustee must not only be aware of the fact that he is to be a trustee for another but also must know who the objects of that trust are. If the testator communicates the existence of the trust without communicating its terms then there is no secret trust in favour of the beneficiaries. The intended trustee, who now having acknowledged that he or she was to be nothing more than a trustee of the testator's property, will be required to hold the property on resulting trust for the testator's estate. This was neatly illustrated in *Re Boyes*[36] where George Boyes informed the intended trustee that he was to receive his property under his will for certain beneficiaries. Boyes did not at this stage inform his solicitor as to whom those beneficiaries were but told him that he would so before his death. No communication of the beneficiaries was made before Boyes's death

---

[34] (1855) 25 LJ Ch. 241.
[35] Although the rule in the case of a half-secret trust is fundamentally different; see later.
[36] (1884) 26 Ch. D 531.

and it was only after his death that documents were found, which directed the intended trustee to use the property for the benefit of a mistress and an illegitimate child. Kay J held that no secret trust had arisen in favour of the mistress and the illegitimate child. The fact that the intended trustee had accepted that he was to be nothing more than a trustee of Boyes's property meant that he held such property on a resulting trust for Boyes's estate. It may well be questioned as to why the court is unwilling to enforce the secret trust in favour of the secret beneficiaries when the intended trustee has indeed acknowledged that he was to be a trustee for them. The rationale behind the rule appears to focus on the right of the intended trustee to reject the trust once he is aware of the nature and terms of the trust. It may well be that the intended trustee, having established exactly whom the trust is for, may feel uncomfortable about the trust. In such a case he should have the right to accept or reject the trust in question.

APPLYING THE LAW

Frances has made a will in which she has left all of her property to Kirsty. During her lifetime Frances told Kirsty that she had left her estate to her absolutely but, that on Frances's death Kirsty was to follow the instructions in a letter which she would find in a steel box belonging to Frances. When Frances died, Kirsty obtained the letter from the steel box and when she read it, it instructed her to give all of Frances's property to charity.

Is Kirsty a legatee of Frances's property or a trustee in favour of charity?

A question which has often been asked in this area of the law is whether the terms of the trust can be communicated by handing over a sealed envelope with the instructions that the envelope is not to be opened until after the testator's death. In light of the decision in **Re Boyes**[37] it is difficult to see how this situation is any different; the trustee will not ascertain the terms of the trust until he opens the letter after the testator's death. However, despite this, in **Re Keen**[38] a testator informed the intended trustee that he was to receive a sum of £10,000 on trust in his will. This made the trust in question a half-secret trust. He then handed over to the trustee a sealed letter with the instructions that the letter was not to be opened until after the testator's death. Lord Wright MR held that there had been communication of the existence of the trust. His Lordship drew an analogy with a ship sailing under sealed order, which 'is sailing under sealed orders even though the exact terms are not ascertained by the captain till later'.[39] Although the facts of **Re Keen** involved a half-secret trust, the principle can equally apply to a fully secret trust. For example, a testator can inform the intended trustee that he is to receive property under his will and that the property should be dealt with in accordance with the sealed letter which is handed over. What is required is evidence of a connection between the knowledge that the intended trustee is to receive property in a will, which is in fact subject to a secret trust, and the letter connected to that will and the secret trust. For example, it is unlikely that a secret trust will arise where a testator makes a will leaving his property to a person absolutely and then many years later hands over an envelope with the instructions 'not to be opened until after my death'. Whatever may be the contents of that letter, the letter in no way indicates to the recipient that he is to be bound as a trustee.

---

[37] (1884) 26 Ch. D 531.
[38] [1937] Ch. 236. See also *Re Bateman's Will Trusts* [1970] 1 WLR 1463.
[39] [1937] Ch. 236 at 242.

It may well be questioned what the difference is between *Re Boyes*[40] and *Re Keen*.[41] In both cases the terms of the trust are ascertained after the testator's death. In *Re Boyes* the rationale for the failure to enforce the secret trust was based on the fact that the secret trustee did not have the opportunity to reject the trust should he find the trust sensitive and uncomfortable. Does the same rationale not apply to the *Re Keen* situation? It is argued that it does not. In the *Re Boyes* situation the intended trustee simply has no possibility of establishing the terms of the trust; the matter is beyond his control. In the case of handing over an envelope with the instructions 'not to be opened until after my death', the intended trustee is agreeing to be bound by something which he does not yet know but knows will only be discovered after the testator's death.

There must be communication of the extent of the trust

A testator must not only communicate the existence and fact of the trust, he must also communicate the true extent of the trust. Thus, if the testator communicates to the intended trustee that he is to receive a sum of £10,000 in his will absolutely which is to be used for a beneficiary but then later increases the gift to £20,000, he must communicate the additional increase in the gift to the trustee. If the trustee is unaware of the increase then he will only be a trustee of the £10,000 and will be entitled to keep the remaining £10,000 absolutely. In *Re Cooper*[42] a testator gave £5000 in his will to two trustees to be applied for purposes which he had communicated to them. The testator later on increased the amount to £10,000, but failed to communicate the increase to the two trustees. On the testator's death the court held that the trustees were only bound by a trust of £5000 in favour of the secret beneficiaries. However, because this was a case of a half-secret trust, that is, the trustees had been left the money in the will on trust, the remaining £5000 had to be returned to the testator's estate under a resulting trust. If this was a case of a fully secret trust then the trustees would have been able to keep the £5000 absolutely.

Communication where there is more than one trustee

Further complications can arise where a testator leaves property in a will to more than one secret trustee, but fails to communicate the trust to all of them. The question arises: who is bound and who is not? Furthermore, should a trustee who has not received any communication be bound on the basis that his co-trustee has in fact been communicated the existence of the trust? These questions were answered by Farwell J in *Re Stead*[43] which concerned a fully secret trust. On the facts of the case a testatrix left her residue to the plaintiff and the defendant as tenants in common, on the understanding that it should be applied for a certain William Collett and the balance for charities which the plaintiff and the defendant in their discretion think fit. The defendant argued that no communication of the secret trust had ever been made to her and therefore she was not bound by the secret trust, but was beneficially entitled to the residuary estate. The plaintiff, on the other hand, accepted that communication of the secret trust had been made to her and that she was bound by the trust. As to whether the defendant was bound by the trust despite the lack of communication to her, Farwell J attempted to answer the question by looking at the existing authorities and drawing a distinction between cases where property was left to the intended secret trustees as joint tenants and cases where the property was left to them as tenants in common. Farwell J explained the matter as follows:

[40] (1884) 26 Ch. D 531.
[41] [1937] Ch. 236. See also *Re Bateman's W.T.* [1970] 1 WLR 1463.
[42] [1939] Ch. 811.
[43] [1900] 1 Ch. 237.

If A induces B either to make a will, or leave unrevoked, a will leaving property to A and C as tenants in common, by expressly promising, or tacitly consenting that he and C will carry out the testator's wishes, and C knows nothing of the matter until after A's death, A is bound but C is not bound: *Tee v Ferris*;[44] the reason stated being, that to hold otherwise would enable one beneficiary to deprive the rest of their benefits by setting up a secret trust. If, however, the gift were to A and C as joint tenants, the authorities have established a distinction between those cases in which the will is made on the faith of an antecedent promise by A and those in which the will is left unrevoked on the faith of a subsequent promise. In the former case, the trust binds both A and C,[45] the reason stated being that no person can claim an interest under fraud committed by another; in the latter case A and not C is bound,[46] the reason stated being that the gift is not tainted with any fraud in procuring the execution of the will.[47]

On this basis, Farwell J held that the defendant was not bound by the trust which had not been communicated to her during the testatrix's lifetime. The principles in *Re Stead*[48] can be explained in the table below. It is submitted that Farwell J's analysis of the cases and the subsequent principles enunciated are not entirely convincing. One commentator has explained that Farwell's analysis of the cases is in fact misleading and the only question that matters in cases where property is left to more than one trustee such as A and C is whether the gift to C was induced by A's promise.[49]

Understanding the communication rules to co-trustees

To whom has communication been made and when?	Who is bound and why?
Property left to A and C as **tenants in common** (e.g. £1000 to A and C in equal shares). Communication is made to A but **not** to C. It is important to remember that under a tenancy in common each tenant in common has a separate share in the property.	In this case A is clearly bound but C is not. The reason for this is that to hold C bound by the trust would deprive C of her rights by allowing a beneficiary to set up a secret trust enforceable against C. Thus in *Tee v Ferris*[50] communication was made to only one of three tenants in common. The court held that the two innocent tenants in common were not bound.
Property is left to A and C as **joint tenants** (e.g. £1000 to A and C). Communication is made to A but **not** to C **before the will**. It is important to remember that under a joint tenancy no joint tenant has any share in the property but both are collectively entitled to the whole.	In this case both A and C are bound by the trust, even though C is unaware of the existence of the trust. The reason behind this rule is that the testator is making a will on an antecedent promise by one joint tenant to carry out the trust. Joint tenants are united in one and both are bound; see *Russell v Jackson*.[51]
Property is left to A and C as **joint tenants** (e.g. £1000 to A and C). Communication is made to A but **not** to C **after the will**.	In this case A is bound but C is not. The reason for this is that the gift to A and C in the will is not tainted with any fraud in procuring the execution of the will. In this case the will is made without any acceptance by any one of the joint tenants to be trustees of the property.

---

[44] (1856) 2 K & J 357.

[45] *Russell v Jackson* (1852) 10 Hare 204; *Jones v Badley* (1868) LR 3 Ch. 362.

[46] *Burney v Macdonald* (1845) 15 Sim. 6; *Moss v Cooper* (1861) 1 John & H 352.

[47] [1900] 1 Ch. 237 at 247.

[48] [1900] 1 Ch. 237.

[49] B. Perrins, 'Can You Keep a Half-secret?' (1972) 88 LQR 225.

[50] (1856) 2 K & J 357.

[51] (1852) 10 Hare 204.

Acceptance of the secret trust

APPLYING THE LAW

In her will, Emma left a sum of £200,000 to Joan, Steve and Connie absolutely. During her lifetime, however, Emma told Joan, Steve and Connie that the money was to be used for the benefit of an animal welfare charity. Joan and Steve agreed to hold the money for the animal welfare charity, but Connie did not say anything. When Emma died, Connie refused to hold the money for the charity and claimed to be entitled to a third of the £200,000.

Can Connie claim one-third of the £200,000?

The final requirement for a fully secret trust is acceptance of the trust. The intended trustee must accept the office of trusteeship. It is the acceptance of the trust which prevents the trustee from claiming what appears to be an absolute gift to him in the will. Acceptance of the trust can be made in one of two ways: firstly, by express agreement that the trustee will so act in accordance with the trust or, secondly, by implication from silence. A good example of an express agreement is found in *Strickland v Aldridge*[52] where a son induced his father to leave him property on the express understanding that he would give a certain sum of money from that property to his elder brother. The court held that there was a trust in favour of the elder brother. If the intended trustee is informed of the secret trust but remains silent then his silence will be taken as amounting to acquiescence of the trust.[53] This point of law was neatly illustrated in *Moss v Cooper*[54] where a testator left property to three individuals in a will but during his lifetime, communicated to all three that the property was to used for certain charitable purposes. Two of the intended trustees expressly accepted the obligation, the other remained silent. Page-Wood VC held that as soon as the legatee learned of the fact that he was to be a trustee of property left in a will to him he was bound to elect whether he would undertake the trust or not.

There is nothing stopping a secret trustee, who has accepted the secret trust, from revoking his acceptance of the trust. The immediate question which arises here is: what happens if he does revoke the trust? The answer very much depends on the timing of the revocation. If the revocation is before the testator's death then the testator should change his will and ask someone else who will accept the trust. If he fails to change his will then under a fully secret trust the legatee will keep the property absolutely. Under a half-secret trust the property left on trust in the will reverts back to the testator's estate under a resulting trust. If the secret trustee revokes the trust after the testator's death then the trust will not fail on the equitable maxim that a trust will never fail for want of a trustee. If the secret trustee does disclaim the trust then the personal representatives will hold the property on trust for the intended beneficiaries. The view is that the rule applies to both half-secret and fully secret trusts.[55]

---

[52] (1804) 9 Ves. 517.
[53] See *Ottaway v Norman* [1972] Ch. 698 at 711.
[54] (1861) 1 John & H 352.
[55] See D.J. Hayton, *Hayton and Marshall, Commentary and Cases on the Law of Trusts and Equitable Remedies* 12th edn (2010) at p. 121.

Requirements for a half-secret trust

The requirements for a half-secret trust are exactly the same as that for a fully secret trust except that the rule of communication is different. In a fully secret trust communication can take place any time before the testator's death and it does not matter whether it is before or after the execution of the will. In the case of a half-secret trust the rule of communication is that it must be before or at the same time as the will. Communication which is made after the execution of the will is ineffective and the half-secret trustee will be required to hold the property on resulting trust for the testator's estate. The basis for this rule was explained by Lord Sumner in **Blackwell v Blackwell**[56] where his Lordship explained that 'a testator cannot reserve to himself a power of making future unwitnessed dispositions by merely naming a trustee and leaving the purposes of the trust to be supplied afterwards . . .'.[57] Similarly in **Re Keen**[58] Lord Wright commented that the trust 'referred to but undefined in the will must be described in the Will as established prior to or at least contemporaneously with its execution'.[59]

It is not entirely clear why there should be a different rule of communication for a half-secret trust and a fully secret trust. It has already been seen that secret trusts operate outside of the Wills Act 1837. They are said to be *inter vivos* trusts which are fully constituted by the testator leaving the subject matter of the trust property in the will to the intended trustees. Given that they are *inter vivos* trusts, surely the declaration of the trust and the communication thereof can come any time up until the testator's death. So what then is the justification for a different rule of communication for half-secret trusts? The justification stems from the doctrine of 'incorporation by reference'. Basically, this doctrine allows a document to be incorporated into a will if it was in existence before the will was made. For example, a testator can make a will which is indeed signed, witnessed and in writing. However, it need not contain all the instruction as to how his property is to be distributed; he may well refer to an earlier document which sets out his intentions. The earlier document can be incorporated into the will and thus form the basis of his intentions and part of the will. The matter is neatly explained by Gorell-Barnes P in **Re Smart's Goods**[60] where he said that:

> if a testator, in a testamentary paper duly executed, refers to an existing unattested testamentary paper, the instrument so referred to becomes part of his will; in other words it is incorporated into; but it is clear that, in order that the informal document should be incorporated in the validly executed document, the latter must refer to the former as a written instrument then existing – that it is at the time of the execution – in such terms that it may be ascertained.[61]

This analogy is employed in the context of secret trusts to the extent that if the testator's will attempts to create a half-secret trust by appointing a trustee, there must also be at the time of the will, or before the will, communication of the terms of the trust to the trustee. In other words, if the will makes reference to a half-secret trust then all manifestations of the trust, including the objects, must be known by the trustee. The will cannot simply refer to a trust which is in fact not communicated to the intended trustee. While

---

[56] [1929] AC 318.
[57] [1929] AC 318 at 339.
[58] [1937] Ch. 236.
[59] [1937] Ch. 236 at 246.
[60] [1902] P 238.
[61] [1902] P 238 at 240.

the doctrine of incorporation by reference has some role to play in the rules of probate, it is not entirely clear why such a doctrine should be employed in the context of secret trusts. As explained before, a secret trust is not created by the will but is created during the lifetime of the testator. Therefore, incorporation by reference does not have any real application to secret trusts when the will is insignificant in so far as the declaration of the secret trust. Other jurisdictions do not distinguish between the different rules of communication for fully secret and half-secret trusts.[62]

Predecease of the secret beneficiary

APPLYING THE LAW

Hilary, who died last year, was a secret beneficiary of £4000 under a trust created in her favour by her uncle, Alfred. The trustee is Jenny, who is left the money absolutely in Alfred's will. Alfred died last year and his executors duly transferred the £4000 to Jenny; however, Hilary's children claim that the £4000, which has been transferred to Jenny, belongs to them on the grounds that Hilary left her entire estate to them.

Does the £4000 belong to Hilary's children?

It has already been observed above that a gift in a will to an individual will lapse should that individual predecease the testator.[63] The gift never vests in that individual, and as such, that individual cannot leave whatever he was to receive under the testator's will in his own will or on his intestacy. This apparently logical state of affairs has not been followed in the context of secret trusts. In *Re Gardner (No. 2)*[64] a testatrix made a will in which she left her property to her husband for his life and then subject to a secret trust for her two nieces and one nephew. On the death of the testatrix she had been predeceased by one of her nieces. The question before Romer J was whether the personal representatives of the deceased niece were entitled to one-third share of the testatrix's property after her husband's death. Romer J explained that as soon as the secret trust was accepted by the secret trustee the secret beneficiary acquired an interest in the property. As such, the niece was capable of leaving her interest to her next of kin. The overwhelming view is that *Re Gardner* is wrongly decided and that, until such time as the secret trust is constituted by the vesting of the trust property in the intended trustees on the decease of the testator, the secret beneficiary acquires no interest in the trust property. It must be remembered that until such time as the testator dies and the will vests the property in the intended secret trustees, the secret trust, whether fully secret or half-secret, is incompletely constituted and as such the beneficiary has no proprietary rights in trust property.

One possible defence of the much criticised decision of Romer J in *Re Gardner (No. 2)*[65] is that the court was actually faced with a situation where the niece had predeceased the

---

[62] For example, in Ireland, see *Riordan* v *Banon* (1876) Ir. 10 Eq. 469 and in Australia, see *Ledgerwood* v *Perpetual Trustee Co. Ltd* (1997) 41 NSWLR 532. See also L.A. Sheridan, 'English and Irish Secret Trusts' (1951) 67 LQR 314.

[63] S. 25 Wills Act 1837.

[64] [1923] 2 Ch. 230.

[65] [1923] 2 Ch. 230.

testatrix who had, before litigation had commenced, also died. In this context, the death of the testatrix would have completely constituted the trust in favour of the niece who, albeit, predeceased her. One leading authority on the subject explains that 'what has to be considered is the effect of completely constituting a trust in favour of a person who is already dead – that is, after all, what actually happened in *Re Gardner (No. 2)'*.[66] The authorities are not decisive on this point and the general view is that the decision in *Re Gardner (No. 2)* is wrongly decided.

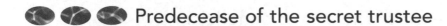

Predecease of the secret trustee

Further complications may arise if the intended secret trustee predeceases the testator. The effect of the predecease of the secret trustee depends very much on whether the trust in question is a fully secret trust or a half-secret trust. In the case of a fully secret trust if the secret trustee dies before the testator then the trust fails altogether. It will be recalled that under a fully secret trust the trust property is left to the intended trustee absolutely in the will as legatee. If the legatee dies then his gift is said to lapse which means that the intended trust will never become completely constituted.[67] On the other hand, in the case of a half-secret trust, the predecease of the secret trustee will not destroy the trust. The fact that the property is given to a person in his capacity as trustee means that if that person dies there is nothing stopping another trustee being appointed. The maxim operating here is that 'equity will not allow a trust to fail for want of a trustee'. Provided the secret beneficiary has the necessary evidence to show the existence of the trust, the personal representatives of the testator will act as trustees who may seek to appoint new trustees to carry out the secret trust.[68]

Can a secret trustee derive a benefit from the secret trust?

One question which has caused some confusion in the case law is whether a secret trustee can derive a benefit under the trust. The secret trustee may be able to derive a benefit in one of two ways. Firstly, the secret trustee may be one of the beneficiaries of the trust. Secondly, the testator may indeed allow the secret trustee to retain any surplus property left once the purpose of the secret trust has been carried out. In *Re Rees' Will Trusts*[69] the Court of Appeal held that a half-secret trustee cannot also be one of the beneficiaries of the trust as this would be inconsistent with terms of the will which clearly states that he takes as trustee. It is not altogether clear why this should be the case, since as already observed earlier in this chapter, a secret trust is not created in the will but is an *inter vivos* trust. On the other hand, in the case of a fully secret trust it has been held that a secret trustee is entitled to retain the surplus of the trust property once the trust had been carried out.[70] This distinction has been questioned by Pennycuick J in *Re Tyler*[71] although the court did not have to decide the issue on the facts.

---

[66] See, A.J. Oakley, *Parker and Mellows: The Modern Law of Trusts* 9th edn (2008) at p. 130.
[67] *Re Maddock* [1902] 2 Ch. 220.
[68] *Mallot v Wilson* [1903] 2 Ch. 494.
[69] [1950] Ch. 204.
[70] *Irvine v Sullivan* (1869) LR 8 Eq. 673.
[71] [1967] 1 WLR 1269 at 1278.

 How are secret trusts classified?

A final issue which needs to be considered is the juridical nature of secret trusts. The question is: what is the nature of secret trusts and how are they classified? Two suggestions have been made about the nature and classification of secret trusts. One suggestion is that secret trusts are express trusts. A testator expressly declares an *inter vivos* by appointing a trustee and communicating the terms of the trust to him. The effect of the will is to simply constitute that trust by vesting the trust property in the trustee. On this basis secret trusts need to comply with all of the formal requirements which apply to express trusts. Thus, if the secret trust relates to land, the testator must, during his lifetime, evidence the trust in writing as required by s. 53(1)(b) of the Law of Property Act 1925.[72] In *Re Baillie*,[73] a case decided under the predecessor of s. 53(1)(b),[74] a half-secret failed for want of compliance with the necessary writing. If the subject matter of the secret trust is a pre-existing equitable interest, the trust will only come into existence if the equitable interest is disposed of in writing and signed by the person disposing of the same.

In the context of a fully secret trust there have many commentators who have argued that such trusts are constructive trusts rather than express trusts. For example, Professor Hayton argues that it is possible to treat 'such trusts as constructive trusts . . . on grounds that such trusts, unlike ordinary express trusts which can be created unilaterally, depend crucially upon the trustee's express or tacit promise to honour the trust in favour of the secret beneficiary'.[75] Professor Hayton's argument centres on the fact that it would be unconscionable for the secret trustee to go back on his agreement and keep the property for himself. It is the element of unconscionability that justifies the imposition of a constructive trust on the secret beneficiary. He cites the judgment of Robert Walker LJ in *Gillett v Holt*[76] where his Lordship explained that 'there must be an agreement between A and B conferring a benefit on C because it is the agreement which would make it unconscionable for B to resile from his agreement'.[77] In *Re Cleaver*[78] Nourse J took the view that secret trusts were constructive trusts.

The question whether secret trusts are indeed a species of constructive trusts is, however, unresolved. It was also observed in Chapter 7 that secret trusts can be of two kinds. In the case of a fully secret trust, the refusal of the apparent legatee to hold the property for the benefit of the secret trustee would clearly amount to a fraud. To prevent the fraud, the legatee will be compelled to hold the property as a constructive trustee for the secret beneficiary. On the other hand, in the case of a half-secret trust, property is left to a trustee on the face of the will without disclosing the identity of the beneficiary. In the case of a half-secret trust, there can be no question of fraud on the part of the half-secret trustee because he has accepted the office of trusteeship. On the basis that a half-secret trust is not prone to fraud, it has been argued that such a secret trust is not imposed as a

---

[72] This section was discussed in Chapter 5.

[73] (1886) 2 TLR 660.

[74] S. 7 Statute of Frauds 1677.

[75] D.J. Hayton, *Hayton and Marshall: Commentary and Cases on the Law of Trusts and Equitable Remedies* 13th edn (2010) at p. 121.

[76] [2000] 2 All ER 289. This case did not concern a secret trust but was dealing with the equitable doctrine of proprietary estoppel, in circumstances where the claimant was promised that he would be given a farm by the defendant in return for working on that farm.

[77] [2000] 2 All ER 289 at 305.

[78] [1981] 2 All ER 1018.

constructive trust, but rather as an express trust declared during the testator's lifetime.[79] The question whether a fully secret trust is enforced as a constructive trust and a half-secret trust is enforced as an express trust if not fully answered yet.[80] If both a fully secret trust and a half-secret trust are said to operate outside the Wills Act 1837, in the sense that they are trusts declared during the lifetime of the settlor, there is much to be said that such trusts are indeed express trusts. However, even though such trusts are declared during the lifetime of the settlor, Professor Alastair Hudson explains that they cannot be express trusts. He writes:

> [A] secret trust is a trust not properly constituted by the settlor but the substance of which was communicated to persons who are named as legatees under the settlor's will. As such, the enforcement of the settlor's promise could not be an express trust because the settlor retains the right to change her will, something which would not be permitted if an express trust had already been created over . . . property. The only viable trust law analysis is therefore that the secret trust must be in the form of a constructive trust.[81]

 ## Mutual wills

APPLYING THE LAW

Sandra and David married in 1977 and executed identical wills in 2001 leaving their respective property to each other on the understanding that the survivor of the two would then leave their property to their daughter Heather. Sandra and David agreed not to revoke or change their wills. Sandra died in 2005 and David duly acquired all of her property. David remarried in 2006 and executed a new will last month leaving his entire estate, including the property he had inherited from Sandra, to his new wife. Heather is not happy that her father has executed a new will and seeks advice as to whether she has any rights to her father's property.

A very similar doctrine to secret trusts is that of mutual wills. Mutual wills are wills created by two or more persons in accordance with an agreement they have made during their lifetimes. Typically, mutual wills take the form of each person leaving his or her property to the other in similar terms in a will. For example, a husband and wife may enter into an agreement to make wills leaving each other's property to the other on the understanding that the survivor will leave the property to some other third party, for example, their daughter. Although a will is revocable up until the testator's death, if the husband dies before his wife, having left all his property to his wife, the wife, although at liberty to revoke her will and make a new one in favour of others, will be bound by the agreement and a constructive trust will be imposed on property subject to the mutual will. In other words, should the wife revoke the will and leave the property to someone other than her daughter, a constructive trust will be imposed and the daughter will benefit from the agreement leading to the execution of the mutual wills. The constructive trust is imposed to prevent the unconscionable conduct of the survivor who has benefited from receiving property on the understanding that it will be dealt with in a particular

---

[79] See, for example, L.A. Sheridan, 'English and Irish Secret Trusts' (1951) 67 LQR 314.

[80] See, for example, D. Hodge, 'Secret Trusts: The Fraud Theory Revisited' (980) Conv. 341.

[81] A. Hudson, *Equity and Trusts* 5th edn (2007) at p. 556.

manner. In this respect, the constructive trust is imposed to prevent fraud. The matter is neatly explained by Lord Camden in *Dufour v Pereira*[82] where the judge explained that:

> the parties by the mutual will do each of them devise, upon the engagement of the other, that he will likewise devise in manner therein mentioned. The instrument is the evidence of the agreement; and he that dies first does by his death carry the agreement on his part into execution. If the other then refuses he is guilty of fraud, can never unbind himself, and becomes a trustee of course. For no man shall deceive another to his prejudice. By engaging to do something that is in his power he is made a trustee for the performance and transmits that trust to those that claim under him.[83]

The operation of mutual wills was considered at length recently by the Court of Appeal in *Olins v Walters*[84] where a husband and wife made identical wills in 1988. In 1998 the husband and wife executed similar codicils and agreed not to revoke their existing wills. The wife died in 2006 and the husband received her estate including a house valued at £1.5 million. The husband then sought to deny the fact that he and his wife had made mutual wills and entered into an agreement not to revoke their wills. One of grandsons, who was also an executor sought to argue that his grandparents had indeed made mutual wills and pointed to the codicils executed in 1998 and the agreement not to revoke their wills. Mummery LJ held that the husband and wife had entered into mutual wills and an agreement not to revoke them. In the course of his judgment the judge explained the principles and requirements for mutual wills. The key elements of Mummery LJ's judgment is reproduced below.

KEY CITATION

Olins v Walters [2009] Ch. 212 (Nature of mutual wills and requirements to enforce the obligation under mutual wills per Mummery LJ at 221–2)

It is a legally *necessary* condition of mutual wills that there is clear and satisfactory evidence of a contract between two testators. However, the argument resting on the alleged insufficiency or uncertainty of the terms of this contract is misconceived. The case for the existence of mutual wills does not involve making a contractual claim for specific performance or other relief. The claimant in a mutual wills case is not even a party to the contract and does not have to establish that he was.

The obligation on the surviving testator is equitable. It is in the nature of a trust of the property affected, so the constructive trust label is attached to it. The equitable obligation is imposed for the benefit of third parties, who were intended by the parties to benefit from it. It arises by operation of law on the death of the first testator to die so as to bind the conscience of the surviving testator in relation to the property affected.

It is a legally *sufficient* condition to establish what the judge described as 'its irreducible core' . . . which he analysed as a contract between two testators, T1 and T2:

> that in return for T1 agreeing to make a will in form X and not to revoke it without notice to T2, then T2 will make a will in form Y and agree not to revoke it without notice to T1. If such facts are established then upon the death of T1 equity will impose upon T2 a form of constructive trust (shaped by the exact terms of the contract that T1 and T2 have

▶

---

[82] (1769) 1 Dick. 419.

[83] (1769) 1 Dick. 419 in 2 Hargraves Juridical Arguments at 304 cited in *Re Goodchild (deceased)* [1996] 1 WLR 694 at 699.

[84] [2009] Ch. 212.

made). The constructive trust is imposed because T1 has made a disposition of property on the faith of T2's promise to make a will in form Y, and with the object of preventing T1 from being defrauded.

In my judgment, that is an accurate and clear statement of the equitable principles. Mr Steinfeld accepted that. He agreed that Mr Walters would be bound by a constructive trust, but only if sufficient terms of the contract were established to raise one.

The answer to the sufficiency point is, I think, summed up in a single sentence in *Snell's Equity*, 31st ed (2005), para 22–31: 'Mutual wills provide an instance of a trust arising by operation of law to give effect to an express intention of the two testators.'

The intentions of Mr Walters and the deceased were sufficiently expressed in the contract to lay the foundations for the equitable obligations that bind the conscience of Mr Walters, as the survivor, in relation to the deceased's estate. The judge found all that he needed to find in order to hold that, contrary to the contentions of Mr Walters, mutual wills existed. Possible, and as yet unexplored, legal consequences of the application of the equitable principles do not negative the existence of the foundation contract or prevent a constructive trust from arising by operation of law on the death of the deceased.

It had been accepted on behalf of Mr Walters in submissions to Norris J that, if there was a valid contract for mutual wills, the doctrine operated by imposing a constructive trust on him as the survivor, because the deceased had performed her promise to leave her estate to him. In my judgment, the trust is immediately binding on him in relation to the deceased's property left to him on the basis of the contract. It is not postponed to take effect only after the death of Mr Walters when the property, or what may be left of it, comes into the hands of his personal representatives.

Disputes about the actual operation of the trust in practice usually turn on construction of the contract in all the relevant circumstances. Of course, the disagreements can be resolved without litigation, if all the beneficiaries are agreed and have legal capacity to do so. If not, the disputes can be determined on an application to the court by Mr Walters in proceedings to which those interested are made parties.

In this case the issues before the judge were the validity of the codicil and the existence of the mutual wills contract, both of which were unsuccessfully contested by Mr Walters. The judge determined those issues against him for sound reasons in an excellent judgment. He was not asked to rule on the possible legal consequences of the declaration for Mr Walters or for the beneficiaries arising on the death of the deceased. The judge prudently declined to be drawn into determining matters, such as the scope or extent of the constructive trust, which were neither raised in the pleadings nor in the submissions of the parties. As Bowen LJ said in Cooke v New River Co (1888) 38 Ch D 56, 71, the teaching of experience is that judgments should be given on points that the judge is bound to decide. Deciding more than is necessary could, 'like the proverbial chickens of destiny', come home to roost sooner or later. Unnecessary opinions can be a source of future embarrassment, or even worse when, as here, no other points have been pleaded, investigated or argued.

The requirements for mutual wills are discussed in more detail in the sections below.

There must be an agreement not to revoke

A claimant will only benefit from a mutual will providing that two individuals entered into a binding agreement not to revoke their wills and that the claimant has been left

their respective property. For example, suppose a husband and a wife agree to leave their respective property to each other on identical terms in two different wills on the understanding that the survivor of the two will then leave the property to their son. In such a case, the son will have an interest in the property which is in the hands of his surviving parent, who cannot revoke his or her will, or indeed, leave the property to any other person. Any purported attempt by one of the survivors to revoke the will or otherwise give the property to any other person will be ineffective on the grounds that the son will have an equitable interest in the property under a constructive trust. The son's interest will prevail over and above any other third party's purported attempt to claim the property on the equitable maxim that 'where the equities are equal, the first in time prevails'.

At the heart of the mutual will doctrine is the requirement of an agreement on the part of those executing mutual wills that they will agree not to revoke their wills. The agreement must be a legally binding agreement.[85] In *Re Cleaver* Nourse LJ explained that:

> the principle of all these cases is that a court of equity will not permit a person to whom property is transferred by way of gift, but on the faith of an agreement or clear understanding that it is to be dealt with in a particular way for the benefit of a third person, to deal with that property inconsistently with that agreement or understanding. If he attempts to do so after having received the benefit of the gift equity will intervene by imposing a constructive trust on the property which is the subject matter of the agreement or understanding.[86]

In *Re Goodchild*[87] Leggatt J explained that a 'key feature of the concept of mutual wills is the irrevocability of the mutual intentions. Not only must they be binding when made, but the testators must have undertaken, and so must be bound, not to change their intentions after the death of the first testator.'[88] On the facts of *Re Goodchild*, a husband and wife had made similar wills leaving their respective property to their son. When the wife died, the husband remarried and made a new will, leaving his property to his second wife. The son purported to argue that his parents had made mutual wills and that he was entitled to a constructive trust over property that his father had acquired from his mother, which was now being claimed by his stepmother. The Court of Appeal held that there was no evidence that the son's parents intended to enter into an agreement to create mutual wills. Therefore, the husband was capable of leaving his entire estate to his new wife. In order to enforce mutual wills the agreement not to revoke must be clearly demonstrated to the court. The court will be entitled to examine extrinsic evidence in order to establish whether in fact the parties intended to make mutual wills. The matter is neatly illustrated by the decision in *Re Goodchild* where, as explained above, despite the fact that a husband and a wife made similar wills leaving property to their son, the evidence was that they were not putting themselves under a legally binding obligation not to revoke their wills. The Court of Appeal examined all the evidence, in particular the evidence of the solicitor advising the husband and wife, and concluded that the parties had not put themselves under a legal obligation not to revoke their wills.

Two recent cases which illustrate that the court will look to all the relevant evidence to establish whether there was an agreement to make mutual wills are *Charles v Fraser*[89] and *Fry v Densham-Smith*.[90] In *Charles v Fraser* the question before the High Court was

---

[85] *Re Cleaver* [1981] 2 All ER 1018.
[86] *Re Cleaver (deceased)* [1981] 1 WLR 939 at 947.
[87] [1997] 1 WLR 1216.
[88] [1997] 1 WLR 1216 at 1225.
[89] [2010] EWHC 2154.
[90] [2010] EWCA Civ 1410.

whether two sisters had executed irrevocable mutual wills. In 1991, Mabel and Ethel, who were 78 and 76, made identical wills benefiting certain individuals including one Mrs Thompson. The beneficiaries of the identical wills were carefully selected by both sisters and were either very close friends of the sisters or relatives. In evidence, Mrs Thompson had explained that when Mabel and Ethel visited her they both explained that they had executed identical wills leaving their property to each other and then to named beneficiaries including Mrs Thompson. Other beneficiaries also gave evidence of a similar nature. Mabel died in 1995 and in 2003 Ethel altered her will, leaving her estate to two named individuals. In 2006 Ethel altered her will once more and left her entire estate to Mrs Fraser. In 2006 Ethel died and Mrs Fraser became entitled to a sum of £300,000 under Ethel's will. Mrs Thompson argued that she was entitled under the will of 1991 and that Ethel's subsequent attempt to revoke the 1991 will was a breach of trust. The question before the court was whether, on all the facts and all the evidence given in court, there was an agreement by Mabel and Ethel not to revoke their identical will. The court held that there was an agreement not to revoke the wills made in 1991 and therefore Mrs Thompson was entitled to the share that she was left in the 1991 will. The following extract from the judgment of Mr Jonathan Gaunt QC neatly explains the role of the court in looking at all of the facts before coming to a conclusion as to whether indeed irrevocable wills had been made:

> In my judgment, a Court has to approach oral evidence of the kind that was given by and on behalf of the Claimants in this case warily and with appropriate scepticism. First, I bear in mind the inherent improbability of a testator being prepared to give up the possibility of changing his or her will in the future, whatever the change of circumstances. Secondly, I take into account that a number of the witnesses who gave evidence that the sisters said they had made an agreement and that the wills could not be changed had a financial interest in the outcome of the case. I do not mean by that that I think for a moment that anybody was being dishonest. My impression of all the ladies who gave evidence before me was that they gave their evidence honestly and scrupulously and, having taken the oath, would have been shocked at any suggestion that they might do otherwise. Nevertheless, one is aware from experience of the ability of the human mind to 'remember' what a person wishes to remember.
>
> Ultimately I am swayed by the following factors to accept that in all probability there was an agreement between the sisters at the time they made their 1991 wills that each would leave her estate to the other and that the survivor would leave what remained of their conjoined estates to the beneficiaries and in the shares stipulated in clause 5 of the wills. They made mutual promises to each other and it was either an explicit or implicit part of those promises that the will of the survivor would not be altered so as to change those gifts. The way in which the shares of the beneficiaries were calculated and divided equally between the friends and relatives of the respective sisters indicates this (though it is not enough on its own). It is clear that each sister was conscious that the assets of the survivor would derive in part from the family of the first to die, in particular the estate of her deceased husband, and ought, in fairness, to be shared equally with that sister's family. Moreover, the evidence of Angela Charles, Anne Thompson, Angela O'Neill, Marilyn Brenard and Iris Rayment as to what the sisters said before Mabel's death and what Ethel said after Mabel's death was largely unshaken in cross-examination, was not shown to contain inconsistencies and was given in a convincing, frank and open manner. The weight of the evidence that there had been an agreement and that part of it was that the wills were not to be changed was such that the Court would need strong grounds for rejecting it.[91]

---

[91] [2010] EWHC 2154 at paras 64 and 68.

The second recent case is *Fry v Densham-Smith*,[92] decided in the Court of Appeal. The facts of this case involved Edwin Densham-Smith (deceased), Laura Densham-Smith and Martin Densham-Smith, who was Edwin's son from his first marriage. Following their second marriage in 1985, Edwin Densham-Smith and Laura Densham-Smith made an oral agreement for mutual wills. Those mutual wills were indeed made, leaving the estate of each other to the survivor and then to their respective sons from their previous marriage in equal shares. A copy of Edwin's will showed that he had left his estate to Laura and then to Martin and Laura's son, Jonathan, in equal shares. There was no direct evidence that this will was made pursuant to an oral agreement to execute mutual wills. After Edwin's death, Laura executed further wills in which she left her estate to her own son, Jonathan, absolutely and cut Martin from the family. Jonathan denied that she had executed a mutual will leaving her estate to Martin and himself in equal shares. On Laura's death Martin contended that he was entitled to a half share of Laura's estate on the grounds that her estate was bound by a trust in his favour as a result of the mutual wills executed after 1985. The Court of Appeal held that on the evidence before it, there was a trust in favour of Martin and that he was entitled to a half share of Laura's estate. Looking at all the evidence, including the fact that Edwin did not get on with Jonathan, the Court of Appeal held that it was inconceivable that Edwin wanted Jonathan to receive all the estate to the exclusion of his own real son. Furthermore, letters written by Laura to her ex-husband as to their previous house referred to the fact that the house would be left to Jonathan but Martin would have to share.

The mere fact that two wills are made on identical terms will not in itself give rise to an agreement to create mutual wills. For example, in *Re Oldham*[93] identical wills were made by a husband and a wife whereby each left their respective property to each other on their decease. There was, however, no evidence of any agreement that these wills were to be irrevocable. When the husband died, the wife remarried and changed her will. The question before the court was whether her first will was valid or whether the second one took priority. The court held that, in the absence of an agreement between her and her former husband that their wills were to irrevocable, the wife's second will was valid. In the course of his judgment, Astbury J explained that the 'fact that the two wills were made in identical terms does not necessarily connote any agreement beyond that of so making them, and they point out that there is no evidence on which I ought to hold that there was an agreement that the trust in the mutual will should in all circumstances be irrevocable by the survivor who took the benefit'.[94]

It is not a prerequisite that the surviving testator should take a benefit from the first testator's will

At one point in time it was thought that the imposition of a constructive trust could only arise if the surviving testator benefited from the first testator's will. In other words, the enforcement of mutual wills required the surviving testator to receive some benefit under the first testator's will in order to subject him to the equitable obligation to leave this property to the ultimate beneficiary of the mutual wills. This line of reasoning was rejected by Morritt J in *Re Dale (deceased)*[95] where a husband and wife agreed to leave

---

[92] [2010] EWCA Civ 1410.
[93] [1925] Ch. 75.
[94] [1925] Ch. 75 at 88.
[95] [1994] Ch. 31.

their respective property to their son and daughter in equal shares. The husband died and left his estate in accordance with the agreement; however, the wife changed her will and left £300 to her daughter and the rest of her estate to her son. The court held that the son, who had been appointed as executor of his mother's will, held the estate on trust for himself and the daughter in equal shares. Morritt J held that it was not necessarily important that the surviving testator receives the first testator's property. The judge explained that the imposition of a constructive trust was justified on the more broad principle of fraud. It would certainly be fraud on the part of a person to encourage a person to act in a particular testamentary manner on the assurance that he too would act in the same way but then refused to do so.

The imposition of a constructive trust in favour of a beneficiary

It has already been observed that the operation of mutual wills gives rise to a constructive trust in favour of the beneficiary to whom the property is ultimately left by the persons making mutual wills. The matter was neatly explained by Dixon J in the Australian case **Birmingham v Renfew**[96] where the judge explained that:

> it has long been established that a contract between persons to make corresponding wills gives rise to equitable obligations when one acts on the faith of such an agreement and dies leaving his will unrevoked so that the other takes property under its dispositions. It operates to impose upon the survivor an obligation regarded as specifically enforceable. It is true that he cannot be compelled to make and leave unrevoked a testamentary document and if he dies leaving a last will containing provisions inconsistent with his agreement it is nevertheless valid as a testamentary act. But the doctrines of equity attach the obligation to the property. The effect is, I think, that the survivor becomes a constructive trustee and the terms of the trust are those of the will he undertook would be his last will.[97]

One question which has arisen in the case law is the timing of the constructive trust. In other words, at what time does the constructive trust arise in favour of the ultimate beneficiary? There are at least three possible dates upon which the constructive trust could potentially arise. The first is the date on which the mutual wills are created. No constructive trust will arise at this stage when both parties are still living. Equity will not intervene at this stage because both parties are free to revoke their will, albeit, that such revocation will amount to a breach of contract. If one of the parties does revoke their will, the other party will have a claim for breach of contract, although, the loss suffered will be nominal at this stage and, therefore, the level of damages will also be nominal. One leading treatise on trusts explains that:

> if the other party discovers such a unilateral revocation before either party has died, he is entitled to recover damages for breach of contract. However, since the only possible loss is the loss of the right to receive an unascertained amount at an unascertained time in the future and since the other party still has unrestricted powers to dispose of his own property, it is relatively unlikely that any substantial damages could be recovered.[98]

A second possible date at which the constructive trust could arise in favour of the ultimate beneficiary entitled under a mutual will is the death of the surviving testator

---

[96] (1936) 57 CLR 666.
[97] (1936) 57 CLR 666 at 683.
[98] A.J. Oakley, *The Modern Law of Trusts* 9th edn (2009) at p. 476.

who executed a mutual will. Again, this is not the stage at which the constructive trust arises because it has been held in **Re Hagger**[99] that once the first testator dies, the interest of a beneficiary entitled under a mutual will does not lapse should that beneficiary predecease the surviving testator. It is for this reason that a constructive trust arises as soon as the first testator dies. For example, in **Re Hagger**[100] a husband and wife made mutual wills leaving property to three named beneficiaries. The three beneficiaries survived the wife's death but predeceased the husband. Clauson J held that the interests of the beneficiaries had not lapsed. In the course of his judgment, Clauson J explained that 'from the death of the wife the husband held the property, according to the tenor of the will, subject to the trusts thereby imposed upon it, at all events if he took advantage of the provisions of the will. In my view he did take advantage of those provisions.'[101]

The extent of the beneficial interest

Although it is clear that a constructive trust arises as soon as the death of the first testator making a mutual will occurs, the more problematic question relates to the subject matter of the constructive trust. In other words, over what property does the trust attach? It will be appreciated that when the first testator dies, the surviving testator will be at liberty to deal with his own property. Given the fact the surviving testator's property will be subject to a constructive trust, and that he will be in a position to not only dissipate his own property but also acquire new property, quantifying the beneficial interest under a constructive trust arising in the case of mutual wills becomes problematic. The ultimate beneficiary under a mutual will certainly does not have conventional equitable rights in the trust property during the lifetime of the surviving testator. The beneficiary cannot compel the surviving testator to transfer the property to him simply because the surviving testator is at liberty to use the property for his own benefit.

Quantification of the beneficial interest under a mutual will is extremely problematic and raises doctrinal problems. To suggest that a constructive trust arises as soon as the first testator dies presupposes that the trust meets all the requirements of trust law, including certainty of subject matter. However, the problem is that, whilst the surviving testator is alive and in a position to deal with the trust property for his own benefit, there can be no certainty of subject matter until his eventual death. The significance of imposing a constructive trust is to allow the ultimate beneficiary to acquire everything that belongs to the surviving testator on his death. Given the fact that the trust arises as soon as the first testator dies, but has significance at the time of the surviving testator's death, one view which seems to have been accepted by the courts is that the constructive trust imposed in the context of mutual wills is a kind of 'floating trust' which crystallises on the death of the second testator. This view was first suggested by Dixon J in the Australian case **Birmingham v Renfew**[102] where the judge explained that:

> it is only by the special doctrines of equity that such a floating obligation, suspended, so to speak, during the lifetime of the survivor can descend upon the assets at his death and crystallise into a trust. No doubt gifts and settlements, inter vivos, if calculated to defeat the intention of the compact, could not be made by the survivor and his right of disposition, inter vivos, is, therefore, not unqualified. But, substantially, the purpose of the

---

[99] [1930] 2 Ch. 190.
[100] [1930] 2 Ch. 190.
[101] [1930] 2 Ch. 190 at 195.
[102] (1936) 57 CLR 666.

arrangement will often be to allow full enjoyment for the survivor's own benefit and advantage upon condition that at his death the residue shall pass as arranged.[103]

The floating trust argument was accepted by Carnwath J in **Re Goodchild (deceased)**[104] where the judge explained that the 'enforceability of the mutual agreement depends, not on the continued existence of the former will as such, but on a species of trust which is held binding in equity, notwithstanding the revocation of the will. It is an unusual form of trust, since it does not prevent the surviving testator using the assets during his lifetime. It is "a kind of floating trust" which finally attaches to such property as he leaves upon his death.'[105]

Although the idea of a 'floating trust' in the context of mutual wills seems to have been accepted by the English courts, the concept is not without problems. Firstly, what is there to stop the surviving testator to dissipate or otherwise deal with his property and that acquired from the first testator during his lifetime, thereby defeating the purpose of the mutual wills. The imposition of the constructive trust is only to prevent the surviving testator from leaving his property on his death to some other third party. The question arises as to whether a court could restrain the surviving testator from dealing with his property during his lifetime, and if so, on what legal basis? A second limitation of the 'floating trust' concept is highlighted by Professor Martin, who writes 'if it is correct that the survivor becomes a trustee of all the property he owns or acquires before his death, the consequence of the doctrine could be draconian for the survivor, for example, if he acquires new dependents after the death of the first testator, or wins the lottery; similarly, if the agreed beneficiary acquires a fortune elsewhere or is guilty of misconduct . . .'[106]

Conclusion

This chapter has examined the equitable doctrines and principles relating to secret trusts and mutual wills. Secret trusts have played an important role in providing for beneficiaries whose identity the testator wishes to keep secret. There are number of reasons why the testator might want to keep the identity of the beneficiaries hidden from the rest of the world. A majority of the cases have concerned provisions for illegitimate children and mistresses. However, it would be wrong to assume that secret trusts only concern such matters; the cases have also shown that a testator may wish to provide for some charitable purposes without wanting his family to know. The real problem with secret trusts relates to the justification for their enforcement. These trusts are said to lie at the boundaries between the laws of succession and the laws of trusts.

The person creating a secret trust intends the trust to come into effect on his death. Given the fact that the trust is intended to take effect on his death, the trust should be created in the will. However, it is obvious why the trust is not declared in the will as this would defeat the purpose of keeping the trust secret. On the other hand, the property left to a legatee in the will, who albeit may well have agreed to hold it on trust for a secret

---

[103] (1936) 57 CLR 666 at 675.
[104] [1996] 1 WLR 694.
[105] [1996] 1 WLR 694 at 700.
[106] J. Martin *Hanbury and Martin: Modern Equity* 18th edn (2009) at p. 353.

beneficiary, should take the property absolutely because under the laws of succession he has been duly made a gift in the will. Equity compels enforcement of the secret trust against the form of the will because not to do so would allow a legatee, who has agreed to hold the property on trust, to benefit from his own fraud. However, more importantly, secret trusts are said to arise independently of the will and are *inter vivos* trusts. They are declared during the lifetime of the testator and his will has only one effect, that is, to constitute the incompletely constituted trusts. Seen in this way, secret trusts do not fly in the face of the Wills Act 1837. However, despite this, as this chapter has illustrated, the apparent demarcation between the laws of succession and the laws of trusts has not always been maintained in some of the decisions which have been made in relation to secret trusts.

Although the doctrine of mutual wills is enforced to prevent the fraud of a surviving testator who has agreed to deal with the property of the first testator and his own property in a particular way, the operation of the doctrine is not without problems. Principally, the imposition of a constructive trust over property, which remains uncertain until the death of the surviving testator, is problematic. One solution to the problem may be more careful drafting of mutual wills with more certainty as to which property the trust is subject to and what rights and duties are imposed on the surviving testator with regards to the property which is ultimately intended for the beneficiary.

●●● Case study

Read and analyse the following case study and answer the specific question set below.

Harriet, who died earlier this year, had made a will in which she had made the following dispositions of her property:

> 'My freehold property to be sold and the proceeds to be held by Derek on trust.
>
> £60,000 to Jenny, Jill and Fiona.
>
> The remainder of my estate to be divided equally amongst my children.'

A few weeks before Harriet's death, she visited Derek and handed him a briefcase with the instructions that the contents of the briefcase were important and that should anything happen to her he should follow the instructions in that briefcase. Harriet explained that the key to the briefcase could be obtained from her executor. When Derek opened the briefcase he found a letter instructing him that the proceeds of sale of Harriet's freehold property should be given to a named charity.

Two months before Harriet's death, Harriet visited Jenny, Jill and Fiona. Fiona was not at home as she had gone to work in Spain for a six-month period. Nevertheless, Harriet told Jenny and Jill that she was leaving £60,000 to them and Fiona and that such money was to be given to Harriet's love child, Natasha. Both Jenny and Jill agreed that they would give the money to Natasha. Fiona was never aware of this arrangement.

Fiona has recently arrived back from Spain and has been made aware that she is entitled to some money under Harriet's will. Jenny and Jill have told Fiona that she, along with them, must hand the money over to Natasha. Fiona is refusing to do so. Furthermore, it has also come to light that Natasha died six months before Harriet, but is survived by a three-year-old daughter.

Advise Derek, Jenny, Jill and Fiona.

Moot points

1 The contemporary justification for the enforcement of secret trusts is that they 'dehor the will': see the judgment of Lord Sumner in *Blackwell* v *Blackwell* [1929] 2 AC 318. What do you understand by the term 'dehor the will' and how far is it true to say that a secret trust is an *inter vivos* trust?

2 In a fully secret trust communication of the secret trust can be made any time up till the testator's death. It does not matter whether the communication is before or after the execution of the will. However, in the case of a half-secret trust communication must be made before or at the same time as the execution of the will. In the words of Lord Sumner, 'a testator cannot reserve to himself a power of making future unwitnessed dispositions by merely naming a trustee and leaving the purposes of the trust to be supplied afterwards . . .' [1929] 2 AC 318 at 339. What does Lord Sumner mean in this statement, and is a different rule of communication justified in the context of a half-secret trust?

3 The decision of Romer J in *Re Gardner (No. 2)* [1923] 2 Ch. 230 suggests that if a secret beneficiary predeceases the testator his interest under the secret trust can pass to his personal representatives. This rule is contradiction to the normal rule of succession, which states if a person receiving under a will predeceases the testator then his gift is said to lapse. Until such time as the testator dies, does a secret beneficiary acquire any interest in the secret trust? Do you think that there may have been something on the facts of *Re Gardner (No. 2)* which led to Romer J's decision which has been widely criticised?

4 Does it really make any difference whether secret trusts are classified as express trusts or constructive trusts?

5 Critically evaluate how effective it is to employ the concept of a 'floating trust' in the context of a constructive trust imposed in mutual will cases.

6 At what stage does a constructive trust arise in the case of mutual wills and to what property does the trust attach?

7 Read the decision of the Court of Appeal in *Fry* v *Densham-Smith* [2010] EWCA Civ 1410 and explain on what basis did the court come to the conclusion that mutual wills had been executed in favour of the contending beneficiary.

Further reading

Critchley, P. 'Instruments of Fraud, Testamentary Dispositions and the Doctrine of Secret Trusts' (1999) 115 LQR 631. Examines the contemporary force of the fraud justification for secret trusts and provides an excellent discussion of secret trusts.

Mathews, P. 'The True Basis of the Half-Secret Trust' [1979] Conv. 360. Examines the nature of half-secret trusts and examines the basis for the enforcement of a half-secret trust.

Meager, R. 'Secret Trusts: Do They Have a Future?' [1995] Conv. 402. Examines the contemporary use of secret trusts.

Perrins, B. 'Secret Trusts: The Key to the Dehors?' [1985] Conv. 248. Examines the 'dehor' theory of secret trusts and explains how the theory works.

Richardson, N. 'Floating Trusts and Mutual Wills' (1996) 10 Trust LI 88. Examines the decision in *Goodchild* v *Goodchild* and the effect of remarriage on mutual wills.

Sheridan, L.A. 'English and Irish Secret Trusts' (1951) 67 LQR 314. Examines some of the different rules governing secrets in England and Ireland and examines whether the different rules of communication for fully secret trusts and half-secret trusts is justified.

Wilde, D. 'Secret and Semi-Secret Trusts: Justifying Distinctions Between the Two' [1995] Conv. 366. Examines the reason for the distinction between fully secret trusts and half-secret trusts.

8

The beneficiary principle

Learning objectives

After reading this chapter you should be able to:

→ understand the rationale behind the beneficiary principle

→ explain the principal objections to private purpose trusts

→ distinguish between private trusts and purpose trusts

→ understand the principle in *Re Denley's Deed Trust* and its extent

→ distinguish between charitable and non-charitable trusts

→ explain the exceptions to the beneficiary principle and their rationale

→ understand how gifts are made to unincorporated associations.

Re Astor's Settlement Trusts [1952] Ch. 534: A trust to preserve the independence of the Observer newspaper

The facts of *Re Astor's Settlement Trust* provide an excellent setting for the discussion which is the subject mater of this chapter. The facts of the case concerned a trust whose objective was to preserve the independence of the *Observer* newspaper. A settlement, which was made in 1945, contained a provision instructing trustees to apply the income from a fund for a number of non-charitable purposes, which included, among other things, the 'maintenance . . . of good understanding . . . between nations,' and 'the preservation of the independence and integrity of newspapers'.

The question before the Court of Appeal was whether this trust was valid. So far in this book it has been observed that a trust must be created in favour of a human beneficiary or a group of human beneficiaries. The beneficiary or beneficiaries can be described by name or by some other description, for example, employees of a company or relatives of a person. Provided that the beneficiary or class of beneficiaries is described with an element of conceptual certainty the trust will be upheld by the court. The problem with *Re Astor Settlement Trust* is that it is not apparent who the main beneficiaries of the trust are. Also, what is meant by some of the terms employed by the settlor? For example, how does the court enforce a trust whose objective is to promote good relations between nation states? What does a settlor mean by the promotion of good relations between nation states?

Re Astor Settlement Trust raises interesting questions for this chapter to address, not least, whether a trust can be created for a purpose rather than for a group of definable beneficiaries. For example, can a settlor create a trust for the promotion of playing darts in his village? If he does create such a trust, who are the beneficiaries of the trust? Further still, can a testator leave his entire property on trust for his favourite pet and leave nothing to his family members? If he does do that, who will enforce the obligation against the trustee? A gift or a trust in favour of a pet is not something which is uncommon in practice. In 2007 a wealthy American left some $12 million to her favourite dog, sparking much media attention: for example, the *Financial Times* reported:

Philanthropy goes to the dogs

By Christopher Caldwell: *Financial Times* 4 July 2008

The last will of the hotel heiress, Leona Helmsley, who died last summer with an estate worth $5bn–$8bn, was like something out of a screwball comedy from the last century. It bestowed a $12m trust (later reduced to $2m by a Manhattan court) on her dog, a Maltese named Trouble. It excluded two of her grandchildren altogether. Helmsley had been stingy in life. It was alleged in a 1989 court case in which she was convicted of tax evasion that she once said: 'We don't pay taxes, only the little people pay taxes.'

She was capricious and vindictive in death. The two grandchildren whom her will did honour will get part of their income from $5m (€3m, £2.5m) trusts – but only so long as they visit the grave of Helmsley's son at least once a year. Otherwise, according to the will, 'the principal of such trust, together with all accrued and undistributed net income, shall be disposed of as if such beneficiary had then died'. What remains of the estate – virtually all of it – will go into one of the largest charitable trusts in the world. On Wednesday, though, the New York Times revealed that Helmsley had cut humanity out of her will, too. If the terms of a 2003 'mission statement' are upheld, her money will go to a charity for dogs.

Source: © The Financial Times.

Introduction

It is an essential requirement of trust law that a trust is created in favour of a human beneficiary. In *Leahy v A-G for New South Wales*[1] Viscount Simmonds explained that 'a trust may be created for the benefit of persons . . . but not a purpose or object'.[2] Where a trust is created for a mere purpose or non-human object, the trust is said to be one of imperfect obligation and prima facie void. Trusts created in favour of non-human beneficiaries are also often referred to as non-charitable purpose trusts. The principal objection to purpose trusts is that there is no one who is capable of enforcing the trust against the trustee. It is an essential ingredient of a trust that the trustee can be compelled to execute the trust and that the court can control the execution of that obligation. For example, in *Re Astor's Settlement Trust*[3] Roxburgh J commented that 'a court of equity does not recognise as valid a trust which it cannot both enforce and control'.[4] To have a trust which imposes no obligation on the trustee is tantamount to ownership. The trust is said to impose an imperfect obligation on the trustee. Good examples of purpose trusts or trusts of imperfect obligation include a trust for a pet or animal, a trust to promote playing darts in the local village or a trust for the upkeep of a monument. The basic problem in all of these examples is one of enforcement. The matter is further explained by Roxburgh J in *Astor's Settlement Trust* where the judge explained that:

> the typical case of a trust is one in which the legal owner of property is constrained by a court of equity so to deal with it as to give effect to the equitable rights of another. These equitable rights have been hammered out in the process of litigation in which a claimant on equitable grounds has successfully asserted rights against a legal owner or other person in control of property. Prima facie, therefore, a trustee would not be expected to be subject to an equitable obligation unless there was somebody who could enforce a correlative equitable right, and the nature and extent of that obligation would be worked out in proceedings for enforcement.[5]

Non-charitable purpose trusts and charitable trusts

The law of trusts makes a distinction between non-charitable purpose trusts and charitable trusts. Non-charitable purpose trusts are prima facie void for lack of enforceability. A good example of a non-charitable purpose trust is provided by *Morice v Bishop of Durham*[6] where a trust was created for such objects of benevolence and liberality as the Bishop of Durham would approve of. It was uncertain as to whom the trust was intended for. It was held that the words 'benevolence and liberality' were much wider than charity and the trust remained a non-charitable purpose trust, and therefore, void. However, a trust which is of some worthy cause and conferring a benefit on the public in general is valid as a charitable trust. Charitable trusts are the only true exceptions to the rule that every trust must have definite objects that can enforce the trust. The reason for this simply relates to the public benefit that such trusts confer and are therefore deemed

---

[1] [1959] AC 457.
[2] [1959] AC 457 at 478.
[3] [1952] Ch. 534.
[4] [1952] Ch. 534 at 547.
[5] [1952] Ch. 534 at 541.
[6] (1804) 9 Ves. 339.

to receive favourable treatment in law. The lack of a definable beneficiary or a group of definable beneficiaries is not fatal to a charitable trust. Provided that the purpose of the trust fits into the recognised categories of charity and the trust confers a benefit on the public, the trust is ultimately enforced by the Attorney General in the name of the Crown.[7] The Attorney General is deemed to be the ultimate beneficiary of a charitable trust, although most of the powers of enforcement of charities are now vested in the Charity Commissioners.[8]

A charitable trust will only be regarded as such if it falls within the definition of charity. One of the fundamental objectives of the Charities Act 2006 was to provide a statutory definition of a charity. In Chapter 22 it will be observed that a charitable trust must fall within one of the thirteen heads of charity as identified by the Charities Act 2006 and now the Charities Act 2011. In addition to falling within the definition of charity, a charitable trust must be for the benefit of the public or a sufficiently important section of the public. Finally, a charitable trust must be one which is exclusively charitable. In **Morice v Bishop of Durham**, although the trust was created in favour of charity, it was denied charitable status on the grounds that its purposes also included non-charitable purposes, that is benevolent purposes.

 ## Is the trust a purpose trust?

Essentially every trust has some purpose to it. For example, a trust of a sum of money for the education of the testator's three children is a trust whose main purpose is to provide for the education of the three children. Given that every trust has some purpose to it, it becomes important to determine whether or not the trust in question is a truly a purpose trust or a private trust in favour of a defined group of beneficiaries. In the example above, it is clear that the trust is in favour of the three children and thus in favour of a defined group of beneficiaries. Such a trust, albeit for the education of the children, is not a purpose trust in the true sense, but one capable of enforcement by the beneficiaries. The primary intention is to benefit a group of individuals and the purpose is merely secondary to that objective, in other words, defining use of the property subject to the trust. On the other hand, where the purpose is the primary objective of the trust and the intended benefactors are merely secondary to the trust, then the trust is truly a purpose trust. For example, if a settlor creates a trust to promote playing darts in his local village, it is clear that the primary function is to promote the playing of darts. As to the potential individuals who may benefit from the trust, it is not clear from the trust itself, that merely being secondary to the trust. Furthermore, such individuals would have prima facie no right to call upon the trust property to be distributed to them, a feature which is fundamental to the nature of a private trust.[9]

A number of authorities have laid down principles which can be applied to determine whether the trust in question is a purpose trust or a private trust. In some cases the courts will construe an absolute gift when the purpose is deemed as merely the motive behind the gift. For example, in **Re Osoba**[10] a testator left a fund on trust for the education of his

---

[7] See generally Chapter 22.

[8] Charities Act 1993, s. 32.

[9] Otherwise known as the rule in *Saunders v Vautier* (1841) 4 Beav. 115 which allows a beneficiary or a group of beneficiaries of majority age and absolutely entitled to the trust property to terminate the trust, and call on the trustees to transfer the subject matter of the trust to them in accordance with the settlor's directions.

[10] [1979] 1 WLR 247. See also *Re Bowes* [1896] 1 Ch. 507 where a sum of money was given to owners of an estate to plant trees on the estate: it was held that the surplus belonged absolutely to the estate owners.

daughter up to university level. When the daughter completed her university education the question was whether she was entitled to the surplus fund or whether the surplus was held upon resulting trust for the testator's estate. It was held that the daughter was entitled to the surplus beneficially since the education purpose was merely a statement of the testator's motive. On the other hand, in **Re Abbott Fund Trusts**[11] a number of friends of two deaf and dumb ladies had contributed to a fund for the maintenance of the deaf and dumb ladies. There was no provision as to how the surplus of the fund was to be held. It was argued that the surplus fund belonged to the survivor of the two ladies. The court held that there was no intention to make an absolute gift to the two ladies and consequently the surplus was held on resulting trust for the contributors.

In **Re Andrew's Trust**[12] a trust was set up for the education of the children of a clergyman. The question was whether the surplus fund was available for distribution to the children. Kekewich J explained that, even though the particular trust in question was directed solely for the education of the children, the surplus belonged beneficially to the children. His Lordship referred to the earlier decision of Wood VC who explained the matter could be resolved in the following way: 'If a gross sum be given, or the whole income of property be given, and a special purpose be assigned for this gift this court regards the gift as absolute and the purpose merely as the motive of the gift, and therefore holds that the gift takes effect as to the whole sum or the whole income as the case may be.'[13]

The beneficiary principle stated

The beneficiary principle was originally articulated by Grant MR in **Morice v Bishop of Durham**.[14] It has already been observed that this case concerned a trust in favour of such objects of 'benevolence and liberality' as the Bishop of Durham shall approve of. Having decided that this trust failed, Grant MR explained that 'there can be no trust over which this Court will assume a control, for an uncontrollable power of disposition would be ownership and not trust'.[15] On appeal in the House of Lords, Lord Eldon LC explained the matter as follows: 'As it is a maxim, that the execution of a trust shall be under the control of the court, it must be of such a nature, that it can be under that control, so that the administration of it can be reviewed by the court; or, if the trustee dies, the court itself can execute the trust.'[16]

Relatively more recent decisions have continued to uphold the beneficiary principle. In **Re Astor's Settlement Trusts**[17] a settlement made in 1945 contained a provision instructing trustees to apply the income from a fund for a number of non-charitable purposes which included, among other things, the 'maintenance . . . of good understanding . . . between nations,' 'the preservation of the independence and integrity of newspapers'. The Court held that the trusts were invalid principally for two main reasons. In the first place, they were not for the benefit of individuals but for a number of non-charitable purposes which no one could enforce. Secondly, these trusts included objects which were void for uncertainty. Roxburgh J explained that, with the exception of the anomalous

---

[11] [1900] 2 Ch. 326.

[12] [1905] 2 Ch. 48.

[13] *Re Sanderson's Trust* (1857) 3 K & J 497 at 503.

[14] (1804) 9 Ves. 399.

[15] (1804) 9 Ves. 399 at 404–5. See also *Chichester Diocesan Fund and Board of Finance v Simpson* [1944] AC 341.

[16] (1805) 10 Ves. 522 at 539.

[17] [1952] Ch. 534.

cases,[18] every trust must have a beneficiary who can enforce the trust. The same view was taken in **Re Endacott**[19] where Harman LJ explained that the anomalous cases were not to be followed as these were 'perhaps merely occasions when Homer has nodded'.[20]

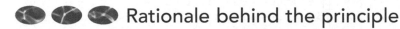 # Rationale behind the principle

The primary rationale behind the beneficiary principle, as already noted above, relates to the question of enforceability. There must be someone who has *locus standi* to enforce the trust. However, as well as enforceability, there are other equally important objections behind the principle.

Uncertainty

Non-charitable purpose trusts are often clouded with uncertainty in terms of their purpose. A good example of this is **Re Endacott**[21] where a testator left a large sum of money to the North Tawton Devon Parish Council 'for the purpose of providing some useful memorial to myself'. The Court of Appeal refused to uphold the gift on the grounds that it was simply too uncertain and vague as to what was meant by 'some useful memorial to myself'. The same reasoning was applied in **Re Astor's Settlement Trusts**[22] where Roxburgh J explained that many of the purposes, for example, the maintenance of good relations between nations, was simply too vague. In his Lordships words: 'but how . . . could I decree in what manner the trusts applicable to income were to be performed? The settlement gives no guidance at all.'[23] In **Morice v Bishop of Durham**[24] you will recall that the trust was set up for such objects of benevolence and liberality as the Bishop of Durham should approve. It was held that these words were just too vague to impose an obligation in favour of a defined group of beneficiaries.

Purpose trusts conflict with the perpetuity rules

Purpose trust in their very nature will violate the common law rules relating to perpetuity. These rules are designed to invalidate certain dispositions of property which have an excessive delay in vesting. The rules have their origins in preventing property being tied up for long periods of time thereby preventing the free flow of it, which is an essential requirement of a free-market economy. The nature and purpose of the perpetuity rules has been described in one leading text as follows.

> Since medieval times, English law has been subjected to the tension between two conflicting influences. Owners of land and of other types of property have generally wished to tie up their property indefinitely, usually for the benefit of their family or for some institution or cause, while the courts and the legislature have always felt that it is in the interest of the nation as a whole that wealth should circulate freely and that property should not be made inalienable. The result has been a compromise. Property may be tied up indefinitely for a purpose which the law wishes to advance, namely a charity. Otherwise property may be

---

[18] These are considered in more detail below.
[19] [1960] Ch. 232.
[20] [1960] Ch. 232 at 250.
[21] [1960] Ch. 232.
[22] [1952] Ch. 534.
[23] [1952] Ch. 534 at 547.
[24] (1804) 9 Ves. 339.

tied up only for a comparatively short period. The rule which enforces this restriction is known as the rule against perpetuities.

Parker and Mellows, The Modern Law of Trusts 9th edn (2009) at p. 255.

The perpetuity rules, as explained above, were originally designed to set a time limit which future dealings with property must occur, this time limit being the perpetuity period. The common law perpetuity period was modified by the Perpetuities and Accumulations Act 1964 and further modified by the Perpetuities and Accumulations Act 2009 which came into force on 6 April 2010. The 2009 Act is not retrospective and will only deal with instruments taking effect after 6 April 2010.

The background to the Perpetuities and Accumulations Act 2009

In March 1998 the Law Commission published a report, *The Rules Against Perpetuities and Accumulations*, suggesting a fundamental reform in relation to the rule against perpetuities and excessive accumulations.[25] The reason for reform in this area was that the rules against perpetuities and accumulations had become out of date with the needs of modern society and restricted the operation of property dealings in commercial areas when in reality the rules were originally designed to deal with family trusts. In a summary of the main report, the Law Commission explained that:[26]

> The Law Commission identified a number of problems with the existing rule against perpetuities and the rule against excessive accumulations. In particular:
>
> The application of the rule against perpetuities has developed over time and is now too wide. It applies to many commercial dealings (such as future easements, options and rights of pre-emption) which have nothing to do with the family settlements that the rule was designed to control. The application of the rule to pension schemes is not consistent with the policy of the rule.
>
> Although there is an exception for most pension schemes from the rule against perpetuities, a small number of pension schemes fell outside of the exemption, and are subject to the rule. The Commission's view was that there was no sound policy basis for this group of pension schemes being subject to the rule against perpetuities.
>
> The existence of multiple methods for calculating the perpetuity period (which includes the use of lives in being at common law, as well as periods of up to 80 years under the 1964 Act) is unnecessarily complex and confusing. In addition, the use of lives in being gives rise to practical difficulties. For example, where a 'royal lives clause' has been used, it may be impossible for the trustees to identify who the last remaining descendants of a monarch are, or indeed whether they are still alive.
>
> In relation to the rule against excessive accumulations, the Law Commission found that there was no longer a sound policy basis for restricting settlors' ability to direct or allow for the accumulation of income, except in the case of charitable trusts (for which there is a public interest in limiting the time for accumulations, so that income is spent for the public benefit, rather than accumulated indefinitely).

As we shall see below, there are a number of aspects to the perpetuity rules, namely the rule against remoteness of vesting, the rule against inalienability and the rule against excessive accumulations. The Law Commission in its report, only considered the rule against remoteness of vesting and the rule against excessive accumulations. It did not consider the rule against inalienability. The following text looks at the relevant aspects of the rules and examines how they have been altered by the Perpetuities and Accumulations Act 2009. It will be observed that the existing rules are a mixture of the old common

---

[25] Law Com No. 251.

[26] http://www.justice.gov.uk/lawcommission/areas/perpetuities-and-excessive-accumulations.htm.

law rule, the Perpetuities and Accumulations Act 1964 and the Perpetuities and Accumulations Act 2009. The Law Commission acknowledged that the law would be a mixture of different rules but nevertheless reform was necessary.

There are a number of aspects to the perpetuity rules:

1 the rule against remoteness of vesting

2 the rule against inalienability

3 the rule against excessive accumulations.

The rule against remoteness of vesting deals with those dispositions of property which have an excessive delay in vesting. Where the rule has been violated, the gift is said to be void. The common law rule on vesting is that no interest is good if it vests, if at all, no later than 21 years after some life or lives in being. The common law perpetuity period measures the perpetuity period by a human life or lives in being plus a further period of 21 years.[27] Where the instrument does not specify any life or lives in being, then the perpetuity period is restricted to 21 years. Thus, any gifts or trusts which do not vest within the perpetuity period will be held void. The Perpetuities and Accumulations Act 1964 reformed the perpetuity period applicable in the case of future interests and estates. Section 1 of the Act allowed a maximum period of 80 years as the perpetuity period provided that the period was specified in the instrument creating the interest. If no perpetuity period was specified in the instrument, then the common law period of 21 years would apply. The Perpetuities and Accumulations Act 2009 makes a fundamental change to the rule against remoteness of vesting. Section 5 of the Act imposes a single mandatory period of 125 years. Thus, future interests and estates that are held on trust must vest within 125 years. There is no longer any need to look at the common law rules in this respect, nor does the Perpetuities and Accumulations Act 1964 have any application here. As part of the reform, the perpetuity period will cease to apply to commercial dealings and rights over property, such as options to purchase, and rights of pre-emption; and also there is an exemption for occupational pension schemes. A trust which is for a purpose will inevitably conflict with the rule against remoteness of vesting. For example, a trust of a large fund of money which is to be invested and the income to be used for the maintenance of a grave or a monument will never vest in any particular individual. The matter is neatly explained in *Mussett v Bingle*[28] where the testator left £300 for building a monument and £200 to be invested and the income to be used for the maintenance of the monument. The court upheld the gift of £300, but declined to uphold the gift of £200 on the grounds that it was void for perpetuity.

The second aspect of the perpetuity rules is the rule against inalienability. This rule invalidates certain dispositions of property which have the effect of tying up property for long periods of time. A gift is said to have become inalienable when it is incapable of being disposed of. The same perpetuity period is applicable to the rule against inalienability and, indeed, where a gift violates the rule against remoteness of vesting, it will inevitably violate the rule against inalienability. Where a trust is created for some purpose rather than for the direct benefit of an individual it will violate the rule against inalienability. For example, a trust of the income of £100,000 to promote fishing in the local village will render the £100,000 inalienable and thus in violation of the rule against inalienability. The rule against inalienability was not affected by the Perpetuities and Accumulations Act 1964 nor the Perpetuities and Accumulations Act 2009. Perpetual trusts, which purpose trusts will inevitably be in their nature, are governed by the common law rule of a life in being plus 21 years.

---

[27] *Re Kelly* [1932] IR 255.

[28] [1876] WN 170.

Rule against accumulations

The rule against excessive accumulations prevents income to be accumulated on capital for long periods of time. Until the enactment of the Perpetuities and Accumulations Act 2009, the time periods governing accumulations of income were extremely complex and were found in the Law of Property Act 1925 and the Perpetuities and Accumulations Act 1964. In its report, the Law Commission suggested that there was no real economic justification for the rule against excessive accumulations except in the case of charitable trusts, where excessive accumulations of income was not in the public interest. In charitable trusts, income and capital should be applied for the wider public good rather than accumulated for long periods of time. Section 13 of the Perpetuities and Accumulations Act 2009 abolishes the time restrictions on accumulations of income; section 14 of the Act restricts accumulation of income in the case of a charitable trust to 21 years.

KEY STATUTE

Perpetuities and Accumulations Act 2009

S. 13 Abolition of restrictions

These provisions cease to have effect –

(a) sections 164 to 166 of the Law of Property Act 1925 (c. 20) (which impose restrictions on accumulating income, subject to qualifications);

(b) section 13 of the Perpetuities and Accumulations Act 1964 (which amends section 164 of the 1925 Act).

S. 14 Restriction on accumulation for charitable trusts

(1) This section applies to an instrument to the extent that it provides for property to be held on trust for charitable purposes.

(2) But it does not apply where the provision is made by a court or the Charity Commission for England and Wales.

(3) If the instrument imposes or confers on the trustees a duty or power to accumulate income, and apart from this section the duty or power would last beyond the end of the statutory period, it ceases to have effect at the end of that period unless subsection (5) applies.

(4) The statutory period is a period of 21 years starting with the first day when the income must or may be accumulated (as the case may be).

(5) This subsection applies if the instrument provides for the duty or power to cease to have effect –

(a) on the death of the settlor, or

(b) on the death of one of the settlors, determined by name or by the order of their deaths.

(6) If a duty or power ceases to have effect under this section the income to which the duty or power would have applied apart from this section must—

(a) go to the person who would have been entitled to it if there had been no duty or power to accumulate, or

(b) be applied for the purposes for which it would have had to be applied if there had been no such duty or power.

(7) This section applies whether or not the duty or power to accumulate extends to income produced by the investment of income previously accumulated.

Excessive delegation of testamentary power

In the case of a will, some commentators have identified that a trust which does not have a beneficiary to enforce it against the trustee will have conferred upon the trustee an excessive delegation of his testamentary power. The main problem here is that it is the trustee who decides the future direction of the testator's property rather than the testator and as such 'the testator has imperfectly exercised his testamentary power; he has delegated it, for the disposal of his property lies with [the trustee] not with him'.[29]

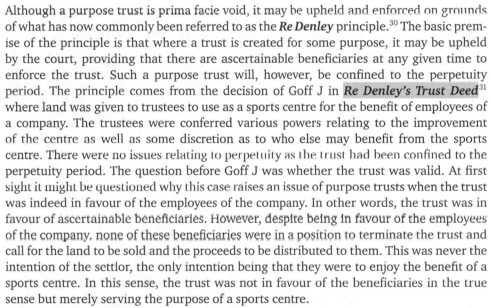

The *Re Denley* principle: a situation outside the beneficiary principle

The principle stated

VISIT CASE NAVIGATOR

Although a purpose trust is prima facie void, it may be upheld and enforced on grounds of what has now commonly been referred to as the **Re Denley** principle.[30] The basic premise of the principle is that where a trust is created for some purpose, it may be upheld by the court, providing that there are ascertainable beneficiaries at any given time to enforce the trust. Such a purpose trust will, however, be confined to the perpetuity period. The principle comes from the decision of Goff J in **Re Denley's Trust Deed**[31] where land was given to trustees to use as a sports centre for the benefit of employees of a company. The trustees were conferred various powers relating to the improvement of the centre as well as some discretion as to who else may benefit from the sports centre. There were no issues relating to perpetuity as the trust had been confined to the perpetuity period. The question before Goff J was whether the trust was valid. At first sight it might be questioned why this case raises an issue of purpose trusts when the trust was indeed in favour of the employees of the company. In other words, the trust was in favour of ascertainable beneficiaries. However, despite being in favour of the employees of the company, none of these beneficiaries were in a position to terminate the trust and call for the land to be sold and the proceeds to be distributed to them. This was never the intention of the settlor, the only intention being that they were to enjoy the benefit of a sports centre. In this sense, the trust was not in favour of the beneficiaries in the true sense but merely serving the purpose of a sports centre.

The facts of **Re Denley's Trust Deed**[32] clearly gave rise to a purpose trust and thus void on the grounds of lack of enforceability. Nevertheless Goff J upheld the trust on the basis that it was an express private trust in favour of ascertainable beneficiaries who could enforce the trust.

> I think there may be a purpose or object trust, the carrying out of which would benefit an individual or individuals, where the benefit is so indirect or intangible or which is otherwise so framed as not to give those persons any *locus standi* to apply to the court to enforce the trust, in which case the beneficiary principle would, as it seems to me, apply to invalidate the trust, quite apart from any question of uncertainty or perpetuity. Such cases can be considered if and when they arise. The present is not, in my judgement, of that

---

[29] Per Viscount Simonds in *Leahy v A-G for New South Wales* [1959] AC 457 at 484.
[30] This principle has often been described as undermining the beneficiary principle; see, for example, G. Moffat, *Trust Law: Text and Materials* 4th edn (2005) at p. 246.
[31] [1969] 1 Ch. 373.
[32] [1969] 1 Ch. 373.

character . . . The beneficiary principle . . . is confined to purpose or object trusts which are abstract or impersonal. The objection is not that the trust is for a purpose or object *per se*, but there is no beneficiary. Where, then, the trust, though expressed as a purpose, is directly or indirectly for the benefit of an individual or individuals, it seems to me that it is generally outside the mischief of the beneficiary principle.[33]

The principle in *Re Denley* is one which relates to the question of enforceability. Provided there are ascertainable beneficiaries who can enforce the trust then it should not be invalidated even if it is a purpose trust. The only limitation is that the benefit should not be so intangible or too indirect. In the case itself, Goff J explained that the employees of the company were an ascertainable group of beneficiaries who could enforce the trust against the trustees. The general impression which comes from the judgment of Goff J in *Re Denley's Deed Trust*[34] is that the main mischief of the beneficiary principle is one of enforceability. Provided that the trust can be enforced by ascertainable beneficiaries then it would seem that there is no violation of the beneficiary principle. Whilst there may be some merit in this view, it is one which does give rise to many conceptual problems.

Conceptual problems with the principle

The main problem with the *Re Denley* type of trust is its nature and its proper classification. A fundamental question is whether the *Re Denley* trust is a private trust in the true sense or whether it is a purpose trust. Clearly, the primary function of the trust in *Re Denley's Deed Trust* was to provide nothing more than the use of a sports centre for the employees. As such it was in its nature nothing more than a non-charitable purpose trust and therefore void. The judgment of Goff J seems to suggest, however, that the trust was a private trust. It was in favour of ascertainable beneficiaries and therefore outside the mischief of the beneficiary principle. The problem with this line of reasoning is that the conditions of the *Re Denley* trust do not fit the normal conditions which are attributable to a private trust. For example, a private trust of land in favour of a group of beneficiaries will have a number of key features. Firstly, the beneficiaries will have an equitable interest in the land enforceable against the trustee. The trust of land will itself be governed by the Trusts of Land and Appointment of Trustees Act 1996. Under this legislation the beneficiaries *inter alia* have the right to occupy the land and certain rights in relation to management. The trustees of land will have power to sell, lease or mortgage the land as they think fit.[35] Furthermore, like any other trust, whether it is land or other property, beneficiaries can terminate the trust under the rule in *Saunders v Vautier*.[36] This rule allows a beneficiary who is of full age, of sound mind and absolutely entitled to the equitable interest in the trust to terminate the trust. The rule extends to two or more beneficiaries who are collectively entitled to the equitable interest in the trust property.

None of the characteristics of a private trust identified above apply to the *Re Denley* type of trust. The facts of *Re Denley's Deed Trust* involved a large fluctuating class of beneficiaries who were never intended to receive any equitable interest in the land. Furthermore, they could not terminate the trust and ask the trustees to sell the land and distribute the proceeds of sale to them. It is this aspect of the *Re Denley* trust which makes it very difficult to justify. A further criticism of the case relates to the question where the beneficial interest lies in the trust. Clearly, the beneficial interest did not belong to the

---

[33] [1969] 1 Ch. 373 at 382.
[34] [1969] 1 Ch. 373.
[35] S. 6 Trusts of Land and Appointment of Trustees Act 1996.
[36] (1841) 4 Beav. 115.

employees of the company. Presumably, the beneficial interest must be suspended during the continuance of the trust. Again, this is difficult to explain within the established trust law principles, in particular, the principle that equity abhors a beneficial vacuum.[37]

The principle endorsed

Despite the criticism of the decision in **Re Denley's Trust Deed** it has been followed and endorsed in subsequent cases. The first of those cases is **Re Lipinski's Will Trusts**[38] where a testator left his estate to an unincorporated association in memory of his wife. The gift was to be applied for the purpose of improving and constructing further buildings which were used primarily for recreation. The problem facing the court was that an unincorporated association, unlike an incorporated company, cannot hold title to property. This matter is explored in further detail below; however for present purposes, the question was how the gift to the association was to be construed. Oliver J proceeded to uphold the gift as a purpose trust in favour of the members of the association who were capable of enforcing the trust on grounds of the principle explained by Goff J in **Re Denley's Trust Deed**.[39] Oliver J explained it as 'a trust which, although expressed as a purpose, was directly, or indirectly for the benefit of an individual or individuals was valid provided those individuals were ascertainable at any given time and the trust was not void for uncertainty'.[40] Although Oliver J seems to endorse the principle in **Re Denley's Trust Deed**, it is submitted that the facts of **Re Lipinski** were rather different from those of **Re Denley**. The facts of **Re Lipinski** involved a gift to an unincorporated association where the rules of the association allowed the members to change their constitution and allow for the distribution of the funds amongst the members. Seen in this way, the equitable interest in the trust was not suspended in the same way it was in **Re Denley's Trust Deed**. The members could alter the constitution and ask for distribution of the funds. Oliver J explained that 'this is a case in which, under the constitution of the association, the members could, by the appropriate majority, alter their constitution so as to provide, if they wished, for the division of the association's assets amongst themselves'.[41]

A rather different interpretation of **Re Denley's Trust Deed** was taken by Vinelott J in **Re Grant's Will Trusts**[42] where land and other property was left to the Chertsey and Walton Constituency Labour Party. This, like in **Re Lipinski's Will Trusts**[43] was a gift left to an unincorporated association. The question before the court was whether the gift was void for uncertainty, breach of the perpetuity rules or otherwise lacking beneficiaries who could receive the gift. The ramifications of this case are considered in much more detail below when this chapter examines the problems associated with making gifts to unincorporated associations; however, for the time being the **Re Denley's Trust Deed**[44] aspect of the case can be considered. Unlike in **Re Lipinski's Will Trusts**[45] where the members of the unincorporated association had the power to change their constitution and distribute the property amongst themselves, no such power existed in this case. The

---

[37] For a more critical analysis of the decision, see L. McKay, 'Trusts for Purposes – Another View' (1979) Conv. 420.
[38] [1976] Ch. 235.
[39] [1969] 1 Ch. 373.
[40] [1976] Ch. 235 at 248.
[41] [1976] Ch. 235 at 249.
[42] [1980] 1 WLR 360.
[43] [1976] Ch. 235.
[44] [1969] 1 Ch. 373.
[45] [1976] Ch. 235.

rules of the constituency party provided for rule-making powers by the annual party conference and the National Executive of the Labour Party. Vinelott J held that the gift was ineffective because the members of the constituency party did not have sufficient control over its property for the gift to take effect. In the course of this judgment Vinelott J. approved the principle in *Re Denley's Trust Deed*.

> That case on a proper analysis, in my judgment, falls altogether outside the categories of gifts to unincorporated associations and purpose trusts. I can see no distinction in principle between a trust to permit a class defined by reference to employment to use and enjoy land in accordance with rules to be made at the discretion of trustees on the one hand, and, on the other hand, a trust to distribute income at the discretion of the trustees amongst a class, defined by reference to, for example, relationship to the settlor. In both cases the benefit to be taken by any member of the class is at the discretion of the trustee, but any member of the class can apply to the court to compel the trustee to administer the trust in accordance with the terms.[46]

Vinelott J explained that it was impossible to construe the gift to the Chertsey and Walton Constituency and Labour Party as a gift to the members of the constituency party, because the constituency party was governed by the National Executive of the Labour Party who could alter the constitution and provide for the property to be transferred elsewhere. In light of this, Vinelott J whilst endorsing the principle in *Re Denley's Trust Deed*, held that the nature of the association did not give rise for an application of that principle. It is submitted, however, that the endorsement of *Re Denley's Trust Deed* by Vinelott J is too extensive. Vinelott J appears to treat the *Re Denley's Trust Deed* as a discretionary trust. He admits that there is no difference in principle between a trust to distribute income at the discretion of a trustee in favour of the relatives of a settlor and a trust to allow the use of some purpose at the discretion of the trustee. With respect to the decision, there is a big difference between the two situations. In the case of a trust to distribute income, albeit at the discretion of the trustee, the beneficiaries can, under the rule in *Saunders v Vautier*[47] call for the trust to be terminated. In the case of land held at the discretion of the trustees for the use of a sports centre, as in *Re Denley's Trust Deed*,[48] the so-called beneficiaries of the trust do not have the same rights to terminate the trust and call for the land to be sold and the proceeds to be distributed amongst them absolutely.

The anomalous cases

Whilst *Re Denley's Trust Deed* is properly classified as a situation which falls outside of the beneficiary principle, in *Re Astor's Settlement Trusts*[49] Roxburgh J identified and reviewed a number of anomalous and exceptional cases which, although lacking a beneficiary to enforce the trust, would nevertheless be enforced by the courts. As to the justification for their enforcement, Roxburgh J explained that they were instances where 'concessions to human weakness and sentiment' had been made.[50] In *Re Endacott*[51] Harman LJ explained that these were anomalous and that they were not to be extended

---

[46] [1980] 1 WLR 360 at 370.
[47] (1841) 4 Beav. 115.
[48] (1969) 1 Ch. 373.
[49] [1952] Ch. 534.
[50] [1952] Ch. 534 at 547.
[51] [1960] Ch. 323.

in the future: that is, decisions 'which are not really to be satisfactorily classified, but are perhaps merely occasions where Homer has nodded, at any rate these cases stand by themselves and ought not be increased in number, nor indeed followed, except where the one is exactly like the other'.[52] The exceptions fall into the following categories:

- trusts for the erection or maintenance of graves and monuments;
- trusts for saying masses;
- trusts for the maintenance and care of specific animals;
- trusts for miscellaneous purposes;
- trusts for the benefit of unincorporated associations.

Whilst these anomalous cases have been accepted by the courts, they must adhere to a number of normal requirements which apply to all trusts. Firstly, they must adhere to the perpetuity rules, in particular, the rule against inalienability. The subject matter of the trust must not be alienated for a period greater than a life in being plus 21 years. Thus, in **Re Denley's Trust Deed**[53] the trust to hold land for the enjoyment as a sports centre for the employees was confined to the perpetuity period specified in the trust instrument. Secondly, the trust, albeit for a purpose, must be framed in a manner which contains an element of certainty. The trustees must know exactly what the purpose of the trust is and how the fund is to be applied for that purpose. Where the trust is framed in such a way that it remains unclear as to what the testator's intention was, then the trust will fail and the property will result back to the testator's estate. For example, in **Re Endacott**[54] you will recall that the testator left a sum of money to be applied to providing some useful memorial to himself. Whilst this trust could possibly fit into the category of trusts for the maintenance of graves and monuments, Harman LJ held that the testator's intention was simply too uncertain and vague.

Finally, with these anomalous cases there does remain the issue of enforceability. The question is whether these trusts are ultimately left to the whim of the trustee. For example, where a testator leaves a sum of money to be applied for the maintenance of a monument, how can he be assured that the trustee will carry out that purpose? It is submitted that, given that these types of trusts will be contained in a will, the court should allow the residuary legatees to apply to court for a direction that, should the trustees fail to carry out the trust, then, the property should result back to them. Seen in this way, there is an indirect method of enforcement and the trustees will have a choice of whether to carry out the trust or be subject to claims from the residuary legatees.

Trusts for the erection and maintenance of graves and monuments

APPLYING THE LAW

In his will Steve left a sum of £100,000 to trustees to be invested indefinitely and the income to be used for the maintenance of his mother's burial site.

Would this be a valid trust and could it continue for ever?

---

[52] [1960] Ch. 232 at 250.
[53] [1969] 1 Ch. 373.
[54] [1960] Ch. 232.

If a testator leaves a sum of money for the maintenance of a particular grave or a particular monument then the trust will be deemed as a trust of imperfect obligation. However, the courts will enforce such a trust of imperfect obligation.[55] For example, a gift for the erection of a monument will be upheld by the courts.[56] In **Trimmer v Danby**[57] the testator left a gift of £1000 to be applied for a monument in memory of the testator at St Paul's Cathedral: this was upheld as valid. Trusts which are for the upkeep of a church in general will be held charitable and thus outside the mischief of the beneficiary principle. These will be upheld as valid charitable trusts and enforceable by the Charity Commissioners acting on behalf of the Attorney General. For example, a trust for the maintenance of a churchyard will be construed as a charitable trust. In **Re Vaughan**[58] North J explained that he 'could not see any difference between a gift to keep in repair what is called God's House and a gift to keep in repair the churchyard round it which is often called God's Acre'.[59]

Although a trust for the maintenance of a grave or monument will be upheld by the court, it must be confined to the perpetuity period. For example, in **Pirbright v Salway**[60] the testator left a sum of £800 and the income thereof to be used for maintenance and upkeep of a child burial enclosure 'for long as law permitted'. The court held that the gift was valid for a period of 21 years. A similar result was found in **Re Hooper**[61] where a trust, set up for the upkeep of various family graves and monuments with the words, 'so long as they could legally do so', was upheld by Maugham J for a period of 21 years. Where the trust is so framed that the property will continue to be alienated beyond the perpetuity period the trust will fail. This is neatly illustrated in **Musset v Bingle**[62] where the testator left a sum of £300 to be applied in erecting a monument in memory of the testator's wife's first husband. A further gift of £200 was made to the trustees to be invested and the income to be used for the maintenance of the monument. The first gift was upheld but the second gift failed as it was possible that this could be applied for a period exceeding 21 years.

Trusts for saying masses

A testator may leave a sum of money to be applied for saying masses or prayers so that, after his death, his soul reaches heaven. It my well be thought that such a trust would be classified as being charitable in nature on the grounds that they fall into the category of advancement of religion. In **Re Hetherington**[63] the court held that a trust for saying prayers would be charitable provided that such prayers were said in public, for example, in a place of worship attended by members of the public at large. Prayers

---

[55] These trusts have their origins in a time when it was impossible for testators to enter into public agreements for the upkeep of graves and burial enclosures. This has now changed under the Parish Councils and Burial Authorities (Miscellaneous Provisions) Act 1970. Under s. 1 of this Act a burial authority or a local authority can enter into a contract for the maintenance of a grave or monument for a period not exceeding 99 years.

[56] *Mitford v Reynold* (1848) 16 Sim. 105.

[57] (1856) 25 LJ Ch. 424.

[58] (1886) 33 Ch. D. 187.

[59] (1886) 33 Ch. D. 187 at 192.

[60] [1896] WN 86.

[61] [1932] 1 Ch. 38.

[62] [1876] WN 170.

[63] [1990] Ch. 1.

which are said in private, for example, by a cloistered religious group will not be held to be charitable.[64] However, in **Bourne v Keane**[65] the court upheld a trust for saying prayers in private as a non-charitable purpose trust. Such a trust will, of course, be confined to the perpetuity period.

Trusts for care and maintenance of specific animals

APPLYING THE LAW

Cecil was a wealthy businessman who had built his business on his own without any help from any of his relatives, including his children. In his will he left half of his residuary estate to charity and the other half for the upkeep of his four horses and his cat Felix. His children have objected to the gift to the horses and the cat and wish to know whether the gift to the horses and the cat is void.

A trust which is created for the welfare of animals in general will be held valid as a charitable trust. Indeed, a trust for the advancement of animal welfare is one of the recognised heads of charity in the Charities Act 2006. However, a trust which is created for the welfare of a specific animal will not be charitable and therefore prima facie void. However, despite this, it has been held that a non-charitable purpose trust for the care of a specific animal will be upheld by the courts. For example, in **Pettingall v Pettingall**[66] a testator left a sum of £50 per annum to his executor for the upkeep of his favourite black mare. The court upheld the gift in favour of the mare on the grounds that the executor had given an assurance that the money would be applied for the upkeep of the mare. Furthermore, Knight Bruce VC in the course of his judgment explained that the residuary beneficiaries of the testator's estate were at liberty to apply to court to challenge the executor should he fail to provide for the mare. Seen in this way, the executor had no choice but to apply the money for the purpose for which it was left. There was no discussion in the case as to whether the gift was to be confined to the perpetuity period. The gift was held to be valid for the lifetime of the animal. A similar result was achieved in **Re Dean**[67] where the testator left his eight horses and hounds to his trustees with a sum of £750 per annum for a period of 50 years for their upkeep and maintenance. Unlike in **Pettingall v Pettingall**[68] where the residuary beneficiaries had the opportunity to challenge the executor should he fail to apply the gift, in this case the residuary beneficiaries were dumb and therefore incapable of seeing that the gift would be so applied by the trustees. Nevertheless, North J upheld the gift in favour of the animals explaining that he did not see the lack of a human beneficiary to enforce the trust as fatal to a trust.[69] As to the lack of any residuary beneficiaries capable of applying to court should the trustees fail to carry out the testator's intention, North J explained that 'if such persons could not

---

[64] See, for example, *Gilmour v Coates* [1949] AC 426.
[65] [1919] AC 815.
[66] (1842) 11 LJ Ch. 176.
[67] (1889) 41 Ch. D. 552.
[68] (1842) 11 LJ Ch. 176.
[69] (1889) 41 Ch. D. 552 at 556.

enforce the trust, still it cannot be said that the trust must fail because there is no one who can actively enforce it'.[70]

Although both *Pettingall v Pettingall*[71] and *Re Dean*[72] hold that a valid non-charitable trust can be created for the welfare of a specific animal, in neither case did the court discuss whether such a trust should be confined to the perpetuity period. It may well be that in many of the cases before the courts the perpetuity period was not at issue because the duration of the animal's life was such that the gift can never offend the perpetuity period. However, horses are certainly capable of living for a period greater than 21 years and such the decisions in both *Pettingall v Pettingall* and *Re Dean* offend the rule against inalienability. It is questionable whether a trust in favour of the upkeep of a specific animal can exceed the perpetuity period of a life in being plus 21 years. It is submitted that such a trust will be confined to the perpetuity period with the consequence that any surplus remaining after the perpetuity period will have to be returned to the residuary legatees of the testator's estate.

● Miscellaneous cases

Like in most cases where the courts devise categories there is always a residual category to cover cases which do not necessarily fit neatly into the others. One such case which is often cited is *Re Thompson*[73] where the testator left a gift of £1000 in his will to be applied for the purpose of promoting fox hunting. The residuary beneficiary was Trinity College in the University of Cambridge. The court upheld the gift on the basis that it could be enforced indirectly by the residuary beneficiary who was at liberty to apply to the court should the trustee fail to carry out the testator intention. On the facts both the trustee and the residuary beneficiary was anxious that the money should be applied for the purpose indicated by the testator. It is not exactly clear as to why the court recognised and enforced a trust for the promotion of fox hunting. The court made an analogy between this trust and the trust in *Pettingall v Pettingall*;[74] however, it is not clear what similarity there is between a trust to maintain a horse and a trust to promote fox hunting. The only connection between the two cases seems to be the indirect means of enforcing the testator's intention, that is, by allowing the residuary beneficiaries to apply to court should the trustee fail in his duty.

There are not too many cases cited in the miscellaneous category; indeed, this reflects the attitude of the courts in not expanding the anomalous cases. Where a non-charitable purpose trusts is deemed to serve no useful purpose, then the court is reluctant to enforce it. For example, in *Brown v Burdett*[75] a testatrix left her house on trust to her trustees with the direction that the windows and the door should be blocked up for a period of 21 years. It is not surprising that the court held that this gift was void on the grounds that this trust served no useful purpose. The trust was described as a capricious trust. A similar result was arrived at in *Re Shaw*[76] where George Bernard Shaw left his residuary estate on trust to be applied in researching the benefits of a 40-letter alphabet. Harman J refused to uphold the gift on the grounds that this trust did not serve any useful purpose.

---

[70] (1889) 41 Ch. D. 552 at 557.
[71] (1842) 11 LJ Ch. 176.
[72] (1889) 41 Ch. D. 552.
[73] [1934] Ch. 342.
[74] (1842) 11 LJ Ch. 176.
[75] (1882) 21 Ch. D. 667.
[76] [1957] 3 K & J 497.

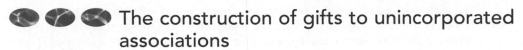

The construction of gifts to unincorporated associations

Definition and problems of ownership of property

Gifts to unincorporated associations present a number of difficulties in law, in particular, how ownership of the property is to be taken by the association. An unincorporated association is nothing more than a group of people who are connected by some common purpose. The connection is usually made through some contract, for example, members of a society are usually bound by the rules of the society. A definition of an unincorporated association was given by Lawton LJ in *Conservative and Unionist Central Office* v *Burrell*[77] where his Lordship explained an unincorporated association as:

> [t]wo or more persons bound together for one or more common purpose, not being business purposes, by mutual undertakings each having mutual duties and obligations, in an organisation which has rules which identify in whom control of it and its funds rests and on what terms . . .[78]

Good examples of unincorporated associations include social and sports clubs. Unlike an association which is incorporated, for example, a limited company, an unincorporated association does not have a separate legal personality which allows it to hold property in its own name. It follows, therefore, that any property which is given to an unincorporated association must be held by the members on trust for the association. In this respect, gifts to unincorporated associations fall squarely in any discussion of the beneficiary principle simply because the property is usually held by certain members of the association in pursuit of some purpose.

Given the fact that an unincorporated association will in most cases continue for long periods of time, and will have a fluctuating group of individuals who will benefit from its purpose, the question arises as to how gifts to unincorporated associations are to be construed.[79] Any property held for the association will inevitably conflict with the perpetuity rules. Furthermore, there is also the question as to how future members of the association can benefit from the property which is held on trust for the members. Over the years the courts have interpreted gifts to unincorporated associations in a number of ways. These interpretations were considered in detail by the court in *Neville Estates Ltd* v *Madden*.[80] Cross J identified a number of ways in which an unincorporated association could receive a gift.

---

[77] [1982] 1 WLR 522.
[78] [1982] 1 WLR 522 at 525.
[79] See, J. Warburton, 'Holding of Property by Unincorporated Associations' [1985] Conv. 318.
[80] [1962] Ch. 832.

The position, as I understand it, is as follows. Such a gift may take effect in one or other of three quite different ways. In the first place, it may, on its true construction, be a gift to the members of the association at the relevant date as joint tenants, so that any member can sever his share and claim it whether or not he continues to be a member of the association. Secondly, it may be a gift to the existing members not as joint tenants, but subject to their respective contractual rights and liabilities towards one another as members of the association. In such a case a member cannot sever his interest. It would accrue to other members on his death or resignation, even though such members include persons who became members after the gift took effect. If this is the effect of the gift, it will not be open to objection on the score of perpetuity or uncertainty unless there is something in its terms or circumstances or in the rules of the association which precludes the members at any given time from dividing the subject of the gift between them on the footing that they are solely entitled to it in equity. Thirdly, the terms or circumstances of the gift or the rules of the association may show that the property in question is not at the disposal of the members for the time being, but it is held upon trust for or applied for the purposes of the association as a quasi-corporate entity. In this case the gift will fail unless the association is a charitable body.[81]

The various ways in which gifts to unincorporated associations are construed by the courts are examined in the next sections.

Gift to present members as co-owners

The simplest way in which a gift can be construed in favour of an unincorporated association is a gift beneficially to the existing member of the association. The members will hold the property as co-owners either as joint tenants or tenants in common. Where they are joint tenants they will be collectively entitled to the property. Should any one member die, the remaining joint tenants will be entitled to the property on the principle of survivorship which holds that the share of each joint tenant passes to the remaining joint tenants. There is nothing stopping any joint tenant from severing his interest and thereby creating a tenancy in common. In the case of tenancy in common, the share of each member will pass under the rules of succession. Whilst this method of holding property is undoubtedly the simplest and avoids any problems of perpetuity, because the property is vested in the members, it does not confer any rights to the property to future members of the association. Furthermore, given that each member is entitled to his share and can pass it to another on death, with the passage of time the property will eventually be used so that it will not be available for the long-term use of the association.

Trust for present members

The second possible construction of a gift to an unincorporated association is that the gift takes effect as a trust for the members of the association. This involves some of the members holding the property on trust for the remaining members. One commentator explains that this method 'would appear to be acceptable from both a conveyancing and the member's point of view'.[82] She explains that 'first the rule, as to certainty of beneficiaries is satisfied because at any one time the beneficiaries can be ascertained by looking at the members of the association. Secondly, provided the beneficiaries are free to dispose

---

[81] [1962] Ch. 832 at 849.
[82] J. Warburton, 'Holding of Property by Unincorporated Associations' [1985] Conv. 318 at p. 321.

of the property, both income and capital, the rules against perpetuities are satisfied.'[83] For example, in **Re Drummond**[84] a testator left his residuary estate to the 'Old Bradfordians Club to be utilised as the Committee of the Club should think best in the interests of the Club'. The gift was held to be valid in favour of the existing members who were free to spend the capital in any manner they thought fit.

However, despite these observations, this method is not without theoretical difficulties. Firstly, although it is quite possible to create a trust for the present members, future members will have no right to the property held by the trustees.[85] Secondly, the trustees will be holding the property on trust for the present members either as tenants in common or joint tenants. In the case of a tenancy in common, the share of each member will, on his death, devolve to his or her next of kin. In the case of a joint tenancy, the share of each member will pass to the remaining members on the grounds of the survivorship principle of a joint tenancy. Finally, there is nothing stopping the members from terminating the trust and calling for the trust property to be distributed to them. In this respect, it is questionable whether such a method is appropriate for an association which is intended to continue for a long period of time. For example, what guarantee does this method give to a testator who wishes his gift to be used by the association for a considerable period of time?

Trust for present and future members applying *Re Denley*

Given the fact that an unincorporated association will wish to continue beyond the perpetuity period and will want to benefit existing as well as future members, one way around this is to create a trust in favour of present and future members. However, the main problem with this method is that it will inevitably violate the perpetuity rules. Where property is to be held for present and future members, it unlikely that the present members will be able to terminate the trust and call for the property to be distributed beneficially amongst them. Seen in this way, such a trust will inevitably fail because the existing and present members will not have true equitable rights to the property subject to the trust. The matter is neatly explained by the decision of the Privy Council in **Leahy v Attorney-General for New South Wales**[86] where a testator left property for 'such orders of nuns of the Catholic Church or the Christian Brothers as my executors and trustees shall select'. The gift could not be construed as charitable because the trustees could select from cloistered nuns.[87] The Privy Council explained that the members capable of benefiting from the property were numerous and located worldwide. Furthermore, given the fact that future members of the order could benefit, it meant that the property would be held by the trustee indefinitely for future members, thereby conflicting with the perpetuity rules. In the opinion of the Privy Council a gift to unincorporated associations could only be construed as a gift to present members. However, on the facts of this case it could never have been the intention that the property in question could be beneficially enjoyed by such a large group of members.

---

[83] *Ibid.* at p. 321. Authorities in support of this view cited by Warburton include *Cocks v Manners* (1871) LR 12 Eq. 574, *Re Clarke* [1901] 2 Ch. 110, *Re Drummond* [1914] 2 Ch. 90 and *Re Ray's Will Trusts* [1936] 1 Ch. 520.

[84] [1914] 2 Ch. 90.

[85] Unless, of course, the existing members assign their equitable interest in accordance with the formal requirements of s. 53(1)(c) of the Law of Property Act 1925. This requires the assignment to be made in writing and signed by the person disposing of such an interest.

[86] [1959] AC 457.

[87] See Chapter 22.

The only possible way in which a trust for present and future members may take effect is if the trust is construed as a trust for a purpose and enforceable under the principle in **Re Denley's Deed Trust**[88] which has already been examined above. It is quite possible under this method to have a trust for a purpose, that is, the purpose of the association, and then to allow the members to enforce the trust against the trustees. Such a trust would have to be confined to the perpetuity period, where a testator leaves the property in his will without specifying any life in being, a period of 21 years. As to present and future members, this would not be an issue since all that is required under the **Re Denley** principle is that there be ascertainable beneficiaries at any given time to enforce the trust against the trustees. Of course, the only limitation with this construction is that the gift is confined to the perpetuity period and as such not conducive to the long-term existence of the association.

Contract holding theory

Given the problems associated with the above methods of making gifts to unincorporated associations, in **Neville Estates v Madden**[89] Cross J identified and explained a more effective way in which a gift may be held by an unincorporated association. He enunciated the principle which has now been referred to as the 'contract holding theory'. In order to understand this theory it is important to appreciate some of the basic features of an unincorporated association. It has already been explained that an unincorporated association is nothing more than a group of individuals bound together for some common purpose. The purpose of the bond is usually defined in the rules of the association, which may also be referred to as the memorandum of the association. For example, most societies will have rules which govern the activities of the society as well as matters relating to rights and duties of the members. Seen in this way, each member who joins the association is bound by the rules of the association and each and every other member is bound with each other, subject to the rules of the association. As to the property belonging to the association, this will in most cases be held by the treasurer of the association on trust for the members in accordance with the rules of the association. The property belongs to the members of the association who are contractually bound with each other to follow the rules of the association, as illustrated in Figure 8.1.

In light of the contractual nature of unincorporated associations, in **Neville Estates v Madden** Cross J bypassed the use of a trust as the principal vehicle to determine the manner in which the property is held by the members and, instead, relied on the contract between the members *inter se* as the means of holding the property. Cross J explained that a gift to an unincorporated association took effect as:

> a gift to existing members not as joint tenants, but subject to their respective rights, contractual rights and liabilities towards one and another as members of the association. In such a case a member cannot sever his share. It will accrue to the other members on his death or resignation, even though such members include persons who became members after the gift took effect. If this is the effect of the gift, it will not be now open to objection on the score of perpetuity or uncertainty unless there is something in the terms or circumstances or in the rules of the association which precludes the members at any given time from dividing the subject matter of the gift between them on the footing that they are solely entitled to it in equity.[90]

---

[88] [1969] 1 Ch. 373.
[89] [1962] Ch. 832.
[90] [1962] Ch. 832 at 849.

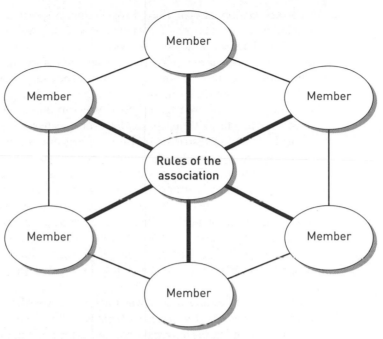

Figure 8.1 Member contractually bound by the rules of the association

The contract holding theory was applied in **Re Recher's Will Trust**[91] where a testatrix left her residuary estate to the 'Anti Vivisection Society, 76 Victoria Street, London SW1'. Shortly before the testatrix's death the society had ceased to exist and gave up its premises in London. The society was then amalgamated with another society and the question before the court was whether the gift could be given to the amalgamated society. The court held that the gift was given to the specific society in Victoria Street and therefore could not be given to the amalgamated society. As a consequence the property was held on resulting trust for the testatrix's estate. In the course of his judgment Brightman J explained that if the society still existed in its form then the gift could take effect as gift to the members, not as joint tenants or tenants in common but as an accretion to the funds of the society. The funds would be held for the members, subject to their contractual rights and duties against each other. Providing that the rules of the association allowed the members to change the rules and call for the property to be vested in them, that is, to wind up the association, then there would be no problems with perpetuity.[92] The same analysis taken in **Re Bucks Constabulary Funds Widows' and Orphans' Fund Friendly Society (No. 2)**[93] where Walton J explained that he could 'see no reason for the thinking that this analysis is any different whether the purpose for which the members

VISIT CASE NAVIGATOR

---

[91] [1972] Ch. 526.

[92] The contract holding theory will not apply where there is something in the rules of the association which prevent the members from changing the rules and calling for the property to be distributed to them. For example, in *Re Grant's Will Trust* [1979] 3 All ER 359, Vinelott J explained that it was impossible to construe the gift to the Chertsey and Walton Constituency and Labour Party as a gift to the members of the constituency party because the constituency party was governed by the National Executive of the Labour Party who could alter the constitution and provide for the property to be transferred elsewhere. The members simply had no power to alter the rules of the association and deal with the property belonging to it.

[93] [1979] 1 All ER 623.

of the association associate are a social club, a sporting club . . . All the assets of the association are held in trust for its members (of course subject to the contractual claims of anybody having a valid contract with the association) save and except to the extent to which valid trusts have otherwise been declared of its property.'[94]

In **Hunt v McLaren**[95] a settlor settled by deed land on trust to secure a sports ground for Horley Football Club. In 2002 the land was sold to a developer for a sum of £4 million. The proceeds were used by the trustees to purchase another piece of land for the purposes of building a Club House. However, because of certain restrictive covenants, the use of the land was restricted to use for sports and leisure. Subsequently, the land was worth less than the amount of money that had been spent on it. Questions arose as to the basis upon which the trustees were holding the assets of the club. The High Court held that the original deed settling the land on trust should be construed as a gift to the members of the club for the time being. This therefore meant that the beneficial interest in the club's property belonged beneficially to the current full members. These members were entitled to the property subject to the rules of the club and could unanimously or by general meeting call for the assets to be transferred. Collins J held that the members could ask for the surplus funds of the club to be divided among the adult members on per capita basis.[96]

The contract holding theory was further endorsed most recently by the High Court in **Hanchett-Stamford v Attorney General**[97] where Lewison J held that, whilst it was accepted that the funds of unincorporated association belonged to the existing members subject to their contract between each other, a sole existing member of a society was equally entitled to the surplus fund irrespective of the fact that he was the sole surviving member. The facts of the case involved an association founded some time in 1914 called the 'The Performing and Captive Animals Defence League' (the League hereafter). Although the League had a formal constitution at the beginning, that constitution had been lost and since 1934 the affairs of the League were conducted by a Director appointed by the members of the League. Although it was very difficult to ascertain the exact purposes of the League, it became evident from a booklet produced for members in 1962 that the objects of the League were to prevent cruelty to animals used in film productions and shows. Thus many of the activities of the League involved preventing travelling circuses and municipal zoos. According to the 1962 booklet the league had two types of members: life members and annual members. At that time there were approximately 250 members and the funds of the League were contributed by gifts and legacies which were duly invested. Towards the end of the 1970s the activities of the League slowed down owing to a decline in the number of travelling circuses. From then onwards the assets of the league were vested in a Mr Hanchett-Stamford who had been an active member of the League and who had worked with a leading vet, Dr Bill Jordan, in educating people about animal welfare. In the early 1990s some of the funds of the League were used to purchase a property which at the time of the case was valued at around £675,000. Title to the property was taken in the name of Mr Hanchett-Stamford and another member both of whom had since died. The property had been occupied by Mrs Hanchett-Stamford until recently when she was moved to a nursing home. In addition to the property, the League also had funds worth some £1.77 million in the form of stocks

---

[94] [1979] 1 All ER 623.

[95] [2006] WTLR 1817.

[96] For a detailed examination of the rules governing the distribution of surplus funds of an unincorporated association, see Chapter 10.

[97] [2009] Ch. 173.

and shares. In the 1990s the League stopped maintaining records of its members and on the advice of the accountant it was decided that the funds of the League be wound up. Mr and Mrs Hanchett-Stamford, the only surviving members, decided that the funds should be donated to the 'Born Free Charity' whose objects included the welfare of animals. However, Mr Hanchett-Stamford died and the question before the Court was whether Mrs Hanchett-Stamford was in a position to give the surplus funds of the League to the Born Free Charity. She could only do this if she was entitled to exercise ownership of the funds and therefore transfer them to the charity. This in turn raised the legal question as to who was entitled to the surplus assets of the League.

Lewison J proceeded to answer the question of ownership of the assets of the league by examining the existing law. Having reviewed the decision in **Neville Estates v Madden**[98] and **Re Recher's Will Trust**[99] he concluded that 'the members for the time being of an unincorporated association are beneficially entitled to "its" assets, subject to the contractual arrangements between them'.[100] On this basis the members could by unanimous agreement or majority vote change the constitution of the unincorporated association and divide the assets equally amongst themselves. On this basis, Mrs Hanchett-Stamford and Mr Hanchett-Stamford being the only existing members of the League were entitled to the ownership of the assets subject to the contract between them.[101] Mr Hanchett-Stamford having died, the assets became vested in Mrs Hanchett-Stamford as the sole surviving member. Lewison J explained that the basis of vesting ownership in the sole surviving member operated akin to the vesting of ownership in a sole surviving joint tenant of a joint tenancy where the rule of survivorship operated. He explained that:

> the thread that runs through all these cases is that the property of an unincorporated association is the property of its members, but that they are contractually precluded from severing their share except in accordance with the rules of the association; and that, on its dissolution, those who are members at the time are entitled to the assets free from any such contractual restrictions. It is true that this is not a joint tenancy according to the classical model; but since any collective ownership of property must be a species of joint tenancy or tenancy in common this kind of collective ownership must, in my judgment, be a sub-species of joint tenancy, albeit taking effect subject to any contractual restrictions applicable as between members. I cannot see why the legal principle should be any different if the reason for the dissolution is the permanent cessation of the association's activities or the fall in its membership to below two.[102]

 ## Reform

The effect of the beneficiary principle is to invalidate a number of non-charitable purpose trusts which do not fall into the recognised exceptions to the principle. Although in the case of unincorporated associations the impact of the beneficiary principle has to some extent been removed by the construction of gifts to such associations on a contractual

---

[98] [1962] Ch. 832.
[99] [1972] Ch. 526.
[100] [2009] Ch. 173 at 183.
[101] Several adverts had been placed in leading newspapers and journals to establish the whereabouts of other possible members but nothing positive developed from these.
[102] [2009] Ch. 173 at 188. See also S. Baughen, 'Performing Animals and the Dissolution of Unincorporated Associations: The Contract Theory Vindicated' Conv. [2010] at 216.

analysis, in the context of other non-charitable purposes the beneficiary principle severely limits the operation of trusts for such purposes. In light of this, there have been several calls for reform in this area akin to the kind of reforms that have already taken place in some offshore jurisdictions.[103] In many offshore jurisdictions, such as Bermuda[104] and the Cayman Islands, statutes have allowed purpose trusts to be recognised and enforced by 'protectors' or 'enforcers'. Such protectors and enforcers are different persons from the settlor or the trustees of the trust. For example, in Bermuda a trust may be created for a non-charitable purpose or purposes provided that certain conditions are met. The trust should be sufficiently certain to carry out; it must be lawful and must not be contrary to public policy. The Supreme Court has the power to make an order for the enforcement of a non-charitable purpose trust. The application for an order can be made by any person who has a sufficient interest in the trust, including the beneficiaries and the settlor. In the Cayman Islands the Cayman Islands Special Trusts (Alternative Regime) Law was introduced in 1997, allowing the creation of non-charitable private purpose trusts which are also exempt from the perpetuity period. Such trusts, also known as STAR trusts are enforced by the enforcer; however, the beneficiaries have no rights against the enforcer and neither do they have any rights in the trust property. The trust property is in effect held merely for the abstract purpose.

In addition to the reforms akin to those in offshore jurisdiction, it has also been suggested that non-charitable purposes can be advanced by legislation which would construe non-charitable purpose trusts as powers rather than trusts. The advantage of this would be that the beneficiary principle would not apply to powers. A non-charitable purpose trust could be construed as a power, giving the donee of the power a right to use the property for the purpose; however, in default of such happening, the property would then result to those entitled in gift over in default of appointment.

Conclusion

This chapter has examined one of the fundamental requirements of a private trust, that is, the need for a human beneficiary to enforce the trust against the trustee. This chapter has shown that a court will not recognise a trust which it cannot both control and execute. An uncontrollable power of disposition is tantamount to giving ownership to the trustee. Except in the case of a trust which is deemed charitable, a trust which is created for a purpose will be held void as a trust of imperfect obligation. The basic problem with such trusts is one of enforceability. The other problem with trusts of imperfect obligation is one of perpetuity. Such trusts are often created for some purpose which is intended to continue for a long period of time. This inevitably involves the subject matter of the trust being inalienated for a long period of time.

Whilst trusts of imperfect obligation are prima facie void, such trusts may be upheld by the courts on two main grounds. Firstly, the trust may fall into one of anomalous

---

[103] See, for example, M. Pawlowski and J. Summers, 'Private Purpose Trusts – A Reform Proposal' (2007) Conv. 440.

[104] Bermuda Trusts (Special Provisions) Amendment Act 1998.

categories recognised by the courts over the years. With the exception of the unincorporated association category, these categories have been described as situations where the courts have given in to human weakness and sentiment. They include trusts for the maintenance of graves and monuments and trust for saying masses. As to the category of unincorporated association, it has been seen in this chapter that trust law has played an instrumental role in construing the manner in which property is held by such associations. The lack of a legal personality means that any property must be held by the members on trust for the association. However, the imposition of a trust in favour of the members has not been without theoretical problems. In more recent times, gifts to such associations have been construed on a contractual basis rather than trust, and in doing so, have allowed those theoretical problems to be overcome. The second way in which a trust of imperfect obligation can be saved is if it falls into a situation which has been described by the courts as falling outside the beneficiary principle. Where a trust is created for a purpose and not necessarily in favour of beneficiaries who are entitled to the trust property, the trust will be valid if the beneficiaries are ascertainable at any given time, capable of enforcing the purpose of the trust against the trustees.

●●● Case study

Read and analyse the following case study and answer the specific question set below.

A testator made a will in which he left his property subject to the following dispositions:

'(i) My real property to be sold and the proceeds to be invested indefinitely for providing holidays for the employees of Alpha Ltd.

(ii) My shares in ICI Ltd to be sold and the proceeds to be used to provide a good memorial to myself and the surplus to be used to erect a statue of myself outside the headquarters of Alpha Ltd.

(iii) The remainder of my property to be sold and the proceeds to be given to my local golf club where I have been a member for the last twenty years.'

The testator died earlier this year and the trustees seek your directions as to the validity of these dispositions.

●● Moot points

1 What are the inherent difficulties in treating a gift to an unincorporated association as a trust for present and future members?

2 Explain why it was not possible to treat the assets of the unincorporated association in *Re Grant's Will Trust* [1979] 3 All ER 359 as being held for the members of that association, subject to their contract rights and duties as determined by the rules of the association.

3 It is trite law that there are a number of so-called exceptions to the beneficiary principle; these exceptions were reconsidered in *Re Astor's Settlement Trusts* [1952] Ch. 534. In all of these exceptional cases there is a clear violation of the beneficiary principle, yet the courts still uphold them as valid non-charitable purpose trusts. What incentive is there for the trustee to carry out the wishes of the person who has created these trusts?

● Further reading

Baughen, S. 'Performing Animals and the Dissolution of Unincorporated Associations: The Contract Theory Vindicated' [2010] Conv. 216: Explores the decision of the court in *Hanchett-Stamford* v *Attorney General*.

Baxendale-Walker, P. *Purpose Trusts* **2nd edn** (2007) Tottel Publishing: Provides a general in-depth analysis of the law relating to purpose trusts and examines other offshore jurisdictions with a view to analysing how purpose trusts are allowed to exist.

Gardner, S. 'A Detail in the Construction of Gifts to Unincorporated Associations' [1998] Conv. 8: Provides a response to Paul Mathews's article in the *Conveyancer* in 1995; (see above).

Mathews, P. 'A Problem in the Construction of Gifts to Unincorporated Associations [1995] Conv. 302: Examines two distinct methods of making a gift to members of an unincorporated association, namely a gift to members as joint tenants and a gift to members subject to their contract with the association.

Panesar, S. 'Surplus Funds and Unincorporated Associations' [2008] Trust and Trustees 698: Examines the decision in Hanchett-Stamford and the destination of surplus funds of an unincorporated association.

Pawlowski, M. and J. Summers, 'Private Purpose Trusts – A Reform Proposal' (2007) Conv. 440: Suggests that reform of purpose trust law in England may take the form of reform which has already been implemented in some offshore jurisdictions.

Sheridan, L.A. 'Trusts for Non-Charitable Purposes' (1953) 17 Conv. (NS) 46: Provides an account of trusts for non-charitable purposes and looks at some of the problems involved with such trusts.

Warburton, J. 'The Holding of Property by Unincorporated Associations' [1985] Conv. 318: Explores the various methods by which an unincorporated association can hold property and examines the limitations involved in each one.

9

Illegality and public policy

Learning objectives

After reading this chapter you should be able to:

→ explain the role of public policy and illegality in trust law

→ explain the public policy grounds upon which a trust will be invalidated

→ understand trusts which interfere with parental duties

→ understand trusts which are in restraint of marriage

→ explain the perpetuity rules and their functions

→ explain the grounds on which a trust may be declared unlawful

→ explain the consequences of a trust which is designed to defraud creditors.

Blathwayt v *Baron Cawley* [1976] AC 397: If I become a Roman Catholic do I lose my right to receive my interest in the trust fund?

The facts of *Blathwayt* v *Baron Cawley* illustrate that a trust which complies with the substantive and formal requirements of trust law may nevertheless be scrutinised by the courts if it is contrary to public policy or is otherwise unlawful. The question in law is essentially: what is public policy and when will a trust be contrary to public policy? Robert Blathwayt made a will in 1934 settling his property in favour of a number of beneficiaries. In clause 6 of the will Robert Blathwayt gave certain property in Somerset and Gloucester on trust to Christopher Blathwayt for his life with remainder to first and other sons of Christopher in succession, and thereafter to Justin Blathwayt for his life and in remainder for the sons of Justin in succession in order of seniority. Clause 9 of the will of Robert Blathwayt declared that the interest of any one of the beneficiaries entitled under the trust would be forfeited should they become Roman Catholics.

Christopher Blathwayt was received into the Roman Catholic Church in 1939 and his eldest son Mark Blathwayt was received into the Roman Catholic Church by baptism in his infancy. Since his baptism Mark had shown adherence to the Roman Catholic Church.

The principal question before the House of Lords was whether Christopher had forfeited his interest in the trust by virtue of becoming a Roman Catholic. For example, can a testator validly discriminate on grounds of religion or is there is a difference between discrimination and choice? *Blathwayt* v *Baron Cawley* is just one example of a situation where a trust may be challenged on grounds of public policy. A trust may also be challenged if it is unlawful, for example if it is created to further some criminal activity or is created to defeat the rights of the creditors of the settlor. This chapter explores these matters in much more detail. The principal focus is on those trusts which are invalidated on grounds of public policy and those trusts which are unlawful.

Introduction

Even where a trust complies with the formal and substantive requirements of trust law it may be struck down by the courts if it contains an element of illegality or is contrary to public policy. It is clear that a trust which is set up for purposes which are illegal will be held void by the courts. Thus, a testator cannot create a trust to advance some criminal purpose such as the murder of another or a trust which encourages or promotes terrorism.[1] However, besides conduct which is criminal, there are many other instances where a trust will be unlawful, for example, where a trust is deliberately created to defraud the creditors of the settlor: in other words, where the settlor settles his property on trust in favour of others for the sole purpose of hiding it from his creditors should he be declared bankrupt or otherwise become insolvent. As to public policy, the courts have long recognised that certain trusts are void on grounds of public policy. For example, a trust which simply serves no useful purpose will be held void on grounds of public policy;

---

[1] In *Thrupp* v *Collett* (1858) 26 Beav. 125 a trust to pay the fines of poachers was held void by the court.

indeed, such a trust will be declared capricious by the courts. What constitutes public policy is a matter for the courts to decide and, as explained in **Blathwayt v Baron Cawley**,[2] 'public policy is a shifting thing and in 1975 one cannot be guided by what happened in 1925. In general, public policy relates to the present time . . .'[3] A good example of the changing nature of public policy is illustrated by trusts which are created in favour of illegitimate children. Before the Family Law Reform Act 1969 trusts which were created either by deed or by will in favour of illegitimate children who were not born were declared void on the grounds that they promoted immorality. The promotion of future immorality was clearly a public policy concern. However, since the enactment of the Family Law Reform Act 1969 such trusts are no longer declared void.[4] This chapter explores the grounds upon which a trust may be declared void on grounds of public policy and illegality.

Freedom of disposition and public policy

At the outset it may be questioned why the law interferes with dispositions of property, whether they be absolute gifts or transfers involving a trust. One of the fundamental features of a system of private property is that there should be private autonomy in property transactions. This simply means that the law views private individuals as having the power to effect changes in their legal relations. This aspect of private autonomy necessarily imports a sense of freedom of disposition in property law. I am able to transfer my things to anyone I want to and in any manner I may wish to do so. Indeed, in relation to transfers after my death by virtue of a will, one of the fundamental axioms of testamentary law is freedom of testamentary disposition.[5] The very fact that individuals have private autonomy in the transfer of things and rights therein to others is crucial to an efficient system of property distribution. In this respect Moffat writes, 'if in a pure liberal market society the market is to carry out its function of allocation of resources amongst various uses, property must be freely alienable. This seems to require a system of property law to sustain freedom of disposition.'[6]

Despite this principle of private autonomy in property law, the State plays a role in 'regulating' transfer of property rights. There is a strong public interest in the private acts of individuals who attempt to dispose of their property to others. It may be questioned why there is such a strong public interest in private acts dealing with acquisition and transfer of property rights. On a theoretical level of analysis, the State interest in private property transactions may be justified by the desire to achieve wider social and economic goals. Property is an important means of liberty and survival; without any property there is no liberty or security. Property is also a fundamental vehicle through which commerce and economic well-being is generated. The State therefore has a strong interest in seeing that property is distributed in a manner that maintains liberty and security, but at the same time generating economic well-being. The level of interest and consequential interference with the private acts of transfer and acquisition depend on the types of distributive justice the State wishes to achieve. In this respect, political theorists have constantly

---

[2] [1976] AC 397.
[3] [1976] AC 397 at 404.
[4] Family Law Reform Act 1969 s. 15(7).
[5] See, J. Finch, L. Hayes, et al., *Wills, Inheritance and Families* (1996) at p. 21.
[6] G. Moffat, *Trust Law: Text and Materials*, 4th edn (2005) at p. 255.

argued in one form or another for state interference in the liberty of individuals to deal with property distribution.[7]

Leaving broader political issues to one side, the law of property does in many ways restrict certain transfers of property. Certain transfers of property rights are said to be void or voidable. The reason given for striking down certain transfers of property is that such transfers are contrary to public policy. Economists have long argued that property should have the characteristics of transferability since it is only through this characteristic that resources can be shifted from a less productive use to a more productive one.[8] However, Moffat explains that within a liberal property system one encounters a basic paradox.[9] Moffat explains this paradox by stating, 'if freedom of disposition conferred upon a person disposing of property means that he or she can regulate the circumstances in which, and the extent to which, the recipients can deal with the property, the recipients do not have freedom of disposition. In this sense unrestricted freedom of disposition cannot logically be permitted and fully maintained.'[10]

Trusts contrary to public policy

Certain trusts will be invalidated on grounds that they are contrary to public policy. As explained earlier, what constitutes public policy is something that changes with time. Trusts which are invalidated on grounds of public policy are generally trusts which offend principles of morality or trusts which offend family values or otherwise question the sanctity of religion. Clearly a trust which is created to promote the activities of pickpockets or prostitutes would be contrary to public policy and morality.[11]

Conditions precedent, conditions subsequent and determinable interests

When a court challenges a trust on grounds of public policy it is usually challenging some clause which is inserted in the trust which is regarded as unlawful on grounds of public policy. Thus, in order to understand the case law governing trusts which may be challenged by the courts on grounds of public policy, it is important to understand the different types of clauses which may be inserted into a trust or a settlement. These clauses may take the form of conditions precedent, conditions subsequent and determinable interests. If the court holds any one of these clauses void on grounds of public policy then the outcome of the trust depends very much on the type of clause that has been held void. For example, a condition precedent will exist where property is given to another, but on the condition that it will only vest in the beneficiary if some event occurs. A good example of a condition precedent is where a settlor settles property on trust for his son providing his son qualifies as a solicitor. If a condition precedent is held void then the effect on the gift or trust will depend very much on the type of property in question. In the case of a gift of land or a trust of land, the gift or trust will simply fail and the property will result back to the settlor. In the case of personal property the gift will

---

[7] See R. Nozick, *Anarchy, State and Utopia* (1974) and J. Rawls, *A Theory of Justice* (1972).
[8] See R. Posner, *The Economic Analysis of Law* (1972) at pp. 10–13.
[9] G. Moffat, *Trust Law: Text and Materials*, 4th edn (2005) at p. 255.
[10] G. Moffat, *Trust Law: Text and Materials*, 4th edn (2005) at p. 255.
[11] As exemplified by Harman LJ in *Re Pinion* [1965] Ch. 85.

take effect notwithstanding that the condition is held void. The condition is effectively ignored.[12] A condition subsequent, on the other hand, is a condition which is inserted into a trust which has the effect of terminating an interest which has already vested in the beneficiary. Where the conditions subsequent is held to be void on grounds of public policy, the conditions fails but the trust remains effective. This is simply because the subject matter of the trust has vested in the beneficiary and he can continue to enjoy his interest. A good example of a condition subsequent is provided by **Re Beard**[13] where a gift was made by a testator to his nephew, but the gift was to be revoked if the nephew was to enter the army or navy. The court held that this condition was void on grounds of public policy and the nephew was entitled to retain the gift absolutely.

Conditional interests are to be distinguished from determinable interests, although the distinction is, indeed, a very fine one. A determinable interest is one which will automatically terminate on the occurrence of some event. If the court holds the determinable interest void on grounds of public policy then the trust will fail and the property will result back to the settlor or the testator's estate. A good example of a determinable interest is where a gift is made to another until such time as he becomes bankrupt. The effect of the bankruptcy of the donee of the gift will automatically terminate his interest in the gift. The event of the bankruptcy of the recipient of the gift is a perfectly valid determinable event and not contrary to public policy. On the other hand, a gift which is given to a wife until such time as the wife lives apart from her husband will be held void.[14]

Trust interfering with parental duties

APPLYING THE LAW

In an *inter vivos* settlement Elizabeth created a trust in favour of her daughter Janet and Janet's two children in equal shares. The terms of the settlement provided that if any of Janet's children live with their father, or otherwise be in any way under his control, they would lose their interest in the trust fund. Janet has split up from her husband; however, one of her children is very close to his father and wishes to live with him.

Does this mean that the child who wishes to live with his father loses his right in the trust fund?

A condition in a trust which prevents a parent from carrying out his parental duties will be struck down by the court. A classic illustration of a condition interfering with parental duties is provided by **Re Sandbrook**[15] where a testatrix left property on trust for her two grandchildren. The terms of the trust provided that if one or both of them lived with their father, or were under any form of custody or control by him, their interest should be forfeited. The court held that this condition was void on grounds of public policy and, because it was condition subsequent, the remainder of the trust was valid. In other words, the property had already vested in the grandchildren who could continue to enjoy their interest free from the condition which had been struck out. In the course of his

---

[12] *Re Elliott* [1952] Ch. 217.
[13] [1908] 1 Ch. 383.
[14] *Re Moore* (1888) 39 Ch. D 116.
[15] [1912] 2 Ch. 471.

judgment Parker J explained that the condition was 'inserted in the will with the direct object of deterring the father of these two children from performing his parental duties with regard to them, because it makes their worldly welfare dependant upon his abstaining from doing what it is certainly his duty to do, namely, to bring his influence to bear and not give up his right to custody, the control and education of his children'.[16] Similarly, in *Re Piper*[17] there was a condition in a will which prevented a child from living with her father. The court held that this was void on grounds of public policy and was simply designed to bring about a separation between parent and child. More importantly, the court held that it did not matter that the parents had separated. The gift took effect in favour of the child irrespective of the condition.

Although it is well established that a total interference with parental duties is contrary to public policy, is it possible to have some partial interference with the carrying out of parental duties? For example, can a trust be created which influences the way in which parental duties are to be exercised? The matter has arisen in the context of religion and, in particular, trusts which encourage a parent to bring their child up according to a particular religion. This issue arose in *Re Borwick*[18] where a trust was created in favour of a child beneficiary, but whose interest was subject to forfeiture if he became a Roman Catholic. The court held that the condition forfeiting the interest on grounds of religion was void on the grounds that it hampered the parents in their parental duties. In the course of his judgment Bennett J explained that a parent's duty should be influenced by the moral and spiritual welfare of the children and not by pecuniary matters.[19]

APPLYING THE LAW

In his will, Josh left his residuary estate on trust to his grandchildren in equal shares on them attaining the age of 25. The terms of the will, however, provided that should any of the grandchildren convert from being Roman Catholics their interest would be terminated.

Is this trust valid?

Despite the decision in *Re Borwick*,[20] the House of Lords in *Blathwayt v Baron Cawley*[21] took a rather different view on the question whether a trust could be created which influenced the religious upbringing of a child. On the facts of the case Robert Blathwayt made a will in 1934 settling his property in favour of a number of beneficiaries. In clause 6 of the will Robert Blathwayt gave certain property in Somerset and Gloucester on trust to Christopher Blathwayt for his life with remainder to first and other sons of Christopher in succession, and thereafter to Justin Blathwayt for his life and in remainder for the sons of Justin in succession in order of seniority. Clause 9 of the will of Robert Blathwayt declared that the interests of any one of the beneficiaries entitled under the trust should be forfeited should they become Roman Catholics. Christopher Blathwayt was received into the Roman Catholic Church in 1939 and his son eldest son Mark Blathwayt was received into the Roman Catholic Church by baptism in his infancy. Mark has since his baptism shown adherence to that church. The principal question before the

---

16 [1912] 2 Ch. 471 at 476.
17 [1946] 2 All ER 503.
18 [1933] Ch. 657.
19 [1933] Ch. 657 at 666.
20 [1933] Ch. 657.
21 [1976] AC 397.

House of Lords was whether Christopher had forfeited his interest in the trust by virtue of becoming a Roman Catholic. The House of Lords held that the condition inserted in the trust, which had the effect of forfeiting the interest of any child who might become a Roman Catholic, was not void on grounds of public policy.

The judgments in **Blathwayt v Baron Cawley** are certainly very interesting and centre on the question whether a clause which seeks to influence a child's religious upbringing amounts to discrimination or simply choice. Lord Wilberforce explained that to suggest 'any condition which might affect or influence the way in which a child is brought up, or in which parental duties are exercised [is invalid] seems to me to state far too wide a rule'.[22] It was argued on behalf of the beneficiaries that the clause was discriminatory in its nature and prevented them from practising the particular religion they wanted to. However, the House of Lords held that there was a big difference between discrimination and choice. In Lord Wilberforce's opinion 'a choice between considerations of material prosperity and spiritual welfare has to be made by many parents for their children – and, one may add, by judges in infants' interests – and it would be cynical to assume that these cannot be conscientiously and rightly made'.[23]

Trusts in restraint of marriage

A trust which is designed to impose a total restraint on marriage will be held void. However, this is only true in so far as the first marriage of a person. A total restraint on a second or any subsequent marriage will be upheld by the court.[24] The rationale behind total restraints of second and subsequent marriages was explained in **Allen v Jackson**[25] where James LJ when dealing with a provision preventing the remarriage of the deceased's widow commented that her husband may well have genuine reason for restraining her subsequent marriage. His Lordship explained that 'if she was a widow with children . . . [her husband] might think that his children would not be so well cared for and protected if his widow formed a second allegiance and became the mother of a second family'.[26]

Although a total restraint on marriage is void, a partial restraint on marriage will be upheld by the courts. For example, in **Jenner v Turner**[27] a testatrix left property to her brother subject to a condition that he did not marry the domestic servant. The court upheld the condition as a partial restraint on marriage; the brother could marry anyone in the world except the domestic servant. In **Hodgson v Halford**[28] a gift was given subject to the condition that the beneficiary should not marry a person who was not practising the Jewish religion and who was not born a Jew. Again the court upheld the condition as being a partial restraint on marriage.[29] However, conditions which do not necessarily restrain marriage as such but require the consent of a third party will be upheld by the courts. For example, in **Re Whiting's Settlement**[30] the court upheld a condition which required a daughter to obtain her mother's consent before she could get married. Furthermore, a gift or a trust which is only to last until marriage will be upheld by the courts.[31] In such a case the trust is not designed to prevent a future marriage: rather the

---

[22] [1976] AC 397 at 426.
[23] [1976] AC 397 at 438.
[24] *Leong v Lim Beng Chye* [1955] AC 648.
[25] (1875) 1 Ch. D 399.
[26] (1875) 1 Ch. D 399 at 403.
[27] (1880) 16 Ch. D 188.
[28] (1879) 11 Ch. D 959.
[29] See also *Perrin v Lyon* (1807) 9 East. 170.
[30] 30 [1905] 1 Ch. 96.
[31] *Morley Rennoldson* (1843) 2 Hare 570; *Re Lovell* [1920] 1 Ch. 122.

assumption is to provide for the beneficiary until such time as marriage takes place. A condition which reduces the gift to a spouse on marriage will be upheld if the court is satisfied that there was some ulterior purpose in reducing that gift. For example, in *Re Hewett*[32] a testator gave a sum of £1200 per annum to a woman with whom he had been cohabiting and then modified the gift to £800 should the woman marry. The understanding was that the £400 reduction would be applied for his son. The court held that the condition in the gift was not one in restraint of marriage: rather the purpose behind this was to make sure that his son was looked after should the woman marry.

It should also be noted that conditions which have the effect of inducing a separation between husband and wife will be held void. The matter is neatly illustrated in *Re Caborne*[33] where a mother left her residuary estate to her son absolutely, but modified the gift so long as his son's wife was alive and married to him. The mother's will continued to the effect that should the son's wife die or the marriage otherwise terminated, the gift was once more to become absolute. The court held that the gift was void on grounds of public policy. The court explained that the desired effect of the gift was to induce a separation of the son's marriage to his wife.[34]

Capricious trusts

A trust which serves no useful purpose or is capricious will be held void by the court. For example, in *Brown v Burdett*[35] a testatrix left a house on trust with the direction that, with the exception of a few rooms for the housekeeper, the house be blocked up for a period of 20 years. The court declined to uphold the trust on the grounds that it served no useful purpose. Bacon VC held that the house remained undisposed of in her will and passed under the intestacy rules to those entitled under intestacy. There are many further examples of trusts which will be held void on grounds of serving no useful purpose. One such example is a trust which is set up to provide a school for pickpockets and prostitutes.[36]

Illegality

Certain trusts will be invalidated on the grounds that they are unlawful by reason of the common law or statute. Clearly a trust which is in furtherance of some criminal activity will be invalidated as will a trust which is in breach of some principle of the common law or statute.[37] The effect of illegality is to render the purported trust void, and the property results back to the settlor or his estate. However, as explained by the Law Commission in its report in this area of the law, the court should have a discretion as to the destiny of the property subject to the purported illegal trust.[38] The court should not automatically

---

[32] [1918] 1 Ch. 458.

[33] [1943] Ch. 224.

[34] See also *Re Johnson's Will Trusts* [1967] Ch. 387 where a much larger gift to a daughter was cut down to a nominal sum as long as she remained married to her husband.

[35] (1882) 21 Ch. D 667.

[36] Explained by Harman LJ *Re Pinion* [1965] Ch. 85.

[37] See, for example, *Re Great Berlin Steamboat Co* (1884) 26 Ch. D 616 where an individual paid into the bank account of a company in order to mislead others as to the creditworthiness of the company. In fact, the money was to be held on trust for the person transferring the money into the account. On the winding-up of the company the court refused to allow the individual to claim the remaining balance in the account on the grounds that the trust was set up for a fraudulent purpose.

[38] Law Com. CP No. 154 (1999) *Illegal Transactions: The Effect of Illegality on Contracts and Trusts*.

return the trust to the settlor but must look to the extent of the illegality. Chapter 11 examines the consequences of illegality in the context of resulting trusts and the extent to which a person's own illegality may prevent him from invoking an interest under a resulting trust. Trusts which also fall into this category include trusts which do not comply with the perpetuity rules, trusts which are unlawful on the grounds that they defraud creditors and finally trusts which are contrary to statutory provisions relating to the provision of dependants. These are explored in more detail in the sections below.

 ## Trusts which contravene the perpetuity rules

APPLYING THE LAW

In his will, Saty left a sum of £500,000 to be invested indefinitely and the income to be used to provide holidays for employees of his company. He also left his house in his will to trustees to be retained indefinitely as he was very fond of his house and could not bear the thought of anyone else living there.

Is this bequest valid?

The classic example of how freedom of disposition may allow an individual to destroy future freedom of disposition is where property is given to another with an excessive delay in vesting of the interest therein. It is quite possible to make a gift to another, or to transfer property to another by other means, which does not immediately vest the property in the hands of the transferee but makes it subject to a time restriction. For example, an individual can purport to make a gift of land today; however, in the document purporting to make the gift he can state that the donee is not entitled to the land until he attains a specified age or meets some other contingency. In such a case he has made a gift but it is said to be subject to a condition precedent. Such a gift can only exist through the medium of a trust since trustees will have to administer the property until the contingency is met. One thing which is striking from this example is that, if it takes a considerably long time for the contingency to be met, the land subject to the gift is not freely alienable; it is in fact tied up and taken out of circulation.

One commentator has explained the purpose behind the perpetuity rules in the following way:

> . . . the most convincing modern explanation of the functions of the Rule [against perpetuities] is the so-called Dead Hand Rationale. According to this doctrine, the Rule is necessary in order to strike a balance between on the one hand the freedom of the present generation and, on the other, that of future generations to deal as they wish with the property in which they have interests. If a settlor or testator had total liberty to dispose of his property among future beneficiaries, the recipients, being fettered by his wishes, would never enjoy that same freedom in their turn. The liberty to make fresh rearrangements of assets is necessary not only in order to be rid of irksome conditions attached by earlier donors to the enjoyment of income but also in order to be able to manoeuvre in the light of new tax laws, changes in the nature of the property and in the personal circumstances of the beneficiaries, unforeseeable by the best intentioned and most perspicacious of donors.'[39]

In order to deal with the problem with excessive delay in vesting (or remoteness of vesting), the common law has long established a rule against remoteness of vesting. The

---

[39] R. Deech 'Lives in Being Revived' (1981) 97 LQR 593 at 594.

rule is described as the 'rule against perpetuities' and was considered in more detail in the previous chapter. The rule finds its origins in social and economic conditions quite different from the ones in which it operates today. Historically, the rule was designed to keep future interests in land within reasonable limits where settlors of land attempted to provide for successive generations.[40]

The modern perpetuity rules are a mixture of the old common law rule, the Perpetuities and Accumulations Act 1964 and the Perpetuities and Accumulations Act 2009. These rules were considered in the previous chapter where it was observed that as far as the rule against remoteness of vesting is concerned, the Perpetuities and Accumulations Act 2009 imposes a maximum perpetuity period of 125 years. As for the rule against inalienability, the common law period of a life in being plus 21 years governs the length of time to which property can be inalienated. Finally, as for the rule against excessive accumulations, the Perpetuities and Accumulations Act 2009 removes any time period preventing excessive accumulations of income except in the case of charitable trusts where the maximum period for accumulations of income is 21 years.[41]

Trusts to safeguard property from creditors

APPLYING THE LAW

Frankie is a photographer; however, his photography business has not been very successful. Frankie has decided to venture out as a second-hand car retailer. He has very little knowledge of the car business; nevertheless he has purchased land with a view to selling cars. He has picked up large amounts of loans from a number of lenders. Two weeks before opening his business he transferred his family home on trust for his three daughters and transferred a number of shares in a private company to his wife for free. He thought this would prevent his creditors from laying their hands on the house and shares should his business fail.

Are the trusts he has created valid?

Sometimes freedom of disposition is interfered with on the grounds that the intended transfer, whether consensual or gratuitous, has taken place simply to avoid a legal consequence. In this respect, the transfer is seen as one that cannot really be regarded as a lawful transfer, but one which seeks to interfere with the due process of particular sets of legal principles. It is trite law that a creditor can demand payment from his debtor out of the debtor's property. Where the debtor's property is insufficient to pay all his debts, the debtor is insolvent and his creditors will remain unpaid. In the case of an insolvent person, or better described as a bankrupt, the legal rules and principles of bankruptcy seek to provide a fair distribution of the bankrupt's property to his creditors. In this background, a person who is about to start a risky business and foresees financial danger is often tempted to put his existing property out of reach of potential creditors. Such property can be transferred to other members of his family or can be settled in other jurisdictions. It is clear that such transfers of property do not represent normal transfers but are ones which are specifically designed to disturb justified legal consequences.

---

[40] See A. Simpson, *A History of the Land Law*, 2nd edn (1986).

[41] In the case of a non-charitable trust, although there is no longer a time period preventing excessive accumulations of income, such a trust is still subject to the rule against remoteness of vesting which requires that the beneficial interest does vest within the perpetuity period.

The common law has long recognised that any such attempts to keep property away from creditors should be disallowed.[42] For example, in **Re Butterworth**[43] Charles Butterworth, who was already a successful baker, decided to purchase a grocery business which he had very little experience of. Prior to the purchase of the business he settled his property in favour of his family. The grocery business turned out to be unsuccessful and he sold it at the same price he had paid for it. Having returned to the bakery business he was subsequently declared bankrupt because that business also failed. The question before the Court of Appeal was whether the creditors of the bakery business could set aside the settlement on the grounds that it was made with the intention to defraud the creditors. In the course of his judgment Jessell MR held that:

> [t]he principle of *Mackay* v *Douglas* ((1872) LR 14 Eq 106), and that line of cases, is this, that a man is not entitled to go into a hazardous business, and immediately before doing so settle all of his property voluntarily, the object being this: 'If I succeed in business, I make a fortune for myself. If I fail, I leave my creditors unpaid. They will bear the loss.' That is the very thing which the statute of Elizabeth was meant to prevent. The object of the settlor was to put his property out of the reach of his future creditors. He contemplated engaging in this new trade and wanted to preserve his property from his future creditors. That cannot be done by a voluntary settlement. That is, to my mind, a clear and satisfactory principle.[44]

Transactions defrauding creditors

The modern rules are to be found in the Insolvency Act 1986. Section 423 of the Insolvency Act allows the court to set aside transactions at undervalue when such transactions are entered into for the purpose of putting assets beyond the reach of creditors.[45] The burden of proving that the transaction was entered with an intention to defraud creditors lies with the applicant who is seeking to set the transaction aside.[46] It is not necessary to prove that the transaction was entered into with a specific intention of defeating the applicant's claim against the debtor.[47] Neither is it important under s. 423 that the person making the transaction was bankrupt at the time of making the transaction. All that is required under the section is that the intention of the person entering into a particular transaction was to put the assets beyond the reach of the applicant. Thus, where a person makes a voluntary settlement of his property in favour of others before entering a business, he will find that such a settlement may be subject to s. 423 and set aside. For example, in **Midland Bank plc v Wyatt**[48] a husband executed a declaration of trust whereby he settled the family home in favour of his wife and daughters. This settlement was made just before the husband was about to start a new business. He retained the trust deed in a safe place with the intention of producing it should his business fail and his creditors seek to claim the house. The court held that this transaction was entered into with the intention of defrauding the creditors.

---

[42] *Re Butterworth, ex p. Russell* (1882) 19 Ch. D 588.

[43] (1882) 19 Ch. D 588.

[44] (1882) 19 Ch. D 588 at 598.

[45] The section requires the court to be satisfied that the transferor intended to defraud his creditors; see, *Barclays Bank plc* v *Eustice* [1995] 4 All ER 511. S. 423 replaced the provisions of s. 172 of the Law of Property Act 1925.

[46] In *Midland Bank plc* v *Wyatt* [1995] 1 FLR 697 the court explained that the more hazardous the business, the more likely the court will be satisfied that there was an intention to put the assets beyond the reach of the creditors.

[47] *Jyske Bank (Gibraltar) Ltd* v *Spjeldnaes (No. 2)* [1999] 2 BCLC 101.

[48] [1995] 1 FLR 696.

Section 423 Insolvency Act 1986 (Transactions defrauding creditors)

(1) This section relates to transactions entered into at an undervalue; and a person enters into such a transaction with another person if –

(a) he makes a gift to the other person or he otherwise enters into a transaction with the other on terms that provide for him to receive no consideration;

(b) he enters into a transaction with the other in consideration of marriage [or the formation of a civil partnership]; or

(c) he enters into a transaction with the other for a consideration the value of which, in money or money's worth, is significantly less than the value, in money or money's worth, of the consideration provided by himself.

(2) Where a person has entered into such a transaction, the court may, if satisfied under the next subsection, make such order as it thinks fit for –

(a) restoring the position to what it would have been if the transaction had not been entered into, and

(b) protecting the interests of persons who are victims of the transaction.

(3) In the case of a person entering into such a transaction, an order shall only be made if the court is satisfied that it was entered into by him for the purpose –

(a) of putting assets beyond the reach of a person who is making, or may at some time make, a claim against him, or

(b) of otherwise prejudicing the interests of such a person in relation to the claim which he is making or may make.

(4) In this section 'the court' means the High Court or –

(a) if the person entering into the transaction is an individual, any other court which would have jurisdiction in relation to a bankruptcy petition relating to him;

(b) if that person is a body capable of being wound up under Part IV or V of this Act, any other court having jurisdiction to wind it up.

(5) In relation to a transaction at an undervalue, references here and below to a victim of the transaction are to a person who is, or is capable of being, prejudiced by it; and in the following two sections the person entering into the transaction is referred to as 'the debtor'.

One important question which arises under s. 423(1) is: what constitutes a transaction at undervalue? S. 423(1) makes it clear that a transaction will be at undervalue if:

- he or she makes a gift or the transaction does not provide the debtor with any consideration;
- the transaction is entered into in consideration of marriage; or
- the transaction is entered into for a consideration which, in money or money's worth, is significantly less than the value, in money or money's worth, of the consideration provided by the debtor.

Clearly a transaction which is made for no consideration or consideration of marriage will be deemed to have been made at undervalue. As to what constitutes consideration which is significantly less than the consideration provided by the debtor will depend on all of the relevant facts. In most cases it will be readily apparent that the consideration provided by the person receiving the debtor's property is of a nominal value. However, in some cases the consideration which is provided by the person receiving the debtor's property may appear to be fair and appropriate; nevertheless, the court may still set aside the transaction. This matter is neatly illustrated by the decision of the Court of Appeal in *Agricultural Mortgage Corporation plc v Woodward*[49] where a farmer who had been declared insolvent granted a tenancy of his farm to his wife at the full market rent. The purpose of this grant was to ensure that the mortgagee of the farm could not get rent-free occupation of the land. Despite the fact that the wife had paid a full rent for the farm, the Court of Appeal set the tenancy aside on the grounds that the sole purpose was to prevent the mortgagee from getting possession of the land. It was held that the wife gave nothing in return for all of the extra benefits she received by the grant of the tenancy, namely the right to live in her house and continue with the business safeguarded from the creditors.

It is important under s. 423 that the person entering into the transaction did so with the intention to defraud his creditors. It has already been mentioned that the court does not have to be satisfied that his primary or dominant purpose was to prejudice a particular creditor from making a claim against him. In *IRC v Hashmi*[50] Arden LJ explained that the purpose of putting assets beyond the reach of creditors must be a real and substantial one rather than one which is simply coincidental. For example, if the court can be shown that the debtor entered in a transaction for a purpose other than to prejudice his creditors, then, even if that transaction does prejudice the claims of creditors, the application will not succeed under s. 423. In the words of Arden LJ: 'for something to be a purpose it must be a real substantial purpose; it is not sufficient to quote something which is a by-product of the transaction under consideration, or show that it was simply a result of it . . . or an element which made no contribution of importance to the debtor's purpose in carrying out the transaction under consideration . . . trivial purposes must be excluded'.[51]

Section 424 of the Insolvency Act 1986 lists those persons who may apply for an order under s. 423. These persons include the official receiver of an insolvent company; the trustees in bankruptcy in the case of an individual who is bankrupt and, in any other case, the victim of the transaction. Once an application is made under s. 423 the court can make an order under s. 425, restoring the position to what it would have been if the transaction had not been entered into.[52] For example, in *Agricultural Mortgage Corporation plc v Woodward*[53] the court set aside the tenancy of a farm granted by a husband to his wife. Section 425 states that the order may affect the property of, or impose any obligation on, any person whether or not he is the person with whom the debtor entered into the transaction. However, such an order is not to prejudice any interest in property which was acquired by a third party who can show that it was a bona fide purchaser.

Bankruptcy provisions

Whereas s. 423 allows the court to set aside transactions made at undervalue with the intention of defrauding creditors, s. 339 of the Insolvency Act allows the court to set aside transactions which were entered into by a bankrupt.[54]

---

[49] [1994] BCC 688. See also *Delane v Chen* [2010] EWCA 1455.
[50] [2002] 2 BCLC 489.
[51] [2002] 2 BCLC 489 at 506.
[52] *National Westminster Bank plc v Jones* [2001] 1 BCLC 98.
[53] [1994] BCC 688.
[54] This section replaced s. 42 of the Bankruptcy Act 1924.

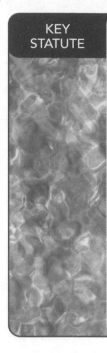

KEY STATUTE

Section 339 Insolvency Act 1986 (Transactions at an undervalue)

(1) Subject as follows in this section and sections 341 and 342, where an individual is adjudged bankrupt and he has at a relevant time (defined in section 341) entered into a transaction with any person at an undervalue, the trustee of the bankrupt's estate may apply to the court for an order under this section.

(2) The court shall, on such an application, make such order as it thinks fit for restoring the position to what it would have been if that individual had not entered into that transaction.

(3) For the purposes of this section and sections 341 and 342, an individual enters into a transaction with a person at an undervalue if –

(a) he makes a gift to that person or he otherwise enters into a transaction with that person on terms that provide for him to receive no consideration,

(b) he enters into a transaction with that person in consideration of marriage [or the formation of a civil partnership], or

(c) he enters into a transaction with that person for a consideration the value of which, in money or money's worth, is significantly less than the value, in money or money's worth, of the consideration provided by the individual.

Section 339 allows the court to set aside transactions at undervalue within certain time limits. It differs from s. 423 in two respects. Firstly, s. 339 does not require the trustees in bankruptcy to prove to the court that the transferor intended to defraud creditors. Secondly, s. 339 operates within certain time restrictions whereas s. 423 applies irrespective of when the transfer took place; the only thing important is that there was an intention to defraud. Section 339 has a five-year time limit attached to it; however, within that five-year time limit, the section distinguishes between two vital time periods.[55] Firstly, a two-year period preceding the date of adjudication of bankruptcy of a person, in which case a transaction at undervalue can be set aside irrespective of the solvency of the transferor. The reason for this is that the person entering into the transaction is presumed to be insolvent. Secondly, the remaining period of three years in which, before a transaction can be set aside, it must be shown that the transferor was insolvent. There is a rebuttable presumption that a person is bankrupt if he enters into a transaction with an associate. An associate is defined by s. 435 as a person including the relative of the bankrupt or of his spouse, his partners, his employers, his employees and any companies which at the time he was related to.

Like s. 423, s. 339 employs the same definition of a transaction at undervalue. Furthermore, the law regards a person as bankrupt in circumstances where the value of his assets are less than his liabilities. In **Re Kumar**[56] a trustee in bankruptcy applied for an order under s. 399 to reverse a transfer of a husband's interest in the matrimonial home. The husband and wife were joint tenants of the matrimonial home which was also subject to a mortgage. The agreement was that the wife would take the absolute title to the house and she would be liable to repay the remainder of the mortgage. The husband's debts could not be made and the wife petitioned for divorce. Under a consent order the wife agreed to forego her right to receive financial provision from her husband on the

55 S. 341 Insolvency Act 1986.
56 [1993] 2 All ER 700.

grounds that she had already received his share in the matrimonial home and receive periodic payments from him. The court allowed the trustee in bankruptcy an order to reverse the transfer of the husband's share in the house. The court explained that, whilst the wife had clearly provided consideration in the form of money and money's worth, the consideration was not relevant for the purposes of s. 339. Ferris J explained that the value of the wife's consideration was insignificant in light of the fact that the husband had already transferred his share in the house before the consent order, and it was not clear that she would make any claim to financial support from her husband. The husband would not have been in a position to meet any such claim to financial provision.

In **Hill v Haines**[57] the Court of Appeal had to decide whether a property adjustment order made on divorce could be set aside under the provisions of s. 339 of the Insolvency Act 1986. The Court of Appeal held that although it was not precluded from setting aside a property adjustment order under the provisions of s. 339, it would not make such an order unless the order had been obtained by fraud, collusion or otherwise by mistake. The facts of **Hill v Haines** involved a property adjustment order under s. 24 of the Matrimonial Causes Act 1973 which had the effect of transferring the husband's share in the matrimonial home to his wife. The husband was subsequently declared bankrupt and his trustees in bankruptcy sought to claim his share in the matrimonial home under s. 339 of the Insolvency Act 1986, on the grounds that it was a transaction at undervalue. In the course of his judgment, Thorpe LJ explained that:

> there is an obvious tension between the statutory scheme for the protection of a bankrupt's creditors and the statutory scheme for the financial protection of the bankrupt's former wife and child. Bankruptcy Acts and Matrimonial Causes Acts may be said to compete for shares in the fund which will always be incapable of satisfying both. Clearly if the act of bankruptcy precedes an order made under the Matrimonial Causes Act the legal and practical outcome is straightforward. Difficulties arise when the order under the Matrimonial Causes Act precedes the bankruptcy.[58]

The Court of Appeal held that a transfer of property under s. 24 of the Matrimonial Causes Act 1973 could not be regarded as a transaction at undervalue. In the course of his judgment Sir Andrew Morritt C explained that:

> [i]f one considers the economic realities, the order of the court quantifies the value of the applicant spouse's statutory right by reference to the value of the money or property thereby ordered to be paid or transferred by the respondent spouse to the applicant. In the case of such an order, whether following contested proceedings or by way of compromise, in the absence of the usual vitiating factors of fraud, mistake or misrepresentation the one balances the other. But if any such factor is established by a trustee in bankruptcy on an application under section 339 of the 1986 Act then it will be apparent that the prima facie balance was not the true one and the transaction may be liable to be set aside.[59]

Finally, under s. 339 of the Insolvency Act 1986 the court may make any order as it thinks fit to restore the position to what it would have been had the transaction not been entered into. As in s. 423, the court may make the same orders; however, no order can be made to prejudice the rights of a third party who has acquired the property in good faith.

---

[57] [2008] Ch. 412.

[58] [2008] Ch. 412 at 429.

[59] [2008] Ch. 412 at 417; see D. Capper, 'Marrying Financial Provisions and Insolvency Avoidance' (2008) LQR 361.

Trusts defeating the rights of the family and dependants

It has already been seen that for a transfer to take effect after the death of the transferor, the transferor must make a valid will. In the will, the transferor, that is the testator, can give his property to anyone he so wishes. He could give all of it to charity and leave nothing for his dependants such as a spouse and children. In such a case the question arises as to whether such freedom of disposition can be interfered with on the grounds that such family members and dependants have not been provided for. Interference with such freedom of testamentary disposition needs to be justified by some State goal or objective. Some commentators explain that in the context of testamentary transfers, the public interest in how people bequeath their property may be justified from the interests of society as a whole.[60] The orderly transfer of property to family and dependants is the means by which family solidarity is achieved. Whether or not the law recognises a general duty on a testator to acknowledge the rights of family members, it does in certain circumstances allow interference with freedom of disposition when family members and dependants are not provided for.

KEY STATUTE	**Section 2 Inheritance (Provision for Family and Dependants) Act 1975: Powers of court to make orders**

(1) Subject to the provisions of this Act, where an application is made for an order under this section, the court may, if it is satisfied that the disposition of the deceased's estate effected by his will or the law relating to intestacy, or the combination of his will and that law, is not such as to make reasonable financial provision for the applicant, make any one or more of the following orders: –

(a) an order for the making to the applicant out of the net estate of the deceased of such periodical payments and for such term as may be specified in the order;

(b) an order for the payment to the applicant out of that estate of a lump sum of such amount as may be so specified;

(c) an order for the transfer to the applicant of such property comprised in that estate as may be so specified;

(d) an order for the settlement for the benefit of the applicant of such property comprised in that estate as may be so specified;

(e) an order for the acquisition out of property comprised in that estate of such property as may be so specified and for the transfer of the property so acquired to the applicant or for the settlement thereof for his benefit;

(f) an order varying any ante-nuptial or post-nuptial settlement (including such a settlement made by will) made on the parties to a marriage to which the deceased was one of the parties, the variation being for the benefit of the surviving party to that marriage, or any child of that marriage, or any person who was treated by the deceased as a child of the family in relation to that marriage.

---

[60] See, J. Finch, L. Hayes, et al., *Wills, Inheritance and Families* (1996) at p. 22.

In order to overcome the problem of family members and dependants who have not been provided, the Inheritance (Provisions for Family and Dependants) Act 1975 was passed. The main purpose of this legislation is to give the court a discretionary power to make an award to a surviving spouse and other dependants on the ground that the disposition of the deceased's estate does not make reasonable financial provision for the applicant. Although the Act originally applied to wills, it now extends to intestacy as well. The basic idea behind this legislation is that an application is allowed to be made by the deceased spouse, a former spouse, a child of the deceased or any other person who, immediately prior to the death of deceased, was being maintained by the deceased.[61] The ground for making an application must be that the deceased's will or the rules of intestacy do not make a reasonable provision for the applicant. The court has a wide discretion in making orders that will seek to provide for such applicants from the deceased's estate. The order may be one requiring the payment of a lump sum or periodic payments from the estate.[62]

More recently, in **Cattle v Evans**[63] an unmarried couple had lived together for 19 years. The male partner died without making a will and under the intestacy rules, his estate fell for his sons. The female partner made a claim under Inheritance (Provision for Family and Dependants) Act 1975 and was awarded a sum from the estate to purchase a house.

Trusts defeating the rights of a spouse

Section 37 of the Matrimonial Causes Act 1973 gives the Family Division a power to set aside dispositions which are made with an intention to defeat the rights of a spouse's claim to financial relief. If the transaction has not yet been entered into the court can make an order preventing the transaction from being made. Section 37(5) provides that such an intention will be presumed if the disposition was made within three years of the application and which has the effect of defeating such a claim. Section 37 of the Matrimonial Causes Act 1973 was at issue in the Court of Appeal's decision in **Kemmis v Kemmis**[64] where a husband, having separated from his wife, bought a house in which his wife and children would live in. The husband moved to Jersey with his new partner. Later on, the husband sold the house and purchased a new house with the proceeds of the sale and with money given by the wife's mother, who also resided with her daughter and her children. In 1980 the husband mortgaged the house to a bank and lived on the proceeds of the mortgage money. In 1983 he asked the wife to sign a licence agreement in respect of her occupation of the house. The wife, suspicious of her husband's actions, commenced divorce proceedings and asked for an order under s. 37 of the Matrimonial Causes Act 1973 in order to set aside the mortgage. At first instance the court held that the bank had constructive notice of the husband's attempt to defeat the rights of the spouse; however, this was overturned by the Court of Appeal. The Court of Appeal held that at the time of the mortgage, the bank was not aware of any pending divorce by the wife and therefore was not put on constructive notice. In the course of his judgment, Purchas LJ explained that:

---

[61] Inheritance (Provision for Family and Dependants) Act 1975 ss. 1(1), 25(1), (4).
[62] Inheritance (Provisions for Family and Dependants) Act 1975 s. 2.
[63] [2011] EWHC 945 (Ch).
[64] [1988] 1 WLR 1307; see J. Fortin, 'Can She Avoid His Diverting Ploys?' (1989) Conv. 204.

the clear purpose of section 37 is to give power to the court to prevent a party acting so as to diminish the assets of the family which would otherwise be available for consideration by the court when making orders for financial relief. It is important to notice that the purpose of this section is to protect the family assets and is not to protect the interest, if any, enjoyed by the applicant party in any of those assets. Although an application under section 37 can only be made after proceedings for financial relief have been instituted, the section embraces dispositions which may have been made at an earlier date.[65]

> **KEY STATUTE**
>
> ## Section 37(2) Matrimonial Causes Act 1973
>
> (2) Where proceedings for financial relief are brought by one person against another, the court may, on the application of the first-mentioned person –
>
> (a) if it is satisfied that the other party to the proceedings is, with the intention of defeating the claim for financial relief, about to make any disposition or to transfer out of the jurisdiction or otherwise deal with any property, make such order as it thinks fit for restraining the other party from so doing or otherwise for protecting the claim;
>
> (b) if it is satisfied that the other party has, with that intention, made a reviewable disposition and that if the disposition were set aside financial relief or different financial relief would be granted to the applicant, make an order setting aside the disposition;
>
> (c) if it is satisfied, in a case where an order has been obtained under any of the provisions mentioned in subsection (1) above by the applicant against the other party, that the other party has, with that intention, made a reviewable disposition, make an order setting aside the disposition.

Like the provisions relating to insolvency, third parties are protected from dealing between a husband and wife. Section 37(4) provides that a transaction cannot be set aside if it is made for consideration, other than marriage consideration, to a bona fide purchaser without notice of the intention to defeat a matrimonial claim. In order for a third party to rely on the defence in s. 37(4), it is important that the party is a bona fide purchaser without notice of one spouse's intention to deprive the other of financial relief. Where the third party has actual or constructive notice of the intention to deprive financial relief to a spouse, that third party cannot rely on the defence in s. 37(4). The matter is neatly illustrated by the decision in **Sherry v Sherry**.[66] where the relationship between a husband and wife had deteriorated to such an extent that the husband had used violence towards his wife. The husband transferred a number of properties to his friend at undervalue. The friend was aware of the breakdown in relationship between the husband and the wife and also knew that the husband was in need of money. When the wife bought an action under s. 37 of the Matrimonial Causes Act 1973, the Court of Appeal held that the friend had constructive notice of the husband's intention to deprive his wife of financial relief and therefore the transfers of property were set aside.[67]

---

[65] [1988] 1 WLR 1307 at 1315.
[66] [1991] 1 FLR 307.
[67] See J. Fortin, 'The Diversions of a Fugitive Husband' (1991) Conv. 370.

 ## The Law Commission's consultation paper

In its consultation paper, the Law Commission has reviewed the effect of illegality on contracts and trusts.[68] In Part III the consultation paper considers that the present rules governing the illegality on trusts are complex and may result in unfair decisions. In particular, Part III of the consultation paper examines the question whether a person should be allowed to benefit from a trust which is set up or has arisen out of some illegality on his part. The provisional proposal of the Law Commission is that the courts should be given a structured discretion to decide whether illegality should act as a defence to normal rights and remedies. In exercising this discretion, the Court is required to take on board a number of factors such as the seriousness of the illegality; the knowledge and intention of the party claiming relief; whether denying the claim would deter illegality; whether denying the claim would further the purpose of the rule which rendered the transaction illegal; and whether denying the claim would be proportionate to the illegality involved.

In 2009 the Law Commission published a further consultation paper[69] and in 2010 published a final report with an attached Draft Bill.[70] The main objective of the Bill is to give a statutory discretion to apply the illegality defence which would prevent a beneficiary from enforcing beneficial rights which have been concealed for fraudulent purposes. The Draft Bill is considered in more detail in Chapter 11 in the context of resulting trusts.

It has already been observed above that in relation to conditions subsequent and conditions precedent which may be held contrary to public policy or illegality, the effect on the trust depends very much on the type of condition and the subject matter of the trust. Where a condition subsequent is held void on grounds of public policy or illegality, the condition is void but the gift takes effect. In contrast, if a condition precedent is held to be unlawful then the outcome depends very much on whether the condition precedent relates to real property or personal property. In the case of real property, if the condition precedent fails then the whole gift fails and there is a resulting trust in favour of the settlor or the testator's estate. In the case of personal property the law distinguishes between conditions which are illegal *malum prohibitum* and *malum in se*, the distinction being something made unlawful by statute only and something being unlawful in itself. For example, something which is *malum in se* is something which is contrary to morality. If the unlawfulness is only *malum prohibitum* then the gift takes effect absolutely. On the other hand, if the condition is held void on ground of *malum in se* the gift fails outright and there is a resulting trust in favour of the settlor or the testator's estate. The Law Commission in its consultation paper recommends the abolition of this distinction.

[68] Law Commission Consultation Paper No. 154 (1999), *Illegal Transactions: The Effect of Illegality on Contracts and Trusts*.

[69] Consultation Paper No. 189, 'The Illegality Defence: A Consultative Report'.

[70] Law Com 320, 'The Illegality Defence' (2010). See, P. Davies 'The Illegality Defence: Turning Back the Clock' [2010] Conv 282.

Conclusion

This chapter has explored some of the public policy and illegality grounds upon which an express trust may be held invalid by the courts. It is clear that an express trust which complies with the substantive and formal requirements of trust law will nevertheless be held invalid if it contravenes public policy or is illegal is some way. At the heart of the debate is the question whether the law should allow absolute freedom in the disposition of a person's private property. Certainly, freedom of disposition seems to be an integral requirement of a society which requires property to be freely alienable amongst competing users. However, as this chapter has highlighted, absolute freedom of disposition can be counter-productive when people attempt to dispose of their property in a manner which goes against public policy or is otherwise illegal. A trust which serves no useful purpose, as for example, keeping a house locked for a long period of time and denying the next of kin any right to it cannot be justified on any grounds. A trust which is to defraud the creditors of the settlor cannot be upheld simply because it goes against the wider concerns of the legal system that the assets of person should be readily available for the creditors should the settlor be unable to pay his debts. Seen in this way, the rules of public policy and illegality ensure that there is sensible balance between freedom of disposition and the effective use of resources in society.

Case study

A couple of years ago George decided to set up his own car-sales business. He borrowed significant amounts of money from a number of lenders in order to purchase cars for sale at his garage. George had very little experience of the car trade and was worried that he might be taking a big risk. A few months before he opened his business he transferred his house on trust for his daughter. The trust deed was duly executed and retained by his solicitor for safe keeping. At the same time he transferred some of his most valuable paintings to his brother, Danny, who paid less than one-third of their value.

In 2006 George created a trust of £300,000 to be invested indefinitely and the income to be used to fund a snooker club in his village.

Over the last few months George's business has not being doing that well and it has had an impact on his marriage. George is intending to separate from his wife but wishes his daughter to remain living with him. He visited his solicitor and asked about the formalities needed for a divorce. After discussing the matter with his solicitor, George decided not to go ahead with the divorce but created a voluntary deed by which he settled a sum of £60,000 on trust for his daughter until she attained the age of 21. The covenant contained a clause to the effect that should his daughter in any way be under the control or guardianship of her mother, she would forfeit any right to the money.

Last month George was declared bankrupt.

- *Can the trustee in bankruptcy claim any of the property on the above facts?*
- *George's daughter wishes to live with her mother but is worried she might lose the £60,000. She wants your advice.*
- *Is the trust for the snooker club valid?*

●● Moot points

1 Why should the law interfere with freedom of disposition?

2 In *Blathwayt* v *Baron Cawley* [1976] AC 397 Lord Wilberforce explained that 'discrimination is not the same thing as choice: it operates over a larger and less personal area, and neither by express provision nor by implication had private selection yet become a matter of public policy' at p. 426. Where a trust fund is created in favour of a beneficiary whose entitlement can be taken away should he practise a particular religion, does that beneficiary have a choice in the matter?

3 Sections 423 and 339 of the Insolvency Act 1986 allow the courts to set aside transactions which defraud creditors. What are the principal differences between these two sections?

4 To what extent can a property adjustment order made under s. 24 of the Matrimonial Causes Act 1973 be set aside under the provision of s. 339 of the Insolvency Act 1986?

● Further reading

Capper, D. 'Marrying Financial Provisions and Insolvency Avoidance' (2008) LQR 361. Looks at the decision of the court in *Hills* v *Haines* and the extent to which a property adjustment order made under s. 24 of the Matrimonial Causes Act can be set aside under the provisions of s. 339 of the Insolvency Act 1986.

Fortin, J. 'Can She Avoid His Diverting Ploys?' (1989) Conv. 204. Examines the decision of the Court of Appeal in *Kemmis* v *Kemmis*.

Fortin, J. 'The Diversions of a Fugitive Husband' (1991) Conv. 370. Examines the decision of the Court of Appeal in *Sherry* v *Sherry* in the context of s. 37 of the Matrimonial Causes Act 1973.

Furey, N. 'Bankruptcy and the Family: The Effect of the Insolvency Act 1986' (1987) 17 Family Law 316. Examines the bankruptcy provisions in the Insolvency Act 1986 and their effect on the family.

Grattan, S. 'Testamentary Conditions in Restraint of Religion', in *Modern Studies in Property Law* Vol. I (2000) (E. Cooke, ed.) (2001). Reviews those conditions in restraint of religion and the extent to which a deceased person can control property after death.

Keay, A. 'Transactions Defrauding Creditors: The Problem of Purpose under s. 423 of the Insolvency Act' [2003] Conv. 272. Examines the operation of s. 423 of the Insolvency Act 1986 with emphasis on the meaning of putting assets beyond the reach of creditors. The author aims to investigate the case law meaning of 'putting assets beyond the reach of creditors'.

Miller, G. 'Transactions Prejudicing Creditors' [1998] Conv. 362. Provides an excellent account of the principles of the Insolvency Act 1986 dealing with transactions prejudicing creditors.

Part III
Trusts implied by law

Part II of this book concentrated primarily on express private trusts, that is, trusts created deliberately by a settlor or a testator. It is not always the case that a trust is created expressly by a settlor or a testator. A trust may arise by implication of law when certain facts give rise to its imposition. Trusts which are implied by the law fall primarily into two categories: namely, resulting and constructive trusts. Unlike express trusts, implied trusts are implied or imputed by the courts as a result of intentions or the conduct of the parties in question. Unlike express trusts, which look to the creation of trusts at some future point in time, implied trusts are normally imposed by the courts as a result of analysing events which have happened in the past. The role of the court is to analyse certain facts that have been presented before it and adjudicate whether on those facts, which have taken place in the past, a trust should be implied.

A resulting trust, like a constructive trust, is imposed by law when certain facts give rise to its implication. The term 'resulting' comes from the Latin word *resalire*: 'to jump back'. The resulting trust operates to 'jump back' interest in property to a donor who transferred it to another person who is now deemed a resulting trustee of property in his hands. It will be seen in Chapter 11 that the facts that give rise to the implication of a resulting trust can be quite diverse. Given the diversity of such facts it is important to provide some general explanation for the implication is of a resulting trust. Chapter 10 explores the nature of a resulting trust and the grounds for imposing such a trust.

Whereas a resulting trust is imposed on the grounds of the intentions of the parties to the trust – normally, the intentions of the person transferring property which becomes subject to a resulting trust – a constructive trust is not necessarily imposed to give effect to the intentions of a person transferring property to another or, indeed, the intentions of the person

▶

receiving the property. Rather, a constructive trust is imposed in circumstances where it would be unconscionable for the legal owner of some property to deny a beneficial interest to some other person. The unconscionability may arise for a number of quite different reasons and these reasons will be explored in more detail in Chapters 13, 14 and 15.

10

Resulting trusts, part I: Nature of resulting trusts

Learning objectives

After reading this chapter you should be able to:

→ understand the nature of a resulting trust

→ understand the theoretical debates surrounding the justifications for the enforcement of resulting trusts

→ explain the role of resulting trusts in circumstances where there is a beneficial vacuum

→ explain the role of resulting trusts in the law of restitution and explain whether the trust is imposed to reverse an unjust enrichment per se or whether it is imposed on grounds of the conscience of the trustee receiving property

→ understand the role of intention in the imposition of a resulting trust, in particular, the intention of the person in whose favour the resulting trust arises

→ explain the extent to which the traditional categories of automatic and resulting trust continue to apply in the modern law.

SETTING THE SCENE

VISIT CASE NAVIGATOR

When does a resulting trust arise?

In *Westdeutsche Landesbank Girozentrale* v *Islington London Borough Council* [1996] AC 669 (HL) Lord Browne-Wilkinson explained at p. 708 of his judgment that:

> Under existing law a resulting trust arises in two sets of circumstances:
>
> (A) Where A makes a voluntary payment to B or pays (wholly or in part) for the purchase of property which is vested either in B alone or in the joint names of A and B, there is a presumption that A did not intend to make a gift to B: the money or property is held on trust for A (if he is the sole provider of the money) or in the case of a joint purchase by A and B in shares proportionate to their contributions. It is important to stress that this is only a *presumption*, which presumption is easily rebutted either by the counter-presumption of advancement or by direct evidence of A's intention to make an outright transfer . . .
>
> (B) Where A transfers property to B *on express trusts*, but the trusts declared do not exhaust the whole beneficial interest . . . Both types of resulting trust are traditionally regarded as examples of trusts giving effect to the common intention of the parties. A resulting trust is not imposed by law against the intentions of the trustee (as is a constructive trust) but gives effect to his presumed intention.

A few years later in *Air Jamaica* v *Charlton* [1999] 1 WLR 1399 Lord Justice Millett explained that:

> Like a constructive trust, a resulting trust arises by operation of law, though unlike a constructive trust it gives effect to intention. But it arises whether or not the transferor intended to retain a beneficial interest – he almost always does not – since it responds to any absence of intention on his part to pass a beneficial interest to the recipient (at p. 1412).

One of the more difficult questions in trust law relates to the theoretical grounds for the imposition of a resulting trust. Unlike an express private trust, which has been the subject matter of discussion in the previous chapters, a resulting trust is implied by law in a number of different factual situations. Whilst the factual situations in which the trust has been implied do not necessarily give rise to much controversy, the question as to why the trust is imposed in the first place does give rise to controversy. It will be seen in this chapter that there have been a number of different theories explaining the grounds for the imposition of a resulting trust. The aim of this chapter is to explore the various theories with a view to establishing the contemporary justifications for the imposition of a resulting trust.

Introduction

The discussion in the previous chapters has focused on trusts which are expressly created by a settlor or a testator. This chapter focuses on one particular type of trust which is not created deliberately but is imposed by law, namely a resulting trust. A resulting trust, like a constructive trust, is imposed by law when certain facts give rise to its implication. The term 'resulting' comes from the Latin word *resalire*: 'to jump back'. The resulting trust operates to 'jump back' interest in property to a donor who transferred it to another person who is now deemed a resulting trustee of property in his hands. It will be seen in Chapter 11 that the facts that will give rise to the implication of a resulting trust can be quite diverse. Given the diversity of such facts it becomes important to provide some general explanation for the implication of a resulting trust. The aims and objectives of this chapter are to explore the nature of a resulting trust and the grounds for imposing such a trust.

It will be seen in the course of this chapter that attempting to provide a general rationale for the imposition of a resulting trust has not been a very simple task. Whilst it has been a relatively straightforward exercise in identifying the various factual situations which have given rise to a resulting trust, identifying a universal principle which explains the grounds for such imposition has been less straightforward. William Swadling wrote that 'the most difficult question one can ask about resulting trusts is why they arise'.[1] The reason for this has been that different judges and different scholars have advocated different justifications for the imposition of a resulting trust. This chapter will attempt to examine the main justifications for the imposition of a resulting trust with a view to identifying the contemporary basis for the imposition of a resulting trust. This chapter will provide the basis for examining the various contexts in which such trusts have been imposed, including the role such trusts have played in determining ownership rights of cohabitees in the family home, all of which are discussed in Chapter 11.

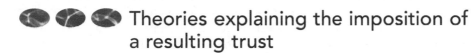

Theories explaining the imposition of a resulting trust

A contemporary staring point for any discussion on the juridical grounds upon which a resulting trust is imposed is the House of Lords' decision in *Westdeutsche Landesbank Girozentrale v Islington LBC*.[2] In this case the House of Lords undertook a comprehensive analysis of the grounds upon which a resulting trust is imposed. The decision in this case, and the important points of law arising from the case, will be discussed in great detail in the course of this chapter. However, before that is done, this section explores the various justificatory theories that have been advanced about the nature and the grounds for imposing a resulting trust. It is important to have some knowledge of the various theories that have been advanced for a number of reasons. Firstly, they will seek to explain the position as it was before the landmark decision of the House of Lords in *Westdeutsche Landesbank Girozentrale v Islington LBC*. Secondly, an understanding of these theories will aid in the understanding of the reasons for direction taken by the House of Lords in that case.

The 'beneficial vacuum' theory

One of the traditional grounds for the imposition of a resulting trust operated around the equitable maxim that 'equity abhors a beneficial vacuum'. The basis of this maxim was that, where a person transferred property to another without identifying who was to enjoy the beneficial interest in such property, the beneficial interest would result back

---

[1] W. Swadling, *Explaining Resulting Trusts* (2008) LQR 72.
[2] [1996] AC 669 (HL).

to the person transferring the property. In **Vandervell v IRC**[3] Lord Reid explained the 'beneficial interest must belong to or be held for somebody; so if it was not to belong to the donee or be held in trust by him for somebody, it must remain with the donor'.[4] This justification went a long way to explain cases such as where a settlor attempted to create a trust, but failed to identify who the beneficiary of the trust was, or had otherwise left the definition of the class of beneficiaries conceptually uncertain.[5] The justification also explained situations where a trust had simply failed for one reason or another, or where the trust had been properly used for its purpose and there then remained a surplus fund. These situations, which are considered in more detail below, have one thing in common, and that is, some property is without a beneficial owner. In such cases, the imposition of a resulting trust has the effect of returning the beneficial ownership back to the person creating the trust.

Whilst the beneficial vacuum theory explains a number of situations in which a resulting trust is imposed, it does not encapsulate all of the situations in which equity imposes a resulting trust. In particular, the theory does not explain a line of cases where a resulting trust is imposed despite the absence of a beneficial vacuum. It will be seen in the course of this chapter that a resulting trust will be imposed when one person voluntarily transfers property in the name of another. A resulting trust will also be imposed when one person purchases property, but the title is taken in the name of another person. In both of these cases the presumption in equity is that the transferor or the person providing the purchase money does not intend to confer absolute ownership on the transferee; rather the presumption is that he intends to retain the beneficial ownership. In **Dyer v Dyer**[6] Eyre CB explained that 'the trust of a legal estate . . . results to the man who advances the purchase money'.[7] Thus, in the absence of a beneficial vacuum, a resulting trust is imposed to reflect the presumed intentions of both the parties. The presumption is made on the equitable maxim that 'equity assumes bargains and not gifts'.[8]

 ## Resulting trusts and a restitutionary justification

Some commentators have argued that the basis upon which a resulting trust is imposed is to reverse an unjust enrichment.[9] You will recall that where a defendant is unjustly enriched at the expense of a claimant, the defendant will be required to effect restitution to the claimant. In this context, the imposition of the resulting trust provides an adequate restitutionary remedy which restores the beneficial interest back to the claimant. In his paper, Professor Birks explained that the law of restitution was divided into two parts.[10] The first part dealt with those situations in which a defendant had been unjustly enriched by some wrong committed against the claimant. This would, for example, cover situations where a fiduciary, such as a trustee, took some property in breach of trust for himself. In

---

[3] [1967] 2 AC 291.

[4] [1967] 2 AC 291 at 308.

[5] A class of objects will be conceptually uncertain where the settlor provides no dictionary meaning of them. For more details, see Chapter 4.

[6] (1788) 2 Cox. Eq. Cas. 92.

[7] (1788) 2 Cox. Eq. Cas. 92 at 93.

[8] Applied in the Canadian case *Goodfriend v Goodfriend* (1972) 22 DLR (3d) 699 by Spence J at p. 703.

[9] See, P. Birks, 'Restitution and Resulting Trusts' in Goldstein (ed.), *Equity and Contemporary Legal Developments* (1992) 335, and R. Chambers, *Resulting Trusts* (1997). See also, P. Birks, 'Equity, Conscience, and Unjust Enrichment' (1999) 23 University of Melbourne LR 1.

[10] *Ibid.* at 364.

such a case the defendant would be required to effect restitution to the claimant. In most cases of breach of fiduciary duty, this would require the court imposing a constructive trust on the property in the hands of the fiduciary.[11]

The second part of the law of restitution dealt with cases where the defendant had been enriched at the expense of the claimant, not because the defendant had necessarily committed a wrong against the claimant but in circumstances where the defendant had innocently received property which he should not have received. Typically, the receipt of property in the hands of the defendant arose by reason of some mistake; or in circumstances where the consideration for the property failed; or where the receipt was under some contract which turned out to be void. Professor Birks argued that in such cases the claimant had been enriched by subtraction from him and in such circumstances the defendant was required to reverse the subtractive enrichment. In his view, the resulting trust provided an appropriate means by which such subtractive restitution could be effected. As soon as the property had been transferred to the defendant in circumstances of mistake, or under a void contract, then a resulting trust was imposed whereby the beneficial interest in the property remained with the transferor. The work of Professor Birks was taken further by Professor Robert Chambers in his seminal work on resulting trusts.[12] Chambers likewise argued that the resulting trust operated to reverse an unjust enrichment in the hands of the defendant. Chambers's work went further in explaining that the grounds for the imposition of a resulting trust in all cases, including those where property had been transferred on grounds of mistake or where the consideration failed, was the intention of the transferor not to pass a beneficial interest in the property. Thus where the property was transferred mistakenly to the defendant, the transferee did not intend the beneficial interest to pass to the recipient.

The work of Professors Birks and Chambers clearly gives the resulting trust a large role to play in the law of restitution. If such a trust is imposed to reverse a subtractive unjust enrichment then it confers upon the claimant a proprietary restitutionary claim. Recognising a proprietary restitutionary claim can have significant consequences for the claimant as well as the defendant. If a resulting trust is imposed in every situation where the defendant is unjustly enriched at the expense of the claimant, then the claimant acquires a proprietary interest in the property in the hands of the claimant. This confers upon the plaintiff a right to trace that property in the hands of the defendant or another third party who cannot show that it has acquired it good faith and without notice of the trust.[13] The recognition of a proprietary right in the property in the hands of the defendant will give the claimant priority over the other unsecured creditors of the defendant. Seen from this perspective, the imposition of a resulting trust to reverse a subtractive enrichment can operate as a powerful tool. However, whether it is entirely accurate for the resulting trust to be used in this restitutionary manner is another matter. Writing extrajudicially Sir Peter Millett explained the grounds upon which a claimant was entitled to a proprietary restitutionary remedy for subtractive enrichment. He explained that where a transferor transferred property to a transferee, which then turned out to have been transferred under mistake, there was no immediate resulting trust arising

---

[11] As in *A-G Hong Kong v Reid* [1994] 1 AC 324 where a constructive trust was imposed on properties in New Zealand which had been purchased with money received as bribes by a public prosecutor in Hong Kong. The constructive trust is examined in more detail in Chapter 11.

[12] R. Chambers, *Resulting Trusts* (1997).

[13] The right to trace equitable property interests is considered in Chapter 21. Suffice to say for the time being that a beneficiary under a trust will have rights binding on everyone except a bona fide purchaser without notice of the equitable interest.

in favour of the transferee. The initial transfer to the transfer had the effect of transferring both the legal and equitable title to the transferee. At the time of the transfer, the intention of the transferee was to make outright transfer of ownership to the transferee. Once the transferee learnt of the mistake, he had a 'mere equity' in his favour entitling him to rescind the contract and ask for a personal restitutionary remedy, or where appropriate, reconveyance of the property. In this sense, the resulting trust has no part to play in granting an immediate equitable interest in the transferee once the property is transferred and where the mistake is yet not known to either party. The matter is neatly illustrated in a passage from Sir Peter Millett's article below.[14]

> The third, intermediate, class of case is where the plaintiff pays away his money by a valid payment, fully intending to part with the beneficial interest to the recipient, but his intention is vitiated by some factor such as fraud, misrepresentation, mistake . . . and so on. In all these cases the beneficial interest passes, but the plaintiff has the right to elect whether to affirm the transaction or rescind it. If he elects to rescind it, it is usually assumed that the beneficial title reverts in the plaintiff, and the authorities suggest that it does so retrospectively. But the recipient cannot anticipate his decision. Pending the plaintiff's election to rescind, the recipient is entitled, and may be bound, to treat the payment as effective. It is well settled that the plaintiff's subsequent rescission does not invalidate or render wrongful transactions which have taken place in the meantime on the faith of the receipt.[15] In the meantime, the plaintiff's right to rescind has been classified as a mere equity.[16] Although this has been criticised[17] there is much to commend it. Pending rescission the transferee has the whole legal and beneficial interest in the property, but his beneficial title is defeasible. There is plainly no fiduciary relationship. The defeasible nature of the transferee's title should not inhibit his use of the property. Any right which the transferor may have to a reconveyance after rescission is best regarded, not as a response to a constructive or resulting trust, but as part of the working out of the equitable remedy of rescission, which is tightly controlled and subject to special defences. It is not inappropriate to describe the transferee as holding the property on a constructive trust for the transferor but only after rescission, in much the same way as we describe the vendor as holding property on a constructive trust for the purchaser but only after the parties have entered into a specifically enforceable contract for sale. If so, the right to reconveyance is a form of specific performance (or 'specific unperformance') which equity makes available because a money judgment is an inadequate remedy. If this is right, then the remedy should be confined to cases of land or other property of special value to the transferor.

Professor Birks's thesis that a resulting trust was imposed to reverse an unjust enrichment in cases such as mistaken payment, or where the consideration under a contract failed, was rigorously attacked by William Swadling.[18] In his own thesis, Swadling argued that the work of Professor Birks failed to take into consideration the nature of the presumptions which were raised when equity imposed a resulting trust.[19] The central aspect of his thesis was that a resulting trust was imposed on grounds of the presumed intentions of the transferor: in particular, a presumed intention on his part that at the time of the transfer he intended to create a trust in his favour. The basic thrust of

---

[14] P. Millett, 'Restitution and Constructive Trusts' (1998) LQR 399 at 416.

[15] *Bolton Partners* v *Lambert* (1889) 41 Ch. D 295 at 307 *per* Cotton LJ; *Lipkin Gorman* v *Karpnale Ltd* [1991] 2 AC 548 at 573 per Lord Goff; *Bristol and West Building Society* v *Mothew* [1996] 4 All ER 698.

[16] *Phillips* v *Phillips* (1862) 4 De GF & J 208 at 218 per Lord Westbury.

[17] See Robert Chambers *Resulting Trusts* (1997) at pp. 172 *et seq.*

[18] W. Swadling, 'A New Role for Resulting Trusts' (1996) 16 *Legal Studies* 110.

[19] For a more critical analysis of the nature of the presumptions raised in resulting trusts, see W. Swadling, 'Explaining Resulting Trusts' (2008) LQR 72.

Swadling's argument is that at the time of transfer in cases where consideration fails, or where there is some mistake, the transferor is intending to make an outright transfer of both legal and equitable ownership to the transferee. In such a case there can be no room for the imposition of a presumed resulting trust simply because the transferee is not intending to create a resulting trust of the property being transferred. In other words, there are no grounds upon which there can be a presumption that, at the time of the transfer, he intended the transferee to hold the property on trust for him. The only real evidence at the time of the transfer is that the transferor intended to transfer absolute ownership to the transferee.

In *Westdeutsche Landesbank Girozentrale* v *Islington LBC*[20] the House of Lords rejected the view that a resulting trust arose to reverse an unjust enrichment in the hands of the defendant. It will be seen below that the case concerned an interest rate swap agreement under which money was transferred to a council under a contract which turned out be void. The question before the court was whether the money paid by the bank to the council had been received subject to a resulting trust, despite the fact that the illegality of the contract was not discovered by the parties until some time later. In the course of his judgment Lord Browne-Wilkinson explained that a resulting trust arose to give effect to the intentions of the transferor, in particular, in transferring property to the transferee, intending to retain a the beneficial interest in the property so transferred. So, in the context of a payment by a bank in circumstances where the bank was unaware that the payment was being made under a void contract, there could be no presumption of an intention that the bank intended to retain the beneficial interest in the money being transferred. In the words of his Lordship:

> any presumption of resulting trust is rebutted, since it is demonstrated that the bank paid, and the local authority received, the upfront payment with the intention that the moneys so paid should become the absolute property of the local authority. It is true that the parties were under a misapprehension that the payment was made in pursuance of a valid contract. But that does not alter the actual intentions of the parties at the date the payment was made . . .[21]

His Lordship also went on to to explain the dangers of a liberal application of a resulting trust to reverse an unjust enrichment as advocated by Peter Birks, in particular, the dangerous consequences it could have on third parties.[22] If a resulting trust arose as soon as money had been received under a void contract it would clearly vest the beneficial interest in the person transferring the money. Although the transferor would clearly have claims against the transferee, he could also have potential claims against any persons receiving the money from the transferee even though no one ever knew that a trust was in place.

The decision in *Westdeutsche Landesbank Girozentrale* v *Islington LBC*[23] clearly rejects a broad restitutionary role to be played by resulting trusts. A resulting trust is imposed to give effect to the presumed intentions of the person transferring property to the transferee. The basis upon which equity will impose a resulting trust, like any other trust, is on the conscience of the recipient of the property. The recipient must realise that he is receiving property subject to a trust and that the person transferring the property to him does not intend to part with the beneficial interest in such property. Although the

---

[20] [1996] AC 669 (HL).
[21] [1996] AC 669 (HL) at 708.
[22] [1996] AC 669 (HL) at 709.
[23] [1996] AC 669 (HL).

broad restitutionary role of a resulting trust was clearly rejected, the judgment of Lord Browne-Wilkinson in respect of the role of intentions in the imposition of a resulting trust is not without its own problems and these are examined in more detail below. Sir Peter Millet has argued that simply because the conscience of a recipient of property has not been affected, it should not preclude the imposition of a resulting trust in order to reverse the subtractive enrichment of the recipient.[24] A resulting trust is quite capable of arising as soon as property is transferred to the recipient, although it is not necessary that the recipient becomes subject to fiduciary duties and liability for breach of trust until such time he becomes aware of the circumstances that will then affect his conscience.

Resulting trusts and the role of intentions

A number of legal scholars and judges have attempted to justify the imposition of a resulting trust on grounds of intention. In **Standing v Bowring**[25] the court explained that 'trusts are neither created nor implied by law to defeat the intentions of donors or settlors; they are created or implied or are held to result in favour of donors or settlors in order to carry out, and give effect to their true intentions, expressed or implied'.[26] When addressing the issue of intention there appear to be two very difficult questions requiring an answer. First of all, whose intention is the court looking to? Secondly, what is the precise nature of that intention? For example, is it an intention on the part of the transferor to create a trust or is it an intention on his part, albeit a presumed intention, that he does not wish to pass a beneficial interest to the recipient? These questions, and in particular the latter, have had a mixed response. In his work, William Swadling took the view that resulting trusts were imposed on grounds that the transferor of property intended to create a presumed intention resulting trust.[27] It is for this reason that he rejected any role for resulting trusts as a general restitutionary response for unjust enrichment. In his view, many of the circumstances leading to an unjust enrichment in the hands of the defendant were not accompanied by an intention on the part of the transferor to create a resulting trust in his favour. The work of Swadling was very much influential in Lord Browne-Wilkinson's judgment in **Westdeutsche Landesbank Girozentrale v Islington LBC**,[28] where it has already been observed that the House of Lords held that a resulting trust responds to the presumed intention of the person transferring property. It only comes into existence when the conscience of the transferee is affected. The conscience of the transferee can only be affected in circumstances where he becomes aware that the transferor did not intend to pass a beneficial interest to him.

The idea that a resulting trust responds to the presumed intentions of the parties and the conscience of the recipient of the property is not, however, without controversy and problems of its own. The presumed intention based justification fails to explain some of the existing authorities in which a resulting trust has been imposed. The first of those authorities is one of the seminal cases on resulting trusts: the decision in **Vandervell v IRC**.[29] The facts of this case clearly show that there was a complete absence of intention, real or presumed, that a settlor, Vandervell, wished to retain any beneficial interest in

[24] P. Millett, 'Restitution and Constructive Trusts' (1998) LQR 399 at 403–4.
[25] (1885) 31 Ch. D 282.
[26] (1885) 31 Ch. D 282 at 289.
[27] W. Swadling, 'A New Role for Resulting Trusts' (1996) 16 *Legal Studies* 110.
[28] [1996] AC 669 (HL).
[29] [1967] 2 AC 291.

shares that he was transferring to the Royal College of Surgeons, and the subsequent option to purchase those shares which were eventually held by the Vandervell Trust Company for the benefit of his children. Indeed, the only intention of Vandervell was to divest himself of any interest in the property being transferred. Despite this, as was observed in Chapter 5, when Vandervell transferred an option to purchase shares from the Royal College of Surgeons to a trust company without defining the benefactors of that option, the court held that the option belonged to Vandervell under a resulting trust.

The requirement that the conscience of the recipient of the property be affected is also problematic. It fails to explain the decision of the court in **Re Vinogradoff**[30] where a testatrix transferred £800 worth of a war loan into the joint account of herself and her granddaughter who was then four years old. The testatrix continued to receive the dividends on the loan until her death. On her death the court held that the granddaughter held the war loan on resulting trust for her grandmother. There is nothing on these facts to suggest that the intentions of the grandmother were to make her granddaughter a trustee of the property she had transferred in their joint names. With regard to her granddaughter, it is not entirely clear how her conscience was affected to constitute her a trustee. In this respect, this decision becomes almost impossible to justify in the context of the modern position enunciated in **Westdeutsche Landesbank Girozentrale v Islington LBC**.[31]

There also appear to be a number of practical problems with linking the imposition of a resulting trust with the conscience of the trustee. Take for example, a situation where a person transfers property to another but does not learn of the fact that the property he has received should in fact be held on trust for the person transferring it to him. This may well happen in a situation where shares or, indeed any other property, are transferred to a recipient who only later on discovers that such shares are not the property of the recipient but are to be held for the transferor. The matter is neatly illustrated by Professor Martin who asks the question: 'Who would be entitled to the beneficial interest, for example dividends on shares, pending the acquisition of knowledge by the trusts?'[32] Professor Martin advocates that a resulting trust should arise as soon as the property is transferred to the transferee but the transferee should not be subject to fiduciary duties and liability for breach of trust until such time as he is acquainted with the knowledge that the property in his receipt cannot consciously be retained by him and must be held for the transferor.[33] Professor Chambers explains that:

> delaying the creation of the trust until the trustees have sufficient notice to affect their consciences may have drastic effect on a number of important matters which depend on the timing of the creation of the resulting [or constructive] trust, such as entitlement to income, liability for taxation, risk and insurance, commencement of limitation periods, transfer and transmission of property interests, and priority of competing claims.[34]

A different approach to the question of intention was taken by Millett LJ in **Air Jamaica v Charlton**[35] where the Privy Council was required to adjudicate on the entitlement to a surplus fund arising in the context of a pension fund. The pension scheme of employees

---

[30] [1935] WN 68. See also *Thavorn v Bank of Credit and Commerce International SA* [1985] 1 Lloyd's Rep. 259.

[31] [1996] AC 669 (HL).

[32] Hanbury and Martin, *Modern Equity* 18th edn (2009) at p. 253.

[33] See, for example, W. Swadling, 'Property and Conscience' (1998) 14 Tru. LI 228 and P. Millett, 'Restitution and Constructive Trusts' (1998) 114 LQR 399.

[34] R. Chambers, *Resulting Trusts* (1997) at p. 206.

[35] [1999] 1 WLR 1399.

of Air Jamaica was terminated in 1994 as a result of privatisation of the company. After the defined benefits under the scheme had been paid out, there remained a surplus of $400. The members of the scheme claimed to be entitled to the surplus by virtue of clause 13 of the scheme which provided that in the event of discontinuance of the scheme any surplus should be used by the trustees to provide additional benefits to the members. Furthermore, clause 4 specifically prohibited the company from reclaiming any money it had contributed into the scheme. The company attempted to amend the scheme so as to be entitled to the surplus fund; however, these amendments proved to be ineffective on grounds of perpetuity. So, the question remained as to who was entitled to the surplus funds. Clearly the scheme intended that the surplus funds would be used for providing additional benefits to the members. Clause 4 clearly prohibited any return of money which the company had contributed towards the scheme. Clause 4, therefore, provided a huge obstacle in the way of finding any resulting trust of the surplus funds in favour of the company. Looked at it from the view of intentions as explained in **Westdeutsche Landesbank Girozentrale v Islington LBC**,[36] it would be impossible to find an intention that the company wished to retain an equitable interest in either all or some of the surplus fund. Despite this, Millett LJ held that the surplus fund belonged to those who had provided it. On the present facts, both the company and the members had provided equally, and despite clause 4 of the scheme, the company was entitled to one-half of the surplus under a resulting trust.

The fundamental question arising from the decision of the Privy Council in **Air Jamaica v Charlton**[37] is: what is the basis for the imposition of the resulting trust in the face of clause 4 of the pension scheme which clearly showed an intention on the part of the company to part with both the legal and beneficial interest in the money contributed to the scheme? Can a resulting trust be imposed even in circumstances where the transferor evidences an intention to part with his beneficial interest? In answering these questions Millett LJ explained that:

> [L]ike a constructive trust, a resulting trust arises by operation of law, though unlike a constructive trust it gives effect to intention. But it arises whether or not the transferor intended to retain a beneficial interest – he almost always does not – since it responds to any absence of intention on his part to pass a beneficial interest to the recipient. It may arise even where the transferor positively wished to part with the beneficial interest, as in *Vandervell* v *IRC*. In that case the retention of a beneficial interest by the transferor destroyed the effectiveness of a tax avoidance scheme which the transferor was trying to implement. The House of Lords affirmed the principle that a resulting trust is not defeated by evidence that the transferor intended to part with the beneficial interest if he has not in fact succeeded in doing so.[38]

There is a lot to be said about the approach of Lord Millett in **Air Jamaica v Charlton**.[39] The idea that a resulting trust is imposed on the basis of an absence of intention to pass a beneficial interest on the part of the transferee avoids many of the theoretical and practical problems of the presumed intentions of the parties and the conscience-based approach in **Westdeutsche Landesbank Girozentrale v Islington LBC**.[40] It also provides the most effective means of explaining the existing line of authorities where a resulting trust has been imposed. For example, it has already been observed how the decision in

---

[36] [1996] AC 669 (HL).
[37] [1999] 1 WLR 1399.
[38] [1999] 1 WLR 1399 at 1412.
[39] [1999] 1 WLR 1399.
[40] [1996] AC 669 (HL).

Westdeutsche fails to explain why a resulting trust was imposed in *Vandervell v IRC*,[41] where the only real intention of the transferor of shares in a private company was to divest himself of both the legal and beneficial interest in order to implement a tax avoidance scheme. When the option to purchase the shares was transferred to the Vandervell Trust Company without any declaration of intention as to whom it was to be held for, the only real intention that could be imputed in such circumstances was an absence of intention on the part of the Vandervell to pass a beneficial interest to the trust company.

The absence of intention on the part of the transferor to pass a beneficial interest to the transferee was further applied by Lord Millett in *Twinsectra Ltd v Yardley*.[42] You will recall from Chapter 3 that a resulting trust was imposed in that case to resolve a long-standing legal debate as to where the beneficial interest lay in money which had been advanced by way of a loan, but only to be used for the specific purposes of the loan. The Court of Appeal in *Twinsectra* was clearly of the opinion that the beneficial interest under a Quistclose trust remained in suspense until the stated purpose of the loan has been carried out or had otherwise failed. This view was rejected in the House of Lords on the grounds that it did not fit comfortably with established principles of equity: in particular, the principle that 'equity abhors a beneficial vacuum' and that the beneficial interest in property must belong to some person at all relevant times. Millett LJ explained that a resulting trust arose in favour of the lender as soon as the loan was made to the borrower. The basis for the imposition of such a trust was on grounds that the lender had an absence of intention that the loan money should belong to any other person. This absence of intention to pass the beneficial interest to any other person meant that it belonged under a resulting trust for the lender. More recently, in *Lavelle v Lavelle*[43] Lord Phillips MR in the Court of Appeal, when considering the purchase of property by a father in his daughter's name, explained that:

> where one person, A, transfers the legal title of a property he owns or purchases to another, B, without receipt of any consideration, the effect will depend on his intention . . . Normally there will be evidence of the intention with which a transfer is made. Where there is not, the law applies presumptions. Where there is no close relationship between A and B, there will be a presumption that A does not intend to part with the beneficial interest in the property.[44]

Although, as will be seen below, the prevailing legal position with regard to the resulting trusts is that such trusts are imposed on the basis of the intentions of the parties, including a requirement that the conscience of the recipient must be affected, it is submitted that the better jurisprudence of such trusts is provided by Lord Millett in *Air Jamaica v Charlton*.[45] As explained above, there is a lot to be gained by the idea that such trusts are imposed in order to reflect an absence of intention on the part of the transferor of property to pass a beneficial interest to the transferee. The requirement that the conscience of the trustee must be affected before a resulting trust can be imposed would, in the words of Professor Chambers, 'be a difficult and dangerous departure from existing law. There is little to be gained by such a move and much to be lost.'[46] With regard to those cases where money has been transferred under mistake or under a contract which is void, the prevailing view is that a resulting trust arises as soon as the money has been

---

[41] [1967] 2 AC 291.
[42] [2002] 2 All ER 377.
[43] [2004] 2 FCR 418.
[44] [2004] 2 FCR 418 at paras 13–14.
[45] [1999] 1 WLR 1399.
[46] R. Chambers, *Resulting Trusts* (1997) at p. 208.

paid over to the transferee. However, the transferee does not become subject to fiduciary duties of trusteeship and liability for breach of trust until such time as his conscience has been affected.[47]

The absence of intention to pass the beneficial interest to the recipient approach as advocated by Millett LJ in **Air Jamaica v Charlton** has received support from a number of writers. For example, Moffat explains that:

> intention here plays an almost negative role in that the focus is on the absence of intention to benefit the recipient or transferee. The onus is on that person to rebut the presumption that the transferor had no intention to benefit him or her. This formulation has certain advantages. One is that it highlights what Professor Birks identifies as 'a fine but important distinction between intent creative of rights as in an express trust . . . and intent conceived as a fact which along with others, calls for the creation of rights by operation of law' (*An introduction to the Law of Restitution* (1989) p. 65). A second feature of the formulation is that it comfortably encompasses the fact situations in both 'automatic' and 'presumed resulting' trusts and, more particularly, may provide a more compelling rationale for the type of resulting trust in *Vandervell* v *IRC*.[48]

Automatic and presumed resulting trusts

**VISIT CASE
NAVIGATOR**

Despite the scholarly and judicial debates surrounding resulting trusts, for a period of some twenty years the judicial classification of resulting trusts by Megarry J in **Re Vandervell's Trusts (No. 2)**[49] remained undisturbed in the textbook tradition.[50] It is important to have some appreciation of the categorisation in **Vandervell**, as many of the existing cases were for a long time explained under those categories. You will recall that the facts of **Re Vandervell (No. 2)** concerned the option to repurchase shares from the Royal College of Surgeons. There were a number to questions before the court, one of those being: to whom did the option belong to once it has been transferred to the trust company without effective declaration of trust in anyone's favour? In attempting to address this question, Megarry J explained that resulting trusts were of two main types:

1 Automatic resulting trusts

2 Presumed resulting trusts

Automatic resulting trusts arose automatically in circumstances where an express trust failed for some reason, such as failure to comply with an appropriate formality or being contrary to the perpetuity rules.[51] An automatic resulting trust was also said to arise in circumstances where some or all of the beneficial interest remained undisposed of under an express trust. Seen in this way, automatic resulting trusts sought to fill in a beneficial

---

[47] See, for example, Hanbury and Martin, *Modern Equity* 17th edn (2005) at p. 241; P. Millett, 'Restitution and Constructive Trusts' (1998) LQR 399 at 416; Hayton and Marshall, *Commentary and Cases on the Law of Trusts and Equitable Remedies* 12th edn (2005) at pp. 292–3.

[48] G. Moffat, *Trust Law: Text and Materials* 4th edn (2005) at p. 187.

[49] [1974] Ch. 269.

[50] Indeed, it still remains undisturbed in some leading texts; see, for example, A. Hudson, *Equity and Trusts* 5th edn (2006) at p. 451 where Professor Hudson admits that to do so is slightly controversial in the context of the decision in *Westdeutsche Landesbank Girozentrale* v *Islington LBC* [1996] AC 669; however, the approach best explains the decided cases.

[51] These rules were considered in Chapter 8. The rules operate to invalidate certain dispositions of property which have an excessive delay in vesting or otherwise inalienate property.

vacuum and operated on the basis that 'equity abhors a beneficial vacuum.' Thus, if a trust was created for A for his life, and thereafter for his oldest son, and then A died without a son, the property subject to the trust would be held by the trustees on resulting trust for A's next of kin. In a majority of the decided cases the question of incomplete disposal of trust property has occurred in the context of subscriptions and contributions to funds for various purposes which cease to be required leaving a surplus fund to be distributed. These cases on incomplete disposal are considered in more detail in the sections below.

A presumed resulting trust was said to arise not on an automatic basis, but rather on the basis of the presumed intentions of the person transferring property to another. Most typically, a presumed resulting trust was said to arise where a person voluntarily transfers property in the name of another or where he purchases property in the name of another. One would have expected that in the case of a voluntarily transferred property in the name of another, he or she is making a gift of that property to the person to whom he is transferring it. Whilst this may be the case, the initial presumption of equity is to presume that the person to whom the property has been transferred is only intended to be a trustee for him. It will be seen in Chapter 11 that the presumption of resulting trusts can be rebutted by evidence which points to a contrary intention, for example, an intention to make a gift to the recipient.

The distinction between automatic and presumed resulting trusts was firmly embedded in the textbook tradition and provided somewhat structured approach in analysing and categorising the situations in which resulting trusts arose. However, despite this it was not entirely correct to assume that an automatic resulting trust was imposed in the absence of any intention on the part of the person to whom the property would eventually result back to. Clearly, in cases where a trust failed for some reason or there remained some surplus fund, the intention of the person creating the trust would be that his intention was not to pass the beneficial interest in that property to whoever may be holding it. If any unexhausted property was to vest in any person other than the person creating the trust then there would be a need to establish some evidence that that was the intention of the person creating the trust. Seen in this way, an automatic resulting trust is better analysed as a response to an absence of intention on the part of the person creating the trust that – given the circumstances, for example, a surplus fund – he did not intend to pass a beneficial interest to whoever may be seeking to claim it.

 *Westdeutsche*: the prevailing view

Some of the sections above have already made extensive reference to the decision of the House of Lords in ***Westdeutsche Landesbank Girozentrale v Islington LBC***,[52] and despite some of the controversies and problems associated with the House of Lords' formulation of resulting trusts in that case, it remains the prevailing view for the imposition of a resulting trust. This section expands on that decision and explains how the House of Lords construed the basis for the imposition of resulting trusts. The case involved what was a very complicated interest rate swap agreement. These agreements became quite popular between banks and local authorities at a time when there were stringent caps on rates which local authorities could charge. It is not necessary to go into the complicated workings of interest rate swap agreement for the purposes of this chapter. It is,

---

[52] [1996] AC 669 (HL).

however, sufficient to say that, as a result of a decision of the House of Lords in **Hazell v Hammersmith and Fulham LBC**,[53] such interest rate swap agreements were declared as void and unenforceable on the grounds that they were entered into beyond the powers of local authorities.

In *Westdeutsche* the claimant bank sought to recover money which it had paid under the agreement. Most of the money advanced by the bank to the local authority had been used: therefore any proprietary claims to money were not possible. Despite the absence of a proprietary claim, it was never doubted that the local authority was under a personal obligation to repay the money back to the bank. The question before the House of Lords was whether the payment of the money was subject to simple or compound interest. Compound interest could only be charged in equity as the common law can only award simple interest. In order to avail themselves of the jurisdiction of equity, it became incumbent on the claimant bank to show that when the money was transferred to the local authority they retained an equitable interest which would allow then to call upon equitable relief. The submission of the bank was that as soon as the money was transferred to the local authority it was held by the local authority on resulting trust for them. It was argued that, even though the swap agreement was declared void retrospectively, there had been a separation of the legal title and equitable title to the money upon receipt by the local authority. It was this argument which was put to the House of Lords in order to argue that the local authority stood in a fiduciary relationship to the bank, and as such was under an obligation to repay the whole amount of money under the agreement with compound interest. So, was the payment of the money under a void contract subject to an immediate resulting trust in favour of the bank?

The majority decision was delivered by Lord Browne-Wilkinson and there are three key aspects to that judgment which need to be analysed here. In attempting to answer the question whether the money paid by the bank had been received on resulting trust, his Lordship firstly explained what he regarded to be the relevant principles of trust law.

KEY CITATION

Westdeutsche Landesbank Girozentrale v *Islington London Borough Council* [1996] AC 669 (HL) (The relevant principles of trust law per Lord Browne-Wilkinson at 705)

(i) Equity operates on the conscience of the owner of the legal interest. In the case of a trust, the conscience of the legal owner requires him to carry out the purposes for which the property was vested in him (express or implied trust) or which the law imposes on him by reason of his unconscionable conduct (constructive trust).

(ii) Since the equitable jurisdiction to enforce trusts depends upon the conscience of the holder of the legal interest being affected, he cannot be a trustee of the property if and so long as he is ignorant of the facts alleged to affect his conscience, i.e. until he is aware that he is intended to hold the property for the benefit of others in the case of an express or implied trust, or, in the case of a constructive trust, of the factors which are alleged to affect his conscience.

(iii) In order to establish a trust there must be identifiable trust property. The only apparent exception to this rule is a constructive trust imposed on a person who dishonestly assists in a breach of trust who may come under fiduciary duties even if he does not receive identifiable trust property.

---

[53] [1990] 2 QB 697.

(iv) Once a trust is established, as from the date of its establishment the beneficiary has, in equity, a proprietary interest in the trust property, which proprietary interest will be enforceable in equity against any subsequent holder of the property (whether the original property or substituted property into which it can be traced) other than a purchaser for value of the legal interest without notice.

These propositions are fundamental to the law of trusts and I would have thought uncontroversial.

Having explained the relevant principles of trust law, in particular the central requirement that before a legal owner of a property can be deemed to be a trustee his conscience must be affected, his Lordship went on to explain when a resulting trust arose.

KEY CITATION

Westdeutsche Landesbank Girozentrale v *Islington London Borough Council* [1996] AC 669 (HL) (When does a resulting trust arise? Per Lord Browne-Wilkinson at 708)

Under existing law a resulting trust arises in two sets of circumstances:

(a) where A makes a voluntary payment to B or pays (wholly or in part) for the purchase of property which is vested either in B alone or in the joint names of A and B, there is a presumption that A did not intend to make a gift to B: the money or property is held on trust for A (if he is the sole provider of the money) or in the case of a joint purchase by A and B in shares proportionate to their contributions. It is important to stress that this is only a *presumption*, which presumption is easily rebutted either by the counter-presumption of advancement or by direct evidence of A's intention to make an outright transfer . . .

(b) Where A transfers property to B *on express trusts*, but the trusts declared do not exhaust the whole beneficial interest . . . Both types of resulting trust are traditionally regarded as examples of trusts giving effect to the common intention of the parties. A resulting trust is not imposed by law against the intentions of the trustee (as is a constructive trust) but gives effect to his presumed intention.

Finally, in respect of the classification of resulting trusts provided by Megarry J in *Re Vandervell's Trusts (No. 2)*,[54] his Lordship explained that 'Megarry J. in *Re Vandervell's Trusts (No. 2)* suggests that a resulting trust of type (B) does not depend on intention but operates automatically. I am not convinced that this is right. If the settlor has expressly, or by necessary implication, abandoned any beneficial interest in the trust property, there is in my view no resulting trust: the undisposed-of equitable interest vests in the Crown as bona vacantia.'[55] Whilst it is true to say that where a person has abandoned an equitable interest in property, such property vests in the Crown as *bona vacantia*, the question whether a person has in fact actually abandoned a beneficial interest in property is not readily answered in the affirmative. It has already been seen in the decision of the Privy Council in *Air Jamaica* v *Charlton*[56] that even where a transferor does not

---

[54] [1974] Ch. 269.
[55] [1996] AC 699 (HL) at 708.
[56] [1999] 1 WLR 1399.

intend to retain any interest in money transferred, a resulting trust will be implied in his favour in circumstances where not to do so would result in an unjust enrichment on the part of the defendant.

Having explained the relevant principles of trust law, the grounds upon which a resulting trust is imposed and whether there existed any real distinction between automatic and presumed resulting trusts, Lord Browne-Wilkinson explained that no immediate resulting trust arose on receipt of the money from the bank. At the time the payment was made by the bank, both parties were unaware that the contract they had entered into was in fact void. The conscience of the local authority could not have been affected until such time as it became aware that the contract was in fact void, and that the money received under it was not capable of being held by it beneficially for itself. The idea that a resulting trust is imposed to reflect the intentions of the parties and the conscience of the transferee remains, however, somewhat problematic. In the previous sections it has already been observed how linking the intentions of the parties and requirement that the transferee's conscience be affected fails to explain some of the earlier authorities. What is more problematic is that the decision in *Westdeutsche Landesbank Girozentrale v Islington LBC*[57] seems to cloud the distinction between resulting trusts and constructive trusts. If a resulting trust is based on the intentions of the parties and the broad requirement of unconscionability on the part of the trustee, then it raises the question as to what the difference is between a resulting and a constructive trust.[58] Sir Peter Millett has explained that a resulting trust does not depend on the unconscionability of the recipient of property, or the so-called resulting trustee: rather the trust is imposed to reflect the intention of the transferor.[59] In this respect, despite the prevailing view in *Westdeutsche Landesbank Girozentrale v Islington LBC*[60] there is much to be said about the absence of intention approach as advocated by Millett LJ in *Air Jamaica v Charlton*.[61] The view adopted in this text is that the absence of intention on the part of the transferor to pass a beneficial interest to the recipient probably best explains the decided cases and is theoretically the soundest justification for the grounds for the imposition of a result trust.

Conclusion

This chapter has explored the nature and operation of resulting trusts. It should become self-evident from this chapter that the resulting trust operates in a number of diverse contexts. It is precisely because of the diversity of its application that has made the search for a universal theory explaining the reasons for its imposition very difficult. It was seen at the outset of this chapter that many theories have been advanced which seek to explain the juridical nature of the resulting trust. Such theories have focused on principles and concepts such as restitution, beneficial vacuums, conscience and intentions. All such principles and concepts have had some role to play in understanding why a resulting trust is imposed; however, each one on its own does not offer a universal

---

[57] [1996] AC 669 (HL).
[58] Considered in more detail in Chapter 11.
[59] P. Millett, 'Restitution and Constructive Trusts' (1998) LQR 399 at 401.
[60] [1996] AC 669 (HL).
[61] [1999] 1 WLR 1399.

explanation for all the possible situations in which a resulting trust will be imposed. It is for this reason that the judicial and academic debates will continue to focus on finding a universal explanation why a resulting trust is imposed. Although the decision of the House of Lords in *Westdeutsche Landesbank Girozentrale v Islington LBC*[62] holds that the resulting trust is imposed on grounds of the conscience and intentions of the parties, there is a lot to be said for the absence of intention to pass a beneficial interest theory advanced by the Privy Council in *Air Jamaica v Charlton*.[63] Having looked at some of the theoretical and doctrinal arguments surrounding the reasons why resulting trusts are imposed, the next chapter explores some of the well-established factual situations which will give rise to a resulting trust.

Moot points

1 The beneficial vacuum theory has long been advocated as the basis for the imposition of a resulting trust. Is it crucial that there be a beneficial vacuum before a resulting trust can be imposed?

2 Resulting trusts and restitution seem to have a natural relationship. The law of restitution seeks to reverse an unjust enrichment in the hands of a defendant. The imposition of a resulting trust has the effect of returning the beneficial interest in property to the transferor. One of the most effective ways to reverse an unjust enrichment is to impose a resulting trust. How far is it appropriate to impose a resulting trust in every case where the defendant is unjustly enriched at the expense of a claimant?

3 In *Westdeutsche Landesbank Girozentrale v Islington LBC* [1996] AC 669 (HL) Lord Browne-Wilkinson explained that a resulting trust is imposed to reflect the presumed intention of the transferor in addition to the conscience of the recipient being affected. How satisfactory is the dual requirement of presumed intention and conscionability in explaining the existing case law where resulting trusts have been imposed?

4 In *Air Jamaica v Charlton* [1999] 1 WLR 1399 Millett LJ advocated that a resulting trust is imposed in circumstances where there is an absence of intention on the part of the transferor of property to pass a beneficial interest to the transferee. What are the advantages of this absence of intention formula?

Further reading

Birks, P. 'Equity, Conscience, and Unjust Enrichment' (1999) 23 University of Melbourne LR 1. Examines the role of equity and conscience in unjust enrichment cases and the imposition of a resulting trust to reverse that unjust enrichment.

Chambers, R. *Resulting Trusts* (1997). Provides a comprehensive analysis of the nature of resulting trusts and the grounds for the imposition of such trusts.

---

[62] [1996] AC 669 (HL).
[63] [1999] 1 WLR 1399.

Millett, P. 'Restitution and Constructive Trusts' (1998) LQR 399. Examines the role of constructive trusts and resulting trusts in effecting proprietary restitution, with emphasis on the circumstances which give rise to the imposition of such trusts in restitutionary claims.

Mitchell, C. (ed.) *Constructive and Resulting Trusts* (2010) (Oxford, Hart Publishing).

Swadling, W. 'A New Role for Resulting Trusts' (1996) 16 *Legal Studies* 110. Examines the role of resulting trusts in the law of restitution, with special reference to mistaken payments and failure of consideration.

Swadling, W. 'Explaining Resulting Trusts' (2008) LQR 72. Examines the nature of the presumptions made in order to give rise to a resulting trust, with specific reference to presumed resulting trusts.

Visit **www.mylawchamber.co.uk/panesar** to access study support resources including interactive multiple choice questions, practice exam questions with guidance, podcasts, weblinks, legal newsfeed all linked to the **Pearson eText** version of Exploring Equity and Trusts which you can **search**, **highlight** and **personalise** with your **own notes** and **bookmarks**.

Use Case Navigator to read in full some of the key cases referenced in this chapter with commentary and questions:

Re Vandervell's Trusts (No. 2) [1974] Ch. 269

Westdeutsche Landesbank Girozentrale v Islington LBC [1996] AC 699 (HL)

11

Resulting trusts, part II: Imposing resulting trusts

Learning objectives

After reading this chapter you should be able to:

→ explain the extent to which the traditional categories of automatic and resulting trust continue to apply in the modern law

→ explain the various situations in which a resulting trust is imposed by law

→ explain the operation of resulting trusts in cases of failure of a trust

→ explain the destination of surplus funds in the contexts of different types of trust

→ explain the destination of surplus funds in the case of unincorporated associations

→ explain the role of resulting trusts in voluntary transfers of property in the name of another and purchase in the name of another

→ understand the presumption of advancement and its contemporary significance

→ explain the extent to which illegality can be used to rebut the presumptions of resulting trust and advancement

→ understand how the resulting trust has played an important role in determining ownership rights in the family home.

Problems requiring a resulting trust solution

Many of the preceding chapters in this book have set the scene by highlighting a case which raises some of the legal issues which will be addressed in the chapter. This chapter takes a rather different approach in setting the scene. Given the diversity of the factual situations which will give rise to the imposition of a resulting trust, this chapter sets the scene by presenting a number of factual situations in which equity may be called upon to impose a resulting trust. Such factual situations will provide a useful starting point for an understanding of resulting trusts.

Situation One

Suppose that a settlor attempts to create a trust by appointing a trustee and transferring the £1000 to him. The settlor explains to the trustee that he will inform him later as to who the beneficiary of the trust is. The settlor fails to inform the trustee as to whom the £1000 was to benefit and a few weeks later dies. To whom does the £1000 belong?

Situation Two

Suppose that a settlor creates a trust by transferring £20,000 on trust to his trustee for the medical costs of his old aunt so long as she is in hospital. The aunt recovers and is discharged from the hospital. The trustee, however, has £12,000 of trust money which was not used for the aunt's medical costs. To whom does the £12,000 belong?

Situation Three

At the beginning of their studies in law, 50 students decided to the form 'Maitland Club'. The main objects of the club were to organise seminars and talks on equity. The club also organised a number of trips. Membership to the club could only be taken on payment of a fee. The club also received some money from the parents of the students by way of voluntary donations and one legacy of £1000. The students are now coming to graduation and wish to end the club. There are 30 members remaining and the club has £1200 in a bank. To whom does the £1200 belong?

Situation Four

Suppose that you secure employment with a firm. The employer provides you with the opportunity to join a private pension payable on your retirement. The scheme requires that you pay a sum of money from your wage every month into the scheme. The employer also agrees to pay a certain sum each year into the scheme so as to make sure that it provides sufficient cover when the employees retire. Your employer has informed you that the business will be closed and that the employees will receive their benefits from the scheme as explained in the scheme should the business cease trading. After payment of the agreed benefits, the pension scheme has a surplus of £200,000. To whom does the £200,000 belong?

Situation Five

Suppose that Michael transfers his house voluntarily in the name of his brother in fear that his new business may fail and his house may be at risk from the claims of creditors. The business, however, is a success, and he wishes his brother to re-convey the house to him. The brother refuses to do so. Michael commences proceedings in court to recover the house on the grounds that the only reason he transferred the house to his brother was to hide it from the creditors. To whom does the house belong? Should the court be concerned with Michael's motive in transferring the house to his brother?

Situation Six
Veronica and David, an unmarried couple, have decided to purchase a house to live in. The legal title is taken in the name of Veronica despite the fact that David contributed £30,000 to the initial deposit price. Do you think David has an interest in the house, and if so, how does it belong to him?

A common feature in all of the situations above is the 'to whom does it belong' question. The answers to these questions can only be arrived at by understanding the equitable rules relating to resulting trusts. This chapter examines the imposition of a resulting trust in a number of diverse situations.

Introduction

VISIT CASE NAVIGATOR

The previous chapter explored the nature of a resulting trust and examined the theoretical grounds for the imposition of a resulting trust. It was observed in that chapter that many theories have been advanced for the grounds on which a court imposes a resulting trust. The prevailing view in the case law is that provided by the House of Lords in *Westdeutsche Landesbank Girozentrale v Islington LBC*,[1] where it was held that a resulting trust responds to the presumed intentions of the person in whose favour the resulting trust is imposed. Additionally, the House of Lords explained that, in order for a resulting trust to be imposed, it was crucial that the conscience of the recipient of the property be affected, in other words, that the recipient be under the knowledge that the property in his hands was not intended for his benefit but was to be held for the transferor. Subsequent analysis in the Privy Council by Millett LJ in *Air Jamaica v Charlton*[2] has adopted a somewhat different and more attractive ground for the imposition of a resulting trust. Millett LJ advocated that a resulting trust responds to an absence of intention on the part of the transferor of property to pass a beneficial interest to the recipient. Although this approach is yet to be fully endorsed by a decision of the Supreme Court, it was explained in the previous chapter that this formulation had much to commend it as it best explained the decided cases. This purpose of this chapter is to explore the factual situations in which resulting trusts have been imposed by the courts.

Failure of the trust

A resulting trust will be imposed in circumstances where an express trust fails. An express trust may fail for a number of reasons, the most simple of them being where a settlor fails to identify the beneficiaries or defines them with some meaning which is not understood by the trustee or the court. A trust will also fail if it contains some element of

---

[1] [1996] AC 669 (HL).
[2] [1999] 1 WLR 1399.

illegality or is otherwise contrary to public policy.[3] The following are some of the circumstances where a resulting trust has been imposed on grounds of failure of the trust.

Failure to declare the beneficial interest

APPLYING THE LAW

Suppose that Adrian transfers certain property to his solicitor on the understanding that it is to be held upon trust for certain individuals. Adrian tells his solicitor that the identity of those individuals will become apparent soon. Adrian never informs his solicitor of the identity of the beneficiaries and dies in the meantime.

What happens with the property in the hands of the solicitor?

Where a settlor attempts to declare an express trust by identifying the trustee and the trust property, but fails to identify the beneficiary of the trust, a resulting trust will be imposed in his favour. If the settlor is dead, the property will be held on resulting trust for those entitled to his estate on his death. A failure to declare the beneficial interest was neatly illustrated in the seminal case of **Vandervell v IRC**.[4] The decision in this case was analysed in more detail in Chapter 5 in the context of the formal requirements needed for a trust. You will recall from Chapter 5 that the case involved a tax-saving scheme devised by Vandervell. On the facts of the case, Vandervell, a wealthy businessman, directed his nominee (National Provincial Bank) to transfer shares held by them for him to the Royal College of Surgeons whose intention it was to endow a chair of pharmacology. Vandervell agreed that the College could have ownership of his shares in his company and use the dividend money to finance the chair. It was also agreed that once the dividends had paid for the purpose of endowing the chair of pharmacology, the College would give an option to purchase the shares for a nominal sum of £5000. The bank duly transferred the legal title to the shares to the College which granted an option to purchase the shares. The option was transferred to the Vandervell Trust Company without any instructions from Vandervell as to whose benefit it was to be held for.

The Inland Revenue claimed surtax from Vandervell on the dividends declared between 1957 and 1961 (this being the period under which the shares remained with the College) on the grounds that Vandervell had not completely divested himself of his beneficial ownership in the shares, even though the legal title to them had been transferred to the college. Two arguments were presented by the Inland Revenue in support of their claim. The argument which succeeded in making a case for liability for surtax related to the grant of the option to purchase the shares which had been transferred to the Vandervell Trust Company. The Revenue claimed that since Vandervell had transferred the option to the trust company without specifying who the benefactor of the option was, the option was held on resulting trust for Vandervell himself. The majority of the House of Lords held that the option was indeed held on resulting trust for Vandervell, who therefore retained some beneficial interest in the shares and therefore was liable to pay surtax on those shares.[5] Lord Wilberforce explained that 'the option is vested in the

---

[3] Illegality and public policy issues were analysed in detail in Chapter 9.
[4] [1967] 2 AC 291.
[5] See Income Taxes Act 1952, s. 415; the current legislation is ICTA 1988 ss. 684, 685.

trustee company as a trustee on trusts, not defined at the time, possibly to be defined later. But the equitable, or beneficial interest, cannot remain in the air: the consequence in law must be that it remains in the settlor.'[6] The issue of liability for surtax was therefore clearly decided on this basis. The decision in **Vandervell v IRC**[7] is perhaps better analysed with the line of reasoning adopted by Lord Millett in **Air Jamaica v Charlton**[8] where, as already observed in Chapter 10, his Lordship explained that a resulting trust is imposed in circumstances where a person transferring property to another has an absence of intention of benefiting the transferee. In **Vandervell** the option was transferred to the trust company with no intention on the part of Vandervell to confer upon it a beneficial interest in the option to the trust company.

Subsequent failure of a trust

APPLYING THE LAW

Suppose that Barry transfers his holiday home in Scotland upon trust for his son and his daughter-in-law for a period of 10 years. One of the conditions of the trust is that his son and his daughter-in-law will only be entitled under the trust so long as they remain married. After two years of setting up the trust, Barry's son and his wife split up. His son is cohabiting with another lady and wishes to use the holiday home.

Can he still do this?

A trust may well be created properly by complying with the formal and substantive requirements of trust law; however, it may subsequently fail for one reason or another. Most typically, a subsequent failure of the trust will occur where the underlying purpose of the trust has failed, or where the very reason for creating the trust no longer exists. The matter is neatly illustrated by the decision in **Re Ames' Settlement**[9] where Louis Ames created a marriage settlement in 1908 in favour of his son and daughter-in-law. The terms of the marriage settlement were to the effect that a sum of £10,000 be provided by Louis Ames to be held on trust, the income to be paid to his son during his life and thereafter to his son's wife for her life or until her remarriage, the remainder to be given to any issue of the marriage. Although the son and his wife lived together until 1926, the wife petitioned for the marriage to be nullified on the grounds of the son's incapacity to consummate the marriage. A decree of nullity was duly granted by the Supreme Court of Kenya with the consequence that the marriage was void *ab initio*. On the death of the son, the question arose as to what should happen with the £10,000 which was initially provided by Louis Ames. The court held that, since the marriage was void, there had been a total failure of consideration and as a result the money was held on resulting trust for Louis Ames' estate.

A somewhat similar result was arrived at in **Re Cochrane**[10] where the purpose of a marriage settlement failed as a result of the wife separating from her husband. On the facts, a husband and wife on their marriage both brought property of their own into the

---

[6] [1967] 2 AC 291 at 329.
[7] [1967] 2 AC 291.
[8] [1999] 1 WLR 1399.
[9] [1946] Ch. 217.
[10] [1955] Ch. 309.

marriage. The terms of the marriage settlement provided that the income was to be paid to the wife so long as she remained married to her husband. The settlement further provided that should either husband or wife die, the entire fund subject to the marriage settlement should vest in the survivor absolutely. The wife left the husband who died shortly thereafter. The question arose as to whether the wife was entitled to the fund subject to the marriage settlement even though she had left her husband. There was nothing in the terms of the trust instrument which covered this eventuality. Harman J could not find any construction in the marriage settlement which could determine whether the wife was entitled to the entire fund subject to the settlement. As a result of this he held that the fund was to be held on resulting trust in proportion to the shares contributed by the husband and wife. Since the wife had left her husband, the husband's share passed to his estate.

Failure due to non-compliance with a substantive or formal requirement

A resulting trust will be imposed in circumstances where a settlor attempts to create an express trust which fails to comply with some substantive or formal requirement needed to create the trust. There are many examples where a trust may fail to comply with the formal and substantive requirements needed for a trust. In this section a few examples can be given to illustrate the general position. It is trite law that a trust must be created for a human beneficiary, which is otherwise known as the beneficiary principle.[11] Where a private trust is not declared in favour of a human beneficiary the property will result back to the settlor or his estate. For example, in *Re Astor's Settlement Trusts*[12] a trust was created whose objective was to preserve the independence of the *Observer* newspaper. The settlement, which was made in 1945, contained a provision instructing trustees to apply the income from a fund for a number of non-charitable purposes which included, among other things, the 'maintenance . . . of good understanding . . . between nations', 'the preservation of the independence and integrity of newspapers'. The court held that this trust was void on grounds of the beneficiary principle and the property resulted back to the settlor's estate.

In the context of charitable trusts, a resulting trust will be imposed where a settlor attempts to declare a charitable trust which, however, includes non-charitable beneficiaries as well as charitable. It will be seen in Chapter 22 that a valid charitable trust will only be recognised if it is exclusively charitable. Where a purported charitable trust has the potential to benefit non-charitable objects it will be declared void, with the consequence that the property results back to the settlor or testator's estate. For example, in *Morice* v *Bishop of Durham*[13] a gift of residue was given to the Bishop of Durham for the benefit of such objects of benevolence and liberality as the Bishop of Durham shall approve of. The court declined to enforce the trust on the grounds that the words 'benevolence and liberality' were much wider than charity. Similarly, in *Re Diplock*[14] a trust created for charitable and benevolent purposes was held to be void, with the consequence that the property transferred to the trustee was held under a resulting trust for the testator's estate.

---

[11] See Chapter 8.
[12] [1952] Ch. 534.
[13] (1804) 9 Ves. 399.
[14] [1948] Ch. 465.

Resulting trusts and Quistclose trusts

APPLYING THE LAW

Harnek is a property developer who buys and sells properties after renovating them. Recently he has experienced some financial problems and is in need of money to continue buying and selling properties. His bank has refused him a loan on the grounds that he is already quite heavily overdrawn. Harnek approaches Quick Money Ltd who are happy to lend him £300,000, but only on the condition that the money be used for the purposes of property development. Quick Money advance the money to Harnek who agrees that the money will only be used for property development. Harnek's solicitor gives an undertaking that Harnek will only use the money for property development. Harnek has been declared bankrupt and none of the £300,000 has been used. His creditors wish to use the £300,000 in his account to meet his liabilities towards them.

To whom does the £300,000 belong?

**VISIT CASE
NAVIGATOR**

In Chapter 3 it was observed that it is quite possible for a loan and trust relationship to coexist. The so-called 'Quistclose' trust, taking its name from the House of Lords' decision in ***Barclays Bank Ltd v Quistclose Investments Ltd***,[15] recognised that a lender could advance money to a borrower whilst at the same time having a resulting trust in his favour should the purpose of the loan fail. Before the decision of the House of Lords in ***Twinsectra Ltd v Yardley***[16] it was appropriate to analyse the imposition of a resulting trust in the context of such 'Quistclose' trusts under the heading of failure of the trust. The reason for this was simply down to the decision of the House of Lords in ***Barclays Bank Ltd v Quistclose Investments Ltd*** in which the general consensus was that a resulting trust was imposed in favour of the lender once the purpose of the loan had failed. You will recall that on the facts of the case Rolls Razor Ltd, who owed a large amount of money to Barclays Bank, borrowed some £209,719 from Quistclose in order to pay dividends which it had declared on its shares. The money was paid into a separate account at Barclays Bank on the understanding that it was only to be used for the specified purpose of paying the dividends. Barclays Bank had full knowledge of the arrangement between Rolls Razor Ltd and Quistclose. Before the dividends had been paid, Rolls Razor Ltd went into liquidation and the question arose whether Barclays Bank could use the money in the separate account to off-set the overdraft that Rolls Razor Ltd had with it, or whether the money belonged to Quistclose on the basis that it was held on trust by Rolls Razor Ltd for them. The House of Lords unanimously held that a loan and trust relationship could coexist. Lord Wilberforce, delivering the unanimous decision of the court, held that the money in the separate account was impressed with a trust in favour of Quistclose as soon as the failure of the primary purpose of the trust occurred.[17] Furthermore, since Barclays Bank had notice of the trust arrangement they were clearly

---

[15] [1970] AC 567.
[16] [2002] 2 All ER 377.
[17] *Ibid.* at 581–2.

bound by the trust in favour of Quistclose.[18] More recently, in **Soutzos v Asombang**[19] the High Court has again emphasised that the lender must show that the money was not freely disposable by the borrower. If there is evidence to suggest that the money is freely disposable then there can be no finding of a Quistclose trust.

Although the existence of a loan and trust relationship was firmly recognised by the House of Lords in **Barclays Bank Ltd v Quistclose Investments Ltd**[20] the main problem with the so-called Quistclose trust related to two things. Firstly, what were the exact terms of the trust, and secondly, what was the nature of the trust in question? These matters fell to be decided by the House of Lords in **Twinsectra Ltd v Yardley**[21] where, until that decision, it was generally understood that the exact terms of the trust depended on the nature of the agreement between the lender and the borrower. It is only from this agreement that the terms of the trust can be construed. In some cases the terms of the trust are to the effect that the money is given to the borrower, who is to hold such money on a primary trust for the purpose of the loan and then on a secondary trust for the lender should the primary trust fail on grounds of some impossibility. This is exactly what happened in **Barclays Bank Ltd v Quistclose Investments Ltd** where the House of Lords held that the loan money had been received by Rolls Razor Ltd on primary trust to pay the dividends to its shareholders and that, in the event of failure of such payment, the money was to be held on a secondary trust for Quistclose Investments Ltd.

The idea that the loan money was held under a primary and then a secondary trust was rejected by Millett LJ in **Twinsectra Ltd v Yardley**.[22] The House of Lords held that the money advanced under a loan for a specific purpose was held under a resulting trust for the lender until such time as it was used for the purposes of the loan. On the facts of the case, Twinsectra Ltd loaned money to a property dealer on the undertaking by the property dealer's solicitors that the money would only be used for property transactions and no other purposes. In breach of this undertaking, the solicitors, at the request of the property dealer, transferred the money to another solicitor who transferred the money at the request of the dealer for purposes other than property transactions. Twinsectra commenced proceedings against the property dealer as well as all of the solicitors involved in the dealings with the loan monies. The claim against the solicitors who had undertaken to make sure that the money would only be used for property transactions was one of breach of trust. As for the solicitor who transferred the loan money for purposes other than that to do with property transaction, the action was one for dishonest assistance in a breach of trust.[23] The success of both of these actions depended crucially on whether there was a trust in favour of Twinsectra. Following the decision in **Barclays Bank Ltd v Quistclose Investments Ltd**[24] the House of Lords accepted that a trust did arise in favour of Twinsectra. The House of Lords then proceeded to examine the nature of the trust

---

[18] The decision of the House of Lords in *Barclays Bank Ltd v Quistclose Investments Ltd* was generally accepted as appropriate by other cases and also academic writings. In *Carreras Rothmans Ltd v Freeman Mathews Treasure Ltd* [1985] Ch. 207 where monies were advanced by one company to another for a specified purpose and to be kept in a separate account, the court explained that 'equity fastens on the conscience of the person who receives from another property transferred for a specific purpose only and not, therefore, for the recipient's own purpose, so that such person shall not be permitted to treat the property as his own or to use it for other than the purpose stated', at p. 222. See Chapter 3 for more detail.

[19] [2010] EWHC 842.

[20] [1970] AC 567.

[21] [2002] 2 All ER 377; see S. Panesar, 'A Loan Subject to a Trust and Dishonest Assistance by a Third Party' (2003) JIBL 18(1), 9.

[22] [2002] 2 All ER 377.

[23] See generally Chapter 14. A person who dishonestly assists in a breach of trust will be liable as a constructive trustee to replace the loss.

[24] [1970] AC 567.

arising in favour of the lender by exploring the possible locations where the beneficial interest in the loan money lay during the time when the money was in the hands of the borrower. Millett LJ identified four possible locations where the beneficial interest in the loan money could exist during the time the loan money was not being used for the purpose for which it was given. His Lordship explained that the beneficial interest could lie with the lender; the borrower; the persons for whom the loan money was taken out, or simply lie in suspense. In coming to a conclusion, Millett LJ explained that, until such time as the loan money was not being used for the purposes of the loan, the beneficial ownership in the money belonged to lender. In his Lordship's words, 'this is the only analysis which is consistent both with orthodox trust law and commercial reality'.[25]

There is much to be said for the line of reasoning taken by Millett LJ in *Twinsectra* simply because it is the only line of reasoning which puts the Quistclose trust comfortably within trust law principles. In so far as the borrower is concerned, there is no intention on the part of the lender that the money should be freely at his disposal. In so far as the intended beneficiary of the purpose of the loan is concerned, it cannot be said that there is a trust in all cases or that there was even an intention on the part of the lender that the advancement of the loan money was directly for the benefit of the beneficiaries of the loan. In some cases such as *Twinsectra* itself the loan money may not be for human beneficiaries. The absence of a human beneficiary would be fatal to the finding of a trust relationship. However, even where there are human beneficiaries who are to benefit from the loan money, for example like the shareholders in *Quistclose*, it is questionable whether it was the lender's intention to create a trust in their favour or whether the real intention was to help the borrower avoid financial problems which might in turn protect the lender who may have a vested interest in the borrower's financial position.

The Court of Appeal in *Twinsectra* was clearly of the opinion that the beneficial interest under a Quistclose trust remained in suspense until the stated purpose of the loan had been carried out or had otherwise failed. This view was rejected in the House of Lords on the grounds that it did not fit comfortably with established principles of equity: in particular, the principle that 'equity abhors a beneficial vacuum' and that the beneficial interest in property must belong to some person at all relevant times. Millett LJ explained that a resulting trust arose in favour of the lender as soon as the loan was made to the borrower. The basis for the imposition of such a trust was on grounds that the lender had an absence of intention that the loan money should belong to any other person. This absence of intention to pass the beneficial interest to any other person meant that it belonged under a resulting trust for the lender.[26]

The decision in *Barclays Bank Ltd v Quistclose Investments Ltd*[27] was applied in *Cooper v Powerhouse Ltd (in liquidation)*[28] where a company received a sum of money from an employee in order to make payment to a finance company in order to discharge the instalments due on a car purchased from a car dealer. The employee had been provided with a Mercedes car which had been purchased by way of a finance agreement with a supplier. The instalments were to be paid by the employers by way of deductions from the employee's salary. When the employee resigned, it was agreed between the employer and the employee that he could purchase the car by discharging the monies due to the car supplier. The employee transferred the monies due to the supplier to his employers who would then make payment on his behalf. Before the payment was made

---

[25] [2002] 1 All ER 377 at 399.
[26] The absence of intention approach was advocated by Millett LJ in the Privy Council in *Air Jamaica v Charlton* [1999] 1 WLR 1399.
[27] [1970] AC 567.
[28] [2008] BCC 588.

by the employers, the employers went into liquidation and the liquidator argued that the employee was an unsecured creditor in respect of the money he had given to his former employers to discharge the instalments due on his company car. The question before Evans-Lombe J was whether the employee was an unsecured creditor or whether the employer held the money under a trust for a purpose, and that, the purpose having failed, the money was held under a Quistclose-type trust for the employee. The court held that the money advanced by the employee to his former employers was indeed transferred, subject to a purpose. The purpose of the loan having failed, the money was held on trust for the employee. The court held that it was not necessary that the money had not been paid into a separate account. It was important, however, that the employers know that the money was advanced for a specific purpose and not for the general availability of the employer. In the course of his judgment, Evans-Lombe J, after a comprehensive review of the principles surrounding Quistclose trusts by Millett J in **Twinsectra Ltd v Yardley**,[29] explained that:

> it seems to me that what emerges from this passage in Lord Millett's speech is that whether or not money has been paid subject to a purpose trust is a question of fact. If a purpose trust is to be established, it is necessary for the payer to show that the arrangement pursuant to which the payment was made defined the purpose for which it was made in such a way that it was understood by the recipient that it was not at his free disposal . . . I have found that Mr Cooper's [the employee] payment was made to the company subject to a purpose trust and that accordingly the company owed him fiduciary duties in respect of it. It follows that rules of equitable tracing apply.[30]

Unexhausted funds

A resulting trust will be implied by the courts where a trust comes to an end with a surplus fund remaining. On a very basic level, if a settlor creates a trust for the maintenance of a child until attaining the age of 18 years and the child attains the age of 18 with a surplus fund held by the trustees, the trust comes to an end with a resulting trust of the surplus fund in favour of the settlor. Despite this apparent simplicity the matter is more complicated in practice and the important question is whether the settlor has indeed divested himself of any interest in the surplus fund. The law in this area is further complicated by the fact that the contexts in which the question of surplus funds arises can be quite diverse with different outcomes. It will be seen in the following sections that the policy considerations can be quite different in each of these different contexts.

The maintenance of individuals

APPLYING THE LAW

Victor, who is a wealthy businessman, transfers £80,000 on trust to his trustees for the education of his brother's children. Victor has no children of his own and has always been fond of his brother's children. The children have all graduated from university and are in full-time employment. The trustees of the trust have a surplus of £20,000 from the trust.

To whom does it belong?

---

[29] [2002] 2 All ER 377.
[30] [2008] BCC 588 at paras 15 and 25.

A trust may be created for a beneficiary in order to provide for some specific purpose. For example, a settlor may provide a sum of money for the education of his nieces. When the purpose of the trust comes to an end, for example the education of the nieces, the question arises as to the destination of the surplus fund. Should the fund to be held on resulting trust for the settlor? The case law in this area is not easily reconcilable as some cases have interpreted a surplus fund as belonging to the beneficiary, on the grounds that the settlor intended to make an absolute gift in the first place. Any reference to the purpose of the trust, for example the education of the beneficiary, has been interpreted as evidence of the motive of the gift with no trust arising in the first place. On the other hand, some cases have decided that the surplus fund belongs to the settlor under a resulting trust, on the grounds the settlor never intended the beneficiary to become the absolute owner of the property transferred on trust for it. For example, in **Re Abbott Fund Trusts**[31] a sum of money was collected mainly through subscriptions from the public in order to be applied for the relief of two ladies who were deaf and dumb. There was no provision made as to what should happen with the £366 surplus fund which remained unexhausted after the death of the two ladies. The question before the court was whether the fund belonged to the survivor of the two ladies and therefore vested in their personal representative or whether the surplus belonged to the subscribers under a resulting trust. It was argued on behalf of the personal representative of the two ladies that the fund belonged to him absolutely, on the grounds that the monies advanced by the various subscribers were intended as absolute gifts and that such subscribers never intended to recall such money advanced to the fund. On the other hand, it was argued on behalf of the subscribers that the surplus was held on resulting trust as it was never intended for the benefit of the relatives of the two ladies. Stirling J held that the surplus fund was indeed held on resulting trust for the subscribers. In the course of his judgment he explained that 'the question is whether, so far as this fund has not been applied for their benefit, there is a resulting trust of it for the subscribers. I cannot believe that it was ever intended to become the absolute property of the ladies so that they should be in a position to demand a transfer of it to themselves, or so that if they became bankrupt the trustee in the bankruptcy should be able to claim it.'[32]

The decision in **Re Abbott Fund Trusts** was not followed some five years later in **Re Andrew's Trust**[33] where friends of a deceased clergyman subscribed to a fund for the education of his children. The terms of the trust made it clear that the money was not for the exclusive use of any one of the children nor for the equal division amongst them; however, the fund could be used for their education. When all of the children had grown up, the question arose as to what should happen with the surplus funds. The court held that there was no resulting trust in favour of the subscribers of the fund and that the surplus fund should be distributed equally amongst the children. In coming to this decision Kekewich J explained that the facts of the present case were very different from the facts that arose in **Re Abbott Fund Trusts**. In particular, Kekewich J paid significant attention to the fact that in **Re Abbott Fund Trusts** the two ladies had died and that no one would ever have intended that the surplus fund was given to them absolutely. On the present facts he explained that the children were still alive and this made a big difference. In coming to the conclusion that the children were entitled to the surplus, the judge explained that the gift was to be construed as an absolute gift and the purpose of the gift, that is the education, was only the motive behind making the gift. In the course of

---

[31] [1900] 2 Ch. 326.
[32] [1900] 2 Ch. 326 at 330.
[33] [1905] 2 Ch. 48.

judgment Kekewich J referred to an earlier decision of Page Wood VC in *Re Sanderson's Trust*[34] where the Vice Chancellor explained that:

> there are two classes of cases between which the general distinction is sufficiently clear, although the precise line of demarcation is occasionally somewhat difficult to ascertain. If a gross sum be given, or if the whole income of the property be given, and a special purpose be assigned for that gift, this Court always regards the gift as absolute, and the purpose merely as the motive of the gift, and therefore holds that the gift takes effect as to the whole sum or the whole income, as the case may be.[35]

The decision in *Re Andrew's Trust*[36] was followed by the Court of Appeal *Re Osoba*[37] where a testator left property on trust for the maintenance of his wife, his mother and for the education of his daughter up to university grade. When the testator's mother had died and his daughter had completed her education, the question arose as to what should happen with the surplus funds in the trust. When the case was heard the testator's wife had also died and the question was whether the daughter was entitled to the surplus fund or whether it was held on resulting trust for the testator's estate. The Court of Appeal held that the testator had intended to make an absolute gift to his wife, mother and his daughter, and the maintenance of his mother and the education of the daughter were merely motives behind making the gift. The fact that his wife and mother had died meant that the daughter was absolutely entitled to the fund.

It is difficult to reconcile the decisions in *Re Andrew's Trust*[38] and *Re Osoba*[39] with the decision in *Re Abbott Fund Trusts*.[40] There appear to be two possibilities where a surplus fund remains in the context of these maintenance cases. Either the court will impose a resulting trust in favour of the settlor or subscribers of the funds or it may hold that the fund is to be construed as an absolute gift in the first instance with the purpose of the fund being construed as merely the motive of making the gift in the first place. The cases do, however, illustrate that where the beneficiaries of the fund are still alive, the court is more inclined to interpret the fund as being given outright as a gift and the purpose of the fund being the motive. This was clearly apparent in the judgment of Megarry VC at first instance in *Re Osoba* where he explained that:

> if a trust is constituted for the assistance of certain persons by certain stated means there is a sharp distinction between cases where the beneficiaries have died and cases where they are still living. If they are dead, the court is ready to hold that there is a resulting trust for the donors; for the major purpose of the trust, that of providing help and benefit for the beneficiaries, comes to an end when the beneficiaries are all dead and so are beyond earthly help, whether by the stated means or otherwise. But if the beneficiaries are still living, the major purpose of providing help and benefit for the beneficiaries can still be carried out even after the stated means have all been accomplished, and so the court will be ready to treat the stated means as being merely indicative and not restrictive.[41]

---

[34] (1857) 3 K & J 497.
[35] (1857) 3 K & J 497 at 503.
[36] [1905] 2 Ch. 48.
[37] [1979] 1 WLR 247.
[38] [1905] 2 Ch. 48.
[39] [1979] 1 WLR 247.
[40] [1900] 2 Ch. 326.
[41] [1978] 1 WLR 791 at 796.

Disaster funds

APPLYING THE LAW

As a result of the recent torrential rain and the consequent flooding, the Mayor of the town has set up a fund to provide relief to those individuals who have been affected by the flooding. The fund was raised by a number of donations by people living in the town as well as street collections. In addition, the Mayor organised a town party where individuals could buy tickets for raffles and sweepstakes and enter the town park at a cost of £5 per person to see various entertainments. The floods have now gone and the residents are resuming normal life. There is a surplus fund of £20,000 held by the treasurers and they seek your advice as to whom the surplus belongs.

The question of ownership of unexhausted funds has commonly arisen in the context of disaster appeals. The contributions towards such disaster appeals may come from a wide variety of sources, for example, legacies left by persons in their will, anonymous street collections, as well as money raised by various forms of entertainment. Furthermore, those persons organising a disaster fund or any other fund may form some sort of club or association whereby members contribute to the fund to further its purposes. When the monies raised for such disaster funds is no loner needed or where the funds of a club are being wound up, the question will arise as to what is to happen with the surplus funds. Is the imposition of the resulting trust the most effective means of determining the ownership of the surplus fund or are there some other means by which the fund is to be distributed? This section explores the development of the case law in the context of the funds for the relief of disasters. The following section looks at the distribution of surplus funds where there is an unincorporated association such as a club. It will be seen that in the context of an unincorporated association a rather different set of rules will apply to determine the ownership of surplus funds.

Before embarking on a discussion of the case law, it is important to have reference to two important doctrines which feature in many of the decided cases. The first doctrine is that of *bona vacantia*, which basically holds that undisposed property which does not belong to anyone will belong to the Crown.[42] The doctrine is commonly employed where a person dies intestate and without any successor to inherit his property. Such property will belong to the Crown. The second doctrine is the cy-près doctrine, which operates in the context of charitable trusts.[43] The cy-près doctrine operates to apply a surplus fund in the context of a charitable trust to purposes which are as close as possible to the original purpose set up by the settlor or a testator. Where the conditions are satisfied for the application of cy-près, the doctrine will operate to displace a resulting trust of the surplus fund and it will be applied to some purpose as near as possible to the original one.

One of the first cases to decide the ownership of a surplus fund in the context of a disaster appeal is *Re Gillingham Bus Disaster Fund*.[44] The facts concerned an appeal by the mayors of three towns to raise money as a result of an accident in which a number of marine cadets were killed and injured in a road traffic accident. The purpose of the fund,

---

[42] Such ownerless property will vest in the Treasury Solicitor.
[43] For a detailed analysis of this doctrine, see Chapter 23.
[44] [1958] Ch. 300.

as advertised in a national newspaper, was towards 'defraying the funeral expenses, caring for the boys who may be disabled, and then to such worthy cause or causes in memory of the boys who lost their lives, as the Mayors may determine'. A sum of £9000 was raised through contributions from identifiable individuals as well as a significant amount of anonymous street collections. The trustees of the fund spent over £2000 in meeting the purposes set out for the fund and then sought directions from the court as to what should be done with the surplus money. There were three possible ways in which the ownership of the surplus fund could be resolved. The first one considered by the court was whether the fund could be applied cy-près. Harman J explained that the fund could not be applied cy-près because in order for that doctrine to operate the fund had to have been charitable in the first place. The present fund was not charitable in nature for the reason that it could be applied for both charitable and non-charitable purposes.[45] This left two possibilities: either the surplus fund went *bona vacantia* or was held under a resulting trust for the persons making the contributions.

Harman J rejected that the surplus fund should be applied *bona vacantia*. In his judgment he concluded that the donors could not have been regarded as having parted outright with their money. It was argued on behalf of the Crown that, whereas it might be possible to impute an intention on the part of those donors who had made large contributions that they did not intend to part outright with their money, such an intention could not be imputed in the case where a person put money in a collection box. In the context of a collection box, the intention of the person contributing is to make an outright gift with no intention for its return should the purpose of the collection fail. Harman J disagreed and held that a resulting trust be applied to all parts of the surplus and it did not matter whether some of the donors made significant contributions whilst others merely made smaller ones. In the course of his judgment he said: 'I see no reason myself to suppose that the small giver who is anonymous has any wider intention than the large giver who can be named. They all give for the one object. If they can be found by inquiry the resulting trust can be executed in their favour. If they cannot I do not see how the money could then . . . change its destination and become bona vacantia.'[46]

Whilst the decision in **Re Gillingham Bus Disaster Fund**[47] applies the resulting trust solution to all surplus funds of a disaster appeal, it is not without practical problems. It is not entirely clear how the resulting trust solution can be applied to those contributing to the collection boxes. There appear to be two major hurdles which prevent the resulting trust from working in that context. The first is the question of determining the exact contribution of the person paying his money into the box. The second is identifying and locating the very persons who made the contributions so as to give them a right to claim back their contribution. In respect of the latter, Harman J explained that it did not matter that the donors could not be found as the money could be paid into court, giving the donors a right to recover it should they appear.

The decision in **Re Gillingham Bus Disaster Fund** was not followed by Goff J in **Re West Sussex Constabulary Benevolent (1930) Fund Trust**[48] where members of the West Sussex Constabulary subscribed to a fund in order to provide for the widows and dependants of deceased members of the constabulary. In 1968 the West Sussex Constabulary

---

[45] A valid charitable trust will only exist if the property subject to it is used exclusively for charitable purposes; see Chapter 19.
[46] [1958] Ch. 300 at 314.
[47] [1958] Ch. 300.
[48] [1971] Ch. 1.

was amalgamated with another constabulary and the question arose as to what should happen with the surplus funds held by the trustees of the fund. The funds came from four distinct sources, namely, contributions from past and present members; collection boxes, entertainments, raffles and sweepstakes; and finally donations and legacies. The question before the court was whether these different contributions were to be held on resulting trust for the donors or whether they were to be applied *bona vacantia*. The court held that, except for the donations and legacies which belonged to the subscribers under a resulting trust, everything else went to the Crown *bona vacantia*. With regard to the contributions made by past and present members Goff J explained that these contributions were made pursuant to a contract and not a trust. By making the contributions to the club they had received all the benefits of being members of the club. As regards the entertainments, raffles and sweepstakes, Goff J explained that these also were governed by contract. For example, a person buying a raffle ticket or a ticket for some other entertainment had received what he had bargained for. Furthermore, the money raised by such raffles and entertainment took the form of a profit rather than a direct contribution to the fund by the person entering a raffle or buying some form of entertainment. On this basis these surplus funds belonged to the Crown. Finally in relation to the street collections, Goff J held that it was impossible to treat such donations as being held on trust for the person making them. Goff J relied on the words of P.O. Lawrence J in **Re Welsh Hospital (Netley) Fund:**[49]

> So far as regards the contributors to entertainments, street collections etc., I have no hesitation in holding that they must be taken to have parted with their money out-and-out. It is inconceivable that any person paying for a concert ticket or placing a coin in a collecting-box presented to him in the street should have intended that any part of the money so contributed should be returned to him when the immediate object for which the concert was given or the collection made had come to an end. To draw such an inference would be absurd on the face of it.

The surplus funds of unincorporated associations

APPLYING THE LAW

Sometime back in 1974 Jack decided to form a club which would promote motorbike racing. In order to start the club, Jack and a number of his friends contributed to the purchase of land in Kenilworth which was to be used to promote the purposes of the club. The land was conveyed in Jack's name; however, the understanding was that it belonged to the club. Over time a considerable number of members joined the club, each having to pay an initial subscription of £30 and then a further £5 each month. In return for their contribution, each member received a monthly update on motor racing as well as unlimited use of the club's racing facilities, which included a racing track and racing cars. The club also received a number of voluntary donations, in some cases of substantial amounts.

Recently there have been complaints about the mismanagement of the club and some members are seeking your legal advice as to their rights, if any, in the club.

---

[49] [1921] 1 Ch. 655 at 659.

The decision in **Re West Sussex Constabulary Benevolent (1930) Fund Trust**[50] illustrates that a surplus fund can often arise in the context of an unincorporated association. You will recall from Chapter 8 that an unincorporated association consists of a group of people connected with some common purpose. An unincorporated association does not have a separate legal entity and as such cannot hold property in its own right. It has been described by Lawton LJ in **Conservative and Unionist Central Office v Burrell**[51] in the following terms: 'Two or more persons bound together for one or more common purpose, not being business purposes, by mutual undertakings each having mutual duties and obligations, in an organisation which has rules which identify in whom control of it and its funds rests and on what terms . . .'[52] Good examples of unincorporated associations include social and sports clubs. When addressing the question as to who is entitled to the surplus funds of an unincorporated association which is being dissolved, there have been three principal approaches taken in the case law:

1 *Bona vacantia*

2 Resulting trust for members

3 Existing members on a contractual basis.

The early case law decided that the surplus funds belonged to the Crown on the basis of *bona vacantia*.[53] The matter is neatly illustrated by the decision in **Cunnack v Edwards**[54] where a society to provide annuities for the widows of its members was set up in 1810. All members of the society had died by 1879 and the last widow entitled to an annuity died in 1892. A surplus of some £1250 remained when the purposes of the society had been exhausted, and the question before the court was whether the personal representatives of the last surviving members were entitled to it. The Court of Appeal held that there was no resulting trust in favour of the personal representatives of the last surviving members. The Court of Appeal proceeded to deal with the matter on the basis that each of the members had contributed their money in return for the protection that was afforded to their widows. On this basis, the money contributed by each member had been abandoned in favour of the society and now belonged to the Crown. The decision in **Cunnack v Edwards** was recently considered by the High Court in **Hanchett-Stamford v Attorney General**[55] where Lewison J explained that the decision rested on the fact that the money contributed by each member was to pay pensions to the widows of the deceased members and not to be held for the benefit of the members themselves. Furthermore, he explained that on the facts of **Cunnack v Edwards** there were no surviving members when the case came before the court and the question whether the members were entitled to the fund did not arise.

The *bona vacantia* approach was rejected some four years later and replaced by a resulting trust approach in favour of members who had contributed to the funds of an unincorporated association. A good illustration of the resulting trust approach is the decision of the court in **Re Printers and Transferrers Society**[56] where a society was set up to provide support for its members, in particular, ensuring that they received

---

[50] [1971] Ch. 1.
[51] [1982] 1 WLR 522.
[52] [1982] 1 WLR 522 at 525.
[53] See S. Panesar, 'Surplus Funds and Unincorporated Associations' (2008) T&T Vol. 14 Issue 10 at 698.
[54] [1896] 2 Ch. 679.
[55] [2009] Ch. 173; this decision in considered in more detail below.
[56] [1899] 2 Ch. 184.

reasonable remuneration for their labour and that they were provided for in times of lockouts and strikes. The level of payment depended on the amount of service provided by each member. Furthermore, the contributions between printers and transferrers differed, with the consequence that the printers received more benefits than the transferrers. When the society was dissolved the question arose as to the entitlement to the surplus fund which stood at some £1000. There was nothing in the rules of the society which covered the distribution of the surplus on dissolution of the society. The court held that the surplus belonged to the members on a resulting trust in proportion of their contributions. A similar approach was taken in *Re Hobourn Aero Components Ltd's Air Raid Distress Fund*[57] where a fund was set up during the Second World War for the benefit of employees of three factories. The purpose of the fund was to provide benefits and relief to those employees who had suffered as a result of the air raids during the war. The principal contributions came from the employees, and it was only those employees who were entitled to benefit from the fund. When the war ended the question arose as to how the surplus fund was to be dealt with. Cohen J held that the fund was not charitable in its nature, on the grounds that it was for the benefit of a private class of persons. Having ruled out charity, Cohen J held that the fund was held on resulting trust for the contributing members, subject to adjustments being made where a member had received some benefit under the fund.

**VISIT CASE
NAVIGATOR**

The more contemporary view is that the surplus funds are held subject to contract between the members. The matter was comprehensively considered by the court in *Re Bucks Constabulary Fund (No. 2)*[58] where a society was created to provide benefits for the widows and orphans of deceased members of a constabulary. The funds of the society were provided by voluntary contributions by its members. In 1968 the Bucks Constabulary was amalgamated with other constabularies with the consequence that the funds of the society were wound up. The question before the court was how the surplus funds of the society should be distributed. The funds of the society came from three main sources: namely, members' subscriptions, outside legacies and donations and money raised from raffles and entertainments (Figure 11.1). You will recall from the decision of Goff J in *Re West Sussex Constabulary Benevolent (1930) Fund Trust*[59] that, except in the case of legacies and donations, the surplus fund of the West Sussex Fund went to the Crown *bona vacantia*. In giving judgment in *Re Bucks Constabulary Fund (No. 2)*, Walton J refused to follow the approach of Goff J and instead came to the conclusion

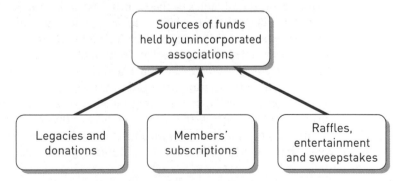

Figure 11.1 Sources of funds of an unincorporated association

---

[57] [1946] Ch. 86.
[58] [1979] 1 WLR 936.
[59] [1971] Ch. 1.

that the existing members of the society were entitled to the surplus fund on an equal basis. Walton J explained that the funds of the society had become vested in the existing members, subject to their contract towards each other. Walton J explained that:

> it is . . . pertinent to observe that all unincorporated societies rest in contract to this extent, but there is an implied contract between all of the members inter se governed by the rules of the society. In default of any rule to the contrary – and it will seldom, if ever, be that there is such a rule – when a member ceases to be a member of the association he ipso facto ceases to have any interest in its funds. Once again, so far as friendly societies are concerned, it is made very clear by section 49(1),[60] that it is the members, the present members, who, alone, have any right in the assets. As membership always ceases on death, past members or the estates of deceased members therefore have no interest in the assets.[61]

The decision of Walton J *Re Bucks Constabulary Fund (No. 2)*[62] clearly establishes that the funds of an unincorporated association are vested in members, subject to their contractual rights and duties towards each other. Collectively, the members can amend the constitution of their association thereby giving them the power to wind up the fund and distribute equally amongst the existing members. The decision was followed in *Hunt v McLaren*[63] where a settlor settled by deed land on trust to secure a sports ground for Horley Football Club. In 2002 the land was sold to a developer for a sum of £4 million. The proceeds were used by the trustees to purchase another piece of land for the purposes of building a clubhouse. However, owing to certain restrictive covenants, the use of the land was restricted to use for sports and leisure. Subsequently, the land was worth less than the amount of money that had been spent on it. Questions arose as to the basis upon which the trustees were holding the assets of the club. The High Court held that the original deed settling the land on trust should be construed as a gift to the members of the club for the time being. This therefore meant that the beneficial interest in the club's property belonged beneficially to the current full members. These members were entitled to the property, subject to the rules of the club, and could unanimously or by general meeting call for the assets to be transferred. Collins J held that the members could ask for the surplus funds of the club to be divided among the adult members on a per capita basis.

The decision in *Re Bucks Constabulary Fund (No. 2)*[64] rules out the possibility that the surplus fund become vested in the Crown *bona vacantia* except where the society becomes moribund, as, for example, where there is only one member: in which case the surplus fund does belong to the Crown. The rationale behind this being that it could never have been the intention of the association to confer a windfall on one existing member. However, this aspect of the decision in *Re Bucks Constabulary Fund (No. 2)* has not been followed in the recent decision of the High Court in *Hanchett-Stamford v Attorney General*[65] where Lewison J held that, whilst it was accepted that the funds of unincorporated association belonged to the existing members subject to their contract between each other, a sole existing member of a society was equally entitled to the surplus fund irrespective of the fact that he was the sole surviving member.

The facts of *Hanchett-Stamford v Attorney General* involved an association founded some time in 1914 called the 'The Performing and Captive Animals Defence League'

---

[60] Friendly Societies Act 1974.
[61] [1979] 1 WLR 936 at 943.
[62] [1979] 1 WLR 936.
[63] [2006] WTLR 1817.
[64] [1979] 1 WLR 936.
[65] [2009] Ch. 173.

(the League hereafter). Although the League had a formal constitution at the beginning, that constitution had been lost and since 1934 the affairs of the League were conducted by a Director appointed by the members of the League. Although it was very difficult to ascertain the exact purposes of the League, it became evident from a booklet produced for members in 1962 that the objects of the League were to prevent cruelty to animals used in film productions and shows. Thus many of the activities of the League involved preventing travelling circuses and municipal zoos. According to the 1962 booklet the league had two types of members: life members and annual members. At that time there were approximately 250 members and the funds of the League were contributed by gifts and legacies which were duly invested. Towards the end of the 1970s the activities of the League slowed down owing to a decline in the number of travelling circuses. From then onwards the assets of the league were vested in a Mr Hanchett-Stamford who had been an active member of the League and who had worked with a leading vet, Dr Bill Jordan, in educating people about animal welfare. In the early 1990s some of the funds of the League were used to purchase a property which at the time of the case was valued at around £675,000. Title to the property was taken in the name of Mr Hanchett-Stamford and another member, both of whom had since died. The property had been occupied by Mrs Hanchett-Stamford until recently when she was moved to a nursing home. In addition to the property, the League also had funds worth some £1.77 million in the form of stocks and shares. In the 1990s the League stopped maintaining records of its members and on the advice of the accountant it was decided that the funds of the League be wound up. Mr and Mrs Hanchett-Stamford, the only surviving members, decided that the funds should be donated to the 'Born Free Charity' whose objects included the welfare of animals. However, Mr Hanchett-Stamford died and the question before the Court was whether Mrs Hanchett-Stamford was in a position to give the surplus funds of the League to the Born Free Charity. She could only do this if she was entitled to exercise ownership of the funds and therefore transfer them to the charity. This in turn raised the legal question as to who was entitled to the surplus assets of the League.

Lewison J proceeded to answer the question of ownership of the assets of the league by examining the existing law. Having reviewed the decisions in **Neville Estates v Madden**[66] and **Re Recher's Will Trust**[67] he concluded that 'the members for the time being of an unincorporated association are beneficially entitled to "its" assets, subject to the contractual arrangements between them'.[68] On this basis the members could by unanimous agreement or majority vote change the constitution of the unincorporated association and divide the assets equally amongst themselves. Therefore, Mrs Hanchett-Stamford and Mr Hanchett-Stamford being the only existing members of the League were entitled to the ownership of the assets subject to the contract between them.[69] Mr Hanchett-Stamford having died, the assets became vested in Mrs Hanchett-Stamford as the sole surviving member. Lewison J explained that the basis of vesting ownership in the sole surviving member operated akin to the vesting of ownership in a sole surviving joint tenant of a joint tenancy where the rule of survivorship operated. He explained that:

> the thread that runs through all these cases is that the property of an unincorporated association is the property of its members, but that they are contractually precluded from severing their share except in accordance with the rules of the association; and that, on its

---

[66] [1962] Ch. 832.
[67] [1972] Ch. 526.
[68] [2009] Ch. 173 at para. 31.
[69] Several adverts had been placed in leading newspapers and journals to establish the whereabouts of other possible members but nothing positive developed from these.

dissolution, those who are members at the time are entitled to the assets free from any such contractual restrictions. It is true that this is not a joint tenancy according to the classical model; but since any collective ownership of property must be a species of joint tenancy or tenancy in common this kind of collective ownership must, in my judgment, be a sub-species of joint tenancy, albeit taking effect subject to any contractual restrictions applicable as between members. I cannot see why the legal principle should be any different if the reason for the dissolution is the permanent cessation of the association's activities or the fall in its membership to below two.[70]

Having established that Mrs Hanchett-Stamford was entitled to the assets whilst a member of the League, that just left one question for the court: what should happen with the surplus fund of the League? You will recall that Mrs Hanchett-Stamford wished to give the money to another welfare animal charity and this could only be possible if she was entitled to the assets. Alternatively, the surplus funds could be claimed by the Crown as *bona vacantia*. There appeared to be two legal obstacles in Mrs Hanchett-Stamford's claim to the surplus funds. First, there was the decision of the Court of Appeal in **Cunnack v Edwards**[71] where the court held that the surplus funds of a society belonged to the Crown. The Court of Appeal held that there was no resulting trust in favour of the personal representatives of the last surviving members. The Court of Appeal proceeded to deal with the matter on the basis that each of the members had contributed their money in return for the protection that was afforded to their widows. On this basis, the money contributed by each member had been abandoned in favour of the society and now belonged to the Crown. Lewison J, however, held that this decision was decided on a rather different set of facts. In particular, he explained that the decision rested on the fact that the money contributed by each member was to pay pensions to the widows of the deceased members and not to be held for the benefit of the members themselves. Furthermore, he explained that on the facts of **Cunnack v Edwards** there were no surviving members when the case came before the court and the question whether the members were entitled to the fund did not arise.

The second obstacle was the decision of Walton J in **Re Bucks Constabulary Fund (No. 2)**[72] where it was held that where an unincorporated association was moribund or where there was only one existing member then there could be no room for the rule that the existing member took the surplus absolutely. In such a case the surplus went to the Crown as *bona vacantia*. The rationale being that it could not have been the intention of the association to confer a windfall on one existing member. Walton J held this to be incorrect and refused to follow the rule. He explained that the sole existing member became entitled to the assets of the association and there could be no justifiable reason to deprive that member of those assets on the winding-up of association. In support of this finding he made reference to Article 1, Protocol 1 of the European Convention for the Protection of Human Rights and Fundamental Freedoms which prevents deprivation of property except in the public interest. Lewison J explained that he could see no public interest being served by the deprivation of a sole member's right to the surplus funds of an association.

Pension fund surpluses

Occupational pension funds are governed primarily by the law of trusts. Although they can take many forms, the most typical arrangement is where both employer and

---

[70] [2009] Ch. 173 at para. 47.
[71] [1896] 2 Ch. 679.
[72] [1979] 1 WLR 936.

employee contribute to the pension scheme. The pension scheme can be either a 'defined benefit scheme' or a 'defined contribution scheme'. The difference between the two is that a defined benefit scheme is usually set up to provide for pensions according to the length of service and salary of a member, whereas a defined contribution scheme is dependent on the amount of contributions of the employee, who is said to take a greater risk in the investment market. Disputes relating to the ownership of the surplus funds of a pension scheme may arise where a pension fund is being wound up; indeed, many of the cases on pension funds have arisen in the context of the ownership of surplus funds. What follows in this section is an analysis of some of the general points of law which have come from some of the decided cases. It must be emphasised that, given the complexity of pension funds, the outcome as to the destination of a surplus fund will very much depend on the terms of each pension scheme. Furthermore, matters may also be influenced by the Pensions Act 1995 and the Pensions Act 2004.

Given the fact that a pension scheme will also have an element of contract to it, the parties to the pension scheme may make some provision in the scheme for the destination of a surplus fund. Normally, the provision will make way for the employer to become entitled to the surplus once all the benefits have been paid out to the employees. It may, however, be the case that the scheme does not make any provision for the surplus fund, in which case the destination of that fund has to be decided by the general law. There are a number of possible destinations where the surplus fund can go:

- Resulting trust for the employer
- Resulting trust for the employees
- *Bona vacantia*
- Resulting trust rateably for the employer and employees.

In the decided cases, the courts have taken a number of different approaches when deciding who is entitled to the surplus fund. This is precisely what happened in ***Davis* v *Richards and Wallington Industries Ltd***[73] where trustees of a pension scheme applied to the court to establish how a surplus fund was to be distributed on its winding up. Prior to the winding up of the scheme, the trustees had executed a deed which allowed the surplus to be paid to the company after pensions had been increased. The question before Scott J was whether the deed had been effectively executed, and if not, how the fund should be distributed. Scott J explained that the deed had been effectively declared and therefore the entitlement to the surplus was to be governed by the deed, which gave the surplus to the employer. However, Scott J proceeded to explain the situation if the deed had been declared ineffective. He explained that, given the fact that a pension fund was a species of unincorporated association on the grounds that the rights of the employees lay in contract, the matter fell to be decided by the general law. Having explained the general law, Scott J proceeded to explain that the overpayments made by the employer were returnable to the employer under a resulting trust; however, the overpayments made by the employees could not be held on resulting trust for them. Instead the contributions of the employees belonged to the Crown as *bona vacantia*. The basis for these findings was primarily on the grounds that, in so far as the employer was concerned, its contributions were rather different from those of the employees. In the opinion of Scott J the employees' contributions were essentially to make sure that the pension scheme met its purpose in paying the pensions. The contributions of the employer were primarily there to make sure that there was no shortfall in the fund. On this basis, even if the

---

[73] [1990] 1 WLR 1511. See, S. Gardner, 'New Angles on Unincorporated Associations' 1992 Conv. 41 and J. Martin, 'Editors Notes' (1991) Conv. 364.

employers had not contributed, the fund would have been sufficient to meet its liabilities. The employers, with hindsight, need not have contributed and any contribution it made was the sole reason that a surplus arose. On this basis their contributions were held on resulting trust whereas any contributions by the employees went to the Crown. Scott J declined to give effect to a resulting trust of the employees' contributions primarily because the employees had received what they had bargained for under the scheme; in any event, a resulting trust would be unworkable given the different contributions and entitlements of the various employees.

> The second question is whether a resulting trust applies to the surplus, or to so much of the surplus as was derived from each of the three sources to which I have referred. As to the surplus derived from the employers' contributions, I can see no basis on which the resulting trust can be excluded. The equity to which I referred in the previous paragraph demands, in my judgment, the conclusion that the trustees hold the surplus derived from the employers' contributions upon trust for the employers. There is no express provision excluding a resulting trust and no circumstances from which, in my opinion, an implication to that effect could be drawn. On the other hand, in my judgment, the circumstances of the case seem to me to point firmly and clearly to the conclusion that a resulting trust in favour of the employees is excluded. The circumstances are these . . . Each employee paid his or her contributions in return for specific financial benefits from the fund. The value of these benefits would be different for each employee, depending on how long he had served, how old he was when he joined and how old he was when he left. Two employees might have paid identical sums in contributions but have become entitled to benefits of a very different value. The point is particularly striking in respect of the employees (and there were several of them) who exercised their option to a refund of contributions. How can a resulting trust work as between the various employees inter se? I do not think it can and I do not see why equity should impute to them an intention that would lead to an unworkable result.[74]

The decision in ***Davis v Richards & Wallington Industries Ltd***[75] adopts a somewhat similar approach of an earlier decision of Millet J in ***Re Courage Group's Pension Schemes***.[76] The facts of this rather complex case involved the takeover of a company and a subsequent sale of it to another company. One of the questions before the court was whether the takeover company was entitled to retain the surplus fund of the pension scheme for the benefit of employees before transferring the employees to a new pension scheme. Millett J took the view that only an employer was entitled to the surplus funds of a pension scheme on the basis that, whilst an employee had no choice other than to contribute to the scheme, the employer's contribution was voluntary and made in good faith to make sure that the scheme met its liabilities to the members of the scheme. In the course of his judgment Millet J explained that 'surplus arises from past overfunding, not by the employer and the employees pro rata to their respective contributions, but by the employer alone to the full extent of its past contributions and only subject thereto by the employees'.[77] The difference between ***Davis v Richards & Wallington Industries Ltd*** and ***Re Courage Group's Pension Schemes*** is that in the former case only the contributions of the employer were held on resulting trust for the employer, the employees' contributions going to the Crown, whereas in the latter case the whole surplus was held to belong to the employer. It is not entirely clear why the whole of the surplus should result back

---

[74] [1990] 1 WLR 1511 at 1544.
[75] [1990] 1 WLR 1511. See S. Gardner, 'New Angles on Unincorporated Associations' 1992 Conv. 41 and J. Martin, 'Editors Notes' (1991) Conv. 364.
[76] [1987] 1 All ER 528.
[77] [1987] 1 All ER 528 at 545.

to the employer. The decision in *Re Courage Group's Schemes* is criticised by Professor Hudson who explains that:

> [t]he logical sense of this argument is not entirely apparent. The surplus arises because there are more assets in the fund than there are obligations to be paid out of it. That surplus exists because *all* of the contributors to the scheme have added so much property that there is more than is needed: not simply that the employer alone has over contributed. The power of the employer to cease making contributions to the scheme has been conflated with the inquiry as to who has contributed the surplus. Suppose two hoses are filling a bucket and that neither tap serving the hoses can be turned off. Suppose that only one of those hoses has a rubber stopper – so, in the same way that it is only the employer which is capable of withholding contributions to the pension scheme in certain circumstances, it is only the hose with the stopper which could cease adding water to the bucket. It is not true to say that it is only the hose with the stopper which causes the full bucket to overspill; rather the water that spills out of the bucket comes from both hoses. It is both sources of water which can claim credit for the overspill. Similarly, the surplus in the scheme property comes from two sources: employer and employee. Therefore, it is not correct to say that only the employer can claim the surplus (or overspill).[78]

A rather different approach to the destination of a surplus fund was taken by Warner J in *Mettoy Pension Trustees Ltd* v *Evans*[79] where a company who had gone into liquidation had a power of appointment in respect of a surplus in a pension fund. The power was held by the company and not the trustees of the fund, which would have made the power fiduciary in its nature. If the power was not exercised then the surplus would in effect belong to the company as it was entitled to the surplus under a gift over in default of appointment. If the money went back to the company it would then become available for the creditors of the company. There were two questions before the court. Firstly, whether the power could be exercised in order to increase the entitlement of the pensioners. Secondly, if the company did not exercise the power, could the court exercise the power? Both of these answers were answered in the affirmative. Warner J held that although the power was held by the company and not the trustees of the pension fund, it was nevertheless fiduciary in its nature. In coming to this conclusion, the judge explained that if the power conferred upon the company was not construed as being fiduciary, then its inclusion in the pension scheme would be meaningless. Warner J went on to say that if it was a mere power then the company would be making gifts of its own absolute property to those entitled under the pension fund. If such was the case, it would be meaningless to have that power in the scheme when the company could, if it wanted, make those payments without recourse to the power. Secondly, Warner J explained that the pensioners under the fund were not volunteers as they had also contributed to the surplus. In such a case, the court explained that the company held a fiduciary power and was subject to the fiduciary duties to consider whether to exercise the power. The court held that, in the absence of the exercise of the power by the company, the court could exercise the power in favour of the pensioners.

The decision in *Mettoy Pension Trustees Ltd* v *Evans*[80] is very much rooted in the application of traditional trust law principles to decide the fate of a surplus pension fund: in particular, the fact that the employer under a pension scheme acquires fiduciary duties towards the employees. The decision was not, however, followed in *Imperial Group*

---

[78] A. Hudson, *Equity and Trusts* 5th edn (2006) at p. 1001.
[79] [1991] 2 All ER 513.
[80] [1991] 2 All ER 513.

Pension Trust Ltd v *Imperial Tobacco Ltd*[81] where Browne-Wilkinson VC took a somewhat novel approach to the determination of the rights and duties of an employer in respect of a pension scheme and the ownership of surplus fund. The decision illustrates that a pension scheme is a rather different species of trust from a normal trust. In the normal trust model, a trustee is usually holding trust property for a beneficiary who in most cases happens to a volunteer. Thus apart from the trust relationship, there is normally no other relationship between the trustee and the beneficiary. In contrast, a pension scheme trust is part and parcel of an employee's contractual relationship with his employer. The payment of benefits under the scheme are dependent on the employee providing services to the employer. In this respect, the decision in *Imperial Group Pension Trust Ltd* v *Imperial Tobacco Ltd* decides that a pension fund cannot be simply governed from a purely trust perspective. Instead, given the fact that a pension fund is an integral part of the employment relationship between the employer and employee, it should be subject to the express and implied contractual duties which govern the employment contract. In particular, it should be subject to the implied contractual duty of good faith as between employer and employee. Although the full extent of this duty is yet to be explored, the basic nature of the duty is to ensure that the employer does not act in a manner which may damage the mutual trust and confidence as between employer and employee in the employment relationship.[82] Equally, the employee is under a duty to recognise that the employer may act in his own self-interest, but subject to the duty to act in good faith towards the employee.

So, how does the contractual analysis in *Imperial Group Pension Trust Ltd* apply to the question of the destination of a surplus fund? The basic tenor of the argument is that where an employer seeks to make any claims to the surplus fund of the scheme, he must show that he has discharged his duty of good faith towards the employees who are also members of the pension scheme. Where, for example, the employer cannot show that in claiming the surplus fund he is acting in good faith, or is otherwise forcing the employees to give up their accrued rights in the fund, then it will not be able to make any such claim to the surplus. The matter is neatly illustrated by the facts of *Imperial Group Pension Trust Ltd* v *Imperial Tobacco Ltd*[83] where Imperial Tobacco Company had been taken over by Hanson. One of the reasons for the takeover by Hanson was to lay claim to the massive surplus fund that had arisen in the pension scheme of Imperial Tobacco Company. On takeover, Hanson agreed to a change in the pension scheme which allowed the benefits to be increased by 5 per cent, but precluded Imperial Tobacco from laying any claim to the surplus fund. When the rate of inflation exceeded 5 per cent the trustees of the pension scheme asked Hanson whether they would agree to an additional increase in benefits to which Hanson refused to consent. Instead, Hanson agreed to set up a new scheme for the employees of Imperial Tobacco with the consequence that it would then become entitled to the surplus funds of the original scheme. The question before the court was whether Hanson was entitled to the surplus or whether, as in *Mettoy Pension Trustees Ltd* v *Evans*[84] it was subject to fiduciary duties to the members of the scheme. Browne-Wilkinson VC held that Hanson's refusal to consent to the increases asked for by the trustees of the original scheme was invalid. Browne-Wilkinson VC held that Hanson

---

[81] [1991] 2 All ER 597.

[82] For an excellent discussion of the exact nature of the duty of good faith in the employment relationship and its application in occupational pension schemes, see M. Thomas and B. Dowrick, 'The Heart of the Matter – Re-Thinking Good Faith in Occupational Pension Schemes' (2007) Conv. 495.

[83] [1991] 2 All ER 597.

[84] [1991] 2 All ER 513.

did not owe a fiduciary duty to the members of the scheme in respect of the surplus. Instead it was held that Hanson was under a contractual duty to act in good faith towards the members of the scheme and not to damage the relationship of employment. In this respect Hanson had failed to show the court that, in taking over Imperial Tobacco Company, it was addressing the efficient running of the scheme or that it was not simply forcing the members to give up their rights in the scheme for some collateral purpose. The approach in *Imperial Group Pension Trust Ltd* rejects the imposition of fiduciary obligations on the employer in respect of the surplus fund of a pension scheme. It does not rule out the possibility that the surplus fund can be claimed by the employer; however, the court has to be satisfied that, whilst the employer can act in his own self-interest, it must have acted in good faith towards the members of the scheme, something very much missing on the facts of *Imperial Group Pension Trust Ltd*.

More recently, in *Air Jamaica v Charlton*[85] the Privy Council has returned to the orthodox principles of trust law to determine the fate of a surplus fund. In doing so Privy Council rejected the approach of Scott J in *Davis v Richards & Wallington Industries Ltd*[86] where the judge held that the contributions of the employees to a pension scheme belonged *bona vacantia* to the Crown.

In 1994 the pension scheme of Air Jamaica's employees was terminated as a result of the company being privatised. After the defined benefits under the scheme had been paid out, there remained a surplus of $400. Clause 13 of the pension scheme provided that, should the scheme discontinue, any surplus should be used by the trustees to provide additional benefits to the members. Consequently, the members claimed that they were entitled to this surplus. In addition, clause 4 of the scheme specifically prohibited Air Jamaica from recovering any contributions it had paid into the scheme (although Air Jamaica tried to alter the scheme in order that they would be entitled to the surplus, but the amendments failed on the basis of perpetuity). So who was entitled to the surplus? It seems obvious that the scheme intended that, in these circumstances, the members should benefit, and clause 4 clearly prohibited the company from reclaiming any money.

However, Millett LJ disallowed the amendments to the scheme, and despite clause 4, he held that the surplus funds belonged to anyone who had paid into it. On the present facts, this meant that the company was entitled to one half of the surplus as it had contributed equally into the scheme.

The fundamental question in *Air Jamaica v Charlton*[87] surrounds the basis for the imposition of the resulting trust in the face of clause 4 of the pension scheme. This clause clearly demonstrated the company's intention to part with both the legal and beneficial interest in the money it contributed to the scheme, so can a resulting trust be imposed even in circumstances where the transferor evidences an intention to part with his beneficial interest? In answering this question Millett LJ explained that:

> Like a constructive trust, a resulting trust arises by operation of law, though unlike a constructive trust it gives effect to intention. But it arises whether or not the transferor intended to retain a beneficial interest – he almost always does not – since it responds to any absence of intention on his part to pass a beneficial interest to the recipient. It may arise even where the transferor positively wished to part with the beneficial interest, as in *Vandervell v IRC*. In that case the retention of a beneficial interest by the transferor destroyed the effectiveness of a tax avoidance scheme which the transferor was trying to

---

[85] [1999] 1 WLR 1399. See C. Harpum, 'Perpetuities, Pensions and Resulting Trusts' (2000) Conv. 170.
[86] [1990] 1 WLR 1511. See S. Gardner, 'New Angles on Unincorporated Associations' 1992 Conv. 41 and J. Martin, 'Editors Notes' (1991) Conv. 364.
[87] [1999] 1 WLR 1399.

implement. The House of Lords affirmed the principle that a resulting trust is not defeated by evidence that the transferor intended to part with the beneficial interest if he has not in fact succeeded in doing so.[88]

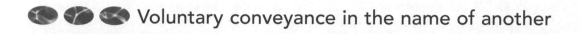 Voluntary conveyance in the name of another

APPLYING THE LAW

Suppose that David voluntarily transfers his house in the name of his sister, Jenny. David then tells Jenny that, although she is the registered proprietor of the house, she will recognise that the house still belongs to David. Jenny agrees to this arrangement, particularly more so as David has voluntarily transferred a sum of £10,000 in her name.

Does David have any interest in the house conveyed to Jenny?

The preceding sections have concentrated on the imposition of a resulting trust where there has been a failure to dispose of the equitable interest. As explained earlier, these cases were once categorised by Megarry J as instances where the courts would impose an 'automatic resulting trust'.[89] Of course, after the decision of the House Lords in **Westdeutsche Landesbank Girozentrale v Islington LBC**,[90] it is no longer appropriate to talk of automatic resulting trusts. The reason is quite simply that all of the circumstances which give rise to the imposition of a resulting trust are based on the presumed intentions of the person in whose favour the resulting trust arises. What follows in the subsequent sections is an analysis of the factual situations in which a traditionally 'presumed resulting trust' is imposed. These situations, also known as the 'apparent gift cases' divide roughly into two, namely: a voluntary conveyance in the name of another and a purchase in the name of another. In both cases, equity imports a presumption of a resulting trust in favour of the person conveying property or purchasing property in the name of another. The apparent basis of this presumption is that equity does not assume gifts but assumes bargains. The basic principle of equity is that a person who voluntarily transfers property to another or who purchases property in the name of another does not intend to part with his beneficial interest in the property so conveyed or purchased.

At the outset it must be emphasised that equity only imports a presumption and, like any presumption, it can be rebutted. The normal basis upon which the presumption will be rebutted is that a person, when purchasing trust property or conveying trust property to another, intended to make an outright gift. Additionally, the presumption of resulting trust could in the past be rebutted by the counter-presumption of advancement.[91] This, rather archaic, presumption operates to impute a donative intent in certain relationships: for example, husband and wife and father and child. The presumption of advancement is discussed in more detail below.

---

[88] [1999] 1 WLR 1399 at 1412.
[89] *Vandervell v IRC (No. 2)* [1974] Ch. 269.
[90] [1996] AC 669 (HL).
[91] The presumption of advancement has been abolished by s. 199 of the Equality Act 2010, which has yet to come into force.

A voluntary conveyance of land in the name of another

This section explores the first instance in which a presumption of resulting trust will be raised, and that is where a person voluntarily conveys property in the name of another. The law distinguishes between voluntary conveyances in the context of land and personal property. The basis of this distinction come from s. 60(3) of the Law of Property Act 1925 which was primarily enacted as a conveyancing device.

In a voluntary conveyance of land in the name of another it is important to have regard to s. 60(3) of the Law of Property Act 1925: 'In a voluntary conveyance a resulting trust for the grantor shall not be implied merely by reason that the property is not expressed to be conveyed for the use or benefit of the grantee.' The precise scope of s. 60(3) has been the subject matter of much academic and judicial discussion.[92] The question is whether the section has the effect of totally excluding the presumption of a resulting trust on a voluntary conveyance of land in the name of another. The words of the section make it clear that a resulting trust shall not be implied simply because the person conveying the property fails to convey it on express terms which confer use and benefit to the transferee. The section was principally enacted as a word-saving section to make effective voluntary conveyances of land to another. Prior to the Law of Property Act 1925 it was essential requirement that in the conveyance of land to another that it be specifically put on use for the benefit of the grantee.[93] Where the land was not conveyed to the grantee with express words indicating that it was for his use and benefit, the equitable interest would result back to the grantor. Section 60(3) was enacted to circumvent the requirement that the conveyance use express terms indicating that the land was conveyed to the grantee for his own use and benefit. If the conveyance was not expressed to be for the use and benefit of the trustee then a resulting trust was not implied. In other words, the grantee would take the absolute ownership in the land conveyed. Despite this the question remains in the law whether the proper impact of s. 60(3) is to abolish the presumption of a resulting trust in a voluntary transfer of land.

The full impact of s. 60(3) remains to be undertaken by a higher court. However, the most comprehensive review of the section was undertaken by Nicholas Strauss QC at first instance in **Lohia v Lohia**[94] where the judge took the view that the full impact of s. 60(3) was to abolish the presumption of a resulting trust in the case of a voluntary transfer of land. He explained that 'on a plain reading of the section the presumption has been abolished. It seems to me that section 60(3) establishes a general rule that a conveyance should be construed according to the words it uses, so that it is possible to tell from it who holds the legal and beneficial estate in the land.' Nicholas Strauss QC explained that, although the presumption of a resulting trust was abolished, it did not mean that a person conveying the property in the name of another could not have a resulting trust in his favour. However, the implication of a resulting trust in such a context would have to be adduced from evidence that the transferor did not intend the transferee to obtain an absolute interest. For example, in **Ali v Khan**,[95] although the Court of Appeal did not find it necessary to decide the issue, it nevertheless said in passing that the decision in **Lohia v Lohia** established 'that the presumption of a resulting trust on a voluntary conveyance of land has been abolished by s. 60(3) Law of Property Act 1925. It was not suggested that this proposition precludes a party to the conveyance from relying on evidence from which a resulting trust may be inferred.'[96]

---

[92] See R. Chambers, *Resulting Trusts*, (1997) at p. 18.
[93] Primarily a requirement of the Statute of Uses 1536.
[94] [2001] WTLR 101.
[95] [2002] EWCA Civ. 974.
[96] [2002] EWCA Civ. 974 at [24].

Does s. 60(3) of the Law of Property Act 1925 alter the substantive law on resulting trusts of voluntary transfers of land? Given the fact that the main objective of s. 60(3) was to operate as a word-saving provision, the general consensus is that the section does not change the substantive law on resulting trusts of voluntary transfers of land. The section merely precludes the automatic presumption of a resulting trust. If the evidence points to the fact that the transferee did not intend to make a gift to the transferee, then a resulting trust will be implied in favour of the transferor. The matter is illustrated by the Court of Appeal's decision in **Hodgson v Marks**[97] where Mrs Hodgson, an elderly lady, had lived in her house since 1939. Around about April 1959 a certain Mr Evans came to live with Mrs Hodgson as a lodger. Over the years Mrs Hodgson became very fond of Mr Evans and entrusted him to sort out many of her financial and other affairs. The nephew of Mrs Hodgson disapproved of Mr Evans and tried to turn him out of the house. It was clear that the nephew did not trust Mr Evans. In response to this, Mrs Hodgson transferred the legal title to the house to Mr Evans on the oral understanding that she would continue to be the beneficial owner of the house. The whole purpose of this arrangement was to protect Mr Evans. Despite the trust and confidence Mrs Hodgson placed in Mr Evans, he transferred the house to Mr Marks, who turned out to be a bona fide purchaser of the legal title without notice. The question before the Court of Appeal was whether Mrs Hodgson was protected against Mr Marks. Such protection could only be recognised if she retained some beneficial interest in the house which would be capable of binding Mr Marks.

The Court of Appeal held that, although the express oral agreement by Mr Evans to the effect that he was holding the land on trust for Mrs Hodgson was unenforceable under s. 53(1)(b) of the Law of Property Act 1925, Mrs Hodgson had acquired a beneficial interest under a resulting trust.[98] The Court of Appeal held that the recognition of a resulting trust in her favour gave rise to a beneficial interest in her favour, and coupled with fact that she was in actual occupation of the land, her interest was binding against Mr Marks.[99] The decision in **Hodgson v Marks**[100] is frequently cited as an example of the imposition of a resulting trust on a voluntary conveyance of land. It must, however, be taken on board that the basis of the decision could easily have been arrived at on two different grounds. The first is under the doctrine of **Rochefoucauld v Boustead**,[101] which was considered in Chapter 5, and prevents a statute to be used as an instrument for fraud. You will recall that Mrs Hodgson transferred the house to Mr Evans on the oral strength that he would hold it for her on trust. Normally, such a declaration of trust would, pursuant to s. 53(1)(b), need to be manifested and proved by some writing. The absence of writing and proof renders the trust merely unenforceable and not void. If Mr Evans could provide the evidence of intention to declare a trust, then the court, under the doctrine of **Rochefoucauld v Boustead**, could enforce the express trust. Secondly, given the unconscionability of Mr Evans and the undue influence exerted over Mrs Hodgson, the court could have considered the possibility of imposing a constructive trust. These matters and the application of s. 60(3) were not considered by the Court of Appeal and the decision in **Hodgson v Marks** remains an example of the imposition of a resulting trust on a voluntary conveyance of land to another.

---

[97] [1971] Ch. 892.

[98] You will recall from Chapter 5 that an express declaration of a trust of land need to be manifested and proved by some writing pursuant to s. 53(1)(b) of the Law of Property Act 1925. Failure to comply with the section renders the intended trust of land unenforceable but not void.

[99] Beneficial interests coupled with actual occupation of land constitute overriding interests in land which bind third parties irrespective of notice; see s. 29 of the Land Registration Act 2002.

[100] [1971] Ch. 892.

[101] [1897] 1 Ch. 196.

It should be further noted that if the effect of s. 60(3) was to alter the substantive law of resulting trusts of voluntary transfers of land, then a rather strange distinction would occur between voluntary transfers of personal property and voluntary transfers of real property. Furthermore, it would be difficult to explain the justification for the imposition of a resulting trust in cases where there is purchase of real property in the name of another (see below) and the exclusion of a resulting trust on a voluntary conveyance of land in the name of another.[102]

A voluntary conveyance in the context of personal property

Clearly s. 60(3) of the Law of Property Act 1925 has no application in the context of personal property, therefore, the rule is that a resulting trust will be presumed where there is a voluntary transfer of personal property into the name of another. The matter is neatly illustrated by the decision in *Re Vinogradoff*[103] where a testatrix transferred £800 worth of a war loan into the joint account of herself and her granddaughter who was four years old. The testatrix continued to receive the dividends on the loan until her death. On her death the court held that the granddaughter held the war loan on resulting trust for her grandmother.

The decision in *Re Vinogradoff* is perhaps one of the more difficult ones to justify in the contemporary law governing the imposition of resulting trusts. You will recall from the earlier discussion in this chapter that in *Westdeutsche Landesbank Girozentrale v Islington LBC*[104] that Lord Browne-Wilkinson explained that a resulting trust arose to give effect to the intentions of the transferor: in particular, the intention that the transferor, in transferring property to the transferee, intended to retain a beneficial interest in the property so transferred. There is nothing on these facts to suggest that the intentions of the grandmother were to make her granddaughter a trustee of the property she had transferred in their joint names. With regard to her granddaughter, it is not entirely clear how her conscience was affected to constitute her a trustee. In this respect, this decision becomes almost impossible to justify in the context of the modern position enunciated in *Westdeutsche Landesbank Girozentrale v Islington LBC*.[105] A more plausible explanation is that the intended transfer of the war loan in the joint names of the grandmother and granddaughter was intended for the benefit of the grandmother for life and thereafter for the granddaughter. Such intention would have had to comply with the provisions of the Wills Act 1837. However, it is not entirely clear why on the facts of *Re Vinogradoff* such intention, albeit not complying with the Wills Act 1837, was not indicative of a gift rather than a resulting trust.

More recently, in *Re Northall (Deceased)*[106] a testatrix left her residuary estate to her five sons in equal shares. She appointed two of her sons, Derek and Christopher, as her executors. The testatrix died in January 2007 at the age of 78 years. The action was bought by two of her other sons who claimed that Christopher had wrongfully withdrawn money soon after their mother's death from a bank account which was in the joint names of the testatrix and Christopher. The money in the account was solely provided by

---

[102] Note, however, the view of D. Hayton and C. Mitchell in *The Law of Trusts and Equitable Remedies*, 12th edn (2005) at p. 321 where it is argued that these inconsistencies are justified from the point of view of the formality rules of transfers of personal and real property.

[103] [1935] WN 68. See also *Thavorn v Bank of Credit and Commerce International SA* [1985] 1 Lloyd's Rep. 259.

[104] [1996] AC 669.

[105] [1996] AC 669.

[106] [2010] EWHC 1448 (Ch).

the testatrix and the evidence before the court was that the account was opened in joint names so that Christopher could make the withdrawals as his mother was too frail to venture out. Christopher, however, argued that his mother (the testatrix) had agreed that the money was his after her death, although this was not supported by any evidence. As to the ownership of the monies in the bank account, Mr Justice David Richards held that the money was held by Christopher on a resulting trust for his mother. The mother had contributed solely to the bank account, and despite the fact that the account was in joint names, the entire beneficial ownership of the account belonged to the mother and now fell into her estate to be divided equally amongst all five brothers. In the course of judgment, the judge explained that 'there is no dispute as to the applicable legal principles. First, where a sum of money belonging to one person is paid into a joint bank account there is a presumption that the owner of the money does not intend to make a gift of it to the other account holder and accordingly the money is held on resulting trust for the provider. The presumption will be rebutted if the circumstances give rise to a presumption of advancement, which is not suggested here, or by evidence that the owner intended to transfer the beneficial interest to the account holders jointly or, as the case may be, to the other account holder solely.'[107]

 ## Purchase in the name of another

APPLYING THE LAW

Six students at university purchase a house to live in during their studies. Each student contributes £15,000 towards the purchase price of the house, but the title is only conveyed in the names of two of the students.

Do the four students, who do not appear on the legal title, have any interest in the house?

A presumption of a resulting trust will arise where a person purchases property and conveys it in the name of another. Thus if A provided the whole purchase price of property which is conveyed in the name of B alone, then a resulting trust of the whole property will be implied in favour of A. The resulting trust will arise irrespective of whether the property is real or personal. The presumption will extend to the situation where the property is taken in the joint names of the purchaser and a third party but the whole purchase price is provided by the purchaser alone. For example, if A provides the whole purchase price of property which is conveyed in the names of A and B, then both A and B hold the property on resulting trust for A alone. The presumption will also apply in cases where there are several purchasers of property, but the title to such property is only taken in one or two of the purchasers. In such a case the legal owners of the property will hold on resulting trust for all of the purchasers according to the contribution made by each of the purchasers. The principle was neatly explained by Eyre CB in ***Dyer v Dyer***[108] in the following terms:

> The clear result of all the cases, without a single exception, is that the trust of a legal estate, whether freehold, copyhold or leasehold; whether taken in the names of the purchasers

---

[107] [2010] EWHC 1448 (Ch) at para. 8.
[108] (1788) 2 Cox. Eq. Cas. 92.

and other jointly, or in the names of other without that of the purchaser; whether in one name or several; whether jointly or successive – results to the man who advances the purchase money.[109]

The presumption of a resulting trust will only arise if there is some contribution to the purchase price. This can be a total contribution by the purchaser of it can be a part contribution to the purchase price. A resulting trust will not be presumed where a person advances money to another by way of a loan to purchase property. For example, in *Re Sharpe (a bankrupt)*[110] Mr and Mrs Sharpe lived with their aunt, Mrs Johnson, who was an elderly lady suffering from a long-term illness. The maisonette in which they lived was purchased in the name of Mr Sharpe for a sum of £17,000. Mrs Johnson had provided £12,000 towards the purchase of the house. In her evidence, she explained that the money was not given to Mr Sharpe by way of a gift: rather it was advanced on the understanding that Mr and Mrs Sharpe would allow Mrs Johnson to reside in the maisonette until such time as the £12,000 be repaid to her. Browne-Wilkinson J held that the money had been advanced by way of loan so that Mrs Johnson did not have an interest under a resulting trust. The same conclusion was arrived at in *Vajpeyi v Yijaf*[111] where the claimant provided the defendant with a sum of £10,000 to purchase a house. The primary purpose of this advance of £10,000 was to help out the defendant who did not have sufficient funds of his own to purchase the house. The claimant, on the other hand, already owned property in her own name. The claimant never objected to the defendant who had collected the rents from the property. Furthermore, for a period of some 21 years the claimant never raised an issue about her purported interest in the house. When the issue arose whether the claimant had an interest in the defendant's property, the court held that the evidence indicated that the money was advanced by way of loan, rather than raising a presumption of resulting trust which would give the claimant a beneficial interest in the house purchased by the defendant.

More recently the question of a loan and a resulting trust arose in the Court of Appeal in *Elithorn v Poulter*[112] where a certain M and E decided to purchase a house in 1995 for cash. The house was transferred in the joint names of M and E although M had provided the entire cash price. The intention was that E would contribute towards half of the purchase price; however, E was unable to sell his previous property in order to raise half the purchase price. M and E agreed that M would loan E half of the purchase price and that he would repay her when he eventually sold his property. It was further agreed that E would only become a true joint owner once he had paid half of the purchase price to M. It was further agreed that E need not pay the loan back until his death. When M died, the question before the court was whether E had a beneficial interest in the house purchased by M and E or whether the house belonged absolutely to M only and therefore to be claimed by her executors. The Court of Appeal held that whilst it was possible to come to the conclusion that M had loaned half the purchase price to E, it was not the case that E did not acquire a beneficial interest in the property. M had indeed loaned the money to E, and E was indebted to M. E was, however, a joint beneficiary of the property as M had only provided half the purchase price whilst E would provide the remaining half. The fact that the title was conveyed in joint names was further evidence of E's beneficial interest in the property.

Questions have arisen, mainly in the context of the family home disputes, as to what will actually constitute a contribution to the purchase price. For example, will an

---

[109] (1788) 2 Cox. Eq. Cas. 92 at 93.
[110] [1980] 1 WLR 219.
[111] [2003] EWHC 2339 Ch.
[112] [2009] 1 P & CR 19.

initial deposit to the purchase of a house be sufficient? Alternatively, will looking after the children and the house be sufficient if it allows a partner to work and discharge a mortgage? These rather controversial questions are discussed below in the section on resulting trusts and the family home. As regards the extent of the interest acquired under a resulting trust in this context, the matter is purely mathematical. The size of the interest resulting back to the purchaser will depend on his contribution.

 ## Rebutting the presumption of a resulting trust

In both cases of a voluntary conveyance and a purchase in the name of another the resulting trust is a mere unrebutted presumption. Like any presumption, the presumption of a resulting trust can be rebutted by evidence which may point to a rather different legal outcome. The matter is explained by Lord Diplock in **Pettitt v Pettitt**[113] where his Lordship explained that 'these presumptions or circumstances of evidence are readily rebutted by comparatively slight evidence'.[114] Lord Diplock in the same case explained the process in the same case as one of:

> imputing an intention to a person wherever the intention with which an act is done affects its legal consequences and the evidence does not disclose what was the actual intention with which he did it. This situation commonly occurs when the actor is deceased. When the act is of a kind to which this technique has frequently to be applied by the courts the imputed intention may acquire the description of a 'presumption' – but presumptions of this type are not immutable. A presumption of fact is no more than a consensus of judicial opinion disclosed by reported cases as to the most likely inference of fact to be drawn in the absence of any evidence to the contrary . . .[115]

The presumption of a resulting trust will be rebutted principally on two grounds: firstly, that the person advancing the purchase money or voluntarily transferring property in the name of another intended to make a gift to the person who has taken the title to property in his own name. The second ground for rebutting the presumption of a resulting trust is where there is counter-presumption of advancement. It will be seen below that this, rather archaic presumption, operates to infer a donative intent in certain types of relationships. Although, when s. 199 of the Equality Act 2010 cames into force, the presumption of advancement will be abolished. This is discussed later.

Evidence of a gift

A presumption of resulting trust will be rebutted where there is evidence that a gift was intended. For example, in **Fowkes v Pascoe**[116] Sarah Baker purchased stocks in the joint names of herself and John Pascoe. John Pascoe was the son of her daughter-in-law who had remarried. In addition to the purchase of the stocks in the joint names of herself and John Pascoe, she held a number of investments in her own name and had also purchased stocks jointly in the name of her partner. In her will she left property to John Pascoe as well as to her daughter-in-law. In light of all of these factors James LJ held that there could only be one conclusion and that was that Sarah Baker intended a gift of the stock

---

[113] [1970] AC 777.
[114] [1970] AC 777 at 814.
[115] [1970] AC 777 at 823.
[116] [1875] 10 Ch. App. 343. See also *Re Young* (1885) 28 Ch. D 705.

to John Pascoe. The judge asked whether it was 'possible to reconcile with mental sanity the theory that she put £250 into the names of herself and companion, and £250 into the names of herself and [John Pascoe], as trustees upon trust for herself? What . . . object is there conceivable in doing this?'[117]

Typically, the presumption of a resulting trust may arise where money is transferred in joint names in a bank account. In such cases, the presumption is much readily rebutted when the mandate of the account makes it clear that the beneficial ownership is to be enjoyed jointly and there is also evidence that such a position was made clear by an official of the bank. The matter is illustrated by the decision in **Aroso v Coutts & Co**[118] where money had been transferred by a wealthy Portuguese into the joint names of himself and his nephew. At the time of opening the account the bank had made it clear that the account had the effect of conferring upon the uncle and nephew joint ownership. In the course of his judgment Collins J explained:

> [T]hat bank has adduced sufficient evidence to displace the presumption of resulting trust, and has proved that the deceased intended to give [the nephew] a beneficial interest in the assets in account A371. First, the terms of the mandate are absolutely clear. The deceased spoke English and was supplied with a translation of the mandate into Portuguese, and the words of the mandate are not capable of being other than an expression of intention that the beneficial interest is to be held jointly, and that the survivor is to take all beneficially. They are at least a representation to the bank that the assets in the account are in their joint beneficial ownership, and are not held on trust for any other person (which would include the deceased solely). Second, I do not think it is right to ignore the terms of the investment agreement which refer to the investments and cash being held for the account holders as beneficial joint tenants.[119]

Where there is no evidence that the person transferring property in the name of another intended to make a gift, then the presumption of a resulting trust remains. For example, in **Re Northall (Deceased)** [2010] EWHC 1448 there was no evidence that a mother had intended to transfer the beneficial interest in a Joint bank account to her son who was a Joint legal owner of the account.

The presumption of advancement

A presumption of resulting trust can be rebutted by the counter-presumption of advancement. The presumption of advancement infers a donative intent on the part of the person transferring property or purchasing property in the name of another. The presumption only applies in special relationships, and these are:

- father and child
- husband and wife
- persons standing *in loco parentis*.

The origins of the presumption of advancement lie in social and economic conditions that no longer exist today. In cases where a father transferred property into the name of his child, or where a husband transferred property into the name of his wife, there was a general presumption that the father or husband was executing his normal duty to provide

---

[117] [1875] 10 Ch. App. 343 at 349.
[118] [2002] 1 All ER (Comm) 241.
[119] [2002] 1 All ER (Comm) 24 at para. 35.

for the child and wife. The presumption of advancement has come under considerable criticism, primarily because of the discriminatory nature in which the presumption operates, for example it applies in cases of transfers from husband to wife but not from wife to husband. Furthermore, the presumption has been attacked on the grounds that it contravenes many of the provisions of the European Convention on Human Rights.[120] The presumption of advancement was criticised by Lord Diplock in *Pettitt v Pettitt*[121] where his Lordship explained that it would be 'an abuse of legal technique for ascertaining or imputing intention to apply to transactions between the post-war generation of married couples "presumptions" which are based upon inferences of fact which an earlier generation of judges drew as the most likely intentions of earlier generation of spouses belonging to the propertied class of a different social era . . .'[122] Despite the archaic nature of the presumption of advancement, it still continues to form part of English law, and therefore it must be analysed alongside any discussion of resulting trusts,[123] although s. 199 of the Equality Act will abolish the presumption of advancement.

The presumption of advancement clearly applies as between husband and wife. In *Re Eykyn's Trusts* the court held that:

> the law of this court is perfectly settled that when a husband transfers money or other property into the name of his wife only, then the presumption is, that it is intended as a gift or advancement to the wife absolutely at once, subject to such marital control as he may exercise, and if a husband invests money, stock, or otherwise, in the names of himself and his wife, then also it is an advancement for the benefit of the wife absolutely if she survives her husband, but if he survives her, then it reverts to him as joint tenant with his wife.[124]

Although the presumption of advancement applies as between transfers to or purchases in the name of the wife, it does not apply if the wife transfers property in the name of her husband or purchases such property in his name. In such a case the presumption of resulting trust will apply.[125] Furthermore, the presumption of advancement will not apply between a man and his mistress[126] or to cohabiting couples.[127]

The presumption of advancement will apply as between father and child but not between mother and child.[128] The fact that the presumption of advancement applies between father and child but not between mother and child is clearly a nonsense. The mother has the same parental duties to provide for a child as does the father.[129] In Australia the presumption of advancement applies equally whether the advancement is from a father of a mother. In a recent decision of the High Court, *Close Invoice Company Ltd v Abaowa*[130] Mr Simon Picken QC was strongly of the opinion that the presumption of advancement should not distinguish whether the advancement was made by a father

---

[120] For an excellent analysis, see G. Andrews, 'The Presumption of Advancement: Equity, Equality and Human Rights' (2007) Conv. 340. The author argues that the presumption clearly violates some of the provisions of the Convention which are enacted in the Human Rights Act 1998 as well as those which have yet to be ratified.

[121] [1970] AC 777.

[122] [1970] AC 777 at 824.

[123] Attempts at abolishing the presumption were made by the Family Law (Property and Maintenance) Bill 2005; however, this private member's bill was dropped owing to insufficient parliamentary time and has not been put before parliament again.

[124] (1877) 6 Ch. D 115 at 118.

[125] *Re Curtis* (1885) 52 LT 244; *Mercier v Mercier* [1903] 2 Ch. 98.

[126] *Diwell v Farnes* [1959] 1 WLR 624.

[127] *Rider v Kidder* (1805) 10 Ves. 360.

[128] *Re Roberts* [1946] Ch. 1.

[129] See, G. Kodilinye, 'Resulting Trusts, Advancement and Fraudulent Transfers' [1990] Conv. 213.

[130] [2010] EWHC 1920 (QB)

or a mother. In the course of his judgment, he explained that 'it seems to me that the modern society in this country is no less egalitarian than the equivalent in Australia, and that there is no question that the presumption of advancement applies in this country in 2010 just as the High Court of Australia held it did some 15 years ago in Australia.'[131] It is perhaps the father and child relationship which is historically regarded as the clearest case where a donative intent should be inferred. The ideology behind this is that a father is naturally bound to provide for and maintain his child and thus any transfers of property to the child only evidence his normal duty to so provide and maintain the child. In Australia the presumption of advancement applies equally to transfers by a husband as well as transfers by a mother to a child.[132] The presumption of advancement can of course be rebutted by a counter-presumption of resulting trust. For example, in **Re Gooch**[133] a father purchased in his son's name stock in a certain company more than sufficient to qualify the son to be a director of the company. The father, however, kept the relevant certificates in an envelope on which he had written 'belonging to me'. Furthermore, the son continued to pay the dividends on those shares to his father. The court held that the evidence before it meant that the legal presumption of gift was rebutted.

Finally, the presumption of advancement will also apply to a person who is standing in a relationship of *in loco parentis*. Such a relationship is said to arise where a person has taken upon himself the duty to provide for a child. A good example is where a person takes upon himself to provide for a stepson.[134]

Abolishing the presumption of advancement

Given the archaic and discriminatory manner in which the presumption of advancement operates, s. 199 of the Equality Act, when it comes into force, will abolish the presumption of advancement. The presumption of advancement is clearly in contravention of Article 5 of the Seventh Protocol to the Convention on Human Rights which provides that 'spouses shall enjoy equality of rights and responsibilities of a private law character between them, and in their relations with their children, as to marriage, during marriage and in the event of its dissolution.'[135]

KEY STATUTE

S. 199 Equality Act 2010

Abolition of presumption of advancement

(1) The presumption of advancement (by which, for example, a husband is presumed to be making a gift to his wife if he transfers property to her, or purchases property in her name) is abolished.

(2) The abolition by subsection (1) of the presumption of advancement does not have effect in relation to –

(a) anything done before the commencement of this section, or

(b) anything done pursuant to any obligation incurred before the commencement of this section.

---

[131] [2010] EWHC 1920 (QB) at para. 96.
[132] *Brown v Brown* (1993) 31 NSWLR 582; *Nelson v Nelson* [1995] 4 LRC 453.
[133] (1890) 62 LT 384.
[134] See, for example, *Re Paradise Motor Co Ltd* [1968] 1 WLR 1125 at 1139.
[135] See, J. Glister, 'How Not to Abolish the Presumption of Advancement' (2010) 73 MLR 807.

Rebutting the presumptions and evidential matters

So far it has been observed that a presumption of resulting trust will arise when there has been a voluntary transfer of property in the name of another or where there has been a purchase in the name of another. It has also been observed that, in some special relationships, a presumption of advancement will apply, thereby conferring upon the transferee a gift rather than a trust in favour of the transferor. Both the presumption of resulting trust and advancement can, of course, be rebutted. In the case of the presumption of a resulting trust, evidence can be put before the court to show that a gift was intended by the person voluntarily transferring or purchasing property in the name of another. In the case of a presumption of advancement, evidence can be put before the court which points to the conclusion that no gift was intended, and that the person transferring or purchasing property in the name of another intended to retain the beneficial ownership in the property. The burden of evidential proof clearly lies with the person against whom the presumption operates. Where a person seeks to rebut the presumption of resulting trust or presumption of advancement, the question arises as to the nature of the evidence that can be put before the court. In recent times, this has become a rather controversial area of law and has attracted many academic and judicial debates.[136] In particular, one question which has troubled the courts is the extent to which a person is entitled to rely on his illegal conduct to rebut the presumptions.

● Evidence of illegality

> **APPLYING THE LAW**
>
> Suppose that Alpha gratuitously transfers his house into the name of his wife, Beta. You will recall from the above discussion that such a transfer will raise the presumption of advancement from husband to wife.
>
> *Can Alpha rebut the presumption by explaining to a court that the only reason he transferred the house to his wife was to preserve the house from his creditors?*

Throughout this book recourse has been made to the well-known equitable maxim that 'he who comes to equity must come with clean hands'. The operation of this maxim is perhaps best illustrated in the context of voluntary transfers and resulting trusts. It is settled law that a person may not rely on his own illegal conduct to rebut the presumption of advancement. The matter is neatly illustrated in ***Gascoigne v Gascoigne***[137] where a husband took a lease of land in his wife's name and built a house on it using his own money. The effect of the purchase of the lease in his wife's name was to raise the presumption of advancement. One of the reasons for the purchase in the wife's name was to prevent the house becoming available to his creditors. On the separation of the husband and wife, the wife refused to assign the lease to the husband. The question before the court was whether the husband was entitled to rely on evidence of his illegality to rebut the presumption of advancement, the illegality being that he transferred the lease into

---

[136] See, F.D. Rose, 'Gratuitous Transfers and Illegal Purposes' (1996) LQR 386.
[137] [1918] 1 KB 223.

his wife's name for the sole purpose of defeating the claims of his creditors. The court held that evidence of illegality was inadmissible to rebut the presumption of advancement. The same principle was applied in **Tinker v Tinker**[138] where a husband, having moved to Cornwall to set up a garage business, purchased a house and conveyed it in the name of his wife. The sole reason for conveying the house into the name of his wife was to protect it from his creditors should his garage business fail. On the subsequent breakdown of the marriage, the husband sought to rebut the presumption of advancement by pointing to the fact that the purpose of the conveyance in his wife's name was to prevent it from being taken by his creditors. The Court of Appeal held that the husband was prevented from using evidence of his illegality to rebut the presumption of advancement. Lord Denning MR explained that it was:

> quite clear that the husband cannot have it both ways . . . He is on the horns of a dilemma. He cannot say that the house is his own and, at one and the same time, say that it is his wife's. As against his wife, he wants to say that it belongs to *him*. As against his creditors, that it belongs to her. That simply will not do. Either it was conveyed to her for her own use absolutely: or it was conveyed to her as trustee for her husband. It must be one or other. The presumption is that it was conveyed to her for her own use: and he does not rebut that presumption by saying that he only did it to defeat his creditors. I think it belongs to her.[139]

Illegality giving rise to the presumption but not to its rebuttal

Authorities such as **Gascoigne v Gascoigne**[140] and **Tinker v Tinker**[141] laid down a very clear principle of law that evidence of an illegal nature will not be admissible to rebut the presumption of advancement. Furthermore, it was generally understood that the court would not intervene even when the evidence of illegality was not needed to rebut any presumption.[142] In other words, the principle in equity was a strict one and no person could benefit in any way from their illegal conduct. Despite this, a rather more liberal approach was adopted by House of Lords in **Tinsley v Milligan**[143] where it was held that where no presumption of advancement arises, but only a presumption of resulting trust, the presumption of resulting trust remains good despite an element of illegal conduct which gives rise to it. This is otherwise known as the 'reliance principle' and is discussed in more detail below. The facts of the case involved two lesbians, Ms Tinsley and Ms Milligan, who purchased a house which was conveyed in the name of Ms Tinsley despite contributions by both of them. The main reason for conveying the house in the sole name of Ms Tinsley was to allow Ms Milligan to make false claims for housing benefit from the Department of Social Security (DSS). Indeed, the evidence before the court showed that both Ms Tinsley and Ms Milligan had made false claims for benefits from the DSS. Ms Milligan subsequently disclosed the fraud to the DSS and settled the matter with

---

[138] [1970] P 136. See also *Re Emery's Investments Trusts* [1959] Ch. 410 where a husband was unable to rely on evidence which pointed to a tax avoidance plan, and *Chettiar v Chettiar* [1962] 1 All ER 494 where a father was unable to rely on evidence that he purchased a rubber plantation in the name of his son only because the law restricted the maximum area of rubber land capable of being owned by one individual.

[139] [1970] P 136 at 141.

[140] [1918] 1 KB 223.

[141] [1970] P 136.

[142] See, for example, the judgment of Lord Eldon in *Muckleston v Brown* (1801) 6 Ves. 52 at 69 where his Lordship said 'let the estate lie, where it falls'.

[143] [1994] 1 AC 340.

the authorities. When the relationship between Ms Tinsley and Ms Milligan broke down, Ms Tinsley moved out. She then later commenced proceedings to recover possession of the house on the grounds that she was the legal owner thereof. Ms Milligan, on the other hand, claimed an order for sale of the land on the grounds that she had a beneficial interest in the house and was therefore entitled to a share on it. The question before the House of Lords was whether Ms Milligan was entitled to a share in the house despite not taking the legal title in order to defraud the DSS.

A bare majority of the House of Lords held that a resulting trust arose in favour of Ms Milligan as soon as the house was purchased in the name of Ms Tinsley. As such Ms Milligan's interest was set up by the resulting trust and the question of illegality was not relevant as she did not require it to be used to set up her claim. The House of Lords affirmed the principle established in cases such as *Gascoigne* v *Gascoigne*[144] that evidence of an illegal purpose was not capable of rebutting the presumption of advancement; however, this was not relevant to the particular facts before the House of Lords. Put simply, Ms Milligan did not need to use evidence of her illegal conduct to set up her claim because that claim had been set up by a resulting trust. *Tinsley* v *Milligan* was subsequently applied in *Silverwood* v *Silverwood*[145] where an old lady was advised by her son to transfer money from her account into the names of her grandchildren. The reason for the transfer was to allow her to claim income support from the DSS, which would otherwise not be available given the funds she had in her account. When she died, her son who was the executor of her will, claimed that the children held the money on resulting trust for the grandmother. The Court of Appeal held that a resulting trust arose in favour of the grandmother and the son and, being the executor of his mother's will, the son was entitled to claim the money from the children. The Court of Appeal affirmed the principle that where no presumption of advancement applied, a claimant was entitled to recover property even though he may have been a party to the illegal conduct, thus proving that illegal conduct was not fatal to set up the claim in the first place. Similarly in *Lowson* v *Coombes*[146] where a man was able to claim property under a resulting trust which had been transferred in the sole name of his mistress in order to defeat any claims by his former wife. Robert Walker LJ held that the principle in *Tinsley* v *Milligan* applied, although at the same time reserving judgment as to its appropriateness. In the course of his judgment he commented that '[t]he importance attached by the majority to the presumption of advancement does to my mind create difficulties, because the presumption has been cogently criticised both as out of date in modern social and economic conditions'.[147]

The so-called 'reliance principle' which comes from the decision of the House of Lords in *Tinsley* v *Milligan*[148] holds that a claimant is entitled to enforce his or her equitable rights despite his illegality in circumstances where he or she does not need to rely on the illegal conduct to prove the interest. Thus in *Tinsley* v *Milligan* Ms Milligan did not need to rely on her illegal conduct to prove that she had an interest in the property. A resulting trust operated in her favour and this was sufficient to establish her equitable interest in the property. In its recent report in this area, the Law Commission explained the reliance principle in the following manner.

---

[144] [1918] 1 KB 223.
[145] (1997) 74 P & CR 453.
[146] [1999] Ch. 373.
[147] [1999] Ch. 373 at 386.
[148] [1994] 1 AC 340.

The Illegality Defence (2010) Law Com Report 320 at 2.2

Explaining the 'reliance principle'

How this principle works in practice can be shown by two straightforward examples.

Example 1: Mr A transfers some business assets to a friend, Mr B. Mr B agrees to hold the assets for Mr A and return them to him when requested. The purpose of the arrangement is to hide the assets from Mr A's creditors. Once the creditors have left empty-handed Mr A asks for the assets back. Mr B refuses to return them, arguing that because of the illegal purpose of the arrangement, the trust in Mr A's favour is unenforceable. However, the law presumes that when Mr A transferred the assets to Mr B for no consideration, a resulting trust arose in Mr A's favour. Mr A can therefore establish this trust by relying on the presumption without any need to plead or lead evidence of the illegality involved. Under the reliance principle Mr A will succeed and the illegality has no effect.

Example 2: Now suppose that Mr A transferred the assets not to a friend but to his wife, Mrs A. Because the transfer is from husband to wife, the law presumes that Mr A intended to make a gift. Generally Mr A would be able to lead evidence of the arrangement which he and Mrs A entered into, in order to rebut this presumption of advancement and show that his intention was to create a trust in his favour. However, this would involve leading evidence of the illegal purpose of his scheme. Under the reliance principle Mr A is not permitted to do this and his claim against his wife will fail.

The approach in *Tinsley* v *Milligan*[149] has been subjected to a number of criticisms. The first and foremost criticism relates to the arbitrary way in which it operates and the discriminatory results that it produces as a result of its application. Clearly the rule operates to prevent a person from relying on illegal conduct when he attempts to rebut the presumption of advancement. However, it allows a person to take the benefit of a resulting trust even though the resulting trust arises as a result of some illegality. A husband who voluntarily transfers property to his wife in order to defeat his creditors cannot use evidence of his illegal motives to rebut the presumption of advancement. However, as the decision in *Lowson* v *Coombes* illustrates, a man can voluntarily transfer or purchase property in his mistress's name with a view to defeating the claims of his former wife and still succeed in retaining the beneficial ownership in the property transferred. Given the fact that the presumption of advancement is clearly out-dated and not relevant to modern day social relationships, it is very difficult to justify these decisions on the discriminatory effect they have.

A second problem with the approach in *Tinsley* v *Milligan* relates to the inflexible way in which it operates. Clearly the case decides that evidence of illegality, whether trivial or extensive, is not admissible to rebut the presumption of advancement. On the other hand, once a resulting trust arises it does not matter that the resulting trust has arisen because of some illegal conduct on the part of the person transferring property. This 'all or nothing' approach can produce some rather bizarre conclusions. Where the illegality on the part of the claimant is trivial, should that be considered by the court before it refuses to rebut the presumption of advancement? Equally, on the other hand, where a

---

[149] [1994] 1 AC 340.

resulting trust arises in favour of a claimant who has been involved in a massive illegal purpose, should the court continue to recognise his equitable interest in the property even though he does not need to rely on that illegal conduct to set up a claim to the property? In this respect there is a lot to be said for the examples given by Goff LJ in his dissenting judgment in *Tinsley* **v** *Milligan*.[150] His Lordship explained that there:

> may be cases in which the fraud is far more serious than that in the present case, and is uncovered not as a result of a confession but only after a lengthy police investigation and a prolonged criminal trial. Again there may be cases in which a group of terrorists, or armed robbers, secure a base for their criminal activities by buying a house in the name of a third party not directly implicated in those activities. In cases such as these there will almost certainly be no presumption of advancement. Is it really to be said that criminals such as these, or their personal representatives, are entitled to invoke the assistance of a court of equity in order to establish an equitable interest in property? It may be said that these are extreme cases; but I find it difficult to see how, in this context at least, it is possible to distinguish between degrees of iniquity. At all events, I cannot think that the harsh consequences which will arise from the application of the established principle in a case such as the present provide a satisfactory basis for developing the law in a manner which will open the door to far more unmeritorious cases, especially as the proposed development in the law appears to me to be contrary to the established principle underlying the authorities.[151]

Instead of the inflexible approach there is something to be said for the 'public-conscience test' advocated by Nicholls LJ the Court of Appeal in *Tinsley* **v** *Milligan*.[152] Although this was subsequently rejected by the House of Lords in *Tinsley* **v** *Milligan* on the grounds that it conferred too wide a discretion on a judge, it requires the court to carry out a cost–benefit analysis when deciding whether to recognise or reject a property claim arising as a result of some illegality. Nicholls LJ explained that 'the court must weigh, or balance, the adverse consequences of granting relief against the adverse consequences of refusing relief. The ultimate decision calls for a value judgment.'[153] Such an approach would, indeed, have given much more discretion to the court to assess each case on its facts. However, it is submitted that this discretionary approach would do more justice on the facts than is currently done under the rather inflexible approach in *Tinsley* **v** *Milligan*. In Australia the High Court in *Nelson* **v** *Nelson*[154] has rejected the approach in *Tinsley* **v** *Milligan*[155] and opted for a more flexible approach based on public policy. On the facts of this case, Mrs Nelson purchased a house in the names of her children in order to take advantage of a subsidy in the purchase of another house under the relevant Australian legislation. A subsidy would only be available to Mrs Nelson if she could show that she did not have any other house in her name. Subsequently after receiving the subsidy, the house, which was conveyed in the name of the children, was sold and one of the children claimed to be entitled to half the proceeds. Such a claim would arise on the grounds that Mrs Nelson, by purchasing the house in the name of her children, had intended to make a gift to them on the grounds that the presumption of advancement applied. The High Court of Australia allowed Mrs Nelson to rebut the presumption of advancement provided that the subsidy was returned to the relevant authorities.

---

[150] [1994] 1 AC 340.
[151] [1994] 1 AC 340 at 362.
[152] [1992] Ch. 310.
[153] [1992] Ch. 310 at 319.
[154] [1995] 4 LRC 453.
[155] [1992] Ch. 310.

⬤ Illegality not carried out

Shortly after the decision in *Tinsley* **v** *Milligan* an interesting question arose in *Tribe* **v** *Tribe*[156] as to whether a claimant was entitled to rely on his illegal conduct to rebut a presumption of advancement in circumstances where the illegal conduct was clearly intended but not carried out in the end. The decision of the Court of Appeal was yet to fuel more controversy over the extent to which the court should recognise property rights in the face of some illegality on the part of a person claiming property. The facts concerned a claimant who held the majority of shares in a private company selling ladies' clothes from a number of shop outlets. The shops were taken out on lease and two of them were in need of substantial repairs and improvements. Fearing that the landlord of the shops would make substantial claims for the dilapidations to the shop premises, the claimant transferred the shares to his son in order to protect them from claims by potential creditors. The company came to an agreement over the lease of the shops with the consequence that no such action would be brought against the claimant. The claimant then requested that the son transfer the shares back to him. The son refused to transfer the shares and the claimant commenced proceeding to recover them. In order to succeed the claimant would have to rebut the presumption of advancement which operated against him.

The Court of Appeal held in favour of the claimant on the grounds that the presumption of advancement was rebutted by a resulting trust in his favour. The principal reason for this was that the illegal purpose, that is the intention to defraud his creditors, had not been carried out. The landlord was not going to make any claims for the dilapidations against the claimant, with the consequence that no creditors would have been deceived. In the course of his judgment Millett LJ explained the state of the law as follows.

KEY CITATION

Tribe v Tribe [1996] Ch. 107 (A statement of the current law on illegality and presumptions of resulting trust and advancement, per Millett LJ at 134)

(1) Title to property passes both at law and in equity even if the transfer is made for an illegal purpose. The fact that title has passed to the transferee does not preclude the transferor from bringing an action for restitution.

(2) The transferor's action will fail if it would be illegal for him to retain any interest in the property.

(3) Subject to (2) the transferor can recover the property if he can do so without relying on the illegal purpose. This will normally be the case where the property was transferred without consideration in circumstances where the transferor can rely on an express declaration of trust or a resulting trust in his favour.

(4) It will almost invariably be so where the illegal purpose has not been carried out. It may be otherwise where the illegal purpose has been carried out and the transferee can rely on the transferor's conduct as inconsistent with his retention of a beneficial interest.

▶

---

[156] [1996] Ch. 107.

(5) The transferor can lead evidence of the illegal purpose whenever it is necessary for him to do so provided that he has withdrawn from the transaction before the illegal purpose has been wholly or partly carried into effect. It will be necessary for him to do so (i) if he brings an action at law or (ii) if he brings proceedings in equity and needs to rebut the presumption of advancement.

(6) The only way in which a man can protect his property from his creditors is by divesting himself of all beneficial interest in it. Evidence that he transferred the property in order to protect it from his creditors, therefore, does nothing by itself to rebut the presumption of advancement; it reinforces it. To rebut the presumption it is necessary to show that he intended to retain a beneficial interest and conceal it from his creditors.

(7) The court should not conclude that this was his intention without compelling circumstantial evidence to this effect. The identity of the transferee and the circumstances in which the transfer was made would be highly relevant. It is unlikely that the court would reach such a conclusion where the transfer was made in the absence of an imminent and perceived threat from known creditors.

Reform

There is no doubt that the current law as exemplified in cases such as **Tinsley v Milligan**[157] and **Tribe v Tribe**[158] does produce some rather unsatisfactory results. Whilst the decisions in both of those cases did justice on the individual facts – for example recognising an ownership interest in a house in circumstances where Ms Milligan had repented to the relevant authorities; and returning shares to a father who intended to leave them to the family rather than half to just one son – the principles which emerge as a result are more problematic. As already explained, the outcomes are purely arbitrary and have a discriminatory effect depending on which presumption is applicable on any given set of facts. For example, a husband who transfers property in the name of his wife cannot use evidence of his illegal conduct to rebut the presumption of advancement. However, a man who transfers property to his mistress in order to defraud his creditors may well get away with defrauding his creditors as well as retaining a beneficial interest under a resulting trust. Furthermore, the law at the moment does not allow the court to take into consideration the seriousness of the illegality. In so far as the decision in **Tribe v Tribe** is concerned, there appears to be an uncomfortable distinction between cases where a person is fortunate enough that his illegality was not carried into effect and cases where the illegality does succeed. The question of intention appears to be wholly irrelevant.

In 1999 the Law Commission reviewed this area of the law and made a number of recommendations.[159] One of the fundamental concerns of the Law Commission was the

---

[157] [1992] Ch. 310.
[158] [1996] Ch. 107.
[159] Law. Com. CP No. 154 (1999) *Illegal Transactions: The Effect of Illegality on Contracts and Trusts.*

arbitrary way in which the current law operates. The thrust of the Law Commission's recommendations is that the courts should enjoy a statutory discretion. Under such discretion a court would decide whether illegality should act as a defence to normal rights and remedies, and would take into account the following factors:

- the seriousness of the illegality involved;
- the knowledge and intention of the party claiming relief;
- whether denying the claim would deter the illegality;
- whether denying the claim would further the purpose of the rule which rendered the transaction illegal;
- whether denying the claim would be proportionate to the illegality involved.

In March 2010 the Law Commission published its Final Report in this area entitled *The Illegality Defence*.[160] The Report was accompanied by a Draft Bill recommending legislative reform in the context of concealment of interests under a trust. Unlike the original reports referred to above, the Final Report does not address legal property rights and those rights in contract and tort. The basic thrust of the Report and the Draft Bill is to give a statutory discretion to apply the illegality defence. The Law Commission recommends that in most cases a beneficiary should be able to enforce his or her normal equitable rights under a trust; however, in exceptional circumstances the court would have discretion to deny the beneficiary a right to enforce those rights. The Draft Bill sets out a list of factors which the court should look to when raising the illegality defence thereby denying the beneficiary a right to his or her equitable interest.[161]

The Law Commission identifies the following factors which the court should take into consideration when exercising the discretion to apply the illegality defence:

1 the conduct and intention of all of the relevant parties;
2 the value of the equitable interest at stake;
3 the effect of allowing the claim on the criminal purpose;
4 whether refusing the claim would act as a deterrent; and
5 the possibility that the person from whom the equitable interest was being concealed may have an interest in the value of the assets of the beneficiary.

In its Final Report the Law Commission explained 'that in each individual case the courts should consider whether the illegality defence can be justified on the basis of the policies that underlie that defence. The law would be clearer, more transparent and easier to understand if judges discussed these policy considerations openly in relation to the facts of the case before them.' In support of this approach, the Law Commission referred to two decisions of the House of Lords which they felt demonstrated the way forward in exercising the statutory defence. These cases were not

---

[160] (2010) Law Com Report No. 320.
[161] For an excellent account of the Report and the Draft Bill, see, P. Davis, 'The Illegality Defence: Turning Back the Clock' Conv (2010) 282.

decided in the context of concealment of interests under a trust but rather in the context of legal rights in tort and contract. The first case is **Gray v Thames Trains**[162] where a claimant suffered injuries as a result of a train crash and these injuries were followed by post traumatic distress. These injuries, and in particular the mental injuries, had a grave effect on his personality. Some two years later, the claimant stabbed to death a stranger and he was convicted of manslaughter on grounds of diminished responsibility. The claimant commenced civil proceedings for damages for loss of earnings from the time of the train crash and general damages for his detention and conviction for manslaughter. The House of Lords held that whilst he was entitled to damages from the time of the rail crash up until the homicide, he was not entitled to general damages thereafter for his conviction and detention. It was not disputed that the claimant may not have killed anyone had he not suffered the mental injuries as a result of the train crash, but in the words of Lord Hoffmann, 'you cannot recover for damage which flows directly from loss of liberty, a fine or other punishment lawfully imposed upon you in consequence of your unlawful act.'[163] The House of Lords explained that it was not possible to recover compensation for losses suffered as a result of one's own criminal conduct. To do so would offend public notions of fairness. The approach adopted in **Gray v Thames Trains** is a much more effective approach than the reliance approach in **Tinsley v Milligan**.[164]

The second decision referred to in the Final Report of the Law Commission is **Stone & Rolls v Moore Stephens**[165] where a company, Stone & Rolls, was controlled by a certain Mr Stojevic. Mr Stojevic used the company to defraud a number of banks by setting up fraudulent letters of credit. The auditors of the company were a firm called Moore Stephens who were not aware of these fraudulent letters of credit. An action was brought by one of the banks and both Mr Stojevic and Moore Stephens were found guilty of deceit and the company, Stone & Rolls, was put into liquidation. The liquidators of Stone & Rolls commenced proceedings against Moore Stephens on the grounds that they had been negligent and in breach of contract in failing to detect the fraud earlier. Moore Stephens counter-argued that the action should fail on the grounds that Stone & Rolls had to rely on their own illegality to prove their case. By a majority of three to two the House of Lords held that the illegality of Mr Stojevic should be attributed to Stone & Rolls and therefore the claim was barred. Unlike the decision in **Gray v Thames Trains**[166] where the House of Lords took the view that the illegality defence should be justified on grounds of public policy, the decision in **Stone & Rolls v Moore Stephens**[167] does not seem to provide any clear guidance as to why the illegality defence should or should not be pleaded.

The suggested reforms of the Law Commission remain to be implemented in legislation, and until such time as that happens, the current law continues to apply.

---

[162] [2009] UKHL 33.
[163] [2009] UKHL 33 at 50.
[164] [1994] 1 AC 340.
[165] [2009] UKHL 39.
[166] [2009] UKHL 33.
[167] [2009] UKHL 39.

Resulting trusts and the family home

Charlie and Simone have been seeing each other for a long time. They do not wish to get married; however, they wish to buy a place where they can live together. They see a lovely cottage and decide to purchase it. The title to the house is taken in the name of Simone. Simone's father provides 20 per cent of the purchase price. Simone picks up a mortgage to cover the remainder of the purchase price. Charlie and Simone move into the house and Charlie, being redundant, spends a lot of time renovating the property. Simone continues to work and she discharges the mortgage. Charlie makes significant renovations to the property which increases its value by 10 per cent. Last year Charlie and Simone's relationship broke down. Charlie claims that he has a substantial interest in the cottage.

Does Charlie have an interest in the cottage?

The final part of this chapter looks at the role resulting trusts have played in resolving ownership interests in the family home. In recent times, the resulting trust, along with the constructive trust,[168] has become a primary vehicle for determining the rights of married and unmarried couples who have taken ownership of a family home. The recourse to resulting and constructive trusts has risen for a number of reasons. Initially the recourse to the doctrines of resulting and constructive trusts became popular in the context of married couples. After the Second World War, the social and economic structure of married couples changed significantly. Whereas at the turn of the twentieth century where ownership of private homes was less significant than it is today, in the middle of the twentieth century private ownership began to increase. The increase was primarily influenced by a number of factors, not least the availability of mortgage finance. Another development was the rise in the number of women securing employment and contributing towards the family home in some way or other, in addition to raising children. Despite these changes, some of the existing trends continued, for example the typical dominance of the husband and the title being taken in most cases in his name. As these social and economic conditions continued to change, husbands and wives rarely made any formal understanding about the ownership of the family home. With the increase in divorce, it soon became apparent to the courts that parties to the marriage, predominantly the wife, would assert ownership claims in the land. The problem facing the courts was essentially finding a means of establishing beneficial ownership in circumstances where the parties had not given any thought to the question of shared ownership at the time of the purchase of the property. In the absence of any special rules governing married couples, the courts had no choice but to apply the general rules of resulting and constructive trusts to resolve ownership disputes. These rules, however, were not always satisfactory in bringing about a just result on the facts of individual cases. As a result of a series of House of Lords' cases decided in the early 1970s, which are discussed below, it soon became apparent that a statutory jurisdiction would be needed to adjust the property rights of married couples in the event of a divorce. The

---

[168] Considered in the next chapter.

statutory jurisdiction came in the form of the Matrimonial Causes Act 1973, which conferred a power on the court to make property adjustment orders in the event of a divorce.

Although the Matrimonial Causes Act 1973 and the Civil Partnership Act 2004 conferred upon the courts a power to make property adjustment orders on separation, it did not mean the end of recourse to resulting and constructive trust doctrines in the context of married couples. In a number of cases coming before the courts, the question was not of divorce, but rather one relating to whether one of the parties to the marriage had an equitable interest which was subsequently binding on a bank that may have provided a mortgage. For example, a husband with legal title to the family home may well have mortgaged it to a bank. On the subsequent default of payment by the husband, the bank would normally exercise its rights to take possession of the land with a view to sale. Typically, a wife would argue that she had acquired a beneficial interest in the land by virtue of a resulting or constructive trust which was binding on the bank.

In the twenty-first century, one of the significant contexts in which resulting and constructive have operated is non-marital cohabitation. In its most recent report on cohabitation, the Law Commission highlighted the significant trends in the growth of non-marital cohabitation.[169] Unlike married cohabitation where there is a statutory framework for making property orders on separation, no such equivalent jurisdiction exists in the case of non-marital cohabitation. It is in the context of such non-marital cohabitation that the courts have had to apply the general principles of resulting and constructive law in order to resolve the ownership disputes between the cohabiting parties.

Purchase money resulting trusts

The principal manner in which a resulting trust will arise in the context of the ownership of a family home is where one cohabiting party purchases property in the name of another cohabitee. You will recall from the earlier discussion in this chapter that 'a trust of a legal estate . . . results to the man who advances the purchase money'.[170] As explained above, the resulting trust will arise in the absence of some express or common intention as to the beneficial ownership of the land. If the parties have expressly declared the extent of their beneficial interest in the family home, then that express declaration will determine their respective rights. If the cohabiting parties have a common intention as to the ownership of the home, then that ownership will be determined by the principles of constructive trusts as applied in the context of family property. These are discussed in more detail in Chapter 13.

What contributions count?

By far the most significant question when addressing resulting trusts in the context of the family home is: what contributions count? The orthodox principle is that only direct contributions to the purchase price at the time of the acquisition of the family home will be sufficient. The matter is neatly explained by one leading treatise on land law, which writes that under 'a resulting trust beneficial shares crystallise in accordance with money contributions made at the date of acquisition of title and are not thereafter capable of variation merely because of supervening reconfigurations of the parties' finances'.[171] A

---

[169] Law Com. No. 307 (2007) *Cohabitation: The Financial Consequences of Relationship Breakdown* (this report is considered in more detail in Chapter 13).

[170] *Dyer* v *Dyer* (1788) 2 Cox. Eq. Cas. 92 at 93.

[171] This quote is taken from the 3rd edition of *Elements of Land Law* (2001) at p. 694; see also K. Gray and S. Gray *Elements of Land Law* 5th edn (2009) at p. 845.

good illustration of a resulting trust arising upon a direct contribution to the purchase price is **Tinsley v Milligan**[172] where it has already been observed that two lesbian partners contributed equally to the purchase of a house. The House of Lords held that Ms Milligan was entitled to half of the beneficial interest in the home under a resulting trust. The extent of the equitable interest under a resulting trust, as will be seen below, will vary according to the level of contribution. In **Arogundade v Arogundade**[173] a flat was purchased for £207,000 and conveyed in the name of the husband. The wife later sought to register an interest in the flat on the grounds that she had contributed to its purchase. After a lengthy review of the sources of the money which enabled the purchase of the flat, the High Court held that the wife was entitled to a 30 per cent interest in the flat by way of resulting trust.

Clearly a direct contribution to the purchase price will be sufficient, for example, a cash payment of 50 per cent. However, it is also clear that other forms of contribution may be sufficient to generate a presumption of resulting trust in the family home. In **Gissing v Gissing**[174] it was explained by Lord Diplock that a contribution in the form of an initial deposit or to the legal costs would be sufficient to generate a beneficial interest under a resulting trust. His Lordship explained that 'the fact that the wife made a cash contribution to the deposit and legal charges not borrowed on mortgage gives rise, in the absence of evidence which makes some other explanation more probable, to the inference that their common intention was that she should share in the beneficial interest in the land conveyed'.[175] In **Midland Bank plc v Cooke**[176] a house was purchased in the sole name of Mr Cooke in 1971. The house was acquired primarily with the aid of a mortgage as well as Mr Cooke's savings and a wedding present of £1100 given to both Mr and Mrs Cooke. The Court of Appeal held that because Mr and Mrs Cooke were jointly entitled to the wedding present, Mrs Cooke had in fact contributed £550 towards the purchase price of the trust. Thus in accordance with the established principles of resulting trusts, she was entitled to 6.47 per cent interest in the home.[177]

Other forms of contributions include a discount available to a tenant of a long lease who wishes to acquire the freehold under the provisions of Part V of the Housing Act 1985. Over the past few years a number of cases have come before the courts illustrating that a discount will count as a contribution to the purchase price. In **Springette v Defoe**[178] the Court of Appeal held that a discount of 41 per cent constituted a contribution to the purchase price of a house in which the tenant had resided for eleven years. In **Oxley v Hiscock**[179] Alan Hiscock and Elayne Oxley had been residing at 35 Dickens Close since 1991. The title to the house was in Mr Hiscock's name alone. According to Mrs Oxley she did not appear on the title because Mr Hiscock had told her that this might prejudice any claims by her former partner. The house was purchased for £127,000 and the purchase price came from a number of sources: firstly, there was a mortgage of £30,000 secured

---

[172] [1992] Ch. 310.

[173] [2005] EWHC 1766 (Ch.).

[174] [1971] AC 886.

[175] [1971] AC 886 at 907.

[176] [1995] 4 All ER 562.

[177] It will be observed in Chapter 13 that Mrs Cooke's interest was eventually held to be 50 per cent; however, that conclusion was based on the fact that she was also entitled to an interest under a common intention constructive trust. The rules for quantification of interests under a constructive trust are fundamentally different from those under a resulting trust.

[178] [1992] 2 FLR 388.

[179] [2004] 3 All ER 703; see S. Panesar, 'Quantifying a Beneficial Interest in Non-Marital Cohabitation' (2004) *Law Teacher* 38(3) at 395.

over the house; secondly, £35,000 of Mr Hiscock's own savings; finally, a sum of £61,500, which represented the sale of a certain 39 Page Close, this being the house that Mrs Oxley had formerly occupied as a secure tenant but which she acquired sometime in 1987 by the exercise of her rights under Part V of the Housing Act 1985. The value of 39 Page Close was put at £45,200; however, because of the right to buy legislation, Mrs Oxley was entitled to a discount of £20,000 and as such was entitled to purchase the property for a sum of £25,200. The Court of Appeal held that the discount constituted a contribution to the purchase price.[180] More recently in *Laskar* v *Laskar*[181] one lady exercised her right to buy a house from the council at a discount. However, unable to finance the whole purchase price, she took the title in her name and the name of another lady. When the relationship subsequently broke down, the question arose before the Court of Appeal as to the extent of the beneficial interests of the two ladies. In respect of the discount, Neuberger LJ explained that the only reason why the property could be purchased in the first instance was that one of the ladies was entitled to a discount which constituted a contribution to the purchase price. It should be emphasised that cases such a *Oxley* v *Hiscock*[182] and *Laskar* v *Laskar*,[183] whilst recognising the nature of a discount as a contribution to the purchase price, have in fact been ultimately resolved by applying the common intention constructive trust principles, which are considered in Chapter 13. The cases illustrate that disputes over the beneficial interests in a family home are more appropriately dealt with under constructive trust principles. The reasons for this development are explained in more detail below.

Mortgage contributions

One particular type of contribution which has caused some difficulties in the law is the contribution to mortgage payments. The difficulty stems from the fact that the payment to mortgage monies, which are usually staggered over a period of time, do not fit neatly into the orthodox ideology of resulting trusts which presumes intentions at the time of the purchase of property. It is the contribution to the purchase price at the time of the acquisition that is the basis for the imputation of intention. However, despite the orthodox position, and given the increased use of mortgage finance, the courts have treated mortgage payments as contributions to the purchase price of property in some circumstances. However, the law is yet to be fully analysed. In *Curley* v *Parkes*[184] Peter Gibson LJ explained that 'the relevant principle is that the resulting trust of a property purchased in the name of another, in the absence of contrary intention, arises once and for all at the date on which the property is acquired. Because of the liability assumed by the mortgagor in a case where monies are borrowed by the mortgagor to be used on the purchase, the mortgagor is treated as having provided the proportion of the purchase price attributable to the monies so borrowed.'[185] Thus where, for example, A purchases land with the aid of a mortgage for £80,000 which he alone pays, and B merely advances £20,000 for the deposit, A's payment of the mortgage will be treated as a contribution to the purchase price. This would give A an 80 per cent interest in the house and B a

---

[180] The decision in this case was eventually resolved by applying principles of constructive trusts based on the common intentions of the parties.
[181] [2008] 1 WLR 2695.
[182] [2004] EWCA Civ. 546
[183] [2008] EWCA Civ. 347.
[184] [2004] EWCA Civ. 1515.
[185] [2004] EWCA Civ. 1515 at [15].

20 percent interest under a resulting trust. If the mortgage is take in the joint names of A and B with the intention that both are to equally discharge the mortgage, then B would have a 60 per cent interest under a resulting trust on the basis that B has made a half contribution to the mortgage.

However, subsequent payments made to a mortgage which were not agreed on between cohabiting parties will not count as contributions to the purchase price. In *Curley v Parkes*[186] Peter Gibson LJ explained that:

> subsequent payments of the mortgage instalments are not part of the purchase price already paid to the vendor, but are sums paid for discharging the mortgagor's obligations under the mortgage . . . By reason of that principle and the modern reliance on mortgage finance the importance of the resulting trust has diminished, and instead reliance is generally placed on a constructive trust where an agreement or common intention can be found or inferred from the circumstances.[187]

The matter is illustrated by the decision in *Cowcher v Cowcher*[188] where a wife, who had already acquired an interest of 30 per cent under a resulting trust, sought to claim a larger interest on the grounds that she occasionally contributed to the mortgage when the husband fell into arrears. Bagnall J refused to increase the entitlement under the resulting trust on the grounds that it had crystallised at the time of the acquisition.[189] The wife was entitled to a personal claim for the money she had paid towards the mortgage but not by way of an interest in the house. Although a subsequent payment towards a mortgage will not be sufficient to raise a presumption of a resulting trust, it will be observed in Chapter 13 that such subsequent payment may play an important part in evidencing a common intention of some shared ownership in the home. Unlike a resulting trust, a constructive trust need not arise contemporaneously with the acquisition of the title to the family home.

Indirect contributions

Indirect contributions to the family home will not be sufficient to raise the presumption of a resulting trust. Where one of the cohabiting partners, usually the one whose name is absent from the legal title, contributes to the household expenses and other domestic endeavour, no resulting trust will arise. This is despite the fact that such a person may have made it easier for the legal owner to discharge the mortgage. For example, a partner who pays the bills and puts the food on the table as well as raising the children will acquire no interest under a purchase price resulting trust. The principle is neatly illustrated in *Gissing v Gissing*[190] where a matrimonial home was conveyed in the sole name of the husband. Both husband and wife had maintained separate finances, but the wife made no direct contribution to the purchase price. The wife did, however, contribute some £220 towards the furnishings and laying down a lawn. The husband left the wife, and the wife sought a declaration as to her interest in the matrimonial home. The House of Lords held that the wife had no interest in the home. Similarly, in *Pettitt v Pettitt*[191] a wife purchased a cottage in her sole name, having provided all of the purchase price. The

---

[186] [2004] EWCA Civ. 1515.
[187] [2004] EWCA Civ. 1515 at [15].
[188] [1972] 1 WLR 425.
[189] See also *McKenzie v McKenzie* [2003] EWHC 601 (Ch).
[190] [1971] AC 886.
[191] [1970] AC 777.

husband, however spent a lot of his own money and labour on improving the property. When the husband and wife separated, the husband commenced proceedings under s. 17 of the Married Women's Property Act 1882 in order to claim an equitable interest in the cottage. The House of Lords held that he had no interest in the cottage: furthermore, that s. 17 of the 1882 Act did not confer a discretion on a court to vary existing property rights in land, but merely to recognise those which had been properly acquired. In the present instance, the husband had not acquired any property interest in the cottage.

Although cases such as *Gissing v Gissing* and *Pettitt v Pettitt* must now be seen in light of the Matrimonial Causes Act 1973,[192] the general law on purchase price resulting trusts remains. In the context of non-marital cohabitation indirect contributions will not confer any interest under a resulting trust. In *Burns v Burns*[193] an unmarried couple had resided in a house which had been purchased in the sole name of the man. The man paid the purchase price and paid off the mortgage using his own money. The female partner raised two children, contributed to the household expenses as well as furnishing the home. When the couple split up, the female partner sought to claim an equitable interest in the home. Unable to rely on the provisions of the Matrimonial Causes Act 1973, the female partner sought to argue that she was entitled under an implied trust in her favour. The Court of Appeal held that, with regard to a resulting trust, the female partner was unable to claim any interest, on the grounds that she had not made any direct contribution to the purchase price.

Quantification

In the case of a purchase price resulting trust, the quantification of the beneficial interest is a purely arithmetical exercise. The size of the equitable interest depends on the level of contribution. Thus where A contributes 50 per cent of the purchase prince to a house which is taken in the sole name of B, A acquires half of the beneficial interest in the house. The matter is neatly illustrated by the decision in *Midland Bank plc v Cooke*[194] where it has already been observed that a house was purchased in the sole name of Mr Cooke in 1971. The house was acquired primarily with the aid of a mortgage as well as Mr Cooke's savings and a wedding present of £1100 given to both Mr and Mrs Cooke. The Court of Appeal held that because Mr and Mrs Cooke were jointly entitled to the wedding present, Mrs Cooke had in fact contributed £550 towards the purchase price of the trust. Thus in accordance with the established principles of resulting trusts, she was entitled to 6.47 per cent interest in the home. As noted earlier, Mrs Cooke was also held to be entitled to an interest under a common intention constructive trust, which actually gave her a 50 per cent interest in the house.[195] This aspect of the case is analysed in more detail in Chapter 13.

Differences between resulting and constructive trusts in the family context

The purchase price resulting trust has not been the only vehicle by which a cohabiting partner is able to secure some beneficial interest in the family home. More recently,

---

[192] In relation to same-sex relationships, see Civil Partnership Act 2004.
[193] [1984] Ch. 317.
[194] [1995] 4 All ER 562.
[195] See also *Drake v Whipp* [1996] 1 FLR 826.

the common intention constructive trust, which is examined in much more detail in Chapter 13, has been frequently invoked in order to set up a claim to some beneficial entitlement to co-owned land. Although the common intention constructive trust is examined in more detail in Chapter 13, it is important at this stage to distinguish between the purchase price resulting trust and the common intention constructive trust. Whilst both the purchase price resulting trust and the common intention constructive trust are, post the developments in **Westdeutsche Landesbank Girozentrale v Islington LBC**,[196] enforced primarily on the grounds of conscience in that it would be unconscionable for the legal owner to deny a beneficial interest to the person claiming it, a number of distinctions do exist.

The first distinction between the resulting trust and the constructive trust, in the context of the family home, is that the constructive trust is based on a bargain between the co-owners of land. The resulting trust, on the other hand, is triggered by one single event – the contribution to the purchase price of a family home. A common intention constructive trust requires some agreement between those cohabiting the family home that they will all have some beneficial interest in the home. This consensus or agreement may be evidenced by express discussions or may be inferred from conduct between the parties. In addition to the agreement to share the beneficial interest in the land, the claimant who seeks to claim an interest under a constructive trust will need to demonstrate to the court that he acted to his detriment by relying on the agreement between the parties. It is such detrimental reliance on the agreement which makes it unconscionable for the legal owner to deny the claimant an equitable interest in the land.

The second distinction between the resulting trust and constructive trust is the time at which the beneficial interest will arise in favour of the claimant. In the case of a resulting trust, the interest of the beneficiary crystallises at the date of acquisition of the property by reason of a contribution to the purchase price. It is for this reason that subsequent payments to the purchase price – for example, the payment towards some mortgage monies – will not be sufficient to raise a presumption of a purchase price resulting trust. In the case of a common intention constructive trust, the beneficial interest claimed under the trust need not arise contemporaneously with the purchase of the property. The trust can arise after the purchase of the property, provided that there is a common intention that the parties to the co-owned land wish there to be an understanding as to the beneficial interest in the land. Furthermore, as we will explore in more detail in Chapter 13, the Supreme Court more recently made it clear in **Kernott v Jones**[197] that a common intention as to the size of the beneficial interest under a constructive trust can over time change with changing circumstances.

The final, and perhaps more important distinction from the claimant's point of view is the manner in which the beneficial interest is quantified under a resulting and constructive trust. It has already been seen that in the context of a resulting trust the quantification question is purely an arithmetical exercise. The extent of the beneficial interest is entirely dependent on the amount of contribution. The constructive trust is, however, much broader when it comes to the question of quantification. Under a common intention constructive trust, the court is required to quantify the beneficial interest in a manner which gives effect to the common intention between the parties. Irrespective of the contribution of the claimant, the court is required to quantify the interest not simply on grounds which look to the relationship between the parties or what may be conceived as 'fair' in the circumstances; rather the court is, as explained by Baroness Hale

**VISIT CASE
NAVIGATOR**

---

[196] [1996] AC 669.
[197] [2011] UKSC 53.

in the decision of the House of Lords in **Stack v Dowden**,[198] required to quantify the interest by looking at the whole course of dealings in respect of the property.

Reform

In the course of this chapter it has been seen that there are a number of anomalies relating to the law of resulting trusts. Primarily, these relate to the nature of presumptions of resulting trusts and advancement. It has already been seen that these presumptions are outdated and do not provide satisfactory results to the contemporary problems facing the courts. The Law Commission has reviewed the area of resulting trusts in a number of reports. In 1988 the Law Commission argued for the presumption of advancement to apply equally amongst husbands and wives.[199] The Equality Act 2000 now calls for the abolition of the presumption of advancement. Additionally, where money is used to purchase property for joint use then such property should be jointly owned by husband and wife. In 2005 the Family Law (Property and Maintenance Bill), a private member's Bill, was provided for the complete abolition of the presumption of advancement; however, owing to insufficient parliamentary time, the Bill had to be shelved. In its most recent report, 'Cohabitation: The Financial Consequences of Relationship Breakdown,'[200] the Law Commission has suggested there ought to be a statutory jurisdiction to adjust property rights of non-married cohabitees. This report is considered in more detail in Chapter 13 under the section on common intention constructive trusts and the family home.

Conclusion

This chapter has explored the various contexts in which a resulting trust has been imposed. It has been observed that the imposition of a resulting trust in the different contexts has achieved a number of different economic and social goals. At the heart of the imposition of a resulting trust is the protection and recognition of the beneficial rights of a transferor of property. The trust is imposed in circumstances where the ultimate intention of the transferor is not to pass a beneficial interest to the recipient. This absence of intention to pass a beneficial interest to the recipient can be seen in a number of examples already explored throughout this chapter: for example, an absence of intention to pass a beneficial interest in circumstances where the trust fails for one reason or the other. In such cases, the intended trustee is not intended to benefit from the trust property, but will hold it for the transferor, that is, the settlor under a resulting trust. The same is true in the context of a purchase in the name of another or a voluntary transfer in the name of another. In such cases, the presumption of equity is that the transferor did not intend to pass a beneficial interest to the recipient and that the recipient holds on resulting trust for the transferor. There is, of course, nothing stopping the transferee from rebutting the presumption of resulting trust, for example, by a counter-presumption of advancement, which as explained in this chapter, applies in certain relationships. Whilst equity will allow the presumptions of resulting trust and advancement to be rebutted,

[198] [2007] 2 AC 432.
[199] Law Com. No. 175 (1988) *Family Law: Matrimonial Property*.
[200] Law Com. No. 307 (2007) *Cohabitation: The Financial Consequences of Relationship Breakdown*.

it will generally not allow evidence of an illegal nature to be used to rebut those presumptions. However, as this chapter has explained, the role of illegality in the field of resulting trusts and the presumptions of advancement remains a controversial area of law and there are several recommendations of the Law Commission in this area, and indeed a new draft Bill in this area.

Finally, this chapter has also highlighted that the imposition of a resulting trust in some contexts has operated alongside other legal categories, for example contract, *bona vacantia* and the cy-près doctrine. As to which of these categories applies to any given facts depends very much on the context in which the issue has arisen. For example, in the context of surplus funds in the case of unincorporated associations, the destination of surplus funds is resolved by contractual means rather than by resulting trusts. In the context of charitable trusts, the doctrine of cy-près allows the surplus funds of a charity to be employed for purposes similar to those of the original charity rather than redirected under a resulting trust to the person creating the trust.

●●● Case studies

Consider the following case studies.

1 Return to the beginning of this chapter and analyse the situations set out in the 'Setting the scene' section.

Explain, with relevant authority, the possible outcomes.

2 The damage caused by an earthquake in Brazil prompted Julian and Carlos to do something to help those affected by the earthquake. Their aim was to help the families who had lost loved ones and also to provide money and other aid to those who had been injured. Julian and Carlos set up the Brazilian Relief Society whose functions were to organise events to raise money for the affected. Julian and Carlos also thought that the society was a good way to encourage people with Brazilian connections to meet up and socialise. The society started out with 20 members who had made substantial donations out of their own pocket. The society also received a legacy of £36,000 from a donor in London. The society organised various social events, raffle ticket sales and street collection boxes. A few months ago Julian and Carlos were told by colleagues in Brazil that public resources and international aid had largely resolved the post-earthquake crisis. Julian and Carlos decided to dissolve the society, which still has substantial amounts of money in the account held in the names of Julian and Carlos as treasurers. There are about 70 existing members of the society.

Advise Julian and Carlos as to what should happen with the surplus money not used for the Brazil earthquake relief efforts.

3 Jason purchased the freehold title to a cottage, Long End, in June 2004 for £150,000. The legal title to the cottage was conveyed in the name of Jason alone. Prior to the purchase Jason had told Alice and Gary that all three of them would reside at the cottage. Gary's father contributed £40,000 towards the purchase price of Long End; Alice contributed to the decorating and general household expenses.

Jason told Alice that she should not appear on the title, as this would prejudice the settlement she was going to receive from her forthcoming divorce. Alice doubted whether Jason's understanding of matrimonial matters was correct. Nevertheless, she decided to accept the arrangement, as Jason had not contradicted her when she asked him if she could live in the cottage for as long as she wished.

Alice spent money decorating the cottage and at times paid the bills. She also paid the mortgage for some six months in 2005 when Jason was ill and laid off work. In 2008, with a view to sell, Jason had the cottage valued at £300,000.

Advise Alice and Gary what rights, if any, they have in the cottage.

●● Moot points

1 Critically explain the extent to which the presumption of resulting trust and the presumption of advancement continue to hold significance in the contemporary law.

2 To what extent should questions of illegality be relevant in any disputes where the presumptions of resulting trust and advancement apply? Do the recommendations of the Law Commission in its Final Report on *The Illegality Defence* [2010] provide a satisfactory way forward when it cames to illegality?

3 Given the fact that a resulting trust will only be imposed in the context of the family home where the non-legal owner makes a direct contribution to the purchase price at the time of the acquisition of the home, is such an approach satisfactory?

● Further reading

Andrews, G. 'The Presumption of Advancement: Equity, Equality and Human Rights' (2007) Conv. 340. Examines the strength of the presumption of advancement in light of human rights law.

Davies, P. 'The Illegality Defence – Two Steps Forward, One Step Back?' (2009) Conv. 182. Examines the Law Commissions' Consultative paper on the illegality defence.

Davies, P. 'The Illegality Defence – Turning Back the Clock' (2010) Conv. 282. Examines the Law Commission's Final Report on *The Illegality Defence*.

Gardner, S. 'New Angles on Unincorporated Associations' (1992) Conv. 41. Examines recent developments in the construction of gifts to unincorporated associations.

Harpum, C. 'Perpetuities, Pensions and Resulting Trusts' (2000) Conv. 170. Examines the decision of the Privy Council in *Air Jamaica* v *Charlton*.

Law. Com. No. 189 The Illegality Defence: A Consultative Report (2009). This consultation paper, which was published in January 2009, looks at the ways forward in dealing with the question of illegality used in the context of trusts as well as other areas of law. In the context of trusts, the Commission recommends a statutory discretion to be used in order to deprive a claimant from relying on illegality to set up a claim.

Law Com. No. 307 (2007) 'Cohabitation: The Financial Consequences of Relationship Breakdown'. For an account of the proposals of the Law Commission in dealing with the rights of co-habitees in relationship breakdown.

Panesar, S. 'Surplus Funds and Unincorporated Associations' (2000) T&T Vol. 14 Issue 10 at 698. Revisits the ways in which unincorporated associations can hold property and examines the decision of the High Court in *Hanchett-Stamford* v *Attorney General*.

Panesar, S. 'A Loan Subject to a Trust and Dishonest Assistance by a Third Party' (2003) JIBL 18(1), 9. Examines the decision of the House of Lords in *Twinsectra* v *Yardley* and examines the nature of a Quistclose trust after that decision.

Panesar, S. 'Quantifying a Beneficial Interest in Non-Marital Co-habitation' (2004) *Law Teacher* 38(3) at 395. Examines the decision in *Oxley* v *Hiscock* and looks at the means of quantifying a beneficial interest under both a resulting and constructive trust.

Rose, F.D. 'Gratuitous Transfers and Illegal Purposes' (1996) LQR 386.

Thomas, M. and Dowrick, B. 'The Heart of the Matter – Re-Thinking Good Faith in Occupational Pension Schemes' (2007) Conv. Examines the surplus funds of pensions funds from the contractual relationship between employer and employee, particularly, in light of the duty of good faith in the employment relationship.

Visit **www.mylawchamber.co.uk/panesar** to access study support resources including interactive multiple choice questions, practice exam questions with guidance, podcasts, weblinks, legal newsfeed all linked to the **Pearson eText** version of Exploring Equity and Trusts which you can **search**, **highlight** and **personalise** with your **own notes** and **bookmarks**.

Use Case Navigator to read in full some of the key cases referenced in this chapter with commentary and questions:

Barclays Bank Ltd v *Quistclose Investments Ltd* [1970] AC 567
Kernott v *Jones* [2010] EWCA Civ 578
Re Bucks Constabulary Widows' and Orphans' Fund Friendly Society (No. 2) [1979] 1 WLR 936
Westdeutsche Landesbank Girozentrale v *Islington LBC* [1996] AC 699 (HL)

12

Constructive trusts, part I: Nature of constructive trusts

Learning objectives

After reading this chapter you should be able to:

→ understand the nature of a constructive trust

→ explain the differences between an institutional and remedial constructive trust

→ understand the grounds for the imposition of a constructive trust in some of the Commonwealth jurisdictions

→ appreciate some of the reasons why a remedial constructive trust is not yet recognised in English law

→ explain the consequences of the imposition of a constructive trust with regard to the constructive trustee, the constructive beneficiary and third parties

→ distinguish between cases where a constructive trust confers both proprietary and personal claims and cases where it only confers a personal claim

→ explain the grounds for the imposition of an institutional constructive trust.

SETTING THE SCENE

Why do we impose constructive trusts?

One leading American judge, Cardozo J, once commented in *Beatty* v *Guggenheim Exploration Co* 225 NY 380 (1919) that 'constructive trust is the formula through which the conscience of equity finds expression. When property has been acquired in circumstances that the holder of the legal title may not in good conscience retain the beneficial interest, equity converts him into a trustee' (at 386).

In the Court of Appeal, Millett LJ explained in *Paragon Finance plc* v *D.B. Thakerar & Co* [1999] 1 All ER 400 that a 'constructive trust arises by operation of law whenever the circumstances are such that it would be unconscionable for the owner of property (usually though not necessarily the legal estate) to assert his beneficial interest in the property and deny the beneficial interest of another' (at 409).

More recently, in a decision of the House of Lords in *Yeoman's Row Management Ltd* v *Cobbe* [2008] 1 WLR 1752 Lord Scott explained that it 'is impossible to prescribe exhaustively the circumstances sufficient to create a constructive trust but it is possible to recognise particular factual circumstances that will do so and also to recognise other factual circumstances that will not' (at 1769).

At the heart of the imposition of a constructive trust is the notion of unconscionability. The constructive trust is not necessarily imposed to give effect to the intention of the trustee or the beneficiary of the constructive trust: rather the trust is imposed because the constructive trustee has conducted himself such that it would be inequitable for him to deny the beneficial interest in property which the beneficiary is seeking to assert.

This chapter explores the nature of the constructive trust in English law and compares it with the notion of a constructive trust as employed in some other jurisdictions. The chapter explores the grounds for the imposition of a constructive trust in addition to the consequences of the imposition of a constructive trust with regard to the constructive beneficiary, the constructive trustee and other third parties.

Introduction

VISIT CASE NAVIGATOR

This chapter explores the second major form of trust which is implied by law, namely a constructive trust. A constructive trust, unlike a resulting trust, is not necessarily imposed to give effect to the intentions of a person transferring property to another or, indeed, the intentions of the person receiving the property. Rather, a constructive trust is imposed in circumstances where it would be unconscionable for the legal owner of some property to deny a beneficial interest to some other person. The unconscionability may arise for a number of quite different reasons and these reasons will be explored in more detail in Chapter 13. For the time being this chapter focuses on the nature and some of the theoretical explanations for the imposition of a constructive trust. In *Westdeutsche Landesbank Girozentrale* v *Islington LBC*[1] Lord Browne-Wilkinson explained the fundamental principles of trust law and in doing so placed the role of conscience at the heart of the enforcement of any trust, including the constructive trust.

---

[1] [1996] AC 669 (HL).

KEY CITATION

Westdeutsche Landesbank Girozentrale v *Islington LBC* [1996] AC 669 (HL) (Constructive trusts and role of conscience per Lord Browne-Wilkinson at 705)

(i) Equity operates on the conscience of the owner of the legal interest. In the case of a trust, the conscience of the legal owner requires him to carry out the purposes for which the property was vested in him (express or implied trust) or which the law imposes on him by reason of his unconscionable conduct (constructive trust).

(ii) Since the equitable jurisdiction to enforce trusts depends upon the conscience of the holder of the legal interest being affected, he cannot be a trustee of the property if and so long as he is ignorant of the facts alleged to affect his conscience, i.e. until he is aware that he is intended to hold the property for the benefit of others in the case of an express or implied trust, or, in the case of a constructive trust, of the factors which are alleged to affect his conscience.

(iii) In order to establish a trust there must be identifiable trust property. The only apparent exception to this rule is a constructive trust imposed on a person who dishonestly assists in a breach of trust who may come under fiduciary duties even if he does not receive identifiable trust property.

(iv) Once a trust is established, as from the date of its establishment the beneficiary has, in equity, a proprietary interest in the trust property, which proprietary interest will be enforceable in equity against any subsequent holder of the property (whether the original property or substituted property into which it can be traced) other than a purchaser for value of the legal interest without notice.[2]

   # When will a constructive trust be imposed?

Searching for a coherent theory which explains the grounds for the imposition of a constructive trust is, as in the case of a resulting trust, not necessarily a straightforward task. The reason for this is that, just like a resulting trust, a constructive trust has been imposed to resolve disputes over property in a wide range of contexts. These contexts, which will be analysed in Chapter 13, involve both commercial and family. Given the diversity of these contexts, it has not always been easy to formulate a theory which explains all of the factual situations which give rise to the imposition of a constructive trust. One commentator writes that a:

> comprehensive review . . . of constructive trusts would require analysis of areas of law as diverse as vendor and purchaser transactions, the perfection of imperfect gifts, fully secret and half secret trusts, breach of fiduciary duty, and accessory liability for breach of trust, among several others. The search for an acceptable, universally acknowledged, principle for the establishment of a constructive trust, which gives coherence to past decisions and provides clear guidance for the future, will certainly prove elusive in relation to many different areas of law and fact which constructive trusts arise.[3]

---

[2] [1996] AC 669 (HL) at 705.
[3] T. Etherton, 'Constructive Trusts: A New Model for Equity and Unjust Enrichment' (2008) CLJ 265.

More recently, in *Cobbe* v *Yeoman's Row Management Ltd*[4] Lord Scott explained that it 'is impossible to prescribe exhaustively the circumstances sufficient to create a constructive trust but it is possible to recognise particular factual circumstances that will do so and also to recognise other factual circumstances that will not'.[5]

It is precisely because of the ability of the constructive trust to operate in such diverse situations that the courts have not attempted to provide a concrete definition which may otherwise confine its application. In *Carl Zeiss Stiftung* v *Herbert Smith (No. 2)*[6] Edmund Davies LJ explained that 'English law provides no clear and all embracing definition of a constructive trust. Its boundaries have been left perhaps deliberately vague, so as not to restrict the court by technicalities in deciding what the justice of a particular case may demand.'[7] A further difficulty has been that the constructive trust has been analysed quite differently in the various jurisdictions in which it has operated. It will be seen below that, unlike in English law, in some jurisdictions the constructive trust has been imposed in circumstances where a defendant has been unjustly enriched at the expense of the claimant. In such jurisdictions the constructive trust has operated as one of a number of potential remedies at the disposal of a court in order to effect a restitution of property which has been unjustly acquired by the defendant. In contrast, in English law the constructive trust has been imposed by the courts in well-defined factual situations where the defendant has acquired property or otherwise dealt with property in an unconscionable way.

One leading and influential American judge once explained that a 'constructive trust is the formula through which the conscience of equity finds expression. When property has been acquired in circumstances that the holder of the legal title may not in good conscience retain the beneficial interest, equity converts him into a trustee.'[8] Whilst there is much to be said about this definition and the broad concerns of equity to deal with the consciences of individuals, good conscience is just too wide a concept to have any meaningful explanation for the grounds for imposition of a constructive trust. Such a wide concept does not offer any real guidance as to when a constructive trust should be imposed. Instead of the broad notion of good conscience, Millett LJ has explained that a 'constructive trust arises by operation of law whenever the circumstances are such that it would be unconscionable for the owner of property (usually necessarily the legal estate) to assert his beneficial interest in the property and deny the beneficial interest of another'.[9] One may question what the difference is between the broad notion of good conscience and the test of unconscionability as advocated by Millett LJ. The answer lies in the fact that good conscience is a much broader notion looking at wider matters of what is and what is not fair on any given facts, whereas the test of unconscionability is much more refined in English law. In English law what is unconscionable and what is not unconscionable has been defined with meaning, depending on the context in which the courts have had to employ the term.

One frequently asked question by students of trust law is: why is a constructive trust called a constructive trust? What does the term 'constructive' mean in the context of a constructive trust?[10] You will recall from the previous chapter that a resulting trust

---

[4] [2008] 1 WLR 1752.
[5] [2008] 1 WLR 1752 at 1769.
[6] [1969] 2 Ch. 276.
[7] [1969] 2 Ch. 276 at 300.
[8] *Beatty* v *Guggenheim Exploration Co* 225 NY 380 (1919) at 386 per Cardozo J.
[9] *Paragon Finance plc* v *D.B. Thakerar & Co* [1999] 1 All ER 400 at 409.
[10] For an excellent discussion, see L. Smith, 'Constructive Trusts and Constructive Trustee' (1999) CLJ 294.

acquired its name from the Latin word *resalire*: 'to jump back'. The resulting trust operates to 'jump back' the interest in property to the person who transferred it to the person who is now deemed a resulting trustee. A trust is termed a 'constructive' trust on the grounds that the courts construe that the defendant should, as result of his unconscionability, be treated as a trustee.

Institutional and remedial constructive trusts

It has already been observed above that the concept of a constructive trust has been analysed quite differently in the various jurisdictions in which it has been recognised. As a result of this, most analyses of a constructive trust make a distinction between an 'institutional constructive trust' and a 'remedial constructive trust'. Despite judicial debates surrounding the remedial constructive trust,[11] English law only recognises an institutional constructive trust. In **Westdeutsche Landesbank Girozentrale v Islington LBC**[12] Lord Browne-Wilkinson explained the distinction between an institutional and remedial constructive trust in the following manner.

> Under an institutional constructive trust, the trust arises by operation of law as from the date of the circumstances which give rise to it: the function of the court is merely to declare that such trust has arisen in the past. The consequences that flow from such trust having arisen (including the possibly unfair consequences to third parties who in the interim have received the trust property) are also determined by rules of law, not under a discretion. A remedial constructive trust, as I understand it, is different. It is a judicial remedy giving rise to an enforceable equitable obligation: the extent to which it operates retrospectively to the prejudice of third parties lies in the discretion of the court.[13]

The distinction between an institutional and remedial constructive trust is explored in more detail in the subsequent sections.

An institutional constructive trust

An institutional constructive trust arises by operation of law on the occurrence of specified events. The trust is not imposed at the discretion of the court: rather the role of the court is to look to certain events which have happened in the past and declare that, as result of those events, the defendant has become a constructive trustee. A good example of a situation in which an institutional constructive trust is imposed is where a fiduciary obtains some unauthorised profit or gain. The ground for the imposition of the constructive trust in such a case is the claim to the unauthorised gain or profit made at the expense of a claimant. In such a case the role of the court is to declare that, as a result of the unauthorised gain, the defendant became a constructive trustee as soon as the gain or profit was made. One of the consequences of the imposition of an institutional constructive trust, as will be explored in more detail below, is that the trust will bind third parties even though it is not declared by the court until judgment. Take for example the very situation identified above, that is, an unauthorised profit made by a

---

[11] See, for example, *Westdeutsche Landesbank Girozentrale v Islington LBC* [1996] AC 669 (HL) at 717.
[12] [1996] AC 669 (HL).
[13] [1996] AC 669 (HL) at 714.

fiduciary. As soon as a fiduciary makes an unauthorised profit, equity will convert him into a constructive trustee[14]. The constructive trust will bind third parties even though the trust is declared much later in time when judgment is given by a court. The effect of this is that if the constructive trustee is declared bankrupt before a judgment of the court declaring the constructive trust, the interest of the constructive beneficiary will nevertheless bind the trustees in bankruptcy of the constructive trustee.[15]

A remedial constructive trust

In contrast to an institutional constructive trust, a remedial constructive trust is imposed by the court and operates as one of a number of remedies available to the court to reverse an unjust enrichment. The basic role of such a trust is to operate as a remedy where the court finds that the defendant has been unjustly enriched at the expense of the claimant, or where it would otherwise be unconscionable not to impose the trust. Unlike an institutional constructive trust, a remedial constructive arises for the first time when the court orders it. The role of the court is to create the constructive trust rather than confirm that, as a result of some conduct in the past, the trust has already arisen. Seen in this way, the remedial constructive operates as a much broader and powerful concept, allowing the court to assess whether, on the basis of the defendant's unjust enrichment, he should be made a constructive trustee of property in his hands. The matter is neatly explained by Slade LJ in *Metall and Rohstoff AG v Donaldson Lufkin & Jenerette Inc*,[16] where the judge explained that 'the court imposes a constructive trust de novo on assets which are not subject to any pre-existing trust as a means of granting equitable relief in a case where it considers it just that restitution should be made'.[17]

The remedial constructive trust has played an important role in jurisdictions outside England such as the United States, Canada and to some extent in Australia and New Zealand, although in the latter two jurisdictions, recent judicial trends indicate that they may be moving away from the recognition of a remedial constructive trust. In such jurisdictions the remedial constructive trust has been employed as one of a number of remedies available to reverse an unjust enrichment. This is not to say that the institutional constructive trust has no role to play in such jurisdictions, rather that both the remedial and institutional constructive trusts have been recognised in these jurisdictions. Where a court is satisfied that the defendant has been unjustly enriched at the expense of the claimant, a constructive trust is imposed on the enrichment. The remedial nature of the constructive trust in the United States is exemplified by the Restatement of the Law of Restitution of 1937. Paragraph 160 states: 'Where a person holding title to property is subject to an equitable duty to convey it to another on the grounds that he would be unjustly enriched if he were permitted to retain it, a constructive trust arises.' In Canada, the remedial trust is perhaps best illustrated by a number of decisions of Dickson CJC, not least the decision of the Supreme Court of Canada in *Pettkus v Becker*[18] which concerned the ownership of property on the breakdown of an unmarried couple. A man and wife had lived together for some twenty years. The woman had supported the

---

[14] See, however, *Sinclair Investments Holding SA* v *Versailles Trade Finance Ltd* [2011] WLTR 1043 where the Court of Appeal required a proprietary base before the gain can be held on constructive trust.

[15] *Re Sharpe (a bankrupt)* [1980] 1 WLR 219.

[16] [1990] 1 QB 391.

[17] [1990] 1 QB 391 at 478.

[18] (1980) 117 DLR (3d) 257.

man in the first five years of their relationship, which allowed the man to save enough money to purchase a farm. Subsequently, the woman helped the man on the farm, in particular, helping him with his bee-keeping business as well as other farming endeavours. The man bought additional land with the profits from the farm. When the man sold the farm, the woman sought a declaration that she was entitled to one-half of the interest in the house and other assets purchased from the proceeds of the farming business. The basis of her claim was that the man was only able to acquire the house and the other assets as result of their joint efforts and that it would be unjust to deny her an interest. The Supreme Court of Canada held that the woman was entitled to a half share in the house under a constructive trust on the grounds of her indirect contribution to money and her direct contribution to labour.[19]

The decision in *Pettkus v Becker*[20] followed the earlier decision of the Supreme Court of Canada in *Rathwell v Rathwell*[21] where the Supreme Court awarded a half share to a wife who had made substantial domestic contributions in the course of her marriage to her husband. In the course of his judgment in *Rathwell v Rathwell*, Dickson J explained that the:

> constructive trust . . . comprehends the imposition of trust machinery by the court in order to achieve a result consonant with good conscience. As a matter of principle, the court will not allow any man unjustly to appropriate for himself the value earned by the labours of another. That principle is not defeated by the existence of a matrimonial relationship between the parties; but, for the principle to succeed, the facts must display an enrichment, a corresponding deprivation and the absence of any juristic reason – such as contract or disposition of law – for the enrichment.[22]

It will be seen in Chapter 13 that the decisions of the Supreme Court of Canada go much further than the English authorities concerning the imposition of a constructive trust in cases of shared ownership of the family home. The English authorities do not recognise mere domestic endeavour as the grounds for the imposition of a constructive trust.[23]

Although the decisions in *Pettkus v Becker* and *Rathwell v Rathwell* illustrate the imposition of a remedial constructive trust on grounds of unjust enrichment, sceptics of the remedial constructive trust have questioned the precise grounds for its imposition. It is entirely for these reasons that the English courts have been reluctant to recognise such a trust which does not provide a clear explanation of the cause of action which will justify its imposition. According to one English judge, the remedial constructive trust serves nothing more than 'palm tree justice'.[24] In particular, questions have arisen as to what exactly is understood by the term 'unjust enrichment' and when a person is unjustly enriched at the expense of another? Judgments in the Canadian cases have sought to dispel such problems by invoking a remedial constructive trust on grounds of unjust enrichment. These decisions illustrate that, despite the broad notion of unjust enrichment, there is criteria for the court to use in deciding whether a particular set of facts

---

[19] It will be observed in Chapter 13 that English law adopts a stricter test for the imposition of a constructive trust in the context of ownership disputes of the family home. Indirect contributions such as domestic endeavour will not provide the basis for the inference of a constructive trust in favour of a claimant.
[20] (1980) 117 DLR (3d) 257.
[21] (1978) 83 DLR (3d) 289.
[22] (1978) 83 DLR (3d) 289 at 306.
[23] The imposition of a constructive trust in the context of family property is examined in Chapter 13.
[24] *Springette* v *Defoe* [1992] 2 FLR 388 at 393 per Dhillon LJ.

gives rise to the imposition of a remedial constructive trust. In other words, the idea that a remedial constructive trust is imposed simply on grounds of fairness at the discretion of the court is ill-founded. For example, in **Sorochan v Sorochan**[25] a man and woman lived together for 42 years. Although they were not married, they had six children and collectively ran a farming business. The woman ran the household, cared for their children and worked long hours on the farm. When the man took on a sales job, the woman took it upon herself to run the farming business. The farm was solely registered in the name of the man. When the relationship deteriorated the woman claimed an interest in the farm. The Supreme Court of Canada allowed the woman an interest in the farm on the grounds of a remedial constructive trust. As for the grounds for the imposition of such a trust the Court explained that such a trust would be imposed where there was proof of an unjust enrichment. Such unjust enrichment consisted of three elements:

1 an enrichment

2 a corresponding deprivation

3 an absence of any juristic reason for the enrichment.

On these grounds, the Supreme Court held that the man clearly benefited from the woman's labour in maintaining and preserving the farm and running the household. As a consequence of the woman's labour on the land, she suffered a corresponding deprivation. The Supreme Court acknowledged that there was no juristic reason for the enrichment: for example, she was not obliged by contract or otherwise to provide the labour which she duly provided. In exercising its discretion to award a remedial constructive trust, the Court explained that it would look into a number of factors: firstly, whether there was a link between the woman's contribution and the disputed property. The Court explained that the link need not be related to the original acquisition of the property. Secondly, consideration in determining whether proprietary relief should be ordered was whether the claimant reasonably expected to receive an actual interest in property and whether the respondent knew or ought reasonably to have known of that expectation. Finally the length of the relationship between the parties to the dispute was also a relevant fact.

The broad restitutionary relief offered to cohabitees in Canada was more recently illustrated by the Supreme Court of Canada in **Kerr v Baranow**.[26] The case involved two appeals involving the breakdown of cohabiting relationships and the subsequent claims to property belonging to the parties. The first appeal was that of **Kerr v Baranow** itself where a relationship between a man and a woman had existed for 25 years. The plaintiff had suffered a massive stroke sometime in 1991 and after years of caring for the plaintiff, the defendant, in whose name the property was taken, terminated the relationship. The plaintiff sought to claim an interest in the house in which the plaintiff and the defendant had resided. The defendant counter-claimed that he had cared for the plaintiff for several years. The trial judge ignored the counter-claim and gave the plaintiff a monetary award of $315,000 on the grounds of a resulting trust and unjust enrichment. The Supreme Court of Canada held that the award should have taken into account the care that had been provided by the defendant. In the second appeal, **Vanasse v Seguin**, the plaintiff and the defendant had a 12-year relationship. The plaintiff had her own career but then

---

[25] (1986) 29 DLR (4th) 1. See, L.I. Rotman, 'Deconstructing the Constructive Trust' (1999) 37 Alta. L. Rev. pp. 133–72. See also *Peter v Beblow* (1993) 101 DLR (4th) 621.

[26] [2011] SCC 10; (2011) 328 DLR (4th) 577 SC (Can).

started a family and looked after the children. Her cohabiting partner continued to successfully build his software company which he sold for a profit. When the relationship broke down, the plaintiff claimed a share in the defendant's profits from the sale of the business. The Ontario Court of Appeal held that the plaintiff could not claim any interest in the business and the profits realised on sale because there was no connection between her efforts and any particular assets in the business belonging to the defendant. The Supreme Court of Canada overruled this decision of the Court of Appeal and held that she was entitled a substantial share of the profits belonging to the defendant. One leading Canadian commentator explains the reasons for the Supreme Court of Canada coming to this rather liberal conclusion. He writes:

> The court offered four (non-exhaustive) indicia of such cases: (1) *mutual effort*, as when finances are pooled and child-rearing responsibilities are divided, (2) *economic integration*, as evidenced by 'common purses' and joint bank accounts, (3) *actual intent*, as suggested by joint ownership of property and public declarations of permanence, and (4) *priority of the family*, as when one partner sacrifices career opportunities in order to build a lasting home. When those criteria are sufficiently met, relief by way of a quantum meruit, which effectively treats the claimant as an employee, is not merely inappropriate, but insulting. Cromwell J accordingly held that even if the claimant did not contribute to the acquisition, maintenance or enhancement of an asset, so as to warrant the imposition of a trust, social justice requires a remedy that reflects the relationship's underlying premise and is calculated as a proportionate share of the couple's accumulated wealth.'[27]

The remedial constructive trust in Canada has been used in resolving disputes not only in the context of family property, but also in the commercial context. For example, in the popularly cited Canadian case, **LAC Minerals Ltd v International Corona Resources Ltd**[28] the Canadian Supreme Court found a fiduciary relationship in circumstances where two companies were negotiating a joint venture to exploit minerals. The land to be mined belonged to the plaintiffs but the defendants, through the course of dealings with the plaintiffs, established that adjacent land also contained minerals. The defendants then mined the adjacent land without the plaintiff's consent. The Court held that the defendants owed fiduciary duties to the plaintiffs because they had obtained confidential information from the plaintiffs. The Supreme Court held that the defendants had been unjustly enriched at the expense of the plaintiffs and therefore held the adjacent land on constructive trust for them. In respect of the unjust enrichment LA Forest J explained that '[t]he determination that the enrichment is "unjust" does not refer to abstract notions of morality and justice, but flows directly from the finding that there was a breach of a legally recognised duty for which the courts will grant relief. Restitution is a distinct body of law governed by its own developing system of rules.'[29]

The Supreme Court of Canada has expanded the remedial constructive trust by holding that such a trust can be imposed even when there is an absence of unjust enrichment and a corresponding deprivation, provided that the court is satisfied that the defendant cannot in 'good conscience' retain property. For example, in **Soulos v Korkontzilas**[30] a very wide application of the remedial constructive trust was involved. The facts of this case concerned a property developer, Korkontzilas, who was in the process of negotiat-

[27] M. McInnes, 'Cohabitation, Trusts and Unjust Enrichment in the Supreme Court of Canada' (2011) LQR 339 at 342.
[28] (1989) 61 DLR (4th) 14.
[29] (1989) 61 DLR (4th) 14 at 45.
[30] (1997) 146 DLR (4th) 214.

ing the purchase of a commercial building for his client. Instead of purchasing the property for his client, Korkontzilas lied to his client that the deal had fallen through and purchased the property for himself. When the client discovered the truth of the matter, he commenced proceedings against Korkontzilas on the grounds of breach of fiduciary duty. The trial judge held that, although Korkontzilas had clearly breached his fiduciary duty to his client, there could be no grounds for the imposition of a constructive trust because the property values had fallen significantly and Korkontzilas had not been enriched at the expense of the client. The Ontario Court of Appeal reversed the decision of the trial judge and the Supreme Court of Canada upheld the reversal. In the Supreme Court, McLaughlin J explained that the principle of 'good conscience' was at the heart of the doctrine of constructive trust. The judge explained that despite the absence of an unjust enrichment, Korkontzilas had acted in breach of duty and in such circumstances was not entitled to the property purchased on the grounds of good conscience. In the course of his judgement, McLaughlin J explained that:

> in Canada, under the broad umbrella of good conscience, constructive trusts are recognized both for wrongful acts like fraud and breach of duty of loyalty, as well as to remedy unjust enrichment and corresponding deprivation. While cases often involve both a wrongful act and unjust enrichment, constructive trusts may be imposed on either ground: where there is a wrongful act but no unjust enrichment and corresponding deprivation; or where there is an unconscionable unjust enrichment in the absence of a wrongful act, as in *Pettkus* v. *Becker* . . . Within these two broad categories, there is room for the law of constructive trust to develop and for greater precision to be attained, as time and experience may dictate.[31]

Like Canada, Australia and New Zealand have also recognised the remedial constructive trust. However, as explained earlier there has been some judicial opinion that such jurisdictions may be drawing back from the recognition of a remedial constructive trust as employed in Canada. Initially, in the context of claims to a beneficial interest in land which has been the subject of cohabitation by unmarried couples, the Australian courts have employed the remedial constructive trust to resolve such disputes. A particular attraction of the remedial constructive trust in this context is that it avoids the finding of a somewhat artificial common intention which is an integral requirement of the institutional constructive trust employed in English law.[32] For example, in **Muschinski v Dodds**[33] Deane J explained that 'in its modern context, the constructive trust can properly be described as a remedial institution which equity imposes regardless of actual or presumed agreement or intention . . . to preclude the retention or assertion of beneficial ownership of property to the extent that such retention or assertion would be contrary to equitable principle'.[34]

Likewise, in **Baumgartner v Baumgartner**,[35] when dealing with the beneficial interest of a cohabitee, Toohey J explained that the:

> object of a constructive trust is to redress a position which otherwise leaves untouched a situation of unconscionable conduct or unjust enrichment. It is equally applicable to persons in a de facto relationship as it is to spouses. In a situation such as the present one, where two people have lived together for a time and made contributions towards the

---

[31] (1997) 146 DLR (4th) 214 at 227.
[32] The common intention constructive trust is analysed in more detail in Chapter 13.
[33] (1985) 160 CLR 583.
[34] (1985) 160 CLR 583 at 614.
[35] (1987) 164 CLR 137.

purchase of land or the building of a home on it, an approach based on unconscionable conduct or one based on unjust enrichment will inevitably bring about the same result. Neither approach necessarily calls for a precise accounting of the contribution to the parties. Equally, the Court cannot ignore disproportionate contributions; especially where one of the parties makes available the proceeds of sale of a property which he or she had acquired prior to the relationship began.[36]

On the facts of **Baumgartner v Baumgartner**[37] an unmarried couple purchased a house in which to live. The title to the house was taken in the man's name; however, all of the outgoings were paid out of the pooled income of the man and woman. When the relationship broke down the High Court of Australia held that the woman was entitled to an interest in the house in proportion to the pooled income she had contributed, which the Court worked out to be 45 per cent. A number of adjustments were made, in particular, an adjustment of the initial contribution which the man had made and the subsequent mortgage payments which he had solely discharged. The High Court held that not to award such an interest would be unconscionable.

Despite the decision in both **Muschinski v Dodds**[38] and in **Baumgartner v Baumgartner** which suggest the recognition of a remedial constructive trust in Australia, the later decision of the High Court of Australia in **Bathurst City Council v PWC Properties**[39] seem to cast doubt on whether the remedial constructive trust is properly recognised in Australian law. In New Zealand, the possibility of a remedial constructive trust was considered in **Fortex Group v MacIntosh**.[40] Up until this decision there was some recognition that a remedial constructive trust existed in the law of New Zealand.[41] However, in the context of whether employees of a superannuation scheme were entitled to a remedial constructive trust on monies in the scheme on the insolvency of their employers, the Court of Appeal held that no such remedial constructive trust arose. In the opinion of the Court of Appeal, to impose a remedial constructive trust would give the employees priority over the other creditors of the company. However, the Court of Appeal did not completely rule out the possibility of a remedial constructive trust. The Court of Appeal suggested that, where there was an element of unconscionability, then there may be grounds for the imposition of a remedial constructive trust. Despite this decision, there does not appear to have been any further developments which suggest that the courts of New Zealand recognise a remedial constructive trust and the grounds upon which such a trust is imposed.

 ## Does English law recognise a remedial constructive trust?

At the present time English law does not recognise a remedial constructive trust. Over the past 40 years or so, there have been numerous occasions when the question has been put before a court whether English law will recognise a remedial constructive trust. Most

---

[36] (1987) 164 CLR 137 at 152.
[37] (1987) 164 CLR 137.
[38] (1985) 160 CLR 583.
[39] (1998) 195 CLR 566.
[40] [1998] 3 NZLR 171.
[41] See, for example, *Elders Pastoral Ltd* v *Bank of New Zealand* [1989] 2 NZLR 180 and also *Liggett* v *Kensington* [1993] 1 NZLR 257.

famously, Lord Denning attempted to introduce the remedial constructive trust in the form of a 'new model constructive trust' in **Hussey v Palmer**.[42] In that case, Lord Denning explained that a constructive trust:

> is imposed by law whenever justice and good conscience require it. It is a liberal process, founded upon large principles of equity, to be applied in cases where the legal owner cannot conscientiously keep the property for himself alone, but ought to allow another to have the property or the benefit of it or a share in it. The trust may arise at the outset when the property is acquired, or later on, as the circumstances may require. It is an equitable remedy by which the court can enable an aggrieved party to obtain restitution.[43]

Lord Denning attempted to use the new model constructive trust as a means by which ownership disputes could be resolved over the family home.[44] However, despite Lord Denning's efforts in the 1970s to introduce the remedial constructive trust into English law, it proved to be unsuccessful. In particular, the new model constructive trust as advocated by Lord Denning proved to be too broad and an uncertain concept to be invoked by the English courts.

Some recognition that a remedial constructive trust was not completely beyond the scope of English law was recognised by the Court of Appeal in **Metall and Rohstoff A.G. v Donaldson Lufkin & Jenrette**[45] where the judges 'were satisfied that there is a good arguable case that such circumstances may arise and, for want of a better description, will refer to a constructive trust of this nature as a "remedial constructive trust"'.[46] In **Re Goldcorp Exchange Ltd (in receivership)**[47] the Privy Council was faced with an appeal from the Court of Appeal in New Zealand on the question whether customers purchasing gold bullion retained proprietary interests in purchased gold bullion which had not been ascertained for each customer. Whilst holding that no individual customer acquired any proprietary interest in the bulk gold, the Privy Council explained that the remedial constructive trust may be grounds for invoking restitutionary remedies.[48]

In **Westdeutsche Landesbank Girozentrale v Islington LBC**,[49] as already explored in the previous chapter, the question arose as to whether a constructive trust could be imposed on money received by a local authority from a bank under a contract that transpired to be **ultra vires**.[50] The House of Lords held in that case that there could be no grounds for the imposition of a constructive trust in the absence of unconscionability; however in the course of his judgment, Lord Browne-Wilkinson explained that:

> [a]lthough the resulting trust is an unsuitable basis for developing proprietary restitutionary remedies, the remedial constructive trust, if introduced into English law, may provide a more satisfactory road forward. The court by way of remedy might impose a constructive trust on a defendant who knowingly retains property of which the plaintiff has been unjustly deprived. Since the remedy can be tailored to the circumstances of the particular case, innocent third parties would not be prejudiced and restitutionary defences, such as change of position, are capable of being given effect. However, whether English law should

[42] [1972] 1 WLR 1286.
[43] [1972] 1 WLR 1286 at 1290.
[44] See, for example, *Eves v Eves* [1975] 1 WLR 1338.
[45] [1990] 1 QB 391.
[46] [1990] 1 QB 391 at 479.
[47] [1995] 1 AC 74.
[48] [1995] 1 AC 74 at 104.
[49] [1996] AC 669 (HL).
[50] For a more detailed analysis of this decision, see Chapter 10.

follow the United States and Canada by adopting the remedial constructive trust will have to be decided in some future case when the point is directly in issue.[51]

Despite such judicial pronouncements to the effect that English law may make some appropriate use of the remedial constructive trust, two English cases provide the strongest rejection that the remedial constructive trust has no role to play in English law. The first is the decision of the Court of Appeal in **Halifax Building Society v Thomas**[52] where the Court was faced with the question whether a mortgagee was entitled to the surplus proceeds of sale of mortgaged land in circumstances where the mortgagor had obtained the mortgage by fraudulent misrepresentation. When the mortgagor defaulted on repayment, the mortgagee sold the mortgaged land. The debt had been paid off and a surplus fund remained to which the mortgagee laid claim under a constructive trust. In holding that the mortgagee was not entitled to the surplus funds on the sale of the mortgaged land, Peter Gibson LJ explained that 'English law has not followed other jurisdictions where the constructive trust has become a remedy for unjust enrichment.'[53] The second decision is that of the Court of Appeal in **Re Polly Peck International plc (in administration)(No. 2)**[54] where the question before the Court was whether a remedial constructive trust could be imposed on assets of a company in administration. The Court of Appeal held that, in the context of the an insolvent defendant, there could be no room for the imposition of a remedial constructive trust which would have the effect of giving the claimants a proprietary interest in the assets thereby defeating the rights of the other creditors of the company. Mummery LJ explained that the imposition of a remedial constructive trust in the context of insolvency would have the effect of interfering with the statutory scheme for the distribution of an insolvent person's assets. In the opinion of his Lordship, there could be no judicial discretion to alter what Parliament had prescribed as to the means of distribution of assets on insolvency. His Lordship explained that the:

> administrators are bound to distribute the assets of the [company] among the creditors on the basis of insolvency. Parliament has, in such an eventuality, sanctioned a scheme for *parri passu* distribution of assets designed to achieve a fair distribution of the insolvent company's property among the unsecured creditors . . . The insolvency road is blocked off to remedial constructive trusts at least when judge-driven in a vehicle of discretion.[55]

Although Mummery LJ was clearly influenced by the insolvency factor, Nourse LJ took a much wider objection to a remedial constructive trust. In the opinion of Nourse LJ property rights could only be varied by Parliament and not by judicial discretion.

The question may well be asked: what are the main reasons why the English courts have been reluctant to recognise a remedial constructive trust in English law? There appear to be a number of reasons for this reluctance. The first and foremost reason relates to the cause of action which gives rise to the imposition of a remedial constructive trust. It has already been observed by one English judge that the English courts are not

---

[51] [1996] AC 669 (HL) at 716.
[52] [1996] Ch. 217.
[53] [1996] Ch. 217 at 229. The Court of Appeal explained that the mortgagee had received exactly what it had contracted to receive. In the absence of a fiduciary relationship, the surplus fund belonged to the mortgagor; however, that fund could be confiscated under the provisions of Part IV of the Criminal Justice Act 1998 which prevented the profits of crime being available for the victim of the crime.
[54] [1998] 3 All ER 812.
[55] [1998] 3 All ER 812 at 827.

prepared to carry out 'palm tree justice'.[56] Although, as seen above, the Canadian courts have been able to apply the principle of unjust enrichment and unconscionability as the grounds for the imposition of a remedial trust, the English courts have not as yet developed the precise grounds which will call upon the court to impose a remedial constructive trust. The matter is elegantly explained by Professor Kevin Gray and Susan Gray:

> The principal demerit of the new-model constructive trust was, almost inevitably, the arbitrary quality of the discretionary allocations of beneficial entitlement to which it gave. Unstructured applications of trusts law are always vulnerable to the objection that they represent a form of palm-tree justice, under which past decisions are worthless as precedent and future decisions are almost entirely unpredictable. The 'new model constructive trust' appeared to allow equitable intervention in property matters as a sheer matter of redistributive justice.[57]

A second reason why a remedial constructive trust has not found a home in English law relates to the effect such a trust can have on the rights of other third parties: in particular, the effect that such a trust can have on the rights of creditors to assets of an insolvent defendant. One of the main reasons why a claimant may ask the court to recognise a remedial constructive trust for the first time on property in the hands of the defendant is to gain a proprietary right to such property, which binds third parties such as his creditors on insolvency. It is precisely in the context of insolvency that a remedial constructive trust becomes an attractive means by which proprietary restitutionary relief can be gained. It has already been seen in cases such as *Re Polly Peck International plc (in administration)(No. 2)*[58] that the courts are not prepared to invoke a remedial constructive trust on the assets of an insolvent defendant, thereby altering the scheme of distribution as prescribed by statute.

Despite the robust rejection for recognition of a remedial constructive trust by the Court of Appeal in *Re Polly Peck International plc (in Administration)(No. 2)*,[59] it appears that the debate over the recognition of a remedial constructive trust in English law is far from closed. More recently, in *London Allied Holdings Ltd v Anthony Lee*[60] Etherton J in the High Court opened the debate whether English law should recognise a remedial constructive trust. The facts of the case concerned a mistaken payment of £1 million by the claimant to the defendant induced by the defendant's fraudulent misrepresentation. Prior to the payment of the money it was clear that no fiduciary relationship existed between the claimant and the defendant. The parties had negotiated at arm's length and, therefore, only a commercial relationship existed between them. One of the questions before Etherton J was whether the payment of money to the defendant was subject to a remedial constructive trust so as to allow the claimant to trace it into the hands of the defendant. Etherton J held that it was not necessary to invoke the remedial constructive trust in favour of the claimant since the fraudulent misrepresentation gave the claimant a right to rescind the contract. The effect of such rescission was to vest the equitable title back in the hands of the claimant under a constructive trust recognised in law.

---

[56] *Springette v Defoe* [1992] 2 FLR 388 at 393 per Dhillon LJ.
[57] K. Gray and S. Gray, *Elements of Land Law* 4th edn (2005) at p. 908; a similar point is made in the 5th edn (2009) at p. 877.
[58] [1998] 3 All ER 812.
[59] [1998] 3 All ER 812.
[60] [2007] EWHC 2061 (Ch.).

However, the judge did question whether the door was closed in England for recognition of a remedial constructive trust. In particular, Etherton J questioned whether, if such a trust was recognised, it would be departing from wide discretion enjoyed by the courts of equity in awarding relief under some other equitable doctrines such as proprietary estoppel. In the course of his judgment Etherton J explained that the very strong language from academic and judicial quarters against the remedial constructive trust was perhaps a little ill-founded.

> An equity lawyer might observe that such language is overly emphatic, having regard, for example, to the strong discretion in the Court to decide upon the appropriate form of relief for proprietary estoppel, including whether it should be personal or proprietary and whether it should be to protect the claimant's expectations or compensate for reliance loss. Moreover, there is no English authority, including *Polly Peck International plc (No. 2)* (in which Mummery LJ, with whom Potter LJ agreed, concentrated on the fact of insolvency), which is binding authority against the remedial constructive trust in principle. Nevertheless, it seems realistic to assume that an English Court will be very slow indeed to adopt the US and Canadian model. On the other hand, there still seems scope for real debate about a model more suited to English jurisprudence, borrowing from proprietary estoppel: namely, a constructive trust by way of discretionary restitutionary relief, the right to which is a mere equity prior to judgment, but which will have priority over the intervening rights of third parties on established principles, such as those relating to notice, volunteers and the unconscionability on the facts of a claim by the third party to priority.[61]

The decision of Etherton J in **London Allied Holdings Ltd v Anthony Lee**[62] illustrates that there remains support for the recognition of a remedial constructive trust which can be imposed to afford proprietary restitutionary remedies to claimants in certain situations where it would be unjust to do so, and where it is often practically impossible to do so because the claimant and defendant do not stand in a fiduciary relationship which may give the claimant to a proprietary claim in equity. It remains to be seen how the higher courts will develop, if at all, the remedial constructive trust in English law. The remainder of this chapter will explore the rules and principles operating in respect of an institutional constructive trust.

 ## Consequences of the imposition of a constructive trust

Where a court declares that a constructive trust has arisen as a result of certain facts which have taken place in the past, the imposition of a constructive trust will have a number of implications. In general the trust will confer upon the beneficiary of the trust both proprietary and personal claims. In some situations, however, a constructive trust may only give rise to a personal claim against the constructive trustee. Furthermore, since the role of the court is to merely declare the trust and not to impose it for the first time, the trust will potentially bind all third parties who cannot show that they acquired the legal title to the constructive trust property without notice of the trust. These matters can be explored in more detail below.

---

[61] [2007] EWHC 2061 (Ch.) at para. 274.
[62] [2007] EWHC 2061 (Ch.).

Proprietary and personal claims

Just as in the case of an express trust, a constructive trust will confer upon the beneficiary of the constructive trust both proprietary and personal claims. A proprietary claim will arise because some property has been subjected to the trust. The beneficiary will be entitled to the property and any interest which is earned on it. For example, if a person standing in a fiduciary relationship breaches his fiduciary duty and acquires some property at the expense of his beneficiary, he will hold such property on constructive trust for the beneficiary. The beneficiary will acquire an equitable property interest in the property acquired in breach of fiduciary duty. So long as that property is in the hands of the fiduciary or some other third party who cannot purport to show that he is a bona fide purchaser of the legal title without notice of the trust, the beneficiary will be able to claim it through the process of tracing and following.[63] The matter is neatly illustrated by the decision of the Privy Council in *A-G for Hong Kong v Reid* where a senior public prosecutor in Hong Kong received large sums of money to obstruct prosecutions. The bribe money was invested in freehold properties in New Zealand, which the Crown sought to recover on the grounds that they were held on constructive trust.[64]

A personal claim will confer upon the beneficiary a right to recover the value of the property which is the subject matter of the constructive trust, along with any income that has been generated on that property. The personal remedy will take the form of an account for the value of the property and the income that has been generated. Where the constructive trustee is solvent it will make no real difference whether the beneficiary elects to pursue a proprietary claim or a personal claim. Where, however, the constructive trustee is insolvent, the beneficiary will elect a proprietary claim to recover the trust property. The advantages of the proprietary claim are that, firstly, the beneficiary will take priority over the other creditors of the constructive trustee; secondly, if there has been any subsequent increase in the value of the property subject to the constructive trust, then the beneficiary will be entitled to take the benefit of any such increase.

Only a personal claim

In some instances where a constructive trust is imposed, the claimant may only be able to pursue a personal claim against the constructive trustee. The reason for this is that the so-called 'constructive trustee' never receives identifiable property over which he assumes control. In this sense it is inappropriate to say that a constructive trust proper has arisen. All that equity is doing here is to treat a defendant as a constructive trustee because of certain conduct on his part. Traditionally equity has imposed liability on a stranger who assists in a breach of trust. Such liability takes the form of converting the stranger into a constructive trustee so as to allow a beneficiary to bring a personal claim against the stranger who assisted in bringing about a breach of trust by another defendant. Constructive trust liability for assisting in a breach of trust is considered in much more detail in Chapter 14. For the time being it should be appreciated that where constructive trusteeship is imposed on a stranger who assists in a breach of trust, the claimant is able to pursue a personal claim against him. This will be of particular significance where the original or primary trustee who has instigated the breach of trust is insolvent, and therefore not in a position to meet any judgment given against him. It will also be significant where the original trust property has found its way into the hands

---

[63] The processes of tracing and following are considered in more detail in Chapter 21.
[64] This decision is analysed in more detail in Chapter 13.

of a bona fide purchaser of the legal title without notice of the trust. There has been some debate as to whether it is entirely appropriate to categorise a stranger who has assisted in a breach of a trust as a constructive trustee.[65] The principal reason for this is that the stranger who assists in a breach of trust never assumes control over any property. It is a fundamental principle of trust law that a trust arises over some identifiable property.

The distinction between cases where a constructive trust arises over identifiable property in the hands of the constructive trustee and cases where a defendant has been classified as a constructive trustee irrespective of having no connection with any trust property was explained by Millett LJ in **Paragon Finance v D.B. Thakerar & Co**.[66] His Lordship explained that there were two categories of constructive trust. The first category arose where a person assumes the role of a trustee even though he was not originally appointed as a trustee. Such cases included, for example, a person who acquired some property in breach of fiduciary duty which he is required to return to the claimant. In the second category a constructive trust arises and attaches constructive trusteeship on a person who has been involved in a fraud, for example, dishonest assistance in a breach of trust. In respect of the second category, whilst expressing inappropriateness of the use of the constructive trust concept to impose liability on the defendant, his Lordship explained that:

> [t]he second class of case is different. It arises when a defendant has been implicated in a fraud. Equity has always given relief against fraud by making any person sufficiently implicated in the fraud accountable in equity. In such a case he is traditionally though I think unfortunately described as a constructive trustee and said to be 'liable to account as a constructive trustee'. Such a person is in fact not a trustee at all, even though he may be liable to account as if he were. He never assumes the position of a trustee, and if he receives the trust property at all it is adversely to the plaintiff by an unlawful transaction which is impugned by the plaintiff. In such a case the expression 'constructive trust' and 'constructive trustee' are misleading, for there is no trust and usually no possibility of a proprietary remedy . . .[67]

The same criticism of the use of the constructive trust language in cases where the defendant never assumes any control over identifiable trust property, for example where he is implicated in a fraud, was made by Millett LJ in **Dubai Aluminium Co Ltd v Salaam**.[68] His Lordship was of the view that 'we should now discard the words "accountable as constructive trustee" in this context and substitute the words "accountable in equity" '.[69] At the present time the courts continue to use the constructive trust language in cases where a defendant dishonestly assists in a breach of trust despite never having any control over identifiable property. In **Westdeutsche Landesbank Girozentrale v Islington LBC**[70] Lord Browne-Wilkinson, having explained that one of the fundamental principles of trust law was that there should be some identifiable property over which a trust was to exist, said that there was an exception in cases where a constructive trust arose in cases of dishonest assistance by a third party.

---

[65] See M. Hemsworth, 'Constructive Trusts and Constructive Trustees – What's in a Name?' (2000) CJQ 154.

[66] [1999] 1 All ER 400.

[67] [1999] 1 All ER 400 at 409.

[68] [2002] 3 WLR 1913.

[69] [2002] 3 WLR 1913 at 1946.

[70] [1996] AC 669 (HL).

The effect on third parties

It has already been observed that an institutional constructive trust arises as soon as the prescribed conduct which gives rise to its implication has taken place. In **Re Sharpe (a bankrupt)**[71] Browne-Wilkinson J held that the role of the court was to recognise that a constructive trust had arisen as a result of conduct that had taken place. The trust arose as soon as the conduct giving rise to it took place, and as a result of this, the right of the constructive beneficiary was binding on third parties in accordance with the principles of equity.[72] The effect of this is that the rights of the constructive beneficiary will be binding on the personal representatives of the constructive trustee as well as his creditors. The constructive beneficiary will have priority ahead of the general creditors of the constructive trustee. The beneficiary will also be able to enforce his or her rights against any other third party which cannot purport to show that it has acquired the legal title to the trust property without notice of the trust. A third party who receives the trust for no consideration will be bound by the interests of the constructive trustee.

The duties of the constructive trustee

It will be seen in the subsequent chapters that the duties of an express trustee can be quite onerous. Express trustees are not only under a duty to safeguard the trust property, but also under positive duties to invest the trust fund. Failure to invest the trust funds will result in a breach of trust and the trustee will be personally liable to compensate the beneficiary for the loss that would otherwise have been avoided had they invested the fund properly. Furthermore, express trustees are under a duty to exercise reasonable care when carrying out their functions as trustees. The duties of a constructive trust have not yet been fully worked out by the courts. The general view appears to be that the duties of a constructive trustee are not necessarily the same as that of an express trustee. Very much depends on the circumstances which give rise to the imposition of the constructive trust. For example, Professor Martin explains that if:

> a person purchases property with constructive but not actual notice of a trust [thereby imposing constructive trusteeship upon himself], the beneficiaries may enforce the trust against him; but if he is not informed of their claims for some time, it seems that he will not be subjected also to liability for failure to invest in trustee investments and to the usual standard of care which is required of express trustees in the performance of their duties.[73]

Conclusion

The focus in this chapter has been on the nature of a constructive trust and an examination of some of the judicial grounds, both in English law and Commonwealth jurisdictions, for the imposition of a constructive trust. The fundamental basis for the imposition of a constructive trust is the unconscionability of the constructive trustee. The constructive trust is imposed in circumstances where it would be unconscionable

---

[71] [1980] 1 WLR 219.
[72] [1980] 1 WLR 219.
[73] Hanbury and Martin, *Modern Equity* 17th edn (2005) at p. 304.

for the constructive trustee not to recognise the beneficial interest of the constructive beneficiary. English law only recognises an institutional constructive trust which arises in the occurrence of certain well-defined events. In a majority of contexts, as will be seen in Chapter 13, a central feature is the constructive trustee's agreement or understanding that he will recognise the beneficial interest of the constructive beneficiary. The constructive trustee's subsequent attempt to resile from the agreement is viewed by the English courts as fraudulent. In contrast, some other jurisdictions such as Canada and the United States have adopted a much wider view of a constructive trust. In such jurisdictions the constructive trust had operated as one of a number of remedies available to a court in order to prevent the unjust enrichment of a defendant at the claimant's expense. Irrespective of agreement, express or implied, and an absence of fraud, the constructive trust is imposed where the defendant is unjustly enriched at the claimant's expense. English law has not yet introduced a remedial constructive trust into its law, primarily because of the uncertainty of the cause of action which gives rise to its imposition and the effect it can have on third parties.

Moot points

1 What do you understand to be the difference between an institutional constructive trust and a remedial constructive trust?

2 What is the relationship between a constructive trust and the principles of unjust enrichment and restitution?

3 Explain the effect of the imposition of an institutional constructive trust with regard to the constructive trustee, the constructive beneficiary and other third parties who may deal with the property subject to a constructive trust.

4 In some situations a constructive trust is imposed without giving the constructive beneficiary a proprietary claim to any trust property but only a personal claim against the trustee. How far is it appropriate to impose a constructive trustee on a defendant without conferring upon the beneficiary a proprietary claim to any trust property? You may wish to return to this question after reading about liability for knowing assistance in Chapter 14.

5 Explain, with examples, how the remedial constructive trust has been imposed in Canada.

6 Why does English law not recognise a remedial constructive trust?

Further reading

Etherton, T. 'Constructive Trusts: A New Model for Equity and Unjust Enrichment' (2008) CLJ 265. Examines the nature of the common intention constructive trust and its relationship with the resulting trust and the equitable doctrine of proprietary estoppel. With specific reference to the joint acquisition of property cases, the article seeks to explain the imposition of a common intention constructive trust from the perspective of unjust enrichment.

Hemsworth, M. 'Constructive Trusts and Constructive Trustees – What's in a Name?' (2000) CJQ 154. Examines the impact of the imposition of a constructive trust in cases of stranger liability and the extent to which such imposition is affected by the Limitation Act 1980.

Millett, P.J. 'Restitution and Constructive Trusts' (1998) LQR 399. Explores the role of constructive trusts in the law of restitution.

Rotman, L.I. 'Deconstructing the Constructive Trust' (1999) 37 Alta. L. Rev. Examines the grounds for the imposition of a constructive trust from an American perspective, with specific reference to the notion of good conscience.

Smith, L. 'Constructive Trusts and Constructive Trustee' (1999) CLJ 294. Examines a number of terminology used in the context of constructive trusts, including addressing the issue about what is constructive about a constructive trust.

Visit **www.mylawchamber.co.uk/panesar** to access study support resources including interactive multiple choice questions, practice exam questions with guidance, podcasts, weblinks, legal newsfeed all linked to the **Pearson eText** version of Exploring Equity and Trusts which you can **search**, **highlight** and **personalise** with your **own notes** and **bookmarks**.

Use Case Navigator to read in full some of the key cases referenced in this chapter with commentary and questions:

Westdeutsche Landesbank Girozentrale v Islington LBC [1996] AC 699 (HL)

13

Constructive trusts, part II: Imposing constructive trusts

Learning objectives

After reading this chapter you should be able to:

→ explain the grounds for the imposition of an institutional constructive trust

→ explain the imposition of a constructive trust in cases where the defendant acquires some property as a result of his criminal wrongdoing

→ understand constructive trusts arising in situations where there is a breach of fiduciary duty

→ understand the role of the constructive trust in resolving ownership disputes in the context of the family home

→ in the context of the family home, explain the difference between the constructive trust and other equitable doctrines such as proprietary estoppel and resulting trusts

→ have some appreciation of other contexts in which a constructive trust arises, for example, constructive trusts arising in the context of specifically enforceable contracts for the sale of property and constructive trusts arising in the context of mutual wills and secret trusts

→ appreciate law reform in some of the contexts in which the constructive trust has been imposed.

Problems requiring a constructive trust solution

Many of the preceding chapters in this book have set the scene by highlighting a case which raises some of the legal issues which will be addressed in the chapter. This chapter, like Chapter 11 on resulting trusts, takes a rather different approach in setting the scene. Given the diversity of the factual situations which will give rise to the imposition of a constructive trust, this chapter sets the scene by presenting a number of factual situations in which equity may be called upon to impose a constructive trust. Such factual situations will provide a useful starting point for an understanding of constructive trusts and the different family and commercial contexts in which constructive trusts are imposed. At this stage it is not important that you have the answers to the questions posed in the relevant situations; it is, however, important that you can appreciate the concerns that are raised and understand that some redress is needed in each of those situations.

Situation One: A trustee taking a benefit for himself

Suppose that a trustee is holding a very profitable lease of a market for a beneficiary. The lease has come to an end and the landlord is quite happy to renew the lease for the trust. However, envious of the fact that the lease of the market is making very good profits for the beneficiary, the trustee lies to the beneficiary and tells him that the landlord has refused to renew the lease. Two months later the trustee renews the lease for himself. The beneficiary finds out what has happened and is not too happy with the situation.

● *Do you think that it is right for the lease to be kept by the trustee?*

Situation Two: Non-marital cohabitation

Gavin and Vicky met sometime in 1998 and started a love relationship. They always intended to get married but never did so, primarily on the grounds that they did not want to commit themselves into a marital relationship. In 2000 Gavin purchased a house which was conveyed in his name only, although he told Vicky that the house was as much hers as it was his. He told Vicky that it would be unwise to put their joint names as this would have certain tax implications. In fact this was just not true as Gavin had no intention of making Vicky the owner of the house at that stage. Gavin and Vicky had two children between 2001 and 2007. Throughout those years, Vicky worked part-time and looked after the children and paid all the costs towards looking after their children, as well as putting food on the table. Vicky's contribution helped Gavin discharge the mortgage on the house which he would not otherwise have been able to do so. Last year, Vicky found out that Gavin was having an affair and has moved out of the house to live with her mother. She has commenced proceedings against Gavin, claiming that the house, which was purchased in his name, belongs to her as well.

● *How can the house belong to Vicky when she is not on the legal title?*
● *Would it be unfair not to give her some interest in the house?*
● *Is unfairness an appropriate ground for helping Vicky?*
● *Is there some other way in which you can explain Gavin's conduct?*

Each of the situations explored above seems to have a common theme in that an individual has attempted to keep some property for himself fraudulently at the expense of an innocent party. It will be observed throughout this chapter that the imposition of a constructive trust is to prevent a person from keeping property for himself in circumstances where it

▶

is unconscionable for him to do so. Although the factual situations giving rise to the imposition of a constructive trust are quite diverse, the basic feature of a constructive trust is to prevent unconscionability in respect of dealings with property. This chapter explores the various factual situations in which English law has imposed a constructive trust.

Introduction

The previous chapter examined the nature of a constructive trust and in doing so attempted to examine some of the theoretical debates surrounding both the nature and the grounds for the imposition of a constructive trust. The purpose of this chapter is to examine some of the principal contexts in which a constructive trust has been imposed by the English courts. It was explained in the last chapter that searching for a coherent theory which explains the grounds for the imposition of a constructive trust is not necessarily a straightforward task. The principal reason for this is that a constructive trust has been imposed to resolve disputes over property in a wide range of contexts. These contexts, as will be illustrated throughout the course of this chapter, involve both commerce and family. Given the diversity of these contexts, it has not always been that easy to formulate a theory which explains all of the factual situations which give rise to the imposition of a constructive trust. As explained earlier, one commentator writes that a:

> comprehensive review . . . of constructive trusts would require analysis of areas of law as diverse as vendor and purchaser transactions, the perfection of imperfect gifts, fully secret and half secret trusts, breach of fiduciary duty, and accessory liability for breach of trust, among several others. The search for an acceptable, universally acknowledged, principle for the establishment of a constructive trust, which gives coherence to past decisions and provides clear guidance for the future, will certainly prove elusive in relation to many different areas of law and fact which constructive trusts arise.[1]

In *Yeoman's Row Management Ltd* v *Cobbe*[2] Lord Scott explained that it 'is impossible to prescribe exhaustively the circumstances sufficient to create a constructive trust but it is possible to recognise particular factual circumstances that will do so and also to recognise other factual circumstances that will not'.[3] In the context of Lord Scott's remarks, this chapter attempts to examine some of the main contexts in which a constructive trust has been imposed.

 ## Acquisition of property as a result of unlawful conduct

A constructive trust will be imposed on a person who acquires the legal title to property by some form of unlawful conduct such as homicide or theft. It is a general principle of

---

[1] T. Etherton, 'Constructive Trusts: A New Model for Equity and Unjust Enrichment' (2008) CLJ 265.
[2] [2008] 1 WLR 1752.
[3] [2008] 1 WLR 1752 at 1769.

English law that an individual should not profit from his crime. The matter was neatly explained by Fry LJ in *Cleaver v Mutual Reserve Fund Life Association*[4] where the judge commented that:

> no system of jurisprudence can with reason include amongst the rights which is enforced rights directly resulting to the person asserting them from the crime of that person. If no action can arise from fraud, it seems impossible to suppose that it can arise from felony or misdemeanour . . . The principle of public policy, like all such principles, must be applied to all cases to which it can be applied without reference to the particular character of the right asserted or the form of its assertion.[5]

Where an individual does acquire the legal title to property through his unlawful conduct, the Forfeiture Rule operates to forfeit the property from the individual. Forfeiture will take place by means of the imposition of a constructive trust on the property acquired as a result of the unlawful conduct. It will be seen later in this section that, where forfeiture is invoked, the defendant may be able to seek relief against forfeiture under the Forfeiture Act 1982.

Acquisition of property by killing

APPLYING THE LAW

Tom discovered that his wife had been cheating on him. In the middle of a heated row with his wife, he pushed her and she hit her head on a concrete floor. His wife died as a result of the fall and Tom has been convicted of manslaughter. Tom's wife had made a will in which she had left all her property to him.

Can Tom claim his wife's property?

The principle of law is that no person may benefit from killing another person. The matter is neatly illustrated in the decision of Sir Samuel Evans P in *In the Estate of Crippen*[6] where Dr Crippen murdered his wife and left the property he would have received from his wife as her intestate successor to his mistress. The question before the court was whether the mistress could receive the property which Dr Crippen acquired as a result of murdering his wife. The Court held that his mistress, being the legatee of his will, was not entitled to the property that he would have received as a result of the death of his wife. In the course of his judgment, Sir Samuel Evans P explained that it 'is clear that the law is, that no person can obtain, or enforce, any rights resulting to him from his own crime; neither can his representative, claiming under him, obtain or enforce any such rights. The human mind revolts at the very idea that any other doctrine could be possible in our system of jurisprudence.'[7] The rule extends to prevent a child of a killer from inheriting, for example, from his grandparents. For example in *Re DWS (deceased)*[8] a killer murdered his parents, both of whom had not made a will. It was not disputed that the killer was prevented from inheriting his parent's property under the intestacy rules. However, the

---

[4] [1892] 1 QB 147.
[5] [1892] 1 QB 147 at 156.
[6] [1911] P 108.
[7] [1911] P 108 at 112.
[8] [2001] Ch. 568.

question arose as to whether the killer's son could inherit his grandparent's property. The court held that since the killer was not dead, the killer's son could not inherit his grandparent's property. One of the reasons for this was the technicality of succession law, which only allows a grandchild to inherit under the intestacy rules if his own parents have died. Since the killer was still alive, the grandson was not entitled to the estate of his grandparents. Instead the property belonging to the grandparents went to other relatives.

One particular area where the forfeiture rule will operate is where land or other property is held by joint tenants and one of the joint tenants kills the other, thereby becoming entitled to the whole of the jointly owned land through the principle of survivorship. It is a cardinal principle of a joint tenancy that where one joint tenant dies, then the remaining joint tenant becomes entitled to the property absolutely on the principle of survivorship. The reason for this is that a joint tenant does not have any specific share in a joint tenancy which he can pass to anyone else. Even where he makes a will purporting to leave his supposed share in the joint tenancy to a third party, the third party will not be able to take any share, as the right of survivorship will take precedence in vesting the entire property which was subject to the joint tenancy in the remaining joint tenant. However, where one joint tenant kills the other joint tenant in order to take advantage of the right of survivorship, the rule of forfeiture will operate to deny him the right to all of the jointly owned property. In such a case, he will hold the once jointly owned property for himself and for the next of kin of the murdered joint tenant. The advantages of the imposition of a constructive trust on the share of the deceased joint tenant is best explained by Professor Kevin Gray and Susan Gray in the following terms.

> The constructive trust approach has major merits. The legal devolution of title is left untouched, whilst the principle of public policy is enforced through the medium of trust. The imposition of a constructive trust efficiently prevents unjust enrichment. The killer is stripped of any profits arising from his crime, but is not otherwise subjected to penalty of forfeiture in respect of his own inchoate interest under the joint tenancy. Moreover, the application of constructive trust principles enables a focus to be placed on the wider question whether the taking of a benefit by the wrongdoer would be so unconscionable as to attract the operation of the public policy rule. Thus, although the devolution of title is allowed to take its normal course, the culpability of the killer's conduct becomes relevant at this secondary stage in determining whether, and if so to what extent, a constructive trust should be imposed on the title-holder.[9]

The forfeiture of an interest under a joint tenancy is neatly illustrated in the judgment of Vinelott J in **Re K**[10] where a wife, who had suffered a series of assaults by her husband, picked up a loaded gun with the intention of scaring her husband. The safety latch on the gun was released, with the consequence that a bullet was fired killing her husband. The wife was charged with the murder of her husband; however, at trial a lesser charge of manslaughter was accepted. The question before the court was whether the wife should forfeit her right to the entire ownership of the matrimonial home on the basis of the right of survivorship. In the course of his judgment Vinelott J, relying on authority from Canada[11] and New Zealand,[12] held that 'there is curiously no reported case on the point in England but it has been held in other jurisdictions where the law was similar to English

---

[9] K. Gray and S. Gray, *Elements of Land Law*, 6th edn (2009) at p. 960.
[10] [1985] Ch. 85.
[11] *Schobelt* v *Barber* (1966) 60 DLR (2d) 519.
[12] *Re Pechar (deceased)* [1969] NZLR 574.

law before 1925 that where one of two joint tenants murders the other while the entire interest vests in the survivor the law imports a constructive trust of an undivided one-half share for the benefit of the next of kin of the deceased other than the offender'.[13]

One question which has not really been answered conclusively in the decided cases is whether the forfeiture rule applies to all types of killing or whether it makes a difference whether the killing was a result of murder or manslaughter. Furthermore, do factors such as the use of violence make any difference in applying the rule? In **Gray v Barr**[14] there was some suggestion that acts not involving violence and lesser forms of manslaughter may not be subject to the forfeiture rule. In this case, the defendant entered the victim's premises with a loaded shotgun, suspecting that the victim was having an affair with his wife. The defendant, whilst threatening his victim, accidentally slipped over, causing the gun to fire a shot at his victim. In holding that the forfeiture rule applied to the present case Salmon LJ explained that:

> although public policy is rightly regarded as an unruly steed which should be cautiously ridden, I am confident that public policy undoubtedly requires that no one who threatens unlawful violence with a loaded gun should be allowed to enforce a claim for indemnity against any liability he may incur as a result of having so acted. I do not intend to lay down any wider proposition. In particular I am not deciding that a man who has committed manslaughter would, in any circumstances, be prevented from enforcing a contract of indemnity in respect of any liability he may have incurred for causing death or from inheriting under a will or upon the intestacy of anyone whom he has killed. Manslaughter is a crime which varies infinitely in its seriousness. It may come very near to murder or amount to little more than inadvertence, although in the latter class of case the jury only rarely convicts.[15]

In **Re H**[16] the defendant, who was suffering from serious depression and on antidepressants, killed his wife. He was later convicted of manslaughter on grounds of diminished responsibility. Peter Gibson J held that the fact that he was not responsible for his actions meant that the forfeiture rule did not apply.

More recently, however, in **Dunbar v Plant**[17] the Court of Appeal has rejected the idea that the application of the forfeiture rule is influenced by factors such as whether violence or threats were used. Rather, the Court of Appeal has explained that the rule applies irrespective of such matters, and that whether a defendant should or should not be subject to the forfeiture rules is more appropriately dealt with under the Forfeiture Act 1982, which confers upon the court a discretion to grant relief against forfeiture.[18] The facts of the case involved a suicide pact between Miss Plant and Mr Dunbar with whom she was in a love relationship. The decision to commit suicide was taken as a result of Miss Plant facing trial for theft and the possibility of a jail sentence. There were a number of different suicide attempts; however, one of them resulted in the death of Mr Dunbar whilst Miss Plant survived. Miss Plant was subsequently found guilty of aiding and abetting suicide under s. 2(1) of the Suicide Act 1961. The question before the court was whether the forfeiture rule applied so as to deny Miss Plant of the benefit of a life insurance which Mr Dunbar had taken out in her favour. The Court of Appeal held that,

---

[13] [1985] Ch. 85 at 100.
[14] [1971] 2 QB 554.
[15] [1971] 2 QB 554 at 581.
[16] [1990] 1 FLR 441.
[17] [1998] Ch. 412. See also *Re Mack (Deceased)* [2009] EWHC 1524.
[18] This Act is discussed in the next section.

even though on the present facts there was no violence, the forfeiture rule did apply in principle. In the course of his judgment, Mummery LJ explained that:

> [i]n my judgment, however, the presence of acts or threats of violence is not necessary for the application of the forfeiture rule. It is sufficient that a serious crime has been committed deliberately and intentionally. The references to acts or threats of violence in the cases are explicable by the facts of those cases. But in none of those cases were the courts legislating a principle couched in specific statutory language. The essence of the principle of public policy is that (a) no person shall take a benefit resulting from a crime committed by him or her resulting in the death of the victim and (b) the nature of the crime determines the application of the principle. On that view the important point is that the crime that had fatal consequences was committed with a guilty mind (deliberately and intentionally). The particular means used to commit the crime (whether violent or non-violent) are not a necessary ingredient of the rule. There may be cases in which violence has been used deliberately without an intention to bring about the unlawful fatal consequences. Those cases will attract the application of the forfeiture rule. It does not follow, however, that when death has been brought about by a deliberate and intentional, but non-violent, act (e.g. poison or gas) the rule is inapplicable.[19]

The Forfeiture Act 1982

Except in the case of murder,[20] the Forfeiture Act confers upon the court a discretion to grant relief against the application of the forfeiture rule. The basic tenet of the Act is as follows.

KEY STATUTE

1—(1) In this Act, the 'forfeiture rule' means the rule of public policy which in certain circumstances precludes a person who has unlawfully killed another from acquiring a benefit in consequence of the killing.

(2) References in this Act to a person who has unlawfully killed another include a reference to a person who has unlawfully aided, abetted, counselled or procured the death of that other and references in this Act to unlawful killing shall be interpreted accordingly.

2—(1) Where a court determines that the forfeiture rule has precluded a person (in this section referred to as 'the offender') who has unlawfully killed another from acquiring any interest in property mentioned in subsection (4) below, the court may make an order under this section modifying the effect of that rule.

(2) The court shall not make an order under this section modifying the effect of the forfeiture rule in any case unless it is satisfied that, having regard to the conduct of the offender and of the deceased and to such other circumstances as appear to the court to be material, the justice of the case requires the effect of the rule to be so modified in that case.

(3) In any case where a person stands convicted of an offence of which unlawful killing is an element, the court shall not make an order under this section modifying the effect of the forfeiture rule in that case unless proceedings for the purpose are brought before the expiry of the period of three months beginning with his conviction.

---

[19] [1998] Ch. 412 at 425. The same principle was more recently applied in *Glover v Staffordshire Police Authority* [2006] EWHC 2414 where the court refused a widow who had been convicted of the manslaughter of her husband to recover pension benefits from her husband's employer.
[20] S. 5 Forfeiture Act 1982.

The question which arises in the context of the Forfeiture Act 1982 is: what criteria will the court apply when deciding to exercise its discretion under s. 2(1) of the Act? Section 2(2) requires that, in order for relief to be given under the Act, the court must look at the conduct of the offender and the deceased and other material circumstances. In **Dunbar v Plant**[21] Mummery LJ explained the manner in which the court will exercise it jurisdiction to grant to relief under the Act.

KEY CITATION	*Dunbar v Plant* [1998] Ch. 412 (Exercising discretion to grant relief under the Forfeiture Act 1982 per Mummery LJ at 427)

[T]he relevant question for the court is: does 'the justice of the case require' that the effect of the forfeiture rule be modified? In my view, the judge erroneously regarded himself as under a duty to try and do 'justice between the parties.' That is not the approach required by section 2(2). The provision requires that the judge should look at the case in the round, pay regard to all the material circumstances, including the conduct of the offender and the deceased, and then ask whether 'the justice of the case requires' a modification of the effect of the forfeiture rule. Having taken the wrong approach, the judge failed, in my view, to give consideration in his reasons to all the factors material to the exercise of his discretion. In those circumstances it is open to this court to exercise the discretion afresh on the basis of the relevant material. On doing that, I have in fact reached the same conclusion as the judge on the limited scope of the modification order. It is difficult to draw the line with confidence. The point at which the judge drew it is not obviously wrong. The court is entitled to take into account a whole range of circumstances relevant to the discretion, quite apart from the conduct of the offender and the deceased: the relationship between them; the degree of moral culpability for what has happened; the nature and gravity of the offence; the intentions of the deceased; the size of the estate and the value of the property in dispute; the financial position of the offender; and the moral claims and wishes of those who would be entitled to take the property on the application of the forfeiture rule.[22]

You will recall from the facts of **Dunbar v Plant** that Miss Plant was part of a suicide pact in which her partner, Mr Dunbar, died. The Court of Appeal allowed full relief from the forfeiture rule on the grounds that suicide cases were tragic and a result of sheer desperation. Relief under the Forfeiture Act 1982 was also given in **Re K**[23] where a wife was found guilty of manslaughter when she accidentally killed her husband who had been extremely violent towards her. In the course of his judgment, Vinelott J explained that, as well as the circumstances of the case, the court could take into consideration the relative financial position of the person claiming relief under the Act and those seeking the application of the forfeiture rule. The court held that the wife, having provided loyal support to her husband as well as giving up a very successful job, was entitled to full relief under the Act.

---

[21] [1998] Ch. 412.
[22] [1998] Ch. 412 at 427.
[23] [1985] Ch. 85.

Law Commission reform

The law relating to the forfeiture rule and succession was reviewed by the Law Commission in 2005.[24] In its report, the Commission concluded that whilst it was right to exclude a murderer from inheriting, it was unfair to exclude the children of the murderer. The Commission concluded that the law in this respect was arbitrary and not based on public policy, but was a by-product of the technical rules of succession. In any event, the Commission concluded that it would not have been the intention of the grandparents to leave the property to other relatives at the expense of their grandchildren. The Commission explained that it was unfair to punish grandchildren for the sins of their parents. In suggesting law reform in this area, the Commission proposed that there be an introduction of a 'deemed predecease rule' which would deem a killer who had killed his parents to have predeceased his parents. This would mean that his predecease would entitle his children to inherit their grandparents' property on the grounds that the killer's interest lapsed and automatically entitled his children to the grandparents' property. In March 2011 a Bill was presented before Parliament entitled 'Estates of Deceased Persons (Forfeiture Rule and the Law of Succession)'. The Bill, when it comes into force, will give effect to the recommendations of the Law Commission in its report of 2005.

Theft

The imposition of a constructive trust has little application in the context of theft simply because a thief does not acquire any legal title to the stolen property, and therefore, cannot pass a good title to a third party. Furthermore, s. 28 of the Theft Act 1968 confers upon the court a power to order a person who has been found guilty of theft to return the property to the rightful owner. Having said this, it is not true to say that the constructive trust has no role in the case of theft. The imposition of a constructive trust on the stolen property may allow the rightful owner of the property to trace his original property into the hands of the thief or some other third party. The possibility of the imposition of a constructive trust on the stolen property was recognised by Lord Browne-Wilkinson in

VISIT CASE
NAVIGATOR

Westdeutsche Landesbank Girozentrale v Islington LBC [25] where his Lordship commented that 'I agree that . . . stolen moneys are traceable in equity. But the proprietary interest which equity is enforcing in such circumstances arises under a constructive, not a resulting, trust.'[26] The advantages of the imposition of a constructive trust on stolen property such as money is that it allows the rightful owner to benefit from the much wider principles of tracing property in equity. Tracing is the process by which an owner of property can lay claim to substituted or mixed property which has been substituted or mixed with his own property. The tracing rules of equity are considered in much more detail in Chapter 21; suffice to say here that where the thief mixes the stolen property with his own property, the rightful owner will not be precluded from tracing into the mixed property. It will be seen in Chapter 21 that the right to trace property at common law is limited to the extent that the property being followed does not become mixed with other property.

Despite the dicta of Lord Browne-Wilkinson in *Westdeutsche Landesbank Girozentrale v Islington LBC*,[27] in *Shalson v Russo*[28] Rimer J questioned whether it was entirely

---

[24] Law Com. No. 295, *The Forfeiture Rule and the Law of Succession* (2005).
[25] [1996] AC 669 (HL).
[26] [1996] AC 669 (HL) at 716.
[27] [1996] AC 669 (HL).
[28] [2005] Ch. 281.

appropriate to impose a constructive trust on stolen property so as to allow the victim of the theft to trace the property under the equitable tracing rules. In the course of his judgment, Rimer J explained he did not find Lord Browne-Wilkinson's passage with reference to the stolen bags of money an:

> easy passage. As to the first paragraph, a thief ordinarily acquires no property in what he steals and cannot give a title to it even to a good faith purchaser: both the thief and the purchaser are vulnerable to claims by the true owner to recover his property. If the thief has no title in the property, I cannot see how he can become a trustee of it for the true owner: the owner retains the legal and beneficial title. If the thief mixes stolen money with other money in a bank account, the common law cannot trace into it. Equity has traditionally been regarded as similarly incompetent unless it could first identify a relevant fiduciary relationship, but in many cases of theft there will be none. The fact that, traditionally, equity can only trace into a mixed bank account if that precondition is first satisfied provides an unsatisfactory justification for any conclusion that the stolen money must necessarily be trust money so as to enable the precondition to be satisfied. It is either trust money or it is not. If it is not, it is not legitimate artificially to change its character so as to bring it within the supposed limits of equity's powers to trace: the answer is to develop those powers so as to meet the special problems raised by stolen money.[29]

Bribes

APPLYING THE LAW

Tom is employed as a planning officer in a local authority council. In the last year or so he has taken a number of bribes from a property development company in return for giving planning permission to the company. The vast majority of the plans submitted by the company have compromised safety standards. Tom has used the bribe money to purchase a house for himself.

Is Tom allowed to keep the money that he has received as bribes? If not, to whom does the money belong?

Until the decision of the Privy Council in **A-G for Hong Kong v Reid**[30] the general principle in English law was that no constructive trust arose in circumstances where a fiduciary, such as an agent, received a bribe. Instead, the agent's principal was confined to a personal remedy against the agent in the form of a personal account. The agent, who had received the bribe, was only under a personal obligation to account and thus stood in a debtor–creditor relationship with his principal. The matter is neatly illustrated by the decision of the Court of Appeal in **Lister & Co v Stubbs**[31] where an employee of Lister & Co received bribes of some £5000 from another company to whom he gave business whilst being employed by Lister & Co. The question before the Court of Appeal was whether the money received by way of bribes was held on constructive trust for Lister & Co. The Court held that the bribe money was not held on constructive trust; instead the relationship between Lister & Co and their employee was one of creditor and debtor.

---

[29] [2005] Ch. 281 at 317.
[30] [1994] 1 AC 324.
[31] (1890) 45 Ch. D 1.

The employee was not a constructive trustee but was only under a personal obligation to account for the money he had received.

The significance of the decision of the Court of Appeal in *Lister & Co* v *Stubbs* was that the principal could not gain any priority over the other creditors of the agent. The fact that no trust arose over the bribe money meant that the principal had no proprietary interest to trace in equity. Despite remaining settled law for over a century, the decision in *Lister & Co* v *Stubbs* was not followed by the Privy Council in *A-G for Hong Kong* v *Reid*.[32] The facts of this Privy Council case concerned a public prosecutor, Reid, employed in Hong Kong by the Crown. In the course of his employment Reid received bribes in excess of NZ$2.5 million which were then used this to purchase properties in New Zealand. The question before the Privy Council was whether the money received by way of bribes was held on constructive trust for the Crown, thereby allowing the crown to trace the money into the properties that Reid had purchased in New Zealand. The Privy Council held that the bribe money received by Reid was held on constructive trust for the Crown and, as a result of this, the Crown was able to trace the bribe money into the freehold properties that Reid had purchased in New Zealand. In coming to this conclusion the Privy Council had to consider whether the decision in *Lister & Co* v *Stubbs* was correct, as well as the grounds for the imposition of a constructive trust on money received by way of a bribe.

The judgment of the Privy Council was delivered by Lord Templeman who provided answers to both of the questions raised in the appeal. In respect of the decision of the Court of Appeal in *Lister & Co* v *Stubbs*,[33] Lord Templeman explained that the decision was:

> not consistent with the principles that a fiduciary must not be allowed to benefit from his own breach of duty, that the fiduciary should account for the bribe as soon as he receives it and that equity regards as done that which ought to be done. From these principles it would appear to follow that the bribe and the property from time to time representing the bribe are held on a constructive trust for the person injured. A fiduciary remains personally liable for the amount of the bribe if, in the event, the value of the property then recovered by the injured person proved to be less than that amount.[34]

With regard to the rationale for the imposition of a constructive trust on the bribe, Lord Templeman was faced with a number of theoretical concerns as well as policy considerations. From a theoretical standpoint, one of the reasons why the decision in *Lister & Co* v *Stubbs* remained unchallenged in English law for some considerable time was that the English courts were not prepared to impose a constructive trust on bribe money when it never formed the property of the principal in the first place. In other words, a constructive trust could not be imposed on property which never once belonged to the principal. In this respect some commentators have required that there be some proprietary base before a constructive trust is imposed allowing a claimant to trace in equity.[35] Policy wise, it was generally thought that the imposition of a constructive trust on bribe money in the hands of an agent gave the principal an unjustified priority over other creditors of the agent.[36] Lord Templeman attempted to reject both the theoretical and policy consideration by offering alternative arguments.

---

[32] [1994] 1 AC 324.

[33] (1890) 45 Ch. D 1.

[34] [1994] 1 AC 324.

[35] P. Birks, *An Introduction to the Law of Restitution* p. 389.

[36] See R. Goode, 'Property and Unjust Enrichment' in *Essays on the Law of Restitution* ed. Burrows (1991); R. Goode, 'Proprietary Restitutionary Claims' in *Restitution: Past, Present and Future* ed. Cornish (1998) and also D. Cowan, '*Lister & Co* v *Stubbs*: Who Profits?' (1996) JBL 22.

In respect of the policy argument, Lord Templeman explained that:

> bribery is an evil practice which threatens the foundations of any civilised society. In particular bribery of policemen and prosecutors brings the administration of justice into disrepute. Where bribes are accepted by a trustee, servant, agent or other fiduciary, loss and damage are caused to the beneficiaries, master or principal whose interests have been betrayed. The amount of loss or damage resulting from the acceptance of a bribe may or may not be quantifiable. In the present case the amount of harm caused to the administration of justice in Hong Kong by the first respondent in return for bribes cannot be quantified.[37]

With regard to the rationale or the theoretical grounds for the imposition of a constructive trust on the bribed money, Lord Templeman explained that as soon as the money was received by the defendant, the defendant was under an immediate obligation to hold it for the claimant. In the words of his Lordship:

> [A]s soon as the bribe was received it should have been paid or transferred instantly to the person who suffered from the breach of duty. Equity considers as done that which ought to have been done. As soon as the bribe was received, whether in cash or in kind, the false fiduciary held the bribe on a constructive trust for the person injured. Two objections have been raised to this analysis. First it is said that if the fiduciary is in equity a debtor to the person injured, he cannot also be a trustee of the bribe. But there is no reason why equity should not provide two remedies, so long as they do not result in double recovery. If the property representing the bribe exceeds the original bribe in value, the fiduciary cannot retain the benefit of the increase in value which he obtained solely as a result of his breach of duty. Secondly, it is said that if the false fiduciary holds property representing the bribe in trust for the person injured, and if the false fiduciary is or becomes insolvent, the unsecured creditors of the false fiduciary will be deprived of their right to share in the proceeds of that property. But the unsecured creditors cannot be in a better position than their debtor. The authorities show that property acquired by a trustee innocently but in breach of trust and the property from time to time representing the same belong in equity to the cestui que trust and not to the trustee personally whether he is solvent or insolvent. Property acquired by a trustee as a result of a criminal breach of trust and the property from time to time representing the same must also belong in equity to his cestui que trust and not to the trustee whether he is solvent or insolvent.[38]

Although the decision of the Privy Council is strictly not binding in English law, it seemed that the decision would be followed and endorsed by the higher courts. The decision was considered in *Daraydan Holdings Ltd v Solland International Ltd*[39] where the claimants Daraydan Holding Ltd commenced proceedings against a former employee who had received an undisclosed commission of some £1.8 million in the course of arranging refurbishment of the claimant's property. One of the questions before Lawrence Collins J was whether the ruling of the Privy Council in *A-G for Hong Kong v Reid*[40] applied to the present case. The judge explained that he was bound to apply the decision of the Privy Council to the present case rather than wait for it to be affirmed by the House of Lords. In the course of his judgment, he explained that:

> the system of precedent would be shown in a most unfavourable light if a litigant in such a case were forced by the doctrine of binding precedent to go to the House of Lords in order

---

[37] [1994] 1 AC 324 at 331.
[38] [1994] 1 AC 324 at 331.
[39] [2005] Ch. 119. See, M. Halliwell 'The Ghost of *Lister & Co v Stubbs*' (2005) Conv. 88.
[40] [1994] 1 AC 324.

to have the decision of the Privy Council affirmed. That would be particularly so where the decision of the Privy Council is recent, where it was a decision on the English common law, where the Board consisted mainly of serving Law Lords, and where the decision had been made after full argument on the correctness of the earlier decision.[41]

VISIT CASE NAVIGATOR

Despite the decision of the Privy Council in *Attorney-General for Hong Kong v Reid*,[42] the Court of Appeal has recently put serious doubt on the correctness of that decision. In particular, the Court of Appeal has rejected that there is a wide principle which holds that bribes and other unauthorised profits are held on a constructive trust thereby giving a claimant a proprietary claim to the profits. The decision is *Sinclair Investments (UK) Ltd v Versailles Trade Finance Ltd (In Administration)*[43] and it has rather left the position in English law very uncertain. The facts of this case are covered in more detail in the next section, but save that it involved a massive fraud by a certain Mr Cushnie who controlled a group of companies called the Versailles Group plc. One of the companies in the group, Versailles Trading Finance Ltd (VTFL) was engaged in trade finance. Despite that, the company was more involved in orchestrating a massive fraud against a number of traders who were encouraged to advance money which would be held by a company called Trading Partners Ltd (TPL) for the purpose of trading activities. In addition, money was also raised through the Versailles Group plc (VGP), in which Mr Cushnie has a substantial holding, and Versailles Trading Finance Ltd (VTFL) which issued debentures to a number of banks, raising money by charges on the assets of that company.

Fraud was carried out against the banks and the traders by Mr Cushnie authorising the use of the money for purposes other than trading. In fact, the money was moved from one company to another, showing profits and thereby increasing the share price of the Versailles Group. Mr Cushnie sold the shares at a considerable profit and purchased personal assets including a house in London. TPL was assigned to an investor called Sinclair Investment Holdings who commenced proceedings to claim proprietary rights to the profits and the house. Sinclair argued that Mr Cushnie owed fiduciary duties to TPL and that the money used from TPL was used in breach of trust. The question before the High Court and eventually the Court of Appeal was whether Mr Cushnie, acting in breach of fiduciary duty, held the profits on a constructive trust, thereby giving the claimant a proprietary right, or whether there was a personal claim only. In the High Court, Lewison J held that TPL was owed fiduciary duties but it had no proprietary claims to the profits and the money realised by Mr Cushnie on the sale of the London property. Lewison J explained that:

> The fiduciary duty relied on in the present case is a duty owed by Mr Cushnie to TPL. The unauthorised profit is a profit realised by Mr Cushnie on the sale of shares in VGP . . . Mr Cushnie acquired those shares before TPL was even incorporated. But at any rate his initial acquisition of the shares could not, in my judgment, have amounted to an acquisition of property that belonged in any sense to TPL. Before his sale of those shares he did not owe trustee-like duties in relation to that specific property. It follows, in my judgment, that the claim by TPL to the profit realised by Mr Cushnie on a sale of those shares is a claim based on the transaction which gave rise to those profits, and the circumstances in which it was made. It is, therefore, a case which falls into [Millett LJ's] second class; and gives rise to a personal remedy only. Since the claim gives rise to a personal remedy only, it is not open to TPL to trace those profits into the proceeds of sale of the Kensington property and

---

[41] [2005] Ch. 119 at 139.
[42] [1994] 1 AC 324.
[43] [2011] EWCA Civ 347.

to assert a proprietary claim to those proceeds. The settlement of personal claims between VTFL and Mr Cushnie cannot be undone by TPL in reliance on a personal claim. That settlement could only be undone by a trustee in bankruptcy or liquidator.[44]

Upholding the decision of Lewison J in the Court of Appeal the matter was explained by the Master of the Rolls Lord Neuberger as follows:

> In a nutshell, the issue between the parties is whether, as it contends, TPL has a proprietary interest in the proceeds of sale of the Shares, or whether, as the defendants argue, TPL has a right to an equitable account to the proceeds of sale. The difference is vital, because, if TPL is correct, it was the beneficial owner of those proceeds, and its beneficial ownership would override, subject to the question of notice, the payments made to the banks in so far as they were made out of the proceeds of sale. On the other hand, if the defendants' case is right, Mr Cushnie's duty is to account to TPL for the proceeds of sale, which is a personal remedy, which would not override the payments already made to the banks.[45]

The Court of Appeal held that Mr Cushnie's breach of fiduciary duty did not give rise to a proprietary claim for the beneficiaries, that is TPL. Lord Neuberger asked the question: 'Why, it may be asked, should the fact that a fiduciary is able to make a profit as a result of the breach of his duties to a beneficiary, without more, give the beneficiary a proprietary interest in the profit? After all, a proprietary claim is based on property law, and it is not entirely easy to see conceptually how the proprietary rights of the beneficiary in the misused funds should follow into the profit made on the sale of the Shares.'[46]

Lord Neuberger was clearly of the opinion that no proprietary claim could arise where a fiduciary had made a profit in breach of his duties, however, where the beneficiaries could not show that the profits represented the property originally belonging to the beneficiaries. In other words, where the beneficiaries could not show a proprietary base to the profits. Lord Neuberger explained that:

> a beneficiary of a fiduciary's duties cannot claim a proprietary interest, but is entitled to an equitable account, in respect of any money or asset acquired by a fiduciary in breach of his duties to the beneficiary, unless the asset or money is or has been beneficially the property of the beneficiary or the trustee acquired the asset or money by taking advantage of an opportunity or right which was properly that of the beneficiary.[47]
>
> For the reasons I have given, previous decisions of this court establish that a claimant cannot claim proprietary ownership of an asset purchased by the defaulting fiduciary with funds which, although they could not have been obtained if he had not enjoyed his fiduciary status, were not beneficially owned by the claimant or derived from opportunities beneficially owned by the claimant. However, those cases also establish that, in such a case, a claimant does have a personal claim in equity to the funds. There is no case which appears to support the notion that such a personal claim entitles the claimant to claim the value of the asset (if it is greater than the amount of the funds together with interest), and there are judicial indications which tend to militate against that notion.[48]

Some may argue that the decision of the Court of Appeal in *Sinclair Investments (UK) Ltd v Versailles Trade Finance Ltd (In Administration)*[49] has introduced some certainty

---

[44] [2010] EWHC 1614 (Civ) at para. 81.
[45] [2011] EWCA Civ 347 at para. 48.
[46] [2011] EWCA Civ 347 at para. 52.
[47] [2011] EWCA Civ 347 at para. 88.
[48] [2011] EWCA Civ 347 at para. 89.
[49] [2011] EWCA Civ 347.

into English law, that is, where a fiduciary makes an unauthorised profit, but the claimant cannot purport to show that the profit belongs to the claimant, there is no proprietary claim to the profit. Furthermore, the decision will be welcome news for creditors of the fiduciary, who, in the event of his insolvency, will find that beneficiaries of the fiduciary will not have prior claims over and above the creditors. However, leading trust lawyers in the field have questioned whether the decision is correct and indeed justified when looked at from the core duties of a fiduciary that are owed to his beneficiaries. From the perspective of the beneficiary, the fiduciary must at all times act in the best interests of that beneficiary. That core duty is an absolute duty which requires the fiduciary to have the exclusive interest of the beneficiary at heart and not to put any of his own interests before that of the beneficiary. With this in perspective, any unauthorised profit or bribe belongs to the beneficiary as it has been made in breach of the core duty to act in the best interests of the beneficiary. The requirement that there be some 'proprietary base', that the bribe or unauthorised gain be linked to the beneficiary's property, becomes irrelevant. In this respect David Hayton comments that:

> . . . a strong case can thus be made that *Sinclair* leaves the law in a most unsatisfactory state and undermines the integrity of the trust concept. At its heart is the fundamental duty of a trustee of property to act exclusively in the best interests of the beneficiaries in fulfilling the role of trustee so as to profit the beneficiaries and not himself (unless duly authorised). To protect the beneficiaries from the trustee's creditors, there is a ring-fenced fund for the beneficiaries that extends beyond the original trust property to property acquired from time to time in the role of trustee. Property acquired in authorised fashion automatically becomes part of the trust fund, while is it not the case that the beneficiaries can also claim that property purportedly acquired howsoever for himself by the trustee through his role of trustee is also part of the authorised trust fund as if acquired in accordance with his core duty? . . . It is accepted that there cannot be ring-fenced security if the trustee could sell trust property and with the proceeds of sale buy assets for his patrimony available to satisfy his creditors' claims, but what if he could sell off trust assets at an undervalue and retain for himself bribes received from the purchasers, or if he could cause the trust to enter into disadvantageous transactions with his alter ego company so that his company could make profits for himself?[50]

The decision of the Privy Council in *A-G for Hong Kong* v *Reid*[51] has significant implications in that it disallows a fiduciary from keeping any unauthorised profit or commission, irrespective of whether the fiduciary's principal has any connection with the profit or commission in the first place. The criticism levelled at the decision of the Privy Council is that it allows a claimant a right to a proprietary remedy against property which was never his or was never capable of reaching his hands. It will be seen later in this chapter that the English courts have traditionally imposed a proprietary claim to property through the vehicle of a constructive trust when the fiduciary has obtained the property at the expense of the claimant. Where the property has not been at the expense of the claimant proper – that is, where some property belonging to the claimant has not reached the hands of the fiduciary – then, despite the fact that the fiduciary has often been labelled a constructive trustee, the duty of such a trustee is to account for the profit.[52] It is this lack of a proprietary connection with the bribe or commission which has been one

---

[50] D. Hayton, 'No Proprietary Liability for Bribes and other Secret Profits?' (2011) Trust Law International 3.
[51] [1994] 1 AC 324.
[52] See, for example, *Boardman* v *Phipps* [1967] 2 AC 46.

VISIT CASE NAVIGATOR

of the fundamental criticisms of the decision in *A-G for Hong Kong v Reid*.[53] The decision did raise questions whether a proprietary claim to follow property would arise in cases such as *Boardman v Phipps*.[54] The facts of the case (considered in more detail in Chapter 17) concerned a solicitor, Boardman, who was providing his services to trustees under a will. The trustees were holding 8000 shares out of an issued 30,000 in a private company. Boardman advised the trustees that there was substantial scope for making a profit on the shares in the private company and therefore they should purchase more of the shares in the company. The trustees refused to purchase the shares, principally because the trust instrument did not allow the acquisition of further shares in the same company. Boardman used the knowledge he had gained from the trust to purchase the remaining shares in the private company. After reorganisation of the private company, the shares he acquired were sold at a profit. He made a profit in the region of £75,000 as well as a benefit to the trust shares in the region of £47,000. The House of Lords held by a majority of 3:2 that Boardman was a constructive trustee of the profits made and as such was required to account for them. In coming to this decision, the House of Lords paid significance to the fact that Boardman had made the profit from knowledge he had acquired of the shares by acting as solicitor to trustees of the trust fund. Furthermore, it was immaterial that the trustees could not have used the information for their own benefit. The fact remained that Boardman made the profit by virtue of his position as solicitor to the trust fund with specific knowledge of the company and the shares within it. Boardman, however, was authorised to retain some of the profit by way of remuneration on the basis of *quantum meruit*. Both the Court of Appeal and the House of Lords were aware that Boardman was a man of great ability and had expended labour in reorganising the company and increasing the value of the shares therein.

In *A-G Reference (No. 1 of 1985)*[55] the Court of Appeal was asked to decide on whether a pub landlord, who was contractually bound to sell only the brewery's beer, held the profits he had made by selling his own beer on constructive trust for the landlord. The Court of Appeal held that the landlord did not hold the money he had received by selling his own beer on constructive trust for the brewery. Instead there was only a personal obligation to account for the money he had received. It is doubtful whether this decision was correct in light of the decision of the Privy Council in *A-G for Hong Kong v Reid*,[56] which holds that where a fiduciary gains some unauthorised profit such profit will belong to the fiduciary's principal as soon as it is received. For the time being the position in English law is that no constructive trust will arise if the gain made by a fiduciary is not connected to the principal's original property.

Fraud

It is a recognised principle of English law that a person who acquires some property as a result of fraud will, in certain circumstances, hold such property on a constructive trust for his victim. In *McCormack v Grogan*[57] Lord Westbury explained that 'a court of equity, proceeding on the ground of fraud, converts the party who has committed it into a trustee for the party who is injured by that fraud'.[58] In *Westdeutsche Landesbank*

---

[53] See A.J. Oakley, 'The Bribed Fiduciary as Constructive Trustee' (1994) 53 CLJ 31.
[54] [1967] 2 AC 46.
[55] [1986] QB 491.
[56] See A.J. Oakley, 'The Bribed Fiduciary as Constructive Trustee' (1994) 53 CLJ 31.
[57] (1896) LR 4 HL 82.
[58] (1986) LR 4 HL 82 at 92.

Girozentrale v Islington LBC[59] Lord Browne-Wilkinson, when explaining the theoretical basis of constructive trusts, commented that a constructive trust was imposed on the trustee 'by reason of his unconscionable conduct'.[60] His Lordship went on to explain that, 'although it is difficult to find clear authority for the proposition, when property is obtained by fraud equity imposes a constructive trust on the fraudulent recipient: the property is recoverable and traceable in equity'.[61] Whilst it is clearly true that in certain circumstances a person who fraudulently acquires property at the expense of his victim holds the property on constructive trust for his victim, the principle is not a universal one and the question whether the trust arises depends on the facts of each case. There appears to be a distinction between two types of cases where property is acquired by a fraud. The first arises where there is an outright acquisition of property by fraud without a person's consent. The second situation arises where property is acquired as a result of some fraudulent misrepresentation and the misrepresentation is not discovered by the victim until some later date.

With regard to an outright acquisition of another's property through fraud, it is clear that the victim of the fraud will be entitled to a constructive trust over the property which is now in the hands of the fraudster. The reason for this is that the beneficial interest in the property never leaves the victim. Where a person fraudulently induces another to transfer property to him on the grounds that he will hold it for another, a constructive trust will arise so as to prevent him from keeping the property for him.[62] Another situation in which a constructive trust arises because of fraud is where a fiduciary pays over his principal's money without his principal's knowledge and consent. In such a case, as explained by Sir Peter Millett:

> the rule of equity is that the beneficial interest is not defeated by a breach of trust or fiduciary duty. It is enforceable against anyone who takes the property in which the interest subsists except a bona fide purchaser for value without notice. Liability to make restitution is strict, for it is not fault based. There is no need for the principal to rescind the transaction in order to revest the beneficial interest; it is as if it never left him, for it never accompanied the legal title.[63]

On a similar principle, it is well established that where a landowner sells land to a purchaser subject to the rights of some other third party, the purchaser cannot later seek to deny the proprietary rights of that third party. Any subsequent denial of the rights of the third party will amount to a fraud on the part of the purchaser and he will be subject to a constructive trust in favour of the third party. The matter is neatly illustrated in *Bannister v Bannister*[64] where A transferred land to B on the oral promise that B would allow A to live on the land for the remainder of his life. When B attempted to evict A from the land, the Court of Appeal held that the land was held by B on constructive trust to give effect to A's beneficial interest. The Court of Appeal held that, whilst there was no fraud when the land was initially conveyed to B, the subsequent denial of A's right in the land was marked with fraud.[65]

---

[59] [1996] AC 669 (HL).

[60] [1996] AC 669 (HL) at 705.

[61] [1996] AC 669 (HL) at 715.

[62] Most typically this will arise under a secret trust where a legatee induces a testator to transfer property to him on the assurance that the legatee will hold the property for a secret beneficiary; see, for example, *McCormick v Grogan* (1896) LR 4 HL 82. For more analysis of secret trusts, see Chapter 7.

[63] Sir Peter Millett, 'Restitution and Constructive Trusts' (1998) LQR 399 at 416.

[64] [1948] 2 All ER 133.

[65] The same principle was applied in *Lyus v Prowsa Developments Ltd* [1982] 1 WLR 1044.

APPLYING THE LAW

Tom is the director of a very successful engineering company. He explains to his best friend Tim that he plans to build an air-conditioning system which will be very energy efficient. Tim agreed to advance £5000 to Tom on the agreement that Tom would sell the first five air conditioning systems to him. In fact, Tom never had any intentions of building a new air-conditioning system and this was a mere fabrication in order to get the money from Tim.

In what capacity does Tom hold the £5000?

Where a person transfers money or some other property to another as a result of some fraudulent misrepresentation, the question has arisen in a number of cases whether the recipient holds the money on a constructive trust as soon as he has received the money.[66] The question certainly raises a number of both theoretical and practical issues of law. As far as the theoretical issue is concerned, the question arises as to how the recipient of money can be treated as a trustee when the transferor intended to transfer both the legal and equitable title to him. On the practical issue, the question arises as to how the recipient can be regarded as a trustee when he is unaware of the existence of any trust; indeed it is questionable as to what duties he is under until such time as the transferor knows of the fraudulent misrepresentation and then attempts to rescind the contract. In this respect, the prevailing judicial position is that, where money has been transferred to a recipient as a result of fraudulent misrepresentation, the recipient acquires both the legal and equitable title to the money. No constructive trust arises as soon as the money is paid over. The transferor does, however, have an equitable right to rescind the contract and, when he does exercise his right to rescind, the recipient will hold the money on resulting trust for the transferor.[67] In *Shalson v Russo*[68] Rimer J explained that he was not convinced that the authorities in English law laid down a principle that, where money was transferred pursuant to a voidable contract induced by fraud, a constructive trust arose immediately on the transfer of the money.[69]

It has already been observed at the outset of this section that whilst the fraud of the defendant can give rise to the imposition of a constructive trust, very much depends on the facts and the context of each case. In *Halifax Building Society v Thomas*[70] the Court of Appeal was faced with the question whether a mortgagee was entitled to the surplus proceeds of sale of mortgaged land in circumstances where the mortgagor had obtained the mortgage by fraudulent misrepresentation. The mortgagor had obtained a mortgage by fraudulent misrepresentation by providing the details of some other person. When the mortgagor defaulted on repayment, the mortgagee sold the mortgaged land. The debt had been paid off and a surplus fund remained to which the mortgage laid claim under a constructive trust. In holding that the mortgagee was not entitled to the surplus funds on the sale of the mortgaged land, Peter Gibson LJ explained that 'English law has not

---

[66] See, for example, *Lonhro plc v Fayed (No. 2)* [1992] 1 WLR 1 and also *Shalson v Russo* [2005] Ch. 281.

[67] See, *Lonhro plc v Fayed (No. 2)* [1992] 1 WLR 1 at 11–12 per Millett J. See also Sir Peter Millett, 'Restitution and Constructive Trusts' (1998) LQR 399 at 416.

[68] [2005] Ch. 281.

[69] [2005] Ch. 281 at 317.

[70] [1996] Ch. 217.

followed other jurisdictions where the constructive trust has become a remedy for unjust enrichment.'[71] With reference to Lord Westbury's dicta in **McCormick v Grogan**[72] that 'a court of equity, proceeding on the ground of fraud, converts the party who has committed it into a trustee for the party who is injured by that fraud',[73] Peter Gibson LJ explained that the statement 'must be read in the context in which it was made, namely the jurisdiction where a secret trust is alleged. It cannot be elevated into a universal principle that wherever there is personal fraud the fraudster will become a trustee for the party injured by the fraud.'[74] Further, his Lordship explained that:

> in considering whether to extend the law of constructive trusts in order to prevent a fraudster benefiting from his wrong, it is also appropriate to bear in mind that Parliament has acted in recent years (notably in Part VI of the Criminal Justice Act 1988) on the footing that without statutory intervention the criminal might keep the benefit of his crime. Moreover, Parliament has given the courts the power in specific circumstances to confiscate the benefit rather than reward the person against whom the crime has been committed.[75]

The question as to whether a constructive trust will be imposed on grounds of fraud was considered by the Court of Appeal in **Sinclair Investment Holdings v Versailles Trade Finance**.[76] This was an earlier Court of Appeal hearing to the one which has recently been heard in **Sinclair Investments (UK) Ltd v Versailles Trade Finance Ltd (In Administration)**.[77] In **Halifax Building Society v Thomas**[78] the Court of Appeal had clearly rejected that there were no grounds in English law for the imposition of a remedial constructive trust in cases of fraud. The decision of the Court of Appeal in **Sinclair Investment Holdings v Versailles Trade Finance** is an interesting one from two perspectives. In the first place, the judgment of Arden LJ opened up the debate as to whether a constructive trust of a remedial character could be imposed in certain cases of fraud. Secondly, the case raised an interesting point of law as to whether a constructive trust could be imposed on profit acquired by the defendant, but in circumstances when the defendant never received any property belonging to the claimant constructive beneficiary. The facts of this case involved an appeal by Versailles Trade Finance Ltd (VTFL) against an order of Mr Nicholas Strauss QC allowing an appeal against an earlier order refusing to strike out claims in the case. The background to the appeal involved VTFL, which was an associated company belonging to a group of companies known as the Versailles Group. An important feature of the case was that a major shareholder in the Versailles Group was a company called Marrlist Ltd, owned by Mr Cushnie, who was also a director of the companies in the Versailles Group. VTFL was a subsidiary of a listed company, Versailles Group plc. The business of the group involved accelerated discount trading. The court did not go into detail about the nature of the business of the Versailles Group, save to say that it involved raising money from third-party investors and investing the money on their behalf in manufactured goods purchased from the manufacturer and sold on to purchasers. Sinclair Investment Holdings SA was one of the third-party investors who had entered into a trader's agreement with VTFL. The terms of the

---

[71] [1996] Ch. 217 at 229. The Court of Appeal explained that the mortgagee had received exactly what it had contracted to receive.
[72] (1896) LR 4 HL 82.
[73] (1896) LR 4 HL 82 at 92.
[74] [1996] Ch. 217 at 228.
[75] [1996] Ch. 217 at 229.
[76] [2006] 1 BCLC 60. See also S. Panesar, 'Fiduciary Relationships and Constructive Trusts in a Commercial Context' (2005) ICCLR 479.
[77] [2011] EWCA 347.
[78] [1996] Ch. 217.

agreement involved, *inter alia*, Sinclair Investments providing VTFL with £2.35 million for the purposes of buying and selling goods for Sinclair Investments.

Despite the terms of the agreement between Sinclair Investments and VTFL, the monies advanced by Sinclair Investments were not used in accordance with that agreement. In fact, the money belonging to Sinclair Investments was used by the Versailles Group to increase its turnover, with the result that Marrlist Ltd was able to sell its shares in the Versailles Group at a profit. In other words, the profits enjoyed by Marrlist, and ultimately Mr Cushnie, were made directly as a result of Sinclair Investment's money. The reason why it can be said that the money still belonged to Sinclair Investments, despite being handed over to VTFL, is that one of the terms of the traders' agreement was that any of the money not used for the purpose of buying and selling goods was to be held on trust in a bank account for Sinclair Investments. This meant that VTFL was holding the money on trust for Sinclair Investments.

The profits made by Marrlist Ltd were used to repay a mortgage on a property in Kensington owned by Mr Cushnie and subsequently sold for £8.6 million. This money had been paid to the receivers of VTFL from whom Sinclair Investments on full trial would attempt to recover. Sinclair Investments sought to recover their money from the £8.6 million on two grounds. First, the profit made by Marrlist Ltd and ultimately Mr Cushnie had been made as a result of a breach of a fiduciary duty owed to Sinclair Investments by Mr Cushnie. Secondly, part of the proceeds of sale were held on constructive trust for Sinclair Investments because the proceeds of the sale of the property in Kensington were made as a result of the fraud of Mr Cushnie, who was responsible for increasing the turnover of the Versailles Group by misusing the money of Sinclair Investments. The judge at first instance held that there was an arguable case on both of these points. VTFL, however, appealed, arguing that there was no fiduciary relationship between Mr Cushnie and Sinclair Investments and nor was there a general principle that a constructive trust should be imposed on a fraudster.

The finding of a fiduciary relationship in Sinclair Investments would itself lead to a possibility that the court could at full trial ask Mr Cushnie to compensate Sinclair Investments for the loss suffered. Alternatively, the court could hold that the profits made by Mr Cushnie on the sale of the property in Kensington were made as a result of a breach of fiduciary duty; the property was purchased by the use of money belonging to Sinclair Investments, and as such the profits were held on constructive trust for Sinclair Investments. However, it was further argued on behalf of Sinclair Investments that there was a general principle on which a constructive trust could be imposed on a fraudster. In this case Mr Cushnie had from the outset instigated a personal fraud and as such received the proceeds of the sale of the shares and then ultimately the house in Kensington on constructive trust for Sinclair Investments. This in turn would allow Sinclair Investments to assert a proprietary claim on the money in the hands of the receivers of VTFL. The question was whether there is a general principle that allows for the imposition of a constructive trust on grounds of personal fraud.

In the opinion of Arden LJ the conduct of Mr Cushnie amounted to actual fraud and the profits made through the sale of the property in Kensington were thus arguably held on constructive trust for Sinclair Investments. There is no doubt on the facts of **Sinclair Investments** that the conduct of Mr Cushnie was fraudulent; however, whether that fraud warranted the imposition of a constructive trust is more doubtful in the absence of direct authority to that effect. It has already been seen that a general discretion to impose a constructive trust on fraud was rejected in **Halifax Building Society v Thomas**.[79] In

---

[79] [1996] Ch. 217.

Sinclair Investments, Arden LJ held that, although counsel for VTFL had shown a powerful dictum to the effect that there was no general principle for the imposition of a constructive trust on grounds of personal fraud, such dicta were *obiter* and not binding on the court. In her Ladyship's opinion the facts in *Sinclair Investments* were more refined and therefore there was an arguable cause of action on trial for the imposition of a constructive trust. Mr Cushnie made a profit out of monies invested in VTFL of which he was not only a director but also a stranger to the trust and thus intermeddling with trust property. Unfortunately, for the sake of further development in the law, the case was presented on a different basis on full trial and it will be some time before it can be said whether English law will recognise a remedial constructive trust to reverse an unjust enrichment induced by the personal fraud of a defendant. Indeed, the recent decision of the Court of Appeal in *Sinclair Investments (UK) Ltd* v *Versailles Trade Finance Ltd (In Administration)*[80] has rather left the position in English law very uncertain. It has clearly rejected that a proprietary claim to unauthorised profits and bribes made in fraud cannot be asserted when the beneficiary cannot purport to show that the gain belongs to the beneficiary. Thus, the imposition of a constructive trust on grounds of fraud is severely limited to those cases where the trust is asserted on those gains which are made directly with the use of the beneficiary's property and the beneficiary's original property can be traced into those gains.

Unauthorised profits gained by a fiduciary

APPLYING THE LAW

Tom and Tim are trustees of a lease of a commercial property which is held upon trust for a beneficiary. The lease has come to an end and the landlord has refused to renew the lease to the trustees in favour of the trust for the beneficiary. Tim is very disappointed about the refusal of the landlord to renew the lease. Some months later Tom renews the lease personally. Both Tim and the beneficiary are not happy with Tom renewing the lease personally. Tom says that he has done nothing wrong as the landlord would not have renewed it for the trust.

Can Tom keep the lease?

One of the common grounds for the imposition of a constructive trust is where a person standing in a fiduciary relationship obtains some unauthorised benefit or profit as result of that position. Much of the discussion relating to unauthorised profits made in breach of fiduciary duty is discussed in Chapter 17 and the following sections of this chapter should be read in conjunction with the discussion in Chapter 17. In *Bristol and West Building Society* v *Mothew*[81] Millett LJ explained that 'a fiduciary is someone who has undertaken to act for or on behalf of another in a particular matter in circumstances which give rise to relationship of trust and confidence. The distinguishing obligation of a fiduciary is the obligation of loyalty. The principal is entitled to the single minded

---

[80] [2011] EWCA Civ 347.
[81] [1998] Ch. 1.

loyalty of his fiduciary . . .'[82] Clearly a trustee stands in a fiduciary relationship with his beneficiary and as such cannot derive any unauthorised personal benefits from his office of trusteeship. However, the principle extends to other fiduciaries such as company directors, agents, solicitors and personal representatives. The principle is a strict one and applies irrespective of the honesty of the fiduciary.

The principle stated

It has been long established in equity that a person who stands in a fiduciary relationship is not allowed to make a secret profit from his office as a fiduciary. In **Bray v Ford**[83] Lord Herschell explained that:

> [i]t is an inflexible rule of a Court of Equity that a person in a fiduciary position . . . is not, unless otherwise expressly provided, entitled to make a profit; he is not allowed to put himself in a position where his interest and duty conflict. It does not appear to me that this rule is, as has been said, founded upon principles of morality. I regard it rather as based on the consideration that human nature being what it is, there is danger, in such circumstances, of the person holding a fiduciary position being swayed by interest rather than by duty, and thus prejudicing those whom he was bound to protect. It has, therefore, been deemed expedient to lay down this positive rule. But I am satisfied that it might be departed from in many cases, without any breach of morality, without any wrong being inflicted, and without any consciousness of wrong-doing. Indeed, it is obvious that it might sometimes be to the advantage of the beneficiaries that their trustee should act for them professionally rather than a stranger, even though the trustee were paid for his services.[84]

More recently, in **Bristol & West Building Society v Mothew**[85] Millett LJ explained that a fiduciary is:

> someone who has undertaken to act for or on behalf of another in a particular matter in circumstances which give rise to a relationship of trust and confidence. The distinguishing obligation of a fiduciary is the obligation of loyalty. The principal is entitled to the single-minded loyalty of his fiduciary. This core liability has several facets: a fiduciary must act in good faith; he must not make a profit out of his trust; he must not place himself in a position where his duty and his interest may conflict; he may not act for his own benefit or the benefit of a third person without the informed consent of his principal. This is not intended to be an exhaustive list, but it is sufficient to indicate the nature of fiduciary obligations.[86]

Examples of unauthorised profits

Clearly a trustee who extracts a personal opportunity for himself which would otherwise belong to the beneficiary is liable to account for the profit he makes. However, the rule also extends to cases where the trustee extracts a profit for himself which could not have been utilised by the beneficiary. The matter is neatly illustrated by the seminal case of **Keech v Sandford**[87] where a lease of a market in Romford was held on trust for an infant beneficiary. On the refusal of the landlord to renew the lease for the infant beneficiary, the trustee renewed the lease for himself in his personal capacity. Lord King LC held that

---

[82] [1998] Ch. 1 at 18.
[83] [1896] AC 44.
[84] [1896] AC 44 at 51.
[85] [1998] Ch. 1.
[86] [1998] Ch. 1 at 18.
[87] (1726) Sel. Cas. Ch. 61.

the trustee must hold the lease on constructive trust for the infant beneficiary. The rule in **Keech v Sandford** is indeed a harsh one and prevents the trustee from renewing for himself a benefit which would not have been available to the beneficiary. The justification for the rule relates to the evidential question of whether the trustee did indeed make all the efforts to renew the lease for the beneficiary or whether he saw this as an opportunity to acquire the lease for himself. Lord King LC explained that 'I very well see, if a trustee, the refusal to renew, might have a lease to himself, few trust estates would be renewed to [beneficiaries]; though I do not say that there is fraud in this case, yet he should have left it to run out, than to have had the lease to himself.'[88] The rule in **Keech v Sandford** extends to cases where the trustee acquires the reversion, that is, the freehold title to the land once the lease expires. The matter is illustrated by the decision of the Court of Appeal in **Protheroe v Protheroe**[89] where a husband was holding a lease on trust for himself and his wife in equal shares. On their separation the husband acquired the freehold for himself. The Court of Appeal held that the freehold must be held on constructive trust for the husband and the wife. The Court of Appeal explained that it was 'a long established rule of equity from **Keech v Sandford** downwards that if a trustee, who owns the leasehold, gets in the freehold, that freehold belongs to the trust and he cannot take the property for himself'.[90]

As explained earlier, questions relating to the honesty and good faith of the fiduciary who does make a profit from his position are irrelevant to the question of liability to account for the profit, or the imposition of a constructive trust on the profit. The irrelevance of the fiduciary's honesty and good faith is illustrated by the House of Lords' decision in **Boardman v Phipps**[91] (discussed earlier in this chapter, see p. 389).

The decision of the House of Lords in **Boardman v Phipps**[92] was applied by the Court of Appeal in **Re Bhullar Brothers Ltd**[93] which concerned a dispute between two sides of a family running a chain of shops managed by Bhullar Bros Ltd. The directors of the company were appointed from both sides of the family. After relations between the two sides of the family had broken down, directors on both sides decided that they should go their separate ways and that no further properties should be acquired by the company. During the period in which the assets of Bhullar Bros Ltd were being wound up, directors from one side of the family purchased land adjacent to the main premises of Bhullar Bros Ltd. The opportunity to purchase this land arose from independent inquiries made by that side of the family. The land was purchased in the name of a separate company. When the other side of the family established that the purchase of the land had been made, they challenged it on the grounds that the purchase was a corporate opportunity vested in Bhullar Bros Ltd.[94] The Court of Appeal held that the directors of the company who had purchased the adjacent land had put themselves in a conflict of interest. They were under a duty to sell the land to the company and account for any profit made. Jonathan Parker LJ explained that it did not matter that the appellants did not have any beneficial interest in the property. All that mattered was that there was a real possibility that there was a

---

[88] (1726) Sel. Cas. Ch. 61 at 62.

[89] [1968] 1 WLR 519.

[90] [1968] 1 WLR 519 at 521. See also, *Thompson's Trustee v Heaton* [1974] 1 WLR 605; A. Hicks, 'The Remedial Principle of *Keech v Sandford Reconsidered*' (2010) CLJ 287.

[91] [1967] 2 AC 46.

[92] *Ibid.*

[93] [2003] 2 BCLC 241. See D.D. Prentice and J. Payne, 'The Corporate Opportunity Doctrine' (2004) LQR 198.

[94] The challenge was made under then s. 459 Companies Act 1985 concerning unfair prejudices to a company. See now, s. 994 Companies Act 2006.

conflict of interest. Furthermore, it is clear from the facts that both sides of the family had agreed that no further land would be bought by Bhullar Bros Ltd, who were in the process of closing their business and winding up the assets. The decision, like the decision in *Boardman* v *Phipps* is indeed a harsh one from the perspective that the purchase of the land by one side of the family was initiated purely by their own efforts, rather than in the course of information they had acquired whilst acting as directors of Bhullar Bros Ltd. The Court of Appeal's decision reaffirms the harshness of the English law on fiduciaries and unauthorised gains. The fact was that at the time of the purchase, the purchasers were directors of a company and there was a possibility that there could have been a conflict of interest.

A final illustration of the principle that a fiduciary cannot obtain a profit from his office of trusteeship is *Regal (Hastings)* v *Gulliver*[95] concerning directors of a company. This case is also a very good example of a fiduciary being unable to keep a benefit which would not have been capable of being utilised by the fiduciary's principal. The facts of the case concerned the purchase of two cinemas by the plaintiff company which already owned one cinema in Hastings. The intention was that the three cinemas would be acquired by the plaintiff company and then sold off together. In order to facilitate the purchase of the cinemas, a subsidiary with a capital of 5000 shares was formed so as to take leases of the cinemas. However, only 2000 of the shares were fully paid, which proved to be fatal because the owner of the cinema was only willing to grant leases of the cinema on the condition that all the shares were fully paid up. The plaintiff did not have any further money to pay into the subsidiary. Four directors and an outsider then acquired the remaining shares and the cinemas were eventually taken over, with the directors making a substantial profit on the respective sale of their shares. The purchaser then brought an action to recover the profits made by the directors on the grounds that it was made in breach of fiduciary duty. The action succeeded in the House of Lords on the grounds that the directors had acquired the shares in their capacity as fiduciaries. The House of Lords were firmly undeterred by the fact that the company could not itself have acquired the shares. The court was firmly of the opinion that the law in *Keech* v *Sandford* laid a strict rule that a fiduciary was not allowed to make an unauthorised profit.

All of the decisions discussed above illustrate a very strict rule of law that a fiduciary is not allowed to make any profit from his position as a fiduciary. The honesty or good faith, or indeed the question of whether the opportunity could not have been utilised by his principal, are not matters which the court will look into to soften what is otherwise strict liability. The strict liability approach was reaffirmed by the Court of Appeal in *Murad* v *Al Saraj*.[96]

Proprietary or personal remedies?

One question which has been the source of much confusion in the case law is: what remedy will the court grant where a fiduciary makes a secret profit or otherwise obtains some unauthorised benefit in his capacity as a fiduciary? There are three possible remedies available to a claimant. The first is the imposition of a constructive trust on the unauthorised profit in the hands of the fiduciary or some other third party who cannot purport to show that he has acquired the legal title to the property as a bona fide purchaser without notice of the trust. The advantage of the imposition of the constructive

---

[95] [1942] 1 All ER 378.
[96] [2005] EWCA Civ. 959, [2005] WTLR 1573. See M. McInnes, 'Account for Profits for Breach of Fiduciary Duty' (2006) LQR 11.

trust is that it allows the claimant to take priority over the other creditors of the fiduciary should he become bankrupt. A further advantage is that the claimant can seek to claim any increase in value to the property which has become subject to the constructive trust. It has already been seen earlier in this chapter that a constructive trust was imposed over bribe money in the hands of a public prosecutor, allowing the Crown to claim properties purchased with the bribe money.[97]

A second remedy available to the court is a personal one requiring the fiduciary to account for the secret profit he has made. An account is an equitable remedy in its own right, requiring the fiduciary to personally account for the profit that has been made. The action is a personal one and will depend very much on the solvency of the fiduciary since, if he is insolvent, any judgment against him to account will be fruitless. Whilst the principle of an equitable account is fairly well established, what is confusing in this area of the law is the question of whether the fiduciary is being asked to account as a constructive trustee. Much of the confusion arises from a number of decisions where the courts have held that a fiduciary who has made an unauthorised profit is a constructive trustee, but nevertheless have gone on to hold that the fiduciary is a under a duty to account for the profits only. This was very much evident in the House of Lords' decision in *Boardman v Phipps*[98] where Boardman was held to be a constructive trustee of profits made in his capacity as a fiduciary, but was nevertheless under a duty to account for the profits that he had made.

Despite the apparent confusion over the nature of a personal account for profits made in breach of fiduciary duty, it is submitted that a duty to account and the imposition of a constructive trust are two different things. An account is a personal remedy granted against the fiduciary, requiring him to pay out of his own pocket the value of the profit he has received. The remedy is restitutionary in the sense that the objective is to reverse an unjust enrichment in the hands of the fiduciary. It is, however, a personal restitutionary claim and is not dependent on the fiduciary being classified as a constructive trustee. On the other hand, the imposition of a constructive trust is a proprietary remedy, giving the claimant a beneficial interest in the profit received by the claimant. The constructive trust is imposed over some identifiable property in the hands of the fiduciary. Where there is no identifiable property, there can by no constructive trust, simply because the constructive trust is a proprietary institution. The only exception to this is where a constructive trust is imposed in the case of liability for knowing assistance, which will be discussed in Chapter 14.

With regard to the question as to which remedy the court should award in situations where there has been a breach of fiduciary duty, there is no definitive answer. The principal reason for this has been that the law has failed to develop clearly established principles which will distinguish whether the remedy should be an account for profits, or whether it should be an imposition of a constructive trust on the profit. In one Australian case Gibbs J explained that:

> the question whether the remedy which the person to whom the duty is owed may obtain against the person who has violated their duty is proprietary or personal may sometimes be one of some difficulty. In some cases the fiduciary has been declared a trustee of the property which he has gained by his breach; in others he has been called upon to account for his profits and sometimes the distinction between the two remedies has not . . . been kept clearly in mind.[99]

---

[97] *A-G for Hong Kong* v *Reid* [1994] 1 AC 324.
[98] [1967] 2 AC 46.
[99] *Consul Development Pty Ltd* v *DPC Estates Pty Ltd* (1975) 5 ALR 231 at 249.

Whether the claimant is awarded a proprietary remedy in the form of a constructive trust or a personal remedy in the form of an account for profits, it will be of significance to the claimant since the proprietary remedy will have further reaching consequences than a personal remedy. It has already been explained that the proprietary remedy will give the claimant priority over the other creditors of the fiduciary should he be insolvent. There has been considerable debate as to the grounds upon which a proprietary remedy should be awarded for breach of fiduciary duty. On many occasions the view has been expressed that a proprietary constructive trust should only be imposed when the profit has been made as a result of the misuse of the claimant's property. Sometimes it has been said that there must a proprietary base which connects the profit with the claimant seeking to lay claim to it.[100] It has been argued in many quarters that the imposition of a constructive trust, in circumstances where there is no proprietary base or connection with the property in the hands of the fiduciary and the claimant seeking to claim it, gives the claimant an unjustified advantage over the creditors of the fiduciary.[101]

However, despite the concerns over the imposition of a proprietary constructive trust in circumstances where the fiduciary has not made the profit as a result of a misuse of the claimant's property, the present position in English law is very uncertain. It has already been observed above in the discussion on bribes in *A-G for Hong Kong v Reid*,[102] where the Privy Council held that a bribe was held on constructive trust for the Crown. In *Daraydan Holding Ltd v Solland International Ltd*[103] Daraydan Holdings Ltd claimed that a former employee had received undisclosed payments. The question before the court was whether the decision in *Lister & Co v Stubbs*[104] was binding on the court. Lawrence Collins J was of the opinion that he would follow the decision of the Privy Council in *A-G for Hong Kong v Reid*[105] on the question whether bribe monies should be held on constructive trust for the principal. However, the recent decision of the Court of Appeal in *Sinclair Investments (UK) Ltd v Versailles Trade Finance Ltd (In Administration)*[106] has rather left the position in English law very uncertain. It has clearly rejected that a proprietary claim to unauthorised profits and bribes made in fraud cannot be asserted when the beneficiary cannot purport to show that the gain belongs to the beneficiary. Thus, the imposition of a constructive trust on grounds of fraud is severely limited to those cases where the trust is asserted on those gains which are made directly with the use of the beneficiary's property and the beneficiary's original property can be traced into those gains.

A final remedy for breach of fiduciary duty is equitable compensation if the claimant has suffered a loss which is caused by a breach of fiduciary duty. The availability of equitable compensation was acknowledged by the House of Lords in *Nocton v Lord Ashburton*.[107] The purpose of equitable compensation is to put the beneficiary back in the position he would have been had the breach not occurred. An example where equitable compensation may be awarded is where a fiduciary enters into a transaction with his principal without full disclosure of the facts. For example, a fiduciary sells some property to his principal without disclosure of the extent of his own interest in the property

---

[100] P. Birks, *An Introduction to the Law of Restitution* (1985), pp. 378–93.
[101] See, for example, P. Birks, 'Proprietary Rights as Remedies' in P. Birks (ed.) *The Frontiers of Liability, Vol. 2* (1994) and G. McCormack, 'The Remedial Constructive Trust and Commercial Transactions' *Company Lawyer* (1996) Vol. 17(1) at 3.
[102] [1994] 1 All ER 1.
[103] [2005] Ch. 119.
[104] (1890) 45 Ch. D 1.
[105] [1994] 1 All ER 1.
[106] [2011] EWCA Civ 347.
[107] [1914] AC 932.

subject to the sale. If the principal suffers any loss, for example, reselling the property at a loss, he may bring an action against the fiduciary. In ***Cavendish Bentinck v Fenn***[108] the House of Lords explained that an agent who sold his own goods to his principal above market price in circumstances when those goods could be obtained at market price would be liable to compensate for the excess charged. Equitable compensation, however, will only be available where the breach of fiduciary duty has caused the principal's loss. For example, in ***Swindle v Harrison***[109] solicitors had made a loan to a principal, who had mortgaged her house to facilitate her sons' hotel restoration, without disclosing their interest in the transaction. Despite the non-disclosure, the principal would have proceeded with the loan in any event and therefore had failed to show that the subsequent loss was caused by the breach of fiduciary duty.[110]

Equitable compensation will also be available where the fiduciary was holding any unauthorised profit on constructive trust for the beneficiary and in breach of trust has dissipated the profit subject to the trust, or otherwise allowed the profit to fall in value.

Constructive trusts and the family home

An important area in which the constructive trust has played a significant role over the past 40 years or so is in the context of family cohabitation disputes concerning land. It will be observed in the remainder of this chapter that the operation of the constructive trust in land disputes can be quite diverse. Whilst this section will concentrate on what has become known as the 'common intention constructive trust', a constructive trust in land will also arise in a number of different contexts; these are explored in the next section. However, it is clear that in many of the situations in which a constructive trust has been imposed in land cases, the common theme has been to prevent the legal owner of land to deny a beneficial interest to a claimant on grounds of unconscionability. The matter was neatly put by Millett LJ in ***Paragon Finance plc v D.B. Thakerar & Co*** where he explained that 'a constructive trust arises by operation of law whenever the circumstances are such that it would be unconscionable for the owner of property (usually but not necessarily the legal estate) to assert his beneficial interest in the property and deny the beneficial interest of another'.[111]

Just like the resulting trust, which was explored in Chapters 10 and 11, the constructive trust has became an important means in which ownership disputes in family cohabitation cases have been resolved. The primary reason for this has been the social and economic changes that took place after a period preceding the middle of the twentieth century in relation to home ownership. Before the Second World War, the English courts did not face the same degree of co-ownership disputes that it did after the War, particularly in the period starting in the late 1960s. With the incidence of divorce being low and title to land taken in the husband's name, there was very little by way of ownership dispute of the family home. The social and economic pattern of home ownership, however, changed significantly in the 1970s.[112] The incidence of divorce increased, thereby giving rise to

---

[108] (1887) 12 App. Cas. 652.

[109] [1997] 4 All ER 705.

[110] See also *Target Holding* v *Redferns* [1996] AC 421.

[111] [1999] 1 All ER 400 at 408.

[112] Some of the more recent trends on cohabitation are identified by the Law Commission in its report, *Cohabitation: The Financial Consequence of Relationship Breakdown* (Law Com. 307) 2007. See also D. Hughes, M. Davies and L. Jacklin, 'Come Live With me and be my Love': a Consideration of the 2007 Law Commission Proposals on Cohabitation Breakdown' (2008) Conv. 197.

ownership disputes of the house once occupied by husband and wife. As well as marital cohabitation, a significant trend which continues today, was the increased non-marital cohabitation. In the context of non-marital cohabitation, where the parties are unable to take advantage of the Matrimonial Causes Act 1973,[113] the recourse to the equitable principles and doctrine of resulting and constructive trust became ever more pressing. A further development which saw a rise in the application of constructive trusts in land was the availability of mortgage finance. Typically, a husband may have taken out a mortgage to purchase the family home or may have remortgaged the family home in order to pick up further monies on the land. In such cases, where the husband defaulted on payment of the mortgage money, the bank sought vacant possession of the land. However, in some cases the wife asserted that a beneficial interest in the land was binding on the bank on the grounds of a constructive trust.

Whilst the Matrimonial Causes Act 1973 affords the court with a power to adjust property rights on divorce of marital cohabitees, no such power exists in relation to non-marital cohabitees.[114] In the context of non-marital cohabitation, ownership disputes can only be resolved by applying the technical and often inflexible rules of resulting and constructive trusts. Litigation in this area continues to test the courts as to the proper application of the principles of resulting and constructive trusts to non-marital and marital cohabitation, the most recent case being *Kernott v Jones* in the court of Appeal.[115]

**VISIT CASE
NAVIGATOR**

The common intention constructive trust

Unlike the purchase price resulting trust, which was explored in Chapter 11, the application of the common intention constructive trust in land is of much wider significance to a claimant who can seek to prove that it has arisen in his favour. You will recall that a purchase price resulting trust of land looks to the pattern of direct financial contributions to the purchase price. If a wife contributes 10 per cent of the purchase price of a house which is conveyed in her husband's name, on any subsequent dispute as to the beneficial ownership of the house, the wife will acquire a 10 per cent interest in the value of the land. A common intention constructive trust is not, as will be explained below, concerned with the pattern of money contributions per se. Rather the common intention constructive trust is imposed to give effect to the common intention of the parties. The quantification of a beneficial interest under a constructive trust can give a claimant significantly more than what he or she may have initially contributed to the purchase price. However, whilst the constructive trust is much broader in this respect, its application is not without criticism, since it will be seen below that the finding of a common intention is not a straightforward process as one would think and in many cases the finding of a common intention is quite artificial.

The common intention constructive trust has its origins in a series of decisions in the early 1970s. One particular decision is that of the House of Lords in *Gissing v Gissing*,[116] which still very much forms the bedrock of the modern law of common intention constructive trusts. The parties in the case were a husband and wife who married in 1935 when they were in the early twenties. The wife worked most of her life as a secretary at

---

[113] This was discussed in Chapter 11 under the context of purchase price resulting trusts.

[114] A similar power does, however, exist for same-sex partnerships registered under the Civil Partnership Act 2004.

[115] [2010] EWCA Civ 578.

[116] [1971] AC 886.

a firm of printers. The husband was in the army until 1946 and thereafter secured a job with the same employers as his wife. In 1951 a house was purchased which was conveyed in the husband's sole name. The house was intended to be the matrimonial home and both the husband and the wife lived in it until 1961 when the husband moved out to live with another woman. The house was purchased with the aid of a mortgage which was duly discharged with the husband's own money. The husband was also lent some £500 by his employers which the husband paid back out of his own money. The husband paid the wife £8 a week for the household expenses and paid for other things such as family holidays. The wife contributed some £200 towards furnishings for the house as well as buying cloths for their son. When the wife was granted a divorce on the grounds of her husband's adultery, she sought a declaration as to her beneficial interest in the house. The House of Lords held that the wife had no interest in the matrimonial home. The wife had made no direct contribution to the purchase of the house which would allow the imposition of a purchase price resulting trust. In so far as to whether a constructive trust arose in her favour, the House of Lords held that there was no common intention as between the wife and the husband which was required for the imposition of a constructive trust. In the course of his judgment, Lord Diplock explained that:

> [a] resulting, implied or constructive trust – and it is unnecessary for present purposes to distinguish between these three classes of trust – is created by a transaction between the trustee and the cestui que trust in connection with the acquisition by the trustee of a legal estate in land, whenever the trustee has so conducted himself that it would be inequitable to allow him to deny to the cestui que trust a beneficial interest in the land acquired, and he will be held so to have conducted himself if by his words or conduct he has induced the cestui que trust to act to his own detriment in the reasonable belief that by so acting he was acquiring a beneficial interest in the land.[117]

The decision of the House of Lords in **Gissing v Gissing**,[118] approved the earlier decision of the House of Lords in **Pettitt v Pettitt**[119] where a wife purchased a cottage in her sole name having provided the entire purchase price. The husband, however, spent a lot of his own money and labour on improving the property. When the husband and wife separated, the husband commenced proceedings under s. 17 of the Married Women's Property Act 1882 in order to claim an equitable interest in the cottage. The House of Lords held that he had no interest in the cottage. Furthermore, that s. 17 of the 1882 Act did not confer a discretion on a court to vary existing property rights in land, but merely to recognise those which had been properly acquired. In the present instance, the husband had not acquired any interest in the land and neither was there any common intention between the wife and the husband to the effect that the husband was to have a beneficial interest in the land.

Requisites for the imposition of a common intention constructive trust

The cumulative effect of the decisions in **Pettitt v Pettitt**[120] and **Gissing v Gissing**[121] was that a constructive trust, in the context of the shared ownership of land, would only arise

---

[117] [1971] AC 886 at 905.
[118] [1971] AC 886.
[119] [1970] AC 777.
[120] *Ibid*.
[121] [1971] AC 886.

where there was a common intention between the cohabiting parties. Furthermore, the party seeking to enforce the trust in his or her favour had to have suffered some detriment, as for example, making some form of direct contribution to the purchase price. Lord Diplock explained the matter when he commented in *Gissing* v *Gissing* that:

> if the court is satisfied that it was the common intention of both spouses that the contributing wife should have a share in the beneficial interest and that her contributions were made upon this understanding, the court in the exercise of its equitable jurisdiction would not permit the husband in whom the legal estate was vested and who had accepted the benefit of the contributions to take the whole beneficial interest merely because at the time the wife made her contributions there had been no express agreement as to how her share in it was to be quantified.[122]

VISIT CASE NAVIGATOR

Whilst *Pettitt* v *Pettitt*[123] and *Gissing* v *Gissing*[124] paved the way for recognition of the common intention constructive trust, it was not until the landmark decision of the House of Lords in *Lloyds Bank plc* v *Rosset*[125] that the precise circumstances giving rise to a common intention and detrimental reliance were clearly spelt out in English law. The facts of the case involved Mr and Mrs Rosset who married in 1972. In 1982, Mr Rosset became entitled to money under a trust fund which had been created in his favour by his grandmother. Mr Rosset decided to use the trust money to purchase a derelict house and renovate it. The house was conveyed in the name of Mr Rosset, this primarily as a result of a request by the trustees of the trust fund who were advancing the trust money to Mr Rosset. Mrs Rosset helped with the renovation works on the property and supervised the builders. Mr Rosset then managed to acquire a mortgage on the property without telling Mrs Rosset. When the relationship broke down, Mr Rosset left the house without paying the mortgage instalments. Lloyds Bank attempted to enforce their security by seeking vacant possession of the land with a view to selling it. Mrs Rosset, however, argued that she had acquired a beneficial interest in the house and as a result the bank was bound by her interest, on the grounds that it was an overriding interest under s. 70(1)(g) of the Land Registration Act 1925.[126] The House of Lords, however, held that Mrs Rosset has no interest in the house.

The leading judgment in *Lloyds Bank* v *Rosset* was delivered by Lord Bridge who explained the grounds for the imposition of a common intention constructive trust. In the course of his judgment, Lord Bridge explained when a common intention would be found on any given set of facts. His Lordship explained that the fundamental question was whether a common intention between the parties had arisen. His Lordship explained that a common intention could arise in one of two situations. Firstly, the parties may well have discussed the matter as to the ownership of the disputed property, in which case they were deemed to have had an express common intention. In the absence of an express common intention, the court could infer a common intention from their conduct. As to the nature of the conduct giving rise to the trust, Lord Bridge explained that anything short of direct contributions to the purchase price would be insufficient for the finding of an implied common intention. The following extract from Lord Bridge's judgment neatly summarises the present state of the law.

---

[122] [1971] AC 881 at 908.
[123] [1970] AC 777.
[124] [1971] AC 886.
[125] [1991] 1 AC 107.
[126] Overriding interests in land bind purchasers and third parties irrespective of notice. See Schedule 3 paragraph 2 of the Land Registration Act 2002 which replaced s. 70(1)(g) of the Land Registration Act 1925.

Lloyds Bank v *Rosset* [1991] 1 AC 107 (Establishing a common intention constructive trust per Lord Bridge at 132)

The first and fundamental question which must always be resolved is whether, independently of any inference to be drawn from the conduct of the parties in the course of sharing the house as their home and managing their joint affairs, there has at any time prior to acquisition, or exceptionally at some later date, been any agreement, arrangement or understanding reached between them that the property is to be shared beneficially. The finding of an agreement or arrangement to share in this sense can only, I think, be based on evidence of express discussions between the partners, however imperfectly remembered and however imprecise their terms may have been. Once a finding to this effect is made it will only be necessary for the partner asserting a claim to a beneficial interest against the partner entitled to the legal estate to show that he or she has acted to his or her detriment or significantly altered his or her position in reliance on the agreement in order to give rise to a constructive trust or a proprietary estoppel.

In sharp contrast with this situation is the very different one where there is no evidence to support a finding of an agreement or arrangement to share, however reasonable it might have been for the parties to reach such an arrangement if they had applied their minds to the question, and where the court must rely entirely on the conduct of the parties both as the basis from which to infer a common intention to share the property beneficially and as the conduct relied on to give rise to a constructive trust. In this situation direct contributions to the purchase price by the partner who is not the legal owner, whether initially or by payment of mortgage instalments, will readily justify the inference necessary to the creation of a constructive trust. But, as I read the authorities, it is at least extremely doubtful whether anything less will do.

At the heart of the common intention constructive trust is the element of a common intention or bargain. Typically, the common intention or bargain will have been made at the time of the acquisition of the property. However, it is possible for the common intention or bargain to have been made after the acquisition of the property. Equally important is the element of detriment or change of position. This requires the claimant to have acted upon or relied on the common intention to his detriment. These matters can be explored in more detail now.

Express common intention

Amy and Peter live at No. 1 Elm Road and the title is conveyed in Amy's name alone. The house was purchased 10 years ago. Although the title is in Amy's name, both Amy and Peter agreed that the house would be their family home. Amy paid for the house out of her own money. Guy and Sharon live at No. 2 Elm Road. The title is conveyed in Guy's name alone. At the time of the purchase Sharon was going through a divorce with her former partner and Guy advised that she should not appear on the title. In fact, Guy never

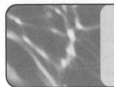

wanted Sharon on the title as he did not want her to have any interest in the house. Both Amy and Peter and Sharon and Guy have broken up. Both couples are not married and Peter and Sharon want to know if they have any interest in the houses they have been living in.

The first category of common intention constructive trusts is the express common intention constructive trust. This type of constructive trust will be imposed where the parties have expressly agreed that the claimant will have a beneficial interest in the land. Most typically this will take the form of a legal owner agreeing with a non-legal owner that the latter is to have some shared ownership in land which is in his name. In **Lloyds Bank v Rosset**[127] Lord Bridge explained that an express common intention could only arise in circumstances where there was evidence that express discussions took place between the parties, albeit that the terms of those discussions were not perfectly remembered. In **Oxley v Hiscock**[128] Chadwick LJ explained that the express common intention need not necessarily relate to the question of the precise beneficial interest of the parties: rather the primary question was whether there was evidence that each were to acquire some beneficial interest in the disputed property.

It is questionable whether situations giving to rise to an express common intention are widespread in cohabitation cases. For example, if the parties had expressly thought about the ownership of the shared property, they probably would have made some formal arrangement as to the recognition of their respective interests in the land. For example, if both parties were to have the joint ownership of the land, the title would be conveyed in both of their names. However, despite this, Lord Bridge identified what he described as outstanding examples of express common intention situations.[129] The first is the decision of the Court of Appeal in **Eves v Eves**[130] where Janet and Stuart decided to reside together as a couple. The house was conveyed in the name of Stuart alone. Stuart informed Janet that she was too young to be named on the title. The Court of Appeal held that Janet was entitled to a share in the house on the grounds that Stuart had led her to believe that she would have an interest in the land. The second decision is that of **Grant v Edwards**[131] where George told his partner, Linda, that the reason why the title to a house was not taken in their joint names was because Linda was going through divorce proceedings with her former husband and that putting her name on the legal title might prejudice her divorce proceedings. The Court of Appeal held that in these circumstances the evidence clearly pointed to the fact that Linda was expressly promised an interest in the land. In the course of his judgment, Nourse LJ explained that '[j]ust as in **Eves v Eves**, these facts appear to me to raise a clear inference that there was an understanding between the plaintiff and the defendant, or a common intention, that the plaintiff was to have some sort of proprietary interest in the house; otherwise no excuse for not putting her name onto the title would have been needed.'[132]

Although the decisions in **Eves v Eves**[133] and **Grant v Edwards**[134] are taken as very good examples of cases where there have been express common intention between the

---

127 [1991] 1 AC 107.
128 [2005] EWCA Civ. 546; see below.
129 [1991] 1 AC 107 at 133.
130 [1975] 1 WLR 1338.
131 [1986] Ch. 638.
132 [1986] Ch. 638 at 649.
133 [1975] 1 WLR 1338.
134 [1986] Ch. 638.

parties as to the shared ownership of a house, the decisions are not without their criticism. One of the main criticisms levelled at both of those decisions relates to the question of whether the intention of the legal owner was indeed genuine or a mere pretence so as to deny the non-legal owner of an interest in the house. For example, there is no question that Stuart's intention in *Eves v Eves* was to trick Janet into believing that she could not take the legal title to the house because she was too young. Stuart never had any intention that she should have an interest in the house. In this respect, the finding of an express common intention in these cases is somewhat artificial. Despite this, Lord Denning MR commented in *Eves v Eves* that 'Stuart should be judged by what he told her – by what he led her to believe – and not by his own intent which he kept to himself.'[135] It is submitted that if this is the case, both *Eves v Eves* and *Grant v Edwards* should have been better analysed as examples of proprietary estoppel rather than constructive trusts. Although, as will be seen below, many of the facts of the cohabitation cases may give rise to both a claim on grounds of proprietary estoppel and constructive trusts, there is a difference between the two concepts. Proprietary estoppel is based on some assurance or reliance given by a legal owner of land which is acted upon by a non-legal owner. A constructive trust, on the other hand is a bilateral process, whereby both the legal owner and the non-legal owner must have some agreement to share the ownership of land in question.

Relatively recent examples of express common intentions in the context of the shared ownership of land include *Hammond v Mitchell*[136] where the legal owner of land informed his partner that the reason why title to a bungalow was put solely in his name was because of tax problems and the conveyance of the bungalow in his name would help resolve those problems. He did tell his partner that the house would be half hers anyway after their marriage. More recently in *Q v Q*[137] a father conveyed his house and other property to his two sons in order to avoid them having to pay inheritance tax. Despite the conveyance, the father continued to control the property in the hands of his sons. Some time later, the father moved out of the house and the sons agreed that one of them would have the absolute ownership in the house as he had married and intended to live there with his wife. Both the father and the other son agreed with the married son that the house would be his beneficially. When the father and the son, who had told his brother that he did not want any interest in the house, sought to resile from the agreement, the question arose as to the ownership of the house which was still in the names of both sons. In the High Court, Black J held that a constructive trust arose in favour of the son, on grounds that there was common intention that the house would belong beneficially to the son who had married and wished to live there with his wife.

Implied common intention

APPLYING THE LAW

Jennifer and Brian, an unmarried couple, have lived at No. 3 Elm Road for 25 years. The house was conveyed in Brian's name and he alone provided the purchase price of the house. Jennifer has looked after their four children and has maintained the house.

---

[135] [1975] 1 WLR 1338 at 1342.
[136] [1991] 1 WLR 1127.
[137] [2009] 1 FLR 935.

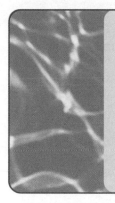

Jennifer has worked part-time and has used her wages to put food on the table. Recently, Jennifer and Brian's relationship has broken down and the question arises as to whether she has any interest in No. 3 Elm Road. Patrick and Beatrice live in No. 4 Elm Road. They are also unmarried and have been living there for 15 years. The title is conveyed in Patrick's name alone and he has provided the purchase price of the house. Patrick and Beatrice did receive a present of £1000 from their friends when they moved into the house and the money was used to pay off the legal costs of purchasing the house. They have no children and their relationship has also broken down.

Does Beatrice have any interest in No. 4 Elm Road?
Does Jennifer have any interest in No. 3 Elm Road.

Where there is an absence of an express common intention, a constructive trust will be imposed if the court can infer a common intention. As to the grounds for the inference of such a common intention, the court is required to look at the conduct of the parties: for example, where they have transferred the legal title in joint names or where one of the parties have directly contributed to the purchase price even though they have not precisely determined their respective shares in the property. In the decision of the House of Lords in **Stack v Dowden**[138] Baroness Hale explained that a conveyance into joint names was prima facie evidence of a common intention of shared ownership in land. The judge commented that:

> the issue is . . . whether a conveyance into joint names indicates only that each party is intended to have some beneficial interest but says nothing about the nature and extent of that beneficial interest, or whether a conveyance into joint names establishes a prime facie case of joint and equal beneficial interests until the contrary is shown. For the reasons already stated, at least in the domestic consumer context, a conveyance into joint names indicates both legal and beneficial joint tenancy, unless and until the contrary is proved.[139]

More recently, in **Fowler v Barron**[140] Miss Fowler and Mr Barron started a relationship in 1983 when Miss Fowler was only 17 years of age and Mr Barron was 47 years old. Mr Barron was employed as a fireman until 1988 when he was discharged from the fire service on grounds of ill health. Mr Barron and Miss Fowler decided to move to Bognor Regis and in June 1988 they purchased a house which was conveyed in both of their names. Although there was no discussion regarding the beneficial ownership of the house, the intention was that this house would be their family home where they would raise their one-year-old son. Six years later they also had a baby girl. The evidence before the court was that the house was purchased with a deposit paid by Mr Barron. A mortgage was taken out in both of their names; however, it was discharged with money belonging to Mr Barron. Miss Fowler and Mr Barron did not hold a joint bank account and Mr Barron paid the council tax and other bills. When the relationship between Miss Fowler and Mr Barron broke down, the question arose as to Miss Fowler's beneficial interest, if any, in the house. Mr Barron argued that, despite the conveyance in both of their names, the house belonged beneficially to him. However, Mr Barron did concede that he agreed with Miss Fowler that should he die before her the house would become hers absolutely. He therefore argued that the only reason for transferring the house in

---

[138] [2007] 2 AC 432.
[139] [2007] 2 AC 432 at 454.
[140] [2008] 2 FLR 831.

joint names was that Miss Fowler would acquire the house on the principle of survivorship which operated in the context of a joint tenancy of land. At first instance, the High court held that the Miss Fowler had no interest in the house and that it belonged to Mr Barron absolutely. The High Court proceeded to address the question on a strictly resulting trust approach. It was held that Mr Barron had contributed 100 per cent towards the purchase of the house and therefore was entitled to a 100 per cent interest under a resulting trust.

The Court of Appeal, however, overturned the decision of the High Court, holding that Miss Fowler had a 50 per cent interest in the house under a constructive trust. Arden LJ explained that the High Court had been wrong to apply a purely resulting trust approach. Applying the decision in **Stack v Dowden**,[141] Arden LJ explained that where property was conveyed in joint names, the starting point was joint beneficial ownership. The burden then shifted on to the person seeking to dispute the joint beneficial interest to show a contrary intention. Having looked at all of the facts, Arden LJ held that Mr Barron had not discharged the burden of proof requiring him to show why the beneficial interest in the house should be any different from the legal title. Arden LJ explained that it was not crucial to the finding of a constructive trust to pay attention to the pattern of money contributions. Even though Miss Fowler did not make any direct contributions to the purchase price, it could not be said that her contributions such as looking after the children were insignificant in terms of the common intention which was to be inferred from the facts. Neither Mr Barron nor Miss Fowler discussed who would pay for what. In this respect Arden LJ explained that the 'parties intended that it should make no difference to their interests in the property which party paid for what expense . . . There was no prior agreement as to who would pay what. The inference from this . . . was that the parties simply did not care about the respective size of each other's contributions.'[142] Furthermore, Arden LJ explained that Miss Fowler was unaware of Mr Barron's secret intentions of leaving the house to her on his death. The only common intention that could be inferred from the facts was that the house was jointly owned.[143]

Where the title is not transferred in joint names but only in the name of one of the parties, the inference of a common intention constructive trust will only be made in circumstances where the non-legal owner has made some contribution to the purchase price. In **Lloyds Bank plc v Rosset**[144] Lord Bridge explained that 'direct contributions to the purchase price by the partner who is not the legal owner, whether initially or by payment of mortgage instalments, will readily justify the inference necessary to the creation of a constructive trust. But, as I read the authorities, it is at least extremely doubtful whether anything less will do.'[145] For example, in **Midland Bank v Cooke**[146] a house was purchased in the sole name of Mr Cooke in 1971. The house was acquired primarily with the aid of a mortgage as well as Mr Cooke's savings and a wedding present of £1100 given to both Mr and Mrs Cooke. Both parties admitted in court that there were no express discussions amongst themselves as to the beneficial ownership of the house. Mrs Cooke did discharge the indirect household expenses out of her own pocket, as well as raising the children. The Court of Appeal held that because Mr and Mrs Cooke were jointly entitled

---

[141] [2007] 2 AC 432.
[142] [2008] EWCA Civ. 377 at [41].
[143] This decision is further analysed below in the context of quantification of the beneficial interest under a common intention constructive trust. However, for an analysis of this case, see N. Piska, 'Two Recent Reflections on Resulting Trust' (2008) Conv. 441.
[144] [1991] 1 AC 107.
[145] [1991] 1 AC 107 at 132.
[146] [1995] 2 FLR 915.

to the wedding present, Mrs Cooke had in fact contributed £550 towards the purchase price of the trust. Thus in accordance with the established principles of resulting trusts, she was entitled to 6.47 per cent interest in the home. However, the Court of Appeal held that Mrs Cooke was also held to be entitled to an interest under a common intention constructive trust, on the grounds that a common intention could be inferred from her direct contribution to the purchase price of the house. With regard to the size of the beneficial interest, the Court of Appeal held that Mrs Cooke was entitled to a 50 per cent interest in the house. In coming to this conclusion, the Court of Appeal explained that a wide range of factors would be taken into consideration when quantifying the beneficial interest under a constructive trust, including contributions to domestic endeavour.

Although it is quite clear that a direct contribution to the purchase price will provide the basis for the inference of a common intention, not every direct contribution will be give rise to a constructive trust. The direct contribution must be made pursuant to a common intention that the claimant was to acquire a beneficial interest in the land. Thus, where the contribution by the claimant is made in the form of a gift or a loan, there can be no room for inferring a common intention constructive trust. For example, in **Driver v Yorke**[147] it was held that occasional payments to a mortgage were not capable of giving rise to a common intention constructive trust. In any event, in that case a son had acted as guarantor on a mortgage and as such had not shown that he would be liable for the mortgage payments. A common intention constructive trust will not be implied where a direct contribution is made without the knowledge of the legal owner. The matter arose in **Lightfoot v Lightfoot-Brown**[148] where a husband discharged the mortgage without the knowledge of his wife. The Court of Appeal held that no common intention constructive trust arose on the facts because of the lack of communication of the common intention to the wife.

Where the parties have no express common intention as to the ownership of a house and the title is not conveyed in joint names, coupled with a failure of the non-legal owner to make some direct contribution to the purchase price, there can be no room for the imposition of a constructive trust. In such cases the non-legal owner's claim to some ownership in the land will be based on the fact that the parties have lived together on the assumption that the non-legal owner is to have some interest in the house. Furthermore, the non-legal owner will desperately point to contributions to domestic endeavour over a long period of time as the basis for the imposition of the constructive trust. However, as the decision in **Lloyds Bank plc v Rosset**[149] illustrates, such contribution to domestic endeavour is not the grounds for inferring a common intention. Furthermore, in cases where the claimant moves into property already belonging to the legal owner, it will become very difficult to infer a common intention simply because of the claimant's lack of direct contribution to the purchase price. For example, in **James v Thomas**[150] the claimant came to live with the defendant after they started a relationship. Both parties were partners in a business and they collectively contributed to the profits made in that business. Some of the profits were used by the defendant to discharge the mortgage on the disputed property. When the claimant made a claim to a beneficial interest in the house belonging to the defendant, the Court of Appeal held that there was no common intention between the claimant and defendant as to the shared ownership of the house. With regard to the claimant's assertion that the profits from the business to which she

---

[147]   [2003] 2 P & CR D30.
[148]   [2005] 2 P & CR D12.
[149]   [1991] 1 AC 107.
[150]   [2007] 3 FCR 696.

contributed in generating were contributions to the purchase price, the Court of Appeal held that the profits from the business were generated to meet all of their outgoings and not just for the discharge of the mortgage. In this respect, the Court of Appeal held that the claimant had not directly contributed to the purchase price and, therefore, no common intention could be inferred.

The decision in **James v Thomas**[151] was more recently, followed in **Morris v Morris**[152] where a son and his mother were the absolute owners of a farm house. The claimant married the son and moved into the farm house where she helped with the farming business. The claimant contributed towards the purchase of an enclosure and started her own horse riding business. The enclosure was purchased with the aid of a loan from the son and his mother. When the relationship between husband and wife broke down, the wife claimed an interest in the farm. The Court of Appeal held that the claimant was not entitled to an interest under a constructive trust on the grounds that there was no evidence of an express intention between the parties. With regard to the question of an inferred conduct, the Court of Appeal held that there were no grounds for implying a common intention. The claimant had received personal benefits from her horse riding business and in this respect there was nothing exceptional which the claimant had done in order to imply a constructive trust in her favour. In the course of his judgment, Sir Peter Gibson held that he could not see that 'the conduct that is relied on by the claimant . . . led to the conclusion that she was acquiring an interest in land. It has been said in a number of cases that the court should be cautious before finding that the activities of a wife or a cohabitant can only be explained on the footing that she believes that she was acquiring an interest in land'.[153] A similar finding was recently made in **Hopton v Miller**.[154]

Although more recent decisions such as **Stack v Dowden**[155] and **Fowler v Barron**[156] illustrate that the English law may well be moving towards a greater appreciation of non-direct financial contributions in assessing the extent of a beneficial interest under a constructive trust, the fact remains that the present law is still subject to criticism. The main criticism is that a common intention will simply not be inferred where the non-legal owner makes no direct contribution to the purchase price but does make a significant contribution to domestic endeavour in the assumption that he or she is entitled to some beneficial ownership in a family home. It is this aspect of the present law of common intention constructive trusts which is the subject of much controversy. However, there are signs that the law may well move further forward by placing less emphasis on the artificiality of implying a common intention only in cases of some direct contribution. In **Stack v Dowden** Lord Walker commented *obiter* that '[w]hether or not Lord Bridge's observation was justified in 1990, in my opinion the law has moved on, and your Lordships should move it a little more in the same direction.'[157] In **Le Foe v Le Foe**[158] a wife who had made a direct contribution to the mortgage by the use of money she had inherited was entitled to a 50 per cent interest in the family home on the grounds that her indirect contributions to the household expenses could be regarded as contributions to the purchase price, allowing her husband to discharge the mortgage. In the High Court Nicholas Mostyn QC explained that although the husband earned more than the wife,

---

[151] [2007] 3 FCR 696.
[152] [2008] EWCA Civ. 257.
[153] [2008] EWCA Civ. 257 at [24].
[154] [2010] EWHC 2232.
[155] [2007] 2 AC 432.
[156] [2008] 2 FLR 1.
[157] [2007] EWCA 432 449.
[158] [2001] 2 FLR 970.

'the family economy depended for its function on [the wife's] earnings. It was an arbitrary allocation of responsibility that [the husband] paid the mortgage, service charge and outgoings, whereas [the wife] paid for day to day domestic endeavour. I have clearly concluded that [the wife] contributed indirectly to the mortgage repayments, the principal of which furnished part of the consideration of the initial purchase price.'[159]

Detriment or change of position

Once a common intention is proved to the court, whether it be in the form of an express common intention or one inferred from the parties' conduct, the claimant must prove to the court that he suffered a detriment or changed his position as a result of that common intention. The requirement of change of position or detrimental reliance requires the claimant to have acted upon the common intention which makes it fraudulent for the defendant to retain the absolute ownership in the disputed land. In this respect, the common intention constructive trust shares many features, as will be seen below, with the equitable doctrine of proprietary estoppel where a successful claimant must demonstrate to the court that he or she has suffered a detriment in reliance on some assurance given by a legal owner of land. The exact nature of the change of position or detrimental reliance will depend very much on whether the common intention is an express common intention or whether it is an implied one. At one time it was thought that a higher degree of detrimental reliance was required in cases where the common intention was implied by conduct: for example, nothing short of acts done which were inherently referable to acquisition of an interest in the land were acceptable. However, in light of more recent case law, it appears that the courts are now recognising that the detrimental reliance in the context of an implied common intention can take the form of contributions to domestic endeavour. These matters can be explored in more detail in the following paragraphs.

In the context of an express common intention, the courts have taken the view that once the claimant has discharged the burden of showing that there was an express common intention as to the shared ownership of land, the claimant need to show that he acted upon that common intention. With regard to the conduct which will be taken as evidence of a change of position, the court is entitled to look at a whole range of conduct including direct and indirect contributions. In **Grant v Edwards**[160] the claimant had not made a direct contribution to the purchase price; however, her indirect contributions allowed the legal owner to meet the mortgage payments. This was, nevertheless, held to be a sufficient change of position and entitled the claimant to an interest in the land. In the course of his judgment in **Grant v Edwards** Browne-Wilkinson VC adopted a rather broad and liberal interpretation of detrimental reliance. He explained that it was:

> impossible to say whether or not the claimant would have done the acts relied on as a detriment even if she thought she had no interest in the house. Setting up house together, having a baby, making payments to general housekeeping expenses (not strictly necessary to enable the mortgage to be paid) may all be referable to the mutual love and affection of the parties and not specifically referable to the claimant's belief that she has an interest in the house. As at present advised, once it has been shown that there was a common intention that the claimant should have an interest in the house, any act done by her to her detriment relating to the joint lives of the parties is, in my judgment, sufficient detriment to qualify.[161]

---

[159] [2001] 2 FLR 970 at 973.
[160] [1986] Ch. 638.
[161] [1986] Ch. 638 at 657.

In the context of an inferred common intention, until relatively recently, the view was that a much stricter test of detrimental reliance was required by the courts. In **Lloyds Bank plc v Rosset**[162] Lord Bridge explained that in cases of an inferred common intention the 'court must rely entirely on the conduct of the parties both as the basis from which to infer a common intention to share the property beneficially and as the conduct relied on to give rise to a constructive trust'.[163] In this respect, only direct contributions to the purchase price of the disputed property were sufficient indicators of a change of position. The direct contribution to the purchase price was both the basis for the inference of a common intention and detrimental reliance. Whilst this remains very much true in the existing law, more recent judicial trends, which are discussed in the following section, illustrate that once a claimant can prove an inferred common intention – for example, where the title is conveyed in joint names or where he or she has made some direct contribution to the purchase price of the disputed property – the court can take into consideration a whole range of factors to determine the size of the beneficial interest arising under the constructive trust. Such factors, as will be discussed below, include direct and indirect contributions in the shared ownership of a house. In this respect, there is at least some movement away from the English law approach which has been described by leading treatise on the land law as being 'slow to acknowledge that domestic partners live in a factual community of goods and their economic activity is generally characterised by constructive cooperation and joint endeavour'.[164]

Quantifying the beneficial interest under a common intention constructive trust

Once a claimant has successfully proved to the court that there was a common intention between the parties and that the claimant has suffered a detriment or has changed his or her position as a result of the common intention, the role of the court is to quantify the beneficial interest. With regard to quantification of the interest, the matter very much depends on whether the parties had an express common intention or whether a common intention is implied on the facts. Where the parties have an express common intention as to the ownership of the land, the court will give effect to the express common intention. If the parties have agreed the size of each other's beneficial interest in the disputed property, the court will give effect to that intention. Thus, where the parties have agreed that they are to have equal shares in the property, the court will give effect to equal shares. For example in **Clough v Killey**[165] Peter Gibson LJ explained that 'the correct starting point was to take the shares established by the parties' express common intention and to depart from this only when there was good cause'.[166] In this case, the express agreement between the parties was to the effect that both would have a 50 per cent share in the property. The legal owner was prevented from arguing that in fact the contribution by the claimant and her detriment was of a value much less than a 50 per cent share in the property.

Where there is some express agreement as to the shared ownership of property but no discussion of the respective shares of the parties, then the court is required to look at the whole course of dealings in order to determine what the parties intended regarding the

---

[162] [1991] 1 AC 107.
[163] [1991] 1 AC 105 at 132.
[164] K. Gray and S. Gray, *Elements of Land Law* 6th edn (2009) at p. 897.
[165] (1996) 72 P & CR D22.
[166] (1996) 72 P & CR D22 at D23.

size of the respective beneficial interests. The same will apply where the agreement is inferred from the conduct of the parties. In both cases, the court is required to look at the whole course of dealings between the parties in order to quantify the beneficial interest which best gives effect to the common intention. In the context of an implied common intention, whilst it is clear that direct contributions to the purchase price will trigger the finding of a common intention, with regard to the question of quantification the court will look to a wide range of factors in order to determine the beneficial interest in the land. These factors will include both direct and indirect contributions to the shared ownership of the disputed property. For example, in *Midland Bank plc v Cooke*,[167] as already explained above, Mrs Cooke was held to have contributed to the purchase of a family home when a wedding present of some £1100 belonging equally to Mr and Mrs Cooke was used to pay for the deposit of the family home. It was accepted in the Court of Appeal that on a purely arithmetical level, Mrs Cooke was entitled to a beneficial interest of 6.47 per cent under a purchase price resulting trust. However, the Court of Appeal held that Mrs Cooke was entitled to a 50 per cent interest in the family home, albeit in the name of Mr Cooke, on the grounds that a constructive trust arose in her favour. In arriving at an interest valued at 50 per cent, the Court of Appeal took into consideration a whole host of factors including Mrs Cooke's contribution to domestic endeavour, as well as bringing up the children. Additionally, Mrs Cooke was consulted and consented to the second mortgage which was taken out on the house. In the course of his judgment, Waite LJ explained that:

> [t]he general principle to be derived from *Gissing v Gissing* and *Grant v Edwards* can in my judgment be summarised in this way. When the court is proceeding, in cases like the present where the partner without legal title has successfully asserted an equitable interest through direct contribution, to determine (in the absence of express evidence of intention) what proportions the parties must be assumed to have intended for their beneficial ownership, the duty of the judge is to undertake a survey of the whole course of dealing between the parties relevant to their ownership and occupation of the property and their sharing of its burdens and advantages. That scrutiny will not confine itself to the limited range of acts of direct contribution of the sort that are needed to found a beneficial interest in the first place. It will take into consideration all conduct which throws light on the question what shares were intended. Only if that search proves inconclusive does the court fall back on the maxim that 'equality is equity'.[168]

Although the decision in *Midland Bank plc v Cooke* was widely regarded by most commentators as a good one on the grounds that it moved away from the purely arithmetical approach to quantification, it did raise the question whether the approach to quantification was rather artificial, on the grounds that it gave effect to a presumed intention which the parties may never have made at the outset. In *Oxley v Hiscock*[169] the Court of Appeal had to consider the extent of the respective beneficial interests in the proceeds of sale of a house in circumstances where there was no evidence of discussions between the parties. The decision of the Court of Appeal suggests that, contrary to what many believed might happen post *Midland Bank plc v Cooke*,[170] the courts are not necessarily manufacturing and giving effect to agreements that the parties never made. Furthermore, neither are they inclined to treat the mere fact that the parties intended to

---

[167] [1995] 4 All ER 562.
[168] [1995] 4 All ER 562 at 574.
[169] [2004] 3 All ER 703.
[170] [1995] 4 All ER 562.

live in the property as a family home, albeit unmarried, as necessarily conclusive that they were intended to be entitled equally.

The facts of *Oxley v Hiscock* concerned two parties, Alan Hiscock and Elayne Oxley, who had been residing at 35 Dickens Close since 1991. The title to the house was in Mr Hiscock's name alone. According to Mrs Oxley she did not appear on the title because Mr Hiscock had told her that this might prejudice any claims by her former partner. The house was purchased for £127,000 and the purchase price came from a number of sources. Firstly, there was a mortgage of £30,000 secured over the house and secondly, £35,000 of Mr Hiscock's own savings. Finally, there was a sum of £61,500, which represented the sale of a certain 39 Page Close, this being the house that Mrs Oxley had formerly occupied as a secure tenant but which she acquired sometime in 1987 by the exercise of her rights under Part V of the Housing Act 1985. The value of 39 Page Close was put at £45,200; however, because of the right to buy legislation, Mrs Oxley was entitled to a discount of £20,000 and as such was entitled to purchase the property for a sum of £25,200. The purchase price money for 39 Page Close was provided by Mr Hiscock through the sale of his former house. The evidence before the court was that the sale of Mr Hiscock's former home was directly linked to the purchase of 39 Page Close, which was never transferred in the joint names of Mr Hiscock and Mrs Oxley: instead the title was in Mrs Oxley's sole name. Mr Hiscock did, however, put a charge on the title to 39 Page Close so as to secure the monies he had provided for its purchase. The net effect of this was that out of the £61,500 provided by Mrs Oxley for the purchase of 35 Dickens Close, Mr Hiscock contributed £25,200 representing his initial outlay in the purchase of 39 Page Close. This also meant that Mrs Oxley's contribution to the purchase of 35 Dickens Close was £36,300 and Mr Hiscock's £60,700 (that being his initial £35,500 own savings and the £25,200 which he had provided for the purchase of 39 Page Close).

Mr Hiscock and Mrs Oxley resided at 35 Dickens Close from 1991 to 2001 until the relationship broke down. The mortgage on the house had been paid off some time ago. In March 2001 the house was sold for £232,000 and Mr Hiscock and Mrs Oxley purchased separate properties. In November 2002 Mr Oxley brought proceedings under s. 14 of the Trusts of Land and Appointment of Trustees Act 1996 (TLATA) seeking a declaration that Mr Hiscock was holding the proceeds of sale of 35 Dickens Close on trust for himself and Mrs Oxley in equal shares. The application of s. 14 of the TLATA 1996 was apparent because Mr Hiscock had an express agreement with Mrs Oxley that she would have a beneficial interest in the property, albeit not quantified, thereby giving rise to a constructive trust. Section 14 of the Act allows a court *inter alia* to make any order it thinks fit declaring the nature or extent of a person's interest in the property subject to a trust.

At first instance the judge held that both Mr Hiscock and Mrs Oxley were entitled to an equal share in the disputed property. The basis for this finding was that, where there was an absence of agreement as to the precise extent of the beneficial interest in the land, the court was required to look at the whole course of dealings in order to come to a conclusion. In support of this the judge cited the decision in *Midland Bank plc v Cooke*[171] where Waite LJ commented that:

> where the court is proceeding in cases like the present where the partner without legal title has successfully established an equitable interest thorough direct contribution, to determine (in the absence of express evidence of intention) what proportions the parties must have intended for their beneficial ownership, the duty of the judge is to undertake a

---

[171] [1995] 4 All ER 562.

survey of the whole course of dealing between the parties relevant to their ownership and occupation of the property and their sharing of its burdens and advantages.[172]

On the present facts the judge came to the conclusion that the course of dealing beginning with the purchase of 39 Page Close and the eventual purchase and occupation of 35 Dickens Close was part of a long-term plan whereby Mr Hiscock and Mrs Oxley were equal owners of both properties.

In particular, the purchase of 39 Page Close by the exercise of the right to buy was advantageous from both Mr Hiscock's point of view as well as Mrs Oxley's. The discount would entitle them to sell the house at a profit and this would enable them to buy a better house where they could live together. Furthermore, in continuing with this long-term plan Mrs Oxley decorated the property, did the gardening and contributed to other outgoings. In other words, there was a pooling of resources sufficient to evince an intention that they were jointly responsible for the benefits and burdens of the property because they regarded themselves as equal owners.

The judge at first instance refused to follow the decision in **Springette v Defoe**[173] where the court held that where two or more persons purchased property without declaring the trusts upon which the property was being held, the property was held on resulting trust for the persons who provided the purchase money in the proportion in which it was provided. You will recall that in this case a sitting tenant was entitled to a discount in the purchase price of her council house. The court held that this was a sufficient contribution to the purchase price, entitling her to an interest under a resulting trust. On this basis it was argued on behalf of Mr Hiscock that Mrs Oxley's share in the disputed property was 22 per cent as representing the discount she received in the purchase of 39 Page Close.

The main issue in the Court of Appeal was whether the judge at first instance was required to follow the decision in **Springette v Defoe**[174] in that where there was an absence of intention as to the exact extent of the beneficial interest in the property, the property was held on resulting trust by the legal owner in proportion to the contributions made by the parties. Or was the judge correct to follow the decision in **Midland Bank plc v Cooke**[175] and look at the course of dealings in order to ascertain the true extent of the beneficial interest in the property? In answering this question Chadwick LJ undertook a comprehensive review of the law pre and post **Midland Bank plc v Cooke**. Having reviewed the existing law, his Lordship came to the conclusion that 'in cases of this nature, that is, (i) property is purchased by unmarried cohabitees; (ii) each having made some contribution to the purchase; (iii) the title is taken in only one of their names; (iv) there is no express declaration of trust; the court was required to answer two questions'.[176] Firstly, whether there is evidence from which to infer a common intention that each shall have a beneficial interest in the property and that such intention has been communicated to each other. In answering this question his Lordship took the approach adopted by Lord Bridge in **Lloyds Bank plc v Rosset**[177] where Lord Bridge held that a common intention could be found either expressly or by implication. Where there was an express common intention, that is, where the parties had some discussion at the time of the purchase, then that would settle the matter. In the present case of **Oxley v Hiscock** Chadwick LJ

---

[172] [1995] 4 All ER 562 at 574.
[173] [1992] 2 FLR 388.
[174] *Ibid.*
[175] [1995] 4 All ER 562.
[176] [2004] 3 All ER 703 at para. 68.
[177] [1991] 1 AC 107.

explained that both Mr Hiscock and Mrs Oxley had an express common intention that both would have a beneficial interest in the disputed property. You will remember that Mr Hiscock advised Mrs Oxley not to go on the title because it might prejudice any claims by her former partner.[178] In the absence of an express common intention, an implied common intention will be readily found by some financial contribution to the purchase price.

Having answered the first question, Chadwick LJ proceeded to answer the second question: 'What is the extent of the parties' respective beneficial interests in the property?' His Lordship identified three strands of law that were capable of answering this question. Firstly, the parties are taken to have agreed at the time of the purchase that their respective shares are to be decided not at the time of the purchase but when the relationship breaks down and the property is sold. In such a case the court is required to come to a conclusion as to what is fair, having regard to the whole course of dealings.[179]

Secondly, there is the strand taken by the Court of Appeal in *Midland Bank plc v Cooke*,[180] whereby the court looks at the whole course of dealings between the parties relevant to their ownership and occupation of the property and then decide what the parties must have assumed to have intended from the outset. In *Midland Bank plc v Cooke* you will remember that Mrs Cooke, who did not feature on the legal title to the property, nevertheless received a joint wedding present of some £1100. The Court of Appeal held that, whilst Mrs Cooke was entitled to a 6.47 per cent interest in the property by reason of her financial contribution, she was entitled to 50 per cent interest by virtue of the whole course of dealings, which evidenced an intention that she was entitled to an equal share from the outset. The Court looked to Mrs Cooke's acts of looking after the house, raising the children and indirectly contributing to the household expenses. The decision is not without problems. In the first place the court does not make it very clear whether the basis of the quantification of the interest is under a resulting trust or a constructive trust. Secondly, it is not altogether clear why subsequent conduct is used to imply an intention that was never agreed from day one.

The final strand identified by Chadwick LJ was that identified in cases such as *Grant v Edwards*[181] and *Yaxley v Gotts*,[182] where the court gives effect to the expectation that has been conveyed by the legal owner to the non-legal owner. This was the approach in the proprietary estoppel cases, which in the opinion of Chadwick LJ were not different to the constructive trust cases in terms of their final outcome.

In the opinion of his Lordship, the strand taken in *Midland Bank plc v Cooke* was the least satisfactory of all. His Lordship explained that it was 'artificial and an unnecessary fiction to attribute to the parties a common intention that the extent of their respective beneficial interests in the property should be fixed as from the time of the acquisition, in circumstances in which all the evidence points to the conclusion that, at the time of the acquisition, they had given no thought to the matter'.[183] In the opinion of the court each

---

[178] This is consistent with the decision in *Grant* v *Edwards* [1986] 1 Ch. 638 where the court found an express common intention on the grounds that the only reason why the non-legal owner did not appear on the title was because it might affect claims by her former partner in divorce proceedings. It is questionable whether pretexts of this nature are conclusive of any common intention at all, for example it has been argued that such pretexts are evidence that the legal owner did not intend the non-legal owner to have any interest at all; see S. Gardner (1993) 109 LQR 263.

[179] As suggested by Lord Diplock in *Gissing* v *Gissing* [1971] AC 886 at 909 and Nourse LJ in *Stokes* v *Anderson* [1991] 1 FLR 391 at 399.

[180] [1995] 4 All ER 562.

[181] [1986] 1 Ch. 638.

[182] [2000] Ch. 162.

[183] [2004] 3 All ER 703 at para. 71.

case had to be decided on the basis of what was fair, having regard to the whole course of dealing between the cohabitees in relation to the property. This required the court to look at the arrangements made between them with regards to the outgoings such as mortgage contributions and council tax. On this basis the court concluded that Mr Hiscock was entitled to a 60 per cent interest in the property and Mrs Oxley 40 per cent. Looking at the whole course of dealings, it could not be said that when Mr Hiscock sold his own house and advanced the proceeds to purchase 39 Page Close (the house which Mrs Oxley bought under her right to buy at a discount) he intended to be an equal owner of that property with Mrs Oxley. Indeed, Mr Hiscock had put a charge on that property for the sums advanced to Mrs Oxley. This naturally meant that when 35 Dickens Close was purchased in Mr Hiscock's name, it could not be imputed that Mr Hiscock and Mrs Oxley were equal owners of that property. Much more of Mr Hiscock's money was used in the purchase of that property, for example the £35,000 of his savings and the £25,200 which he had advanced to Mrs Oxley for the purchase of her council house.

The decision in **Oxley v Hiscock**[184] went a long way to addressing the question of quantification by looking at the whole course of dealings between the parties and arriving at a result which was fair to both the parties. You will recall that the facts of **Oxley v Hiscock** concerned a situation where the title to the disputed property was taken in the sole name of the legal owner. More recently, in the much celebrated decision of the House of Lords in **Stack v Dowden**[185] the House of Lords has approved of the approach taken in **Oxley v Hiscock**. However, as clarified by Baroness Hale, the role of the court in quantifying the beneficial interest is not necessarily to achieve fairness between the parties, but rather 'to ascertain the parties' shared intentions, actual, inferred or imputed, with respect to the property in the light of their whole course of conduct in relation to it'.[186] In other words, the quantification must give effect to the presumed intentions between the parties. The decision of the House of Lords makes a significant breakthrough in joint ownership cases, where in the past the quantification of the beneficial interests of the joint owners had been decided on a purely resulting trust approach by looking at the level of each other's direct contribution to the purchase of the jointly owned property.

The facts of **Stack v Dowden** concerned an unmarried couple who started their relationship in 1975 when they were in their teens. In 1983 Ms Dowden purchased a property which was conveyed in her sole name. The evidence before the court was that the property was purchased solely with money belonging to Ms Dowden. A mortgage of £22,000 was taken out and this was paid by Ms Dowden along with the initial £8000 down payment. It was clear on the facts that Ms Dowden earned much more than Mr Stack. Mr Stack did carry out substantial repairs and improvements in the house. During the period between 1986 and 1991 Ms Dowden and Mr Stack had four children. In 1993, the house was sold for almost three times the value it had been purchased and a new house was purchased which was conveyed in the joint names of Ms Dowden and Mr Stack without express declaration of trust. Ms Dowden contributed 65 per cent of the purchase price by making available money from the sale of the previous house which was in her sole name. The remaining purchase price was met by a mortgage which was taken

---

[184] [2004] 3 All ER 703.

[185] [2007] 2 AC 432. See T. Etherton, 'Constructive Trusts: A New Model for Equity and Unjust Enrichment' (2008) CLJ 265. For a critique of the House of Lords' decision, see N. Piska, 'Intention, Fairness and the Presumption of Resulting Trust after *Stack v Dowden*' (2008) 71 MLR 120 and W. Swadling, 'The Common Intention Constructive Trust in the House of Lords: An Opportunity Missed' (2007) LQR 511.

[186] [2007] 2 AC 432 at 455.

out in their joint names and two endowment policies. The mortgage interest and endowment premiums were paid by Mr Stack totalling £34,000 whilst the mortgage loan was paid back by Mr Stack and Ms Dowden, each contributing £27,000 and £34,435 respectively. All the other outgoings were paid by Ms Dowden, and the evidence before the court was that the parties had kept separate bank accounts and separate investments and savings. When the relationship between the parties broke down, the question arose as to the beneficial interest of the parties in the house which had been jointly conveyed in their names. Mr Stack claimed to be entitled to a 50 per cent interest in the house. In the Court of Appeal, Chadwick LJ applying the approach adopted in *Oxley v Hiscock*[187] held that, in light of the whole course of dealing, in particular, the fact that Ms Dowden had contributed significantly more than Mr Stack, Mr Stack was entitled to 35 per cent interest in the house whilst Ms Dowden was entitled to 65 per cent interest.[188] Chadwick LJ explained that this was a fair result for both the parties.

On appeal to the House of Lords, the House of Lords upheld the decision of the Court of Appeal, although arriving at the same conclusion on rather different grounds. The decision of the majority in *Stack v Dowden* has been described by Professor Kevin Gray and Susan Gray in their treatise on land law as constituting a 'truly remarkable translation of judicially formulated (and perfectly laudable) social agenda into judge made law'.[189] This is not surprising when one considers the jurisprudence within the judgments of the majority. Baroness Hale proceeded to address the issue by holding that the starting point in any discussion of the joint ownership of land was a presumption of joint ownership. On the principle that equity follows the law, the beneficial interest in the land is the same as the legal title, so that where there is joint ownership, both parties are entitled to equal shares. The onus then shifted on to the joint owner who was seeking to claim a greater share in the land to show why the beneficial ownership in the land should be any different from the legal ownership. Baroness Hale explained that 'It should only be expected that joint transferees would have spelt out their beneficial interests when they intended them to be different from their legal interests. Otherwise, it should be assumed that equity follows the law and that the beneficial interests reflect the legal interests in the property.'[190] Furthermore, Baroness Hale explained that:

> just as the starting point where there is sole legal ownership is sole beneficial ownership, the starting point where there is joint legal ownership is joint beneficial ownership. The onus is upon the person seeking to show that the beneficial ownership is different from the legal ownership. So in sole ownership cases it is upon the non-owner to show that he has any interest at all. In joint ownership cases, it is upon the joint owner who claims to have other than a joint beneficial interest.[191]

Having established that joint ownership raised a presumption of joint ownership both at law and in equity, Baroness Hale explained that the onus shifted on to the joint owner who claimed a greater share in the disputed property to explain why and to what extent the beneficial interest in the property should be different from the legal title. Baroness Hale explained that in addressing the question of quantification the court, as in *Oxley v Hiscock*,[192] was entitled to look at a whole range of factors. However, such factors were not examined in order to arrive at what was a fair result: rather the role of the court was to arrive at a conclusion which gave effect to the intentions of the parties.

---

[187] [2004] 3 All ER 703.
[188] [2005] 2 FCR 739.
[189] K. Gray and S. Gray, *Elements of Land Law* 6th edn (2009) at p. 903.
[190] [2007] 2 AC 432 at para. 54.
[191] [2007] 2 AC 432 at para. 56.
[192] [2004] 3 All ER 703.

KEY CITATION	*Stack v Dowden* [2007] 2 AC 432 (Factors relevant in determining the common intention of joint owners and quantifying the beneficial interest, per Baroness Hale at paragraphs 69–70)

Each case will turn on its own facts. Many more factors than financial contributions may be relevant to divining the parties' true intentions. These include:

(i) any advice or discussions at the time of the transfer which cast light upon their intentions then;

(ii) the reasons why the home was acquired in their joint names;

(iii) the reasons why (if it be the case) the survivor was authorised to give a receipt for the capital moneys;

(iv) the purpose for which the home was acquired; the nature of the parties' relationship;

(v) whether they had children for whom they both had responsibility to provide a home;

(vi) how the purchase was financed, both initially and subsequently;

(vii) how the parties arranged their finances, whether separately or together or a bit of both;

(viii) how they discharged the outgoings on the property and their other household expenses.

(ix) When a couple are joint owners of the home and jointly liable for the mortgage, the inferences to be drawn from who pays for what may be very different from the inferences to be drawn when only one is owner of the home. The arithmetical calculation of how much was paid by each is also likely to be less important. It will be easier to draw the inference that they intended that each should contribute as much to the household as they reasonably could and that they would share the eventual benefit or burden equally.

(x) The parties' individual characters and personalities may also be a factor in deciding where their true intentions lay. In the cohabitation context, mercenary considerations may be more to the fore than they would be in marriage, but it should not be assumed that they always take pride of place over natural love and affection. At the end of the day, having taken all this into account, cases in which the joint legal owners are to be taken to have intended that their beneficial interests should be different from their legal interests will be very unusual.

This is not, of course, an exhaustive list. There may also be reason to conclude that, whatever the parties' intentions at the outset, these have now changed. An example might be where one party has financed (or constructed himself) an extension or substantial improvement to the property, so that what they have now is significantly different from what they had then.

Having looked at all of these factors, Baroness Hale concluded that the facts of **Stack v Dowden**[193] were quite unique and that Ms Dowden had rebutted the presumption of joint ownership which arose when the house was jointly conveyed in her and Mr Stack's name. Ms Dowden had contributed significantly more than Mr Stack and by looking at a

---

whole range of factors, including how they had kept their finances separate, it was clear that the intention was not to have equal ownership in the land. Baroness Hale explained that:

> this was, therefore, a very unusual case. There cannot be many unmarried couples who have lived together for as long as this, who have had four children together, and whose affairs have been kept as rigidly separate as this couple's affairs were kept. This is all strongly indicative that they did not intend their shares, even in the property which was put into both their names, to be equal (still less that they intended a beneficial joint tenancy with the right of survivorship should one of them die before it was severed). Before the Court of Appeal, Ms Dowden contended for a 65% share and in my view she has made good her case for that.[194]

Lord Neuberger disagreed with the approach of the majority and gave a critical dissenting judgment. His Lordship agreed with the outcome of the case, but disapproved of the presumption of joint equal ownership in every situation where the legal title was conveyed in the joint names of cohabitees. His Lordship preferred to adopt the resulting trust approach as the means for settling the beneficial entitlements in co-owned land. In the opinion of Lord Neuberger, it was wrong to impute intentions as to the beneficial ownership of the land on principles of fairness which did not necessarily mirror the parties' agreed intentions, or for intentions to be inferred from their conduct. In the course of his judgment Lord Neuberger explained that:

> to impute an intention would not only be wrong in principle and a departure from two decisions of your Lordships' House in this very area, but it also would involve a judge in an exercise which was difficult, subjective and uncertain. (Hence the advantage of the resulting trust presumption). It would be difficult because the judge would be constructing an intention where none existed at the time, and where the parties may well not have been able to agree. It would be subjective for obvious reasons. It would be uncertain because it is unclear whether one considers a hypothetical negotiation between the actual parties, or what reasonable parties would have agreed.[195]

Lord Neuberger went on to to explain that the mere fact that the parties were living together did not necessarily provide any basis for an inference that they were to be entitled equally to the beneficial ownership in the co-owned land. His Lordship explained that he was:

> unimpressed, for instance, by the argument that, merely because they have already lived together for a long time sharing all regular outgoings, including those in respect of the previous property they occupied, the parties must intend that the beneficial interest in the home they are acquiring, with differently sized contributions, should be held in equal shares. Particularly where the parties have chosen not to marry, their close and loving relationship does not by any means necessarily imply an intention to share all their assets equally. There is a large difference between sharing outgoings and making a gift of a valuable share in property; outgoings are relatively small regular sums arising out of day-to-day living, but an interest in the home is a capital asset, with a substantial value. I am similarly unconvinced that the ownership of the beneficial interest in a home acquired in joint names is much affected by whether the parties have children at the time of acquisition. While it justifies the obvious inference that it is to be used for the children as well as the parties, it says nothing on its own as to the intended ownership of the beneficial interest.[196]

---

[194] [2007] 2 AC 432 at para. 92.
[195] [2007] 2 AC 432 at para. 125.
[196] [2007] 2 AC 432 at para. 132.

Despite Lord Neuberger's preference for a more orthodox and traditional application of resulting trust doctrine to resolve the quantum of beneficial interests in jointly owned land, the decision in **Stack v Dowden**[197] is a much welcome development in this area of the law. By placing less significance on the purely arithmetical approach under a resulting trust, the decision goes a long way in recognising that parties who jointly own land do not generally direct the finances towards the family home in a directly structured way, with a clear understanding that each is making separate and individual contributions. The economic reality of shared ownership is that the finances of the parties are pooled together in order to pay for the family home, to pay for domestic endeavour, to pay for utilities and raise the children, and so on. It is highly artificial to look at the direct contributions as the sole means of determining the beneficial interests in the land. In this respect, the decision of the majority is to be commended as giving effect to the social and economic reality of modern shared ownership. It is only in exceptional and unusual circumstances where the parties will have structured their finances so strictly that it would be inappropriate to confer equal joint ownership in such a case. The very facts of **Stack v Dowden** are illustrative of the unusual situation in which the parties kept their finances very separate indeed.

The decision in **Stack v Dowden** was subsequently applied in two cases, both of which provide excellent examples of how the decision operates to give effect to the common intention of the parties. The first is the decision **Adekunle v Ritchie**[198] where a house was conveyed in the joint names of a mother of and her son. The property was conveyed in the son's name because the mother could not afford to purchase the property without her son's assistance. The mother had nine other children and the evidence before the court was that the mother and son had kept their finances separate. The son married and moved out of the house but returned when his marriage had broken down. The mother died and the son claimed to be entitled to the house, on the grounds that he and his mother were joint tenants of the land and that, as a result of the right of survivorship, he was absolutely entitled to the house. It was further argued that the decision in **Stack v Dowden** only applied to cases of sexual or platonic relationships. The court held that the decision in **Stack v Dowden** did apply so as to raise a presumption of joint ownership at law and in equity; however, like **Stack v Dowden** the facts of the case were very unusual. The only reason why the mother had transferred the house in joint names was because she was unable to finance the purchase herself. Whilst it was not disputed that the son would get some beneficial interest in the land, it was not clear that her intention was to make him an equal owner. Furthermore, the mother and son had kept separate finances and, the fact that she had nine other children; it could not have been her intention to leave the entire house to the one son only.

The second case is that of **Fowler v Barron**[199] which has already been discussed above. You will recall that Miss Fowler and Mr Barron were the joint owners of a house in Bognor Regis. Although Mr Barron had paid all the direct contributions to the purchase price, Miss Fowler, who after all had been in the relationship with him since the age of 17, raised two children and looked after the domestic endeavour. Neither party discussed how their finances were to be spent. Mr Barron paid for the family home whilst Miss Fowler provided the running of the house as well as other costs and looking after their two children. In the absence of any further evidence, the Court of Appeal held that Miss Fowler was entitled to a 50 per cent interest in the house. Again the decision in this case

---

[197] [2007] 2 AC 432.
[198] [2007] 2 P & CR DG 20.
[199] [2008] 2 FLR 1.

appears to be a most satisfactory result, given what other common intentions, albeit presumed, could be inferred in so far as Miss Fowler was concerned.

Jones v Kernott in the Supreme Court: further clarification of Stack v Dowden

Although **Stack v Dowden**[200] was applied with relative ease in **Adekunle v Ritchie**[201] and **Fowler v Barron**,[202] the real test came in the **Jones v Kernott** litigation which attracted a considerable amount of attention amongst lawyers and the media. The **Jones v Kernott** litigation, which was recently resolved by the Supreme Court, once again raised the question as to how to quantify the beneficial interests in land where title to the disputed property had been taken in joint names but where the common intention was not exactly clear. In particular, the litigation raised the rather difficult question as to whether, if there had once been a common intention that the joint owners had equal shares in the disputed property, that common intention could change over time, thereby giving one party a substantially greater share than the other.

The facts of the case concerned an unmarried couple who had a relationship for some 23 years. In 1985 the couple purchased a house for some £30,000 with a contribution of £6000 from Ms Jones and the rest was financed through an endowment mortgage. Although the conveyance of the property was taken in the joint names of Ms Jones and Mr Kernott, there was no evidence that the parties had really given any thought or taken advice as to the significance of the title being in their joint names. The couple had two children during the course of their relationship. In 1993 the couple separated and Ms Jones took over the sole responsibility of the outgoings of the property and the maintenance of the two children. Mr Kernott purchased another property for himself, which he was able to finance as a result of not having to pay for the property in which Ms Jones was living and neither having to contribute to the maintenance of the children. In fact, Mr Kernott refused to provide any child support maintenance. Ms Jones made several improvements to the disputed property. In 2006, more than 12 years after the separation, Mr Kernott sought to claim his half share in the disputed property by severing the joint tenancy. The trial judge, applying the principles laid out by Baroness Hale of Richmond in **Stack v Dowden**, held that Ms Jones had made a much larger contribution than Mr Kernott and that she was entitled to a 90 per cent interest in the property and Mr Kernott was entitled to 10 per cent. This was what the trial judge thought was fair and just as between the parties by applying the law as laid down in **Stack v Dowden**. The judge explained that because of the events of 1993, that is, when Mr Kernott moved out of the disputed property, the common intention between Ms Jones and Mr Kernott had indeed changed; they could no longer be thought to have been joint equal beneficial owners of the disputed property. As their common intentions had become unclear, it was for the court to take a holistic approach to determine what was fair on the facts. In coming to that conclusion, the court was required to take on board a whole set of factors in determining what was fair. Those factors included Ms Jones's payment of the mortgage and the improvements to the property, along with the fact that Ms Jones continued to live there and support her children with no assistance from Mr Kernott. Additionally, Mr Kernott was able to purchase another property in which he would live and that was only possible

---

[200]   [2007] AC 432.
[201]   [2007] 2 P & CR DG 20.
[202]   [2008] 2 FLR 1.

because he was not contributing to the disputed property and maintaining the children. Ms Jones did not seek to claim any interest in the subsequent property that Mr Kernott had purchased. In the course of his judgment, Nicholas Strauss QC held that:

> in my view, despite the absence of any communication by either party to the other of any actual intention, the judge was right to impute to the parties an intention that their beneficial interests should be altered to take account of changes in the circumstances from how they stood at the time that they parted, and that, in the absence of any indication by words or conduct as to how they should be altered, the appropriate criterion was what he considered to be fair and just. The parties' interests were 'ambulatory': their respective interests could be quantified at any given time, but until this was done they changed over time to take account of the increasing contribution of Ms Jones and the ever more distant relationship between Mr Kernott and the property. Since the parties had no discernible intentions as to the amount of the adjustment, they must be taken to have intended that it should be whatever was fair and reasonable, as the judge held. In so holding, he did not override any different intention which, from their words or conduct, could reasonably have been attributed to them. Therefore, in my opinion, his approach can be justified as being in accordance with the common intention of the parties. Alternatively, if this is to be regarded as a fiction, it can be justified as the only option available to the court on quantification, once he had rightly decided that the parties intended their respective beneficial interests to change.[203]

Mr Kernott appealed on the grounds that the judge was wrong to imply any intention that the parties' beneficial interests should change after their separation. The decision of the High Court was reversed by the Court of Appeal. In the Court of Appeal Wall LJ explained that the:

> case raises a short but . . . difficult issue, which can . . . be formulated in the following way. Where; (1) an unmarried couple has acquired residential accommodation in joint names, which by common agreement was held by them beneficially in equal shares as at the date of their separation, and; (2) one party (here the respondent) thereafter; (a) continues to live in the property; and; (b) assumes sole responsibility for its continuing acquisition and maintenance – i.e. not only supports herself and the parties' children but pays the mortgage and all the outgoings (including repairs and improvements) – can the court properly infer an agreement post separation that the parties' beneficial interests in the property alter or (to use the phrase coined by Lord Hoffman in argument in **Stack v Dowden** [2007] UKHL 17; [2007] 2 AC 432) become 'ambulatory', thereby enabling the court – as here – to declare that, as at the date of the hearing before the court, the beneficial interests in the property are held other than equally?[204]

VISIT CASE NAVIGATOR

With this in mind Wall LJ sought to examine the decisions in **Oxley v Hiscock**[205] and **Stack v Dowden**.[206] In so far as the decision in **Oxley v Hiscock** Wall LJ explained that the position in that case was essentially one of finding what was fair in the circumstances when the parties had not given thought to the matter. Wall LJ cited the following extract from the judgment of Chadwick J in **Oxley v Hiscock**:

> Chadwick LJ identifies 'three strands of reasoning' which have led the courts away from what he describes as 'a traditional, property-based approach'. They are: (1) the proposition that the interests of the parties are left by them to be determined either when their

---

[203] [2010] 1 P & CR DG 4 at para. 49.
[204] [2010] EWCA Civ 578 at para. 6.
[205] [2004] EWCA Civ 546.
[206] [2007] AC 432.

relationship comes to an end or the property is sold on the basis of what is then fair: (2) the fact that the court undertakes a survey of the whole course of dealing between the parties in order to determine what proportions the parties must be assumed to have intended from the outset for their beneficial ownership: and (3) the court makes such order as the circumstances require; this is a form of estoppel and is required to prevent a denial by the legal owner of the other party's beneficial interest . . .

But it can be said that, if it were their common intention that each should have some beneficial interest in the property – which is the hypothesis upon which it becomes necessary to answer the second question – then, in the absence of evidence that they gave any thought to the amount of their respective shares, the necessary inference is that they must have intended that question would be answered later on the basis of what was then seen to be fair.[207]

In so far as the decision in **Stack v Dowden**[208] Wall LJ made extensive reference to Baroness Hale's judgment requiring a holistic approach to be taken into consideration when determining the extent of the beneficial interest in cases where the non-married cohabitees had not given thought to the extent of the beneficial interest despite the title being conveyed in joint names. Wall LJ in particular referred to the following passage of Baroness Hale's judgment: 'If the question really is one of the parties' "common intention", we believe that there is much to be said for adopting what has been called a "holistic approach" to quantification, undertaking a survey of the whole course of dealing between the parties and taking account of all conduct which throws light on the question what shares were intended.'[209]

Having looked at the decisions in both **Oxley v Hiscock** and **Stack v Dowden** Wall LJ proceeded to take a detailed examination of the dissenting judgment of Lord Neuberger in **Stack v Dowden**. It will be recalled that Lord Neuberger took a very conservative approach in finding an imputed intention by looking at all the relevant facts over the course of the relationship between the parties. His Lordship was at pains to suggest that it was wrong in principle to arrive at an imputed intention which would be fair on the facts. He explained that there was a real difference between an inferred intention and an imputed one looking at all relevant facts and then imputing what the parties might have intended. In the course of his dissenting judgment in **Stack v Dowden** Lord Neuberger explained that:

An inferred intention is one which is objectively deduced to be the subjective actual intention of the parties, in the light of their actions and statements. An imputed intention is one which is attributed to the parties, even though no such actual intention can be deduced from their actions and statements, and even though they had no such intention. Imputation involves concluding what the parties would have intended, whereas inference involves concluding what they did intend.

To impute an intention would not only be wrong in principle and a departure from two decisions of your Lordships' House in this very area, but it also would involve a judge in an exercise which was difficult, subjective and uncertain. (Hence the advantage of the resulting trust presumption.) It would be difficult because the judge would be constructing an intention where none existed at the time, and where the parties may well not have been able to agree. It would be subjective for obvious reasons. It would be uncertain because it is unclear whether one considers a hypothetical negotiation between the actual parties, or what reasonable parties would have agreed. The former is more logical, but

---

[207] [2004] EWCA Civ 546 at paras 70 and 71.
[208] [2007] 2 AC 432.
[209] [2007] 2 AC 432 at para. 61.

would redound to the advantage of an unreasonable party. The latter is more attractive, but is inconsistent with the principle, identified by Baroness Hale at para. 61, that the court's view of fairness is not the correct yardstick for determining the parties' shares.

Having carefully analysed the dissenting judgment of Lord Neuberger in **Stack v Dowden**[210] Wall LJ held that on the facts of **Kernott v Jones**[211] the title to the disputed property had been conveyed in the joint names of both partners. Although his Lordship accepted that the beneficial interest in property could change over time, there would need to be compelling evidence that the parties intended that beneficial interest to change. There had to be evidence of discussions to the effect that the beneficial interest was to change. In his conclusion, his Lordship explained that the 'critical question is whether or not I can properly infer from the parties' conduct since separation a joint intention that, over time, the 50–50 split would be varied so that the property is currently held 90% by the respondent and 10% by the appellant. Presumably, if the beneficial interests are "ambulatory" and the ambulation continues in the same direction, the appellant's interest in the property will at some point be extinguished.'[212] His Lordship continued and held that 'this is a point which I have considered anxiously, and at the end of the day I simply cannot infer such an intention from the parties' conduct. In my judgment, the conveyance into joint names, following **Stack v Dowden** created joint beneficial interests, and the parties agreed that when they separated they had equal interests. There has to be something to displace those interests, and I have come to the conclusion that the passage of time is insufficient to do so, even if, in the meantime, the appellant has acquired alternative accommodation, and the respondent has paid all the outgoings. In my judgment, the appellant has a 50% interest in the property, and both the judge and the deputy judge were wrong to conclude otherwise.'[213]

On the facts of **Kernott v Jones** the title to the disputed property was taken in the names of both partners as beneficial joint tenants and that was the understanding right up and until their separation. In the opinion of the Court of Appeal, there was nothing on separation and post separation to suggest that they intended to change their beneficial interest in the property. The appellant, Mr Kernott, was therefore entitled to a 50 per cent interest in the property. The decision of the Court of Appeal in **Kernott v Jones**[214] represented a very conservative and cautious approach to the quantification of the beneficial interests where property is taken in joint names. The decision had attracted much debate and controversy for the reason that some perceived this as a rejection of the more liberal approach adopted by the House of Lords in **Stack v Dowden**.[215] It was therefore inevitable that the matter would eventually have to be resolved by the highest court in the country and the opportunity to do so arose when Ms Jones appealed to the Supreme Court. The much eagerly awaited decision of the Supreme Court was handed down in November 2011 and is discussed in the paragraphs below.

On appeal to the Supreme Court, **Jones v Kernott**,[216] the Supreme Court overruled the decision of the Court of Appeal and reinstated the order of the High Court. The Supreme Court held that Ms Jones had a 90 per cent interest in the disputed property whilst Mr Kernott's share was 10 per cent despite the fact that the title to the disputed property

---

[210] [2007] AC 432.
[211] [2010] EWCA Civ 578.
[212] [2010] EWCA Civ 578 at para. 57.
[213] [2010] EWCA Civ 578 at para. 58.
[214] [2010] EWCA Civ 578.
[215] [2007] 2 AC 432.
[216] [2011] UKSC 53.

was taken in joint names. The decision of the Supreme Court has been welcomed by family lawyers and certain parts of the media as doing justice on the facts. However, for property and trust lawyers, it was not so much the quantification of the respective beneficial interests of Ms Jones and Mr Kernott that they were eagerly awaiting from the Supreme Court, but rather the principles on which that quantification of those beneficial interests was arrived at in the light of joint ownership of the property. The leading judgment was delivered by Lord Walker and Lady Hale and a number of principles emerge from a reading of that judgment.

In the first place, both Lord Walker and Lady Hale were at pains to explain what they thought were the established and orthodox principle of quantification of beneficial interests where title had been taken in joint names and where the title was only taken in the name of one of the co-owners. Both judges were at pains to explain that the case before the court was extraordinary on its facts. Firstly, both judges explained that there was indeed a single regime to determine how beneficial interests under constructive trusts would be quantified. Although the starting point in quantifying beneficial interests was different in the case of property which was jointly owned and that which was owned by one person, the single regime was the common intention constructive trust.[217] As for those instances where the title was taken in the sole name of one of the cohabitees, the question or starting point was 'whether it was intended that the other party have any beneficial interest in the property at all. If he does, the second issue is what that interest is. There is no presumption of joint beneficial ownership. But their common intention has once again to be deduced objectively from their conduct. If the evidence shows a common intention to share beneficial ownership but does not show what shares were intended.'[218]

The Supreme Court explained that the present case was not one where the title had been taken in the sole name of one of the cohabitees. Instead this was a situation where the title had been taken in joint names at the time of the acquisition. With this in mind equity would follow the law and hold that the parties were joint tenants in law and in equity. That having been said, the court explained that where the parties had not given real thought to their beneficial interests despite the joint ownership of the property, or where the circumstances had so fundamentally changed, then it was imperative to ask what reasonable and just people would have thought about their beneficial interests at the time circumstances had changed. The court explained that the events in 1993 when Ms Jones and Mr Kernott had split up were fundamental in changing the common intention that once may have thought to exist between the parties. The disputed property no longer became the family home as it was originally purchased for in 1985. Mr Kernott has cashed in a life insurance policy which allowed him to purchase a new property for himself and he discontinued to look after the disputed property and the family that once centred on that property. In such circumstances the intentions that once formed in 1985 were no longer in existence. It was for the court then to look at what the new common intention was by taking on board what was fair in the circumstances.

In the course of their judgment, Lord Walker and Lady Hale explained that 'in a case such as this, where the parties already share the beneficial interest, and the question is what their interests are and whether their interests have changed, the court will try to deduce what their actual intentions were at the relevant time. It cannot impose a solution upon them which is contrary to what the evidence shows that they actually

---

[217] [2011] UKSC 53 at para. 16.
[218] [2011] UKSC 53 at para. 52.

intended. But if it cannot deduce exactly what shares were intended, it may have no alternative but to ask what their intentions as reasonable and just people would have been had they thought about it at the time. This is a fallback position which some courts may not welcome, but the court has a duty to come to a conclusion on the dispute put before it.'[219]

KEY CITATION	*Jones* v *Kernott* [2011] UKSC 53: The principles of quantification in joint ownership disputes, per Lord Walker and Lady Hale at para. 51

In summary, therefore, the following are the principles applicable in a case such as this, where a family home is bought in the joint names of a cohabiting couple who are both responsible for any mortgage, but without any express declaration of their beneficial interests.

(1) The starting point is that equity follows the law and they are joint tenants both in law and in equity.

(2) That presumption can be displaced by showing (a) that the parties had a different common intention at the time when they acquired the home, or (b) that they later formed the common intention that their respective shares would change.

(3) Their common intention is to be deduced objectively from their conduct: 'the relevant intention of each party is the intention which was reasonably understood by the other party to be manifested by that party's words and conduct notwithstanding that he did not consciously formulate that intention in his own mind or even acted with some different intention which he did not communicate to the other party' (Lord Diplock in *Gissing* v *Gissing* [1971] AC 886, 906). Examples of the sort of evidence which might be relevant to drawing such inferences are given in *Stack* v *Dowden*, at para. 69.

(4) In those cases where it is clear either (a) that the parties did not intend joint tenancy at the outset, or (b) had changed their original intention, but it is not possible to ascertain by direct evidence or by inference what their actual intention was as to the shares in which they would own the property, 'the answer is that each is entitled to that share which the court considers fair having regard to the whole course of dealing between them in relation to the property': Chadwick LJ in *Oxley v Hiscock* [2005] Fam 211, para. 69. In our judgment, 'the whole course of dealing . . . in relation to the property' should be given a broad meaning, enabling a similar range of factors to be taken into account as may be relevant to ascertaining the parties' actual intentions.

(5) Each case will turn on its own facts. Financial contributions are relevant but there are many other factors which may enable the court to decide what shares were either intended (as in case (3)) or fair (as in case (4)).

Constructive trusts, proprietary estoppel and resulting trusts

The analysis of the case law on common intention constructive trusts illustrates that common intention constructive trusts have a number of similarities with the equitable doctrine of proprietary estoppel. Indeed, many of the cases which appear before the

---

[219] [2011] UKSC at para. 47.

courts are usually argued on both grounds. The essence behind proprietary estoppel is to prevent a legal owner of land from denying a proprietary right in land which he has led the claimant to believe will become his. The doctrine is neatly explained by one leading commentary on land law which explains that 'the doctrine of proprietary estoppel gives expression to a general judicial distaste for any attempt by a legal owner unconscientiously to resile from assumptions which were previously understood, and acted upon, as the basis of relevant dealings in respect of his land. In curtailing the unconscionable disclaimer of such underlying assumption, the estoppel principle is ultimately directed against the abuse of power.'[220] Judicially, Oliver J explained the doctrine as one which:

> requires a very much broader approach which is directed rather at ascertaining whether, in particular individual circumstances, it would be unconscionable for a party to be permitted to deny that which, knowingly, or unknowingly, he has allowed or encouraged another to assume to his detriment than to inquiring whether the circumstances can be fitted within the confines of some preconceived formula serving as a universal yardstick for every form of unconscionable behaviour.[221]

A successful claim to an interest under proprietary estoppel requires that the defendant make some assurance or representation that the claimant will acquire an interest in the defendant's land. Secondly, the claimant must have relied on the assurance or representation by changing his position. Finally, as a result of the representation and subsequent change of position, the claimant must have suffered a detriment which makes it unconscionable for the defendant to deny the very rights in the land which he led the claimant to believe would be his.

Although the common intention constructive trust is often argued alongside proprietary estoppel, there are some fundamental differences between the two doctrines.[222] A common intention constructive trust is essentially imposed on grounds of a bargain between a claimant and a defendant whereas a claim for estoppel is based on some assurance given by the legal owner to a claimant on which the claimant has relied. Another difference lies in the remedies that are given in both cases. In the context of a common intention constructive trust, the appropriate remedial response is to recognise that a trust has arisen in the past, conferring upon the claimant a beneficial interest in the land. The role of the court, as seen above, is to quantify that beneficial interest. In the context of proprietary estoppel, the role of the court is firstly to establish whether an equity has arisen in favour of the claimant. Secondly, the court, at its discretion, seeks to satisfy the equity by either conferring upon the claimant the property right which he was led to believe would be his, or awarding him compensation for loss he has suffered as a result of relying on the defendant's representation or assurance. Finally, in the case of a common intention constructive, the claimant acquires a beneficial interest in the land as soon as the common intention is made and acted upon by the claimant. In this respect, the role of the court is to merely recognise that the claimant became entitled to a beneficial interest sometime in the past, which is capable of binding third parties who have notice of it. In the case of proprietary estoppel, the claimant will only acquire an interest in the land after the court, if it decides to do so, awards a proprietary right in the land.

Finally, some reflections must be made on purchase price resulting trusts and common intention constructive trusts. In Chapter 11 it was observed that a purchase price resulting

---

[220] K. Gray and S. Gray, *Elements of Land Law* 6th edn (2009) at p. 1197.
[221] *Taylor Fashions Ltd* v *Liverpool Victoria Trustees Co Ltd* [1982] QB 133 at 151.
[222] See T. Etherton, 'Constructive Trusts and Proprietary Estoppel: The Search for Clarity and Principle' (2009) Conv. 104.

trust arises where a claimant makes a direct contribution to the purchase price of land. The beneficial interest under a purchase price resulting trust is equivalent to the amount contributed by the claimant. A common intention constructive trust gives effect to the common intentions between typically a legal owner of land and a non-legal owner claimant. In quantifying the beneficial interest under a common intention constructive trust, the court gives effect to the common intention as between the parties. One of the significant developments, and particularly more so after the decision of the House of Lords in **Stack v Dowden**,[223] is the role of resulting trusts in determining the beneficial interests of co-owners of land. Given the fact that a direct contribution, which would normally give rise to a resulting trust in favour of a claimant, will also provide the grounds for the inference of a common intention, most claimants would seek to argue that a common intention constructive trust has arisen in their favour. The advantage of the common intention constructive trust is that the quantification of the beneficial interest in the land is not dependent solely on the pattern of direct contributions to the purchase price; rather, as seen in the above sections, the court is to look at a whole range of factors including direct and indirect contributions. The question arises as to what future role resulting trusts have in the context of co-ownership of land.

Criticism of the present law and law reform in the context of cohabitation

There is no doubt that the law relating to the common intention constructive trust has moved significantly forward in the last few years. Notably, decisions such as those in **Oxley v Hiscock**[224] and **Stack v Dowden**[225] have, at least in the context of quantifying beneficial interest under the trust and in the cases of joint ownership of land, allowed the courts to examine a whole range of factors in determining the extent of the beneficial interest of the parties disputing the ownership of shared land. However, it is equally true to say that the law remains problematic in a number of areas. Fundamentally, there is still a problem in the way in which the law seeks to identify a common intention between the parties.[226] With regard to finding a common intention, there still remains an element of artificiality in the process by which a common intention is found. In respect of an express common intention, cases such as **Eves v Eves**[227] and **Grant v Edwards**[228] have generally been cited as good examples of where the parties have had a common intention as to the shared ownership of land despite the legal title only being conveyed in the name of one of the parties. However, as was observed earlier in this chapter, in both cases it is questionable whether there was any genuine and honest intention on the part of the legal owner to share the beneficial interest in the land with the cohabiting partner. In both cases, the excuses given by the legal owner for not putting the claimant on the legal title were attempts to prevent the claimant from having some interest in the land in the future.[229]

---

[223] [2007] 2 AC 432.

[224] [2004] 3 All ER 703.

[225] [2007] 2 AC 432.

[226] For a critical analysis of the common intention in common intention constructive trust cases, see S. Gardner, 'Re-thinking Family Property' (1993) LQR 263; S. Gardner, 'Family Property Today' (2008) LQR 422; R. Lee, 'Stack v Dowden: A Sequel' (2008) LQR 209.

[227] [1975] 1 WLR 1383.

[228] [1986] Ch. 638.

[229] As explained earlier, these cases are perhaps better analysed as factual situations giving rise to a claim based on proprietary estoppel.

In respect of an inferred common intention, there are further problems. Despite the decisions in *Oxley v Hiscock*[230] and *Stack v Dowden*,[231] which allows the courts to take on board a whole range of factors when quantifying the beneficial interest under a constructive trust, with regard to the initial inquiry into inferring a common intention, only direct contributions to the purchase will be sufficient to infer a common intention. Whilst there have been many *obiter* statements to the effect that a whole range of factors, including direct and non-direct contributions to land, may also be the basis for inferring a common intention, there is no direct authority to the point. In *Stack v Dowden* Lord Walker, when addressing the observations of Lord Bridge as to the grounds that an inferred common intention would only arise where the claimant had made some direct contribution to the purchase price, his Lordship commented 'whether or not Lord Bridge's observation was justified in 1990, in my opinion the law has moved on, and your Lordships should move it a little more in the same direction'.[232] It is unfortunate that, whilst the discussion of the House of Lords in *Stack v Dowden* made significant developments in the area of joint ownership of land, their Lordships did not address in detail the position as regards sole ownership of the shared land. The opportunity did, however, arise before the Judicial Committee of the Privy Council in *Abbot v Abbot*,[233] where membership of the Committee included three of the Law Lords who heard *Stack v Dowden*. Unfortunately for the development of the law in this area, the facts of the case involved a direct contribution by the wife to the purchase price of a house and the husband admitted in evidence that he had agreed with the wife that she would have some beneficial interest in the land; as a result the decision offers little guidance on the relevance of indirect contributions to the finding of a common intention. The case involved an appeal from the Eastern Caribbean Court of Appeal. On the facts, the legal title to a matrimonial home in Antigua and Barbuda was taken in the sole name of the husband. Unlike English law, Antigua and Barbuda does not have property adjustment legislation such as that existing under the Matrimonial Causes Act 1973. Ownership disputes are settled by applying the general common law principles. Despite the conveyance in the husband's name, the wife had undertaken joint liability for the mortgage and this was partly discharged from her own wages, although not necessarily equally. As explained earlier, the husband had admitted to the court that he and his wife were to have some shared ownership in the land. The question before the Committee was essentially one relating to the size of the beneficial interest in the house. Applying the decision of the House of Lords in *Stack v Dowden*[234] the Privy Council held that the wife was entitled to an equal share in the property. Baroness Hale explained that it was important to survey the whole course of dealings between the parties. In particular, her Ladyship explained that on the facts the parties had organised their finances jointly and were jointly liable for the repayment of the mortgage. Furthermore, the land upon which the house was built was given to the husband and wife as a gift. In the course of her judgment, Baroness Hale again reiterated what Lord Walker had said in *Stack v Dowden* about Lord Bridge's observations of an implied common intention. Her Ladyship explained that the 'the law has indeed moved on since then. The parties' whole course of conduct in relation to the property must be taken into account in determining their shared intentions as to its ownership.'[235] It remains to be

---

[230] [2004] 3 All ER 703.
[231] [2007] 2 AC 432.
[232] [2007] 2 AC 432 at para. 26.
[233] [2008] 1 FLR 1451.
[234] [2007] 2 AC 432.
[235] [2008] 1 FLR 1451 at para. [19].

seen when a case will arise before the courts where a common intention constructive trust will is inferred on grounds of conduct which falls short of some direct contribution to the purchase price.

Law reform in the area of shared ownership was considered by the Law Commission in 1992.[236] In its report that Commission concluded that whilst reform in this area was needed, such reform could not be achieved through statutory means. In the opinion of the Commission, it would be difficult to devise a statutory scheme which would produce fairness in all situations of cohabitation. Instead the Commission, having concluded that the approach to the finding of a common intention was somewhat artificial in many cases, suggested that the courts should adopt a much broader approach, both in relation to initial finding of a common intention and the subsequent quantification of the beneficial interests of the parties in the land. In particular, the Commission suggested that indirect contributions to the purchase of the property should be taken into consideration. Since the Commission's report in 1992, some of the suggestions have already been taken on board in the decided case law. For example, post *Oxley* v *Hiscock*[237] the courts are now taking into consideration a whole range of factors and course of dealings when quantifying the beneficial interest under a common intention constructive trust.

The Law Commission revisited this area of the law in 2007 and this time opted for a statutory regime which would address the problem of shared ownership.[238] The basic feature of the Commission's proposal is the enactment of a statutory regime which would allow the adjustment of property rights between cohabiting couples on separation. The reasons for reform are highlighted in the following extract from the Commission Report.[239]

KEY CITATION

Law Com. No. 307 (*Cohabitation: the financial consequences of relationship breakdown (2007), paragraphs 2.15–2.16 (footnotes omitted))*

The law of common intention constructive trusts, to which resort is had in the absence of an express declaration of trust, is based on the parties' intentions regarding the ownership of the asset in dispute. While those intentions may change over time, the constructive trust cannot accommodate 'contingent' intentions. It cannot simultaneously provide that the parties hold the property in particular shares while they stay together but will hold in different shares should they separate. Moreover, since the parties' shares are to be determined by reference to their intentions . . . the court cannot substitute its own view of what is the fair outcome on separation.

▶

---

[236] Law Com. No. 278, *Sharing Homes: A Discussion Paper* (2002).

[237] [2004] 3 All ER 703.

[238] Law Com. No. 307, *Cohabitation: The Financial Consequences of Relationship Breakdown* (2007). For an excellent account of the Commission's proposals, see D. Hughes, M. Davis and L. Jacklin, '"Come Live with me and be my Love" – Consideration of the 2007 Law Commission Proposals on Cohabitation Breakdown' (2008) Conv. 197. See also S. Bridge, 'Cohabitation: Why Legislative Reform is Necessary' [2007] *Fam. Law* 911.

[239] Note, footnotes are omitted from the extract.

> The general law, therefore, is not equipped to provide a comprehensive solution to problems arising on separation, responding to the economic consequences of the parties' contributions to their relationship. Moreover, since it is limited to addressing the beneficial ownership of individual assets, the general law of property and trusts offers very little remedial flexibility. It provides no scope for orders that take effect, for example, over parties' pension funds. It offers no assistance where parties do not own the home that they have shared and do not have capital assets. A coherent set of statutory remedies providing financial relief between cohabitants would provide a way of doing better justice between the parties on separation, while respecting the interests of affected third parties.

Under the statutory scheme suggested by the Commission certain cohabitants would have rights on separation. With regard to the question as to who is a cohabitee, the Commission's definition includes those who have been cohabiting for a period to be specified between two and five years and have a child from the relationship. As regards the rights of the cohabitee, the Commission proposes that the court be given a discretion to award financial relief based on the contributions of the parties. The mere fact that the parties have lived together is not the basis for the financial relief. Instead the Commission proposes that the contribution of the parties, including the welfare of the children, be looked at before awarding some sort of financial relief. In particular the court would look to the question whether the applicant under the scheme suffered some economic disadvantage such as loss of earnings as a result of looking after children in the relationship, and the contribution to childcare costs. Equally, the court would be required to look at any benefits retained by a partner as a result of the other's contributions. With regard to the nature of the relief, the Commission proposes that the court be given the power to make lump sum payments, property transfers or settlements and orders for sale. Finally the Commission's proposal is that the scheme is to apply to the general exclusion of the law of trusts, estoppel and contract. The Law Commission's proposals have been shelved by the present Coalition government. It is no surprise as the government seeks to promote family solidarity as the bedrock of modern society. It therefore remains to be seen whether the proposals of the Law Commission will one day become law.

Miscellaneous situations giving rise to a constructive trust

It was explained at the outset of this chapter that the situations giving rise to the imposition of a constructive trust are quite wide and diverse. A number of the more popular situations have already been discussed above; however, this chapter would remain incomplete without reference to the following situations in which a constructive trust has also been imposed. The first three situations relate to constructive trusts in land and should be appreciated as an addition to the common intention constructive trusts discussed in the preceding section. The final situation looks at the operation of constructive trusts in the context of secret trusts and mutual wills.

Specifically enforceable contract for the sale of property

A constructive trust will arise where two parties enter into a contract which is capable of specific performance. A decree of specific performance will be available where a purchaser cannot adequately be compensated for his loss by an award of damages. Thus, where a purchaser enters into a contract for the purchase of a unique item, such as an antique or some rare painting or some shares in a private company, damages are not necessarily adequate. In such a case, the purchaser will demand that the vendor specifically performs the contract by delivering the subject matter of the contract to him. The ability of equity to decree specific performance stems from the application of the equitable maxim that 'equity regards that as done which ought to be done'. As soon as the contract is entered into, the vendor becomes a constructive trustee for the purchaser. This means that the beneficial interest in the property, which is subject to the contract, passes to the purchaser as soon as the contract is made. The matter is neatly explained by Jessel MR in *Lysaght v Edwards*[240] where he explained that:

> the effect of a contract for sale has been settled for more than two centuries; certainly it was completely settled before the time of Lord Hardwicke, who speaks of the settled doctrine of the Court as to it. What is that doctrine? It is that the moment you have a valid contract for sale the vendor becomes in equity a trustee for the purchaser of the estate sold, and the beneficial ownership passes to the purchaser, the vendor having a right to the purchase-money, a charge or lien on the estate for the security of that purchase-money, and a right to retain possession of the estate until the purchase-money is paid, in the absence of express contract as to the time of delivering possession. In other words, the position of the vendor is something between what has been called a naked or bare trustee, or a mere trustee (that is, a person without beneficial interest) . . .[241]

A contract can be specifically enforceable in respect of both personal and real property. In the context of personal property, for example the sale of shares in a private company, the contract can be made orally. For example, in *Oughtred v IRC*[242] where a mother and her son entered into a contract for the sale of shares in a private company, the House of Lords recognised that the contract was one capable of specific performance. In the context of real property, that is the sale of land, the contract will only be capable of specific performance if it is in writing, incorporating the terms of the contract and signed by the parties.[243]

Whilst it is trite law that a constructive trust will arise in favour of a purchaser who enters into a specifically enforceable contract for the sale of property, it must be emphasised that the nature and the duties owed by the constructive trustee are very different from those of a normal trustee. The reason for this stems from the fact that, until completion of the contract, the vendor, whilst being regarded as having transferred the beneficial interest to the purchaser (under the maxim 'equity regards that as done which ought to be done'), retains a vested interest in the property should the contract fall through for some reason or another. He certainly cannot be said to have divested himself of all self-interest in the property. The matter is particularly acute in the context of the sale of land where the vendor is under a duty to provide a good title, and the purchaser is waiting to see what title is deduced and whether he is willing to go ahead with the purchase in light of the title that is deduced. Certainly it cannot be said that the vendor is a constructive trustee proper until such time as both parties have agreed the title which is being conveyed. Until the title has been agreed, it can be said that the vendor is some form of quasi trustee. The matter is neatly illustrated by Mason J in *Chang v Registrar of Titles*[244] where the judge explained that:

---

[240] (1876) 2 Ch. D 499.

[241] (1876) 2 Ch. D 499 at 506.

[242] [1960] AC 206, see also *Neville v Wilson* [1996] 3 All ER 171.

[243] Section 2(1) Law of Property (Miscellaneous Provisions) Act 1989.

[244] (1976) 137 CLR 177, quoted in D. Hayton and C. Mitchell, *Hayton v Marshall: Cases and Commentary on the Law of Trusts and Equitable Remedies* 12th edn (2005) at p. 377.

there has been controversy as to the time when the trust relationship arises and as to the character of that relationship. Lord Eldon considered that a trust arose on execution of the contract.[245] Plumer MR thought that until it is known whether the agreement will be performed the vendor 'is not even in the situation of constructive trustee; he is only a constructive trustee *sub modo*, and providing nothing happens to prevent it. It may turn out to that the title is not good, or the purchaser may be unable to pay.'[246] Lord Hatherley said that a vendor becomes a trustee for the purchaser when the contract is completed, as by payment of the purchase money.[247] Jessel MR held that a trust *sub modo* arises on the execution of the contract but that the constructive trust comes into existence when the title is made out by the vendor or is accepted by the purchaser.[248]

The matter has more recently been considered by the House of Lords in *Jerome v Kelly*[249] where Lord Walker, having reviewed the authorities, explained the position of both vendor and purchaser under a specifically enforceable contract way.

KEY CITATION

Jerome v Kelly (Inspector of Taxes) [2004] 1 WLR 1409 (Vendor and purchaser under a specifically enforceable contract for sale of land per Lord Walker at 32)

It would therefore be wrong to treat an uncompleted contract for the sale of land as equivalent to an immediate, irrevocable declaration of trust (or assignment of beneficial interest) in the land. Neither the seller nor the buyer has unqualified beneficial ownership. Beneficial ownership of the land is in a sense split between the seller and buyer on the provisional assumptions that specific performance is available and that the contract will in due course be completed, if necessary by the court ordering specific performance. In the meantime, the seller is entitled to enjoyment of the land or its rental income. The provisional assumptions may be falsified by events, such as rescission of the contract (either under a contractual term or on breach). If the contract proceeds to completion the equitable interest can be viewed as passing to the buyer in stages, as title is made and accepted and as the purchase price is paid in full.

Whilst it is clear from the judgment of Lord Walker in *Jerome v Kelly*[250] that the vendor under a specifically enforceable contract for the sale of land is entitled to the enjoyment of the land and any profit deriving thereunder, the vendor is, however, under a duty to take reasonable care to preserve the property.[251]

Undertaking by purchaser to recognise the right of another

The constructive trust has become a very useful means by which certain proprietary and personal rights in land may become binding on a purchaser who has purchased land in the acknowledgment that he will respect those rights. Typically in the case of proprietary

---

[245] *Paine v Meller* (1801) 6 Ves. 349; *Broome v Monck* [1803–1818] All ER 631 (1805).
[246] *Wall v Bright* (1820) 1 Jac. & W 494.
[247] *Shaw v Foster* (1872) LR 5 HL 321.
[248] *Lysaght v Edwards* (1876) 2 Ch. D 499, accepted in *Rayner v Preston* (1881) 18 Ch. D 1.
[249] [2004] 1 WLR 1409.
[250] [2004] 1 WLR 1409.
[251] *Clarke v Ramuz* [1891] 2 QB 456.

rights in land, where the title to land is registered, equitable proprietary interests will bind subsequent purchasers only in so far as they have been registered on the land register. However, in some exceptional cases, an equitable interest will bind a third party despite an absence of registration when that third party has purchased the land subject to the rights of the third party. The matter is illustrated by the decision in **Lyus v Prowsa Developments**[252] where Mr and Mrs Lyus entered into a contract with a building company for the purchase of a plot of land on which they were intending to build a house. The effect of this contract was to create an equitable interest in favour of Mr and Mrs Lyus in the form of an estate contract capable of registration by notice on the land register. The building company had initially borrowed money from a bank by way of mortgage and the bank had a registered charge over all of the land belonging to the building company. When the building company went into liquidation, the bank sought to sell the land to another development company. The bank was able to sell the land free of Mr and Mrs Lyus's caution on the land, on the grounds that it had been registered after their legal charge on the land and therefore not binding on them. The bank sold the land to Prowsa Developments who expressly agreed to buy the land subject to Mr and Mrs Lyus's estate contract. When the issue arose as to whether Mr and Mrs Lyus's estate contract was binding on the Prowsa Developments, Dillon J held that is was on the grounds of a constructive trust. The development company had purchased the land expressly subject to the rights of Mr and Mrs Lyus. In the course of his judgment Dillon J explained that:

> it seems to me that the fraud on the part of the defendants in the present case lies not just in relying on the legal rights conferred by an Act of Parliament, but in the first defendant reneging on a positive stipulation in favour of the plaintiffs in the bargain under which the first defendant acquired the land. That makes, as it seems to me, all the difference. It has long since been held, for instance, in **Rochefoucauld v Boustead**,[253] that the provisions of the Statute of Frauds 1677 now incorporated in certain sections of the Law of Property Act 1925, cannot be used as an instrument of fraud, and that it is fraud for a person to whom land is agreed to be conveyed as trustee for another to deny the trust and relying on the terms of the statute to claim the land for himself. *Rochefoucauld v Boustead* was one of the authorities on which the judgment in **Bannister v Bannister**[254] was founded.[255]

However, it must be emphasised that a case such as **Lyus v Prowsa Developments**[256] is confined to its fact; in particular, the interest of Mr and Mrs Lyus bound the development company on the grounds that they had expressly agreed to purchase the land with the full knowledge and acceptance of Mr and Mrs Lyus's estate contract. What is crucial for the imposition of a contractive trust in cases such as **Lyus v Prowsa Developments**[257] is that the purchaser's conscience has been affected.

The decision in **Lyus v Prowsa Developments**[258] is illustrative of an unregistered proprietary interest in land binding a third party on the basis of a constructive trust. The principle is, however, not limited to unregistered proprietary interests. It is possible for a mere personal right in land, for example an occupational licence to occupy land, to bind a third party who purchases the land subject to the rights of the contractual licensee. An occupational licence typically arises where an owner of land contracts with another for

---

[252] [1982] 1 WLR 1044.
[253] [1897] 1 Ch. 196. This decision was considered in more detail in Chapter 5.
[254] [1948] 2 All ER 133.
[255] [1982] 1 WLR 1044 at 1054.
[256] [1982] 1 WLR 1044.
[257] *Ibid.*
[258] [1982] 1 WLR 1044.

the occupation of land in return for some consideration. For example, an owner of land may allow parents to live rent-free in his house in return for upkeeping the house in some form or other. Clearly the right of occupation is conferred by the owner and only binds the owner. Should the owner of the land sell the land to a third party, the third party will not be bound by the contractual licence. In *Ashburn Anstalt v Arnold*[259] the Court of Appeal held that a contractual licence was not a proprietary interest in land; however, such a licence could bind a subsequent purchaser of land in circumstances where the purchaser purchased the land expressly subject to the rights of the contractual licensee in situations where the conscience of the purchaser is affected. With regard to the question as to when the conscience of the purchaser will be affected, factors such as a purchase below market price will become relevant. In *IDC Group Ltd v Clark*[260] Browne-Wilkinson VC explained that a constructive trust would only be imposed on a purchaser with notice of the licence where there were very special circumstances showing that the transferee of the property undertook a new liability to give effect to provisions for the benefit of third parties.

A neat illustration of an occupational licence binding a purchaser under a constructive trust is found in the Court of Appeal's decision in *Binions v Evans*[261] where trustees of an estate agreed with one of the estate's employee's widow, Mrs Evans, that she could reside in a cottage on the estate for the rest for her life. This agreement, which was put into writing, required the widow to keep the cottage in a state of repair. The agreement constituted a contractual licence to occupy the land for the remainder of Mrs Evans's life. The trustees subsequently sold the land to Mr and Mrs Binions subject to the right of Mrs Evans in the cottage. Owing to the fact that Mrs Evans was to reside in the cottage, Mr and Mrs Binions negotiated a lower price than that asked by the trustees. After the title to the estate was conveyed to Mr and Mrs Binions, they brought an action to recover the cottage from Mrs Evans, who at the time was almost 80 years of age. In the Court of Appeal, Lord Denning MR held that Mr and Mrs Binions were bound by Mrs Evans's interest in the cottage on the grounds of a constructive trust. The constructive trust arose because it would have been unconscionable for Mr and Mrs Binions to deny Mrs Evans her right in the cottage which they clearly had knowledge of at the time of the purchase of the estate at a reduced price. The decision in *Binions v Evans*[262] along with a number of earlier decisions[263] did raise the question whether a contractual licence binding upon a purchaser by way of a constructive trust had the effect of elevating a personal right in land to a proprietary one. However, as explained by the Court of Appeal in *Ashburn Anstalt v Arnold*,[264] a contractual licence to occupy land does not confer a proprietary interest in land. The imposition of the constructive trust is a vehicle by which the purchaser is bound by the personal right of the contractual licence, on the grounds that not to do so would allow the purchaser to get away from a fraud. The matter is neatly summed up by one leading commentary on trust law, which states that:

> the constructive trust, used to protect [the contractual licensee's] interest in cases of this sort is probably not a trust at all. The court finds [the purchaser's] conscience to be person-ally affected by an obligation to give effect to [the contractual licensee's] interest, and therefore treat him constructively as though he were a trustee, to the limited extent that it

---

[259] [1989] Ch. 1.
[260] [1992] EGLR 187.
[261] [1972] Ch. 359.
[262] [1972] Ch. 359.
[263] *Errington v Errington Woods* [1952] 1 KB 290.
[264] [1989] Ch. 1.

is necessary to place him under a personal obligation to [the contractual licensee]. This does not mean that [the contractual licensee] acquires an equitable interest in the land, for otherwise his contractual license would be a valid equitable interest binding the land . . .[265]

Failure to comply with formality requirements for interests in land

Equity has long established the maxim that a person cannot use a statute to set up his own fraud. This maxim has already been covered in a number of the preceding chapters. For example, in Chapter 5, in the context of the formalities required for the creation of trusts, it was observed that a declaration of trust of land should be manifested and proved in writing pursuant to s. 53(1)(b) of the Law of Property Act 1925. Failure to comply with the section renders the intended trust unenforceable, but not void. Where the intended beneficiary can prove by some other evidence the existence of the trust of land, equity will enforce the trust. The trust is enforced on the grounds that it would be fraudulent for a person to take land absolutely in circumstances where he has orally agreed to hold it for the beneficiary. The view taken in this book is that in such a case the intended trustee will be become a constructive trustee for the intended beneficiary.[266]

Another area where the constructive trust has been imposed in circumstances where there has been an absence of statutory compliance is in the context of contracts for the sale of or other dispositions of an interest in land. The relevant formality is found in s. 2(1) of the Law of Property (Miscellaneous Provisions) Act 1989, which states: A contract for the sale or other disposition of an interest in land can only be made in writing and only by incorporating all the terms which the parties have expressly agreed in one document or, where contracts are exchanged, in each. Where a contract for the sale of an interest in land or some other disposition of land is not in writing, the contract is void. Section 2(5)(c) of the 1989 Act holds that the existence and operation of constructive trusts is not affected by s. 2(1). It is, therefore, possible for an oral agreement for the sale or disposition of an interest in land to be capable of being enforced by the imposition of a constructive trust. For example, in *Yaxley v Gotts*[267] the plaintiff wished to purchase land for development purposes with the intention of building flats for letting out. The land was, however, purchased by the defendant who orally agreed with the plaintiff that the plaintiff would be entitled to the ground floor flats in return for working on the upper floor flats as well as acting as a letting manager for the defendant. The agreement was not put into writing as required by s. 2(1) of the Law of Property (Miscellaneous Provisions) Act 1989 and therefore technically void. Despite the absence of writing, the Court of Appeal held that a proprietary estoppel arose in favour of the plaintiff who had been assured an interest in land and had relied on the assurance by suffering a detriment in developing the land. You will recall from the discussion above in the context of the common intention constructive trust that the doctrine of proprietary estoppel operates

---

[265] D. Hayton and C. Mitchell, *Hayton and Marshall Commentary and Cases on The Law of Trusts and Equitable Remedies* 12th edn (2005) at p. 380.

[266] *Rochefoucauld v Boustead* [1897] 1 Ch. 196. It is debatable whether a trust of land which fails to comply with s. 53(1)(b) is enforced as an express trust or as a constructive trust. In *Rochefoucauld v Boustead* Lindley LJ was of the opinion that the trust being enforced was essentially an express trust. The view in this book is that trust cannot be express simply on the grounds that the intended trustee has refused to honour the trust has fraudulently claimed the land for himself. The constructive trust argument has been applied in a number of cases; see, for example, *Bannister v Bannister* [1948] 2 All ER 133.

[267] [2000] Ch. 162.

to prevent a person from denying some interest in land which he has assured to the claimant.[268] A claimant will be able to establish an equity based on estoppel provided that he has relied on some assurance made by the defendant and has, as a result of such reliance, suffered a detriment. Where the claimant successfully establishes an equity in his favour, the court satisfies the equity by the award of remedy. In most cases, the award of the remedy is to give effect to the interest which the defendant has led the claimant to believe would be given. In the Court of Appeal Lord Walker held that the proprietary estoppel also gave rise to a constructive trust imposed on the defendant as a result of his unconscionable conduct. Lord Walker explained that the doctrine of proprietary estoppel was very similar to the common intention constructive trust, discussed above. He explained that a 'constructive trust of that sort is closely akin to, if not indistinguishable from, proprietary estoppel. Equity enforces it because it would be unconscionable for the other party to disregard the claimant's rights. Section 2(5) expressly saves the creation and operation of a constructive trust.'[269] This point of law was more recently confirmed in **Whittaker v Kinnear** [2011] EWHC 1479 where the High Court held that proprietary estoppel had survived the enactment of s. 2 of the Law of Property (Miscellaneous Provisions) Act 1989.

The House of Lords in **Yeoman's Row Management Ltd v Cobbe**[270] took the opportunity to review the circumstances when proprietary estoppel and constructive trusts would arise in the context of an oral contract for the sale of an interest in land or some other disposition of an interest in land. The facts of this case involved an appeal by Yeoman's Row Management Ltd (Yeoman's hereafter) against a decision of the Court of Appeal which held that the claimant, Mr Cobbe, had established a proprietary estoppel against Yeoman's arising out of an oral agreement between Yeoman's and Mr Cobbe.[271] The essence of the agreement, which was made with one of the directors of Yeoman's, was to the effect that Mr Cobbe would seek planning permission out of his own pocket to develop land belonging to Yeoman's, and that if permission was obtained, Yeoman's would sell the land to Mr Cobbe for a sum of £12 million. The agreement also made provision for Mr Cobbe to receive vacant possession of the land in order to erect six town houses. Additionally the agreement made allowance for Yeoman's to receive further profits from the sale of the town houses should Mr Cobbe succeed in making a profit in excess of £24 million. This agreement which was concluded 'in principle' did not cover all the matters relating to the sale of the land to Mr Cobbe, for example, matters relating to timescales regarding completion and building of the flats and so on. Planning permission was duly granted by the local authority; however, Yeoman's withdrew from the original agreement and claimed that Mr Cobbe has incurred expenditure on the land at his own risk. Mr Cobbe, however, commenced proceedings against Yeoman's on the grounds that they estopped from denying the interest in the land they had promised to give him; furthermore, that he had incurred the expenditure as a result of the assurances

---

[268] The requirements for a successful claim to proprietary estoppel were laid out in *Taylor Fashions* v *Liverpool Victoria Trustees Co Ltd* [1982] QB 133. More recently, see *Thorner v Majors* [2009] 1 WLR 776.

[269] [2000] Ch. 162 at 180. Although Lord Walker expressed the view that constructive trusts and proprietary estoppel are very similar, there are some fundamental differences between the two concepts. Fundamentally, proprietary estoppel involves the defendant making some representation to the claimant which is then relied on by the claimant at his detriment. The constructive trust imposed in common intention cases requires a common intention as to the shared ownership of land. These matters have been discussed above in the section on common intention constructive trusts.

[270] [2008] 1 WLR 1752. See M. Pawlowski, 'Oral Agreements: Estoppel, Constructive Trusts and Restitution' (2008) LT Review 163; S. Panesar, 'Enforcing Oral Contracts to Develop Land' (2009) ICCLR Vol. 20 Issue 5 at 165.

[271] [2006] 1 WLR 2964.

given by Yeoman's to him. Additionally, Mr Cobbe sought to argue that a constructive trust arose in his favour on the grounds of the unconscionability of Yeoman's conduct in withdrawing from the oral agreement.

At first instance, Etherton J held that a proprietary estoppel arose in favour of Mr Cobbe on the grounds that an assurance was made that he would have an interest in land belonging to Yeoman's and thereby suffered a detriment in expending money in reliance on that assurance.[272] In the course of his judgment, Etherton J held that the proprietary estoppel was sufficient grounds for the enforcement of the terms of the oral contract. This aspect of the decision of Etherton J is significant in that – despite s. 2(5) of the 1989 Act, which states that nothing affects the operation of constructive trusts – the judge was clearly of the view that an independent proprietary estoppel, without any reference to a constructive trust, could nevertheless be invoked to give effect to an oral contract for the sale of an interest in land. Unlike in *Yaxley v Gotts*,[273] Etherton J explained that, although the facts could give rise a constructive trust, the case was best decided on the grounds that an estoppel, independent of a constructive trust, arose in favour of Mr Cobbe. The judge explained that:

> Yeoman's had encouraged Mr Cobbe to believe that, if Mr Cobbe succeeded in obtaining planning permission in accordance with the second agreement, that agreement would be honoured, even though it was not legally binding, and that, in reliance on that belief, Mr Cobbe, to [the knowledge of Yeoman's] and with [its] encouragement, acted to his detriment. I have also concluded that, in all the circumstances, [Yeoman's] took an unconscionable advantage of him.[274]

On the basis of the estoppel, Etherton J held that Mr Cobbe was entitled to a half share in the increased value of the property as a result of the planning permission. The decision of Etherton J was approved by the Court of Appeal.

The House of Lords, however, overruled the decision of the Court of Appeal which had affirmed the decision of the Etherton J at first instance. There are three significant aspects to the decision of the House of Lords. Firstly, the House of Lords emphasised that proprietary estoppel was not a vehicle by which the formality requirements of s. 2(1) Law of Property (Miscellaneous Provisions) Act 1989 could be ignored. In other words, proprietary estoppel could not be used as a mechanism by which an oral contract for the sale of an interest in land could be enforced. Lord Scott held that 'proprietary estoppel cannot be prayed in aid in order to render enforceable an agreement that statute has declared to be void. The proposition that an owner of land can be estopped from asserting that an agreement is void for want of compliance with the requirements of section 2 is, in my opinion, unacceptable. The assertion is no more than the statute provides. Equity can surely not contradict the statute.'[275] This aspect of the decision of the House of Lords clearly rejects that proprietary estoppel can provide the basis of the enforcement of an oral agreement for the sale of an interest in land.

The second important feature of the decision in *Yeoman's Row Management Ltd* v *Cobbe*[276] related to the question of whether a case for proprietary estoppel arose on the facts. At first instance, and in the Court of Appeal, it was held that Mr Cobbe had established a successful claim to a remedy on the grounds of estoppel. In the House of Lords, Lord Scott attempted to address the question of estoppel by simply asking the question as

---

[272] *Yeoman's Row Management Ltd* v *Cobbe* [2005] WTLR 625.

[273] [2000] Ch. 162.

[274] *Yeoman's Row Management Ltd* v *Cobbe* [2005] WTLR 625 at para. 123.

[275] [2008] 1 WLR 1752 at 1769.

[276] [2008] 1 WLR 1752. See M. Pawlowski, 'Oral Agreements: Estoppel, Constructive Trusts and Restitution' (2008) LT Review 163.

to what exactly were the grounds for invoking the doctrine of estoppel. It has already been observed above that a successful claim on grounds of proprietary estoppel requires the claimant to establish that an equity has arisen in his or her favour, in particular, that the defendant made some assurance to the claimant that the claimant would have some interest in the land. Lord Scott held that the facts did not give rise to any estoppel, on the grounds that Yeoman's had not made any concrete assurance that Mr Cobbe was to be given some interest in the land. The oral agreement which had been entered into was nothing more than an agreement 'in principle'. There was still room for further negotiations and the agreement did not refer to all the terms which the parties would have wanted to include. In this respect Mr Cobbe could not be heard to be asserting that the oral agreement was enforceable but for the absence of writing. Lord Scott explained that the oral agreement did not profess to create an expectation that Mr Cobbe would be granted an interest in land. At most the expectation Mr Cobbe had was that there would be further negotiations which would lead to a formal agreement. In this respect, the decision in **Yeoman's Row Management Ltd v Cobbe** illustrates that an oral agreement 'subject to contract' is repugnant to a finding of proprietary estoppel. Lord Scott explained that 'the reason why, in a "subject to contract" case, a proprietary estoppel cannot ordinarily arise is that the would-be purchaser's expectation of acquiring an interest in the property in question is subject to a contingency that is entirely under the control of the other party to the negotiations . . .'[277]

Finally, in relation to the question of whether a constructive trust arose in favour of Mr Cobbe, the House of Lords held that no such trust had arisen on the facts despite what may have been perceived as unconscionable conduct on the part of Yeoman's. In the course of his judgment, Lord Scott explained that, whilst there were instances where a constructive trust arose when two or more parties negotiated the joint venture to develop land, also known as the 'equity in **Pallant v Morgan**',[278] the facts of the present case were very different from those cases where a constructive trust arose in the joint venture to develop land. The so called 'equity in **Pallant v Morgan**' was explained by Lord Scott in the following manner.

> A particular factual situation where a constructive trust has been held to have been created arises out of joint ventures relating to property, typically land. If two or more persons agree to embark on a joint venture which involves the acquisition of an identified piece of land and a subsequent exploitation of, or dealing with, the land for the purposes of the joint venture, and one of the joint venturers, with the agreement of the others who believe him to be acting for their joint purposes, makes the acquisition in his own name but subsequently seeks to retain the land for his own benefit, the court will regard him as holding the land on trust for the joint venturers. This would be either an implied trust or a constructive trust arising from the circumstances and if, as would be likely from the facts as described, the joint venturers have not agreed and cannot agree about what is to be done with the land, the land would have to be resold and, after discharging the expenses of its purchase and any other necessary expenses of the abortive joint venture, the net proceeds of sale divided equally between the joint venturers.[279]

The constructive trust arising under the 'equity in **Pallant v Morgan**' is part and parcel of the much wider ground for the imposition of a constructive trust that a defendant is not entitled to keep absolutely for himself in circumstances where he has agreed to

---

[277] [2008] 1 WLR 1752 at 1767. See also the earlier decision of the Privy Council in *Attorney-General of Hong Kong v Humphrey's Estate (Queen's Gardens) Ltd* [1987] AC 114.

[278] [1952] 2 All ER 951.

[279] [2008] 1 WLR 1752 at 1769.

respect the beneficial interest therein of the claimant. The matter was neatly explained by Millett J in *Lonrho plc v Fayed (No. 2)*[280] where the judge commented that:

> equity will intervene by way of constructive trust, not only to compel a defendant to restore the plaintiff's property to him, but also to require a defendant to disgorge property which should have acquired, if at all, for the plaintiff. In the latter category of case, the defendant's wrong lies not in the acquisition of the property, which may or not have been lawful, but in his subsequent denial of the plaintiff's beneficial interest. For such to be the case, however, the defendant must either have acquired property which but for his wrongdoing would have belonged to the plaintiff, or he must have acquired property in circumstances in which he cannot conscientiously retain it against the plaintiff.[281]

The facts of *Pallant v Morgan*[282] involved two parties who agreed, prior to the auction of a piece of land in which both were interested, that one would bid for the land whilst the other would refrain from bidding. The agreement was to the effect that if the bid was successful, the land would be divided between both parties. The party who bid for the land was successful in acquiring it but subsequently failed to agree the terms of division of the land between the parties. When the party who had acquired the land sought to claim absolute ownership of the land, the court held that the land was held on constructive trust for the both parties jointly and that if the parties disagreed as to the division of the land, it was to be divided equally between them.[283] On the facts of *Yeoman's Row Management Ltd v Cobbe*[284] Lord Scott held that the 'equity in *Pallant v Morgan*' did not arise. Unlike the facts of *Pallant v Morgan*, in the present case, the land was already owned by Yeoman's and there was no joint venture agreement to develop the land before the land was purchased by Yeoman's. The basis of the imposition of a constructive trust in cases such as *Pallant v Morgan* is that it would be inequitable for the defendant to retain absolute ownership in property when he purchased the property knowing that he was to jointly exploit it with the claimant. Having dismissed the 'equity in *Pallant v Morgan*', Lord Scott proceeded to question what other grounds there could be for the imposition of a constructive trust in favour of Mr Cobbe. Having not found any grounds for the imposition of a constructive trust on the facts, Lord Scott questioned whether a constructive trust could be simply imposed in favour of the party who had failed to receive an expected benefit under an unenforceable oral agreement 'in principle'. To this question, his Lordship explained that 'a claim for the imposition of a constructive trust in order to provide a remedy for a disappointed expectation engendered by a representation made in the context of incomplete contractual negotiations is, in my opinion, misconceived and cannot be sustained by reliance on unconscionable behaviour on the part of the representor'.[285]

Secret trusts and mutual wills

In Chapter 7 it was observed that a secret trust arose in circumstances where a person was left property in a will on the understanding that he or she would hold it on trust for

---

[280] [1992] 1 WLR 1.

[281] [1992] 1 WLR 1 at 9–10.

[282] [1952] 2 All ER 951.

[283] See also *Banner Homes Group plc v Luff Developments Ltd* [2000] Ch. 372 and *Kilcarne Holdings Ltd v Targetfollow (Birmingham) Ltd* [2005] 2 P & CR 105.

[284] [2008] 1 WLR 1752. See M. Pawlowski, 'Oral Agreements: Estoppel, Constructive Trusts and Restitution' (2008) LT Review 163.

[285] [2008] 1 WLR 1752 at 1773.

another person. Thus, a legatee receiving money in a will on the understanding that it was for the benefit of some secret beneficiary was bound to hold it for the benefit of that other person, the secret beneficiary. Despite the apparent conflict of secret trusts with the testamentary formalities contained in s. 9 of the Wills Act 1837, one of the reasons why secret trusts are enforced is to prevent fraud. Clearly a legatee who derives some benefit under a will on the understanding that he will hold it for the benefit of another person cannot rely on s. 9 of the Wills Act 1837 to claim the property for himself. To do so would encourage a statute to be used as an instrument for fraud. Where the legatee refuses to comply with the oral or otherwise written agreement that he will hold for the secret beneficiary, equity will impose a constructive trust, preventing the legatee from benefiting from his fraud and thereby being unjustly enriched at the expense of the secret beneficiary.

Despite what has been said in the preceding paragraph, the question whether secret trusts are indeed a species of constructive trusts is, however, unresolved. It was also observed in Chapter 7 that secret trusts can be of two kinds. The first kind is a fully secret trust, which arises where on the face of the will a person receives the trust property absolutely as a legatee, but on the understanding that he will hold it for the secret beneficiary. In such a case, the refusal of the apparent legatee to hold the property for the benefit of the secret trustee would clearly amount to a fraud. To prevent the fraud, the legatee will be compelled to hold the property as a constructive trustee for the secret beneficiary. On the other hand, in the case of a half-secret trust, property is left to a trustee on the face of the will without disclosing the identity of the beneficiary. In the case of a half-secret trust, there can be no question of fraud on the part of the half-secret trustee because he has accepted the office of trusteeship. It was observed in Chapter 7 that despite the absence of fraud in the case of a half-secret trust, the half-secret trust was enforced on the grounds that the trust was declared during the lifetime of a testator. The effect of the will was to merely constitute the *inter vivos* trust.[286] On the basis that a half-secret trust is not prone to fraud, it has been argued that such a secret trust is not imposed as a constructive trust: rather the express trust declared during the testator's lifetime is being imposed.[287] The question whether a fully secret trust is enforced as a constructive trust and a half-secret trust is enforced as an express trust if not fully answered yet.[288] If both a fully secret trust and a half-secret trust are said to operate outside the Wills Act 1837, in the sense that they are trusts declared during the lifetime of the settlor, there is much to be said that such trusts are indeed express trusts. However, even though such trusts are declared during the lifetime of the settlor, Professor Alastair Hudson explains that they cannot be express trusts. He writes:

> [A] secret trust is a trust not properly constituted by the settlor but the substance of which was communicated to persons who are named as legatees under the settlor's will. As such, the enforcement of the settlor's promise could not be an express trust because the settlor retains the right to change her will, something which would not be permitted if an express trust had already been created over . . . property. The only viable trust law analysis is therefore that the secret trust must be in the form of a constructive trust.[289]

In the case of mutual wills, which were considered in Chapter 7, it is trite law that a constructive trust will be imposed preventing a person from revoking his will in breach

---

[286] ***Blackwell v Blackwell*** [1929] AC 318 in which a secret trust was said to 'dehor' the will, that is operate outside the provisions of the Wills Act 1837.

[287] See, for example, L.A. Sheridan, 'English and Irish Secret Trusts' (1951) 67 LQR 314.

[288] See, for example, D. Hodge, 'Secret Trusts: The Fraud Theory Revisited' (980) Conv. 341.

[289] A. Hudson, *Equity and Trusts* 5th edn (2007) at p. 556. See also A. Hudson, *Equity and Trusts* 6th edn (2010).

of the agreement which was concluded by the parties making mutual wills. Mutual wills are wills created by two or more persons in accordance with an agreement they have made during their lifetimes. Typically, mutual wills take the form of each person leaving his or her property to the other under similar terms in a will. For example, a husband and wife may enter into an agreement to make wills leaving each other's property to the other on the understanding that the survivor will leave the property to some other third party, for example their daughter. Although a will is revocable up until the testator's death, if the husband dies before his wife, having left all his property to his wife, the wife, although at liberty to revoke her will and make a new one in favour of others, will be bound by the agreement and a constructive trust will be imposed on property subject to the mutual will. In other words, should the wife revoke the will and leave the property to someone other than her daughter, a constructive trust will be imposed and the daughter will benefit from the agreement, leading to the execution of the mutual wills. The constructive trust is imposed to prevent the unconscionable conduct of the survivor who has benefited from receiving property on the understanding that it will be dealt with in a particular manner. In this respect, the constructive trust is imposed to prevent fraud. The matter is neatly explained by Lord Camden in **Dufour v Pereira**[290] where the judge explained that:

> the parties by the mutual will do each of them devise, upon the engagement of the other, that he will likewise devise in manner therein mentioned. The instrument is the evidence of the agreement; and he that dies first does by his death carry the agreement on his part into execution. If the other then refuses he is guilty of fraud, can never unbind himself, and becomes a trustee of course. For no man shall deceive another to his prejudice. By engaging to do something that is in his power he is made a trustee for the performance and transmits that trust to those that claim under him.[291]

Conclusion

The focus in this chapter has been on identifying some of the contexts in which English law imposes a constructive trust. What is self-evident from this chapter is that the constructive trust has been imposed in a number of quite different contexts. A remarkable feature of the constructive trust has been its ability to resolve ownership disputes in both commercial and family contexts. However, what is equally clear from the existing law on constructive trusts is that it has often become very difficult to define with exact precision the grounds for the imposition of a constructive trust. The reason for this is that each context brings with it different policy concerns. However, it is fair to say that in attempting a broad rationalisation of these contexts the constructive trust is imposed to prevent the unconscionability of the constructive trustee. Within the commercial context, a constructive trust has been imposed to prevent a fiduciary from benefiting from unauthorised profits, to attach liability to individuals who have assisted in breach of trust or some other

---

[290] (1769) 1 Dick 419.

[291] (1769) 1 Dick 419 in 2 Hargraves Juridical Arguments at 304 cited in *Re Goodchild (deceased)* [1996] 1 WLR 694 at 699. More recently, in *Re Cleaver (deceased)* [1981] 1 WLR 939 at 947 Nourse LJ explained that 'the principle of all these cases is that a court of equity will not permit a person to whom property is transferred by way of gift, but on the faith of an agreement or clear understanding that it is to be dealt with in a particular way for the benefit of a third person, to deal with that property inconsistently with that agreement or understanding. If he attempts to do so after having received the benefit of the gift equity will intervene by imposing a constructive trust on the property which is the subject matter of the agreement or understanding.'

fiduciary duty, or where some commercial third party, such as a bank, has received property transferred in breach of trust. In the family context, the constructive trust has operated to resolve ownership disputes over the family home where, as observed in this chapter, the law has been both controversial and fast developing in the past few years. In other areas, the constructive trust has been imposed where there has been an absence of strict formality, thereby preventing the constructive trustee from taking a benefit, on the grounds that 'equity will not allow a statute to be used as an instrument for fraud'.

Case studies

1   Suppose that a trustee is holding a very profitable lease of a market for a beneficiary. The lease has come to an end and the landlord is quite happy to renew the lease for the trust. However, envious of the fact that the lease of the market is making very good profits for the beneficiary, the trustee lies to the beneficiary and tells him that the landlord has refused to renew the lease. Two months later the trustee renews the lease for himself. The beneficiary finds out what has happened and is not too happy with the situation.

- *Do you think that it is right for the lease to be kept by the trustee?*
- *Would your answer be different if the landlord had refused to renew the lease for the beneficiary. In other words, there was no chance of the beneficiary ever getting a renewal of that lease.*

2   Gavin and Vicky met sometime in 1998 and started a love relationship. They always intended to get married but never did so, worried about committing themselves into a marital relationship. In 2000 Gavin purchased a house which was conveyed in his name only, although he told Vicky that the house was as much hers as it was his. In fact, he told Vicky that it would be unwise to put the house into both their names as this would have certain tax implications. In fact this was just not true as Gavin had no intention of making Vicky the owner of the house. Gavin and Vicky had two children between 2001 and 2007. Throughout those years, Vicky worked part-time and looked after the children and paid all the costs towards looking after their children, as well as putting food on the table. Vicky's contribution helped Gavin discharge the mortgage on the house which he would not otherwise have been able to do so. Last year, Vicky found out that Gavin was having an affair and has moved out of the house to live with her mother. She has commenced proceedings against Gavin, claiming that the house which was purchased in his name belongs to her as well as Gavin.

- *How can the house belong to Vicky when she is not on the legal title?*
- *Would it be unfair not to give her some interest in the house?*
- *Is unfairness an appropriate ground for helping Vicky?*

3   Harry and Laura married a few years ago and have since been living in a flat. Recently they decided a buy a house of their own. They saw a house in Warwick, which was advertised for £210,000. They very much liked the house but realised that they could not afford it. Harry inquired into the possibility of getting a mortgage from Midwest Bank. The bank was prepared to advance up to £150,000, which left a shortfall of £60,000.

Harry's father agreed to advance £20,000 to Harry. The remaining £40,000 was secured by the sale of Harry's flat in Kenilworth. The legal title to the house in Warwick was conveyed in Harry's name only, although he had assured Laura that this was going to be their family home and one day when they got married a place to bring their children up. The legal costs of the conveyance came to £1200 and this was paid by Laura.

Advise Laura and Harry's father if they have any interest in the house which is in Harry's name.

Moot points

1 What criteria will a court use when exercising its discretion to grant relief against forfeiture of property under s. 2(1) of the Forfeiture Act 1982?

2 It is well established that a fiduciary who makes an unauthorised profit cannot keep it. He will either have to account for the profit or hold the profit on constructive trust for his principal. Liability in this respect is strict and the court is not swayed by the honesty of the fiduciary and neither is it concerned with the fact that the profit utilised by the fiduciary could never have been utilised by the principal. What is the rationale of disallowing a fiduciary from keeping profits which would not otherwise have been capable of being utilised by the principal?

3 Where a fiduciary makes an unauthorised profit at his principal's expense he will be required to either account for the profit or the profit will be held on a constructive trust for the principal. What principles, if any, govern whether the court will order an account for profits or impose a constructive trust on the profit? Should a constructive trust be imposed on profits in circumstances when they have not being acquired by the use of the principal's own property? Amongst other decisions, you are advised to read the decision in *Attorney General of Hong Kong* v *Reid* [1994] 1 AC 324.

4 The decision of the House of Lords in *Stack* v *Dowden* [2007] 2 AC 432 has generally been regarded as a welcome development in the law relating to constructive trusts and the joint ownership of a family home. What do you regard to be the salient features of the decision in that case? Does the decision afford any guidance as to the quantification of a beneficial interest under a constructive trust where the title is taken in the sole name of a person who is cohabiting with another?

5 What do you understand by the 'equity in *Pallant* v *Morgan*' arising from the decision in *Pallant* v *Morgan* [1952] 2 All ER 951 and explain why it was not applied in the House of Lords in *Yeoman's Row Management Ltd* v *Cobbe* [2008] 1 WLR 1752.

6 In its report, Law Com No. 307, *Cohabitation: The Financial Consequences of Relationship Breakdown*, (2007), the Law Commission has proposed a statutory regime to govern the breakdown of relationships in the context of shared ownership of land. What are the key features of the proposal and what type of relationships will be covered by the Law Commission's proposal?

7 Critically evaluate how the decision of the Supreme Court in *Kernott* v *Jones* [2011] UKSC 53 further clarifies how the court should quantify the beneficial interests in land where property is taken in joint names but where the beneficial interests have not been decided by the parties.

8 The decision of the Court of Appeal in *Sinclair Investments (UK) Ltd* v *Versailles Trade Finance Ltd (In Administration)* [2011] EWCA Civ. 347 marks a fundamental change from what was thought to be the position regarding proprietary claims to bribes and other unauthorised gains made by fiduciaries. Critically evaluate the extent to which the need for a proprietary base linking the unauthorised profit to the beneficiaries' original property is a perquisite for a proprietary claim to such unauthorised profits.

● **Further reading**

Bridge, S. 'Cohabitation: Why Legislative Reform is Necessary' [2007] Fam. Law 911. Examines the reasons why legislation is needed in the context of breakdown in cohabitation cases and looks at financial relief and the interests of children.

Cowan, D. '*Lister & Co* v *Stubbs*: Who Profits?' (1996) JBL 22. Examines the imposition of a constructive trust in *A-G Hong Kong* v *Reid* and argues that the imposition of a constructive trust in cases of bribes undermines the distinction between personal and proprietary claims, and gives certain creditors an unfair advantage over others in the case of the insolvency of the person receiving the bribe.

Etherton, T. 'Constructive Trusts: A New Model for Equity and Unjust Enrichment' (2008) CLJ 265. Examines the decision in *Stack* v *Dowden* with a view to arguing a restitutionary basis for the imposition of a common intention constructive trust.

Etherton, T. 'Constructive Trusts and Proprietary Estoppel: The Search for Clarity and Principle' (2009) Conv. 104. Examines the relationship between the doctrine of proprietary estoppel and the common intention constructive trust.

Gardner, S. 'Family Property Today' (2008) LQR 422. Provides a critical assessment of the case law on common intention constructive trusts, including the decision in *Stack* v *Dowden* and decisions after that case.

Halliwell, M. 'The Ghost of *Lister & Co* v *Stubbs*' (2005) Conv. 88. Examine the decision of the Privy Council in *A-G for Hong Kong* v *Reid*.

Haytan, D. 'No Proprietary Liability for Bribes and other Secret Profits?' (2011) Trust Law International 3. Examines the decision of the Court of Appeal in *Sinclair Investments (UK) Ltd* v *Versailles Trade Finance Ltd (In Administration)*.

Hicks, A. 'The Remedial Principle of *Keech* v *Sandford* Reconsidered' (2010) CLJ 287. Re-examines whether the decision in *Keech* v *Sandford* was intended to lay down such a wide principle of law.

Hughes, D., M. Davis and L. Jacklin, 'Come Live with Me and be my Love – Consideration of the 2007 Law Commission Proposals on Cohabitation Breakdown' (2008) Conv. 197. Examines the proposals of the Law Commission on cohabitation breakdown, in addition to offering other ways forward to resolve the problems of cohabitation breakdown.

McCormack, G. 'The Remedial Constructive Trust and Commercial Transactions' Company Lawyer (1996) Vol. 17(1). Considers the remedial constructive trust and its operation in family and commercial cases, with particular reference to the insolvency of the constructive trustee and the rights of the constructive beneficiary over those of other creditors of the constructive trustee.

Oakley, A.J. 'The Bribed Fiduciary as Constructive Trustee' (1994) 53 CLJ 31. Examines the decision of the Privy Council in *A-G for Hong Kong* v *Reid* and the extent to which a bribed fiduciary should hold the bribe on constructive trust for its principal.

Panesar, S. 'Enforcing Oral Contracts to Develop Land in English Law' (2009) Vol. 20 165. Examines the decision of the House of Lords in *Yeoman's* v *Cobbe*.

Pawlowski, M. 'Oral Agreements: Estoppel, Constructive Trusts and Restitution' (2008) LT Review 163. Examines the decision in *Yeoman's* v *Cobbe* in respect of the imposition of a constructive trust in cases of oral contracts to develop land.

Piska, N. 'Intention, Fairness and the Presumption of Resulting Trust after *Stack* v *Dowden*' (2008) 71 MLR 120. Critically evaluates the decision of the House of Lords in *Stack* v *Dowden*.

Swaddling, W. 'The Common Intention Constructive Trust in the House of Lords: An Opportunity Missed' (2007) LQR 511. Critically evaluates the decision of the House of Lords in *Stack* v *Dowden* and argues that the House of Lords missed an opportunity to analyse the common intention trust in detail and its relationship with the remedial constructive trust in addition to the resulting trust and the equitable doctrine of proprietary estoppel.

Visit **www.mylawchamber.co.uk/panesar** to access study support resources including interactive multiple choice questions, practice exam questions with guidance, podcasts, weblinks, legal newsfeed all linked to the **Pearson eText** version of Exploring Equity and Trusts which you can **search**, **highlight** and **personalise** with your **own notes** and **bookmarks**.

Use Case Navigator to read in full some of the key cases referenced in this chapter with commentary and questions:

Kernott v *Jones* [2010] EWCA Civ 578
Lloyds Bank plc v *Rosset* [1991] 1 AC 107
Sinclair Investments (UK) Ltd v *Versailles Trale Finance Ltd (In Administration)* [2011] EWCA 347
Stack v *Dowden* [2007] UKHL 17
Westdeutsche Landesbank Girozentrale v *Islington LBC* [1996] AC 699 (HL)
Boardman v *Phipps* [1967] 2 AC 46

14

Constructive trusts, part III: Imposing constructive trusts – intermeddling with trust property

Learning objectives

After completing this chapter you should be able to:

→ understand the nature of liability for intermeddling with trust property

→ understand the consequences of the imposition of a constructive trust in cases of intermeddling with a breach of trust

→ understand the difference of constructive liability for knowing assistance in a breach of trust and knowing receipt of trust property

→ understand the requisite ingredients for liability for knowing assistance

→ understand case law development regarding the test of dishonesty applied in liability for knowing assistance cases

→ understand the requirements for liability for knowing receipt of trust property

→ explain how the test of unconscionability works in the case of liability for knowing receipt of trust property

→ assess whether strict liability for knowing receipt of trust property is a more effective way forward.

SETTING THE SCENE

Royal Brunei v *Tan* [1995] 2 AC 378: Money held on trust by an airline agent, a breach of trust by that company and dishonest assistance by the director of the company

The facts of the decision of the Privy in *Royal Brunei* v *Tan* illustrate the concerns of this chapter. Royal Brunei Airlines appointed Borneo Leisure Travel (BLT) as its agent for both passenger and cargo transportation. The agency agreement stipulated that BLT was to hold all monies received from the sale of passenger and cargo transportation for the airline until accounted for. The effect of this was to constitute BLT a trustee for the airline company. The money received by BLT by sale of airline tickets and cargo transportation was not put into a separate account: instead the money was put into the general account of BLT. The defendant, who was the principal shareholder and managing director of BLT, allowed the money accountable to the airline company to be used for BLT's own purposes. When asked by the airline company to account for the money received, BLT had insufficient funds in order to do so. The airline company terminated the agency agreement and commenced proceedings against the defendant to recover the money on the grounds that he had knowingly assisted in a breach of trust by BLT.

The facts of *Royal Brunei* v *Tan* illustrate that third parties may acquire liability for intermeddling with trust property. In the case, BLT had agreed to act as a trustee for the Royal Brunei Airlines. The trust relationship was between the Airline and BLT. Despite this, the case illustrates that, as well as the primary trustee of a trust, other parties may become liable for helping to bring about a breach of trust, or for receiving trust property with the requisite knowledge that the property in question is subject to a trust. In *Royal Brunei* the claim was against the director of BLT who had allowed trust property to be used in breach of trust.

This chapter explores the liability of third parties who intermeddle with trust property. There are two principal ways in which such intermeddling may take place. Either the third party knowingly assists in breach of trust or knowingly receives trust property in breach of trust. In both cases, equity imposes constructive trust liability on third parties who intermeddle with trust property. This chapter explores the constructive trust liability for knowing assistance in a breach of trust and knowing receipt of trust property. This area of law has been the source of much litigation in recent years and the courts have had to entertain questions relating to the precise state of mind of a third party that assists in a breach of trust or receives property in breach of trust.

Introduction

So far it has been observed that the trust relationship is primarily between trustee and beneficiary. Where the trustee acts in breach of trust he will liable to replace the loss caused to the trust estate.[1] Where the trustee is insolvent, the beneficiary may be able to follow his or her equitable interest into the hands of any third parties who acquire the trust property and are not bona fide purchaser of it. Whilst the beneficiaries clearly have a claim against the original trustee of the trust for breach of trust, the general rule is that

---

[1] Liability for breach of trust is analysed in Chapter 20.

other third parties who may deal with the trust property do not automatically become liable as trustees. For example, an agent employed to deal with the trust property in a particular manner does not automatically become a trustee. Provided that such agent complies with his normal duties he does not become liable to the beneficiary. Even where an agent acts in breach of his normal duties, his liability will arise under normal principles of law and not in trust. For example, where an agent who is employed to deal with investment of the trust property, negligently invests the trust property, his liability will be in the law of contract or in the tort of negligence and the trustee will have a claim against him. For example, in **Mara v Browne**[2] a solicitor who was acting on behalf of trustees wrongfully invested the trust funds, thereby causing a loss to the trust estate. The court held that the trustee was liable for breach of contract, but was a not a constructive trustee. On the facts of the case, the claim failed on the grounds that it was time barred.

The general rule that third parties do not automatically acquire trust liability can be displaced when those third parties exceed their authority and intermeddle with the trust property. Where they do intermeddle with the trust property they acquire liability in the form of a constructive trustee. Intermeddling with trust property can take two principal forms. The third party either knowingly assists in a breach of trust or knowingly receives trust property in breach of trust. In both cases, the imposition of a constructive trust liability gives the beneficiary a right to bring action against that third party. Liability for assisting in a breach of trust or receiving trust property in breach of trust has long been recognised in trust law. Where a stranger assists in a breach of trust by the primary trustee he will acquire secondary liability to make good the loss that he has caused as a result of the breach of trust. Liability will only arise where the stranger dishonestly assists in the breach of trust. Lord Selborne LC explained in **Barnes v Addy**[3] that 'strangers are not to be made constructive trustees merely because they act as the agents of trustees in transactions within their legal powers, transactions, perhaps of which the Court of equity may disapprove, unless those agents receive and become chargeable with some part of the trust property, or unless they assist with the knowledge in a dishonest and fraudulent design on the part of the trustees'.[4] The secondary liability of a stranger who assists in a breach of trust arises by virtue of the imposition of a constructive trust on him. It is sometimes said that the stranger who is made liable as a constructive trustee is a trustee *de son tort*. The idea of trusteeship *de son tort* was explained by A.L. Smith LJ in **Mara v Browne**[5]: 'It appears to me if one, not being a trustee and not having authority from a trustee, takes it upon himself to intermeddle with trust matters or to do acts characteristic of the office of trustee, he may thereby make himself what is called in law a trustee of his own wrong – *i.e.*, a trustee *de son tort*, or, as it is also termed, a constructive trustee.'[6]

Nature of liability for knowing assistance

One particular context in which a constructive trust operates is where a third party (stranger) assists in bringing about a breach of trust committed by the primary trustee. It is a generally recognised principle of trust law that a person who assists in bringing about a breach of trust will be held accountable as a constructive trustee.

---

[2] [1986] 1 Ch. 199.
[3] (1874) 9 Ch. App. 244.
[4] (1874) 9 Ch. App. 244 at 251.
[5] [1896] 1 Ch. 199.
[6] [1896] 1 Ch. 199 at 209.

APPLYING THE LAW

Thomas is holding a sum of £300,000 on trust for Victor's children on their attaining the age of 25 years. Thomas is also a wine merchant and his business has not been doing well and he finds himself in financial difficulty. His accountant tells him that he needs £100,000 as soon as possible in order to keep the business running. Thomas transfers £100,000 from the trust account to the accountant in order to keep the business running. Unfortunately, the business collapses and the £100,000 is all used up. Thomas is bankrupt; however, the beneficiaries seek to make the accountant liable to replace the loss on the grounds that he was aware that the money was used from the trust account.

Is the accountant liable?

Although there is no real doubt that a person who does assist in bringing about a breach of trust should be made accountable in some way in equity, the appropriateness of converting such a person into a constructive trustee is more controversial. There are two reasons for this criticism. In the first place, the person assisting in the breach of trust may not in many cases have any control over ownership of property belonging in equity to another person bringing the claim against him. In this respect, the question has arisen whether it is wholly appropriate to confer constructive trusteeship on someone who never had trust property in his control. Secondly, in the most typical case where a trust is imposed, the beneficiary acquires both a personal claim against a defaulting trustee as well as a proprietary claim to follow his or her equitable interest into the hands of the trustee or any other party who cannot purport to show that he or she is a bona fide purchaser of the legal title without notice of the trust.[7] In the context of a constructive trust imposed on a person who assists in a breach of trust, there is no proprietary claim since there is no property in question in so far as the constructive trustee is concerned. The imposition of the constructive trust only gives rise to a personal claim against the constructive trustee to replace the loss which has been caused to the trust estate. It is because of these criticisms that some have questioned whether it is wholly appropriate to discuss the liability of a person who assists in a breach of trust as one arising under a constructive trust. It is therefore not surprising that some texts avoid constructive trust language and prefer to describe the liability of a person who assists in a breach of trust as 'accessory liability'. The courts have explained on a number of occasions the undesirability of using the constructive trust language in cases where there has been a dishonest assistance in a breach of trust. For example, in *Dubai Aluminium Co Ltd v Salaam*[8] Millett LJ was of the view that 'we should now discard the words "accountable as constructive trustee" in this context and substitute the words "accountable in equity"'.[9] However, at the present time the courts continue to use the constructive trust language in cases where a defendant dishonestly assists in a breach of trust despite never having had any control over identifiable property. In *Westdeutsche Landesbank Girozentrale v Islington LBC*[10] Lord Browne-Wilkinson, having explained that one of the fundamental principles of trust law was that there should be some identifiable property over which a

VISIT CASE NAVIGATOR

---

[7] The beneficiary will of course have to elect between a personal or a proprietary claim.
[8] [2002] 3 WLR 1913.
[9] [2002] 3 WLR 1913 at 1946.
[10] [1996] AC 669 (HL).

trust was to exist, said that there was an exception in cases where a constructive trust arose in cases of dishonest assistance by a third party.

A more contemporary explanation of constructive trust liability for dishonestly assisting in a breach of trust was provided by the Privy Council in *Royal Brunei Airlines* v *Tan*.[11] The decision of the Privy Council remains the basis of the modern law on liability for assisting in a breach of trust[12] and, as will be seen below, has been further clarified and elaborated upon by more recent decisions. In *Royal Brunei Airlines* v *Tan* Lord Nicholls explained the rationale for constructive trust liability for knowing assistance in the following manner:

> The rationale is not far to seek. Beneficiaries are entitled to expect that those who become trustees will fulfil their obligations. They are also entitled to expect, and this is only a short step further, that those who become trustees will be permitted to fulfil their obligations without deliberate intervention from third parties. They are entitled to expect that third parties will refrain from intentionally intruding in the trustee–beneficiary relationship and thereby hindering a beneficiary from receiving his entitlement in accordance with the terms of the trust instrument. There is here a close analogy with breach of contract. A person who knowingly procures a breach of contract, or knowingly interferes with the due performance of a contract, is liable to the innocent party. The underlying rationale is the same.[13]

Requisites for liability for knowing assistance

In order for a stranger to be held liable for assisting in a breach of trust a number of requirements must be met before liability is attached. These requirements were identified by Mance LJ in *Grupo Torras SA* v *Al-Sabah*:[14]

- A breach of trust or fiduciary duty by someone other than the defendant
- Assistance by the defendant
- Dishonesty on the part of the defendant
- Resulting loss to the claimant.

It will be seen that these general requirements have over the years been refined, particularly in relation to the question of dishonesty on the part of the defendant who assists in the breach of trust. These matters are explored in more detail in the subsections below.

A breach of trust or fiduciary duty by someone other than the defendant

The most typical situation in which a stranger will be held liable for dishonestly assisting in a breach of trust is where an express trustee breaches the trust and the stranger assists in bringing about that breach of trust. For example, in *Royal Brunei Airlines* v *Tan*[15]

---

[11] [1995] 2 AC 378.
[12] Affirmed by the House of Lords in *Twinsectra Ltd* v *Yardley* [2002] 2 All ER 377.
[13] [1995] 2 AC 378 at 387. See also P. Ridge, 'Justifying the Remedies For Dishonest Assistance' (2008) 124 LQR 445.
[14] [1999] CLC 1469.
[15] [1995] 2 AC 378.

Royal Brunei Airlines appointed Borneo Leisure Travel (BLT) as its agent for both passenger and cargo transportation. The agency agreement stipulated that BLT was to hold all monies received from the sale of passenger and cargo transportation for the airline until accounted for. The effect of this was to constitute BLT a trustee for the airline company. The money received by BLT by sale of airline tickets and cargo transportation was not put into a separate account: instead the money was put into the general account of BLT. The defendant, who was the principal shareholder and managing director of BLT, allowed the money accountable to the airline company to be used for BLT's own purposes. When asked by the airline company to account for the money received, BLT had insufficient funds in order to do so. The airline company terminated the agency agreement and commenced proceedings against the defendant to recover the money on the grounds that he had knowingly assisted in a breach of trust by BLT. The Privy Council held that the defendant had indeed assisted in a breach of trust which had been committed by the primary trustee, BLT, and therefore was liable to account for the loss it had suffered. The decision of the Privy Council was a landmark case as it attempted to formulate the requirement of dishonesty on the part of the defendant that was in order needed to find liability for assisting in a breach of trust. This aspect of the judgment is explored in the section on dishonesty below.

Although liability for assisting in a breach of trust arises when an express trustee breaches a trust, it will equally arise when a trustee under a constructive or resulting trust breaches the trust. The matter is neatly illustrated by the decision of the House of Lords in *Twinsectra Ltd v Yardley*[16] where Twinsectra agreed to lend £1 million on a short-term loan to Mr Yardley who, amongst other things, was involved in a series of property transactions. Twinsectra was only prepared to advance the loan money to Mr Yardley on the understanding that his solicitor gave an undertaking that the monies should be used for the specific property transaction in question and not for any other purpose. The property transaction in question was the purchase of some residential land in Apperley Bridge, Bradford. The solicitor dealing with the sale of the land was a certain Mr Paul Leach, the appellant in the case. Mr Leach refused to give an undertaking that the monies would be solely used for the purposes of the purchase of the land in Bradford. This, however, did not prevent Mr Yardley from securing the loan because another firm of solicitors, Sims and Roper of Dorset, agreed to give the undertaking that the monies advanced to Mr Yardley would only be used for the purpose of the specific property transaction in question. At the same time as Twinsectra agreed to advance the money, Barclays Bank agreed to loan the money for the purchase of the property in Bradford.

Although the loan money from Twinsectra was no longer needed, Mr Yardley and Mr Sims (the solicitor from Sims and Roper acting on behalf of Mr Yardley) nevertheless agreed to proceed with the loan from Twinsectra. The agreement between Mr Sims and Mr Yardley was to the effect that Mr Sims would take up the loan on his own account and use it to repay his personal indebtedness to Mr Yardley. Neither Mr Yardley nor Mr Sims disclosed this fact to Twinsectra because it would naturally put the loan at risk. On the understanding that the money would be used for the purpose of the property transaction in Bradford, Twinsectra advanced the loan to Sims and Roper, who accepted on the undertaking that the loan monies will be retained by Twinsectra until such time as they are applied in the acquisition of property on behalf of Mr Yardley.

Despite the undertaking by Mr Sims that the monies advanced by Twinsectra would only be used for the specific purpose, Mr Sims advanced the monies to Mr Leach who in

---

[16] [2002] 2 All ER 377.

turn informed Mr Sims that the money would be used for certain property transactions including the purchase of the property in Bradford. He also told Mr Sims that Mr Yardley was fully aware of what was going on and that this arrangement was at his request. The money was transferred to Mr Leach's firm and it was used according to Mr Yardley's instructions. Over half of the money had been used in relation to various property transactions, including the purchase of property in Bradford, and as such was not in dispute because it was within the spirit of the loan. However, the remaining monies were transferred according to Mr Yardley's instruction, and they were not used in connection with any property transactions.

The loan was not subsequently repaid to Twinsectra. Twinsectra sued all the parties including Mr Leach. The claim against Mr Leach was one for dishonest assistance in a breach of trust by Sims and Roper. The loan money had been given on trust to Sims and Roper who had transferred it in breach of trust and Mr Leach had knowingly assisted in the breach of trust. In the House of Lords, Millett LJ explained that loan money advanced to Sims and Roper was held on a resulting trust for Twinsectra and that, having transferred the money in breach of trust, Mr Leach was liable for dishonestly assisting in that breach.[17] The decision of the House of Lords in *Twinsectra Ltd* v *Yardley*[18] is further examined below in the context of the requirement of dishonesty on the part of the stranger assisting in the breach of trust.

Liability for assisting in a breach of trust will extend to situations where there may not have been a trust at all in the strict sense but where there has been a breach of some fiduciary duty, for example, by an agent or a director of a company. In *Royal Brunei Airlines* v *Tan* Lord Nicholls explained that:

> increasingly plaintiffs have recourse to equity for an effective remedy when the person in default, typically a company, is insolvent. Plaintiffs seek to obtain relief from others who were involved in the transaction, such as directors of the company, or its bankers, or its legal or other advisers. They seek to fasten fiduciary obligations directly onto the company's officers or agents or advisers, or to have them held personally liable for assisting the company in breaches of trust or fiduciary obligations.[19]

Assistance by the defendant

In order to be establish liability for dishonestly assisting in a breach of trust, the defendant must have assisted in the breach of trust. In most cases this requirement is not too difficult to prove as it is simply a question of fact whether the stranger did assist in the breach of trust. It has already been seen in *Royal Brunei Airlines* v *Tan*[20] that the defendant allowed trust money belonging to an airline company to be used for the primary trustees' own purposes. In *Twinsectra Ltd* v *Yardley*[21] the defendant, a solicitor, allowed trust monies to be used for purposes not allowed by the terms of the original loan, in circumstances when the loan money was held on resulting trust for the lender.

---

[17] The decision in *Twinsectra Ltd* v *Yardley* [2002] 2 All ER 377 holds that, where loan money is transferred for a specific purpose, the beneficial interest in the money remains with the lender until such time as the money is used for the specific purpose of the loan. The coexistence of a loan and trust relationship was examined in Chapter 3.

[18] [2002] 2 All ER 377.

[19] [1995] 2 AC 378 at 382.

[20] [1995] 2 AC 378.

[21] [2002] 2 All ER 377.

APPLYING THE LAW

Suppose Charlie is holding £400,000 on trust and, in breach of trust, he closes the account in which the money is held and asks for bank notes representing the money. Charlie then decides to leave the country in his car with the money in a suitcase. Charlie's wife is a little suspicious but she does not question anything. Charlie is later arrested.

Do you think that Charlie's wife had anything to do with the breach of trust?

One question which has arisen in the case law is whether a person can be held to have dishonestly assisted in a breach of trust where he or she merely acquiesces in conduct involving a breach of trust, but without knowledge of the breach of trust. The matter fell to be decided in ***Brinks Ltd v Abu-Saleh (No. 3)***[22] where the plaintiff, Brinks Ltd, suffered a major loss as a result of a robbery at one of their warehouses at Heathrow. The robbery had been facilitated by one of the employees of Brinks Ltd who had betrayed his trust to the company by providing a key to the warehouse along with photographs of where gold bullion had been stored. The stolen gold had been melted and sold and the proceeds of sale had been laundered. The question before the court was whether the defendant was liable for dishonestly assisting in a breach of trust in circumstances where she had travelled with her husband who was carrying the stolen money to Switzerland on behalf of one of the robbers. The defendant thought that her husband was involved in some tax evasion scheme and had accompanied him on various trips to Switzerland carrying the money. Rimer J held that the defendant could not be liable for dishonestly assisting in a breach of trust in circumstances where she was unaware of the existence of trust in the first place. In the course of his judgment, Rimer J explained that the:

> only conclusion which I consider that I can properly draw from the evidence is that Mrs Elcombe went on such trips as she did in the capacity of Mr Elcombe's wife, providing him with welcome company on what were long and no doubt tiring drives and in the happy knowledge that the expenses of herself and her children were all being paid for by her husband's rich and benevolent employer, whose benevolence was also explained by the fact that he was part of the family. Whilst not for one moment wishing to minimise the benefit to a husband of being able so to enjoy the company of his wife, I do not regard Mrs Elcombe's presence on such trips as constituting relevant 'assistance' in furtherance of the breach of trust of which Brinks complain.[23]

It is not entirely true to say that the defendant wife in ***Brinks Ltd v Abu-Saleh (No. 3)*** was clearly unaware that her husband was involved in some sort of scheme to misappropriate money. Indeed, in her own evidence, the defendant had admitted that she thought that her husband was involved in some sort of unlawful tax evasion scheme. In the course of his judgment Rimer J held that she 'believed that her husband was engaged in an unlawful and dishonest tax-evasion exercise. An honest wife who knew that her husband was so engaged would counsel him to wash his hands of it immediately and, if he refused, would not wish to have any association with the operation, and certainly not as an all expenses paid passenger.'[24] However, despite this, the fact that she was unaware of the

[22] [1996] CLC 133.
[23] [1996] CLC 133 at 149.
[24] *Ibid.*

existence of the trust meant that she could not be liable for dishonestly assisting in a breach of trust. It is not entirely clear why knowledge of the existence of the trust should be make a difference when the defendant is clearly aware, or even suspicious, that what she or he is doing is participating in involves some misappropriation of property. The decision of Rimer J in **Brinks Ltd v Abu-Saleh (No. 3)**[25] has had cast doubt over it by the decision of the Privy Council in **Barlow Clowes International v Eurotrust International**[26] where Lord Hoffmann commented that '[i]n **Brinks Ltd v Abu-Saleh (No. 3)**[27] Rimer J expressed the opinion that a person cannot be liable for dishonest assistance in a breach of trust unless he knows of the existence of the trust or at least the facts giving rise to the trust. But their Lordships do not agree. Someone can know, and can certainly suspect, that he is assisting in a misappropriation of money without knowing that the money is held on trust or what a trust means . . .'[28]

VISIT CASE NAVIGATOR

Dishonesty on the part of the stranger

By far the most controversial requirement of liability for dishonestly assisting in a breach of trust is the requirement of dishonesty on the part of the stranger. The courts have over the years debated over the exact state of mind needed for a stranger to be found liable for dishonestly assisting in a breach of trust. The central question has turned on the meaning of the 'dishonesty' in this context. The matter has also been debated extensively amongst academic circles.[29]

Liability for assisting in a breach of trust requires the defendant to have some sort of state of mind that he is actually assisting in a breach of trust. Until the decision of the Privy Council in **Royal Brunei Airlines v Tan**,[30] the requisite state of mind of the defendant remained very unclear and controversial. In **Baden Delvaux v Société Générale pour Favoriser le Développement du Commerce et du l'Industrie en France SA**[31] Peter Gibson J held that knowledge sufficient to impose constructive trusteeship for knowing assistance could comprise any one of five different mental states as follows:[32]

(1) actual knowledge;

(2) wilfully shutting one's eyes to the obvious;

(3) wilfully and recklessly failing to make the inquiries as an honest and reasonable person would make;

(4) knowledge of the circumstances which would indicate the facts to an honest and reasonable person; and

(5) knowledge of the circumstances which would put honest and reasonable persons on inquiry.

Ever since this formulation by Peter Gibson J considerable academic and judicial opinion centred on its meaning and, in particular, exactly what must be shown under each of these categories in order for the defendant to be fixed with constructive trusteeship. In attempting to generalise this formulation it may be stated that knowledge can

---

[25] [1996] CLC 133.

[26] [2006] 1 WLR 1476, considered in more detail below.

[27] [1996] CLC 133.

[28] [2006] 1 WLR 1476 at 1484.

[29] Amongst the dearth of literature, see S. Gardner, 'Knowing Assistance and Receipt: Taking Stock' (1996) 112 LQR 56; S.B. Elliot and C. Mitchell, 'Remedies for Dishonest Assistance' (2004) 67 MLR 16; P.D. Finn, 'The Liability of Third Parties for Knowing Receipt or Assistance' in D. Waters (ed.), *Equity and Fiduciaries* (1993) and C. Harpum, 'Accessory Liability for Procuring or Assisting in a Breach of Trust' (1995) 111 LQR 545.

[30] [1995] 2 AC 378.

[31] [1992] 4 All ER 161.

[32] [1992] 4 All ER 161 at 236.

range from actual to imputed knowledge. Categories (1), (2) and (3) are examples of dishonesty and are thus subjective inquiries while categories (4) and (5) represent something akin to negligence and are thus objective inquiries. It was not so much categories (1), (2) and (3) which caused difficulty but rather categories (4) and (5). The problem in respect of these categories had been in defining exactly the nature of the defendant's state of mind. It is quite clear that a defendant would not have actual knowledge as in the case of categories (1), (2) and (3). The nature of actual knowledge under the first three categories was neatly explained by Millett J in **Agip Africa (Ltd) v Jackson**[33] where he explained that:

> [i]f a man does not draw the obvious inferences or make the obvious inquiries, the question is: why not? If it is because, however foolishly, he did not suspect wrongdoing or, having suspected it, had his suspicions allayed, however unreasonably, that is one thing. But if he did suspect wrongdoing yet failed to make inquiries because he 'did not want to know' (category (2)) or because he regarded it as 'none of his business' (category (3)), that is quite another. Such conduct is dishonest, and those who are guilty of it cannot complain if, for the purpose of civil liability, they are treated as if they had actual knowledge.[34]

In respect of categories (4) and (5), until the decision of the Privy Council in **Royal Brunei Airlines v Tan**,[35] debate centred on two concepts, namely constructive notice and imputed knowledge. In respect of constructive notice, the question was whether it was entirely appropriate to speak of constructive notice in the context of commercial dealings where it was not the common practice to investigate title to property as in the case of land dealings. In respect of imputed knowledge, the question was whether a defendant could be held liable for being negligent in not making the necessary enquiries. In **Selangor United Rubber Estates Ltd v Craddock (No. 3)**[36] company funds were transferred by the defendant in order to purchase shares in the same company controlled by the plaintiffs. The process by which the transfer took place was that the national bank drew two drafts in favour of the defendant's bank (district bank) to be placed in the plaintiff's new account with that bank. Subsequently a further cheque was drawn on that account in favour of Woodstock Trust Ltd, by way of a loan to the defendant, Craddock. Craddock used the money to obtain a majority shareholding in the plaintiff company. The court held that the district bank was liable as constructive trustee for its part in honouring a cheque drawn on the plaintiff's account without sufficient inquiry as to the purpose for which it was applied. On the basis of an objective inquiry a reasonable bank would have been aware of the fraud instigated by Craddock. The decision in **Selangor United Rubber Estates Ltd v Craddock (No. 3)** suggested that liability could extend to a defendant who negligently assisted in a breach of trust, albeit honestly.

The test of dishonesty in *Royal Brunei v Tan*

In 1995, in what can be described as a landmark decision, the Privy Council in **Royal Brunei Airlines v Tan**[37] rejected the approach taken in **Selangor United Rubber Estates**

---

[33] [1990] Ch. 265.

[34] [1990] Ch. 265 at 293.

[35] [1995] 3 WLR 64. See, M. Halliwell, 'The Underlying Concept of Accessory Liability for Breach of Trust' (1995) Conv. 339 and G. Griffiths, 'A Matter of Principle – The Basis of Secondary Liability for Knowing Assistance' (1996) JBL 281.

[36] [1968] 1 WLR 1555.

[37] [1995] 3 WLR 64. See M. Halliwell, 'The Underlying Concept of Accessory Liability for Breach of Trust' (1995) Conv. 339 and G. Griffiths, 'A Matter of Principle – The Basis of Secondary Liability for Knowing Assistance' (1996) JBL 281.

Ltd v *Craddock (No. 3)*.[38] Instead, Lord Nicholls in the Privy Council attempted to reformulate the requirements needed for establishing liability for assisting in a breach of trust. The facts, which have been rehearsed in more detail above, involved an agent who allowed money held on trust by a company to be used for purposes not authorised by the terms of the trust. Two questions arose before the Privy Council: firstly, whether liability for dishonestly assisting in a breach of trust required a finding that the breach by the primary trustee should be dishonest and, secondly, what state of mind was required of the defendant who had assisted in the breach of trust.

In respect of the question whether it was crucial in finding liability for dishonest assistance that the defendant must have participated in a dishonest breach of trust by the primary trustee, the Privy Council held that accessory liability was not dependent on a finding that the primary trustee was also acting dishonestly. In the opinion of Lord Nicholls, the requirement in *Barnes* v *Addy*,[39] that the defendant assist with knowledge in a dishonest and fraudulent design on the part of the trustee which had been established in that case, could not be applied literally to all cases involving dishonest assistance. His Lordship explained that 'dishonesty on the part of the third party would seem to be a sufficient basis for his liability, irrespective of the state of mind of the trustee who is in breach of trust. It is difficult to see why, if the third party dishonestly assisted in a breach, there should be a further prerequisite to his liability, namely that the trustee also must have been acting dishonestly.'[40]

In respect of the state of mind required of a defendant to be affixed with constructive trust liability for knowing assistance in a breach of trust, Lord Nicholls, after reviewing a range of possibilities, opted for a test based on dishonesty alone. In his Lordship's opinion, the categories of knowledge as identified by Peter Gibson J in *Baden* v *Société Générale*[41] were best forgotten, and liability for assisting in a breach of trust should be dependent on whether the defendant had dishonestly assisted in a breach of trust. In the words of Lord Nicholls, 'dishonesty on the part of the third party would seem to be a sufficient basis for his liability'.[42] In so far as the meaning of dishonesty is concerned the Privy Council held that 'for the most part dishonesty is to be equated with conscious impropriety'.[43]

So how does the test of dishonesty work in this context? The Privy Council's understanding of dishonesty entails a twofold test having both an objective and subjective element to it. In the first stage of inquiry, the court has to be satisfied whether the defendant acted honestly in the circumstances. This is an objective inquiry: the court has to examine the circumstances and the standards of behaviour expected of honest people in the given facts. This seems somewhat difficult to comprehend at first, since a test based on dishonesty has a strong flavour of subjectiveness. However, this first inquiry is designed to prevent people from setting their own standards of behaviour to avoid liability. In this context Lord Nicholls explained that 'honesty is not an optional scale, with higher or lower values according to the moral standards of each individual. If a person knowingly appropriates another's property, he will not escape a finding of dishonesty simply because he sees nothing wrong in such behaviour.'[44]

---

[38] [1968] 1 WLR 1555.
[39] (1874) 9 Ch. App. 244.
[40] [1995] 3 WLR 64 at 70.
[41] [1983] 1 WLR 509.
[42] [1995] 3 WLR 64 at 69.
[43] [1995] 3 WLR 64 at 73.
[44] [1995] 3 WLR 64 at 73.

In the second stage of the inquiry, the court is to examine the accessory's behaviour, that is, whether he was conscious of the impropriety of his acts or omissions. This is essentially a subjective inquiry. The obvious attraction of **Royal Brunei** is its departure from the **Baden** categories and the associated problems of defining the nature of the five heads of knowledge. If the assistant to the breach is honest in the circumstances, having regard to what is expected of reasonably honest people, and is not conscious of the impropriety of his acts, he attracts no liability. This second stage of inquiry is not objective, that is, the court cannot judge the defendant's own behaviour by what may subsequently appear to the court as being reasonable. If the defendant acts honestly as within the first stage of inquiry, he cannot be liable on a subsequent basis that the court thinks he acted unreasonably. This analysis avoids the necessity to refer to negligent assistance which in light of **Royal Brunei** cannot be an adequate basis for liability in equity for knowing assistance. Only dishonest acts of third parties will attract equitable liability; honest assistance which turns out to be negligent is not a sufficient basis of liability. This is understandably so, since the very basis of equitable intervention is unconsciousness which cannot be equated with carelessness. If a defendant, such as an agent or some other third party does act negligently, then of course, liability may arise at common law for negligence, but not in equity.

The test of dishonesty in *Twinsectra* v *Yardley*

The decision of the Privy Council in **Royal Brunei Airlines v Tan**[45] was generally regarded by most commentators as setting the appropriate test for deciding the state of mind of a defendant who had assisted in a breach of trust. It was only a question of time when the decision would be approved by an English court and the test of dishonesty as formulated by Lord Nicholls would finally be recognised in English law. The opportunity to approve the decision in **Royal Brunei Airlines v Tan** presented itself in the House of Lords in **Twinsectra Ltd v Yardley**.[46] The decision of the House of Lords in that case did, however, give rise to more controversy than was initially expected. In particular, Lord Hutton's interpretation of dishonesty marked a significant departure from the interpretation adopted by Lord Nicholls.

You will recall that on the facts of **Twinsectra v Yardley** that a firm of solicitors, Sims and Roper, had received loan money on the understanding that Mr Yardley would use it only in connection with the acquisition of property. Having already established that this gave rise to a trust relationship whereby Sims and Roper held the money on trust for Twinsectra, Mr Sims proceeded to transfer the money to Mr Leach in breach of trust. Mr Leach was made fully aware by Mr Sims that the money was held by his firm on the undertaking that it would only be used in connection with certain property acquisitions. Mr Leach, however, proceeded to transfer the money to Mr Yardley as and when he requested it. Although some part of the money was used in the acquisition of property, other parts of the money were advanced to Mr Yardley for purposes other than the acquisition of property. One would have thought that, given that Mr Leach had full knowledge that such money was only to be used in connection with the acquisition of property, any advances of that money to Mr Yardley were clearly in breach of trust. Applying the test of

---

[45] [1995] 3 WLR 64. See M. Halliwell, 'The Underlying Concept of Accessory Liability for Breach of Trust' (1995) Conv. 339 and G. Griffiths, 'A Matter of Principle – The Basis of Secondary Liability for Knowing Assistance' (1996) JBL 281.

[46] [2002] 2 All ER 377. See T.M. Yeo, 'Knowing What is Dishonesty' (2002) LQR 502 and P. Jenny, 'Helping to Break an Undertaking' [2002] 303.

dishonesty formulated in ***Royal Brunei Airlines v Tan***,[47] the House of Lords nevertheless held that Mr Leach's conduct did not amount to knowing assistance in a breach of trust. It is this aspect of the decision which is by far the most controversial and it is questionable whether the principles of dishonest assistance in ***Royal Brunei Airlines v Tan***,[48] as explained by Lord Nicholls and understood by many commentators, had been properly applied.

In respect of the requirement of dishonesty, the majority of the House of Lords held that Mr Leach's conduct was not dishonest: in other words, his transfer of the money to Mr Yardley as and when requested did not amount to dishonesty on his part even though he was fully aware of the nature of the undertaking made by Sims and Roper to Twinsectra Ltd. Lord Millett gave a powerful dissenting judgment and held that Mr Leach's conduct was dishonest. Applying the above principles, there is little doubt that Mr Leach's conduct was dishonest. Although honest and reasonable people would have thought that Mr Leach was simply handing over money in the course of his employment as a solicitor to his client, Mr Leach had actual knowledge that such monies should only be advanced in connection with the acquisition of property. Mr Leach failed to ensure that this was the case and was therefore acting dishonestly. The majority in ***Twinsectra*** held that Mr Leach's conduct was not dishonest whilst Lord Millett held that it was. It is submitted that the majority, although purporting to apply the test of dishonesty, did so incorrectly and confused it with the test of dishonesty in the context of criminal liability.

On the question of dishonesty, Lord Hutton delivered the majority judgment. In an attempt to apply the test of dishonesty formulated by Lord Nicholls, Lord Hutton explained that the courts often drew a distinction between subjective and objective dishonesty and in doing so applied three possible standards that could determine whether a person had acted dishonestly.[49] In the first place, there is a purely subjective standard, described by his Lordship as occurring when a person 'transgresses his own standard of dishonesty, even if that standard is contrary to that of reasonable and honest people'.[50] His Lordship explained that the courts had rejected this standard. Secondly, at the other end of the spectrum is a purely objective standard 'whereby a person acts dishonestly if his conduct is dishonest by the ordinary standards of reasonable and honest people, even if he does not realise this'.[51] Finally there is a standard which combines both the subjective and objective tests. This requires the defendant's conduct to be dishonest by the ordinary standards of reasonable and honest people and that the defendant himself realised that by those standards his conduct was dishonest. Lord Hutton referred to this last standard as the combined test of dishonesty. In the opinion of Lord Hutton, Lord Nicholls in ***Royal Brunei Airlines***[52] was advocating a combined test for determining whether a person had acted dishonestly. On the facts of the case, Mr Leach, by transferring money to Mr Yardley, did not regard that his conduct in doing so would be regarded as dishonest by the standards of honest and reasonable people.

It is true to say that Lord Nicholls did adopt a test of dishonesty incorporating both subjective and objective elements. However, the manner in which Lord Hutton applied the test of dishonesty does not accord with the manner in which Lord Nicholls suggested that it should apply, and furthermore, failed to distinguish between dishonesty for the

[47] [1995] 3 WLR 64.
[48] *Ibid.*
[49] [2002] 2 All ER 377 at 384.
[50] *Ibid.*
[51] *Ibid.*
[52] [1995] 3 WLR 64.

purpose of criminal liability and that for civil liability. Lord Hutton approached the concept of dishonesty in the manner used in the context of criminal liability. In the context of criminal liability, the test laid down in **R v Ghosh**[53] by Lord Lane CJ requires that the defendant himself must have realised that what he was doing was dishonest by the ordinary standards of reasonable and honest people. Applying this test, his Lordship was able to come to the conclusion that Mr Leach was not dishonest because he did not consider that reasonable and honest people would regard his conduct as dishonest. It is submitted that this conclusion does not fit neatly with the test of dishonesty formulated in **Royal Brunei Airlines v Tan**.[54] In **Royal Brunei Airlines v Tan** Lord Nicholls was at pains to distinguish the test of dishonesty in the context of knowing assistance and that for criminal liability. His Lordship commented at one stage in his judgment that 'whatever may be the position in some criminal and other contexts . . . in the context of accessory liability principle dishonestly, or with a lack of probity, which is synonymous, means simply not acting as an honest person would in the circumstances'.[55]

Applying the test of dishonesty in **Royal Brunei Airlines v Tan**, Mr Leach's conduct, it has to be said, was dishonest for the following reasons. The application of the test of dishonesty requires the court to examine what reasonable and honest people would have thought about the conduct of Mr Leach on the facts. Initially, honest people may well have thought that Mr Leach, a professional solicitor, was simply acting honestly by giving over money to his client in the course of certain property transactions. However, such a finding leads to the grave conclusion that Mr Leach, knowing full well that the money was held by Sims and Roper for use in connection with the purchase of property only, escapes liability when he gives the money to Mr Yardley in the full knowledge that it should not have been given to him. This, therefore, requires the court to examine the subjective element and that is basically Mr Leach's knowledge of the facts of the case. Lord Nicholls referred to the actual knowledge of the defendant as opposed to what a reasonable person would have known and appreciated. Lord Nicholls was again at pains to argue that the subjective and objective elements were designed to avoid people from setting their own standards. His Lordship commented that 'honesty is not an optional scale, with higher and lower values according to the moral standards of each individual. Therefore, a person who knowingly appropriates a person's property will not escape a finding of dishonesty simply because he sees nothing wrong in such behaviour.'[56]

Lord Millett's powerful dissenting judgment provides an excellent example of the way in which the test of dishonesty ought to be applied to a knowing assistance claim. It also explains how the objective and subjective elements of the test of dishonesty work together. Having dismissed the concept of dishonesty in the context of criminal liability, his Lordship explained that the test of dishonesty formulated by Lord Nicholls is essentially an objective one. In so far as the subjective element is concerned, his Lordship explained that this element requires the court to examine external factors such as the defendant's experience and actual knowledge at the time when he acted. His Lordship commented that:

> Lord Nicholls was adopting an objective standard of dishonesty by which the defendant was expected to attain the standard which would be observed by an honest person placed in similar circumstances. Account must be taken of subjective considerations such as the defendant's experience and intelligence and his actual state of knowledge at the relevant

---

[53] [1982] 2 All ER 689.
[54] [1995] 3 WLR 64.
[55] [1995] 3 WLR 64 at 75.
[56] [1995] 1 WLR 64 at 73.

time. But it is not necessary that he should actually have appreciated that he was acting dishonestly; it is sufficient that he was.[57]

It is submitted that this and only this interpretation of the test of dishonesty properly explains the test of dishonesty formulated by Lord Nicholls and, furthermore, is the only test which sits neatly in the field of trust law. In Mr Leach's case dishonesty had clearly been shown because a reasonable solicitor with the knowledge that Mr Leach had should not have transferred monies over to Mr Yardley for purposes which were not related to the acquisition of property.

The test of dishonesty after *Twinsectra* v *Yardley*

The apparent confusion and uncertainty which arose from the decision of the House of Lords in *Twinsectra Ltd v Yardley*[58] was revisited by the Privy Council in *Barlow Clowes International v Eurotrust International*.[59] The facts of this case concerned a fraudulent offshore investment scheme operated in Gibraltar by Peter Clowes. The money which had been invested by the investors had been fraudulently misappropriated through payment into bank accounts maintained by the defendants in the Isle of Man. The defendants were the principal directors of companies which had been formed in the Isle of Man by one of Peter Clowes's associates. The involvement of the directors of these companies with Peter Clowes and his investment scheme was clearly explained by Lord Hoffmann in his judgment in the Privy Council; suffice to say here that these directors had become quite involved with Peter Clowes and his associates and were fully acquainted with knowledge of the operations of Barlow Clowes International. The scheme collapsed sometime in 1988 and Peter Clowes was convicted and imprisoned for his fraudulent activity. The action against the defendants, in particular a certain Mr Henwood, was commenced on the grounds that they had dishonestly assisted Peter Clowes in misappropriating the money belonging to the investors. The claim was principally on the grounds that they knew or strongly suspected that the monies that were being passed through the companies of which they were directors was the money belonging to the investors. In proceedings in the Isle of Man, at first instance, the court held that the defendants, and in particular Mr Henwood, were liable for dishonestly assisting in a breach of trust. The court explained that Mr Henwood must have been under a strong suspicion that the money being transferred through the companies of which he was a principal director, was money belonging to the public investors of the investment scheme run by Barlow Clowes. On appeal, the staff of the Government Division of the High Court in the Isle of Man held that the defendants were not liable for dishonestly assisting in a breach of trust. With reference to Mr Henwood, it was held that, although reasonable people may have thought that what he was doing was dishonest, Mr Henwood did not have a subjective state of mind to the effect that he knew that the money that he was dealing with was the money belonging to the investors; Furthermore, that he himself believed that ordinary honest reasonable people would not regard his conduct as dishonest.

The proceedings before the Privy Council were an appeal from the Isle of Man and the question was whether Mr Henwood had dishonestly assisted in a breach of trust by allowing money to pass through the companies of which he was a director. The Privy Council

---

[57] [2002] 2 All ER 377 at 408.

[58] [2002] 2 All ER 377. See T.M. Yeo, 'Knowing What is Dishonesty' (2002) LQR 502 and P. Jenny, 'Helping to Break an Undertaking' [2002] 303.

[59] [2006] 1 WLR 1476. See J.E. Penner, 'Dishonest Assistance Revisited: *Barlow Clowes International (in liquidation) and others* v *EuroTrust International*' (2006) TLI 122.

held that Mr Henwood was liable for dishonestly assisting in a breach of trust. With reference to the claim on behalf of Mr Henwood – that he did not regard that his conduct would be regarded as dishonest by ordinary standards and, therefore, on the basis of the decision in **Twinsectra Ltd v Yardley**,[60] he should escape liability – Lord Hoffmann attempted to put right the confusion caused in **Twinsectra Ltd v Yardley**. Delivering the advice of the Board, Lord Hoffmann, who was in the majority in the decision of the House of Lords in **Twinsectra Ltd v Yardley**, explained:

> Their Lordships accept that there is an element of ambiguity in these remarks which may have encouraged a belief, expressed in some academic writing, that the *Twinsectra* case had departed from the law as previously understood and invited inquiry not merely into the defendant's mental state about the nature of the transaction in which he was participating but also into his views about generally acceptable standards of honesty. But they do not consider that this is what Lord Hutton meant. The reference to 'what he knows would offend normally accepted standards of honest conduct' meant only that his knowledge of the transaction had to be such as to render his participation contrary to normally acceptable standards of honest conduct. It did not require that he should have had reflections about what those normally acceptable standards were. Similarly in the speech of Lord Hoffmann, the statement . . . that a dishonest state of mind meant 'consciousness that one is transgressing ordinary standards of honest behaviour' was in their Lordships' view intended to require consciousness of those elements of the transaction which make participation transgress ordinary standards of honest behaviour. It did not also require him to have thought about what those standards were.[61]

In the view of the Privy Council, Mr Henwood could not escape liability on the grounds that he considered that his actions would not be considered dishonest by ordinary standards of reasonable people. According to the Privy Council, by ordinary standards, a person would have regarded that the monies passing through the companies, of which Mr Henwood was a principal director, was suspicious. On this objective test of dishonesty, Mr Henwood was dishonest. Lord Hoffmann explained that 'someone can know, and can certainly suspect, that he is assisting in a misappropriation of money without knowing that the money is held on trust or what a trust means . . .'[62] The decision of the Privy Council in **Barlow Clowes International v Eurotrust International**[63] confirms that the test of dishonesty is essentially an objective one. Lord Hoffmann explained that the decision of the judge at first instance in **Barlow Clowes International v Eurotrust International** was correct and that the judge was right when she concluded that:

> liability for dishonest assistance requires a dishonest state of mind on the part of the person who assists in a breach of trust. Such a state of mind may consist in knowledge that the transaction is one in which he cannot honestly participate (for example, a misappropriation of other people's money), or it may consist in suspicion combined with a conscious decision not to make inquiries which might result in knowledge . . . Although a dishonest state of mind is a subjective mental state, the standard by which the law determines whether it is dishonest is objective. If by ordinary standards a defendant's mental state would be characterised as dishonest, it is irrelevant that the defendant judges by different standards.[64]

---

[60] [2002] 2 All ER 377. See T.M. Yeo, 'Knowing What is Dishonesty' (2002) LQR 502 and P. Jenny, 'Helping to Break an Undertaking' [2002] 303.

[61] [2006] 1 WLR 1476 at 1481.

[62] [2006] 1 WLR 1476 at 1484.

[63] [2006] 1 WLR 1476.

[64] [2006] 1 WLR 1476 at 1479.

The decision of the Privy Council in *Barlow Clowes International* v *Eurotrust International*[65] restores the principle of dishonesty as explained by Lord Nicholls in *Royal Brunei Airlines* v *Tan*.[66] The test of dishonesty is essentially an objective one which looks to see whether the defendant's conduct was dishonest by ordinary standards. In *Royal Brunei Airlines* v *Tan* Lord Nicholls did not rule out a subjective element to the test of dishonesty; however, this subjective element only refers to the question of whether a defendant, having been judged to have acted in accordance with ordinary standards, was nevertheless aware of the impropriety of his own acts. The subjective element does not, however, mean that a defendant can escape liability simply on the grounds that he was of the view that he did not regard his conduct to be dishonest by ordinary standards, even though on an objective ground it was.

The decision in *Barlow Clowes International* v *Eurotrust International* has subsequently been considered in one case and applied in another. The decision was considered in *Abou-Rahmah* v *Abacha*[67] which involved a massive and complicated fraud perpetrated by the first, second and third defendants who persuaded a Kuwaiti trading company and its lawyer to advance sums of money to be invested in a family trust worth some $65 million. The defendants agreed with the claimants that, in return for their assistance, they would receive 40 per cent of the capital of the trust and 15 per cent of the income which would be earned on the trust. The family trust money was actually in Benin, and the agreement with the claimants was that the money they were to advance would be used to pay various regulatory agencies in Benin to seek approval for the family trust money to be moved to Kuwait. Trusting the defendants, the claimants paid the money into City Express Bank of Lagos (CEB), the account to be held for Trust International, this being the payee as directed by the defendants. The defendants never transferred the trust fund to the claimants and instead disappeared, having withdrawn the money from CEB. The question before the Court of Appeal was whether CEB was liable for dishonestly assisting in a breach of trust on the grounds that it had a suspicion that the defendants were involved in a fraud.

At first instance, Treacy J held that the agreement between the fraudsters and the claimants was in the nature of a joint venture that gave rise to fiduciary duties, including a mutual duty on the parties to act in good faith in their dealings with each other. The frauds perpetrated on the claimants were in clear breach of that duty.[68] Treacy J clearly applied the law as explained by Lord Hoffmann in *Barlow Clowes International* v *Eurotrust International*[69] when he commented that the law on dishonest assistance as he understood it required the following constituent elements:

> (i) A dishonest state of mind on the part of the person assisting is required in the sense that that person's knowledge of the relevant transaction had to be such as to render his participation contrary to normally acceptable standards of honest conduct.
>
> (ii) Such a state of mind may involve knowledge that the transaction is one in which he cannot honestly participate (e.g. a misappropriation of other people's money), or it may involve suspicions combined with a conscious decision not to make enquiries which might result in knowledge.

---

[65] [2006] 1 WLR 1476.
[66] [1995] 3 WLR 64. See M. Halliwell, 'The Underlying Concept of Accessory Liability for Breach of Trust' (1995) Conv. 339 and G. Griffiths, 'A Matter of Principle – The Basis of Secondary Liability for Knowing Assistance' (1996) JBL 281.
[67] [2006] EWCA Civ. 1492; [2007] 1 Lloyd's Rep. 115. See N. Kiri, 'Dishonest Assistance: Latest Perspective From the Court of Appeal' (2007) JIBLR 305.
[68] [2006] 1 Lloyd's Rep. 484.
[69] [2006] 1 WLR 1476.

(iii) It is not necessary for the claimants to show that the person assisting knew of the existence of a trust or fiduciary relationship between the claimants and defendants . . . It was sufficient that he should have entertained a clear suspicion that this was the case.[70]

Applying these requisites to the present case Treacy J held that the CEB was not liable for assisting in a breach of trust or fiduciary duty. The judge explained that the bank may have had a general suspicion that from time to time the defendants might have been laundering money, but on the present facts there was no specific suspicion that the money being paid by the bank was specifically in connection with the fraud perpetrated in respect of the family trust.

The Court of Appeal upheld the decision of Treacy J at first instance. However, the judgments of all three judges in the Court of Appeal illustrate that the controversy over the application of the test of dishonesty for knowing assistance was far from over. In particular, the decision illustrates that the question whether subjective dishonesty is a prerequisite for liability is not yet fully answered in the case law. Judgments were given by Rix LJ, Pill LJ and Arden LJ. All three judges came to the conclusion that the bank (CEB) was not liable for dishonestly assisting in a breach of trust, on the grounds that the bank's general suspicion fell short of the particular or specific suspicion that the defendants were involved in a fraud in respect of the money that the claimants had paid into its account. Despite this, the judgments of Rix LJ and Pill LJ reintroduce the notion of subjective dishonesty as a possible requirement for finding liability for dishonest assistance. On the other hand, the decision of Arden LJ is perhaps the strongest endorsement of the decision of the Privy Council in **Barlow Clowes International v Eurotrust International**[71] and the objective test of dishonesty as originally explained by Lord Nicholls in **Royal Brunei Airlines v Tan**.[72] Arden LJ explained that:

> it is unnecessary to show subjective dishonesty in the sense of consciousness that the transaction is dishonest. It is sufficient if the defendant knows of the elements of the transaction which make it dishonest according to normally accepted standards of behaviour. This is the first opportunity, so far as I am aware, that this court has had an opportunity of considering the decision of the Privy Council, and in my judgment this court should follow the decision of the Privy Council.[73]

Rix LJ, in summarising the law as it stood, explained that:

> a claimant in this area needs to show three things: first, that a defendant has the requisite knowledge; secondly, that, given that knowledge, the defendant acts in a way which is contrary to normally acceptable standards of honest conduct (the objective test of honesty or dishonesty); and thirdly, **possibly**, that the defendant must in some sense be dishonest himself (a subjective test of dishonesty which might, on analysis, add little or nothing to knowledge of the facts which, objectively, would make his conduct dishonest).[74]

The judgment of Rix LJ clearly demonstrates that a subjective element plays a part in determining liability for dishonest assistance. It was unfortunate that Rix LJ did not venture further on this question as his Lordship explained that the present appeal only centred on CEB's knowledge and suspicion. The judgment of Pill LJ is perhaps the most

---

[70] [2006] 1 Lloyd's Rep. 484 at 492.

[71] [2006] 1 WLR 1476.

[72] [1995] 3 WLR 64. See M. Halliwell, 'The Underlying Concept of Accessory Liability for Breach of Trust' (1995) Conv. 339 and G. Griffiths, 'A Matter of Principle – The Basis of Secondary Liability for Knowing Assistance' (1996) JBL 281.

[73] [2007] 1 Lloyd's Rep. 115 at 127.

[74] [2007] 1 Lloyd's Rep. 115 at 119.

difficult one in respect of the role of subjective dishonesty and one which leaves the question open as to whether the defendant must himself be aware that his conduct fell short of ordinary standards. In the course of his judgment, his Lordship explained that the Privy Council in **Barlow Clowes International v Eurotrust International**[75] did not reject the notion of subjective dishonesty. His Lordship explained that:

> [t]he Privy Council in Barlow Clowes did not find that the decision of the House of Lords in *Twinsectra* was, on its facts, wrong. What determined the outcome in that case was, in the view of the majority, as described by Lord Hoffmann in Barlow Clowes the honest belief of the defendant solicitor in a certain view of the law. As Lord Hoffmann explained 'If he [the defendant] honestly believed, as the judge found, that the money was at Mr Yardley's disposal, he was not dishonest.' The case turned, it appears to me, on the view taken of the honesty of the defendant's conduct in the transaction. The majority all took the view that the trial judge's conclusion that the defendant had not been dishonest should be upheld. Whether a defendant's belief is honest or dishonest involves an assessment of his mental state.[76]

It is submitted that the decision of the Privy Council in **Barlow Clowes International v Eurotrust International**[77] was an attempt to accept that the decision of Lord Hutton in **Twinsectra Ltd v Yardley**[78] may simply have wrongly applied the test of dishonesty as understood in **Royal Brunei Airlines v Tan**.[79] In doing so, the Privy Council was at pains to make it clear that the test of dishonesty was an objective one, requiring the court to establish whether the conduct of the defendant had transgressed normally accepted standards of behaviour. Lord Hoffmann attempted to re-rationalise the basis of the decision in **Twinsectra Ltd v Yardley** by saying that the conduct of the solicitor in that case was not dishonest because it had not transgressed normally accepted standards of behaviour; in fact the real basis of the decision of the House of Lords in that case was that the solicitor was not liable because he did not think that his conduct would have been regarded by ordinary honest people to be dishonest.[80] In this respect, the judgment of Pill LJ is somewhat difficult to accept simply because the Privy Council, whether admittedly or not, did find that the wrong test had been applied and that the decision may simply have been wrongly decided on the facts.

Where does this leave the state of the law? The view taken in this text is that the test of dishonesty as originally explained by Lord Nicholls in **Royal Brunei Airlines v Tan**,[81] and subsequently endorsed by the Privy Council in **Barlow Clowes International v Eurotrust International**,[82] represent the law in respect of liability of a defendant who dishonestly assists in a breach of trust. The test of dishonesty is essentially an objective one, which requires the court to establish whether the conduct of the defendant went beyond the normally accepted standards of behaviour. If the defendant's conduct does

---

[75] [2006] 1 WLR 1476.

[76] [2007] 1 Lloyd's Rep. 115 at 134.

[77] [2006] 1 WLR 1476.

[78] [2002] 2 All ER 377. See T.M. Yeo, 'Knowing What is Dishonesty' (2002) LQR 502 and P. Jenny, 'Helping to Break an Undertaking' [2002] 303.

[79] [1995] 3 WLR 64. See M. Halliwell, 'The Underlying Concept of Accessory Liability for Breach of Trust' (1995) Conv. 339 and G. Griffiths, 'A Matter of Principle – The Basis of Secondary Liability for Knowing Assistance' (1996) JBL 281.

[80] [2006] 1 WLR 1476 at 1481.

[81] [1995] 3 WLR 64. See M. Halliwell, 'The Underlying Concept of Accessory Liability for Breach of Trust' (1995) Conv. 339 and G. Griffiths, 'A Matter of Principle – The Basis of Secondary Liability for Knowing Assistance' (1996) JBL 281.

[82] [2006] 1 WLR 1476.

transgress normally accepted standards of behaviour, then he will be personally liable to account for the loss suffered by the claimant. As to the question of whether the subjective state of mind of the defendant is important, it is submitted that much of the confusion centres on exactly what is meant by the subjective state of mind of the defendant. Subjective dishonesty may have some role to play in determining the liability of a defendant who has assisted in a breach of trust; however, the subjective enquiry is of a secondary and particular nature. It does not require the defendant to appreciate that what he was doing was within the normally accepted behaviour of such a person. Rather the enquiry is whether the defendant, having being adjudicated not to have conducted himself beyond normal standards of behaviour, nevertheless was aware for some reason or another as to the impropriety of his own acts. In such a case, even though the conduct of the defendant was seen as being normally accepted, he cannot escape liability because of the subjective dishonesty he is affixed with. The matter can be best illustrated by the facts of **Abou-Rahmah v Abacha**[83] where the conduct of the bank was not seen to be beyond the normally accepted practices of a bank.[84] Having established that the conduct of the bank was not objectively dishonest, the subjective enquiry would only apply where the bank, for some reason or another, was specifically aware that the money that it was transferring at the request of the defendants was indeed money advanced by the claimants and fraudulently being laundered by the defendants. In the absence of such a state of mind, the bank could not be liable for merely having some general suspicion.

The decision of the Privy Council has been applied by Evans-Lombe J in **Statek Corp v Alford**[85] where a defendant assisted two directors of a company to misappropriate money belonging to a company. The defendant had been a very close business associate of the two directors and, indeed, was involved in some respect with the running of the company. The High Court held that the defendant was liable for dishonestly assisting in a breach of trust on grounds of his knowledge and participation in the company. In other words, he must have known that the monies being transferred into his account and subsequently transferred by him elsewhere were money belonging to the company. In the course of his judgment, Evans-Lombe J held that 'in this area the law is now authoritatively found in two decisions of the Privy Council, **Royal Brunei Airlines v Tan** and **Barlow Clowes International v Eurotrust International**'.[86] In doing so, the judge explained that liability for dishonest assistance required a dishonest state of mind on the part of the defendant. Whether the defendant acted honestly in the circumstances required an objective enquiry.

The most recent endorsement of the test of dishonesty as clarified by the Privy Council in **Barlow Clowes International v Eurotrust International**[87] has been made in the Court of Appeal decision in **Starglade Properties Ltd v Nash**.[88] On the facts Starglade Properties Ltd instructed Technograde Ltd to produce a site investigation report as to the suitability for developing a sloping site which was known as Hillside Nursery in Kent. Technograde Ltd reported back on 14 December 1998, explaining that the site was

---

[83] [2006] EWCA Civ. 1492; [2007] 1 Lloyd's Rep. 115. See N. Kiri, 'Dishonest Assistance: Latest Perspective From the Court of Appeal' (2007) JIBLR 305.

[84] Although, what is the normally accepted behaviour and practices of a bank, or indeed any other commercial context, is not always clear. See R. Lee, 'Dishonesty and Bad Faith After *Barlow Clowes*: *Abou-Rahmah v Abacha*' (2007) JBL 209.

[85] [2008] EWHC 32 (Ch.).

[86] [2008] EWHC 32 (Ch.) at para. 98.

[87] [2006] 1 WLR 1476.

[88] [2010] EWCA 1314.

suitable for development of a number of two-storey houses. On 21 June 1999 Starglade sold the site to a company called Larkstore Ltd which duly commenced its development. Unfortunately, in 2001 there was a landslip causing substantial damage to properties uphill from the site. In 2003 the owners of those properties commenced proceedings against Larkstore Ltd. An agreement was made on 23 February 2004 between Starglade Properties Ltd and Larkstore Ltd in which Starglade Properties Ltd assigned to Larkstore Ltd the full benefits, interests and rights of Starglade in the report provided by Technograde Ltd. This essentially gave Larkstore the right to sue Technograde.

On the same date, Mr Nash, the sole director of Larkstore, undertook to pay to Starglade half of the net monies it would receive from Technograde Ltd from the action it would commence against it. The net effect of this was that Larkstore Ltd declared itself a trustee for half of the money for the benefit of Starglade Ltd. Larkstore did indeed succeed in suing Technograde and received substantial damages. Mr Nash used all of the monies received in damages to pay Larkstore's creditors. It is important to note that this was done despite the fact that Mr Nash knew that half of the money was held for Starglade; this was a very important fact in the Court of Appeal. Starglade commenced proceedings against Mr Nash for dishonestly assisting in a breach of trust. It was contended that the money was held by Larkstore Ltd on trust for Starglade Ltd and that the money was given in breach of trust to the creditors and that Mr Nash had assisted in that breach of trust.

At first instance, the trial judge Mr Nicholas Strauss QC held that Mr Nash had not been guilty of dishonestly assisting a breach of trust. The judge explained that the case raised 'two main issues. First, it being frankly admitted that Mr Nash did deliberately prefer other creditors, was this dishonest? Secondly, is it necessary for the purposes of a dishonest assistance claim that the dishonesty should relate to the breach of trust? Or, to put it another way, is the fact that Mr Nash did not know that half the money belonged to Starglade fatal to the claim?'[89] As to the first question, the judge held that Mr Nash did know, at the time that he caused Larkstore Ltd to pay its creditors in preference to Starglade, that the money was held by Larkstore on trust for Starglade Ltd. In so far as whether Mr Nash had acted dishonestly, the judge explained what he understood the authorities suggested as the appropriate test of dishonesty. He explained that:

> The authorities suggest that it will usually be obvious in cases of dishonest assistance that the conduct in question is at least objectively dishonest; it is conduct which would be regarded as dishonest by any right-thinking person. However, as indicated, it is not always just a question of looking at the conduct and deciding whether, objectively, it was dishonest. There may be subjective questions: see also *Abou-Rahmah* at 66 per Arden LJ. Further, there may be cases in which different views could reasonably be held: some might think the conduct dishonest, others not. In such a case, in my view, the defendant is not liable for dishonest assistance. The tenor of the speeches of Lord Hoffmann in *Barlow Clowes* and Lord Nicholls in *Royal Brunei Airlines* is that the defendant must be guilty of conduct which transgresses normally accepted standards of conduct i.e. conduct which all normal people would regard as dishonest.[90]

Looking at the conduct of Mr Nash in paying his creditors, Mr Nicholas Strauss QC held that his conduct could not have been described as conduct which transgressed generally accepted standards of commercial behaviour of persons in a similar role as Mr Nash. In the course of his judgment he explained that:

---

[89] [2010] EWHC 148 (Ch) at para. 19.
[90] [2010] EWHC 148 9Ch) at para. 51.

The question whether a company director may prefer some creditors over others is not one to which most people would know the answer as a matter of law, nor in my judgment would there be a general view as to what was honest or dishonest in this connection. It might well be dishonest to prefer creditors in the face of advice that it was unlawful, or personal knowledge of the decided cases referred to above establishing that it was unlawful, but not in my view otherwise. Therefore, in my opinion, Mr Nash's conduct was not conduct which would have transgressed generally accepted standards of commercial behaviour on the part of a person in his position, even if he had had greater commercial experience. His lack of experience and lack of understanding as to the legal position are additional relevant factors.[91]

On appeal, the Court of Appeal reversed the decision of Nicholas Strauss QC. The Court of Appeal held that the trial judge had erred in applying the proper test of dishonesty as understood in the Privy Council in **Barlow Clowes International v Eurotrust International**.[92] The Lord Chancellor Morritt LJ explained that the deputy judge's comments were apt to mislead: 'The relevant standard, described variously in the statements I have quoted, is the ordinary standard of honest behaviour. Just as the subjective understanding of the person concerned as to whether his conduct is dishonest is irrelevant so also is it irrelevant that there may be a body of opinion which regards the ordinary standard of honest behaviour as being set too high. Ultimately, in civil proceedings, it is for the court to determine what that standard is and to apply it to the facts of the case.'[93] The Lord Chancellor went on to find that 'Mr Nash knew that Larkstore was insolvent but that the obligation of Larkstore to Starglade was binding. Thus he could only "frustrate" Starglade if he left Starglade to pursue its remedy against an insolvent company without assets. He could only remove Larkstore's assets by paying its other creditors. This is what he did. He cannot, in my view, be protected from the consequences of that course of conduct by the advice of Mr Twining. Mr Twining was not asked, and expressed no view, as to the legality or otherwise of the payments actually made in view of either the undoubted insolvency of Larkstore or the purpose or intention of Mr Nash in making them.'[94]

The decision of the Court of Appeal in **Starglade Properties Ltd v Nash**[95] illustrates the proper application of the test of dishonesty in a personal claim for knowing assistance in a breach of trust. As explained above, there is a single test of dishonesty with no sliding scale. If by ordinary standards a defendant's mental state and conduct would be regarded as dishonest, it does not matter that the defendant thought that his conduct was indeed accepted as normal practice. A further illustration of the application of the test of dishonesty was recently provided by the High Court decision in **Secretary of State for Justice v Topland Group plc**.[96] The facts concerned the Secretary of State for Justice who had a lease on a property. The Secretary engaged a property agent to represent him in a rent review and a surrender of the lease with a view to negotiation of a new lease on the same property. The property in question was in fact being purchased by the defendant who had paid a secret profit to the claimant's agents in order to negotiate a regeared/restructured lease. The claimant Secretary of State argued that the defendants had not only given the claimant's agent a bribe, but had dishonestly assisted in a breach

[91] [2010] EWHC 148 (Ch) at para. 54.
[92] [2006] 1 WLR 1476.
[93] [2010] EWCA Civ 1314 at 32.
[94] [2010] EWCA 1314 at para. 35.
[95] [2010] EWCA 1314.
[96] [2011] EWHC 983.

of trust, the agents acting on trust for the claimant. The payment of the bribe was regarded by the claimant as dishonest conduct on the part of the defendant. However, the defendant argued that the payment of the secret commission was not a bribe and that it was known to both the agent and the defendant that this was normal practice in the real estate market. The question, therefore, was whether the conduct of the defendant was indeed dishonest. Most ordinary honest people may think that the acceptance of a secret commission for the negotiation of a lease would be regarded as honest. However, the High Court found that whilst at the first level of inquiry the court might come to the conclusion that honest people would regard the conduct of the defendant as being honest, it was important to look at the subjective question of whether the defendant, knowing what he knew, would be regarded as being dishonest by ordinary standards of normal people. In answering this question, King J explained that both the agent and the defendant's conduct was what was normal practice in the real estate market. To people working in the real estate market, the acceptance of such a commission would be normal. In such a case it would be difficult to conclude that the defendant's conduct was dishonest. In light of this, King J explained that:

> the pleaded market practice must in my judgment be arguably relevant to the court's determination of whether the Defendants' conduct was objectively dishonest since again on authority in the context of a commercial transaction the court has to determine, amongst other things, whether the conduct was 'commercially unacceptable conduct' (see Lord Nicholls in *Tan* at 390F-G; the Chancellor in *Starglade* at paragraph 24 *'The advice of the Privy Council . . . clearly identified dishonesty as the touchstone of liability, and as synonymous with a want of probity and commercially unacceptable conduct'*).[97]

Receipt of trust property in breach of trust

APPLYING THE LAW

William operates a small investment company in which investors can invest money. The terms of the investment are that William holds all monies belonging to investors on a trust for them. Recently, his company has been experiencing financial difficulties and one particular creditor remains unpaid. This creditor helped William set up the company and is aware of the activities of the company. William transfers money from the trust account to the creditor in order to discharge the debt he owes. The creditor subsequently wastes the money with nothing to account for it

Clearly, William has acted in breach of trust; however, should the creditor be liable in any way?

A constructive trust will be imposed on a person who knowingly receives trust property transferred to him in breach of trust. If the recipient of the property subsequently disposes of the property to a bona fide purchaser without notice of the trust, or otherwise dissipates the trust property, he will be personally liable to the beneficiary of the trust property to replace the loss. Such liability is referred to as liability for knowing receipt of

---

[97] [2011] EWHC 983.

trust property. It is the element of knowing receipt which triggers the personal liability of the recipient who is deemed a constructive trustee. Constructive trust liability for knowing receipt is often considered alongside liability for dishonest assistance in a breach of trust. There are two reasons for this nexus. In the first place, both knowing receipt of trust property and dishonest assistance in a breach of trust involve third parties, otherwise known as strangers, intermeddling in a breach of trust by a primary trustee. The second reason relates to the fact that until more recent times, the requisite degree of knowledge required on the part of the third party intermeddler was thought to be governed by the same principles.[98] When discussing the liability for knowing receipt of trust property, it is important to appreciate that a potential claimant may also have a proprietary claim to the trust property which is in the hands of the third party who has knowingly received it in breach of trust. Such a proprietary claim will take the form of tracing the trust property into the hands of the third party, or indeed, any other party who cannot purport to show that it has received it as bona fide purchaser without notice of the trust.

Significance of knowing receipt liability and requisites for liability

When will liability for knowing receipt of trust property be important? As already mentioned above, a claimant who has lost property as a result of a breach of trust or some other fiduciary duty will be able to trace his beneficial interest in equity into the hands of third parties who have received the trust property with knowledge of the breach. The personal liability of the third party who has received the trust property will be important when the trust property has been dissipated or where it has subsequently depreciated in value. In this context, the purpose of making the third party liable is to allow the claimant to recover the value of the property which he has been deprived of. The matter was neatly explained by Collins J in *Re Loftus*[99] where the judge explained that 'the main purpose of seeking to establish constructive trust liability on the basis of knowing receipt is when the alleged constructive trustee has disposed of the property so that a personal remedy for its value is sought against him'.[100]

The requirements needed to find constructive trust liability for knowing receipt of trust property were laid out by Hoffmann LJ in *El Ajou v Dollar Land Holdings*:[101]

- a disposal of assets in breach of fiduciary duty
- the beneficial receipt by the defendant of assets which are traceable as representing the assets of the claimant
- knowledge on the part of the defendant that the assets he received are traceable to a breach of fiduciary duty.

Disposal of assets in breach of trust or fiduciary duty

The first requirement for establishing liability for knowing receipt is that there has been a disposal of assets in breach of fiduciary duty. In the simplest case, a trustee may seek

---

[98] *Baden v Société Générale* [1983] 1 WLR 509.
[99] [2005] 1 WLR 1890.
[100] [2005] 1 WLR 1890 at 1921.
[101] [1994] BCC 143 at 154.

to transfer the trust property to the third party in breach of trust. However, just as in the case of liability for dishonest assistance, the assets need not necessarily have been subject to a formal trust; it suffices that the assets are transferred by some person in breach of fiduciary duty. For example, liability will extend to situations where a director transfers company property to third parties who receive it with the requisite knowledge that it has been transferred in breach of fiduciary duty. The matter is neatly illustrated by the Court of Appeal's decision in *Polly Peck International plc v Nadir (No. 2)*[102] where the facts of the case involved a transfer of funds belonging to a company, Polly Peck International, by the then reputable Asil Nadir (chief executive of the company) to the Central Bank of Cyprus (CBC) in exchange for the Turkish lira. The question was whether the CBC could be held liable as constructive trustee of the sterling funds transferred in breach of a fiduciary relationship by the chief executive Nadir. The Court of Appeal held that the bank was not liable for knowing receipt of money transferred in breach of trust, on the grounds that there was no reason for the bank to be suspicious of receiving and exchanging large amounts of sterling against the Turkish lira.[103]

Liability for knowing receipt will extend to cases where the recipient has received property which represents the traceable product of the original property. For example, a trustee may exchange the original trust property for some other property and then transfer it into the hands of the recipient. In such a case it does not matter that the property which is in the hands of the recipient is not in its original form, provided that it represents the original property.

Receipt of assets transferred in breach of trust or fiduciary duty

The second requirement for liability for knowing receipt is that the recipient receives property transferred in breach of trust or fiduciary duty. There are a number of aspects to this requirement. In the first place, it is clear that the receipt of property need not originate from a formal trust but may originate from some breach of fiduciary duty. For example, in *Belmont Finance Corporation Ltd v Williams Furniture Ltd (No. 2)*[104] Buckley LJ explained that 'if the directors of a company in breach of their fiduciary duties misapply the funds of their company so that they come into the hands of some stranger to the trust who receives them with knowledge (actual or constructive) of the breach, he cannot conscientiously retain those funds against the company unless he has some better equity. He becomes a constructive trustee for the company.'[105]

The second aspect to the requirement that the recipient must have received property transferred in breach of trust or breach of fiduciary duty is that the property received must be the identical trust property or its traceable product. In this respect, it can be said that the tracing and following rules of property, which are considered in Chapter 20, apply equally in this context. However, it is worth noting that in *El Ajou v Dollar Land Holdings*[106] Millett J suggested that the following and tracing rules may be less stringent in the context of liability for knowing receipt. The case involved a complex fraud whereby an agent of a very wealthy investor was persuaded by bribes to invest in Dutch companies

---

[102] [1992] 4 All ER 769.
[103] See N. Clayton, 'Banks as Constructive Trustees: The English Position' (1993) JIBL 191.
[104] [1980] 1 All ER 393.
[105] [1980] 1 All ER 393 at 405.
[106] [1993] 3 All ER 717.

operated by three Canadians. In fact these companies held no other assets and carried out no trade other than providing a vehicle for the Canadians to carry out their fraud by a fraudulent share-selling scheme. The monies were channelled by the Canadians through a number of different jurisdictions, including jurisdictions where the concept of the trust was not recognised. It was also clear on the facts that the money had gone missing whilst in Panama before appearing again in Geneva. The money was eventually invested in England in a property development by a company called Dollar Land Holding Ltd. One of the non-executive directors of Dollar Land Holding Ltd was instrumental in making contact with the Canadians and introducing them to Dollar land Holding Ltd. The plaintiff commenced proceedings against Dollar Land Holding on the grounds that it had received property in breach of fiduciary duty. At first instance, Millett J held that the money which Dollar Land Holding had received was indeed the money belonging to the plaintiff, although, he concluded that Dollar Land Holding did not have sufficient knowledge of the breach of fiduciary duty. The Court of Appeal, however, overturned the decision of Millett J on the grounds that the non-executive director of Dollar Land Holding had knowledge that the money had been acquired by the Canadians in breach of fiduciary duty and that such knowledge could be imputed to Dollar Land Holding Ltd. The Court of Appeal, whilst reversing the decision of Millett J in respect of the knowledge on the part of Dollar Land Holding Ltd, seem to have accepted that the money received by Dollar Land Holding Ltd was indeed representative of money belonging to the plaintiff despite passing through several jurisdictions and having been converted into different currencies and mixed with other money. The fact that the money went missing in Panama with no immediate connection when it was found it Geneva clearly illustrates a much relaxed application of the following and tracing rules, which otherwise require a direct connection between the original property and the final traceable product, albeit that the original property has been mixed with other property.

A third and final aspect of the requirement that the recipient must have received property in breach of trust or fiduciary duty is that it must have received the property beneficially. In most cases this will be simply a question of fact whether the defendant has indeed received the trust property beneficially. However, much confusion has arisen in the context of a bank and whether a bank can be said to have received property in breach of fiduciary duty, thereby making it liable as a constructive trustee. In **Polly Peck v Nadir (No. 2)**[107] the facts of which have already been rehearsed above, one of the questions before the Court of Appeal was whether a bank could be liable for knowing receipt of money in circumstances where it accepted money from its client and then exchanged the currency for other currency. Scott LJ proceeded to answer this question on the grounds that a bank could be liable for knowing receipt of money deposited into an account. The decision has been criticised on the grounds that although, as between a bank and its customer, the relationship is essentially one of debtor and creditor, the bank merely acts as an agent for the customer. In this respect one commentator writes that 'a currency exchange should not be treated as a knowing receipt, because it is not materially different from merely crediting the customer's account with a deposit. It is generally a purely ministerial receipt by the bank in its capacity as an agent, and should not attract the liability of a constructive trustee.'[108]

---

[107] [1992] 4 All ER 769.
[108] J. O'Donovan, *Lender Liability* (2005) at p. 385.

● Knowledge

As in the case of knowing assistance in a breach of trust, by far the most controversial aspect of liability for knowing receipt of trust property is the requisite degree of knowledge of the breach of trust by the recipient. It is clear that the recipient need not be dishonest or be privy to a fraud perpetrated by the person transferring the property to him. For example, in *Eagle Trust plc v SBC Securities Ltd*[109] Vinelott J explained that 'in a "knowing receipt" case it is only necessary to show that the defendant knew that the money paid to him were trust moneys and of circumstances which made the payment a misapplication of them. Unlike a "knowing assistance" case it is not necessary, and never has been necessary, to show that the defendant was in any sense a participator in the fraud.'[110] Although it is not necessary for the defendant to be dishonest, the question arises as to the degree of knowledge that he must have in order to be found liable for knowing receipt. As explained before, it is a question which has been the fertile source of much controversy in recent times. The question was succinctly put by Nourse LJ in *Bank of Credit and Commerce International (Overseas Ltd) (in Liquidation) v Akindele*[111] in the following terms:

**VISIT CASE
NAVIGATOR**

> With the proliferation in the last 20 years or so of cases in which the misapplied assets of companies have come into the hands of third parties, there has been a sustained judicial and extrajudicial debate as to the knowledge on the part of the recipient which is required in order to found liability in knowing receipt. Expressed in its simplest terms, the question is whether the recipient must have actual knowledge (or the equivalent) that the assets received are traceable to a breach of trust or whether constructive knowledge is enough.[112]

At one time the requisite degree of knowledge required on the part of the defendant for liability for knowing receipt was governed by the decision in *Baden v Société Générale*[113] where Peter Gibson J held that knowledge sufficient to impose constructive trusteeship for knowing receipt as well as knowing assistance could comprise any one of five different mental states as follows:[114]

(1) actual knowledge;

(2) wilfully shutting one's eyes to the obvious;

(3) wilfully and recklessly failing to make the inquiries as an honest and reasonable person would make;

(4) knowledge of the circumstances which would indicate the facts to an honest and reasonable person; and

(5) knowledge of the circumstances which would put honest and reasonable persons on inquiry.

You will recall from the earlier discussion on knowing assistance that ever since this formulation by Peter Gibson J considerable academic and judicial opinion centred on its meaning and, in particular, exactly what must be shown under each of these categories in order for the defendant to be fixed with constructive trusteeship. In attempting to

---

[109] [1992] 4 All ER 488.
[110] [1992] 4 All ER 488 at 501. See also *Bank of Credit and Commerce International (Overseas Ltd) (in liquidation) v Akindele* [2001] Ch. 437 at 449.
[111] [2001] Ch. 437.
[112] [2001] Ch. 437 at 450.
[113] [1983] 1 WLR 509.
[114] [1983] 1 WLR 509 at 575.

generalise this formulation it may be stated that knowledge can range from actual to imputed knowledge. Categories (1), (2) and (3) are examples of actual knowledge and are thus subjective inquiries while categories (4) and (5) represent something akin to negligence and are thus objective. It was not so much categories (1), (2) and (3) which caused difficulty but rather categories (4) and (5) which constitute constructive knowledge or as it is often described 'constructive notice'. It is, however, preferable to use the term 'constructive knowledge' rather than 'constructive notice' since constructive notice has developed primarily in the context of land-based transactions and has acquired a special meaning, where a person is affixed with constructive notice of interests in land where there is an opportunity to investigate title to the land. In the context of non-land-based transactions there is usually no opportunity to investigate title to property which may be received by a person. The matter is illustrated by the famous words of Lindley LJ in **Manchester Trust v Furness**:[115]

> The equitable doctrines of constructive notice are common enough when dealing with land and estates, with which the court is familiar; but there have been repeated protests against the introduction into commercial transactions of anything like an extension of these doctrines, and the protest is founded on good sense. In dealings with estates in land title is everything, and it can be leisurely investigated; in commercial transactions possession is everything, and there is no time to investigate title, and if we were to extend the doctrine of constructive notice to commercial transactions we should be doing infinite mischief and paralysing the trade of the country.

Returning to the question posed by Nourse LJ in **Bank of Credit and Commerce International (Overseas Ltd) (in Liquidation) v Akindele**[116] as to the requisite degree of knowledge required on the part of the knowing recipient, the following principles emerge from the existing case law. In the first place, a recipient who has actual knowledge that money or other property received by him has been transferred in breach of trust or fiduciary duty will clearly be liable as a constructive trustee to account for the loss suffered by the claimant. A defendant will have actual knowledge under the first three categories of the **Baden** classification. It is sometimes said that categories (2) and (3) constitute 'Nelsonian' and 'naughty' knowledge respectively. Nelsonian knowledge refers to the defendant's actual knowledge obtained by deliberately shutting his eyes to the obvious as Admiral Nelson did by putting a telescope to his blind eye to avoid signs to withdraw from battle. Naughty knowledge refers to that of a person who deliberately fails to make inquiries which an honest person would make in the circumstances. In the case of categories (1) to (3) the defendant will have actual knowledge and he will be liable. For example, in **Belmont Finance Corporation v Williams Furniture (No. 2)**[117] directors of a company allowed one of its wholly owned subsidiaries to be purchased with its own money contrary to the then s. 54 of the Companies Act 1948. The parent company was held to be liable as constructive trustee of the money it had received on the sale of the subsidiary, on the grounds that the company had actual knowledge that the money used to purchase the subsidiary was transferred in breach of fiduciary duty.

Whilst it is not disputed that actual knowledge will attract constructive trust liability for knowing assistance, the question is whether constructive knowledge will suffice. In **Nelson v Larholt**[118] Denning J was of the opinion that constructive knowledge was a

---

[115] [1895] 2 QB 539.
[116] [2001] Ch. 437.
[117] [1980] 1 All ER 393.
[118] [1948] 1 KB 339.

sufficient basis for liability for knowing receipt. In this case eight cheques had been drawn by an executor on the estate's bank account in favour of the defendant who had cashed them in good faith. The court held the defendant liable for knowing receipt of the money from the executor in breach of trust. Although the defendant had no actual knowledge that the funds were being transferred in breach of trust, the defendant was found to be foolish in not inquiring as to why eight consecutive cheques had been used by the executor from the estate which he was administering.

Whether or not on the facts of **Nelson v Larholt** the defendant should have been liable to account, subsequent judicial opinion has rejected the concept of constructive notice as being the basis of liability. In **Re Montagu's Settlement Trusts**[119] Megarry VC reconsidered the question of knowledge required for the imposition of constructive trusteeship in knowing receipt liability. The facts concerned a settlement whereby property was settled on trust for the tenth Duke of Manchester absolutely. Trustees of the settlement transferred certain property to the tenth Duke in breach of trust who in turn disposed of the property during his lifetime. An action was commenced by the eleventh Duke of Manchester on the grounds that the tenth Duke had become a constructive trustee of the property he had received and subsequently disposed of in breach of trust. The question before the court was whether the tenth Duke was liable as a constructive trustee. It was not disputed that the tenth Duke's solicitor was aware that certain property should not have been transferred to the Duke; however, could it be said that the Duke was also aware that the property he had received was indeed property transferred in breach of trust? One of the arguments presented to the court was that the Duke must have at one time understood the terms of the settlement and therefore could be said to have had constructive knowledge of the fact that the property he received should not have been transferred to him. Megarry VC held that the tenth Duke was not liable as a constructive trustee for the property he had received. The fact that the solicitor may have been aware was not sufficient to impute notice on the part of the Duke. Furthermore, the fact that the Duke may, at one point, have known of the terms of the settlement did not mean that he was aware when the property was actually received by him. There are two important statements in Megarry VC's judgment which explain the relevance of categories (4) and (5) of the **Baden** classification and the concept of constructive notice. First, with regard to the categories (4) and (5) of knowledge, Megarry VC commented that 'knowledge is not confined to actual knowledge, but includes knowledge of types (2) and (3) in the **Baden** case for in such cases there is a want of probity which justifies imposing a constructive trust. Whether knowledge of the **Baden** types (4) and (5) suffices for this purpose is at best doubtful; in my view it does not for I cannot see that the carelessness involved will normally amount to a want of probity.'[120] Therefore, what is required is a want of probity or conscious impropriety and this cannot be equated with an objective based negligence standard for the purposes of equitable liability. As regards the concept of constructive notice, Megarry VC explained that 'the cold calculus of constructive and imputed notice does not seem to me to be an appropriate instrument for deciding whether a man's conscience is sufficiently affected for it to be right to bind him of the obligation of a constructive trustee'.[121]

The notion of constructive notice or constructive knowledge as the basis for liability was further rejected in a number of decisions decided after **Re Montagu's Settlement**

---

[119] [1987] Ch. 264.
[120] [1987] Ch. 264 at 285.
[121] *Ibid.*

Trusts.[122] In *Agip (Africa)* v *Jackson Agip* a firm of accountants were liable to account to the plaintiff company because they had knowingly participated in the laundering of money defrauded by their chief accountant. Millett J's reasoning at first instance rejected the application of categories (4) and (5) of the *Baden* classification as appropriate constituents of the test of knowledge. The judgment of Millett J did not reject the need for the defendant to be affixed with knowledge: rather knowledge is to be equated with dishonesty irrespective whether constructive trust liability was being imposed for knowing assistance or knowing receipt.[123] In so far as dishonesty is concerned Millett J explained that this could be established under any one of the first three categories of the *Baden* classification: in other words, what is required is actual knowledge as opposed to inferred knowledge. Millett J held that 'there is no sense in requiring dishonesty on the part of the principal while accepting negligence as sufficient for his assistant. Dishonest furtherance of a dishonest scheme of another is an understandable basis for liability, negligent but honest failure that someone's scheme is dishonest is not.'

The decision of Millett J in *Agip (Africa)* v *Jackson*[124] suggested that what was required on the part of the defendant was dishonesty on the grounds that categories (1)–(3) of the *Baden* classification constituted dishonesty. It has to be noted, however, that the decision in *Agip (Africa)* v *Jackson* predates the decision in *Royal Brunei Airlines* v *Tan*,[125] where Lord Nicholls adopted a primarily objective test of dishonesty requiring the defendant to have failed to have acted like an honest person. It is seems clear that the test of dishonesty as established in the context of knowing assistance does not apply to cases of knowing receipt, which is essentially based on the knowledge of the recipient and, therefore, requiring a subjective inquiry into his state of mind.

The notion of constructive notice or knowledge was further rejected in *Eagle Trust plc* v *SBC Securities Ltd*[126] where Vinelott J explained that constructive notice in the context of financial transactions was not easy to accommodate. He explained that the doctrine of constructive notice had its roots firmly in land-based transactions and that 'the courts have been particularly reluctant to extend the doctrine of constructive notice to cases where moneys are paid in the ordinary course of business to the defendant in discharge of a liability. Unlike a "knowing assistance" case it is not necessary, and never has been necessary, to show that the defendant was in any sense a participator in the fraud.'[127] In *Polly Peck International plc* v *Nadir (No. 2)*[128] Scott LJ took the opportunity to point out further that constructive notice was an insufficient basis for liability under the head of knowing receipt. The facts of the case concerned a transfer of Polly Peck International

---

[122] [1987] Ch. 265.

[123] [1987] Ch. 265 at 273 where Millett J explained that 'it does not matter whether the plaintiffs' claim is treated as "knowing receipt" or as "knowing assistance" since, (a), if there was a breach of trust it was a fraudulent breach of trust on any view of the matter, and the only issue remaining is the issue as to the defendants' state of mind. (b) The degree of knowledge required under each of the two heads of constructive trusteeship is the same . . . The plaintiffs must show a want of probity of one of categories (i) to (iii), set out by Peter Gibson J in *Baden, Delvaux and Lecuit* v *Société General pour Favoriser le Dévelopement du Commerce et de l'Industrie en France S.A.* [1983] B.C.L.C. 325, i.e. (i) "actual knowledge," (ii) wilfully shutting ones eyes to the obvious, or (iii) wilfully and recklessly failing to make such inquiries as an honest and reasonable man would make . . .'

[124] [1987] Ch. 265.

[125] [1995] 2 AC 378.

[126] [1992] 2 All ER 488 at 507.

[127] [1992] 4 All ER 488 at 501. See also *Bank of Credit and Commerce International (Overseas Ltd) (in Liquidation)* v *Akindele* [2001] Ch. 437 at 449.

[128] [1992] 4 All ER 769

funds by the then reputable Asil Nadir to the Central Bank of Cyprus (CBC) in exchange for the Turkish lira. The question was whether the CBC could be held liable as constructive trustee of the sterling funds transferred in breach of a fiduciary relationship by the chief executive Nadir. Scott LJ approached the issue on the basis that personal liability of the CBC could only be shown to exist if the CBC had knowledge under the first three heads of the *Baden* classification. Essentially, what the court is looking for is a want of probity or conscious impropriety which can be established under the first three headings of *Baden*.

The opportunity to revisit the question of knowledge for receipt-based liability presented itself to the Court of Appeal in *Bank of Credit and Commerce International (Overseas Ltd) (in Liquidation) v Akindele*.[129] The facts of the case involved employees of BCCI (Overseas Ltd) who entered in a fraudulent loan agreement with the defendant, a Nigerian. The facts of the case are very complex; however, it is sufficient to explain that the defendant advanced to the bank a sum of £10 million on which he was to receive a return of some £6.8 million. At the time of the transfer of the £10 million there was nothing to suggest that BCCI was operating a fraudulent banking service. The sum was advanced under an artificial loan agreement designed to give the impression that certain dummy loans were performing as normal: this was clearly in breach of fiduciary duty by the employees of the bank. In 1991 the BCCI group of companies went into liquidation and the liquidator of the companies commenced proceedings against the defendant to recover their losses on the grounds that the defendant had become a constructive trustee of the money received under the fraudulent loan agreements. The basis of the liquidators' claims were that the defendant had knowingly assisted in a breach of fiduciary duty and that the sum of £6.8 million, which was an exceptionally high rate of return, was a knowing receipt of money in breach of fiduciary duty. The question before the Court of Appeal was essentially one relating to the state of mind of the defendant.

Nourse LJ undertook a review of the existing authorities with a view to finding exactly what state of mind was required on the part of a defendant in order to incur liability for knowing assistance. From what has been observed so far, the existing case law was not entirely clear. Possibilities ranged from the fivefold classification in *Baden v Société Générale*[130] to the 'want of probity' requirement in *Re Montagu's Settlement Trusts*[131] to the question of dishonesty as explained in *Agip (Africa) v Jackson*.[132] Having reviewed the authorities Nourse LJ explained that dishonesty on the part of the recipient was not a prerequisite for liability for knowing receipt. Furthermore, Nourse LJ rejected that the fivefold classification by Peter Gibson J in the *Baden* case should serve as a yardstick to measure the levels of knowledge for knowing receipt. Nourse LJ explained that:

> just as there is now a single test of dishonesty for knowing assistance, so ought there to be a single test of knowledge for knowing receipt. The recipient's state of knowledge must be such as to make it unconscionable for him to retain the benefit of the receipt. A test in that form, though it cannot, any more than any other, avoid difficulties of application, ought to avoid those of definition and allocation to which the previous categorisations have led. Moreover, it should better enable the courts to give commonsense decisions in the commercial context in which claims in knowing receipt are now frequently made . . .[133]

---

[129] [2001] Ch. 437.
[130] [1983] 1 WLR 509.
[131] [1987] Ch. 264.
[132] *Ibid.*
[133] [2001] Ch. 437 at 455.

Applying the test of 'unconscionability' Nourse LJ held that a defendant would only incur knowing receipt liability in circumstances where the state of mind of the defendant makes it unconscionable for him to retain the property. On the facts of **Bank of Credit and Commerce International (Overseas Ltd) (in Liquidation) v Akindele**,[134] Nourse LJ explained that the relevant question was 'whether the judge's findings, though made in the course of an inquiry as to the defendant's honesty, are equally supportive of a conclusion that his state of knowledge was not such as to make it unconscionable for him to retain the benefit of the receipt?'[135] Having made the inquiries into the defendant's state of mind, Nourse LJ concluded that at the time of the payment of the £10 million by the defendant to the bank, the defendant did not have any reason to suspect the integrity of the bank and that it was possibly operating fraudulent practices. Furthermore, the fact that the defendant was obtaining an unusually high rate of return on his investment did not necessarily mean that he would be put on inquiry as to the propriety of the bank's conduct.

The decision in **Bank of Credit and Commerce International (Overseas Ltd) (in liquidation) v Akindele** has subsequently been applied by the Court of Appeal in **Criterion Properties plc v Stratford UK Properties LLC**[136] and **Charter plc v City Index Ltd (Gawler and others, Part 20 defendants)**[137] where the claimants, Charter plc, were defrauded of large sums of money by one of their employees working in the foreign exchange department. The employee, Mr Chu, transferred the money to City Index Ltd in order to finance his betting addiction. Charter plc commenced proceeding against City Index Ltd on the grounds that they had knowingly received money transferred in breach of fiduciary duty by one of their employees. Charter plc argued that it would be unconscionable for City Index Ltd to use and transfer the money to aid Mr Chu's betting habits. In the Court of Appeal Carnwath LJ explained that 'liability for "knowing receipt" depends on the defendant having sufficient knowledge of the circumstances of the payment to make it "unconscionable" for him to retain the benefit or pay it away for his own purposes'.[138] Liability was admitted by City Index Ltd, who in turn argued under the Civil Liability (Contribution) Act 1978 that other defendants, namely auditors and directors of Charter plc, were liable to contribute on the grounds that they had allowed the money to be transferred by Mr Chu undetected from Charter plc. The Court of Appeal ordered that the issue proceed to full trial, but gave permission for an appeal to the House of Lords, primarily to resolve the interpretation of the 1978 Act.[139]

More recently two further cases have applied the decision in **Bank of Credit and Commerce International (Overseas Ltd)**. The first is **Hollis v Rolfe**[140] where land subject to a charitable trust had been transferred to the defendant. It was contended that the transfer was a breach of trust and that the defendant had knowingly received the land in breach of trust. Evans-Lombe J held that the disputed land had not been transferred in breach of trust and, applying the principle of unconscionability endorsed by Nourse LJ in **Bank of Credit and Commerce International (Overseas Ltd) (in liquidation) v Akindele**, it was not unconscionable for the defendant to retain the land transferred to

---

[134] [2001] Ch. 437.
[135] [2001] Ch. 437 at 456.
[136] [2003] 1 WLR 2108, affirmed by the House of Lords [2004] 1 WLR 1846.
[137] [2008] Ch. 313.
[138] [2008] Ch. 313 at 321.
[139] At the time of writing the House of Lords had not given their decision. It will be interesting, however, to see how the House of Lords will interpret the nature of liability for knowing receipt. See S. Gardner, 'Moment of Truth for Knowing Receipt' (2009) LQR 20.
[140] [2008] EWHC 1747 (Ch.).

him. The second case is the decision of the Court of Appeal in **Uzinterimpex JSC v Standard Bank plc**[141] which involved a complex international sales contract for the purchase of cotton by an English buyer from an Uzbek seller. To facilitate the sale of sale, Standard Bank plc acted as a correspondent bank to an Uzbek bank agreeing to act as a guarantor under the sales contract. The Uzbek seller experienced problems in getting the appropriate documentation to the buyer in order to take delivery of the cotton from the warehouses. The English buyer managed to take delivery of the cotton without the appropriate documentation and subsequently sold it to sub-buyers. The effect of this was that the Uzbek seller remained unpaid. When the English buyer deposited the proceeds of sale of the cotton with Standard Bank plc, the Uzbek buyer commenced litigation against Standard Bank plc on a number of grounds, one of them being knowing receipt of the money as a result of the sub-sale of the cotton. The Court of Appeal held that there were no evidential grounds for finding that the bank had received the money unconscionably. More recently, in **Horler v Rubin**[142] a claim for knowing receipt was found when a trustee in bankruptcy who had known that there was an outstanding claim that the bankrupt had been in a partnership distributed the proceeds of sale of assets of the claimed partnership to creditors of the bankrupt who were not creditors of the partnership. Given the fact that the trustee in bankruptcy knew that the assets possibly belonged to the partnership meant that he was liable as a constructive trust on the basis of knowing receipt of trust property.

Although the decision in **Bank of Credit and Commerce International (Overseas Ltd) (in Liquidation) v Akindele** firmly establishes that the test for liability for knowing receipt is founded on 'unconscionability', it is very difficult to explain how the test works in practice. The term 'unconscionability' has a wide meaning and there are number of very different factual situations which may render a person's conduct unconscionable. It is not disputed that 'unconscionability' is the very foundation upon which equitable relief is given;[143] however, there must be certain 'triggering events' which lead one to conclude that a person's conduct is unconscionable. For example, in the case of the imposition of a constructive trust where a person acquires property in breach of fiduciary duty, it is fairly well established that it is the breach of fiduciary duty, coupled with the absence of authority to retain the property acquired, which is the basis for the imposition of the constructive trust. In the context of knowing receipt, it is unfortunate that Nourse LJ did not expand further on the basis of what makes it unconscionable for the recipient to be converted into a constructive trustee. Clearly, as explained in the judgment of Nourse LJ, dishonesty is not a requirement; however, short of dishonesty, what exactly makes the receipt of property unconscionable? There are a number of events and circumstances that the court may look into: for example, whether the recipient should have been suspicious of the receipt or whether he should have undertaken some further inquiry. In its present form, the test of unconscionability seems to give the court a very loose notion to apply on individual factual situations. Some may argue that this flexible approach is much more suited in applying knowing-receipt liability to a wide range of factual circumstances. On the other hand, the absence of defined criteria leads to questions whether the constructive trust in such a case is more akin to a remedial constructive trust, discussed in Chapter 12, which is imposed in circumstances where it would be simply unconscionable for the defendant to retain property.

---

[141] [2008] 2 Lloyd's Rep. 456.
[142] [2011] EWHC 453 (Ch.).
[143] As explained by Lord Browne-Wilkinson in *Westdeutsche Landesbank Girozentrale v Islington LBC* [1996] AC 669 at 705.

Strict liability?

A question which has been raised on more than one occasion is whether liability for knowing receipt should take the form of strict liability subject to certain defences. The reason for this suggestion stems from the fact that, where a defendant receives property transferred in breach of fiduciary liability, the remedies against that defendant may be quite diverse, with different requisite elements needed to find liability in each instance. In some cases the defendant may be strictly liable to return money received; in other cases he may be liable for assisting in the breach but only in circumstances where he has been guilty of dishonesty; whilst in the case of knowing receipt he may incur liability if it was unconscionable for him to retain the property received. The question is whether different degrees of liability for acts carried out in the same set of facts is justified. The problem is best illustrated by A.J. Oakley in the following manner.

> The imposition of the obligations of trusteeship on the recipient of property disposed of in breach of trust is generally known as 'liability for knowing receipt'. The imposition of liability is, however, only one of a number of claims which may be available to the person from whom the property has been abstracted. If the property or its product is still identifiable in the hands of the recipient or of any third party to whom it is has been subsequently transferred, he will also have the possibility of bringing a proprietary claim, either at law or in equity to enable him to follow the property into the hands of its present holder. Additionally he may be able to bring a personal action at law for money had and received against the recipient, a personal action in equity against whoever was responsible for initiating the misapplication, and a claim to make accountable in equity anyone who has been guilty of dishonest assistance.

> *Parker and Mellows: The Modern Law of Trusts*, A.J. Oakley ed. 9th edn (2008) at pp. 424–5

Where a claimant pursues a proprietary claim to follow property into the hands of a defendant, he can do so provided that the defendant has not acquired the title to the property as a bona fide purchaser without notice. Other than that, the claimant will be entitled to follow the property even though the defendant has no knowledge that the property was transferred in breach of trust. With regard to the common law action for money had and received, again liability will be imposed irrespective of the notice on behalf of the defendant.[111] In the context of knowing receipt, as explained in the preceding sections, liability is based on fault and requires knowledge on the part of the recipient. In this context, the question is whether liability for knowing receipt should be strictly subject only to the defences of a bona fide purchaser for value without notice and change of position. The defence of a bona fide purchaser without notice has been rehearsed many times in the previous chapters; the defence of change of position is considered in more detail in Chapter 20. The defence operates to prevent a claimant from seeking a restitution of property where the defendant has so fundamentally changed his position since the receipt of property.

Although it has been contended that liability for receipt should be strict,[145] this has not been supported by other commentators and judges. A.J. Oakley in his work argues that strict liability would subject innocent volunteers to the strict liability of constructive trusteeship in the absence of fault on their part.[146] For example, a charity receiving property innocently but in breach of trust would have to account as a constructive trustee.

---

[144] See *Lipkin Gorman v Karpnale Ltd* [1991] 2 AC 548.

[145] See, for example, Lord Nicholls in *Restitution – Past, Present and Future* (Cornish ed. 1998) at p. 231.

[146] A.J. Oakley, *Parker and Mellows: The Modern Law of Trusts* 9th edn (2008) at p. 440.

In *Bank of Credit and Commerce International (Overseas Ltd) (in Liquidation)* v *Akindele*[147] Nourse LJ undertook an inquiry into strict liability for knowing receipt but rejected it on the grounds that it would be impractical to do so:

> We must continue to do our best with the accepted formulation of the liability in knowing receipt, seeking to simplify and improve it where we may. While in general it may be possible to sympathise with a tendency to subsume a further part of our law of restitution under the principles of unjust enrichment, I beg leave to doubt whether strict liability coupled with a change of position defence would be preferable to fault-based liability in many commercial transactions, for example where, as here, the receipt is of a company's funds which have been misapplied by its directors. Without having heard argument it is unwise to be dogmatic, but in such a case it would appear to be commercially . . . that, simply on proof of an internal misapplication of the company's funds, the burden should shift to the recipient to defend the receipt either by a change of position or perhaps in some other way. Moreover, if the circumstances of the receipt are such as to make it unconscionable for the recipient to retain the benefit of it, there is an obvious difficulty in saying that it is equitable for a change of position to afford him a defence.[148]

Conclusion

This chapter has looked at the constructive liability of third parties who either knowingly assist in a breach of trust or knowingly receive trust property in breach of trust. It is clear from this chapter that, whilst agents and other third parties who deal with trust property do not automatically acquire trust liability for their dealings with the trust property, they will attract constructive trust liability if they exceed their duties and intermeddle with the trust property. In the context of a knowing assistance, it was observed that the imposition of constructive trust liability is doctrinally difficult to justify on the grounds that the third party in most cases does not assume control over the trust property. Despite this, equity has long established that the third party will be liable as a constructive trustee to replace the loss if it does assist in a breach of trust. By far the most controversial aspect of liability for knowing assistance has centred on the state of mind of the third party. Recent judicial analysis has required that the third party be guilty of dishonesty before he or she can be held liable for knowing assistance. However, despite the requirement of dishonesty, there still remains an element of uncertainty as to exactly how the test of dishonesty operates in this context. With regard to liability for knowing receipt, again the imposition of a constructive trust gives a potential beneficiary another source to claim the loss it has suffered. Where a third party knowingly receives trust property which is then dissipated, the beneficiary will have a claim against that third party to replace the loss. As in the case of knowing assistance, the biggest problem in determining whether a third party is liable for knowing receipt has turned on his or her state of mind. At the present time the courts have adopted a test of unconscionability to determine liability for knowing receipt; however, exact scope of that test remains to be fully articulated by the courts.

---

[147] [2001] Ch. 437.
[148] [2001] Ch. 437 at 456.

● ● ● Case study

Michael is a senior partner in a firm of accountants, Alpha Ltd. Michael is authorised to access funds belonging to the firm. Michael is bored with working in the firm and has decided to set up his own company. Michael instructs Midwest Bank, which is the bank with whom Alpha Ltd bank with, to transfer almost two-thirds of the money in the account of Alpha Ltd into the name of a company in Jersey. When the transfer request is put through, the bank manager raises some suspicion about the transfer but, since he was a very good friend of Michael, allowed the funds to be transferred. Michael has left Alpha Ltd without informing anyone and has used some of the money transferred to the company in Jersey to buy properties in Jersey. Some of the money has been gambled at a casino and about £40,000 still remains in the account of the company in Jersey, whose director is Michael's brother.

Having discovered what has happened, Alpha Ltd has commenced proceedings against the following people:

● Michael for breach of his duty owed to the company;

● Midwest Bank for allowing the money to be transferred to Jersey without any investigation;

● The company in Jersey to recover the money that was transferred to it;

● A claim against the properties purchased by Michael with money belonging to Alpha Ltd.

In each of these claims, Alpha Ltd claims that property belonging to it has been unjustly transferred into the names of others as a result of Michael's fraud.

How are these issues to be resolved?

● ● Moot points

1 In *Barlow Clowes International* v *Eurotrust International* [2006] 1 WLR 1476 the Privy Council explained that the test of dishonesty, in the context of liability for knowing assistance in a breach of trust, is essentially an objective one. It requires the court to be satisfied that the defendant's conduct was dishonest by ordinary standards. Is it true to say that the test of dishonesty is purely objective, or is there a subjective element in the enquiry as to the defendant's state of mind?

2 Read the decision of the Court of Appeal in *Storglade Properties Ltd* v *Nash* [2010] EWCA 1314 and explain why the court held that the defendant's conduct had transgressed the normal standards of honest behaviour.

3 Read the judgment of the Court of Appeal in *Abou-Rahmah* v *Abacha* [2006] EWCA Civ. 1492 and explain how the test of dishonesty was interpreted by the judges.

4 In *Bank of Credit and Commerce International (Overseas Ltd) (in Liquidation)* v *Akindele* [2001] Ch. 437 the Court of Appeal held that a defendant will be liable for knowing receipt of property in circumstances where it would be unconscionable for the defendant to retain the property. How does the test of 'unconscionability' work? What exactly makes the receipt of property unconscionable?

5 It is sometimes argued that liability for knowing receipt should be strictly subject to certain defences, such as change of position on the part of the recipient. What are the advantages and disadvantages of strict liability?

Further reading

Clayton, N. 'Banks as Constructive Trustees: The English Position' (1993) JIBL 191. Examines the extent to which banks can acquire constructive trust liability for knowing assistance and knowing receipt.

Elliot, S.B. and C. Mitchell, 'Remedies for Dishonest Assistance' (2004) 67 MLR 16. Looks at the type of claims that can be made against third parties who dishonestly assist in a breach of trust.

Finn, P.D. 'The Liability of Third Parties for Knowing Receipt or Assistance' in D. Waters (ed.), *Equity and Fiduciaries* (1993). Explores the nature of third party liability for knowing assistance and knowing receipt of trust property.

Gardner, S. 'Knowing Assistance and Receipt: Taking Stock' (1996) 112 LQR 56. Examines a series of decisions decided in the 1990s which contribute to the decided case law on knowing assistance and knowing receipt. Amongst such cases analysed are *Polly Peck* v *Nadir* and *Royal Brunei* v *Tan*.

Gardner, S. 'Moment of Truth for Knowing Receipt' (2009) LQR 20. Looks at the nature of liability of knowing receipt with reference to the decision in *Charter plc* v *City Index Ltd* and suggests possible ways forward.

Griffiths, G. 'A Matter of Principle – The Basis of Secondary Liability for Knowing Assistance' (1996) JBL 281. Examines the decision of the Privy Council in *Royal Brunei* v *Tan*.

Halliwell, M. 'The Underlying Concept of Accessory Liability for Breach of Trust' (1995) Conv. 339. Examines the decision of the Privy Council in *Royal Brunei* v *Tan*.

Harpum, C. 'Accessory Liability for Procuring or Assisting in a Breach of Trust' (1995) 111 LQR 545. Case comment on the decision of the Privy Council in *Royal Brunei* v *Tan*.

Panesar, S. 'A Loan Subject to a Trust and Dishonest Assistance' (2003) JIBL 18(1) at 9. Explores the decision in *Twinsectra* v *Yardley* and evaluates the test of dishonesty advocated in that case.

Ridge, P. 'Justifying the Remedies for Dishonest Assistance' (2008) 124 LQR 445. Examines the remedies available for third parties who dishonestly assist in a breach of trust, with particular reference to the position in Australia.

Ryan, D. 'Royal Brunei Dishonesty: Clarity at Last' (2006) Conv. 188. Explores the decision of the Privy Council in *Barlow Clowes International* as a welcome development in clarifying the test of dishonesty.

Visit **www.mylawchamber.co.uk/panesar** to access study support resources including interactive multiple choice questions, practice exam questions with guidance, podcasts, weblinks, legal newsfeed all linked to the **Pearson eText** version of Exploring Equity and Trusts which you can **search**, **highlight** and **personalise** with your **own notes** and **bookmarks**.

premium
mylawchamber
unrivalled support for legal education

Use Case Navigator to read in full some of the key cases referenced in this chapter with commentary and questions:

Bank of Credit and Commerce International (Overseas Ltd) (in Liquidation) v *Akindele* [2001] Ch. 437

Westdeutsche Landesbank Girozentrale v *Islington LBC* [1996] AC 699 (HL)

Barlow Clowes International v *Eurotrust International* [2006] 1 WLR 1476

POWERED BY LexisNexis

Part IV
The administration of trusts

Part IV of this book examines the law relating to the administration of trusts. Once a trust is fully set up, it is the role of the trustee to administer the trust in accordance with the trust instrument and trust law in general. In the office of trusteeship, a number of powers and duties are conferred on trustees, which allow them to administer the trust in the best interests of the beneficiaries. Chapter 15 explores the office of trusteeship and, in doing so, examines a number of aspects connected with the office of trusteeship. This chapter looks at some of the reasons why an individual may wish to take up the office of trusteeship; it explores the general nature of the office of trusteeship and addresses questions relating to the appointment, retirement and removal of trustees. Chapter 16 explores one of the fundamental duties of trusteeship, that is, the investment of the trust funds. Where the trust property consists of a fund, it is the duty of the trustee to invest the trust fund so as to preserve its value in line with inflationary pressures. It will be observed in Chapter 16 that investment in modern financial markets is a very complex matter for trustees. Unless a trustee is a professional trustee acquainted with financial knowledge, a trustee will be best advised to delegate his investment duty and discretion to a qualified investment manager.

Chapter 17 explores the fiduciary nature of trusteeship. A trustee stands in a fiduciary relationship to his beneficiary, and it will be seen in this chapter that a fiduciary is a person who owes a duty of loyalty to his beneficiary. The duty of loyalty and confidentiality arises because of the special relationship between the fiduciary and the beneficiary. As a general rule, a fiduciary will not be able to extract any personal benefits for himself in the course of his office as a fiduciary. In this respect, it will be observed in Chapter 17 that a trustee must at all times act in the best interests of his beneficiary and cannot take benefits for himself which duly belong to the beneficiary.

Chapter 18 explores the various powers that are conferred upon trustees. Unlike duties, which are imperative, powers are discretionary in the sense that the trustee is not obliged to exercise them, although if he does exercise them they must be exercised in good faith and within reason. Three important powers are considered in this part of the book: firstly, the power of delegation, which allows the trustees to delegate certain duties and discretions upon agents; secondly, the power of maintenance, which allows the trustee to pay income to an infant beneficiary for his or her maintenance, education or other benefit; and finally, the power of advancement, which allows payment of capital sums from the trust fund to a beneficiary who is entitled to the capital. It will be observed that the powers of maintenance and advancement are important powers which allow the release of trust funds before the trust has come to an end.

Finally, Chapter 19 explores the question whether a trust, which is once created by a settlor or a testator, can be varied. There may be instances where a deviation from the existing terms of the trust may be in the interests of the beneficiaries. Such a deviation may be requested by the settlor or the existing beneficiaries. One of the more common instances where a deviation from the original terms of the trust will be important is in the context of taxation. It will be appreciated that many trusts will continue for long periods of time, and over the course of that time there will be many changes in the fiscal regime of the jurisdiction in which the trust is being administered. Certainly a settlor will not be able to cover for every contingency or change in the tax structure that may affect the trust. It may well be that, as a result of certain changes in the taxation structure, the trust is administered, or the beneficial interests of the beneficiaries are changed, so that the trust attracts a more favourable tax treatment. Although it is a fundamental rule of trust law that the trustees give effect to the settlor's or testator's intentions, it is equally clear that a settlor or testator will have intended that his beneficiaries pay the least amount of tax where possible.

15

Introduction to trusteeship appointment, removal and retirement

Learning objectives

After reading this chapter you should be able to:

→ explain who can be a trustee

→ explain when new trustees can be appointed

→ explain when a trustee can retire from a trust

→ explain the circumstances in which a trustee can be removed from office

→ understand the different types of trustees

→ understand some of the initial duties of trustees on appointment and the vesting of the trust property in the trustees

→ explain how the duties and discretions of trustees are controlled.

SETTING THE SCENE

Klug v *Klug* [1918] 2 Ch. 67: A mother appointed as a trustee for her children; the daughter beneficiary marrying without mother's consent; the mother refusing to pay trust monies to the daughter

The facts of *Klug* v *Klug* illustrate some of the themes which form the subject matter of this chapter. A testator made a will in 1907 in which he settled a sum of money on trust for his wife for her life and thereafter for his two sons and daughter. The remainder of his estate was settled in equal shares upon trust for his children on the condition that the sons attain the age of 30 years and the daughter 21 years. The will also provided that should the daughter marry, her interest would go to her children. The mother of the children was appointed a trustee of that trust along with a public trustee. The testator died in 1910 when all three children were infants. In 1915, Frida Klug, the daughter of the testator, became entitled to her interest in the trust fund. However, owing to various circumstances surrounding her birth, Frida became liable to pay tax on her interest. In order to pay the tax, she mortgaged her interest to an insurance company in order to pay the Inland Revenue. However, the money received was not enough to pay the whole amount of the tax.

In 1916 Frida married Jean Moro against the wishes of her mother. In 1917 Frida found it difficult to make payments to the Inland Revenue and the question was whether she could ask for an advancement of money from the capital, on the grounds that this was specifically authorised by her father. In other words, Frida's mother had a discretion to make the payment if she so wished. Frida's mother, who was also a trustee, refused to make any advancement of capital to her, on the grounds that she had married against her wishes. The public trustee, on the other hand, had no problems with making the advancement in her favour.

The facts of *Klug* v *Klug* raise interesting questions regarding the office of trusteeship. Clearly a trust had been created in favour of a daughter beneficiary. The trustee refused to exercise a discretion in favour of her on the grounds that the daughter married without her consent. Can a trustee take on board improper reasons when considering whether to exercise the discretion? What is the position when a beneficiary is not happy with the way in which a trust is being administered by the trustee? Can a trustee be removed from office? Can the court interfere with the administration of a trust? The mother was clearly appointed as a trustee in *Klug* v *Klug*; however, why was there a public trustee? What is a public trustee?

The answers to these questions and how the issue was dealt with in *Klug* v *Klug* will be investigated in this chapter.

Introduction

This chapter explores the office of trusteeship, and in doing so, examines a number of aspects connected with the office of trusteeship. It looks at some of the reasons why an individual may wish to take up the office of trusteeship; it explores the general nature of the office of trusteeship and addresses questions relating to the appointment, retirement and removal of trustees. At the outset of this chapter it has to be emphasised that the office of trusteeship is an onerous one. The Law Reform Committee once wrote that 'there is much to be said about the duties and obligations of a trustee, little of his rights'.[1] Writing in the *Law Times* in 1854 Lord Chancellor Cottenham is said to have described 'any man who accepted trusteeship a second time fit only for a lunatic asylum'.[2] The reasons for this relates to the onerous duties that are placed on trustees. A trustee must at all times act in the best interests of his beneficiaries. He is not allowed to put himself in a position where there is a conflict between his duty to the trust and his own personal interests. Unless there is some express authorisation in the trust instrument or statute, a trustee acts voluntarily and is not paid for his services. It will be seen, however, that in contemporary trust law most trustees will have the right to be remunerated by the trust instrument or by statute. In the exercise of his duties, a trustee must act prudently and reasonably in the circumstances. It is no defence to say that he was not competent to do the job or that whatever he did he thought was appropriate in the circumstances. In other words, his state of mind is irrelevant. Equity does not look to whether he acted in good faith or whether he was honest in the circumstances. Even where his breaches of trust are innocent or merely technical, he will be liable for breach of trust.[3]

If the office of trusteeship is indeed an onerous one, the question arises as to why an individual may want to act as a trustee. Historically, trustees acted out of a sense of moral obligation rather than legal duty. In the typical trust of the eighteenth and nineteenth centuries, where land would be settled by way of trust in favour of a succession of beneficiaries in the family, a trustee would be a close member of the family acting out of a sense of responsibility. Today, most trustees will act out of contractual rather than moral duty. For example, professional trustees such as banks, solicitors and other financial organisations will provide their professional services in return for remuneration. Other trustees will act because of a special role that has been assigned to them by statute or by the court. For example, the public trustee is a trustee set up by the Public Trustee Act 1906 to deal with small estates or, as a last resort, where no one is capable of dealing with the property of an individual, for example, the property of a mental patient.[4] The court may appoint a judicial trustee in circumstances where there has been a breakdown in the administration of a trust. The role of the judicial trustees is to work closely with the court and investigate the breakdown in the administration of the trust and put right what has gone wrong.[5] In **Re Ridsdel** Jenkins J explained that the object of a judicial trustee was to 'provide a middle course in cases where the administration of the estate by the ordinary trustees had broken down and it was not desired to put the estate to the expense of a full administration. In these circumstances, a solution was found in the appointment of a judicial trustee who acts in close contact with the court and under conditions enabling the court to supervise his transactions.'[6]

 ## Capacity and numbers

Except in the case of charity or a pension trust[7] the basic rule is that any person who is capable of holding the legal title to property can act as a trustee. Section 20 of the Law of

[1] 23rd Report, *Powers and Duties of Trustees* (Cmnd 8733), (1982) para. 12.
[2] Quoted in G. Moffat, *Trust Law: Text and Materials*, 4th edn (2005) at p. 406.
[3] Matters relating to breach of trust are examined in Chapters 20 and 21.
[4] Public Trustee and Administration of Funds Act 1986.
[5] Judicial Trustee Act 1896.
[6] [1947] Ch. 597 at 605.
[7] Discussed later in the chapter.

Property Act 1925 provides that 'the appointment of an infant to be a trustee in relation to any settlement or trust shall be void . . .' An infant will never be able to act as a trustee of land because s. 1(6) of the Law of Property Act 1925 provides that a minor cannot hold the legal title to land. If, in the case of pure personal property, an infant is found to have been appointed as a trustee, there are statutory mechanisms in place to remove and replace that infant from trusteeship.[8] It is quite possible, however, to find an infant as trustee of personal property under a resulting trust. For example, in **Re Vinogradoff**[9] a lady transferred a sum of £800 jointly into the names of herself and her four-year-old granddaughter. The court held that a voluntary transfer of personal property to another gave rise to a presumption of a resulting trust in favour of the donor.[10] The grandmother having died, the granddaughter held the money on resulting trust for her grandmother's estate.

With regard to numbers, there is no restriction on the number of trustees of personal property. However, it is not advisable to have too many trustees as this can hamper the effective administration of the trust, especially in cases where the consent of all trustees is required before certain administrative tasks can be performed. In the case of land, s. 34 of the Trustee Act 1925 limits the number of trustees to four. It is advisable to have at least a minimum of two trustees in the case of land for two main reasons. Firstly, it allows the trust to benefit from the principle of overreaching which requires payment to at least two trustees of land.[11] Overreaching is that process by which equitable interests in land are lifted from the land and shifted to the proceeds of sale. It does not matter that the purchaser of land has notice of the equitable interest: payment to two trustees is sufficient to overreach the equitable interests. Secondly, in the case of a trust of land it is impossible for a sole trustee to give a valid receipt for the proceeds of sale or any other capital monies arising under the trust.

Appointment of initial trustees

The first trustees will inevitably be appointed by the settlor in the trust instrument or in the will which purports to create the trust. A trust will not fail for want of a trustee. Thus, if the original trustee disclaims the trust, is unfit to act, or has predeceased the testator, the trust will not fail. In the case of an *inter vivos* trust where the trustee disclaims the trust, the trust property will revert to the settlor who will hold such property subject to the trust.[12] It may well be that the settlor has in fact died before the trustee disclaims the trust. If this is the case, the trust property will revest in the personal representatives of the settlor, who will likewise be required to hold it subject to the trusts that were declared by the settlor. The personal representatives may then apply for the appointment of new trustees.

Different rules will apply if the intended trust is created in the will. If the intended trustee dies before the testator, the personal representatives of the deceased trustee will hold the property subject to the trust.[13] The personal representatives may then take

---

[8] Section 36(1) Trustee Act 1925, discussed in much more detail below.
[9] [1935] WN 68.
[10] The presumption of a resulting trust was considered in greater detail in Chapter 10.
[11] Sections 2 and 27 Law of Property Act 1925.
[12] *Mallot v Wilson* [1903] 2 Ch. 494.
[13] *Re Willis* [1921] 1 Ch. 44.

steps to appoint new trustees in accordance with the statutory powers discussed in the next section.

Appointment of new trustees

Suppose a trust is created and trustees are duly appointed by the settlor. What is the position if one of the trustees is unfit to act or has gone abroad for a long period of time? What if the trust has become administratively burdensome and extra trustees are required to administer it? Can new trustees be appointed? Who has the power to appoint them and who can be appointed as a trustee?

Although the initial trustees will be appointed by the trust instrument, it will become inevitable that new trustees will have to be appointed at some time in the lifespan of a trust. The need for new appointments may vary from the simple fact that the trust is continuing for a long time and new replacement trustees are required, owing to the fact that a trustee wishes to disclaim the trust or is unfit to act as trustee. The appointment of new trustees might also be needed if the workload of the trust has increased. There are two questions which arise when there is a need to appoint new trustees:

1 Is there a power to appoint new trustees?

2 Who can exercise the power to appoint new trustees?

The power to appoint new trustees may be found either in the trust instrument, in which case there is an express power of appointment, or, in the absence of the trust instrument, in statute.

Express power to appoint a new trustee

It may well be that the trust instrument confers upon certain individuals the power to appoint new trustees. One question that arises in the context of an express power to appoint is whether the donee of such a power can appoint himself. In **Montefiore v Guedalla**[14] the court held that there was no rule that a donee of a power to appoint new trustees could not appoint himself. Buckley J went on to to comment that the court could sanction such an appointment in special circumstances. However, although the court can sanction the appointment of the donee, it should be borne in mind that the donee should not appoint himself, because such a power to appoint will be fiduciary in nature. For example, in **Re Skeats' Settlement**[15] an express power to appoint trustees was conferred upon certain individuals who sought to exercise the power by appointing themselves. The court held that this was an improper exercise of the power because it was fiduciary in nature. In the course of his judgment Kay J explained the justification behind the rule by saying that:

---

[14] [1903] 2 Ch. 723.
[15] (1889) 42 Ch. D 522.

naturally no human being can be imagined who would not have some bias one way or the other as to his own personal fitness, and to appoint himself among other people, or excluding them to appoint himself would certainly be an improper exercise of any power of selection of a fiduciary character such as this is. In my opinion it would be extremely improper for a person who has a power to appoint or select new trustees to appoint himself.[16]

The statutory power in s. 36 Trustee Act 1925

The fact that there is an absence of an express power to appoint new trustees is not fatal, since there are number of statutory powers which can be invoked to appoint new trustees. The first of those powers is found in section 36(1) of the Trustee Act 1925.

KEY STATUTE

S. 36(1)(2) Trustee Act 1925

(1) Where a trustee, either original or substituted, and whether appointed by a court or otherwise, is dead, or remains out of the United Kingdom for more than twelve months, or desires to be discharged from all or any of the trusts or powers reposed in or conferred on him, or refuses or is unfit to act therein, or is incapable of acting therein, or is an infant, then subject to the restrictions imposed by this Act on the number of trustees –

(a) the person or persons nominated for the purpose of appointing new trustees by the trust instrument, if any, creating the trust; or

(b) if there is no such person, or no such person able and willing to act, then the surviving or continuing trustees or trustee for the time being, or the personal representatives of the last surviving or continuing trustee;

may, by writing, appoint one or more other person (whether or not being the persons exercising the power) to be a trustee or trustees in the place of the trustee so deceased, remaining out of the United Kingdom, desiring to be discharged from the trust, and the provisions of this section shall apply accordingly, but subject to the restrictions imposed by this Act on the number of trustees.

(2) Where a trustee has been removed under a power contained in the instrument creating the trust, a new trustee or new trustees may be appointed in the place of the trustee who is removed, as if he were dead, or, in the case of a corporation, as if the corporation desired to be discharged from the trust, and the provisions of this section will apply accordingly, but subject to the restrictions imposed by this Act on the number of trustees.

Section 36 of the Trustee Act 1925 lays down seven well-defined circumstances in which a new trustee can be appointed:

1 The trustee is dead

2 The trustee remains out of the United Kingdom for more than 12 months

3 The trustee wishes to be discharged from the trust

4 The trustee refuses to act

---

[16] (1889) 42 Ch. D 522 at 527.

5 The trustee is unfit or incapable of acting

6 The trustee is an infant

7 The trustee has been removed under an express power.

With regard to the persons who may exercise the power, s. 36(1) identifies three types of person. The first person or persons who may exercise the power are those named in the trust instrument. The power is only exercisable by such persons if it is general in nature. Such persons will not be able to exercise the power if it is specific or otherwise narrowed down to special circumstances. The matter is neatly illustrated in *Re Wheeler and De Rochow*[17] where a power to appoint a new trustee was given to certain individuals in circumstances where one of the initial trustees should become incapable of acting. One of the trustees was declared bankrupt and later absconded. The question was whether a new trustee could be appointed under s. 36(1)(a). The court held that the persons nominated in the trust instrument did not have the power to appoint a new trustee because the bankrupt trustee was not incapable of acting but merely unfit to act. The court, however, held that the continuing trustees could appoint a new trustee under s. 36(1)(b).[18]

Where there is no person or persons nominated to appoint new trustees then the appointment has to be made by the surviving or continuing trustee or trustees. One question which has arisen in this context is: who are the surviving or continuing trustee or trustees? Section 36(8) of the Trustee Act 1925 makes it clear that the surviving or continuing trustee or trustees includes a trustee who has refused to act or wishes to retire from the trust. The net effect of this is that such a trustee can be allowed to join in the appointment of a new trustee. Section 36(8) does raise an interesting point of law in that if a trustee, who refuses to act or wishes to retire from the trust, does not participate in the appointment of the new trustee, is the appointment void? Although the case law is not conclusive on this point, the courts have taken a somewhat narrow construction of the words 'a refusing or retiring trustee'. For example, in *Re Stoneham Settlement Trust*[19] a new trustee was appointed in circumstances where one of the original trustees remained outside the United Kingdom for a period greater than 12 months. When the original trustee returned to the United Kingdom, he sought to have the appointment set aside, on the grounds that he was not consulted. The court held that his participation was not required because he was not a 'refusing or retiring trustee' but a removed trustee, on the grounds that he had been absent from the United Kingdom for more than 12 months.[20]

If there are no continuing or surviving trustees to make the appointment of a new trustee then the power to appoint is conferred on the personal representatives of the last surviving trustee. The personal representatives may make the appointment before the grant of probate; however, the new trustee will not be able to take up office until after the grant of probate.[21]

So far it has been observed that s. 36(1) allows the appointment of new trustees in circumstances where one or more of the original trustees are ceasing to continue with his duties. Section 36(6) goes further and allows for the appointment of additional trustees without necessarily any one of the original trustees being removed from office. The section, however, will only apply where there are less than three trustees. Additional

---

[17] [1896] 1 Ch. 315.
[18] Followed in *Re Sichel's Settlements* [1916] 1 Ch. 358.
[19] [1953] Ch. 59.
[20] The same view was taken in *Re Coates to Parsons* (1886) 34 Ch. D 370.
[21] *Re Crowhurst Park* [1974] 1 WLR 583.

trustees may be appointed, but the total number of trustees must not exceed four. Thus, where there are two original trustees under a trust, they can appoint two further trustees under s. 36(6). The power may be exercised by the person or persons nominated in the trust instrument, or the trustee or trustees for the time being.

The statutory power in s. 41 Trustee Act 1925

APPLYING THE LAW

Tom has been appointed as a trustee under a trust created some time ago. In the last few years the beneficiaries have been concerned with they way in which he has administered the trust. Some of his decisions have had a detrimental effect on the trust. Tom has been diagnosed as suffering from clinical depression and has visited a mental institute on some occasions. He refuses to retire from the trust, saying that he is fit to act.

Can the beneficiaries ask for him to be removed from office?

Section 41 of the Trustee Act 1925 confers upon the court a power to appoint new trustees.

KEY STATUTE

S. 41 Trustee Act 1925 (The power of the court to appoint new trustees)

(1) The court may, whenever it is expedient to appoint a new trustee or new trustees, and if it is found inexpedient difficult or impracticable so to do without the assistance of the court, make an order appointing a new trustee or new trustees either in substitution for or in addition to any existing trustee or trustees, or although there is no existing trustee.

The section allows for the appointment of new trustees in circumstances when it would be inexpedient or difficult to do so without assistance of the court. The section is not used widely by the courts and, in particular, the court will require, where possible, for the appointment to be made under an express power of appointment or the statutory power in s. 36(1). The assistance of the court will be required as a last resort, for example, where there has been a breakdown in the administration of the trust between the existing trustees, and one or more trustees refuse to cooperate to get a new trustee appointed under the statutory power in s. 36(1). Other examples, where the assistance of the court may be required is where the trustee has been declared bankrupt or is mentally incapable of acting as a trustee. It is well established under s. 41(1) that the court can displace a trustee against his will.[22]

---

[22] *Re Henderson* [1940] Ch. 764.

With regard to the exercise of its discretion under s. 41(1), the court will have regard to three criteria. These criteria were laid down in **Re Tempest**,[23] a case decided under the predecessor of s. 41(1). Turner LJ explained that the court would have regard to the wishes of the settlor, the interests of the beneficiaries and, finally, regard to the effective administration of the trust. A good example where the court may deem the appointment not to be in the interest of the due administration of the trust is when the appointment is of a trustee who is abroad. Turner LJ explained it in the following way.

First, the Court will have regard to the wishes of the persons by whom the trust has been created, if expressed in the instrument creating the trust, or clearly to be collected from it. I think this rule may be safely laid down, because if the author of the trust has in terms declared that a particular person, or a person filling a particular character, should not be a trustee of the instrument, there cannot, as I apprehend, be the least doubt that the Court would not appoint to the office a person whose appointment was so prohibited, and I do not think that upon a question of this description any distinction can be drawn between express declarations and demonstrated intention. The analogy of the course which the Court pursues in the appointment of guardians affords, I think, some support to this rule. The Court in those cases attends to the wishes of the parents, however informally they may be expressed.

Another rule which may, I think, safely be laid down is this – that the Court will not appoint a person to be trustee with a view to the interest of some of the persons interested under the trust, in opposition either to the wishes of the testator or to the interests of others of the *cestuis que trusts*. I think so for this reason, that it is of the essence of the duty of every trustee to hold an even hand between the parties interested under the trust. Every trustee is in duty bound to look to the interests of all, and not of any particular member or class of members of his *cestuis que trusts*.

A third rule which, I think, may safely be laid down, is, – that the Court in appointing a trustee will have regard to the question, whether his appointment will promote or impede the execution of the trust, for the very purpose of the appointment is that the trust may be better carried into execution.[24]

The matter is neatly illustrated in **Re Weston's Settlement Trust**[25] where the court refused to appoint a non-resident trustee in Jersey. The case involved an attempt to move a trust from England to Jersey primarily for tax reasons. One of the reasons for not appointing the non-resident trustee was because of the inadequacy of trust law in Jersey and thus its consequential impact on the effective administration of the trust.[26]

In the exercise of its power under s. 41 of the Trustee Act 1925 the court will appoint someone whom they think will act in the best interests of the trust. Particular types of person who may not be appointed include those who might favour one particular beneficiary against another.[27] Although in the past the courts have been reluctant to appoint a beneficiary as a trustee, the modern trend is to do so on the grounds that the beneficiary will have a vested interested in the due administration of the trust. Perhaps, the best person to be appointed is a professional trustee, such as a solicitor, if this is what the beneficiary would prefer. One particular question which does arise is whether the court can be influenced by the other trustees as to the appointment, particularly in circumstances where the other trustees may not wish to work with or cooperate with

---

[23] (1866) 1 Ch. App. 485.

[24] (1866) 1 Ch. App. 485 at 488.

[25] [1969] 1 Ch. 223.

[26] The decision in this case is considered in more detail in Chapter 19, which looks at the extent to which the terms of a trust may be varied.

[27] *Re Parsons* [1940] Ch. 973.

the proposed new trustee. The matter was addressed in **Re Tempest**[28] where Turner LJ explained that:

> I think it would be going too far to say that the court, ought, on that ground alone, to refuse to appoint the proposed trustee: for this would, as suggested in the argument, be to give the continuing or surviving trustee a veto upon the appointment of the new trustee. In such a case I think it must be the duty of the court to inquire and ascertain whether the objection of the surviving or continuing trustee is well founded or not, and to act or refuse to act upon it accordingly.[29]

Section 41 of the Trustee Act 1925 is wide enough to remove a trustee against his or her will. The statutory power was used by Bennett J in **Henderson v Henderson**[30] to remove a trustee and replace her with a public trustee. The court exercised its discretion primarily as a result of the breakdown in the administration of the trust by the existing trustees. One of the trustees asked to be replaced by a public trustee but then changed her mind and demanded certain conditions before the public trustee was appointed in place of her. In the course of his judgment, Bennett J explained that:

> [I] do not think that it is open to doubt that on the language of the sub-section the Court has jurisdiction to displace a trustee against his will and to appoint a new trustee in substitution for him. Take the case of a trustee who is a convicted felon or a bankrupt whom the beneficiaries desire to have replaced by a new trustee. On the language of the sub-section, in my judgement, the Court has a discretion, which it can exercise, if it regards it as expedient so to do, by appointing a new trustee in place of the trustee who has been convicted of the felony, or who is bankrupt.[31]

The application of s. 41 of the Trustee Act 1925 was more recently illustrated by the decision of the High Court in **Alkin v Raymond**[32] where two executors who were also trustees had put themselves in a position of conflict of interest. The facts concerned two trustee executors appointed by the testator. They had been very good friends of the testator and had done some property development work for him when he was alive. The beneficiaries included a number of different individuals including the testator's wife, Mrs Alkin, and the testator's daughter, Mrs Price. One of the executors, a certain Mr Whelan, was also a builder by trade and had done some development work with the testator. Mr Whelan backdated an invoice from his company and presented the bill to the estate. Both the executors accepted the bill and proceeded to pay upon it without checking the legitimacy of the invoice. The bill made no reference to any extra work that had been carried out by Mr Whelan's firm and it was described by the court as not being in accordance with normal industry standards. Indeed, when scrutinised by the court it became obvious that those additional costs mentioned in the bill would have eliminated any profit that the testator would have made on the properties that were worked on by Mr Whelan's firm. The court held that both executor trustees had failed to discharge their duties in the administration of the estate. The court held that they could be removed under s. 41 of the Trustee Act 1925 as they could not be trusted to act in the best interests of the beneficiaries when they had put their own interests first. As to the appointment of new trustees, the court appointed two new trustees despite representations by Mrs Price, the testator's daughter, that she should be replaced as a trustee. The court examined the principles in **Re Tempest**[33] and explained that Mrs Price was not best placed to become a trustee as

---

[28] (1866) 1 Ch. App. 485.
[29] (1866) 1 Ch. App. 485 at 490.
[30] [1940] Ch. 764.
[31] [1940] Ch. 764 at 767.
[32] [2010] WTLR 1117.
[33] [1866] LR 1 Ch 485.

this is not what her father would have wanted and that it would be difficult for her to objectively balance the competing claims to the estate.

Appointment under the Trusts of Land and Appointment of Trustees Act 1996

The preceding statutory powers confer a power to appoint new trustees either in the continuing or surviving trustees of the court. There is nothing in those powers which confer any right on the beneficiaries to make an appointment. This position was rectified by s. 19 of the Trusts of Land and Appointment of Trustees Act 1996. The power also allows the beneficiaries to request that a trustee retires from the trust.

KEY STATUTE

S. 19 of the Trust of Land and Appointment of Trustees Act 1996 (The beneficiaries' right to appoint new trustees)

(1) This section applies in the case of a trust where –

(a) there is no person nominated for the purpose of appointing new trustees by the instrument, if any, creating the trust, and

(b) the beneficiaries under the trust are of full age and capacity and (taken together) are absolutely entitled to the property subject to the trust.

(2) The beneficiaries may give a direction or directions of either or both of the following descriptions –

(a) a written direction to a trustee or trustees to retire from the trust, and

(b) a written direction to a trustee or trustees for the time being (or, if there are none, to the personal representatives of the last person who was a trustee) to appoint by writing to be a trustee or trustees the person or persons specified in the direction.

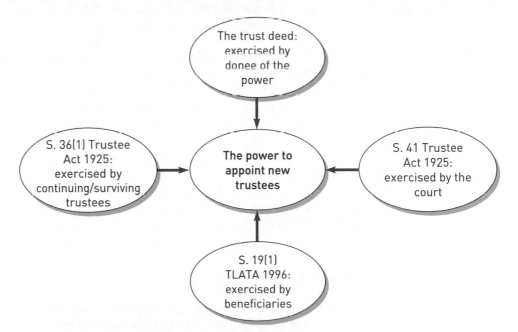

Figure 15.1 The powers to appoint new trustees

As can be observed from the section, the power is only exercisable when there is no one in the trust instrument with a power to appoint new trustees. Furthermore, the beneficiaries must be of full age and collectively entitled to the trust property. The section allows for the appointment of new trustees as well as retirement at the direction of the beneficiaries.

   ## The retirement of trustees

It may well be that once a potential trustee finds out that he has been appointed as a trustee that he wishes to retire from the trust. There are a number of circumstances under which the trustee may retire from the trust. Firstly, there may be an express power in the trust instrument which allows the trustee to retire from the office of trusteeship. Alternatively, a trustee may retire from the trust where the continuing or surviving trustees appoint a new trustee under s. 36 of the Trustee Act 1925. For example, this would cover a situation where the trustee wishes to be discharged and the continuing or surviving trustee exercises the power by appointing a new trustee. A trustee may also be allowed, indeed instructed, to retire under s. 19 of the Trusts of Land and Appointment of Trustees Act 1996 if the direction is given in writing by adult beneficiaries who are collectively entitled to the trust property. These sections have been examined above; however, s. 39 of the Trustee Act 1925 gives an extra facility to a trustee who wishes to be discharged from the office of trusteeship.

KEY STATUTE

S. 39 of the Trustee Act 1925 (The retirement of trustees)

(1) Where a trustee is desirous of being discharged from the trust, and after his discharge there will be either a trust corporation or at least two persons to act as trustees to perform the trust, then, if such trustee as aforementioned by deed declares that he is desirous of being discharged from the trust, and if his co-trustees and such other persons, if any, as is empowered to appoint trustees, by deed consent to the discharge of the trustee, and to the vesting in the co-trustees alone of the trust property, the trustee desirous of being discharged shall be deemed to have retired from the trust, and shall by deed, be discharged therefrom under this Act, without any new trustee being appointed in his place.

Section 39 of the Trustee Act 1925 allows for the retirement of a trustee without the need for a new appointment being made. The requirements are that the retirement must be made by deed and that the other trustees consent to the retirement. More importantly, however, a trustee will only be able to invoke s. 39 in circumstances where he is leaving behind a trust corporation of at least two trustees. Where there are only two trustees to start off with, the trustee desiring to be released from the office of trusteeship cannot use s. 39 but will have to use s. 36 of the Trustee Act, thereby asking to be discharged with the appointment of an additional trustee(s).

   ## Removal of a trustee

A trustee can, of course, retire from a trust in the circumstances which have been discussed above. The question arises whether a trustee can be removed from the office of trusteeship against his own will. It has already been seen that s. 41 of the Trustee Act 1925 confers upon the court a power to appoint new trustees as well as a power to remove a trustee against his will. As well as s. 41 of the Trust Act 1925, the court has an inherent jurisdiction to remove a trustee from office. The court's inherent jurisdiction is exercised primarily in the interests of the beneficiaries. For example, the inherent juris-diction will be exercised where the trustee to be removed has been guilty of a criminal offence, has been dishonest or has been declared bankrupt. However, despite this, there does not appear to be too much by way of authority explaining the extent to which the inherent jurisdiction will be exercised. For example, will the court exercise its inherent jurisdiction on the grounds that the beneficiaries do not particularly like a trustee? Equally, will the court exercise its inherent jurisdiction where there has been a complete breakdown with the existing trustees? Presumably, in the latter example, the interests of the beneficiaries may require the removal of one or more of the trustees. In **Re Wrightson**[34] the beneficiaries complained of mismanagement with the trust property and the inappropriateness of certain investments. The court held that it had the power to remove a trustee, on the grounds that it would not be in the best interests to leave the property in the original trustees. The absence of any guidelines in the exercise of the court's inherent jurisdiction has been attributed to the fact that each case must depend on its facts.[35]

Special types of trustees

So far this chapter has looked at the appointment, removal and retirement of trustees in general. Regard must also be had to special types of trustees.

Public trustee

APPLYING THE LAW

Alf has been living by himself for many years. He is an elderly individual and has been diagnosed as suffering from a mental condition. He has no family and there are concerns as to how his property affairs are to be managed. There is nobody willing to act as a trustee for him.

What is the position of such an individual where no one is willing to act as a trustee?

In some circumstances it may well be that no one is willing to acts as a trustee or there may not be anyone who can deal with the estate of a deceased person. The Public Trustee Act 1906 introduced the office of public trustee. The function of such a trustee is to manage the property of an individual as a last resort. There are many advantages of employing a public trustee. In the first place, a public trustee is a corporation solely and its office is not confined to a particular named individual. Thus, where an individual who is acting in the office of public trustee dies, the office nevertheless continues. The second

---

[34] [1908] 1 Ch. 789.
[35] See, for example, *Letterstedt* v *Broers* (1884) 9 App. Cas. 371.

advantage is that the Lord Chancellor's department is liable for any loss which is caused by the public trustee.[36] Thirdly, the public trustee cannot set his own fees because the fees are set up by the Lord Chancellor's department. Once appointed, a public trustee has the same powers and duties as a private trustee and will have the same liabilities. Although a public trustee may refuse to act as a trustee, he cannot do so simply on the grounds of the low value of trust property. A public trustee is, however, restricted from accepting a charitable trust and dealing with trusts which involve arrangements with creditors.

A public trustee may be appointed as a custodian trustee by the court or any other person who has the power to appoint new trustees. Indeed, a public trustee can be appointed as a normal private trustee by persons who have the power to appoint new trustees. Furthermore, such a trustee can act in the administration of an estate when requested to do so and usually as a last resort. In practice the office of public trustee is not used that often and its role is confined to cases where there is absolutely no one else willing to act as trustee.

Judicial trustee

In some cases the management of a trust may well fall apart and issues may arise as to what went wrong and how things can be put right. The court has a power under the Judicial Trustee Act 1896 to appoint a judicial trustee to investigate the matter and try and ascertain exactly what went wrong before litigation commences. The judicial trustee becomes an officer of the court and works closely with the court. The judicial trustee can be an individual or in most cases a corporation. Such a trustee will work closely with the court and will seek direction from the court as to the best way to proceed with the trust management. Such directions from the court can be obtained at any time and informally. A judicial trustee will be entitled to receive remuneration from the trust fund; however, he must prepare annual accounts for the court to see.[37] A good example of the use of a judicial trustee is where there has been a dispute between the beneficiaries and the trustees as to the proper administration of the trust. The court can appoint an accountant or someone similar to investigate the matter where the complaint deals with the trust funds.

Trust corporations

In more recent times, much of trust administration is undertaken by trust corporations. Most typically a trust corporation will be a bank which has decided to provide a specialist service in the administration of a trust. Other commercial companies may also provide specialist trust management services. The advantage of a trust corporation is that it provides the settlor or testator with specialist trust management skills. Another advantage of a trust corporation is that it can act alone in cases where it would be a minimum requirement that there be at least two trustees. For example, in the case of land, at least two trustees are needed before a valid receipt can be given for money arising from the sale of land.[38] Furthermore, payment to a trust corporation will allow any beneficial interests in land to be overreached.[39] Overreaching, the process by which equitable interests in land are moved to the purchase money, otherwise requires payment to a minimum of two trustees.

---

[36] S. 7 Public Trustee Act 1906.
[37] Judicial Trustee Rules 1983.
[38] Section 14(2) Trustee Act 1925.
[39] Section 27(2) Law of Property Act 1925.

Vesting of the trust property in trustees

In the case of original trustees of a trust, the trust property will be vested by the settlor or the testator's personal representatives by whatever formality is required for the type of property in question. On the other hand, once a new trustee has been appointed, it is important that the trust property is vested in the new trustee or trustees. The vesting of the trust property in new trustees is dealt with in s. 40(1) of the Trustee Act 1925 which provides that the vesting of the trust property will automatically take place provided the trust was created by deed. There is no need for an express conveyance or an assignment. The reason for this is that post 1925 every deed appointing a new trustee will be assumed to contain a vesting declaration. There are three situations when s. 40(1) will not have the effect of vesting the trust property in the trustees. The first instance is where land is held by the trustees by way of mortgage for securing money loaned from the trust funds. The reason for this is to avoid bringing the trust on to the title. If s. 40(1) is applied the mortgagor would have to investigate the title of every new trustee and, indeed, make sure that he was paying to the right trustee. The second exception is where land is held under a lease and consent is required of the legal owner before there can be an assignment of the lease. In such a case, the exception is there to prevent an unintended breach of covenant which would otherwise occur if s. 40(1) was applied. The final exception relates to stocks and shares where the title can only be transferred by effective registration in the shareholders register.

Conducting the office of trusteeship

APPLYING THE LAW

Tom has been a trustee under a trust created by his brother. Tom has no specialist knowledge of trust law and has very little understanding of financial matters. In a separate trust, Tim, who is a trust practitioner with several years of trust experience has also been appointed. Tom is worried that he does not have the same expertise as Tim.

Are Tom and Tim expected to conduct the office of trusteeship with the same degree of skill?

**VISIT CASE
NAVIGATOR**

Once appointed, the basic requirement of a trustee is to act in the best interests of the beneficiaries. In ***Westdeutsche Landesbank Girozentrale v Islington LBC***[40] Lord Browne-Wilkinson explained that at the heart of the imposition of a trust is good conscience. Given the fact that the trustee is bound in equity on the grounds that he has promised to hold the property for the beneficiary, it is the element of conscience arising from the promise that binds him. There are a number of duties and power conferred upon trustees and these are considered in the chapters which follow. However, for the time being it is important to understand the basic duty of care and prudence which must be observed by all trustees.

The general duty of care is to be found in Part I of the Trustee Act 2000. The duty of care applies to trustees whether they are carrying out their functions under the statute or the trust instrument. The general duty is defined in s. 1 of the Act as follows.

---

[40] [1996] AC 669 (HL).

KEY STATUTE

S. 1 of the Trustee Act 2000 (The duty of care imposed on trustees)

(1) Whenever the duty under this subsection applies to a trustee, he must exercise such care and skill as is reasonable in the circumstances, having regard in particular –

(a) to any special knowledge or experience that he has or holds himself out as having, and

(b) if he acts as trustee in the course of a business or profession, to any special knowledge or experience that it is reasonable to expect of a person acting in the course of that kind of business or profession.

(2) In this Act the duty under subsection (1) is called 'the duty of care'.

The general duty of care provides that a trustee must exercise such care and skill as is reasonable in the circumstances, making allowance for his special knowledge, experience or professional status.[41] The general duty of care, whilst creating an objective standard of care, does have a subjective element to it. Whilst a trustee is expected to demonstrate standards expected of a reasonable man of business, s. 1 requires that the experience and skills of the individual trustee be taken into account when applying the duty of care. The general duty of care in s. 1 of the Trustee Act 2000 reflects the now displaced common law duty of care formulated in some of the nineteenth century cases. For example, in **Speight v Gaunt**[42] Lord Blackburn commented that 'as a general rule a trustee discharges his duty if he takes in the management of trust affairs all those precautions which an ordinary prudent man of business would take in managing similar affairs of his own'.[43] Similarly, in the context of making investments, Lindley LJ explained that the duty of a trustee is to 'take such care as an ordinary prudent man of business would take if he were under a duty to make the investments for other persons for whom he felt morally bound to provide'.[44] The duty of care in s. 1 is, however, slightly different from common law duty. Firstly, the common law duty of care requires the trustee to act as a prudent man of business, whereas the duty in s. 1 of the Trustee Act 2000 requires the trustee to act reasonably. There is a difference between acting prudently and acting reasonably. Prudent behaviour under the common law duty requires the trustee to act cautiously. For example, in the very context of trustee investments, a trustee must not take any risks at all. Under s. 1, the trustee is expected to act reasonably and is therefore entitled to take a risk in the investment of the trust funds, provided that the risk is reasonable in all of the circumstances.

A second difference between the duty of care in s. 1 of the Trustee Act 2000 and the common law duty is that s. 1 requires the court to take into consideration the specific skills and experience of the individual trustee. One question which arises in this context is whether this subjective criterion lowers the level of care required of a lay trustee. For example, it is possible for a lay trustee to argue that he is subject to a very low duty of care because he is simply not competent or experienced in trust matters. The answer to this is that, despite the fact that the court is required to take on board the specific skills and experience of the trustee, a trustee must observe a minimum standard of competency.

---

[41] Schedule 1 of the Trustee Act 2000 makes provision for the general duty of care to be excluded in the trust instrument.

[42] (1883) 9 App. Cas. 1.

[43] (1883) 9 App. Cas. 1 at 19.

[44] *Re Whiteley* (1886) 33 Ch. D 347.

Section 1 of the Trustee Act 2000 specifically requires a higher duty of care from a professional trustee. However, one thing which remained unclear prior to the enactment of the Trustee Act 2000 was whether a higher duty of care was also required of a paid trustee. In **Re Waterman's Will Trust**[45] Harman J commented that a 'paid trustee is expected to exercise a higher standard of diligence and knowledge than an unpaid trustee, and . . . a bank which advertises itself largely in the public press as taking charge of administrations is under a special duty'.[46] Whilst there is no doubt that a professional trustee should owe a higher duty of care based on his knowledge, skill and experiences, not all paid trustees are necessarily professional trustees. What Harman J was envisaging was a professional trustee and not just a paid trustee. The general duty of care in s. 1 allows for a higher duty of care to be expected from a professional trustee without necessarily a higher duty of care from a paid trustee who happens to be a lay trustee. Thus, a lay trustee may be paid for his services; however, the duty of care required from him is to be measured in the circumstances of the case making allowance for his special knowledge and experience.

 ## Control of trustees' discretions

APPLYING THE LAW

The trust instrument or statute may confer upon a trustee a discretion to act in a particular way. For example, the trustee may be given a discretion to make some payment of income or capital to a beneficiary before the beneficiary is in a position to terminate the trust.

What is the position if the trustee refuses to exercise the discretion on grounds of an improper motive?

In the course of the administration of a trust, a trustee will not only be subject to certain duties, but will also be conferred a number of powers by the trust instrument, statute as well as case law. It has already been observed that duties impose an imperative obligation on the part of the trustee to act. For example, the general duty of care considered in the preceding section requires the trustees to act reasonably in the circumstances. In the subsequent chapters it will be seen that other imperative duties include the duty to invest the trust funds and the duty not to put a conflict of interest between the trustees' personal interest and the interests of the beneficiaries.

Powers, on the other hand, are discretionary in the sense that they confer upon the trustee an authority to act. Unlike a duty, which must be exercised, the exercise of a power is not imperative. The exercise of a power needs only to be considered and in most cases there is no obligation on the part of the trustee to exercise the power at all. One particular concern of the law of trusts is the extent to which the courts can control the exercise of powers conferred on trustees.[47] For example, what if a trustee simply fails to consider the exercise of a power, or having considered it, refrains from exercising it, on

---

[45] [1952] 2 All ER 1054.
[46] [1952] 2 All ER 1054 at 1055.
[47] See N.D.M. Parry, 'Control of Trustees' Discretions' Conv. [1985],

grounds which the beneficiary is not in agreement with. The answers to these questions depend on the type of power or discretion that has been conferred upon the trustees. Powers can be divided into two types: dispositive powers and administrative powers.

Dispositive discretions

A dispositive discretion is a discretion conferred upon a trustee allowing him to dispose, at his discretion, any part of the capital or income subject to a trust. Good examples of dispositive discretions include the power to distribute property under a discretionary trust,[48] the power to apply income and capital under the powers of maintenance and advancement[49] and the power to appoint amongst objects under a power of appointment.[50] In the case of a discretionary trust, trustees must exercise their discretion and distribute the trust property amongst the beneficiaries or class of beneficiaries. Failure to exercise the discretion will amount to a breach of trust and the court will intervene and execute the settlor's intentions either by appointing new trustees or directing certain persons to prepare a scheme for distribution.[51] In exercising their discretion under a discretionary trust, the trustees must show that they acted in good faith and reasonably. They must demonstrate to the court that they applied their mind to the size of the potential class of beneficiaries before making individual distributions of the trust money. In *Re Hay's Settlement Trusts*[52] Megarry VC explained the extent of a trustee's duty under a discretionary trust. In the course of his judgment he explained that:

> the trustee must not simply proceed to exercise the power in favour of such of the objects as happen to be at hand or claim his attention. He must first consider what persons or classes of persons are objects of the power . . . what is needed is an appreciation of the width of the field, and thus whether a selection is to be made merely from a dozen or, instead, from thousands and millions . . . Only when the trustee has applied his mind to the size of the problem should he consider individual cases . . .[53]

In the case of a power of appointment, or the power to make advancements or maintenance payments, the trustees are under no imperative duty to exercise the discretion. They are, however, under a duty to consider from time to time whether or not to exercise the power.[54] In the absence of some fraud or bad faith on the part of a trustee, the court will not interfere in the exercise of trustee discretions. For example, in *Re Beloved Wilkes' Charity*[55] trustees of a charitable trust had the power to select a boy to be educated at Oxford as a minister for the Church of England. Preference was given to four named parishes if, in the judgment of the trustee, a fit and proper candidate was forthcoming. The trustees chose a candidate from outside the preferred parishes and, when challenged, the court refused to intervene. Lord Truro LC explained that:

> it is to the discretion of the trustee that the execution of the trust is confided, that discretion being exercised with an entire absence of indirect motive, with honesty of intention, and with a fair consideration of the subject. The duty of supervision on the part of the court will

---

VISIT CASE NAVIGATOR

48 Discussed in Chapter 4.
49 See Chapter 18.
50 Discussed in Chapter 3.
51 *McPhail v Doulton* [1971] AC 424, see Chapter 4.
52 [1982] 1 WLR 202.
53 [1982] 1 WLR 202 at 209–10.
54 *Re Hay's Settlement Trusts* [1981] 3 All ER 786.
55 (1851) 3 Mac. & G 440.

thus be confined to the question of the honesty, integrity, and fairness with which the deliberation has been conducted, and will not be extended to the accuracy of the conclusion arrived at . . .

Despite the general rule that the courts will not intervene in the exercise of a trustee's discretion, over the years a number of principles have emerged which seek to explain the circumstances in which a court may intervene in the exercise of a power. The precise extent and limits of some of these principles remain uncertain.

The courts will intervene in the exercise of a trustee's discretion if the trustee simply fails to consider the exercise of the power or where the power is exercised improperly. For example, in *Tempest v Lord Camoys*[56] Jessel MR explained that '[i]t is settled law that when a [settlor] has given a pure discretion to trustees as to the exercise of a power, the court does not enforce the exercise against the wishes of the trustees, but it does prevent them from exercising it improperly.'[57] Clearly, if the trustee fails to consider exercising his discretion the court will intervene. In *Tempest v Lord Camoys* the trustees had a power to invest in land and raise money by way of mortgage. One of the trustees objected to the purchase of a particular property, on the grounds that he did not consider it to be suitable. The court refused to intervene, on the grounds that the trustee had considered the discretion to invest in the land; and having considered it, in the absence of any impropriety, the court would not compel him to exercise the discretion. Similarly, in *Gisborne v Gisborne*[58] trustees were given an absolute and uncontrollable discretion to apply income for the maintenance and benefit of the testator's widow. The widow was also entitled to income under her marriage settlement. When the question arose whether the trustees should pay income from the trust fund set up by her husband or from the marriage settlement, the House of Lords held that the matter lay entirely in the hands of the trustees and, provided that they did not act in bad faith, the court would not intervene and direct them in the manner they exercised their discretion. Lord Chancellor Cairns, referring to the trustees' discretion, explained that 'always supposing that there is no mala fides with regard to its exercise, [it] is to be without check or control from any superior tribunal'.[59]

Where a discretion is simply not considered or is exercised on some improper grounds, then the court will intervene. For example, the power of maintenance confers upon a trustee the power or discretion to pay income to an infant beneficiary for his or her maintenance. What is the position if the trustee blatantly refuses to exercise the power or refuses to exercise the power on grounds that are totally irrelevant? For example, let us say that a trustee refuses to exercise the power, on the grounds that the beneficiary should not be considered because she married against the wishes of the trustee. In such a case the court will intervene and either remove the trustee from office or direct that a payment should be made. A total omission to consider the exercise of the power or the refusal to exercise the discretion on a ground which is taken in bad faith will be open to challenge in the courts. For example, in *Klug v Klug*[60] a mother, who was also a trustee, refused to exercise the power of advancement, on the grounds that her daughter (the beneficiary) has married against her will. Neville J held that the court could order payment, on the grounds that the trustee had not properly considered the exercise of the power.

---

[56] (1882) 21 Ch. D 571.
[57] (1882) 21 Ch. D 571 at 578.
[58] (1877) 2 App. Cas. 300.
[59] (1877) 2 App. Cas. 300 at 305.
[60] [1918] 2 Ch. 67.

In more recent times the courts have suggested that public law principles may be the way forward to determine whether the court should or should not intervene in the exercise of discretions. Students of public law will be aware of the doctrine of **Wednesbury unreasonableness**[61] which allows a court or tribunal to challenge the decision of a public body if the court comes to the conclusion that the decision arrived at by the public body is one which no reasonably informed body could have reached. The suggestion was made in **Dundee General Hospitals v Walker**[62] which involved an appeal from Scotland to the House of Lords. The case involved a discretion conferred upon trustees to apply a legacy in favour of a hospital. The legacy could be applied so long as the trustees were satisfied that the hospital was not in state control. The trustees decided that the hospital was in state control and therefore refused to apply the legacy. The hospital challenged the exercise of the discretion, although, conceding that the trustees had not acted in bad faith, but rather, had not considered all of the facts. When the question arose as to the proper exercise of the discretion, the House of Lords proceeded to determine the matter on the principle of unreasonableness. That is, the decision arrived at by the particular trustees was one that no reasonable trustee could have arrived at in light of the expectations of the beneficiaries. In the course of Lord Reid's judgment, his Lordship explained that: '[i]f it can be shown that the trustees considered the wrong question, or that, although they purported to consider the right question, they did not really apply their minds to it or perversely shut their eyes to the facts, or that they did not act honestly or in good faith, then there was no true decision and the court will intervene . . .'[63] Lord Reid's statement illustrates that the court may intervene in circumstances where the trustees act in bad faith or where they only consider legal relevant factors at the expense of the relevant facts. More recently, in **Edge v Pensions Ombudsman**[64] Scott VC explained that, '[t]he judges may disagree with the manner in which the trustees have exercised their discretion, but unless they can be seen to have taken into account irrelevant, improper or irrational factors, or unless their decision can be said to be one that no reasonable body of trustees properly directing themselves could have reached, the judge cannot interfere.'[65]

Whilst the public law principle of unreasonableness clearly appears to be an attractive means by which the courts can intervene in the exercise of trustees' discretions, it is questionable whether such a public law principle is apt in the private law of trusts. The real concern relates to the fact that, unlike public bodies such as a local authority, a private trustee is under no duty to give reasons for coming to a particular conclusion. Provided that the trustee does consider the exercise of a discretion, he is not obliged to explain why he did not wish to exercise the discretion or why he exercised the discretion in a particular manner. The matter is neatly explained by Professor David Hayton and C. Mitchell as follows.

> In public law, the judicial review principles require the public body to afford the claimants an opportunity to make their case so that both sides' arguments can be fully considered. In trust law, trustees are only under a duty to ensure that they have adequate factual and/or legal background information to enable them to reach an informed decision. They do not, for example, need to inform the objects of powers or default beneficiaries that the trustees are contemplating doing something that may affect them and, *a fortiori*, do not need to give a hearing to objects of a power of appointment and those beneficiaries entitled in default of exercise of the power. Once in possession of such information they cannot

---

[61] Enunciated in *Associated Provincial Picture Houses* v *Wednesbury Corporation* [1948] 1 KB 223.
[62] [1952] 1 All ER 896.
[63] [1952] 1 All ER 896 at 910.
[64] [1998] Ch. 512.
[65] [1998] Ch. 512 at 534.

exercise their discretions in a way that is capricious, irrational or perverse to any sensible expectation of the settlor. In light of such traditional terminology that creates rights under private trust law there is surely no need by analogy with public law to hold that trustees cannot exercise their discretions in a way that no reasonable body of trustees would have done. After all, is it not perverse to any sensible expectation of the settlor to permit trustees to make a decision that no adequately informed reasonable body of trustees could possibly have made?

D. Hayton and C. Mitchell, Commentary and Cases on the Law of Trusts and Equitable Remedies, 12th edn (2005, Sweet & Maxwell, London) at p. 657

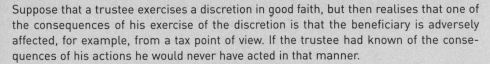

APPLYING THE LAW

Suppose that a trustee exercises a discretion in good faith, but then realises that one of the consequences of his exercise of the discretion is that the beneficiary is adversely affected, for example, from a tax point of view. If the trustee had known of the consequences of his actions he would never have acted in that manner.

Can the court reverse the exercise of that discretion?

The rule in *Re Hastings-Bass (Deceased)*

Although it yet remains to be seen how far the public law principle of **Wednesbury unreasonableness** will be universally applied by the courts, there is one principle which allows the courts to intervene in the exercise of a discretion on grounds that the trustees failed to take account of relevant factors. The principle is often referred to as the **Hastings-Bass** principle and emanates from the decision in **Re Hastings-Bass**[66] where trustees exercised the power of advancement to resettle property on trust for the purpose of avoiding estate duty.[67] The effect of the settlement, unknown to the trustees, was to make void the interests of a number of remainder beneficiaries on grounds of perpetuity. The Court of Appeal explained that it could intervene in the exercise of a discretion even though the trustees acted in good faith, provided that the exercise of the discretion produced a result which was clearly not intended by them because of the application of some rule of law or other event.

KEY CITATION

[W]here a trustee is given a discretion as to some matter under which he acts in good faith, the court should not interfere with his action, notwithstanding that it does not have the full effect which he intended, unless

(1) what he has achieved is unauthorised by the power conferred upon him, or

(2) it is clear that he would not have acted as he did

(a) had he not taken into account considerations which he should not have take into account, or

(b) had he not failed to take into account considerations which he ought to have taken into account.[68]

---

[66] [1975] Ch. 25. See T. Hang Wu, 'Rationalising *Re Hastings-Bass*: A Duty to Act on Proper Bases', *Trust Law International* (2007). See also R. Walker, 'The Limits of the Principle in *Re Hastings-Bass*' [2002] PCB 226.

[67] The power of advancement is examined in detail in Chapter 18.

[68] [1975] Ch. 25 at 41.

The *Hastings-Bass* principle has been primarily used in cases where trustees have exercised a discretion without fully understanding the fiscal consequences of the exercise of the discretion. In such circumstances the beneficiaries have sought to overturn the decisions of trustees on the grounds that, had they considered the full consequences of their actions, they would not have acted in the way in which they did. The principle has been applied in a number of cases although its precise extent seems to vary from case to case. In *Mettoy Pension Trustees Ltd v Evans*[69] Warner J explained the rule by explaining that 'where a trustee acts under a discretion given to him by the terms of the trust, the courts will interfere with his action if it is clear that he would not have acted as he did had he not failed to take into considerations which he ought to have taken into account'.[70] In *AMP (UK) v Barker*[71] the court held that it was sufficient to invoke the principle in *Hastings-Bass*, provided that the court could be shown that the trustee might have acted differently and not necessarily would have acted differently. More recently, in *Abacus Trust Company v Barr*[72] Lightman J proceeded to apply the principle only in circumstances where the trustees had acted in breach of trust. Lightman J explained that the principle could not simply be invoked where the trustees had made a mistake: rather the court would need to be satisfied that the trustee had failed to take into consideration something which they were under a duty to consider. The mere element of mistake or failure to appreciate the full extent of their decision is insufficient. Until recently, it was not altogether clear whether the breach of duty is indeed a requirement before the principle in *Hastings-Bass* can be invoked. In *Sieff v Fox*[73] Lloyd LJ explained that there was no requirement to show that there had been a breach of duty before the principle could be invoked.[74]

Over the years the rule in *Re Hastings-Bass* had caused much uncertainty and controversy. The controversy related to the appropriateness of relieving trustees of liability in circumstances where they had taken professional advice as to the exercise of a power. In addition, there was the question as to why such trustees and their beneficiaries could avoid fiscal implications in the backdrop of having taken such professional advice. As to the uncertainty with the rule, the legal question which remained troublesome was whether there was a need for the proof of a breach of duty on the part of the trustee before the rule could be invoked or whether it was just sufficient to show that had the trustees understood the consequences of their actions, they would have acted differently. These matters have been the subject of lengthy and careful scrutiny by the Court of Appeal in *Pitt v Holt*[75] where Lloyd LJ redefined what was the true ambit of the rule. Before the decision of the Court of Appeal is analysed, it is important to look at the two High Court cases which afforded the opportunity on appeal to resolve the much needed uncertainty.

The first case is *Pitt v Holt*[76] where the High Court applied the rule to undo a decision made by a receiver appointed under the Mental Health Act 1984. The facts of the case concerned a settlement made by a certain Mrs Pitt (the claimant) in her capacity as a receiver for the benefit of her husband. Mrs Pitt's husband had been seriously brain

---

[69] [1990] 1 WLR 1587.
[70] [1990] 1 WLR 1621.
[71] [2001] 1 WTLR 1237.
[72] [2003] 2 WLR 1362.
[73] [2005] 1 WLR 3811.
[74] See, M. Thomas and B. Dowrick, 'The Odd Couple? *Hastings-Bass* and Mistake' [2006] Conv. 91.
[75] [2011] EWCA Civ 197.
[76] [2010] WTLR 269.

damaged as a result of a road accident. The damages that Mr Pitt received were put into a settlement in order to provide for his future care. Although Mrs Pitt did take advice from specialists, neither Mrs Pitt nor her advisers considered the tax implications of the settlement. If they did take into consideration the tax implications, it would have become clear to them that the settlement would become liable to inheritance tax and, therefore, adversely affect Mr Pitt's money. It was also clear that if Mrs Pitt and her advisers had considered the tax implications, they would have executed a different settlement which would not have been so adversely affected by tax. Mrs Pitt sought a declaration setting aside the settlement on two principle grounds, namely the rule in *Re Hastings-Bass* and mistake.

The High Court held that the settlement could be set aside under the rule in *Re Hastings-Bass* but not on grounds of mistake. In so far as the rule in *Re Hastings-Bass*, Robert Englehart QC, after reviewing the rule in detail, held that the rule applied in the present case. It was argued on behalf of HM Revenue & Customs that the rule in *Re Hastings-Bass* should not be applied in the present case because of two reasons. In the first place, the rule in *Re Hastings-Bass* had only ever been applied in the context of dispositions made by trustees. On the facts of the present case Mrs Pitt was not a trustee but a receiver, albeit in a fiduciary capacity. Secondly, it was argued that the existing line of authorities, where the court did unravel dispositions on the grounds that they produced unfavourable tax consequences, were wrongly decided. It was contended that fiscal consequences were irrelevant when applying the rule in *Re Hastings-Bass*. Robert Englehart QC declined to accept these arguments. In so far as the contention that the rule only operated in the context of dispositions made by trustees, the learned judge commented that '. . . in principle there is no material distinction between a trustee exercising a power for the benefit of a beneficiary under a trust instrument and a receiver exercising a power for the benefit of a patient pursuant to the Mental Health Act 1983. In each case the power is, as is common ground, a fiduciary one. In each case, the person exercising the power is doing so in the interests of another but is not acting on the instructions of that other.'[77] In so far as the contention that the existing line of authorities were wrongly decided in that they were wrong to take into consideration fiscal consequences, Robert Englehart QC explained that he 'would be most reluctant to depart from such a consistent line of authority unless perhaps I were persuaded that some critical error had been made and thereafter overlooked.'[78]

The second High Court decision which was also heard on appeal in the joined appeal of *Pitt v Holt*[79] was *Futter v Futter*[80] where Norris J had to decide whether the rule in *Re Hastings-Bass* could be invoked to invalidate the decisions of trustees who had executed a number of offshore life interest settlements with the intention of off-setting certain 'stockpiled gains' of the beneficiary. Unfortunately, unknown to the trustees, this was not possible as a result of s. 2(4) of the Taxation of Chargeable Gains Act 1992. In deciding whether the life interest settlements were void or merely voidable, Norris J revisited a number of first instance decisions where the question had arisen as to the effect on a disposition made by trustees but subsequently caught by the rule in *Re Hastings-Bass*. The first of those decisions was that of Lightman J in *Abacus Trust Company v Barr*[81] where the learned judge took the view that the disposition was merely voidable and not void.

---

[77] [2010] WTLR 269 at para. 39.
[78] [2010] WTLR 269 at para. 42.
[79] [2011] EWCA Civ 197.
[80] [2010] EWHC 449.
[81] [2003] 2 WLR 1362.

Lightman J based his view on the grounds that a breach of fiduciary duty in equity gave rise to a voidable disposition and not a void disposition.[82] The reasoning of Lightman J was not followed by Lloyd J in *Sieff v Fox*[83] who, albeit recognising the potential practical advantages of holding a particular disposition voidable, was more inclined to follow the line of reasoning in *Re Abraham's WT*[84] where Cross J held that the exercise of a power of advancement was void on grounds of perpetuity. What is crucial in the judgment of Lloyd J in *Sieff v Fox* is that a disposition would be void even in circumstances where there was no breach of duty on the part of the trustee. So long as there was an invalid exercise of the power, the disposition would be held void. In *Futter v Futter* Norris J opted to follow *Sieff v Fox*, in particular the arguments advanced by Mr Taube QC in holding that the effect of invoking the rule in *Re Hastings-Bass* was to render a disposition void and not voidable. In so far as the impracticalities and harshness of holding a particular disposition void, Norris J explained that these could be mitigated by the application of the defence of change of position in addition to laches or acquiescence. In the words of the learned judge '. . . (in relation to private family trusts of the type with which this case is concerned) the consequence of invoking "the Rule in *Hastings-Bass*" is to make the deed or transaction void. The rigours of this analysis may be mitigated in particular cases. First, there must in my view be a "change of position" defence (not advanced by any defendant in the case before me). Second . . . since the remedy lies in equity, and the grant of a declaration is discretionary, matters affecting the conscience of the parties, including laches or acquiescence, can be taken into account by the Court in deciding what (if any) relief to grant . . .'[85]

Although, the decision of Norris J in *Futter v Futter*[86] was thought to remove an element of uncertainty over the consequences of finding a settlement void in so far as beneficiaries and third parties are concerned, it did not remove the uncertainty relating to the grounds for holding such a disposition void in the first place. Beneficiaries and innocent third parties may well be able to plead the defence of change of position or the equitable defences of laches or acquiescence; however, the fundamental question remains as to whether a court should hold void the actions of trustees, or indeed any other fiduciaries, who have not acted in breach of their duty. In the absence of a fraudulent exercise of a power, it is not clear what the grounds are for holding that a mere invalid exercise of a power, that is, for failing to take into consideration facts which they should have taken into consideration, is void.

Pitt v Holt in the Court of Appeal: redefining the rule in *Re Hastings-Bass*

Given the uncertainties created by the decisions in *Pitt v Holt*[87] and *Futter v Futter*[88] the Court of Appeal took the opportunity in a joined appeal to which HMRC was also joined to revisit the so-called rule in *Hastings-Bass*.[89] The leading judgment was given by Lloyd

---

[82] As, for example, a breach of the self-dealing rule which gives rise to a voidable transaction and not a void one *per se*.

[83] [2005] 1 WLR 1362.

[84] [1969] 1 Ch. 463.

[85] [2010] EWHC 449 at para. 33.

[86] [2010] EWHC 449.

[87] [2010] WTLR 269.

[88] [2010] EWHC 449.

[89] *Pitt v Holt* [2011] EWCA Civ 197. See generally, R. Nolan and A. Cloherty, 'The Rule in *Pitt v Holt*?' (2011) LQR 499; P. Davies, 'Correcting Mistakes: With the Rule in *Re Hastings-Bass*' (2011) Conv 406; M. Conaglen, 'Reviewing the Review of Fiduciary Discretions' (2011) CLJ 301; R. Chambers, 'The Rule in *Hastings-Bass (Deceased)*: *Pitt v Holt*' (2011) Trust Law International 17.

LJ after a much detailed analysis of the decision in *Re Hastings-Bass (Deceased)*.[90] Lloyd LJ explained that 'two questions arise in these appeals. The first can be stated, broadly, in this way. Trustees of a settlement exercise a discretionary power intending to change the beneficial ownership of trust property, but the effect of what they do turns out to be different from that which they intended. Can their act be set aside by the court? If so, what is the correct legal test to determine in what circumstances and on what basis the court can intervene? The second question concerns the correct legal test to be applied if a donor seeks to have a voluntary disposition set aside as having been made under a mistake.'[91]

In so far as the first question, Lloyd LJ proceeded to analyse the decision of the Court of Appeal in *Re Hastings-Bass (Deceased)*. Lloyd LJ explained the correct principle arising from the rule in *Re Hastings-Bass* as follows.

KEY CITATION

Re Hastings-Bass: The correct principle per Lloyd LJ in *Pitt* v *Holt* [2011] EWCA Civ 197 at para. 127

The cases which I am now considering concern acts which are within the powers of the trustees but are said to be vitiated by the failure of the trustees to take into account a relevant factor to which they should have had regard – usually tax consequences – or by their taking into account some irrelevant matter. It seems to me that the principled and correct approach to these cases is, first, that the trustees' act is not void, but that it may be voidable. It will be voidable if, and only if, it can be shown to have been done in breach of fiduciary duty on the part of the trustees. If it is voidable, then it may be capable of being set aside at the suit of a beneficiary, but this would be subject to equitable defences and to the court's discretion. The trustees' duty to take relevant matters into account is a fiduciary duty, so an act done as a result of a breach of that duty is voidable. Fiscal considerations will often be among the relevant matters which ought to be taken into account. However, if the trustees seek advice (in general or in specific terms) from apparently competent advisers as to the implications of the course they are considering taking, and follow the advice so obtained, then, in the absence of any other basis for a challenge, I would hold that the trustees are not in breach of their fiduciary duty for failure to have regard to relevant matters if the failure occurs because it turns out that the advice given to them was materially wrong. Accordingly, in such a case I would not regard the trustees' act, done in reliance on that advice, as being vitiated by the error and therefore voidable.

The above passage from Lloyd LJ's judgment offers the clearest and correct principle of law as to when the rule in *Re Hastings-Bass* can and should be invoked to unravel the discretions of trustees. It is of utmost importance that there is a breach of duty on the part of the trustee which gives rise to the application of the rule. Where trustees have taken professional advice before embarking on a course of action, they are not deemed to acting in breach of their duties. Lloyd LJ was at pains to explain that trustees who take professional advice and then later discover that their actions produced consequences not intended, for example adverse fiscal consequences, were not acting in breach of duty. In this respect, any attempt to hold the exercise of a discretion voidable in such

---

[90] [1975] Ch. 25.
[91] [2011] EWCA Civ 197 at para. 1.

circumstances was not justified in law. Lloyd LJ explained that 'in my judgment, in a case where the trustees' act is within their powers, but is said to be vitiated by a breach of trust so as to be voidable, if the breach of trust asserted is that the trustees failed to have regard to a relevant matter, and if the reason that they did not have regard to it is that they obtained and acted on advice from apparently competent advisers, which turned out to be incorrect, then the charge of breach of trust cannot be made out.'[92] The decision of the Court of Appeal in *Pitt v Holt*[93] brings much needed certainty into this area of the law. Trustees acting within their powers and taking professional advice cannot have their decisions then unravelled simply because of unintended fiscal consequences. Of course, trustees and beneficiaries are at liberty to sue those very professional advisers for negligence. The full implication of the decision of the Court of Appeal in *Pitt v Holt* will be felt amongst such professional advisers who have long escaped the consequences of negligent advice. Of course, the decision will be welcomed by HMRC.

Lloyd LJ then proceeded to answer the second question, that is, what is the correct legal test to be applied if a donor seeks to have a voluntary disposition set aside as having been made under a mistake? In particular, the question whether failure to understand the fiscal consequences of the exercise of a particular discretion in circumstances of having taken professional advice. In *Gibbon v Mitchell*[94] Millett J explained the grounds upon which a court could set aside a voluntary disposition on grounds of mistake. The learned judge explained that a voluntary transaction '. . . will be set aside for mistake whether the mistake is a mistake of law or of fact, so long as the mistake is as to the effect of the transaction itself and not merely as to its consequences or the advantages to be gained by entering into it.'[95] The test advocated by Millett J is stricter than that advocated in the nineteenth century by Lindley LJ in *Ogilvie v Littleboy*[96] where the learned judge explained that a voluntary settlement could be set aside on grounds of mistake where the mistake was 'of a serious character to render it unjust on the part of the donee to retain the property given to him'.[97] Whilst it is possible to include tax consequences as being mistakes of a serious character under *Ogilvie v Littleboy* so as to set aside the transaction, under the formula adopted in *Gibbon v Mitchell*[98] tax consequences are not sufficient grounds for setting aside a transaction. The 'effect and consequences' approach advocated by Millett J in *Gibbon v Mitchell* was endorsed by Englehart QC in the High Court in *Pitt v Holt*[99] who was of the opinion that taxation mistakes were mistakes relating to consequences and not effects and therefore not capable of being set aside on grounds of mistake. It will be seen below that in *Pitt v Holt* the claimant, Mrs Pitt, had entered into a settlement with professional advice as to its effect. The settlement subsequently became liable to inheritance tax and Mrs Pitt sought to have the settlement set aside under the rule in *Re Hastings-Bass* as well as under the courts equitable jurisdiction to set aside the settlement on grounds of mistake. The High Court held that Mrs Pitt had fully intended the settlement to come into effect and was under no mistake as to its legal effect. As for the consequences of inheritance tax, Mrs Pitt never

---

[92] [2011] EWCA Civ 197 at para. 125.

[93] [2011] EWCA Civ 197.

[94] [1990] 1 WLR 1304.

[95] [1990] 1 WLR 1304 at 1309. The decision of Lindley LJ was endorsed by the House of Lords; see *Ogilvie v Allen* (1899) 15 TLR 294.

[96] (1897) 13 TLR 399.

[97] (1897) 13 TLR 399 and 400.

[98] [1990] 1 WLR 1304.

[99] [2010] WTLR 269.

thought about that issue and could never have been under any mistake as to its effects. Englehart QC refused to set aside the settlement on grounds of mistake.

In **Pitt v Holt**[100] the Court of Appeal held that 'for the equitable jurisdiction to set aside a voluntary disposition for mistake to be invoked, there must be a mistake on the part of the donor either as to the legal effect of the disposition or as to an existing fact which is basic to the transaction. (I leave aside cases where there is an additional vitiating factor such as some misrepresentation or concealment in relation to the transaction.) . . . Moreover the mistake must be of sufficient gravity as to satisfy the **Ogilvie v Littleboy** test 13 TLR 399, 400, which provides protection to the recipient against too ready an ability of the donor to seek to recall his gift. The fact that the transaction gives rise to unforeseen fiscal liabilities is a consequence, not an effect, for this purpose, and is not sufficient to bring the jurisdiction into play.'[101]

In upholding the joined appeals in **Pitt v Holt** the Court of Appeal has introduced much needed certainty in this area of the law. Trustees acting within their powers and duties and taking professional advice cannot have their discretions set aside simply because of unintended fiscal consequences.

Administrative discretions

Whereas a dispositive discretion refers to a discretion relating to the distribution of trust property, an administrative discretion is conferred upon a trustee in relation to the way in which the trust property is administered. For example, a trustee will be conferred a power of investment by the trust instrument or, in the absence of the trust instrument, by the Trustee Act 2000.[102] Whilst the trustee is under a duty to invest, how he invests and in what types of investments will depend primarily on the extent of the power of investment that is conferred upon him. He need not act in a particular way or choose any particular types of investment. The statutory power of investment confers upon a trustee a wide power to choose any investments as he was absolutely entitled to the trust property. Despite the breadth of this power, the trustee must show that he acted reasonably. Administrative powers are more easily controlled because they are subject to the overriding general duty of care found in s. 1 of the Trustee Act 2000.

Do trustees need to give reasons?

One of the key factors which will allow a beneficiary to challenge the decisions made by trustees is access to information. Unless the beneficiaries have information and reasons why a particular course of action was taken, it becomes extremely difficult if not impossible to challenge the decisions that have been made. The question then is whether the trustees need to provide any reasons for the way in which they acted. The general rule in English law is that beneficiaries are not entitled to confidential information, such as the reason why a particular discretion was exercised in a particular way. Beneficiaries are, however, entitled to inspect other trust documents such as accounts and other information relating to the day-to-day management of trust matters.[103]

---

[100] [2011] EWCA Civ 197.
[101] [2011] EWCA Civ 197 at para. 210.
[102] Section 3 of the Trustee Act 2000; see generally, Chapter 13.
[103] *Re Londonderry's Settlement* [1965] 1 Ch. 918.

The right to inspect trust documents

A distinction is drawn between the requirement of a trustee to give reasons for the way in which he acted and the right to inspect trust documents. In respect of the latter Lord Wrenbury once commented that a beneficiary 'is entitled to see all the trust documents because they are trust documents and because he is a beneficiary. They are in a sense his own. Action or no action, he is entitled to access them. This has nothing to do with discovery. The right to discovery is a right to someone else's documents. A proprietary right is a right to access documents which are your own.'[104] Lord Wrenbury views the right to see the trust documents as a proprietary right flowing from the fact that they relate to the property in which the beneficiary has a proprietary interest. Despite this statement, there has been much controversy over exactly who is entitled to see the trust documents and which documents. For example, it makes perfect sense for a single beneficiary entitled to all of the trust fund to see the trust documents. What is the position if there are more than one beneficiaries, for example, beneficiaries entitled under a fixed or discretionary trust? Further still, what is the position of an object of a power of appointment that may become entitled on the exercise of the power? Prior to the decision in *Schmidt* **v** *Rosewood Trust*[105] it was settled that beneficiaries of both a fixed and discretionary trust were entitled to inspect trust documents relating to matters such as dealings with the trust property and its present state.

However, there were doubts whether beneficiaries of a potentially large discretionary trust could inspect the trust documents or objects of a power of appointment. In *Schmidt* **v** *Rosewood Trust*[106] the Privy Council explained that the right to access trust information was entirely at the court's inherent jurisdiction rather than on the basis of a proprietary entitlement. Lord Walker commented that:

> a beneficiary's right to seek disclosure of trust documents, although sometimes not inappropriately described as a proprietary, is best approached as one aspect of the court's inherent jurisdiction to supervise (and where appropriate intervene in) the administration of trusts. There is therefore in their Lordships' view no reason to draw any bright dividing line either between transmissible and non-transmissible (that is, discretionary) interests, or between the rights of objects of a discretionary trust and those of the object of a mere power.[107]

Disclosure of the reasons for acting in a particular way

Although the beneficiaries are entitled to inspect trust documents, albeit after the decision in *Schmidt* **v** *Rosewood Trust* at bequest of the court, beneficiaries do not have a right to demand that the trustee explains why they exercised a particular discretion. In *Re Londonderry's Settlement*[108] trustees were conferred a discretion to distribute the trust property amongst a number of beneficiaries. One of the beneficiaries complained that she had not received enough and therefore demanded that she inspect a number of trust documents in order to commence an action against the trustees. The trustees objected to the disclosure of the documents, on the grounds that this would reveal the reasons why they had acted in the manner they did in relation to the distribution of the

---

[104] *O'Rourke* v *Darbishire* [1920] AC 581 at 626.
[105] [2003] 2 AC 709.
[106] *Ibid.*
[107] [2003] 2 AC 709, para. 66. See also *Foreman* v *Kingstone* [2004] 1 NZLR 841.
[108] [965] Ch. 918.

trust property. The Court of Appeal held that the beneficiary did not have a right to inspect the document which gave reasons for the way in which the trustees had acted. The Court of Appeal was of the view that such disclosures would cause unnecessary problems and arguments amongst family members and would ultimately mean that trustees would not be in a position to do their job.[109]

The decision of Court of Appeal in **Re Londonderry's Settlement**[110] was carefully analysed by Briggs J in the High Court decision in **Breakspear v Ackland**[111] where the question before the court was whether a wish letter, which had been executed alongside the trustee deed by the settlor, could be inspected by the beneficiaries. The beneficiaries were entitled under a discretionary trust and the wish letter contained information relating to the way in which the trustees should exercise their dispositive discretion. The court described a wish letter as 'a mechanism for the communication by a settlor to trustees of the settlement of non-binding requests by him to take stated matters into account when exercising their discretionary powers. Typically, wish letters are concerned with the exercise of dispositive discretions, but they may include wishes in relation to the exercise of powers of investment, or of other purely administrative powers. For present purposes I am concerned with a wish letter which is substantially contemporaneous with the settlement itself.'[112]

KEY CITATION	**What is a wish letter?** *Breakspear* v *Ackland* [2008] EWHC 220 at paras 6 and 7 per Briggs J

The large increase in the use of wish letters has gone hand in hand with the rise in the popularity of discretionary trusts, in preference to the more detailed fixed interest trust. The combination of a broad discretionary trust accompanied by a wish letter may be said to have two particular advantages. The first, an advantage which it enjoys over the old-fashioned fixed interest trust, is that it preserves flexibility for the trustees in responding to changes in the beneficiaries' circumstances which are not or cannot be foreseen by the settlor. The second advantage, which stems from the placing of the trusts affecting the property and the settlor's non-binding wishes into separate documents, is that the settlor may make use of a confidential wish letter as the medium for the written expression of facts, beliefs, expectations, concerns and (occasionally) prejudices about the beneficiaries which it would or might be hurtful, impolitic or simply undesirable for him to include in a document which the beneficiaries had a right to inspect. That advantage may be summarised in the word confidentiality, so long as it is appreciated that the word has both a subjective and an objective connotation. Confidentiality may serve a purely selfish desire of the settlor to keep his wishes, beliefs and the communication of certain facts secret from the family. Objectively speaking, that secrecy may in many cases be thoroughly beneficial, since it may tend to preserve family harmony and mutual respect, while enabling trustees to be briefed as to matters relevant to the exercise of their discretionary powers, rather than kept in ignorance of them.

▶

---

[109] See also *Wilson* v *Law Debenture Trust Corp* [1995] 2 All ER 337.
[110] [1965] Ch. 918.
[111] [2008] EWHC 220 (Ch.).
[112] [2008] EWHC 220 at para. 5.

The use and advantages of wish letters in conjunction with broad discretionary trusts is not confined to family trusts. For example, the advantage of flexibility may be equally applicable to an employee trust. Nonetheless, the advantage of confidentiality is at its most obvious in relation to a family trust, and it is in the effect upon that advantage which any uncertainty or change in the law relating to disclosure of wish letters at the request of beneficiaries is at its most acute. Plainly, if the law is that, generally, wish letters are not disclosable, settlors will be encouraged to use them as the medium for the communication of valuable but confidential information relevant to the exercise of the trustees' discretionary powers. If by contrast wish letters are generally disclosable, that potential advantage is likely to be wholly closed off for the future, and the disclosure of genuinely confidential information in existing wish letters at the request of beneficiaries is likely to risk causing precisely the harm which led to that information being included in a wish letter in the first place, and to defeat what may to date have been real expectations of confidentiality in the minds both of settlors and trustees.

Having explained the very nature of a wish letter, Briggs J held that the beneficiaries had no right to inspect the wish letter. Briggs J held that the very nature of a wish letter fell within the grounds of the principle enunciated in **Re Londonderry's Settlement**. In particular, Briggs J paid emphasis on a wish letter in the context of a family trust and the confidential nature of such a letter. The judge explained that the wish letter fell squarely in the Londonderry principle which he explained as follows:

> At the heart of the Londonderry principle is the unanimous conclusion (most clearly expressed by Danckwerts LJ) that it is in the interests of beneficiaries of family discretionary trusts, and advantageous to the due administration of such trusts, that the exercise by trustees of their dispositive discretionary powers be regarded, from start to finish, as an essentially confidential process. It is in the interests of the beneficiaries because it enables the trustees to make discreet but thorough inquiries as to their competing claims for consideration for benefit without fear or risk that those inquiries will come to the beneficiaries' knowledge. They may include, for example, inquiries as to the existence of some life-threatening illness of which it is appropriate that the beneficiary in question be kept ignorant. Such confidentiality serves the due administration of family trusts both because it tends to reduce the scope for litigation about the rationality of the exercise by trustees of their discretions, and because it is likely to encourage suitable trustees to accept office, undeterred by a perception that their discretionary deliberations will be subjected to scrutiny by disappointed or hostile beneficiaries, and to potentially expensive litigation in the courts.'[113]

---

[113] [2008] EWHC 220 (Ch.).

Conclusion

This chapter has examined some of the important principles relating to the office of trusteeship. In particular, emphasis has been placed on the persons who may become trustees and how they can be replaced by new trustees. The chapter has illustrated that there are various statutory mechanisms in place for the appointment and removal of trustees. Once new trustees are appointed statutory provisions in the Trustee Act 1925 vest the trust property in the new trustees. As well as matters relating to appointment, removal and retirement, this chapter has touched upon some of the key issues in the administration of trusts: in particular, the manner in which the office of trusteeship should be conducted and the position of the beneficiaries with regard to the improper exercise of discretions. Whilst these matters are to be explored in much more depth in the subsequent chapters, for the time being, it should be clear that trustees must observe the duties that are imposed upon them and consider the proper exercise of discretions. The most basic duty is the duty of care requiring the trustee to act reasonably in the circumstances. With regard to discretions, the trustee must, in the case of a dispositive discretion, consider the exercise of the discretion. The court will intervene in the exercise of that discretion if it can be shown that he acted in bad faith or took on board irrelevant considerations. The law in this area is, however, developing and there are judicial variations as to what precise grounds give rise to intervention by the court. With regard to administrative discretions, the trustees must comply with the paramount duty of care enshrined in s. 1 of the Trustee Act 2000.

Case study

Sarah and Sarina are two trustees of a trust. Sarah also happens to be one of the beneficiaries under the trust. The trust property consists of £20,000 and a collection of paintings and a freehold house, all of which is settled for Paul and Mathew for life and thereafter for Sarah.

Sarah and Sarina are constantly in dispute over the management of the trust property. Sarah is of the opinion that Sarina is not giving her full devoted attention to the trust and has neglected the £20,000 which has remained in a bank account. Sarah has advised Sarina to retire from the trust but Sarina is refusing to do so.

Last month, Paul, who is 16 years of age, asked for money from the trust fund to pay for a school trip to America. The purpose of the trip is to visit American universities with a view to studying there. Sarah is quite happy for him to have some money but Sarina has told him that she will not give him the money because he is never going to make it to university. Paul is upset with this, particularly in light of the fact that he has secured excellent results at school.

Advise Paul and Sarah, who both feel that Sarina is suffering from some mental disorder.

Moot points

1 What factors should the court take on board when removing a trustee under s. 41 of the Trustee Act 1925 and replacing him or her with a new one?

2 Can an express power to appoint new trustees be exercised in favour of the donee of such a power?

3 Explain the role of a Public Trustee and investigate how far such a trustee is used in modern trust practice.

4 What do you understand by the *Hastings-Bass* principle considered in this chapter. Can the principle be invoked to relieve a trustee from breach of trust? Explain how the decision of the Court of Appeal in the co-joined appeals in *Pitt v Holt* and *Futter v Futter* [2011] EWCA (Civ) 197 redefines the so-called rule in *Re Hastings-Bass*.

5 It has been suggested on a number of occasions that the effective way of controlling trustees' discretions is by using the public law principle of *Wednesbury* unreasonableness. How far is such a public law principle effective in the private law of trusts? In debating this question, you may wish to consider the fact that the test of unreasonableness is objective whereas discretionary decision-making is purely subjective.

6 Read the decision in *Breakspear v Ackland* [2008] EWHC 220 (Ch) and explain what is a wish letter and why it is beneficial to a discretionary trust.

Further reading

Davies, P. 'Correcting Mistakes with the Rule in *Re Hastings-Bass*' [2011] Conv 406.

Parry, D.M. 'Control of Trustees' Discretions' Conv. [1985]. Examines the way in which the courts can control both dispositive and administrative discretions conferred upon trustees.

Tang, H.W. 'Rationalising *Re Hastings-Bass*: A Duty to Act on Proper Bases', *Trust Law International* (2007). Examines the basis upon which the *Hastings-Bass* principle is applied and argues that the principle is based on the duty of a trustee to act prudently and cannot be applied simply in cases of mistakes made by the trustee.

Thomas, M. and B. Dowrick, 'The Odd Couple? *Hastings-Bass* and Mistake' [2006] Conv 9. Examines the *Hastings-Bass* principle in light of the High Court decision in *Sieff* v *Fox*.

Walker, R. 'The Limits of the Principle in *Re Hastings-Bass*' [2002] PCB 226. Sir Robert Walker explains the limits of the principle in *Hastings-Bass* and argues that it is not a panacea in all cases of mistake by trustees.

Visit **www.mylawchamber.co.uk/panesar** to access study support resources including interactive multiple choice questions, practice exam questions with guidance, podcasts, weblinks, legal newsfeed all linked to the **Pearson eText** version of Exploring Equity and Trusts which you can **search**, **highlight** and **personalise** with your **own notes** and **bookmarks**.

premium mylawchamber
unrivalled support for legal education

Use Case Navigator to read in full some of the key cases referenced in this chapter with commentary and questions:

McPhail v Doulton [1971] AC 424

Westdeutsche Landesbank Girozentrale v Islington LBC [1996] AC 699 (HL)

POWERED BY LexisNexis®

16

Investment of trust funds

Learning objectives

After reading this chapter you should be able to:

→ understand the objective of trustee investment

→ understand how trustee investment has changed with time

→ distinguish between an express power of investment and the statutory power of investment found in the Trustee Act 2000

→ explain the relationship between an express power of investment and the statutory power of investment

→ explain the common law and statutory duties imposed on trustees when they exercise the power of investment

→ explain the operation of the statutory power of investment

→ understand the delegation of investment powers

→ explain trust investment in land

→ explain the extent to which investment powers can be extended

→ understand pre-investment duties such as conversion and apportionment.

Nestlé v *National Westminster Bank plc* [1993] 1 WLR 1260: A beneficiary who claims to be entitled to four times more than what she actually received: did the trustees invest properly?

The facts of *Nestlé* v *National Westminster Bank plc* illustrate some of the issues which are the subject matter of discussion in this chapter. In his will, William David Nestlé, who died in 1922 settled a number of investments on trust. The trustees of the settlement were National Westminster Bank and they were instructed to hold a portfolio of equities firstly for William Nestlé's wife, then their children and then their grandchildren. The fund invested at the start of the settlement was worth some £54,000. In 1986, Miss Nestlé (granddaughter of William Nestlé) became absolutely entitled to the fund settled by her granddad. In 1986 the fund was worth £269,000; however, Miss Nestlé, not happy with this amount, argued that had the trustees invested the money more wisely she would have received four times more than its current value. Miss Nestlé argued that the trustees had failed to diversify the equities, failed to periodically review the trust investments and favoured other beneficiaries at her expense. Were the trustees at fault?

The facts of the Nestlé litigation neatly illustrate the investment aspect of a trustee's duty and the dilemma faced by trustees when investing the trust funds. Miss Nestlé obviously felt that she was entitled to four times more than she received. Indeed, her lawyers were able to point to various financial data proving that if the investments had been made differently she would have received more money. The trustees, on the other hand, did not only have Miss Nestlé to think about, but also needed to generate sufficient income for her grandmother, mother and brothers and sisters.

So, should the trustees have invested more in high-capital-growth investments or were they right in investing in income-producing investments? Given the fact that this trust continued for a long period of time, should the trustees have periodically reviewed the trust investments?

This chapter explores one of the most important duties of a trustee: namely, the duty to invest the trust funds. In doing so it looks to the duty of investment and the way in which that duty should be discharged by trustees.

Introduction

One of the more important aspects of trust administration is the investment of trusts funds. Except in the most simple of trusts, for example, where trustees are given a direction to simply hold and retain a particular asset, like an expensive antique or a painting, it is the duty of trustees to invest the trust fund for the benefit of their beneficiaries. Where the subject matter of the trust is money, there is no question that trustees must invest such money in order to get the best returns for their beneficiaries. Where the subject matter consists of things other than money – for example, other items of personal property – then unless the trustees have been given specific directions to retain such items, trustees will invariably have to convert such items into money and then invest the money accordingly. Investment is important for a number of reasons. In the first place, given that a trust normally has a lifespan of many years, it is not sufficient for the trustees to merely retain the trust fund, awaiting the day when the beneficiary calls for the termination of the trust and the receipt of the trust money. The effect of inflation may mean that the initial money subject to the trust is not worth what it was at the time of the creation of the trust. It is therefore important for the trustees to invest the trust fund and preserve its real value in line with inflationary pressures. Secondly, and again related to the issue of the lifespan of the trust, it is only through proper investment that beneficiaries will be able to receive financial benefits and interim payments of income. Indeed, it may be that some of the beneficiaries are only entitled to income, for example a beneficiary entitled to a life interest only. Income for such a beneficiary can only be paid through careful investment of the trust funds.

The duty of investment and the power of investment

The investment aspect of trust administration comes under the umbrella of trustees' duties. Given the importance of investment outlined above, it is paramount and imperative that trustees invest the trust funds. When a trustee is under some imperative obligation to act, he is said to be subject to a duty. The scope or the range of permitted investments available to the trustee will be ascertained from the investment power that is conferred upon the trustee. An investment power is an administrative power which determines the scope of the possible investments that a trustee can legitimately make. Where can the trustee find these investment powers? The first and most obvious place is the trust instrument which purports to create the trust. In most modern trusts, and certainly in trusts created by professional trustees and other professional persons, it is common to insert into the trust instrument a clause which confers upon the trustees an investment power which will allow them to invest the funds for the best interests of the beneficiaries. Such clauses, which might typically read, 'that the trustees have the power to invest the trust funds in any manner they think and as if they were the absolute owners of the fund' are called express powers of investment. However, it is not always the case that a purported trust is accompanied with an elaborate investment power. In home-drawn trusts and in the case of wills, it is not necessarily obvious to the person making the trust or the will to incorporate an investment clause. Where there is no express power of investment, it is not fatal to the trust; in such a case the trustees will find that the power of investment is conferred by statute. Since the nineteenth century, statutes have from time to time conferred investment powers on trustees. The modern statutory power of investment is to be found in the Trustee Act 2000 which repealed the statutory power of investment in the Trustee Investment Act 1961.

The starting point for any discussion on trustee investment should be made clear. Whilst trustees are under a duty to invest the trust funds, what they invest in is determined by the power of investment which is conferred upon them. The power of investment may be in the form of an express power of investment or a statutory power of investment.

The objectives of trust investment

The objectives of trust investment change both in respect of time and with the needs of individual trusts. In respect of time, trustee investment has been influenced by social and economic factors. Changes in social and economic patterns greatly influence the function of trustee investment, and history shows that one type of investment ideology does not neatly provide the framework for investment in different period of time. It is also for this reason that the law is constantly under pressure for law reform, because rules relating to one particular investment climate do not satisfactorily resolve problems arising in totally different social and economic contexts, where the needs of trustee investment may have changed.[1]

At the end of the nineteenth century the trust operated primarily in the context of wills and family settlements. The primary function of trustees in such a context was to preserve the trust fund over a long period of time for the benefit of beneficiaries entitled in succession. Whilst investment of the trust funds was important, the paramount duty was to preserve the trust fund and this meant that trustees were generally not allowed to invest in risky investments. In such a context investment was not necessarily a complex matter for trustees. Today, whilst the trust does have a role to play in wills and in the context of family arrangements, the express private trust finds itself operating more and more in a financial and commercial context requiring trustees to meet different social and economic objectives. Furthermore, the economic and financial conditions under which trustees invest today are much different from those that existed in times gone by. In this respect Dhillon LJ in *Nestlé v National Westminster Bank plc*[2] explained that 'what the prudent man should do at any time depends on the economic and financial conditions of that time and not on what judges of the past, however, eminent, have held to be the prudent course of conditions of 50 or 100 years before . . . when investment conditions were different'.[3] In many modern trusts the paramount duty of the trust is not only to preserve the trust fund but also to make sure that the fund grows and meets inflationary pressures.[4] In trusts where capital growth is of the essence, for example in trusts governing pension and investment funds, the trustees duty is to make sure that there is satisfactory growth in the capital value of the fund. Therefore, unlike the trustee of the nineteenth and early twentieth century, the modern trustee's duty to invest is an extremely important matter, requiring knowledge of complex investment matters. The transition of trusteeship from the type that existed at the end of the nineteenth century to a more modern one was best explained by one commentator as far back as 1951.[5] Shattuck writes:

> To be sure, a hundred years before the time of Victoria's death trusteeship had passed, somewhat nervously, from the concept of safe conduct of a specific *res* into the concept of maintenance of a stated set of values. During that transition the duty of the English trustee had transformed itself from the relatively restricted obligations related to care, custody and operation of family agricultural real estate and its appurtenances to the more intricate task of trading in commercial and financial markets and to the attempted maintenance, through the life of the trust, of a value which had been stated to exist at the time of the opening of the inventory.[6]

---

[1] An excellent account of the changing nature of trusteeship is examined by Lord Nicholls in 'Trustees and Their Broader Community: Where Duty, Morality and Ethics Converge' (1995) Trust LI Vol. 9 No. 71.

[2] [1994] 1 All ER 118.

[3] [1994] 1 All ER 118 at 126.

[4] An excellent account of the changing economic and financial condition under which modern trustees manage trust funds is provided by A. Duckworth, 'Legal Aspects of Trustee Investment – Is the Prudent Man Still Alive and Well?' 1997 PCB Issue No. 122.

[5] Shattuck, 'The Development of the Prudent Man Rule for Fiduciary Investments in the Twentieth Century' (1951) 12 Ohio State LJ 491 at 491–2.

[6] *Ibid.*

Not only do the functions and objectives of trust instrument change with time, but they also change in respect of particular types of trusts. Not all trusts have the same objectives; some trusts are merely short-term trusts whilst others are for much longer periods of time. The amount of the trust fund in many trusts varies form trust to trust. In the case of pension and unit trusts the potential trust fund may run into millions of pounds. Obviously in such cases the trustees' investment strategy may well be different from a trust of a few thousand pounds to be held over a very short period of time. In the case of a pension fund trust the duty of the trustees will be to invest the trust funds over a long period of time in a carefully selected portfolio of investments, which protect the value of the fund against inflationary pressures but at the same time produces sufficient accumulations of income and capital to meet the needs of the beneficiaries. Further still, the type of beneficiaries for which the trust is providing for may well determine the objectives of trust investment. Where the trust is for beneficiaries entitled in succession, the trustees must ensure that their investment carefully provides a balance between income and capital so that both the life tenant and the remainderman are equally treated. Thus, in **Nestlé v National Westminster Bank plc**,[7] where a remainderman argued that she would have been entitled to much more of the capital of the trust fund had the trustees invested properly, the Court of Appeal held that the trustees were entitled to take into account the relative wealth of the life tenant and the remainderman. If after taking account of these matters the trustees decided to invest in high income as opposed to high-capital-growth investments there would be no breach of trust, even though had they invested in another way a much greater return of capital may have been provided for the remainderman.

The underlying objective of modern trustee investment is therefore clear. The trustees duty is confer the best financial return for their beneficiaries, or as one judge has put it, 'when the purpose of the trust is to provide financial benefits for the beneficiaries, as is usually the case, the best interests of the beneficiaries are normally their best financial interests'.[8] How the trustees provide the best financial returns cannot, however, be reduced to a single formula. In each case the trustees must have regard to the type of trust in question and the nature of beneficial interests for which they are under a duty to provide.

 ## Historical note and contemporary trends in trustee investment

Matters of legal history do not often appeal to the minds of those engaged in the study of contemporary rules of law. This habit, however, is something that a trust lawyer should avoid falling into at all costs. In its long history, the trust has been used as a tool to achieve various social and legal goals; it has operated in different contexts ranging from family to commercial. It is because of these changing contexts that rules from one period of trust law do not neatly provide the framework for the proper administration of trusts in another period of time. One is reminded of the precious words of Lord Devlin who wrote that:

> in truth it is only with much effort that law and practice upon any subject can be kept together, and that is because, though they have the same origin, they are in their motions

---

[7] [1993] 1 WLR 1260.
[8] *Cowan* v *Scargill* [1984] 2 All ER 750 at 760, per Megarry VC.

attracted by different objects. Rigidity and a regular patter are pleasing to the legal mind, and as soon as he can the lawyer sets up a system of principles and rules from which he is reluctant to depart. He may start close to his subject, but because it is alive, illogical and contrary, it is likely to slip and slither out of the pattern he devises for it. The danger in any branch of law is that it ossifies.[9]

Rules should be appreciated in the contexts in which they have developed and this requires an appreciation of the changing contexts. The need to understand the historical and contextual matters is especially important in the area of trustee investment. Such an inquiry will help to explain why the law relating to trustee investment has changed and continues to change under modern conditions.

The history of trustee investment illustrates that social, economic and financial factors have all influenced investment law and practice.[10] Before the bursting of the South Sea Bubble in 1720 the Court of Chancery did not regulate trustee investment with the degree to which it did after 1720. Trustees were permitted to invest the trust funds freely and in any manner they thought fit. The bursting of the South Sea Bubble, however, played an important role in tightening the rules on trustee investment. Until the bursting of the South Sea Bubble, trustees, like many other investors, had taken advantage of the emergence of the joint stock company and the speculative investments which this form of organisation bought with it.[11] In the first place, the Court of Chancery heavily clamped down on the types of investments which trustees were authorised to invest in. Secondly, the Court began the process of ensuring that the capital value of the trust fund was preserved and that trustees should refrain from taking risks. This underlying objective to preserve the trust fund and avoid risky investments was clearly manifested in a series of nineteenth-century cases, which are examined in the next section.

The bursting of the South Sea Bubble also gave rise to the concept of 'authorised investment', which until the Trustee Act 2000 dominated trustee investment law. Trustees were not allowed to invest freely, unless of course there was an express power of investment authorising them to do so.[12] The first authorised trustee investment around 1720 was the Bank of England 3 per cent Consolidated Annuities.[13] The list of authorised investments was expanded some hundred years later by the Lord St Leonard's Act 1859 to include, *inter alia*, stock of the Bank of England, first mortgages of freehold land, and colonial stock. There then followed a series of Acts in the latter part of the nineteenth century which sought to expand the list as new investments arose.[14] The list of investments in these statutes reflected the early Court of Chancery approach, which was one of safe investment and therefore confined primarily to fixed-rate investments. The first

---

[9] P. Devlin, 'The Relationship Between Commercial law and Commercial Practice', (1951) 14 MLR 249 at p. 250.

[10] On trustee investment history, see Chesterman, 'Family Settlements on Trusts: Land Owners and the Rising Bourgeoisie' in *Law, Economy and Society, 1750–1914: Essays in the History of English Law*, Rubin and Sugarman edn, London, Professional Books Limited (1984) pp. 157–64; G. Moffat, *Trust Law: Text and Materials* 4th edn (2005) pp. 456–59.

[11] On the bursting of the South Sea Bubble, see *Farrar's Company Law* 4th edn, Butterworths (1998) pp. 17–19.

[12] However, even where there was an express power of investment, such a power was construed by the courts with restriction to safe and authorised investments. It was not until the middle of the twentieth century that the restrictive interpretation of express investment clauses was abandoned. This is explored later on in the chapter.

[13] See F.W. Maitland, *Equity: A Course of Lectures* (J. Brunyate edn) 1936 at p. 95; also see A. Duckworth, 'Legal Aspects of Trustee Investment – Is the Prudent Man Still Alive and Well? 1997 PCB Issue No. 122 at p. 23.

[14] For example, Trustee Investment Act 1889 and then the Trustee Act 1893.

twentieth-century statute listing authorised investment was the Trustee Act 1925, which followed the safe investment policy of its predecessors.

In the twentieth century, and particularly after the Second Word War, trustee investment became influenced by other factors. In the first place, the trust began to operate in contexts far different from those that existed at the close of the nineteenth century. The settlement type of trust, which had for a long time provided the framework and model for trustee investment, had been displaced by trusts of a different kind. Rather than settling property in favour of a series of beneficiaries entitled in succession, property owners saw the trust as a useful tool for investment. Investment could be achieved simply by the provision of a future gift for a beneficiary or the redistribution of family property so as to avoid taxation. Still further, the trust could be employed as a means of investing in a unit fund or a pension fund for employees of a company. In these types of the trust the purpose of trust investment was not the same as that under a settlement type of trust. In particular, trustees did not have the same concerns about the interests of different beneficiaries, for example the life tenant and remainderman, which existed under a settlement. The overriding function of trustees in these new types of trust was to get the best financial returns for the beneficiaries. This function could only be discharged by a careful portfolio of investments which would produce a good financial return.

A second factor influencing trustee investment in the twentieth century was inflation. It became absolutely imperative from the beneficiaries' point of view that the trust fund preserved real value and not just the value at the time of trust coming into effect. Higher rates of inflation coupled with growing taxation meant that investment in safe authorised fixed-rate investments were not in the best interests of the beneficiaries. What was needed was investment in equities which would allow the fund to grow with inflation, thereby giving the beneficiaries a real value when the trust was terminated.

The courts were not oblivious to the concerns which have been outlined above. In 1949 Jenkins J when construing an express power of investment in a trust instrument held that there was no justification for giving a restricted interpretation to such a clause. Instead, he went on to say that 'so, construing the words "in or upon such investments as to them may seem fit", I see no justification for implying any restriction. I think the trustees have, under the plain meaning of those words to invest in any investments which . . . they honestly think are desirable . . .'[15] Statutory intervention came, however, in the form of the Trustee Investment Act 1961, which attempted to provide some compromise between the underlying objective of safe investment and the growing need to meet inflationary pressure. This Act, which is discussed in more detail below in the context of the statutory power of investment, allowed for the first time equities to be included in the list of authorised investments. The Act allowed investment in shares in public companies, subject to limitations, and providing that at least half of the trust fund was investment in the traditional safe fixed-rate investments. This was seen as a compromise between preservation and growth in inflationary terms. Despite the change in the division of the fund between equities and fixed-rate investments, so that up three-quarters of the fund could be invested in equities, the Trustee Investment Act 1961 became heavily criticised as being too restrictive. Amongst the main criticisms were firstly, that the requirement of division between fixed-rate investments and equities was too burdensome, and secondly, that the concept of equities for the purposes of the 1961 Act was in fact too restrictive.[16]

Trustee investment has entered yet another phase in the twenty-first century. The modern trustee investment framework is influenced by concerns about the changing

---

[15] *Re Harari's Settlement Trusts* [1949] 1 All ER 430 at 432; see below.
[16] *Trustee Power and Duties* Law. Com. 260.

functions of the trust and its important role in commercial and financial matters. Trustees are aware of the needs of the trust fund to grow in line with inflationary pressures; furthermore, that there should be capital growth in trust funds where the beneficiaries are not necessarily interested in income and capital preservation. But, what is a more notable feature of influencing modern investment law and practice is the range and complexity of investment opportunities. The range of investment opportunities and the conditions under which they operate raise concerns whether the average trustee can properly invest trust funds for his beneficiaries. Given the diversity of investments, this new phase of trustee investment has shifted from the concept of authorised investments to complete freedom.[17] Instead, there is now recognition that it is primarily the type of trust in question and portfolio of the total investment that govern the choice of investments. Furthermore, unlike in the past, trustee investment is not necessarily something which has to be discharged by trustees, but more so by investment managers offering specialised skills. The modern statutory rules on investment are to be found in the Trustee Act 2000, which is discussed in more detail in this chapter.

Common law and statutory duties when investing

The general duty of care in the Trustee Act 2000

Part I of the Trustee Act 2000 imposes a statutory duty of care applicable to trustees when carrying out their functions under the Act: for example, investment and appointment of agents, nominees and custodians. The general duty of care extends to trustees carrying out similar functions under the trust instrument. The general duty is defined in s. 1 and basically provides that a trustee must exercise such care and skill as is reasonable in the circumstances, making allowance for his special knowledge, experience or professional status. Schedule 1 to the Act makes provision for this general duty to be excluded in the trust instrument. The general duty of care, whilst creating an objective standard of care, does have a subjective element to it. Whilst a trustee is expected to behave as a prudent businessman, s. 1 specifically requires that the experience and skills of the individual trustee be considered when applying the duty of care. There are a couple of points to note about the general duty of care in s. 1 of the Act.

Firstly, the general duty of care replaces the 'prudent man of business' test which had on many occasions been applied in the common law. The common law imposed a duty on trustees when carrying out their administrative functions under the trust. In *Speight v Gaunt*[18] Lord Blackburn explained that 'as a general rule a trustee sufficiently discharges his duty if he takes in managing trust affairs all those precautions which an ordinary prudent man of business would take in managing similar affairs of his own'.[19] In the context of trustee investment the leading case is that of *Learoyd v Whiteley*[20] where both the Court of Appeal and then the House of Lords explained how the ordinary prudent man of business test was to be applied. In the Court of Appeal, Lindley LJ commented that, 'the duty of a trustee is not to take such care only as a prudent man would take if he had only himself to consider; the duty rather is to take such care as an ordinary prudent man would take if he were minded to make an investment for the benefit of other people

---

[17] Subject, of course, to all the duties imposed by common law and statute; see below.
[18] (1883) 9 App. Cas. 1.
[19] *Ibid.* at 19.
[20] (1897) 12 App. Cas. 727.

for whom he felt morally bound to provide'.[21] This prudent man of business had been described as 'counterpart of the reasonable man who is so ubiquitous in the common law'.[22] Lindley LJ spoke of a prudent man of business as someone investing for another person for whom he felt morally obliged to provide for. This test requires more than acting as a prudent business person simply because a trustee is not allowed to invest in risky or hazardous investments. Prudent men of business do often take risks in investment; however, a trustee was not required to take such risky investments at the expense of the beneficiaries. In this respect Lord Watson in the House of Lords commented that, 'businessmen of ordinary prudence may, and frequently do, select investments which are more or less of a speculative character; but it is the duty of trustees to confine himself to the class of investments which are permitted by the trust, and likewise to avoid all investments of that class which are attended with hazard'.[23]

Whilst the prudent businessman test served as the yardstick to measure the liability of a trustee investing trust funds, in recent times there had been concerns about the adequacy of the test in modern conditions of trust investment. There appeared to be two issues which remained problematic. The first related to whether the prudent businessman test was completely redundant in judging the standard of care expected of modern trustees in the context of trustee investment. The second issue related to the question of whether the test was not in itself redundant but should be interpreted in light of contemporary investment practices. The answers to these questions had attracted a mixed response. In respect of whether the prudent businessman test is redundant, some writers had suggested that changes in trustee investment practice had made it impossible to have a notion of a prudent businessman for the purposes of trust investment. Given the complexity of modern investments, not even professional advisers can claim they have expertise in financial markets and types of investment. Once such writer comments that the 'ordinary prudent man of business standard of care is largely meaningless in modern conditions. It is a fact that prudent businessmen invest in all sorts of radically different ways, they have different objectives, and they have widely differing levels and areas of investment skill. This so-called standard is now nothing more than a conventional formula which serves to lend an air of objectivity to judge's notions of appropriate conduct.'[24] However, writing extrajudicially Lord Nicholls had rejected the idea that the prudent man of business test has become redundant; instead he has explained that its interpretation must be influenced by contemporary investment practices.[25]

It is submitted that the modern application of the prudent man of business test would require trustee investments to be judged in light of the modern portfolio theory. This means that individual investments must not be considered in isolation but must be

---

[21] *Re Whiteley* (1886) 33 Ch. D 347 at 355. A similar approach has been followed in the United States where in one case Judge Putnam stated that 'all that can be required of a trustee to invest, is, that he shall conduct himself faithfully and exercise a sound discretion. He is to observe how men of prudence, discretion, and intelligence manage their affairs, not in regard to speculation, but in regard to the permanent disposition of their funds, considering the probable income as well as the probable safety of the capital to be invested,' *Harvard College* v *Amory* 9 Pick. 446 (Mass. Sup. Jud. Ct 1830) at 461. See D. Grosh, 'Trustee Investment: English Law and the American Prudent Man Rule', 1974 ICLQ 748.

[22] Lord Nicholls, at p. 73, *op. cit.* see note 1.

[23] (1897) 12 App. Cas. 727 at 733.

[24] A. Duckworth, 'Legal Aspects of Trustee Investment – Is the Prudent Man Still Alive and Well? 1997 PCB Issue No. 122 at p. 27.

[25] Lord Nicholls in 'Trustees and Their Broader Community: Where Duty, Morality and Ethics Converge' (1995) Trust LI Vol. 9 No. 71 at p. 73.

viewed in light of the portfolio of investments. What may appear as a high-risk investment in isolation may appear to be totally adequate in a low-risk portfolio of investments. In this respect Hoffmann J was able to comment at first instance in *Nestlé v National Westminster Bank plc* [26] that, 'modern trustees acting within their investment powers are entitled to be judged by the standards of current portfolio theory, which emphasises the risk level of the entire portfolio rather than the risk attaching to each investment taken in isolation'.

Section 1 of the Trustee Act 2000 replaces the prudent man of business test and requires the trustee to exercise a duty of care as is reasonable in the circumstances, making allowance for the trustee's specific knowledge and experience. The difference between the duty of care in s. 1 of the Trustee Act 2000 and the previous prudent man of business test is that s. 1 of the Act requires the court to take into consideration the specific skills and experience of the individual trustee. The question arises as to whether this subjective element lowers the standard of care required of a lay trustee who may not have the knowledge which a reasonable businessman may have. It is doubtful that it does lower the standard of care; all that it appears to be saying is that reasonableness must be measured in the light of different trustees. Of course, it would be absurd to suggest that a professional trustee must be expected to exercise the same degree of care and skill as that required of a lay trustee. Equally on the other hand, a lay trustee cannot be expected to exercise the same care and skill which a professionally trustee claims to have. However, this does not mean that a lay trustee is necessarily subject to a lower duty of care; he must exercise such care and skill required of a person in a similar situation. In other words, reasonableness must now be measured in light of all the circumstances of the trust.

Secondly, the general duty of care makes it absolutely clear that a professional trustee owes a higher duty of care than a normal trustee. Prior to the Trustee Act 2000 there was no doubt in the minds of many that a professional trustee should exercise a higher duty of care than that of a reasonable businessman. However, with regard to the case law, the matter was far from clear and much confusion centred on the question as to whether the higher duty of care was required from a paid trustee or professional trustee. In one case Harman J explained that a 'paid trustee is expected to exercise a higher standard of diligence and knowledge than an unpaid trustee, and . . . a bank which advertises itself largely in the public press as taking charge of administrations is under a special duty'.[27] Whilst there is no doubt that a professional trustee should owe a higher duty of care based on his knowledge, skill and experience,[28] not all paid trustees are necessarily professional trustees. What Harman J was envisaging was a professional trustee and not just a paid trustee. The general duty of care in s. 1 of the Trustee Act 2000 allows for a higher duty of care to be expected from a professional trustee, not necessarily from a paid trustee who happens to be a lay trustee. Although a lay trustee may be paid for his services, the duty of care required of him is to be measured in the circumstances of the case, making allowance for his special knowledge and experience.

Balance the financial interests of all the beneficiaries

When investing the trust funds, trustees must act impartially among all the beneficiaries. This means that they must not confer greater financial advantages on one beneficiary at

---

[26] 29 June 1988, unreported.
[27] *Re Waterman's Will Trust* [1952] 2 All ER 1054 at 1055.
[28] *Bartlett* v *Barclays Bank Trust Co Ltd* [1980] 1 All ER 139.

the expense of another when the trust instrument does not so authorise. In the case of consecutive interests in a trust fund, as for example in the case of a settlement in favour of beneficiaries entitled in succession, the trustees must ensure that they maintain a balance between the interests of the life tenant and the remainderman. It is the trustee's duty to deal fairly between both types of beneficiary so that the life tenant receives a reasonable income during his lifetime whilst the remainderman has a reasonable capital return.

APPLYING THE LAW

In his will, Samuel settled a sum of £300,000 upon trust for his wife for life and thereafter for his three children equally upon their attaining the age of 21 years. Samuel died a few years ago and the trustees have invested the money in a number of high interest bank accounts. The children have complained to the trustees that the money in these accounts is not allowing the capital to grow and that they should consider investing in stocks and shares.

Should the trustees diversify the investments?

In *Nestlé v National Westminster Bank plc*[29] William Nestlé left some £54,000 in the form of equities by way of settlement for his wife for life, thereafter for his children and grandchildren. In 1986 Miss Nestlé, his granddaughter, became entitled to the trust fund, which at that time was worth £269,000. National Westminster Bank had managed the portfolio of equities as trustees. Miss Nestlé alleged that the trust fund would have been worth over £1 million had the trustees properly invested the trust funds. Thus, in attempting to make the trustee liable for breach of trust, she argued, *inter alia*, that the bank had failed to diversify the initial equities, failed periodically to review the investments and that the bank had favoured the income beneficiaries at her expense. The Court of Appeal held that, although the trustees had failed to periodically review the trust investment and also the extent of their investment power, they were not in breach of trust. The Court of Appeal held that the bank was under a duty to balance the needs of the life tenant and the remainderman, and if that meant that the trustees retained investments which did not necessarily provide greater capital growth they were not in breach of trust. Staughton LJ commented that, 'a life tenant may be anxious to receive the highest possible income while the remainderman will wish the real value of the fund to be preserved. If the life tenant is living in penury and the remainderman already has ample wealth common sense suggests that a trustee should be able to take into account, not necessarily be seeking the highest possible income at the expense of capital but by inclining in that direction.'[30]

The decision in *Nestlé v National Westminster Bank plc*[31] also illustrates the immense difficulty faced by a plaintiff like Miss Nestlé in establishing breach of trust in the context in which the case arose. Where trustees are investing, for example over a period of 60 years, and considering the interests of the life tenant and the remainderman, it becomes a difficult task to prove that particular investments, which appear objectively appropriate

---

[29] [1994] 1 All ER 118.
[30] [1994] 1 All ER 118 at 137.
[31] [1994] 1 All ER 118. See, M. Stauch and G. Watt, 'Is there liability for Imprudent Trustee Investment?' Conv. (1998) 352.

at the given time, are necessarily a breach of trust when looked at with hindsight. In ***Nestlé v National Westminster Bank plc*** Miss Nestlé's counsel may well have shown the court elaborate financial statistics showing equity growth; however, unless the trustee failed to make investments or made the wrong investments resulting in loss, no liability could attach even if they had not appreciated the extent of their investment power. The matter was elegantly put by Leggatt LJ who commented that the 'bank's engagement was as trustee; and as such, it is to be judged not so much by success as by absence of proven default'.[32] In the course of his judgment Straughton LJ explained that:

> the misunderstanding of the investment clause and the failure to conduct periodic reviews do not by themselves, whether separately or together, afford the plaintiff a remedy. They were symptoms of incompetence or idleness – not on the part of National Westminster Bank but of their predecessors; they were not, without more, breaches of trust. The plaintiff must show that, through one or other or both of those causes, the trustees made decisions which they should not have made or failed to make decisions which they should have made. If that were proved, and if at first sight loss resulted, it would be appropriate to order an inquiry as to the loss suffered by the trust fund.[33]

The duty not to have regard to non-financial considerations

The duty of trustees is to act in the best financial interests of their beneficiaries. With this primary objective in mind, the question has arisen whether trustees can, when investing the trust funds, have regard to non-financial considerations? These non-financial considerations may range from social, political, moral and ethical issues. For example, trustees may be opposed to investing in alcohol or arms related companies because they have strong views about alcohol or arms, but does this justify abstention from investing in such companies if the actual investments will be in the best financial interests of the beneficiaries? This question has been the subject matter of both judicial and academic debate.[34] Docking and Pittaway have distinguished between social investment and social disinvestment.[35] Social investment has been described as the 'selection of investments for a social or political objective rather than solely for reasons of a strictly commercial nature . . . the social objective may include investing in particular groups within society . . . investing in companies with a sound record on environmental control'.[36] Social disinvestment, on the other hand, occurs when there is a deliberate decision not to invest in a particular investment, for example, where the investment is in a company which is in competition with the company which is administering a trust for its employees. The fact that a trustee may be influenced by social, political and moral issues should come as no surprise. A prudent man of business is not necessarily immune to issues of morality, society and ethics. Lord Nicholls explains that whether 'an expert or not, the ordinary prudent person is not to be regarded as wholly lacking in moral sensitivity'.[37]

---

[32] [1994] 1 All ER 118 at 142.
[33] [1994] 1 All ER 118 at 134.
[34] See Docking and Pittaway, 'Social Investment by English Pension Funds: Can it be done?' (1990) *Trust Law and Practice* Vol. 4 No. 125; Lord Nicholls, 'Trustees and Their Broader Community: Where Duty, Morality and Ethics Converge' (1995) Trust LI Vol. 9 No. 71. An excellent account is provided in G. Moffat, *Trust Law: Text and Materials*, 4th edn (2005) at pp. 465–72.
[35] Docking and Pittaway, 'Social Investment by English Pension Funds: Can it be done?' (1990) *Trust Law and Practice* Vol. 4 No. 125.
[36] *Ibid.* at p. 25.
[37] Lord Nicholls, 'Trustees and Their Broader Community: Where Duty, Morality and Ethics Converge' (1995) Trust LI Vol. 9 No. 71 at p. 73.

APPLYING THE LAW

Bill, Bob and Fred are three trustees of a fund worth £500,000 held in favour of employees of a company payable on their retirement. All three trustees have consulted an investment adviser who has provided them with an investment plan for the next five years which will make sure the fund achieves optimum growth. Bill has objected to the plan on the grounds that a number of the investments in the plan are in companies producing alcohol and tobacco. He refused to consent to the investment even though it would produce a very high return for the beneficiaries.

Can Bill object to the investment plan on his personal views?

The issue of non-financial consideration was considered by Megarry VC in **Cowan v Scargill**.[38] The facts of this case concerned the mineworkers' pension fund which was being administered by ten trustees. Five of those trustees had been appointed by the National Union of Mineworkers whilst the other five were appointed by the National Coal Board. In 1982 the trustees were presented with a portfolio of investments which included investment in overseas energy companies which were in direct competition with the coal industry in England. Naturally, the five trustees appointed by the National Union of Mineworkers objected to the investment in such overseas energy companies. Investment in overseas energy companies was against the policy of the National Union of Mineworkers, which was to protect the coal industry in the United Kingdom. Meggary VC held that the duty of the trustees was to act in the best interests of the beneficiaries, and in the present context, their best financial interests. Taking on board the declining nature of the coal industry in the United Kingdom and the fact that the value of the pension fund was worth more than the assets of the industry, he went on to say that the trustees would be in breach of trust if they did not accept the proposed investments, which included overseas companies.

In the course of his judgment Megarry VC made an important statement about the relevance of non-financial consideration in trustee investment. He commented that:

> [t]rustees may have strongly held social and political views. They may be firmly opposed to investment in South Africa or other countries, or they may object to any form of investment in companies concerned with alcohol, tobacco, armaments or many other things. In the conduct of their own affairs, of course, they are free to abstain from making such investments. Yet under a trust, if investment of this type would be more beneficial to the beneficiaries than other investments, the trustees must not refrain from making the investments by reason of the view they hold.[39]

Whilst the decision in **Cowan v Scargill** illustrates that non-financial consideration should not undermine the duty of the trustees to act in the best financial interests of their beneficiaries, the decision does not categorically rule out the relevance of non-financial considerations. In the first place, a settlor can make it a term of the investment power in the trust instrument that investment in particular types of organisation is not allowed. Secondly, where all the beneficiaries are in agreement as to the desirability or otherwise of a particular proposed investment, their views must surely override the views of the

---

[38] [1985] Ch. 270.
[39] [1985] Ch. 270 at 287.

trustees. Thirdly, and perhaps more importantly, trustees may to some extent take on board non-financial consideration, providing that the proposed investment plan does not prejudice the financial interests of their beneficiaries. So, a trustee may have strong views about investment in portfolio A because this portfolio contains tobacco industries; however, if he decides to invest in portfolio B which does not contain such industries, there will be no breach of duty if the financial returns from both portfolios is the same. This is something which can happen in practice, given the scope of investments that are available to trustees.[40]

A different type of problem can occur when an investment plan is proposed, but is totally against the purposes of the trust. The problem is particularly acute in the context of a charitable trust: for example, one which is for the cure of lung cancer. In such a case, it would be totally incompatible with the trust objectives to invest in tobacco-related industries. So whilst the possibility exists for trustees in such a trust to avoid investments on social grounds, the court will closely control the extent to which they can do so. The matter will ultimately be one of assessing the extent of the financial detriment to the beneficiaries and the objectives of the trust. Thus, in **Harries v Church Commissioners for England**,[41] the Bishop of Oxford, whose objective was to promote the Christian faith through the Church of England, challenged the investment policy of the Church Commissioners. The Bishop along with other clergy argued that the Commissioners should not select investments which were incompatible with the purposes they were promoting, even if it involved financial detriment to the trust funds. Nicholls VC, whilst accepting that non-financial considerations may sometimes be relevant in charitable trusts, nevertheless held that the view put forward by the Bishop and others was far too restrictive. It involved significant detriment to the trust fund.

Review of the trust investments

Once the trust funds have been invested, the trustees are under a continuing duty to review those investments and consider whether they are appropriate at the particular time and for the purposes of the trust. Although in **Nestlé v National Westminster Bank plc**[42] the bank was not found to be in breach of trust, the court held that the trustees were under an ongoing duty to periodically review the trust investments. The trustees' duty to review the trust investments was more recently considered by Mr Blohm QC in the High Court decision in **Jeffrey v Gretton**[43] where trustees were holding a Grade II dilapidated property on trust for a life tenant and thereafter for two remaindermen. As a result of a deed of variation, the life tenant ceased to live in the property. The trustees allowed one of the remaindermen to live in the property despite suggestions by the other that it was more beneficial to sell the property in 2002. The trustees attempted to refurbish the property without taking professional advice as to the suitability of such refurbishments and that such refurbishments would run over their time. The property was eventually

---

[40] This point is neatly illustrated by a Scottish decision, *Martin v City of Edinburgh District Council* 1988 SLT 329. In this case a council administering trust funds reinvested the funds away from investment in South African companies because they were opposed to apartheid in South Africa. This reinvestment was not done pursuant to any professional advice, and neither had the trustees considered the financial interests of the beneficiaries. Lord Murray held, *inter alia*, trustees were under a duty not to fetter their investment discretions by any predetermined decision.

[41] [1992] 1 WLR 1241.

[42] [1994] 1 All ER 118.

[43] [2011] WTLR 809.

sold in 2008 and the claimant, Mrs Jeffrey, one of the remainder, commenced proceedings against the trustees, alleging that they had acted in breach of trust by failing to review the trust investment. If they had properly reviewed the trust investment they would have sold the property much earlier than they did. Mr Blohm QC held that the trustees had indeed breached their duty to regularly review the trust investment. In the course of his judgment the learned judge explained that 'a trustee who fails to exercise a power that he ought to exercise will be in breach of trust. A trustee owes his beneficiaries a duty to review the trust holding from time to time – see Section 4(2) Trustee Act 2000 which states:

> "(2) A trustee must from time to time review the investments of the trust and consider whether, having regard to the standard investment criteria, they should be varied."

and if appropriate to alter the investment of the trust. That duty to review applied to the Defendants. Although the will trusts confer on the trustees the power to invest of a beneficial owner, such a provision does not exclude the trustees' duty to review their investment from time to time.'[44]

The decision in *Jeffrey v Gretton* is also considered in Chapter 20 on breach of trust. Mrs Jeffrey claimed that the trustees had acted in breach of trust, which the court clearly accepted; however, she needed to show the court that she actually suffered a loss as result of the breach of trust. These matters are analysed in more detail in Chapter 20.

Express powers of investment

It has already been observed above that it is the duty of a trustee to invest the trust funds. How the trustee invests the funds will be determined by the power of investment which is conferred upon him or her. The power may be in the form of an express power in the trust instrument or, in the absence of an express power, the statutory power in the Trustee Act 2000. This section explores the scope of an express power of investment.

The nature of an express power of investment

APPLYING THE LAW

In an *inter vivos* settlement Jill settled a sum of £100,000 on trust for her three children in equal shares until they all attain the age of 21 years. The settlement confers upon the trustees in clause 15 of the settlement a power to invest in any investments as if they were the absolute owners of the fund. The trustees seek your advice as to the proper scope of clause 15.

Although trustees are under a duty to invest the trust funds, the range of investments they can invest in is governed by the power of investment that is conferred upon them. In most modern and carefully drawn-up trusts the trust deed will invariably incorporate a wide power of investment. An example of such a wide power of investment is where the trust deed says something to the effect that the trustees have the power to invest in such

---

[44] [2011] WTLR 809, Lawtel judgment at para. 69.

investments as if they were the beneficial owner of the trust fund. Whilst this type of power appears to be extremely wide, the trustees cannot literally do what they like, because they are still subject to the duties outlined above. In particular they are subject to the general duty of care. This type of wide power does, however, give the trustees an unrestricted range of investments in which they can invest in, providing they exercise the duties imposed upon them by common law and statute. Where there is no express power of investment the trustees will find that the power is conferred by statute. The modern statutory power is found in Part II of the Trustee Act 2000 which came into force on 1 February 2001. This Act repealed the former statutory power of investment found in the Trustee Investment Act 1961. At one time the distinction between an express power of investment and the statutory power of investment was vital. Until the Trustee Act 2000 came into force, the statutory power of investment found in the Trustee Investment Act 1961 gave only restricted powers of investment to trustees.[45] Where a trust instrument failed to incorporate an express power of investment, for example, most typically in home-drawn-up trusts and wills, trustees of such a trust found themselves with restricted powers of investments compared to those trustees exercising an express power of investment. In the modern law the difference between an express power and the statutory power is not as vital as it was before, because the statutory power, as will be seen later, confers wide powers of investment on trustees.[46]

Interpreting express investment clauses

In the law relating to express powers of investment, the following points should be noted. The power must, in the first place, be drafted with a degree of certainty so as to make it clear to the trustees the scope of their power and be capable of control by the court.[47] With regard to the extent of an express power of investment, the courts are required to give the express power its natural and plain meaning. The matter is neatly illustrated by the decision in **Re Harari's Settlement Trusts**[48] where a settlor gave the power to his trustees to retain or, with his daughter's consent, invest the trust money 'in or upon such investments as to them may seem fit'. The existing investments included Egyptian bonds and securities. These investments were not investments authorised by the law at the time. Jenkins J had to decide whether an express investment clause of this nature restricted the trustees to invest only in the usual range of trustee investments or whether the trustees could invest outside that range. Prior to this case the general position in law was that an express clause should be construed restrictively and should only allow investments in those types of investments which were authorised by law.[49] For practical

---

[45] These matters are explored in more detail in the next section.

[46] The distinction, however, has not altogether disappeared; it is still the case that a carefully drafted express power of investment may confer a very broad power of investment which is not to be found under the Trustee Act 2000. For example, the settlor can relieve the trustees from balancing appreciation between income and capital, which would otherwise apply under the statutory power.

[47] See, for example, *Re Kolb's Will Trust* [1962] Ch. 531 where investment in 'blue chip' companies and other investments, which would have been approved by the settlor, was held to be void for uncertainty. Where the power is void for uncertainty the court has the power to widen the trustees' power of investment. The basis upon which the power will be enlarged was considered by Meggary VC in *Trustees of the British Museum* v *A-G* [1984] 1 All ER 337; see later.

[48] [1949] 1 All ER 430.

[49] A good example of this restrictive approach can be seen in *Bethell* v *Abraham* [1873] LR 17 Eq. 24, where Jessel MR held that a clause which purported to give the trustees a power to change securities from time to time only determined that securities could be changed from time to time and not that there could be substantive changes in the type of securities themselves.

purposes in *Re Harari's Settlement Trust* this meant the very restricted and safe investments under the then s. 1 of the Trustee Act 1925. Jenkins J, however, held that there was no justification for giving a restricted interpretation to an express investment clause. Instead, he went on to say that 'so, construing the words "in or upon such investments as to them may seem fit", I see no justification for implying any restriction. I think the trustees have, under the plain meaning of those words to invest in any investments which . . . they honestly think are desirable . . .'[50]

The meaning of investment

One question, which has often been discussed in the case law, is the meaning of investment for the purposes of an express power of investment, indeed, for any investment power. Does the employment of the word 'investment' in the context of trustee investment require that there be income and capital gains or can there simply be capital gains from a particular investment? For example, are trustees of a fund allowed to purchase a valuable painting in the knowledge that such painting will be worth considerably more in years ahead? In this type of investment there is no income during the term of the investment,[51] but only an increase in its capital value. Of course this type of investment would be totally unsatisfactory for a trust for beneficiaries entitled in succession. In such a case, as seen above, the trustees would be required to maintain a balance between income and capital growth so that both the life tenant and the remainderman would benefit.[52] However, where the trust is one that is not in succession it is not altogether clear why a non-income-producing investment should not be allowed. Until relatively recently, the common law position was that such an investment, which does not yield income, will not be authorised. The reason for this stemmed from the widely used judicial definition of investment found in *Re Wragg*[53] where P.O. Lawrence J commented, in the course of construing a clause allowing investment in 'stock funds shares and securities or other investments' that investment meant 'property . . . purchased in order to be held for the sake of the income which it will yield'.[54] It is submitted that this is no longer a limitation in the modern law and that a trustee can purchase a non-income-producing investment if that is more suitable for the trust.[55] The Trustee Act 2000 in s. 3 allows the trustee to make any kind of investment that he could make if he were absolutely entitled to the trust fund. Moreover, in *Harries v Church Commissioners*[56] Sir Donald Nicholls VC interpreted 'investment' to mean to hold property 'for the purpose of generating money, whether from income or capital growth, with which to further the work of the trust'.[57]

---

[50] *Ibid.* at p. 432.
[51] Unless the painting is to be put, for example, in a museum.
[52] *Nestlé* v *National Westminster Bank plc* [1994] 1 All ER 118.
[53] [1919] 2 Ch. 58.
[54] *Ibid.* at p. 64.
[55] This was certainly the view of the Law Commission; see *Trustees Powers and Duties* Law. Com. No. 260 at p. 22. Furthermore, the Explanatory Notes to the Trustee Act 2000 make it clear that investment can include income or capital-related profit; see note 22.
[56] [1992] 1 WLR 1241.
[57] *Ibid.* at 1246.

Statutory power of investment

Where there is an absence of an express power of investment, trustees must invest the trust funds in accordance with the power conferred by law. In other words, they must look to the power of investment conferred by statute. The modern statutory power of investment is to be found in the Trustee Act 2000 which came into force on 1 February 2001. The power is contained in Part II of the Act and its enactment had the effect of repealing the former statutory power of investment which was found in the Trustee Investment Act 1961.

Background to the investment power in the Trustee Act 2000

Reforming the law relating to trustee investment was at the heart of the Trustee Act 2000. The Trustee Investment Act 1961, which contained the statutory power of investment, had become so out of date with investment practice that its repeal had been argued for over two decades. The Trustee Investment Act 1961 allowed trustees to invest in equities without totally abandoning the policy of safe investments. The 1961 Act restricted trustees to authorised investments. The Act divided investments into 'narrow range' and 'wide range' investments. Narrow-range investments consisted primarily of fixed-rate investments whilst wide-range investments consisted of shares in public companies. Trustees could, if they wanted, invest the whole of the trust fund in the narrow range; however, if they wanted to invest in the wide range they were required to divide the trust fund into two parts. Initially trustees were required to divide the fund equally and make sure that one half was invested in the narrow range, allowing the other half to be invested in equities. At the time of its repeal, that division had changed so that trustees were only required to invest 25 per cent of the trust fund in the narrow range, allowing up to 75 per cent to be invested in the wide range.

Whilst the Trustee Investment Act 1961 was seen as generous at the time of its enactment, it had clearly become out of date with modern investment practices. The manner in which financial markets operate and the functions of the modern trust had made it impossible in many cases for the ordinary trustee to invest trust funds in the best interests of the beneficiaries. In many cases it is far more appropriate for such trustees not to be restricted to authorised investments such as those which existed under the Trustee Investment Act 1961, but rather to delegate the entire process of selecting and implementing investment decisions to professional persons. The requirement to divide the fund between the narrow range and the wide range had been criticised as been unduly restrictive.[58] In the case of trusts which consist of very large funds, investment, which can produce substantial growth in the capital, requires the employment of nominees to deal with securities. The use of nominees is absolutely essential to the investment because it is only through this medium that the investment of the trust fund can produce the best results. Nominees are not only in the best position to determine the adequacy of a particular portfolio of investment but they can also manage the fund, provide paperwork for the Inland Revenue and also facilitate the electronic transfer of and settlement in securities.

---

[58] See P. Milner and J. Holmes, 'Trust Law Reforms: Are We Nearly There Yet?' PCB Vol. 2 (2000) pp. 114–29.

The general power of investment

Where there is no wide power of investment conferred by the trust instrument, trustees must adhere to the power of investment in Part II of the Trustee Act 2000. The general power is to be found in s. 3(1) and it provides that a 'trustee may make any kind of investment that he could make if he were absolutely entitled to the assets of the trust'. The general power does not extend to trustees making investments in land other than in loans secured on land. Investment in land is, however, dealt with by s. 8 of the Act.[59] Unlike the Trustee Investment Act 1961, the new power in the Trustee Act 2000 does not restrict trustees to specified investments; instead the power is a wide one which allows any investments, subject of course to compliance with any common law and statutory duties which are imposed upon them. Section 7(1) of the Act states that the new power of investment applies to trusts created before the commencement of the Act, so is therefore retrospective in application. The fact that the general power is retrospective will make it particularly important in trusts created before the commencement of the Act: for example, in contexts such as wills and home-drawn-up trust deeds. It is precisely in these contexts that people fail to give appropriate investment powers to the trustees. The general power of investment is a default provision, which means that it can be excluded or restricted in some way or another.[60]

Standard investment criteria

When exercising the general power of investment, trustees are required to have regard to what is described in the Act as the 'standard investment criteria'.[61] Trustees are required to review the trust investments from time to time, having regard to the standard investment criteria, and consider whether those investments should be varied.[62] The standard investment criteria are to be found in s. 4(3) of the Act.

KEY STATUTE

S. 4 Trustee Act 2000 (Standard investment criteria)

(1) In exercising any power of investment, whether arising under this Part or otherwise, a trustee must have regard to the standard investment criteria.

(2) A trustee must from time to time review the investments of the trust and consider whether, having regard to the standard investment criteria, they should be varied.

(3) The standard investment criteria, in relation to a trust, are –

(a) the suitability to the trust of investments of the same kind as any particular investment proposed to be made or retained and of that particular investment as an investment of that kind, and

(b) the need for diversification of investments of the trust, in so far as is appropriate to the circumstances of the trust.

---

[59] See below.
[60] Trustee Act 2000 s. 6(1).
[61] Trustee Act 2000 s. 4(1).
[62] Trustee Act 2000 s. 4(2).

Some aspects of the criteria were to be found in the Trustee Investment Act 1961 and as such there does not appear to be a major change in the law in this respect. Other aspects of the criteria were already discussed in the case law and trustees, even before the Trustee Act 2000, were bound by such criteria. The standard investment criteria requires the trustees to have regard to suitability to the trust of the investments in question; secondly, the extent to which they are appropriate in the circumstances and finally the need for diversification if appropriate for the trust. The fact that trustees are under a duty to periodically review the trust investments had been made clear in the case law.[63] The need to have regard to suitability and diversification was found in s. 6(1) of the Trustee Investment Act 1961. In this respect, this aspect of the Trustee Act 2000 codifies the existing law. A trustee who fails to review the trust investments with regard to the standard investment criteria will be in breach of trust.

The need for advice

KEY STATUTE

S. 5 Trustee Act 2000 (The need to take advice)

(1) Before exercising any power of investment, whether arising under this Part or otherwise, a trustee must (unless the exception applies) obtain and consider proper advice about the way in which, having regard to the standard investment criteria, the power should be exercised.

(2) When reviewing the investments of the trust, a trustee must (unless the exception applies) obtain and consider proper advice about whether, having regard to the standard investment criteria, the investments should be varied.

(3) The exception is that a trustee need not obtain such advice if he reasonably concludes that in all the circumstances it is unnecessary or inappropriate to do so.

(4) Proper advice is the advice of a person who is reasonably believed by the trustee to be qualified to give it by his ability in and practical experience of financial and other matters relating to the proposed investment.

The need to take proper advice is an important aspect of trustee investment. Under the old law, that is, under the Trustee Investment Act 1961, trustees were only required to take advice in respect of certain types of investments.[64] Under the Trustee Act 2000 the requirement for advice is not restricted to particular investments, but it is a general requirement which can be dispensed with only when the trustee concludes that it is reasonable not to take advice. The issue of advice is dealt with by s. 5 of the Act, which requires the trustee to take advice before exercising any power of investment[65] or when reviewing the investments of the trust.[66] Advice must be considered in conjunction with the standard investment criteria. It is important to note that the taking of advice in s. 5 is not restricted to the exercise of the power of investment in the Act. It is made clear by

---

[63] See, for example, *Nestlé* v *National Westminster Bank plc* [1993] 1 WLR 1260 at 1282 and also *Bartlet* v *Barclays Bank Trust Co Ltd* [1980] 1 All ER 139.

[64] Advice was only needed for those types of investment which were regarded as more risky than others because they had fluctuations in their capital value; they included narrow-range Part II and wide-range investments.

[65] Trustee Act 2000 s. 5(1).

[66] Trustee Act 2000 s. 5(2).

s. 1 that advice must be taken when exercising any power of investment and not just the general power in the Act. Where a trustee reasonably concludes that the circumstances do not require advice to be taken, then s. 5(3) of the Trustee Act 2000 allows for the taking of advice to be dispensed with. This, of course, would apply in the more simple cases where there is very little risk in the investment to be taken: for example, putting money into an ordinary bank account pending a more detailed investment plan would not require advice. However, a decision to lend money by way of a loan over land would necessarily entail advice from a qualified person, such as a surveyor. In *Jeffrey v Gretton* [2011] WTLR 809 the High Court held that trustees holding a dilapidated property should have sought professional advice as to the suitability of carrying out repairs or whether to sell the property.

As to what constitutes proper advice, s. 5(4) states that 'proper advice is the advice of a person who is reasonably believed by the trustee to be qualified to give it by his ability in and practical experience of financial and other matters relating to the proposed investment'. This section is modelled on the definition of proper advice which used to exist in s. 6 of the Trustee Investment Act 1961. Trustees are required to have a reasonable belief that a particular person is qualified to give the advice; this means that they will be judged on an objective standard and their subjective opinion will not matter.

Delegation of investment powers and asset management

APPLYING THE LAW

Sasha and Nikita are two trustees of a trust arsing under Georgina's will. The trust fund consists of a considerable amount of money settled in favour of a number of different beneficiaries. Sasha and Nikita have very little knowledge of investment matters and seek your advice whether they can simply ask some expert to deal with the investment of the trust money.

The conditions in which modern day investment of funds takes place are very complex and technical. Investing trust funds in such complex and technical financial markets requires specialist knowledge of not only the types of investment that are available but also the mechanisms by which such investments are put into effect in order to get the best returns for their beneficiaries.[67] Given the much specialised nature of modern investments, trustees will often lack the necessary expertise to invest trust funds with a view to getting the best returns for their beneficiaries. In an ideal world trustees would be much better off delegating not only their duty to invest the trust funds but also the power of selecting which types of investments are appropriate to the trust. Until the Trustee Act 2000 came into force, trustees were not generally allowed to delegate their discretions but could delegate their duties or ministerial functions in accordance with the criteria

---

[67] It has been argued that trustees should have some basic understanding of principles of investment; however, it is doubtful whether all types of trustees will have such an understanding. For example, Legair writes that 'a basic understanding of the mathematics of percentages and yields is not enough. Trustees should now be able to cope with and understand concepts such as normal distribution, standard deviation, covariance and many other such terms, and they must have a full appreciation of the lexicon used by investment analysts'. See I.N. Legair, 'Modern Portfolio Theory: A Primer', *Trust Law International* Vol. 14 No. 275 at p. 75.

laid out in the Trustee Act 1925.[68] Trustees of pension funds were in a different position because they had been given the power to delegate their investment powers by s. 34 of the Pensions Act 1995. The absence of a power to delegate discretions meant that a trustee could not employ a specialised fund manager to decide which investments to invest in and when such investments should be changed. This had been seen as a major obstacle in the trustees' path in ensuring that the best returns were obtained for the beneficiaries. The Trustee Act 2000 allows for the delegation of administrative discretions. This means that trustees can now employ discretionary trust managers to manage substantial investments on their behalf.

KEY STATUTE

Section 15 Trustee Act 2000 (Asset management)

(1) The trustees may not authorise a person to exercise any of their asset management functions as their agent except by an agreement which is in or evidenced in writing.

(2) The trustees may not authorise a person to exercise any of their asset management functions as their agent unless –

(a) they have prepared a statement that gives guidance as to how the functions should be exercised ('a policy statement'), and

(b) the agreement under which the agent is to act includes a term to the effect that he will secure compliance with –

(i) the policy statement, or

(ii) if the policy statement is revised or replaced under section 22, the revised or replacement policy statement.

(3) The trustees must formulate any guidance given in the policy statement with a view to ensuring that the functions will be exercised in the best interests of the trust.

(4) The policy statement must be in or evidenced in writing.

(5) The asset management functions of trustees are their functions relating to –

(a) the investment of assets subject to the trust,

(b) the acquisition of property which is to be subject to the trust, and

(c) managing property which is subject to the trust and disposing of, or creating or disposing of an interest in, such property.

Where a trustee delegates his investment power to an investment manager, the Trustee Act 2000 imposes special restriction on such asset management. Section 15 of the Act gives the trustees authority to employ an agent in the form of an asset manager, providing the terms of the agency is in writing or evidenced by writing. It is not sufficient for an agent to be employed as an asset manager unless there is also a 'policy statement' prepared by the trustees which explains how the functions of the agent, i.e. the asset manager, are to be exercised.[69] The policy statement is really a statement which identifies the objectives of the particular trust investments to be managed by the assets manager. For example, the policy statement could make specific reference to the need for a balance

---

[68] The Trustee Act 2000 has repealed this criteria, found in s. 23 and s. 30 Trustee Act 1925. Trustee delegation is considered in Chapter 18 in more detail.

[69] Trustee Act 2000 s. 15(2)(a).

between income and capital if the trust is one for successive beneficiaries. The policy statement must be prepared before the commencement of the agency and it must be referred to in the terms of the agency to the effect that the agent is to have regard to the policy statement.[70] The policy statement must be in or evidenced in writing and can be changed as and when the purpose or objective of the trust investment changes. Trustees are then required to have regard to the revised or replaced policy statement.

Purchase of land as an investment

Until the Trustee Act 2000 came into force, trustees had no general power to purchase land as an investment. There were only two exceptions to this. Firstly, where the trust instrument authorised the trustees to purchase land as an investment, they could do so for the purpose of generating income. The application of this rule was shown in *Re Power*[71] where the court refused the purchase of land for the rent-free occupation of the beneficiaries. The rule has its origins in the judicial definition of investment for trust law purposes, which requires the production of income rather than simple capital growth. In *Re Wragg*[72] Lawrence J commented that the word 'invest' includes as one of its meanings 'to apply money in the purchase of some property from which interest or profit is expected and which property is purchased in order to be held for the sake of income which it will yield'.[73]

Secondly, where the trustees were trustees of land and so governed by the Trusts of Land and Appointment of Trustees Act 1996, s. 6 of the 1996 Act confers upon trustees of land a power to purchase land as an investment, for occupation by the beneficiary or for any other reason. The net effect of the absence of a general power to purchase land was that trustees of pure personalty had no power to acquire land for the rent-free occupation of their beneficiaries. However, trustees who held personalty as well as land on trust for their beneficiaries could give rent-free occupation to their beneficiaries by virtue of the 1996 Act. This produced an unsatisfactory result since, if by chance the subject matter of a trust consisted of personalty as well as realty, trustees could invest in land and give rent-free occupation. On the other hand, personal property subject to a trust could not be converted into real property for the rent-free occupation of the beneficiaries.

Under the Trustee Act 2000 trustees can now purchase land in the United Kingdom. Part III of the Trustee Act 2000 gives the trustees a power to purchase land as an investment, for occupation by the beneficiaries or for any other reason.[74] This new power is based upon that which is contained in the Trusts of Land and Appointment of Trustees Act 1996. Once trustees have acquired land they will be vested with the same powers as an absolute owner of land. Trustees will be able to sell, lease and mortgage the land. The new power to purchase land is a default provision, which means that it can be excluded subject to a contrary provision in the trust instrument.[75] Moreover, the new power is retrospective so applies to trusts created before the commencement of the Act.[76]

---

[70] Trustee Act 2000 s. 15(2)(b).
[71] [1947] Ch. 572.
[72] [1919] 2 Ch. 58.
[73] [1919] 2 Ch. 58 at 64.
[74] Trustee Act 2000 s. 8(1).
[75] Trustee Act 2000 s. 9(1).
[76] Trustee Act 2000 s. 10.

Mortgages of land as an investment

The general power of investment in s. 3 of the Trustee Act 2000 allows trustees to invest in land by means of a loan secured on the land. Section 8 of the Act specifically allows for investment in land. At one time a popular form of trust investment in land was a mortgage of land. The Trustee Act 1925 gave trustees a power to invest in 'real securities' in the United Kingdom and the Trustee Investment Act 1961 included mortgages of land as an authorised narrow-range Part II investment.[77] Despite their historical attraction to trust investments, in more recent times other forms of investment such as stocks and shares have displaced mortgages of land as popular forms of trust investment. Trustees can if they so wish invest trust funds in return for a mortgage of land; however, their decision to do so must be impartial and must be made reasonably. They will, of course, be subject to the statutory duty of care embodied in s. 3 of the Trustee Act 2000.

The early cases decided that only first legal mortgages could be authorised mortgages, and other inferior types of mortgages such as equitable and second mortgages could not.[78] However, it is doubtful whether this is the modern day position because the Trustee Act 1925 and the Trustee Investment Act 1961 did not differentiate between legal and equitable mortgages. The definition of a mortgage in the Trustee Act 1925 relates to 'every estate and interest regarded in equity as merely a security for money'.[79] Accordingly, it has been argued that, given that one of objectives of the Trustee Investment Act 1961 was to increase trustees' powers, it is doubtful whether the pre-1925 cases still represent the true position as regards equitable and second mortgages and that the definition of mortgage in the Trustee Act 1925 must also be the same for the Trustee Investment Act 1961:[80] in other words, capable of extending to equitable mortgages of land. Furthermore, the concerns that an equitable mortgage was no good because it might be defeated by the sale of the mortgaged land to a bona fide purchaser of the legal title without notice of the equitable mortgage do not exist after 1925. An equitable mortgage, which is not protected by deposit of title deeds, is capable of being registered as an equitable charge under the Land Charges Act 1972. In the case of registered land, such a mortgage would be protected by the entry of a notice or caution on the title land.

Trustees investing trust funds on mortgages of land should note that s. 8 of the Trustee Act 1925 provides guidance as to the amount of loan that should be made and the circumstances in which the loan should be made. Although compliance with s. 8 is not mandatory, a trustee is best advised to comply with the guidance therein simply because it sets out the standards of reasonable behaviour. A trustee complying with the guidance will have a good defence in any breach of trust proceedings. The guidance in s. 8 consists of three interrelated aspects. If the guidance is observed then the trustee will 'not be chargeable with breach of trust by reason only of the proportion borne by the amount of loan to the value of the property at the time when the loan was made'. Firstly, a trustee must not advance more than two-thirds of the value of the property. Secondly, that in making the loan the trustee was acting upon a report as to the value of the property made by a person whom he reasonably believed to be qualified as a practical surveyor or valuer, and that such a person was appointed independently of the owner of the land. Finally, that the loan was made under the advice of the surveyor or valuer.

---

[77] Mortgages of land were authorised by s. 1(1)(a) Trustee Act 1925 and also by the Trustee Investment Act 1961 as narrow-range Part II investments.

[78] *Chapman* v *Browne* [1902] 1 Ch. 785.

[79] Trustee Act 1925 s. 68(7).

[80] *Lewin on Trusts*, (1964) 16th edn at pp. 370–1.

KEY STATUTE

S. 8 Trustee Act 1925

A trustee lending money on the security of any property on which he can properly lend shall not be chargeable with breach of trust by reason only of the proportion borne by the amount of the loan to the value of the property at the time when the loan was made, if it appears to the court –

(a) that in making the loan the trustee was acting upon a report as to the value of the property made by a person whom he reasonably believed to be an able practical surveyor or valuer instructed and employed independently of any owner of the property, whether such surveyor or valuer carried on business in the locality where the property is situate or elsewhere; and

(b) that the amount of the loan does not exceed two third parts of the value of the property as stated in the report; and

(c) that the loan was made under the advice of the surveyor or valuer expressed in the report.

Where a trustee fails to comply with the guidance in s. 8 of the Trustee Act 1925 he will be liable to replace the whole loss incurred to the trust estate. Thus, where he fails to employ a surveyor or valuer independently of the owner of the property he will be liable.[81] Where the trustee advances more than the authorised amount in s. 8, but the mortgage would have been a proper mortgage for a lesser sum of monies, the trustee is only required to make good the sum advanced in excess with interest.[82] The decision in **Shaw v Cates**[83] provides a good example of this. Here the trustees had loaned some £4400 when in fact the maximum they could advance was only £3400. Parker J held that the trustee's liability was confined to making good the excess of the amount, which in this case was £1000 with interest.

Enlargement of investment powers: the return of the *Re Kolb* principle

Trustees may feel that the power of investment conferred upon them is too narrow and that the court should widen the power. This can happen by a variation of the power authorised by all the beneficiaries who are of age and competent to do so. If this is not forthcoming, the trustees may ask the court to vary the investment power under s. 57 of the Trustee Act 1925 or the Variation of Trusts Act 1958.[84] Given the fact that the Trustee Act 2000 confers upon trustees a very wide power of investment, requests for the extension of investment powers will not be problematic in modern trust law. The principle in **Re Kolb's Will Trust**[85] is that, whilst the court can widen a power of investment, it should not do so beyond the established law, in particular, the relevant statutory power of

---

[81] *Re Solomon* [1912] 1 Ch. 261; *Re Somerset* [1894] 1 Ch. 231 which were decided under s. 8(1) of the Trustee Act 1893.

[82] Trustee Act 1925 s. 9.

[83] [1909] 1 Ch. 389.

[84] The Variation of Trusts Act 1958 and the general law regarding variation of trusts is considered in Chapter 19.

[85] [1962] Ch. 531.

investment unless a special case can be made for a more extensive power. Application of this principle in light of the Trustee Act 2000 would give trustees a very wide power of investment, and it is difficult to imagine why and how a greater power of investment than that under the Trustee Act 2000 would be required.

> **KEY STATUTE**
>
> ## S. 57 Trustee Act 1925
>
> Where in the management or administration of any property vested in trustees, any sale, lease, mortgage, surrender, release or other disposition, or any purchase, investment, acquisition, expenditure, or other transaction, is in the opinion of the court expedient, but the same cannot be effected by reason of the absence of any power for that purpose vested in the trustees by the trust instrument, if any, or by law, the court may by order confer upon the trustees, either generally or in any particular instance, the necessary power for the purpose, on such terms, and subject to such provisions and conditions, if any, as the court may think fit and may direct in what manner any money authorised to be expended, and the costs of any transaction, are to be paid or borne as between capital and income.

Prior to the Trustee Act 2000, the principle in *Re Kolb's Will Trust* was undermined by a series of cases which highlighted the shortcomings of the power of investment conferred either by a trust instrument or by statute. In such cases, trustees sought to argue that the court should extend the powers beyond the power established by law. For example, in *Mason v Farbrother*[86] the court approved an extension beyond the power conferred by the Trustee Investment Act 1961. In this case the trust fund was one belonging to a pension fund and the concerns of the trustees were that the present power of investment did not allow them to hedge against inflation. More importantly, in *Trustees of the British Museum v A-G*[87] Trustees of the British Museum sought an application for extension of the power of investment that had been conferred upon them by Pennycuick J in 1960. Sir Robert Megarry VC approved an extension of the investment power beyond that which existed under the Trustee Investment Act 1961 and explained that the principle in *Re Kolb's Will Trust* should no longer be followed. The judge went on to comment that changes in investment practices and the types of trust in modern practice inevitably meant that trustees would need wider powers than those conferred by the present law. With regard to the factors which would influence the court when exercising its discretion to widen the power of investment, Sir Robert Megarry VC commented that the court would look to, *inter alia*, the size of the fund and the object of trust. In the present case the trustees sought to invest abroad as well as investing a greater proportion of the fund in capital appreciation investments. This was justifiable because of the soaring price of acquisitions for the museum. More recently, in *Alexander v Alexander*[88] Morgan J in the High Court ordered the sale of land under s. 57 of the Trustee Act 1925 when no such power existed and indeed was excluded in the trust instrument. The facts concerned a cottage which the trustees were holding on trust for several beneficiaries. The cottage had fallen into a bad state of disrepair and was uninhabitable. The trustees wished to sell the cottage; however, the trust instrument

---

[86] [1983] 2 All ER 1078.
[87] [1984] 1 WLR 418.
[88] [2011] EWHC 2721 (Ch.).

expressly prohibited this. This therefore meant that the trustees were left with no power of sale which would normally have existed under s. 6 of the Trusts of Land and Appointment of Trustees Act and s. 8 of the Trustee Act 2000. Nevertheless, having looked at the power in s. 57 and the existing authorities, Morgan J held that the trustees could sell the property as it was expedient to do so and would not alter the beneficial interests of the beneficiaries. In the course of judgment he held that:

> The court has a discretion under section 57(1). Normally, where a transaction is expedient within the subsection, the court would exercise its discretion to confer power on the trustees to effect the transaction. However, as was pointed out in *Royal Melbourne Hospital* v *Equity Trustees*, the court can take into account the wishes of the settlor when deciding whether, in the exercise of its discretion, to confer the relevant power on the trustees. In the present case, the testator's wishes were expressed in his will in March 2006. He plainly thought that the cottage would be suitable for Ms Shuker to live in and that she would want to live in it. It is now clear that the cottage is not suitable for her and she does not want to occupy it. The present position is that the cottage has remained empty, neglected and uninsured. It is hard to think that the testator would want that state of affairs to continue. Further, this is not a case where the beneficiaries are divided in their opinion and the testator's wishes would allow me to favour one point of view over another. The proposed transaction is in the interests of all the beneficiaries and there is no opposition to the proposed transaction.'[89]

The duty to act fairly amongst the beneficiaries

This chapter has focused on the investment duty of the trustee, which, as explained at the outset of this chapter, imposes an imperative obligation on the trustee to invest the trust funds in accordance with the power of investment that is conferred upon the trustee. Before a trustee invests the trust property, he may be subject to other imperative duties in respect of the trust property. One of those duties is the duty to preserve equality between the beneficiaries. The duty will arise most typically in the context of a trust which is created for beneficiaries who are entitled in succession: for example, a trust for A for life and thereafter for B absolutely. Where the trust property consists of certain types of property, the trustee may be subject to the rules of conversion and apportionment before they invest the property. There are two rules which the trustees may be subject to:

1 The Rule in *Howe* v *Earl of Dartmouth*.
2 The Rule in *Re Earl of Chesterfield's Trust*.

The rule in *Howe* v *Earl of Dartmouth*: the duty to convert

APPLYING THE LAW

Suppose that a testator leaves £20,000, a car, a painting, a copyright in a book and a future interest on trust for Tom for life and thereafter for Tim absolutely. In such trust,

---

[89] [2011] EWHC 2721 (Ch.) at para. 33.

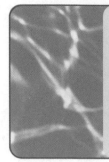

Tom, the life tenant, would be entitled to the income on the trust property and Tim would be entitled to the capital on Tom's death. The trustees can invest the £20,000 and pay the income to Tom and hold the capital value for Tim. The problem with the painting is that it does not produce any income and is therefore no good to Tom. The problem with the copyright in a book and the car is that they are assets which are depreciating in value and therefore no good to Tim. The problem with the future interest is that it is not yet producing income for Tom.

What should the trustees do about this situation?

The rule in ***Howe v Earl of Dartmouth***[90] imposes upon a trustee a duty to convert certain assets which are left in succession to a life tenant and a remainderman. The basis of the rule is that, subject to a contrary intention in a will, where residuary personalty is settled in favour of beneficiaries entitled in succession, a trustee is under a duty to convert all such parts of it which are:

- of a wasting nature;
- of a future or reversionary nature;
- non-income producing;
- unauthorised investments.

The rule in ***Howe v Earl of Dartmouth*** only applies in the case of residuary personalty left in a will. The trustee must convert all such parts which are of a wasting nature, future or reversionary nature, non-income producing or are otherwise unauthorised under the terms of the trust instrument or statute. For example, where a car is left on trust for A for life and thereafter for B, the trustees must sell the car and invest the money so that income can be paid to A and the capital value can be held for B. Where the property in question is a future interest, the trustee must where possible convert such property so that it produces an income for the life tenant. In the case of a reversionary interest, that is, some property which cannot fall into possession until some time in the future, the trust will have to apportion the reversionary property when it does fall into possession. The rule of apportionment is considered in the next section.

The rule in *Re Earl of Chesterfield's Trust*: the duty to apportion

Where a trustee is under a duty to convert trust property he or she will invariably be under a duty to apportion the converted fund. The principal reason for this is that the life tenant will either have missed out on income in the case of non-income producing assets or may have received too much income in the case of hazardous and risky investments at the expense of the remainderman. The duty to apportion the trust funds ensures that the life tenant receives the missed income on those assets which were not income-producing, for example, a car. The same will apply to a future or a reversionary interest which does not fall into possession until some future date.

The rule in ***Re Earl of Chesterfield's Trust***[91] is that the converted fund is apportioned at an interest rate of 4 per cent. The principal way in which a converted fund is apportioned was explained by Chitty J in ***Re Earl of Chesterfield's Trust***.

---

[90] (1802) 7 Ves. Jr. 137.
[91] (1883) 24 Ch. D 643.

[T]he proper mode of calculation is as follows: each item of receipt should be taken separately, deducting in the case of the policy moneys the amounts repaid on account of the premiums; and as regards each item of receipt, it should be calculated what sum invested at the death of the seventh Earl at 4 per cent. interest, with yearly rests, would have produced the amount actually received: then the aggregate of the principal sums arrived at by this calculation ought to be treated as capital, and the rest ought to be treated as income.[92]

The basic effect of the application of the rule in *Re Earl of Chesterfield's Trust* is that the converted funds, whether they are funds converted from non-income-producing assets or future interests, represent a combination of part interest and part capital.

The contemporary application of the rules of conversion and apportionment and law reform

The rules of conversion and apportionment have to some extent lost the importance they once occupied in trust law. There are a number of reasons for this, not least the fact the conditions giving rise to their application have changed in contemporary trust law. Although it is still possible for testators to leave property by way of settlement in favour of a series of life tenants and remaindermen, such settlements are indeed rare. Furthermore, with regard to the duty to apportion the trust funds, the duty is almost always excluded by the trust instrument. The reason for this is that the application of the duty can be very expensive and complicated. In a consultation paper in 2004 the Law Commission reviewed the conversion and apportionment rules and advocated that rules in *Howe v Earl of Dartmouth*[93] and *Re Earl of Chesterfield's Trust*[94] should be abolished.[95] On 7 May 2009 the Law Commission published its report and recommended that the equitable and statutory rules of apportionment be abolished.[96] Instead the Law Commission has suggested that trustees be given greater flexibility in maximising the trust fund, without having to maintain a balance between capital and income returns.

KEY CITATION

Law Commission Report 315 (2009) *Capital and Income in Trusts: Classification and Apportionment*, at pp. 84–5

In the CP we criticised the apportionment rules individually, but the main thrust of the criticisms was that the rules are routinely excluded in professionally drafted trusts, and for trusts where the rules still technically apply, they are honoured more in their breach than in their application. The second limb of *Howe v Earl of Dartmouth* and the rule in *Re Earl of Chesterfield's Trusts* were criticised for being overly complex. In many cases they are disproportionately expensive to apply. It was also pointed out that changing economic circumstances, and the changes brought about by the Trustee Act 2000 . . . have undermined the rationale of these rules. Although the justice of the rule in *Allhusen v Whittell* was not doubted, there was concern that the rule requires cumbersome calculations, in many cases affecting only small sums of money. Similar criticisms to those made of the rule in *Allhusen v Whittell* were noted in relation to

---

[92] (1883) 24 Ch. D 643 at 648.
[93] (1802) 7 Ves. Jr. 137.
[94] (1883) 24 Ch. D 643.
[95] Law Com. CP 175 (2004), *Capital and Income in Trusts: Classification and Apportionment*.
[96] Law Com. 315 (2009), *Capital and Income in Trusts: Classification and Apportionment*.

the apportionment of deficient securities. The CP provisionally proposed that all the existing equitable rules of apportionment should be abolished, an approach already taken in relation to the second limb of the rule in *Howe v Earl of Dartmouth* in Western Australia and New Zealand, and in relation to the rule in *Allhusen v Whittell* in New Zealand and in a number of states and provinces in Australia and Canada. This was also in line with the Law Reform Committee, Trust Law Committee and Scottish Law Commission's recommendations.

On 17 January 2011 the government annontced its decision to take formaed reforms suggested in the Law Commission Report. The Trusts (Capital and Income) Bill will be introduced in Parliament.

Conclusion

The investment functions of trusteeship are undoubtedly the most important of all. As the *Nestlé* litigation illustrates, beneficiaries will be keen to get a good return on the trust fund and ensure that it has kept in line with inflation. Trustees, on the other hand, have a primary obligation to preserve the trust fund as well as balancing the needs of all of the beneficiaries under the trust. Where a trust is for successive beneficiaries they need to ensure that the life tenants receive adequate income whilst the remaindermen have capital growth.

In most professionally drafted trust instruments the trustees will be conferred wide powers of investment. However, where there is no express power of investment, such as under a home-made will, the trustees will be conferred a statutory power of investment by the Trustee Act 2000. Today there is very little difference between an express power of investment and the statutory power of investment found in the Trustee Act 2000. The modern statutory power of investment, unlike its predecessors, confers upon the trustee a very broad power of investment. Trustees can make any investments they like as if they were the absolute owners of the fund. However, whether the trustees are exercising an express power or the statutory power, they are subject to common law and statutory duties. Most importantly, they must act reasonably in the circumstances. Trustees must have regard to the standard investment criteria, which includes suitability, diversification and appropriateness. They are generally not allowed to make ethical investments, that is, investments influenced by their ethical views.

Finally, an important development in modern trustee investment law is the ability of trustees to delegate both their duty to invest and their discretion to invest. The Trustee Act 2000 recognises that investment markets and processes are quite complex and that ordinary trustees with little investment knowledge are not necessarily best placed to made investment decisions. The Trustee Act 2000 allows for the appointment of an investment manager to select and make the investments which are most suitable and appropriate for the particular trust in question.

●●● Case studies

Consider the following case studies.

1 In an *inter vivos* settlement created two years ago, a settlor created a trust of £500,000 in favour of his son for life and thereafter for his daughter absolutely.

The trust instrument gave trustees the power 'to invest in securities of any kind as if the trustees were the beneficial owners thereof'. They thereupon invested trust money in the following manner:

(a) In the purchase of a freehold house for the rent-free occupation of the beneficiaries.

(b) In mortgage of free households to the amount of two-thirds the value of the property, relying exclusively upon their own judgement. The property depreciated to half the value it had at the time of the loan.

(c) In loans to a trading company guaranteed by a director of the company. The company went into compulsory liquidation and the director was adjudicated bankrupt.

(d) The trustees also exchanged certain shares in private companies and lost £500.

One of the trustees has decided that much more of the funds should be invested in shares, but the other remaining trustees refuse to accept the investment in shares because most of the companies suggested by the one trustee are involved in the production of cigarettes.

Are the trustees in breach of trust in respect of any of these investments?

2 By his will, Thomas, who died last year, after appointing Charles and Amanda to be his executors and trustees, left all his residuary estate to Charles and Amanda upon trust to pay the income thereof to Thomas's widow, Sylvia, for life and subject thereto upon trust for Thomas's two sons Bill and Fred in equal shares. After paying all the funeral expenses, legacies and debts, Thomas' residuary estate consists of:

(i)   a copyright in an unpublished novel

(ii)   £2500 in a 'capital growth' unit trust (under which no income is payable)

(iii)   a future interest in a trust fund of £50,000, expectant on the death of Thomas's brother

(iv)   two original paintings by Picasso

(v)   a sum of £500,000 in a high-interest bank account.

Advise Charles and Amanda how they should determine the income to be paid to Sylvia and how they should invest the trust property.

●● Moot points

1 What do you consider to be the main objective of trustee investment?

2 How does the general duty of care in s. 1 of the Trustee Act 2000 differ from the prudent man of business test applied by the common law in cases such as *Re Whiteley* (1886) 33 Ch. D 347 and *Speight* v *Gaunt* (1883) 9 App. Cas. 1.

3 What were the main reasons for reforming the statutory power of investment in the Trustee Act 2000?

4 What is the rationale behind employing an 'asset manager' under s. 15 of the Trustee Act 2000? Where such an asset manager is employed, what role do the trustees play in the investment of trust funds?

5 What was the rationale behind the rules of apportionment and conversion found in the rules in *Howe* v *Earl of Dartmouth* and *Re Earl of Chesterfield's Trust* and explain why the Law Commission in its report in 2009 Law. Com. 315 *Capital and Income in Trusts: Classification and Apportionment* has suggested the abolition of these rules.

● Further reading

Chesterman, M.R. 'Family Settlements on Trusts: Land Owners and the Rising Bourgeoisie' in *Law, Economy and Society, 1750–1914: Essays in the History of English Law*, Rubin and Sugarman edn, London, Professional Books Limited (1984) pp. 157–64.

Docking, P. and Pittaway, I. 'Social Investment by English Pension Funds: Can it be Done?' (1990) *Trust Law and Practice* Vol. 4 No. 1 25. Explains the extent to which pension trustees can engage in social investments.

Duckworth, A. 'Legal Aspects of Trustee Investment – Is the Prudent Man Still Alive and Well? 1997 PCB Issue No. 1 22. Examines the contemporary significance of the prudent man of business test which was replaced by the Trustee Act 2000.

Grosh, D. 'Trustee Investment: English Law and the American Prudent Man Rule', 1974 ICLQ 748. Provides a comparative account of English and American trustee investment, with particular reference to the prudent man rule.

Milner, P. and J. Holmes, 'Trust Law Reforms: Are We Nearly There Yet?' PCB Vol. 2 (2000) pp. 114–29. Explores the position of trustee delegation and investment pre Trustee Act 2000 and suggests law reform by the Trustee Act 2000 will resolve some of the inadequacies of the law pre Trustee Act 2000.

Lord Nicholls, 'Trustees and Their Broader Community: Where Duty, Morality and Ethics Converge' (1995) Trust LI Vol. 9 No. 71. Explores ethical investing, issues of morality in trustee investment and the extent of the trustee investment.

Panesar, S. 'The Trustee Act 2000' (2001) ICCLR 151. Explores the fundamental changes introduced by the Trustee Act 2000, including the reform of trustee investment law.

Shattuck, M.A. 'The Development of the Prudent Man Rule for Fiduciary Investments in the Twentieth Century' (1951) 12 Ohio State LJ 491 at 491–2.

Thornton, R. 'Ethical Investments: A Case of Disjointed Thinking' (2008) Conv. 396. Examines the notion of ethical investments and considers the extent to which trustees are allowed to engage in ethical investments.

Visit **www.mylawchamber.co.uk/panesar** to access study support resources including interactive multiple choice questions, practice exam questions with guidance, podcasts, weblinks, legal newsfeed all linked to the **Pearson eText** version of Exploring Equity and Trusts which you can **search**, **highlight** and **personalise** with your **own notes** and **bookmarks**.

premium
mylawchamber
unrivalled support for legal education

17

Fiduciary nature of trusteeship

Learning objectives

After reading this chapter you should be able to:

→ understand the nature of a fiduciary relationship

→ explain when a fiduciary relationship arises

→ understand the nature of fiduciary liability and the rationale thereof

→ understand the fiduciary nature of trusteeship

→ explain trustee remuneration

→ explain the rules relating to purchase of trust property by trustees

→ understand how trustees may abuse their position and make unauthorised incidental profits

→ explain the remedies available for breach of fiduciary duty

→ explain whether the strict liability approach of fiduciary law is justified in modern trust law.

SETTING THE SCENE

Keech v *Sandford* (1726) Sel. Cas. Ch. 61: A lease of Romford market, the infant beneficiary's renewal of the lease and his trustee taking a lease of the market for himself

The facts in the seminal case of *Keech* v *Sandford* neatly illustrate the concerns raised in this chapter. On the facts, a trustee held a lease and the profits thereof on trust for an infant beneficiary. When the lease came up for renewal the landlord refused to renew the lease in favour of the infant beneficiary. The apparent reason for this was that the landlord was concerned about enforcing the lease against the minor. Although the landlord was reluctant to renew the lease in favour of the minor, albeit through the trustee, he was prepared to renew the lease in favour of the trustee in his personal capacity. The trustee duly renewed the lease in his personal capacity. When the infant beneficiary established that the trustee had renewed the lease for himself he brought an action in court to have the lease assigned to him with an account for profits.

The Court of Chancery held in favour of the infant beneficiary on the grounds that there had been a conflict of interest between that of the trustee's own interest and that owed to the beneficiary. Lord Chancellor King held that the lease must be assigned to the infant beneficiary with an account for profits. His Lordship explained that 'I very well see, if a trustee, on the refusal to renew, might have a lease to himself, few trust estates would be renewed to [beneficiaries]; though I do not say there is a fraud in this case, yet he should have left it to run out, than to have had the lease to himself' (at p. 62).

A number of interesting questions arise from the decision in *Keech* v *Sandford*. Why was the trustee required to account for profits and assign the lease to the infant? If the infant was never going to have the lease renewed in his favour, why did this prevent the trustee renewing for himself? The facts of *Keech* v *Sandford* are often used to illustrate the point that a trustee stands in a fiduciary relationship to his beneficiary, and as such, he should at all times put the interests of his beneficiary ahead of his personal interests. A person standing in a fiduciary relationship must not profit from his position as a fiduciary, and if he does, he must account for such profits to his beneficiary. On the facts of this case, the trustee was able to renew the lease for himself by virtue of having knowledge of the lease in his capacity as trustee. Although on the facts the infant beneficiary was never in a position to renew the lease for himself, the concern of the court of equity was whether the trustee had really considered the interests of the beneficiary, or extracted a benefit for himself which duly belonged to the beneficiary. This chapter examines the concept of a fiduciary relationship and looks at some the basic fiduciary rules governing trustees. It further addresses the question whether the strict liability of fiduciary law is justified in the modern law of trusts.

Introduction

This chapter explores the fiduciary nature of trusteeship. It is trite law that a trustee stands in a fiduciary relationship to his beneficiary, and because of this relationship, a trustee owes his beneficiary a number of fiduciary duties. Unlike the duty of investment considered in the last chapter, which normally involves the trustee to take positive steps to deal with the trust property, fiduciary duties in their nature tend to be negative. They are negative in the sense that the trustee is required to refrain from doing certain things. The paramount fiduciary duty of a trustee is not to allow there to be a conflict of interest between his duty and his own interest. The trustee must at all time act in the best interests of his beneficiary and must not, at any point in time, allow his own interests to take precedent over the interests of those of the beneficiary. For example, a trustee cannot derive any benefits for himself which belong to the beneficiary. The rationale for this lies principally on the grounds that a trustee stands in a position of loyalty to his beneficiary and is reposed with confidence. Breach of confidence has long been one of the traditional heads of jurisdiction in the Court of Chancery. Any breach of that position of loyalty and confidence will ultimately allow the trustee to make a profit at the expense of his beneficiary, which equity will not allow the trustee to retain.

The position in equity is well established: where a trustee makes an unauthorised profit at the expense of his beneficiary, he will be required to return that profit to the beneficiary. The trustee will be required to reverse his unjust enrichment by effecting restitution. Restitution is the process by which a person who is unjustly enriched at the expense of another is required to return those unjust gains to that other person. It will be seen later in this chapter that restitution can be effected in one of two ways. Firstly, the beneficiary may require the trustee to account for profits made as a result of the breach of fiduciary duty, or secondly, may ask the court to impose a constructive trust on the profits or any other property acquired by the use of those profits. In ordering the trustee to effect restitution the court will not generally look to questions of whether the trustee acted honestly or in subjective good faith. If there is a real possibility of a conflict of interest between his duty and own interest, the court will intervene. A trustee, however, will not be required to effect restitution of any gains made in circumstances with the full consent of the beneficiary or where they have been authorised by the trust instrument.

● ● ● Defining fiduciary relationships

● Problems of definition

Although the abuses of fiduciary relationship have long been one of the major concerns of equitable jurisdiction, the concept of a fiduciary is far from clear. In *LAC Minerals v International Corona Ltd*[1] La Forest J in the Supreme Court of Canada explained that 'there are few legal concepts more frequently invoked but less conceptually certain than that of the fiduciary relationship'.[2] In his seminal work Professor Finn described a fiduciary relationship as 'one of the most ill-defined, if not altogether misleading terms

---

[1] (1989) 61 DLR (4th) 14.
[2] (1989) 61 DLR (4th) 14 at 26.

in our law'.[3] It is, perhaps this lack of a comprehensive definition that has made the law of fiduciaries not only an interesting area for legal scholars but also a difficult one when asked to define the circumstances in which such a relationship will arise. English law categorises certain relationships as fiduciary per se. This is no more than saying that certain relations are by their very nature fiduciary per se, that is, without further inquiry. Thus the settled categories of fiduciary relationships include solicitor and client,[4] agent and principal,[5] company director and the company,[6] and trustee and beneficiary.[7] However, despite certain relationships being categorised as fiduciary per se, the list of fiduciary relationships is not closed. The courts have, from time to time, admitted into the category of fiduciary relationships those which are not traditionally fiduciary per se. For example, in **O'Sullivan v Management Agency and Music Ltd**[8] a manager was held to owe fiduciary duties to a singer. On the facts of the case a new and inexperienced pop singer had entered into a contract on grounds of undue influence. The court held that, by virtue of his inexperience and the undue influence asserted by the manager, the facts gave rise to a fiduciary relationship.

When will a fiduciary relationship arise?

Although certain relationships are fiduciary per se, the real question is: when will the court find a fiduciary relationship in circumstances when it does not fit into the recognised categories of fiduciary relationships? The problem is that the English courts have not provided a universal definition of a fiduciary relationship; instead, the approach has been very much one of judicial flexibility. Academics have attempted to address the matter by identifying certain factors which justify the imposition of a fiduciary relationship. For example, Sealy, after having reviewed the existing authorities argued in 1962 that there were essentially four categories of fiduciary relationship.[9] Sealy argued that the first two classes were reasonably capable of definition whilst the third and fourth classes were concerned with the application of certain presumptions which justified the imposition of fiduciary duties, thereby giving rise to a fiduciary relationship between the parties. The first category deals with the situation where one person has control over property for the benefit of another. Included in this category are persons such as trustees, guardians and bailiffs. Also included in this category is a donee of a power of appointment in circumstances when that power is imposed in the office, for example, of trusteeship.[10] The second category deals with those situations where a plaintiff entrusts to the defendant to perform a job in the best interests of the plaintiff. What is clear with Sealy's second classification is that there is no requirement that the defendant is actually dealing with property belonging to the plaintiff. Thus, whilst the majority of fiduciary relationships will involve some control over property belonging to another, according to Sealy's classification it is not crucial that there be some control over property. A good example of a situation falling into this category is the decision of the House of Lords in **Reading v A-G**.[11] In this case, a British army sergeant stationed in Cairo allowed, by virtue of his

---

[3] P.D. Finn, *Fiduciary Obligations* (1977), p. 1.
[4] *Bristol and West Building Society v Mothew* [1998] Ch. 1.
[5] *Kelly v Cooper* [1993] AC 205.
[6] *Guinness v Saunders* [1990] 2 AC 663.
[7] *Keech v Sandford* (1726) Sel. Cas. Ch. 61
[8] [1985] 1 QB 428.
[9] S. Sealy, 'Fiduciary Relationships' [1962] CLJ 69.
[10] *Re Hay's Settlement Trusts* [1981] 3 All ER 786.
[11] [1949] 2 KB 232.

position as an army sergeant, civilian lorries carrying contraband goods to pass through checkpoints without any checks. The House of Lords held that the sergeant, by virtue of being employed by the Crown, stood in a fiduciary relationship to the Crown and thus was required to account for the bribes he had received from the smugglers. Whilst Sealy's second category does not require that the fiduciary be in control of property, it is questionable whether this is correct in light of a recent judicial pronouncement that a fiduciary relationship requires some control over property belonging to another.[12]

The third and fourth categories of Sealy's classification are more complicated and work on the presumption that certain events have occurred which call for the imposition of fiduciary duties thereby giving rise to a fiduciary relationship. In the third category are situations where a person who is already in a fiduciary relationship and who is controlling property for another then acquires property for himself as a result of his position as a fiduciary. Any new property acquired will be deemed as an accretion to the original property. Sealy gives as an example the seminal case of **Keech v Sandford**[13] where, as will be seen in more detail later, a trustee, having failed to renew a lease of a market for an infant beneficiary, renewed the lease personally. The court held that the new lease was to be held on the same terms and conditions of the original lease in favour of the infant.

VISIT CASE NAVIGATOR

Another example which could be classified as falling into this category, albeit in categories one and two also, is the decision of the House of Lords in **Boardman v Phipps**.[14] On the facts of this case, a solicitor who was acting in connection with a trust, advised the trustees, who were already holding shares in a private company, that they should acquire more shares in the same company with a view to exerting greater control in that company. The trustees refused to purchase further shares on the basis that the trust instrument did not authorise them to do so. After consultation with some of the trustees, the solicitor acquired a controlling interest in the company and made a substantial profit for himself as well as restructuring the company and profiting the beneficiaries. The House of Lords held by a bare majority that the solicitor was required to account for those profits made in his capacity as a fiduciary. Despite the absence of dishonesty on his part, those profits had been made in his capacity as a fiduciary and thus belonged to the beneficiaries. The decision of the House of Lords in **Boardman v Phipps**[15] illustrates the strict rule of equity that questions of good faith and honesty are generally not an issue in deciding whether the fiduciary is entitled to retain any property made in his capacity as a fiduciary. This matter is discussed in more detail below. The final classification deals with the imposition of a fiduciary relationship where one party exerts undue influence on another. The existence and possibility of undue influence is sufficient to generate a fiduciary relationship.

Despite Sealy's categorisation, and indeed that of other academics writing in this field,[16] the courts have not yet given a comprehensive definition of a fiduciary. Instead, judicial flexibility has resulted in the courts working on the premise that the central defining features of a fiduciary relationship is where one party is acting in the best interests of the other party and therefore is required to owe a duty of loyalty to the other. Judicial pronouncements of these features can be found in a number of English law cases. In **White**

---

12 *Sinclair Investment Holding SA v Versailles Trade Finance Ltd* [2006] 1 BCLC 60. This decision is explored in more detail below.

13 (1726) Sel. Cas. Ch. 61

14 [1967] 2 AC 46.

15 *Ibid.*

16 See, for example, Finn, *Fiduciary Obligation* (1977); Sheperd, *The Law of Fiduciaries* (1981) and Sheperd, 'Towards a Unified Concept of Fiduciary Relationships' (1981) 97 LQR 51.

v *Jones*[17] Lord Browne-Wilkinson commented that 'the paradigm of the circumstances in which equity will find a fiduciary relationship is where one party, A, has assumed to act in relation to the property or affairs of another, B'.[18] In ***Bristol and West Building Society*** **v *Mothew***[19] Millett LJ explained that 'a fiduciary is someone who has undertaken to act for or on behalf of another in a particular matter in circumstances which give rise to relationship of trust and confidence. The distinguishing obligation of a fiduciary is the obligation of loyalty. The principal is entitled to the single minded loyalty of his fiduciary . . .'[20] In other jurisdictions such as Australia and Canada the courts have employed concepts such as 'undertaking to act on behalf of another' or 'the exercise of a power or discretion so as to affect the principal's legal position' in order to find a fiduciary relationship.[21]

Although certain relationships have been described as fiduciary per se, the courts are not precluded from finding a fiduciary relationship in circumstances which justify the imposition of such a relationship and the corresponding duties that follow it. The reason for this, as Millett LJ explained in ***Bristol and West Building Society*** v ***Mothew***, is that a fiduciary 'is not subject to fiduciary obligations because he is a fiduciary; it is because he is subject to them that he is a fiduciary'.[22] In other words, it is the particular circumstances which give rise to the finding of a fiduciary relationship, rather than the nature of the primary relationship of the parties. What the court is required to do is to examine whether any particular set of facts have the features that are identified by Millett LJ in ***Bristol and West Building Society*** v ***Mothew***:

- an element of undertaking by the fiduciary to act for or on behalf of another to procure the best terms for that person
- an element of reliance by the principal that the fiduciary will act in his or her best interest
- an element of vulnerability that the fiduciary may be in a position to negatively affect the interests of that other person.

Using these criteria the courts have found fiduciary relationships beyond the recognised categories identified above. Thus it has been possible for professional advisers, bank managers, mortgagees, doctors and employees to be subject to fiduciary obligations even though they do not fit into the recognised relationships which are fiduciary per se.

Fiduciary relationships in a commercial context

The extent to which fiduciary relationships can be imposed in a purely commercial context has been the subject matter of much debate in recent times. There appear to be a number of reasons as to why the debate is more acute in the commercial context than any other. In the first place, there has been the long standing debate as to the proper application of equitable doctrines in a purely commercial context. In ***New Zealand and***

---

[17] [1995] 2 AC 207.
[18] *Ibid.* at 728. This statement echoes the opinion of Asquith LJ in the Court of Appeal in *Reading* v *A-G* [1949] 2 KB 232, where his Lordship explained that 'a fiduciary relationship exists (a) whenever the plaintiff entrusts to the defendant property . . . and relies on the defendant to deal with such property for the benefit of the plaintiff or purposes authorised by him, and not to do otherwise, and (b) whenever the plaintiff entrusts to the defendant a job to be performed . . . and relies on the defendant to procure for the plaintiff the best terms available . . .' at p. 236.
[19] [1998] Ch. 1.
[20] [1998] Ch. 1 at 18.
[21] See G. Moffat, *Trust Law: Text and Materials* 3rd edn (2005) at pp. 802–6.
[22] [1998] Ch. 1 at 16.

Australian Land Co v *Watson*[23] Bramwell LJ explained that he would be very sorry to see 'the various intricacies and doctrines connected with trusts into commercial transaction'.[24] Similarly, writing extrajudicially Millett LJ commented that 'it is of the first importance not to impose fiduciary obligations on parties to a purely commercial relationship'.[25] The reasoning behind this relates to the nature of commercial transactions and the relationships created thereby. Unlike the relationship of trust, where the trustee undertakes to act in the best interests of the beneficiary, the assumption in commercial relationships is that each party is bargaining at arm's length and is not acting in the best interests of the other but has its own interests foremost. In the words of Snell 'it is normally inappropriate to expect a commercial party to subordinate its own interest to those of another commercial party'.[26]

A second reason for the reluctance to have a liberal application of fiduciary law in a commercial context relates to the remedies which are available in cases of breach of fiduciary duty. Where a fiduciary breaches his duty of loyalty to his beneficiary, the beneficiary will have a right to equitable compensation in circumstances in which he has suffered a loss; or where the fiduciary has made a profit, he will be entitled to restitution. Restitution can be effected in one of two ways: firstly, by requiring the fiduciary to account for the profit or, secondly, by imposing a constructive trust on the profit so as to allow the beneficiary a proprietary claim to such profit. It is the imposition of the constructive trust which is more controversial in recent times. The reason for this relates to the fact that the imposition of such a trust gives a particular commercial party, which is the principal of a fiduciary relationship, priority over property of an insolvent fiduciary. Leading academics have warned against the imposition of a constructive trust in such circumstances so as to adjust property rights on insolvency.[27] This matter is explored in more detail towards the end of this chapter.

Despite the reservations about the proper role of fiduciary law in a commercial context, it would be nonsense to say that commercial transactions do not lend themselves to fiduciary obligations. Parties in a commercial relationship may well have intended to bring about a fiduciary relationship so that one party is acting in the interests of the other, or the course of conduct between the parties may show that they are under a duty of loyalty to the other. Many agency relationships involve a commercial context where one company is acting in the interests of another. In other situations, the circumstances will themselves import a fiduciary relationship. For example, in the popularly cited Canadian case, *LAC Minerals Ltd* v *International Corona Resources Ltd*[28] the Canadian Supreme Court found a fiduciary relationship in circumstances where two companies were negotiating a joint venture to exploit minerals. The land to be mined belonged to the plaintiff but the defendants, through the course of dealings, established that adjacent land also contained minerals. The defendants then mined the adjacent land without the plaintiff's consent. The Court held that the defendants owed fiduciary duties to the plaintiffs because they had obtained confidential information from the plaintiffs.

In *Sinclair Investment Holding SA* v *Versailles Trade Finance Ltd*[29] the Court of Appeal had the opportunity revisit the grounds for the imposition of a fiduciary

---

[23] [1881] 7 QBD 374.
[24] *Ibid.* at 382.
[25] P. Millett, 'Equity's Place in the Law of Commerce' (1998) 14 LQR 214 at 217.
[26] *Snell's Equity* 31st edn (2004) at p. 149.
[27] See, for example, P. Birks, *The Frontiers of Liability* Vol. 2 (1994) at 218.
[28] (1989) 61 DLR (4th) 14.
[29] [2005] EWCA Civ. 722.

relationship in a commercial context. This case involved an appeal by Versailles Trade Finance Ltd (VTFL) against an order of Mr Nicholas Strauss QC, allowing an appeal against an earlier order refusing to strike out claims in the case. VTFL was an associated company belonging to wider group – Versailles Group PLC. Crucially in this case, a major shareholder in Versailles Group was another company called Marrlist Ltd. Marrlist was owned by a Mr Cushnie who also happened to be a director of the Versailles Group companies. The Versailles Group was in the business of accelerated discount trading,[30] although the court did not go into detail about the nature of the Group's business, save to say that it involved raising money from third parties and investing it on their behalf in manufactured goods. These goods were bought direct from the manufacturer at a discount, and sold on to purchasers at the full sale price.

One such third party investor was Sinclair Investment Holdings SA who entered a trading agreement with VTFL, the terms of which involved, *inter alia*, Sinclair Investments providing VTFL with £2.35 million for the purposes of buying and selling goods for Sinclair Investments. However, the money advanced by Sinclair Investments was not used in accordance with the terms of the agreement. Instead, it was used by the Versailles Group to increase its own turnover and improve its share value. Consequently, Marrlist Ltd was able to sell its shares in the Versailles Group at a profit. In other words, the profits enjoyed by Marrlist, and ultimately Mr Cushnie, were made as a direct result of Sinclair Investment's money. These profits were used to repay a mortgage on a property in Kingston, owned by Mr Cushnie, and subsequently sold for £8.6 million.

Despite the fact that Sinclair Investments had handed the sum over to VTFL, the money could still be said to belong to them because under the terms of the traders' agreement VTFL were bound to hold on trust any money *not* used for the purpose of buying and selling goods, in a bank account for Sinclair Investments. There were two grounds on which Sinclair Investments sought to recover their money from the £8.6 million proceeds of the property sale. Firstly, the profit made by Marrlist (and ultimately, Mr Cushnie) resulted from a breach of a fiduciary duty owed to Sinclair Investments by Mr Cushnie. Secondly, that part of the proceeds of sale from the Kensington property be held in constructive trust for Sinclair Investments because these proceeds were made as a result of Mr Cushnie's fraud. The judge at first instance held that there was an arguable case on both of these points. VTFL, however, appealed arguing that there was no fiduciary relationship between Mr Cushnie and Sinclair Investments, and neither was there a general principle that a constructive trust should be imposed on a fraudster. These points can be examined in more detail.

Whilst it is trite law that a director owes fiduciary duties to the company in which he is employed,[31] does a director owe fiduciary duties beyond that of his company? The general position is that a director does not owe fiduciary duties beyond those owed to the company: thus, a director does not owe such duties to the shareholders generally. Mr Cushnie may well have been a director of the companies belonging to the Versailles Group and thus owing fiduciary duties to VTFL, but did he also owe fiduciary duties to Sinclair Investments? It was argued on behalf of VTFL that Mr Cushnie could not owe parallel duties to VTFL as well the Sinclair Investments for whom VTFL had become a trustee. This would simply put Mr Cushnie in a position of 'hopeless conflict'.[32] In support of this argument counsel for VTFL cited a powerful passage from Millett LJ's judgment in **Bristol and West Building Society v Mothew**[33] where his Lordship, when commenting

---

[30] Also known as *accelerated payment trading*.
[31] *Guinness plc v Saunders* [1990] 2 AC 663.
[32] [2005] EWCA Civ. 722 at para. 14.
[33] [1998] Ch. 1.

on the features of a fiduciary relationship, explained that 'a fiduciary must act in good faith; he must not make a profit out of his trust; he must not place himself in a position where his duty and interest may conflict; he may not act for his own benefit or the benefit of third person without the informed consent of his principal'.[34] In the opinion of counsel for VTFL, Mr Cushnie simply did not give any undertaking, express or implied, to Sinclair Investments of loyalty.

Although on the facts Mr Cushnie's relationship with Sinclair Investments could not be categorised as fiduciary in the sense of belonging to the recognised categories of fiduciary relationships, Arden LJ in the Court of Appeal proceeded to answer the question whether Mr Cushnie could have acquired fiduciary obligations towards Sinclair Investments. In her Ladyship's judgment, 'if it is alleged that a person who does not fall within the usual categories of a fiduciary relationship, such as trustee and director, made manifest his intention to enter into a fiduciary relationship – that is, to undertake to the other a duty of loyalty – there would be a sufficient pleading of fiduciary relationship'.[35] Having identified that a fiduciary relationship could arise where a person had undertaken a duty of loyalty to another, Arden LJ proceeded to examine whether it was a necessary prerequisite to the finding of a fiduciary relationship that the fiduciary should have a relationship with any item of property belonging to the principal. This question was important on the facts because Mr Cushnie did not have legal title over the money advanced by Sinclair Investments to VTFL. Normally, in most other fiduciary relationships which are fiduciary per se, the fiduciary is exercising control over property for the benefit of another, for example the trustee–beneficiary relationship. In her Ladyship's opinion there was nothing in the authorities to suggest that there was a need for fiduciary to have a particular relationship with any property. However, on the present facts this was a contentious issue because, although Mr Cushnie did not have legal title to the money advanced by Sinclair Investments, he was a director of VTFL, and was in a position to control the exercise by VTFL of its powers over the money belonging to Sinclair Investments. In the opinion of the Court of Appeal, Mr Cushnie, although a director of VTFL and as such not owing fiduciary duties to the traders investing with VTFL, nevertheless had by his own conduct given an undertaking of loyalty to the relevant traders that their sums advanced would be safeguarded and invested in an appropriate manner. This conduct was sufficient for the finding of a fiduciary relationship between Mr Cushnie and the traders.

The nature and standard of fiduciary liability

The most basic duty of a fiduciary is not to allow himself to be put in a position where there is a conflict between his personal interest and that of his principal. This, often referred to as the 'no conflicts rule', will be applied rigorously by the courts. If the fiduciary allows there to be a conflict then inevitably it will result in him making an unauthorised or secret profit at the expense of his principal, or in the case of a trust, his beneficiary. Sometimes it is also said that fiduciary law is concerned with the law against secret profits. The matter is neatly summed up by Lord Herschell in **Bray v Ford**:[36]

> It is an inflexible rule of a Court of Equity that a person in a fiduciary position . . . is not, unless otherwise expressly provided, entitled to make a profit; he not allowed to put himself in a position where his duty and interest conflict. It does not appear to me that this rule is, as has been said, founded upon principles of morality. I regard it rather as based on the

---

[34] [1998] Ch. 1 at 18.
[35] [2005] EWCA Civ. 722 at para. 22.
[36] [1896] AC 44.

consideration that, human nature being what it is, there is a danger, in such circumstances, of the person holding a fiduciary position being swayed by interest rather than by duty, and thus prejudicing those whom he was bound to protect. It has, therefore, been deemed expedient to lay down this general rule. But I am satisfied that it might be departed from in many cases, without any breach of morality, without any wrong being inflicted, and without any consciousness of wrong-doing.[37]

The nature of fiduciary liability was extensively considered by Millett LJ in *Bristol & West Building Society* v *Mothew*.[38] The question before the Court of Appeal was whether a solicitor, who was acting both for a lender and borrower, was in breach of a fiduciary duty in circumstances where the solicitor had given incorrect advice to the lender. In holding that negligent advice given by the solicitor was a breach of duty, albeit not a breach of fiduciary duty, Millett LJ explained the core elements of the basic fiduciary duty of no conflict of interest:

> A fiduciary is someone who has undertaken to act for or on behalf of another in a particular matter in circumstances which give rise to a relationship of trust and confidence. The distinguishing obligation of a fiduciary is the obligation of loyalty. The principal is entitled to the single-minded loyalty of his fiduciary. This core liability has several facets: a fiduciary must act in good faith; he must not make a profit out of his trust; he must not place himself in a position where his duty and his interest may conflict; he may not act for his own benefit or the benefit of a third person without the informed consent of his principal. This is not intended to be an exhaustive list, but it is sufficient to indicate the nature of fiduciary obligations.[39]

It has been suggested that the paramount duty of loyalty comprise two related themes.[40] The first comprises a general prohibition of a fiduciary allowing there to be a conflict of interest between his duty and interest. The second is a prohibition on the fiduciary making a secret profit from his position as a fiduciary. However, the two themes are interrelated because the very possibility of a conflict of interest will invariably result in the fiduciary making an unauthorised profit at the expense of his principal.[41]

It is clear that a person standing in a fiduciary relationship owes fiduciary obligations to his principal or beneficiary. However, it should be noted that not all of the duties of a person categorised as a fiduciary are necessarily fiduciary duties. In other words, a fiduciary may owe parallel duties. For example, it is possible for a fiduciary to be subject to contractual duties or duties arising in tort whilst at the same time being subordinated to fiduciary duties.[42] The matter is neatly explained by the decision in *Bristol & West Building Society* v *Mothew*[43] where a solicitor was not in breach of a fiduciary duty in circumstances where he had given negligent advice to his client. Although the negligent advice was a breach of duty, it could not be properly categorised as a breach of his fiduciary duty. In the course of his judgment Millett LJ explained that 'the expression fiduciary duty is properly confined to those duties which are peculiar to fiduciaries and

---

[37] [1896] AC 44 at 51.
[38] [1998] Ch. 1.
[39] [1998] Ch. 1 at 18.
[40] See Snell, *Principles of Equity* 31st edn (J. McGhee) at p. 150.
[41] See, for example, *Boardman* v *Phipps* [1967] 2 AC 46 at 123.
[42] For a critical insight into the relationship between fiduciary and non-fiduciary duties, see M. Conaglen, 'The Nature and Function of Fiduciary Loyalty' (2005) 121 LQR 453 and also R. Lee, 'In Search of the Nature and Function of Fiduciary Loyalty: Some Observations on Conaglen's Analysis' (2007) 27 OJLS 327.
[43] [1998] Ch. 1.

the breach of which attracts legal consequences differing from those consequent upon the breach of other duties. Unless the expression is so limited it is lacking in practical utility. In this sense it is obvious that not every breach of duty by a fiduciary is a breach of fiduciary duty.'[44]

There are many examples of the concurrency of fiduciary and non-fiduciary duties imposed on a particular individual. For example, it is trite law that a trustee owes fiduciary duties to his beneficiary. However, a trustee who fails to invest the trust funds will be liable for breach of trust and not for breach of fiduciary duty. His failure to invest the trust funds arises from trust law and not from the fact that he stands in a fiduciary relationship to the beneficiary. The concurrency of fiduciary and non-fiduciary relationships is illustrated in the decision of the Court of Appeal in **A-G v Blake**.[45] The facts of this case concerned a certain Blake who was a member of the Crown Secret Intelligence Service from 1933 to 1961. In 1951 he because an agent for the former Soviet Union and was eventually convicted and sentenced to 42 years in prison for communicating information contrary to the Official Secrets Act 1911. In 1966 he managed to escape from prison and went to live in Moscow. In 1990 he published a book *No Other Choice* which detailed his activities as a member of the secret service. This publication was without permission from the Crown who subsequently sought to recover profits he had made as a result of the publication of the book. The Attorney-General acting for the Crown argued that the profits on the book had been made as a result of breach of his fiduciary duty of loyalty owed to the Crown. The basis of the argument was that Blake was a former servant of the Crown and as such owed fiduciary duties to the Crown. Furthermore, the information he had acquired about the secret service was imparted to him in his capacity as a servant of the Crown and that this information was now being used to make a profit.

The Court of Appeal accepted that when Blake was employed by the Crown he owed the Crown a core fiduciary obligation of loyalty. His Lordship explained that 'the core obligation of a fiduciary of this kind is the obligation of loyalty. The employer is entitled to the single-minded loyalty of his employee. The employee must act in good faith; he must not make a profit out of his trust; he must not place himself in a position where his duty and his interest may conflict; he must not act for his own benefit or the benefit of a third party without the informed consent of his employer.'[46] However, the Court of Appeal held that Blake was not acting in breach of fiduciary duty when the book was published. Lord Woolf MR explained that whilst Blake was employed by the Crown he undoubtedly owed fiduciary duties to the Crown. However, these duties only lasted as long as the relationship giving rise to it lasted. The fact that Blake was no longer employed by the Crown when the book was published meant that he no longer stood in a fiduciary relationship with the Crown. The Court of Appeal did, however, hold that although there had been no breach of fiduciary duty, Blake had committed a breach of contract, on the grounds that his contract of employment required clearance before writing the book.

It is clear now that a fiduciary owes onerous duties to his principal. It should also be made clear that the standard of liability is strict. The courts will not entertain questions of honesty or whether the fiduciary acted in good faith. If there is a possibility of a conflict of interest and the fiduciary allows that conflict to occur then he will be liable and subject to the remedies for breach of fiduciary duty. For example, in **Bray v Ford**[47] the

---

[44] [1998] Ch. 1 at 16. See also *Lloyds TSB Bank plc v Markandan & Uddin (A firm)* [2010] EWHC 2517 (Ch.).
[45] [1998] 1 All ER 833, affirmed by the House Lords [2001] 1 AC 268.
[46] [1998] 1 All ER 833 at 842.
[47] [1896] AC 44.

court explained that a breach of fiduciary duty 'may be attended with perfect good faith'[48] and furthermore that the conflict rule 'might be departed in many cases, without any breach of morality, without any wrong being inflicted, and without any consciousness of wrong doing'.[49] The same view was echoed in **Regal (Hastings) Ltd v Gulliver**[50] where Lord Russell of Killowen, when dealing with the fiduciary duties of a director, explained that:

> [t]he rule of equity, which insist on those, who by use of a fiduciary position make a profit, being liable to account for that profit, in no way depends on fraud, or absence of bona fides; or upon such questions or considerations as whether the profit would or should otherwise have gone to the plaintiff, or whether the profiteer was under a duty to obtain the source of the profit from the plaintiff, or whether he took a risk or acted as he did for the benefit of the plaintiff, or whether the plaintiff has in fact been damaged or benefited by his action. The liability arises from the mere fact of a profit having, in the stated circumstances, been made. The profiteer, however, honest and well intentioned, cannot escape the risk of being called upon to account.[51]

Perhaps a good illustration of the lack of dishonesty and the absence of bad faith being irrelevant factors in determining liability is the decision of the House of Lords in **Boardman v Phipps**.[52] You will recall that in this case Boardman was a solicitor providing his services to trustees under a will. The trustees were holding 8000 shares out of an issued 30,000 in a private company. Boardman advised the trustees that there was a substantial scope of making a profit on the shares in the private company and therefore they should purchase more of the shares in the company. The trustees refused to purchase the shares because the trust instrument did not allow the acquisition of further shares in the same company. Boardman used the knowledge he had gained from the trust to purchase the remaining shares in the private company. After reorganisation of the private company, the shares he acquired were sold at a profit. He made a profit in the region of £75,000 as well as a benefit to the trust shares in the region of £47,000. The House of Lords held by a majority of 3:2 that Boardman was a constructive trustee of the profits made and as such was required to account for them. In coming to this decision, the House of Lords paid significance to the fact that Boardman had made the profit by virtue of the fact that he had acquired knowledge of the shares while acting as solicitor to trustees of the trust fund. Furthermore, it did not matter that the trustees could not have used the information for their own benefit. The fact remained that Boardman made the profit by virtue of his position as solicitor to the trust fund with specific knowledge of the company and the shares within it. Boardman, however, was authorised to retain some of the profit by way of remuneration on the basis of *quantum meruit*. Both the Court of Appeal and the House of Lords were aware that Boardman was a man of great ability and had expended labour in reorganising the company and increasing the shares therein.

The absence of bad faith being an irrelevant factor in determining the liability of the fiduciary was also illustrated in the decision of the House of Lords in **Guinness v Saunders**.[53] On the facts of this case, a director of a company received a sum of £5.2 million under a contract he had entered into to provide his services in relation to a takeover bid. Thomas Ward, a former non-executive director of Guinness, was employed to provide his services to Guinness in relation to the takeover bid for Distillers. Ward had

[48] [1896] AC 44 at 48.
[49] [1896] AC 44 at 52.
[50] [1967] 2 AC 134.
[51] [1967] 2 AC 134 at 150.
[52] [1967] 2 AC 46.
[53] [1990] 2 AC 663.

been a former non-executive director of Guinness and, despite the absence of any bad faith on his part, the House of Lords held that he had failed to disclose his former interest to the Company Board. On this basis the House of Lords held that he was liable to account for the money he had received.

The rationale for the strict approach

Why does fiduciary law adopt a very strict approach to the no-profit rule? It has been observed that where a profit is made by a fiduciary the court will require that the profit be returned to the principal or beneficiary, despite the honesty or good faith of the fiduciary. Furthermore, the strict approach in English law is further illustrated by the fact that the courts will require the fiduciary to return any profits made in circumstances when the opportunity to make such profits could not be utilised by the beneficiary. For example, it has been seen in **Boardman v Phipps**[54] that the beneficiaries were never in a position to acquire further shares in the private company, albeit through their trustees: nevertheless, Boardman was required to account for the profit he made on the shares. Similarly, in **Keech v Sandford**[55] it was observed at the outset of this chapter that the infant beneficiary was not in a position to renew the lease of Romford Market: nevertheless, the trustee was required to assign the lease to him and account for profits. The rationale for the strict approach hinges on a delicate matter of evidence. From the early nineteenth century the Court of Chancery preferred a deterrence approach because of the evidential difficulties involved in determining the motive of the fiduciary and establishing whether he did act honestly and in good faith. Honesty and good faith are by their very nature subjective criteria in law and involve determining the individual state of mind of the fiduciary. The ultimate question is whether the fiduciary has really put the interests of the beneficiary first or whether he has clouded his decision with the fact that he sees the opportunity to make a profit for himself. The matter is neatly explained by Moffat who writes: 'The courts of equity in the nineteenth century, particularly, under the early guiding influence of Lord Eldon, favoured the deterrent approach. This was in large measure because of concern over evidentiary difficulties facing a court in determining a trustee's motives where a possible conflict existed.'[56] In more recent times, it has been doubted whether this strict approach adopted in some of the eighteenth-century cases is justified in modern fiduciary law. The matter is examined in a little more detail in the next section.

Is the strict liability approach in fiduciary law justified in the modern law?

In a decision of the House of Lords, Lord Browne-Wilkinson commented that it is 'wrong to lift wholesale the detailed rules developed in the context of traditional trusts and seek to apply them to trusts of quite a different kind'.[57] This observation has been quite interestingly used by one leading treatise on the law of trusts to question whether the strict liability approach of fiduciary law is justified in the modern law of trusts.[58] So far it has been observed that where a fiduciary makes an unauthorised profit, he will be required

---

[54] [1967] 2 AC 46.
[55] (1726) Sel. Cas. Ch. 61.
[56] G. Moffat, *Trust Law: Text and Materials* 4th edn (2005) at pp. 418–20.
[57] *Target Holdings v Redferns* [1996] 1 AC 421.
[58] A.J. Oakley, *Parker and Mellows: The Modern Law of Trust* 9th edn (2009) at p. 394.

to return it to his principal, irrespective of his good faith and honesty. Fiduciary law, however, goes further and holds that a fiduciary will be under a duty to effect restitution even when the profit he has made could never have been made by his principal. For example, cases such as **Keech v Sandford**,[59] **Boardman v Phipps**[60] and **Regal (Hastings) v Gulliver**[61] all make it clear that a profit which is made in circumstances where the principal could not have utilised the opportunity to make the profit for himself must nevertheless be returned to the principal. Historically, the justification for the strict rule related to the evidential issues involved in establishing the true motive of the fiduciary. Essentially, the question was whether the fiduciary had put the interests of the principal before his own interest.[62]

In a number of modern cases the evidential issues which concerned the early Court of Chancery do not arise. The cases involve situations where there is no possibility that the principal could have utilised the opportunity for himself. Take, for example, **Regal (Hastings) v Gulliver**,[63] the facts of which concerned the purchase of two cinemas by the plaintiff company which already owned one cinema in Hastings. The intention was that the three cinemas would be acquired by the plaintiff company and then sold off together. In order to facilitate the purchase of the cinemas, a subsidiary with a capital of 5000 shares was formed so as to take leases of the cinemas. However, only 2000 of the shares were fully paid, which proved to be fatal because the owner of the cinema was only willing to grant leases of the cinema on the grounds that all the shares were fully paid up. The plaintiff did not have any further money to pay into the subsidiary. Four directors and an outsider then acquired the remaining shares and the cinemas were eventually taken over, with the directors making a substantial profit on the respective sale of their shares. The purchaser then brought an action to recover the profits made by the directors on the grounds that it was made in breach of fiduciary duty. The action succeeded in the House of Lords on the grounds that the directors had acquired the shares in their capacity as fiduciaries. The House of Lords were firmly undeterred by the fact that the company could not itself have acquired the shares. The court was firmly of the opinion that the law in **Keech v Sandford** laid a strict rule that a fiduciary was not allowed to make an unauthorised profit.

The decision in **Regal (Hastings) v Gulliver**[64] exemplifies the strictness of the common law. However, it is questionable whether this strict approach is justified in circumstances where there are no real evidential issues as regards the fiduciaries' motives. For example, in **Regal (Hastings) v Gulliver** the company was never in a position to acquire the shares in the subsidiary. The directors did not abuse their position in order to get the shares, and the profit was made in good faith. A.J. Oakley makes reference to a number of cases from other jurisdictions where a more flexible approach has been adopted.[65] The Supreme Court of Canada in **Peso-Silver Mines v Cropper**[66] a director was entitled to retain profits made from certain mining claims which the company on whose board he sat had initially

---

[59] (1726) Sel. Cas. Ch. 61.
[60] [1967] 2 AC 46.
[61] [1942] 1 All ER 378.
[62] See I. Samet, 'Guarding the Fiduciary's Conscience: A Justification of a Stringent Profit-Stripping Rule' (2008) OJLS 763, where the author defends the strict rule that unauthorised gains should not be kept by fiduciaries.
[63] [1967] 2 AC 134.
[64] [1967] 2 AC 46.
[65] Parker and Mellows: *The Modern Law of Trusts* 9th edn (2008) at p. 397.
[66] (1966) 58 DLR (2d) 1.

declined to take. Likewise in *Consul Development* v *DPC Estates*[67] the High Court of Australia was of the view that a manager of a company could purchase property for himself which the company for whom he was working for did not want to purchase themselves. A.J. Oakley concludes by commenting that 'if Lord Browne-Wilkinson's remarks cause judges to think twice before they automatically apply conclusions reached in totally different legal and economic contexts to modern conditions, English Law may indeed one day adopt the more flexible attitudes already manifested in other jurisdictions'.[68]

The opportunity to debate the question whether English law should adopt a more lenient approach to gains made by fiduciaries, particularly where those gains could not have been utilised by the principal, arose in the Court of Appeal in *Murad* v *Al-Saraj*.[69] The facts involved the purchase of a hotel in London by two sisters and a certain Mr Al-Saraj by way of a joint venture. The sisters were to contribute £1 million cash and the Mr Al-Saraj £500,000. The purchase price of the hotel was £4.1 million and was to be purchased through a company in which the sisters and Mr Al-Saraj had two-thirds and one-third share respectively. It later transpired that Mr Al-Saraj did not contribute a cash sum of £500,000 and further that the hotel was in fact only purchased for £3.6 million. The reason for the discrepancy between the figure of £4.1 million and £3.6 million was that the vendor was indebted to Mr Al-Saraj and the reduced price was a means of discharging his debts to Mr Al-Saraj. When the sisters discovered the non-disclosure of the vendor's reduced price and the fact that Mr Al-Saraj did not contribute a sum of £500,000 cash, they sought to make him accountable for profits made in the joint venture. The Court of Appeal held that Mr Al-Saraj did owe a fiduciary duty to the sisters in the joint venture and therefore, in breach of fiduciary duty by not disclosing the true state of affairs, was liable to account for the profits. In the course of her judgment Arden LJ hinted that English law might adopt a less stringent test in cases of fiduciary gains made by a defendant when the gains could not have been utilised by the principal, but held that the question was for another court to decide. In the course of her judgment her Ladyship explained that:

> it may be that the time has come when the court should revisit the operation of the inflexible rule of equity in harsh circumstances, as where the trustee has acted in perfect good faith and without any deception or concealment, and in the belief that he was acting in the best interests of the beneficiary. I need only say this: it would not be in the least impossible for a court in a future case, to determine as a question of fact whether the beneficiary would not have wanted to exploit the profit himself, or would have wanted the trustee to have acted other than in the way that the trustee in fact did act. Moreover, it would not be impossible for a modern court to conclude as a matter of policy that, without losing the deterrent effect of the rule, the harshness of it should be tempered in some circumstances. In addition, in such cases, the courts can provide a significant measure of protection for the beneficiaries by imposing on the defaulting trustee the affirmative burden of showing that those circumstances prevailed. Certainly the Canadian courts have modified the effect of equity's inflexible rule (see *Peso-Silver Mines Ltd* v *Cropper* (1966) 58 DLR (2d) 1; see also the decision of the Privy Council on appeal from Australia in *Queensland Mines* v *Hudson* (1978) 52 AJLR 399), though I express no view as to the circumstances in which there should be any relaxation of the rule in this jurisdiction. That sort of question must be left to another court.[70]

---

[67] (1975) 5 ALR 231.
[68] Parker and Mellows: *The Modern Law of Trusts* 9th edn (2008) at p. 402.
[69] [2005] EWCA Civ. 959; see M. McInnes, 'Account for Profit for Breach of Fiduciary Duty' (2006) LQR 11.
[70] [2005] EWCA Civ. 959 at para. 82.

The purchase of trust property

What follows in the remainder of this chapter is an examination of the specific fiduciary rules which apply to trustees. The first of those rules considered here relates to the purchase of trust property. In *Tito v Waddell (No. 2)*[71] Megarry VC explained that there are two rules which relate to the purchase of trust property: namely, the self-dealing rules and the fair-dealing rule. These rules were described by Megarry VC as follows:

> The self-dealing rule is (to put it very shortly) that if a trustee sells the trust property to himself, the sale is voidable by any beneficiary *ex debito justitiae*, however, fair the transaction. The fair dealing rule is . . . that if a trustee purchases the beneficial interest of any of his beneficiaries, the transaction is not voidable *ex debito justitiae*, but can be set aside by the beneficiary unless the trustee can show that he has taken no advantage of his position and has made full disclosure to the beneficiary, and that the transaction is fair and honest.[72]

These rules are often interpreted to mean that trustees should not purchase trust property. However, the rule is not that the trustees must not purchase trust property: rather, the rule is that if trustees do purchase trust property of one form of another, then they are liable to have the sale set aside, depending on which of the two rules has been violated. Breach of the self-dealing and fair-dealing rules has rather different outcomes and they are considered separately in the following sections.

The self-dealing rule

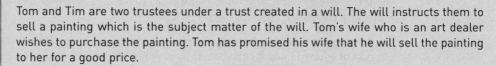

APPLYING THE LAW

Tom and Tim are two trustees under a trust created in a will. The will instructs them to sell a painting which is the subject matter of the will. Tom's wife who is an art dealer wishes to purchase the painting. Tom has promised his wife that he will sell the painting to her for a good price.

Can the trustee do this?

The self-dealing rule relates to the situation where the trustee is purchasing the trust property for himself. For example, suppose that a trustee is under a duty to sell land under the terms of the trust instrument and decides to purchase the land for himself. In such a situation, the scope for a conflict of interest cannot be more obvious, given the fact that the trustee is vendor and purchaser at the same time. As vendor, the duty of the trustee is to obtain the best price for his beneficiaries; and as purchaser, the trustee has a personal interest in obtaining the lowest price for his purchase. If the trustee does proceed to purchase trust property then the beneficiaries can ask the court to set the sale aside, in other words rescind the transaction and restore the position to its original state. In doing so, the court is not concerned with questions of honesty of the trustee or

---

[71] [1977] Ch. 106.
[72] [1977] Ch. 106 at 241.

whether a full and fair price was paid for the trust property.[73] The sale is said to be voidable per se, provided that the beneficiaries choose to set it aside within a reasonable time.[74] It should be noted that the sale is not void *ab initio*, merely voidable at the request of the beneficiaries. Furthermore, the right to set the sale aside is good against any third party who has purchased the property with notice of the circumstances. The limited exceptions to the rule include situations where the trust instrument allows for the trustee to purchase the property and where there is some statutory provision enabling such a purchase.[75]

The self-dealing rule cannot be avoided by a trustee who has retired from the trust with the specific intention of purchasing the trust property. An exceptional case, however, is that of *Holder v Holder*[76] where an executor who had ineffectively renounced his executorship was nevertheless allowed to keep property he had purchased from the estate that he was originally administering. On the facts of the case, a testator appointed his widow, daughter and one of his sons, Victor, to be his executors and trustees. Victor was also a tenant of some of the farms which the testator had instructed to be sold by the executors. After some minor acts, Victor took no further part in the administration of his father's estate. One of farms was ordered for sale at auction and Victor made a successful bid. It was clear that Victor had paid a proper price for the farm which had been independently valued. Later on, Victor's brother applied to the court to have the sale set aside on the grounds of self-dealing. The court refused to set the sale aside on the grounds that Victor had not participated in the administration of his father's estate. Harman LJ explained that there was no conflict of interest, simply because the other beneficiaries were not looking to Victor to protect their interest. Furthermore, information about the sale of the farm had been acquired by Victor in his capacity as a tenant and not necessarily as an administrator. The decision in *Holder v Holder* is, therefore, an exceptional one and limited to the facts. It is clear that a trustee who retires from his office will be subject to the self-dealing rule for a long period of time.

The self-dealing rule cannot be avoided by a sale to a nominee of the trustee or to a company in which the trustee has an interest. For example, in *Re Thompson's Settlement*[77] leases which were taken in the name of a company and partnership in which the trustees were a shareholder and partner respectively. Vinelott J set aside the leases on the grounds that this was a breach of the self-dealing rule. He explained that the rule 'is applied stringently in cases where a trustee concurs in a transaction which cannot be carried out into effect without his concurrence and who also has an interest in or holds a fiduciary duty to another in relation to the same transaction'.[78] Similarly, a trustee who creates a company with the specific intention of purchasing trust property will find that such a purchase by the company will be set aside.[79] According to *Snell's Equity*, 'a sale by a trustee to his wife is probably not within the rule, especially if the wife has made the purchase on her own initiative, rather than at the instigation of the trustee, and has paid for it out of her own funds'.[80] Such a sale to the wife of a trustee will be viewed with

---

[73] See, for example, *ex p. James* (1803) 8 Ves. 337; *Aberdeen Railway Co v Blaikie Bros* (1854) 1 Macq. 461; *Movitex Ltd v Bulfield* [1988] BCLC 104.

[74] *Campbell v Walker* (1800) 5 Ves. Jr. 678; *Re Sherman* [1954] Ch. 653.

[75] For example, s. 68 Settled Land Act 1925 allows for the tenant for life to purchase the settled land.

[76] [1968] Ch. 353.

[77] [1986] Ch. 99.

[78] [1986] Ch. 99 at 115.

[79] *Silkstone and Haigh Moor Coal Co v Edey* [1900] 1 Ch. 167.

[80] *Snell's Equity* (31st edn Sweet & Maxwell, London) 2004 at p. 159. See also *Burrell v Burrell's Trustees* 1915 SC 333 at 337.

caution and if there is any evidence that the sale benefits her husband then it will be set aside.

The fair-dealing rule

Harry and Veronica are beneficiaries under a trust of Ivy Cottage. The trustees of the cottage are Tom and Tim. Veronica wishes to sell her beneficial interest in the cottage to Tom. Tom is not sure whether as a trustee he can purchase her beneficial interest.

Whereas the self-dealing rule concerns the purchase of trust property by the trustee, the fair-dealing rules governs the position where the trustee purchases the beneficial interest of the beneficiary. For example, suppose a beneficiary has a beneficial interest in a painting and that the painting is held on trust by trustees for three beneficiaries. It may well be that one of the beneficiaries wishes to sell his share in the painting. The question arises as to whether one of the trustees can purchase his beneficial interest. Such a sale of the beneficiary's interest would, of course, amount to a disposition of the beneficiary's interest and would need to comply with the written requirements of s. 53(1)(c) and the Law of Property Act 1925.[81] The fair-dealing rule allows the trustee to purchase the beneficial interest of a beneficiary; however, the court will scrutinise the sale and make sure that the trustee paid a fair price and that all relevant disclosure was made to the beneficiary. In one case the court explained that it will 'examine such a transaction and ascertain that full value was paid by the trustee, and will throw upon the trustee the onus of proving that he gave full value and that all the information was laid before the beneficiary when it was sold'.[82] In this respect, the sale is not said to be voidable per se but the court will investigate into whether fair price was paid. As well as ascertaining whether a fair price was paid and that all information was laid before the beneficiary, the court will also investigate whether there was any element of undue influence.

Trustee remuneration

Historically, the rule has been that a trustee acts voluntarily and is not paid for his services.[83] This rule applies despite the fact that a trustee expends a considerable amount of time and energy into the administration of a trust. An early illustration of the rule can be found in *Barrett* v *Hartley*[84] where a trustee had successfully managed a business belonging to the beneficiaries, thereby allowing a substantial profit to be received by those beneficiaries. When the trustee asked the court for remuneration for his efforts it was turned down on the grounds that what he had done was a normal part of his duty as a trustee. A trustee is, however, entitled to be reimbursed for out-of-pocket expenses

---

[81] This section was considered in Chapter 5.
[82] *Thomson* v *Eastwood* (1877) 2 App. Cas. 215 at 236. See also *Coles* v *Trecothick* (1804) 9 Ves. 234 at 244.
[83] *Robinson* v *Pett* (1734) 3 P Wms. 249.
[84] [1866] LR 2 Eq. 789.

incurred in the administration of a trust.[85] Furthermore, a trustee is entitled to recover any money he has had to pay out as a result of liabilities arising to the trust. For example, in **Benett v Wyndham**[86] a trustee was sued as a result of someone suffering injury on the trust land. The trustee paid the compensation out of his own pocket but was later entitled to recover the money paid from the trust fund.

The apparent justification for the no-remuneration rules lies in the fact that the Court of Chancery has historically been concerned with claims by trustees for work carried out which is not essential to the trust. In **Re Duke of Norfolk's Settlement Trusts** Fox LJ explained in one case that the court would always be careful to protect beneficiaries with claims by trustees for remuneration which, after all, would be paid out of the trust funds.[87] Another possible reason behind the no-remuneration rule is that historically trustees acted out of moral rather than contractual duty. The typical eighteenth and nineteenth century trusts involved a member of the family who would act as a trustee out of moral duty. The right to be paid for his services would not have been an issue in taking of the office of trusteeship. The image of trusteeship in this period of time has been described by Moffat as one 'of disinterested devotion to the gratuitous administration of a friend's or relative's property – and a burden undertaken usually out of a sense of obligation'.[88] However, with changes in social and economic condition, the no-remuneration rule has become very difficult to justify in modern trust law. Unlike in early trust law, modern trustees usually act out of contractual rather than moral duty. For example, many modern trustees take the form of professional trustees or solicitors who profess to have special knowledge of the administration of trusts.[89] So what then is the modern position with regards to trustee remuneration? In **Dale v I.R.C**[90] the court explained that 'it is not that reward for services is repugnant to the fiduciary duty, but that he who has the duty shall not take any secret remuneration or any financial benefit not authorised by the law, or by his contract, or by the trust deed under which he acts'.[91] Thus, in the modern law the right to receive remuneration depends on whether it has been authorised, and authorisation may come from a number of different sources. These are examined in the following subsections (see Figure 17.1).

The trust instrument

The most obvious place where a trustee may claim remuneration is from the trust instrument. In most professionally drafted trust instruments the settlor will make provision for the trustee to be remunerated for his services. Such a provision is often referred to as a charging clause. Historically, such clauses were construed strictly against the trustee. For example, in the absence of a very wide charging clause, a solicitor-trustee was not entitled to be remunerated for work done in the administration of a trust which could have been done by a lay trustee.[92] The matter is now governed by s. 28 of the Trustee Act 2000 which applies when there is an express charging clause in the trust instrument.

---

[85] *Stott v Milne* (1884) 25 Ch. D 710. The right to be reimbursed for out-of-pocket expenses is now to be found in s. 31(1)(a) of the Trustee Act 2000 which states that a trustee is entitled to receive from the trust funds 'expenses properly incurred by him when acting on behalf of the trust'.

[86] (1862) 4 De GF & J 259.

[87] *Re Duke of Norfolk's Settlement Trusts* [1982] Ch. 61. This case is dealt with in more detail below.

[88] G. Moffat, *Trust Law: Text and Materials* 4th edn 2005 at p. 406.

[89] See G.W. Keeton 'The Selection of Trustees' in *Modern Developments in the Law of Trusts* (1971) p. 13.

[90] [1954] AC 11.

[91] [1954] AC 11 at 27.

[92] *Re Chapple* (1884) 27 Ch. D 584.

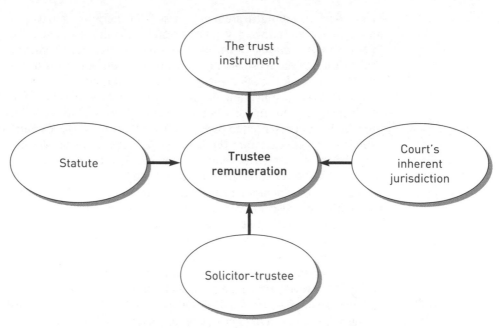

Figure 17.1 Sources of trustee remuneration

With regard to trust corporations and professional trustees, the section provides that trustees may claim remuneration for work done even when that work could have been done by a lay trustee.[93]

The court's inherent jurisdiction

A settlor created a trust some 25 years ago and authorised the trustees to receive remuneration at an agreed rate per annum. In the last few years the trust administration has grown substantially and the trustees cannot afford to continue administering the trust at the agreed remuneration.

How can the remuneration be increased?

The court has an inherent jurisdiction to award remuneration in circumstances where there is no provision for remuneration. The jurisdiction also extends to situations where there is some express provision for remuneration but the trustees wish to increase the scale of fees which were agreed at the commencement of the trust. The matter is neatly illustrated in ***Re Duke of Norfolk's Settlement Trusts***[94] where a trust corporation was administering a trust on a fee agreed at the commencement of the trust. In the course of administering the trust the trustees became involved in an extensive development in

---

[93] Section 28(1) allows for the section to be excluded by the trust instrument.
[94] [1982] Ch. 61.

London. This generated much more work than what was conceived at the beginning of the trust. The trustees applied to the court to have the fees, which were agreed at the outset, to be increased. The Court of Appeal allowed for the increase in the fees on the grounds that it had an inherent jurisdiction to do so. Fox LJ explained that, in the exercise of its inherent jurisdiction, the court would balance two different factors. Firstly, the office of trusteeship is gratuitous and the court would be careful to protect the interests of the beneficiaries against claims to remuneration by the trustees. Secondly, it is of utmost importance to the beneficiaries that the trust is efficiently administered, and if the trustees are to be remunerated for doing that work efficiently, then the court will authorise it. In the words of his Lordship, 'if the court concludes, having regard to the nature of the trust, the experience and skill of a particular trustee and to the amounts which he seeks to charge when compared with what other trustees might require to be paid for their services and to all the other circumstances of the case, that it would be in the interests of the beneficiaries to increase the remuneration, then the court may properly do so'.[95]

Examples of where the court has exercised its inherent jurisdiction include *O'Sullivan v Management Agency and Music Ltd*[96] where a contract between a fiduciary and a musician was set aside on grounds of undue influence. However, the fiduciary, who was the agent of the singer, was allowed to claim remuneration and some of the profits made by the singer on the grounds that he had contributed significantly to the success of the musician. Similarly, it has already been observed that in *Boardman v Phipps*[97] a solicitor who had made a profit in his capacity as a solicitor to a trust was entitled to retain some of the profits by way of a *quantum meruit* (reasonable sum) for the services he had rendered in allowing that profit to be made. In *Foster and Others v Spencer*[98] two trustees of a run-down cricket club were involved in selling the ground. The sale proved to be particularly troublesome because the land was subject to a local authority provision that no buildings were to be erected on the land. Furthermore, there were a number of squatters on the land who had to be removed before the sale could go ahead. The two trustees embarked on obtaining planning permission and removing the squatters from the land. When the trustees asked for remuneration for the work they had done it was authorised by the court. The court explained that, although there had been no express provision for remuneration, the work done by the two trustees was exceptional. The court was of the view that the beneficiaries would been unjustly enriched if the trustees were not given any reward for their exceptional efforts in getting the land sold at a price higher than it would have been had the trustees not have done what they did.

The inherent jurisdiction of the court to award remuneration will not, however, be exercised in circumstances where it would encourage the fiduciary to put himself in a position where his interest and duty would conflict. The matter is neatly illustrated in the decision of the House of Lords in *Guinness v Saunders*[99] where, as already observed, a director received an unauthorised payment of some £5.2 million as a result of a takeover bid. The director's subsequent claim for remuneration was turned down by the court on the grounds that he had put himself in a position of conflict. As a director, he was under a duty to obtain the best price for his company; this conflicted with his personal interest, which was the award of a sum of money depending on the value of the bid. The higher the bid, the higher the amount he would receive. Therefore, although he had offered his

---

[95] [1982] Ch. 61 at 79.
[96] [1985] QB 428.
[97] [1967] 2 AC 46.
[98] [1996] 2 All ER 672.
[99] [1990] 2 AC 663.

services in relation to the takeover bid, the court would not award remuneration in this instance. It was further doubted whether the court had the power to order remuneration to a director when to do so would be intermeddling with the company's affairs.

Statute

Statute has from time to time authorised certain types of trustees to receive remuneration. For example, the Judicial Trustee Act 1896 empowers a person appointed as Judicial Trustee to receive remuneration. Similarly, the Public Trustee Act 1906 allows for remuneration to be paid to a person who is appointed as Public Trustee. It has already been observed that s. 28 of the Trustee Act 2000 entitles a professional trustee who has been given an express charging clause to claim remuneration for work done which could have been done by a lay trustee. Section 29 of the same Act goes further and allows trust corporations to receive reasonable remuneration for services provided to a trust. This section applies where there has been no provision in the trust instrument or any other legislation. Section 29 extends to any other professional trustee, provided that he is not a sole trustee and that there has been agreement in writing between the other trustees. The section makes it clear that the remuneration is payable even if the services could have been provided by a lay trustee. Section 29(3) defines reasonable income as one which is reasonable for the provision of those services to the trust by the particular trustee.

Solicitor-trustees

Prior to the Trustee Act 2000 trustees who were also solicitors were not entitled to claim remuneration for their services to the trust. The only exception to this was where there was some express authorisation in the trust instrument. Even then, as observed above, the express charging clause would be construed strictly thereby preventing the solicitor-trustee from claiming for work done which could have been done by a lay trustee. The matter, as observed above, has now been resolved by ss. 28 and 29 of the Trustee Act 2000. It is worth noting, however, two rather strange rules which governed solicitor-trustees. The first was the rule in *Cradock v Piper*[100] which allowed a solicitor-trustee, when acting as a solicitor for himself and his co-trustees in matters relating to litigation on behalf of the trust, to recover the usual cost of litigation. The rule had been criticised as being curious and without any justification. Upjohn J described the rule in one case as 'exceptional, anomalous and not to be extended'.[101] The basic criticism levelled at this rule related to the question of why it was proper for a solicitor-trustee to recover for the cost of litigation work and not for non-litigation work.[102] The second rule allowed a solicitor-trustee to employ his own firm of solicitors when it was proper to employ an outside solicitor, provided that he did not benefit from the work done.[103]

Incidental profits

In the course of the administration of a trust, trustees may take advantage of a number of situations, thereby allowing them to make incidental profits. If they do make such profits

---

[100] (1850) 1 Mac. & G 664.
[101] *Re Worthington* [1954] 1 All ER 677 at 678.
[102] In *Re Corsellis* (1887) 34 Ch. D 675 Cotton LJ attempted to justify the rule on the grounds that the court, in awarding the costs of litigation, would be careful to disallow costs which were too excessive.
[103] *Clack v Carlon* (1866) 30 LJ Ch. 639.

they will be liable to account for such profits to their beneficiaries. The opportunity to make such profits may arise in a number of context and these are examined in the sub-sections below. Where such profits are made, the courts are not concerned with the questions whether the trustee acted in good faith. Furthermore, the strictness of the common law is demonstrated in the fact that the courts are not influenced by the fact that the profit which the trustee has made could never have been utilised by the beneficiary.

Renewal of a lease

Clearly a trustee who extracts an opportunity for himself which would otherwise belong to the beneficiary is liable to account for the profit he makes. However, the rule extends to cases where the trustee extracts a profit for himself which could not have been utilised by the beneficiary. The seminal case is *Keech v Sandford*[104] where, as observed earlier in the chapter, a lease of a market in Romford was held on trust for an infant beneficiary. On the refusal of the landlord to renew the lease for the infant beneficiary, the trustee renewed the lease for himself in his personal capacity. Lord King LC held that the trustee must hold the lease for the infant beneficiary. The rule in *Keech v Sandford* is indeed a harsh one and prevents the trustee from renewing for himself a benefit which would not have been available to the beneficiary. The justification for the rule relates to the evidential question of whether the trustee did indeed make all the efforts to renew the lease for the beneficiary or whether he saw this as an opportunity to acquire the lease for himself. Lord King LC explained: 'I very well see, if a trustee, the refusal to renew, might have a lease to himself, few trust estates would be renewed to [beneficiaries]; though I do not say that there is fraud in this case, yet he should have left it to run out, than to have had the lease to himself.'[105] The rule in *Keech v Sandford* extends to cases where the trustee acquires the reversion, that is, the freehold title to the land once the lease expires. The matter is illustrated by the decision of the Court of Appeal in *Protheroe v Protheroe*[106] where a husband was holding a lease on trust for himself and his wife in equal shares. On their separation the husband acquired the freehold for himself. The Court of Appeal held that the freehold must be held on constructive trust for the husband and the wife. The Court of Appeal explained that it was 'a long established rule of equity from *Keech v Sandford*, downwards that if a trustee, who owns the leasehold, gets in the freehold, that freehold belongs to the trust and he cannot take the property for himself'.[107]

Directors' fees

APPLYING THE LAW

Michael is a trustee of a trust consisting of a number of shares in a private company. In fact the majority of the shares are held by Michael on trust for the beneficiaries. Recently, there has been a need to appoint a new director in the company in which the shares are held. By using his majority shareholding, Michael has appointed himself as director and is now receiving payment for being a director.

Can he become a director?

---

[104] (1726) Sel. Cas. Ch. 61.
[105] (1726) Sel. Cas. Ch. 61 at 62.
[106] [1968] 1 WLR 519.
[107] [1968] 1 WLR 519 at 521. See also *Thompson's Trustee v Heaton* [1974] 1 WLR 605.

It is quite possible for a trustee to be holding shares in a company on trust for the beneficiaries. Where the trustee is holding a substantial number of shares in the company, he may purport to exercise his controlling interest by appointing himself a director and receive director's remuneration. Alternatively, the trustee may be vested with a power to appoint new directors and in doing so he appoints himself in order to receive the director's remuneration. The question arises as to whether a trustee can receive directors' remuneration in such circumstances. In **Re Francis**,[108] trustees were holding a large number of shares in a private company on behalf of a trust. The articles of the association of the company gave shareholders a specified number of shares to vote themselves as directors of the company. The trustees, having sufficient shares to avail themselves to this opportunity, voted themselves as directors. However, the court subsequently held that they were to account for the fees they had received as directors. Similarly in **Re Macadam**,[109] trustees had the power under the articles of the association of a company to appoint two directors. The trustees exercised the power by appointing themselves as directors. The court, following the decision in **Re Francis**, held that they were liable to account for the remuneration they had received as directors.

Trustees will be allowed to retain directors' fees when they have been appointed independently of the fact that they were holding shares in the company. A good example of this is the decision of the Court of Appeal in **Re Dover Coalfield Extension Ltd**,[110] where a company, Dover Coalfield Extension, held shares in Consolidated Kent Collieries Corporation. One of the directors of Dover Coalfield Extension was appointed as a director of Kent Collieries Corporation. Under the terms of his appointment he was entitled to claim remuneration for the work he was charged with overseeing. However, one of the terms of articles of association of Kent Collieries Corporation required all directors to acquire 1000 shares in the company within a month of their appointment. Dover Coalfield Extension transferred the 1000 shares to the director on the grounds that they would be held on trust for that company. When the question arose whether the director was entitled to retain the remuneration he had received since becoming director, the court held that he could. The Court of Appeal held that he had been appointed by an independent board of directors and had acquired the shares after his appointment.

Finally, it should be noted that a trustee will be entitled to retain directors' fees if he was already a director before his appointment as a trustee. Furthermore, a trustee will be entitled to retain directors' fees if the trust instrument allows him to be appointed as a director and receive the fees.[111]

● Competing and doing business with the trust business

A trustee must not enter into business which is in direct competition with the trust business. For example, in **Re Thomson**[112] an executor of a will was under the instruction to continue running the yacht business of the testator. He then decided to set up his own yacht business within the same town. The court granted an injunction preventing him setting up his own business, on the grounds that this would amount to a conflict of interest with his duty to ensure that the executor's business was efficiently run and profits maximised.

---

[108] (1905) 74 LJ Ch. 198.
[109] [1946] Ch. 73.
[110] [1908] 1 Ch. 65.
[111] *Re Llewellin's Will Trusts* [1949] Ch. 225.
[112] [1930] 1 Ch. 203.

Although a trustee cannot compete with the business of the trust which he is managing, the question arises as to whether he can conduct business with the trust business and thereby make some profit. For example, if he is managing a public house on trust, can he supply the public house with drinks made by his own firm and thereby make some profit? The general rule is that if the trustees do make a profit in this way then they are liable to account for the profit.[113] The trust instrument may, however, entitle the trustees to retain profits as in *Re Sykes,*[114] where trustees were appointed to manage a public house on trust. The terms of the trust instrument allowed them to supply wine to the public house. The court held that in such circumstances they were entitled to retain the usual profits made in supplying such wine.

Remedies for breach of fiduciary duty

Throughout this chapter it has been observed that a trustee who puts his interests ahead of those of his beneficiary will inevitably end up making a profit at the expense of his beneficiary. Where such a profit is made, the trustee will have been unjustly enriched at the expense of the beneficiary. To reverse the unjust enrichment the law requires the trustee to effect restitution to the trust estate. Restitution may be effected in one of two ways: firstly, the court may require the trustee to account for the profits he has made and, secondly, the court may impose a constructive trust on the profits. The beneficiary may also be able to claim equitable compensation in circumstances where the breach of fiduciary duty has caused some loss to the trust estate. These remedies can be examined in more detail in the following subsections.

Account for profits

An account for profits is a personal remedy requiring the trustee to account for the profits he has made. This requires him to personally pay over to the beneficiary the monetary value of the profit he has received. For example, where a trustee purchases trust property in breach of the self-dealing rule and then sells that property to a bona fide purchaser of the legal title without notice, he will be ordered to account for any profits he makes on the sale of that property. As it is a personal claim against the trustee, its success very much depends on whether the trustee is solvent.

A constructive trust imposed on the profits

It is possible for the court to impose a constructive trust on the profits which have been received by the fiduciary. The imposition of a constructive trust takes the form of a proprietary remedy and gives the beneficiaries certain proprietary claims in respect of the profits made by the trustee. The effect of the imposition of a constructive trust on the profits is that the beneficiary acquires an equitable interest in the property as soon as the profit is received. The effect of this is that it allows the beneficiary to follow the profits into the hands of third parties who cannot purport to show that they are bona fide purchasers of the legal title without notice of the trust. The further advantage of the imposition of a constructive trust is that the insolvency of the trustee is immaterial,

---

[113] *Re Sykes* [1909] 2 Ch. 241.
[114] [1909] 2 Ch. 241.

as the beneficiaries will be making claim to specific property rather than the trustee himself. Examples where constructive trusts have been imposed include **Boardman v Phipps**[115] where the solicitor was required to hold the profits made on the sale of shares in a private company on constructive trust for the beneficiaries. In **Keech v Sandford**[116] the lease which was renewed personally by the trustee was held on constructive trust for an infant beneficiary and in **Guinness v Saunders**[117] the House of Lords held that a payment of £5.2 million to a director was held on constructive trust for the company.

Although English law clearly recognises that a constructive trust will be imposed on profits made as a result of breach of fiduciary duty, there is, however, a debate as to when a constructive trust should be imposed. The question is whether every situation in which a fiduciary makes an unauthorised profit should give rise to the imposition of a constructive trust on the profit. In order to understand the debate it is important to bear in mind that the imposition of a constructive trust is a very powerful remedy. It takes the form of a proprietary claim and gives the beneficiary an immediate equitable interest in the profit. The consequence of this is that the beneficiary has an equitable proprietary interest which binds third parties who cannot purport to show that they are bona fide purchasers of the legal title without notice of the trust. More importantly, the equitable interest binds the creditors of the fiduciary and, on his insolvency, the beneficiaries have an immediate claim to the property which is subject to the trust. It has been argued in many quarters that the imposition of a constructive trust gives the beneficiaries of the fiduciary in certain cases an unjustified advantage over the creditors of the fiduciary.[118]

One particular decision that has fuelled the debate is that of the Privy Council in **A-G for Hong Kong v Reid**[119] where the court was faced with the issue of bribes received by a fiduciary. Prior to the decision in **A-G for Hong Kong v Reid** the position in English law was that a fiduciary who obtained a bribe was only liable to account for the money received. The bribe monies received were not held on constructive trust for the principal whose confidence had been betrayed.[120] The facts of **Reid** concerned a senior public prosecutor in Hong Kong who received large sums of money to obstruct prosecutions. The bribe money was invested in freehold properties in New Zealand, which the Crown sought to recover on the grounds that they were held on constructive trust. The Privy Council, overruling the decision in **Lister & Co v Stubbs**,[121] held that as soon as the fiduciary received a bribe he was under a duty to transfer the bribe money to his principal. Applying the equitable maxim that 'equity sees that as done which ought to be done' the bribe money belonged in equity to the principal by virtue of a constructive trust. In the words of Lord Templeman 'as soon as the bribe was received it should have been paid or transferred instantly to the person who suffered from the breach of duty. Equity considers as done which ought to have been done. As soon as the bribe was received, whether in cash or in kind, the false fiduciary held the bribe on a constructive trust for the person injured.'[122] It is clear from Lord Templeman's judgment that the Privy Council

---

[115] [1967] 2 AC 46.
[116] (1726) Sel. Cas. Ch. 61.
[117] [1990] 2 AC 663.
[118] See, for example, P. Birks, 'Proprietary Rights as Remedies' in P. Birks (ed) *The Frontiers of Liability, Vol. 2* (1994) and G. McCormack, 'The Remedial Constructive Trust and Commercial Transactions' Company Lawyer (1996) Vol. 17(1) at 3.
[119] [1994] 1 All ER 1.
[120] *Lister & Co v Stubbs* (1890) 45 Ch. D 1.
[121] (1890) 45 Ch. D 1.
[122] [1994] 1 All ER 1 at 5.

adopted the view that a constructive trust should be imposed in all situations where a fiduciary makes a secret profit.

The decision in *A-G for Hong Kong* v *Reid*[123] was regarded by many as a case where there has been an unjustified extension of the imposition of a constructive trust. In the case of bribes received by a fiduciary, one of the major reasons why there was only a duty to account and no constructive trust of the bribe was to prevent the unsecured creditors of the fiduciary from losing out on claiming the bribe money to meet what was owed to them. In *A-G for Hong Kong* v *Reid* the Privy Council rejected this argument, on the grounds that the unsecured creditors could not gain a better position than their debtor. Lord Templeman explained that the authorities showed that:

> property acquired by a trustee innocently but in breach of trust and the property from time to time representing the same belong in equity to the [beneficiary] and not the trustee personally, whether he is solvent or insolvent. Property acquired by a trustee as a result of criminal breach of trust and the property from time to time representing the same must also belong in equity to the [beneficiary] and not to the trustee whether he is solvent or insolvent.[124]

Despite this observation, some commentators have explained that the imposition of a constructive trust requires some connection between the principal and the unauthorised profit made by the fiduciary.[125] This connection can be, for example, where the fiduciary makes a profit through the use of some property belonging to the principal. A good example of this would be the case of *Boardman* v *Phipps*[126] where it has already been observed that a solicitor had used confidential information belonging to a trust for his own benefit. Support for a proprietary connection between the principal and the profit has been made by Professor Peter Birks, who has called for a 'proprietary base' connecting the principal and the profit before a constructive trust is imposed.[127]

VISIT CASE NAVIGATOR

The need for a 'proprietary base' linking the authorised profit to the claimant was more recently endorsed by the Court of Appeal in *Sinclair Investments (UK) Ltd* v *Versailles Trade Finance Ltd (In Administration)*.[128] In doing so, the Court of Appeal has put serious doubt on the correctness of the decision in *A-G for Hong Kong* v *Reid*.[129] In particular, the Court of Appeal has rejected that there is a wide principle which holds that bribes and other unauthorised profits are held on a constructive trust thereby giving a claimant a proprietary claim to the profits. The facts of this case are covered in more detail in the next section, but save that it involved a massive fraud by a certain Mr Cushnie who controlled a group of companies called the Versailles Group plc. One of the companies in the group, Versailles Trading Finance Ltd (VTFL) was engaged in trade finance. Despite that, the company was more involved in orchestrating a massive fraud against a number of traders who were encouraged to advance money which would be held by a company called Trading Partners Ltd (TPL) for the purpose of trading activities. In addition money was also raised through two further companies in the group, the first called Versailles Group plc (VGP) in which Mr Cushnie has a substantial holding and another called Versailles Trading Finance Ltd (VTFL) which issued debentures to a number of banks, raising money by charges on the assets of that company.

[123] [1994] 1 All ER 1.
[124] [1994] 1 All ER 1 at 5.
[125] See R. Pearce and J. Stevens, *The Law of Trusts and Equitable Obligation* (4th edn, 2006) at p. 813.
[126] [1967] 2 AC 46.
[127] P. Birks, *An Introduction to the Law of Restitution* (1985), pp. 378–95.
[128] [2011] EWCA Civ 347.
[129] [1994] 1 AC 324.

Fraud was carried out against the banks and the traders by Mr Cushnie authorising the use of the money for purposes other than trading. In fact, the money was moved from one company to another, showing profits and thereby increasing the share price of the Versailles Group. Mr Cushnie sold the shares at a considerable profit and purchased personal assets including a house in London. TPL was assigned to an investor called Sinclair Investments Holdings which commenced proceedings to claim proprietary rights to the profits and the house. Sinclair argued that Mr Cushnie owed fiduciary duties to TPL and that the money used from TPL was used in breach of trust. The question before the High Court and eventually the Court of Appeal was whether Mr Cushnie, acting in breach of fiduciary duty, held the profits on a constructive trust thereby giving the claimant a proprietary right or whether there was a personal claim only. In the High Court, Lewison J held that TPL was owed fiduciary duties but it had no proprietary claims to the profits and the money realised by Mr Cushnie on the sale of the London property. Lewison J explained that:

> The fiduciary duty relied on in the present case is a duty owed by Mr Cushnie to TPL. The unauthorised profit is a profit realised by Mr Cushnie on the sale of shares in VGP . . . Mr Cushnie acquired those shares before TPL was even incorporated. But at any rate his initial acquisition of the shares could not, in my judgment, have amounted to an acquisition of property that belonged in any sense to TPL. Before his sale of those shares he did not owe trustee-like duties in relation to that specific property. It follows, in my judgment, that the claim by TPL to the profit realised by Mr Cushnie on a sale of those shares is a claim based on the transaction which gave rise to those profits, and the circumstances in which it was made. It is, therefore, a case which falls into [Millett LJ's] second class; and gives rise to a personal remedy only. Since the claim gives rise to a personal remedy only, it is not open to TPL to trace those profits into the proceeds of sale of the Kensington property and to assert a proprietary claim to those proceeds. The settlement of personal claims between VTFL and Mr Cushnie cannot be undone by TPL in reliance on a personal claim. That settlement could only be undone by a trustee in bankruptcy or liquidator.[130]

Upholding the decision of Lewison J in the Court of Appeal the matter was explained by the Master of the Rolls Lord Neuberger as follows:

> In a nutshell, the issue between the parties is whether, as it contends, TPL has a proprietary interest in the proceeds of sale of the Shares, or whether, as the defendants argue, TPL has a right to an equitable account to the proceeds of sale. The difference is vital, because, if TPL is correct, it was the beneficial owner of those proceeds, and its beneficial ownership would override, subject to the question of notice, the payments made to the banks in so far as they were made out of the proceeds of sale. On the other hand, if the defendants' case is right, Mr Cushnie's duty is to account to TPL for the proceeds of sale, which is a personal remedy, which would not override the payments already made to the banks.[131]

The Court of Appeal held that Mr Cushnie's breach of fiduciary duty did not give rise to a proprietary claim for the beneficiaries, that is TPL. Lord Neuberger asked the question: 'Why, it may be asked, should the fact that a fiduciary is able to make a profit as a result of the breach of his duties to a beneficiary, without more, give the beneficiary a proprietary interest in the profit? After all, a proprietary claim is based on property law, and it is not entirely easy to see conceptually how the proprietary rights of the beneficiary in the misused funds should follow into the profit made on the sale of the Shares.'[132]

---

[130] [2010] EWHC 1614 (Civ) at para. 81.
[131] [2011] EWCA Civ 347 at para. 48.
[132] [2011] EWCA Civ 347 at para. 52.

The Court of Appeal and Lord Neuberger were clearly of the opinion that no proprietary claim could arise where a fiduciary had made a profit in breach of his duties where the beneficiaries could not show that the profits represented the property originally belonging to the beneficiaries. In other words, where the beneficiaries could not show a proprietary base to the profits. Lord Neuberger explained that:

> a beneficiary of a fiduciary's duties cannot claim a proprietary interest, but is entitled to an equitable account, in respect of any money or asset acquired by a fiduciary in breach of his duties to the beneficiary, unless the asset or money is or has been beneficially the property of the beneficiary or the trustee acquired the asset or money by taking advantage of an opportunity or right which was properly that of the beneficiary.[133]
>
> For the reasons I have given, previous decisions of this court establish that a claimant cannot claim proprietary ownership of an asset purchased by the defaulting fiduciary with funds which, although they could not have been obtained if he had not enjoyed his fiduciary status, were not beneficially owned by the claimant or derived from opportunities beneficially owned by the claimant. However, those cases also establish that, in such a case, a claimant does have a personal claim in equity to the funds. There is no case which appears to support the notion that such a personal claim entitles the claimant to claim the value of the asset (if it is greater than the amount of the funds together with interest), and there are judicial indications which tend to militate against that notion.[134]

Some may argue that decision of the Court of Appeal in *Sinclair Investments (UK) Ltd* v *Versailles Trade Finance Ltd (In Administration)*[135] has introduced some certainty into English law, that is, where a fiduciary makes an unauthorised profit, but the claimant cannot purport to show that the profit belongs to the claimant, there is no proprietary claim to the profit. Furthermore, the decision will be welcome news for creditors of the fiduciary who, in the event of his insolvency, will find that beneficiaries of the fiduciary will not have prior claims over and above the creditors. However, leading trust lawyers in the field have questioned whether the decision is correct and indeed justified when looked at from the core duties of a fiduciary that are owed to his beneficiaries. From the perspective of the beneficiary, the fiduciary must at all times act in the best interests of that beneficiary. That core duty is an absolute duty which requires the fiduciary to have the exclusive interest of the beneficiary at heart and not to put any of his own interests before that of the beneficiary. With this in perspective, any unauthorised profit or bribe belongs to the beneficiary as it has been made in breach of the core duty to act in the best interests of the beneficiary. The requirement that there be some 'proprietary base', that the bribe or unauthorised gain to be linked to the beneficiary's property, becomes irrelevant. In this respect David Hayton comments that:

> a strong case can thus be made that *Sinclair* leaves the law in a most unsatisfactory state and undermines the integrity of the trust concept. At its heart is the fundamental duty of a trustee of property to act exclusively in the best interests of the beneficiaries in fulfilling the role of trustee so as to profit the beneficiaries and not himself (unless duly authorised). To protect the beneficiaries from the trustee's creditors, there is a ring-fenced fund for the beneficiaries that extends beyond the original trust property to property acquired from time to time in the role of trustee. Property acquired in authorised fashion automatically becomes part of the trust fund, while is it not the case that the beneficiaries can also claim that property purportedly acquired howsoever for himself by the trustee through his role of trustee is also part of the authorised trust fund as if acquired in accordance with his core

---

133 [2011] EWCA Civ 347 at para. 88.
134 [2011] EWCA Civ 347 at para. 89.
135 [2011] EWCA Civ 347.

duty? . . . It is accepted that there cannot be ring-fenced security if the trustee could sell trust property and with the proceeds of sale buy assets for his patrimony available to satisfy his creditors' claims, but what if he could sell off trust assets at an undervalue and retain for himself bribes received from the purchasers, or if he could cause the trust to enter into disadvantageous transactions with his alter ego company so that his company could make profits for himself?[136]

Equitable compensation

A beneficiary will be entitled to equitable compensation if he suffers a loss which is caused by a breach of fiduciary duty. The availability of equitable compensation was acknowledged by the House of Lords in **Nocton v Lord Ashburton**.[137] The purpose of equitable compensation is to put the beneficiary back in the position he would have been had the breach not occurred. An example where equitable compensation may be awarded is where a fiduciary enters into a transaction with his principal without full disclosure of the facts. For example, a fiduciary sells some property to his principal without disclosure of the extent of his own interest in the property subject to the sale. If the principal suffers any loss, for example, reselling the property at a loss, he may bring an action against the fiduciary. In **Cavendish Bentinck v Fenn**[138] the House of Lords explained that an agent who sold his own goods to his principal above market price in circumstance when those goods could be obtained at market price would be liable to compensate for the excess charged. Equitable compensation, however, will only be available where the breach of fiduciary duty has caused the principal's loss. For example, in **Swindle v Harrison**[139] solicitors had made a loan to a principal who had mortgaged her house to facilitate her son's hotel restoration, without disclosing their interest in the transaction. Despite the non-disclosure, the principal would have proceeded with the loan in any event and therefore had failed to show that the subsequent loss was caused by the breach of fiduciary duty.[140]

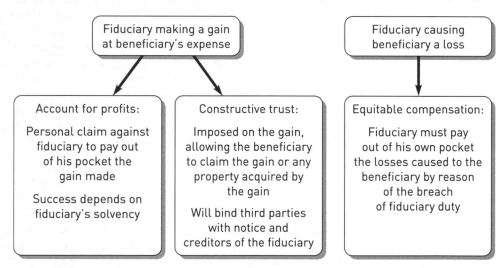

Figure 17.2 Remedies for breach of fiduciary duty

---

[136] D. Hayton, 'No Proprietary Liability for Bribes and other Secret Profits?' (2011) Trust Law International 3.
[137] [1914] AC 932.
[138] (1887) 12 App. Cas. 652.
[139] [1997] 4 All ER 705.
[140] See also *Target Holding v Redferns* [1996] AC 421.

Conclusion

This chapter has analysed the fiduciary nature of trusteeship. In doing to so it has shown that trustees stand in a fiduciary relationship to the beneficiary, and in doing so, owe strict duties. The core duty of a fiduciary is to prevent there being a conflict of interest between the duty owed to the beneficiary and the personal interests of the fiduciary. The basic rule is that a fiduciary must not make any unauthorised profits from his position as a fiduciary.

Where such profits are made, the fiduciary is under a duty to effect restitution to the principal's or beneficiary's estate. Restitution can be effected by either an account for profits or the imposition of a constructive trust on the profit itself. These two remedies have rather different outcomes and, as this chapter has shown, the imposition of a constructive trust offers a powerful way in which the beneficiary can claim a proprietary interest in the profit binding third parties who cannot purport to show that they are bona fide purchasers of the property which is in the form of a profit. However, recent trends in English law suggest that a constructive trust will only be imposed in circumstances where a claimant can show a connection with the unauthorised gain; that is, the gain was made by the use of the claimant's property rather than a breach of fiduciary duty per se.

The chapter has also encouraged the reader to think about some of the wider concerns of fiduciary law: firstly, the precise circumstances which give rise to the finding of a fiduciary relationship; secondly, the question whether the strict liability approach founded in English law is justified in the modern cases that come before the courts; finally, the appropriate remedial response to deal with breaches of fiduciary duty.

●●● Case study

Consider the following case study.

Blackwell and Bardolph were two trustees of a trust arising under the will of Blackwell's uncle. Blackwell was also a partner in the firm of Blackwell and Jones, solicitors, which had for many years acted on behalf of Blackwell's uncle. Blackwell was also one of the five beneficiaries under his uncle's will.

From the death of Blackwell's uncle, the firm of Blackwell and Jones acted for the trustees in the administration of the estate, and, in the course of it transferred a good deal of the property on behalf of the trustees, and also acted for the trustees in an action in which the trustees received a debt of £5000 due to the trust estate.

Blackwell secured Bardolph's agreement to the purchase by Blackwell's wife of a house forming part of the trust estate for £17,000. The house was worth £20,000 and Blackwell's wife has contracted to sell it to Prospect for that sum. The firm of Blackwell and Jones acted for the trustees in connection with the conveyance to Blackwell's wife.

Blackwell and Jones have now presented a bill of costs to the trustees, covering the whole of the work done on behalf of the trust. The tenant for life of the estate, Wise, has objected to the payment of this bill, and also to the sale of the house to Blackwell's wife.

Advise Blackwell, Bardolph and the firm of Blackwell and Jones.

●● Moot points

1 The case law on fiduciary liability makes it clear that the courts will not entertain questions of good faith and honesty in deciding whether the fiduciary made a profit in his position as a fiduciary. What is the rationale for this strict approach taken by the courts of equity?

2 Read the judgment of Lord Cohen in *Boardman* **v** *Phipps* [1967] 2 AC 46 and explain why his Lordship was not influenced by the fact that the information which Boardman used to make the profit could never have been used by the trustees or their beneficiaries for their own advantage. Do you think the decision in *Boardman* **v** *Phipps* is based on the fact that the information Boardman acquired was the property of the trust? Is information property? See (1968) 84 LQR 472.

3 What are the main differences with an account for profit and the imposition of a constructive trust?

4 When imposing a constructive trust on profits received by a fiduciary, should the court be influenced by the question of whether the fiduciary is solvent or insolvent?

● Further reading

Conaglen, M. 'The Nature and Function of Fiduciary Loyalty' (2005) 121 LQR 453. Examines the function of the fiduciary duty of loyalty and explains how this duty is different from other legal duties.

Finn, P.D. *Fiduciary Obligations* (1977). Provides a seminal account on the law relating to fiduciary obligations.

Hicks, A.D. 'The Remedial Principle of *Keech* v *Sandford* Reconsidered' [2010] CLJ 287. Considers the extent to which the decision in *Keech* v *Sandford* (1726) Sel. Cas. Ch. 61 was intended to set a universal principle of law.

Lee, R. 'In Search of the Nature and Function of Fiduciary Loyalty: Some Observations on Conaglen's Analysis' (2007) 27 OJLS 327. Provides a further analysis on Conaglen's work on the nature of fiduciary loyalty.

McInnes, M. 'Account for Profit for Breach of Fiduciary Duty' (2006) LQR 11. Examines the decision of the Court of Appeal in *Murad* v *Al Saraj*.

Millett, P. 'Equity's Place in the Law of Commerce' (1998) 14 LQR 214. Examines the proper role of equity in a commercial context, including the imposition of fiduciary obligations in commercial transactions.

Samet, I. 'Guarding the Fiduciary's Conscience: A Justification of a Stringent Profit-Stripping Rule' (2008) OJLS 763. Where the author defends the strict rule that unauthorised gains should not be kept by fiduciaries.

Sealy, S. 'Fiduciary Relationships' [1962] CLJ 69. Explores the circumstances in which fiduciary relationship should arise; in particular, articulates four different situations in which the fiduciary relationship arises.

Sheperd, C. *The Law of Fiduciaries* (1981). Provides a general account of the law of fiduciaries.

Visit **www.mylawchamber.co.uk/panesar** to access study support resources including interactive multiple choice questions, practice exam questions with guidance, podcasts, weblinks, legal newsfeed all linked to the **Pearson eText** version of Exploring Equity and Trusts which you can **search**, **highlight** and **personalise** with your **own notes** and **bookmarks**.

Use Case Navigator to read in full some of the key cases referenced in this chapter with commentary and questions:

Sinclair Investments (UK) Ltd v *Versailles Trade Ltd (In Administration)* [2011] EWCA 347
Boardman v *Phipps* [1967] 2 AC 46

18
Powers of trustees

Learning objectives

After reading this chapter you should be able to:

→ understand the difference between administrative powers and administrative duties

→ explain the extent to which a trustee can delegate his functions to another

→ explain when a trustee will be liable for the acts of an agent employed

→ explain the power of maintenance

→ explain the power of advancement

→ understand other miscellaneous powers which are conferred on trustees.

Re Pauling's Settlement Trusts [1964] Ch. 303
The spendthrift parents, the children with trust money
and a little help from the trustees

The seminal facts of *Re Pauling's Settlement Trusts* decided in 1963 illustrate some of the concerns raised in this chapter. Trustees were holding a fund for a wife for her life and thereafter for her children. The trust deed contained an express power of advancement. The children's father, who lived beyond his means, sought to claim some of the trust fund from the trustees vis-à-vis his children. The trustees made a number of advancements to the children; however, the money was used for different purposes, including the purchase of a house and another to pay off the mother's overdraft. When the validity of these advancements was questioned, the trustees argued that they had given the money to the children and what then subsequently happened with that money was not a concern of the trustees. The Court of Appeal rejected this argument, on the grounds that the trustees were under a duty to see that the advancement was for the benefit of the beneficiary and that the money advanced was applied for the purpose stipulated.

The facts of *Re Pauling's Settlement Trusts* raise interesting questions. For example, can an infant or a beneficiary who is not yet entitled to the trust fund ask for money to be paid out of that fund? Unlike what happened in *Re Pauling's Settlement Trusts*, what if the request for money is to pay for the welfare of the child? Can trustees in the administration of the trust release some of the capital or income to a beneficiary? In other words, do they have a power to do so and when can it be exercised?

This chapter explores some of the powers conferred on trustees in the course of the administration of a trust.

Introduction

In the course of the office of trusteeship, trustees are conferred a number of powers. These powers may be conferred either by the trust instrument or by law. A power is to be distinguished from a duty in the sense that a power is discretionary whereas a duty imposes an imperative obligation on the trustee. For example, the last two chapters have looked at the duties of trustees, including the duty of investment and the general fiduciary duty of loyalty. A trustee has no choice but to invest the trust fund. Powers are conferred on trustees so as to allow them to effectively administer the trust in favour of the beneficiaries. If they decide not to exercise the power, the beneficiaries, prima facie, have no say in the matter unless the refusal to exercise is unreasonable or taken out of bad faith and therefore capable of being challenged on those grounds. Although a trustee need not exercise a power, they are under a duty to consider whether to exercise it or not. Chapter 15 explored the grounds on which the court will intervene in the exercise of a discretion, and the reader is encouraged to return to that chapter when exploring the powers which are examined in this chapter.

This chapter explores three important powers conferred on trustees as well as miscellaneous other powers. The three powers examined are the power to delegate, the power of maintenance and the power of advancement. These are known as administrative and dispositive powers. An administrative power is one which confers upon the trustee authority to administer the trust property in a particular way. For example, the power to delegate aspects of the management of trust property is an administrative power. Another good example of an administrative power is a power of investment, which confers upon the trustee a discretion in the types of investments he may make. On the other hand, a dispositive power confers upon the trustee an authority to distribute the trust property or any part of it at the discretion of the trustee. The powers of advancement and maintenance, as will be seen below, confer upon the trustee an authority to distribute or dispose of some aspect of the trust property. The trustees need not exercise the power; however, they must consider the exercise of the power if the circumstances give rise to a possibility that the power is capable of being exercised.

The power to delegate

APPLYING THE LAW

Tim and Tom have been appointed trustees under a will created last year. The will leaves property subject to a number of trusts which are expected to run for a number of years. Tim and Tom have very little knowledge of trust law and are worried about how to manage the trust property. They have a sum of £500,000 which needs to be invested; however, they are not sure how to do this.

Can they delegate their work to an agent? Will they be liable for the agent they employ?

Given the fact that a trust involves confidence being placed in a trustee, to entertain the question of delegation in the context of trusteeship does at first sight seem rather paradoxical. The basic premise of a trust is that a settlor is putting trust in another to carry out his instructions or, in the case of the exercise of some discretion, that the trustee and he alone exercise the discretion. It is for this reason that historically the rule in equity was that a trustee could not delegate his duties or his discretions to another person. If he delegated his duties to another the trustee remained liable for the acts of the agent. The position was summarised by the Latin expression: *Delegatus non potest delegare*. The matter was neatly explained by Lord Langdale in **Turner v Corney**[1] where his Lordship explained that 'trustees who take on themselves the management of property for the benefit of others have no right to shift their duty on other persons; and if they employ an agent, they remain subject to the responsibility toward their [beneficiaries] for whom they have undertaken the duty'.[2]

In the context of some of the very early trusts, where trustees had very little or no duties in relation to the trust property, the rule of delegation worked well. However, it soon became apparent that some work in connection with the trust may require some specialist help in the form of a solicitor or stockbroker. The question then arose as to whether the trustee was justified in delegation aspects of his management functions to an agent. The modern rule of delegation is fundamentally different and the question is

---

[1] (1841) 5 Beav. 515.
[2] (1841) 5 Beav. 515 at 517.

not whether the trustee can delegate, but whether the trustee has authority to delegate. In addressing the modern question whether trustees can delegate their functions to an agent, the law is concerned essentially with two main questions:

1 Does the trustee have the authority to delegate?

2 Once delegation has taken place, how far is the trustee liable for the acts of the agents employed?

The modern position with regard to trustee delegation is now to be found in Part IV of the Trustee Act 2000. However, in order to understand the modern rules it is important to revisit the principles pre-Trustee Act 2000 and see how the law responded to the two questions raised above. It will be seen that there are three stages in the development of the law relating to trustee delegation: the principles pre-1925, the principles between 1925 and 2000 and finally, the present position to be found in the Trustee Act 2000. It will be seen that some of the principles of delegation found in the Trustee Act 2000 involve a return somewhat to the principles of prudent behaviour found in some of the pre-1925 cases. Although prudency has now been replaced by reasonable conduct by the Trustee Act 1925, the modern rules of delegation nevertheless impose higher standards of care than those imposed by the Trustee Act 1925.

Principles of delegation pre-1925

Prior to the Trustee Act 1925, there was a limited right conferred on trustees to delegate their functions to another. This right was recognised in light of the fact that the trustee would need to use the services of a specialists such as a stockbroker, solicitor or a surveyor. Therefore, in relation to the question whether a trustee could delegate, the court explained in *Re Parsons, ex parte Belchier*[3] that trustees were justified in delegating their duties to another on grounds of necessity or where a prudent man of business would.

Thus, it was quite possible for trustees to delegate some aspects of their ministerial functions, such as implanting certain investments such a stocks and government bonds, or requiring a solicitor to execute a conveyance on their behalf. It was, however, clear that trustees were not allowed to delegate their discretions to an agent. For example, if a trustee was empowered with an investment clause, it was the trustee alone who could decide which investments he would make. Similarly, a trustee conferred a power of sale or a power to mortgage or lease land could only make that decision himself and could not confer that decision on an agent.

In respect of the question whether the trustee was liable for the acts of the agent employed, the law took the view that the trustee would not be liable for the acts of the agent employed, provided that the agent was employed in the normal scope of business and that the trustee acted prudently when making the appointment. The matter is illustrated in a number of pre-1925 cases such as *Fry v Tapson*[4] and *Speight v Gaunt*.[5] In *Fry v Tapson* trustees decided to lend money by way of mortgage. Instead of appointing an independent valuer themselves, they delegated the duty to appoint the valuer on their solicitor. The solicitor appointed a valuer who had no knowledge of the area where the land was situated and who was also an agent of the mortgagor with a pecuniary interest should the mortgage be granted. The money was duly lent by the trustees; however, the

---

[3] (1754) Amb. 218.
[4] (1884) 28 Ch. D 268.
[5] (1883) 22 Ch. D 727.

mortgagor defaulted on payment and when the trustee sought to sell the land it was found to be not worth the money they had lent. The court held that the trustees were liable to replace the loss to the trust fund because it was not in the ordinary course of business for a solicitor to appoint a valuer.

Where a trustee employed an agent in the ordinary course of business and in doing so acted like a prudent man of business, the law made it clear that he was not liable for the acts of the agents employed. The point is nicely illustrated in *Speight* v *Gaunt* where a trustee wishing to invest the trust fund in certain stocks approached a reputable stock-broker. The stockbroker received the trust money but never purchased the stocks for the trustee. When the stockbroker later absconded with the money the question was whether the trustee was liable. The Court of Appeal held that the trustee had employed the stock-broker in the ordinary course of business and in circumstances where it was reasonably necessary to employ. The appointment had been made reasonably and, therefore, the trustee was not liable when the stockbroker absconded with the money.

It was also clear that once the trustee did delegate his duties to the agent, he was under a duty to supervise the activities of the agent. The trustee was not allowed to sit back and assume that the agent was executing the function that had been delegated to him. For example, in *Rowland* v *Witherden*[6] the management of the trust had been placed in the hands of a solicitor who misapplied the trust property. In short, the trustees had failed to invest the money and lend money by way of mortgage despite giving the trustees assurances that they would do so. The court held that the trustees were liable to replace the loss, on the grounds that they failed to oversee that the solicitor had indeed carried out the functions that were delegated to him.

Principles of delegation under the Trustee Act 1925

The principles of delegation pre-1925 presented a fairly high standard in relation to the question of delegation. The incorporation of the principle of prudency meant that the trustee's conduct would be decided by what would be expected of a reasonable prudent man of business. The Trustee Act 1925 enacted a statutory right to delegate the functions of trusteeship to an agent. The Trustee Act 1925 was a consolidating statute and the expectation was that it would consolidate the existing law rather than revolutionise it. As for consolidating the common law of delegation, nothing could be further from the truth. In the words of Maugham J in *Re Vickery*,[7] 'it is hardly too much to say that [the Trustee Act 1925] revolutionises the position of a trustee . . . so far as regards the employment of agents. He is no longer required to do any actual work himself, but he may employ a solicitor or other agent to do it, whether there is any real necessity or not.'[8]

The Trustee Act 1925 enacted s. 23 and s. 30, and in doing so, set the grounds for what was to be the most criticised sections in the Act and fuelled a debate on the adequacy of trustee delegation for the remainder of the twentieth century. Section 23 addressed the question of whether the trustee could delegate his functions to an agent. Section 23 allowed the trustee to delegate in quite general terms and concluded that the trustee would not be liable for the acts of the agent if employed in good faith. Section 30 addressed the question of the liability of the trustee for the acts of the agent. The need for s. 30 did appear to be rather puzzling in light of the fact that s. 23 made it quite clear that if the agent was appointed in good faith then the trustee would not be liable. Nevertheless, s. 30 made it possible for the trustee to be responsible for the acts of the

---

[6] (1851) 3 Mac. & G 568.
[7] [1931] 1 Ch. 572.
[8] [1931] 1 Ch. 572 at 581.

agent is they were directly a result of the trustee's 'wilful default'. The relationship between ss. 23 and 30 fell to be decided in *Re Vickery* where an executor, in the course of winding up a small estate, appointed a solicitor. Unknown to the executor, the solicitor had been twice suspended from practice. The beneficiaries, when they established this fact, asked for a new solicitor to be appointed. The executor failed to appoint a new solicitor and when the solicitor absconded with the trust money, the beneficiaries sought to make the executor liable for the loss to the estate. Maugham J found that the executor was not liable for the loss, on the grounds that the executor had appointed the solicitor in good faith. Good faith, being a subjective criterion, only required proof of honesty and the executor did honestly believe at the time of the appointment that the solicitor was able and competent to carry out the work. As for his subsequent refusal to appoint a new solicitor, the executor was on the understanding that the solicitor would indeed fulfil his obligations and therefore was not guilty of wilful default. Maugham J equated wilful default with conscious wrongdoing, meaning intending to commit a breach of his duty, of being recklessly careless, in the sense of not caring whether his acts or omissions amounted to a breach of duty.[9] In the circumstances, the executor had been assured by the solicitor that he would deal with the estate effectively. The net effect of ss. 23 and 30 and the decision in *Re Vickery*[10] was to set a very low standard of care in the appointment and supervision of an agent. Provided that the agent was appointed in good faith, something that could be done by an honest fool, then the trustee would not liable unless he consciously became aware of the impropriety of the agent's acts. The matter was clearly seen as unsatisfactory by the Law Commission.[11]

Principles of delegation under the Trustee Act 2000

The present rules on trustee delegation are to be found in Part IV of the Trustee Act 2000. Three important sections in Part IV are ss. 11, 22 and 23.

KEY STATUTE

Sections 11, 22 and 23 of the Trustee Act 2000 (The trustee's power to delegate)

11(1) Subject to the provisions of this Part, the trustees of a trust may authorise any person to exercise any or all of their delegable functions as their agent.

(2) In the case of a trust other than a charitable trust, the trustees' delegable functions consist of any function other than –

(a) any function relating to whether or in what way any assets of the trust should be distributed,

(b) any power to decide whether any fees or other payment due to be made out of the trust funds should be made out of income or capital,

(c) any power to appoint a person to be a trustee of the trust, or

(d) any power conferred by any other enactment or the trust instrument which permits the trustees to delegate any of their functions or to appoint a person to act as a nominee or custodian.

▶

---

[9] This definition was borrowed from *Re City Fire Equitable Insurance Co Ltd* [1925] Ch. 407 where Romer J was considering the liability of a director at common law.

[10] [1931] 1 Ch. 572.

[11] The Law Commission Consultation paper No. 146: *'Trustee's Powers and Duties'*.

22(1) While the agent, nominee or custodian continues to act for the trust, the trustees –

(a) keep under review the arrangements under which the agent, nominee or custodian acts and how those arrangements are being put into effect,

(b) if circumstances make it appropriate to do so, must consider whether there is a need to exercise any power of intervention that they have, and

(c) if they consider that there is a need to exercise such a power, must do so.

23(1) A trustee is not liable for any act or default of the agent, nominee or custodian unless he has failed to comply with the duty of care applicable to him, under paragraph 3 of Schedule 1 –

(a) when entering into the arrangements under which the person acts as agent, nominee or custodian, or

(b) when carrying out his duties under section 22.

Section 11 of the Trustee Act 2000 confers a very wide power of delegation to trustees and provides that they can delegate any or all of their delegable functions to an agent. In the case of non-charitable trust the trustee's delegable functions consist of any function except for four. These are:

- any function relating to whether or in what way any assets of the trust should be distributed;
- any power to decide whether any fees or other payment due to be made out of the trust funds should be made out of income or capital;
- any power to appoint a person to be a trustee of the trust; or
- any power conferred by any other enactment or the trust instrument which permits the trustee to delegate any of their functions to appoint a person to act as a nominee or custodian.

In the case of charitable trusts, the trustee's delegable functions consist of:

- any function consisting of carrying out a decision that the trustees have taken;
- any function relating to the investment of assets subject to the trust (including, in the case of land held as an investment, managing the land and creating or disposing of an interest in the land);
- any function relating to the raising of funds for the trust other than by means of profits of a trade which is an integral part of carrying out the trust's charitable purpose;
- any other function prescribed by an order made by the Secretary of State.

The Trustee Act 2000 allows a trustee to distribute both his ministerial duties as well as his ministerial discretions. The only exceptions are where, for example, the discretion relates to the distribution of the trust property or the appointment of new or custodian trustees. In such cases it is only the appointed trustees that can perform those functions. In the context of charitable trusts, the power to delegate is much more restrictive. Whilst the trustees may delegate functions, such as the collection and generation of income for charity, they cannot delegate their functions in relation to the application of income for charitable purposes. The role of the charitable trustees is simply too integral and important for such to be delegated to another.

The trustees have a very broad power of delegation under s. 11 and can delegate on such terms as they think fit. However, when it comes to the delegation of an administrative function, for example, the delegation of investment decisions, trustees are subject to s. 15 of the Trustee Act 2000. Section 15(1) requires the terms of the agreement which authorises the delegation to be put in writing or at least to be evidenced in writing. This agreement, which is otherwise known as the 'policy statement' must give guidance as to how the functions should be exercised and should also seek an undertaking from the agent that such agent will secure compliance with the policy statement. In a typical example, where the trust settles property for the benefit of beneficiaries in succession – for example, for A for life and thereafter for B – the policy statement must refer to the standard investment criteria in s. 4 of the Act, as well as requiring the investments to provide a balance between income and capital growth for the life tenant and remainderman.[12]

Section 12 of the Trustee Act 2000 covers who can be appointed an agent. In general there are no restrictions on the persons who may be appointed as agents, but it does prevent the appointment of a beneficiary as an agent. The rule preventing a beneficiary from acting as an agent is to avoid such a trustee from putting his own interests ahead of those of other beneficiaries. The only exception to this is a beneficiary entitled under a trust of land, for example, a life tenant of the land. In such cases s. 9 of the Trusts of Land and Appointment of Trustees Act 1996 allows the trustees to delegate to a beneficiary any of their functions as trustees which relate to the land. This is a common-sense and practical exception where, for example, land is settled for A for life and thereafter for B, it is A who has occupation of the land. The section does not, however, allow the trustees to delegate any function relating to the proceeds from any dealings with the land. Where two or more persons are appointed, s. 12 requires that they exercise their function jointly. Apart from these restrictions, a trustee can delegate to another trustee, nominee or custodian.

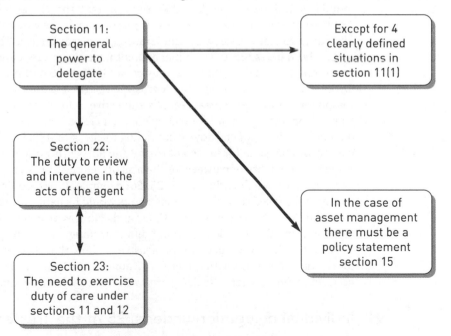

Figure 18.1 Delegation of trustee duties and discretions

---

[12] The standard investment criteria in s. 4 of the Trustee Act are considered in Chapter 16.

Sections 21, 22 and 23 provide for the review by the trustee of the appointment of agents, nominees and custodians and also the liability of the trustee for the acts of such persons employed. Collectively these sections repeal ss. 23 and 30 of the Trustee Act 1925. In doing so, they impose an objective standard of care on trustees rather than the very low subjective standards imposed under the old law. Section 21 identifies the circumstances when ss. 22 and 23 apply. Basically, these sections will apply when the trustee appoints agents, nominees and custodians under the Act or under similar provisions in the trust instrument.

Section 22 of the Act imposes upon trustees who delegate their functions to agents, nominees and custodians a duty consisting of three parts. Firstly, the trustees are required to keep under review the terms of the appointment and make sure that the person who is appointed is suitable for the purposes for which he is employed. Once the agent is appointed, the trustee cannot simply sit back and assume that the agent will continue to execute the terms of the delegation. There is a proactive duty on the trustee to ensure that the agent remains suitable at all times. Secondly, trustees are required to consider whether to intervene in the appointment if the circumstances make it appropriate to do so. Finally, trustees are expected to intervene if the circumstances require intervention. In so far as the delegation of administrative functions are concerned, s. 22(2) of the Trustee Act 2000 requires the trustees to consider whether there is any need to revise the policy statement, and if so, to do so. Furthermore, the trustees are under a duty to make sure that the policy statement is being complied with.

With regard to the liability for the acts of an agent employed, the matter is addressed by s. 23 of the Trustee Act 2000. Section 23 deals with the question of liability both in respect of the initial appointment of the trustee and the subsequent supervision by the trustee. Section 23 provides that a trustee will not be liable for the acts of agents, nominees and custodians, provided that the trustee complies with the general duty of care found in s. 1 of the Trustee Act 2000. You will recall that the general duty of care imposes a duty on trustees to act with care as is reasonable in the circumstances, making special allowance for the trustee's special knowledge and expertise. The general duty of care applies both in respect to the initial appointment of the agent and his subsequent supervision. Unlike ss. 23 and 30 of the Trustee Act 1925, s. 23 of the Trustee Act 2000 imposes an objective standard of care on the trustee. The trustee must demonstrate that he acted reasonably in the circumstances. His subjective state of mind is irrelevant. Thus, if a trustee appoints an agent, for example a financial adviser, honestly believing him to be qualified to give financial advice but failing to check that he is indeed a professional, the trustee will be liable for breach of trust if the adviser is not what he claims to be. In this respect, the liability of trustees for the acts of their agents is very similar to the common law principles of delegation pre-1925. For example, it was observed in that context that trustees who failed to supervise their agents would be liable, although trustees appointed agents in the ordinary course of business and acting as prudent businessmen would not.[13] However, one thing which is clearly different under the principles of delegation after 2000 is that there is no need for the trustee to show that there was any reasonable need for the delegation in the first place. The power to delegate is a general one and there is no need to demonstrate the delegation was reasonable in the first place.

Individual delegation under s. 25 of the Trustee Act 1925

In addition to the general power to delegate under the Trustee Act 2000, trustees have an individual power of delegation under s. 25 of the Trustee Act 1925. The section allows a

---

[13] *Speight* v *Gaunt* (1883) 9 App. Cas. 1.

trustee to delegate his duties and discretions by power of attorney for a period not exceeding 12 months. There are, however, no restrictions on the number of delegations that can be made under the section. The original intention behind the section was to allow a trustee to delegate in circumstances where he was going to be abroad for some period of time, but equally it allowed a trustee to delegate in circumstances where the trust property was abroad and the trustee was in the UK.

> **KEY STATUTE**
>
> **S. 25 of the Trustee Act 1925 as amended by the Trustee Delegation Act 1999 (Delegation of trustee's functions by power of attorney)**
>
> (1) Notwithstanding any rule of law or equity to the contrary, a trustee may, by power of attorney, delegate the execution or exercise of all or any of the trusts, powers and discretions vested in him as trustee either alone or jointly with any other person or persons.
>
> (2) A delegation under this section –
>
> (a) commences as provided by the instrument creating the power or, if the instrument makes no provision as to the commencement of the delegation, with the date of the execution of the instrument by the donor; and
>
> (b) continues for a period of twelve months or any shorter period provided by the instrument creating the power.
>
> (3) The persons who may be donees of a power of attorney under this section include a trust corporation.

Section 25(1) requires not only that the delegation must be made by power of attorney, but also that the trustee give written notice of the delegation to each of the other trustees and to any other person who have the power to appoint new trustees.[14] The written notice must state the terms of the power of attorney including its commencement date and the duration. It must also give reasons for the delegation and clearly identify the donee of the power of appointment. Once the power of attorney is created, the donee will be able to exercise the functions of the delegating trustee; however, the delegating trustee will liable for the acts of the donee. In this respect, it may be asked what purpose there is in delegating under s. 25(1) of the Trustee Act 1925 when the delegating trustee remains liable for the acts of the donee. The truth of the matter is that the section is not a widely invoked compared to the other statutory powers of delegation. Section 25(1) was further amended by the Trustee Delegation Act 1999 and allows for the delegation to be made in favour of any person.

The power of maintenance

> **APPLYING THE LAW**
>
> Mary is entitled to £20,000 under a trust created in her favour by her father. Mary is 14 years of age; her father died last year and her mother is on a very modest income. Mary is desperate for money to pay for her school fees and wishes to know whether the trustees can give her some money.

---

[14] Section 25(4) Trustee Act 1925.

The power of maintenance confers upon the trustee the right to pay income arising from a trust fund to an infant beneficiary. In the absence of such a power a trustee is not authorised to pay any income to an infant beneficiary on the grounds that a beneficiary under the age of 18 is not capable of giving a valid receipt for the income. However, trust law recognises that in certain circumstances an infant beneficiary may need recourse to income during his or her infancy.[15] For example, take an infant beneficiary whose worldly welfare is dependant on a trust fund. In such a case, it may well be that income from the trust fund is needed for maintenance and education. The power to release income from the trust fund will often be expressly provided in the trust instrument; however, failure to include it is not fatal as there is a power conferred by statute.

Express powers of maintenance

A professionally drafted trust instrument may contain an express power of maintenance. Questions often arise as to the construction to be given to an express power of maintenance. Sometimes, what may appear to be a power to maintain an infant during his infancy may indeed be construed as an imperative trust to apply the income during the child's infancy. For example, in **Wilson v Turner**[16] Jessel MR explained that 'a trust to apply the whole or part as the trustees may think fit of the income for the maintenance of the children is an obligatory trust and compels the trustees to maintain the children where the trust occurs in the marriage settlement to which the father is a party'.[17] In **Re Peel**[18] the trust instrument gave a fund 'upon trust to pay or apply the same in manner thereinafter provided to or for the benefit of the children'. Given the imperative language in the trust instrument, the court construed this as a trust and not a power. In other words, the trustees were obliged, and not merely conferred discretion, to use the income for the maintenance of the children.

The court will not interfere with the exercise of an express power of maintenance, provided it is exercised in the best interest of the infant. The trustee must, however, show that he did exercise discretion rather than make income payments as and when they accrue. For example, in **Wilson v Turner**[19] property was settled for Mrs Wilson for life and thereafter for her children. The trustees were conferred an express power of maintenance where, after Mrs Wilson's decease, they used to give payment to Mr Wilson (the father), without making any decisions as to why it was being handed over. In such circumstances, the court held that the trustees had failed to exercise any discretion at all. The money was recoverable from the father's estate. Equally, a trustee who simply fails to exercise a discretion or refuse to exercise a discretion by not making any income payments at all will find that the beneficiaries can apply to court for an appropriate order. One thing is clear, however: where a trustee does exercise the power in the interests of the infant, it does not matter that one of the parents of the infant may incidentally benefit from the exercise of the power. The matter is neatly illustrated in **Fuller v Evans**[20] where trustees exercised the power of maintenance by paying the school fees of children. It so happened that the children's father was required to pay such fees by reason of a consent order in divorce

---

[15] The paternal concerns of infants was recognised by equity as long ago as 1860 in the Lord Cranworth's Act which authorised payments of income to infants.
[16] (1883) 22 Ch. D 521.
[17] (1883) 22 Ch. D 521 at 515 at 525.
[18] [1936] Ch. 161.
[19] (1883) 22 Ch. D 521.
[20] [2000] 1 All ER 636.

proceedings. The question was whether the trustees were precluded from paying the school fees in circumstances where it would confer a benefit on the father. The court held that, provided the trustees honestly considered that the exercise of the power would be in the best interests of the children then the fact that it conferred an incidental benefit on the father was not crucial. Lightman J said: 'I find it very difficult to read the settlement as paralysing the trustees in this situation, barring them from exercising the powers conferred on them merely because a by-product of their exercise is an advantage to the settlor . . . if the trustees reach the conclusion that it is in the best interests of the beneficiaries to make such provisions out of the trust funds, they are free to do so.'[21]

The statutory power of maintenance in s. 31 Trustee Act 1925

The fact that the trust instrument does not contain an express power of investment is not fatal, as the Trustee Act confers a statutory power of maintenance.

KEY STATUTE

S. 31 of the Trustee Act 1925 (The power of maintenance)

(1) Where any property is held by trustees in trust for any person for any interest whatsoever, whether vested or contingent, then, subject to any prior interests or charges affecting that property –

(i)   during the infancy of any such person, if his interest so long continues, the trustees may, at their sole discretion, pay to his parent or guardian, if any, or otherwise apply for or towards his maintenance, education, or benefit, the whole or such part, if any, of the income of that property as may, in all the circumstances, be reasonable, whether or not there is –

(a) any other fund applicable to the same purpose; or

(b) any person bound by law to provide for his maintenance or education, and

(ii) if such person on attaining the age of eighteen years has not a vested interest in such income, the trustees shall thenceforth pay the income of that property and of any accretion thereto under subsection (2) of this section to him, until he either attains a vested interest therein or dies, or until failure of his interest . . .

The statutory power of maintenance allows the trustee to pay income to an infant beneficiary regardless of whether the interest of that infant is vested or contingent. Thus a trust of £1000 for the benefit of a beneficiary on him attaining the age of 25 creates a contingent interest. The trustees are not precluded in making a maintenance payment in such a trust when the beneficiary is still an infant. However, it must be observed that the statutory power of maintenance can be modified or even excluded by a contrary intention. For example, in **Re Turner's Will Trusts**[22] a trust entitled the beneficiary a vested interest on him attaining the age of 28 years. At the age of 24 the question arose whether he could ask for maintenance from the trust fund. The Court of Appeal held that since the settlor had directed that the income be accumulated, there was no right to the income. A similar result was achieved in **Re Erskine's Settlement Trusts**[23] where a settlor created

---

[21] [2000] 1 All ER 636 at 638.
[22] [1937] Ch. 15.
[23] [1971] 1 WLR 162.

a settlement for his grandson. The grandson was entitled to the capital on him attaining the age of 22; however, the settlor expressly required that the income on the capital should be accumulated until the grandson attained the age of 22 and that the power of maintenance should not apply. The court, following *Re Turner* held that the grandson was not entitled to any income.

Exercising the statutory power of maintenance

There are a number of key features in the statutory power of maintenance in s. 31(1). The power is only exercisable in favour of an infant beneficiary who is entitled to the income. The section makes it clear that the trustees must have regard to circumstances and see whether it is reasonable under those circumstances. It does not matter whether the interest of the beneficiary is vested or contingent. Furthermore, the power of maintenance can be exercised even where there is some other fund applicable for the same purpose or where there is some other person who is responsible for the maintenance of the infant. The income must be applied for the maintenance, education and benefit of the infant. Thus, the payment of income can cover a vast range of things, including the payment of school fees,[24] the purchase of a house[25] as well as payment of the beneficiary's debts.[26] It has already been observed in *Wilson v Turner*[27] that the trustees must consciously exercise the discretion rather than just handing over the income as and when it accrues on the trust fund. On the other hand, where the trustees do honestly believe that the payment will be for the benefit of the infant, they should not be deterred by the fact that there may be some other person who might or should be providing for the infant. The matter is illustrated in *Re Lofthouse*[28] where a female infant was entitled contingently on her attaining 21, or marrying, to a fund of which her deceased mother had been tenant for life. The trustees had power 'to apply all or any part' of the income for her maintenance and education. In considering the exercise of the power of maintenance, Cotton LJ:

> said that the trustees in exercising their discretion must consider what is most for the benefit of the infant. In considering that, they should take into account that the father is not of sufficient ability properly to maintain his child, and that it is for her benefit not merely to allow him enough to pay her actual expenses, but to enable him to give her a better education and a better home. They must not be deterred from doing what is for her benefit because it is also a benefit to the father, though, on the other hand, they must not act with a view to his benefit apart from hers.[29]

Accumulations of income and attaining majority

Whilst the statutory power allows the payment of income to an infant beneficiary, one question which arises is: what should be done with the income that is accruing on the trust property during the infancy of the beneficiary? The answer to this is found in s. 31(2), which explains not only what should be done with the income but also how that income is to be held during the course of the trust. The subsection is extremely complex,

[24] *Fuller* v *Evans* [2000] 1 All ER 636.
[25] *Re Heyworth's Contingent Reversionary Interest* [1956] Ch. 364.
[26] *Re Spencer* [1935] Ch. 533.
[27] (1883) 22 Ch. D 521.
[28] (1885) 29 Ch. D 921.
[29] (1885) 29 Ch. D 921. at 932.

but the matter can be explained as follows. Firstly, as to income which is accruing during the infancy of the beneficiary, the subsection requires the trustees to accumulate the income. Such accumulated income is then available for maintenance throughout the infancy of the beneficiary. The trustees may or not exercise the power of maintenance. As to what happens with the accumulations of income, this depends on whether the beneficiary has a vested interest in the trust or a contingent interest. Where his interest is vested, that is, there are no conditions on his right to terminate the trust at 18 years of age, the beneficiary is entitled to the accumulations of income from that day onwards as well as income that accrues from that day. Such a beneficiary can, of course, terminate the trust if he so chooses.[30] Where the interest of the beneficiary is contingent, for example, on attaining the age of 21 years, the accumulations of income are treated as if they are part of the capital. Such accumulations will only be payable when the contingency is satisfied. Thus, where a beneficiary has to attain 21 years of age, the entitlement to the accumulations will arise when the beneficiary is 21 years. The beneficiary will be entitled to the intermediate income from the age of 18 years unless there is a contrary intention to the effect that the intermediate income must be accumulated throughout the contingency.[31]

The power of advancement

Whereas the power of maintenance allows the trustees to pay income to an infant beneficiary, the power of advancement allows them to give some of the capital to the beneficiary. The power is not dependent on the age of the beneficiary. Provided that the beneficiary is entitled to the capital, the trustees can pay some of that capital by way of advancement for the benefit of the beneficiary.

APPLYING THE LAW

Harry is entitled £120,000 under a trust created in his favour by his father. However, the terms of the trust provide that he should qualify as a solicitor before he is entitled to the money. Harry has just completed his law degree at university and now wishes to study for the professional course needed to qualify as a solicitor. He has very little funds to finance the course and wishes to know whether he can get £10,000 from the trustees.

In most professionally drafted trust instruments there will often be an express power of advancement; however, given the extent of the statutory power of advancement in s. 32 of the Trustee Act 1925, it is not necessary to include an express power unless the settlor wishes to modify the power in s. 32. If the settlor does incorporate a provision in the trust instrument which is inconsistent with the statutory power, then the statutory power will be deemed as being excluded. For example, in **Re Evans's Settlement**[32] the trust instrument authorised the trustees to advance up to £5000. Stamp J held that, since the trustees could only advance £5000, a sum much less than the amount possible under

---

[30] *Saunders* v *Vautier* (1841) 4 Beav. 115.
[31] For example, the conclusion reached in *Re Turner Will Trusts* [1936] Ch. 15, discussed above. See also, *Re McGeorge* [1963] Ch. 544.
[32] [1967] 1 WLR 1294.

the statutory power, the statutory power had been excluded by implication. A settlor can, of course, extend the statutory power of advancement by allowing a sum greater than the statutory sum to be advanced.

KEY STATUTE

S. 32 of the Trustee Act 1925: The power of advancement

(1) Trustees may at any time or times pay or apply any capital money subject to a trust, for the advancement or benefit, in such manner as they may, in their absolute discretion, think fit, of any person entitled to the capital of the trust property or of any share thereof, whether absolutely or contingently on his attaining any specified age or on the occurrence of any other event, or subject to a gift over on his death under any specified age or on the occurrence of any other event, and whether in possession or in remainder or reversion, and such payment or application may be made notwithstanding that the interest of such person is liable to be defeated by the exercise of a power of appointment or revocation, or to be diminished by the increase of the class to which he belongs:

Provided that –

(a) the money so paid or applied for the advancement or benefit of any person shall not exceed altogether in amount one-half of the presumptive or vested share or interest of that person in the trust property; and

(b) if that person is or becomes absolutely and indefeasibly entitled to a share in the trust property the money so paid or applied shall be brought into account as part of such share; and

(c) no such payment or application shall be made so as to prejudice any person entitled to any prior life or other interest, whether vested or contingent, in the money paid or applied unless such person is in existence and of full age and consents in writing to such payment or application.

The nature of s. 32 Trustee Act 1925

The power of advancement in s. 32 is only exercisable in circumstances where the beneficiary is entitled to the capital. For example, where a trust is created in favour of Barry for life and thereafter for Harry, Barry would not be entitled to an advancement under s. 32 of the Trustee Act because he is not entitled to the capital sum. Barry's interest is only in the income for the duration of his life. Harry, however, is entitled to the capital and, therefore, entitled to an advancement. Such an advancement, if possible, will of course affect the income with is payable to Barry. In such circumstances, the section requires the consent of Barry before such an advancement can be made. This matter is discussed in more detail below. It should be further noted that the power is exercisable even when the beneficiary's interest is contingent or otherwise liable to be defeated by the exercise of a power of appointment. For example, if the beneficiary must reach a specified age before he or she is entitled to the trust property, the power of advancement remains available to that beneficiary should the trustees decide to exercise it. It does not matter that the beneficiary never satisfies the contingency or the interest if defeated later on by the exercise of a power of appointment. The trustees cannot ask for the return of any money advanced should the interest be defeated.[33] In this respect making an advancement to a contingently entitled beneficiary may well defeat the interests of other potential beneficiaries who may become absolutely and indefeasibly entitled to the capital.

The meaning of advancement

Perhaps the most important aspect of s. 32 of the Trustee Act 1925 is the meaning of advancement. In other words, when will the trustee be justified in making advancement? The section requires that the money be applied for the advancement or benefit of the beneficiary. The exact meaning of these words fell to be decided by the House of Lords in *Pilkington v IRC*[34] where the trustees attempted to advance a sum of money in order to create new trusts for the beneficiary, thereby avoiding the incidence of death duties. Lord Radcliffe explained that advancement meant the 'use of money which will improve the material situation of the beneficiary'.[35] There must be some benefit in the form of establishing the particular beneficiary in life. A number of good examples can be provided where the advancement has been for the material benefit of the beneficiary. In *Re Williams' Will Trust*[36] advancement was made to buy business premises for a doctor. In *Roper-Curzon v Roper-Curzon*[37] advancement was made to a beneficiary who wished to pursue a career as a barrister. Other examples, include setting someone up in trade[38] and payment for the education of a beneficiary.[39]

An advancement under s. 32 of the Trustee Act 1925 which seeks to improve the situation of somebody other than the beneficiary will be an improper exercise of the power. In such circumstances the trustees will be liable to repay the loss to the trust estate or require the person receiving the money to return it to the trust estate. In *Molyneux v Fletcher*[40] trustees advanced some money to a beneficiary so that she could pay off her father's debt. To make matters worse, the debts were owed by the father to one of the trustees. The court held that this was an improper exercise of the power of advancement. In *Re Pauling's Settlement Trusts*[41] trustees were holding a fund for a wife for her life and thereafter for her children. The trust deed contained an express power of advancement. The children's father, who lived beyond his means, sought to claim some of the trust fund from the trustees vis-à-vis his children. The trustees made a number of advancements to the children; however, the money was used for different purposes, including the purchase of a house and another to pay off the mother's overdraft. When the validity of these advancements was questioned, the trustees argued that they had given the money to the children and what then subsequently happened with that money was not a concern of the trustees. The Court of Appeal rejected this argument on the grounds that the trustees were under a duty to see that the advancement was for the benefit of the beneficiary and that the money advanced was applied for the purpose stipulated. The court explained that:

---

[33] *Hardy v Shaw* [1975] 2 All ER 1052.
[34] [1964] AC 612.
[35] [1964] AC 612 at 635.
[36] [1953] Ch. 138.
[37] (1871) LR 11 Eq. 452.
[38] *Re Kershaw's Trusts* (1868) LR 6 Eq. 322.
[39] *Re Breed's Will* (1875) 1 Ch. D 226.
[40] [1898] 1 QB 648.
[41] [1964] Ch. 303.

the power can be exercised only if it is for the benefit of the child or remoter issue to be advanced or, as was said during argument, it is thought to be 'a good thing' for the advanced person to have a share of capital before his or her due time . . . A power of advancement can be exercised only if there is some good reason for it. That good reason must be beneficial to the person to be advanced; it cannot be exercised capriciously, or with some other benefit in view.[42]

It is relatively clear that the advancement under s. 32 of the Trustee Act 1925 must be for the material benefit of the beneficiary. The case law requires some tangible material benefit, such as education of the beneficiary or setting the beneficiary in trade or business. A case which does not necessary fit into the definition of material benefit is *Re Clore's Settlement Trusts*,[43] where a request was made for an advancement by a beneficiary who felt a moral obligation to donate to charity. The court sanctioned the advancement primarily on the ground that the payment out of the trust fund would relieve the beneficiary from having to withdraw the money from his own funds. The court explained that the beneficiary must have a genuine moral obligation to provide for charity. On the facts of the case, the beneficiary was entitled to a substantial sum of money because he genuinely felt obliged to provide for charity.

An advancement under s. 32 of the Trustee Act 1925 must be for the benefit of the beneficiary. One question which has arisen in the case law is whether an advancement can be made in order to resettle trust property on trusts which are more beneficial from a fiscal or some other point of view. In *Re Wills' Will Trust* Upjohn J explained that 'trustees cannot under the guise of making an advancement create new trusts merely because they think they can devise better trusts than those which the settlor has chosen to declare. They must honestly have in mind some particular circumstances making it right to apply funds for the benefit of an object or objects of the power.'[44]

The provisos in s. 32 Trustee Act 1925

There are three main provisos to s. 32 of the Trustee Act 1925. The first proviso is that the trustee must not advance more that one-half of the presumptive share of a beneficiary. For example, if a beneficiary is entitled to £10,000 under a trust, the maximum amount that can be advanced is £5000. One question which has arisen in this context is whether the trustees, having advanced up to one-half of the presumptive share of the beneficiary, can make further advancements on the grounds that the value of the capital has risen. Suppose a beneficiary is entitled to £50,000 and receives £25,000 in the form of an advancement. If the remaining £25,000 increases in value, can the beneficiary ask for further advancement on the grounds that the total value of the capital has gone up? The matter fell to be decided in *Re Marquess of Abergavenny's Estate Act Trusts*[45] where trustees had advanced the maximum one-half presumptive share to the beneficiary. When the beneficiary asked for a further advancement, the trustee sought the direction of the court. In the High Court Goulding J held that the trustees did not have any further power to make an advancement in circumstances where the value of the capital had risen. On the other hand, where the trustees do not advance the maximum half presumptive share,

---

[42] [1964] Ch. 303 at 333.
[43] [1966] 1 WLR 955.
[44] [1959] Ch. 1 at 14; see N. Hassall, 'Power of Advancement: How Far Can Pilkington be Stretched?' (2007) PCB 282.
[45] [1981] 2 All ER 643.

there is nothing stopping them from making further advances should the capital increase in value.

The second proviso under s. 32 of the Trustee Act 1925 is that the advancement must be brought into account when the beneficiary becomes absolutely entitled to the trust fund. For example, suppose James and Harry are entitled to £100,000 equally on attaining the age of 30 years and the trustees have made an advancement to Harry of £25,000. When James and Harry attain the age of 30 years, James will be entitled to £50,000 and Harry £25,000 on the grounds that he has already received the remaining £25,000 by way of an earlier advancement.

APPLYING THE LAW

A trust fund worth £200,000 is settled in favour of Jason for life and thereafter for Julie absolutely. Julie wished to start her own business and asks the trustees whether she is entitled to any part of the trust fund.

Can the trustees advance any capital to Julie, and if so, what should they make sure before they advance the money to her?

The third and final proviso under s. 32 of the Trustee Act is that no payment shall be made which will prejudice the interests of any prior beneficiary. This proviso principally deals with the situation where there is a prior life interest in the trust. For example, suppose that there is a trust of £100,000 for Emily for life and thereafter for William absolutely. William could potentially ask for an advancement of £50,000; however, such an advancement will have a knock on effect on Emily. Instead of receiving income on £100,000, Emily would only receive income on £50,000. In such circumstances the trustees cannot make any advancement to William unless there is written consent by Emily.

Reforming the statutory power of advancement and maintenance

In May 2011 the Law Commission published a Consultation Paper calling for the reform of the statutory power of maintenance and advancement found in s. 31 and s. 32 of the Trustee Act 1925. The Supplementary Consultation Paper is part and parcel of the wider reform relating to intestacy and family provision claims on death. The Law Commission calls for widening the statutory power of advancement in s. 32 of the Trustee Act 1925 and reforming s. 31 of the same Act.

KEY STATUTE

Intestacy and Family Provision Claims on Death: Sections 31 and 32 of the Trustee Act 1925

A Supplementary Consultation Paper: Consultation Paper No. 191 (Supplementary) 26 May 2011
(Edited version)

PART 1 INTRODUCTION

Section 32 of the Trustee Act 1925 enables trustees to 'pay or apply' capital 'for the advancement or benefit' of a beneficiary who has a recognised entitlement to the capital of the trust fund but is not entitled to have it paid over outright. For example, it may be appropriate to release capital for the benefit of a young child who is a beneficiary under the statutory trusts created on a parent's intestacy. However, the scope of section 32 is limited: the trustees can use only one-half of the beneficiary's capital share in this way.

1.7 We proposed removing that one-half limit in relation to the statutory trusts arising on intestacy for three main reasons.

First, it would bring the provisions which apply to such trusts into line with what we understand to be standard practice in drafting wills and lifetime trusts.

Secondly, it would reduce administrative difficulties in calculating and keeping within the one-half limit. Thirdly, it would increase trustees' flexibility and reduce the need for court applications to be made in order to permit advances.

1.8 Statistics on the size of intestate estates suggest that they are often of relatively modest size compared to estates where the deceased left a will: analysis carried out by HM Revenue & Customs for the Consultation Paper shows that 64% of intestate estates have a net value of less than £100,000, half of these being less than £25,000. We considered that in such cases there might be particularly good reasons to advance the whole fund to the beneficiaries outright to simplify the administration of the trust or to make provision for them at a time when it may be particularly needed . . .

1.12 Secondly, we felt that we should consult again as to whether it would be appropriate to reform section 31, again for all trusts. Section 31 includes restrictions on the trustees' power to use income for the benefit of trust beneficiaries. In the context of a consultation on a general relaxation of the restrictions on trustees' power to make payments of capital under section 32, we think it appropriate to examine again section 31. This is supported by the fact that, as one consultee noted, it is also common to modify the effect of section 31 when drafting wills and trust documents . . .

PART 3 REFORM

INTRODUCTION

3.1 In this Part we ask consultees to comment on reforms to sections 31 and 32 of the Trustee Act 1925 and on transitional provisions for those reforms.

3.2 We begin by considering reform of section 32, having already made a provisional proposal on that topic in the Consultation Paper.

SECTION 32: THE RESTRICTION TO ONE-HALF OF A BENEFICIARY'S SHARE

The proposal in the Consultation Paper

3.3 We remain of the view we expressed in the Consultation Paper that it would be appropriate to amend the section 32 power so that it is exercisable over the whole of a beneficiary's prospective share under the statutory trusts. We expressed that view only in the context of a discussion of the trusts arising on intestacy, but the arguments in favour of reform are relevant to other trusts.

3.4 While beneficiaries are under 18 there are many reasons why this increased flexibility would help to support them in the most appropriate way, particularly if the trust fund is small. Indeed it may be appropriate for the whole fund to be used for those purposes, in which case it can be wound up, thus saving administration expenses.

3.5 This reform will not affect trustees' duties to exercise the power properly. Their use of the power must be for the benefit of the particular beneficiary. It has been said that: This . . . follows from a consideration of the fact that the parties to a settlement intend the normal trusts to take effect, and that a power of advancement be exercised only if there is some good reason for it. That good reason must be beneficial to the person to be advanced; it cannot be exercised capriciously or with some other benefit in view. The trustees, before exercising the power, have to weigh on the one side the benefit to the proposed advancee, and on the other hand the rights of those who are or may hereafter become interested under the trusts of the settlement. (*Re Pauling's ST* [1964] Ch 303, 333 by Willmer LJ.)

Miscellaneous powers of trustees

The power of sale

Section 6(1) of the Trusts of Land and Appointment of Trustees Act 1996 confers upon a trustee of land all the powers of an absolute owner including the power to sell the land. Section 12 of the Trustee Act 1925[46] confers upon a trustee a power to sell the whole or part of the trust property at public auction. In relation to property other than land, trustees have the power to sell such property. The power to sell such property may be expressly provided in the trust instrument or it may be implied by operation of some rule. For example, under the rule in *Howe v Lord Dartmouth*[47] trustees have the power to sell property which is of a wasting, non-income or reversionary nature in circumstances when it is settled by will in favour of successive beneficiaries. Indeed, in such a case the power arises from the fact that the trustees are under a duty to maintain a fair balance between the income and the capital entitled to the beneficiaries. Section 16 of the Trustee Act 1925 confers upon trustees a power to sell any property subject to a trust in circumstances when they are authorised to pay capital or apply capital money for any purpose connected with the trust. In *Re Suenson-Taylor's Settlement*[48] the power in s. 16 was confined to instances where the money was required to preserve the trust assets or to make advancement of capital to the beneficiaries. The power does not allow the trustees to raise money on the security of the trust property, thereby allowing them to make further purchases of land by way of investment.

The power to insure

Section 19 of the Trustee Act 1925 confers upon trustees the power to insure the trust property. The section has been substituted by s. 34 of the Trustee Act 2000 and

---

[46] As amended by the Trusts of Land and Appointment of Trustee Act 1996.
[47] (1802) 6 RR 96, discussed in Chapter 14.
[48] [1974] 3 All ER 397.

provides that trustees have the power to insure the trust property and can pay the premiums for such insurance out of the income or capital funds of the trust. Prior to s. 19 of the Trustee Act, there was no power conferred upon trustees to insure the trust property, or a common law obligation on a trustee to insure the trust property. It is still the case that trustees are not under a duty to insure the trust property.[49] The general reluctance on the part of English law to impose a duty to insure the trust property primarily relates to practical problems. In the case where property is settled in favour of a tenant for life and thereafter for someone else, Eve J in *Re McEacharn*[50] held that insurance was not to be paid out of trust money belonging to the tenant for life, but did not decide whether trustees were under a duty to insure. It may well be that there may be no trust funds available from which to insure the trust property. The present position in s. 34 of the Trustee Act 2000 is that a trustee may insure the trust property.

KEY STATUTE

S. 34 of the Trustee Act 2000 (The power to insure)

(1) For section 19 of the [1925 c. 19.] Trustee Act 1925 (power to insure) substitute –

19 Power to insure

(1) A trustee may –

(a) insure any property which is subject to the trust against risks of loss or damage due to any event, and

(b) pay the premiums out of the trust funds.

(2) In the case of property held on a bare trust, the power to insure is subject to any direction given by the beneficiary or each of the beneficiaries –

(a) that any property specified in the direction is not to be insured;

(b) that any property specified in the direction is not to be insured except on such conditions as may be so specified.

(3) Property is held on a bare trust if it is held on trust for –

(a) a beneficiary who is of full age and capacity and absolutely entitled to the property subject to the trust, or (b) beneficiaries each of whom is of full age and capacity and who (taken together) are absolutely entitled to the property subject to the trust.

Although under s. 34 trustees are not under a duty to insure the trust property, they may find themselves liable for breach of trust in circumstances where they have failed to exercise their power to insure when it would have been reasonable to do so. It must be remembered that trustees are under a paramount duty to act in the best interests of their beneficiaries, and if it would have reasonable in the circumstances to insure the trust property, then their omission to exercise the power in s. 34 will be deemed as

---

[49] The Law Commission Consultation Paper No. 146, 'Trustees' Powers and Duties', which led to the enactment of the Trustee Act 2000, did recommend that all trustees should be under a duty to insure the trust property; however, this recommendation did not evidence itself in s. 34 of the Trustee Act 2000.

[50] (1911) 103 LT 900.

unreasonable. Section 19 of the Trustee Act 1925, as substituted by s. 34 of the Trustee Act 2000, however, does not require a trustee to insure the trust property held under a bare trust if the beneficiaries direct that the property subject to the trust is not to be insured. The reason for this exception relates to the fact that under a bare trust the beneficiaries are in a position to terminate the trust. The section defines property as held on a bare trust when the beneficiaries are of full age and absolutely entitled to the trust fund.

The power to give receipts

Section 14 of the Trustee Act 1925 confers upon trustees a power to give receipt for any money security and property which is given to them.

KEY STATUTE

S. 14 of the Trustee Act 1925 (The power to give receipts)

(1) the receipt in writing of a trustee for any money, securities, investments, or other personal property or effects payable, transferable, or deliverable to him under any trust or power shall be a sufficient discharge to the person paying, transferring, or delivering the same and shall effectually exonerate him from seeing to the application or being answerable for any loss or misapplication thereof.

Subsection 2 of s. 14 provides that the general power to give a receipt for money does not affect any other statutory provisions relating to the payment of money to trustees. For example, s. 14 does not alter the fact that under a trust of land, the payment of capital monies must be made to a minimum of two trustees or a trust corporation.[51]

The power to compound liabilities and compromise

Section 15 of the Trustee Act 1925 confers power upon trustees to compound liabilities. This power allows the trustees to pay debts or otherwise entering into some form of a compromise settling the debt or other disputes arising from the trust.

KEY STATUTE

S. 15 of the Trustee Act 1925 (The power to compound liabilities)

(1) A personal representative, or two or more trustees acting together, or, subject to the restrictions imposed in regard to receipts by a sole trustee not being a trust corporation, a sole acting trustee where by the instrument, if any, creating the trust, or by statute, a sole trustee is authorised to execute the trusts and powers reposed in him, may, if and as he or they think fit –

(a) accept any property, real or personal, before the time at which it is made transferable or payable; or

(b) sever and apportion any blended trust funds or property; or

(c) pay or allow any debt or claim on any evidence that he or they think sufficient; or

(d) accept any composition or any security, real or personal, for any debt or for any property, real or personal, claimed; or

▶

---

[51] S. 27(2) Law of Property Act 1925.

> (e) allow any time of payment of any debt; or
>
> (f) compromise, compound, abandon, submit to arbitration, or otherwise settle any debt, account, claim, or thing whatever relating to the testator's or intestate's estate or to the trust;
>
> and for any of those purposes may enter into, give, execute, and do such agreements, instruments of composition or arrangement, releases, and other things as to him or them seem expedient, without being responsible for any loss occasioned by any act or thing so done by him or them [if he has or they have discharged the duty of care set out in section 1(1) of the Trustee Act 2000].

The trustees' power to compromise is neatly illustrated by the Court of Appeal decision in **Re Earl of Strafford**[52] where the Earl of Strafford left his property to beneficiaries entitled successively, that is, one after the other. After a variation of the initial trusts the trusts were transferred to a company, Wrotham Park Settled Estates. Subsequently a dispute arose between the trustees and the beneficiaries with regard to some of the trust property and the allocation of it: In particular, whether some of the property in question belonged to the Earl of Strafford and therefore were part of the variation of the trust. If they did not belong to the Earl they would certainly belong to his wife, the Countess of Strafford. A compromise was reached whereby the beneficiaries of the Countess's will offered to surrender a life interest, providing that the trustees of the Earl's will abandon their claim to the property they initially thought was included in the variation of the Earl's settlement. The Court of Appeal held that the compromise was perfectly justified under s. 15 of the Trustee Act 1925. Megarry VC held that the proposed compromise was within the trustees' power and it did not matter that some of the beneficiaries objected. Buckley LJ explained the matter by commenting that:

> the language of s.15 is, it appears to me, very wide. It would, I think, be undesirable to seek to restrict its operation in any way unless legal principles require this, for it seems to me to be advantageous that trustees should enjoy wide and flexible powers of compromising and settling disputes, always bearing in mind that such a power, however wide, must be exercised with due regard for the interests of those whose interests it is the duty of the trustees to protect. I see nothing in the language of the section to restrict the scope of the power.[53]

It is important to note that the trustees' power to compromise is concerned with external factors affecting the trust and not with internal disputes that may arise between the beneficiaries as to entitlement amongst them. The trustee must show that he has exercised a discretion and has acted in the best interests of the beneficiaries. The statutory power to compromise must be exercised in accordance with the general duty of care that is found in s. 1 of the Trustee Act 2000. Furthermore, in the exercise of the power there is no need for the trustee to show that had there been no compromise then the claim against the trust would certainly have succeeded.[54]

---

[52] [1979] 1 All ER 513.
[53] [1979] 1 All ER 513 at 520.
[54] *Re Ridsdel* [1947] Ch. 597.

Conclusion

This chapter has explored some of the more important powers that are conferred upon trustees in the administration of a trust. Powers confer upon the trustees an authority to act in a particular way; sometimes, they are equated with discretions. Powers, whether conferred by the trust instrument or statute, allow for the effective administration of a trust. The power of delegation allows the trustees to delegate both the duties and discretions to agents, nominees and custodians. The reform of the law of delegation in the Trustee Act 2000 was a welcome development. Prior to the Act, the law of delegation set a hopelessly low standard of care on trustees when appointing agents and then subsequently supervising their acts. Trustees who delegated honestly and in good faith, but in circumstances where they did not exercise due care, were held not to be liable. The Trustee Act 2000 confers a very broad power of delegation and, in doing so, puts in place a duty of care in the appointment and supervision of such agents. The Act allows for the delegation of discretions as well as duties and this, whilst suggesting that the trustee need not do anything himself, is in fact a development which recognises that some trustees may not be the best persons to execute some of the discretions conferred upon them. For example, in the context of trustee investment, a lay trustee may not be the best person to make investment decisions in complex financial markets. Surely in such a case it is in the best interests of the trust beneficiaries that the investments are taken by experts who will get the best return for the beneficiaries.

In relation to the other powers examined in this chapter, the powers of maintenance and advancement play an important role in allowing some parts of the trust fund to be released to a beneficiary in circumstances where it would be appropriate to do so. For example, an infant will be perfectly entitled to some income where that infant's welfare is entirely dependent on the trust fund. The release of capital to a beneficiary who is about to start a business is a good example of the exercise of the power of advancement. The law of trusts will, however, scrutinise and hold improper payments of trust funds under the powers of maintenance and advancement which benefit some person other than the beneficiary. Finally, the chapter has explored some of the miscellaneous powers conferred on trustees in areas such as sale, receipt and insurance. These powers allow the trustees to deal with the trust property in one form or another in the best interests of the beneficiaries.

●●● Case studies

Consider the following case studies.

1 By his will, Barry, who died last year, after appointing Charles and Amanda to be his executors and trustees, left all his residuary estate to Charles and Amanda upon trust to pay the income thereof to Barry's widow, Sylvia, for life and subject thereto upon trust for Barry's two sons, Bill and Fred, in equal shares. After paying all the funeral expenses, legacies and debts, Barry's residuary estate consists of:

● a copyright in an unpublished novel
● £2500 in a 'capital growth' unit trust (under which no income is payable)

- a future interest in a trust fund of £50,000, expectant on the death of Barry's brother
- two original paintings by Picasso.

Advise Charles and Amanda how they should determine the income to be paid to Sylvia and whether they can advance any part of the capital for the benefit of Bill and Fred.

2 You are consulted by Edith (a widow) and Henry who are the trustees of a mixed fund of personalty and realty held on trust for sale. Edith is entitled to the income for her life and her two sons (Richard and Edward, aged 16 and 19 respectively) are entitled to the capital contingently upon them attaining the age of 21 years. In addition, Richard is entitled to a sum of £2000 under the will of his late uncle on reaching the age of 21 years and Edith and Henry are also trustees in this case.

Edward is about to get married and Edith wishes to know whether it will be possible to provide all or part of the purchase money of a house for Edward and his fiancée out of the first trust fund. In view of the fact that Edith will now be living on her own she also wishes to leave the rented house in which she is at present residing and to buy a smaller house. She asks whether it will be possible to use any of the trust fund of which she is entitled to the income to provide all or any of the purchase price.

What is your advice to Edith?

Moot points

1 How far does the present law on trustee delegation allow the trustees to act in the best interests of their beneficiaries?

2 There is no doubt that trustees have wide powers of delegation under the Trustee Act 2000. They can delegate both their duties as well as their administrative discretions. Is such an excessive power to delegate not repugnant to the idea of a trust which involves placing confidence and trust in a trustee?

3 In order to make an advancement to a beneficiary under s. 32 of the Trustee Act 1925 the beneficiary must show that the advancement is for his or her material benefit. What is meant by material benefit and is the judicial definition satisfactory? Would an advancement to a child to pay her mother's overdraft be possible if the mother had run up a very high overdraft as a result of undergoing treatment for a serious illness?

4 Explain how accumulations of income under s. 31 of the Trustee Act 1925 are dealt with in relation to beneficiaries entitled under both a vested and a contingent interest.

5 Read the Law Commission's Supplementary Consultation Paper: Consultation Paper No. 191, 26 May 2011, and explain why and how the powers of maintenance and advancement found in ss. 31 and 32 of the Trustee Act 1925 should be reformed.

6 What is the justification for allowing trustees a power to compromise disputes? What type of dispute avail themselves to a compromise and how should a compromise be exercised by a trustee?

● Further reading

Hassall, N. 'Power of Advancement: How Far Can Pilkington be Stretched?' (2007) PCB 282. Looks at the meaning of benefit in *Pilkington* v *IRC* and considers how far the requirement of benefit in making an advancement can be extended to resettling trust property of trusts better, perhaps from a fiscal pint of view, for the beneficiaries.

Law Commission, 'Trustees' Powers and Duties' Report No. 260. Explains the inadequacies of some of the rules governing trustees' powers and duties and suggesting reform which eventually came in the form of the Trustee Act 2000.

Law Commission Supplementary Consultation Paper: Consultation Paper 191, 'Intestacy and Family Provision Claims on Death: Sections 31 and 32 of the Trustee Act 1925,' 26 May 2011.

Panesar, S. 'The Trustee Act 2000' [2001] ICCLR. Looks at some of the key sections of the Trustee Act 1925, including the power of delegation.

Visit **www.mylawchamber.co.uk/panesar** to access study support resources including interactive multiple choice questions, practice exam questions with guidance, podcasts, weblinks, legal newsfeed all linked to the **Pearson eText** version of Exploring Equity and Trusts which you can **search**, **highlight** and **personalise** with your **own notes** and **bookmarks**.

premium
mylawchamber
unrivalled support for legal education

19

Variation of trusts

Learning objectives

After reading this chapter you should be able to:

→ understand the reasons why the terms of a trust may need to be varied

→ understand the nature and the extent of the rule in *Saunders* v *Vautier*

→ explain the court's inherent jurisdiction to vary the terms of a trust and its contemporary importance

→ explain the statutory provisions allowing a variation of the terms of a trust

→ understand the reasons for the enactment of the Variation of Trusts Act 1958

→ explain the principles involved in a variation of trust under the Variation of Trusts Act 1958.

SETTING THE SCENE

Re Weston's Settlements [1969] 1 Ch. 233: Can you change the terms of a trust if it makes the beneficiary richer?

The facts of this case concerned two settlements made by Stanley Weston in 1964 in favour of his two sons and their children. Stanley Weston came to England from Russia in 1894 and, despite a short education, he went straight into business opening as a sole trader. His sole trade business proved to be successful and he subsequently opened a chain of retail shops. In 1964 the business was turned into a public company, The Stanley Western Group Ltd, and Stanley Weston took his office as Chairman. Both settlements in favour of his two sons were created over substantial shares in the company. At the time when the settlements were created there was no capital gains; however, as a result of the enactment of the Finance Act 1965, capital gains tax would be payable on the shares. As a result of these changes, the Weston family decided to move to Jersey in order to avoid being subject to the tax. The Finance Act 1965 did not apply if the majority of the trustees were outside the United Kingdom and the beneficiaries were also not resident in the United Kingdom. Additionally, the administration of the trust should be carried outside the United Kingdom. Stanley Weston moved to Jersey in 1966 and his older son followed in 1967. Three months later Stanley Weston sought to appoint new trustees in Jersey with a view to moving the settlements made in the United Kingdom to the new trustees, subject to new but identical trusts to be administered in Jersey by Jersey trustees. The question before the Court of Appeal was whether the variations proposed by Stanley Weston would be approved under the Variation of Trusts Act 1958. In other words, should the court consent on behalf of the children and any future unborn children?

The Court of Appeal refused to sanction the arrangement proposed, on the grounds that it was not for the benefit of the children. Lord Denning MR accepted that the proposed variation was undoubtedly for the financial benefit of all the parties, but emphasised that the court should also look to the wider social and moral benefits. In the course of his judgment, Lord Denning MR explained that:

> [t]he court should not consider merely the financial benefit to the infants or unborn children, but also their educational and social benefit. There are many things in life more worth while than money. One of these things is to be brought up in this our England, which is still 'the envy of less happier lands'. I do not believe it is for the benefit of children to be uprooted from England and transported to another country simply to avoid tax . . . Children are like trees: they grow stronger with firm roots (at p. 245).

The facts and decision in *Re Weston's Settlement* raise interesting issues, which are the subject matter of discussion in this chapter. The central theme is the extent to which the terms of an existing trust can be varied. As the facts of *Re Weston's Settlement* illustrate, a settlor cannot possibly cater for contingencies which may arise in the future. For example, if the tax regime changes with the effect that the trust is subject to higher tax, why cannot the settlor, or indeed beneficiaries, change the terms of the trust? Should a court frustrate the settlor's or beneficiaries' attempts to change the terms of the trust?

This chapter looks at the principal ways in which the terms of an existing trust may be varied.

Introduction

It is a fundamental principle of trust law that a trustee complies with and executes the terms of the trust in accordance with the settlors's intentions which are manifested in the trust instrument. If a trustee fails to comply with the terms of the trust, or otherwise attempts to administer the trust contrary to the terms of the trust, he will be liable for breach of trust. However, there may be instances where a deviation from the existing terms of the trust may be in the interests of the beneficiaries. Such a deviation may be requested by the settlor or the existing beneficiaries. One of the more common instances where a deviation from the original terms of the trust will be important is in the context of taxation. It will be appreciated that many trusts will continue for long periods of time and, over the course of that time, there will be many changes in the fiscal regime of the jurisdiction in which the trust is being administered. Certainly a settlor will not be able to cover for every contingency or change in the tax structure that may affect the trust. It may well be that, as a result of certain changes in the taxation structure, the trust is administered, or the beneficial interests of the beneficiaries are changed, so that the trust attracts a more favourable tax treatment. Although, it is a fundamental rule of trust law that the trustees give effect to the settlor's or testator's intentions, it is equally clear that a settlor or testator will have intended that his beneficiaries pay the least amount of tax where possible.

The main issue in this chapter is the extent to which the terms of an original trust can be varied. In most professionally drafted trusts instruments it will be common to see quite wide powers allowing for variation of the beneficial interests under the trust. However, in the absence of such express powers to vary the terms of a trust, the question arises as to how the terms of a trust can be varied. In this chapter it will be observed that, until the enactment of the Variation of Trusts Act 1958, the ability to vary the terms of a trust was very restricted. This chapter explores some of the principal means by which the terms of a trust can be varied.

The rule in *Saunders* v *Vautier*

The nature of the rule

Where a beneficiary is absolutely entitled to a trust fund and has attained the age of majority he or she can of course terminate the trust. The beneficiary may well resettle the property on further trusts. Where there is more than one beneficiary, for example where property is settled for A for life and thereafter for B absolutely, collectively A and B can terminate the trust and call for the property to be vested in A and B, provided they are both of majority age. In such a case, termination of the trust by A and B may be to avoid paying inheritance tax on A's death. The ability of a beneficiary, or group of beneficiaries, who are collectively entitled to the whole of the trust fund to terminate the trust comes from what has become known as the rule in *Saunders* v *Vautier*.[1]

The rule in *Saunders* v *Vautier* extends to situations where an absolute gift is made to a beneficiary, but with a direction that the trustees accumulate the income and pay over

---

[1] (1841) 4 Beav. 115.

the capital at some future date. In such a case, when the beneficiary attains majority and is absolutely entitled to the fund, he or she can ask the trustee to transfer the trust property to them. The beneficiary need not wait until the future date before the trust can be terminated. The matter is neatly illustrated by the facts of **Saunders v Vautier** where a testator created a trust of certain stocks for his great nephew until he attained the age of 25 years. In the meantime, the trustees were directed to accumulate the income on the stocks. When the great nephew attained the age of 21, which at that time was the age of majority, he asked the court whether he was entitled to call for the whole trust property to be transferred to him. Lord Langdale MR held that the great nephew was entitled to the whole of the trust property on his attaining the age of majority. Lord Langdale MR noted that an immediate gift of the stock had been made by the great uncle subject only to a duty to accumulate and that, furthermore, the nephew was the only beneficiary entitled to the fund even if he died. In the course of his judgment, Lord Langdale MR explained that 'I think that principle has been repeatedly acted upon; and where a legacy is directed to accumulate for a certain period, or where the payment is postponed the legatee, if he has an absolute indefeasible interest in the legacy, is not bound to wait until the expiration of that period, but may require payment the moment he is competent to give a valid discharge.'[2]

Justifications for the rule

As a general rule, the law allows great freedom in the manner in which a person disposes of his property to other persons. This freedom of disposition is only interfered with where the disposition of property is contrary to public policy or it otherwise unlawful. In Chapter 9 it was observed that certain trusts were held to be void on grounds of illegality and public policy. For example, a trust or some other form of gift which has an excessive delay in vesting will be invalidated on the grounds that it contravenes the perpetuity rules, which require that dispositions of property vest within specified periods of time.[3] The rationale behind the perpetuity rules is that in a liberal market economy, property must be freely alienable so as to allow maximum utilisation of it. In this respect, interfering with dispositions of property on the grounds of the perpetuity rules is justified on policy grounds. With regard to the rule in **Saunders v Vautier**,[4] the question arises as to the basis for interfering with a testator's intention. Put simply, what is the basis for allowing a beneficiary who has attained the age of majority, and who is absolutely entitled to the trust fund, to terminate the trust even though the testator may have postponed the right to terminate the trust until some future date? The rationale behind the rule lies in the fact that, where a testator makes an absolute gift to a beneficiary, with the intention that the property belongs to the beneficiary and no one else but the beneficiary, he cannot impose limitations which are inconsistent with the absolute gift. In other words, if he intends nothing more than an absolute gift, then why should he restrict the beneficiary's right to call for the absolute gift?[5] The rationale behind the rule was further explained in **Gosling v Gosling**[6] where the court held that, provided that a beneficiary had reached

---

[2] Quoted in D. Hayton and C. Mitchell, *Cases and Commentary on the Law of Trusts and Equitable Remedies* 12th edn (2005) at p. 601.

[3] The common law rule being that no interest is good if it vests, if at all, no later than 21 years after some life in being. See Chapter 9 for more detail.

[4] (1841) 4 Beav. 115.

[5] The rule has its origins in cases involving wills where an absolute gift has been conferred upon a legatee; see, for example, *Green v Spicer* (1830) 1 Russ. & M 395.

[6] (1859) Gosling v Gosling (1859) 70 ER 423.

the age of 21 years (today this would be 18 years), and the property was to belong to the beneficiary and no other person, then there could be no justification for a testator or a settlor to impose any fetters on the enjoyment of the property. In this respect it can be said that there are no policy reasons why a person should be able to control property which is absolutely given to another individual who has attained the age of majority. Once that individual has attained the age of majority, he is legally capable of dealing with his or her own affairs.

The basis of the rule in **Saunders v Vautier** can also be explained on the grounds that a trust involves a fragmentation of ownership between the trustee and the beneficiary. The trustee has a mere nominal title to the trust property whereas the beneficiary is entitled to the full beneficial interest in the trust property. The person creating the trust, that is the settlor or the testator, falls out of the picture. The settlor or testator does not retain any rights in the trust property. The fruits of the ownership lie essentially with the beneficiary, who on attaining the age of 18, and becoming absolutely entitled to the trust fund, is entitled to deal with his or her property as he or she wishes to do so. As explained in the preceding paragraph, any attempt by the settlor to control the equitable ownership of the beneficiary who is nevertheless entitled to the property absolutely is not justified.

Application to different types of trust

In order to take advantage of the rule in **Saunders v Vautier**[7] it is not necessary to seek approval of the court before terminating the trust. It is important, however, that the beneficiaries seeking to terminate the trust are ascertained of majority age and absolutely entitled to the whole of the trust property. The rule in **Saunders v Vautier** has no application to a bare trust, which can be terminated by a beneficiary at any time. You will recall from Chapter 2 that a bare trust arises where a trustee, also often referred to as a nominee, holds the equitable interest for a single beneficiary absolutely entitled to the trust property. The beneficial interest of the beneficiary is not subject to any contingency and the beneficiary, having attained the age of 18, can call for the trust property to be transferred to him. The rule in **Saunders v Vautier** will, however, apply to situations where, for example, a testator has given property on trust to a beneficiary absolutely, but has postponed the enjoyment until some future date beyond the majority age of the beneficiary. The rule will also apply where a testator has made an absolute gift of property to the beneficiary but subject to a direction that the trustees accumulate the income until a date beyond the majority age of the beneficiary.

APPLYING THE LAW

A trust is created for the benefit of Maria for her life and thereafter for the benefit of her son Victor. The trust consist of shares in a private company. Maria has been told that if she is the absolute owner of the shares she can be appointed director. Maria and Victor have decided to terminate the trust and transfer the shares to Maria absolutely.

Is this possible?

One of the questions which arises when discussing the rule in **Saunders v Vautier** is the extent to which is applies where there may be more than one beneficiary in question. There are at least three situations in which there may be more than one beneficiary. In

---

[7] (1841) 4 Beav. 115.

the first place, a trust may be settled for two or more beneficiaries entitled in succession: for example, a trust for A for life and thereafter for B absolutely. In such a case the rule will apply allowing both A and B to terminate the trust, providing that both A and B have reached the age of majority. Collectively, A and B are absolutely entitled to the property subject to the trust and can deal with it in any manner they think fit.

A second situation in which there may be more than one beneficiary is where the testator or settlor has created a fixed trust for a number of beneficiaries. For example, suppose that a testator creates a trust for A, B, C and D in equal shares. Whilst there is no doubt that collectively A, B, C and D can terminate the trust if they have attained the age of majority, a more difficult question arises as to whether any one of them can call for his or her share to be paid out of the trust fund. A potential problem arises if the share of one of the beneficiaries is paid, thereby having detrimental effects on the shares of the other beneficiaries. For example, the rate of return on the fund held in favour of the beneficiaries may fall as a result of the fund depreciating in value because one of the beneficiaries has taken his or her interest. The matter was explored in *Stephenson v Barclays Bank Trust Co Ltd*[8] where beneficiaries became absolutely and jointly entitled to a testator's residuary estate. The question before the court was whether one of the beneficiaries was entitled to take her share out of the trust fund which was jointly owned by the beneficiaries. In holding that the beneficiary was so entitled to take a share, Walton J explained that:

> when the situation is that a single person who is sui juris has an absolutely vested beneficial interest in a share of the trust fund, his rights are not, I think, quite as extensive as those of the beneficial interest holders as a body. In general, he is entitled to have transferred to him (subject, of course, always to the same rights of the trustees as I have already mentioned above) an aliquot share of each and every asset of the trust fund which presents no difficulty so far as division is concerned. This will apply to such items as cash, money at the bank or an unsecured loan, Stock Exchange securities and the like. However, as regards land, certainly, in all cases, as regards shares in a private company in very special circumstance . . . the situation is not so simple, and even a person with a vested interest in possession in an aliquot share of the trust fund may have to wait until the land is sold, and so forth, before being able to call upon the trustees as of right to account to him for his share of the assets.[9]

Finally, the question arises in the context of a discretionary trust as to whether the beneficiaries of a discretionary trust are capable of invoking the rule in *Saunders v Vautier*[10] in order to terminate a discretionary trust. At the outset, the potential problems with the application of rule in *Saunders v Vautier* to a discretionary trust is that, until such time as the exercise of the discretion by the discretionary trustee, the discretionary beneficiaries have no proprietary interest in the trust property. Despite this, the general position is that beneficiaries under a discretionary trust are entitled to collectively terminate the trust, provided that all of the beneficiaries of the trust act together and that collectively they are entitled to the trust property. It is an important requirement that the discretionary trust in question is an exhaustive discretionary trust in that all of the trust property is to be distributed at the trustees' discretion amongst the objects of the discretionary trust. The matter was explained by Romer J in *Re Smith*[11] where the judge asked:

> [W]hat is to happen where the trustees have a discretion whether they will apply the whole or only a portion of the fund for the benefit of one person, but are obliged to apply the rest

---

[8] [1975] 1 All ER 625.
[9] [1975] 1 All ER 625 at 891.
[10] (1841) 4 Beav. 115.
[11] [1928] Ch. 915.

of the fund, so far as not applied for the benefit of the first named person, to or for the benefit of a second named person? There, two people together are the sole objects of the discretionary trust and, between them, are entitled to have the whole fund applied to them or for their benefit.[12]

Limits to the rule in *Saunders* v *Vautier*

Although the rule in **Saunders v Vautier**[13] allows an adult beneficiary or beneficiaries to terminate a trust in circumstances when the trust property belongs absolutely to them, the rule cannot to be invoked to vary the terms of an existing trust. The rule does not allow a beneficiary to compel the trustee of the trust to administer the trust on terms different from those imposed by the settlor. For example, the rule in **Saunders v Vautier** does not allow beneficiaries to order trustees to exercise a particular discretion in a particular way and neither does the rule allow the beneficiaries to impose new duties on the trustees. The matter is neatly illustrated by the decision in **Re Brockbank**[14] where a trustee wished to exercise the statutory power of appointment under s. 36 of the Trustee Act 1925 and appoint a particular trustee. The beneficiaries of the trust, however, wanted to appoint a trustee of their own choice and the question before the court was whether the beneficiaries could direct the trustee to exercise a discretion to appoint a new trustee in a way in which he did not wish to exercise it. Vaisey J explained that the beneficiaries could not rely on the rule in **Saunders v Vautier** to compel the trustee to appoint a new trustee of their choice. In the course of his judgment, the judge explained that:

> it is said that where all the beneficiaries concur, they may force a trustee to retire, compel his removal and direct the trustees, having the power to nominate their successors, to appoint as such successors such persons or person or corporation as may be indicated by the beneficiaries, and it is suggested that the trustees have no option but to comply.
>
> I do not follow this. The power of nominating a new trustee is a discretionary power, and, in my opinion is no longer exercisable and, indeed, can no longer exist if it has become one of which the exercise can be dictated by others. But then it is said that the beneficiaries could direct the trustees to transfer the trust property either to themselves absolutely, or to any other person or persons or corporation, upon trusts identical with or corresponding to the trusts of the testator's will. I agree, provided that the trustees are adequately protected against any possible claim for future death duties and are fully indemnified as regards their costs, charges and expenses.[15]

The court's inherent jurisdiction to order variation

Whilst the rule in **Saunders v Vautier**[16] allows an adult beneficiary absolutely entitled to the trust fund to terminate the trust, it does not allow the beneficiary to vary the terms of an existing trust, thereby requiring the trustees to act in a manner not prescribed by the trust instrument. At most, the minimal variation that occurs under the rule in **Saunders v Vautier**[17] is the divergence from a testator's intention, for example, to

---

[12] [1928] Ch. 915 at 918.
[13] (1841) 4 Beav. 115.
[14] [1948] Ch. 206.
[15] [1948] Ch. 206 at 208.
[16] (1841) 4 Beav. 115.
[17] (1841) 4 Beav. 115.

postpone the right to capital beyond the majority age of a beneficiary who is absolutely entitled to the trust fund. Leaving the rule in **Saunders v Vautier** to one side, the question arises whether there is a power to vary the terms of an existing trust. In other words, does a court, for example, have a power to vary the terms of an existing trust, which essentially involves a departure from the intentions of a settlor or testator expressed in a trust instrument of a will? In **Re New**,[18] which is discussed in more detail below, Romer J explained that '[a]s a rule, the court has no jurisdiction to give, and will not give, its sanction to the performance by trustees of acts with reference to the trust estate which are not, on the face of the instrument creating the trust, authorised by its terms.'[19] Similarly, in **Re Walker**[20] the judge expressed the view held that 'I decline to accept any suggestion that the court has an inherent jurisdiction to alter a man's will because it thinks it to be beneficial. It seems to me that is quite impossible.'[21]

Although some of the early decisions in trust law had made it clear that the court did not have a general power to vary the terms of an existing trust or a will, the House of Lords in **Chapman v Chapman**[22] explained that the court had an inherent jurisdiction to authorise a variation of a trust. Lord Morton identified four situations in which the court would exercise an inherent power to order a variation. The House of Lords' decision in **Chapman v Chapman** illustrates that, whilst the court does possess an inherent jurisdiction to authorise a variation of trust, the court's inherent power is extremely limited. Furthermore, it will be seen below that some of the situations identified by the House of Lords have become redundant as a result of changes in law and various statutory enactments. The limited inherent jurisdiction of the court, which was exposed by the House of Lords in **Chapman v Chapman**, was the principal reason for the enactment of the Variation of Trusts Act 1958, which is explored in greater detail later in this chapter.

Conversion

The first situation in which the court has an inherent jurisdiction to authorise a variation is in the case of conversion. This situation, which has lost its contemporary significance as a result of changes to succession laws, allowed the court to change the nature of an infant's estate from realty to personalty and vice versa where it was for the benefit of the infant. Without the court exercising its inherent jurisdiction, the trustees of an infant's estate were not entitled to change real property to personal property and personal property to real because it would interfere with the laws of succession, which treated the devolution of real and personal property differently. It is not intended to examine this category in any more detail than this, simply because it has lost any contemporary significance.

Emergency

The second situation in which the court had a power to sanction a variation from the existing terms of the trust was in cases of emergency. This situation did not authorise the court to vary the beneficial interests of the beneficiaries: rather it allowed the court

---

[18] [1901] 2 Ch. 534.
[19] [1901] 2 Ch. 534 at 544.
[20] [1901] 1 Ch. 879.
[21] [1901] 1 Ch. 879 at 885.
[22] [1954] AC 429.

to authorise dealings with the trust property where it was required as a matter of emergency, and there was no provision in the trust instrument. The exercise of the court's inherent jurisdiction in the case of emergency is neatly illustrated by the decision in *Re New*[23] where the question before the Court of Appeal was whether trustees holding shares in a company were able to take part in the reconstruction of a company in which the shares were held. The reconstruction involved a subdivision of the shares at a lower value, thereby making them more marketable. The Court of Appeal held that as a matter of emergency the trustees were authorised to take part in the reconstruction even though this was not authorised by the terms of the trust instrument. In the course of his judgment, Romer J explained that:

> in the management of a trust estate, and especially where that estate consists of a business or shares in a mercantile company, it not infrequently happens that some peculiar state of circumstances arises for which provision is not expressly made by the trust instrument, and which renders it most desirable, and it may be even essential, for the benefit of the estate and in the interest of all the cestuis que trust, that certain acts should be done by the trustees which in ordinary circumstances they would have no power to do. In a case of this kind, which may reasonably be supposed to be one not foreseen or anticipated by the author of the trust, where the trustees are embarrassed by the emergency that has arisen and the duty cast upon them to do what is best for the estate, and the consent of all the beneficiaries cannot be obtained by reason of some of them not being sui juris or in existence, then it may be right for the Court, and the Court in a proper case would have jurisdiction, to sanction on behalf of all concerned such acts on behalf of the trustees . . .[24]

The court's inherent jurisdiction to authorise a deviation from the terms of the trust has been replaced by s. 57 of the Trustee Act 1925 which is discussed in more detail below.

Maintenance

One of the more common situations in which the court's inherent jurisdiction has been invoked is in the case of maintenance of an infant beneficiary. Thus, where a trust is created for an infant beneficiary with a direction that the income be accumulated rather than be available for the benefit of the infant, the court can sanction that maintenance be available for the infant. A neat illustration of the court exercising its inherent jurisdiction under the head of maintenance is illustrated by the decision in *Re Collins*[25] where a testator directed that income be accumulated for a period of 21 years and then the accumulations to be paid to his sister for her life and thereafter for her sons. The question before the court was whether it could sanction a deviation from the will in order to allow the trustees to make income payment to the sister so as to maintain and educate her three sons. Farwell J held that the court had an inherent power to authorise the payment of income to the sister, on the grounds that the testator could not possibly have intended the children to go without education and maintenance. In the course of his judgment the judge explained that:

> where a testator has made a provision for a family, using that word in the ordinary sense in which we take the word, that is the children's particular stirps in succession, but has postponed the enjoyment, either for a particular purpose or generally for the increase of the estate, it is assumed that he did not intend that these children should be left un-provided

---

[23] [1910] 2 Ch. 534.
[24] [1910] 2 Ch. 534 at 544.
[25] (1886) 32 Ch. D 229.

for or in a state of such moderate means that they should not be educated properly for the position and fortune which he designs them to have, and the court has accordingly found from the earliest times that where an heir-in-law is un-provided for, maintenance ought to be provided for him.[26]

It should be noted that, unlike the previous two heads discussed already, the maintenance head allows the court to vary the beneficial interests of the beneficiaries.

Compromise

The final situation in which the court may exercise an inherent jurisdiction to change the terms of a trust is in cases of compromise. The basis for the court intervening in such cases is that there is some dispute as to the rights of the beneficiaries. It is questionable whether the so-called 'compromise jurisdiction' is indeed a variation of trust. The reason for this is that the court is not really changing the terms of a trust: rather, in the face of uncertainty and doubt, the court is agreeing a compromise which defines the terms of the trust from that point in time. The matter was explained by Lord Morton in **Chapman v Chapman**[27] where his Lordship said that there are 'many cases to be found in the reports in which the Court of Chancery, and its successor the Chancery Division, have approved compromises of disputed rights of infants interested under a will or settlement and on behalf also of possible after-born beneficiaries . . . Where rights are in dispute, the court approves a compromise, it is not altering the trusts, for the trusts are, ex hypothesi, still in doubt and unascertained.'[28]

One of the more difficult questions which has arisen in the context of the compromise jurisdiction is: what is a compromise? For example, does the compromise have to take the form of a resolution of the disputed rights of the beneficiaries; or can compromise cover a situation where there is no dispute between the rights of the trust beneficiaries? This important question was the subject matter of discussion in the Court of Appeal in three conjoined appeals in **Re Downshire Settled Estates, Re Blackwell's Settlement Trusts** and **Re Chapman's Settlement Trusts**.[29] In the first two cases, the court was requested to sanction variations which involved the interests of life tenants and the remaindermen. The principal reason for the variation was to accelerate the interests of the remainder-man and avoid tax by a surrender of some of the interest in the trust property by the life tenant. In the final case the court was requested by trustees of three family settlements to transfer the trust funds to trustees of a new settlement on similar terms, but omitting a provision from one of the original trusts which provided for unequal and selective maintenance of the beneficiaries. The principal reason for the resettlement was that it would reduce the possibility of estate duty claims in the future. The trustees argued that the court should exercise its inherent power to give effect to the proposed resettlements, on the grounds that this would amount to a compromise between the beneficiaries of the trust. Lord Evershed MR explained that:

> in each of the present cases a principal object of the scheme presented to the court has been to achieve (so far as foresight could achieve it) a limitation of the future liability of the corpus of the trust property to serious diminution from estate duty. The high rates of taxation, in

---

[26] (1886) 32 Ch. D 229 at 232.
[27] [1954] AC 429.
[28] [1954] AC 429 at 457.
[29] [1953] Ch. 218.

the form both of income tax and of death duties, is a phenomenon of the present generation. It must be taken as notorious that many persons, having families and free estates, so dispose of their estates as to reduce, within the law, liability for income tax during their lives . . . It follows, in our judgment, that it is not an objection to the sanction by the court of any proposed scheme in regard to trust property that its object or effect is or may be to reduce liability for tax (including death duties).[30]

The Court of Appeal sanctioned the proposed schemes in *Re Downshire Settled Estates* and *Re Blackwell's Settlement Trusts*,[31] but failed to give effect to the scheme proposed in *Re Chapman's Settlement Trusts*.[32] Both Lord Evershed MR and Romer LJ took the view that the 'compromise' should not be restricted to cases where there was a dispute between the beneficiaries, but extended to cases where there was an arrangement between the life tenant and the remainderman. Both judges took the view that in *Re Downshire Settled Estates* and *Re Blackwell's Settlement Trusts* one beneficiary, that is the life tenant, was giving up something uncertain in return for something definite. The arrangement was in the interests of all the beneficiaries even though the purpose behind such a compromise was to avoid future estate duty. On other hand, the Court of Appeal, Denning LJ dissenting, refused to sanction the scheme in *Re Chapman's Settlement Trusts*, principally on the grounds that the proposed scheme was a completely new trust which had the effect of varying the beneficial interests of the beneficiaries in a manner not intended by the settlor. Denning LJ dissented on the grounds that the court had a much wider jurisdiction to authorise a variation. He explained that the 'jurisdiction is not confined to cases where there is a dispute about the extent of the beneficial interests, nor to cases of emergency or necessity, but extends wherever there is a bargain about the beneficial interests which is for the benefit of the infants or unborn persons.'[33]

It will be seen below that the trustees in *Re Chapman's Settlement Trusts*[34] appealed to the House of Lords who unanimously rejected the appeal, with the consequence that the law remained, until the enactment of the Variation of Trusts Act 1958, rather controversial and somewhat illogical.[35] The House of Lords held that the word 'compromise' was to be given a narrow meaning. Lord Simonds explained that 'compromise' certainly did not extend to cases where there was no dispute between the beneficiaries. The net effect of this was that, whilst cases such as *Re Downshire Settled Estates* and *Re Blackwell's Settlement Trust*[36] allowed trustees to implement schemes as between life tenants and remaindermen to avoid tax, no such scheme could be proposed where there was no dispute even though a proposed scheme was beneficial to future beneficiaries.[37] The decision of the House of Lords in *Chapman v Chapman*[38] did leave the question wide open as to whether the Court of Appeal was right in approving the schemes in *Re Downshire Settled Estates*, and *Re Blackwell's Settlement Trust*.

---

[30] [1953] Ch. 218 at 233.
[31] [1953] Ch. 218.
[32] [1954] AC 429.
[33] [1953] Ch. 218 at 274.
[34] [1954] AC 429.
[35] *Chapman v Chapman* [1954] AC 429.
[36] [1953] Ch. 218. Although, Lord Simonds did cast doubt whether the authorities used to justify these decisions were indeed appropriate. For example, in *Re Downshires Settled Estates* [1953] Ch. 218, Lord Evershed MR relied on the decision in *Re Trenchard* [1902] 1 Ch. 378 which was regarded by Lord Simonds as being an isolated case.
[37] For a more detailed analysis, see O.R. Marshall, 'Deviations from the Terms of a Trust' [1954] 17 MLR 420.
[38] [1954] AC 429.

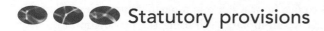 # Statutory provisions

Although a very wide statutory power to authorise variations of a trust is now found in s. 1 of the Variation of Trusts Act 1958, there are a number of other statutory enactments which confer upon the courts a power to make variation of trusts. This section looks at the various statutory provisions before analysing the Variation of Trusts Act 1958.

Section 53 of the Trustee Act 1925

Section 53 of the Trustee Act 1925 confers upon the court a power to make an order in favour of an infant beneficiary who is absolutely entitled to any property. An order can be made for the capital or income to be applied in favour of the infant beneficiary. The section is much wider than s. 31 of the Trustee Act 1925[39] which confers upon the trustees a power to make income payments to an infant beneficiary entitled to the income. Under s. 31 the payment of income must be for the maintenance of the infant and maintenance is construed strictly to include material benefit. Under s. 53, however, benefit has been construed widely to include amongst maintenance and education wider benefits such as tax avoidance.[40]

> **KEY STATUTE**
>
> ### S. 53 of the Trustee Act 1925 (Vesting orders in relation to infant's beneficial interest)
>
> (1) Where an infant is beneficially entitled to any property the court may, with a view to the application of the capital or income thereof for the maintenance, education, or benefit of the infant, make an order –
>
> (a) appointing a person to convey such property; or
>
> (b) in the case of stock, or a thing in action, vesting in any person the right to transfer or call for a transfer of such stock, or to receive the dividends or income thereof, or to sue for and recover such thing in action, upon such terms as the court may think fit.

The ambit of s. 53 of the Trustee Act 1925 was explored by Upjohn J in **Re Heyworth**[41] where the question before the court was whether the section could be applied to allow a life tenant to purchase a reversionary interest from reversionary beneficiaries, one of whom was an infant. The court held that the section could only be invoked for the maintenance, education or benefit of an infant. The court held that the sale of an infant's reversionary interest could not be ordered by the court under s. 53 since it was not for the infant's benefit. The effect of the proposed transaction was to merely enlarge the interest of the life tenant, thereby putting an end to the trust. In the course of his judgment, Upjohn J explained that benefit 'covers not merely expenditure but capital investment

---

[39] Considered in detail in Chapter 18.
[40] *Re Meux' Will Trusts* [1958] Ch. 154.
[41] [1956] Ch. 364.

such as the purchase of a house to live in or a share in a partnership, or even in some cases placing of money on deposit for an infant . . . to bring the jurisdiction into play, there must be "a view to the application" of the capital or income for the maintenance, education or benefit of the infant'.[42] Upjohn J went on to explain that the effect of the proposed transaction between the life tenant and the infant remainderman was to change the beneficial interest of the infant. In his view s. 53 of the Trustee Act 1925 did not confer upon the court a power to alter beneficial interests. The judge explained that '[t]he deed is not in the least degree entered into with a view to the application of, or for the purpose of applying, any capital or income of the infant for her benefit . . . If I sanctioned this scheme on behalf of the infant I should be reading the section as though it empowered the court to convey the property of an infant whenever it was for her benefit. Unfortunately, the section only confers a more limited jurisdiction.'[43]

Section 57 of the Trustee Act 1925

Section 57 of the Trustee Act allows the court to sanction variations from the terms of the trust in cases where it is 'expedient' to do so. The section governs the management and administrative functions of a trust and does not give the court a right to vary the beneficial interest of the beneficiaries. Section 57 has many similarities to the emergency jurisdiction which exists under the court's inherent jurisdiction; however, the section is much wider, as it covers expediency which is broader than emergency.

KEY STATUTE

S. 57 of the Trustee Act 1925 (Power of court to authorise dealings with trust property)

(1) Where in the management or administration of any property vested in trustees, any sale, lease, mortgage, surrender, release, or other disposition, or any purchase, investment, acquisition, expenditure or other transaction, is in the opinion of the court expedient, but the same cannot be effected by reason of the absence of any power for that purpose vested in the trustees by the trust instrument, if any, or by law, the court may by order confer upon the trustees, either generally or in any particular instance, the necessary power for the purpose, on such terms, and subject to such provisions and conditions, if any, as the court may think fit and may direct in what manner any money authorised to be expended, and the costs of any transaction, are to be paid or borne as between capital and income.

(2) The court may, from time to time, rescind or vary any order made under this section, or may make any new or further order.

(3) An application to the court under this section may be made by the trustees, or by any of them, or by any person beneficially interested under the trust.

(4) This section does not apply to trustees of a settlement for the purposes of the Settled Land Act 1925.

---

[42] [1956] Ch. 364 at 370.
[43] [1956] Ch. 364 at 371.

APPLYING THE LAW

Tom and Tim are two trustees of a trust created in the will of the testator. The terms of the will provide that the trust property can only be invested in banks, building societies and government securities. The beneficiaries have complained that the trust should be invested in a wider range of investments. Tom and Tim want to know whether they can enlarge the investment power.

In *Re Downshire Settled Estates*[44] Evershed MR explained that the:

> object of section 57 was to secure that trust property should be managed as advantageously as possible in the interests of the beneficiaries and, with that object in view, to authorize specific dealings with the property which the court might have felt itself unable to sanction under the inherent jurisdiction, either because no actual 'emergency' had arisen or because of inability to show that the position which called for intervention was one which the creator of the trust could not reasonably have foreseen; but it was not part of the legislative aim to disturb the rule that the court will not rewrite a trust, or to add to such exceptions to that rule as had already found their way into the inherent jurisdiction.[45]

Section 57 of the Trustee Act was invoked in *Mason v Farbrother*[46] where the question before the court was whether trustees of a pension scheme could expand the range of investment in which they were entitled to invest. The court used s. 57 to extend the trustees' investment powers.[47]

Section 57 of the Trustee Act does not allow the court to vary the beneficial interests of the trust. The section only allows a variation to the terms of a trust when it is expedient to do so in the management and administration of it. The section cannot be invoked simply because it is in the interests of one beneficiary to do so despite the absence of any real expediency. The matter is neatly illustrated by the decision *Re Craven's Estate (No. 2)*[48] where a testatrix had left money to her son as well as other named beneficiaries. The trustees were given an express power of advancement; however, the advancement could only be made for limited purposes of buying a business. The testatrix's son wished to become a member of Lloyd's of London and needed a sum of money to make the initial deposit. Clearly, the limited power of advancement could not be exercised to advance payment of money to become a member of Lloyd's of London, as this was not strictly the purchase of a business. The question before the court was whether s. 57 could be invoked to vary the limited power of advancement, thereby allowing the payment to the son. Farwell J declined to invoke s. 57 on the grounds that, although the payment of money would be for the benefit of the son, it was not expedient to the other beneficiaries. In the course of his judgment, Farwell J explained that 'the word "expedient" there quite clearly

---

[44] [1953] Ch. 218.
[45] [1953] Ch. 218 at 248.
[46] [1983] 2 All ER 1078.
[47] See also *Anker-Petersen* v *Anker-Petersen* [2000] WTLR 581.
[48] [1937] Ch. 431.

must mean expedient for the trust as a whole. It cannot mean that however expedient it may be for one beneficiary if it is inexpedient from the point of view of the other beneficiaries concerned the Court ought to sanction the transaction. In order that the matter may be one which is in the opinion of the Court expedient, it must be expedient for the trust as a whole.'[49]

More recently, in **_Alexander_ v _Alexander_**[50] Morgan J in the High Court ordered the sale of land under s. 57 of the Trustee Act 1925 when no such power existed and indeed was excluded in the trust instrument. The facts concerned a cottage which the trustees were holding on trust for several beneficiaries. The cottage had fallen into a bad state of disrepair and was uninhabitable. The trustees wished to sell the cottage; however, the trust instrument expressly prohibited this. This therefore meant that the trustees were left with no power of sale which would normally have existed under s. 6 of the Trusts of Land and Appointment of Trustees Act and s. 8 of the Trustee Act 2000. Nevertheless, having looked at the power in s. 57 and the existing authorities, Morgan J held that the trustees could sell the property as it was expedient to do so and would not alter the beneficial interests of the beneficiaries. In the course of judgment he held that:

> The court has a discretion under section 57(1). Normally, where a transaction is expedient within the subsection, the court would exercise its discretion to confer power on the trustees to effect the transaction. However, as was pointed out in _Royal Melbourne Hospital_ v _Equity Trustees_, the court can take into account the wishes of the settlor when deciding whether, in the exercise of its discretion, to confer the relevant power on the trustees. In the present case, the testator's wishes were expressed in his will in March 2006. He plainly thought that the cottage would be suitable for Ms Shuker to live in and that she would want to live in it. It is now clear that the cottage is not suitable for her and she does not want to occupy it. The present position is that the cottage has remained empty, neglected and uninsured. It is hard to think that the testator would want that state of affairs to continue. Further, this is not a case where the beneficiaries are divided in their opinion and the testator's wishes would allow me to favour one point of view over another. The proposed transaction is in the interests of all the beneficiaries and there is no opposition to the proposed transaction.[51]

Section 64 of the Settled Land Act 1925

Section 64 confers upon the court a relatively wide jurisdiction to authorise any transaction which would be for the benefit of the settled land. Although the significance of this provision will eventually diminish as a result of the fact that no further settlements can be made under the Settled Land Act 1925 by virtue of the Trusts of Land and Appointment of Trustees Act 1996,[52] the section can be used in cases of altering management as well as beneficial interests. The word 'transaction' in the section is not limited to management and administration functions.

---

[49] [1937] Ch. 431 at 436.
[50] [2011] EWHC 2721 (Ch.).
[51] [2011] EWHC 2721 (Ch.) at para. 33.
[52] See s. 2(1) of the Trusts of Land and Appointment of Trustees Act 1996.

APPLYING THE LAW

In a settlement created in 1940 Lord Simpleton left his stately home and the surrounding land for the Duke of Simpleton for life and thereafter for the son of the Duke absolutely. The Duke realises that his son is irresponsible and not fit to own the land absolutely. He wishes to vary the settlement by creating a protective trust for his son with discretionary interests in favour of the issue of his son.

Can this be done?

KEY STATUTE

S. 64 of the Settled Land Act 1925 (General power for the tenant for life to effect any transaction under an order of the court)

(1) Any transaction affecting or concerning the settled land, or any part thereof, or any other land (not being a transaction otherwise authorised by this Act, or by the settlement) which in the opinion of the court would be for the benefit of the settled land, or any part thereof, or the persons interested under the settlement, may, under an order of the court, be effected by a tenant for life, if it is one which could have been validly effected by an absolute owner.

In *Re Scarisbrick Resettlement Estates*[53] s. 64 was used by a life tenant of Scarisbrick Hall, a stately home, to order trustees to sell investments and raise some £10,000 for the repair of the Hall, which without such repair was not capable of being occupied. The investments were also held on trust for the life tenant and remaindermen, but the income was simply insufficient to maintain the Hall. Cohen J authorised the sale of the investments under s. 64 as this would be for the benefit of the settled land. Section 64 of the Settled Land Act 1929 was further explored by Morrit J in the High Court in *Hambro v Duke of Marlborough*.[54] The facts of this case involved a proposed scheme by trustees of the Blenheim Estates who were holding land on trust for the Duke of Marlborough and the then Marquess of Blandford, who was the oldest son of the 11th Duke of Marlborough. The trustees of the settlement sought to argue that the Marquess of Marlborough, who was entitled to the land after the death of the 11th Duke of Marlborough, was not fit to take control of the land because of lack of responsibility. The trustees proposed a scheme which would entitle them to hold the land on trust for the Duke and then on protective trusts for the Marquess. On the eventual death of the Marquess, the trustees proposed to hold the land under the terms of the original settlement. The proposed scheme was to protect the settled land. Morrit J held that s. 64 could be invoked in the present case so as to implement the new trusts in favour of the settled land. Morrit J explained that it did not matter that the Marquess of Blandford objected to the new trusts. In concluding his judgment Morrit J explained that 'powers conferred by section 64, like all others conferred by the Settled Land Act 1925 on a tenant for life, are exercisable by the tenant

---

[53] [1944] Ch. 229.
[54] [1994] 3 All ER 332. See, E. Cooke, 'What to do with an Unbarrable Tail' (1994) Conv. 492.

for life of the Parliamentary Estates even if such exercise would "hinder, bar or disinherit" a subsequent tenant for life from holding or enjoying the Parliamentary Estates'.[55]

Section 24 of the Matrimonial Causes Act 1973

Section 24 of the Matrimonial Causes Act 1973 confers upon the court a power to make property adjustment order on divorce. The section confers upon the court a very wide power to order the payment of cash or the transfer of property for the benefit of the other spouse and children. The order under s. 24 is most commonly invoked in the context of the matrimonial home. A spouse can be ordered to transfer the matrimonial home to the other in return for the other giving up some other right, for example, the right to receive maintenance.

KEY STATUTE

S. 24 of the Matrimonial Causes Act 1973 (Property adjustment orders in connection with divorce proceedings, etc.)

(1) On granting a decree of divorce, a decree of nullity of marriage or a decree of judicial separation or at any time thereafter (whether, in the case of a decree of divorce or of nullity of marriage, before or after the decree is made absolute), the court may make any one or more of the following orders, that is to say—

(a) an order that a party to the marriage shall transfer to the other party, to any child of the family or to such person as may be specified in the order for the benefit of such a child such property as may be so specified, being property to which the first-mentioned party is entitled, either in possession or reversion;

(b) an order that a settlement of such property as may be so specified, being property to which a party to the marriage is so entitled, be made to the satisfaction of the court for the benefit of the other party to the marriage and of the children of the family or either or any of them;

(c) an order varying for the benefit of the parties to the marriage and of the children of the family or either or any of them any ante-nuptial or post-nuptial settlement (including such a settlement made by will or codicil) made on the parties to the marriage;

(d) an order extinguishing or reducing the interest of either of the parties to the marriage under any such settlement . . .

A good illustration of an order under s. 24 of the Act varying a settlement is provided by *E v E (financial provision)*.[56] On the facts of this case, the matrimonial home was settled upon discretionary trust for the husband, wife and their children. The husband was a very wealthy individual and when the relationship broke down between the husband and wife, the question was whether the wife was entitled to money from the trust. The court ordered that the wife and the children receive a sum of £1.25 million from the discretionary trust, this order being made under s. 24(1)(b) of the Act.

---

[55] [1994] 3 All ER 332 at 346.
[56] [1990] 2 FLR 233.

Section 24(1) of the Matrimonial Causes Act 1923 allows the court to vary both ante-nuptial and post-nuptial settlements. A variation of a post-nuptial settlement was ordered by the House of Lords in **Brooks v Brooks**,[57] which concerned a pension scheme of a husband which provided that part of his benefit could be paid to his wife on his death, and furthermore, a lump sum should be made to the wife and children should he die prematurely. It is important to note on the facts that the husband was the sole member of the pension scheme. The question before the House of Lords was whether the husband's pension scheme was a settlement for the purposes of s. 24(1)(c), which provides that the court can make any order varying an ante-nuptial or post-nuptial settlement. The House of Lords held that the pension constituted a post-nuptial settlement for purposes of s. 24(1) of the Act. The House of Lords directed that the pension scheme be varied so as to provide an immediate annuity and then an eventual pension for the wife.[58] More recently, s. 24(1) of the Matrimonial Causes Act 1973 was invoked in **Ben Hashem v Ali Shayif**[59] where a wife was granted a limited right to occupation of a matrimonial home. It was held that the wife's right to reside in a property which belonged to a company and her children was a settlement for the purposes of the Act.

The Variation of Trusts Act 1958

The remaining part of this chapter focuses on the provision of the Variation of Trusts Act 1958. It was observed above that the inherent jurisdiction of the court to vary the terms of a trust is very limited in its application. The jurisdiction certainly does not give the court any wide powers to authorise variations which may be for the benefit of certain beneficiaries. For example, there is no general power to vary the terms of a trust if they are in fiscal interests of the beneficiaries. The enactment of the Variation of Trusts Act 1958 gave the courts a wide discretion to vary the terms of the trust.

The background to the Act

The principal reason for the enactment of the Variation of Trusts Act 1958 was because of the limited inherent jurisdiction of the court to authorise variation of trusts. As explained above, the limited jurisdiction of the court was exposed by the House of Lords' decision in **Chapman v Chapman**[60] where trustees of three family settlements proposed to transfer the trust funds to trustees of a new settlement on similar terms, but omitting a provision from one of the original trusts which provided for unequal and selective maintenance of the beneficiaries. The principal reason for the resettlement was that it would reduce the possibility of estate duty claims in the future. The trustees argued that the court should exercise its inherent power to give effect to the proposed resettlements, on the grounds that this would amount to a compromise between the beneficiaries of the trust. The Court of Appeal refused to sanction the proposed settlements, on the grounds that there was no issue of compromise in the true sense of the word. The Court of Appeal held that the facts of **Chapman v Chapman**[61] did not give rise to a dispute between

---

[57] [1996] AC 375. See, M. Thomas, 'Divorce and Pension Funds' (1997) Conv. 52.
[58] The decision in *Brooks v Brooks* will not apply to pension schemes where there are numerous members. Such schemes are governed by the Welfare Reform and Pensions Act 1999.
[59] [2009] 1 FLR 115.
[60] [1954] AC 429.
[61] *Ibid.*

the beneficiaries as to their respective rights: rather, what was being proposed was a variation from the intentions of the settlor. The House of Lords affirmed the decision of the Court of Appeal and, whilst accepting that it had an inherent jurisdiction to sanction a departure from the terms of a trust, the House of Lords held that the facts of the present case did not warrant a departure from the terms of the trust.

The decision of the House of Lords in *Chapman v Chapman* made it clear that the courts were not in a position to sanction variations of trust simply because the proposed variations were beneficial to the beneficiaries from a fiscal point of view. As to whether this limited jurisdiction was wholly appropriate, Lord Simonds explained that 'it is for the legislature . . . to determine whether there should be a change in the law and what that change should be'.[62] Given the severely limited jurisdiction of the court, it is not surprising therefore that in 1957 the Law Reform Committee was sanctioned to review the law and consider proposals for change. The Committee reported that the inherent jurisdiction of the court had become so restrictively applied by the courts that it was time to implement a much wider discretionary power on the courts to sanction variations of trust. The Law Reform Committee took the view that the court should not shy away from making variations of trust which were designed to avoid tax liability arising in the future. In the view of the Committee, a proposed resettlement of a trust on grounds of tax should be allowed by the courts.

The wide discretion in s. 1 of the Variation of Trust Act 1958

A wide discretion to vary the terms of a trust is provided in s. 1 of the 1958 Act.

> **KEY STATUTE**
>
> **1.— Jurisdiction of courts to vary trusts**
>
> (1) Where property, whether real or personal, is held on trusts arising, whether before or after the passing of this Act, under any will, settlement or other disposition, the court may if it thinks fit by order approve on behalf of –
>
> (a) any person having, directly or indirectly, an interest, whether vested or contingent, under the trusts who by reason of infancy or other incapacity is incapable of assenting, or
>
> (b) any person (whether ascertained or not) who may become entitled, directly or indirectly, to an interest under the trusts as being at a future date or on the happening of a future event a person of any specified description or a member of any specified class of persons, so however that this paragraph shall not include any person who would be of that description, or a member of that class, as the case may be, if the said date had fallen or the said event had happened at the date of the application to the court, or
>
> (c) any person unborn, or
>
> (d) any person in respect of any discretionary interest of his under protective trusts where the interest of the principal beneficiary has not failed or determined,
>
> any arrangement (by whomsoever proposed, and whether or not there is any other person beneficially interested who is capable of assenting thereto) varying or revoking all

---

[62] [1954] AC 429 at 444.

or any of the trusts, or enlarging the powers of the trustees of managing or administering any of the property subject to the trusts:

provided that except by virtue of paragraph (d) of this subsection the court shall not approve an arrangement on behalf of any person unless the carrying out thereof would be for the benefit of that person.

The Variation of Trusts Act 1958 applies to trusts of both real and personal property. Furthermore, the Act is retrospective and therefore applies to trusts created before and after the commencement of the Act. The central feature in s. 1 of the Variation of Trusts Act 1958 is that the court can approve on behalf of four categories of persons 'any arrangement . . . varying or revoking all or any of the trusts, or enlarging the powers of the trustees managing or administering any of the property subject to the trusts'. The section was described by Evershed MR in **Re Steed's W.T.** as a 'very wide and, indeed revolutionary discretion'.[63] Although the application can be made by any interested party, for example, the settlor, trustee or beneficiary, the court can only make an arrangement in favour of four classes of persons, which are listed in s. 1(1)(a)–(d). Essentially, these are persons who are unborn, unascertained or infants. Additionally, the section confers upon the court a power to make an order on behalf of a person who has a discretionary contingent interest under a protective trust. Where that person's interest has not failed or determined, the court can make an order against the wishes of that person. With the exception of discretionary beneficiaries under a protective trust, the principal beneficiaries on whose behalf the court is acting and consenting are beneficiaries who cannot give their consent. In this respect, it has often been said that the operation of s. 1 of the Variation of Trusts Act 1958 is a statutory extension of the rule in **Saunders v Vautier**,[64] which has already been discussed earlier in the chapter. For example, in **Goulding v James**[65] Mummery LJ explained that jurisdiction in s. 1 of the Variation of Trusts Act 1958 was 'a statutory expansion of the consent principle embodied in the rule in **Saunders v Vautier**'.[66]

A number of different types of arrangements have been approved under the Variation of Trusts Act 1925. The Act has been used to expand the investment powers of trustees[67] even though the power to do so coexists under s. 57 of the Trustee Act 1925. In **Re Lister's Will Trusts**[68] Buckley J authorised a variation of a trust to include a power of advancement which did not exist in the original trust instrument. Of course, the majority of applications made under the 1958 Act have involved schemes attempted to avoid tax liability. However, it will be observed below that, although taxation benefits are clearly benefits which the court can take into consideration when approving a scheme for the benefit of a person, taxation is not the only factor the court will look to. In **Goulding v James**[69] a proposed variation of the terms of a trust was authorised where it increased the possible interests of unborn children fivefold.

---

[63] [1960] Ch. 407 at 420.
[64] (1841) 4 Beav. 115.
[65] [1997] 2 All ER 239. See P. Luxton, 'Variations of Trusts: Settlor's Intentions and the Consent Principle in *Saunders* v *Vautier*' (1997) MLR 719.
[66] [1997] 2 All ER 239 at 427. See also *Wyndham* v *Egremont* [2009] EWHC 2076 (Ch.).
[67] *Re Byng's Will Trusts* [1959] 1 WLR 375.
[68] [1962] 1 WLR 1441.
[69] [1997] 2 All ER 239.

It has been mentioned that Variation of Trust Act 1958 applies to trusts of personal and real property. Whilst the Act applies to most types of trust, it was held not to apply to a trust of money paid into court by the manufacturers of a drug that caused defects in children born to mothers who had taken thalidomide. The matter arose in **Allen v Distillers Co (Biochemicals)**[70] where an application was made to vary the terms of the money which was held for the benefit of children. Under the original agreement the money was to be paid to the children on their attaining the age of majority. Under the terms of the proposed scheme, the payment was to be deferred beyond majority. Eveleigh J held that the Variation of Trusts Act 1958 did not extend to the type of trust in question. The judge explained that the 'Act contemplates a situation where a beneficial interest is created which did not previously exist and probably one which is related to at least one other beneficial interest. Moreover, the Act is designed to deal with a situation where the original disposition was intended to endure according to its terms but which in the light of changed attitudes and circumstances it is fair and reasonable to vary.'[71]

The persons on whose behalf an arrangement can be made

Section 1(1) of the Variation of Trusts Act 1958 allows the court to consent on behalf of four categories of persons when making an arrangement which has the effect of varying the original trusts. These individual categories require a little more analysis as some of them are rather complicated.

KEY STATUTE

S. 1(1)(a) – any person having, directly or indirectly, an interest, whether vested or contingent, under the trusts who by reason of infancy or other incapacity is incapable of assenting.

The first category is relatively straightforward and covers infants and those with some other incapacity such as insanity. Thus a court can consent on behalf of an infant beneficiary as well as a beneficiary who is suffering from insanity.

KEY STATUTE

S. 1(1)(b) – any person (whether ascertained or not) who may become entitled, directly or indirectly, to an interest under the trusts as being at a future date or on the happening of a future event a person of any specified description or a member of any specified class of persons, so however that this paragraph shall not include any person who would be of that description, or a member of that class, as the case may be, if the said date had fallen or the said event had happened at the date of the application to the court.

This category is by far the most complicated one in terms of its construction. It envisages those beneficiaries who are unascertained by reason of the fact that the event which ascertains them has not yet occurred. A good example is where consent is given on behalf of beneficiaries entitled under a discretionary trust. For example, in **Re Clitheroe's**

---

[70] [1974] QB 384.
[71] [1974] QB 384 at 394.

Settlement Trusts[72] a settlement was created in 1954 in favour of a specified class by Lord Clitheroe. The settlement conferred upon the trustees a discretion to apply the property in favour of descendants of the settlor's father including any spouse; however, the settlor was excluded from the settlement. As a result of the introduction of the Finance Act 1958 it became apparent that if the settlor married and his wife received any interest under the settlement then such income would be treated as the income of the husband for tax purposes. The settlor proposed to vary the trust by assigning his and his wife's interest under the settlement to his daughter. In return he covenanted to pay another sum of money to his wife. The question before Danckwerts J was whether the court could consent on behalf of his wife who was a discretionary beneficiary, but who had not been appointed as such by the discretionary trustees. Danckwerts J approved the variation on the grounds that it was for the benefit of the settlor, his wife and any unborn beneficiaries. In the course of his judgment, the judge explained that under:

> section 1 of the Variation of Trusts Act, 1958, I have to be satisfied, except in the case of protective trusts, that the person on whose behalf I have to approve a variation procures a benefit. In the present settlement there are no protective trusts because it is not a case of a determinable life interest, but of an immediate discretionary trust under which certain persons are benefiting. Accordingly, I must be satisfied that the proposed variation is not only for the benefit of the infant beneficiaries who have been joined in this application, but also for the benefit of any future spouses of Lord Clitheroe whose interests are going to be excluded by the proposed deed of variation.[73]

This category, however, does not include persons who have an existing contingent interest in the trust no matter how remote it may be. The matter is neatly illustrated by the decision of the court in **Knocker v Youle**[74] where a trust was created in favour of a daughter and then in default to cousins of the daughter. The daughter had numerous cousins and some of them were in Australia. A variation of the trust was presented to the court and, given the impracticalities of getting the consent of all of the cousins, the question before the court was whether consent could be given on their behalf by the court. Warner J refused to sanction the variation on behalf of the cousins, on the grounds that they were not within s. 1(1)(b) of the Variation of Trusts Act 1958. The judge explained that the sister's cousins, although having the remotest of interests, were persons who were nevertheless entitled to an interest and not persons who may become entitled to an interest. Warner J explained that a person who has an 'actual interest directly conferred upon him or her by a settlement, albeit a remote interest, cannot properly be described as one who "may become" entitled to an interest'.[75]

Finally, in respect to the persons identified in s. 1(1)(b) of the Variation of Trusts Act 1958, the court cannot consent on behalf of persons who would become entitled to the trust property if the future date or event had already occurred at the date of the application to the court. This is a rather complicated area of law and is sometimes referred to as the 'double contingency test', which means that the section requires that the persons on whose behalf the court is consenting must be persons who may become entitled to an interest at some future date; however, they must not be persons who would become entitled to the trust property if the future event had occurred at the time of the application.

---

[72] [1959] 1 WLR 1159.
[73] [1959] 1 WLR 1159 at 1162.
[74] [1986] 1 WLR 934. See J.G. Riddall, 'Does it or Doesn't It? – Contingent Interests and the Variation of Trusts Act 1958' (1987) Conv. 144.
[75] [1986] 1 WLR 934 at 937.

Basically, whilst the court can consent on behalf of those persons who may become entitled to an interest at some future date or event, the court cannot consent on behalf of those persons who are in existence and who would definitely become entitled had the event or future date occurred at the time of the application. This is, perhaps, best explained with reference to the decided cases. The first case is the decision in *Re Suffert's Settlement*[76] where a settlement was made by a settlor in 1935 whereby property was settled upon trust for the settlor for life and thereafter on protective trusts[77] for her daughter. When the settlor died, the daughter became entitled to the trust property under the protective trust. The settlement ultimately provided that the property should go to her statutory next of kin. A variation of the settlement was proposed by the daughter, and at the time of the application, she had three cousins who were her next of kin. One of the cousins consented to the variation, but the other two did not. The question before Buckley J was whether the court could consent on behalf of the other two cousins. The court held that whilst a variation could be sanctioned, it could not consent of behalf of the two cousins who would be entitled as the statutory next of kin.

A similar decision was reached in *Re Moncrieff's Settlement Trusts*[78] where the settlor created a trust for the benefit of her daughter, Ann Moncrieff, and then for her issue and in default of appointment for those entitled on intestacy. Although Ann Moncrieff had a daughter, the daughter died at the age of 14 and was never appointed under the trust. Ann Moncrieff and her husband adopted a son in 1946 and in 1961 summoned for a variation of the trust. At that time her adopted son was of majority age and she also had some next of kin in the form of maternal cousins. Buckley J held that he could not consent on behalf of the adopted son, on the grounds that he was the next of kin of Ann Moncrieff and would become entitled on her death. Buckley J was, however, prepared to sanction the variation on behalf of the maternal cousins as they were not entitled to Ann's estate on her death. Buckley J held that 'none of the other persons who might become entitled to participate in the estate of the settlor were she to survive the first respondent and then die intestate is excluded because none of them would be within the class of next-of-kin if she died today. Therefore, I am in a position to approve the arrangement on behalf of all persons whether ascertained or not who might become interested in the settlor's estate at a future date with the exception of the first respondent (that is, the adopted son).'[79]

The third category of persons on whose behalf the court can consent are unborn persons. This category is relatively straightforward; the court's consent will not be required where it is clear that there will be no unborn persons on whose behalf consent is being sought. For example, in *Re Pettifor's Will Trust*[80] a variation was proposed with the effect that any future child of a lady would be excluded under the terms of the variation. The woman was 78 years of age and the trustees applied to the court to get the consent of an unborn child of the woman. Pennycuick J held that the Variation of Trusts Act 1958 was not designed to deal with impossible contingencies and that it would be a waste of money for trustees to seek to get consent for contingencies which were impossible. In the

---

[76] [1961] Ch. 1.

[77] Protective trusts were analysed in Chapter 3. Protective trusts are created by settlors for irresponsible beneficiaries and protect the trust property from being wasted by the beneficiary. Typically, property is settled in favour of the protective beneficiary with a forfeiture of the property should the beneficiary become bankrupt. The forfeiting event has the effect of providing for others named by the settlor, for example a class of discretionary beneficiaries.

[78] [1962] 1 WLR 1344.

[79] [1962] 1 WLR 1344 at 1346.

[80] [1966] Ch. 257.

course of his judgment, the learned judge explained that 'in the case of a woman in the seventies, not only would trustees be authorised to distribute a fund on that footing without any doubt or question, but the court would, I think, normally consider it an unnecessary waste of money for the trustees to come to the court and ask for leave so to distribute. Trustees can with complete safety and propriety deal with their funds on the basis that a woman of 70 will not have a further child.'[81]

The final category of persons includes persons who have a discretionary interest under a protective trust where the interest of the principal beneficiary has not yet failed. For example, where property is settled on protective trust for A, but then on a discretionary trust for B, the court may consent of behalf of B. This category does not require that the arrangement which is being approved is for the benefit of B. Even where it may be disadvantageous, the court can approve the arrangement. In such a case, given the restricted interest conferred upon the protective beneficiary, any variation sought is most frequently for the benefit of the protective beneficiary, for example, an enlargement of the beneficiary's interest. Where the protective trust serves no useful purpose any more, because of the change of circumstances surrounding the beneficiary in whose favour it was created, there is no need for the property to vest in any other person such as another discretionary beneficiary. Although it is not necessary to show benefit for the person on whose behalf the court is consenting, the requirement of benefit is not totally dispensed with. For example, in *Re Baker's Settlement Trust*[82] an arrangement was sought to convert a protective life interest into an absolute one to both capital and income. Ungoed-Thomas J adjourned proceedings on the grounds that 'where property was held on protective life trusts and an application was made to the court to vary those trusts, evidence, including evidence of the financial position of the applicant and her husband, must be laid before the court to show to what extent the protective trusts continued to serve any useful purpose'.[83]

The requirement of benefit

At the heart of the court's power to sanction a variation of trusts under s. 1 of the Variation of Trusts Act 1958 is the requirement of benefit. An arrangement can only be approved if it is for the benefit of the person on whose behalf the court is consenting.[84] Most typically, the benefit will be financial, for example a reduction in tax liability. However, financial benefit is not the only thing that the court will inquire into. In addition to any financial benefits, the proposed variation must be on the whole beneficial. For example, in *Re Van Gruisen's Will Trust*[85] Ungoed-Thomas J explained that the:

> court is not merely concerned with this actuarial calculation, even assuming that it satisfies the statutory requirement that the arrangement must be for the benefit of the infants and unborn persons. The court is also concerned whether the arrangement as a whole, in all the circumstances, is such that it is proper to approve it. The court's concern involves, inter alia, a practical and businesslike consideration of the arrangement, including the total amounts of the advantages which the various parties obtain, and their bargaining strength.[86]

---

[81] [1966] Ch. 257 at 260.
[82] [1964] 1 WLR 336.
[83] [1964] 1 WLR 336 at 337.
[84] The only exception being s. 1(1)(d); this has been discussed above.
[85] [1964] 1 WLR 449.
[86] [1964] 1 WLR 449 at 450.

In *Re Holt's Settlement Trusts*[87] a scheme was authorised whereby the interests of infant beneficiaries were deferred until they were 30 years old. The scheme was thought to be beneficial on the grounds that it was for their social and moral benefit. The fact that that the children had to wait for a longer period meant that they could not just sit back idly on the assumption that they were financially provided for.

APPLYING THE LAW

Some 25 years ago a settlor created a trust for the benefit of his wife for life, thereafter for his children equally and thereafter for the issue of his children. The trust property consists of a fund in excess of £5 million. The settlor died a few years ago and his children who are aged 20, 23 and 27 respectively wish to resettle the money on new trusts in the Isle of Man where all of them have been living for the last few years. The trust in the Isle of Man would certainly attract less taxation.

Can the court approve the resettlement?

A very good example of a non-financial benefit is provided by the decision in *Re Remnant's Settlement Trusts*[88] where a trust fund was created in favour of the children of two sisters. The terms of the trust provided that if any of the children practised Roman Catholicism or married a Roman Catholic their interest would be forfeited in favour of the children of the other sister. One sister's children were Roman Catholics whilst the other were Protestants. The question before the court was whether the original trust could be varied so as remove the forfeiture clause. Pennycuick J approved the removal of the forfeiture clause on the grounds that it was for the overall benefit of all of the beneficiaries. In the course of his judgment, he explained that 'it remains to consider whether the arrangement is a fair and proper one. As far as I can see, there is no reason for saying otherwise, except that the arrangement defeats this testator's intention. That is a serious but by no means conclusive consideration. I have reached the clear conclusion that these forfeiture provisions are undesirable in themselves in the circumstances of this case and that an arrangement involving their deletion is a fair and proper one.'[89]

Although financial benefits are clearly taken into account by the court when sanctioning a variation of trust, the mere fact that a financial benefit accrues to a person on whose behalf the court is consenting means that the court will also look to moral and social benefits. If moral and social benefits outweigh the financial benefits, the court will not approve a variation. This matter is neatly illustrated by the decision of the Court of Appeal in *Re Weston's Settlements*.[90] The facts of this case concerned two settlements made by Stanley Weston in 1964 in favour of his two sons and their children. Stanley Weston came to England from Russia in 1894 and, despite a short education, he went straight into business opening as a sole trader. His sole trade business proved to be successful and he subsequently opened a chain of retail shops. In 1964 the business was turned into a public company, The Stanley Western Group Ltd, and Stanley Weston took his office as Chairman. Both settlements in favour of his two sons were created over substantial shares in the company. At the time when the settlements were created there was

---

[87] [1969] 1 Ch. 100. Discussed in more detail below.
[88] [1970] Ch. 560.
[89] [1970] Ch. 560 at 566.
[90] [1969] 1 Ch. 223.

no capital gains; however, as a result of the enactment of the Finance Act 1965, capital gains tax would be payable on the shares. As a result of these changes, the Weston family decided to move to Jersey in order to avoid being subject to the tax. The Finance Act 1965 did not apply if the majority of the trustees were outside the United Kingdom and the beneficiaries were also not resident in the United Kingdom. Additionally, the legislation required that the administration of the trust should be carried outside the United Kingdom. Stanley Weston moved to Jersey in 1966 and his older son followed in 1967. Three months later Stanley Weston sought to appoint new trustees in Jersey with a view to moving the settlements made in the United Kingdom to the new trustees subject to new, but identical trusts to be administered in Jersey by Jersey trustees. The question before the Court of Appeal was whether the variations proposed by Stanley Weston would be approved under the Variation of Trusts Act 1958. In other words, should the court consent on behalf of the children and any future unborn children?

The Court of Appeal refused to sanction the arrangement proposed, on the grounds that it was not for the benefit of the children. Lord Denning MR accepted that the proposed variation was undoubtedly for the financial benefit of all the parties, but emphasised that the court should also look to the wider social and moral benefits.

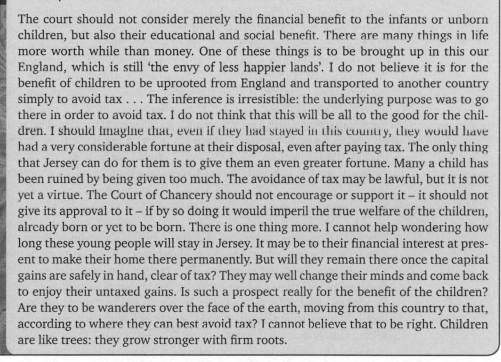

KEY CITATION

Re Weston's Settlements [1969] 1 Ch. 223 (per Lord Denning MR at 445–6)

The court should not consider merely the financial benefit to the infants or unborn children, but also their educational and social benefit. There are many things in life more worth while than money. One of these things is to be brought up in this our England, which is still 'the envy of less happier lands'. I do not believe it is for the benefit of children to be uprooted from England and transported to another country simply to avoid tax . . . The inference is irresistible: the underlying purpose was to go there in order to avoid tax. I do not think that this will be all to the good for the children. I should imagine that, even if they had stayed in this country, they would have had a very considerable fortune at their disposal, even after paying tax. The only thing that Jersey can do for them is to give them an even greater fortune. Many a child has been ruined by being given too much. The avoidance of tax may be lawful, but it is not yet a virtue. The Court of Chancery should not encourage or support it – it should not give its approval to it – if by so doing it would imperil the true welfare of the children, already born or yet to be born. There is one thing more. I cannot help wondering how long these young people will stay in Jersey. It may be to their financial interest at present to make their home there permanently. But will they remain there once the capital gains are safely in hand, clear of tax? They may well change their minds and come back to enjoy their untaxed gains. Is such a prospect really for the benefit of the children? Are they to be wanderers over the face of the earth, moving from this country to that, according to where they can best avoid tax? I cannot believe that to be right. Children are like trees: they grow stronger with firm roots.

The decision in *Re Weston's Settlements*[91] should be contrasted with the decision in *Re Seale's Marriage Settlement*[92] where a trust was created in England for the benefit of a husband and wife and their children. The children were all born in the United Kingdom;

---

[91] [1969] 1 Ch. 223.
[92] [1961] 3 All ER 136.

however, when they were very small the whole family emigrated to Canada. The children grew up as Canadians and the family sought to appoint Canadian trustees as well as moving the trust to Canada to be held by the Canadian Trustees on the same terms of the English trust. Buckley J authorised this arrangement to take place. Lord Denning MR distinguished the decision in *Re Seale's Marriage Settlement* in *Re Weston's Settlements* on the grounds that the family in *Re Seale's Marriage* had moved to Canada long before the variation was proposed. It was not a variation for pure tax reasons whereas the variation proposed in *Re Weston's Settlements* was deemed by Lord Denning MR as a pure tax ploy.

One question which has arisen before the courts is whether the court can sanction an arrangement to vary a trust which is certainly beneficial, but may involve some risk to future beneficiaries. The matter was explored in *Re Cohen's Settlement Trusts*[93] where the proposed arrangement was to distribute the trust fund at an earlier date in order to avoid paying estate duty. Property had been settled upon trust until all of the settlor's sons should have died and then the fund was to be divided between such of the settlor's grandchildren as were then living, who attained 21 or being female married under that age; and the issue then living of any grandchild who should then have died, who attained 21 or being female married under that age, in equal shares per capita, the issue of a grandchild taking the shares which their parent would have taken if living at the material date. The proposed arrangement was to distribute the trust property in June 1973; however, this was not sanctioned by the court on grounds that this would not be for the benefit of future unborn beneficiaries. However, the court can sanction an arrangement even where there is an element of risk, provided that it is for the overall benefit of the beneficiaries. For example, in another case bearing the same name as the one just discussed, the court explained that a risk was allowed if it was a type of risk that an adult would be prepared to take. The case in question in *Re Cohen's Will Trusts*[94] where the proposed variation was on the whole beneficial to the parties; however, there was potential risk that should any of the testator's children die before the testator's widow then the scheme arrangement would be disadvantageous. The testator's widow was 80 years of age at the time and the court was prepared to sanction the arrangement despite the element of risk. Dankwerts J held that 'if it is a risk that an adult would be prepared to take, the court is prepared to take it on behalf of an infant'.[95]

The wishes of the settlor

When making an arrangement under s. 1 of the Variation of Trusts Act 1958, the question arises as to whether the court should take the wishes of the settlor into account when approving an arrangement. This matter was explored by the Court of Appeal in *Re Steed's Will Trusts*[96] where a testator left property, including a farm, on protective trust for the plaintiff for her life and after her death as she should appoint. The trustees had the power to make capital payments to the plaintiff as and when they thought appropriate by selling the farm. It was the intention of the settlor that the plaintiff would be adequately provided for during her life because of her loyalty as a long-serving housekeeper. The testator was also wary of the fact that he did not want the plaintiff to have an absolute interest in the farm, given the real threat that the plaintiff's brother would take advantage

---

[93] [1965] 3 All ER 139. See also *Re Tinker's Settlement* [1960] 1 WLR 1011.
[94] [1959] 1 WLR 865.
[95] [1959] 1 WLR 865 at 868.
[96] [1960] Ch. 407.

of her. The farm, which had been let out to the plaintiff's brother, was decided to be sold by the trustees. The plaintiff sought to appoint herself as the person entitled to the farm on her death and sought a variation of the existing trust by removing the protective trust. The net effect of this would be to make her absolute owner of the farm. The arrangement was refused by the Court of Appeal on the grounds that the court should take into consideration the settlor's intentions. Lord Evershed MR explained that 'the court must regard the proposal as a whole, and so regarding it, then ask itself whether in the exercise of its jurisdiction it should approve that proposal on behalf of the person who cannot give a consent, because he is not in a position to do so. If that is a right premise, then it follows that the court is bound to look at the scheme as a whole, and when it does so, to consider, as surely it must, what really was the intention of the [settlor].'[97]

The question of the settlor's intention arose in **Goulding v James**[98] where a testatrix left property for her daughter, June Goulding, for life, remainder to June's son, Marcus Goulding, provided that he attained the age of 40. The will provided that should Marcus fail to attain that age or should he die before June, the children of Marcus living at his death should take the capital. The testatrix died in 1994 leaving an estate worth £1.14 million. June and Marcus proposed that there be a variation of the existing trust to the effect that the estate be held on trust for June and Marcus in shares of 45 per cent each and the remaining 10 per cent to be held for Marcus's children. Actuarial evidence showed that the proposed scheme would in fact increase the interests of the children by fivefold. Marcus who had married an American wife, lived in the United States, but did not as yet have any children. Marcus was aged 32 at the time of the proposed variation. The proposed variation could only be sanctioned if the court could give approval on behalf of Marcus's unborn children. The trustees of the will, however, pointed out that the proposed arrangement was clearly inconsistent with the testatrix's intentions. In particular, the trustees pointed out to the court that June's mother did not want June to have any interest in the capital, on the grounds that she did not trust June's husband. The evidence showed that he had mistreated June physically. As to the reasons for delaying Marcus's right to the capital until he was 40, the trustees pointed out that the testatrix knew that he was unlikely to settle down until much later in life. At first instance, the proposed arrangement was not authorised by the court applying the principle in **Re Steed's Will Trust**[99] because it was inconsistent with the intention of the testatrix. The Court of Appeal, however, sanctioned the proposed arrangement and distinguished **Re Steed's Will Trust**. In the Court of Appeal, Mummery LJ did not seem to think it was appropriate to pay significance to the testatrix's intention. The judge explained that 'the intentions and wishes of [the testatrix], expressed externally to her will in relation to the adult beneficiaries and an adult non-beneficiary, had little, if any, relevance or weight to the issue of approval on behalf of future unborn great grandchildren, whose interest in the residue was multiplied fivefold under the proposed arrangement'.[100] With regard to the decision in **Re Steed's Will Trust** Mummery LJ explained that it was very different on its facts. There the testator had provided intrinsic evidence in the will that he did not want the plaintiff to have an absolute interest in the trust property. Furthermore, given the fact that a protective trust was created in favour of the plaintiff in **Re Steed's Will Trust** the court was not required to consider the element of benefit for persons entitled

---

[97] [1960] Ch. 407 at 421.
[98] [1997] 2 All ER 239.
[99] [1960] Ch. 407.
[100] [1997] 2 All ER 239 at 251.

to a discretionary interest on failure of the protective interest. In **Goulding v James**[101] the proposed scheme was for the benefit of the unborn children. The case clearly lays down the principle that, provided the benefit test is satisfied, the intentions of the settlor are irrelevant. Sir Ralph Gibson explained that he could not see why 'evidence of the intention of the testator can be of any relevance whatever if it does no more than explain why the testator gave the interests set out in the will and the nature and degree of feeling with which such provisions were selected'.[102]

Variation or resettlement

In making an 'arrangement' under s. 1 of the Variation of Trusts Act 1958 the court is empowered with a very wide discretion. However, despite this wide discretion, the court is only entitled to vary the terms of an existing trust and not to completely resettle the trust property. Despite the distinction, there is a blurred line between a resettlement and a variation. The test to establish whether an arrangement amounts to a resettlement or a variation was explained by Megarry J in **Re Ball's Settlement**.[103] Megarry J explained that:

> [i]f an arrangement changes the whole substratum of the trust, then it may well be that it cannot be regarded merely as varying that trust. But if an arrangement, while leaving the substratum, effectuates the purpose of the original trust by other means, it may still be possible to regard that arrangement as merely varying the original trusts, even though the means employed are wholly different and even though the form is completely changed.[104]

An example of a variation of trust is provided by **Re Holt's Settlement Trusts**[105] where a settlement was created in favour of a lady for her life and thereafter for her children provided that they attained the age of 21 years. A scheme was proposed whereby the mother would surrender her interest in half of the income and that the children's right to the capital be postponed until they were 30 years of age. This proposed scheme was sanctioned by the court as a genuine variation of the trust. On the other hand, in **Re T's Settlement Trusts**[106] a variation was not sanctioned where the proposed scheme was to put the interest of a beneficiary upon protective trust. On the facts, an infant was entitled to a 25 per cent interest to income under a trust on her attaining the age of majority. The infant's mother sought to transfer the share of that infant to new trustees to be held upon protective trust for the daughter for life with remainder to her issue. Wilberforce J refused to sanction the variation, on the grounds that this would amount to a new trust rather than a variation of the existing trust. The judge explained that:

> it is obviously not possible to define exactly the point at which the jurisdiction of the court under the Variation of Trusts Act stops or should not be exercised. Moreover, I have no desire to cut down the very useful jurisdiction which this Act has conferred upon the court. But I am satisfied that the proposal as originally made to me falls outside it. Though presented as 'a variation' it is in truth a complete new resettlement. The former trust funds were to be got in from the former trustees and held upon wholly new trusts such as might be made by an absolute owner of the funds. I do not think that the court can approve this.[107]

---

[101] [1997] 2 All ER 239.
[102] [1997] 2 All ER 239 at 252.
[103] [1968] 1 WLR 899.
[104] [1968] 1 WLR 899 at 905.
[105] [1969] 1 Ch. 100.
[106] [1964] Ch. 158.
[107] [1964] Ch. 158 at 162.

● The effect of a variation

Once the court orders a variation of the terms of the trust, the question arises as to whether the variation of the beneficial interests takes effect as a result of the order or as a result of the arrangement. The question is of significance from the point of view of formality requirements. If the beneficial interests are varied as a result of the arrangement and not the court order, then with regard to the beneficiaries who have consented, surely their interests will not move unless they comply with s. 53(1)(c) of the Law of Property Act 1925, which requires that they be put in writing.[108] In *Re Holmden's Settlement Trusts*.[109] Lord Reid explained that the:

> beneficiaries are not bound by variations because the court has made the variation. Each beneficiary is bound because he has consented to the variation. If he was not of full age when the arrangement was made he is bound because the court was authorised by the Act to approve of it on his behalf and did so by making an order. If he was of full age and did not in fact consent he is not affected by the order of the court and he is not bound. So the arrangement must be regarded as an arrangement made by the beneficiaries themselves. The court merely acted on behalf of or as representing those beneficiaries who were not in a position to give their own consent and approval.[110]

The question of whether the variations of beneficial interests required compliance with the formality requirement in s. 53(1)(c) of the Law of Property Act 1925 was considered by Megarry J in *Re Holt's Settlement Trusts*.[111] The judge was of the opinion that 'Parliament in the Act of 1958 had provided by necessary implication an exception from section 53(1)(c).'[112] With regard to variations which involved a beneficiary forfeiting some beneficial right in return for some other right, Megarry J explained that:

> where, as here, the arrangement consists of an agreement made for valuable consideration, and that agreement is specifically enforceable, then the beneficial interests pass to the respective purchasers on the making of the agreement. Those interests pass by virtue of the species of constructive trust made familiar by contracts for the sale of land, whereunder the vendor becomes a constructive trustee for the purchaser as soon as the contract is made, albeit the constructive trust has special features about it. Section 53(2) provides that 'This section does not affect the creation or operation of resulting, implied or constructive trusts.' Accordingly, because the trust was constructive, section 53(1)(c) was excluded.[113]

Conclusion

This chapter has looked at the principles and rules governing variations of trusts. Whilst the trustee is expected to execute the terms of the trust as laid down by the settlor, there may be occasions when a departure from the original terms of a trust may be beneficial to the beneficiaries. Many trusts have lifespans of many years, and whilst the settlor can attempt to cater for possible future contingencies that may affect the trust, inevitably a

---

[108] See Chapter 5.
[109] [1968] AC 685.
[110] [1968] AC 685 at 701.
[111] [1969] 1 Ch. 100.
[112] [1969] 1 Ch. 100 at 115.
[113] [1969] 1 Ch. 100 at 116.

settlor cannot cater for all of them. Changes in social and economic conditions may mean that the terms of the original trust no longer serve their purpose; furthermore, changes in fiscal practice may mean that the trust and its beneficiaries may be subject to a higher taxation than originally envisaged. In this chapter it has been observed that, until the enactment of the Variation of Trusts Act 1958, the courts had a very limited inherent jurisdiction to sanction departures from the original terms of a trust. Although numerous statutory provisions were embedded in various pieces of legislation, such provisions were very specific and operated in the specifically identified contexts.

It has been observed that the limitations of the inherent jurisdiction of the court, which was exposed by the House of Lords' decision in *Chapman* v *Chapman*,[114] led to the enactment of the Variation of Trusts Act 1958. This chapter has explored the wide jurisdiction under this Act, which confers upon the court a discretion to consent on behalf of a number of persons when making an arrangement which is for their benefit. Although the Act has been primarily invoked to confer upon beneficiaries financial benefits, it has been observed that the court is not solely influenced by such considerations. The court will look to a proposed variation in its entirety and decide whether, despite the financial benefit that may accrue to the beneficiaries, the proposed variation is in their moral and social interests. What is interesting in this process is the question of how far a court should be able to dictate what is in the moral and social interests of, for example, children, when the family have decided to vary a trust which confers greater financial benefits on their children. The courts have on many occasions explained that they represent a form of statutory attorney exercising consent on behalf of persons such as children; this may be so, but does the statutory attorney give them a power to decide the moral and social welfare of children which is clearly the duty of their parents?

●● Moot points

1 Can the rule in *Saunders* v *Vautier* be used to vary the terms of an existing trust so that the trustees are subject to different duties?

2 The 'compromise jurisdiction' which is one of grounds for invoking the court's inherent power to vary the terms of a trust requires that there must be genuine dispute as to the rights of the beneficiaries before a compromise can be sanctioned. The jurisdiction was successfully applied in *Re Downshire Settled Estates* and *Re Blackwell's Settlement Trusts* but not in *Re Chapman's Settlement Trusts*. All three cases can be read at [1953] Ch. 216. Explain why the compromise jurisdiction was invoked in the first two cases and not in *Re Chapman's Settlement Trusts*.

3 Where would the enlargement of an investment power in a trust instrument be made?

4 Explain the reasons for the enactment of the Variation of Trusts Act 1958?

5 On whose behalf can the court consent under s. 1 of the Variation of Trusts Act 1958 and what types of benefit will suffice for an arrangement to be made on behalf of the persons to which consent is being given?

---

[114] [1954] AC 429.

6 Read the decision of the Court of Appeal in *Re Weston's Settlements* [1969] 1 Ch 233 and explain why the court refused to approve the scheme of variation proposed by the settlor. Do you think the courts are right in making decisions about the moral and social welfare of children when those decisions should be made by their parents? Do you think that the refusal of the court to sanction a variation of the trust in this case was an undue interference in the freedom of members of a family to decide where they live?

Further reading

Luxton, P. 'Variations of Trust: Settlor's Intention and the Consent Principle in *Saunders* v *Vautier*' (1997) MLR 719. Provides an account of the decision of the Court of Appeal in *Goulding* v *James* [1997] 2 All ER 239.

Marshall, O.R. 'Deviations from the Terms of a Trust' [1954] 17 MLR 420. Provides an excellent account of the limited inherent jurisdiction of the court to vary the terms of a trust and examines the decision in *Chapman* v *Chapman* [1954] AC 429.

Riddall, J.G. 'Does it or Doesn't it? – Contingent Interests and the Variation of Trusts Act 1958' (1987) Conv. 144. Provides an account of the decision in *Knocker* v *Youle* [1986] 1 WLR 1159 and explores those persons on whose behalf the court cannot give consent under s. 1 of the Variation of Trusts Act 1958.

Thomas, M. 'Divorce and Pension Funds' (1997) Conv. 52. Provides an account of the decision of the House of Lords in *Brooks* v *Brooks* [1966] AC 375 where the House of Lords had to consider whether a husband's pension scheme was a post-nuptial settlement capable of variation under the Matrimonial Causes Act 1973.

Visit **www.mylawchamber.co.uk/panesar** to access study support resources including interactive multiple choice questions, practice exam questions with guidance, podcasts, weblinks, legal newsfeed all linked to the **Pearson eText** version of Exploring Equity and Trusts which you can **search**, **highlight** and **personalise** with your **own notes** and **bookmarks**.

premium
mylawchamber
unrivalled support for legal education

Part V
Breach of trust and remedies

Part IV explored some of the major issues relating to the administration of the trusts. It will be recalled that a number of powers and duties are conferred on a trustee which allow him to administer the trust in accordance with the trust instrument or trust law in general. The trustee's powers and duties will be ascertained from the terms of the trust or, in the absence of the trust instrument, from trust law as defined by the common law and statute. Should the trustee fail to comply with the duties that are imposed upon him or improperly exercise a power, the trustee will be liable for breach of trust and make good the loss to the trust instrument.

It will be observed in Chapters 20 and 21 that there are primarily two main remedies available to a beneficiary should the trustee breach the trust. The beneficiary's first remedy will be to bring a personal action against the trustee to replace the loss out of his own pocket. The nature of the personal remedy is essentially compensatory and the trustee will be liable for those losses which have been caused by the trustee's own breach. The trustee may have certain defences in a personal claim that has been brought against him, for example, the consent of a beneficiary to the breach of trust. The success of a personal claim will primarily depend on whether the trustee is solvent and in a position to meet the judgment that has been given against him.

Where a trustee is insolvent, the beneficiary may pursue a proprietary claim against the trust property which is in the hands of the trustee or some other third party who has not acquired the property in good faith and without notice of the trust. Such a remedy will take the form of asserting ownership of an asset which is in the hands of the trustee or some other third party. In most cases it will involve the imposition of a constructive trust on the asset. The imposition of a constructive trust will mean that the trustee or some other third party is denied absolute ownership of the asset being traced and will be compelled to recognize the equitable interest of the beneficiary in that asset. In this respect the proprietary claim is a more powerful remedy than the

▶

personal one since it will allow the beneficiary to claim any subsequent increase in value to the trust property after its misuse by the trustee or some other third party. In other cases, the beneficiary may be awarded a lien on the asset which is in the hands of the trustee or some third party. The effect of a lien is give the beneficiary security for the value of the original trust property which it has lost as a consequence of it being wrongfully in the hands of the trustee or third party. This chapter explores the principles of tracing at common law and in equity and examines the rather technical rules of equity which allow a beneficiary to trace into mixed property. It also examines those circumstances when the right to trace may be lost as against a third party.

20

Breach of trust and personal remedies

Learning objectives

After reading this chapter you should be able to:

→ explain when a breach of trust occurs

→ identify the principal remedies available for breach of trust

→ explain the nature of the personal liability of a trustee

→ explain liability of the trustee for his own acts and liability of the acts of co-trustees

→ understand the difference between compensatory claims and restitutionary claims

→ explain some of the established principles governing measure of liability

→ identify principal defences for breach of trust

→ understand the limitation periods for breach of trust claims

→ understand when the equitable doctrine of laches will apply.

SETTING THE SCENE

Target Holdings v *Redferns* [1996] AC 421: A massive mortgage fraud and a defaulting trustee: who bears the loss?

The facts in the decision of the House of Lords in *Target Holdings* v *Redferns*[1] illustrate some of the concerns which will be the subject of discussion in this chapter. Target Holdings agreed to lend a sum of just over £1.7 million to Crowngate Development Ltd who were seeking to purchase land from a company called Mirage Properties Ltd. Unknown to Target Holdings, the land was actually being purchased for some £775,000; however, because of a combination of an over-valuation and a series of sales from a number of connected companies the land was actually valued at £2 million. Redferns, a firm of solicitors, agreed to act for Crowngate in connection with the sale of the land. Additionally, Redferns agreed to act for Target Holdings in connection with the loan which was to be secured by a charge on the land being purchased by Crowngate. On 28 June 1989, Target Holdings transferred some £1.5 million into the client account of Redferns to be held on bare trust until completion of the sale and mortgage. Only then could the money be released to the sellers. On 29 June 1989, without the consent of Target Holdings, Redferns transferred some £1.25 million into the account of the sellers. Completion of the sale did not take place until a few days later and the charge was not registered until 4 July 1989. Crowngate defaulted on payment and Target, as mortgagees of the land, exercised their power of sale and sold the land for £500,000, clearly well short of the sum they had advanced to Crowngate.

Being the victims of a mortgage fraud, Target Holdings commenced proceedings against Redferns as well the valuers for giving a negligent valuation. However, proceedings against the valuers was meaningless since they were insolvent and in liquidation. The proceedings against Redferns were on the grounds that they had acted in breach of trust by transferring the loan money into the account of the sellers before completion of sale and the execution of the charge. It was established that Redferns were holding the loan money advanced to them by Target Holdings in their client account under a bare trust for Target Holdings.

Clearly, Redferns had acted in breach of trust by transferring property held on trust for Target Holdings before completion of the sale and mortgage. The breach committed by Redfern's gave rise to a number of questions for a trust lawyer:

● Was the breach of trust by Redfern's intentional? Would it make any difference if it was not intentional?

● Did the breach by Redfern's cause Target's loss?

● If Refern's did cause the loss, what remedies would be available to Target?

● Where a trustee does commit a breach, are there any defences for breach of trust?

---

[1] [1996] 1 AC 421. See D. Capper, 'Compensation for Breach of Trust' Conv. 1997, 14, and also C.E.F. Rickett, 'Equitable Compensation: The Giant Stirs' 1996, 112 LQR 27. Rickett argues that the decision highlights the similarity between common law compensation and equitable compensation for breach of trust.

Introduction

This chapter focuses on breach of trust and the personal liability of a trustee for such a breach. At a very basic level a breach of trust will occur where a trustee fails to comply with a duty or improperly exercises a power conferred upon him. It has been seen in the previous chapters that duties and powers are conferred upon trustees either by the trust instrument or by trust law in general as found in relevant statutes[2] and cases decided by the courts. In **Target Holdings v Redferns**[3] Lord Browne-Wilkinson explained that it was 'the basic right of a beneficiary to have the trust duly administered in accordance with the provisions of the trust instrument, if any, and the general law'.[4] A breach of trust will occur when it is deliberately intended by the trustee, for example, where the trustee gambles the trust fund. A breach of trust will also occur when it not deliberate but is merely innocent or technical. In **Armitage v Nurse**[5] Millett LJ explained that 'a breach of trust may be deliberate or inadvertent; it may consist of an actual misappropriation or misapplication of the trust property or merely of an investment or other dealing which is outside the trustee's powers; it may consist of a failure to carry out a positive obligation of the trustees or merely of a want of skill and care on their part in the management of the trust property; it may be injurious to the interests of the beneficiaries or be actually to their benefit'.[6] If the breach does turn out to be a technical breach or an innocent breach, the trustee may have certain defences in his favour.[7]

There are three principal remedies available for breaches of trusts by a trustee:

1 an injunction;
2 a personal claim against the trustee, otherwise known as a personal remedy;
3 a right to trace the trust property, otherwise known as a proprietary claim.

An injunction will be an important remedy where the trustee has not yet committed a breach but the beneficiary anticipates that the trustee may well do so. Where a breach has taken place then the beneficiary may seek to make the trustee personally liable to replace the loss. A personal claim against the trustee normally requires the trustee to compensate the beneficiary for any losses that have been caused to the trust estate. Such compensatory liability, as will be discovered in more detail during the course of this chapter, requires the beneficiary to show that the breach has caused a loss to the trust fund, which the trustee must now replace by paying out of his own pocket. In some cases, however, the personal claim against the trustee need not be compensatory but restitutionary. It has already been observed in Chapter 17 that a restitutionary claim is pursued in order to reverse an unjust enrichment. Thus, where a trustee breaches a trust, for example purchasing trust property for himself with a view to making a profit, the beneficiary will make a personal claim against the trustee. Although the purchase of the trust property may result in some initial loss to the trust, for example where the trustee does not pay a proper price for the property, the beneficiary will seek to claim the profit made, particularly, where the profit is much greater than the initial loss caused to the beneficiaries. Such a personal claim will not be in the form of demanding compensation

---

[2] For example, the Trustee Act 2000.
[3] [1996] 1 AC 421.
[4] [1996] 1 AC 421 at 434.
[5] [1998] Ch. 241.
[6] [1998] Ch. 241 at 250.
[7] These are examined in more detail later on in this chapter.

but rather an account for the profit that the trustee has made at the expense of the beneficiary. It is important to note here that where a beneficiary has the possibility of either a compensatory claim or a restitutionary claim, he or she must elect one of them. The beneficiary cannot sue for compensation as well as demanding an account for profit. To do so would allow the beneficiary to double recovery from the same wrong.[8]

The success of any personal claim against the trustee will depend on whether he is solvent. If the trustee is insolvent then pursuing a judgment against him may be a fruitless exercise. In such a case the beneficiary may consider pursuing a proprietary claim against the trust property. The nature of tracing and proprietary claims is considered in more detail in Chapter 21. For the time being, suffice to say that a proprietary remedy is a claim against a specific thing rather than a specific person. Where the beneficiaries can identify and locate their beneficial interest then they may seek to claim it back. This proprietary claim is pursued through a process called tracing. Tracing is essentially an evidential process which allows the beneficiary to show to the court that the property in the hands of the trustee or some other third party is in fact the beneficiary's property or is the property which has been acquired by use of the beneficiary property. The advantage of a proprietary claim is that it does not depend on the insolvency of the trustee or any other third party. The beneficiary is not suing any particular individual; rather he is seeking to argue that the property in the hands of the trustee or some third party is in fact his property and that it must be returned to the beneficiary. A further advantage of the proprietary claim is that it allows the beneficiary to take advantage of any increases in value of the property in the hands of a trustee or some other third party. For example, suppose that a trustee is holding a gold ring on trust for a beneficiary who then sells that ring and uses the money to buy a diamond. If the diamond is worth twice as much as the gold ring the beneficiary is entitled to that value because it has been purchased with the beneficiary's money. The proprietary remedy is essentially restitutionary in its nature. What the beneficiary is asking the court to do is to recognise that some property in the hands of the trustee or some other third party is indeed the property of the beneficiary and should be duly restored to him. Failure to order such a return would amount to an unjust enrichment on the part of the trustee. The process of tracing is recognised both at common law and in equity.

 ## The personal liability of the trustee

Where the trustee causes a loss to the trust fund or trust estate he will be liable to replace the loss. The juridical nature of the personal liability of the trustee was, until the decision of the House of Lords in *Target Holdings* v *Redferns*,[9] rather confusing. Much of the debate focused on whether the liability of the trustee was restitutionary or compensatory. In one case Street J explained that the 'obligation of a defaulting trustee is essentially one of

---

[8] See, *Tang Min Sit* v *Capacious Investments* [1996] AC 514, where a loss as well as a gain was made by one company at the expense of another. The claimant company requested an account for the profit which was duly paid by the defendants. When the claimant company sought to claim damages for loss caused by the defendant's breach, the Privy Council held that where the claimant had the possibility of both a compensatory and restitutionary remedy, the claimant had to elect between the two. On the facts, the claimant company was allowed to sue for damages because, in the opinion of the Privy Council, no proper election had been made.

[9] [1996] 1 AC 421.

effecting a restitution to the trust estate. The obligation is of a personal character and its extent is not to be limited by common law principles governing remoteness of damage.'[10] In the Court of Appeal in **Target Holdings v Redferns** Peter Gibson LJ stated that 'it is not in dispute or in doubt that the obligation of a trustee who commits a breach of trust is to account for and to restore to the trust fund that which has thereby been lost to it. The remedy afforded to the beneficiary by equity is compensation in the form of restitution of that which has been lost to the trust estate, not damages.'[11] Whilst there is no doubt that a defaulting trustee is under a duty to restore the trust fund to what its value would have been had there been no breach of trust, to describe the liability of the trustee as strictly restitutionary is rather misleading. Furthermore, it is not clear how, as according to Peter Gibson LJ, the liability can be compensatory and restitutionary at the same time. It is either compensatory or restitutionary as these remedies are very different in their nature. Other commentators have explained that compensation in this sense takes the form of a restorative compensation. Restitution in its proper sense is a response to an unjust enrichment. The claimant must show that the defendant has been unjustly enriched at his expense and that he must return that enrichment to the claimant. In most breaches of trust the trustee does not necessarily make a gain at the expense of the beneficiary: rather, the trustee ends up causing a pure loss to the trust. In such a case it is not appropriate to refer to the liability of the trustee as restitutionary as there is no gain which has been made at the beneficiary's expense.

The proceedings against Redferns were commenced on two grounds. Firstly, Redferns had been negligent in not alerting Target of the suspicion of fraud, particularly, as Redferns were also acting for Crowngate and were aware of the series of sub-sales from Mirage Properties to Crowngate Development. Secondly, Redferns had acted in breach of trust by transferring the loan money into the account of Panther Ltd before completion of sale and the execution of the charge. It is the second of these claims that is particularly relevant for the purposes of this chapter. Target Holdings' basic argument before the court was that Redferns had committed a breach of trust by transferring the loan money before completion and, by applying the existing law, there was an immediate duty to

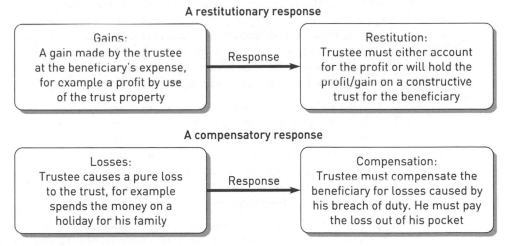

A restitutionary response

| Gains:
A gain made by the trustee at the beneficiary's expense, for example a profit by use of the trust property | → Response → | Restitution:
Trustee must either account for the profit or will hold the profit/gain on a constructive trust for the beneficiary |

A compensatory response

| Losses:
Trustee causes a pure loss to the trust, for example spends the money on a holiday for his family | → Response → | Compensation:
Trustee must compensate the beneficiary for losses caused by his breach of duty. He must pay the loss out of his pocket |

Figure 20.1

[10] *Re Dawson* [1966] 2 NSWR 211 at 214.
[11] [1994] 1 WLR 1089.

effect restitution to the trust estate. It was argued on behalf of Target that principles of foreseeability and remoteness of damage were not relevant to the question whether Redferns should make good the loss. It was argued that the established cases had decided that causation was not a relevant question and that there was an immediate duty to restore the fund once a breach had been established. The approach in the older authorities is best summed up by Professor Alastair Hudson.

> The older authorities imposed principally a personal liability on the trustee, the aim of which was to place the trust fund in the position it would have occupied if there had been no breach of trust. However, there was no question of foreseeability nor remoteness of damage nor the claimant's contributory negligence involved in that personal liability. The trustee's potential liability was expanded by the lack of any foreseeability test. For the defaulting trustee, there was only the defence of acquiescence on the part of the beneficiaries under the trust, such that it was possible to preclude any entitlement to an equitable remedy for breach of trust.
>
> A. Hudson, *Equity and Trusts* 6th edn (2010) Routledge at p. 776

Target Holdings Ltd succeeded in the Court of Appeal, where Peter Gibson LJ held that there was an immediate duty on a trustee to restore the trust fund.[12] The House of Lords, however, reversed the decision of the Court of Appeal, principally on the grounds that the breach of trust was not the cause of Target Holdings' loss and that Target would still have been in the same position had there been no breach of trust. The principal judgment was delivered by Lord Browne-Wilkinson. In the course of his judgment his Lordship attempted to address the approach adopted in some of the older authorities and also the nature of equitable compensation and how it differed from common law compensation. As to the approach of strict and immediate restoration as established in the context of some of the older authorities decided in the context of family trusts, his Lordship commented that it was 'wrong to lift wholesale the detailed rules developed in the context of traditional trusts and then seek to apply them to trusts of quite a different kind'.[13] His Lordship explained that in the more traditional type of trust property would often be settled for one beneficiary for life and thereafter for another: typically, for example, to A for life and thereafter for B in remainder. In such a case the basic duty of the trustee was to preserve the trust property and make sure that it was available for B when B's interest fell into possession. In such a context, any wrongful payment by the trustee of the trust fund required an immediate duty to restore it so that B would get his entitlement. In such a traditional trust the requirement of immediate restoration of the fund was justified. However, his Lordship went on to explain that:

> in the modern world the trust has become a valuable device in commercial and financial dealings. The fundamental principles of equity apply as much to such trusts as they do to the traditional trusts in relation to which those principles were originally formulated. But in my judgment it is important, if the trust is not to be rendered commercially useless, to distinguish between the basic principles of trust law and those specialist rules developed in relation to traditional trusts which were applicable only to such trusts and the rationale of which has no application to trusts of quite a different kind.[14]

On the immediate facts of Target, the House of Lords explained that this case involved a bare trust quite different from the settlement type of trust where property was settled for beneficiaries in succession. Whilst there was no doubt that the money advanced by

---

[12] [1994] 1 WLR 1089.
[13] [1996] 1 AC 421 at 435.
[14] *Ibid.*

Target was held on trust by Redferns, the House of Lords held that a beneficiary was only entitled to be compensated for losses he would not have suffered but for the breach. In other words, there must be a causal relationship between the breach of trust and the loss which has been suffered by the beneficiary. On the present facts, Target Holdings had failed to show the court that the breach by Redferns was the primary cause of their loss. Assuming that the loan monies had been paid once there had been completion of the sale and the execution of the charge, Target would still have been in the same position. The actual loss was caused by the mortgage fraud rather than the breach of trust by Redferns. In the opinion of the House of Lords, a trustee was liable to pay equitable compensation for breaches of trust which had been caused by the breach of trust. With regard to the nature of equitable compensation and how it differs from common law compensation, an important part of Lord Browne-Wilkinson's judgment is reproduced below.

| KEY CITATION | *Target Holdings* v *Redferns* [1996] AC 421 (The nature of equitable compensation per Lord Browne-Wilkinson at 423 and 435) |

At common law there are two principles fundamental to the award of damages. First, that the defendant's wrongful act must cause the damage complained of. Second, that the plaintiff is to be put 'in the same position as he would have been in if he had not sustained the wrong for which he is now getting his compensation or reparation': *Livingstone* v *Raywards Coal Co*. (1880) 5 App. Cas. 25, 39, *per* Lord Blackburn. Although, as will appear, equity approaches liability for making good a breach of trust from a different starting point, in my judgment those two principles are applicable as much in equity as at common law. Under both systems liability is fault-based: the defendant is only liable for the consequences of the legal wrong he has done to the plaintiff and to make good the damage caused by such wrong. He is not responsible for damage not caused by his wrong or to pay by way of compensation more than the loss suffered from such wrong. The detailed rules of equity as to causation and the quantification of loss differ, at least ostensibly, from those applicable at common law. But the principles underlying both systems are the same . . .

The equitable rules of compensation for breach of trust have been largely developed in relation to such traditional trusts, where the only way in which all the beneficiaries' rights can be protected is to restore to the trust fund what ought to be there. In such a case the basic rule is that a trustee in breach of trust must restore or pay to the trust estate either the assets which have been lost to the estate by reason of the breach or compensation for such loss. Courts of Equity did not award damages but, acting in personam, ordered the defaulting to restore to the trust estate . . . If specific restitution of the trust property is not possible, then the liability of the trustee is to pay sufficient compensation to the trust estate to put it back to what it would have been had the breach not been committed . . . Even if the immediate cause of the loss is the dishonesty or failure of a third party, the trustee is liable to make good the loss to the trust estate if, but for the breach, such loss would not have occurred . . . Thus the common rules of remoteness of damage and causation do not apply. However, there does have to be some causal connection between the breach of trust and the loss to the trust estate for which compensation is recoverable, viz. the fact that the loss would not have occurred but for the breach.

The judgment of Lord Browne-Wilkinson concentrates on the distinction between traditional family trusts and commercial trusts. The key emphasis in his judgment is undesirability of applying principles of traditional trusts to trusts operating in a more contemporary context, and in particular, a commercial context. This distinction has not, however, been met with the same degree of acceptance amongst certain quarters. Writing extrajudicially, Sir Peter Millett, whilst agreeing with the decision in **Target Holdings v Redferns**,[15] has questioned whether it is satisfactory to distinguish traditional trusts from commercial trusts.[16] As Professor Martin explains, the same principles enunciated in **Target Holdings** would apply if a trustee of a family trust investing in a mortgage had committed the same breach.[17] Both commentators suggest that a more appropriate distinction should be made between breach of fiduciary duty by a trustee and breach of duty by a trustee which is not necessarily categorised a fiduciary breach. There is a lot to be said for this line of reasoning.

You will recall from Chapter 17 that a trustee is subject to a number of fiduciary duties, for example, not to allow a conflict between his duty and interest. In addition to fiduciary duties, a trustee is subject to other duties, for example, the duty to take care in the administration of the trust. In Chapter 17 it was observed that fiduciary duties could exist concurrently with other duties arising, for example, those arising under contract or in tort. As Millett LJ explained in **Bristol & West Building Society v Mothew**[18] 'The expression "fiduciary duty" is properly confined to those duties which are peculiar to fiduciaries and the breach of which attracts legal consequences differing from those consequent upon the breach of other duties. Unless the expression is so limited it is lacking in practical utility. In this sense it is obvious that not every breach of duty by a fiduciary is a breach of fiduciary duty.'[19] With this in mind, restitutionary remedies should only be available in situations where a trustee has breached a fiduciary duty, and compensatory remedies should be available to cases where there has been some maladministration by a trustee causing loss to the trust, for example, an improper investment of the trust funds. Thus where a trustee breaches a fiduciary duty, for example, purchasing trust property for himself, the beneficiary should be entitled to a resitutionary remedy in the form of either an account for profits or, where possible, a proprietary right to claim the trust property.[20] Where a trustee breaches the trust, for example, by an unauthorised payment or investment, then the beneficiary has the right to equitable compensation for such breach, but only if such breach has caused the loss to the trust estate.

Whilst causation is clearly an important factor in determining whether equitable compensation is available, questions of foreseeability and remoteness of damage seem to be irrelevant in such an enquiry. Once it is established that the breach of trust has caused the loss, the question for the court is to quantify the level of compensation. With regard to the question of quantification, Lord Browne-Wilkinson referred to the decision of the Supreme Court of Canada in the **Canson Enterprises Ltd v Boughton and Co**,[21] where McLachlin J explained that 'a related question which must be addressed is the time of assessment of the loss. In this area tort and contract law are of little help . . . The basis of compensation at equity, by contrast, is the restoration of the actual value of the thing lost through the breach. The foreseeable value of the items is not in issue. As a result, the losses are to be assessed at the time of the trial, using the full benefit of hindsight.'[22]

---

[15] [1996] AC 421.

[16] Sir Peter Millet, 'Equity's Place in the Law of Commerce' 114 LQR 214. See also R. Nolan, 'A Targeted Degree of Liability' [1996] LMCLQ 161.

[17] Hanbury and Martin, *Modern Equity* 18th edn (2009) at p. 686.

[18] [1998] Ch. 1.

[19] [1998] Ch. 1 at 16.

[20] The right to trace the trust property into the hands of the trustee or any other third party who cannot purport to show that it is a bona fide purchaser. Equitable tracing is discussed in more detail below.

[21] (1991) 85 DLR (4th) 129.

[22] (1991) 85 DLR (4th) 129 at 162.

In this respect, equitable compensation is to restore the value of the trust fund or as one commentator describes it, to make reparative compensation.[23] It must, however, be noted, as pointed out by Professor Hudson, that in the context of investment of trust funds even where a beneficiary may be able to show that a trustee has failed to review the trust investments or has failed to generate profit or keep the trust fund to its real value, establishing loss can be very difficult.[24] For example, in *Nestlé* v *National Westminster Bank plc*[25] the claimant beneficiary complained that the trustee had failed to invest the trust funds in a manner which would have generated a return four times more than that which was returned. She was able to show this to the court by illustrating how comparable investment indices had performed over the previous years. Although the trustee was held not have periodically reviewed the investments, the trustee would have acted in the same way it had acted by virtue of all of the other factors that had to be considered, including the interests of previous beneficiaries entitled to the income.

Target Holdings v *Redferns*[26] was followed by the Court of Appeal in *Swindle* v *Harrison*[27] where Mrs Harrison, on the advice of her son, decided to mortgage her house so as to purchase a hotel which would be run as a restaurant business by her and her son. The mortgage money was to be loaned by a brewery and on the mistaken belief that the brewery would provide the loan, Mrs Harrison instructed her solicitors to exchange contracts. Unfortunately, the brewery decided not to go ahead with the loan and, fearing that she would lose her deposit on the hotel, Mr Swindle, her solicitor, agreed to provide a bridging loan secured by a first charge on the property. Furthermore, Mr Swindle was expected to make a hidden profit from the loan and was clearly aware that the brewery would not make the loan. Mrs Harrison's business proved to be unsuccessful and when she defaulted on both mortgages, the mortgage lenders took possession of her house. Mrs Harrison commenced proceedings against Mr Swindle on the grounds that he had breached his fiduciary duty in not disclosing all of the relevant facts when the bridging loan was made. She claimed to be entitled to compensation for the lost equity in her house. The Court of Appeal dismissed her claim on the grounds that she had failed to show the court that she would not have accepted the loan had she been aware of the breach by Mr Swindle. The Court of Appeal explained that she would still have gone ahead with the loan from Mr Swindle in order to finance her business venture and, in such circumstances, the cause of her loss was not Mr Swindle's breach, but rather the fact that the business failed to succeed. Evans LJ explained that:

> [Mr Swindle's] failure to disclose cannot be said to have led to the making of the loan, even on a but for basis, precisely because disclosure of the true facts would not have affected her decision to accept it. Since she would have accepted the loan and completed the purchase, even if full disclosure had been made to her, she would have lost the value of the equity in her home in any event. She cannot recover damages or compensation for that loss, in my judgment, except on proof either that the plaintiffs acted fraudulently or in a manner equivalent to fraud or that she would not have completed the purchase if full discourse had been made, i.e. if the breach of duty had not occurred.[28]

---

[23] C. Rickett, 'Equitable Compensation: Towards a Blueprint?' [2003] Syd. L. Rev.

[24] A. Hudson, *Equity and Trusts* 5th edn (Routledge, 2007) at p. 752.

[25] [1994] 1 All ER 118, discussed in detail in Chapter 15.

[26] [1996] 1 AC 421. See D. Capper, 'Compensation for Breach of Trust' Conv. 1997, 14 and also C.E.F. Rickett, 'Equitable Compensation: The Giant Stirs' 1996, 112 LQR 27. Rickett argues that the decision highlights the similarity between common law compensation and equitable compensation for breach of trust.

[27] [1997] 4 All ER 705; see T. Yeo, 'Limited Liability for Breach of Fiduciary Duty' (1998) LQR 181.

[28] [1997] 4 All ER 705 at 718; see also *Nationwide Building Society* v *Balmer Radmore* [1999] Lloyd's Rep. PN 241.

In *Swindle* v *Harrison*[29] the Court of Appeal did, however, decide that if the breach of fiduciary duty was a result of a fraud then a special principle would apply, allowing the beneficiary to benefit from purely restitutionary remedies such as account for profit or rescission on facts similar to *Swindle* v *Harrison*. In such a case the fiduciary could not plead to the court that the beneficiary would have acted in the same way despite the fraudulent non-disclosure. More recently, in *Lloyds TSB Bank Plc* v *Markandan & Uddin (a firm)*[30] a bank was entitled to the return of money advanced to a firm of solicitors in circumstances where one of the solicitors had wrongfully paid the money over to fraudsters. On the facts, the money had been advanced subject to a mortgage; however, the solicitors who were holding the money under a bare trust paid the money in breach of their instructions and authority. The court held that this was a breach of trust entitling them to the return of such money.

 ## Liability for co-trustees

Tom and Tim are two trustees of a trust fund which consists of a house held on trust for two beneficiaries. Tom has decided to sell the house to his wife at a considerable under-value. Tim realises that this would constitute a breach of trust and is not happy with the sale, but nevertheless is urged by Tom to complete the conveyance to Tom's wife. Tom is later declared bankrupt and the beneficiaries now wish to commence an action for breach of trust against Tim. Tim has explained that it was not his intention to sell the house to Tom's wife.

Would the beneficiaries be able to commence a personal claim against Tim?

Although it is clear post *Target Holdings* v *Redferns*[31] that the liability of a trustee who breaches a trust is to pay compensation in the form of restoring or repairing the loss that the beneficiary has suffered, a trustee is only liable for his own acts and not for those of any other co-trustee or agent. Liability is essentially primary and not vicarious. However, in practice a trustee may find himself liable for the acts of his co-trustees in circumstances where he fails to participate in the effective administration of the trust. It is often said that there is no such thing in trust law as a sleeping trustee. The general rule is that where there is more than one trustee they must act jointly in the administration of the trust. The rationale behind this requirement is to prevent individual trustees from failing to participate in the management of the trust and then later escaping liability. The matter is neatly illustrated by the rather old case of *Townley* v *Sherborne*[32] where two trustees were holding a lease on trust. The rent was paid to both trustees; however, one of the trustees made no attempts to ensure that the money was thereafter properly invested. When the trustee who had retained control of the money misappropriated it, the trustee who had failed to ensure that that it was safeguarded was held to be liable for breach of trust, on the grounds that he had taken no steps to ensure that his co-trustee had properly invested the trust money. Similarly, in *Booth* v *Booth*[33] a trustee was held to be liable

29 [1997] 4 All ER 705.
30 [2010] EWHC 2517 (Ch.).
31 [1996] 1 AC 421.
32 (1643) J Bridg. 35.
33 (1838) 1 Beav. 125.

for the acts of his co-trustee who had allowed the trust business to be used for his own personal benefit. When the business failed and the trustee became insolvent, the other trustee was held to be liable for breach of trust. Cases like *Townley* v *Sherborne* illustrate that where there are two or more trustees of a trust, when one trustee breaches the trust, the other(s) will become liable in two distinct situations:

1 Where T1 breaches the trust and T2 in full knowledge of the breach sits back and does nothing about it. In such a case T2 will have acquiesced in the breach and will be liable along with T1.

2 Where T1 breaches the trust, but T2 simply fails to take any interest in the effective administration of the trust. In such a case it can be said that T2 is recklessly careless in the sense of not caring whether his acts or omissions amount to a breach. Since trustees must jointly act in the administration of the trust, T2 will be held liable along with T1 for breach of trust.

A new trustee will not be liable for the acts of existing trustees and will be entitled to take office on the assumption that the existing trustees have up until his appointment effectively administered the trust.[34] If a new trustee does, however, discover that previous breaches of trust have been committed he will not be liable for those. However, when he does discover that there have been previous breaches, he must like any other trustee obtain satisfaction from the previous trustees that steps are being taken to make good the loss. If he sits back in the knowledge that no attempt is being made to redress those breaches, then he will be liable to make good the loss even though they were committed before he took office.[35] A trustee who has retired from the trust will not be liable for breaches of trust committed by the remaining trustees unless it can be shown that his retirement was undertaken in order to facilitate the breach of trust.[36]

 ## Joint liability, contribution and indemnity

Once it is clear that two or more trustees are liable for the same breach of trust, their liability is said to be joint and several. This means that any one of the trustees can be sued for the entire loss.[37] The matter is neatly illustrated by the decision in *Bishopsgate Investment Management Ltd* v *Maxwell (No. 2)*[38] where two trustees of a pension fund allowed certain pension monies to be transferred in breach of trust. The Court of Appeal held that both trustees were jointly and severally liable to replace the loss.

APPLYING THE LAW

Suppose in the question posed above, Tom failed to disclose to Tim that the sale was to his wife and Tim failed to establish that a fair price was being paid for the house. Furthermore, that Tom put considerable pressure on Tim to go ahead with the sale to his wife. Clearly, Tom is instigating the breach.

If Tim does get sued, is it fair that he pays the whole compensation?

---

[34] *Re Strahan* (1856) 8 De GM & G 291.
[35] *Hobday* v *Peters (No. 3)* (1860) 28 Beav. 603.
[36] *Head* v *Gould* [1898] 2 Ch. 250.
[37] *Fletcher* v *Green* (1864) 33 Beav. 426.
[38] [1994] 1 All ER 261.

In circumstances where liability is joint and several, it has been seen that one trustee may be liable to meet the whole of the liability. A question arising in such a situation is whether such a trustee is entitled to any contribution or indemnity. Contribution may become relevant where one trustee argues that he should not have to meet the whole of the liability alone and that his co-trustee(s) should contribute to it. Equity has long recognised that where two or more trustees are jointly and severally liable for the same loss then the trustee who has had to meet the liability is entitled to contribution from the other trustee who has not been sued by the beneficiary. Prior to the enactment of the Civil Liability (Contribution) Act 1978 the rule in equity was that where two or more trustees were liable in respect of the same loss they were equally liable for the loss irrespective of their blameworth. Thus if T1 was the one sued, he could claim an equal contribution from T2 irrespective of whether T1 or T2 was more at fault.[39] The matter is now governed by the Civil Liability (Contribution) Act 1978.

> ### KEY STATUTE
>
> ## S. 1 of the Civil Liability (Contribution) Act 1978 (The right to contribution)
>
> (1) Subject to the following provisions of this section, any person liable in respect of any damage suffered by another person may recover contribution from any other person liable in respect of the same damage (whether jointly with him or otherwise).
>
> 2 (1) Subject to subsection (3) below, in any proceedings for contribution under section 1 above the amount of the contribution recoverable from any person shall be such as may be found by the court to be just and equitable having regard to the extent of that person's responsibility for the damage in question.

It is fairly clear from s. 2(1) of the Act that the court enjoys a wide discretion to apportion liability when two or more trustees are liable for the same breach of trust.

A trustee may be entitled to an indemnity from either a co-trustee or a beneficiary. Entitlement to an indemnity means that he will not have to meet the liability that is being exerted against him. Indemnity can work in a number of situations. With regard to an indemnity from a co-trustee, there appear to be three well-established situations in which a co-trustee will have to indemnify his fellow trustee from liability for breach of trust. The first situation arises where the co-trustee is a professional, for example a solicitor, and the other trustee relies on the professional opinion of that co-trustee and then finds that both trustees are liable for breach of trust. In such a case the professional co-trustee will have to give full indemnity to the other trustee. The matter is nicely illustrated in **Re Partington**[40] where there were two trustees, one being a solicitor. The solicitor-trustee advised the other trustee that it would be appropriate to invest the trust monies by way of mortgage. However, the fact was that this was not an appropriate investment for the trust. When both trustees became liable for breach of trust, the court held that the solicitor-trustee was liable to indemnify the other trustee who had relied on his professional opinion. The second situation arises where two trustees are liable for breach but one of the trustees takes a personal benefit from the breach.[41] In such a case the trustee who benefits from the breach must give an indemnity to his co-trustee. Finally, where one of the trustees is also a beneficiary and has personally benefited from

---

[39] *Bahin v Hughes* (1886) 31 Ch. D 390.
[40] (1887) 57 LT 654.
[41] *Bahin v Hughes* (1886) 31 Ch. D 390.

the breach of trust, he will be liable to indemnify his co-trustee from liability. For example, in **Chillingworth v Chambers**[42] a trustee who was also a beneficiary encouraged the other trustee that they should invest in mortgages which eventually provided insufficient security. One of the reasons for the investment in mortgages was that it would give a high rate of return on the trust, thereby ultimately benefiting that trustee beneficiary. When a loss of some £1500 was incurred to the trust, the court held that it should be made good from the beneficial interest of the trustee beneficiary and that the other trustee had an indemnity from breach of trust.

As well as an indemnity from a co-trustee, a trustee may be able to obtain an indemnity from a beneficiary. The principal ground upon which a trustee will be indemnified by a beneficiary is where the beneficiary instigated or acquiesced in the breach of trust. Although the courts of equity had for a long time an inherent jurisdiction to indemnify a trustee where the breach was instigated by the beneficiary[43] the matter is now dealt with by s. 62 Trustee Act 1925.

KEY STATUTE

S. 62 of the Trustee Act 1925 (The right to indemnity)

(1) Where a trustee commits a breach of trust at the instigation or request or with the consent in writing of a beneficiary, the court may, if it thinks fit . . . make such order as to the court seems just, for impounding all or any part of the interest of the beneficiary in the trust estate by way of indemnity to the trustee or persons claiming through him.

Section 62 of the Trustee Act 1925 provides a trustee with an indemnity in circumstances where the beneficiary has requested or instigated the breach of trust. The way in which the indemnity works is by impounding the beneficial interest of the beneficiary who has instigated the breach of trust. Thus where a trustee finds himself liable to pay £1000 to the trust estate because of a breach instigated by a beneficiary, the court can impound the interest of the beneficiary to the extent of £1000. So, where the beneficiary's interest was initially worth £2000, it would now only be worth £1000. The discretion to impound the interest of the beneficiary under s. 62 of the Trustee Act will only be exercised provided that the court is satisfied that the beneficiary fully understood what he was consenting to. In **Re Somerset**[44] Smith LJ commented that 'upon the true reading of this section, a trustee to obtain the benefit conferred thereby, must establish that the beneficiary knew the facts which rendered what he was instigating, requesting or consenting to in writing a breach of trust'.[45] It will, however, be seen later in this chapter that the beneficiary does not need to know that what he or she is consenting to is a breach of trust, provided that he or she fully understands what is being consented to.[46]

 # Established principles when assessing liability

Having established that the liability of a defaulting trustee is to compensate the beneficiaries for the loss suffered as a result of the breach, this section explores some of the settled categories of liability and the principles governing restorative compensation.

---

[42] [1896] 1 Ch. 865.
[43] *Booth v Booth* (1838) 1 Beav. 125.
[44] [1894] 1 Ch. 231.
[45] [1894] 1 Ch. 231 at 266.
[46] *Re Pauling's Settlement Trust (No. 2)* [1963] Ch. 576.

● Making an unauthorised investment

APPLYING THE LAW

Tim and Tom have been given an express power of investment which prevents investment in private companies. Despite this prohibition, both trustees invest in a private company. The beneficiary has objected to the investment and has asked Tom and Tim to sell the shares in the private company. They duly sell them making a loss of £1000 to the trust fund. The beneficiary brings an action to recover the loss to the trust fund. At the time of the hearing the shares in the private company double in value and Tom and Tim say that they would have made a profit to the trust fund if they had been retained.

Should Tom and Tim replace the loss?

The general rule is that where a trustee makes an unauthorised investment he is liable for any losses that incur on sale of that unauthorised investment. For example, if a trustee invests £30,000 of trust money without taking advice when it would have been appropriate to take advice, he will be liable for any loss that has been incurred to the £30,000. It is no defence for a trustee to say that, had he in fact retained the unauthorised investment, he would in fact have made a profit for the trust. The matter is neatly illustrated in *Knott v Cottee*[47] where an executor of a will invested trust money in foreign stocks, contrary to the terms of the will, which only authorised investments in government stocks. The foreign stocks were sold at a loss by an order of the court pending a full hearing of the case. The court held that the executor was liable to replace the loss even though had they been retained up until the hearing they would have made a profit. The principle here is that the trustee makes an unauthorised investment and as a result deliberately causes loss to the trust estate which he must now replace by way of compensation. It is no defence for him to look back with hindsight and show the court that, had he in fact retained the unauthorised investment, he would have produced a profit for the beneficiaries.

● Improperly retaining an investment

APPLYING THE LAW

In Chapter 16 it was observed that where a trustee is holding a wasting asset, for example a car, on trust for A for life and thereafter for B, the trustee must sell the car because it is not producing an income for A and its capital value is depreciating at the expense of B.

What if the trustee does not sell that car or delays the sale for a long time? He would be retaining an unauthorised investment. How is loss assessed?

A trustee may find himself in a position where he is under a duty to sell a particular investment. The duty to sell may arise from the trust instrument where, for example, the testator may provide that the trustee is to sell a specific investment and distribute the proceeds equally amongst the beneficiaries. The duty to sell may also arise from the operation of some rule of law. It has already been observed in Chapter 16 that a trustee will be under a duty to sell certain assets which are of a wasting nature when they are settled

---

[47] (1852) 16 Beav. 77.

in favour of beneficiaries entitled in succession. For example, where a testator leaves a car on trust for A for life and thereafter for B, a trustee will be under a duty to convert the car into money so as to produce an income for A and preserve the capital for B.[48] Where a trustee is under a duty to sell a specific investment, he will be liable for breach of trust if he fails to sell. The general rule is that the trustee will be liable to replace the difference between what he would have got had he sold at the right time and what he actually receives when he sells much later on. The matter is neatly illustrated by the decision in *Fry v Fry*[49] where trustees were instructed by the terms of the trust to sell a certain inn as soon as it was convenient to do so. The trustees received one offer of £900 some two years later but refused to accept it. The value of the inn dropped considerably thereafter as a result of the opening of a railway line. Romilly MR held that the trustees were liable to replace the difference between £900 and the value that was actually received when the inn was eventually sold.

The decision in *Fry v Fry*[50] can produce a harsh result especially if the trustee's refusal to sell is to obtain a higher price for the beneficiary. After all, the trustee is under a duty to act in the best interests of the beneficiary. Provided that the trustee has not acted negligently in delaying the sale, he may have a defence under s. 61 of the Trustee Act 1925; this is explored in more detail below. Where, of course, the beneficiary does not suffer a loss as a result of the delay in selling trust property, there will be no compensation. The matter is neatly illustrated by the decision in *Jeffrey v Gretton*[51] where trustees had failed to review the trust investments by retaining trust property longer than necessary. However, when the beneficiaries commenced proceedings, they were not able to show that they had suffered any loss by the retention of the property.

Improperly selling an authorised investment

Where a trustee improperly sells an investment which is authorised he will be liable to replace the loss caused to the trust. However, unlike in the situation where a trustee simply makes an unauthorised investment, in the case of an improper sale of an authorised investment the rule is slightly different.

APPLYING THE LAW

Suppose that Tom and Tim have correctly invested the trust money in a public company quoted on the stock exchange. They then improperly sell the shares in the public company and invest them in a private company in breach of trust. The beneficiary objects and orders that the private company shares be sold. Tom and Tim duly sell the shares in the private company without any loss to the trust fund. The beneficiary does, however, discover that if the shares in the private company had been retained they would be worth three times as much today than they were worth when they were sold.

How would the loss be calculated here?

The rule is that the trustee must either account for the proceeds of sale of the investment, which he should never have made, or to replace the existing investment depending on which is higher. Take, for example, a trustee who is holding 2000 authorised shares in a public company. Suppose that the trustee sells the shares and improperly invests

---
[48] Otherwise known as the rule in *Howe* v *Earl of Dartmouth* (1802) 6 RR 96.
[49] (1859) 27 Beav. 144.
[50] (1859) 27 Beav. 144.
[51] [2011] WTLR 809.

them in a private company without taking advice. Clearly the investment in the private company shares constitutes a breach of trust and the trustee will be ordered to sell the shares in the private company (unless of course the beneficiaries wish to adopt them by consenting to such an investment). When the shares in the private company are sold, the trustee must account for the proceeds of sale. If the private company shares are sold for £3000, then the trustee must account for £3000. However, this is not the end of the matter; the beneficiaries may require the trustee to replace the existing investment. This means that they can ask the trustee to replace the existing investment by showing to the court that, had the trustee retained the existing investment they would in fact have received much more than £3000. This would occur where, for example, if the 2000 shares in the public company would in fact be worth £5000. The trustee would have to pay another £2000 out of his pocket. The principle is neatly illustrated in *Re Massingberd's Settlement* [52] where trustees were authorised to invest in certain government stocks. The trustees sold the government stocks and invested the money in mortgages which were not authorised. The unauthorised mortgages were eventually sold and no money had been lost on them; however, the Court of Appeal held that the trustees must replace the government stocks which were worth a much higher price.

A trustee who simply fails to invest the trust fund

A trustee is under a duty to invest the trust funds and failure to do so will amount to a breach of trust. Pending any full investment decision a trustee is under a statutory duty to pay the trust money into an interest-bearing account.[53] Where a trustee simply fails to invest the trust funds the measure of liability will depend on whether he was instructed by the trust instrument to make a specific investment or whether he was given a discretion to choose from a range of investments. In the case of a direction to make a specific investment, if the trustee fails to make that investment and that investment subsequently increases in value, he will be required to purchase as much of that specific investment.[54] Take for example, a trustee who is directed to invest the trust fund £2000 in specified shares in a company which are worth £1 when the investment should be made. If he simply fails to invest and the shares in the company double in price, he will have to make good a further £2000, which the beneficiaries would have made if he had invested the money in the first place. Where there is no specific direction to invest the trust funds, the trustee will have to replace the trust fund with interest only. The justification for this rule lies in the impracticalities of assessing loss in circumstances when the trustee could have chosen from several investments. The matter is explained by Wigram VC in *Shepherd v Mouls* [55] where he commented that 'the discretion given to the trustee to select an investment among several securities makes it impossible to ascertain the amount of the loss (if any) which has arisen to the trust from the omission to invest, except, perhaps, in the possible case (which has not occurred here) of a particular security having been offered to the trustees, in conformity with the terms of the trust'.[56]

Assessment of compensation and interest

Two important, and often problematic questions, arise in the context of assessing equitable compensation in breach of trust cases. The first question is: what is the proper time

---

[52] (1890) 63 LT 296.
[53] Sections 16–24 Trustee Act 2000.
[54] *Byrchall* v *Bradford* (1822) 6 Madd. 235.
[55] (1845) 4 Hare. 500.
[56] (1845) 4 Hare. 500 at 504.

for calculating compensation? Is it the date of the breach or is it the date of the judgment? The question becomes particularly acute in the context where the trust property fluctuates in value between the time of the breach and the time of the judgment. The second question is: does the trustee have to replace the loss with interest? What is particularly relevant in respect of the second question is the rate of interest to be charged and whether the interest to be charged should be simple or compound interest.

In respect of the proper time at which compensation should be assessed Lord Browne-Wilkinson explained in *Target Holdings v Redferns*[57] that the proper time of the assessment was the date of the judgment and not the date of the breach.[58] This aspect of the decision in *Target Holdings v Redferns* overruled the 'highest intermediate balance' principle established in *Jaffray v Marshall*,[59] which held that a trustee was liable to compensate the beneficiaries to the level of the highest price that would have been available to the trust property which remained unrestored. The basis for this rule was that everything was presumed against the defaulting trustee. Thus in *Jaffray v Marshall* the use of trust money to purchase a house proved to be a breach of trust. At the time of the writ the house was actually valued at some £160,000; however, at the time of the judgment it had fallen considerably in value. The High Court held that compensation was to be assessed at the time of the writ when the property could have been sold at a much higher price. In the opinion of Lord Browne-Wilkinson the decision in *Jaffray v Marshall* had been wrongly decided on the grounds that it applied wrongly applied principles relating to account for profits to claims for compensation. His Lordship explained that:

> the principles applicable in an action for account for profits were, to my mind wrongly applied to a claim for compensation for breach of trust. In my judgment [*Jaffray v Marshall*] was wrongly decided not only because the wrong principle was applied but also because the judge awarded compensation by assessing the quantum on an assumption (viz that the house in question would have been sold at a particular date) when he found as a fact that such a sale would not have taken place even if there had been no breach of trust.[60]

With regard to the question of interest, the rule has always been that a trustee is liable to pay compensation with interest from the day of the breach of trust. The justification for awarding interest was explained by Buckley LJ in *Wallersteiner v Moir (No. 2)*[61] where his Lordship explained that it was well 'established in equity that a trustee who in breach of trust misapplies trust funds will be liable not only to replace the misapplied principal fund but also to do so with interest from the date of the misapplication. This is on the notional ground that the money so applied was in fact the trustee's own money and that he has retained the misapplied trust money in his own hands and used it for his own purposes.'[62] The rate of interest is at the discretion of the court;[63] however, the traditional rate of interest has been 4 per cent.[64] However, the fact that the rate of interest is at the discretion of the court means that the court may impose a higher rate of interest in times of high inflation.[65] A higher rate of interest may also be charged where the trustee has been fraudulent[66] or where he was expected to receive a return higher than

---

[57] [1996] 1 AC 421.

[58] His Lordship relied on the Canadian judgment of McLachlin J in *Canson Enterprises Ltd* v *Boughton and Co* (1991) 85 DLR (4th) 129.

[59] [1994] 1 All ER 143.

[60] [1994] 1 All ER 143 at 154.

[61] [1975] QB 373.

[62] [1975] QB 373 at 397.

[63] *Attorney General* v *Alford* (1855) 4 De GM & G 843.

[64] *Fletcher* v *Green* (1864) 33 Beav. 426.

[65] *Bartlett* v *Barclays Bank Trust Co (No. 2)* [1980] Ch. 515.

[66] *Attorney General* v *Alford* (1855) 4 De GM & G 843.

4 per cent.[67] In practice, the rate of interest is usually that of the court's short-term investment account as established under s. 6(1) of the Administration of Justice Act 1965.

As to whether the trustee is to pay simple or compound interest, the matter is at the discretion of the court. Unlike the common law jurisdiction, equity does enjoy a jurisdiction to award simple or compound interest.[68] The general rule is that the trustee will only be charged with simple interest; however, the court may exercise its discretion and award compound interest. As to the basis of exercising the discretion, the matter is far from clear. In some cases it was argued that compound interest would be awarded where the trustee had been guilty of fraud and the award of compound interest was to punish the trustee.[69] In other cases, compound interest was awarded when the trustee was under a duty to accumulate the trust income.[70] In *Wallersteiner v Moir (No. 2)*[71] Lord Denning MR held that the award of compound interest was not to punish the trustee but rather to reflect the benefit that the trustee had received by misapplying the trust property for his own benefit. In other words, compound interest would be awarded to reflect what the trustee has received personally as a result of the breach of trust, for example, by the use of the trust money for his own purposes.

Setting off profits and losses in two or more breaches

APPLYING THE LAW

Tim and Tom have an express power to invest in public company shares only. In breach of trust they invest half of the trust fund in one private company and the other half in another private company. The shares in one of the private companies fall in value whilst the shares in the other make a substantial gain. The beneficiary brings an action to recover the loss in value to that part of the trust which was invested in the company whose shares have fallen in value. Tom and Tim refuse to accept liability, arguing that the fund has not lost any value overall as the shares in the other private company have made a considerable profit.

Are Tom and Tim liable for the loss caused by the shares in the private company which have fallen in value?

In some cases a trustee may well be guilty of more than one breach of trust in respect of the same trust. In such a case the question arises whether the trustee can offset a loss in one breach of trust by a gain made in another breach of trust. The general position in equity is that each breach of trust is to be assessed individually. The matter was neatly explained by Brightman J in *Bartlett v Barclays Bank Trust Co (No. 2)*[72] where he explained that 'the general rule . . . is that where a trustee is liable in respect of distinct breaches of trust, one of which resulted in a loss and the other in a gain, he is not entitled

[67] *Jones v Foxall* (1852) 15 Beav. 388.
[68] Although the Law Commission has proposed changes to the award of compound interest on debts and damages at common law, see Law Com. No. 287 (2004), *Pre Judgment Interest on Debts and Damages*.
[69] *Jones v Foxall* (1852) 15 Beav. 388.
[70] *Re Barclay* [1899] 1 Ch. 674.
[71] [1975] QB 373.
[72] [1980] Ch. 515.

to set the gain against the loss, unless they arise in the same transaction'.[73] A good illustration of the application of the rule disallowing an offset of a loss by a gain is **Dimes v Scott**[74] where trustees failed to sell an unauthorised investment as required by the terms of the trust and to invest them in government stocks. When the unauthorised investments were eventually sold the price of the government stocks had dropped in value, thereby allowing the trustees to purchase much more than they would had they sold the unauthorised investment earlier. The trustees attempted to offset the gains made on the government stocks against the loss they had suffered by virtue of retaining the unauthorised investments. The court held that the trustees were not able to offset the loss by the gains made by the governments stocks. In the opinion of the court, the failure to sell the unauthorised investment and the subsequent investment in government stocks were two distinct transactions. A similar decision was reached in **Wiles v Gresham**[75] where trustees committed a breach of trust by failing to recover a sum of £2000 from a husband under a marriage settlement. The trustees then invested some of the other trust money in the purchase of land despite having no authority to do so. The husband improved the land with his own funds and it was worth much more than the value the trustees had paid for it. The trustees then attempted to offset the gain in the purchase of the land against their failure to recover the £2000. The court held that they were unable to do so as the failure to recover the £2000 and the subsequent unauthorised investment in the land were two separate transactions.

On the other hand, if the breach of trust occurs in the context of one single transaction, then the trustees may be able to offset a loss made by a subsequent gain. What is crucial here is that the breach occurs in the context of one indivisible transaction. Whether the transaction is indeed a single indivisible one is often very difficult to determine. For example, in **Fletcher v Green**[76] trustees committed a breach of trust by lending money by way of mortgage to a company in which one of the trustees had a personal interest. The mortgaged property was eventually sold at a loss and the money was paid into court and then invested in consols. The consols subsequently rose in value thereby realising the loss that had been made on the unauthorised mortgage. The court held that the subsequent rise in the consols were allowed to be offset against the loss made on the mortgage as they were part of the same transaction.

A somewhat more liberal approach was taken in **Bartlett v Barclays Bank Trust Co (No. 2)**[77] where trustees embarked upon two speculative property development projects. The trustees failed to ensure that the operations were properly supervised and had failed to obtain sufficient information from the board of directors. One of the projects, namely the 'Old Bailey' project, made a loss whilst the other, the 'Guildford' project, made a profit. Brightman J having conceded that the authorities were very difficult to reconcile, held that the trustees were able to offset the loss in the 'Old Bailey' project against the profit made in the 'Guildford' project. In the course of his judgment he explained that:

> [t]he relevant cases are, however, not altogether easy to reconcile. All are centenarians and none is like the present. The Guildford development stemmed from exactly the same policy and (to a lesser degree because it proceeded less far) exemplified the same folly as the Old Bailey project. Part of the profit was in fact used to finance the Old Bailey disaster. By sheer luck the gamble paid off handsomely, on capital account. I think it would be

---

[73] [1980] Ch. 515 at 538.
[74] (1828) 4 Russ. 195.
[75] (1854) 2 Drew. 258; 24 LJ Ch. 264.
[76] (1864) 33 Beav. 426.
[77] [1980] Ch. 515.

unjust to deprive the bank of this element of salvage in the course of assessing the cost of the shipwreck. My order will therefore reflect the bank's right to an appropriate set-off.[78]

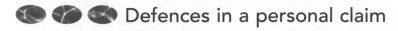 Defences in a personal claim

Where a trustee has committed a breach of trust there may be a number of defences which may relieve him wholly or partly from the breach. Three principal defences that a trustee may rely on are firstly, an exemption clause in the trust instrument excusing liability; secondly, concurrence by the beneficiaries and, finally, s. 61 of the Trustee Act 1925.

Trustee exemption clauses

Tim and Tom's trust instrument contains a clause which reads 'No trustee shall be liable for any loss or damage which may happen to the fund or any part thereof or the income thereof at any time or from any other cause whatsoever unless such loss or damage shall be caused by the trustee's own actual fraud . . .' Tim and Tom want to know exactly what types of conduct this covers.

A trust instrument may contain an exemption clause relieving a trustee from liability for breach of trust. Whilst it is settled law that a trustee cannot exclude liability for breaches which occur through his own fraud,[79] the question does arise as to the extent to which a trustee can exclude liability for breaches of trust. Thus, where a very wide exemption clause is inserted into a trust instrument, the question is how far that clause can be construed. Before the substantive law on trustee exemption clauses is examined, it is important to understand that trustee exemption clauses have proved to be a source of much controversy in trust law.[80] There are a number of reasons for that controversy. In the first place, there is the 'repugnancy argument' which centres on the fact that such clauses are repugnant to the notion of trusteeship. It is inevitable that where a very wide trustee exemption clause is inserted into a trust instrument, the substantive duties with which the trustee needs to comply with are reduced. If the beneficiaries have no rights enforceable against the trustee then there is no trust. For example, where a trust instrument contains a clause excluding the trustee's liability for breach of trust unless it is caused by the trustee's own fraud, it is quite possible that the trustee will not be liable for breaches of trust which happen through his own negligence. Thus, it is quite possible for a trustee to escape liability for want of his own care and diligence. In substance, the trustee need only act in good faith and honestly and thereby set a very low standard of care towards the trust. The second reason relates to the extent to which professional trustees should be allowed to escape liability for professional negligence.

---

[78] [1980] Ch. 515 at 538.
[79] *Wilkins* v *Hogg* (1861) LJ Ch. 41.
[80] See S. Panesar, 'Actual Fraud and Gross Negligence: The Scope of Trustee Exemption Clauses' 1998 Bus LR 19(1) 8 and Paul Mathews, 'The Efficacy of Trustee Exemption Clauses in English Law' [1989] Conv. 42.

VISIT CASE NAVIGATOR

The efficacy of a widely drafted trustee exemption clause was considered by the Court of Appeal in *Armitage v Nurse*[81] which concerned a settlement of 1984 in which the appellant was the principal beneficiary. The settlement arose as a result of a variation of a marriage settlement under the Variation of Trusts Act 1958[82] made by the appellant's grandfather. Under the marriage settlement the appellant's mother was the tenant for life and the appellant, Paula, aged 17 in 1984 was entitled to the remainder. The subject matter of the marriage settlement consisted primarily of farm land and some money. The land had been farmed by the family company called G.W. Nurse and Co Ltd of which the sole director and shareholder were Paula's mother and grandmother. The variation had the effect of partitioning the subject matter of the marriage settlement between Paula and her mother. Paula's mother took part of the land together with a sum of £230,000 free from the terms of the marriage settlement. Paula was allocated the remainder of the land together with a sum of £30,000; however, because Paula was only 17 at the time of the 1984 settlement her share was held by trustees on a new settlement prepared for her. It was this settlement and its terms which were the subject matter of discussion in the Court of Appeal. Paula's action for breach of trust was based on the following grounds. First, the trustees of the settlement had appointed G.W. Nurse and Co to farm Paula's land in breach of trust. Secondly, the trustees had failed to properly supervise the company's management of Paula's land. Thirdly, the trustees had failed to make proper inquiry into the reasons why Paula's land had fallen in value. Finally, the trustee failed to obtain proper payment of interest in respect of a loan made by the trustees to Paula's mother. In defence to these claims, the trustees pointed to clause 15 of the settlement which provided that '[n]o trustee shall be liable for any loss or damage which may happen to Paula's fund or any part thereof or the income thereof at any time or from any other cause whatsoever unless such loss or damage shall be caused by his own actual fraud . . .'

In the Court of Appeal Millett LJ held that this clause was effective to exclude liability for breach of trust other than those breaches occurring as a result of the actual fraud of the trustee. With regard to the definition of actual fraud, his Lordship equated this with proof of dishonesty on the part of the trustee. In the course of his judgment he commented that actual fraud 'connotes at the minimum an intention on the part of the trustee to pursue a particular course of action, either knowing that it is contrary to the interests of the beneficiaries or being recklessly indifferent whether it is contrary to their interests or not'.[83] With regard to conduct falling short of dishonesty such as negligence or imprudency, Millett LJ held that a widely drafted exemption clause was sufficient to exclude liability for such conduct. In the opinion of his Lordship, whilst there was an irreducible core of obligations owed by a trustee to a beneficiary, those obligations did not include the duties of care and skill. His Lordship commented that:

> I accept the submission made on behalf of Paula that there is an irreducible core of obligations owed by trustees to the beneficiaries and enforceable by them which is fundamental to the trust. If the beneficiaries have no rights enforceable against the trustees there are no trusts. But I do not accept the further submission that these core obligations include the duties of care and skill, prudence and diligence. The duty of the trustees to perform the trusts honestly and in good faith for the benefit of the beneficiaries is the minimum necessary to give substance to the trust, but in my opinion is sufficient.[84]

---

[81] [1997] 2 All ER 705.
[82] Variation of trusts and the Variation of Trust Act was considered in more detail in Chapter 19.
[83] [1997] 2 All ER 705 at 711.
[84] [1997] 2 All ER 705 at 713.

The test of dishonesty was further considered in **Walker v Stones**[85] where the question was whether a solicitor-trustee could be held to be dishonest in circumstances where he subjectively believed that what he was doing was in the best interests of the beneficiaries, even though no reasonable solicitor would have considered it to be honest. With regard to the meaning of dishonesty, the Court of Appeal approved the definition of Rattee J at first instance, where it was held that a trustee is guilty of dishonesty where he intends to do something which is not in the interests of the beneficiary, or is recklessly careless in the sense of not caring whether his acts or omissions are in the interests of the beneficiaries. The Court of Appeal further held that a trustee could be guilty of dishonesty in circumstances where he might have honestly believed that what he was doing was in the interests of the beneficiaries, but where no reasonable trustee would have come to the same conclusion. The decision in **Walker v Stones** adopts both a subjective and objective test of dishonesty, akin to the test of dishonesty employed by the courts when examining the liability of third parties who dishonestly assist in a breach of trust.[86]

The current law and practice relating to trustee exemption clauses was considered by the Law Commission in a paper 'Trustee Exemption Clauses'.[87] The Law Commission does not propose that there be a total prohibition in the use of trustee exemption clauses as this would unduly restrict the flexible nature of the trust and the obligations created thereunder. The Law Commission does, however, propose that a distinction be made between professional and lay trustees and that, as far as professional trustees are concerned, they should not be allowed to exclude liability for breaches of trust arising from their negligence. The Commission further proposes that those drafting exemption clauses should make it clear to the settlor the extent of a particular clause. With regard to implementing these proposals, the Law Commission does not suggest that there should be new legislation: rather, the proposals are best implemented by the trust industry through the promotion of good practice.

Consent from the beneficiaries

Where a beneficiary acquiesces or consents to a course of conduct which will amount to a breach of trust, the beneficiary cannot later successfully sue the trustee for breach of trust. The trustee will have a defence and if all the beneficiaries have given consent his defence will be complete. If it is one beneficiary out of a number of beneficiaries, then the trustee may not have a complete defence but will certainly be indemnified by the consenting trustee. The issue of consent in the context of a breach of trust was considered in **Re Pauling's Settlement Trust**[88] where trustees were holding a fund for a wife for her life and thereafter for her children. The trust deed contained an express power of advancement. The children's father, who lived beyond his means, sought to claim some of the trust fund from the trustees vis-à-vis his children. The trustees made a number of advancements to the children; however, the money was used for different purposes, including the purchase of a house and another to pay off the mother's overdraft. When the validity of these advancements was questioned, the trustees argued that they had given the money to the children and what then subsequently happened with that money was not a concern of the trustees. The Court of Appeal rejected this argument on the grounds that the trustees were under a duty to see that the advancement was for the benefit of the beneficiary and that the money advanced was applied for the purpose

[85] [2001] QB 902.
[86] This was examined in detail in Chapter 14.
[87] Law. Com No. 301 *Trustee Exemption Clauses* (July 2006).
[88] [1964] Ch. 303.

stipulated. The trustees further argued that the beneficiaries had consented to the advancements which turned out to be made in breach of trust. The trustee argued that the beneficiaries were fully aware that the money advanced was being used for the benefit of their mother.

In coming to the conclusion that the trustees were not liable for breach of trust, the Court of Appeal held that a valid consent from the beneficiaries would only be accepted by the court, provided a number of requirements were met. Firstly, that the beneficiary was of majority age. An infant beneficiary is incapable of giving a valid consent to a breach of trust.[89] However, an infant beneficiary who consents by fraudulently misrepresenting his age cannot then plead that his consent was ineffective.[90] Secondly, that the consent was given freely. This requires proof that the beneficiary was under no undue influence. For example, in *Re Pauling's Settlement Trust* one of the arguments was that the trustees were unable to rely on consent because the beneficiaries were under the influence of their parents. The trustees, however, argued that where a beneficiary had attained majority age the presumption of undue influence ceased to apply. The Court of Appeal accepted the argument that a presumption of undue influence arose as between child and parent, but, without specifying the exact period of time, held that the presumption continued beyond attaining the age of majority. Provided that the trustee knew or ought to have known that the beneficiary was acting under undue influence then it could not be said that the consent was freely given. The third requirement is that the consent was given in the full knowledge of all of the facts. The beneficiary must understand what he or she is consenting to. This requires the trustee to disclose all relevant information which may affect his decision whether or not to give consent. It does not, however, matter that the beneficiary understands that what he or she is consenting to actually amounts to a breach of trust. The matter is neatly explained by Lord Wilberforce in *Re Pauling's Settlement Trust*[91] where his Lordship explained that:

> the court has to consider all the relevant circumstances in which the concurrence of the [beneficiary] was given with a view to seeing that it was fair and equitable that, having given his concurrence, he should afterwards turn around and sue the trustees: that, subject to this, it is not necessary that he should know what he is concurring in is a breach of trust, provided that he fully understands what he is concurring in, and that it is not necessary that he should have directly benefited by the breach of trust.[92]

The defence of consent normally applies where the trustee is about to commit a breach of trust. In some cases the trustee may well have already committed the breach of trust and the question then arises whether the beneficiary has acquiesced in the breach of trust or otherwise released the trustee from liability for the breach which has taken place. It is perfectly well established that a beneficiary can acquiesce or otherwise release a trustee from a breach which has already taken place. In *Walker v Symonds*[93] Lord Eldon commented that 'either concurrence in the act, or acquiescence without original concurrence, will release the trustees; but that is only a general rule, and the court must inquire into circumstances which induced concurrence and acquiescence'.[94] As in the case of consent before a breach of trust, acquiescence after the breach has taken place will only be effective, provided the beneficiary is fully acquainted with the all facts

---

[89] *Lord Montfort v Lord Cadogen* (1810) 19 Ves. 635.
[90] *Overton v Bannister* (1844) 3 Hare. 503.
[91] [1964] Ch. 303.
[92] [1964] Ch. 303 at 339.
[93] (1818) 3 Swans. 1.
[94] (1818) 3 Swans. 1 at 64.

involved in the breach. A release does not necessarily have to take any particular form; however, it is clear that the mere passage of time alone will be insufficient to infer a release. There must be some additional conduct on the part of the beneficiary which demonstrates an intention to waive his rights to bring an action for breach of trust. However, where a long time has passed since the breach took place, then small acts on the part of the beneficiary will be taken as evidence of an intention to release the trustee. In *Life Association of Scotland* v *Siddal*[95] Campbell LC explained that 'although the rule be that the onus lies on the party relying on acquiescence to prove the facts from which the consent of the [beneficiary] is to be inferred, it is easy to conceive cases in which, from the great lapse of time, such facts might and ought to be presumed'.[96]

Section 61 Trustee Act 1925

Section 61 of the Trustee Act 1925 confers upon the court a discretion to relieve a trustee wholly, or partly, from a breach of trust.

KEY STATUTE

S. 61 of the Trustee Act 1925 (A statutory defence for breach of trust)

If it appears to the court that a trustee, whether appointed by the court or otherwise, is or may be personally liable for any breach of trust, whether the transaction alleged to be a breach of trust occurred before or after the commencement of this Act, but has acted honestly and reasonably, and ought fairly to be excused for the breach of trust and for omitting to obtain the directions of the court in the matter in which he committed such breach, then the court may relieve him either wholly or partly from personal liability for the same.

APPLYING THE LAW

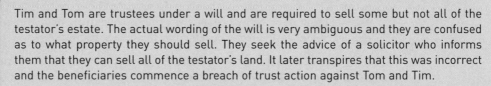

Tim and Tom are trustees under a will and are required to sell some but not all of the testator's estate. The actual wording of the will is very ambiguous and they are confused as to what property they should sell. They seek the advice of a solicitor who informs them that they can sell all of the testator's land. It later transpires that this was incorrect and the beneficiaries commence a breach of trust action against Tom and Tim.

Are Tim and Tom liable for the whole loss?

Whilst s. 61 confers a discretion to relieve a trustee from personal liability for breach of trust, the section is not as easy to apply as it first appears. The main reason for this is that the court is required to exercise its discretion by looking at three different factors, namely: the trustee's honesty, whether he acted reasonably, and whether he ought fairly to be excused. All three factors are very different in their nature and require the courts to make rather different enquires into the trustee's conduct. For example, in respect of whether a particular trustee acted honestly, the requisite enquiry is into the subjective frame of mind of the trustee and whether he acted in good faith. On the other hand, when looking at the reasonableness of the trustee's conduct, the court is required to look to whether the trustee acted in accordance with the standards expected of a reasonable

---

[95] (1861) 3 De GF & J 58.
[96] (1861) 3 De GF & J 58 at 77.

trustee. Thus, even though a particular trustee may have acted honestly, that is, in good faith, his conduct may nevertheless be unreasonable because it falls short of what would have been expected of a reasonable trustee in the very same circumstances. As to the question of fairness, this appears to be a much wider factor which allows the court to look at all of the facts and decide whether on such facts the trustee ought to be relieved of liability. It is because of these different factors that there has been a lack of a uniform set of principles which determine when and how the court will exercise its jurisdiction. In **Re Turner**[97] Byrne J explained that it was impossible to 'lay down any general rules or principles to be acted on in carrying out the provisions of the section, and I think each case must depend on its own circumstances'.[98] The onus is on the trustee to show that he did in fact act honestly and reasonably in the circumstances.

Despite the absence of a comprehensive set of principles explaining the grounds for the exercise of the court's discretion, there are a series of cases, primarily decided on the predecessor of s. 61, which attempt to provide some examples of when and how the court might invoke s. 61 to relieve a trustee from liability. Firstly, in relation to the question of honesty, the decided cases suggest that the court is primarily looking at conduct which is not dishonest in the first instance. Clearly, a trustee who has acted dishonestly will not be able to escape liability for breach of trust. Therefore, in relation to the question of honesty, the court's main concern is with dishonesty and not with the question of whether the trustee simply acted in good faith, albeit, as an honest fool. In one decided case, Byrne J explained that the provisions of the section 'were intended to enable the court to excuse breaches of trust where the circumstances of the particular case showed reasonable conduct, but it was never meant to be used as a sort of general indemnity clause for honest men who neglect their duty'.[99]

The focal point in the decision of a court to exercise its discretion under s. 61 is whether the trustee acted reasonably. In **Perrins v Bellamy**[100] Kekewich J explained that 'the legislation has made the absence of all dishonesty a condition precedent to the relief of the trustee from all liability. But that is not the grit of the section. The grit is in the words "reasonably and ought fairly to be excused for the breach of trust" . . .'[101] In order to show the court that he acted reasonably the trustee will need to demonstrate that his conduct, albeit conduct leading to a breach of trust, was conduct which would have been expected of a reasonable trustee. He must show that he complied with the statutory duty of care imposed upon him by s. 1 of the Trustee Act 2000. In assessing whether the trustee did act reasonably in the circumstances the courts have looked to a number of factors. One of the factors is whether or not the trustee took advice. The taking of advice is an important factor but it is not sufficient on its own. A good example of where the taking of advice was considered relevant in relieving liability under s. 61 is **Perrins v Bellamy**, where trustees were wrongly advised by a solicitor that they had a power to sell certain trust land. When a surveyor advised the trustees that it would be best to sell the trust land the trustees did so relying on the advice they had received from the solicitor. In fact, it later transpired that the trustees never had any power to sell the land and the beneficiary commenced proceedings against them. The court held that the trustees acted reasonably in taking the advice of a solicitor.[102] However, as mentioned previously, the

---

[97] [1897] 1 Ch. 536.
[98] [1897] 1 Ch. 536 at 542. The fact that each case depends on its own circumstances was also echoed by Lord Upjohn in *Re Pauling's Settlement Trusts* [1964] Ch. 303 at 359.
[99] *Williams* v *Byron* (1901) 18 TLR 172 at 176.
[100] [1898] 2 Ch. 521.
[101] [1898] 2 Ch. 521 at 527.
[102] See also *Re Allsop* [1914] 1 Ch. 1.

taking of advice does not automatically guarantee that the trustee will have a defence under s. 61. For example, in **National Trustees Co of Australasia v General Finance Co of Australasia**[103] the trustees were wrongly advised by a solicitor. Despite the advice of the solicitor, the court refused to relieve the trustees from liability. One of the reasons for this was that, given the very size of the trust fund, the trustees should have taken advice from some higher person such as Queen's Counsel. More recently in **Jeffrey v Gretton**[104] trustees had failed to take advice as to the suitability of an investment. They were held not to be able to rely on s. 61 of the Trustee Act 1925.

Another factor taken into account by the courts is whether the trustee would have acted in the same manner had he been dealing with his own property. For example, in **Re Stuart**[105] a trustee invested the trust money by way of lending money on a mortgage of land. Although the trustee had the power to invest the money by way of mortgage, the security proved to be insufficient and the trustee failed to comply with the then statutory requirements of s. 8 Trustee Act 1925, which required the trustee not to advance more than two-thirds of the loan money. In coming to the conclusion that the trustee should not be relieved of liability, Stirling J held that it was fair to consider whether the trustee would have acted in the same way had he been dealing with his own property. Similarly, in **Ward-Smith v Jebb**[106] a solicitor-trustee and his co-trustee made payments to a beneficiary which they thought the beneficiary was entitled to under the Adoption of Children Act 1949. In fact the particular beneficiary was not entitled to any payments. In refusing to relieve the trustees of liability the court held that any prudent person whose affairs were affected by a statute would either make sure that he understood the full implications of the statute or seek legal advice.

With regard to the question of whether the trustee ought fairly to be excused, it is not entirely clear about the exact extent of this requirement. It seems to give the court a general discretion to look at the case and refuse relief even where the trustee has acted honestly and reasonably because there are some other factors that are important. For example, in **Perrins v Bellamy**[107] Kekewich J was of the view that 'in the absence of special circumstances, a trustee who has acted "reasonably" ought to be relieved and that it is not incumbent on the Court to consider whether he ought "fairly" to be excused, unless there is evidence of a special character showing that the provisions of the section ought not to be applied in his favour'.[108] In **Re Evans**[109] an administratrix took out insurance to cover the share of a missing beneficiary. She was of the honest belief that the beneficiary was in fact dead and also took legal advice in obtaining the insurance. Later on, the missing beneficiary appeared and claimed his share from the property she was administering. The insurance covered only the capital sum and not interest. When the missing beneficiary claimed for interest against her, the court held that she could rely on s. 61 of the Trustee Act 1925 and be relieved of liability for not insuring for interest as well. The court was influenced by the fact that she had taken advice and also that she was a lay trustee who was administering a small estate. Although s. 61 applies to both professional and lay trustees, a professional trustee is expected to exercise a higher duty of care, and will therefore find it more difficult to invoke the relief of s. 61.[110]

[103] [1905] AC 373.
[104] [2011] WTLR 809.
[105] [1897] 2 Ch. 583.
[106] [1964] 108 Sol. Jo. 919.
[107] [1898] 2 Ch. 521.
[108] [1898] 2 Ch. 521 at 529.
[109] [1999] 2 All ER 777.
[110] *Re Pauling's Settlement Trusts* [1964] Ch. 303.

Limitation of actions

The general limitation period

A beneficiary must bring an action for breach of trust within the prescribed limitation period. The general rule is that any action for breach of trust will become statute barred after the expiry of six years from the date on which the right of action arose. The principal s. is 21(3) of the Limitation Act 1980.

KEY STATUTE

S. 21(3) of the Limitation Act 1980 (Limitation period in breach of trust cases)

Subject to the preceding provisions of this section, an action by a beneficiary to recover trust property or in respect of any breach of trust, not being an action for which a period of limitation is prescribed by any other provision of this Act, shall not be brought after the expiration of six years from the date on which the right of action accrued.

For the purposes of this subsection, the right of action shall not be treated as having accrued to any beneficiary entitled to a future interest in the trust property until the interest fell into possession.

There are a number of key aspects to s. 21(3) which need to be understood. Firstly, the limitation period in s. 21(3) clearly applies to breaches of trust which have been committed by trustees; it does not, however, apply to breaches of fiduciary such as self-dealing and fair-dealing by a trustee.[111] Such breaches of fiduciary duty continue to be governed by the equitable doctrine of laches which is explored below. Secondly, the definition of trustees is governed by s. 38(1), which basically provides that the same definition of trustees in the Trustee Act 1925 will apply. Under s. 68(17) of the Trustee Act 1925, trustees include express trustees, trustees under resulting and constructive trusts and personal representatives. Finally, in the case of a beneficiary with a future interest, the right of action does not begin until his interest falls into possession.

Exceptions to the limitation period

There are two exceptions to the limitation period in the cases of breaches of trust. These are covered by s. 21(1) of the Limitation Act 1925.

KEY STATUTE

S. 21(1) of the Limitation Act 1980 (Exceptions to the limitation period in breach of trust cases)

No period of limitation prescribed by this Act shall apply to an action by a beneficiary under a trust, being an action –

(a) in respect of any fraud or fraudulent breach of trust to which the trustee was a party or privy; or

(b) to recover from the trustee trust property or the proceeds of trust property in the possession of the trustee, or previously received by the trustee and converted to his use.

---

[111] *Tito v Waddell (No. 2)* 1977 Ch. 106.

The exception in s. 21(1)(a) covers breaches of trust which are fraudulent. Thus where a trustee's breach of trust is fraudulent, there is no limitation period. As to the meaning of fraud, in **Armitage v Nurse**[112] Millett LJ equated fraud with proof of dishonesty. The exception in s. 21(1)(a) will only apply where the trustee was party to the fraud; it will not apply where some other party was fraudulent and the trustee was unaware of that fraud, albeit, negligently. For example, in **Thorne v Heard**[113] a trustee negligently left trust property in the hands of a solicitor who misappropriated the money. The Court of Appeal held that the claimant's action was statute barred because the trustee had not in the present case been guilty of fraud. The exception in s. 21(1)(b) covers breaches of trust where the trustee has converted the trust property for his own purpose. Where the trustee does use the trust property for his own purposes there is no additional requirement to show that he also acted dishonestly. Dishonesty is only applicable under s. 21(1)(a). A good example of the application of s. 21(1)(a) is **Re Howlett**[114] where a trustee who was also a beneficiary remained in possession of the trust property beyond his entitlement. When the trustee died the remainderman was able to sue the representatives of the trustees for occupational rent.

It has already been observed that the definition given to the word 'trustees' for the purposes of the Limitation Act 1980 covers not only express trustees, but also implied and constructive trustees. Having said this, it is very important to appreciate that s. 21(1) does not extend to all types of constructive trusts. The exception in s. 21(1) applies only when there is a proper trustee/beneficiary relationship. You will recall from Chapter 14 that a constructive trust may be imposed on a person who dishonestly assists in a breach of trust. Such a person will not have received trust property and will not have been in a trustee relationship in the context of holding trust property for a beneficiary. The imposition of such a constructive trust on a person who assists in a breach of trust is done primarily to make that person personally liable to compensate the beneficiary for the loss. In contrast to this type of situation, a constructive trust is imposed on someone who has assumed fiduciary duties to a beneficiary before a breach of trust has occurred: for example, a solicitor who receives trust property knowing that it belongs to a beneficiary. In such a case the solicitor will have assumed the relationship of a trustee proper and will be treated as holding the property for the beneficiary. In **Paragon Finance plc v D.B. Thakerar**[115] Millett LJ explained that only those constructive trusts which arose by virtue of the trustee agreeing to hold trust property, or assuming fiduciary duties before the conduct complained of by the claimant, were covered by the exception in s. 21(1). Millett LJ explained that those constructive trusts which were imposed in cases such as dishonest assistance in a breach of trust 'were not in reality trusts at all, but merely a remedial mechanism by which equity gave relief for fraud'.[116] A good illustration of the type of constructive trust which is covered by s. 21(1) is **JJ Harrison (Properties) Ltd v Harrison**,[117] where a company director misused his fiduciary powers and converted company property for himself. The court held that the director had become a constructive trustee as a result of his breach of fiduciary duty and as such was a constructive trustee of property belonging to the company. As such, he was prevented by s. 21(1) of the Limitation Act 1980 from raising a defence based on limitation.

---

[112] [1997] 2 All ER 705.
[113] [1894] 1 Ch. 599.
[114] [1949] Ch. 767.
[115] [1990] 1 All ER 400.
[116] [1990] 1 All ER 400 at 409.
[117] [2002] 1 BCLC 162.

Finally, the Law Commission has recently reviewed the limitation rules in respect of civil wrongs and has suggested a number of changes in relation to the existing rules.[118] The Commission explained that the existing rules were unfair, complex and out of date with modern law. The Law Commission's view is that there is no justification in making distinctions between different forms of action. Furthermore, the Commission is of the view that sometimes hardship can be caused where the claimant is unaware that the right of action has accrued. The basic recommendation is that a single core limitation period is applicable to all actions. The suggested limitation period is three years from the time the claimant knows, or ought reasonably to know of the facts that give rise to the action. The basic structure of the core limitation regime is reproduced below.

KEY CITATION

Law Com. 270 (2001) 'Limitation of actions'

In this Report we recommend that these problems should be resolved by the introduction of a single, core limitation regime, which will apply, as far as possible, to all claims for a remedy for a wrong, claims for the enforcement of a right and claims for restitution. This regime will consist of:

1 A primary limitation period of three years starting from the date on which the claimant knows, or ought reasonably to know (a) the facts which give rise to the cause of action; (b) the identity of the defendant; and (c) if the claimant has suffered injury, loss or damage or the defendant has received a benefit, that the injury, loss, damage or benefit was significant.

2 A long-stop limitation period of 10 years, starting from the date of the accrual of the cause of action or (for those claims in tort where loss is an essential element of the cause of action, or claims for breach of statutory duty) from the date of the act or omission which gives rise to the cause of action (but for personal injuries claims see below).

We recommend that the above core regime should apply without any qualification to the following actions: the majority of tort claims, contract claims, restitutionary claims, claims for breach of trust and related claims, claims on a judgment or arbitration award, and claims on a statute.

The equitable doctrine of laches

Where no statutory period of limitation applies, for example, s. 21(1) of the Limitation Act 1980 and actions for breach of self-dealing and fair-dealing, the equitable doctrine of laches will continue to apply as a defence to such actions. The basic tenet of this doctrine is that a beneficiary, who has knowledge of the breach of trust, has nevertheless acquiesced in the breach by virtue of delaying in bringing an action. The classical statement of the doctrine was made by Lord Selbourne in *Lindsay Petroleum Co v Hurd*.[119] His Lordship explained that:

> the doctrine of *laches* in courts of equity is not an arbitrary or a technical doctrine. Where it would be practically unjust to give a remedy, either because the party has by his conduct, done that which might fairly be regarded as a waiver of it, or where by his conduct and neglect he has, though perhaps not waiving that remedy, yet put the other party in a situation

---

[118] Law Com. 270 (2001) 'Limitation of Actions'.
[119] (1874) LR 5 PC 221.

in which it would not be reasonable to place him if the remedy were afterwards to be asserted, in either of these cases, lapse and delay are most material.[120]

Whilst delay is an important factor in raising the defence of laches, it is not the only crieria that the court will take into consideration. In **Nelson v Rye**[121] the court explained that other relevant factors included the extent to which the defendant's position has been prejudiced by the delay in bringing the action and the extent to which the claimant had contributed to the defendant's position. More recently, in **Patel v Shah**[122] claimants who deliberately failed to bring an action to recover land at a time when the propety markets were depressed could not do so when the property markets picked up. The Court of Appeal held that the only reason for not asserting their rights much earlier was to put the defendants in a position where they would have to deal with keeping the properties afloat in a depressed property market.

Conclusion

This chapter has focused on the personal remedy available to a beneficiary for breaches of trust committed by a trustee administering a trust. This remedy will take the form of a personal claim against the trustee to compensate the beneficiary for losses that have been caused to the trust. A personal claim requires the trustee to pay out of his own pocket the loss which has been suffered by the beneficiary. It has been observed in this chapter that the nature of the personal liability of the trustee has in the past been the subject of much debate. Questions have centred on whether the defaulting trustee is to effect a restitution of the trust estate or whether he is required to compensate the beneficiary. It should be clear from this chapter that the personal liability of the trustee is to compensate the beneficiary for losses which have been caused by the breach of trust. The trustee is required to effect some form of restorative compensation. The primary duty of the trustee is not to effect restitution because in most cases the acts of a defaulting trustee will have caused a loss to the estate rather than a gain at the expense of the beneficiary. Restitution is a response to unjust enrichment at the beneficiary's expense. Some breaches of trust will, however, result in an unjust enrichment and these will occur primarily in the context of breach of fiduciary duties. Where there is a breach of fiduciary duty, the trustee will have to effect restitution by way of an account for profits.

Case study

Consider the following case study.

Thomas by his will appointed John and Bert to be his executors and trustees. The will contained, *inter alia*, the following provisions:

- Clause 5 provided that the trustee was to hold the residue of the estate upon trust 'for my wife, Jenny during her lifetime and thereafter for my daughter, Simone'.
- Clause 6 authorised the trustee to invest the money in any manner he thought fit as if he were the absolute owner thereof, provided he took professional advice.

---

[120] (1874) LR 5 PC 221 at 239.
[121] [1996] 2 All ER 186.
[122] [2005] EWCA Civ. 157.

The residuary estate was initially valued at £50,000. Bert invested the sum of £20,000 in Manhattan Ltd without taking advice. He used £20,000 as a deposit for a house for his family. The house needed renovation and he spent a lot of his own money for that purpose. The house is now valued at £87,000. The remaining £10,000 was paid into his bank account where he already had £14,000. A few months ago his stockbroker told Bert that the shares in Manhattan had halved in price. Bert sold the shares in Manhattan Ltd for £10,000 and invested them in Horse and Rider Ltd: they are now valued at £30,000. Bert used £14,000 from his own bank account to buy more shares in Manhattan Ltd for himself. The remaining £10,000 he gambled at a casino and lost everything.

Advise the beneficiaries as to the remedies available to them for breach of trust.

Moot points

1 What do you understand to be the difference between equitable compensation, common law damages and restitution?

2 What is the proper time at which the court should assess equitable compensation?

3 How far is it possible for a trustee to offset a loss made in one breach by a gain made in another breach of trust? Read the case *Bartlett* v *Barclays Bank Trust Co (No. 2)* [1980] Ch. 515 and explain why the court thought that the 'Old Bailey' project and the 'Guildford' project were part of the same project. What other points of trust law does this case decide?

4 What do you consider to be the principal factor which will influence the court to award a defence to a trustee under s. 61 of the Trustee Act 1925?

5 To what type of breaches of trust will the equitable doctrine of laches continue to apply?

Further reading

Capper, D. 'Compensation for Breach of Trust' Conv. 1997, 14. This article considers the decision of the House of Lords in *Target Holdings* v *Redferns* [1996] AC 421.

Nolan, R. 'A Targeted Degree of Liability' [1996] LMCLQ 16. A casenote on the decision in *Target Holdings*.

Rickett, C. 'Equitable Compensation: Towards a Blueprint?' [2003] Syd. L. Rev. A very comprehensive account of the nature of equitable compensation.

Rickett, C.E.F. 'Equitable Compensation: The Giant Stirs' 1996, 112 LQR 2. This article examines the nature of equitable compensation in *Target Holdings*.

Visit **www.mylawchamber.co.uk/panesar** to access study support resources including interactive multiple choice questions, practice exam questions with guidance, podcasts, weblinks, legal newsfeed all linked to the **Pearson eText** version of Exploring Equity and Trusts which you can **search**, **highlight** and **personalise** with your **own notes** and **bookmarks**.

Use Case Navigator to read in full some of the key cases referenced in this chapter with commentary and questions:

Armitage v *Nurse* [1998] 2 All ER 705

21

Tracing and a proprietary claim

Learning objectives

After reading this chapter you should be able to:

→ understand the advantages of pursuing a proprietary remedy over a personal one

→ understand the nature of tracing and following as distinct from claiming property

→ understand the restitutionary and proprietary basis of tracing

→ understand the differences and limitations of tracing at common law and tracing in equity

→ understand the common law action for money had and received

→ understand the rules of mixing trust property with other property

→ understand the limitations and defences for tracing in equity.

Re Diplock [1948] Ch. 465: Invalid charitable trusts, wrongful payments to innocent third parties and the beneficiaries' right to recover property

The facts of the seminal case of *Re Diplock* illustrate the issues which will be explored in this chapter. By the will dated 3 November 1919 of Caleb Diplock, who died on 23 March 1936, his executors were directed to apply his residuary estate 'for such charitable institution or institutions or other charitable or benevolent object or objects in England'. After the will was proved in 1936, the executors made a series of payments to a number of charities including the Dr Barnardo's Charity and the Royal Sailors Orphan Girls' School. Many of these charities had mixed the money with their own money in order to improve their property. It later transpired that Caleb Diplock's will did not in fact create a valid charitable trust and that in such circumstances his next of kin were the true beneficiaries of his estate and not the charities.

The question before the court was whether the next of kin beneficiaries could trace their property into the hands of the charities who had mistakenly and innocently received property which did not belong to them. The facts of *Re Diplock* nicely illustrate the problems that may occur when property is wrongly transferred by a trustee to a third party. Some of the questions which arise in this chapter include:

- Does a beneficiary have a right to trace property into the hands of a third party?
- What happens if the third party mixes the trust property with his own property?
- What would be the position if the third party uses the money to pay off its debts or otherwise improves its land? Would it be fair to follow property into its hands?

These matters relating to tracing and proprietary claims are investigated in this chapter.

Introduction

In the previous chapter the personal liability of the trustee for breach of trust was explored. In addition to a personal remedy a beneficiary may also seek a proprietary remedy. Whereas a personal claim against a trustee requires the trustee to compensate the beneficiary out of his own pocket for the loss that has been caused to the trust estate, a proprietary claim allows the beneficiary to claim property in the hands of a trustee or some other third party as his own. Provided that such property is not in the hands of a bona fide purchaser of the legal title without notice of the trust, the beneficiary can assert his or her right to the property in question. Such a remedy will take the form of asserting ownership to an asset which is in the hands of the trustee or some other third party. In most cases it will involve the imposition of a constructive trust on the asset. The imposition of a constructive trust will mean that the trustee or some other third party is denied absolute ownership of the asset being traced and will be compelled to recognise the equitable interest of the beneficiary in that asset. In other cases, the beneficiary may be awarded a lien on the asset which is in the hands of the trustee or some third party. The effect of a lien is to give the beneficiary security for the value of the original trust property which it has lost as a consequence of it being wrongfully in the hands of the trustee or third party. The matter was neatly explained by Keene LJ in **Director of Serious Fraud Office v Lexi Holdings plc (In Administration)**[1] where his Lordship explained that 'where misappropriated trust assets are thereafter applied in the acquisition of other property the beneficiary is entitled at his option either (a) to assert, via a constructive trust, beneficial ownership of the proceeds (or a commensurate part of them) or (b) to make a personal claim against the defaulting trustee, if need be enforcing an equitable charge or lien over the proceeds in question to secure restoration by the defaulting trustee of the misappropriated assets. These are true alternatives. In the first kind of claim, the beneficiary is in effect saying: "Those proceeds (or part of them) belong to me." In the second, alternative, kind of claim the beneficiary is in effect saying "The trustee is obliged to account personally to me for his misappropriation and those proceeds stand charged as security for his personal obligation to me".' This chapter explores the principles of tracing at common law and in equity and examines the rather technical rules of equity which allow a beneficiary to trace into mixed property. It also examines those circumstances when the right to trace may be lost as against a third party.

Proprietary claims and tracing

The process by which a beneficiary will seek to assert a right to property is called tracing or following. In other words, the beneficiary is seen to be tracing his or her ownership into the trust property, either in its original form, some other substituted form, or a form where the trust property has become mixed with some other property. Seeking a proprietary claim over and above a personal claim has two distinct advantages. Firstly, a proprietary claim does not depend on the question whether the trustee is solvent or not. The success of a personal claim against the trustee very much depends on whether he is solvent and in a position to meet the judgment that has been given against him. In contrast, where a beneficiary asserts some proprietary claim over property through following or tracing, he is simply asking the court to recognise his ownership in that property and restore it back to him. It is for this reason, as will be explored in more detail below, that the rules of tracing and following are deeply embedded in the law of restitution. The second advantage of tracing is that it allows a beneficiary to take advantage of any increase in value of the trust property. For example, suppose that a trustee in breach of trust gives trust property to his wife. Let's assume that the trust property was a diamond worth £50,000 and the wife sells it for that much and then buys a painting with the proceeds of the sale. The beneficiaries discover the breach of trust and also become aware that the painting is now worth £100,000. If the beneficiaries were to bring a personal claim against the trustee, that claim would be for the loss they have suffered, which would be a diamond worth £50,000. However, if they sought a proprietary claim, they could claim the painting as their property because it has been purchased with the proceeds of their diamond. It would be unlikely that the wife would be able to refute such a claim as she would not be regarded as a bona fide purchaser of the diamond without notice of the beneficiaries' interest.

The process of tracing and following has attracted considerable debate and discussion.[2] There appear to be three important questions which arise when discussing tracing and

---

[1] [2008] EWCA Crim 1443 at para. 36.

[2] See, for example, L. Smith, *The Law of Tracing* (1997); R.H. Maudsley, 'Proprietary Remedies for the Recovery of Money' (1959) 75 LQR 234; P. Birks, 'Mixing and Tracing Property and Restitution' (1992) CLP 69; P. Millett, 'Tracing the Proceeds of Fraud' (1991) 107 LQR 71 and C. Rickett and R. Grantham, 'Tracing and Property Rights: The Categorical Truth' (2000) 63 MLR 6.

following. The first question relates to the nature of the process of tracing and following. The second question focuses on the basis upon which tracing is founded: in particular, is tracing inherently restitutionary in nature or is it founded upon some proprietary principle? The final question is whether the two separate principles of tracing at common law and equity are founded on principle. In addressing the first question, students of trust law often regard tracing as a remedy when in reality tracing is a process by which a personal claim may be made against a defendant or a proprietary claim may be asserted over a particular asset. Tracing allows a beneficiary to identify that he is the owner of some trust property and that the trust property has now found itself in the hands of another person who is not entitled to assert absolute ownership to it. The nature of tracing and following is best explained by one leading treatise on equity.

> The rules of following and tracing are artificial rules of evidence which allow a claimant to identify misapplied property or its proceeds. Following is the process of identifying the same property as it is transferred from one person to another. Tracing is the process of identifying a new asset as the substitute for an original asset which was misappropriated from the claimant. Where one asset is exchanged for another, the claimant may elect to treat the substituted asset as representing the value contained in the original asset into the substituted asset. He is said to trace the value represented in the original asset into the substituted asset.
>
> In the strict sense, the processes of following and tracing are not claims or remedies. They merely lay the evidential foundation necessary to prove some claim against the defendant which the claimant then enforces by a remedy. The remedy may be personal or proprietary. So for example the claimant may follow money which the trustee paid in breach of trust to a third party. The claimant's motive may be to establish the personal liability in a claim for knowing receipt. In such a case the process of following merely proves the identity of the money received by the third party with that misapplied from the trust. It is common, however, that a claimant relies on the rules of following and tracing to prove his entitlement to a proprietary remedy against the defendant.

Snell's Principles of Equity, J.A. McGhee (ed.) 31st edn (2005) at p. 683

VISIT CASE NAVIGATOR

Tracing and following are concepts which are sometimes used interchangeably; however, it is important to note that they are different in nature. In ***Foskett v McKeown***[3] Millett LJ explained that 'following is the process of following the same asset as it moves from hand to hand. Tracing is the process of identifying a new asset as a substitute for the old.'[4]

With regard to the second question, which is essentially whether tracing is part of the law of restitution or the law of property, there have been two main schools of thoughts, both of which seek to provide compelling justifications for the basis upon which tracing is allowed. One school of thought is that tracing is deeply embedded in the law of restitution.[5] Restitution is a term that has appeared in many parts of this book and primarily governs that area of law which seeks to reverse an unjust enrichment at the claimant's expense.[6] The process of tracing enables a beneficiary to establish that property retained or received by the defendant is retained or received at the expense of the beneficiary. Whilst it is not doubted that tracing and following are restitutionary in nature in that the function of tracing is to identify property in the hands of the defendant which should be restored to the claimant, there has been some debate as to the 'proprietary' basis of

---

[3] [2001] 1 AC 102.

[4] [2001] 1 AC 102 at 127.

[5] See generally P. Birks, *The Law of Restitution* (1985) and A. Burrows, *The Law of Restitution* 2nd edn (2002).

[6] See A. Burrows, 'Proprietary Restitution: Unmasking Unjust Enrichment' (2002) 117 LQR 412.

tracing. Most notably, Pearce and Stevens in their text explain that it cannot be said that tracing is a mere process, albeit one to reverse an unjust enrichment, without proprietary implications.[7] Whilst both commentators accept that the process of tracing is to reverse an unjust enrichment, they argue that such enrichment is reversed because, through the process of tracing, the claimant has shown that property which once belonged to him still belongs to him despite being in some other form or shape. They argue that title to property claimed through tracing has essentially descended from the claimant's original title. Restitutionary lawyers had rejected the descent of title argument on the basis that the claimant would gain property interests in every exchange that resulted from the claimant's original property. Pearce and Stevens give an example of a trustee who takes £5000 from a trust fund and then buys a ring which is then sold for £10,000 in order to purchase a car. The argument is that the beneficiary would have an interest in the ring, the £10,000 and the car at the same time. Whilst rejecting the idea of a multiple number of claims in the exchanges that may have taken place with the claimant's original property, both commentators reject the idea that the tracing is without a proprietary basis. There is much to be said for this line of reasoning and the following extract from their text neatly summarises their argument.

> Whilst the use of tracing as means of identifying the receipt of enrichment is unquestioned, it is submitted that the relegation of tracing to a mere process without proprietary implications is unduly reductionist and at odds with both authority and principle. Whilst tracing may functionally operate to demonstrate receipt, and thus as the foundation for a personal claim to restitution at common law or in equity, the process of tracing is intrinsically proprietary in nature. Value cannot exist in the abstract but only in the form of specific assets or property. The leading cases concerning the right to trace at common law and in equity support the view that tracing operates by 'descent of title' so that the [claimant] can trace his property through mixtures and substitutions. At every stage of the chain of events he continues to be the owner, whether at law or in equity, of the assets identified by the rules of tracing. If at any time he ceases to be the owner, his right to trace comes to an automatic end, as when trust property is acquired by a bona fide purchaser.
>
> R. Pearce and J. Stevens, *The Law of Trusts and Equitable Obligation* 5th edn (2010) at p. 1017

The final question concerning the nature of tracing revolves around whether the historical distinction between tracing at common law and tracing in equity is justified. It will be seen in the sections below that tracing is recognised at common law and in equity. The right to trace at common law is restricted when compared with the right to trace in equity. Whilst the common law recognises the right to trace property which has been substituted for another, it does not recognise a right to trace property which has been mixed with other property. In equity, mixing of trust property has never been a problem; however, the right to trace in equity depends very much on whether the claimant can prove the existence of equitable interest in the property being traced and a prior fiduciary relationship. The requirement of a fiduciary relationship is deeply rooted in the historical basis that equitable relief would be granted. However, the requirement has unduly restricted the types of claimants that are able to seek the equitable jurisdiction to trace property. In a series of relatively recent cases Millett LJ has questioned whether the distinction between tracing at common law and tracing in equity is justified. His Lordship has called for a uniform set of rules which set out the rules of tracing. Such uniform rules would be applied in all cases with the court then being required to give an appropriate

---

[7] R. Pearce and J. Stevens, *The Law of Trusts and Equitable Obligation* 5th edn (2010) at p. 1017.

remedial response, whether that be in the form of a personal claim or a proprietary claim. In **Foskett v McKeown**[8] Millett LJ explained that:

> given its nature, there is nothing inherently legal or equitable about the tracing exercise. There is no sense in maintaining different rules for tracing at law and in equity. One set of tracing rules is enough . . . There is certainly no logical justification for allowing any distinction between them to produce capricious results in cases of mixed substitutions by insisting on the existence of a fiduciary relationship as a precondition for applying equity's tracing rules. The existence of such a relationship may be relevant to the nature of the claim which the plaintiff can maintain, whether personal or proprietary, but that is a different matter.[9]

It is generally understood that the rules of tracing will gradually become uniform in identifying what property the claimant may seek to make a remedial claim. As to the remedial response, the court will decide on the facts of each case exactly what remedy to afford the claimant, whether it is in the form of a personal one or a proprietary one.[10] For the time being the distinction between tracing at common law and in equity remains and the sections below consider some of the key principles of both sets of tracing rules.

Tracing and proprietary claims at common law

Historically, the common law did not recognise a general right of a person to recover his property in the event of wrongful interference. The only exception to this was in the case of land where the claimant was able to bring a real action to recover the land. If a claimant's property had been wrongfully interfered with by a defendant then he was entitled to damages for the tort of conversion.[11] The matter is now governed by the Torts (Interference with Goods) Act 1977, which preserves the tort of conversion but gives the court under s. 3 a discretion to order specific delivery of the claimant's property. Where the subject matter of the property was money, then provided that the claimant could prove his entitlement to the money, the common law also recognised an action for money had and received. This action, which was primarily in the form of a restitutionary claim, entitled the claimant to return of the money.[12] The action for money had and received is a personal restitutionary claim and not one which takes the form of a proprietary claim. The rules of tracing in this respect establish that the defendant received money which belonged to the claimant and that upon receipt that money did not belong to any person other than the claimant. The matter is neatly illustrated by the decision of the House of Lords in **Lipkin Gorman v Karpnale Ltd**[13] where a partner in a firm of solicitors wrongfully withdrew money from the partnership account and gambled the money at the Playboy Club. The partners had suffered a loss of some £220,000 as result of the money

---

[8] [2001] 1 AC 102.

[9] [2001] 1 AC 102 at 113. This echoed very much what his Lordship had said in *Jones (FC) & Sons* v *Jones* [1996] 3 WLR 703 where his Lordship commented that 'there is no merit in having distinct and different tracing rules at law and in equity, given that tracing is neither a right nor a remedy but merely a process by which the plaintiff establishes what has happened to his property and make good his claim that the assets which he claims can properly be regarded as representing his property' at 712.

[10] See P. Birks, 'The Necessity of a Unitary Law of Tracing' in *Making Commercial Law, Essays in Honour of Roy Goode* (1997).

[11] See R. Hickey, 'Wrongs and the Protection of Personal Property' Conv. (2011) 48.

[12] *Lipkin Gorman* v *Karpnale Ltd* [1991] 2 AC 548.

[13] [1991] 2 AC 548.

being gambled at the club. The Playboy Club had made a net profit of some £155,000 from the misappropriated money, the remainder of the sum having being paid out to the partner by way of winnings. The firm of solicitors commenced proceedings against the Club to recover the sum of £155,000 as money had and received. The House of Lords upheld their action for money had and received on the grounds that the Club had been unjustly enriched at the expense of the firm of solicitors.

Unmixed property

It is clear that the common law does recognise the right of a claimant to trace and claim his property, provided that such property has not been mixed with any other property. The right to trace at common law belongs to the legal owner of the property.[14] The leading case here is *Taylor v Plumer*[15] where the defendant, Sir Thomas Plumer, entrusted his stockbroker, Walsh, with a bank draft for £22,000 with the express instructions that Walsh invest the money in Exchequer bills. Walsh, having become insolvent, invested some of the money in bills and the remainder in US securities and bullion, with the intention of absconding with the money to America. Just as Walsh was about to board a ship at Falmouth destined for America, Plumer's agent intercepted him and seized the securities and bullion. The claimants, Walsh's assignees in bankruptcy, commenced proceedings against Plumer on the grounds of trover (now the tort of conversion), that the bullion and securities belonged to Walsh. Lord Ellenborough CJ held that the money which Sir Thomas Plumer had given to Walsh could be traced into the securities and bullion and therefore was property of Sir Thomas Plumer. The central point in the judgment of Lord Ellenborough CJ was that provided that the money had not been mixed with other money it could be traced. It did not matter that the money had been substituted for something else. In the course of judgment his Lordship explained that:

> it makes no difference in reason or law into what other form, different from the original, the change may have been made, whether it be into that of promissory notes for the security of the money which was produced by the sale of the goods of the principal . . . or into other merchandise, for the product of or substitute for the original thing still follows the nature of the thing itself, as long as it can be ascertained as such, and the right only ceases when the means of ascertainment fail, which is the case when the subject is turned into money, and mixed and confounded in a general mass of the same description.[16]

Unmixed property and profits

Taylor v Plumer[17] firmly decides that the right to trace at common law will exist providing that what the claimant seeks to trace does not become mixed with other property. The rule was applied in *Banque Belge pour L'Etranger v Hambrouck*[18] where a certain Hambrouck forged a number of cheques worth £6000 from his employers and paid them into his own account. He then withdrew sums of money from his account and paid them to his mistress for no consideration. The mistress paid the money into her account at a different bank. A sum of £315 was in the account of Hanbrouck's mistress and the claimant bank commenced proceedings to claim that money. The Court of Appeal held

---

[14] *MCC Proceeds v Lehman Brothers International (Europe)* (1998) *The Times*, 14 January 1998.
[15] (1815) 3 M & S 562.
[16] (1815) 3 M & S 562 at 575.
[17] (1815) 3 M & S 562.
[18] [1921] 1 KB 321.

that the money remained identifiable at every stage; it had not been mixed with any other money and therefore the bank was entitled to trace the money into the account. The rule in **Taylor v Plumer** was taken one step further in **Jones (FC) & Sons v Jones**[19] where the question arose whether a legal owner could trace property not only into its product, that is, the exchange value of the property but also the profits made on it. On the facts of the case a sum of £11,700 was loaned from a partnership account to the wife of one of the partners. The wife paid the cheque into a new account and began trading with commodity brokers. The wife made a profit of some £50,000 with the use of the original loan money. It later transpired that under the Bankruptcy Act 1924 the partnership was bankrupt before the payment of the loan money was made to the partner's wife. The effect of this being that the wife was never entitled to the money. Instead all of the assets were to pass to the official receivership. The official receivership commenced proceedings to trace the money from the partner's wife. It was not disputed that the official receiver was the proper owner of the £11,700 at the time it was transferred to the wife and therefore entitled to trace that amount into the hands of the wife. At common law this would take the form of an action for money had received. Essentially this would require the wife returning what she had received in the first place, that is the £11,700. However, the real question was whether the official receiver was also entitled to the profit that the wife had made as a result of the commodity trading.

The Court of Appeal held that the official receiver was entitled to the profit that was made through the use of the £11,700. In other words, the official receiver could trace the £50,000. Clearly this demonstrated a further expansion of the common law action for money had and received. Millett LJ sought to justify the decision on the grounds that the cheque paid to the wife remained in a separate account at all times and the profit she made was likewise paid into a different account. There had been no mixing of the trust property at any stage. His Lordship explained that the money at all time belonged to the official receiver and was identifiable as belonging to it at every stage. Nourse LJ agreed with Millett LJ's conclusion but suggested that the basis of the decision turned on the grounds that it would be unjust enrichment for the wife to retain the profit. His Lordship accepted that the decision in this case went further than the decided cases; however, he explained that 'the defendant cannot in conscience retain the profit any more than the original £11,700. She had no title to the original. She could not have made the profit without her use of it. She cannot, by making a profit through the use of the money to which she had no title, acquire some better title to the profit.'[20]

Mixed property

A significant factor in the decision of the Court of Appeal in **Jones (FC) & Sons v Jones**[21] was that original cheques were paid the partner's wife and she paid those cheques into separate accounts. What is more, when she received a cheque from the commodity brokers representing the profits, this cheque was paid into a separate account. In the view of Millett LJ this was sufficient to show that the money had not been mixed at any stage and the official receiver could identify his property at every stage. What would have been crucial in that case is if the money had indeed been mixed with other money.

---

[19] [1996] 3 WLR 703. See J. Beatson and N. Andrews, 'Common Law Tracing: Springboard or Swan Song?' (1997) LQR 21.
[20] [1901] 2 Ch. 534.
[21] [1996] 3 WLR 703.

As **Taylor v Plumer**[22] decides, the right to trace will be lost if the property or money becomes mixed with other property before it is received by the defendant. The matter is neatly illustrated by the decision of the Court of Appeal in **Agip (Africa) Ltd v Jackson**[23] where the claimant's accountant forged payment orders in order to launder money from Tunis to London. The defendant had created a number of dummy companies in London. One such company was Baker Oil Ltd which held an account at a Lloyds branch in London. The accountant fraudulently changed the name of one payment order of some $518,000 to be payable to Baker Oil Ltd in London. Agip's bankers in Tunis arranged for Baker Oil Ltd's account at London to be credited with a sum of $518,000 by arranging with a New York clearing bank where they held an account to credit the account of Lloyds correspondent bank in New York and debit their account. The sum paid to into the account of Baker Oil Ltd in London was then transferred into the defendant's account in the Isle of Man. Only a sum of £45,000 remained in the account belonging to the defendants. The question was whether Agip could trace the payment order into the account of the defendants in the Isle of Man. In the High Court Millett J held that Agip were unable to trace the payment order of $518,000 into the account of the defendants in the Isle of man, as nothing belonging to Agip had passed to the defendants. Millett J explained that nothing but a series of electrons had been transferred amongst the various banks. In his words, 'nothing passed between Tunisia and London but a stream of electrons. It is not possible to treat the money received by Lloyds Bank in London or its correspondent bank in New York as representing the proceeds of the payment order or of any other physical asset previous in its hands and delivered by it in exchange for the money.'[24] In the Court of Appeal, whilst affirming the decision of Millett J at first instance, Fox LJ placed emphasis on the fact that money which has been transferred through an inter-bank clearing system could never be traced because the money would inevitably be subject to mixing with other money.[25]

In summary, the right to trace at common law is dependent on whether the claimant can show that the property being traced retains the identity of his original property. It does not matter that the property has been substituted for another property, provided that the property has not been mixed with other property. In most cases the process of tracing at common law is to bring a personal restitutionary action against the defendant for money had and received, in circumstances where the claimant can prove that the money received by the defendant belonged to the claimant. Cases such as **Jones (FC) & Sons v Jones**[26] extend the principles of common law tracing to include the right to claim any profits that are made by the use of the claimant's property. However, as the decision in **Agip (Africa) Ltd v Jackson**[27] illustrates, the right to trace at common law will be lost in circumstances when the claimant seeks to trace property which has been the subject matter of mixing. If the claimant's property becomes mixed with that of the defendant's property then the right to trace at common law will be lost. At the present time it is impossible to trace money that is paid through an inter-clearing bank system simply on the grounds that any payment out of an inter-bank clearing system will represent money paid out of a mixed account. This is obviously a major limitation in the right to trace at common law, although it will be seen below that such a limitation does not prevent the right to trace in equity.

---

[22] (1815) 3 M & S 562.
[23] [1991] Ch. 547.
[24] [1990] Ch. 265 at 399.
[25] See also *Bank Tejarat* v *Hong Kong and Shanghai Banking Corpn* [1995] 1 Lloyd's Rep. 239.
[26] [1996] 3 WLR 703. See J. Beatson and N. Andrews, 'Common Law Tracing: Springboard or Swan Song?' (1997) LQR 21.
[27] [1991] Ch. 547.

 # Tracing and proprietary claims in equity

A beneficiary under a trust will essentially trace its beneficial interest in property under the rules of equitable tracing. Unlike at common law, the rules of tracing in equity are much more flexible and, as will be seen in the course of the following sections, the right to trace in equity is not defeated where the property has been mixed with other property. Historically, the right to trace in equity depended on whether the claimant had a distinct equitable interest or title in the property being traced. This was easily satisfied in the context of a typical trust where the trust would fragment legal and equitable title between the trustee and the beneficiary. In such a case the trustee would be standing in a fiduciary relationship to the beneficiary and any misapplication of the beneficiary's property would generate a right to follow it in equity. One of the consequences of the requirement of a distinct equitable title meant that a person who had both legal and equitable title before his property had been misapplied could not use the rules of equitable tracing to claim property. Whilst this is still the case today, it will be seen that the courts have in the past liberally construed the notion of a fiduciary relationship. These and other matters are explored in more detail in the sections which follow.

The right to trace in equity

The requisites for tracing in equity were considered in the **Re Diplock**.[28] The facts of the case involved a will in which Diplock left his residuary estate to such 'charitable and benevolent objects' as his personal representatives think fit. On the understanding that this created a valid charitable disposition, the personal representatives distributed his residuary estate to a number of charities. The next of kin of Diplock successfully challenged the nature of the disposition and sought to recover the money from the charities. In the Court of Appeal Lord Greene MR held that they were entitled to trace the money into the hands of the charities. In the course of his judgment his Lordship explained that 'equity may operate on the conscience not merely of those who acquire a legal title in breach of some trust, express or constructive, or of some other fiduciary obligation, but of volunteers provided that as a result of what has gone before some equitable proprietary interest has been created and attaches to the property in the hands of the volunteer'.[29] The decision in **Re Diplock** is usually taken as having decided that the right to trace in equity is dependant upon the proof of:

- an initial fiduciary relationship;
- a prior equitable interest.

Where a claimant does stand in a fiduciary relationship and does have an equitable interest he can trace property into the hands of everyone except a bona fide purchaser of the legal title without notice of the equitable interest.

Although a beneficiary under a trust, whether it is an express trust or an implied trust, clearly can demonstrate that he or she has an equitable interest by virtue of being in a fiduciary relationship, the insistence on the need for a proper fiduciary relationship has been the subject matter of much criticism and debate. The main concern over the requirement of a fiduciary relationship is that it severely restricts the type of claimants that may

---

[28] [1948] Ch. 465.
[29] [1948] Ch. 465 at 530.

seek the benefit of the rules of equitable tracing. It has already been seen that, given the very restricted scope of tracing at common law, the need to invoke the equitable rules becomes even more pressing. Where a claimant does not benefit from standing in a fiduciary relationship there is no right to trace in equity. However, despite this, the courts have in the past adopted a very liberal approach to finding a fiduciary relationship which will generate the right to trace in equity. For example, in a number of cases it has become clear that the fiduciary relationship need not exist before the transfer of the claimant's property into the hands of the defendant. It is sufficient that the transfer itself generates the finding of a fiduciary relationship. In *Agip (Africa) v Jackson*[30] Millet J explained that 'it is not necessary that the fund to be traced should have been the subject of fiduciary obligation before it got into the wrong hands . . . it is sufficient that the payment to the defendant itself gives rise to a fiduciary relationship'.[31] For example, in *El Ajou v Dollar Land Holdings plc*[32] the court held that a claimant who pays money to another as result of a fraudulent misrepresentation retains an equitable interest under a resulting trust so as to trace the money in equity. In *Westdeutsche Landesbank Girozentrale v Islington Borough Council*[33] Lord Browne-Wilkinson explained that a thief who steals from a victim holds the stolen money on constructive trust for the victim who is entitled to trace in equity. His Lordship commented that 'the stolen moneys are traceable in equity. But the proprietary interest which equity is enforcing in such circumstances arises under a constructive, not a resulting, trust. Although it is difficult to find clear authority for the proposition, when property is obtained by fraud equity imposes a constructive on the fraudulent recipient; the property is recoverable and traceable in equity . . . Money stolen from a bank account can be traced in equity.'[34]

VISIT CASE NAVIGATOR

The liberal finding of a fiduciary relationship can be seen in a number of the decided cases. Firstly, in *Sinclair v Brougham*[35] a building society was held to be acting outside its powers by operating a banking business. When the society was being wound up, the question arose as to whether the depositors could trace their money into the funds of the society. The House of Lords held that the building society had received the depositors' money in the capacity as a fiduciary and as such the money was held under a trust entitling them to trace in equity. The decision in *Sinclair v Brougham* was overruled in *Westdeutsche Landesbank Girozentrale v Islington Borough Council*[36] where the House of Lords held that payment made under a void contract does not generate an equitable interest in the transferor. In *Chase Manhattan Bank v Israeli-British Bank (London)*[37] one bank, because of a clerical error, made two payments of the same amount into the account of another bank. When the receiving bank became insolvent the question arose whether the bank that had paid the money by mistake was entitled to trace in equity. Goulding J held that 'a person who pays money to another under a factual mistake retains an equitable property in it and the conscience of that other is subjected to a fiduciary duty to respect his proprietary right'.[38] Although not overruled, the decision in this case was doubted by Lord Browne-Wilkinson in *Westdeutsche Landesbank Girozentrale v Islington Borough Council*.

---

[30] [1990] Ch. 265.
[31] [1990] Ch. 265 at 270.
[32] [1993] 3 All ER 717.
[33] [1996] AC 669 (HL).
[34] [1996] AC 669 at 716.
[35] [1914] AC 398.
[36] [1999] AC 669 (HL).
[37] [1981] Ch. 105.
[38] [1981] Ch. 105 at 119.

Tracing original property and clean substitutions

APPLYING THE LAW

Tim and Tom are holding a painting on trust for a beneficiary. They have auctioned the painting and received a sum of £100,000. They have used this money to purchase a house which is now valued at £200,000.

Can the beneficiary trace into the house?

The rules and precise extent of equitable tracing was examined in detail in **Re Hallett's Estate**.[39] The simplest case of tracing will arise where the trustee in breach of trust transfers the trust property to a third party. For example, let us assume the trustee gives a gold necklace held on trust for a beneficiary to his wife as a gift. In such a case the beneficiary can trace and claim the necklace from the trustee's wife who will not be regarded as a bona fide purchaser of the necklace without notice of the beneficiary's interest. More typically, however, the trustee may take the necklace and exchange it for another asset, for example, a gold watch. In such a case the beneficiary has potentially two options. The first option is trace the necklace into the hands of the third party who has received it. The success of this claim will depend very much on whether the necklace is still in the hands of the third party and that the third party is not a bona fide purchaser of the legal title to the necklace without notice of the beneficiary's interest in it. If the third party can show that it has acquired a 'clean' title to the necklace by virtue of giving consideration and being without notice of the trust then the beneficiary has no right to claim the necklace. Instead, in such a situation, the beneficiary will seek to trace the substituted asset in the hands of the trustee, that is, the gold watch. If the beneficiary does decide to trace into the gold watch, the court can award one of two proprietary remedies. Firstly it can award an equitable lien on the substituted property to the value of the necklace. Secondly, if the beneficiary does elect to take the substituted property, that property will be held under a constructive trust for him. The effect of this is to hold the substituted property as security for the value of the original property. In **Re Hallett's Estate**[40] Jessel MR explained that the beneficiary may 'elect either to take the property purchased, or to hold it as security for the amount of the trust property laid out in the purchase; or, as we generally express it, he is entitled to his election either to take the property, or to have a charge on the property for the amount of the trust property'.[41] If the beneficiary does elect to take the substituted property, that property will be held under a constructive trust for him.

Tracing trust property which has been mixed with the trustee's property

In most cases it is going to be rare that there has been a clean substitution of the beneficiary's property. Typically, the beneficiary's property will have become mixed with property belonging to another. The property may become mixed with the trustee's own property or property belonging to some other third party. It is when such mixing occurs

---

[39] (1879) 13 Ch. D 696.
[40] *Ibid.*
[41] (1879) 13 Ch. D 696 at 709.

that the rules of equitable tracing become particularly relevant. This section explores the situation where the beneficiary's property is mixed with the trustee's property. For example, the trustee may use £30,000 from a trust fund and use £10,000 of his own money to purchase a house for himself. He may then spend further money in renovating the house which is now valued at £200,000. Clearly, as can be seen from this example, the beneficiary's money has become mixed with that of the trustee. What is the position of the beneficiary regarding his right to trace and claim his property? In such a case the trustee has clearly acted wrongfully, and because of this, the rules of tracing raise presumptions against the trustee. If the trustee does mix trust property with his own property then the rules will operate harshly against him. The beneficiary will have a first charge over the mixed asset or fund in question. If the trustee cannot prove what part of the mixed asset is his, the beneficiary can claim the whole amount. The matter was explained in *Re Tilley's Will Trusts*[42] where Ungoed-Thomas J explained that 'if a trustee mixes trust assets with his own, the onus is on the trustee to distinguish the separate assets, and to the extent that he fails to do so, they belong to the trust'.[43]

APPLYING THE LAW

Tim and Tom are holding £100,000 in trust for a beneficiary. They withdraw the trust money from the bank and use it to purchase a house. The house is in need of a lot of renovation. They use their own money to renovate the house; however, they have kept all receipts for the materials and work expended from their own money. The house is now worth £300,000 and the beneficiary claims to be entitled to it, whilst accepting that he will reimburse the trustees for the amount of money used to renovate the house. Tim and Tom, however, claim to be entitled to a proportionate share in the house.

Can the beneficiary claim the house worth £300,000?

Where the trustee does mix trust property with his own property and is in a position to prove to the court what part of the mixed property was his own, it would be unfair to give the beneficiary a right to claim the whole of the mixed property. In such a case the beneficiary is entitled to a lien over the mixed property to the value of the trust property originally mixed with the trustee's property or he is entitled to a proportional beneficial interest in the mixed property. The advantage of a lien is that he will be entitled to claim back his share from the mixed property and any depreciation in the value of the property will have to be met by the trustee. The advantage of electing to have a proportional share is that, should the mixed property increase in value, he will be entitled to a proportional increase. The matter is neatly illustrated by the decision in *Foskett v McKeown*[44] where a trustee took out a life insurance for himself and paid the first three annual instalments out of his own money. The next two annual premiums were paid by using money that the trustee was holding on trust for a group of beneficiaries. The insurance policy was expected to pay a death benefit of £1 million and this was settled in favour of the trustee's children. The trustee committed suicide in 1991 and the benefits of the life insurance were duly paid out to the children. The beneficiaries, whose money had been used to pay two of the five instalments, argued that they were entitled to 40 per cent of the death

---

[42] [1967] 1 Ch. 1179.
[43] [1967] 1 Ch. 1179 at 1183.
[44] [2001] 1 AC 102.

benefit paid out, as representing a proportionate share of their money used to purchase the life insurance. The children counter-argued that they were only entitled to the value of the instalments paid with interest. The House of Lords held that the beneficiaries were entitled to a pro-rata share in the death benefit, on the grounds that their money had been mixed with that of the trustee's money. Furthermore, the children could not reject such a claim on the grounds that they were mere volunteers and, therefore, could not prove that they were bona fide purchasers of the death benefit.[45]

Tracing trust money which has been mixed with the trustee's money in a bank account

In most cases the mixing of the beneficiary's money with the trustee's money will occur in the context of a current bank account. Because everything is presumed against the trustee, the rule of equity is that where a trustee mixes trust funds with his own funds in a bank account, he is presumed to have withdrawn his money first. Thus where the trustee mixes £1000 of trust money with £1000 of his own money and then makes a withdrawal of £1000, he is deemed to have drawn his £1000 out first. It makes no difference that the trust money was in the account before he put his own money into that account.[46] The rule is designed to protect the beneficiary. The rule that the trustee withdraws his money first can, however, produce a rather strange result. Take for example a trustee who pays £1000 into his account and the pays a further £1000 of trust money into the same account. He then withdraws £1000 and purchases shares which are now worth £5000. He then uses the remaining £1000 on a holiday. If the rule is strictly applied, the trustee purchases the shares with his own money so that he now has shares worth £5000. As for the beneficiaries, they have nothing as their £1000 is dissipated on a holiday. Despite the rule that the trustee withdraws his money first, the rule is modified to the extent that everything is presumed against him. In such a case the beneficiary has an equitable lien on the shares purchased to the extent of his money which has now been dissipated. The matter is neatly illustrated by the decision of the court in *Re Oatway*[47] where a trustee wrongly mixed £3000 of trust money with £4000 of his own money in a bank account. He then withdrew a sum of £2137 from the account to purchase shares in a private company. The remainder of the balance in the company was dissipated. On his death the question arose whether the trustees could trace their money into the shares in the private company which were now worth £2475. Joyce J held that the beneficiaries were entitled to trace into the shares in the private company and were, therefore, entitled to claim the shares over and above the creditors of the trustee.

APPLYING THE LAW

Tim and Tom are holding £1000 on trust for a beneficiary. Tom deposits the £1000 into his own bank account where he has £1000 of his funds. He then withdraws £1500 which he gambles at the casino, leaving a balance of £500 in the account. At the end of the month he gets paid £1000 which is credited into his account, which is now showing a balance of £1500.

Can the beneficiary trace into the account and claim his £1000 back?

---

[45] See also *Shalson v Russo* [2005] 2 WLR 1213.
[46] *Re Hallett's Estate* (1880) 13 Ch. D 696.
[47] [1903] 2 Ch. 356.

One further issue, which arises in the context of a trustee who mixes his own money in a bank account with that of the beneficiary, relates to the question of what happens when the trustee deposits additional money into the account after he has made withdrawals from the mixed fund. For example, a trustee deposits £1000 of his own money into an account and deposits £1000 of trust money. He then withdraws a sum of £1500 from the account. From what has been said above, the remaining balance of £500 in the account belongs to the beneficiary. What would be the position if the trustee was to deposit a further £1000 into the account? Is there a presumption that, by depositing further money of his own into the account that he intends to replenish the claimant's money? The answer is that there is no such presumption and the 'lowest intermediate balance' principle will apply. This principle holds that, in the absence of an intention that the trustee intended to replenish the beneficiary's money, the beneficiary can only trace into the lowest intermediate balance. Thus in the example above, the beneficiary would only be able to trace into the £500 and not into the additional £1000 which the trustee has deposited later on. The matter was neatly explained in **Roscoe v Winder**[48] where the court explained that:

> in a case where the account into which the moneys are paid is the general trading account of the debtor on which he has been accustomed to draw both in the ordinary course and in breach of trust when there are trust funds standing to the credit of that account which were convenient for that purpose, I think it is impossible to attribute to him that by the mere payment into the account of further moneys which to a large extent he subsequently used for purposes of his own he intended to clothe those moneys with a trust in favour of the plaintiffs.[49]

Tracing trust property which has been mixed with other trust property or that of an innocent volunteer

A trustee may not mix the trust property with his own property but might mix the trust property with property belonging to another trust or some other innocent third party. For example, a trustee administering two trusts for two separate beneficiaries may mix the property of each trust and end up with a new asset representing the mixed property. For example, a trustee might use £40,000 from trust one and £60,000 from trust two to purchase a house which is now worth £200,000. In such a case both sets of beneficiaries are said to share *pari passu* in the mixed asset. This simply means that they will share the value of the mixed fund proportionally. So, in the example given, beneficiaries of trust one will have a 40 per cent interest in the £200,000 and beneficiaries of trust two will have a 60 per cent share. Both sets of beneficiaries will have to bear the depreciation in the value of the mixed asset as well as gaining any increases to it.

However, where the mixing of two trusts or money belonging to an innocent volunteer occurs in the context of a bank account, then a rather different rule applies. The traditional rule applying to the distribution of mixed funds in a bank account was laid out in **Devaynes v Noble**, otherwise known as the rule in Clayton's case.[50] The rule lays down that the first payment into the account is presumed to the first payment out of the account, the so called 'first in, first out' rule. The rule is based on the presumed intentions of the person operating the account, but has been described by some commentators as 'capricious and arbitrary'.[51] In one American case Judge Learned Hand commented on

---

[48] [1915] 1 Ch. 62.
[49] [1915] 1 Ch. 62 at 69.
[50] (1816) 1 Mer. 572.
[51] Goff and Jones, *The Law of Restitution* (5th edn, 1998), p. 108.

the rule, saying, '[T]o throw all the loss upon one, through the mere chance of his being earlier in time, is irrational and arbitrary, and is equally a fiction as the rule in Clayton's case. When the law adopts a fiction, it is, or at least it should be, for some purpose of justice. To adopt it here is to apportion a common misfortune through a test which has no relation whatever to the justice of the case.'[52]

In other jurisdictions the rule has been rejected and restricted to appropriate situations.[53] However, despite the criticisms of the rule, the Court of Appeal in ***Barlow Clowes International Ltd v Vaughan***[54] confirmed the rule but held that it applied subject to a contrary intention that could be express or presumed. The facts of ***Barlow Clowes*** concerned investments by a number of investors in schemes operated by Barlow Clowes International Ltd. The money in these schemes had been wrongfully dissipated and the question was whether the rule in Clayton's case applied or whether the money was held rateably for the investors. Whilst holding that the rule in Clayton's case was binding on the Court of Appeal, Woolf LJ held that here there was a shared misfortune and as such the intention of the investors was that the rule did not apply so that the fund should be shared rateably. On the other hand Dillon LJ did not think that it would be unjust to apply the rule in Clayton's case. In his view, later investors might well feel that it would be unfair for their claims to be ranked rateably with the earlier investors.

An alternative solution to the rule in Clayton's case is the rolling-charge method used in North America. This method was considered at length by the Court of Appeal in ***Barlow Clowes*** and operates on the following basis. Where money has been mixed in an account, the beneficiaries should share a loss in proportion to their interest in the account immediately before each withdrawal. Woolf LJ described the rule by commenting that it was a solution whereby 'credits to a bank account made at different times and from different sources are treated as a blend or cocktail with the result that when a withdrawal is made from the account it is treated as a withdrawal in the same proportions as the different interests in the account (here of the investors) bear to each other at the moment before the withdrawal is made'.[55] Although the rolling-charge method does appear to be a much fairer solution to the distribution of the fund, it is one that is not always practical in the case of large collective investments.

The application of the rule in Clayton's case was further considered in ***Russell-Cooke Trust Co v Prentis***[56] where the facts concerned an investment scheme run by a solicitor, which in June 2000 ceased to operate as a result of intervention by the Law Society, with substantial shortfalls in the funds owed to the contributors. Custodian trustees were appointed and the question was: how should the remaining funds be distributed amongst the contributors under the scheme? The investment scheme was called the 'Secured Property Investment Plan' (the SPIP) and worked on the following premises. The plan offered investors a fixed rate of 15 per cent per annum return on sums invested. Monies received by the solicitor were paid into the solicitor–client account called the 'Prentis no. 2 client account'. The money (belonging to more than one investor) was then to be loaned to a borrower by way of a charge over his property at an interest rate of 15 per cent

[52] *Re Walter J Schmidt & Co ex p. Feuerbach* (1923) 298 F 314 at 316.
[53] *Re Registered Securities Ltd* [1991] 1 NZLR 545 (New Zealand approach). In this case the Court of Appeal in New Zealand refused to apply the rule in Clayton's case where it was not possible to trace investors' money into mortgages allocated to them. Instead a *pari passu* method was employed to achieve a result which would do more justice on the facts.
[54] [1992] 2 All ER 22.
[55] [1992] 4 All ER 22 at 35; see S. Panesar, 'Collective Investment Scheme, Breach of Trust and Distribution of Funds' (2003) ICCLR 289.
[56] [2003] 2 All ER 478.

per annum. Save in one case, the investors were not consulted on matters relating to the type of property over which the loans were being made by the solicitor operating the scheme. As and when interest became due it was paid into the 'Prentis no. 3 client account', which was intended as the account to be used to pay the investors the sums due to them under the plan. The plan attracted some £6 million by way of investment. However, subsequently a number of irregularities was found in the conduct of the operation of the SPIP. There was no correlation between interest received or deducted in advance from a particular borrower and interest paid to an investor or investors to whom a charge from that borrower had been allocated. Neither Mr Prentis nor his firm kept a cash book for any of the relevant bank accounts or a complete list of investors. There were substantial shortfalls in both income and capital to meet the claims of individual investors. It was established there was a shortfall of some £3.66 million in the fund needed to meet the claims of the investors. On 2 June 2000 the Law Society intervened and Mr Prentis was struck off the roll of solicitors of the Supreme Court. The consequence of this was that Mr Prentis and his firm were incapacitated from acting as trustees in relation to trusts conducted by them. By instructions of the Court, Russell-Cooke Trust Co, a custodian trustee was appointed to control the assets of the SPIP scheme. One of the questions before the court was how the money in the client account should be distributed.

In deciding how the Prentis no. 2 client account should be distributed to the investors, Lindsay J, whilst recognising the criticisms of the rule in Clayton's case, nevertheless held that the rule was binding on the court but could be distinguished by the facts of the particular case. In particular the rule could be dispensed with where there was an express or presumed counter-intention that the rule was not intended to apply. In the words of Lindsay J, 'the modern approach in England has generally not been to challenge the binding nature of the rule but rather to permit it to be distinguished by the reference to the facts of the particular case'.[57] In support of this the judge referred to the Court of Appeal's decision in **Barlow Clowes International Ltd v Vaughan**[58] where the rule was not applied because it could not have been the intention of the investors that this was the contemplated way in which the funds would be distributed in the event of the collapse of the investment scheme. Certainly, such a distribution would do no justice on the facts of that case. On the facts of **Russell-Cooke Trust v Prentis** Lindsay J found that there was significant evidence that the rule in Clayton's case was not intended to apply. In particular the facts illustrated that the payments made into the account were not always paid out in the same sequence. The allocation of money from the account was completely out of sequence with the payments made into the account. In the words of Lindsay J:

> whilst the brochures (given to the investors under the SPIP) made it plain that investments might be combined, nothing indicated combinations would be made up in a strict temporal sequence . . . It is, as I see it, one thing to apply a 'first in, first out', rule where it might have been expected or intended by the investors to be applied and where nothing is known inconsistent with its being so expected or intended but quite another to presume it to be an intention where both a reasonable contemplation of what was intended and the known facts can be seen to be inconsistent with it.

As regards the North American rolling-charge method, the court did not feel the need to consider it, as the rule in Clayton's case did not apply on the facts. The rolling charge was only an alternative means of distribution which would do more justice on the facts as compared with the 'first in, first out' method. Lindsay J did, however, comment that

---

[57] [2003] 2 All ER 478 at 984.
[58] [1992] 4 All ER 22.

the rolling-charge method was in any event very complicated and expensive to apply in a situation where there were many investors and the payments into and out of the account were made without much temporal sequence. Unlike some other jurisdiction, English law has yet to decide the fate of the rule in Clayton's case. Whilst recognising the injustices that can arise from a system of 'first in, first out', English law continues to hold good the rule yet adopts a rather different test in its application to given factual situations. The approach suggested both in the Court of Appeal's decision in **Barlow Clowes International Ltd v Vaughan**[59] and in the High Court in **Russell-Cooke Trust Co v Prentis** is to distinguish the rule by particular reference to the facts of a given case. In both of these cases, where investors had pooled their investments, nothing on the facts could have suggested that the equitable solution in the distribution of the remaining funds after the collapse of the investment scheme was intended to be on the basis of a 'first in, first out' method.

Whilst the decision in **Russell-Cooke Trust Co v Prentis** is a sensible and practicable one on the facts of the case, there are some who may argue whether the rule in Clayton's case is simply an unnecessary point of law which has no significance in the modern law. Although the rule has not been applied to large investment schemes where it would produce an unfair and inequitable outcome in the distribution of funds remaining in a current account, the same result is achieved in a current account with a small number of investors or beneficiaries. For the meantime the rule in Clayton's case remains good law, only to be quickly dispensed with when the facts do not contemplate its application.

Loss of the right to trace

The right to trace trust property may be lost in a number of situations. The first situation is fairly well recognised in equity and will arise when the trust property is in the hands of a bona fide purchaser without notice of the equitable proprietary interest. If a purchaser is unaware of the existence of the beneficiary's equitable interest he will not be bound by it. It is imperative that he is a purchaser in the sense of providing consideration, and acts in good faith without notice. Clearly, where the recipient of the trust property is a volunteer, that is, not having provided consideration, then he will be bound irrespective of his good faith and lack of notice.

The second situation where the right to trace will be lost is where the beneficiary's property has been destroyed or dissipated. In such a case there will be no specific property identifiable as representing the beneficiary's property in order to pursue a proprietary claim. Thus if the trustee uses the trust money in order to finance a holiday for himself, there will be no property into which the beneficiary will be able to trace.

APPLYING THE LAW

Tim has an overdrawn account at Midwest Bank. He withdraws a further £1000 and buys himself a car. Two weeks later he withdraws money from the trust account and pays it into his overdrawn account at Midwest thereby clearing the overdraft. The beneficiary, not pleased with this, seeks to trace into the car and claim it as being purchased with trust property.

Can the beneficiary do this?

---

[59] [1992] 4 All ER 22.

Trust money which is used to pay a debt will cease to be traceable.[60] The reason for this is that a debt is a liability and not an asset and the payment of the debt is simply to reduce the liability.[61] Similarly, in ***Bishopsgate Investment Management Ltd v Homan***[62] it was held that money paid by a trustee into an overdrawn bank account ceases to be traceable in equity. It has been questioned whether a claimant can effectively 'trace backwards', a process known as backward tracing. This situation will arise where, for example, a trustee uses money from his overdrawn account to purchase a specific asset. Clearly the trustee has used borrowed money to finance the purchase of the asset. Assume that he then pays his overdraft with the deposit of trust money. Clearly, the general rule will prevent the beneficiary from tracing into an overdrawn account. However, can the claimant beneficiary trace into the asset which the trustee has purchased with the borrowed money? In ***Bishopsgate Investment Management Ltd v Homan*** Leggatt LJ explained that 'there can be no equitable remedy against an asset acquired before misappropriation of money takes place, since ex hypothesi it cannot be followed into something which existed and so had been acquired before the money was received and therefore without its aid'.[63]

Finally, the right to trace will be lost where the defence of change of position is raised by the defendant. The defence of change of position is a relatively new defence in restitutionary claims based on unjust enrichment.[64] The basis of the defence is that, given the fact that the defendant's position has changed significantly since the receipt of the claimant's property, it would be inequitable for the claimant to trace the property. You will recall from the facts of ***Re Diplock***[65] that the personal representatives had distributed some of Diplock's estate to a number of charities. Such charities had used the money to improve their property. If the claimants were entitled to trace into those properties, they could technically have put a charge on them with the consequence of forcing a sale of them. Given that these properties belonged to charities, it would have been inequitable in such a case to allow the claimants to trace. The defence of change of position will only apply where the defendant acted innocently and in good faith. Where the defendant changes his position in the knowledge that he should not be in receipt of the claimant's property then the defence will not be available.

Conclusion

This chapter has focused on the rules of tracing which allow a beneficiary to ask the court to award a proprietary remedy where there has been a breach of trust. The rules of tracing take the form of asserting ownership of some asset which is in the hands of the trustee or some other third party who cannot purport to show that he is a bona fide purchaser of the beneficiary's property without notice of the beneficiary's interest. In this chapter it has been observed that the rules of tracing are rules of evidence used to identify where property belonging to a potential claimant lies at any given time. Once a particular rule of tracing is successful in identifying the claimant's property, the claimant

---

[60] *Re Diplock* [1948] Ch. 465.
[61] See *Shalson v Russo* [2005] 2 WLR 1213.
[62] [1995] Ch. 211.
[63] [1995] Ch. 211 at 221. See M. Conaglen, 'Difficulties with Backwards' Tracing (2011) LQR 432.
[64] Recognised by the House of Lords in *Lipkin Gorman v Karpnale Ltd* [1991] 2 AC 548.
[65] [1948] Ch. 465.

will then seek the return of that property through the imposition of an appropriate proprietary remedy, for example, the imposition of a constructive trust. It has been observed that the rules of tracing are recognised both at common law and in equity. At common law the legal owner of property may trace his legal ownership, provided that his property does not become mixed with other property. The principal remedy at common law will be restitutionary claim for money had and received where the claimant's money has been received by another. The right to trace in equity is much wider and is not defeated by the fact that the claimant's property has been mixed with other property belonging to the defendant or some other third party. The right to trace in equity will, however, be lost when it is has been dissipated, has found itself in the hands of a bona fide purchaser without notice, or where it would be inequitable to trace.

Case study

Consider the following case study.

Sunita, in her will, appointed Betty and Celia as her executors and trustees. The will contained, *inter alia*, the following provisions:

- To retain indefinitely shares valued at £20,000 in Auto Products until my youngest attains the age of 21 years.
- Orchard House to be held upon trust for my children until the youngest attains the age of 21 and thereafter to be sold and the proceeds to be distributed equally amongst them.
- The remainder of my estate to be invested in any manner deemed fit by my trustees as if they were the absolute owners thereof.

  Sunita died in July 2004. In January 2005 Celia advised the beneficiaries, Timothy, Graham and Jill, then aged 20, 19 and 17 respectively that since none of them wanted to reside in Orchard House it would be better to sell it. Timothy and Graham agreed to the sale but Jill was not too happy about the situation. The House was sold to Celia's husband in March 2005 for £100,000.

  Celia's husband converted the house into a bed-and-breakfast hotel and it is now valued at £239,000. Recently, Jill discovered that the true value of the house in March 2005 was around £175,000.

  In March of this year the trustees sold the shares in Auto Products and invested them in Fancy Foods Ltd, a private company owned by Celia. Celia did not offer any advice to the beneficiaries about the nature of the shares in Fancy food Ltd. Within a month the shares lost 60 per cent of their value.

Advise the beneficiaries as to their remedies for breach of trust.

Moot points

1 What is the basis upon which a claimant is allowed to trace property into the hands of a third party? Is the basis restitutionary or does it arise by virtue of the fact that the property being traced still belongs to the claimant?

2 What do you understand by the common law action for money had and received?

3 What is the basis for the insistence on the existence of a fiduciary relationship before a claimant can trace in equity?

4 If someone steals your £100 and buys a gold watch, can you trace in equity?

5 What do you understand by backward tracing? In *Bishopsgate Investment Management Ltd v Homan* Leggatt LJ explained that 'there can be no equitable remedy against an asset acquired before misappropriation of money takes place, since ex hypothesi it cannot be followed into something which existed and so had been acquired before the money was received and therefore without its aid' [1995] Ch. 211 at 221. Does this statement help you in arriving at an answer to question 1 above?

● Further reading

Beatson, J. and N. Andrews, 'Common Law Tracing: Springboard or Swan Song?' (1997) LQR 21. Examines the extent of equitable tracing into substituted assets and profits.

Birks, P. 'The Necessity of a Unitary Law of Tracing' in *Making Commercial Law, Essays in Honour of Roy Goode* (1997). This paper examines whether the two different rules of tracing at common law and equity are justified and whether a unified system of rules of tracing can be applied.

Burrows, A. 'Proprietary Restitution: Unmasking Unjust Enrichment' (2002) 117 LQR 412. An account of the juridical basis of tracing, whether tracing is proprietary or restitutionary based.

Conaglen, M. 'Difficulties with Backward Tracing' (2011) LQR 432. Looks at the problems of tracing into an overdrawn account.

Panesar, S. 'Collective Investment Scheme, Breach of Trust and Distribution of Funds' (2003) ICCLR 289. Examines the High Court decision in *Russell-Cooke Trust Co* v *Prentis* and the application of the rule in Clayton's case.

Smith, L. 'Tracing into the Payment of Debt' [1995] CLJ 290. Examines the extent to which it is possible to trace into a debt, and backward tracing.

Visit **www.mylawchamber.co.uk/panesar** to access study support resources including interactive multiple choice questions, practice exam questions with guidance, podcasts, weblinks, legal newsfeed all linked to the **Pearson eText** version of Exploring Equity and Trusts which you can **search**, **highlight** and **personalise** with your **own notes** and **bookmarks**.

premium
my**law**chamber
unrivalled support for legal education

Use Case Navigator to read in full some of the key cases referenced in this chapter with commentary and questions:

Foskett v *McKeown* [2001] 1 AC 102

Westdeutsche Landesbank Girozentrale v *Islington LBC* [1996] AC 699 (HL)

POWERED BY ● LexisNexis·

Part VI
Charities and charitable trusts

The final part of this book explores the law relating to charities and charitable trusts. It will be observed in the remaining chapters that the law of charities is heavily underpinned by trust law. This is as a result of historical factors: in particular, charities were historically controlled by the ecclesiastical courts, primarily because social welfare and charitable giving was carried out through the Church. The work of the ecclesiastical courts, including the administration of charities, was then taken over by the Court of Chancery. The law of charities has also undergone changes as a result of the Charities Act 2006, whose main function was to modernise the law of charities.

Chapter 22 looks at some of these historical factors which have shaped modern charity law and then proceeds to examine the changes that have been brought about by the Charities Act 2006 and the Charities Act 2011, including the provision of a statutory definition of charity, and a requirement that all charitable trusts must demonstrate public benefit, in addition to changes in the administration and regulation of charities. This chapter will look at the definition of charity as provided by the Charities Act 2006 and the Charities Act 2011 and the case law which continues to provide guidance as to what can or cannot be regarded as a charitable purpose. It then focuses on the public benefit requirement which applies to all charities today, including trusts for the relief of poverty. It also looks at the requirement that a charitable purpose must be exclusively charitable and the extent to which charities and charitable trustee can engage in campaigning and political activity in order to further their charitable purposes.

Chapter 23 explores the cy-près doctrine which has a special application to charitable trusts. It has already been observed in Part III of this book that where an express private trust fails, the trust property will, as a general rule, revert back to the settlor or the testator's estate. In the case of a charitable trust which fails for some reason – for example, where the gift made has ceased to exist before the testator's death – it is not always the case that

▶

the subject matter of the gift reverts back to the testator's estate. It may be possible to apply the gift for another charitable purpose by virtue of the cy-près rule. The term cy-près, which comes from French, means 'as near as possible'. The rule allows a charitable gift that has failed to be applied for other purposes which are as near as possible to those intended by the settlor or testator. The cy-près rule has been further modified by the Charities Act 2006 and these modifications are explored in detail in Chapter 23.

22

Charities and charitable trusts

Learning objectives

After reading this chapter you should be able to:

→ explain the difference between charitable trusts and private trusts

→ explain the advantages enjoyed by charitable trusts

→ explain the requirements needed to establish a charitable trust

→ explain the key features of the Charities Act 2006, including changes made to the administration of charities

→ explain the definition of charity in light of the Charities Act 2006 and the Charities Act 2011

→ explain the various heads of charity with relevant case law

→ explain the public benefit requirement needed for a charitable trust

→ explain the consequences where a charitable trust is not exclusively charitable

→ understand the extent to which trustees of a charitable trust can engage in campaigning and political activity.

SETTING THE SCENE

IRC v *McMullen* [1981] AC 1 House of Lords: The Football Association promotes the playing of association football in schools – is that education and therefore charitable in nature?

In 1972 the Football Association sought to set up a charitable trust. Its objects were stated, in clause 3 (a), to be, inter alia: organise or provide or assist in the organisation and provision of facilities which will enable and encourage pupils of schools and universities in any part of the United Kingdom to play association football or other games or sports and thereby to assist in ensuring that due attention is given to the physical education and development of such pupils as well as to the development and occupation of their minds and with a view to furthering this object:

(i) to provide or assist in the provision of association football or games or sports equipment of every kind for the use of such pupils as aforesaid

(ii) to provide or assist in the provision of courses lectures demonstrations and coaching for pupils of schools and universities in any part of the United Kingdom and for teachers who organise or supervise playing and coaching of association football or other games or sports at such schools and universities as aforesaid

(iii) to promote, provide or assist in the promotion and provision of training colleges for the purpose of training teachers in the coaching of association football or other games or sports at such schools and universities as aforesaid

(iv) to lay out, manage, equip and maintain or assist in the laying out, management equipment and maintenance of playing fields or appropriate indoor facilities or accommodation (whether vested in the trustees or not) to be used for the teaching and playing of association football or other sports or games by such pupils as aforesaid.

The question before the House of Lords was whether this trust was a charitable trust.

The facts of the *IRC* v *McMullen* raise some very interesting issues which are the subject matter of discussion in this chapter.

In the preceding chapters it has been observed that a trust must be for identifiable beneficiaries and that there must be certainty of objects. Looking at the facts of *IRC* v *McMullen* can you identify with certainty who the beneficiaries of the trust set up by the Football Association were?

It has been observed in the preceding chapters that a trust for a purpose is prima facie void. The objects of the Football Association seem to be merely promoting the playing of football. Should the trust, therefore, not fail?

Do you think that a trust which promotes a young person to engage in a sport is beneficial to that person? Do you think that a trust which promotes the general health of young people is beneficial to the community?

Property which is the subject matter of trust is, like any other type of property, subject to taxation. Do you think that, as a matter of policy, if property is utilised for the benefit of the community or public at large it should enjoy special privileges such as exemption from taxation?

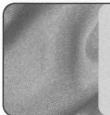

In *IRC v McMullen* the House of Lords held that the trust created by the Football Association was a charitable trust and therefore valid and exempt from taxation. This chapter explores a special category of trusts, otherwise known as charitable trusts, and in doing so many of the questions raised in the *IRC v McMullen* are discussed. In addition, the chapter looks at the changes bought about by the Charities Act 2006 which, amongst other things, expands the range of purposes which can be charitable in law.

Introduction

This chapter explores the legal issues surrounding charities and charitable trusts. Although the law of charities is an extensive area of law and a subject in its own right, charities and charitable trusts have traditionally been studied in the context of trust law and equity. There are a number of reasons for the connection between charities and trust law. In the first place, although historically charities were controlled by the ecclesiastical courts, primarily because social welfare and charitable giving was carried out mainly through the Church, the work of the ecclesiastical courts was taken over by the Court of Chancery. As a result, charities began to be administered by the Court of Chancery. Secondly, and perhaps more importantly, one of the principal ways in which a fund for charitable purposes could be administered, and indeed still is the case today, was through the vehicle of a trust. Money or other property could be transferred by an individual donor to trustees to be used for the furtherance of some charitable purpose. In early times, this would happen where a wealthy person left money during his lifetime, or in his will, for the furtherance of some charitable cause. Although this may still happen today, where for example a settlor or testator in his will attempts to leave a fund to be applied for charitable purposes, a more contemporary way of administering a charity is through an unincorporated association or a company limited by guarantee, both of which are explored later in the chapter. The Charities Act 2006 introduces a new form of administering a charity known as the Charitable Incorporated Association, which is also explored later in the chapter.

This chapter looks at some of the historical factors that have shaped modern charity law and then proceeds to examine the changes which have been brought about by the Charities Act 2006 and the Charities Act 2011. These Acts have made a number of changes to charity law, including the provision of a statutory definition of charity, a requirement that all charitable trusts must demonstrate public benefit in addition to changes in the administration and regulation of charities. The chapter will look at the definition of charity as provided by the Charities Act 2006 and the case law which continues to provide guidance as to what can or cannot be regarded as a charitable purpose. The chapter then focuses on the public benefit requirement which applies to all charities today, including trusts for the relief of poverty. It will also look at the requirement that a charitable purpose must be exclusively charitable. Finally, the chapter looks to the extent to which charities and charitable trustees can engage in campaigning and political activity in order to further their charitable purposes.

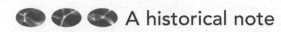 A historical note

Developments in charitable giving

Charities and charitable giving is not something of a new phenomenon in the society in which we live. We are very familiar with fund-raising events that are screened on the television such as Children in Need, Comic Relief and so on; however, charitable giving can be traced back to the Middle Ages. A detailed history of charities and the law of charities is beyond the scope of this book; the historical note here is a brief explanation of some of the key developments in charities and the law of charities.[1] In the Middle Ages the endowed charity was the most common method by which a person could set up a fund for the benefit of, for example, the poor. Typically, such an endowment would take effect under a trust whereby property, for example land, would be used as an almshouse for the poor. Other forms of endowments included the repair of churches and the saying of prayers for the dead. The fact that that many of these endowments were made through the Church, The Roman Catholic Church served as a important provider of social welfare before the Reformation of the Church. It is also for this reason that such endowed charities were administered by the ecclesiastical courts. After the Reformation the role of the church declined with regard to social welfare, and the State became more involved in the provision of social welfare. As well as the State, private philanthropy played an important role in providing for purposes such as the advancement of education, the repair of roads and bridges and other municipal works. The late eighteenth century and the nineteenth century, however, witnessed a decline in state intervention for social welfare. There appear to be a number of reasons for this development. One principal reason is the changes taking place in society and the movement to a more economic driven policy of laissez-faire.[2] The encouragement to provide for the poor, for example, was seen as not conducive to a system of economic efficiency in the marketplace. In other words, the policy of the state was to encourage people to engage in productive work rather than encourage idleness. The twentieth century witnessed yet another change in policy with the introduction of the welfare state, which took over many of the existing charitable purposes such as relief of the aged, sick and poor as well as the provision of education. In the context of state welfare, private charitable provision took on a more subsidiary and secondary role.[3]

---

[1] For a more detailed analysis of the history of charities see G. Jones, *History of Charity Law 1532–1827* (1969) and P. Luxton, *Charity Fund Raising and the Public Benefit: An Anglo-American Perspective* (1990). See also G. Moffat, *Trust Law: Text and Materials* 4th edn (2005) Chapter 18.

[2] Explained by the Nathan Committee in *Report of the Committee on the Law and Practice Relating to Charitable Trusts*, Nathan Report (1952) (Cmnd 8710) at para. 40.

[3] For an excellent and more detailed analysis of these developments see G. Moffat, *Trust Law: Text and Materials* 4th edn Chapter 18.

Developments in the law relating to charity

With regard to the development of charity law, up until the enactment of the Charities Act 2006, there were a number of legislative enactments dealing with all aspects of charity.[4] The following key enactments provide some idea of the statutory development:

- The Statute of Charitable Uses 1601: Although this statute received more fame for its preamble, which provided a list of charitable purposes, the main objectives of this legislation was to iron out abuses by charitable trustees. The Act empowered Charity Commissioners to investigate and deal with breaches of trust. The objectives of the legislation were frustrated by the Civil War in the middle of the seventeenth century.

- The Charitable Trusts Act 1853: Given the problems in regulating charities, this legislation sought to introduce new procedures to deal with the administration and regulation of charities. Amongst the key developments were newly formed Charity Commissioners and the right of the Attorney General to instigate proceedings against abuses of charity. The Charity Commissioners were empowered to obtain accounts from charity trustees.

- The Charities Act 1960: This piece of legislation repealed the Charitable Trusts Act 1853. The Act sought to provide a comprehensive system for the administration and regulation of charities. The Act introduced a mandatory requirement that charities seek registration. The Act also sought to deal with the cy-près doctrine, which as will be seen in Chapter 23, allows a charitable purpose to be applied for another similar purpose if the original purpose cannot be carried out. The 1960 Act sought to expand the grounds for invoking the cy-près scheme.

- The Charities Act 1993: This legislation took the form of a consolidation statute with the objective of increasing the supervision of charities. The Act sought to increase the reporting and accounting duties of trustees in addition to making provisions for the disqualification of charity trustees. The Act consolidated the cy-près scheme and imposed tougher controls on fund-raising and public charitable collections. The Act empowered the Charity Commission the same powers as the Attorney General to instigate proceedings against charity trustees.

- The Charities Act 2006: The most recent reform of the law of charity. The Act which has come into force over the past two years, makes a number of changes to charity law. The origins behind the legislation lie in a review commissioned by the Labour government to investigate the strengths and weaknesses of the then current legal and regulatory framework of charities. To this end, the purpose of the Charities Act 2006 was to modernise charity law with particular emphasis on the delivery of public benefit. The key features of the Act are considered in more detail below; for the time being, it is sufficient to say that the Act provides a statutory definition of charity, requires that all charitable trusts demonstrate public benefit and finally introduces changes to the administration and regulation of charities.

- At the time of writing this edition the Charities Act 2011 further consolidates the definition of charity.

The structure of charity

Charities may take a number of different legal forms. This chapter is primarily concerned with charitable trusts which arise where a settlor or a testator creates a trust for a

---

[4] For an excellent account see P. Luxton, *Charity Fund Raising and the Public Benefit: An Anglo-American Perspective* (1990) Ch. 2.

charitable purpose. A typical example of this is a transfer of some money, perhaps in a will, to be used to further the education of the needy children in the testator's town. Such trusts were very common in the nineteenth century where the trust would be created by a very wealthy person. In the middle of the twentieth century, typically a testator would provide for the education of the employees of his company.[5] Whilst the trust has played an important role in the devise of charitable gifts, two other legal forms have played an important role in facilitating charitable giving. The first of these forms is the unincorporated association. Unincorporated associations, which were considered in more detail in Chapter 8, involve the grouping of individuals for some common purpose. Unincorporated associations do not have a separate legal identity and they cannot hold property in their own right. Property of such associations is usually held by one or more of the members acting as either board of governors or some other form of treasurers. Unincorporated charitable associations are particularly common where there is no single individual donor but a group of members who contribute to the purposes of the associa-tion. Members are bound by the contract between each other as governed by their con-stitution. As well as member contributions, contributions to the funds of the association are also made by outside persons in the form of legacies and other donations. Charitable unincorporated associations were particularly common in the 1800s for providing for schools and hospitals.[6] One commentator describes that the:

> basic method of contribution was the annual subscription: a subscriber of a specified minimum sum would frequently obtain certain rights in the running of the charity – perhaps a place on the board of governors. Subscriptions would be supplemented by other fund raising activities, such as annual charity dinners, admission to which was often secured through the purchase of tickets at extravagant prices, and benefit performances of a musical or dramatic nature.[7]

The unincorporated association still continues to be a form that as a charity may take although, as will be seen below, the Charities Act 2006 has introduced new legal forms for charities with many advantages compared to the unincorporated association.

In addition to charitable unincorporated associations, charities can also take the form of companies limited by guarantee. Such companies are particularly suitable for charities and other non-profit-making organisations. Unlike a company which is limited by shares, a company which is limited by guarantee enables its members to agree that, in the event of liquidation, they will pay up an agreed sum. A company limited by guarantee has a number of advantages. In the first place, it places a smaller financial obligation on its members because it is not a profit-making organisation. A second advantage is that it allows its members to easily resign from the company and makes it easier for new members to join. The principal reason for this is that each member has no shares which he has to assign to another third party. In the case of a company limited by shares, a new member cannot join unless a new share is being issued or an existing shareholder is prepared to assign him.[8]

Although the trust, the unincorporated association and the company limited by guar-antee have all played an important role in the provision of charitable giving, they do all have their own shortcomings. As a result of these shortcomings, the Charities Act 2006

---

[5] See, for example, *Oppenheim v Tobacco Securities Trusts Company* [1951] AC 297. This decision is considered at more length later in the chapter.

[6] P. Luxton, *Charity Fund Raising and the Public Benefit: An Anglo-American Perspective* (1990) at p. 22.

[7] *Ibid.* at p. 22.

[8] For a more detailed analysis of companies limited by guarantee, see P. Davies, *Gower and Davies Principles of Modern Company Law* (2008) 8th edn at p. 8.

has introduced a more effective vehicle for the administration of a charitable fund, namely through something called the Charitable Incorporated Association (CIO).[9] The need for a new legal form for charities had been on the agenda for some time. In 2001 the Advisory Group to the Charity Commission delivered a report outlining the basic structure of the CIO.[10] The CIO has a number of advantages over and above the existing charitable forms. The deficiencies of the existing forms have been highlighted by one commentator who explains that in so far as the trust vehicle is concerned, the trust lacks a distinct legal entity from its trustees and therefore exposes them to unlimited liability.[11] In so far as the unincorporated association is concerned, like the trust, it lacks a separate legal personality and exposes the trustees and members to unlimited liability. Whilst the company limited by guarantee avoids unlimited liability, it is not without it own problems. Cross explains that:

> structurally the guarantee company is regulated primarily by companies legislation[12] which takes no particular cognisance of the activities undertaken by the company or the fact that it has charitable status. This bifurcated approach to status and structure means that charities which are also companies limited by guarantee will have been subject to registration with Companies House, the Charity Commission . . . The burden of dual regulation also extends to the preparation and submission of accounts and annual returns.[13] More broadly in relation to company law it has been argued that there is uncertainty as to how the fiduciary duties applicable to company directors by virtue of company law relate to and potentially overlap with the duties which bind charity trustees and concern as to which prevails in the event of uncertainty.[14] The application of charity law and company law also gives rise to the possibility of confusion on the part of trustees as to the potential extent of personal liability arising from issues such as wrongful trading. More broadly there are ongoing concerns as to the present or future applicability of EU company law directives to charitable companies.[15] The creation of a new legal form which addresses these and other issues is what lies behind the proposals for the CIO.[16]

The first and foremost advantage of the CIO is that it avoids dual registration with Companies House and the Charity Commission. In addition, the CIO will not be regulated by company law as is the case with companies limited by guarantee. Company law imposes onerous requirements on companies registered with Companies House. However, being a corporate body, the CIO will only require registration with the Charity Commission. A second advantage of the CIO is that is avoids the onerous requirements of preparing accounts and reports under existing company law. In essence the CIO provides a simpler, less bureaucratic and cheaper method of administering a charity.

---

[9] For an excellent account see S. Cross, 'New Legal Forms for Charities in the United Kingdom' (2008) JBL 662.

[10] http://www.charity-commission.gov.uk/common/incorporg.asp.

[11] S. Cross, 'New Legal Forms for Charities in the United Kingdom' (2008) JBL 662 at 666.

[12] The principal regulation is now to be found in a combination of the Companies Act 1985 and the Companies Act 2006 as that Act increasingly comes into effect.

[13] Presently dealt with in relation to private companies by Pt VII (in particular, Chs I, II and III) and Ch.III of Pt XI respectively of the Companies Act 1985.

[14] For more detailed comments see *Private Action, Public Benefit* (2002), p. 5.

[15] *Private Action, Public Benefit* (2002), p. 5 fn. 4 discusses the application of Art. 58 of the EC Treaty. Article 58 defines companies as meaning: 'companies or firms constituted under civil or commercial law, including cooperative societies, and other legal persons governed by public or private law, save *for those which are non-profit making*' [emphasis added]. The uncertainty arises from concerns over the use of an incorporation regime which is also applicable to for-profit organisations, particularly when not-for-profit guarantee companies are not subjected to any statutory lock on reconstitution as a commercial body.

[16] S. Cross, 'New Legal Forms for Charities in the United Kingdom' (2008) JBL 662 at 666.

The Charities Act 2006

The Charities Act 2006, which has come into force over the past two years, makes a number of changes to charity law. The origins behind the legislation lie in a review commissioned by the Labour government to investigate the strengths and weaknesses of the then current legal and regulatory framework of charities. To this end, the purpose of the Charities Act 2006 was to modernise charity law with particular emphasis on the delivery of public benefit. The Act received Royal Assent on 8 November 2006. In a guidance document relating to the Charities Act 2006, the Cabinet Office of the Third Sector, which is primarily responsible for charity law and charity regulation, explained the main purposes of the Act as follows.

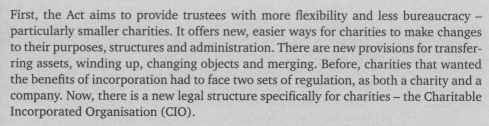

| KEY CITATION | Charities Act 2006 (*What trustees need to know*, Cabinet Office of the Third Sector, May 2007) |

First, the Act aims to provide trustees with more flexibility and less bureaucracy – particularly smaller charities. It offers new, easier ways for charities to make changes to their purposes, structures and administration. There are new provisions for transferring assets, winding up, changing objects and merging. Before, charities that wanted the benefits of incorporation had to face two sets of regulation, as both a charity and a company. Now, there is a new legal structure specifically for charities – the Charitable Incorporated Organisation (CIO).

Second, the Act modernises the definition of 'charitable purposes', bringing it up to date to reflect how charity has evolved and developed over many years. All purposes that were recognised as charitable before the Act are covered by the new definition. The Act ensures that the test of 'public benefit' remains a cornerstone of charity, underlining the requirement that all charities must be for the benefit of the public. It also addresses the need to make the public aware of the ways in which charities deliver public benefit, and charges the Charity Commission with making sure this happens.

Third, the Act protects public trust. Confidence in charity is vital, and it is something we cannot take for granted. The Act strengthens the charity sector's accountability and transparency. It will bring around 13,000 larger charities, which were previously exempt or excepted, onto the register of charities. It thereby ensures that these charities are regarded in the same way as other charities. The Commission itself has been given updated objectives and powers to support its role as a modern and effective regulator. It will be cheaper and easier for charities to challenge the Commission's decisions through the Charity Tribunal. As well as improving the Commission's accountability, this will help charity law develop more flexibly over time.

Differences between charitable trusts and private trusts

Charitable trusts are different from private trusts in a number of respects. Whereas a private trust is for the direct benefit of ascertainable beneficiaries, a charitable trust is essentially a trust for a purpose which will benefit individuals at large. The key features of a charitable trust were explained by Mummery LJ in ***Gaudiya Mission Brahmachary***[17] where the judge explained that:

> under English law charity has always received special treatment. It often takes the form of a trust; but it is a public trust for the promotion of purposes beneficial to the community, not a trust for private individuals. It is therefore subject to special rules governing registration, administration, taxation and duration. Although not a state institution, a charity is subject to the constitutional protection of the Crown as parens patriae, acting through the Attorney-General, to the state supervision of the Charity Commissioners and to the judicial supervision of the High Court. This regime applies whether the charity takes the form of a trust or of an incorporated body.[18]

There are four important differences between a private trust and a charitable trust and these are explored further in the following sections.

APPLYING THE LAW

Charitable trusts are trusts for the public benefit rather than for private individuals.

Given the fact that charitable trusts confer wider benefit to society, should these trusts receive privileges which do not apply to private trusts?

Fiscal advantages

Charities and charitable trusts receive numerous exemptions from the fiscal regime in which they operate. A more detailed analysis of the specific fiscal exemptions can be found in specialists texts, but a few examples can be given here. Charities are exempt from paying income tax on their investments and they are not subject to corporation tax. If money or other property is inherited by a charity, then it is not subject to inheritance tax. Additionally, charities are exempt from paying capital gains tax and stamp duty.[19]

Non-compliance with the beneficiary principle

A charitable trust is essentially a purpose trust rather than a trust for identifiable beneficiaries. You will recall from Chapter 8 that purpose trusts, otherwise also known as trusts of imperfect obligation, are prima facie void for want of a human beneficiary to enforce them. It is sometimes said that there is no one with *locus standi* to enforce a purpose trust. The same is very much true of a charitable trust in the sense that, although certain people may benefit from a charitable trust, no individual person has any standing to enforce the trust.[20] However, despite being purpose trusts, charitable trusts are nevertheless enforced by the Attorney General on behalf of the Crown. The Attorney General can be regarded as the guardian of charitable trusts and, therefore, the overall beneficiary of a charitable trust who enforce the trust in court. The general administration of charitable trusts is today overseen by the Charity Commissioners through the Charity Commission. The role of the Charity Commission is explored in a little more detail below.

---

[17] [1998] Ch. 341.

[18] [1998] Ch. 341 at 350.

[19] For a more detailed analysis of the tax exemptions see A. J. Oakley, *The Modern Law of Trusts* 9th Edition (2008) at p. 489.

[20] Under s. 33 of the Charities Act 1993 no individual has standing to enforce a charitable trust but proceedings must be initiated through the Charity Commissioners.

The perpetuity rules

It is often said that charitable trusts need not comply with the perpetuity rules. The perpetuity rules, which were examined in Chapter 8, attempt to invalidate certain dispositions of property which have an excessive delay in vesting. There are two aspects to the perpetuity rules. The first relates to what is known as the 'rule against remoteness of vesting'; the second relates to what is known as the 'rule against inalienation'. It is only the rule against inalienation which does not apply to a charitable trust. A charitable trust can be perpetual and it is possible to inalienate property for a long period of time. Indeed, many charities have existed for many years because they are permitted to hold their assets perpetually. The rule against remoteness of vesting applies to a charitable trust in as much as it does to any other type of trust. This means that where a gift is made to a charity, it must vest within the charity within the perpetuity period.[21] The rationale for exempting charitable trusts from the perpetuity rules was explained by Lord Macnaghten in *Commissioners for Special Purposes of Income Tax v Pemsel*[22] where his Lordship explained that the:

> Court of Chancery has always regarded with peculiar favour those trusts of a public nature which, according to the doctrine of the court derived from the piety of early times, are considered to be charitable. Charitable uses or trusts form a distinct head of equity. Their distinctive position is made the more conspicuous by the circumstance that owing to their nature they are not obnoxious to the rule against perpetuities, while a gift in perpetuity not being a charity is void.[23]

Although the rule against remoteness of vesting will apply to a charitable trust, there is one exception where the rule will not apply and that will occur where a gift is being made from one charity to another charity.[24] The matter is neatly illustrated by the decision in *Re Tyler*[25] where Sir James Tyler, by his will, left certain property to the London Missionary Society with the instructions that they should upkeep his family vault in a certain cemetery. The will provided that, if the London Missionary Society failed to maintain the family vault, the property be given to the Bluecoat School. One of the questions before the Court of Appeal was whether the gift to the Bluecoat School was void on the grounds that it could well vest outside the perpetuity period. Lindley LJ explained that the gift to the London Missionary Society with a gift over to the Bluecoat School was not void on grounds of perpetuity since the property was vested in charitable purposes throughout and, therefore, it did not matter whether the Bluecoat might receive the property outside the normal perpetuity period. What mattered was that the property was vested in charitable purposes throughout. In the course of judgment, Lindley LJ explained that 'it is common knowledge that the rule as to perpetuities does not apply to property given to charities; and there are reasons why it should not . . . A gift to a charity for charitable purposes, with a gift over on an event which may be beyond the ordinary limit of perpetuities to another charity – I cannot see that there is anything illegal in this.'[26]

Although a charitable trust need not comply with the rule against inalienability, a charitable trust does need to comply with the rule against excessive accumulations. The

---

[21] Discussed further in Chapter 8 above.
[22] [1891] AC 531.
[23] [1891] AC 531 at 580.
[24] *Christ's Hospital* v *Grainger* (1849) 1 Mac. & G 460.
[25] [1891] 3 Ch. 252.
[26] [1891] 3 Ch. 252 at 254–5. The principle was confirmed by the House of Lords in *Royal College of Surgeons* v *National Provincial Bank* [1952] AC 631.

rule against excessive accumulations prevents income to be accumulated on capital for long periods of time. Until the enactment of the Perpetuities and Accumulations Act 2009, the time periods governing accumulations of income were extremely complex and were found in the Law of Property Act 1925 and the Perpetuities and Accumulations Act 1964. In its report, the Law Commission suggested that there was no real economic justification for the rule against excessive accumulations except in the case of charitable trusts where excessive accumulations of income was not in the public interest. However, in charitable trusts, income and capital should be applied for the wider public good rather than being allowed to be accumulated for long periods of time. Section 13 of the Perpetuities and Accumulations Act 2009 abolishes the time restrictions on accumulations of income in all trusts except charitable; section 14 of the Act restricts accumulation of income in the case of a charitable trust to 21 years.

KEY STATUTE

Perpetuities and Accumulations Act 2009

S. 13 Abolition of restrictions

These provisions cease to have effect –

(a) sections 164 to 166 of the Law of Property Act 1925 (c. 20) (which impose restrictions on accumulating income, subject to qualifications);

(b) section 13 of the Perpetuities and Accumulations Act 1964 (which amends section 164 of the 1925 Act).

S. 14 Restriction on accumulation for charitable trusts

(1) This section applies to an instrument to the extent that it provides for property to be held on trust for charitable purposes.

(2) But it does not apply where the provision is made by a court or the Charity Commission for England and Wales.

(3) If the instrument imposes or confers on the trustees a duty or power to accumulate income, and apart from this section the duty or power would last beyond the end of the statutory period, it ceases to have effect at the end of that period unless subsection (5) applies.

(4) The statutory period is a period of 21 years starting with the first day when the income must or may be accumulated (as the case may be).

(5) This subsection applies if the instrument provides for the duty or power to cease to have effect –

(a) on the death of the settlor, or

(b) on the death of one of the settlors, determined by name or by the order of their deaths.

(6) If a duty or power ceases to have effect under this section the income to which the duty or power would have applied apart from this section must –

(a) go to the person who would have been entitled to it if there had been no duty or power to accumulate, or

(b) be applied for the purposes for which it would have had to be applied if there had been no such duty or power.

(7) This section applies whether or not the duty or power to accumulate extends to income produced by the investment of income previously accumulated.

The cy-près doctrine

Charitable trusts enjoy the benefit of the cy-près doctrine, which basically means that if a charitable trust fails on grounds that it has become impossible to carry out the purposes of the gift, then the gift can be applied for purposes as close as possible to the original one intended by the settlor or testator. The doctrine is considered in much more detail in Chapter 23; suffice to say here that in the case of a private trust which fails for some reason or another, for example, uncertainty of objects, the normal rule is that the intended trust property results back to the settlor or testator's estate under a resulting trust. In the case of a charitable trust, the cy-près doctrine allows the gift to be directed to another similar cause because of the impending impossibility in applying it for the original purpose. The trust may become impossible for reasons relating to some sort of initial failure, as for example, the charity to whom the gift was made has ceased to exist before the testator's death; or due to some subsequent failure, as where the charity ceases to exist after the gift has been received by it. In both cases the Charity Commissioners have the power to apply the original gift for some other purpose. The grounds for applying the cy-près doctrine were broadened by the Charities Act 1960 as amended by the Charities Act 1993. Further amendments have been made by the Charities Act 2006.[27]

Regulation and supervision of charities

Charities are regulated and supervised by the Charity Commission for England and Wales.[28] The roots of the modern Charity Commission can be traced back to the Statute of Charitable Uses 1601, which conferred upon commissioners power to investigate and deal with abuses of charitable trusts. Although in the middle years of the seventeenth century the role of the commissioners became somewhat abandoned, it was resurrected by the Charitable Trusts Act 1853 which conferred new powers on Charity Commissioners. The Charities Act 1960 paved the way for the establishment of a Charity Commission and the Charities Act 1993 increased the supervision of charities by the Charity Commission. Amongst other things, the Charities Act 1993 increased the obligation on charity trustees to prepare accounts, provided a central register for charities, provide for the disqualification of charity trustees as well as confer certain powers on the Charity Commissioners to devise schemes for the better administration of charities. This section explores some of the more important changes which have been bought into effect by the Charities Act 2006 in respect of the regulation and supervision of charities.

The Charity Commission

The Charities Act 2006 makes a number of changes to the administration, supervision and regulation of charities. In this respect the 2006 Act amends the Charities Act 1993 in a number of respects. Until the 2006 Act, the Charity Commission did not have a separate legal personality; however, s. 6 of the Charities Act 2006 now provides that the Charity Commission will be a body corporate called the Charity Commission for England and Wales. The objectives of the Charity Commission are set out in s. 1 of the 2006 Act as follows.

---

[27] For a more detailed analysis of this doctrine see later Chapter 23.
[28] S. 6 Charities Act 2006.

KEY STATUTE

1 The public confidence objective is to increase public trust and confidence in charities.

2 The public benefit objective is to promote awareness and understanding of the operation of the public benefit requirement.

3 The compliance objective is to promote compliance by charity trustees with their legal obligations in exercising control and management of the administration of their charities.

4 The charitable resources objective is to promote the effective use of charitable resources.

5 The accountability objective is to enhance the accountability of charities to donors, beneficiaries and the general public.

With regard to the functions of the Charity Commission, s. 7 identifies six main functions.

1 Determining whether institutions are or are not charities.

2 Encouraging and facilitating the better administration of charities.

3 Identifying and investigating apparent misconduct or mismanagement in the administration of charities and taking remedial or protective action in connection with misconduct or mismanagement therein.

4 Determining whether public collections certificates should be issued, and remain in force, in respect of public charitable collections.

5 Obtaining, evaluating and disseminating information in connection with the performance of any of the Commission's functions or meeting any of its objectives.

6 Giving information or advice, or making proposals, to any Minister of the Crown on matters relating to any of the Commission's functions or meeting any of its objectives.

Registration

The Charities Act 2006 makes certain changes in respect of the registration of charities. Section 9 of the Act[29] continues to provide for the registration of all charities except for three descriptions of charity which do not require registration. The first class is the so-called 'exempt charities' which have their own supervision and regulation. Examples of exempt charities include some universities and colleges as well as museums and voluntary-aided schools. The second class of charities which do not require registration are the so-called 'excepted charities', which consist of two groups. Firstly, those excepted by the Charity Commission and those excepted by some other regulation. These include organisations such as the Boy Scout and Girl Guide charities. It should be noted that, in both the case of exempt charities and excepted charities, registration is compulsory if their annual income exceeds £100,000. The third description of charities which do not require registration are those whose annual income do not exceed £5000. Before the Charities Act 2006 the threshold was £1000. The rationale for exempting such charities from registration is to release them from their duties of registration and maintaining their registered details, but allowing them to benefit from charitable status.

---

[29] This inserts a new s. 3A in the Charities Act 1993.

Auditing and accounting

In addition to changes to registration, the Charities Act 2006 makes changes to the auditing and accounting responsibilities of charities. Charities which are incorporated as companies must have their accounts prepared by accountants in accordance with company law legislation where the annual income is between £90,000 and £500,000 and with assets worth £2.8 million or less. Where the annual income of a charitable company is over £500,000 with assets over £2.8 million, the company must have a professional audit.[30] Under s. 43 of the Charities Act 1993, an unincorporated charity was required to have its accounts professionally audited if its gross income or total expenditure exceeded £250,000 in the financial year, or its gross income or total expenditure exceeded £250,000 in either of the two years preceding that financial year. The Charities Act 2006 changes this threshold to £500,000 and introduces an additional asset value threshold of £2.8 million.[31]

Remuneration of charity trustees

The Charities Act 2006 retains the general principle that charity trustees act voluntarily and are not paid for their work. However, s. 36 of the Charities Act does provide a new power on a charity to pay trustee remuneration for work which is carried out not in the office of trusteeship or some other contract of employment.[32] The remuneration is allowed for additional services that are provided by the trustee to the charity. Remuneration under this section must only be awarded if the charity thinks that it would be in the best interests to do so. A good example where the power to award remuneration may be used is where the trustee has some professional skill which he could use and offer to the charity at a price lower than some other similar professional. For example, suppose that the trustee of the charity also happens to be an electrician and the charity is in need of an electrician. It seems wholly inappropriate not to allow the trustee to carry out the work at a cheaper price than that of some other similar electrician. However, before the power in s. 36 can be used, the charity must make sure that the number of trustees receiving the remuneration is in the minority. Furthermore, the amount paid must be reasonable and is set out in a written agreement between the charity and the trustee.

The Charity Tribunal

One of the many roles of the Charity Commission is to make decisions on matters affecting charities and charitable trusts. For example, one of the foremost decisions that the Charity Commission has to make is whether a particular purpose is indeed charitable. This requires the Commission to consider whether the purpose of the proposed charity or charitable trust fits in with the definition of a charity and is also for the public benefit. Inevitably decisions made by the Commission will be appealed against by individuals. Prior to the Charities Act 2006, a right of appeal to the High Court existed in relation to decisions made by the Commission. The Charities Act 2006 creates a new Charity Tribunal which has jurisdiction to hear appeals against decisions of the Charity Commission.[33] The jurisdiction of the Tribunal extends to hearing matters referred to it by the Attorney General and the Charity Commission on points of charity law.

---

[30] Companies Act 2006.
[31] S. 28 Charities Act 2006 inserting a new s. 43(1) Charities Act 1993.
[32] S. 36 of the Charities Act amends s. 73 of the Charities Act 1993.
[33] S. 8 Charities Act 2006.

Charities Bill 2011

On 4 March 2011 the Charities Bill 2011 was introduced with the objective of consolidating charity law. At the moment the key statutory principles governing charities are to be found in the Charities Act 1993; the Charities Act 2006 amends the Charities Act 1993 and also amends the definition of charity. Additionally, the Recreational Charities Act 1958 governs recreational charities. The Charities Bill 2011 is a consolidating statute and will not make any substantial changes to the law; however, it will put the law in one single statute. In addition, the Bill will make the Charity Commission the official regulator of public charity collections which will require the permission for door to door charity collections. The Bill is a welcome and much needed consolidation of charity law found in the various statutes mentioned above. On 14 March 2012 the Bill was accepted in Parliament and is now the Charities Act 2011.

Requirements for a charitable trust

The preceding sections have looked at the many different ways in which charities are administered. The remaining focus and discussion in this chapter centres on charitable trusts and the requirements needed for a charitable trust to be recognised in law. You will recall from the earlier discussion that a trust will only be deemed charitable where it can be shown that the purposes of the trust fall into the definition of charity, that the purpose of the trust is for the public benefit and that the trust is exclusively charitable. It is also important that a charitable trust does not have political objects. Of course, all of the requirements will equally apply to any other form of charity, for example a charitable company, an unincorporated charity or a charitable incorporated association.

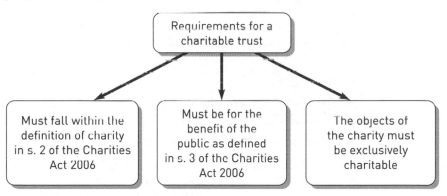

Figure 22.1 Requirements for a charitable trust

The definition of charity

A charitable trust will only be regarded as such if it falls within the definition of charity. One of the fundamental objectives of the Charities Act 2006 was to provide a statutory definition of a charity. In order to understand the modern definition of charity it is important to have some understanding of the position before the Charities Act 2006. It will be seen that, whilst the Charities Act 2006 provides a new statutory definition of charity, the definition incorporates most if not all of the pre-existing definition of charitable purposes as understood and explained by the decided case law. Indeed, the decided case law is still relevant in interpreting the various purposes which are defined in s. 2 of the Charities Act 2006. In March 2012 the Charities Act 2011 consolidated the definition of charity.

Defining a charitable purpose pre-Charities Act 2006

Prior to the enactment of the Charities Act 2006 and the Charities Act 2011, there was no statutory definition of what constituted a charitable purpose. Instead, the courts confined their inquiry into establishing whether or not a particular purpose was charitable by reference to the preamble to the Charitable Uses Act 1601,[34] which listed a number of charitable purposes as understood in 1601. The preamble listed the following purposes as charitable:

KEY CITATION

Preamble to the Charitable Uses Act 1601 (Defining charity)

The relief of the aged, impotent and poor people; the maintenance of sick and maimed soldiers and mariners, schools of learning, free schools and scholars in universities; the repair of bridges, ports, havens, causeways, churches, sea-banks and highways; the education and preferment of orphans; the relief, stock or maintenance of houses of correction; the marriages of poor maids, the supportation, aid and help of young tradesmen, handicraftsmen and persons decayed; the relief or redemption of prisoners or captives; and the aid or ease of any poor inhabitants concerning payment of fifteens, setting out of soldiers and other taxes.

Although the preamble to the 1601 Act provided a list of charitable purposes, it was never intended to act as a precise definition of a charity. Instead, the main purpose of the 1601 Act was to correct certain abuses of trusts which had become commonplace in the administration of trusts. Despite the repeal of the Charitable Uses Act 1601 by the Mortmain and Charitable Uses Act 1888, which in turn was repealed by the Charities Act 1960, the preamble remained an important starting point when deciding whether a purpose was charitable or not. In the somewhat famous ***Pemsel's case***[35] Lord Macnaghten explained that the 1601 preamble consisted essentially of four categories of charitable purposes, namely:

- The relief of poverty
- The advancement of education
- The advancement of religion
- Other purposes beneficial to the community.

Despite the fact that the preamble had clearly become outdated in the twentieth century, for example, many of the purposes within the preamble was taken over by the State, the preamble remained an important factor in determining whether a particular purpose was charitable or not. For example, in ***William's Trustees v IRC***[36] the question before the House of Lords was whether a trust to promote the interests of Welsh people living in London was charitable. Amongst the purposes of the trust were things such as allowing the Welsh community in London to meet up and discuss Welsh art and music as well as promoting the Welsh language. Whilst it was not disputed that the trust in question was beneficial to the community in some way, the House of Lords held that it was not beneficial to the community as required for purposes of charity. Delivering the leading judgment, Lord Simmonds explained that 'it is still the general law that a trust is not

---

[34] Also known as the Statute of Elizabeth I.
[35] *Commissioners for Special Purposes of Income Tax* v *Pemsel* [1891] AC 531.
[36] [1947] AC 447.

charitable and entitled to the privileges which charity confers, unless it is within the spirit and intendment of the preamble to the statute of Elizabeth'.[37] A similar approach was adopted by the Court of Appeal in **Re Strakosch**[38] where a testator directed that part of his residuary estate should be held by his trustees upon trust to be applied 'to a fund for any purpose which in their opinion is designed to strengthen the bonds of unity between the Union of South Africa and the Mother Country and which incidentally will conduce to the appeasement of racial feeling between the Dutch and English speaking sections of the South African community'. The Court of Appeal, whilst recognising the public benefit that may arise out of such a trust, held that the trust was not beneficial in a way the law deemed it be beneficial. In the course of his judgment, Lord Greene MR explained that 'though undoubtedly of benefit to the community the purpose under consideration is not "charitable" in the sense in which the benefits to the community instanced in the preamble are charitable'.[39]

Given the fact that, until the enactment of the Charities Act 2006, the requirement that a purpose be within the spirit and intendment of the 1601 preamble played an important role in determining whether a purpose was charitable or not, the question arose as to how the law developed to accommodate new purposes which were not necessarily within the preamble. The answer to this was that the courts proceeded to incorporate new purposes into the category of charity on the basis of making analogies with those purposes within the preamble and placing them in the fourth head of charity as identified by Lord Macnaghten in **Pemsel's case**.[40] The matter is neatly illustrated by the decision of the House of Lords in **Scottish Burial Reform and Cremation Society v Glasgow City Corporation**[41] where the question before the House of Lords was whether a society set up to provide crematorium facilities was charitable. The provision of crematorium facilities was clearly not a purpose listed within the preamble; however, the House of Lords were able to make an analogy with the burial grounds within churchyards, which were clearly within the spirit and intendment of the preamble. The analogy approach is neatly exemplified in the judgment of Lord Upjohn who proceeded to analyse the existing authorities.[42] His Lordship explained that in **Re Vaughan**[43] a trust for the repair of the parish churchyard was held to be charitable. In **Re Manser**[44] a trust for keeping in good order burial grounds for members of the Society of Friends was held to be charitable. Warrington J explained that there was no difference between the upkeep of burial grounds and the repair of a church, which was clearly within the preamble. Furthermore, Lord Upjohn referred to the decision of the court in **Re Eighmie**[45] where a trust for the maintenance of a cemetery owned and managed by a local authority as a public burial ground was held to be charitable. In light of these analogies, Lord Upjohn held that 'if a trust for such a burial ground is charitable why (even if, contrary to the facts of this case, it is used for burials not in accordance with religious rites) is not the provision of a crematorium? In my view, the appellant company qualifies as a charity.'[46]

---

[37] [1947] AC 447 at 455.
[38] [1949] Ch. 529.
[39] [1949] Ch. 529 at 538.
[40] *Commissioners for Special Purposes of Income Tax v Pemsel* [1891] AC 531.
[41] [1968] AC 138.
[42] [1968] AC 138 at 152.
[43] (1886) 33 Ch. D 187.
[44] [1905] 1 Ch. 68.
[45] [1935] Ch. 524.
[46] [1968] AC 138 at 153.

Lord Wilberforce, whilst reinforcing the charity by analogy approach explained by Lord Upjohn, explained what he perceived to be the modern test for whether a particular purpose was charitable or not. In doing so, whilst recognising the importance of the preamble, his Lordship also explained the need for the law to change with time. Lord Wilberforce explained:

> On this subject, the law of England, though no doubt not very satisfactory and in need of rationalisation, is tolerably clear. The purposes in question, to be charitable, must be shown to be for the benefit of the public, or the community, in a sense or manner within the intendment of the preamble to the statute 43 Eliz. 1, c. 4. The latter requirement does not mean quite what it says; for it is now accepted that what must be regarded is not the wording of the preamble itself, but the effect of decisions given by the courts as to its scope, decisions which have endeavoured to keep the law as to charities moving according as new social needs arise or old ones become obsolete or satisfied. Lord Macnaghten's grouping of the heads of recognised charity in Pemsel's case is one that has proved to be of value and there are many problems which it solves. But three things may be said about it, which its author would surely not have denied: first that, since it is a classification of convenience, there may well be purposes which do not fit neatly into one or other of the headings, secondly, that the words used must not be given the force of a statute to be construed; and thirdly, that the law of charity is a moving subject which may well have evolved even since 1891.[47]

The analogy approach to defining charitable purposes is retained by the Charities Act 2006 in s. 2(4) of the Act. It will be observed below that the Charities Act 2006 lists 13 heads of charity; however, s. 2(4) allows purposes that are analogous to or within the spirit of any other recognised charitable purposes to be recognised. This includes any of the 13 heads of charity listed in s. 2 of the Act and any other purposes which have been recognised as charitable on grounds of analogy with existing charitable purposes. The objective behind s. 2(4) of the Charities Act 2006 is to allow the law to expand in the future by allowing new charitable purposes to be recognised.[48] Despite the fact that the Charities Act 2006 envisages that, by adopting the analogy approach, the law of charities will be able to move with social change, it is questionable whether the analogy approach will in fact move with social change. The reason for this is that, whilst the analogy approach allows new purposes analogous with existing purposes to be recognised, what is the position where no such analogy can be made? Does this mean that any new purpose, which may be deemed as deserving charitable status, will not be recognised until such time as Parliament recognises it in legislation? The question is returned to later in the chapter.

One of the advantages of the position before the enactment of the Charities Act 2006 was that the courts were able, as will be seen in the next paragraph, to recognise new purposes which were not necessarily analogous to the preamble. Furthermore, they were also able to recognise purposes as charitable which may have at some earlier time been held not be charitable. For example, in **Funnell v Stewart**[49] the court held that a trust to promote faith healing was charitable despite the fact that some 73 years earlier the court held that it was not charitable.[50] Conversely, the courts were also able to declare purposes

---

[47] [1968] AC 138.
[48] As explained in the *Charities Act 2006: Explanatory Notes* at p. 5.
[49] [1996] 1 WLR 288.
[50] *Re Hummeltenberg* [1923] 1 Ch. 237.

which were once deemed as charitable not to be charitable at some later date. For example, in *National Anti-Vivisection Society v IRC*[51] the House of Lords held that a society whose purpose was to prevent animals used for medical research was not charitable even though some 50 years earlier the law recognised that a similar charity was indeed charitable.[52] In the course of his judgment Lord Simmonds explained that '[a] purpose regarded in one age as charitable may in another be regarded differently . . . I conceive that an anti-vivisection society might at different times be differently regarded.'[53] The House of Lords held that benefits to the public of medical research outweighed the advantages of reducing cruelty to animals.

Before the enactment of the Charities Act 2006, although the analogy approach allowed the courts to recognise new purposes which were not necessarily specifically mentioned within the preamble to the 1601 Act, the question did appear before the courts as to how purposes, which were not analogous to those in the preamble, could be recognised in law. In *Incorporated Council of Law Reporting for England and Wales v A-G*[54] the question before the Court of Appeal was whether a company limited by guarantee with the object of producing law reports was charitable. One of the main issues before the Court was whether the production of law reports sold at a price to professional persons in order to carry out their profession could be charitable. It was argued that this purpose was not within the spirit and intendment of the preamble of 1601. In holding that the production of law reports was charitable under the fourth head of Pemsel's case, Lord Russell LJ explained that if 'a purpose is shown to be so beneficial or of such utility it is prima facie charitable in law . . . [and] the proper question to ask is whether there are any grounds for holding it to be outside the equity of the Statute'.[55] Russell LJ explained that the production of a comprehensive and complete set of law reports was in the interests of the public and certainly in the interests of the government in ensuring the due administration of law. In the course of his judgment, Russell LJ criticised the approach by analogy with the preamble, which he described 'to be too narrow or refined an approach'.[56]

The approach adopted by Russell LJ in *Incorporated Council of Law Reporting for England and Wales v A-G*[57] has been subsequently approved by the Privy Council, in particular, in the judgment of Lord Browne-Wilkinson who commented that 'Russell LJ's approach has much to commend it in deciding whether or not a purpose specified by the donor falls within the spirit and intendment of the preamble to the Statute of Elizabeth I . . .'[58] After the enactment of the Charities Act 2006, is the approach adopted by Russell LJ an appropriate test to establish whether a purpose is indeed debatable? Can a court simply proceed to assume that where a trust is beneficial to the community, it should be deemed to be charitable unless there are other reasons why it should not be charitable? The Charities Act 2006, as will be seen very shortly, lists 13 heads of charity in s. 2 of the Act. It then goes on to explain in s. 2(4) of the Act that other purposes which are analogous to the purposes listed in s. 2 of the Act, or otherwise analogous to purposes which have been held charitable in law will be deemed charitable. If the approach is purely one

---

[51] [1948] AC 31.
[52] *Re Foveaux* [1895] 2 Ch. 501.
[53] [1948] 1 WLR 288 at 73.
[54] [1972] Ch. 73.
[55] [1972] Ch. 73 at 88.
[56] *Ibid.*
[57] [1972] Ch. 73.
[58] *A-G of the Cayman Islands v Wahr-Hansen* [2001] 1 AC 75 at 82.

by analogy between purposes which have been recognised as charitable either by statute or by decided cases, then it is questionable how any new purpose can be simply assumed to be charitable under the approach suggested by Russell LJ in *Incorporated Council of Law Reporting for England and Wales v A-G*.[59] The answer to this question may be purely one of interpretation of s. 2(4) of the Charities Act 2006. If s. 2(4) is interpreted quite liberally, thereby giving effect to the fourth head of Pemsel's case, that is, other purposes beneficial to the community, then there is no reason why the decision in *Incorporated Council of Law Reporting for England and Wales v A-G*, which was decided under the fourth head, should not remain good law. The view taken in this text is that 'any other purposes beneficial to the community' continues to remain a category of charity despite not being listed in the 13 heads of charity in s. 2(1) of the Charities Act 2006, because s. 2(4) of the Act preserves existing charity law. To suggest that the approach in *Incorporated Council of Law Reporting for England and Wales v A-G* has been removed by the Charities Act 2006 would produce a rather strange and restricted definition of charity, which would not allow new purposes to be admitted into the category of charity because of an insufficient analogy between existing ones. This would then leave it up to Parliament to enact further legislation to expand the definition of charity. This matter is discussed in more detail.

The definition of charitable purposes post Charities Act 2006

The definition of charity is today found in s. 2 of the Charities Act 2006. Reforming the definition of charitable purposes was one of the key aims of the Charities Act 2006, prior to which it had been clearly accepted that the definition of charity by reference to the preamble to the Statute of Elizabeth 1601 was clearly out of date. The Act seeks to do away with the preamble and expands the four heads of charitable purposes identified in Pemsel's case. In order for a purpose to be charitable, it must fall within one of the 13 heads listed in s. 2 of the Act. However, despite what might be perceived to be a new definition of charity in s. 2 of the Act, the 'old' law of charity is not completely removed. Indeed, it is questionable whether the reform of the definition of charity in the Charities Act 2006 is indeed novel. There are a number of reasons for this, not least, that at the heart of s. 2 of the Act there are many references to the old law of charity. Firstly, the fourfold classification in Pemsel's case[60] is retained in the s. 2 of Act. The first three purposes are identical to the first three purposes identified in Pemsel's case and the fourth category in Pemsel's case is retained in the thirteenth head when read in conjunction with s. 2(4) of the Act. Secondly, s. 2(4) of the Act explicitly says that other purposes which are within the spirit of the Act as well as analogous to purposes already recognised as charitable will continue to be charitable. Finally, s. 2(5) of the Charities Act 2006 preserves the existing meanings of terms used in s. 2 of the Act. It will be seen below that many of the new purposes identified in s. 2 of the Act are indeed a refinement of purposes which have already been held by the courts to be charitable under the fourth head of charity in Pemsel's case. In this respect, the definition of charity in the Charities Act 2006 is more of a consolidation of and refinement of the existing definition rather than a novel definition of charity. It is also for these reasons that an appreciation of the definition of charity in the Charities Act 2006 requires an analysis of cases decided prior to the

---

[59] [1972] Ch. 73.
[60] *Commissioners for Special Purposes of Income Tax* v *Pemsel* [1891] AC 531. See also now the Charities Act 2011 which provides the most recent definition of charity.

enactment of the Act. It is only from an analysis of the decided case law that a proper understanding of the scope of the purposes listed in s. 2(2) of the Charities Act can be appreciated.

KEY STATUTE

S. 2 of the Charities Act 2006 (Meaning of 'charitable purpose')

(1) For the purposes of the law of England and Wales, a charitable purpose is a purpose which –

(a) falls within subsection (2), and

(b) is for the public benefit (see section 3).

(2) A purpose falls within this subsection if it falls within any of the following descriptions of purposes –

(a) the prevention or relief of poverty;

(b) the advancement of education;

(c) the advancement of religion;

(d) the advancement of health or the saving of lives;

(e) the advancement of citizenship or community development;

(f) the advancement of the arts, culture, heritage or science;

(g) the advancement of amateur sport;

(h) the advancement of human rights, conflict resolution or reconciliation or the promotion of religious or racial harmony or equality and diversity;

(i) the advancement of environmental protection or improvement;

(j) the relief of those in need by reason of youth, age, ill-health, disability, financial hardship or other disadvantage;

(k) the advancement of animal welfare;

(l) the promotion of the efficiency of the armed forces of the Crown, or of the efficiency of the police, fire and rescue services or ambulance services;

(m) any other purposes within subsection (4).

Subsection 4 provides

(4) The purposes within this subsection (see subsection (2)(m)) are –

(a) any purposes not within paragraphs (a) to (l) of subsection (2) but recognised as charitable purposes under existing charity law or by virtue of section 1 of the Recreational Charities Act 1958 (c. 17);

(b) any purposes that may reasonably be regarded as analogous to, or within the spirit of, any purposes falling within any of those paragraphs or paragraph (a) above; and

(c) any purposes that may reasonably be regarded as analogous to, or within the spirit of, any purposes which have been recognised under charity law as falling within paragraph (b) above or this paragraph.

Charitable purposes under the Charities Act 2006

The relief of poverty

APPLYING THE LAW

In his will Alf left his residuary estate to be applied for the building of a centre consisting of 50 self-contained flats for providing short-term accommodation for individuals on low incomes. The trustees are not sure who individuals on low income are.

Is this a charitable trust?

The first category in s. 2 of the Charities Act 2006, just like in Pemsel's case,[61] covers the prevention or relief of poverty. Although, s. 2(2)(a) of Charities Act 2006 makes reference to the prevention as well as the relief of poverty, the words 'prevention or relief of poverty' imply that they are to be read disjunctively; therefore, a trust will be held to be charitable if it either relieves poverty or prevents poverty from arising in the future. The section does not define what is meant by poverty, and therefore, its interpretation is to be governed by the existing law. The preamble to the 1601 Act spoke of the relief of 'aged, impotent and poor'. Despite the reference to the relief of the aged, impotent and poor, these words were construed disjunctively by the court in *Joseph Rowntree Memorial Trust Housing Association Ltd v Attorney General*.[62] Section 2(2)(a) refers to the prevention and relief of poverty alone; however, the relief of the aged and impotent has been removed to s. 2(2)(j) of the Charities Act 2006 and this matter is explored later on.

The question in the context of the prevention or relief of poverty centres on what is meant by poverty. When is a person deemed to be poor? The decided case law does not provide an absolute definition of when a person is deemed to be poor; instead each case has turned on its own facts and the courts have interpreted poverty as being a relative term. In *Re Coulthurst*[63] a trust was created for the benefit of widows and orphans of deceased officers of a bank who in the opinion of the trustee were deserving of such money by reason of their financial situation and hardship. In coming to the conclusion that this created a valid charitable trust for the relief of poverty, Evershed MR explained that 'poverty does not mean destitution; it is a word of wide and somewhat indefinite import; it may not unfairly be paraphrased for present purposes as meaning persons who have to "go short" in the ordinary acceptation of that term, due regard being had to their status in life, and so forth'.[64] It is clear from this definition that 'poverty' does not require

---

[61] *Commissioners for Special Purposes of Income Tax* v *Pemsel* [1891] AC 531.

[62] [1983] Ch. 159. The decision in *Joseph Rowntree Memorial Trust Housing Association* v *Attorney General* is considered more appropriately under s. 2(2)(j) of the Charities Act 2006, which covers purposes for the relief of those in 'need by reason of youth, age, ill health, disability, financial hardship or other disadvantage'.

[63] [1951] Ch. 661.

[64] [1951] Ch. 661 at 666.

absolute destitution but is a term of relative import. In **Mary Clark Homes Trustees v Anderson**,[65] in the context of whether a home for ladies of reduced means was charitable or not, Channell J observed that 'the expression "poor person" in a trust for the benefit of poor persons does not mean the very poorest, the absolutely destitute; the word "poor" is more or less relative. The difficulty in such a case as the present is to determine from which point of view the question is to be looked at, for obviously very different views may be held as to what is poverty and what is riches.'[66] One leading treatise on the law of charities provides a number of examples where a trust has been held charitable despite the absence of destitution.[67] For example, trust for the benefit of distressed gentlefolk,[68] trusts for the benefit of persons of moderate means[69] and tradesmen of a particular kind[70] have all been held to be charitable. More recently, in **AITC Foundation's Application for Registration as a Charity**[71] the Charity Commissioners registered a foundation for the benefit of some 300 investors who had suffered hardship as a result of investments they had made in certain split-capital investment companies. The benefits were available to the investors pending full compensation when liability was admitted by the companies in which the investments were made.

APPLYING THE LAW

As a result of the recent hardship caused by the recession, a group of settlors have created a trust to relieve the financial hardship caused to investment bankers who have lost their jobs.

Is this a charitable trust to relieve poverty?

In its draft supplementary guidance for consultation on public benefit and the prevention and relief of poverty, the Charity Commission regarded poverty as meaning something akin to financial hardship.[72] Although the Commission recognised that people of all walks of life, including those more affluent than others, may experience financial hardship in some form or another, the Commission explained that financial hardship meant lacking something in the nature of a necessity which the majority of the population regarded as necessary for a modest, but adequate standard of living. The Commission in its latest guidance on poverty and public benefit defined poverty as follows.

---

[65] [1904] 2 KB 645.
[66] [1904] 2 KB 645 at 654.
[67] See *Tudor on Charities* 9th edn (2003) at p. 39.
[68] *A-G v Power* (1809) 1 Ball & B 145, quoted in *Tudor on Charities* 9th edn (2003) at p. 39.
[69] *Re Clarke* [1923] 2 Ch. 407.
[70] *Re White's Trusts* (1886) 33 Ch. D 449.
[71] [2005] WTLR 1265.
[72] Charity Commission, *Public Benefit and the Prevention or Relief of Poverty: Draft Supplementary Guidance for Consultation* February 2008, http://www.charity-commission.gov.uk/Library/publicbenefit/pdfs/pbprpsum.pdf. See also Charity Commission, *The Prevention or Relief of Poverty for the Public Benefit* (December 2008).

KEY CITATION

Charity Commission: *The prevention or relief of poverty for the public benefit* (December 2008)

Defining Poverty:

'People in poverty' does not just include people who are destitute, but also those who cannot satisfy a basic need without assistance. The courts have avoided setting any absolute criteria to be met in order for poverty to be said to exist, although they have been prepared to state in specific cases whether or not a particular level of income or assets meant that a person was 'poor'. In essence, 'people in poverty' generally refers to people who lack something in the nature of a necessity, or quasi-necessity, which the majority of the population would regard as necessary for a modest, but adequate, standard of living.

Although a trust for the prevention or relief of poverty need not be for the benefit of those who are destitute, there appear to be a number of principles which emerge from the existing case law. Firstly, it is no bar to the creation of a charitable trust for the poor which benefits the poor, but excludes certain individuals who may be deemed to be more deserving than the ones within the trust or gift. In other words, it is not fatal to the validity of a charitable trust for the poor if the poorest are excluded from the gift. The matter is neatly illustrated by the decision in **Re de Carteret**[73] where a trust was created in the will of the Bishop of Jamaica, which provided 'annual allowances of forty pounds each to widows or spinsters in England whose income otherwise shall not be less than eighty or more than one hundred and twenty pounds per annum . . . preference shall be given to widows with young children dependent on them . . .' Maugham J held that this created a valid charitable trust for the relief of poverty, and because preference was given to widows with young children, it did not matter that the trust excluded widows whose income was less that eighty pounds per annum. Maugham J commented that 'I should have hesitated to hold that it was a good charitable gift had it been merely for "widows and spinsters": but I think that, in confining it, as I do, in effect, to widows with young children dependent on them, I am within the decisions to which I have referred.'[74]

The second principle emerging from the decided case law is that a trust which benefits the 'poor' as well as the more affluent will not be held to be charitable. The matter is neatly illustrated by the decision in **Re Gwyon**[75] where a testator directed that his residuary property be sold and the proceeds used to set up a fund, called the Gwyon's Boys Clothing Foundation, to provide a particular type of trousers for schoolboys in the Farnham area. The terms of the will did not impose any particular preference in favour of children of poor parents, although, the will clearly barred boys of black origin from benefiting from the trust. Eve J held that the trust was not a trust for the relief of the poor. In the course of his judgment, the judge explained that:

> the question is whether the testator has effectively created such a charity as he contemplated, a charity in the legal sense of the word. Is the object of his benefaction the relief of poverty, are the gifts for the benefit of the poor and needy? I do not think they are. Apart from residential and age qualifications, the only conditions imposed on a recipient are (1.) that he shall not belong to or be supported by any charitable institution, (2.) that neither he nor his parents shall be in receipt of parochial relief, (3.) that he shall not be black, (4.)

---

[73] [1933] Ch. 103.
[74] [1933] Ch. 103 at 114.
[75] [1930] 1 Ch. 255.

that on a second or subsequent application he shall not have disposed of any garment received within the then preceding year from the Foundation and that when he comes for a new pair of knickers or trousers the legend 'Gwyon's Present' shall still be decipherable on the waist band of his old ones.[76]

With regard to reference to the colour bar in this case, this would now be governed by the provisions of s. 34(1) of the Race Relations Act 1976 which prevents a colour bar being used in a charitable trust in favour of a class. More recently, in **Gibbs v Harding**[77] a charitable trust which was confined to the 'black community' of a particular part of London took effect as a charitable trust without reference to the colour bar.

A third principle which has emerged from the decided case law is that a trust for the relief of a certain social class, such as the working class, is not necessarily a trust for the relief of poverty; however, each case must be determined on its own facts. For example, in **Re Sanders' Will Trusts**[78] a testator directed that a certain amount of his residuary estate be used to provide or assist in the provision of dwellings for the working class of a certain part of Pembrokeshire in Wales. Harman J explained that the working class were not to be classed as poor persons. In the course of his judgment, Harman J explained that changes in society over the past fifty years had made it inappropriate to regard working class people as a section of poor persons. The judge explained that:

> working classes fifty years ago denoted a class which included men working in the fields or the factories, in the docks or the mines, on the railways or the roads, at a weekly wage. The wages of people of that class were lower than those of most of the other members of the community, and they were looked upon as a lower class. That has all now disappeared. The social revolution in the last fifty years has made the words 'working classes' quite inappropriate today. There is no such separate class as the working classes. The bank clerk or the civil servant, the school teacher or the cashier, the tradesman or the clergyman, do not earn wages or salaries higher than the mechanic or the electrician, the fitter or the mineworker, the bricklayer or the dock labourer. Nor is there any social distinction between one or the other. No one of them is of a higher or a lower class.[79]

Although, the decision in **Re Sanders' Will Trusts** held that 'working class' did not constitute poor persons, the question arose in **Re Niyazi's Will Trust**[80] whether a trust for the construction of a working men's hostel was charitable? The testator, a Turkish Cypriot living in England, left his residuary estate to his trustees with the directions that it be paid over to an official of the town of Famagusta in Northern Cyprus and be used for the 'purposes only of the construction of or as a contribution towards the cost of the construction of a working men's hostel'. Megarry VC held that the trust in question was a charitable trust for the relief of poverty. It may be questioned what difference there is between 'working classes' as used in **Re Sanders' Will Trusts** where the trust was not charitable and 'working men's in the present case where the trust was held to be charitable. The answer to this question lies not so much in the terms 'working class' or 'working men' as in the nature of the gift. In **Re Niyazi's Will Trust** Megarry VC placed significance on the fact that this was a provision of a hostel for working men and that a hostel denoted a place of living for men with a low income. In the course of his judgment, Megarry VC explained that:

> the word 'hostel' has to my mind a strong flavour of a building which provides somewhat modest accommodation for those who have some temporary need for it and are willing to

---

[76] [1930] 1 Ch. 255 at 260.
[77] [2008] 2 WLR 361.
[78] [1954] Ch. 265.
[79] [1954] Ch. 265 at 270.
[80] [1978] 1 WLR 910.

accept accommodation of that standard in order to meet the need. When 'hostel' is prefixed by the expression 'working men's,' then the further restriction is introduced of the hostel being intended for those with a relatively low income who work for their living, especially as manual workers. The need, in other words, is to be the need of working men, and not of students or battered wives or anything else. Furthermore, the need will not be the need of the better paid working men who can afford something superior to mere hostel accommodation, but the need of the lower end of the financial scale of working men, who cannot compete for the better accommodation but have to content themselves with the economies and shortcomings of hostel life. It seems to me that the word 'hostel' in this case is significantly different from the word 'dwellings' in *In re Sanders' Will Trusts* . . . a word which is appropriate to ordinary houses in which the well-to-do may live, as well as the relatively poor.[81]

Finally, reference must be made to the change of emphasis in s. 2(2)(a) of the Charities Act 2006 in respect of trusts which concern the relief of poverty. Section 2(2)(a) of the Charities Act 2006 states that a purpose will be charitable if it is for the 'prevention or relief of poverty'. So whilst purposes which are for the relief of poverty will clearly be charitable, purposes which have the objective of preventing future poverty will also be held to be charitable. It remains to be seen how this will be interpreted by the courts and the Charity Commissioners. In its draft guidance on public benefit and the prevention or relief of poverty, the Charity Commission gives a number of examples of the ways in which a charity may be regarded as preventing poverty.

KEY CITATION

Charity Commission: *The prevention or relief of poverty for the public benefit* (December 2008)

Ways of Relieving Poverty:

The prevention or relief of poverty in [insert geographical area of operation] by providing: grants, items and services to individuals in need and/or charities, or other organisations working to prevent or relieve poverty.

To relieve poverty [or financial hardship] among refugees, asylum seekers, migrant workers and their dependants living in [insert geographical area] by providing interpreting/translating/advocacy/health/housing advice and education.

The prevention or relief of poverty [or financial hardship] anywhere in the world by providing or assisting in the provision of education, training, healthcare projects and all the necessary support designed to enable individuals to generate a sustainable income and be self-sufficient.

To prevent or relieve poverty through undertaking and supporting research into factors that contribute to poverty and the most appropriate ways to mitigate these.

To prevent or relieve poverty by awarding a 'fair trade mark' to products, the sale of which relieves the poverty of producers by ensuring they receive at least a fair price for their goods and advising such producers of the best ways in which to engage in the trading process.

To relieve the poverty of young people by the provision of grants to enable them to participate in healthy recreational activities that they could not otherwise afford.

---

[81] [1978] 1 WLR 910 at 915.

The advancement of education

Section 2(2)(b) of the Charities Act 2006 provides that a trust for the advancement of education will be charitable. Trusts for the advancement of education have for a long time been held to be charitable. The preamble to the Statute of Elizabeth in 1601 referred to schools of learning, free schools and scholars in universities. The advancement of education was categorised in Pemsel's case[82] as the second head of charity. As in the context of the prevention or relief of poverty, there is no exact definition of what constitutes education for the purposes of charity. Education is construed quite broadly for the purposes of charity and it is not confined to a pupil–teacher relationship in a classroom. Furthermore, given the fact that schools of learning and universities have been under the control of State provision, the legal definition of education for charity encompasses a much wider range of activities. In its draft consultation guide on public benefit and the advancement of education the Charity Commission listed a number of examples of education.[83]

KEY CITATION

Charity Commission: *Public Benefit and the Advancement of Education: Draft Supplementary Guide for Consultation* (March 2008, page 13)

Education today includes:

- formal education;
- community education;
- physical education and development of young people;
- training (including vocational training) and life-long learning;
- research and adding to collective knowledge and understanding of specific areas of study and expertise;
- the development of individual capabilities, competencies, skills and understanding.

Types of charities that advance education include:

- educational establishments, such as schools, colleges and universities;
- charities supporting the work of educational establishments, or associated with them, such as parent–teacher organisations, prize funds, standard-setting organisations, teacher training organisations, student unions, examination boards;
- pre-school education and out of school education, such as playgroups, Saturday schools, summer schools, homework clubs;
- physical education of young people, such as youth sporting facilities;
- life skills training, such as Duke of Edinburgh award scheme, Scouts & Guides, Woodcraft Folk;
- research projects, think tanks, etc;

▶

---

[82] *Commissioners for Special Purposes of Income Tax* v *Pemsel* [1891] AC 531.

[83] Charity Commission *Public Benefit and the Advancement of Education: Draft Supplementary Guide for Consultation* March 2008, http://www.charity-commission.gov.uk/Library/publicbenefit/pdfs/phaesum.pdf. The latest guidance is found in Charity Commission, *Analysis of the Law Underpinning the Advancement of Education and Public Benefit* December 2008.

- learned societies, such as the Royal Geographical Society;
- museums, galleries, libraries, scientific institutes;
- professional education bodies;
- organisations that educate the public in a particular subject, for instance in human rights, climate change, physics, personal financial management;
- organisations that educate the public in particular skills and competences, such as surgery, carpentry, electronic engineering;
- internet, radio, television, libraries, information centres, university presses, seminars, conferences, lectures, and so on.

Established charitable purposes that come under the heading of education include, for example, traditional purposes which have been regarded as advancing education, for example, gifts given to schools[84] or money given to endow a chair at a university.[85] Professional bodies such as the Royal College of Surgeons[86] as well as the Royal College of Nursing[87] have been held to be charitable. However, as explained earlier, the courts have construed the notion of education for charitable purposes in a broad way. What is meant by education will be continued to be influenced by the existing case law, and the case law provides guidance which can be explained in a series of points. The first point which emerges from the decided case law is that education is not confined to a teacher–pupil relationship in a classroom. This matter was explored by the House of Lords in **IRC v McMullen**[88] where a trust was set up by the Football Association. One of the purposes of the trust was 'to organise or provide or assist in the organisation or provision of facilities which will enable and encourage pupils at schools and universities in any part of the United Kingdom to play association football or other games or sports and thereby to assist in ensuring that due attention is given to the physical education and development and occupation of their minds . . .' The question before the House of Lords was whether this trust was a charitable for the advancement of education. In holding that this was a charitable trust, Lord Hailsham explained that education was:

> a balanced and systematic process of instruction, training and practice containing . . . both spiritual, moral, mental and physical elements, the totality of which in any given case may vary with, for instance, the availability of teachers and facilities, and the potentialities, limitations and individual preferences of the pupils. But the totality of the process consists as much in the balance between each of the elements as in the enumeration of the things learned or the places in which the activities are carried on. I reject any idea which would cramp the education of the young within the school or university syllabus, confine it within the school or university campus, limit it to formal instruction, or render it devoid of pleasure in the exercise of skill.[89]

The promotion of playing sports would now be covered under s. 2(2)(g), which covers the advancement of amateur sport.

---

[84] *Abbey Malvern Wells Ltd* v *Ministry of Local Government* [1951] Ch. 728.
[85] *A-G* v *Margaret and Regius Professors in Cambridge* (1682) 1 Vern. 55.
[86] *Royal College of Surgeons* v *National Provincial Bank Ltd* [1952] AC 631.
[87] *Royal College of Nursing* v *St Marylebone Corporation* [1959] 1 WLR 1077.
[88] [1981] AC 1.
[89] [1981] AC 1 at 18.

A very good illustration of an educational purpose which does not necessarily involve a teacher–pupil relationship is the decision of the Court of Appeal in *Incorporated Council of Law Reporting for England and Wales* v *A-G*,[90] where the Court was asked whether a company limited by guarantee and producing law reports of the decisions of the courts in England and Wales was charitable. The Court of Appeal held that the production of law reports by the Incorporated Council of Law Reporting for England and Wales was charitable on the grounds that it was disseminating important educational materials for the study of law. Although the Court of Appeal held that the purposes of the Council were also within the fourth head of charity identified in Pemsel's Case,[91] the majority were also of the view that the purposes fell within the advancement of education. In the course of his judgment, Buckley LJ explained that the 'council was established for the purpose of recording in a reliably accurate manner the development and application of judge-made law and of disseminating the knowledge of that law, its development and judicial application, in a way which is essential to the study of the law'.[92] Buckley LJ explained that education extended to the improvement of a useful branch of knowledge and its public dissemination. Buckley LJ referred to two decisions in support of this point of law. The first is the decision in *Re Lopes*[93] which concerned the London Zoological Society, the objective of which were the advancement of zoology and animal physiology and the introduction of new and curious subjects of the animal kingdom. Farewell J in holding that the objectives of the Society were charitable, explained that '[i]ts first object is the advancement of zoology and animal physiology. That is clearly educational, for the advancement of scientific knowledge, and therefore charitable.'[94] The second is the decision in *Re British School of Egyptian Archaeology*[95] which involved an association whose objectives were to discover knowledge related to ancient Egypt through excavations and so forth, Harman J held that the objectives of the association were charitable. In the course of his judgment, Harman J commented that 'I cannot doubt that this was a society for the diffusion of a certain branch of knowledge, namely, knowledge of the ancient past of Egypt; and that it also had a direct educational purpose, namely, to train students in that complicated branch of knowledge known as Egyptology. In my view this is clearly a charity from the educational aspect.'[96]

A second point which emerges from the decided case law is that advancement of education includes the promotion of artistic, cultural and aesthetic education, although such purposes are now found in the Charities Act 2006 s. 2(2)(f). In *Royal Choral Society* v *Inland Revenue Commissioners*[97] the Court of Appeal held that a society whose object was to form and maintain a choir to promote choral works was charitable. It was argued that the formation and maintenance of a choir could not be education, on the grounds that it did not involve teaching in the traditional sense. Lord Greene MR rejected this argument on the grounds that 'a body of persons established for the purpose of raising the artistic taste of the country and established by an appropriate document which confines them to that purpose, is established for educational purposes, because the education of artistic taste is one of the most important things in the development of

---

[90] [1972] Ch. 73.
[91] *Commissioners for Special Purposes of Income Tax* v *Pemsel* [1891] AC 531.
[92] [1972] Ch. 73 at 103.
[93] [1931] 2 Ch. 130.
[94] [1931] 2 Ch. 130 at 135.
[95] [1954] 1 WLR 546.
[96] [1954] 1 WLR 546 at 551.
[97] [1943] 2 All ER 101.

a civilised human being.'[98] In *Re Delius*[99] the wife of Frederick Delius (a composer) left property in her will for the advancement of her husband's music. The question before Roxburgh J was whether this trust was charitable. Roxburgh J, following the decision in *Royal Choral Society v Inland Revenue Commissioners*, held that this was a charitable trust. Further discussion of artistic and cultural work is undertaken below in the context of s. 2(2)(f) of the Charities Act 2006.

APPLYING THE LAW

Alf, who had been a train spotter all of his life, has left his entire residuary estate upon trust to apply the income to gathering data about how many train stations there are in England and how many trains call at such stations per day. Once the data is completed, he wishes findings to be published in a book.

Is this a charitable trust?

A third point under this head which requires discussion is does research qualify as being charitable purpose and, if so, what constitutes research for the purpose of charity law? Although research inherently involves the furtherance of knowledge, the definition of research in the context of charity law involves more than just the acquisition of further knowledge. A trust which involves research will only be recognised as charitable if the subject of the research is a useful one and is in the interests of the public. Furthermore, it is important that the research is disseminated to the public or a sufficiently large section of the public. Clearly, a trust to promote research into an illness such as cancer and the effective prevention thereof will qualify as being in the interests of the public. A trust to promote, for example, the gathering of factual information is not prima facie charitable. For example, a trust set up to investigate how many five-star hotels there are in London is not charitable. On the other hand, a trust which is set up to investigate how many people in London are below a certain income in order to establish the level of poverty in London is prima facie charitable, as such information would be in the public interest in attempting to tackle poverty.

Research is inherently subjective; what one person thinks is a useful subject to study may be regarded by another not to be the case. For example, in *Re Pinion*[100] Russell LJ commented that 'a school to teach people how to be pickpockets or prostitutes would be educational in a sense, but not beneficial to the public, since it would be contrary to public policy and morality'.[101] In this context, the question arises as to how a court makes a value judgment when presented with a purpose which is deemed by a settlor or testator to be charitable. Despite the subjective nature of research and the need to make value judgments, the courts have approached the question of research primarily by focusing on public benefit. Whether a particular proposed subject of research is charitable or not depends on whether the courts view the research and the dissemination of the findings thereof as being in the interest of the public. The matter was explored in detail by Slade J in *McGovern v Attorney-General*[102] which concerned the charitable status of Amnesty

---

[98] [1943] 2 All ER 101 at 104.
[99] [1957] Ch. 299.
[100] [1965] Ch. 85.
[101] [1965] Ch. 85 at 100.
[102] [1982] Ch. 321.

International. One of the purposes of Amnesty International was to carry out research into human rights. Although the court held that Amnesty International was not a charity on the grounds that its purposes involved political objects, which as will be explained below cannot be incorporated into a charity, the court held that carrying research into human rights would ordinarily have been charitable. In the course of his judgment, Slade J referred to an earlier judgment of his in *Re Besterman's Will Trusts*[103] where the judge explained the principles which govern whether a trust to promote research would be charitable.

KEY CITATION	*Re Besterman's Will Trust* (1980) *Times*, 21 January, per Slade J (see *McGovern* v *Attorney-General* [1982] Ch. 321 at 352)

When will a trust to promote research be charitable?

(1) A trust for research will ordinarily qualify as a charitable trust if, but only if:

(a) the subject matter of the proposed research is a useful subject of study; and

(b) it is contemplated that knowledge acquired as a result of the research will be disseminated to others; and

(c) the trust is for the benefit of the public, or a sufficiently important section of the public.

(2) In the absence of a contrary context, however, the court will be readily inclined to construe a trust for research as importing subsequent dissemination of the results thereof.

(3) Furthermore, if a trust for research is to constitute a valid trust for the advancement of education, it is not necessary either

(a) that a teacher/pupil relationship should be in contemplation, or

(b) that the persons to benefit from the knowledge to be acquired should be persons who are already in the course of receiving 'education' in the conventional sense.

(4) In any case where the court has to determine whether a bequest for the purposes of research is or is not of a charitable nature, it must pay due regard to any admissible extrinsic evidence which is available to explain the wording of the will in question or the circumstances in which it was made.

There are a number of cases which illustrate the types of research that will qualify as being charitable. For example, in *Re Besterman's Will Trusts*[104] a trust set up to carry out research on Voltaire and Rousseau, two famous philosophers, was held to be charitable in nature. Similarly, in *Re Hopkins Will Trusts*[105] a testatrix by her will left some of her residuary estate to the Francis Bacon Society 'to be earmarked and applied towards finding the Bacon–Shakespeare manuscripts and in the event of the same having been discovered by the date of my death then for the general purposes of the work and propaganda of the society'. The question before the court was whether this gift created a charitable trust. Wilberforce J held that this gift created a valid charitable purpose, on the grounds that 'the discovery of such manuscripts, or of one such manuscript, would be of

---

[103] (1980) *Times*, 21 January.
[104] (1980) *Times*, 21 January.
[105] [1965] Ch. 669.

the highest value to history and to literature'.[106] In the course of his judgment Wilberforce J explained that education:

> must be used in a wide sense, certainly extending beyond teaching, and that the requirement is that, in order to be charitable, research must either be of educational value to the researcher or must be so directed as to lead to something which will pass into the store of educational material, or so as to improve the sum of communicable knowledge in an area which education may cover – education in this last context extending to the formation of literary taste and appreciation.[107]

As explained earlier, where the purpose of a proposed research is merely to increase knowledge without any educational value, the gift will not be construed as charitable in nature. The matter is neatly illustrated in *Re Shaw*[108] where George Bernard Shaw left his residuary estate to be used to research the benefits of a 40-letter alphabet. In addition, his will directed the trustees to convert one of his plays, 'Androcles and the Lion' into the 40-letter alphabet. Harman J held that this did not create a valid charitable trust. In the course of his judgment he explained that 'if the object be merely the increase of knowledge, that is not in itself a charitable object unless it be combined with teaching or education'.[109] Although Harman J took a rather restricted view of research in this case, that is, confining it to teaching and education, the main reason why the trust failed in *Re Shaw* was that Harman J could not find any reason why such a purpose would be beneficial to the public. Later in his judgment, Harman J explained that 'the research and propaganda enjoined by the testator seem to me merely to tend to the increase of public knowledge in a certain respect, namely, the saving of time and money by the use of the proposed alphabet. There is no element of teaching or education combined with this, nor does the propaganda element in the trusts tend to more than to persuade the public that the adoption of the new script would be "a good thing," and that, in my view, is not education.'[110] The decision in *Re Shaw* illustrates that, in order to qualify as charitable, a proposed gift or trust to promote research must be of some value to the public at large or an important section of the public. If the research merely increases knowledge or is not in the interests of the public, it will not charitable in nature.

The advancement of religion

Section 2(2)(c) of the Charities Act 2006 lists the advancement of religion as a charitable purpose. The advancement of religion used to be the third head of charity as identified by Lord Macnaghten in Pemsel's case.[111] Section 2(3) of the Charities Act 2006 explains that religion includes a religion which involves belief in more than one god, and a religion which does not involve belief in a god. This emphasis on the belief in more than one god and a religion which does not involve a belief in god is deliberately inserted into the Charities Act 2006 to reflect the contemporary understanding of religion which was not necessarily reflective in the existing case law. For example, in *Bowman v Secular Society*[112] Lord Parker took the view that only those religions which believed in one god would qualify as being charitable. In the course of his judgment Lord Parker explained

---

[106] [1965] Ch. 669 at 679.
[107] [1965] Ch. 699 at 680.
[108] [1957] 1 WLR 729.
[109] *Ibid.*
[110] [1957] 1 WLR 729 at 738.
[111] *Commissioners for Special Purposes of Income Tax* v *Pemsel* [1891] AC 531.
[112] [1917] AC 406.

that 'It would seem to follow that a trust for the purpose of any kind of monotheistic theism would be a good charitable trust.'[113] However, the decision in this case was decided at a time when there was not the same degree of religious diversity that exists in modern society. Despite the decision of the court in **Bowman v Secular Society**, it was never doubted that Hinduism was a religion for the purposes of charity, even though those practising Hinduism believe in more than one god. Section 2(3) of the Charities Act establishes that religions, which believe in more than one god, will be charitable.

APPLYING THE LAW

Sometime in 1997 Stephen created the Coventry Ethical Society. The objectives of the society were to encourage good ethical living. The Society has 100 members who meet each week to discuss a number of issues such as honest living, respect for fellow individuals as well encouraging all members to practise whatever faith they believe in. The Society is seeking to register as a charity.

Do you think it is advancing religion?

One of the features of the case law on religion prior to the Charities Act 2006 was that there should be some belief in god or some spiritual supreme being. Organisations which did not believe in a god or some supreme being were held not charitable under the heading of religion. For example, in **Re South Place Ethical Society**[114] the question before Dillon J was whether a society whose objects were to promote the 'study and dissemination of ethical principles and the cultivation of a rational religious sentiment'. Dillon J held that the objects of the society were not advancing religion, on the grounds that there was no connection with a divine supreme being: instead, the purposes of the society were to advance good ethical values. With regard to ethical values, Dillon J equated these with love, beauty and truth. In the course of his judgment Dillon J explained that religion 'is concerned with man's relations with God, and ethics are concerned with man's relations with man'.[115] Similarly in **United Grand Lodge of Ancient Free and Accepted Masons of England v Holborn Borough Council**[116] the question arose whether freemasonry was charitable on the grounds of advancement of religion. Although freemasons do not reject any belief in god, their main objects are to encourage good morals in life. In holding that the freemasonry was not charitable, Lord Donovan explained that 'to advance religion means to promote it, to spread its message ever wider among mankind; to take some positive steps to sustain and increase religious belief; and these things are done in a variety of ways which may be comprehensively described as pastoral and missionary'.[117]

The decision in **Re South Place Ethical Society**[118] must now be read in light of s. 2(3) of the Charities Act 2006, which defines religion as including a religion which does not believe in a god. The purpose behind this section is to include certain religions which, although not believing in a god as such, nevertheless believe in some divine being or entity. The most obvious example is Buddhism, which does not believe in a god, but nevertheless believes that individuals should follow the life led by the Buddha, which in itself can lead

---

[113] [1917] AC 406 at 449.
[114] [1980] 1 WLR 1565.
[115] [1980] 1 WLR 1565 at 1571.
[116] [1957] 1 WLR 1080.
[117] [1957] 1 WLR 1080 at 1090.
[118] [1980] 1 WLR 1565.

to spiritual enlightenment. It is now also clear that a society whose objects are to promote faith healing[119] will be held charitable as will a society whose objects are spiritual healing. For example, in ***Sacred Hands Spiritual Centre's Application for Registration as a Charity***[120] the Charity Commission registered as a charity an organisation that was spiritual healing, on the grounds that the beliefs of spiritualists in the spirit world and the existence of a supreme being were a belief system and could be characterised as a faith.

It is important in the case of advancement of religion that it involves worship of some supreme being such as a god or some supreme entity. In this context, the question has arisen as to what is exactly meant by the notion of worship. In ***R v Registrar General ex p Segerdal***[121] Buckley LJ explained that worship 'must have some at least of the following characteristics: submission to the object worshipped, veneration of that object, praise, thanksgiving, prayer or intercession'. It is for this reason that the Church of Scientology, which proclaims to be one of the fastest growing religions, particularly in the United States where it is recognised as a charity, is not a charity for the purposes of English law. The Church of Scientology, which has its origins in the works of Ron Hubbard, believe in the practice of one-to-one understanding of the past life of an individual as a means to attaining spiritual enlightenment. Those who adhere to the Church of Scientology believe that, through a process of auditing and training, individuals can understand that they are immortal and that through scientology they can understand themselves spiritually.[122] A particular problem with the Church of Scientology is that its activities are carried out in private and as a result it becomes very difficult to satisfy the public benefit requirement. In its recent draft consultation paper on Public Benefit and the Advancement of Religion, the Charity Commission gave the following explanation.

KEY CITATION

Charity Commission *Public Benefit and the Advancement of Religion: Draft Supplementary Guide for Consultation* (February 2008, page 14)

The process in which followers or adherents take part in acts or practices expressing their belief in the 'supreme being or entity' by showing reverence for, or veneration of, the personal or non-personal 'supreme being or entity' is often called 'worship', but different religions use other concepts. Reverence and veneration are characterised by qualities including deep respect, homage, adoration, devotion, obeisance, submission, prayer and meditation.

As with 'supreme being or entity', we think the term 'worship' may not be considered appropriate with regard to some religious belief systems, such as those that do not involve belief in a personal creator god or gods, or where the belief system is based on a belief that followers or adherents can attain a state of purity or oneness after death from living good lives.[123]

In its draft consultation paper the Charity Commission identifies Jainism as a good example of where there is worship even though there is no belief in a god. Those who adhere to Jainism, which incidentally has a long history, believe that living a certain life

---

[119] *Funnell* v *Stewart* [1996] 1 WLR 288.
[120] [2006] WTLR 873, West Law Summary.
[121] [1970] 2 QB 697.
[122] In the context of a breach of confidence, Lord Denning described material relating to the Church of Scientology as 'dangerous material'; see *Hubbard* v *Vosper* [1972] 2 QB 84 at 96.
[123] The most recent guidance is provided by the Charity Commission, *Analysis of the Law Underpinning the Advancement of Religion for the Public Benefit* December 2008.

detached from materialistic things in life can lead to 'god consciousness'. Although there is no god as such, followers of Jainism believe that each individual, through good deeds and detachment from the world, can leave the cycle of life and death. The belief is that each individual is born and lives a particular life because of his past deeds, otherwise known as 'karma'. A person can change the destiny of his life when he is reborn by doing better deeds in this life and through this process he can eventually move out of the cycle of life and death by attaining 'god consciousness'. As a result of the change of emphasis implemented in s. 2(3) of the Charities Act 2006, a wider range of religions will be accepted into the category of charity provided that there is, in the words of the Charity Commission, some 'worship or have reverence or respect for . . . or a connection with the supreme being or entity'.[124]

In order for a purpose to be one which is for advancement of religion, it is important that it does involve an element of advancement of religion. This can be achieved in a number of ways: for example, the building of a place of worship, the maintenance of public churchyards, the conducting of ceremonies such as weddings, saying of prayers in public and so on. Clearly, saying a prayer in private has an element of religion attached to it; however, the saying of prayers in private are not for the advancement of religion.[125] In **Re Hetherington**[126] a testatrix left £2000 to the Roman Catholic Bishop of Westminster for 'masses for the repose of the souls of my husband and my parents and my sisters and also myself when I die'. The court held that, the fact that the masses were to be said in public by the Bishop of Westminster, the gift was charitable in nature on the grounds of advancement of religion. In respect of private prayers, Lord Denning explained that 'when a man says his prayers in the privacy of his own bedroom, he may truly be concerned with religion but not with the advancement of religion'.[127] The notion of advancement of religion was the subject matter of much discussion in **United Grand Lodge of Ancient Free and Accepted Masons of England** v **Holborn Borough Council**,[128] where as noted above, the issue was whether freemasonry was to be regarded as a purpose for advancing religion. Although freemasonry did not reject the idea of respect for a supreme being such as a god, the main purpose of freemasonry was to advance good morals and ethical ways of living. In this context, Donovan J explained that the objects of the Grand Lodge of Ancient Free and Accepted Masons of England were not to advance religion. In the course of his judgment, the judge explained that 'to advance religion means to promote it, to spread its message ever wider among mankind; to take some positive steps to sustain and increase religious belief; and these things are done in a variety of ways which may be comprehensively described as pastoral and missionary'.[129]

It has already been explained that religion can be advanced in a number of different ways, for example, the conducting of ceremonies in places of worship, the building of a place of worship, supporting religious officers in their office and so forth. The advancement of religion can most obviously be advanced by making a particular religion reach out to new converts. Curiously, and indeed misguidedly, the Charity Commission explained in its draft consultation paper 'Public Benefit and the Advancement of Religion' that one particular religion in which religion is not advanced by seeking new followers or adherents is Sikhism. In the words of the Charity Commission 'in some cases (e.g. Sikhism) followers or adherents are born into the religion and people who are not

---

[124] Charity Commission, *Public Benefit and the Advancement of Religion: Draft Supplementary Guide for Consultation* February 2008 at page 15.
[125] *Gilmour* v *Coats* [1949] AC 426.
[126] [1990] Ch. 1.
[127] *National Deposit Friendly Society Trustees* v *Skegness UDC* [1959] AC 293 at 322.
[128] [1957] 1 WLR 1080.
[129] [1957] 1 WLR 1080 at 1090.

born into the religion are not able to convert to it. In those cases, the "advancement" of the religion will not be concerned with encouraging people to join the religion, since that is determined by birth, but may be concerned with the personal and social consequences of the religion being practised by such followers or adherents.'[130] However, this is in fact not true as there are many individuals who, despite not being born into a Sikh family, have converted to Sikhism. There are a growing number of individuals of European origin which now follow Sikhism.[131]

Finally, in relation to the advancement of religion, it will be seen from the decided case law that the courts do not entertain questions regarding the relative worth of one religion as compared to another. Provided that the religion in question conforms to the principles examined above, that is, a belief in some supreme being or supreme entity, the court will not question whether a particular religion is either right or better than another. For example, in *Neville Estates Ltd v Madden*[132] Lord Cross explained that 'as between different religions the law stands neutral, but it assumes that any religion is at least likely to be better than none'.[133] It is for this reason that certain religious sects and cults have been recognised as being charitable despite not being amongst the mainstream religions of the world. For example, in *Thornton v Howe*[134] a trust was created to advance the works of Joanna Southcote who claimed to be the mother of the second messiah. Sir John Romilly MR, whilst of the opinion that she was 'a foolish, ignorant woman, of an enthusiastic turn of mind, who had long wished to become an instrument in the hands of God to promote some great good on earth',[135] nevertheless held the trust to be charitable. In the course of his judgment the judge explained that:

> a trust 'for printing, publishing and propagating the sacred writings' of Joanna Southcote is a charitable trust, which if given out of pure personalty will be enforced and regulated. In respect to charitable trusts for printing and circulating works of a religious tendency, this court makes no distinction between one sect and another, unless their tenets include doctrines adverse to the foundation of all religion or be subversive of all morality, in which case this court will declare the bequest void.[136]

The decision in *Thornton v Howe* was applied in *Re Watson*[137] where a trust was created to promote the works of a certain H.G. Hobbs who had published a number of books on an alternative view of Christianity. Although experts had found no intrinsic value in the publications, the court held that the trust was charitable.

More recently, the Charity Commission has recognised that the Druid Network is a religion.[138] The objectives of the Druid Network, otherwise known as Druidry, are set out 'to provide information on all principles of Druidry for the benefit of all and to inspire and facilitate that practice for those who have committed themselves to the spiritual path.' Druids believe in public rituals at places such as Stonehenge and at solstices. The basic tenor of Druidry is the belief in nature as being the Supreme Being. Everything in the natural environment, such as the plants, animals, mountains etc. have a spirit. The gods worshiped within Druidry include Saxon and Nordic gods.

---

[130] Charity Commission, *Public Benefit and the Advancement of Religion: Draft Supplementary Guide for Consultation* February 2008 at page 16.
[131] For more information, see www.sikhnet.com.
[132] [1962] Ch. 832.
[133] [1962] Ch. 832 at 853.
[134] (1862) 31 Beav. 14.
[135] (1862) 31 Beav. 14 at 18.
[136] *Ibid.*
[137] [1973] 1 WLR 1472.
[138] *Druid Network*, Ch Com Decision, September 21, 2010. See, P. Luxton and N. Evans, 'Cogent and Cohesion: Two Recent Charity Commission Decisions on the Advancement of Religion' (2011) Conv 144.

The advancement of health or saving lives

The fourth category of charitable purposes under the Charities Act 2006 is the advancement of health or saving lives. Section 2(3)(b) of the Charities Act 2006 states that the advancement of health includes the 'prevention or relief of sickness, disease or human suffering'. Although this category appears to be a new one, it is in fact a refinement of a number of purposes which would have fallen into either the first category of Pemsel's case,[139] namely the relief of poverty, or the fourth category, which included other purposes beneficial to the community. With regard to the relief of poverty, it will be recalled from the earlier discussion in this chapter that the poverty category was formulated by Lord Macnaghten from the 1601 preamble of the Statute of Elizabeth, which referred to the relief of the 'aged, impotent and the poor'. A disjunctive reading of these words meant that any purposes which relieved impotent persons, that is, persons suffering from illnesses or other ailments, would be classified as the relief of poverty.

So what types of purposes are or will be included under the advancement of health or saving lives? The most obvious example from the older case law is the opening of a hospital. Although the provision of hospital care has been undertaken by the National Health Service, the decided case law illustrates that a gift to a hospital run on voluntary contributions and not for profit will be held to be charitable. For example, in **Re Smith's Will Trust**[140] a testator left property to his trustees to be given to hospitals which, in the opinion of the trustees, were charitable. The Court of Appeal upheld the gift as being charitable for hospitals which were run on a voluntary contributions basis rather than private hospitals or private nursing homes which would not be charitable. Today, purposes which advance health or save lives is interpreted in a broad way to cover a wide range of things which promote health and the saving of lives. This category will include conventional means by which lives are saved and health is promoted in addition to non-conventional methods. For example, alternative and complementary treatment and medicines will be covered under this category as will spiritual and faith healing which was decided under the fourth head of Pemsel's case.[141] The definition of the advancement of health is wide enough to cover purposes which provide some support and relief to those who administer healthcare. For example, a trust to provide accommodation for nurses will be charitable. In **London Hospital Medical College v IRC**[142] a students' union at a medical school was granted charitable status on the grounds that it promoted the efficient running of the medical school.

The saving of lives includes rescue charities such as lifeboats,[143] mountain rescue, fire and ambulance services, to name but a few. A trust which is created to deal with a national disaster will be held to be charitable as will a trust to promote the donation of blood.

The advancement of citizenship or community development

The fifth category in the definition of charitable purposes under s. 2 of the Charities Act 2006 is the advancement of citizenship or community development. Section 2(3) of the Charities Act explains that the advancement of citizenship or community development includes 'rural and urban regeneration and the promotion of civic responsibility, volunteering, the voluntary sector of the effectiveness or efficiency of charities . . .' This

---

[139] *Commissioners for Special Purposes of Income Tax v Pemsel* [1891] AC 531.
[140] [1962] 2 All ER 563. See also the Privy Council's decision in *Re Resch's Will Trust* [1969] 1 AC 514.
[141] *Funnell v Stewart* [1996] 1 WLR 288.
[142] [1976] 1 WLR 613.
[143] For example, the Royal National Lifeboat Association, which has already been given charitable status.

category covers a wide range of purposes which are directed primarily at the community rather than the individual.

With regard to rural and urban regeneration, the Charity Commission issued in 1999 its own guidance as to what rural and urban regeneration involved. An extract of the guidance is reproduced below.

KEY CITATION

Charity Commission: *Review of the Register: Promotion of rural and urban regeneration* (RR2) March 1999

Regeneration organisations may do some, or all, of the following:

- provide financial or other assistance to people who are poor;
- provide housing to those people in need and help to improve housing standards generally in those parts of an area of deprivation where poor housing is a problem;
- help unemployed people find work;
- provide education, training and re-training opportunities and work experience, especially for unemployed people;
- provide financial or technical assistance or advice to new businesses or existing businesses where it would lead to training and employment opportunities for unemployed people;
- provide land and buildings on favourable terms to businesses in order to create training and employment opportunities for unemployed people;
- provide, maintain, and improve roads and accessibility to main transport routes;
- provide, maintain and improve recreational facilities;
- preserve buildings in the area which are of historic or architectural importance;
- provide public amenities.

With regard to the question of advancement of citizenship, there is no real definition of what is meant by citizenship for the purposes of the Charities Act 2006. Citizenship incorporates a wide number of meanings, including social and ethnic integration in a country in which a person lives. However, because s. 2(2)(h) covers the advancement of racial harmony and equality and diversity, which would cover purposes promoting diversity in society, the notion of citizenship in the Charities Act 2006 must cover a wider range of citizenship activities. For example, organisations such as the Guides and the Scouts would fall under this heading as promoting better citizenship. Equally, voluntary work within the community would be seen as an example of citizenship.

The advancement of arts, culture, heritage, or science

Trusts which promote art and culture have long been recognised by the Charity Commission and the courts as being charitable in nature: for example, museums, archaeology, written works and dramatic performances have been recognised as charitable purposes. Prior to the Charities Act 2006, trusts promoting artistic and cultural works were considered to fall into the second category of Pemsel's case,[144] that is, the advancement of education. It has already been seen above, in the context of advancement of education, that a trust to create a choir and promote choral works was considered by the court to be charitable on the grounds that it encouraged the education of artistic taste.[145] Trusts

---

[144] *Commissioners for Special Purposes of Income Tax* v *Pemsel* [1891] AC 531.
[145] *Royal Choral Society* v *IRC* [1943] 2 All ER 101.

which promote the works of a famous composer have also been deemed to be charitable on the grounds that they advance artistic values.[146] The advancement of art and culture encompasses a wide range of things covering visual and performance art, as well as conceptual and figurative art. By its very nature, art is a very subjective concept, and what is art in the eyes of one person may indeed be a load of nonsense in the eyes of another. Given the very subjective nature of art, the question arises as to what types of purposes promoting art will qualify as attracting charitable status. Does a court make an objective evaluation, that is examine the artistic value or merit of the proposed art, or does the court take the subjective opinion of the person creating a trust which seeks to promote art?

Unlike in the context of the advancement of religion, where it has been observed that the courts do not generally entertain questions about the relative worth of different religions, in the context of the advancement of art the courts have in the past adopted an objective assessment to establish whether the proposed art is of genuine artistic merit. Clearly, very bad art or poor acting will not attract charitable status; neither will productions which are contrary to public policy and immorality: for example, pornography. Where there is an element of doubt, the court can always call upon expert opinion to resolve the matter. For example, in **Re Pinion**[147] a testator, who had been a collector of paintings, furniture, china as well as other objects of art, left his collections of art to his trustees to be displayed in a museum. The question before the court was whether this was a valid charitable purpose on the grounds of advancing art. The court held that, whilst the testator was indeed a prolific collector of art, nothing which he had collected was of any artistic value. Expert opinion was so critical that one of the experts commented that he was surprised that the testator had not collected anything of value even by accident. In holding that the trust was not charitable, Harman LJ commented that '[I] can conceive of no useful object to be served in foisting upon the public this mass of junk.'[148] The Charity Commission has issued guidance on the criteria that it will use in determining whether museums and galleries will be afforded charitable status.[149]

KEY CITATION

Charity Commission, RR10: *Museums and Art Galleries* (August 2002)

General requirements for charitable status:

7. We have concluded that in order to be charitable, museums and art galleries will need to demonstrate that their collections or exhibits –

(i) **are set up for the benefit of the public,** that is:

they provide sufficient public access;

any private benefit gained by individuals is incidental and properly regulated;

they are not used for non-charitable purposes, such as trading; and

(ii) **they satisfy a criterion of merit,** that is, there is sufficient evidence that the collections and exhibits and the use made of them either will educate the minds of the public whom the museum or art gallery intends to serve, or at least will be capable of doing so. What is conveyed to the public is an idea, emotion or experience which is enlightening and which is, or is capable of being, of value to them.

---

[146] *Re Delius* [1957] Ch. 299.
[147] [1965] Ch. 85.
[148] *Ibid.*
[149] Charity Commission, RR10: *Museums and Art Galleries* (August 2002).

With regard to the advancement of culture, a trust which promotes cultural values – for example, historic building, the ways in which people have lived in the past, morris dancing or craftsmanship, to name but a few – would certainly be charitable. The matter is neatly illustrated by the decision in **IRC v White**[150] where the principal object of the Clerkenwell Green Association for Craftsmen was 'to promote any charitable purpose which will encourage the exercise and maintain the standards of crafts both ancient and modern, preserve and improve craftsmanship and foster, promote and increase the interest of the public therein'. In order to promote craftsmanship, the Association had converted buildings to be used for craftsmen such as hand engravers, antique furniture restorers, glass polishers and watch repairers. The purposes of the Association were held by Fox J to be charitable. In the course of his judgment, Fox J explained that 'the word craftsmanship, in its general use in the English language, suggests a degree of quality of workmanship . . . There is, in my opinion, a substantial range of activity which would foster, promote and increase the interest of the public in craftsmanship and which would itself be charitable . . . It seems to me that there is a wide field of high-quality craftsmanship where there could be no doubt as to the educative value to the public of increased information.'[151]

In so far as heritage is concerned, it has been recognised for a long time that purposes and organisations which promote heritage, for example the National Trust, are charitable in nature. A trust or gift to erect a monument of a famous and important person in history, for example Earl Mountbatten of Burma, will be charitable on the grounds of advancement of heritage.[152] A trust, however, for a monument or some other memorial or a private individual will not be charitable. For example, in **Re Endacott**[153] the court refused to recognise a trust to 'provide some useful memorial' to the testator. Finally, in respect to science, purposes such as those of the Royal College of Surgeons or the Royal College of Nursing will clearly now fall into this category.

KEY CITATION	Charity Commission: *Commentary of the descriptions of charitable purposes in the Charities Act 2006*, March 2007

Examples of charities and charitable purposes advancing art, culture, heritage and science.

Art galleries, arts festivals and arts councils;

Charities that promote, or encourage high standards of, the arts of drama, ballet, music, singing, literature, sculpture, painting, cinema, mime, etc, e.g. theatres, cinemas and concert halls; choirs; orchestras; music, operatic and dramatic societies;

The promotion of crafts and craftsman;

Local or national history or archaeology societies;

Local arts societies;

Charities that preserve ancient sites or buildings;

---

[150] [1980] TR 155. This case analysis is taken from E. Burn and J. Virgo, *Maudsley and Burn's Trusts and Trustees* 7th edn (2008) at p. 485.

[151] [1980] TR 155 at 158, quoted in E. Burn and J. Virgo, *Maudsley and Burn's Trusts and Trustees* 7th edn (2008) at p. 485.

[152] See, for example, Report of the Charity Commissioners for England and Wales 1981, paras 68–70.

[153] [1960] Ch. 232.

Charities that preserve a specified monument, building or complex of historic/ architectural importance, or the preservation of historic buildings in general, such as building preservation trusts;

The preservation of historical traditions, such as carnivals, country/folk dancing societies, Scottish country dancing and highland dancing societies, eisteddfords, folk clubs, etc.;

Scientific research projects;

Charities connected with various learned societies and institutions, e.g. the Royal College of Surgeons; Royal College of Nursing; Royal Geographical Society.

The advancement of amateur sport

Before the enactment of the Charities Act 2006 trusts to promote sport were not charitable per se. For example, in **Re Nottage**[154] a testator left money on trust to provide annually for a prize to be given to the most successful yacht of the season, stating that his object in giving the cup was to encourage the sport of yacht-racing. The court held that a trust to promote a mere sport was not charitable in nature. Kekewich J commented that:

> I cannot bring myself to hold that the sport of yacht-racing is beneficial to the community in the sense in which that phrase is used by Lord Macnaghten in the case in the House of Lords and by other learned judges. I cannot see that the benefit of the community is the natural direct and necessary result of this gift; and though I am far from saying that the result of the gift is not beneficial, I must hold that it is not beneficial to the community so as to constitute this a charitable gift. The consequence is that the gift fails.[155]

APPLYING THE LAW

In his will, Michael left his entire residuary estate to be applied for the furtherance of playing snooker in Warwickshire. The fund was directed to building snooker rooms and encouraging youngsters to play snooker and pool. Admission to the snooker rooms would be free. The trustees seek charitable status.

Is this trust charitable?

Although prior to the Charities Act 2006 the advancement of sport was not charitable per se, a trust to advance sport could be charitable under one of two of the heads of charity as identified by Lord Macnaghten in Pemsel's case.[156] The first is under the head of advancement of education. In **IRC v McMullen**[157] the Football Association sought to set up a charitable trust. Its objects were stated, in clause 3(a), to be, inter alia, 'to organise or provide or assist in the organisation or provision of facilities which will enable and encourage pupils at schools and universities in any part of the United Kingdom to play association football or other games or sports and thereby to assist in ensuring that due

---

[154] [1885] 2 Ch. 649.
[155] [1885] 2 Ch. 649 at 653.
[156] *Commissioners for Special Purposes of Income Tax* v Pemsel [1891] AC 531.
[157] [1981] AC 1.

attention is given to the physical education and development and occupation of their minds . . .' The trust was registered by the Charity Commission as charitable in nature; however, the Inland Revenue successfully appealed against the decision of the Charity Commission, arguing that the trust was not charitable in law. The question before the House of Lords was whether a trust to promote playing football in schools in the United Kingdom was charitable. The House of Lords held that it was, on the grounds that it fell under the head of advancement of education. Lord Halisham explained that education consisted of 'a balanced and systematic process of instruction, training and practice containing . . . both spiritual, moral, mental and physical elements'.[158]

Other than sport in the context of education, a trust to promote a sport could fall into the fourth head of charity in Pemsel's case, that is, other purposes beneficial to the community. It has already been observed earlier in this chapter that, for a purpose to fall within the fourth head, the particular purpose in question would be presumed to be beneficial to the community unless there was a reason why it should not be. Prior to the decision in *Incorporated Council of Law Reporting for England and Wales* v *A-G*[159] the approach of the courts was to look to whether the purpose was within the spirit and intendment of the preamble to the Statute of Elizabeth 1601. A good example of a trust to promote sport, which fell under the fourth head of charity under Pemsel's case is *Re Gray*[160] where, by his will, a testator gave money to a regiment 'for the promotion of sport (including in that term only shooting, fishing, cricket, football and polo)'. The court held that this was a valid trust, on the grounds that it promoted the efficiency of the armed forces.[161] Romer J explained that the present case could be distinguished from the decision in *Re Nottage*[162] on the grounds that the testator's intention was to 'benefit the officers and men of the Carabiniers by giving them an opportunity of indulging in healthy sport. It is to be observed that the particular sports specified were all healthy outdoor sports, indulgence in which might reasonably be supposed to encourage physical efficiency.'[163]

In addition to the certain purposes of a sporting nature which could fall under the heads of advancement of education or other purposes beneficial to the community, some purposes promoting sport could, and still can today, fall to be governed by the Recreational Charities Act 1958, which is considered in more detail below. Sporting facilities provided in the interests of social welfare, with the object of improving the conditions of life of the people using them, will be held to be charitable.

In 2003 the Charity Commission recognised that single-sports clubs could register as charities provided that they demonstrated sufficient public benefit.[164] The Charity Commission recognised that community amateur sports clubs (CASCs) could be charitable provided that:

● the sport in question is capable of improving the physical health and fitness of a person;

● the club must have an open membership, that is, access to the club's facilities must be genuinely available to anyone who wishes to take advantage of them.

---

[158] [1981] AC 1 at 18.

[159] [1972] Ch. 73.

[160] [1925] Ch. 362.

[161] The decision in this case must now be interpreted in light of s. 2(2)(l) of the Charities Act 2006, which specifically provides that a trust for the promotion of the efficiency of the armed forces will be charitable. This is discussed below.

[162] [1885] 2 Ch. 649.

[163] [1925] Ch. 362 at 365.

[164] See Charity Commission RR11: *Charitable Status and Sport* (April 2003).

With reference to the question as to what sport is regarded as capable of improving the physical health and fitness of a person, the Charity Commission explained in its guidance that sports that are capable of providing 'healthy recreation' are those sports which, 'if practised with reasonable frequency, will tend to make the participant healthier, that is, fitter and less susceptible to disease. Fitness includes elements of stamina, strength and suppleness (there may be others), but it will be enough if a sport contributes to just one of these elements.'[165] In the view of the Charity Commission in 2003, sports which do not promote physical health and fitness are angling, snooker, pool, crossbow, flying and gliding, to name but a few.

The advancement of amateur sport is now clearly a separate head of charity under s. 2(2)(g) of the Charities Act 2006. Section 2(3)(d) makes it clear that only sports which involve 'physical skill and exertion' are charitable. In this respect the same guidance which is given in the context of community amateur sports clubs applies to s. 2(3). With regard to the types of organisations which are capable of being charitable, the guidance of the Charity Commission in respect of community amateur sports clubs will apply. The guidance provides that there must be open membership, which can only be legitimately restricted in limited situations, for example, on the medical condition of an individual, or where there is maximum use and someone has to be put on a waiting list, or on other safety grounds. The Act does not define what is meant by 'amateur sport', presumably, in accordance with the existing approach of the Charity Commission, sports facilities which do not promote the fitness of professional individuals, such as playing snooker, will not attract charitable status.

The advancement of human rights, conflict resolution or reconciliation, or the promotion of religious harmony or equality and diversity

The eighth category of charity under the Charities Act 2006, which is embedded in s. 2(2)(h) of the Act, is the advancement of human rights, conflict resolution and equality. Unlike many of the categories already discussed above, this category is a new one in the sense that there is very little existing case law which puts light on its meaning and extent.

KEY CITATION

Charity Commission: *Commentary on the descriptions of charitable purposes in the Charities Act 2006* (March 2007, para. 26)

The advancement of conflict resolution or reconciliation includes the resolution of international conflicts and relieving the suffering, poverty and distress arising through conflict on a national or international scale by identifying the causes of the conflict and seeking to resolve such conflict. It includes the promotion of restorative justice, where all the parties with a stake in a particular conflict or offence come together to resolve collectively how to deal with its aftermath and its implications for the future. It also includes purposes directed towards mediation, conciliation or reconciliation as between persons, organisations, authorities or groups involved or likely to become involved in dispute or inter-personal conflict.

One of the fundamental problems with a trust to promote human rights is that it inevitably involves a campaign to bring about a change in the law of a country. It will be seen below that a trust which has a political objective behind it will not attract charitable

---

[165] Charity Commission RR11: *Charitable Status and Sport* (April 2003) at para. 9.

status, on the grounds that it involves bringing about a change in the law. Despite this, the Charity Commission in its guidance on the promotion of human rights in 2005 has explained that:

> Charities are able to engage in political campaigning in order to further their charitable purposes. Charity law draws a distinction between political purposes and political activities. An organisation which has purposes which include the promotion of human rights by seeking a change in the law, or a shift in government policy, or a reversal of a government decision has (at least in part) political purposes and cannot be a charity. However, the trustees of a charity may nonetheless use political means without jeopardising charitable status. What is important for charitable status is that political means should not be the dominant method by which the organisation will pursue its apparently charitable objects.[166]

With regard to the promotion of religious or racial harmony or equality and diversity, there is very little by way of case law which will aid in the interpretation of its meaning. In the past, trusts which have sought to promote religious or racial harmony have inevitably been construed as being political in nature. For example, in **Re Strakosch**[167] a testator directed that part of his residuary estate should be held by his trustees upon trust to be applied 'to a fund for any purpose which in their opinion is designed to strengthen the bonds of unity between the Union of South Africa and the Mother Country and which incidentally will conduce to the appeasement of racial feeling between the Dutch and English speaking sections of the South African community'. The Court of Appeal, whilst recognising the public benefit that may arise out of such a trust, held that the trust was not beneficial in a way the law deemed it be beneficial. In the course of his judgment, Lord Greene MR explained that 'though undoubtedly of benefit to the community the purpose under consideration is not "charitable" in the sense in the sense in which the benefits to the community instanced in the preamble are charitable'.[168] Lord Greene MR explained that a trust which has the object of bringing about a change in government policy or a change in the law of another country could not be charitable.

Section 2(2)(h) of the Charities Act 2006, which allows purposes which advance human rights, conflict resolution and equality, truly marks a change in the law on charities. Whilst the interpretation of s. 2(2)(h) by the courts will not allow purposes, which have as their main goals political objectives and activities, to adopt what the Charity Commission says is a cautionary approach, charities which seek to advance human rights and racial harmony and diversity will be allowed charitable status, providing that the political objectives are not the dominant objectives of the charity. The Charity Commission identifies the following types of charities and purposes falling into this category.

KEY CITATION

Charity Commission: *Commentary on the descriptions of charitable purposes in the Charities Act 2006* (March 2007, para. 29)

Charities concerned with the promotion of human rights, at home or abroad, such as relieving victims of human rights abuse, raising awareness of human rights issues, securing the enforcement of human rights law;

Charities concerned with the promotion of restorative justice and other forms of conflict resolution or reconciliation;

---

[166] Charity Commission RR12: *The Promotion of Human Rights* (January 2005) at para. 33.
[167] [1949] Ch. 529.
[168] [1949] Ch. 529 at 538.

Charities concerned with the resolution of national or international conflicts;

Mediation charities;

Charities promoting good relations between persons of different racial groups;

Charities promoting equality and diversity by the elimination of discrimination on the grounds of age, sex or sexual orientation;

Charities enabling people of one faith to understand the religious beliefs of others.

The advancement of environmental protection or improvement

Increasingly over the years the Charity Commission has recognised that organisations concerned with the protection of the environment deserve charitable status. The protection and improvement of the environment covers a wide range of activities relating to conservation of the natural environment. For example, organisations which protect animals, birds, wildlife, plant species, natural beauty spots and the environment generally will fall into this category. A trust to promote sustainable development will fall into this category as will trusts or organisations which promote recycling and waste management. There is very little by way of decided case law to illustrate the judicial interpretation of this category; however, the Charity Commission produced guidance in 2001 on preservation and conservation.[169] In its guidance, the Charity Commission explained that a trust to promote preservation or conservation must satisfy the criterion of merit and must be for the public benefit. With regard to the question of merit, the trust must seek to conserve and preserve something which deserves protection. Whether something deserves protection can be adduced by expert evidence: for example, in the context of the preservation of a historic building, expert evidence can be looked at to see whether the building is worthy of preservation. In the case of a listed building, production of the listing and the reasons for the listing of the building will normally be sufficient to obtain charitable status. With regard to the question of public benefit, the purposes of the trust must not be for non-charitable purposes, such as trading: rather, the benefits of the trust must be available to the public.

The relief of those in need, by reason of youth, age, ill health, disability, financial hardship or other disadvantage

Section 2(2)(j) of the Charities Act 2006 provides that a trust to provide relief of those in need by reason of youth, age, ill health, disability, financial hardship or other disadvantage will be charitable. This category, unlike some of the categories discussed above, is not entirely new but encapsulates purposes which have in the past been decided under the head of relief of poverty and under the Recreational Charities Act 1958. The existing case law decided under the relief of poverty and some of the cases decided under the Recreational Charities Act 1958 will apply in the context of this category. The Recreational Charities Act 1958 will still govern recreational facilities which are provided in the interests of social welfare, which is discussed below. In this respect many purposes falling under s. 2(2)(j) will also fall under the Recreational Charities Act 1958.[170]

---

[169] Charity Commission, RR9: *Preservation and Conservation* (February 2001).
[170] This is specifically provided for by s. 5 of the Charities Act 2006.

Under the head of relief of poverty, you will recall that the relief of poverty took its place from the preamble to the Statute of Elizabeth 1601, which spoke of the relief of the aged, impotent and poor. In *Joseph Rowntree Memorial Trust Housing Association Ltd v A-G*[171] the court held that the words 'aged, impotent and poor' were to be read disjunctively, so that a trust to provide housing for the aged was clearly within the ambit of the advancement of poverty. The facts of the case involved a charitable housing association who, along with trustees of a charitable housing trust, wished to build dwellings especially for the elderly. The scheme, which was put forward by the association involved the elderly paying a capital sum in return for a long lease of the dwellings, in addition to the service charge. The Charity Commission refused to register the scheme as being charitable, on the grounds that the scheme was based on contract: that is, the payment of money for the dwellings. Additionally, the dwellings were available to private individuals only and the association was making a profit. The question before the court was whether the purposes of the housing association were charitable. Peter Gibson J held that the purposes of the housing association were charitable, on the grounds that they relieved the needs of a particular group of people, namely the elderly, who needed the facilities by reason of their age. In interpreting the words 'aged, impotent and poor' Peter Gibson explained that:

> first, the words 'aged, impotent and poor' must be read disjunctively. It would be as absurd to require that the aged must be impotent or poor as it would be to require the impotent to be aged or poor, or the poor to be aged or impotent. There will no doubt be many cases where the objects of charity prove to have two or more of the three qualities at the same time. Second, essential to the charitable purpose is that it should relieve aged, impotent and poor people. The word 'relief' implies that the persons in question have a need attributable to their condition as aged, impotent or poor persons which requires alleviating and which those persons could not alleviate, or would find difficulty in alleviating, themselves from their own resources. The word 'relief' is not synonymous with 'benefit'.[172]

The types of purposes falling into this category include, for example, purposes which provide for the care of children in children's homes. Although, prior to the enactment of the Charities Act 2006, an organisation such as the National Society for the Prevention of Cruelty to Children was clearly charitable, there remained some decisions of the courts which doubted whether a trust for the general welfare of children was charitable. One decision which remained controversial was that of the Court of Appeal in *Re Cole*[173] where a testator left property to be used for the general benefit and general welfare of children at a children's home run by a council. Without any further limitation on the gift, Romer LJ held that the gift could not be charitable as it could be used for purposes which were not charitable within the spirit of the preamble to the Statute of Elizabeth I 1601. Of particular concern to Romer LJ was that the money could be used to provide benefits which were not of a charitable nature. For example, in the course of his judgment, Romer LJ explained that 'I cannot regard the provision of television sets, etc., for the benefit of such persons as juvenile delinquents and refractory children in Southdown House as coming within any conception of charity which is to be found in the preamble.'[174] It is not altogether clear why the provision of a television set for delinquent children should necessarily not be within the spirit of charity. The very reason why the children may be

---

[171] [1983] Ch. 159.
[172] [1983] Ch. 159 at 171.
[173] [1958] Ch. 877.
[174] *Ibid.*

in the state they are in is because of their upbringing. In this respect there is much to be said for the dissenting judgement of Evershed MR who commented that 'the care and upbringing of children, who for any reason have not got the advantage or opportunity of being looked after and brought up by responsible and competent persons, or who could, for these or other reasons, properly be regarded as defenceless or "deprived", are matters which prima facie qualify as charitable purposes'.[175] The decision in *Re Cole*[176] no longer holds any weight by virtue of s. 2(2)(k) which clearly provides for the relief of persons in need by reason of youth as well as other disadvantages.

The advancement of animal welfare

Section 2(2)(k) provides that purposes which advance animal welfare are charitable. Formerly, purposes promoting the welfare of animals were decided under the fourth head of Pemsel's case,[177] that is, other purposes beneficial to the community. It has long been recognised that a trust which promotes the welfare of animals in general is charitable. The leading case is *Re Wedgwood*[178] where a testatrix left property on secret trust for the protection and benefit of animals in general. The Court of Appeal held that the trust was charitable in nature. In the course of his judgment Swinfen Eady LJ explained that:

> a gift for the benefit and protection of animals tends to promote and encourage kindness towards them, to discourage cruelty, and to ameliorate the condition of the brute creation, and thus to stimulate humane and generous sentiments in man towards the lower animals, and by these means promote feelings of humanity and morality generally, repress brutality, and thus elevate the human race. That such purposes are eminently charitable, in the accepted legal sense of that term, is amply established by the cases . . .[179]

A trust for the advancement of animal welfare must demonstrate that it does in fact advance the welfare of animals. If the purpose of the trust is to merely protect animals from the human race by providing a sanctuary which does not within itself seek to protect the welfare of the animals, the trust will not be charitable. The matter is neatly illustrated by the decision of the Court of Appeal in *Re Grove-Grady*[180] where a lady left her residuary estate upon trust to purchase land and establish the 'Beaumont Animals Benevolent Society'. The objects of the Society were to provide 'a refuge of refuges for the preservation of all animals, bird or other creatures not human . . . and so that all such animals, birds or other creatures not human shall there be safe from molestation or destruction by man . . .' The Court of Appeal held that this trust to provide a sanctuary was not charitable, on the grounds that it was not for the public benefit. Whilst the Court of Appeal acknowledged that a trust to provide a sanctuary was capable of being a charity, as for example the protection of some endangered species,[181] the facts of the present case failed to show what benefit could be achieved from a sanctuary in which animals were left to defend for themselves. In the course of his judgment, Lord Hanworth MR explained that:

---

[175] [1958] Ch. 877 at 892.

[176] [1958] Ch. 877.

[177] *Commissioners for Special Purposes of Income Tax* v *Pemsel* [1891] AC 531.

[178] [1915] 1 Ch. 113.

[179] [1915] 1 Ch. 113 at 122. See also *Re Green's Will Trust* [1985] 3 All ER 455.

[180] [1929] 1 Ch. 557.

[181] A purpose which would also fit into the category of the advancement of environment protection or improvement under s. 2(2)(i) Charities Act 2006.

in this proposed refuge all creatures are to find freedom and safety from molestation or destruction by man . . . It is not a sanctuary for any animals of a timid nature whose species is in danger of dying out: nor is it a sanctuary for birds which have almost entirely left our shores and may be attracted once more by a safe seclusion to nest and rear their young. No such purpose is indicated, nor indeed possible. The one characteristic of the refuge is that it is free from the molestation of man, while all the fauna within it are to be free to molest and harry one another. Such a purpose does not, in my opinion, afford any advantage to animals that are useful to mankind in particular, or any protection from cruelty to animals generally. It does not denote any elevating lesson to mankind.[182]

APPLYING THE LAW

For most of her life Sarah had been a strong campaigner for the protection and welfare of animals. In her will, she left property to trustees to build a sanctuary for animals suffering from cruelty. Additionally her will directed trustees to campaign against cruelty to animals.

Is this a charitable trust?

The decision in **Re Grove-Grady** illustrates that the objects of a trust to promote the advancement of animal welfare must indeed promote animal welfare, which in turn, is for the general benefit of mankind. One line of cases, which have in the past proved to controversial, are those concerned with anti-vivisection. Is a trust to prevent the vivisection of animals charitable on the grounds that it advances the welfare of animals? In **Re Foveaux**[183] a lady gave her residuary estate to her executors with a power to apply the estate in favour of a number of organisations concerned with the suppression of anti-vivisection, that is, the use of animals for medical and scientific research. The executors gave some of the estate to the International Society for the Total Suppression of Anti-Vivisection and the London Anti-Vivisection Society. The question before Chitty J was whether the gifts to these societies were gifts to charitable purposes. Chitty J held that a gift to a society whose objects were to prevent antivivisection was a gift for a charitable purpose. In the course of his judgment the judge explained that:

> if a society for the prevention of cruelty to animals is a charitable society, it would seem to follow that an institution for the prevention of a particular form of cruelty to animals is also charitable . . . Cruelty is degrading to man; and a society for the suppression of cruelty to the lower animals, whether domestic or not, has for its object, not merely the protection of the animals themselves, but the advancement of morals and education among men. The purpose of these societies, whether they are right or wrong in the opinions they hold, is charitable in the legal sense of the term.[184]

The decision in **Re Foveaux**[185] was, however, overruled in the later decision of the House of Lords in **National Anti-Vivisection Society v IRC**[186] which concerned the question whether the National Anti-Vivisection Society whose objects were the total suppression

---

[182] [1929] 1 Ch. 557 at 573.
[183] [1895] 2 Ch. 501.
[184] [1895] 2 Ch. 501 at 507.
[185] [1895] 2 Ch. 501.
[186] [1948] AC 31.

of anti-vivisection was charitable. The House of Lords held that the objects of the Society were not charitable. Two reasons were given by the House of Lords in coming to this conclusion. Firstly, it was held that the benefits to the public in carrying out research by experimenting on animals outweighed the harm that was caused to the animals used in such experiments. Secondly, it was held that, because the objects of the Society were to bring about a change in the law, the Society's objects were political and therefore could not be deemed to be charitable. This second grounds for refusing charitable status is examined in much more detail later in this chapter. For the time being, emphasis is placed on the argument in the House of Lords that the benefits of vivisection outweighed the harm caused to animals used in the process. In the course of this judgment Lord Wright commented that:

> it is impossible to apply the word cruelty to efforts of the high-minded scientists who have devoted themselves to vivisection experiments for the purpose of alleviating human suffering . . . But I put against that the benefit to humanity . . . The scientist who inflicts pain in the course of vivisection is fulfilling a moral duty to mankind which is higher in degree than the moralist or sentimentalist who thinks only of the animals. Nor do I agree that animals ought not to be sacrificed to man when necessary. A strictly regulated amount of pain to some hundreds of animals may save and avert incalculable suffering to innumerable millions of mankind. I cannot doubt what the moral choice should be.[187]

It remains interesting to see how the decision of the House of Lords in **National Anti-Vivisection Society v IRC**[188] is affected, if at all, by the statutory recognition in s. 2(2)(k) of trusts, which advance animal welfare as being charitable in nature. For the time being, the decision in **National Anti-Vivisection Society v IRC** remains good law.

Finally, although a trust for the advancement of animal welfare will be held to be charitable, if the objects of the trust involve political objects, it will be denied charitable status. This has been recently illustrated by the decision in **Hanchett-Stamford v Attorney General**[189] the facts of the case involved an association founded sometime in 1914 called the 'The Performing and Captive Animals Defence League' (the League hereafter). Although the League had a formal constitution at the beginning, that constitution had been lost and since 1934 the affairs of the League were conducted by a Director appointed by the members of the League. Although it was very difficult to ascertain the exact purposes of the League, it became evident from a booklet produced for members in 1962 that the objects of the League were to prevent cruelty to animals used in film productions and shows. Thus many of the activities of the League involved preventing travelling circuses and municipal zoos. According to the 1962 booklet the league had two types of members: life members and annual members. At that time there were approximately 250 members and the funds of the League were contributed by gifts and legacies which were duly invested. Towards the end of the 1970s the activities of the League slowed down, owing to a decline in the number of travelling circuses. From then onwards the assets of the league were vested in a Mr Hanchett-Stamford who had been an active member of the League and who had worked with a leading vet, Dr Bill Jordan, in educating people about animal welfare. In the early 1990s some of the funds of the League were used to purchase a property which at the time of the case was valued at around £675,000. Title to the property was taken in the name of Mr Hanchett-Stamford and

---

[187] [1948] AC 31 at 48.
[188] [1948] AC 31.
[189] [2009] Ch. 173. See S. Panesar, 'Surplus Funds and Unincorporated Associations' *Trusts and Trustees*, Vol. 14 Issue 10 (2008) 698.

another member, both of whom had since died. The property had been occupied by Mrs Hanchett-Stamford until recently when she was moved to a nursing home. In addition to the property, the League also had funds worth some £1.77 million in the form of stocks and shares. In the 1990s the League stopped maintaining records of its members and, on the advice of the accountant, it was decided that the funds of the League be wound up. Mr and Mrs Hanchett, the only surviving members, decided that the funds should be donated to the 'Born Free Charity' whose objects included the welfare of animals. However, Mr Hanchett died and the question before the Court was whether Mrs Hanchett was in a position to give the surplus funds of the League to the Born Free Charity. She could only do this if she was entitled to exercise ownership of the funds and therefore transfer them to the charity. One of the questions before the court was whether the objects of the League were charitable.

Lewison J held that the purposes and objects of the League prevented it from being a charity. He explained that the purposes of the society were to bring about a change in the law and that as a result of the House of Lords' decision in *National Anti-Vivisection Society v IRC*[190] a trust with purposes intended to bring about a change in the law could not be charitable.

> Looking at the statement of the League's objectives there can be little doubt, in my judgment, that at least one of its significant purposes was to change the law. It is true that it asserted that the particular acts of cruelty against which it was campaigning were already illegal as a result of the Prevention of Cruelty to Animals Act 1911, but plainly its founders considered that that Act was not enough and that more legislation was needed. It seems probable that the members of the League had a wider conception of cruelty than the law did. The booklet also asserted that it was impossible to train any performing animal without cruelty and it is clear, in my judgment, that the League's aim was to ban performing animals completely (hence the reference to 'just compensation to the trade'). This would undoubtedly represent a change in the law just as much as banning fox-hunting or the farming of mink. In my judgment this has the consequence that at its inception the League was not a charitable organisation.[191]

The promotion of the efficiency of the armed forces of the Crown

Section 2(2)(l) of the Charities Act 2006 provides that a trust to promote the efficiency of the armed forces of the Crown, of the efficiency of the police, fire and rescue services or ambulance services is charitable in nature. It has already been observed above that a trust to provide sporting facilities to a regiment will be deemed as being charitable in nature.[192] This category includes a wide range of purposes which improve the fitness of members of a particular service, recruiting new members, increasing technical know-how, as well as providing specialist equipment to deal with emergency situations. The key element in this category is the promotion of efficiency of the armed forces and so forth. A trust which does not promote efficiency will not be deemed charitable in nature. For example, in *IRC v City of Glasgow Police Athletic Association*[193] it was held by the House of Lords that an athletic association whose objects were to provide sporting and recreational and past time facilities in the form of a sports club was not charitable.

---

[190] [1948] AC 31.
[191] [2008] EWHC 330 (Ch.).
[192] *Re Gray* [1925] Ch. 362.
[193] [1953] AC 380.

Although the decision in **IRC v City of Glasgow Police** will not be deemed to be charitable on the grounds of improving the efficiency of the police force, the decision will have to be considered in the light of s. 2(2)(g), which provides that a trust to advance amateur sport will be charitable in nature.

Any other purposes

The final category of charity to be listed in s. 2 of the Charities Act is 'any other purposes' within subsection 4 of s. 2.

KEY STATUTE

S. 2(4) Charities Act 2006

(4) The purposes within this subsection (see subsection (2)(m)) are –

(a) any purposes not within paragraphs (a) to (l) of subsection (2) but recognised as charitable purposes under existing charity law or by virtue of section 1 of the Recreational Charities Act 1958 (c. 17);

(b) any purposes that may reasonably be regarded as analogous to, or within the spirit of, any purposes falling within any of those paragraphs or paragraph (a) above; and

(c) any purposes that may reasonably be regarded as analogous to, or within the spirit of, any purposes which have been recognised under charity law as falling within paragraph (b) above or this paragraph.

This final category of charity at first instance looks very similar to the fourth head of charity as once identified by Lord Macnaghten in Pemsel's case,[194] namely, 'other purposes beneficial to the community'. However, despite the obvious similarity in that it appears to suggest that it is a catch-all category for purposes which do not fit into any of the preceding twelve heads of charity, it remains to be seen how it will be interpreted by the courts and the Charity Commission. Subsection 4 of s. 2 of the Act gives specific guidance as to how it should be applied. Firstly, subsection 4 makes it clear that any purpose which is not within the preceding 12 heads in s. 2 of the Act will nevertheless be deemed charitable if that purpose has already been held to be charitable in law. Most notably purposes which have been deemed to be charitable under the Recreational Charities Act 1958 will be charitable and, indeed, s. 5 of the Charities Act makes it clear that purposes falling under Recreational Charities Act will also fall under the heading of the advancement of amateur sport in s. 2(2)(g) of the Charities Act 2006.

The second key feature of s. 2(4) of the Charities Act 2006 is that it allows in s. 2(4)(b) for purposes, which are analogous and within the spirit of the existing heads of charity, in s. 2 of the Act to be recognised. Additionally, s. 2(4)(c) allows purposes that may reasonably be regarded as analogous to, or within the spirit of, any purposes which have been recognised under charity law as being charitable. The net effect of s. 2(4) is to consolidate the existing law by providing that charitable purposes not falling within s. 2(2)(a)–(l) are charitable in nature. In this respect, although, s. 2(2)(m) provides for 'any other purpose', given the fact that the old law is not repealed, the fourth head in Pemsel's case[195] is not changed. Although many of the purpose decided under the fourth

---

[194] *Commissioners for Special Purposes of Income Tax v Pemsel* [1891] AC 531.
[195] *Commissioners for Special Purposes of Income Tax v Pemsel* [1891] AC 531.

head, that is, 'other purposes beneficial to the community' will now fall under many of the new heads identified in s. 2 of the Charities Act 2006, it does not mean that the category has been eradicated. Furthermore, the section leaves room for new purposes to be accepted as charitable by reference to the spirit of s. 2 of the Act in addition to analogous purposes to those within s. 2 of the Act, as well as those decided under charity law.

One of the more interesting questions which arises from s. 2(4) of the Charities Act 2006 is: what approach will a court take when deciding whether a new purpose is to be accepted as being charitable? Clearly, the guidance in s. 2(4) is that the purpose should be within the spirit of the Charities Act 2006. Also the court may decide the matter by way of making analogies with purposes within s. 2 of the Act. Additionally, the court can make analogies and follow the approach taken under the existing cases decided. In this respect, the decision in *Incorporated Council of Law Reporting for England and Wales* v *A-G*[196] remains unchanged by the Charities Act 2006. You will recall from the earlier discussion in this chapter that the question before the Court of Appeal was whether a company limited by guarantee with the object of producing law reports was charitable. One of the main issues before the Court was whether the production of law reports sold at a price to professional persons in order to carry out their profession could be charitable. It was argued that this purpose was not within the spirit and intendment of the preamble of 1601. In holding that the production of law reports was charitable under the fourth head of Pemsel's case, Lord Russell LJ explained that if 'a purpose is shown to be so beneficial or of such utility it is prima facie charitable in law . . . [and] the proper question to ask is whether there are any grounds for holding it to be outside the equity of the Statute'.[197] Russell LJ explained that the production of a comprehensive and complete set of law reports was in the interests of the public and certainly in the interests of the government in ensuring the due administration of law. In the course of his judgment, Russell LJ criticised the approach by analogy with the preamble, which he described, 'to be too narrow or refined an approach'.[198]

The approach adopted by Russell LJ in *Incorporated Council of Law Reporting for England and Wales* v *A-G*[199] has been subsequently approved by the Privy Council, in particular, in the judgment of Lord Browne-Wilkinson who commented that 'Russell L.J.'s approach has much to commend it in deciding whether or not a purpose specified by the donor falls within the spirit and intendment of the preamble to the Statute of Elizabeth I . . .'[200] Earlier in this chapter it was questioned, whether after the enactment of the Charities Act 2006, the approach adopted by Russell LJ remains an appropriate test to establish whether a purpose is indeed charitable. Can a court simply proceed to assume that where a trust is beneficial to the community it should be deemed to be charitable unless there are other reasons why it should not be charitable? The answer to this question may be purely one of interpretation of s. 2(4) of the Charities Act 2006. If s. 2(4) is interpreted quite liberally, thereby giving effect to the fourth head of Pemsel's case, that is, other purposes beneficial to the community, there is no reason why the decision in *Incorporated Council of Law Reporting for England and Wales* v *A-G*, which was decided under the fourth head, should not remain good law. The view taken in this text is that 'any other purposes beneficial to the community' as interpreted by the courts before the enactment of the Charities Act 2006 continues to remain a category of charity

---

[196] [1972] Ch. 73.
[197] [1972] Ch. 73 at 88.
[198] [1972] Ch. 73 at 88.
[199] [1972] Ch. 73.
[200] *A-G of the Cayman Islands* v *Wahr-Hansen* [2001] 1 AC 75 at 82.

in its own right. In other words, the courts can follow the approach adopted under the old law in addition to the thirteen heads under s. 2(2) of the Charities Act 2006. To suggest that the approach in *Incorporated Council of Law Reporting for England and Wales* v *A-G* has been removed by the Charities Act 2006 would produce a rather strange and restricted definition of charity, which would not allow new purposes to be admitted into the category of charity because of an insufficient analogy between existing ones. This would then leave it up to Parliament to enact further legislation to expand the definition of charity.

 ## Recreational charities

Before the enactment of the Charities Act 2006, trusts which sought to promote recreational facilities were governed by two distinct principles. Firstly, as explained above, if recreational facilities were provided in the context of education then they could be seen as advancing education.[201] Additionally, if recreational facilities were provided so as to improve, for example, the efficiency of the armed forces they could be deemed to be charitable under the fourth head of Pemsel's case,[202] that is, other purposes beneficial to the community.[203]

Secondly, recreational facilities could be regarded as charitable if they were caught by the Recreational Charities Act 1958. The 1958 Act was enacted primarily as a result of the decision of the House of Lords in *IRC* v *Baddeley*[204] where land was conveyed to a Methodist Mission with the instruction that:

> the trustees shall permit the said property to be appropriated and used by the leaders for the time being of the Stratford Newtown Methodist Mission for the promotion of the religious social and physical well-being of persons resident in the County Boroughs of West Ham and Leyton . . . by the provision of facilities for religious services and instruction and for the social and physical training and recreation of such aforementioned persons who for the time being are in the opinion of such leaders members or likely to become members of the Methodist Church and of insufficient means otherwise to enjoy the advantages provided by these presents and by the provision of facilities for religious social and physical training and recreation and by promoting and encouraging all forms of such activities as are calculated to contribute to the health and well-being of such persons . . .

The question before the House of Lords was whether this created a valid charitable trust. The House of Lords held by a majority four to one that this was not a valid charitable trust. There appear to be two principal reasons why the trust was not held to be charitable. In the first place, the House of Lords explained that the inclusion of social purposes was not within the definition of charity. Viscount Simonds explained that 'the moral, social and physical well-being of the community or any part of it is a laudable object of benevolence and philanthropy, but its ambit is far too wide to include only purposes which the law regards as charitable'.[205] The second reason why the trust in *IRC* v *Baddeley* was not held to be charitable was that it did not satisfy the public benefit test. It will be seen below that, in addition to falling within the definition of charity, a trust must be for the benefit of the public or a sufficiently important section of the public. The

---

[201] *IRC* v *McMullen* [1981] AC 1.
[202] *Commissioners for Special Purposes of Income Tax* v *Pemsel* [1891] AC 531.
[203] See, for example, *Re Gray* [1925] Ch. 362.
[204] [1955] AC 572.
[205] [1955] AC 572 at 589.

House of Lords held that Methodists in the West Ham and Leyton were not a section of the public or a sufficiently important section of the public. In the course of his judgment, Viscount Simonds explained that it was important to distinguish between 'a form of relief extended to the whole community yet by its very nature advantageous only to the few and a form of relief accorded to a selected few out of a larger number equally willing and able to take advantage of it'.[206] In the opinion of the majority the trust in **IRC v Baddeley**[207] was beneficial to a class within a class, and therefore, did not demonstrate a sufficient public benefit.

The decision of the House of Lords in **IRC v Baddeley**, which endorsed an earlier decision of the House of Lords in **Williams' Trustee v IRC**[208] where it was held that a trust to promote the interests of Welsh people living in London was not charitable on the grounds that the Welsh people in London were not a sufficient section of the public, gave rise to serious uncertainty about the charitable nature of certain village halls, women's institutes and other similar organisations. In order to resolve the uncertainty, the Recreational Charities Act 1958 was enacted.

KEY STATUTE

S. 1 of the Recreational Charities Act 1958 (General provision as to recreational and similar trusts, etc.)

(1) Subject to the provisions of this Act, it shall be and be deemed always to have been charitable to provide, or assist in the provision of, facilities for recreation or other leisure-time occupation, if the facilities are provided in the interests of social welfare:

Provided that nothing in this section shall be taken to derogate from the principle that a trust or institution to be charitable must be for the public benefit.

(2) The requirement in subsection (1) that the facilities are provided in the interests of social welfare cannot be satisfied if the basic conditions are not met.

(2A) The basic conditions are –

(a) that the facilities are provided with the object of improving the conditions of life for the persons for whom the facilities are primarily intended; and

(b) that either –

(i) those persons have need of the facilities by reason of their youth, age, infirmity or disability, poverty, or social and economic circumstances, or

(ii) the facilities are to be available to members of the public at large or to male, or to female, members of the public at large.

(3) Subject to the said requirement, subsection (1) of this section applies in particular to the provision of facilities at village halls, community centres and women's institutes, and to the provision and maintenance of grounds and buildings to be used for purposes of recreation or leisure-time occupation, and extends to the provision of facilities for those purposes by the organising of any activity.

The central feature of the Recreational Charities Act 1958 is that recreational and leisure-time facilities will be deemed to be charitable if they are provided in the 'interests of social welfare'. In addition to social welfare, the trust must be for the benefit of the

---

[206] [1955] AC 572 at 592.
[207] [1955] AC 572.
[208] [1947] AC 447.

public, and in this respect the Act does not affect the decisions *IRC v Baddeley*[209] and *Williams' Trustees v IRC*,[210] where the beneficiaries of the trust were deemed to be a class within a class. What is, however, important under s. 1 of the 1958 Act is the meaning of 'interests of social welfare'. When are recreational and other leisure-time facilities provided in the interests of social welfare? Section 2(a) of the 1958 Act states that facilities are provided in the interests of social welfare when they are provided with the object of improving the conditions of life of the persons for whom they are intended. Furthermore, those persons have need of the facilities by reason of their youth, age, infirmity or disability, poverty, or social and economic circumstances, or the facilities are to be available to members of the public at large or to male, or female, members of the public at large. In *IRC v McMullen*[211] the Court of Appeal took the view that a trust to promote the playing of football in schools was not a facility provided in the interests of social welfare because it was not designed to improve the conditions of life of children playing football. In *IRC v McMullen* the House of Lords held that a trust to promote playing football fell under the head of advancement of education and, therefore, did not consider the meaning of social welfare for the purposes of the Recreational Charities Act 1958. This did, therefore, leave open the question whether a trust with recreational objectives had to be provided for persons suffering some social disadvantage or deprivation.

The opportunity to put light on the meaning of 'social welfare' and 'improving the conditions of life persons' presented itself to the House of Lords in *Guild v IRC*.[212] The facts of this case concerned a gift made by a testator to North Berwick Town Council 'for . . . use in connection with the Sports Centre in North Berwick or some similar purpose in connection with sport . . .' In the context of a tax issue, the question before the House of Lords was whether this gift was charitable. The leading judgment was delivered by Lord Keith, who held that this created a valid charitable gift within s. 1 of the Recreational Charities Act 1958. In the course of his judgment, his Lordship explained that he did not consider that:

> the reference to social welfare in subsection (1) can properly be held to colour subsection (2)(a) to the effect that the persons for whom the facilities are primarily intended must be confined to those persons who suffer from some form of social deprivation . . . If it suffices that the facilities are to be available to the members of the public at large, as sub-paragraph (ii) provides, it must necessarily be inferred that the persons for whom the facilities are primarily intended are not to be confined to those who have need of them by reason of one of the forms of social deprivation mentioned in sub-paragraph (i) . . . The fact is that persons in all walks of life and all kinds of social circumstances may have their conditions of life improved by the provision of recreational facilities of suitable character.[213]

Therefore, a recreational trust which is intended to promote the welfare of persons in the community in general will be held to be charitable. Recreational charities are now within the general definition of charity found in the Charities Act 2011.

 ## Public benefit

As well as falling into one of the recognised categories of charity under s. 2 of the Charities Act 2006, a charitable trust or charitable purpose must be for the benefit of the

---

[209] [1955] AC 572.
[210] [1947] AC 447.
[211] [1979] 1 WLR 130.
[212] [1992] 2 AC 310. See H. Norman, 'Sporting Charities – Social Welfare Defined' (1992) Conv. 361.
[213] [1992] 2 AC 310 at 322.

public or a sufficiently important section of the public. The public benefit requirement has undergone some changes as a result of the enactment of the Charities Act 2006.[214] The public benefit test is found in s. 3 of the Act. Section 3(3) preserves the existing law governing the definition of public benefit; however, unlike the position before the Act, there is no longer a presumption that trusts for the relief or prevention of poverty, or the advancement of education and religion are for the public benefit.[215] Instead, such trusts must demonstrate that the public do indeed benefit from the trust. Furthermore, the Charity Commission has explained that the public benefit must be determined in light of modern social conditions.[216] This is to reflect economic and social changes, and whilst the courts are not dictated by public opinion, they can have regard to public opinion in deciding whether a particular purpose is for the public benefit or not. The courts have in the past shown that changes in society will influence their decisions. For example, at one time it was thought that a trust to promote faith healing was not charitable;[217] however, 70 years later the court held that such a trust was charitable, given changes in public opinion which regarded faith healing as a genuine activity of public benefit.

KEY STATUTE

S. 3 of the Charities Act 2006 (The 'public benefit' test)

(1) This section applies in connection with the requirement in section 2(1)(b) that a purpose falling within section 2(2) must be for the public benefit if it is to be a charitable purpose.

(2) In determining whether that requirement is satisfied in relation to any such purpose, it is not to be presumed that a purpose of a particular description is for the public benefit.

(3) In this Part any reference to the public benefit is a reference to the public benefit as that term is understood for the purposes of the law relating to charities in England and Wales.

(4) Subsection (3) applies subject to subsection (2).

The public benefit principles: principle 1 – identifiable benefit

In its most recent guidance on public benefit and charities the Charity Commission identified two principles relating to public benefit.[218] These are:

1 There must be an identifiable benefit or benefits

2 Benefit must be to the public, or a section of the public.

---

[214] The latest guidance on public benefit was issued by the Charity Commission in December 2008. See Charity Commission, *Analysis of the Law Underpinning Charities and Public Benefit*, December 2008.

[215] See, however, J. Hackney, 'Charities and Public Benefit' (2008) LQR 347, who explains that it is questionable whether the courts ever presumed trusts for the relief of poverty or trusts for the advancement of education or religion as being charitable. Instead, he argues that it was an unchallengeable assumption rather than a presumption that such trusts were charitable.

[216] Charity Commission, *Analysis of the Law Underpinning Charities and Public Benefit*, December 2008 at p. 6.

[217] *Re Hummeltenburg* [1923] 1 Ch. 237.

[218] Charity Commission, *Analysis of the Law Underpinning Charities and Public Benefit*, December 2008 at p. 9.

The first principle is that there must be an identifiable benefit or benefits. There are a number of sub-principles to this principle. In the first place, in order to satisfy the test of public benefit, a purpose must be beneficial in a manner recognised by law. This is no more than saying that the benefit to the public must be a benefit recognised in law: for example, benefiting in an educational way, benefiting in a religious way, benefiting the armed forces and so forth. It has already been mentioned above that the new law makes no presumption that a trust to relieve poverty, or a trust to advance education or religion is for the public benefit. Instead, in each of these categories, as well as the other categories in s. 2(2) of the Charities Act 2006, the benefit to the public must be capable of proof, by evidence where necessary. For example, a trust for the advancement of education must demonstrate what educational benefits arise from the trust. In order to establish the public benefits arising from the trust, the court is able to consult expert opinion to help decide the matter.[219] However, it is not always necessary for the public benefit to be demonstrated as a matter of fact. The reason for this is that the benefit may be so apparent that it goes without saying that the purpose is for the public benefit. The matter is neatly illustrated by the decision in *Incorporated Council of Law Reporting for England and Wales v A-G*[220] where, you will recall from the earlier discussion, the court was asked whether a company limited by guarantee and producing law reports of the decisions of the courts in England and Wales was charitable. The Court of Appeal held that the production of law reports by the Incorporated Council of Law Reporting for England and Wales was charitable, on the grounds that it was disseminating important educational materials for the study of law. In the course of his judgment Russell LJ explained that:

> there are some matters which require no proof . . . It cannot be doubted that dissemination by publication of accurate copies of statutory enactments is beneficial to the community as a whole: and this is not the less so because at least in many instances the ordinary member of the public either does not attempt to, or cannot by study, arrive at a true conclusion of their import, or because the true understanding is largely limited to persons engaged professionally or as public servants in the field of any particular enactment, or otherwise interested in that field.[221]

Connected to the first principle that a trust must have identifiable benefits, it is important that the benefits must be related to the aims. Where the benefits are merely incidental, they will not count as being for the public benefit thereby rendering a trust or other purpose charitable. There must be a real connection between the charitable purpose and the benefits derived thereunder. For example, a trust to advance education of children living in a particular area is clearly charitable. The benefits to the public flow directly from the trust whose purpose is to promote education. On the other hand, where the benefits are merely accidental or adventitious, then there can be no room for the argument that the trust is for the public benefit. The matter was explored by the House of Lords in *Oppenheim v Tobacco Securities Trust Co Ltd*[222] where a testator left securities to be

---

[219] See, for example, *Re Pinion* [1965] Ch. 85 where the court consulted expert opinion to establish whether a trust to promote the 'artistic collections' of a testator was indeed the advancement of art for the public benefit. Harman J, having consulted expert opinion, held that he could not see any useful object 'in foisting upon the public this mass of junk', at 107.

[220] [1972] Ch. 73.

[221] [1972] Ch. 73 at 86.

[222] [1951] AC 297.

invested and held upon trust for providing 'for . . . the education of children of employees or former employees' of British American Tobacco or any of its subsidiary or allied companies. The company employed over 110,000 employees and the question before the House of Lords was whether the trust was for the advancement of education. The House of Lords held that, although the trust was clearly within the definition of advancement of education, it was not for the benefit of the public as understood by charity law. In particular, the House of Lords held that the beneficiaries were not a section of the public, but rather connected to the testator by reason of employment in British American Tobacco. In this respect the House of Lords explained that there was a 'personal nexus' between the testator and the beneficiaries (this matter is explored in more detail below). One of the arguments put before the Court was that, even though the trust was not for the public benefit, there were wider benefits flowing from the trust in that it educated a large class of individuals. This argument was rejected by Lord Normand who explained that '[i]f there is no public element to be found in the bare nexus of common employment all attempts to build up the public element out of circumstances which have no necessary relation with it but are adventitious, accidental and variable must be unavailing when the truster has chosen to define the selected class solely by the attribute of common employment'.[223]

Finally, in respect to identifiable benefit or benefits, the Charity Commission in its guidance has confirmed the position in the decided case law that the benefits must be balanced against any detriment or harm.[224] For example, as observed earlier in this chapter, one of the questions before the House of Lords in *National Anti-Vivisection Society v IRC*[225] was whether a gift to an antivivisection society was charitable. In the House of Lords, Lord Wright held that the benefits from vivisection outweighed the harm caused to animals used in the process.[226]

The public benefit principles: principle 2 – benefit must be to the public, or a section of the public

The second principle identified by the Charity Commission in its guidance on public benefit is that the benefit must be to the public, or a section of the public.[227] This second principle has a number of manifestations to it:

- the beneficiaries must be appropriate to the purpose;
- where the benefit is to a section of the public, the opportunity to benefit must not be unreasonably restricted;
- people in poverty must not be excluded from the opportunity to benefit;
- private benefits must be incidental.

These aspects are considered in more detail in the following sections.

---

[223] [1951] AC 297 at 310.
[224] Charity Commission, *Analysis of the Law Underpinning Charities and Public Benefit*, December 2008 at p. 15.
[225] [1948] AC 31.
[226] [1948] AC 31 at 48.
[227] Charity Commission, *Analysis of the Law Underpinning Charities and Public Benefit*, December 2008 at p. 16.

The nature of the public benefit test

It is a requirement that the beneficiaries of a charitable trust are the public or an important section of the public. This matter has been well settled in the decided case law. For example, in **Verge v Sommerville**[228] Lord Wrenbury commented that 'to ascertain whether a gift constitutes a valid charitable trust so as to escape being void on the ground of perpetuity, a first inquiry must be whether it is public – whether it is for the benefit of the community or of an appreciably important class of the community. The inhabitants of a parish or town, or any particular class of such inhabitants, may, for instance, be the objects of such a gift, but private individuals, or a fluctuating body of private individuals, cannot.'[229] Although the benefits of a charitable trust must be available to the public or a sufficiently important section of the public, it is no bar to the validity of the trust that the benefits are available only to a few by reason of their need. For example, a trust for the benefit of the blind people in Coventry is charitable even though there may be just one blind person in Coventry who benefits from the trust. The fact is that the trust is available to the blind people in Coventry. On the other hand, as will be observed below, a trust for the education of the children of the employees of a university will not be charitable. The trust is not for the benefit of the public or a sufficiently large section of the public because it is confined to a particular group connected with private individuals employed by the university.

What is also clear from the decided case law is that the test of public benefit is not necessarily applied in a uniform manner across the range of charitable purposes. It may well be that, what is a sufficient section of the public for the purposes of the advancement of education may not be for the purposes of advancement of religion. With regard to the relief of poverty, it will be seen that the public benefit test has been reduced to a minimal requirement.[230] The matter is neatly explained by Lord Simonds in **Gilmour v Coats**[231] where the question before the House of Lords was whether a trust of money for the benefit of a group of cloistered nuns who dedicated their lives to prayer was charitable. The House of Lords held that the trust was not for the public benefit, on the grounds that the nuns had dedicated their lives to prayer in cloistered conditions. Prayers said in cloistered conditions were not susceptible to proof and therefore were not for the public benefit. In the course of his judgment, Lord Simonds, however, explained that 'it would not, therefore, be surprising to find that, while in every category of legal charity some element of public benefit must be present, the court had not adopted the same measure in regard to different categories, but had accepted one standard in regard to those gifts which are alleged to be for the advancement of education and another for those which are alleged to be for the advancement of religion, and it may be yet another in regard to the relief of poverty'.[232] Although prayers said in private are not charitable, prayers said in public at a place of worship are charitable, regardless of how many people actually attend the place of worship.[233] In **Neville Estates v Madden**[234] a trust for the benefit of members of a synagogue was held to be charitable even though it benefited only a small number of members.

---

[228] [1924] AC 496.

[229] [1924] AC 496 at 499.

[230] Although it remains to be seen how far the poverty cases, which are discussed below, survive after the Charities Act 2006.

[231] [1949] AC 426.

[232] [1949] AC 426 at 449.

[233] See, for example, *Re Hetherington* [1990] Ch. 1.

[234] [1962] Ch. 832.

Class within a class

A trust which benefits a class within a class cannot be held to be for the public benefit. The two leading cases which illustrate this point of law are *IRC v Baddeley*[235] and *Williams' Trustee v IRC*.[236] You will recall that in *IRC v Baddeley*[237] land was conveyed to a Methodist Mission for various social and recreational purposes. The question before the House of Lords was whether this created a valid charitable trust. The House of Lords held by a majority of four to one that it was not. The House of Lords explained that the trust did not satisfy the public benefit test, principally on the grounds that Methodists in the West Ham and Leyton were not a section of the public or a sufficiently important section of the public. In the course of his judgment, Viscount Simonds explained that it was important to distinguish between 'a form of relief extended to the whole community yet by its very nature advantageous only to the few and a form of relief accorded to a selected few out of a larger number equally willing and able to take advantage of it'.[238] In the opinion of the majority the trust in *IRC v Baddeley*[239] was beneficial only to a few out of a larger class and therefore did not demonstrate a sufficient public benefit. The decision of the House of Lords in *IRC v Baddeley* followed an earlier decision of the House of Lords in *Williams' Trustee v IRC*,[240] where it was held that a trust to promote the interests of Welsh people living in London was not charitable, on the grounds that the Welsh people in London were not a sufficient section of the public.

APPLYING THE LAW

In his will, Gustavo left his entire residuary estate upon trust to provide a centre in Kenilworth for the Spanish people living in Warwickshire. The purpose of the centre was to allow Spanish people to meet up and socialise and organise various events, such as Spanish music and dance.

Can the trustees obtain charitable status for the centre?

It may well be questioned why a trust for the benefit of members of a synagogue in *Neville Estates v Madden*[241] was held to be charitable, whereas a trust to provide recreational and social facilities for Methodists or Welsh people living in London was not. Are not members of a synagogue a 'class within a class' just as much as Methodists in a particular area are a 'class within a class' or indeed as much as Welsh people in London? The answer to this lies not so much in the fact that the intended beneficiaries of the trust are a class within a larger class: rather the reason, as explained by the Charity Commission in its recent guidance, is that there appears to be no rational link between

---

[235] [1955] AC 572.
[236] [1947] AC 447.
[237] [1955] AC 572.
[238] [1955] AC 572 at 592.
[239] [1955] AC 572.
[240] [1947] AC 447.
[241] [1962] Ch. 832.

the purpose of the trust and restriction on the beneficial class.[242] The matter is explained by Viscount Simonds in *IRC v Baddeley*[243] where the judge explained that:

> the difficulty has sometimes been increased by failing to observe the distinction . . . between a form of relief extended to the whole community yet by its very nature advantageous only to the few and a form of relief accorded to a selected few out of a larger number equally willing and able to take advantage of it . . . Somewhat different considerations arise if the form, which the purporting charity takes, is something of general utility which is nevertheless made available not to the whole public but only to a selected body of the public – an important class of the public it may be. For example, a bridge which is available for all the public may undoubtedly be a charity and it is indifferent how many people use it. But confine its use to a selected number of persons, however numerous and important: it is then clearly not a charity. It is not of general public utility: for it does not serve the public purpose which its nature qualifies it to serve . . . Who has ever heard of a bridge to be crossed only by impecunious Methodists?[244]

Personal nexus

APPLYING THE LAW

Midwest University has set up a fund for the education of the children of employees and ex-employees of the University. The scheme offers grants to the children, with preference to those children whose parents' annual income is less that £50,000 per annum. Midwest University is seeking charitable status for this fund.

Is this a charitable purpose?

In order to satisfy the test of public benefit, it is important that the benefits of a charitable trust are not confined to a class of beneficiaries who are connected to the person creating the trust in a private way. For example, in *Re Compton*[245] a trust was created for the advancement of education of the three named relatives of the testatrix. The Court of Appeal held that this did not create a charitable trust, but rather a family trust. The benefits of the trust were confined to beneficiaries who were related to the testatrix and, therefore, because of the connection between the beneficiaries and the testatrix, the benefits did not extend to the public. This so-called 'personal nexus rule', was considered at length by the House of Lords in *Oppenheim v Tobacco Securities Trust Co Ltd*[246] where a testator left securities to be invested and held upon trust for providing 'for . . . the education of children of employees or former employees' of British American Tobacco or any of its subsidiary or allied companies. The company employed over 110,000 employees and the question before the House of Lords was whether the trust was for the advancement of education. The House of Lords held that, although the trust was clearly

---

[242] Charity Commission, *Analysis of the Law Underpinning Charities and Public Benefit*, December 2008 at p. 18.
[243] [1955] AC 572.
[244] *Ibid.*
[245] [1945] Ch. 123.
[246] [1951] AC 297.

within the definition of advancement of education, it was not for the benefit of the public as understood by charity law. In particular, the House of Lords held that the beneficiaries were not a section of the public, but were connected to the testator by reason of their employment in British American Tobacco. In this respect the House of Lords explained that there was a 'personal nexus' between the testator and the beneficiaries. Lord Simonds explained that the:

> beneficiaries must not be numerically negligible, and secondly, that the quality which distinguishes them from other members of the community, so that they form by themselves a section of it, must be a quality which does not depend on their relationship to a particular individual. It is for this reason that a trust for the education of members of a family or of a number of families cannot be regarded as charitable. A group of persons may be numerous but, if the nexus between them is their personal relationship to a single propositus or to several propositi, they are neither the community nor a section of the community for charitable purposes. I come, then, to the present case where the class of beneficiaries is numerous but the difficulty arises in regard to their common and distinguishing quality. That quality is being children of employees of one or other of a group of companies. I can make no distinction between children of employees and the employees themselves. In both cases the common quality is found in employment by particular employers.[247]

One question which has arisen in the case law is whether it is possible to create a trust in favour of a much wider class of beneficiaries, for example the public at large, but to then give preference to a limited class, such as the relations or employees of the person creating the trust? This matter arose in *IRC v Educational Grants Association Ltd*[248] where the Educational Grants Association Ltd, a company limited by guarantee, was set up 'to advance education in such ways as shall from time to time be thought fit and in particular by making grants to or for the benefit of and for the education of all such persons as shall be considered likely to benefit from education at a preparatory, public or other independent school, including boarding-schools, and at technical colleges'. Despite the rather broad definition of beneficiaries capable of benefiting from this educational trust, the Association made between 76 and 85 per cent of the grants to the children of the Metal Box Ltd. This was not surprising given the fact that the members of the Association were connected with the Metal Box Ltd. The Court of Appeal held that the Association was not charitable, on the grounds that its funds had not been applied for the benefit of the public and was therefore not exclusively charitable. A similar result was achieved in *Caffoor v Income Tax Commissioner for Columbo*[249] where a trust for the advancement of education was created in favour of a section of the public, but preference was given to the relatives of the settlor. The Privy Council held that this did not create a charitable trust.

Although the decision in *IRC v Educational Grants Association Ltd*[250] is correct in the sense that it should not make any difference if a trust is framed for the benefit of a very broad range of beneficiaries, but then is confined to a private class, the question does arise as to the extent to which a preference can be given without destroying the public nature of the trust. In *Re Koettgen's Wills Trusts*[251] a testatrix left her estate upon trust for the furtherance of commercial education. The will directed that 'the persons eligible as beneficiaries under the fund shall be persons of either sex who are British born subjects

---

[247] [1951] AC 297 at 306.
[248] [1967] Ch. 993.
[249] [1961] AC 584.
[250] [1967] Ch. 993.
[251] [1954] Ch. 252.

and who are desirous of educating themselves or obtaining tuition for a higher commercial career but whose means are insufficient or will not allow of their obtaining such education or tuition at their own expense . . .' The will then directed that the trustees give a preference of up to 75 per cent to the employees of a particular company. The court held that this created a valid charitable trust despite the preference to employees of the company.

Although the personal nexus rule is fairly well established in the law of charity, the question has arisen on more that one occasion as to whether an arbitrary application of it is justified. Certainly, in one respect, the rule is justified on the grounds that it prevents the benefits of charitable status to be extended to trusts created, for example by a company to give tax-free benefits to a private group of individuals. On the other hand, it is also questionable whether the arbitrary classification of individuals into 'personal' and 'impersonal groups' is satisfactory. For example, in his dissenting judgment in **Oppenheim v Tobacco Securities Trust Co Ltd**,[252] Lord MacDermott explained that:

> there was much difficulty in dividing the qualities or attributes, which may serve to bind human beings into classes, into two mutually exclusive groups, the one involving individual status and purely personal, the other disregarding such status and quite impersonal. As a task this seems . . . no less baffling and elusive than the problem to which it is directed, namely, the determination of what is and what is not a section of the public for the purposes of this branch of the law.[253]

The view of the Charity Commission in its recent guidance is that the 'personal nexus rule' should be retained; however, 'it should be cautious and flexible in the application' of the test.[254] The Charity Commission's view is exemplified in the following statement.

KEY CITATION

Charity Commission: *Analysis of the law underpinning charities and public benefit* (December 2008, p. 25)

It would appear that a class whose distinguishing feature is an impersonal quality may be a sufficient section of the public even though its constituent members also happen to share some personal characteristics (e.g. being tenants of a single landlord). This means that:

— on this view there may be a sufficient section of the public in a case where (even though all potential beneficiaries might actually be connected by kin or contract);

— on a general survey of the circumstances and considerations regarded as relevant it is clear that a public class is suggested; and

— that the class can be (and, as a rule, is in fact) described otherwise than by reference to kin or contractual relationship;

— if it is difficult to describe a class using objective and impersonal terms, that would suggest that the body concerned is established for private rather than public benefit; and

— in those cases where the conclusion is that private benefits are intended for a group of individuals who are not together fairly describable as a section of the public, the 'personal nexus' rule applies to deny the benefits of charitable status.

---

[252] [1951] AC 297.
[253] [1951] AC 297 at 317.
[254] Charity Commission, *Analysis of the Law Underpinning Charities and Public Benefit*, December 2008 at p. 25.

● Poverty and poor relations cases

APPLYING THE LAW

In his will, Barry left certain property upon two trusts:

(i) to be applied for relieving poverty amongst my four nieces; and

(ii) to be applied for relief of poverty amongst any of my relatives.

Are these charitable trusts?

Before the enactment of the Charities Act 2006 it was fairly well established in the case law that the public benefit test did not apply in the same way to trusts for the relief of poverty.[255] In particular, it was established in ***Dingle v Turner***[256] that the 'personal nexus rule' did not apply to trusts for the relief of poverty. In other words, it was possible for a trust to retain charitable status even though the beneficiaries of the intended trust were related to the person creating the trust by some blood or contractual tie, provided that the trust was not so framed as to confer a benefit on specifically named individuals.[257] These so-called 'poor relations' cases were not really justified on grounds of any principle other than the fact that they had been established in the decided cases for a long time. In ***Re Scarisbrick***[258] Evershed MR attempted to justify the 'poor relations' cases on the grounds that 'the relief of poverty is of so altruistic a character that the public element may necessarily be inferred thereby; or they may be accepted as a hallowed, if illogical, exception'.[259] On the facts of ***Re Scarisbrick*** a testatrix left her property on trust for the needy relatives of her son and daughters. The court held that this created a valid charitable trust in favour of the relatives of the son and daughters. In ***Oppenheim v Tobacco Securities Trust Co Ltd***[260] Lord Simonds explained that the 'poor relations' cases had been recognised for some considerable period of time and felt that there was no need to overrule a long line of cases which had established the rule. In the course of his judgment Lord Simonds commented 'how unwise it would be to cast any doubt upon decisions of respectable antiquity in order to introduce a greater harmony into the law of charity as a whole'.[261]

The opportunity to consider the public benefit in the context of the relief of poverty presented itself to the House of Lords in ***Dingle v Turner***[262] where a testator directed the trustees of his will to pay the income of his residuary estate to his wife for her life and thereafter to invest £10,000 in the names of trustees on trust 'to apply the income thereof

---

[255] *Spiller v Maude* (1881) 32 Ch. D. 158 where a fund for relief of orphans of deceased members of a society by means of medical help and other financial help was held to be charitable despite the preference to a limited class.

[256] [1972] AC 601.

[257] *Re Segelman* [1996] Ch. 171 where a trust was created in favour of six named relatives and their issue. Chadwick J explained that in substance the trust was potentially for the benefit of 26 relatives and possibly more. On this basis the trust was not just for the benefit of named individuals but for a wider class of relatives.

[258] [1951] Ch. 622.

[259] [1951] Ch. 622 at 639.

[260] [1951] AC 297.

[261] [1951] AC 297 at 309.

[262] [1972] AC 601.

in paying pensions to poor employees of E Ltd., a company jointly owned by him'. The question before the House of Lords was whether this created a valid charitable trust despite the preference given to the employees of the company. At the time of the testator's death there were about 600 employees, including ex-employees. The House of Lords held that this created a valid charitable trust. With regard to the question of 'personal nexus', Lord Cross explained that:

> the 'poor members' and the 'poor employees' decisions were a natural development of the 'poor relations' decisions and to draw a distinction between different sorts of 'poverty' trusts would be quite illogical and could certainly not be said to be introducing 'greater harmony' into the law of charity. Moreover, though not as old as the 'poor relations' trusts 'poor employees' trusts have been recognised as charities for many years; there are now a large number of such trusts in existence; and assuming, as one must, that they are properly administered in the sense that benefits under them are only given to people who can fairly be said to be, according to current standards, 'poor persons,' to treat such trusts as charities is not open to any practical objection. So as it seems to me it must be accepted that wherever else it may hold sway the [personal nexus] rule has no application in the field of trusts for the relief of poverty.[263]

Although the application of the 'personal nexus rule' was clearly rejected by the House of Lords in *Dingle v Turner*,[264] the question, which has arisen on more than one occasion, is whether the exception is justified. It has already been explained above that one of the justifications for the exception is that the mere fact that a trust relieves property is sufficient on the grounds that it is so altruistic in character. On the other hand, in *IRC v Educational Grants*[265] Harman J emphasised that 'the word "public" there runs through all the charity cases. But . . . the "poverty" cases . . . stick out like a sore thumb from the general rule.'[266] In *Dingle v Turner* Lord Cross attempted to explain the poverty cases on the grounds that, unlike in the context of education, there was little or no scope for a testator or a settlor to take advantage of fiscal benefits. For example, in the case of education, there was a genuine possibility that the person creating the trust was motivated by fiscal advantages arising from the trust. On the other hand, in the context of poverty, the relief of poverty being so altruistic in nature prevented the existence of any wider motives on the part of the testator to take advantage of fiscal advantages. In the course of his judgment, Lord Cross explained that:

> to establish a trust for the education of the children of employees in a company in which you are interested is no doubt a meritorious act; but however numerous the employees may be the purpose which you are seeking to achieve is not a public purpose. It is a company purpose and there is no reason why your fellow taxpayers should contribute to a scheme which by providing 'fringe benefits' for your employees will benefit the company by making their conditions of employment more attractive. The temptation to enlist the assistance of the law of charity in private endeavours of this sort is considerable . . . and the courts must do what they can to discourage such attempts.[267]

Given the enactment of the Charities Act 2006, which now abolishes any presumption of public benefit, the question which will need to be decided by the Charity Commission and the courts is whether a trust for the relief of poverty must satisfy the public benefit

---

[263] [1972] AC 601 at 623.
[264] [1972] AC 601.
[265] [1967] Ch. 993.
[266] [1967] Ch. 993.
[267] [1972] AC 601 at 625.

test. The matter is not as simple as it first appears. Section 3(3) of the Charities Act 2006 provides that the 'reference to public benefit is a reference to the public benefit as that term is understood for the purposes of the law relating to charities'. In this respect, Professor Hudson explains that this provision:

> should, it is suggested, be understood to mean that the requirement for a public benefit under the statute is to be interpreted in accordance with the understanding of the term public benefit as applied in the case law on charities before 2006. The understanding of the public benefit requirement before the 2006 Act came into force was that the public benefit requirement did not apply to poverty trusts. Thus, s. 3(3) should be interpreted to mean that no public benefit is required in relation to a trust for the relief of or prevention of poverty.[268]

This view, however, does not seem to prevail in any of the guidance issued by the Charity Commission. In it its latest guidance, the Commission wrote that the 'poor relations trusts in the past have been accepted as charitable. We consider that there has to be a rational link between the beneficial class and the purpose which makes clear it is for the public benefit. Given that all trusts must now have to establish they are for the public benefit, it may be the case that a poor relations trust or family poverty trust would be unable to show this.'[269] In February 2011 the Attorney General's Office explained that it had received a number of enquiries regarding the status of those trusts for the relief of poverty which involved some personal nexus between the person creating the trust and the ultimate beneficiaries. The Office explained that such a question would have to be decided by a tribunal or the courts; however, the Office commented that:

> The object of the Reference is to seek clarification of the charity law concept of 'public benefit' as it applies to the purposes of certain kinds of trust for the relief of poverty. They are trusts where the class of potential objects of the trust's bounty are defined by reference to:
>
> - their personal relationship to one or more individuals (e.g. trusts for the relief of poverty amongst 'my poor relations') or;
> - their or a member of their family's employment by a specified commercial company (e.g. a trust for the relief of poverty amongst the poor employees or poor former employees of the XYZ Company Ltd) or;
> - their membership of an unincorporated association (e.g. a trust for the relief of poverty amongst the poor members of the PQR Benevolent Association).

In addition to the three classes listed above, certain other types of charity, which are similar in character and so may be affected, have been identified. One category is utility trusts where the beneficiaries are defined by being customers of a particular utility company. Another is trusts for the relief of poverty among former players of a particular football club.

Before the Charities Act 2006 came into force, case law established that the purposes of trusts of the kind in question were charitable. The Charity Commission and others have been concerned that the effect of the Charities Act 2006 may have been to cause such purposes to cease to be charitable. Essentially the Reference asks the Tribunal to determine whether that has been the effect of the 2006 Act.

The outcome of the Reference may be either:

- that the Tribunal decides that Charities Act 2006 has not materially altered the law as to the charitable nature of the purposes of the kind in question, or;

---

[268] A. Hudson, *Equity and Trusts* 5th edn (2007) at p. 1033.

[269] Charity Commission, *Analysis of the Law Underpinning the Prevention or Relief of Poverty for the Public Benefit* December 2008 at p. 15.

- that it has done so, with the consequence that generally (and subject to any appeal or other proceedings) purposes of the kind in question will have ceased to be charitable.

The Attorney General considers that, if the Charities Act 2006 has caused such purposes to cease to be charitable:

(a) Charities with purposes of the kind in question which were in existence before 1 April 2008 (the date the relevant provisions of the Charities Act 2006 came into force) would not cease to be charities. Generally, s. 13(1)(e)(ii) Charities Act 1993 would apply to them, and their trustees would be bound by s. 13(5) Charities Act 1993 to apply for a cy-près scheme; that is to say a scheme whereby their assets became applicable for, broadly speaking, the nearest practicable charitable purposes to their pre-existing purposes.

(b) Trusts or institutions with purposes of the kind in question which came into existence on or after 1 April 2008 would not be charities.

Although the determination of the charitable nature of their purposes would ultimately be a matter for the Tribunal or the courts, the Attorney General considers that trusts for the benefit of needy serving or former military personnel and their families should generally not be affected by the Reference or its determination, whichever way it is decided. This is because the promotion of military efficiency and esprit de corps can be inferred as the primary purpose, even where this is not expressly stated in the objects. Further the Attorney General considers that there is a distinction in charity law between:

(i) a trust for the benefit of the employees of a particular employer and;

(ii) a trust for the benefit of persons working in a particular industry or for the benefit of a particular profession or occupation, even if the two classes are in practice virtually identical. Generally an otherwise charitable trust expressed to be for the benefit of the latter is charitable and is not within the terms of the reference, whilst one expressed to be for the benefit of the former is within the terms of the reference.

Exclusively charitable

So far it has been observed that a charitable trust will only be recognised if the purpose of the trust is within the definition of charity, now to be found in s. 2(2) of the Charities Act 2006, and that the purpose is for the benefit of the public or an important section of the public. In addition to these requirements, it is of utmost importance that a charitable trust is exclusively charitable. If the purposes of the trust can be applied for charitable and non-charitable purposes then the trust will fail to succeed as a charitable trust. In the past trusts such as the one in *IRC v Baddeley*,[270] where the purpose was to promote the interests of Methodists living in Leyton by providing social and recreational faculties, was held not to be charitable on the grounds that the inclusion of social and recreational facilities was not exclusively charitable. In *IRC v City of Glasgow Police Athletic Association*[271] the question before the House of Lords was whether a police athletic association which was intended to benefit policemen was charitable. The objects of the association included athletic as well as many other activities including general pastime activities. The House of Lords held that the objects of the association were not exclusively charitable; indeed the activities increasing the efficiency of the policemen were held to be merely incidental.

---

[270] [1955] AC 572.
[271] [1953] AC 380.

The question whether a trust is exclusively charitable often requires a close construction of the terms of the gift. A subtle change in language used in the gift may determine whether the trust is exclusively charitable or not. For example, in **Farley v Westminster Bank**[272] a testatrix left the residue of her estate in equal shares to two charities and to the respective vicars and churchwardens of two named churches 'for parish work'. The question before the House of Lords was whether this was a charitable gift. The House of Lords held that the words 'for parish work' included objects which were not exclusively charitable. In the course of his judgment, Lord Atkin explained that:

> 'parish work' seems to me to be of such vague import as to go far beyond the ordinary meaning of charity, in this case in the sense of being a religious purpose. The expression covers the whole of the ordinary activities of the parish, some of which no doubt fall within the definition of religious purposes, and all of which no doubt are religious from the point of view of the person who is responsible for the spiritual care of the parish in the sense that they are conducive, perhaps, to the moral and spiritual good of his congregation. But that, I think, quite plainly is not enough; and the words are so wide that I am afraid that on no construction can they be brought within the limited meaning of 'charitable' as used in the law.[273]

The decision of the House of Lords in **Farley v Westminster Bank**[274] can be contrasted with the decision in **Re Simson**[275] where a testatrix, by her will, gave the residue of her estate to the vicar of a named church 'to be used for his work in the parish'. Romer J held that this was a valid charitable gift, on the grounds that the gift was given to the vicar in connection with his work as a vicar. Romer J explained that:

> gift to a vicar and churchwardens for parish work is a general phrase covering a multitude of activities, and, as such, was held to be too wide; but a gift to a vicar for his work in the parish, seems to me to be totally different and involving a totally different conception, and merely means that it is to be used for the purposes of such part of his work (that is to say, his functions connected with the cure of souls in the particular district) as lies within the particular parish. In my judgment, such work is both sufficiently definite and is charitable.[276]

Is the non-charitable purpose merely incidental?

It is, however, possible for a trust to remain charitable in nature despite the inclusion of a non-charitable purpose, provided that the non-charitable purpose is merely incidental or subsidiary to the main purpose. For example, in **Re Coxen**[277] the Mayor of London left a sum of money to the Court of Aldermen for the benefit of orthopaedic hospitals, but directed the trustees to use a sum not greater than 100 pounds for organising an annual dinner for the Court of Aldermen to discuss trust business. The court held that the provision of the dinner was merely incidental to the main purpose of the trust and, therefore, the trust was valid as a charitable trust. In **London Hospital Medical College v IRC**[278] the question before the court was whether a student union was a charitable trust where its main purpose was to promote the purposes of a college, but also included personal private personal benefits to the students. The court held that the private personal benefits, for example to individual students selected as union members and using the

---

[272] [1939] AC 430.
[273] [1939] AC 430 at 435.
[274] [1939] AC 430.
[275] [1946] Ch. 299.
[276] [1946] Ch. 299 at 305.
[277] [1948] Ch. 747.
[278] [1976] 1 WLR 613.

facilities, were merely incidental to the main objective of the union which was to further the objectives of the college.[279] Finally, in *Incorporated Council of Law Reporting for England and Wales v A-G*[280] where the question was whether the Incorporated Council of Law, whose main purpose was the publication of law reports at a moderate price available to everyone, was charitable. The Court of Appeal held that the Council was charitable in nature even though the production of law reports benefited practitioners who used the reports in the course of their profession to make money.

The 'and/or' cases

In some instances a trust which refers to non-charitable purposes may be construed exclusively charitable depending on the way in which the settlor's or testator's words are interpreted. The matter is essentially one of construction and the rules that follow here are merely prima facie points of law. Ultimately, the court will have to look at all the relevant facts in order to establish the settlor's intention. The courts have distinguished between a line of cases called the 'and/or' cases. If a settlor uses words to the effect that property subject to a trust can be applied for charitable and benevolent purposes, or charitable and public purposes, the trust remains a good charitable trust despite the reference to the non-charitable purpose. The reason for this is that the words 'charitable and benevolent' are read conjunctively so as to mean that the property must only be applied for benevolent charitable purposes. The matter is neatly illustrated in a number of cases, for example, in *Re Sutton*[281] where a gift was made for 'charitable and deserving objects'. The gift was held to be exclusively charitable on the grounds that the words 'charitable and deserving' were to be construed conjunctively so that the gift could only be applied for deserving charitable objects. A similar conclusion was arrived at in *Re Best*[282] where a gift made to charitable and benevolent purposes was held to be exclusively charitable. As explained above, the mere fact that a settlor uses the words 'charitable and benevolent' is only a prima facie finding that the words are to be read conjunctively. A court may refuse to read the words conjunctively if this would lead to a finding that would be inconsistent with the settlor's intention. For example, in *Attorney General of the Bahamas v Royal Trust Co*[283] a trust was created for the education and welfare of Bahamian children. The Privy Council held that the words were to be read disjunctively as the trust intended to create two purposes: namely, the education of the Bahamian children as well as their general welfare. The trust could not be construed to mean the educational welfare of the children.

APPLYING THE LAW

In her will, Vicky left £300,000 to be applied for educating people in Warwickshire about the dangers of drug abuse. She directed that the trustees could spend no more than 5 per cent of the annual income to organise an annual dinner party for the trustees. In addition she left £30,000 to be applied for similar educational and benevolent purposes. The trustees seek your advice as to whether this is a charitable trust.

---

[279] See also *Royal College of Surgeons v National Provincial Bank* [1952] AC 631.
[280] [1972] Ch. 73.
[281] (1885) 28 Ch. D 464.
[282] [1904] 2 Ch. 354.
[283] [1986] 1 WLR 1001.

Where a settlor uses words to the effect that property subject to a trust can be applied for charitable or non-charitable purposes then the trust will fail on the grounds that the words are to be given a disjunctive meaning. For example, suppose a settlor creates a trust for 'charitable or public purposes', the trust will not be charitable, on the grounds that the trust can be applied for purposes charitable as well as purposes which are not charitable. For example, in **Blair v Duncan**[284] where a testatrix created a trust for 'such charitable or public purposes as my trustee thinks proper', the House of Lords held that this did not create a charitable trust, on the grounds that the trust could be applied for charitable as well as non-charitable purposes. In the course of his judgment, Lord Davey explained that 'the words we have here are "charitable or public purposes", and I think these words must be read disjunctively. It would, therefore, be in the power of the trustee to apply the whole of the fund for purposes which are not charitable though they might be of a public character.'[285] In **Chichester Diocesan Fund and Board of Finance v Simpson**[286] a trust was created for charitable and benevolent purposes. The trustees, on their understanding that this created a valid charitable trust, distributed the property to a large number of charities. It was held that this was not a charitable trust, on the grounds that the words were to be given a disjunctive meaning.

Severance

If a trust contains both charitable and non-charitable purposes, the question arises as to whether a court can sever the charitable from the non-charitable. If severance is possible, the charitable purposes can stand good even if it means that the non-charitable purposes fail or are otherwise applied for the non-charitable purposes. Severance was applied by the court in **Salusbury v Denton**[287] where a testator left money to his widow to be applied partly for 'the foundation of a charity school, or such other charitable endowment for the benefit of the poor of Offley as she may prefer, and under such restrictions as she may prescribe, and the remainder to be at her disposal among testator's relatives as she may direct'. When the widow died without having distributed any of the money, the court directed that the fund be divided equally between the charitable purposes and the testator's relatives. Severance is not, however, a possibility in every case and certainly not a possibility where the settlor or testator directs that a fund be used for charitable or non-charitable purposes. In **Salusbury v Denton**[288] Page-Wood VC explained that 'it is one thing to direct a trustee to give *a part* of a fund to one set of objects *and the remainder* to another, and it is a distinct thing to direct him to give "either" to one set of objects "or" to another . . . This is a case of the former description. Here the trustee was bound to give a part to each.'[289]

Charitable Trusts (Validation) Act 1954

The Charitable Trusts (Validation) Act 1954, which applies to trusts taking effect before 16 December 1952, renders 'imperfect trust provisions' valid even though under the common law they are invalidated. An imperfect trust provision is a provision which

---

[284] [1902] AC 37.
[285] [1902] AC 37 at 44.
[286] [1944] AC 341.
[287] (1857) 3 K & J 529.
[288] *Ibid.*
[289] (1857) 3 K & J 529 at 539.

allows the trust to be applied for charitable or non-charitable purposes, for example, charitable or benevolent purposes. Clearly, such a trust would fail on the grounds that it is not exclusively charitable. The 1954 Act, however, stipulates that such a trust is to be construed as applying exclusively for charity. It was observed above that in **Chichester Diocesan Fund and Board of Finance v Simpson**[290] a trust was created in favour of charitable and benevolent objects. The trustees distributed the money to a large number of charities only to discover, as a result of litigation by the testator's next of kin, that the trust was not charitable. Clearly, the 1954 Act would have had the effect of rendering the trust in this case as being valid in favour of charitable objects only.

One of the main problems which has arisen in the application of the Charitable Trusts (Validation) Act 1954 is the meaning to be attributed to an 'imperfect trust provision'. In **Re Gillingham Bus Disaster Fund**[291] Harman J took a rather restrictive view as to the circumstances which would give rise to an imperfect trust provision. The facts concerned an appeal by the mayors of three towns to raise money as a result of an accident in which a number of marine cadets were killed and injured in a road traffic accident. The purpose of the fund, as advertised in a national newspaper, was for 'defraying the funeral expenses, caring for the boys who may be disabled, and then to such worthy cause or causes in memory of the boys who lost their lives, as the Mayors may determine'. According to Harman J reference to 'worthy cause' was not grounds for the application of the Charitable Trusts (Validation) Act 1954 because it was not an imperfect trust provision. Harman J took the view that, in order for a trust to be regarded as an imperfect trust provision, it was important that there was some reference to charitable as well as non-charitable purposes. For example, had the fund in **Re Gillingham Bus Disaster Fund**[292] been available for charitable or worthy causes, then the 1954 Act would have applied in rendering the trust exclusively charitable. Despite, the rather restrictive approach of Harman J in **Re Gillingham Bus Disaster Fund**, subsequent decisions have not followed the approach of Harman J. For example, in **Re Wykes' Will Trusts**[293] a trust was created for benevolent and welfare purposes. Buckley J preferred to construe the word 'welfare' as having a strong flavour of charity to it and therefore, following the approach of Cross J in **Re Mead's Trust Deed**,[294] held that the trust could be applied exclusively for charity.

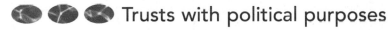

Trusts with political purposes

The general rule against political purposes

It is a general rule of charity law that a trust which has political objects, or which includes political purposes, cannot be held to be charitable. The principle was explained by Lord Parker in **Bowman v The Secular Society**[295] where his Lordship explained that 'a trust for the attainment of political objects has always been held invalid, not because it is illegal, for every one is at liberty to advocate or promote by any lawful means a change in the law, but because the Court has no means of judging whether a proposed change in the

---

290 [1944] AC 341.
291 [1958] Ch. 300.
292 *Ibid.*
293 [1961] 1 Ch. 229.
294 [1961] 1 WLR 1244.
295 [1917] AC 406.

law will or will not be for the public benefit, and therefore cannot say that a gift to secure the change is a charitable gift'.[296] Similarly, in **National Anti-Vivisection Society v IRC**[297] Lord Normand explained that if 'the leading purpose of [a] society was to promote legislation in order to bring about a change of policy towards field sports or the protection of wild birds it would follow that the society should be classified as an association with political objects and that it would lose its privileges as a charity'.[298] The question before the House of Lords in **National Anti-Vivisection Society v IRC**[299] was whether a gift to the National Anti-Vivisection Society was a gift to a charitable purpose. The House of Lords held that, since the purpose of the Society was to bring about a change in the law, the objects of the Society were political.

When will a trust be deemed to have political objects?

In *McGovern* v *Attorney-General* Slade J had to consider whether the objects of Amnesty International were charitable. There were four principal objects of Amnesty International: namely, the relief of prisoners of conscience, the release of prisoners of conscience throughout the world, procurement of changes in nations' laws and governmental decisions and finally, research into observance of human rights. Slade J held that the objects of Amnesty International were political and could not, therefore, be regarded as being charitable. As to the question when a trust would be deemed as being charitable, Slade J explained it in the following way.

KEY CITATION	*McGovern* v *Attorney-General* [1982] Ch. 321: (When is a trust for a political purpose? per Slade J at 330)

Trusts for political purposes falling within the spirit of this pronouncement include, inter alia, trusts of which a direct and principal purpose is either

(i) to further the interests of a particular political party; or

(ii) to procure changes in the laws of this country; or

(iii) to procure changes in the laws of a foreign country; or

(iv) to procure a reversal of government policy or of particular decisions of governmental authorities in this country; or

(v) to procure a reversal of government policy or of particular decisions of governmental authorities in a foreign country.

In finding that the objects of Amnesty International were not charitable, Slade J explained that:

indisputably, laws do exist both in this country and in many foreign countries which many reasonable persons consider unjust. No less indisputably, laws themselves will from time

---

[296] [1917] AC 406 at 442.
[297] [1948] AC 31.
[298] [1948] AC 31 at 76.
[299] [1948] AC 31.

to time be administered by governmental authorities in a manner which many reasonable persons consider unjust, inhuman or degrading. Amnesty International, in striving to remedy what it considers to be such injustices, is performing a function which many will regard as being of great value to humanity. Fortunately, the laws of this country place very few restrictions on the rights of philanthropic organisations such as this, or of individuals, to strive for the remedy of what they regard as instances of injustice, whether occurring here or abroad . . . the elimination of injustice has not as such ever been held to be a trust purpose which qualifies for the privileges afforded to charities by English law. I cannot hold it to be a charitable purpose now.[300]

Applications of the rule in the decided cases

The application of the rule, that a charitable trust must not have political objectives, is illustrated in a number of cases. The decision in **National Anti-Vivisection Society v IRC**[301] is illustrative of the fact that where the objective of an organisation is to bring about a change in the law of this country, it cannot be charitable. The decision was followed more recently in **Hanchett-Stamford v Attorney General**,[302] which concerned an association founded sometime in 1914 called the 'The Performing and Captive Animals Defence League' (the League hereafter). Although the League had a formal constitution at the beginning, that constitution had been lost and since 1934 the affairs of the League were conducted by a Director appointed by the members of the League. Although it was very difficult to ascertain the exact purposes of the League, it became evident from a booklet produced for members in 1962 that the objects of the League were to prevent cruelty to animals used in film productions and shows. Thus many of the activities of the League involved preventing travelling circuses and municipal zoos. Lewison J explained that the purposes of the society were to bring about a change in the law and that as a result of the House of Lords' decision in **National Anti-Vivisection Society v IRC**[303] a trust with purposes intended to bring about a change in the law could not be charitable.[304]

It is likely that in some cases the political objectives are disguised as educational objectives so as to validate purposes as educational trusts. Despite the disguise as an educational trust, the court will look to substance, and where the education amounts to nothing more than political propaganda masquerading, the trust will be deemed as having political objects. For example, in **Re Hopkinson**[305] a trust was made 'for the advancement of adult education with particular reference to . . . the education of men and women of all classes (on the lines of the Labour Party's memorandum headed "A note on Education in the Labour . . .") to higher conception of social, political and economic ideas and values and of the personal obligations of duty and service which are necessary for the realisation of an improved and enlightened social civilisation'.[306] Vaisey J held that this was not a charitable trust, on the grounds that there was a big difference between education for the purposes of charity and political propaganda masquerading.

---

[300] [1982] Ch. 321 at 354.
[301] [1948] AC 31.
[302] [2009] Ch. 173. See S. Panesar, 'Surplus Funds and Unincorporated Associations' *Trust and Trustees* (2008) Vol. 14 Issue 10 at 698.
[303] [1948] AC 31.
[304] [2009] Ch. 173.
[305] [1949] 1 All ER 346.
[306] Quoted in E.H. Burn and J. Virgo, *Trust and Trustees: Cases and Materials* 7th edn, (2008) at p. 524.

A similar result was achieved in **Re Bushnell**[307] where a testator left his residuary estate 'to pay the same to the Socialist Medical Association, the Haldane Society, the Labour Research Department and the Marx Memorial Library and Workers School' as endowment trustees. The endowment trustees were to use the fund 'for the advancement and propagation of the teaching of socialised medicine'. Goulding J held that the purposes of the trust were political and, therefore, could not be charitable. In the course of his judgment he explained that 'there is no doubt that in this country in 1941 the establishment of a state health service, or of anything that could fairly be identified with the testator's scheme of socialised medicine, required major legislative changes, and a trust for that purpose would accordingly fail as one for a political object'.[308]

On the other hand, the mere fact that there is an element of political debate within a purpose does not necessarily invalidate the trust as being charitable. For example, an organisation can enter into discussions and debates which are political; however, the organisation must not seek to further those political ideas. The matter is neatly illustrated by the decision in **Re Koeppler's Will Trusts**[309] where the question before the Court of Appeal was whether an organisation founded by a testator in 1946 in Buckinghamshire was charitable. The purposes of the organisation were to carry out research into foreign affairs including subjects such as security, ecology and the environment. The organisation held a number of conferences annually which were attended by members of organisations such as the OECD and the European Union. The Court of Appeal held that although there was no doubt that the activities of the organisation involved research into matters which were of a political nature, the organisation was not furthering the political objects of any party and neither was it seeking to advocate changes in the law. In the course of his judgment, Slade LJ explained that the activities of the organisation 'are not of a party political nature. Nor, so far as the evidence shows, are they designed to procure changes in the laws or governmental policy of this or any other country: even when they touch on political matters, they constitute, so far as I can see, no more than genuine attempts in an objective manner to ascertain and disseminate the truth.'[310]

Is political activity and campaigning totally disallowed?

APPLYING THE LAW

A few months ago, Asylum 2000, was set up in the West Midlands. The objectives of the organisation are to provide education and other help for asylum seekers. The organisation is very concerned about the lack of government initiatives to help asylum seekers. It is planning to devote most of its resources on campaigning for greater rights for asylum seekers.

Will this affect their charitable status?

---

[307] [1975] 1 WLR 1596.
[308] [1975] 1 WLR 1596 at 1603.
[309] [1986] Ch. 423.
[310] [1986] Ch. 423 at 437.

It has been long recognised that charitable organisations inevitably seek to participate in debates which further their aims and objectives. For example, a charity concerned with the relief of poverty will inevitably wish to get involved with any discussions at a political level which have some effect on its aims and objectives. The question arises as to what level of campaigning and involvement in political activity is allowed before a charity is stripped of its charitable status. This is a matter which the Charity Commission has provided guidance from time to time and the most recent guidance was issued in March 2008.[311] The recent guidance provided by the Charity Commission has been well received by most parties involved in the debate on the level of political activity capable of being undertaken by a charity. The guidance has generally been described as providing much needed clarity.[312] The most recent guidance establishes that any charity, unless prohibited by its own governance rules, can become involved in political campaigning in order to support its charitable purposes. There must be a reasonable likelihood that the campaigning and political activity is to further or support is own charitable purposes. An important feature of the recent guidance is that a charity can carry out political activity in order to bring about a change in law provided if supports the charity's own purposes. However, the guidance makes it equally clear that a charity cannot have, as one of its charitable purposes, an objective to change the law in the UK or abroad.

So how does this work in practice and how does this change, if at all, the position in the decided case law, for example the decision of the House of Lords in *National Anti-Vivisection Society* v *IRC*?[313] In *National Anti-Vivisection Society* v *IRC* a gift to the National Anti-Vivisection Society was not a gift for charitable purposes because the Society's objectives were to bring about a change in the law on animal cruelty. The answer is that the decision in *National Anti-Vivisection Society* v *IRC* remains good law; and a distinction is to be drawn between organisations with charitable purposes which involve a change in the law and organisations with charitable purposes which do not involve a change in the law. In the former case, there can be no charitable status whereas in the latter the organisation retains charitable status with the scope to get involved in political campaigning. The matter is neatly illustrated by an example given within the guidance provided by the Charity Commission. The guidance states that:

> [a]n organisation was set up to campaign for an end to all animal experimentation in the UK. This was considered by the courts not to be charitable, because the only way of achieving its purpose was to seek a change in the law, thus its reason for existing would not come under any of the charitable purposes defined in charity law. It was also considered that an end to animal experimentation could well be against the public interest, as medical research would thus be curtailed. However, it is possible that a charity with wider animal welfare objects could campaign for amendments to the law on animal experimentation, where it could show that such amendments would be likely to support the delivery of its charitable purposes.[314]

The recent guidance provided by the Charity Commission is quite extensive; below is an extract of some of the questions and answers which the guidance has provided in the context of campaigning and political activity.

---

[311] Charity Commission, *CC9 – Speaking Out – Guidance on Campaigning and Political Activity by Charities*, March 2008.

[312] See, R. McCarthy, 'Charities and Campaigning' (2008) PCB 235.

[313] [1948] AC 31.

[314] Charity Commission, *CC9 – Speaking Out – Guidance on Campaigning and Political Activity by Charities*, March 2008.

FURTHER THINKING

Charity Commission, *CC9 – Speaking Out – Guidance on campaigning and political activity by charities*, March 2008

1 Can a charity carry out campaigning and political activity?

Yes – any charity can become involved in campaigning and in political activity which further or support its charitable purposes, unless its governing document prohibits it.

2 Must a charity campaign and engage in political activity?

The short answer

No – trustees have discretion to decide how best to use the resources of their charity to achieve its purposes. Trustees are not required to campaign, nor should they feel under external pressure to do so.

3 Can a charity have a political purpose?

The short answer

A charity cannot have a political purpose. Nor can a charity undertake political activity that is not relevant to, and does not have a reasonable likelihood of, supporting the charity's charitable purposes.

   Whilst a charity cannot have political activity as a purpose, the range of charitable purposes under which an organisation can register as a charity means that, inevitably, there are some purposes (such as the promotion of human rights) which are more likely than others to lead trustees to want to engage in campaigning and political activity.

4 Can a charity have campaigning or political activity in its governing document?

The short answer

Yes – providing it is explained in its governing document that this campaigning or political activity will be a means of furthering or supporting its charitable purposes.

5 Can a charity carry out political activity?

The short answer

Although a political organisation cannot be a charity, a charity can, in support of its charitable purposes, undertake a range of political activities. However these cannot be the only activities that the charity carries out.

6 Can a charity carry out political activity for a change in the law?

The short answer

Yes – charities may carry out political activity for a change in the law if it supports their own charitable purpose.

In more detail

Political activity, including campaigning for a change in the law, is an entirely legitimate activity and can be an effective means of supporting a charitable purpose. However . . . it is not a charitable purpose to campaign for changes to the law whether in the UK or overseas.

7 Can a charity campaign or carry out political activity to influence government or other bodies?

The short answer

Yes – a charity can seek to influence government or other public bodies, providing it is in support of their charitable purposes. However trustees must take care to avoid an approach which is purely focused on political activity as this could call into question the propriety of their actions, or ultimately, their charitable status.

8 Can a charity support a political party?

The short answer

No – a charity must not give its support to any one political party. It may express support for particular policies which will contribute to the delivery of its own charitable purposes so long as its independence is maintained, and perceptions of its independence are not adversely affected.

9 Can a charity engage with a political party?

The short answer

Yes – a charity may engage with a political party in ways that supports its own charitable purposes. In doing so, it must remain politically neutral and should consider working with other parties to help ensure public perceptions of neutrality. Trustees should be as open and transparent as possible about any engagement their charity has with a political party.

Conclusion

This chapter has focused on the law relating to charities and charitable trusts. Such trusts are trusts created for the benefit of the public or an important section of the public. Given their importance in conferring upon the general public benefits recognised by law, such trusts enjoy special privileges which do not apply to the private trusts which have been analysed in the preceding chapters. The privileges range from fiscal advantages, for example, exemption to capital gains tax and income tax, to exemptions from the rigour of strict trust law, for example the need to have identifiable trust beneficiaries and the need to comply with the perpetuity rules. The fact that a charitable trust enjoys so many privileges would have led one to assume that English law has provided a comprehensive definition of when a particular trust is given charitable status. However, the fact is that, until the enactment of the Charities Act 2006, there had been no comprehensive definition of a charity. Instead, as observed in this chapter, the definition of charity was more or less controlled by the courts by reference to a preamble to a statute enacted in 1601, which had been subsequently refined by a decision of the House of Lords in Pemsel's case. Despite the reference to the preamble, it cannot be questioned that the courts developed and allowed the law of charity to meet with new social and economic conditions. The absence of a rigid definition allowed the courts a degree of flexibility in order to allow the law to develop to meet new conditions in society.

The enactment of the Charities Act 2006 has introduced many changes in the law of charities and charitable trusts. Firstly, as observed throughout this chapter, the Act introduces a statutory definition of charity comprising thirteen categories. This definition of charity has been consolidated in the Charities Act 2011. It has been frequently said that the Act introduces a new definition of charity; however, caution should be exercised before making such a broad statement. Whilst the Act expands the categories of charitable heads which were identified by Lord Macnaghten in Pemsel's case, many, if not all of the new heads under the Charities Act 2006 and the Charities Act 2011 are a consolidation of categories which were already identified in the existing case law. Furthermore, the Charities Act 2006 makes it clear that the definition of charity is to be interpreted in light of existing case law. The definition of charity in the Act is more of a consolidation exercise rather than a complete change in definition and the courts and the Charity Commission will continue to have the flexibility to consider new purposes as and when they arise. What is, however, a change in direction in the Act is the removal of the presumption of public benefit which once applied to charitable trusts for the relief or prevention of poverty and the advancement of education and religion. All charitable purposes must now demonstrate that they are for the benefit of the public or an important section of the public. The biggest impact of this change will be in relation to charitable trusts for the relief or prevention of poverty where it has been firmly established in case law that trusts for poor relations are charitable. It remains to be seen how far such poor relation cases survive now that that Act is in force. Finally, the Act makes a number of changes relating to the administration of charities, notably, the introduction of a new form of charitable organisation called the Charitable Incorporated Association as well as a new Charity Tribunal to hear appeals from the decisions of the Charity Commissioners. The Charities Act 2011 has not only consolidated the definition of charity, but has unified many statutory principles governing charities into one single Act.

●●● Case studies

Consider the following case studies.

1   Harvey Gibson was an artist and collector of antiques. He owned a shop in his local village that sold many of his paintings and antiques. However, no one ever bought anything from this shop and Harvey spent most of his time alone in that shop until his death earlier this year. In his will Harvey made the following dispositions of his property:

(i)   £20,000, which is in my bank account, to be given at the discretion of my trustees to children in the Coventry area who are seeking a place at University to study arts, with preference given to the children of the Red School in Coventry.

(ii) My shop and the contents therein to be turned into a museum for the benefit of tourists visiting Coventry.

(iii) My shares in ICI Ltd to be sold and the proceeds to be used for such benevolent and deserving objects in the Coventry area.

(iv) The remainder of my estate to be sold and the proceeds to be invested by my trustees with a discretion to apply the income for any regeneration schemes they see fit in my neighbourhood.

Advise the executors of Harvey's will as to the validity of the dispositions in his will.

2   In his will a testator made the following dispositions:

My real property to be sold and the proceeds to be invested to provide scholarships for the children of the employees of Barney Ltd as well as the needy children living in Coventry.

£50,000 to be invested by my trustees and the income to be used to campaign against the government cuts in higher education funding.

£30,000 to be used to provide holidays for the terminally ill living in Coventry.

£40,000 to be used by my trustees for such public or charitable purposes they see fit.

The remainder of my estate to be sold and the proceeds to be used to build a hostel for those in need of accommodation.

Advise on the validity of the dispositions in the will.

●● Moot points

1 Explain the main reasons behind the enactment of the Charities Act 2006.

2 To what extent has the Charities Act 2006 redefined the legal definition of charity? Does the Act create new categories of charity which did not exist before the Act came into force?

3 The Charities Act 2006 introduces a new form of charitable organisation called the Charitable Incorporated Association (CIO). What are the advantages of using the CIO as a means of administering a charity?

4 Do the perpetuity rules apply to charitable trusts?

5 Section 2(2) of the Charities Act 2006 lists a number of charitable purposes. If a settlor attempts to create a charitable trust, but is unable to demonstrate that his purpose falls into one of the recognised categories in s. 2(2), does it mean that the suggested purpose cannot be recognised as charitable?

6 Trusts to promote artistic works are clearly charitable. However, given the fact that art is by its very nature very subjective, how does a court make an evaluation whether something is artistic or not?

7 Explain what criteria will be used by a court or the Charity Commission to determine whether a particular purpose is charitable if it does not fit under one of the heads of charitable purposes identified in s. 2(2)(a)–(l).

8 What are the principal objections to a charitable trust which has political objects? Can a charity get involved in political activities and campaigning? If so, what advice would you give the trustees so that they avoid losing charitable status for the charity they are administering?

9 What do you understand by the concept of 'interests of social welfare' as used in section 1 of the Recreational Charities Act 1958?

10 A trust must be for the benefit of the public or an important section of the public; it cannot be for a class within a class. What is meant by a class within a class?

11 Whist the 'personal nexus rule' has some justification in that it prevents fiscal advantages to be enjoyed by private individuals, how effective is the rule? Read in particular the judgment of Lord MacDermott explaining that 'there was much difficulty in dividing the qualities or attributes, which may serve to bind human beings into classes, into two mutually exclusive groups, the one involving individual status and purely personal, the other disregarding such status and quite impersonal. As a task this seems . . . no less baffling and elusive than the problem to which it is directed, namely, the determination of what is and what is not a section of the public for the purposes of this branch of the law.' [1951] AC 297 at 317.

12 Consider the extent to which political campaigning is allowed under a charitable trust.

13 Explain the purposes and functions of the Charities Act 2011.

● Further reading

Cross, S. 'New Legal Forms for Charities in the United Kingdom' (2008) JBL 662. Provides a discussion of the nature of the newly introduced charitable incorporated association and its benefits over and above other forms of charitable organisation such as the trust and the company limited by guarantee.

Hackney, J. 'Charities and Public Benefit' (2008) LQR 34. Looks at public benefit presumption and questions whether the courts ever made a presumption in relation to charitable trusts for the relief of poverty or the advancement of education or religion.

McCarthy, R. 'Charities and Campaigning' (2008) PCB 235. Looks at the recent guidance on political campaigning by trustees issued by the Commission.

Moffat, G. *Trust Law: Text and Materials* (2005) CUP, Chapter 18. Provides an excellent account of some of the historical factors governing charities and their relationship with the state.

23

The cy-près doctrine

Learning objectives

After reading this chapter you should be able to:

→ understand the meaning of the cy-près doctrine

→ distinguish the cy-près doctrine from the doctrine of resulting trusts

→ explain the grounds for invoking the cy-près doctrine

→ understand reasons for the statutory widening of the cy-près doctrine

→ understand the requirement of a general charitable intent

→ distinguish between initial and subsequent failure of charitable gifts

→ explain the circumstances in which a charitable gift is deemed to have initially failed

→ explain why the application of cy-près is much broader in cases of subsequent failure

→ explain the reasons for the further widening of the cy-près doctrine by the Charities Act 2006.

SETTING THE SCENE

Re Rymer [1895] 1 Ch. 19 and Re Slevin [1891] 2 Ch. 236: Two very similar cases but two very different outcomes – what's it all about?

It is appropriate to begin this chapter with a brief look at two somewhat similar cases, yet differently decided, in order to understand the nature of the enquiry in this chapter.

In *Re Rymer* a testator bequeathed a sum of money to St Thomas' Seminary for the education of priests in the diocese of Westminster. The testator died in 1893; however, St Thomas' Seminary had ceased to exist before the testator's death and the priests who had been studying there had been transferred to another seminary in Birmingham. The court held that it had become impossible to apply the testator's gift for its original purpose. As to whether the gift could be given to the seminary in Birmingham, the court held that it could not be given.

In *Re Slevin* a testator left a number of monetary gifts to various charitable organisations. One of those organisations was an orphanage which ceased to exist shortly after the testator's death. The question before the Court of Appeal was whether the gift failed and resulted back to the testator's estate, or whether the Attorney General could apply the gift for another similar purpose. The Court of Appeal held that the monetary gift which had been made to the orphanage could be taken by the Attorney General and applied for other purposes as close as possible to the original purposes intended by the testator.

The facts of *Re Rymer* and *Re Slevin* are similar on their facts in that in both cases testamentary gifts were left to charitable organisations which then ceased to exist. The only apparent difference between the two cases is that in *Re Rymer* the charity to whom the gift was made ceased to exist before the testator's death whereas in *Re Slevin* the charity ceased to exist after the testator's death. In *Re Rymer* the gift resulted back to testator's estate whereas in the *Re Slevin* the Attorney General (who is the overall guardian of charitable trusts) was able to take the gift and apply it for other purposes as close as possible to those originally intended by the testator. The facts and decisions of both cases raise a number of important questions which are the subject matter of discussion in this chapter. Amongst those questions are the following.

- In *Re Rymer*, why could the gift not be applied for the benefit of priests who had moved to the seminary in Birmingham? Why did it result back to the testator?

- In *Re Slevin* why was the Attorney General able to claim the gift which was made specifically to an orphanage which had ceased to exist? Following *Re Rymer*, why did the gift not result back to the testator's estate?

Finally, you will recall from Chapters 10 and 11 on resulting trusts, that where the objects of a trust fail, the subject matter of the trust results back under a resulting trust to the person creating the trust. The question arises as to whether the same principles apply to charitable trusts.

This chapter explores what is known as the cy-près doctrine, which has a special application to charitable trusts. Put simply, the doctrine allows the courts and the Charity Commission to apply failed charitable gifts for purposes similar to those intended by the settlor, provided that the conditions for its operation have been met.

Introduction

Where a private trust fails for one reason or another, for example where there is uncertainty of objects, the trust property results back to the settlor or the testator's estate under an implied resulting trust. Similarly, when a non-exhaustive trust has carried out its purpose and is left with some surplus funds, the surplus funds are held on resulting trust for the settlor or the testator's estate.[1] On the other hand, where a charitable trust fails for some reason, for example the charity to which the gift was made has ceased to exist before the testator's death, it is not always the case that the subject matter of the gift results back to the testator's estate. It may be possible to apply the gift for another charitable purpose by virtue of the cy-près rule. The term 'cy-près' is taken from the French, meaning 'as near as possible'. The rule allows a charitable gift which has failed to be applied for other purposes as near as possible to those intended by the settlor or testator.

Before the statutory modifications of the cy-près rule in the form of the Charities Act 1960, the Charities Act 1993 and more recently the Charities Act 2006, the courts possessed a somewhat limited inherent jurisdiction to apply failed charitable gifts cy-près. The inherent jurisdiction could only be exercised in circumstances where it had become 'impossible' or 'impracticable' to carry out the original purposes of the gift. Whilst the courts attempted to construe impossibility and impracticability quite widely, these requirements did severely restrict the grounds for applying failed gifts under the cy-près rule. It will be observed in the course of this chapter that the statutory modifications of the rule have expanded the grounds for applying charitable gifts cy-près. The Charities Act 2006 provides that, when altering the purposes of a charity or a charitable trust, the Charity Commission and the courts should take into account the social and economic circumstances prevailing at the time. The basic objective of the Charities Act 2006, like its predecessors, is to make sure that charitable property is utilised in the most efficient way in the light of modern social and economic situations. These matters are explored in more detail throughout the course of this chapter.

The court's inherent jurisdiction to apply cy-près

Before the Charities Act 1960, the court could only consider applying charitable gifts under the cy-près rule if it had become impossible or impracticable for the purposes of the charity or charitable trust to be carried out. An example of impossibility would arise, for example, where the testator attempts to provide a charitable gift to a charity which simply never existed or which has ceased to exist before the testator's death. For example, in **Re Rymer**[2] a testator bequeathed a sum of money to St Thomas' Seminary for the education of priests in the diocese of Westminster. The testator died in 1893; however, St Thomas' Seminary had ceased to exist before the testator's death and the priests who had been studying there had been transferred to another seminary in Birmingham. The court held that it had become impossible to apply the testator's gift for the original purpose. As to whether the gift could be applied for the seminary in Birmingham, the court held that it could not, on the grounds that the testator had not manifested a general

---

[1] See Chapters 10 and 11 on resulting trusts.
[2] [1895] 1 Ch. 19.

charitable intent, which as will be observed below, is a prerequisite for the application of property cy-près. An example of a nonexistent charity is provided by the decision in **Re Harwood**[3] where the testatrix left property to two institutions: the first was the 'Wisbech Peace Society, Cambridge' and the second was the 'Peace Society of Belfast'. The 'Wisbech Peace Society, Cambridge' had ceased to exist before the testatrix's death. The 'Peace Society of Belfast' had never existed. The court held that both of these gifts had become impossible to apply for their original purposes. The former gift was held to be specific with no general charitable intent, which, therefore, resulted back to the testatrix's estate. The latter gift, however, was construed to evidence a general charitable intent on the part of the testatrix and was, therefore, applied cy-près to other societies promoting peace.

Impossibility and impracticality, whilst serving as a useful starting point for the application of property cy-près, did give rise to a number of problems before the enactment of s. 13 of the Charities Act 1960 which was re-enacted in the Charities Act 1993. The fundamental problem with the requirement of impossibility or impracticality was that it did not allow the law to adapt to changes in social and economic conditions. For example, prior to the enactment of the Charities Act 1960, a trust to distribute food to the poor people of a certain locality was not necessarily impossible, although the fund could be used in a more effective way to relieve poverty. Furthermore, the requirement of impossibility did often produce results which were not necessarily appropriate when the spirit of the gift was examined in more detail. For example, before the Charities Act 1960, a trust to provide education for children of a particular colour would be very difficult to changed under the cy-près principle simply because it was not impossible for the trust to carry out its purposes, albeit offensive on the grounds of the colour bar. Given these problems, it was not surprising that the courts construed the words 'impossibility' and 'impracticality' in a very broad way. The matter is illustrated by the decision in **Re Dominion's Student's Hall Trust**[4] where a company limited by guarantee had been set up to promote community of citizenship, culture and tradition among all members of the British Commonwealth of Nations. One of the objects of the charity was to maintain a hostel for boys of the overseas dominions of the British Empire; however, a colour bar was imposed which restricted the benefits of the hostel for those boys of European origin. The company sought to change the terms of the charity by removing the colour bar, on the grounds that this would antagonise students of all races. The question before Evershed J was whether the cy-près doctrine could be invoked to remove the colour bar. Strictly speaking, the objects of the charity were not impossible or impractical since it was not impossible to apply the colour bar. However, Evershed J held that the cy-près doctrine could be applied to remove the colour bar.[5] The judge explained that the word 'impossibility' was to be interpreted widely and that the inclusion of the colour bar in the objects of the charity would certainly antagonise boys of both European and non-European origin thereby defeating the main purpose of the charity. In the course of his judgment Evershed J explained that whilst it was true that 'a particular charitable purpose cannot be applied cy-près by the court unless it has been shown to be impossible

---

[3] [1936] Ch. 285.

[4] [1947] Ch. 183.

[5] Discrimination on grounds of race, colour, nationality and ethnic origin in the context of charities is governed by s. 34 of the Race Relations Act 1976. This section makes it unlawful to discriminate on such grounds, and any provision which is inserted into a charity which has the effect of such discrimination will be treated as non-operational. For example, a charitable trust for the education of white children only will be treated as a trust for the education of children in general, irrespective of their colour.

to carry out the testator's intention . . . It is not necessary to go to the length of saying that the original scheme is absolutely impracticable. Were that so, it would not be possible to establish in the present case that the charity could not be carried on at all if it continued to be so limited as to exclude coloured members of the Empire.'[6]

The court's inherent jurisdiction was applied in *Re J.W. Laing Trust*[7] which concerned a settlement of shares created in 1922, whereby the trustees of the settlement were directed by the settlor to distribute the income or capital to certain charities during his lifetime or not later than 10 years after his decease. The settlor died in 1978 and the investment in the shares was worth around £24 million. The charities who were the immediate benefactors of the settlement were certain Christian evangelical causes; however, none of them had become part of some central umbrella organisation. None of the causes were fit to receive large amounts of money which had now accrued in the settlement. The question before the court was whether the terms of the settlement could be altered so as to remove the condition that the fund should be distributed within ten years of the settlor's death. Peter Gibson J held that the terms of the settlement could be changed under the cy-près doctrine. In the course of his judgment he explained that 'there is a particular difficulty in relation to providing for the future work of the Christian Brethren because they do not accept any organisation as a governing or controlling body but operate on an individual basis. There would be severe practical inconveniences and difficulties in distributing the very large sums of capital now held by the plaintiff in a way that would ensure continuance of the causes which the settlor wished to support by the charity.'[8] It should be noted that the decision in *Re J.W. Laing Trust*[9] was made at a time when the Charities Act 1960 had already been in force for many years. It will be seen from the discussion below that the Charities Act 1960 had significantly widened the grounds for applying charitable gifts cy-près; however, the Act did not cover an alteration to a charitable gift simply because such alternation was sought on administrative grounds. The alteration of the settlement in *Re J.W. Laing Trust* was primarily to allow the trustees to continue administering funds beyond a time period originally indicated by the settlor.

The court's inherent jurisdiction to apply charitable gift cy-près has been largely superseded by a statutory power to apply charitable gifts cy-près. The statutory power was introduced in s. 13 of the Charities Act 1960 as a result of the recommendations of the Nathan Committee, which reported that the requirements of impossibility and impracticality had proved to be unduly restrictive.[10] Section 13 of the Charities Act 1960, which provided a power to apply charitable gifts cy-près in five situations, was re-enacted in the Charities Act 1993. The Charities Act 2006 has further expanded the grounds for applying charitable gift cy-près. The most significant change, which will be discussed below, is that the power to apply charitable gifts is not necessarily confined to making alterations to a charitable gift which is within the spirit of the original gift. Instead, where the original purposes of the gift have ceased to provide a suitable and effective method of using the property, the courts will be allowed to authorise cy-près schemes by having regard to appropriate considerations. Appropriate considerations include not only the spirit of the gift but also social and economic circumstances prevailing at the time of the proposed alteration of the original purposes. The Charities Bill 2011 will consolidate the Charities Act 1993 and the Charities Act 2006 along with other relevant statutory provisions into one single piece of legislation.

---

[6] [1947] Ch. 183 at 186.
[7] [1984] Ch. 143.
[8] [1984] Ch. 143 at 154.
[9] [1984] Ch. 143.
[10] *Report of the Committee on the Law and Practice Relating to Charitable Trusts* (1952) (Cmmd 8710).

 A general charitable intent

The question whether property can be applied cy-près depends on a number of factors. First of all, as explained in the preceding section, the purposes of the original gift must be covered by one of the grounds in s. 13 of the Charities Act 1993 as amended by the Charities Act 2006. In addition, there must be evidence of a general charitable intention on the part of the donor of the gift. It is only when the donor has manifested a general charitable intention that the original gift can be applied for different purposes. Whether the donor has manifested a general charitable intention depends on the construction of the document purporting to make the charitable gift. The role of the court is to construe whether the donor manifested a general charitable intent or whether his intention was more specific in favour of a particular donee only. The matter is neatly explained by Parker J in **Re Wilson**[11] where the judge explained that:

> the authorities must be divided into two classes. First of all, we have a class of cases where, in form, the gift is given for a particular charitable purpose, but it is possible, taking the will as a whole, to say that, notwithstanding the form of the gift, the paramount intention, according to the true construction of the will, is to give the property in the first instance for a general charitable purpose rather than a particular charitable purpose, and to graft on to the general gift a direction as to the desires or intentions of the testator as to the manner in which the general gift is to be carried into effect. In that case, though it is impossible to carry out the precise directions, on ordinary principles the gift for the general charitable purpose will remain and be perfectly good, and the Court, by virtue of its administrative jurisdiction, can direct a scheme as to how it is to be carried out. In fact the will be read as though the particular direction had not been in the will at all, but there had been simply a general direction as to the application of the fund for the general charitable purpose in question.
>
> Then there is the second class of cases, where, on the true construction of the will, no such paramount general intention can be inferred, and where the gift, being in form a particular gift – a gift for a particular purpose – and it being impossible to carry out that particular purpose, the whole gift is held to fail. In my opinion, the question whether a particular case falls within one of those classes of cases or within the other is simply a question of the construction of a particular instrument.[12]

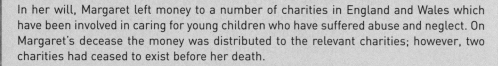

APPLYING THE LAW

In her will, Margaret left money to a number of charities in England and Wales which have been involved in caring for young children who have suffered abuse and neglect. On Margaret's decease the money was distributed to the relevant charities; however, two charities had ceased to exist before her death.

Can the share of those charities be applied for other purposes? Throughout her life Margaret had campaigned for the protection of vulnerable children.

---

[11] [1913] 1 Ch. 314.
[12] [1913] 1 Ch. 314 at 320.

The cases in which a general charitable intention was found include **Biscoe v Jackson**[13] and **Re Woodhams**.[14] In **Biscoe v Jackson** a testator made a gift in his will for providing a soup kitchen and a hospital in Shoreditch. The gift failed on the grounds that it was not possible to carry out these intentions. Nevertheless, despite the specific instructions to provide a soup kitchen and a hospital, the court was able to find a general charitable intention on the part of the testator to benefit the sick and poor people of Shoreditch. In **Re Woodhams** a music teacher left some of his estate to the London College of Music to fund annual scholarships for boys. The terms of the gift, however, restricted the scholarships to boys from two specific orphanages: namely, Dr Barnado's and England Children's Society. The London College of Music was not willing to accept the gift subject to the restrictions imposed by the testator. The question before Vinelott J was whether the gift failed and resulted back to his next of kin on the grounds that the testator had manifested a specific intention or whether the testator had manifested a general charitable intent to further musical education. Vinelott J held that the testator had indeed manifested a general charitable intention and that the reference to these specific orphanages was only evidence of an intention to benefit those more deserving, although not confined to them. In the course of his judgment Vinelott J explained that:

> the testator wanted to further musical education and to do so by means of founding scholarships at colleges with which he had a long and . . . a valued connection. He chose absolute orphans from homes run by well known charities as those most likely to need assistance. But it was not, as I see it, an essential part of this scheme that the scholarships should be so restricted, whatever needs might present themselves in changed circumstances. That being so, that part of the scheme or mode of achieving a charitable purpose can be modified without frustrating his intention.[15]

APPLYING THE LAW

Thomas, who died last year, was a very successful businessman. In his will he directed his trustees that a sum of money be used to erect a business school in his home town and a further sum of money be invested to run the school for underprivileged youngsters wanting to do short courses in how to run their own businesses. The sums of money he has left are insufficient to carry out his objectives and the question is what should be done with the money?

A general charitable intention was not found in **Re Rymer**[16] where a testator bequeathed a sum of money to St Thomas' Seminary for the education of priests in the diocese of Westminster. The testator died in 1893; however, St Thomas' Seminary had ceased to exist before the testator's death and the priests who had been studying there had been transferred to another seminary in Birmingham. The court held that it had become impossible to apply the testator's gift for the original purpose. As to whether the gift

---

[13] (1887) 35 Ch. D 460.
[14] [1981] 1 WLR 493.
[15] [1981] 1 WLR 493 at 505.
[16] [1895] 1 Ch. 19.

could be applied for the seminary in Birmingham, the court held that it could not, on the grounds that the testator had not manifested a general charitable intent. Similarly, in **Re Good's Will Trust**[17] a testator directed that a sum of money be used to erect six rest homes in Hull. The testator had provided specific details, including plans for the management and the running of the homes once they were erected. In particular, the testator had provided certain regulations with regard to the inmates of the houses and then carefully defined the powers and duties of the trustees. The money, however, proved to be insufficient for erecting the six houses in accordance with the specific instructions of the testator. The question before Wynn-Parry J was whether the money could be applied for other similar purposes. The court held that the testator had a specific intention and therefore the money could not be used for other purposes.

Initial failure

In deciding whether to apply charitable gifts cy-près the original purposes of the gift must generally have failed. Although, as will be explored in more detail below, under the Charities Act 1993 as amended by the Charities Act 2006, it is not a prerequisite that, before funds are applied cy-près, there must be a complete failure of the original purposes, the question has arisen as to what amounts to an initial failure of a charitable trust or gift. It may be the case that what at the outset looks like a potential failure of the purposes of the original gift may indeed not be a failure at all. The decided cases have provided a number of principles which are examined in the following subsections.

Gifts to a specific institution

Clearly, where a gift is made with a high degree of precision in respect to the donee of the gift, there will be initial failure of the purposes of the gift if the donee of the gift ceases to exist. For example, it has already been observed in **Re Rymer**[18] that a gift made to a specific seminary that eventually ceased to exist made it impossible for the gift to be applied for its original purposes. In such a case there was a clear initial failure of the gift. It could only be applied cy-près provided that the testator had manifested a general charitable intention which, as observed above, was not present because of the testator's intention to benefit a specific donee. A similar result was arrived at in **Re Harwood**[19] where the testatrix left property to two institutions, the first being the 'Wisbech Peace Society, Cambridge' and the second the 'Peace Society of Belfast'. The 'Wisbech Peace Society, Cambridge' had ceased to exist before the testatrix's death. The 'Peace Society of Belfast' had never existed. The court held that both of these gifts had become impossible to apply for their original purposes. The former gift was held to be specific with no general charitable intent, which, therefore, resulted back to the testatrix's estate. The latter gift, however, was construed to evidence a general charitable intent on the part of the testatrix and was, therefore, applied cy-près to other societies promoting peace.

---

[17] [1950] 2 All ER 653.
[18] [1895] 1 Ch. 19.
[19] [1936] Ch. 285.

A gift to a specific institution without a general charitable intention was more recently found in the decision of the High Court in **Kings v Bultitude**.[20] A certain Mrs Schroder, who had died in 2008, had left the residue of her estate in her will in the following terms:

> to the person who at the time of the payment of the same shall be or act as the Trustee of the Ancient Catholic Church known as the Church of the Good Shepherd at present meeting at Rookwood Road London N16 in the London Borough of Hackney for the general purposes of the said Church and the receipt of such Trustee or the person acting as such shall be a sufficient discharge to my trustees.

The church was described as Mrs Schroder's life and she had devoted all of her time and energies in financing it. Although the church had a long history starting around the 1940s and being affiliated to the Catholic Apostolic Church, from the 1970s Mr and Mrs Schroder were mainly in charge and after Mr Schroder's death in 1985, Mrs Schroder acted as Reverend and she was the only one conducting services and running the church on a day to day basis. She was indeed the sole custodian of the church. After Mrs Schroder's death the church closed and the question before the court was whether there had been an initial failure of the gift in the will which could be applied cy-près if there was a general charitable intent on the part of Mrs Schroder. After looking at all of the evidence, in particular the evidence that the church in question revolved around Mrs Schroder and that her existence was fundamental to the furtherance of the activities of the church, Proudman J held that there had been an initial failure of the trust with no general charitable intention. In the course of his judgment, Proudman J explained that 'there is nothing in the Will to indicate a general charitable intention which might save the gift: contrast **Re Harwood** [1936] 1 Ch 285 with **Re Finger** (below). The Will contains no other charitable gift. The Church was constituted in accordance with the personal idiosyncratic beliefs of its founder, and continued by Mrs Schroder in accordance with her own particular idiosyncrasies.'[21]

Amalgamation with another charity

Sarah executed a will in 2001 in which she left some money to Midland Bright Futures, a registered charity with educational objectives. Sarah died in June 2009 and the executors of her will have discovered that Midland Bright Futures does not exist any more but has amalgamated with another charity called Central Education UK. The executors are not sure what to do with the money left to Midland Bright Futures.

In some cases what may appear to be an initial failure of the gift, for example, where the charity to whom the gift is conferred has ceased to exist, may not in fact be an initial failure because the ceased charity has continued in some other form or has amalgamated with some other charity. The matter is neatly illustrated by the facts of **Re Faraker**[22]

---

[20] [2010] EWHC 1795 (Ch.).
[21] [2010] EWHC 1795 (Ch.) at para. 53. See also, J. Picton, 'Kings v Bultitude – A Gift Lost to Charity' (2011) Conv 69.
[22] [1912] 2 Ch. 488.

where Mrs Faraker, who died in 1911, left property in her will to 'Mrs Bailey's Charity, Rotherhithe'. A charity matching that description had been founded by Mrs Hannah Bayly in 1756 for the relief of poor widows of Rotherhithe. In 1905 the Charity Commission had approved a scheme whereby this charity was consolidated with a number of other charities in the area for the relief of poverty. The question before the Court of Appeal was whether the charity founded by Mrs Hannah Bayly had ceased to exist. The Court of Appeal held that the charity had not ceased to exist, but was amalgamated with other charities. In the course of his judgment Cozens-Hardy MR explained that:

> Hannah Bayly's Charity is not extinct, it is not dead, and I go further and say it cannot die. Its objects may be changed, though not otherwise than in accordance with law: they may be changed either by the Court of Chancery in its own jurisdiction over charities or by schemes formed by the Charity Commissioners, to whom Parliament has entrusted that particular duty. Subject to that lawful alteration by competent authority of the objects, Hannah Bayly's Charity is not extinct, it exists just as much as it did when the testatrix died in 1756, as it did when there were changes made in 1814, and as it does to-day. Now it is to be remembered, as has been pointed out by Kennedy L.J., that this legacy was not given to Mrs. Bayly's Charity for widows; it was simply given to a charity which is identified by name. It was given to an ancient endowed charity, and in my opinion a gift of that kind carries with it the application of it according to the lawful objects of the charity funds for the time being.[23]

The Charities Act 2006 introduces some new measures to deal with the merger of two or more charities.[24] The 2006 Act requires the Charity Commission to keep a register of those mergers which are notified to the Commission.[25] There are two types of mergers that can be registered with the Commission.[26] The first is where, for example, charity A transfers all of its property to charity B and then ceases to exist. The second type of merger is where, for example, charity C and charity D decide to create a new charity – charity E – and then transfer the property of charities C and D to E and then charities C and D cease to exist. The Charities Act 2006 as inserted a new s. 75F into the Charities Act 1993, which deals with the situation where a gift is made to a charity, for example charity A, which has merged with charity B; in such a case the fact that charity A has ceased to exist will not prevent charity B from receiving the gift.

Non-existent charity

It was observed earlier that where a gift is made to a charity which did not exist, the courts are more likely to find a general charitable intent on the part of the donor of the gift. In such a case the gift will not fail but will be available for another purpose as close as possible to the original one. A similar result was arrived at in **Re Harwood**,[27] the facts of which have already been observed earlier in the chapter. The 'Peace Society of Belfast' had never existed. The court held that both of these gifts had become impossible to apply for their original purposes. The former gift was held to be specific with no general charitable intent, which, therefore, resulted back to the testatrix's estate. The latter gift, however, was construed to evidence a general charitable intent on the part of

---

[23] [1912] 2 Ch. 488 at 494.

[24] See S. White, 'The Protection of Legacies and Gifts Upon Merger Under the Charities Act 2006' (2007) PCB 375.

[25] New s. 75C of the Charities Act 1993.

[26] See s. 75C Charities Act 1993.

[27] [1936] Ch. 285.

the testatrix and was, therefore, applied cy-près to other societies promoting peace. A similar result was reached in *Re Satterthwaite's Will Trusts*[28] where a testatrix left her residuary estate to nine animal welfare organisations. One of the organisations, namely the 'London Animal Hospital' did not exist as a charity; however, a veterinary surgeon had practised under that trade name. The question before the Court of Appeal was whether the gift could be claimed by the veterinary surgeon. The Court of Appeal held that the testatrix had made a gift to a non-existent charity and not to the veterinary surgeon. The fact that the testatrix had made a substantial number of gifts to charitable organisations involved in animal welfare was sufficient to show a wide charitable intent. On these grounds the Court of Appeal ordered that the gift be applied cy-près.

Gifts to unincorporated and incorporated charitable associations

When determining whether there has been an initial failure of a gift, it is important to distinguish between gifts which are made to unincorporated charitable associations and gifts which are made to incorporated associations. The reason for this is that every gift to an unincorporated charitable association will take effect as a gift for a charitable purpose and will not fail for want of a trustee. Thus, where a gift is made in favour of an unincorporated charitable association, it will not fail if that association has ceased to exist because the gift will be applied for similar purposes. In such situations the maxim 'a trust will not fail for want of a trustee' is applied to save the gift for other similar purposes. On the other hand a gift to an incorporated charity takes effect as a gift to that incorporated charity. If the incorporated charity has ceased to exist, the gift cannot be applied cy-près unless there is a general charitable intent on the part of the donor. The leading case is *Re Vernon's Will Trust*[29] where a testatrix left her residuary estate to be divided amongst a number of charities in a will created in 1937. One of those charities was the 'Coventry Crippled Children's Guild' which at the time of the execution of the will existed as the 'Coventry and District Crippled Children's Guild'. This charity had been incorporated under the then Companies Act 1919 and provided orthopaedic clinics and other services for crippled children. As a result of the enactment of the Health Service Act 1946, the assets of the company were vested in the Minister of Health and a clinic and hospital was operated at another location in Coventry by a management committee operating under the Health Services Act 1946. The Coventry and District Crippled Children's Guild was dissolved in 1952; however, in 1949 another, unincorporated, charity known as the 'Coventry and District Crippled Guild' was formed. The question before Buckley J in the High Court was whether the estate of the testatrix belonged to the management committee who were running a hospital under the Health Service Act 1946 or whether the estate could be taken by the unincorporated 'Coventry and District Crippled Guild', which was formed after the testatrix's will. Buckley J held that the estate belonged to the management committee who had taken the assets of the incorporated guild. The judge explained that the testatrix had made a specific gift to the incorporated guild and that the work of the incorporated guild continued to be carried out by the management committee of the hospital and clinic operating under the Health Service Act 1946. As such, the management committee was entitled to the estate. In the course of his judgment, Buckley J drew a distinction between charitable gifts to unincorporated and incorporated associations.

---

[28] [1966] 1 WLR 277.
[29] [1972] Ch. 300.

Re Vernon's Will Trust [1972] Ch. 300 (Construing charitable gifts to unincorporated and incorporated associations per Buckley J at 303)

Every bequest to an unincorporated charity by name without more must take effect as a gift for a charitable purpose. No individual or aggregate of individuals could claim to take such a bequest beneficially. If the gift is to be permitted to take effect at all, it must be as a bequest for a purpose, viz., that charitable purpose which the named charity exists to serve. A bequest which is in terms made for a charitable purpose will not fail for lack of a trustee but will be carried into effect either under the Sign Manual or by means of a scheme. A bequest to a named unincorporated charity, however, may on its true interpretation show that the testator's intention to make the gift at all was dependent upon the named charitable organisation being available at the time when the gift takes effect to serve as the instrument for applying the subject matter of the gift to the charitable purpose for which it is by inference given. If so and the named charity ceases to exist in the lifetime of the testator, the gift fails . . . A bequest to a corporate body, on the other hand, takes effect simply as a gift to that body beneficially, unless there are circumstances which show that the recipient is to take the gift as a trustee. There is no need in such a case to infer a trust for any particular purpose. The objects to which the corporate body can properly apply its funds may be restricted by its constitution, but this does not necessitate inferring as a matter of construction of the testator's will a direction that the bequest is to be held in trust to be applied for those purposes: the natural construction is that the bequest is made to the corporate body as part of its general funds, that is to say, beneficially and without the imposition of any trust. That the testator's motive in making the bequest may have undoubtedly been to assist the work of the incorporated body would be insufficient to create a trust.[30]

APPLYING THE LAW

William, who was a retired surgeon, left money in his will to two charitable organisations involved in furthering research into advanced surgery. The first was Alpha Surgery which was an unincorporated association; the second was Beta Surgery Research which was incorporated. William died last month and the executors have established that both institutions had been wound up six months before his death.

What should happen with the money that was left to them?

The principles enunciated by Buckley J were neatly illustrated and applied in **Re Finger's Will Trust** [31] where a testatrix left her residuary estate to a number of different charities. Amongst those charities were the 'National Radium Commission' and the 'National Council for Maternity and Child Welfare'. No institution in the name of the 'National Radium Council' existed; however, an unincorporated association known as the 'Radium Commission' had existed until 1947 when it was wound up and the work taken over by the Minister of Health. The 'National Council for Maternity and Child

---

[30] [1972] Ch. 300 at 303.
[31] [1972] Ch. 268.

Welfare' had existed as an incorporated body but was wound up in 1948 and its assets were transferred to the National Association for Maternity and Child Welfare. The question before Goff J was whether the gifts to 'National Radium Council' and the 'National Council for Maternity and Child Welfare' failed or whether they could be applied cy-près. Goff J held that the gift to the 'National Radium Council' was to be construed as a gift for a purpose and that, because the purposes of the 'National Radium Council' were still very much being carried out, the gift could be applied under a scheme for similar purposes. On the other hand, Goff J construed the gift to the 'National Council for Maternity and Child Welfare' as a gift to a specific incorporated body. The fact that the 'National Council for Maternity and Child Welfare' had ceased to exist normally meant that the gift would result back to the testatrix's estate unless there was a general charitable intent on the part of the testatrix. As to whether there was a general charitable intention on the part of the testatrix, Goff J held that there was a general charitable intent, on the grounds that a construction of the testatrix's will indicated a general intention to devote her estate to charitable causes.

The distinction between gifts to unincorporated and incorporated charitable organisations was applied in **Re ARMS (Multiple Sclerosis Research) Ltd**[32] where the issue before the court was whether the liquidator of an incorporated charitable company was entitled to a number of gifts made by a testator, or whether those gifts could be applied cy-près. On the facts, a testator had made a number of gifts to ARMS (Multiple Sclerosis Research) Ltd, which was an incorporated company researching into the cure and prevention of multiple sclerosis. When the company ran into financial problems it was wound up, owing money to a number of preferential and ordinary creditors. Neuberger J held that the money which had been given by the testator belonged to the company and was not impressed with any purpose trust. The judge explained that, although testators did not as a matter of intention donate money to charities in order for it be used to meet the needs of creditors, there was a clear distinction between gifts to charitable incorporated associations and charitable unincorporated associations. In respect of incorporated associations, Neuberger J adopted a rather strict approach in holding that the mere fact that the incorporated association was a charity did not mean that the testator intended that the gifts were made for charitable purposes rather than belonging specifically to the incorporated association.

The distinction between construing gifts to incorporated and unincorporated associations is a rather problematic one. It is not absolutely clear why a gift to an unincorporated charitable association should be construed as a gift for a purpose whilst a gift to an incorporated association is construed as a gift specifically for the incorporated association. Certainly it cannot be the case that the distinction is based on the intentions of the donor. For example, when making a charitable gift to an association, whether incorporated or unincorporated, can it truly be said that the testator had two different intentions in respect of gifts made to the two different associations? Surely, in both cases the intention of the donor is to make a gift for charitable purposes which would be carried out by the association irrespective of its legal status. The apparent difficulty with this distinction was explained by Harman J in **Re Meyers**[33] where a testator had made a series of gifts to a number of hospitals, some of which were incorporated and others unincorporated. All these hospitals had been taken over by the Minister of Health under the Health Services

---

[32] [1997] 2 All ER 679. See A. Dunn, 'Construing Bequests to Charitable Companies in the Course of Winding Up' (1997) *Company Lawyer* 213.
[33] [1951] 1 All ER 538.

Act 1946. The question before the court was whether these gifts could be continued to be applied by the Minister of Health or whether they failed. With regard to the gifts made to the unincorporated associations, Harman J found no problem in construing these as gifts for the purposes of the work of the hospital which continued under the auspices of the Minister of Health. With regard to the gifts to the incorporated hospitals, Harman J likewise construed the gifts as gifts for purposes and therefore available to the Minister of Health. In the course of his judgment Harman J explained: 'I am doing no violence to the language which the testator has used, in the context in which he has used it, in saying that in every case when he gave money to a hospital he did not regard the fact whether it was corporate or not, but he gave to the work that that hospital was carrying on.'[34]

Discriminatory conditions

A court is unlikely to find initial failure in cases where a charitable gift is accompanied by a condition precedent which the court deems as being discriminatory, offensive or otherwise unnecessary in light of the spirit of the gift. The matter is illustrated by the decision in **Re Lysaght**[35] where a testatrix left money in her will to the Royal College of Surgeons to provide medical studentships. The terms of the gift, however, restricted the studentships to those students who were male and sons of qualified British born men. The terms of the gift did not allow such studentships to be conferred upon students of Jewish or Roman Catholic faith. The Royal College of Surgeons refused to accept the gift subject to the conditions imposed by the testatrix, on the grounds that this would be inconsistent with the work and objectives of the College. The question before Buckley J was whether the gift to the Royal College of Surgeons failed on the grounds that the College, being the trustee of the gift, was not prepared to accept the gift. Buckley J held that the gift did not fail and the Royal College of Surgeons were able to take the money free from the conditions imposed by the testatrix as regards students being male and sons of British qualified doctors in addition to not being of Jewish or Roman Catholic faith. Buckley J concluded that the testatrix had manifested a general charitable intention to further the work of the Royal College of Surgeons and that the conditions imposed in her will as regards the gift did not form part of her paramount intention. It has already been observed above that a similar result was arrived at in **Re Woodhams**[36] where a music teacher left some of his estate to the London College of Music to fund annual scholarships for boys. The terms of the gift, however, restricted the scholarships to boys from two specific orphanages. The court concluded that the reference to the two specific orphanages was not part of the paramount intention of the testator, rather only evidence of the testators' desire to benefit those more deserving than others.

Subsequent failure

As a general rule, the application of gifts cy-près is broader in cases of subsequent failure. Subsequent failure occurs in cases where a gift to a charitable organisation has been received by the organisation and, after receipt of the gift, the charitable organisation ceases to exist. The general position in charity law is that once property is received by

---

[34] [1951] 1 All ER 538 at 542.
[35] [1966] Ch. 191.
[36] [1981] 1 WLR 493.

charity it remains in the pot of the charity. Thus, where there is subsequent failure, the gift or any surplus does not as a matter of general principle result back to the donor of the gift. Instead, the gift is applied cy-près for purposes close to the original ones. The relevant time for determining whether the property results back or is applied cy-près is on the death of the testator. If at the time of the testator's death the property is capable of being applied for the intended charitable purposes then it will be applied cy-près, even though it may become impracticable or impossible after the testator's death. The matter is neatly illustrated by the decision in *Re Slevin*[37] where a testator left a number of pecuniary legacies to various charitable organisations. One of those organisations was an orphanage which ceased to exist shortly after the testator's death. The question before the Court of Appeal was whether the gift failed and resulted back to the testator's estate or whether the Attorney General could apply the gift cy-près. The Court of Appeal held that the crucial time to determine whether the gift resulted back to the testator's estate or whether it was applied cy-près was on the testator's death. If at the time of the testator's death the charity was still in existence, then it became the property of the charity. In such a case there could be no room for a resulting trust; instead the gift would be applied cy-près, irrespective of any general charitable intention on the part of the testator. In the course of his judgment Kay LJ explained that the gift should be applied cy-près 'not on the ground that there is such a general charitable intention that the fund should be administered cy-près even if the charity had failed in the testator's lifetime, but because, as the charity existed at the testator's death, this legacy became the property of that charity, and on its ceasing to exist its property falls to be administered by the Crown, who will apply it, according to custom, for some analogous purpose of charity . . .'[38] A similar conclusion was arrived in *Re Wright*[39] where a testatrix directed that her residuary estate be given to a tenant for life and thereafter used as a convalescent home for impecunious gentlewomen. The testatrix died in 1933 and the tenant for life died in 1942. In 1942 it became impracticable to provide a convalescent home and the question was whether the property resulted back to the testatrix's next of kin. The Court of Appeal held that the relevant time of determining whether the testatrix's property resulted back to her next of kin was on the testatrix's death. At the time of her death in 1933 her residuary estate had been dedicated to the tenant for life and the provision of a convalescent home and, as this was practicable in 1933, the property became that of charity. The property was therefore ordered to be applied cy-près.

APPLYING THE LAW

Katherine made a number of gifts to charitable organisations in her will. One gift was made to 'Attack Poverty' which had been registered as a charity in the West Midlands but ceased to exist a year after her death, with a surplus of funds. Another gift was to a charitable project undertaken in the Midlands to assess the factors contributing to poverty. That project came to an end a year after her death, leaving £30,000 in unexhausted funds. Katherine was the sole contributor to the fund.

What should be done with the surplus funds?

[37] [1891] 2 Ch. 236.
[38] [1891] 2 Ch. 236 at 343.
[39] [1954] Ch. 347.

Whilst the application of charitable gifts cy-près is much easier in cases of subsequent failure – for example, it is not necessary to show that the donor of the charitable gift had a general charitable intention – it should be noted that the position with regards to surplus funds is rather more complicated. In **Re King**[40] a testatrix left a sum of money in the region of £1,500 to provide a stained-glass window in a church in memory of her parents, her sister and herself. The cost of the window was in fact only £800 and the question before Romer J was what should happen with the surplus fund. Romer J held that the whole of the £1,500 had been dedicated to charity and, therefore, the surplus could be applied cy-près for the provision of a second window. The same conclusion, however, was not arrived in **Re Stanford**[41] where a surplus existed after the completion of a dictionary. Eve J declined to order the surplus fund to be used cy-près, on the grounds that the testator had not manifested a general charitable intention that the property should be dedicated outright to charity. In the course of his judgment, the judge explained:

> I cannot bring myself to hold that in making this bequest he had any general charitable intention or indeed any intention beyond the obvious one of getting one or other of the Universities to produce the work. In these circumstances I do not think there is any case for the application of the cy-près doctrine; there is a resulting trust for the testator, and those claiming under him, of the surplus moneys, and they fall to be dealt with as part of his residuary estate.[42]

Eve J distinguished **Re King**[43] on the grounds that in that case the testatrix had manifested a general charitable intention.

In the context of surplus fund it seems undecided in the case law whether surplus fund will automatically be applied cy-près or whether there is a need for general charitable intent on the part of the donor that he intended the property to be given to charity outright. In **Re Stanford**[44] the court took the view that the gift was so specific that the surplus fund could not be applied cy-près because of the absence of a general charitable intention. In most cases, however, the finding of general charitable intention in cases of a surplus fund will be readily inferred by the court. This is particularly so in the context of public appeals. For example, in **Re Welsh Hospital (Netley) Fund**[45] a hospital was built in Wales after the outbreak of the First World War to provide relief to the sick and injured soldiers in Wales. A few years later, the hospital was wound up and the question arose as to what should be done with the surplus funds. The court held that the surplus fund could be applied cy-près, on the grounds that the contributors had manifested a general charitable intent and did not want the donated money to be returned under a resulting trust. In **Re Wokingham Fire Brigade Trusts**,[46] however, Danckwerts J took the view that it was not necessary to establish a general charitable intention in cases of a surplus fund. On the facts, a fire brigade had been purchased by the National Fire Service and the question before the court was what should be

---

[40] [1923] 1 Ch. 243.
[41] [1924] 1 Ch. 73.
[42] [1924] 1 Ch. 73 at 77.
[43] [1923] 1 Ch. 243.
[44] [1924] 1 Ch. 73.
[45] [1921] 1 Ch. 655.
[46] [1951] Ch. 373.

done with the proceeds of sale. Danckwerts J held that the money had been held for charitable purposes in general and therefore could be applied cy-près. It should be noted here that, although s. 14 of the Charities Act 1993 as modified by the Charities Act 2006 provides for destination of charitable collections cy-près, the section does not apply to cases of surplus funds. This section is discussed in more detail below; for the present time, the law relating to the destination of surplus charitable funds remains to be clearly established in case law.

 ## The Charities Act 1993

Earlier in this chapter it was observed that the court's inherent jurisdiction to authorise charitable gifts to be applied cy-près was limited in cases where the original gift had become impossible or impractical to be applied. Impossibility and impracticality, whilst serving as a useful starting point for the application of property cy-près, did give rise to a number of problems. The fundamental problem with the requirement of impossibility or impracticality was that it did not allow the law to adapt to changes in social and economic conditions. For example, prior to the enactment of the Charities Act 1960, a trust to distribute food to the poor people was not necessarily impossible, although the fund could be used in a more effective way to relieve poverty. Furthermore, the requirement of impossibility did often produce results which were not necessarily appropriate when the spirit of the gift was examined in more detail. For example, before the Charities Act 1960, a trust to provide education for children of a particular colour would be very difficult to change under the cy-près principle, simply because it was not impossible for the trust to carry out its purposes, albeit offensive on the grounds of the colour bar.[47] Although the courts did adopt a liberal approach in the interpretation of the words 'impossibility and impracticality',[48] it was clearly recognised that the grounds for invoking cy-près should be expanded.[49]

The present grounds for invoking the cy-près jurisdiction is found in s. 13 of the Charities Act 1993 as amended by s. 15 of the Charities Act 2006.[50] Section 13 of the Charities Act provides a much wider jurisdiction for invoking cy-près. The section provides for five situations in which charitable gifts can be applied cy-près. As will be seen in the next section, the fundamental change implemented by the Charities Act 2006 is that, when exercising the jurisdiction in s. 13 of the Charities Act 1993, the court or the Charity Commission can have regard to the spirit of the gift as well as prevailing social and economic circumstances before authorising a gift to be applied cy-près.

---

[47] Although, as mentioned earlier, discrimination on grounds of race and colour would now be governed by s. 34 of the Race Relations Act 1976 which makes such discrimination unlawful.

[48] See, for example, *Re Dominion's Hall Trust* [1947] Ch. 183 where reference to a colour bar was removed even though it was not impossible or impractical for the trust to be administered with the colour bar in place.

[49] These recommendations coming from the Nathan Committee; see *Report of the Committee on the Law and Practice Relating to Charitable Trusts* (1952) (Cmmd 8710).

[50] Section 13 was first introduced in the Charities Act 1960.

KEY STATUTE

S. 13 of the Charities Act 1993 as amended by the Charities Act 2006 (Occasions for applying property cy-près)

(1) Subject to subsection (2) below, the circumstances in which the original purposes of a charitable gift can be altered to allow the property given or part of it to be applied cy-près shall be as follows –

(a) where the original purposes, in whole or in part –

(i) have been as far as may be fulfilled; or

(ii) cannot be carried out, or not according to the directions given and to the spirit of the gift; or

(b) where the original purposes provide a use for part only of the property available by virtue of the gift; or

(c) where the property available by virtue of the gift and other property applicable for similar purposes can be more effectively used in conjunction, and to that end can suitably, regard being had to [the appropriate considerations], be made applicable to common purposes; or

(d) where the original purposes were laid down by reference to an area which then was but has since ceased to be a unit for some other purpose, or by reference to a class of persons or to an area which has for any reason since ceased to be suitable, regard being had to [the appropriate considerations], or to be practical in administering the gift; or

(e) where the original purposes, in whole or in part, have, since they were laid down, –

(i) been adequately provided for by other means; or

(ii) ceased, as being useless or harmful to the community or for other reasons, to be in law charitable; or

(iii) ceased in any other way to provide a suitable and effective method of using the property available by virtue of the gift, regard being had to [the appropriate considerations].

(1A) In subsection (1) above 'the appropriate considerations' means –

(a) (on the one hand) the spirit of the gift concerned, and

(b) (on the other) the social and economic circumstances prevailing at the time of the proposed alteration of the original purposes.

It is clear from a reading of s. 13 of the Charities Act 1993 that the modern grounds for invoking cy-près are much broader. For example, it is now possible to invoke cy-près where the original purposes of the gift have been adequately fulfilled by other means or where the original purposes cannot be carried out in light of the spirit of the gift. One of the very first cases to be decided under s. 13 was ***Re Lepton's Charity***[51] where a testator, in a will executed in 1715, directed trustees to pay a sum of £3 per annum

---

[51] [1972] Ch. 276, decided under s. 13. Charities Act 1960.

to a Protestant Minister in order to preach in Pudsey and also to pay the overplus of profits from land to the poor people of Pudsey. In 1715 the income from the land was £5 per annum, but in 1970 that income had increased to some £800 per annum. The question before Pennycuick J was whether the income of the Minister could be increased from £3 per annum to £100 per annum. Pennycuick J ordered that the income be increased, on the grounds that s. 13 applied. In the first place, the judge explained that the original purposes in whole could not be carried out in the spirit of the gift under s. 13(1)(a)(i). Additionally, it was held that a change in the Minister's income could be authorised under s. 13(1)(e)(iii) in that the original purposes ceased in any other way to provide a suitable and effective method of using the property available by virtue of the gift. Section 13(1)(e)(iii) was invoked in **Varsani v Jesani**[52] where a Hindu sect, having split up into two parties, could not resolve their differences. On the question whether members of one party could remove trustees belonging to the other party, the court held that, in the absence of having jurisdiction to resolve their differences, they could resolve the matter under s. 13(1)(e)(iii) of the Charities Act 1993. The Court of Appeal held that under that section the original purposes of the charity ceased in any other way to provide a suitable and effective method of using the property within the spirit of the gift. The Court of Appeal ordered that the assets of the charity be divided equally amongst the two parties.

The approach taken by the Court of Appeal was recently endorsed by the High Court in **White v Williams**[53] where trustees of an ecclesiastic charity claimed by way of cy-près a large Victorian place of worship situated in Lewisham. The building formed part of the assets of the Bibleway Trust. The Bibleway Trust in fact owned four church buildings, the Lewisham building as well as church buildings in Bethnal Green, Mitcham and Cambridge. The trustees of the Bibleway trust were entirely from the Cambridge congregation. Due to a schism the Bibleway Trust was split into two different factions. Both the Mitcham and Bethnal Green congregations went their separate ways and decided not to have any affiliation to the Bibleway Trust UK. The Lewisham congregation also split away from the two factions and decided to operate independently of the Bibleway Trust. The pastor of the Lewisham congregation, who was also a trustee of what was known as the Tabernacle Trust, claimed the property in Lewisham from the trustees of the Bibleway Trust on two main grounds. In the first place, the existing trustees of the Lewisham building had no connection with the Lewisham congregation. Secondly, the purported use of the Lewisham building by the trustees of the Bibleway Trust were inconsistent with the spirit of the gift, which was to provide a place of worship in Lewisham. Indeed, the existing trustees had threatened to sell the building.

The High Court held that it had jurisdiction under s. 13(1)(e)(iii) and s. 14B of the Charities Act 1993 to transfer the Lewisham Building to the claimant trustees of the Tabernacle Trust. It will be recalled that under s. 13(1)(e)(iii) the court can make a scheme when the original purposes, in whole or in part, have, since they were laid down, ceased in any other way to provide a suitable and effective method of using the property available by virtue of the gift, regard being had to appropriate considerations. Subsection 1A defines appropriate considerations as the spirit of the gift and social and economic circumstances prevailing at the time of the proposed alteration of the original purposes. The Court held that since the spirit of the original gift was to

---

[52] [1999] Ch. 219.
[53] [2010] EWHC 940.

provide places of worship in the respective localities, that purpose still continuing, the properties could be vested in the respective trustees of the congregations of Mitcham, Bethnal Green and indeed Lewisham. In the course of his judgment, Briggs J explained that:

> I have no doubt that the matters which have engaged the court's jurisdiction under section 13, considered together with the additional matters set out in section 14B of the Act, are such as to require the making or direction of a scheme. The present situation, under which the Bibleway Trust's places of worship are controlled by trustees who are as the result of the schism unable meaningfully to communicate with the congregations who worship and witness there, should not be allowed to continue. The eviction of the congregations, as threatened by the defendant Trustees, cannot be an appropriate solution. Nor should each congregation be required, as the defendants have demanded, in effect to re-purchase their own place of worship, after having raised the funds for its acquisition in the first place. Since the three relevant congregations are, although in friendly relations with each other, now independent and autonomous, the replacement of the defendants by a single set of new trustees is unlikely to be a satisfactory solution either, at least in the long term. A scheme or schemes whereby each place of worship is transferred to separate trustees whose role is directed to the fulfilment of purposes specific to the congregation or locality associated with it seems to me to be plainly the best solution.'[54]

Section 13 was further applied in **Peggs v Lamb**[55] where the cy-près doctrine was invoked to enlarge the class of persons who were capable of benefiting from a charitable gift. The facts concerned land which was enjoyed by the freemen and their widows in the area of Huntingdon for a long period of time. Income from the land was generally paid to the needy and poor freemen in Huntingdon. The freemen received rent from the land, and despite the fact that the land had been acquired by the Huntingdon Corporation by virtue of the Municipal Corporations Act 1835, the freemen continued to receive the benefits from the land. The Charity Commission recognised the freemen's right to take income from the land as being charitable, on the grounds that it was an anomalous locality case. Although in the past there had been a substantial number of freemen in the area, that number had dropped substantially so that by the time of the litigation that number had dropped to as low as fifteen. The fifteen freemen claimed the income, which would entitle them to over £30,000 per annum, irrespective of their need. The question before Morritt J was whether the class to benefit had since ceased to be a suitable class under s. 13(1)(d). Morritt J held that the original purposes of the charity had ceased to be suitable with regard to the spirit of the gift and ordered that the benefits of the charity be extended to all the inhabitants of Huntingdon and not just the freemen. The judge explained that '[t]he original basic intention or spirit of the gift was the benefit of the borough of Huntingdon. It would, in my judgment, be entirely consistent with that, that in 1993 the class of persons by reference to which the charitable purposes are laid down should be enlarged from the freemen to the inhabitants as a whole.'[56]

---

[54] [2011] EWHC 494 at para. 108.
[55] [1994] Ch. 172.
[56] [1994] Ch. 172 at 197.

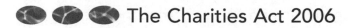 # The Charities Act 2006

Regard to social and economic circumstances

As mentioned earlier in this chapter, the Charities Act 2006 has made further changes to the grounds for the application of charitable gifts cy-près. Whereas s. 13 of the Charities Act 1993 required the courts and the Charity Commission to have regard to 'the spirit of the gift' before it authorised property to be applied cy-près under s. 13(1)(c), (d) and (e), the Charities Act 2006 substitutes 'the spirit of the gift' for 'appropriate considerations'. When authorising a cy-près scheme the courts must have regard to 'appropriate considerations' which, as can be seen from the newly inserted s. 1A of the Charities Act 1993, requires the courts and the Charity Commission to have regard, not only to 'the spirit of the gift', but also the 'prevailing social and economic circumstances'.

KEY STATUTE

S. 15 of the Charities Act 2006 (Amending s. 13 of the Charities Act 1993 – application of cy-près by reference to current circumstance)

(1) Section 13 of the 1993 Act (occasions for applying property cy-près) is amended as follows.

(2) In subsection (1)(c), (d) and (e)(iii), for 'the spirit of the gift' substitute 'the appropriate considerations'.

(3) After subsection (1) insert –

'(1A) In subsection (1) above "the appropriate considerations" means –

(a) (on the one hand) the spirit of the gift concerned, and

(b) (on the other) the social and economic circumstances prevailing at the time of the proposed alteration of the original purposes.'

Although the Charities Act 2006 has amended s. 13 of the Charities Act 1993 by requiring the courts and the Charity Commission to have regard to the social and economic circumstances prevailing at the time of the proposed alteration of a charitable gift, it is not quite true to say that this is something which is new in terms of the practice of the Charity Commission and the approach of the courts. Although the requirement to have regard to prevailing social and economic circumstances now firmly finds itself embedded in s. 13 of the Charities Act 1993, the courts and the Charity Commission did indeed have regard to prevailing social and economic circumstances in the past. For example, the decision in **Re Lepton's Charity** [57] is a very good example where the court authorised the increase in payment to a Minister to reflect modern economic circumstances. Likewise, the decision in **Peggs v Lamb** [58] is a very good example where the court had regard to the changed social and economic circumstances with regard to freemen in Huntingdon. You will recall from above that the court altered the original charitable gift to allow a larger community to enjoy the benefits of a charity which had become socially and economically obsolete.

---

[57] [1972] Ch. 276, decided under s. 13 Charities Act 1960.
[58] [1994] Ch. 172.

Charity Commission guidance on 'social and economic circumstances'

In its recent guidance, the Charity Commission has explained what it means by 'prevailing social and economic conditions'.

KEY CITATION	The Charity Commission: *Application of property cy-près: the law and how it should be applied* OG2 1A (March 2008)

Before the implementation of the 2006 Act, our main consideration was the spirit of the original gift. Under the new provisions we will also take into account current social and economic circumstances when considering cases that fall within s. 13(1)(c), (d) and (e).

The 'spirit of the gift' in the context of s. 13 means the basic intention underlying the original gift as a whole: *Re Lepton's Charity* [1972] Ch 276. The intention may be clear from the terms of the governing document of the charity: if not, records available at the time the charity was established, or even the way in which the charity has been administered and managed over the years, may be relevant.

The meaning of 'social and economic circumstances prevailing at the time of the proposed alteration' is not defined, but is about evaluating the ongoing usefulness of the charity's trusts. This provision enables the Commission to consider other relevant factors alongside the spirit of the original gift in deciding whether a cy-près occasion has arisen, placing equal emphasis on the wording of the original purposes and the needs and circumstances of current beneficiaries. It is clear from the Parliamentary debates on the Charities Bill that the phrase 'social and economic circumstances' is intended to be interpreted broadly, and to encompass all relevant circumstances that the trustees or the Commission might need to take into account when deciding how or whether the purposes of the charity should be altered. Other authorities have suggested that this could therefore include environmental, legal, scientific or technological considerations.

We might take into account, for example, the following:

In some cases the provision of specific articles such as food or fuel may no longer be the most practical means of relieving financial hardship or other forms of disadvantage.

Provision of care for people with disabilities is now generally based around enabling them to live in their own homes rather than housing them in institutions.

In some cases the social or economic circumstances that led to the setting up of a charity (e.g. to provide education or housing) for members of one sex only may have changed over time.

The objects of some charities may imply outdated social or moral judgements about potential beneficiaries, such as 'deserving poor' (historically, poor people who could work but didn't were officially classed as 'idle' and therefore undeserving). These may unnecessarily restrict the beneficiary class. Some objects contain language that could now be offensive or off-putting to potential beneficiaries or donors, such as 'crippled', 'handicapped', 'invalid' or 'insane'.

Current social and economic circumstances are not an entirely new consideration in charity law. In the case of *Re Hanbey's Will Trusts* [[1956] Ch 264] . . . the court considered the 'social utility' of the charity's objects as well as the intentions of the founder.

Cy-près when there are primary and secondary trusts

One question which has been the subject matter of recent discussion by the Charity Commission relates to the extent to which the courts and the Charity Commission can authorise the use of property cy-près where there are primary and secondary trusts attached to the same property.[59] For example, suppose that property is dedicated to charity A which, in the event of failure, is then dedicated to charity B. The question raised by the Charity Commission is whether cy-près is available in the event of charity A failing without the need to give the property to charity B. In its guidance, the Charity Commission has explained that it is possible to order charitable property to be applied cy-près where there has been a failure of the primary trust and even where the secondary trust is workable. In exercising the discretion to order the property to be applied cy-près, thereby defeating the secondary trust, the court or the Charity Commission must have regard to the intentions of the founder and social utility in addition to prevailing social and economic circumstances. The effect of this is to allow property to be applied more effectively than simply allow it to be given over to the secondary trust which may not be as advantageous as the scheme proposed by applying the property cy-près.

In its operational guidance, the Charity Commission explained that:

> in situations where the primary trust has failed, trustees may ask us to make a cy-près Scheme under s. 13(1) of the 1993 Act to change the objects, even though there are second-ary trusts which are still workable. We should consider such a request very carefully, as we have to weigh up whether the intentions of the founder, and social utility, are better served by modifying the primary trusts, or by requiring the beneficiaries of the secondary trust to be preferred . . . Ascertaining the intentions of the founder (the spirit of the original gift) may be complicated where there are secondary trusts. It might appear that simply allowing the secondary trust to take effect would always be more consistent with the intention of the founder, rather than allowing the primary trust to continue in a different form. But normally, the founder would be more concerned with the primary trust than with the secondary one. If the primary trust could be amended without altering it in any real substance, that might seem more consistent with the founder's intentions than allowing the secondary trust to take effect, particularly if the secondary trust was substantially different to the primary one.[60]

With regard to the question of 'social utility' which is analogous to 'prevailing current social and economic circumstances, the Charity Commission referred to the decision in **Re Hanbey's Will Trusts**[61] where property had been settled in favour of two charitable trusts. In 1786, by his will, a testator directed that a sum of money be invested and the annual income given to various charitable causes with a gift over to the Christ Hospital. Since 1917 the trustees had found it increasingly difficult to give the annual income to beneficiaries of the primary trust and the question was whether the gift over to the School took effect or whether the original trust could be altered by making a new scheme. The court held that it had a power either to make or refuse a scheme altering the original trusts and in exercising that power it would take into consideration the intentions of the settlor as well as social utility. In the course of his judgment Danckwerts J explained:

> first, has the court power to direct a scheme? It seems to me that the court has power to direct a scheme. Secondly, if the court does direct a scheme, will that scheme, continuing

---

[59] See Charity Commission, *Application of Property Cy-près: The Use of the Cy-près Doctrine Where There are Secondary Trusts*, OG 2 B2 March 2008.

[60] Charity Commission, *Application of Property Cy-près: The Use of the Cy-près Doctrine Where There are Secondary Trusts*, OG 2 B2 March 2008 at pp. 1–2.

[61] [1956] Ch. 264.

the original trusts in a different form, have the effect of defeating the gift over? It seems to me that the answer to that must also be in the affirmative, that is to say, that such a scheme will defeat the gift over because the original trust will continue although it will be in an altered form which is authorized by law.[62]

Charity donations and unidentifiable donors

So far this chapter has explored the grounds for applying the cy-près doctrine where the purposes of the original trust fail or are otherwise caught by s. 13 of the Charities Act 1993. Where property has been collected through, for example, donations, collections in boxes or the proceeds of entertainments, the question arises as to what should be done with such collections should the purposes for which the collections were made become impossible to carry out. Before the enactment of s. 14 of the Charities Act 1960, now s. 14 of the Charities Act 1993, the law was in a rather unsatisfactory state. Certainly, it was not possible to apply the collected funds, which had now become impossible for their original purposes, for other purposes as close as possible under the cy-près doctrine. Instead, the law required that the money be returned to the original donors, and if they could not be found, that the money be paid into court. Alternatively, in the case of money raised by entertainment such as raffle tickets, the money was ordered *bona vacantia*. Section 14 of the Charities Act 1993 allows property, which has been given for specific charitable purposes which have failed, to be applied cy-près. The section imputes a general charitable intention, provided that certain conditions are met. Essentially, the requirements under s. 14 are that property must belong to donors who, after advertisements and inquiries as prescribed by the Charity Commission have been made, cannot be found or identified. In such a case the property can be applied for other purposes as close as those to the original ones, taking into consideration the spirit of the gift and prevailing social and economic considerations. Additionally, s. 14 allows property, which has been given for specific charitable purposes, to be applied cy-près where a donor has executed a disclaimer to the effect that he does not want the property returned to him.

Section 14(3) of the Charities Act 1993 states that property will be presumed to belong to unidentifiable donors where it consists of proceeds of collections boxes, lottery, competitions, entertainment or similar fund-raising activities. In such a case, there is no need for any advertisements and inquiries as to the identity of the donors. In this sense, s. 14(3) makes it much easier for the proceeds of collections boxes and the like to be applied cy-près.

KEY STATUTE

S. 14 of the Charities Act 1993 (Application cy-près of gifts of donors unknown or disclaiming)

(1) Property given for specific charitable purposes which fail shall be applicable cy-près as if given for charitable purposes generally, where it belongs –

(a) to a donor who after –

(i) the prescribed advertisements and inquiries have been published and made, and

---

[62] [1956] Ch. 264 at 274.

(ii) the prescribed period beginning with the publication of those advertisements has expired, cannot be identified or cannot be found; or

(b) to a donor who has executed a disclaimer in the prescribed form of his right to have the property returned.

(2) Where the prescribed advertisements and inquiries have been published and made by or on behalf of trustees with respect to any such property, the trustees shall not be liable to any person in respect of the property if no claim by him to be interested in it is received by them before the expiry of the period mentioned in subsection (1)(a)(ii) above.

(3) For the purposes of this section property shall be conclusively presumed (without any advertisement or inquiry) to belong to donors who cannot be identified, in so far as it consists –

(a) of the proceeds of cash collections made by means of collecting boxes or by other means not adapted for distinguishing one gift from another; or

(b) of the proceeds of any lottery, competition, entertainment, sale or similar money-raising activity, after allowing for property given to provide prizes or articles for sale or otherwise to enable the activity to be undertaken.

The Charities Act 2006 has made further reforms in the context of money raised in response to a solicitation or an appeal. A new s. 14A is inserted into the Charities Act 1993 by the Charities Act 2006. The essence of the newly inserted s. 14A is that it allows money raised in the context of a public appeal to be applied cy-près in circumstances where the money cannot be used or where the money has not been totally exhausted. In such a case there is no need to make inquiries as to the identity of the donors, provided that the appeal is accompanied with a general statement that, unless the donor makes a declaration that he wants the money to be returned to him, it will be deemed as given for charitable purposes generally. If the donor does make a declaration to the effect that he does want the property returned to him in the event that it cannot be applied for the purposes for which it is given, then s. 14A(5) requires trustees to take appropriate steps to find the donor before the money can be applied cy-près.

S. 14A of the Charities Act 1993 (Application cy-près of gifts made in response to certain solicitations)

(1) This section applies to property given –

(a) for specific charitable purposes, and

(b) in response to a solicitation within subsection (2) below.

(2) A solicitation is within this subsection if –

(a) it is made for specific charitable purposes, and

(b) it is accompanied by a statement to the effect that property given in response to it will, in the event of those purposes failing, be applicable cy-près as if given for charitable purposes generally, unless the donor makes a relevant declaration at the time of making the gift.

(3) A 'relevant declaration' is a declaration in writing by the donor to the effect that, in the event of the specific charitable purposes failing, he wishes the trustees holding the property to give him the opportunity to request the return of the property in question (or a sum equal to its value at the time of the making of the gift).

(4) Subsections (5) and (6) below apply if –

(a) a person has given property as mentioned in subsection (1) above,

(b) the specific charitable purposes fail, and

(c) the donor has made a relevant declaration.

(5) The trustees holding the property must take the prescribed steps for the purpose of –

(a) informing the donor of the failure of the purposes,

(b) enquiring whether he wishes to request the return of the property (or a sum equal to its value), and

(c) if within the prescribed period he makes such a request, returning the property (or such a sum) to him.

(6) If those trustees have taken all appropriate prescribed steps but –

(a) they have failed to find the donor, or

(b) the donor does not within the prescribed period request the return of the property (or a sum equal to its value),

section 14(1) above shall apply to the property as if it belonged to a donor within paragraph (b) of that subsection (application of property where donor has disclaimed right to return of property).

 ## Cy-près schemes

Section 14B of the Charities Act 1993[63] sets out the factors which the court or the Charity Commission must have regard to when exercising its power to make a cy-près scheme. Section 14B requires the court or Charity Commission to have regard to:

- the spirit of the original gift;
- the desirability of securing that the property is applied for charitable purposes which are close to the original purposes;
- the need to ensure that the charity has purposes which are suitable and effective in the light of current social and economic circumstances.

Where a scheme is made by which the assets of one charity are transferred to another, s. 14B(4) requires the trustees of the receiving charity to ensure that the property is used for purposes as similar and practicable as the original purposes for which the property was held. The aim of the section is to ensure that the property is used as close as possible to the original purposes in circumstances where the transfer to the new charity was not necessarily to alter the original purposes but merely to allow the new charity to administer the property more effectively.

---

[63] Inserted by s. 17 of the Charities Act 2006.

Conclusion

This chapter has explored the cy-près doctrine which confers upon the courts and the Charity Commission a power to apply failed charitable gifts for purposes as close as possible to the ones intended by the person making the gift in the first place. The doctrine serves as a useful basis for the application of property for charitable purposes rather than its return to the donor of the gift or, where he has deceased, to his estate. Although the doctrine confers upon the courts and the Charity Commission a wide power to apply failed charitable gifts for other purposes, it would be wrong to think that that its application is axiomatic. Fundamentally, what is a required is that the donor of the original charitable gift manifested a general charitable intent to benefit charity. In cases where the donor's intention was to benefit a specific charity and no more, there are no grounds for invoking the doctrine. However, what has been illustrated in this chapter is that questions of whether the donor has indeed manifested a general charitable intent, and whether the charitable gift has indeed failed in the first instance are much more complicated in practice. Certainly, in some cases, what may appear to be an initial failure of a charitable gift may indeed not be the case because the original charity has continued in some other form.

It has been observed in the chapter that the modern grounds for invoking the cy-près doctrine are much wider than they originally were. For example, it was observed in the chapter that, before the enactment of the Charities Act 1993 as amended recently by the Charities Act 2006, the ground for invoking the cy-près doctrine were limited to situations where the original gift had become impossible or impracticable to be applied for its purposes. The requirement that the gift become impossible or impractical severely hampered the use of charitable gifts for more socially and economically useful purposes. The reason for this was where a gift could be applied for its original purposes despite no real social or economic utility in its application, the gift could not be changed because it was not impossible or impracticable. The Charities Act 1993 as amended by the Charities Act 2006 allows the courts and the Charity Commission to apply cy-près doctrine to be applied in a number of situations where the gift has not necessarily failed or has become impossible or impracticable. Section 13 of the Charities Act 1993 allows charitable gifts to be applied cy-près, taking into consideration prevailing social and economic circumstances, and in this respect, allows the more effective use of charitable gifts.

Case study

Consider the following case study.

In her will Janet directed that her real property be sold and be divided equally amongst the following charities:

- The ABC Education Charity in Kenilworth
- The Western Animal Sanctuary in Kenilworth
- The Divine Church Movement in Birmingham.

The residuary legatees of the will were Janet's children.

Additionally, when Janet was alive, she directed that a sum of £500,000 be invested and the income used to provide school uniforms for the needy children of Hampden. For a number of years the needy children have benefited from this trust fund. Throughout her life, Janet had made a number of charitable donations to educational charitable causes in Hampden and Kenilworth.

Janet died a few months ago and the executors of her estate have discovered that the ABC Education Charity in Kenilworth, which was an unincorporated association, no longer exists. The assets of the charity were transferred to the Warwickshire Educational Trust.

The executors have transferred the share of the proceeds of the sale of Janet's real property to the Western Animal Sanctuary; however, they have also learnt that this charity, which operated as an incorporated association, has been adjudicated bankrupt and is in the process of winding up its assets.

The Divine Movement in Birmingham received their share of Janet's property; however, a dispute has arisen amongst the religious sect about their spiritual leader. A large number of followers of the sect have asked for the assets to be transferred to new trustees.

Finally, in respect the trust fund of £500,000 for the needy children in Hampden and the provision of school uniform, the trustees have not made any payments to any children for a number of years. This is primarily because the schools in Hampden have not required a specific uniform.

Advise:

- *The executors of Janet's will as to what should be done with the share of the proceeds of sale of Janet's freehold property which was given to ABC Education Charity in Kenilworth.*
- *The creditors of Western Animal Sanctuary as to whether they can use the money they have received under Janet's will to meet their debts.*
- *The Divine Church Movement as to what should happen with the assets of the Church.*
- *The trustees of the trust of £500,000 who have not made any payments of income and are unlikely to do so.*

●● Moot points

1 The Charities Act 2006 further expands the grounds for applying charitable gifts cy-près by allowing the Charity Commission and the courts to have regard to 'appropriate considerations' when authorising an alternation to a charitable gift. What do you understand by the term 'appropriate considerations' and explain how far such considerations allow the courts and the Charity Commission to discard the original intentions of the donor of the charitable gift, i.e. the original settlor or testator in the case of a charitable trust.

2 How satisfactory is the distinction that is made between charitable gifts made to charitable unincorporated associations and charitable incorporated associations? In particular, where a gift is made to a charitable unincorporated association, it is construed as a gift for a purpose which can be applied cy-près even if the unincorporated association has ceased to exist. On the other hand, a gift made to an incorporated charitable association is construed as a gift for the incorporated association, which cannot be generally applied cy-près should the association cease to exist before the testator's death. Is the distinction based on the testator's true intentions?

3 Whilst it is generally accepted that the application of property cy-près is much easier in cases of subsequent failure, primarily because gifts once donated to charity are regarded as belonging to the pot of charity, is this always true in cases of surplus funds which remain after a charitable purpose has been exhausted?

4 How far is it possible to apply a gift cy-près when it is given to two charities in succession and only the first charity has failed but not the second in line?

5 Critically distinguish the decisions in *Kings* v *Bultitude* [2010] EWHC 1795 (Ch) with *White* v *Williams* [2010] EWHC 940.

Further reading

Dunn, A. 'Construing Bequests to Charitable Companies in the Course of Winding Up' (1997) *Company Lawyer* 213. Provides a discussion of the decision in *Re ARMS (Multiple Sclerosis Research) Ltd* [1997] 2 All ER 679 and examines the distinction between gifts made to charitable unincorporated associations and charitable incorporated associations.

Luxton, P. 'In Pursuit of Purpose Through s. 13 of the Charities Act 1960' [1985] Conv. 313. Provides an account of the ambit of s. 13 of the Charities Act 1960.

White, S. 'The Protection of Legacies and Gifts upon Merger under the Charities Act 2006' (2007) PCB 375. Provides an account of the changes introduced by the Charities Act 2006 in respect of gifts made to a charity which has merged with another charity.

Visit **www.mylawchamber.co.uk/panesar** to access study support resources including interactive multiple choice questions, practice exam questions with guidance, podcasts, weblinks, legal newsfeed all linked to the **Pearson eText** version of Exploring Equity and Trusts which you can **search, highlight** and **personalise** with your **own notes** and **bookmarks**.

Index